The Contemporary Reader

S0-AEU-634

The Contemporary Reader

FIFTH EDITION

Gary Goshgarian

Northeastern University

HarperCollins*CollegePublishers*

Acquisitions Editor: Patricia Rossi
Project Editor: Brigitte Pelner
Photo Researcher: Corrine Johns
Text/Cover Designer: Wendy Ann Fredericks
Cover Photo: Keith Tishken
Electronic Production Manager: Valerie A. Sawyer
Manufacturing Manager: Helene G. Landers
Electronic Page Makeup: BookMasters, Inc.
Printer and Binder: RR Donnelley & Sons Company
Cover Printer: Phoenix Color Corp.

For permission to use copyrighted material, grateful acknowledgment is made to the copyright holders on pp. 563–566, which are hereby made part of this copyright page.

The Contemporary Reader, Fifth Edition

Copyright © 1996 by Gary Goshgarian

All rights reserved. Printed in the United States of America. No part of this book may be used or reproduced in any manner whatsoever without written permission, except in the case of brief quotations embodied in critical articles and reviews. For information address HarperCollins College Publishers, 10 East 53rd Street, New York, NY 10022. *For information about any HarperCollins title, product, or resource, please visit our World Wide Web site at **http://www.harpercollins.com/college.***

ISBN: 0-673-52412-4 (Student Edition)
ISBN: 0-673-52413-2 (Instructor Edition)

95 96 97 98   9 8 7 6 5 4 3 2 1

This book is dedicated to my sons,
Nathan and David

Contents

· 1 ·

Personal Discoveries   1

On Keeping a Notebook   3
Joan Didion

> "It is a good idea, then, to keep in touch, and I suppose that keeping in touch [with your-self] is what notebooks are all about."

Shame   10
Dick Gregory

> Everybody's got a Helene Tucker—a symbol of everything one wants. But when Dick Gregory realized that his classmates and teacher pitied him, shame hurt even more than longing.

Graduation   14
Maya Angelou

> Graduation epidemic strikes; both young and old are nervous and jubilant. But it's not until the ceremony almost goes amiss that this community of blacks feels truly proud.

Salvation   24
Langston Hughes

> "I was saved from sin when I was going on thirteen. but not really saved," confesses the celebrated American author.

The Eye of the Beholder   27
Grace Suh

> This young Asian-American woman learns the price of conforming to Western standards of beauty by paying the vanity fare.

•2•
Family Matters   49

•3•
Changing Times 83

·4·
Consumer Culture 122

•5•

Advertising   157

•6•
Male/Female   222

Why Do We Need Celebrities?   339
Christina Kelly

> "Once TV started, the whole celeb-creation and -worship thing careened out of control. . . . TV gives you the false impression that celebrities are talking right to you . . . like they're your friends."

The Wrong Examples   345
David L. Evans

> "A foreigner watching American TV would probably conclude that most successful black males are either athletes or entertainers."

In Praise of Roseanne   349
Elayne Rapping

> "Roseanne is not a descendant of the pristine line of virginal wife/mothers who have set the norms for such characters from the days of June Cleaver to the present."

Don't Blame TV   356
Jeff Greenfield

> The rise in crime? Increased divorce rate? Lower voter turnout? Falling SAT scores? Greater sexual promiscuity? The collapse of the family? The decline of Western civilization? Don't blame TV, says this network reporter.

Why I Quit Watching Television   360
P. J. O'Rourke

> "Well, I was nuzzling her ear, making little kissy noises. . . . Then, all of a sudden, I experienced one of those devastating realizations: She was watching a *Star Trek* rerun over my shoulder."

•9•
Crime and Punishment   364

Pilgrimage to Nonviolence   366
Martin Luther King, Jr.

> While violence threatens the very nature of American life, here is a plea for human love from one of this century's most charismatic and influential opponents of violence.

The Culture of Violence   372
Myriam Miedzian

> "Like many warrior societies, we have a long tradition of raising our boys to be tough, emotionally detached, deeply competitive, and concerned with dominance."

•10•

Censorship Versus Free Speech   413

POLITICALLY CORRECT LANGUAGE

•13•

Education   512

·14·
Death and Dying   544

Rhetorical Contents

DESCRIPTION: USING YOUR SENSES

DIVISION AND CLASSIFICATION: SORTING THINGS OUT

DEFINITION: DETERMINING THE NATURE AND LIMITS OF SOMETHING

Preface

The Contemporary Reader is a collection of essays chosen to challenge today's college students—essays on subjects students can relate to, essays that talk about the times and culture of which students are a part. Moreover, these are essays that inspire thought, stimulate class discussion, and serve as writing models.

By its very nature, a book on contemporary matters must be kept up to date. Therefore, for the fifth edition I have made some major changes, several at the suggestions of instructors and students who used the fourth edition. These changes include the following.

New Topics and New Essays.   Naturally, material that was dated or that was no longer useful to students and instructors has been dropped. And many new topics have been added to the already broad spectrum covered in past editions. Some of the new topics are safe sex, consumerism, date rape, the law, being gay, street gangs, computers, mall culture, "healthism" advertising, TV violence, celebrities, adolescent crimes, political correctness, censorship and free speech, and college course work, to name a few. In fact, of the 95 selections, 53 are new to this edition, and most were written since 1993 and never before reprinted.

New Chapters.   Four new chapters have been added: Consumer Culture, Multicultural America, Crime and Punishment, and Censorship Versus Free Speech.

Increased Number of Women Writers.   Women composed 46 of the 95 selections in this edition.

Increased Number of Minority Writers.   Members of minority groups composed 24 out of the 95 selections in this edition.

ABOUT THE ESSAYS AND ADVERTISEMENTS

Diversity

The fifth edition still reflects the wide range of student interests: television, movies, music, advertising, race relations, multiculturalism, drug control, morality, free speech, the media, crime, sports, the natural world, abortion, dating, sexual roles, education, death and dying, and more.

This edition also contains the writings of some of the most respected authors of our time: Alice Walker, Maya Angelou, Martin Luther King, Jr., Langston Hughes, Joan Didion, Arthur Schlesinger, Jr., Edward Hoagland, Lewis Thomas, and Cornel West. Many of the authors are well-known journalists and columnists: Jeff Greenfield, Anna Quindlen, Barbara Ehrenreich, Nat Hentoff, Jonathan Alter, Deborah Baldwin, Alan Lupo, and Gwynne Dyer. There are also pieces by familiar humorists such as Dave Barry, P. J. O'Rourke, and Garrison Keillor.

The writing styles and techniques are as diverse as are the authors and subjects. Contained in this collection are examples of the "basic" essay as well as editorials, satirical narratives, parodies, journal entries, news reports, descriptive narratives, pointed arguments, commercial ads, and more. They vary in length from 500 words to 2000—a range most writing assignments fall within.

Debates

Essays on controversial topics are a special feature of *The Contemporary Reader*. As in the first four editions, many contemporary issues are examined from opposing points of view. In fact, most of the fourteen chapters contain a few essays that debate each other. They might be indirect as in Chapter 8, Television, where Jeff Greenfield's article "Don't Blame TV" argues against some of the viewpoints that precede it on the dangers of television. Or they might be more pointed as in Chapter 5, Advertising, where Deborah Baldwin's lament on the inescapable roar of commercials is juxtaposed with Michael Schudson's defense of advertising in "Delectable Materialism." Because the debate format has proven so popular, we have in this fifth edition devoted Chapter 10, Censorship Versus Free Speech, to essays that are paired, pro and con, on four specific First Amendment issues: politically correct language, pornography, rap music, and hate speech.

Humor

There is no reason why the writing experience should not be fun, nor is there any reason why writing models cannot be entertaining. As you will discover, many of the selections are quite funny; at the same time, they have something serious to say. Nearly every section contains some humorous pieces. Even Chapter 3, Changing Times, contains Pulitzer Prize–winning humorist Dave Barry's hilarious reflection, "You Have to Be a Real Stud Hombre Cybermuffin to Handle 'Windows.'"

Advertisements

Because of the strong response to past use of magazine ads in the chapter Advertising, we have included nine new ads with specific questions to help students closely analyze how advertising works on us—and to spark some lively class discussions.

APPARATUS

This book is not just a collection of interesting thoughts on contemporary experience. The selections offer varied but solid assistance to composition students trying to develop their own writing abilities. First, each chapter has an introduction outlining the rationale behind the selections. Second, the essays serve as models of many different expository techniques and patterns. Third, each selection is preceded by a headnote containing thematic and biographic information as well as clues to writing techniques and strategies. Fourth, each piece is followed by a series of review questions covering both thoughts and themes (Topical Considerations) and compositional features (Rhetorical Considerations)—questions designed to help students think analytically about the content and form of the essays. Each essay is followed by several writing assignments to suggest how students might relate the essays to other selections and to their own experience. Suggested research topics are also included. A rhetorical table of contents groups the essays according to particular writing strategies.

ACKNOWLEDGMENTS

Many people behind the scenes are, at the very least, deserving of acknowledgment and gratitude. It would be impossible to thank all of them, but there are some for whose help I am particularly grateful. First, I would like to thank all the instructors and students who used the first four editions of *The Contemporary Reader*. Their continued support has made possible this latest edition. Also, I would like to thank those instructors who spent hours answering lengthy questionnaires on the effectiveness of the essays and who supplied many helpful comments and suggestions. They are Connie Adair, Marshalltown Community College; Brenda Ayers Hajec, Merrimack College; John Bremer, Moorhead State University; Mattie Collins, Angelina College; Gordon Dossett, Santa Monica College; Rob Israel, Palomar College; W. David Lenoir, Western Kentucky University; Carde Permar, Marshalltown Community College; John Philibert, Massasoit Community College; Georgeanne Ross, Middle Tennessee State University; Jan Strever, Gonzaga University; Richard Trama, Stockton State College; Joette T. Waddle, Roane State Community College; Thomas A. Westerfield, University of Northern Iowa. A special thanks goes to Pamela Childers of The McCallie School, Richard Elia of Salem State College, and Mary Lee Donahue of Glassboro State College;

also to my colleagues Ruth Lepson, Maryemma Graham, and Kathleen Kelly for their suggestions; and to Stuart Peterfreund for his support. Thanks also to Jeanne Phoenix Laurel, Elizabeth Swanson, Phebe Jensen, Paul Crumbly, and Catherine Anderson for their expert assistance in writing the study questions and answers for the essays. I am also very grateful to Charles O'Neill and George Felton for updating their fine essays for this edition, and to Michael Eric Dyson for refashioning "Bum Rap" to fit our needs.

Very special thanks to the people of HarperCollins, especially my ever-helpful, ever-supportive editor, Patricia Rossi, her assistant, Lynne Cattafi, Development Editor, Leslie Taggart, and Project Editor, Brigitte Pelner.

Finally, thanks again to my wife Kathleen for her keen insight, her many hours of assistance, and her encouragement.

GARY GOSHGARIAN

S elf-discovery, the ancient philosophers tell us, is the greatest virtue. The high premium, of course, implies the difficulty of attainment. For some, self-discovery constantly evades. For others, it brings pain. For others still, the experience is enlightening. In some measure we all come to know ourselves as we move from childhood to old age. More often than not, discovery arises from a particular experience. Whether big or small, accidental or sought, good or bad—it is a moment that forever marks the souls. Nearly every essay in this chapter describes such a moment in the life of the respective author. Some stories are recounted by men looking back on childhood, others by women in middle age. Four of the authors are white, three are black, and one is Asian-American. But universal is the experience, for it declares to us who we are in the world.

The first essay addresses one of the surest ways we can learn who we are: writing. "On Keeping a Notebook" was written when its author, Joan Didion, was a young woman at the beginning of her famed career as a professional writer. Characteristically anecdotal, the piece explains the importance of keeping a journal, for it records who we used to be long after we've forgotten.

The next two essays look back to grade-school experiences that ignited personal and racial consciousness for the authors. In "Shame," Dick Gregory describes a profoundly painful moment in second grade when a teacher's comment suddenly defines his place in the classroom and the world outside. For Maya Angelou and her classmates, eighth-grade graduation promised to be "the hush-hush magic time" of their young lives. But as described in "Graduation," ugly racial insensitivity during the ceremony turned the young black woman's expectations into bitter pain and anger. Then an epiphany turns the moment into a triumphant celebration of the proud heritage out of which she was born.

An epiphany of a different sort is the motivation behind Langston Hughes's brief narrative, "Salvation." In this flashback to a church revival meeting in his childhood, Hughes poignantly illustrates how he failed to live up to adult-world demands to be saved.

Self-discovery doesn't always burst in key moments. Sometimes intense soul-searching is required, as we see in the next two pieces. In "The Eye of the Beholder," Grace Suh reports how on an impulse she decided to do something about her looks. So, she headed for a cosmetic counter to have her face made over. After the extensive application of various cleansers, paints, and glosses, she discovers a side of beauty that isn't so pretty. The discovery for Linda Bird Francke is clearly stated in the title of her essay, "The Ambivalence of Abortion." In a powerful piece of introspection, the author explains how her mind and heart tore at each other when faced with an unwanted pregnancy.

A different kind of ethical dilemma faced Sam Benson. In his essay "Why I Quit Practicing Law," the author explains how one day he decided that despite his fancy office and salary he had had it with being an attorney. And the reasons he names tell as much about him as they do about the profession.

Our final piece is a touching recollection of a man who at fourteen realized that he was attracted to other boys—an attraction that he was certain would subject him to a lifetime of scorn. In "A Clack of Tiny Sparks: Remembrance of a Gay Boyhood," Bernard Cooper describes how he dealt with his awareness, trying variously to submerge, deny, even redirect his yearnings. But as he looks back, he is struck by regret that his secret had kept him from being who he was.

On Keeping a Notebook
Joan Didion

Writing might be the only means we have of preserving who we are. More than photography or even home videos, a personal journal keeps the past alive and, more importantly, keeps us in touch with someone we used to be. That is the message in this first essay—a message about making personal discoveries that never end. And it comes from a woman whose distinguished literary career as a novelist, essayist, and short-story writer spans 40 years.

Joan Didion began writing professionally in 1956 when she was hired as a staff writer at *Vogue* magazine. She is the author of four novels including the bestselling *Democracy* (1984) and several other nonfiction books including *The White Album* (1979), *Salvador* (1983), and most recently *After Henry* (1992). This essay comes from her collection, *Slouching Towards Bethlehem* (1968).

1 "'That woman Estelle,'" the note reads, "'is partly the reason why George Sharp and I are separated today.' *Dirty crepe-de-Chine wrapper, hotel bar, Wilmington RR, 9:45 a.m. August Monday morning.*"

2 Since the note is in my notebook, it presumably has some meaning to me. I study it for a long while. At first I have only the most general notion of what I was doing on an August Monday morning in the bar of the hotel across from the Pennsylvania Railroad station in Wilmington, Delaware (waiting for a train? missing one? 1960? 1961? why Wilmington?), but I do remember being there. The woman in the dirty crepe-de-Chine wrapper had come down from her room for a beer, and the bartender had heard before the reason why George Sharp and she were separated today. "Sure," he said, and went on mopping the floor. "You told me." At the other end of the bar is a girl. She is talking, pointedly, not to the man beside her but to a cat lying in the triangle of sunlight cast through the open door. She is wearing a plaid silk dress from Peck & Peck, and the hem is coming down.

3 Here is what it is: The girl has been on the Eastern Shore, and now she is going back to the city, leaving the man beside her, and all she can see ahead are the viscous summer sidewalks and the 3 A.M. long-distance calls that will make her lie awake and then sleep drugged through all the steaming mornings left in August (1960?

1961?). Because she must go directly from the train to lunch in New York, she wishes that she had a safety pin for the hem of the plaid silk dress, and she also wishes that she could forget about the hem and the lunch and stay in the cool bar that smells of disinfectant and malt and make friends with the woman in the crepe-de-Chine wrapper. She is afflicted by a little self-pity, and she wants to compare Estelles. That is what that was all about.

4   Why did I write it down? In order to remember, of course, but exactly what was it I wanted to remember? How much of it actually happened? Did any of it? Why do I keep a notebook at all? It is easy to deceive oneself on all those scores. The impulse to write things down is a peculiarly compulsive one, inexplicable to those who do not share it, useful only accidentally, only secondarily, in the way that any compulsion tries to justify itself. I suppose that it begins or does not begin in the cradle. Although I have felt compelled to write things down since I was five years old, I doubt that my daughter ever will, for she is a singularly blessed and accepting child, delighted with life exactly as life presents itself to her, unafraid to go to sleep and unafraid to wake up. Keepers of private notebooks are a different breed altogether, lonely and resistant rearrangers of things, anxious malcontents, children afflicted apparently at birth with some presentiment of loss.

5   My first notebook was a Big Five tablet, given to me by my mother with the sensible suggestion that I stop whining and learn to amuse myself by writing down my thoughts. She returned the tablet to me a few years ago; the first entry is an account of a woman who believed herself to be freezing to death in the Arctic night, only to find, when day broke, that she had stumbled onto the Sahara Desert, where she would die of the heat before lunch. I have no idea what turn of a five-year-old's mind could have prompted so insistently "ironic" and exotic a story, but it does reveal a certain predilection for the extreme which has dogged me into adult life; perhaps if I were analytically inclined I would find it a truer story than any I might have told about Donald Johnson's birthday party or the day my cousin Brenda put Kitty Litter in the aquarium.

6   So the point of my keeping a notebook has never been, nor is it now, to have an accurate factual record of what I have been doing or thinking. That would be a different impulse entirely, an instinct for reality which I sometimes envy but do not possess. At no point have I ever been able successfully to keep a diary; my approach to daily life ranges from the grossly negligent to the merely absent, and on those few occasions when I have tried dutifully to record a day's events, boredom has so overcome me that the results are mysterious at best. What is this business about "shopping, typing piece, dinner with E, depressed"? Shopping for what? Typing what piece? Who is E? Was this "E" depressed, or was I depressed? Who cares?

7   In fact I have abandoned altogether that kind of pointless entry; instead I tell what some would call lies. "That's simply not true," the members of my family frequently tell me when they come up against my memory of a shared event. "The party was *not* for you, the spider was *not* a black widow, *it wasn't that way at all.*" Very likely they are right, for not only have I always had trouble distinguishing between what happened and what merely might have happened, but I remain unconvinced that the distinction, for my purposes, matters. The cracked crab that I recall

having for lunch the day my father came home from Detroit in 1945 must certainly be embroidery, worked into the day's pattern to lend verisimilitude; I was ten years old and would not now remember the cracked crab. The day's events did not turn on cracked crab. And yet it is precisely that fictitious crab that makes me see the afternoon all over again, a home movie run all too often, the father bearing gifts, the child weeping, an exercise in family love and guilt. Or that is what it was to me. Similarly, perhaps it never did snow that August in Vermont; perhaps there never were flurries in the night wind, and maybe no one else felt the ground hardening and summer already dead even as we pretended to bask in it, but that was how it felt to me, and it might as well have snowed, could have snowed, did snow.

8   *How it felt to me:* that is getting closer to the truth about a notebook. I sometimes delude myself about why I keep a notebook, imagine that some thrifty virtue derives from preserving everything observed. See enough and write it down, I tell myself, and then some morning when the world seems drained of wonder, some day when I am only going through the motions of doing what I am supposed to do, which is write—on that bankrupt morning I will simply open my notebook and there it will all be, a forgotten account with accumulated interest, paid passage back to the world out there: dialogue overheard in hotels and elevators and at the hatcheck counter in Pavillon (one middle-aged man shows his hat check to another and says, "That's my old football number"); impressions of Bettina Aptheker and Benjamin Sonnenberg and Teddy ("Mr. Acapulco") Stauffer; careful *aperçus*[1] about tennis bums and failed fashion models and Greek shipping heiresses, one of whom taught me a significant lesson (a lesson I could have learned from F. Scott Fitzgerald, but perhaps we all must meet the very rich for ourselves) by asking, when I arrived to interview her in her orchid-filled sitting room on the second day of a paralyzing New York blizzard, whether it was snowing outside.

9   I imagine, in other words, that the notebook is about other people. But of course it is not. I have no real business with what one stranger said to another at the hatcheck counter in Pavillon; in fact I suspect that the line "That's my old football number" touched not my own imagination at all, but merely some memory of something once read, probably "The Eighty-Yard Run."[2] Nor is my concern with a woman in a dirty crepe-de-Chine wrapper in a Wilmington bar. My stake is always, of course, in the unmentioned girl in the plaid silk dress. *Remember what it was to be me:* that is always the point.

10   It is a difficult point to admit. We are brought up in the ethic that others, any others, all others, are by definition more interesting than ourselves; taught to be diffident, just this side of self-effacing. ("You're the least important person in the room and don't forget it," Jessica Mitford's[3] governess would hiss in her ear on the advent

---

[1]*aperçus:* Summarizing glimpse or insight (French).—Ed.

[2]*"The Eighty-Yard Run"*: Popular short story by Irwin Shaw.—Ed.

[3]*Jessica Mitford* (b. 1917): British satirical writer and essayist.—Ed.

of any social occasion; I copied that into my notebook because it is only recently that I have been able to enter a room without hearing some such phrase in my inner ear.) Only the very young and the very old may recount their dreams at breakfast, dwell upon self, interrupt with memories of beach picnics and favorite Liberty lawn dresses and the rainbow trout in a creek near Colorado Springs. The rest of us are expected, rightly, to affect absorption in other people's favorite dresses, other people's trout.

11 And so we do. But our notebooks give us away, for however dutifully we record what we see around us, the common denominator of all we see is always, transparently, shamelessly, the implacable "I." We are not talking here about the kind of notebook that is patently for public consumption, a structural conceit for binding together a series of graceful *pensées;*[4] we are talking about something private, about bits of the mind's string too short to use, an indiscriminate and erratic assemblage with meaning only for its maker.

12 And sometimes even the maker has difficulty with the meaning. There does not seem to be, for example, any point in my knowing for the rest of my life that, during 1964, 720 tons of soot fell on every square mile of New York City, yet there it is in my notebook, labeled "FACT." Nor do I really need to remember that Ambrose Bierce liked to spell Leland Stanford's[5] name "£eland $tanford" or that "smart women almost always wear black in Cuba," a fashion hint without much potential for practical application. And does not the relevance of these notes seem marginal at best?:

> In the basement museum of the Inyo County Courthouse in Independence, California, sign pinned to a mandarin coat: "This MANDARIN COAT was often worn by Mrs. Minnie S. Brooks when giving lectures on her TEAPOT COLLECTION."

> Redhead getting out of car in front of Beverly Wilshire Hotel, chinchilla stole, Vuitton bags with tags reading:

> MRS LOU FOX
> HOTEL SAHARA
> VEGAS

13 Well, perhaps not entirely marginal. As a matter of fact, Mrs. Minnie S. Brooks and her MANDARIN COAT pull me back into my own childhood, for although I never knew Mrs. Brooks and did not visit Inyo County until I was thirty, I grew up in just such a world, in houses cluttered with Indian relics and bits of gold ore and ambergris and the souvenirs my Aunt Mercy Farnsworth brought back from the Orient. It is a long way from that world to Mrs. Lou Fox's world, where we all live now, and is it not just as well to remember that? Might not Mrs. Minnie S. Brooks help me to remember what I am? Might not Mrs. Lou Fox help me to remember what I am not?

---

[4]*pensées:* Thoughts or reflections (French)—Ed.

[5]*Bierce . . . Stanford's:* Ambrose Bierce (1842–1914?), American journalist and short-story writer known for his savage wit; Leland Stanford (1824–1893), wealthy railroad builder who was a governor of California and the founder of Stanford University.—Ed.

14   But sometimes the point is harder to discern. What exactly did I have in mind when I noted down that it cost the father of someone I know $650 a month to light the place on the Hudson in which he lived before the Crash? What use was I planning to make of this line by Jimmy Hoffa:[6] "I may have my faults, but being wrong ain't one of them"? And although I think it interesting to know where the girls who travel with the Syndicate have their hair done when they find themselves on the West Coast, will I ever make suitable use of it? Might I not be better off just passing it on to John O'Hara?[7] What is a recipe for sauerkraut doing in my notebook? What kind of magpie keeps this notebook? *"He was born the night the Titanic went down."* That seems a nice enough line, and I even recall who said it, but is it not really a better line in life than it could ever be in fiction?

15   But of course that is exactly it: not that I should ever use the line, but that I should remember the woman who said it and the afternoon I heard it. We were on her terrace by the sea, and we were finishing the wine left from lunch, trying to get what sun there was, a California winter sun. The woman whose husband was born the night the *Titanic* went down wanted to rent her house, wanted to go back to her children in Paris. I remember wishing that I could afford the house, which cost $1,000 a month. "Someday you will," she said lazily. "Someday it all comes." There in the sun on her terrace it seemed easy to believe in someday, but later I had a low-grade afternoon hangover and ran over a black snake on the way to the supermarket and was flooded with inexplicable fear when I heard the checkout clerk explaining to the man ahead of me why she was finally divorcing her husband. "He left me no choice," she said over and over as she punched the register. "He has a little seven-month-old baby by her, he left me no choice." I would like to believe that my dread then was for the human condition, but of course it was for me, because I wanted a baby and did not then have one and because I wanted to own the house that cost $1,000 a month to rent and because I had a hangover.

16   It all comes back. Perhaps it is difficult to see the value in having one's self back in that kind of mood, but I do see it; I think we are well advised to keep on nodding terms with the people we used to be whether we find them attractive company or not. Otherwise they turn up unannounced and surprise us, come hammering on the mind's door at 4 A.M. of a bad night and demand to know who deserted them, who betrayed them, who is going to make amends. We forget all too soon the things we thought we could never forget. We forget the loves and the betrayals alike, forget what we whispered and what we screamed, forget who we were. I have already lost touch with a couple of people I used to be; one of them, a seventeen-year-old, presents little threat, although it would be of some interest to me to know again what it feels like to sit on a river levee drinking vodka-and-orange-juice and listening to Les Paul and Mary Ford[8] and their echoes sing "How High the Moon" on the car radio.

---

[6]*Jimmy Hoffa* (1913–1975?): Controversial leader of the Teamsters Union who disappeared in the mid-seventies.—Ed.

[7]*John O'Hara* (1905–1970): American novelist who wrote several books about gangsters.—Ed.

[8]*Les Paul and Mary Ford:* Husband-and-wife musical team of the forties and fifties who had many hit records.—Eds.

(You see I still have the scenes, but I no longer perceive myself among those present, no longer could even improvise the dialogue.) The other one, a twenty-three-year-old, bothers me more. She was always a good deal of trouble, and I suspect she will reappear when I least want to see her, skirts too long, shy to the point of aggravation, always the injured party, full of recriminations and little hurts and stories I do not want to hear again, at once saddening me and angering me with her vulnerability and ignorance, an apparition all the more insistent for being so long banished.

17   It is a good idea, then, to keep in touch, and I suppose that keeping in touch is what notebooks are all about. And we are all on our own when it comes to keeping those lines open to ourselves: your notebook will never help me, nor mine you. *"So what's new in the whiskey business?"* What could that possibly mean to you? To me it means a blonde in a Pucci bathing suit sitting with a couple of fat men by the pool at the Beverly Hills Hotel. Another man approaches, and they all regard one another in silence for a while. "So what's new in the whiskey business?" one of the fat men finally says by way of welcome, and the blonde stands up, arches one foot and dips it in the pool, looking all the while at the cabaña where Baby Pignatari is talking on the telephone. That is all there is to that, except that several years later I saw the blonde coming out of Saks Fifth Avenue in New York with her California complexion and a voluminous mink coat. In the harsh wind that day she looked old and irrevocably tired to me, and even the skins in the mink coat were not worked the way they were doing them that year, not the way she would have wanted them done, and there is the point of the story. For a while after that I did not like to look in the mirror, and my eyes would skim the newspapers and pick out only the deaths, the cancer victims, the premature coronaries, the suicides, and I stopped riding the Lexington Avenue IRT because I noticed for the first time that all the strangers I had seen for years—the man with the seeing-eye dog, the spinster who read the classified pages every day, the fat girl who always got off with me at Grand Central—looked older than they once had.

18   It all comes back. Even that recipe for sauerkraut: even that brings it back. I was on Fire Island when I first made that sauerkraut, and it was raining, and we drank a lot of bourbon and ate the sauerkraut and went to bed at ten, and I listened to the rain and the Atlantic and felt safe. I made the sauerkraut again last night and it did not make me feel any safer, but that is, as they say, another story.

■ TOPICAL CONSIDERATIONS

1. Didion begins her essay with an entry from her notebook and wonders about its significance in the next three paragraphs. What is the content of the entry? Does Didion's memory of the event make sense to you? What does Didion say about this entry that relates to the main theme of the essay? Why did Didion write it in her notebook? What meaning does it have for her? Where in the essay do you know the meaning of the entry?

2. Didion remembers her first writing tablet and what she wrote in it. What was the entry? How does her five-year-old writing resemble her adult writing? Do you recall your first writings? Did you keep a notebook or diary? Do you see any resemblance in that early writing to how you write or think today?

3. What happened when Didion tried to keep a conventional diary? What reason does she give for abandoning that for her own kind of notebook? How does her family react to her memories? Do your memories conflict with those of your family? Recall a scene from childhood or from a shared experience and state the significance of the memory for you.

4. Didion states that writing "how it felt to me" is "closer to the truth" (paragraph 8). Why is writing one's own personal version of the truth more difficult than recording factual details? What distinction does Didion make between the personal notebook and *pensées?* Do you agree with her?

5. Didion reveals a darker side of her personality in paragraph 15. What notebook entry triggers her memory? What does she reveal about herself in the illustration? What reasons does she give for recording this incident and her feelings?

■ RHETORICAL CONSIDERATIONS

1. From a rhetorical point of view, Didion makes heavy use of illustration throughout the essay. Why does she resort to so much illustration? How does she make use of the illustrations? Are some illustrations more effective than others? If so, which seem to work well, and which do not?

2. Didion uses the present tense in most of her illustrations. What purpose does the present tense serve in her essay?

3. Look at the opening sentences of paragraphs 6, 7, 8, 9, 10, and 11. Didion begins most of these paragraphs with a declarative sentence. How would you characterize the tone of these sentences? How is the declarative sentence useful in connecting the paragraphs to each other? How do these sentences contrast with Didion's other sentences, such as her use of questions and descriptions?

■ WRITING ASSIGNMENTS

1. In her essay, written thirty years ago, Didion claims that our culture teaches us to pay more attention to what others think than what we believe is personally true. Do you think this perception is still true today? Do we still care about what our neighbors think? What our family thinks? What our community values? Using examples from your own experience growing up, write a paper exploring these questions. What was more important, your own personal insight or the viewpoint of your community and family?

2. Keep a notebook for one week in which you record not factual details you observe but what your imagination dictates, in the manner of Didion. The next week, keep a factual notebook, recording what happens around you. What did you learn about the personal truth of your experience from this exercise? Which approach was more rewarding for you? Explain your response.

3. Many artists have kept a notebook of their creative and spiritual lives. Using your library, research the notebooks of the artist Paul Klee, the German artist Paula Modersohn Becker, or Georgia O'Keefe. What personal record-

ings convey their awareness of family conflict, political events of the day, sadness or beauty?

4. In paragraph 4, Didion writes: "Keepers of private notebooks are a different breed altogether, lonely and resistant rearrangers of things, anxious malcontents, children afflicted apparently at birth with some presentiment of loss." Do you agree with her? Write an essay in which you describe the kind of person who chooses to write about personal issues, or who writes in a private notebook no one sees.

Shame

Dick Gregory

Dick Gregory is a well-known satirist, whose humor cuts below the surface of comedy. As a stand-up comic, he was a regular on a variety of television shows during the 1960s and 1970s. He continues to be active in the Civil Rights Movement. Additionally, Gregory has become a noted nutritionist, devoting his efforts to helping people suffering from obesity. The essay below is a sensitive narrative of a childhood experience that taught Gregory the meaning of shame. The selection comes from Gregory's 1964 autobiography, *nigger*.

1   I never learned hate at home, or shame. I had to go to school for that. I was about seven years old when I got my first big lesson. I was in love with a little girl named Helene Tucker, a light-complexioned little girl with pigtails and nice manners. She was always clean and she was smart in school. I think I went to school then mostly to look at her. I brushed my hair and even got me a little old handkerchief. It was a lady's handkerchief, but I didn't want Helene to see me wipe my nose on my hand. The pipes were frozen again, there was no water in the house, but I washed my socks and shirt every night. I'd get a pot, and go over to Mister Ben's grocery store, and stick my pot down into his soda machine. Scoop out some chopped ice. By evening the ice melted to water for washing. I got sick a lot that winter because the fire would go out at night before the clothes were dry. In the morning I'd put them on, wet or dry, because they were the only clothes I had.

2   Everybody's got a Helene Tucker, a symbol of everything you want. I loved her for her goodness, her cleanness, her popularity. She'd walk down my street and my brothers and sisters would yell, "Here comes Helene," and I'd rub my tennis sneakers on the back of my pants and wish my hair wasn't so nappy and the white folks' shirt fit me better. I'd run out on the street. If I knew my place and didn't come too close, she'd wink at me and say hello. That was a good feeling. Sometimes I'd follow her all the way home, and shovel the snow off her walk and try to make friends with her Momma and her aunts. I'd drop money on her stoop late at night on my way back

from shining shoes in the taverns. And she had a Daddy, and he had a good job. He was a paper hanger.

3   I guess I would have gotten over Helene by summertime, but something happened in that classroom that made her face hang in front of me for the next twenty-two years. When I played the drums in high school it was for Helene and when I broke track records in college it was for Helene and when I started standing behind microphones and heard applause I wished Helene could hear it, too. It wasn't until I was twenty-nine years old and married and making money that I finally got her out of my system. Helene was sitting in that classroom when I learned to be ashamed of myself.

4   It was on a Thursday. I was sitting in the back of the room, in a seat with a chalk circle drawn around it. The idiot's seat, the troublemaker's seat.

5   The teacher thought I was stupid. Couldn't spell, couldn't read, couldn't do arithmetic. Just stupid. Teachers were never interested in finding out that you couldn't concentrate because you were so hungry, because you hadn't had any breakfast. All you could think about was noontime, would it ever come? Maybe you could sneak into the cloakroom and steal a bite of some kid's lunch out of a coat pocket. A bite of something. Paste. You can't really make a meal of paste, or put it on bread for a sandwich, but sometimes I'd scoop a few spoonfuls out of the paste jar in the back of the room. Pregnant people get strange tastes. I was pregnant with poverty. Pregnant with dirt and pregnant with smells that made people turn away, pregnant with cold and pregnant with shoes that were never bought for me, pregnant with five other people in my bed and no Daddy in the next room, and pregnant with hunger. Paste doesn't taste too bad when you're hungry.

6   The teacher thought I was a troublemaker. All she saw from the front of the room was a little black boy who squirmed in his idiot's seat and made noises and poked the kids around him. I guess she couldn't see a kid who made noises because he wanted someone to know he was there.

7   It was on a Thursday, the day before the Negro payday. The eagle always flew on Friday. The teacher was asking each student how much his father would give to the Community Chest. On Friday night, each kid would get the money from his father, and on Monday he would bring it to the school. I decided I was going to buy me a Daddy right then. I had money in my pocket from shining shoes and selling papers, and whatever Helene Tucker pledged for her Daddy I was going to top it. And I'd hand the money right in. I wasn't going to wait until Monday to buy me a Daddy.

8   I was shaking, scared to death. The teacher opened her book and started calling out names alphabetically.

9   "Helene Tucker?"

10   "My daddy said he'd give two dollars and fifty cents."

11   "That's very nice, Helene. Very, very nice indeed."

12   That made me feel pretty good. It wouldn't take too much to top that. I had almost three dollars in dimes and quarters in my pocket. I stuck my hand in my pocket and held onto the money, waiting for her to call my name. But the teacher closed her book after she called everybody else in the class.

13   I stood up and raised my hand.

14 "What is it now?"

15 "You forgot me."

16 She turned toward the blackboard. "I don't have time to be playing with you, Richard."

17 "My Daddy said he'd . . . "

18 "Sit down, Richard, you're disturbing the class."

19 "My Daddy said he'd give . . . fifteen dollars."

20 She turned around and looked mad. "We are collecting this money for you and your kind, Richard Gregory. If your Daddy can give fifteen dollars you have no business being on relief."

21 "I got it right now, I got it right now, my Daddy gave it to me to turn in today, my Daddy said . . . "

22 "And furthermore," she said, looking right at me, her nostrils getting big and her lips getting thin and her eyes opening wide, "we know you don't have a Daddy."

23 Helene Tucker turned around, her eyes full of tears. She felt sorry for me. Then I couldn't see her too well because I was crying, too.

24 "Sit down, Richard."

25 And I always thought the teacher kind of liked me. She always picked me to wash the blackboard on Friday, after school. That was a big thrill, it made me feel important. If I didn't wash it, come Monday the school might not function right.

26 "Where are you going, Richard?"

27 I walked out of school that day, and for a long time I didn't go back very often. There was shame there.

28 Now there was shame everywhere. It seemed like the whole world had been inside that classroom, everyone had heard what the teacher had said, everyone had turned around and felt sorry for me. There was shame in going to the Worthy Boys Annual Christmas Dinner for you and your kind, because everybody knew what a worthy boy was. Why couldn't they just call it the Boys Annual Dinner; why'd they have to give it a name? There was shame in wearing the brown and orange and white plaid mackinaw the welfare gave to three thousand boys. Why'd it have to be the same for everybody so when you walked down the street the people could see you were on relief? It was a nice warm mackinaw and it had a hood, and my Momma beat me and called me a little rat when she found out I stuffed it in the bottom of a pail full of garbage way over on Cottage Street. There was shame in running over to Mister Ben's at the end of the day and asking for his rotten peaches, there was shame in asking Mrs. Simmons for a spoonful of sugar, there was shame in running out to meet the relief truck. I hated that truck, full of food for you and your kind. I ran into the house and hid when it came. And then I started to sneak through alleys, to take the long way home so the people going into White's Eat Shop wouldn't see me. Yeah, the whole world heard the teacher that day, we all know you don't have a Daddy.

■ TOPICAL CONSIDERATIONS

1. Gregory tried so hard to impress Helene Tucker that he often got sick from wearing wet clothes that couldn't dry because the fire had gone out in the night. When you were growing up, was there any one person for whom you

went to such extremes to impress? What did you do? What was he or she like? Do you know any adults who would go (or have gone) to such extremes?

2. Helene Tucker seems to have been a success symbol for Gregory when he was a child. He comments: "Everybody's got a Helene Tucker, a symbol of everything you want" (paragraph 2). What does Gregory's description of Helene tell you about what success meant to him? What influenced his view? Describe a person who represents success to you. What influences have shaped this view?

3. What do you think of the way Gregory handled himself in school the day the teacher embarrassed him? Would you have responded in the same way? Was his refusal to go to school after this incident the only way he could deal with his shame? What would have been your answer?

4. Why did the memory of Helene Tucker's presence the day he was shamed in class motivate Gregory to excel as a teenager? Do you think this is a useful motivational device? What other incentives can be effective?

5. Gregory remarks that he wasn't able to get Helene Tucker out of his system for twenty-two years. Why was he finally able to forget her? Do you think that if he were confronted with the same kind of experience now, he would respond in the same way? Why? Is there anything about Gregory's experience that you can relate to your own life?

6. How sensitive was the teacher? How else might she have responded to Gregory?

7. Do you think most welfare recipients are like Gregory and do not want to be on welfare? Give reasons for your answer.

■ RHETORICAL CONSIDERATIONS

1. Where does Gregory state his thesis? Is this the best place for it? Explain.
2. What adjectives does Gregory use in his description of Helene Tucker in the first paragraph? Does he use too many? Not enough? Are they essential to the development of his thesis? Why or why not?
3. What is the primary rhetorical pattern Gregory uses in this essay? Are others used as well? Cite sample passages.
4. Does Gregory *tell* or *show* his reader how he feels about Helene Tucker? What rhetorical patterns does he use to accomplish this?
5. What can you say about Gregory's conclusion? Does it tie in with his thesis? Is it an effective ending? Why or why not?

■ WRITING ASSIGNMENTS

1. Have you ever had an experience that caused you to feel shame? Write an essay describing the incident. Include concrete details, illustrations, and dialogue (as Gregory does) that will show your reader exactly what happened.
2. What does success mean to you? In an essay, analyze your own answer to this question. Discuss the influences that have shaped your view.

3. Write an essay describing someone you idealize and would like to impress. Narrate some of the things you would do or have done to gain this person's esteem.

	Graduation
	Maya Angelou

One of the most important events in a young person's life is graduation day. This selection, a vivid recollection of one such day and the events leading up to it, is by the famous black author, Maya Angelou. Born Marguerita Johnson in 1928, Angelou survived some terrible childhood experiences—a broken home, being raped at the age of eight, becoming an unwed mother at sixteen. As an adult, she involved herself in theater, television, and journalism. She also served as a coordinator of Martin Luther King's Southern Christian Leadership Conference.

Today Ms. Angelou is Reynolds Professor of American Studies at Wake Forest University. At the 1993 Inauguration of President Clinton, Angelou performed her poem "On the Pulse of Morning." She is perhaps best known for her autobiographical books, including *I Know Why the Caged Bird Sings* (1970), from which this piece was taken, and *The Heart of a Woman* (1981), a memoir.

1 The children in Stamps trembled visibly with anticipation. Some adults were excited too, but to be certain the whole young population had come down with graduation epidemic. Large classes were graduating from both the grammar school and the high school. Even those who were years removed from their own day of glorious release were anxious to help with preparations as a kind of dry run. The junior students who were moving into the vacating classes' chairs were tradition-bound to show their talents for leadership and management. They strutted through the school and around the campus exerting pressure on the lower grades. Their authority was so new that occasionally if they pressed a little too hard it had to be overlooked. After all, next term was coming, and it never hurt a sixth grader to have a play sister in the eighth grade, or a tenth-year student to be able to call a twelfth grader Bubba. So all was endured in a spirit of shared understanding. But the graduating classes themselves were the nobility. Like travelers with exotic destinations on their minds, the graduates were remarkably forgetful. They came to school without their books, or tablets, or even pencils. Volunteers fell over themselves to secure replacements for the missing equipment. When accepted, the willing workers might or might not be thanked, and it was of no importance to the pre-graduation rites. Even teachers were respectful of the now quiet and aging seniors, and tended to speak to them, if not as equals, as beings only slightly lower than themselves. After tests were returned and grades given, the student body, which

acted like an extended family, knew who did well, who excelled, and what piteous ones had failed.

2   Unlike the white high school, Lafayette County Training School distinguished itself by having neither lawn, nor hedges, nor tennis court, nor climbing ivy. Its two buildings (main classrooms, the grade school and home economics) were set on a dirt hill with no fence to limit either its boundaries or those of bordering farms. There was a large expanse to the left of the school which was used alternately as a baseball diamond or a basketball court. Rusty hoops on the swaying poles represented the permanent recreational equipment, although bats and balls could be borrowed from the P.E. teacher if the borrower was qualified and if the diamond wasn't occupied.

3   Over this rocky area relieved by a few shady tall persimmon trees the graduating class walked. The girls often held hands and no longer bothered to speak to the lower students. There was a sadness about them, as if this old world was not their home and they were bound for higher ground. The boys, on the other hand, had become more friendly, more outgoing. A decided change from the closed attitude they projected while studying for finals. Now they seemed not ready to give up the old school, the familiar paths and classrooms. Only a small percentage would be continuing on to college—one of the South's A & M (agricultural and mechanical) schools, which trained Negro youths to be carpenters, farmers, handymen, masons, maids, cooks, and baby nurses. Their future role heavily on their shoulders, and blinded them to the collective joy that had pervaded the lives of the boys and girls in the grammar school graduating class.

4   Parents who could afford it had ordered new shoes and ready-made clothes for themselves from Sears and Roebuck or Montgomery Ward. They also engaged the best seamstresses to make the floating graduating dresses and to cut down secondhand pants which would be pressed to a military slickness for the important event.

5   Oh, it was important, all right. Whitefolks would attend the ceremony, and two or three would speak of God and home, and the Southern way of life, and Mrs. Parsons, the principal's wife, would play the graduation march while the lower-grade graduates paraded down the aisles and took their seats below the platform. The high school seniors would wait in empty classrooms to make their dramatic entrance.

6   In the Store I was the person of the moment. The birthday girl. The center. Bailey[9] had graduated the year before, although to do so he had had to forfeit all pleasures to make up for his time lost in Baton Rouge.

7   My class was wearing butter-yellow piqué dresses, and Momma launched out on mine. She smocked the yoke into tiny crisscrossing puckers, then shirred the rest of the bodice. Her dark fingers ducked in and out of the lemony cloth as she embroidered raised daisies around the hem. Before she considered herself finished she had added a crocheted cuff on the puff sleeves, and a pointy crocheted collar.

8   I was going to be lovely. A walking model of all the various styles of fine hand sewing and it didn't worry me that I was only twelve years old and merely graduat-

---

[9]Angelou's brother.—Ed.

ing from the eighth grade. Besides, many teachers in Arkansas Negro schools had only that diploma and were licensed to impart wisdom.

9 The days had become longer and more noticeable. The faded beige of former times had been replaced with strong and sure colors. I began to see my classmates' clothes, their skin tones, and the dust that waved off pussy willows. Clouds that lazed across the sky were objects of great concern to me. Their shiftier shapes might have held a message that in my new happiness and with a little bit of time I'd soon decipher. During that period I looked at the arch of heaven so religiously my neck kept a steady ache. I had taken to smiling more often, and my jaws hurt from the unaccustomed activity. Between the two physical sore spots, I suppose I could have been uncomfortable, but that was not the case. As a member of the winning team (the graduating class of 1940) I had outdistanced unpleasant sensations by miles. I was headed for the freedom of open fields.

10 Youth and social approval allied themselves with me and we trammeled memories of slights and insults. The wind of our swift passage remodeled my features. Lost tears were pounded to mud and then to dust. Years of withdrawal were brushed aside and left behind, as hanging ropes of parasitic moss.

11 My work alone had awarded me a top place and I was going to be one of the first called in the graduating ceremonies. On the classroom blackboard, as well as on the bulletin board in the auditorium, there were blue stars and white stars and red stars. No absences, no tardinesses, and my academic work was among the best of the year. I could say the preamble to the Constitution even faster than Bailey. We timed ourselves often: "WethepeopleoftheUnitedStatesinordertoformamoreperfect union . . . " I had memorized the Presidents of the United States from Washington to Roosevelt in chronological as well as alphabetical order.

12 My hair pleased me too. Gradually the black mass had lengthened and thickened, so that it kept at last to its braided pattern, and I didn't have to yank my scalp off when I tried to comb it.

13 Louise and I had rehearsed the exercises until we tired out ourselves. Henry Reed was class valedictorian. He was a small, very black boy with hooded eyes, a long, broad nose and an oddly shaped head. I had admired him for years because each term he and I vied for the best grades in our class. Most often he bested me, but instead of being disappointed I was pleased that we shared top places between us. Like many Southern Black children, he lived with his grandmother, who was as strict as Momma and as kind as she knew how to be. He was courteous, respectful, and soft-spoken to elders, but on the playground he chose to play the roughest games. I admired him. Anyone, I reckoned, sufficiently afraid or sufficiently dull could be polite. But to be able to operate at a top level with both adults and children was admirable.

14 His valedictory speech was entitled "To Be or Not to Be." The rigid tenth-grade teacher had helped him to write it. He'd been working on the dramatic stresses for months.

15 The weeks until graduation were filled with heady activities. A group of small children were to be presented in a play about buttercups and daisies and bunny rabbits. They could be heard throughout the building practicing their hops and their little songs that sounded like silver bells. The older girls (non-graduates, of course)

were assigned the task of making refreshments for the night's festivities. A tangy scent of ginger, cinnamon, nutmeg, and chocolate wafted around the home economics building as the budding cooks made samples for themselves and their teachers.

16   In every corner of the workshop, axes and saws split fresh timber as the woodshop boys made sets and stage scenery. Only the graduates were left out of the general bustle. We were free to sit in the library at the back of the building or look in quite detachedly, naturally, on the measures being taken for our event.

17   Even the minister preached on graduation the Sunday before. His subject was, "Let your light so shine that men will see your good works and praise your Father, Who is in Heaven." Although the sermon was purported to be addressed to us, he used the occasion to speak to backsliders, gamblers, and general ne'er-do-wells. But since he had called our names at the beginning of the service we were mollified.

18   Among Negroes the tradition was to give presents to children going only from one grade to another. How much more important this was when the person was graduating at the top of the class. Uncle Willie and Momma had sent away for a Mickey Mouse watch like Bailey's. Louise gave me four embroidered handkerchiefs. (I gave her three crocheted doilies.) Mrs. Sneed, the minister's wife, made me an underskirt to wear for graduation, and nearly every customer gave me a nickel or maybe even a dime with the instruction "Keep on moving to higher ground," or some such encouragement.

19   Amazingly the great day finally dawned and I was out of bed before I knew it. I threw open the back door to see it more clearly, but Momma said, "Sister, come away from that door and put your robe on."

20   I hoped the memory of that morning would never leave me. Sunlight was itself still young, and the day had none of the insistence maturity would bring it in a few hours. In my robe and barefoot in the backyard, under cover of going to see about my new beans, I gave myself up to the gentle warmth and thanked God that no matter what evil I had done in my life He had allowed me to live to see this day. Somewhere in my fatalism I had expected to die, accidentally, and never have the chance to walk up the stairs in the auditorium and gracefully receive my hard-earned diploma. Out of God's merciful bosom I had won reprieve.

21   Bailey came out in his robe and gave me a box wrapped in Christmas paper. He said he had saved his money for months to pay for it. It felt like a box of chocolates, but I knew Bailey wouldn't save money to buy candy when we had all we could want under our noses.

22   He was as proud of the gift as I. It was a soft-lather-bound copy of a collection of poems by Edgar Allan Poe, or, as Bailey and I called him, "Eap." I turned to "Annabel Lee" and we walked up and down the garden rows, the cool dirt between our toes, reciting the beautifully sad lines.

23   Momma made a Sunday breakfast although it was only Friday. After we finished the blessing, I opened my eyes to find the watch on my plate. It was a dream of a day. Everything went smoothly and to my credit. I didn't have to be reminded or scolded for anything. Near evening I was too jittery to attend to chores, so Bailey volunteered to do all before his bath.

24 Days before, we had made a sign for the Store and as we turned out the lights Momma hung the cardboard over the doorknob. It read clearly: CLOSED. GRADUATION.

25 My dress fitted perfectly and everyone said that I looked like a sunbeam in it. On the hill, going toward the school, Bailey walked behind with Uncle Willie, who muttered, "Go on, Ju." He wanted him to walk ahead with us because it embarrassed him to have to walk so slowly. Bailey said he'd let the ladies walk together, and the men would bring up the rear. We all laughed, nicely.

26 Little children dashed by out of the dark like fireflies. Their crepepaper dresses and butterfly wings were not made for running and we heard more than one rip, dryly, and the regretful "uh uh" that followed.

27 The school blazed without gaiety. The windows seemed cold and unfriendly from the lower hill. A sense of ill-fated timing crept over me, and if Momma hadn't reached for my hand I would have drifted back to Bailey and Uncle Willie, and possibly beyond. She made a few slow jokes about my feet getting cold, and tugged me along to the now-strange building.

28 Around the front steps, assurance came back. There were my fellow "greats," the graduating class. Hair brushed back, legs oiled, new dresses and pressed pleats, fresh pocket handkerchiefs and little handbags, all homesewn. Oh, we were up to snuff, all right. I joined my comrades and didn't even see my family go in to find seats in the crowded auditorium.

29 The school band struck up a march and all classes filed in as had been rehearsed. We stood in front of our seats, as assigned, and on a signal from the choir director, we sat. No sooner had this been accomplished than the band started to play the national anthem. We rose again and sang the song, after which we recited the pledge of allegiance. We remained standing for a brief minute before the choir director and the principal signaled to us, rather desperately I thought, to take our seats. The command was so unusual that our carefully rehearsed and smooth-running machine was thrown off. For a full minute we fumbled for our chairs and bumped into each other awkwardly. Habits change or solidify under pressure, so in our state of nervous tension we had been ready to follow our usual assembly pattern: the American National Anthem, then the pledge of allegiance, then the song every Black person I knew called the Negro National Anthem. All done in the same key, with the same passion and most often standing on the same foot.

30 Finding my seat at last, I was overcome with a presentiment of worse things to come. Something unrehearsed, unplanned, was going to happen, and we were going to be made to look bad. I distinctly remember being explicit in the choice of pronoun. It was "we," the graduating class, the unit, that concerned me then.

31 The principal welcomed "parents and friends" and asked the Baptist minister to lead us in prayer. His invocation was brief and punchy, and for a second I thought we were getting back on the high road to right action. When the principal came back to the dais, however, his voice had changed. Sounds always affected me profoundly and the principal's voice was one of my favorites. During assembly it melted and lowed weakly into the audience. It had not been in my plan to listen to him, but my curiosity was piqued and I straightened up to give him my attention.

32   He was talking about Booker T. Washington, our "late great leader," who said we can be as close as the fingers on the hand, etc. . . . Then he said a few vague things about friendship and the friendship of kindly people to those less fortunate than themselves. With that his voice nearly faded, thin, away. Like a river diminishing to a stream and then to a trickle. But he cleared his throat and said, "Our speaker tonight, who is also our friend, came from Texarkana to deliver the commencement address, but due to the irregularity of the train schedule, he's going to, as they say, 'speak and run.'" He said that we understood and wanted the man to know that we were most grateful for the time he was able to give us and then something about how we were willing always to adjust to another's program, and without more ado—"I give you Mr. Edward Donleavy."

33   Not one but two white men came through the door offstage. The shorter one walked to the speaker's platform, and the tall one moved over to the center seat and sat down. But that was our principal's seat, and already occupied. The dislodged gentleman bounced around for a long breath or two before the Baptist minister gave him his chair, then with more dignity than the situation deserved, the minister walked off the stage.

34   Donleavy looked at the audience once (on reflection, I'm sure that he wanted only to reassure himself that we were really there), adjusted his glasses, and began to read from a sheaf of papers.

35   He was glad "to be here and to see the work going on just as it was in the other schools."

36   At the first "Amen" from the audience I willed the offender to immediate death by choking on the word. But Amens and Yes, sir's began to fall around the room like rain through a ragged umbrella.

37   He told us of the wonderful changes we children in Stamps had in store. The Central School (naturally, the white school was Central) had already been granted improvements that would be in use in the fall. A well-known artist was coming from Little Rock to teach art to them. They were going to have the newest microscopes and chemistry equipment for their laboratory. Mr. Donleavy didn't leave us long in the dark over who made these improvements available to Central High. Nor were we to be ignored in the general betterment scheme he had in mind.

38   He said that he had pointed out to people at a very high level that one of the first-line football tacklers at Arkansas Agricultural and Mechanical College had graduated from good old Lafayette County Training School. Here fewer Amen's were heard. Those few that did break through lay dully in the air with the heaviness of habit.

39   He went on to praise us. He went on to say how he had bragged that "one of the best basketball players at Fish sank his first ball right here at Lafayette County Training School."

40   The white kids were going to have a chance to become Galileos and Madame Curies and Edisons and Gauguins, and our boys (the girls weren't even in on it) would try to be Jesse Owenses and Joe Louises.

41   Owens and the Brown Bomber were great heroes in our world, but what school official in the white-goddom of Little Rock had the right to decide that

those two men must be our only heroes? Who decided that for Henry Reed to become a scientist he had to work like George Washington Carver, as a boot-black, to buy a lousy microscope? Bailey was obviously always going to be too small to be an athlete, so which concrete angel glued to what county seat had decided that if my brother wanted to become a lawyer he had to first pay penance for his skin by picking cotton and hoeing corn and studying correspondence books at night for twenty years?

42 The man's dead words fell like bricks around the auditorium and too many settled in my belly. Constrained by hard-learned manners I couldn't look behind me, but to my left and right the proud graduating class of 1940 had dropped their heads. Every girl in my row had found something new to do with her handkerchief. Some folded the tiny squares into love knots, some into triangles, but most were wadding them, then pressing them flat on their yellow laps.

43 On the dais, the ancient tragedy was being replayed. Professor Parsons sat, a sculptor's reject, rigid. His large, heavy body seemed devoid of will or willingness, and his eyes said he was no longer with us. The other teachers examined the flag (which was draped stage right) or their notes, or the windows which opened on our now-famous playing diamond.

44 Graduation, the hush-hush magic time of frills and gifts and congratulations and diplomas, was finished for me before my name was called. The accomplishment was nothing. The meticulous maps, drawn in three colors of ink, learning and spelling decasyllabic words, memorizing the whole of *The Rape of Lucrece*—it was nothing. Donleavy had exposed us.

45 We were maids and farmers, handymen and washerwomen, and anything higher that we aspired to was farcical and presumptuous. Then I wished that Gabriel Prosser and Nat Turner had killed all whitefolks in their beds and that Abraham Lincoln had been assassinated before the signing of the Emancipation Proclamation, and that Harriet Tubman had been killed by that blow on her head and Christopher Columbus had drowned in the *Santa Maria*.

46 It was awful to be Negro and have no control over my life. It was brutal to be young and already trained to sit quietly and listen to charges brought against my color with no chance of defense. We should all be dead. I thought I should like to see us all dead, one on top of the other. A pyramid of flesh with the whitefolks on the bottom, as the broad base, then the Indians with their silly tomahawks and teepees and wigwams and treaties, the Negroes with their mops and recipes and cotton sacks and spirituals sticking out of their mouths. The Dutch children should all stumble in their wooden shoes and break their necks. The French should choke to death on the Louisiana Purchase (1803) while silkworms ate all the Chinese with their stupid pigtails. As a species, we were an abomination. All of us.

47 Donleavy was running for election, and assured our parents that if he won we could count on having the only colored paved playing field in that part of Arkansas. Also—he never looked up to acknowledge the grunts of acceptance—also, we were bound to get some new equipment for the home economics building and the workshop.

48   He finished, and since there was no need to give any more than the most perfunctory thank-you's, he nodded to the men on the stage, and the tall white man who
was never introduced joined him at the door. They left with the attitude that now they
were off to something really important. (The graduation ceremonies at Lafayette
County Training School had been a mere preliminary.)

49   The ugliness they left was palpable. An uninvited guest who wouldn't leave. The
choir was summoned and sang a modern arrangement of "Onward, Christian
Soldiers," with new words pertaining to graduates seeking their place in the world.
But it didn't work. Elouise, the daughter of the Baptist minister, recited "Invictus,"
and I could have cried at the impertinence of "I am the master of my fate, I am the
captain of my soul."

50   My name had lost its ring of familiarity and I had to be nudged to go and receive my diploma. All my preparations had fled. I neither marched up to the stage
like a conquering Amazon, nor did I look in the audience for Bailey's nod of
approval. Marguerite Johnson, I heard the name again, my honors were read, there
were noises in the audience of appreciation, and I took my place on the stage as
rehearsed.

51   I thought about colors I hated: ecru, puce, lavender, beige, and black.

52   There was shuffling and rustling around me, then Henry Reed was giving his
valedictory address, "To Be or Not to Be." Hadn't he heard the whitefolks? We
couldn't *be,* so the question was a waste of time. Henry's voice came out clear and
strong. I feared to look at him. Hadn't he got the message? There was no "nobler in
the mind" for Negroes because the world didn't think we had minds, and they let us
know it. "Outrageous fortune"? Now, that was a joke. When the ceremony was over
I had to tell Henry Reed some things. That is, if I still cared. Not "rub," Henry,
"erase." "Ah, there's the erase." Us.

53   Henry had been a good student in elocution. His voice rose on tides of promise
and fell on waves of warnings. The English teacher had helped him to create a sermon winging through Hamlet's soliloquy. To be a man, a doer, a builder, a leader, or
to be a tool, an unfunny joke, a crusher of funky toadstools. I marveled that Henry
could go through with the speech as if we had a choice.

54   I had been listening and silently rebutting each sentence with my eyes closed;
then there was a hush, which in an audience warns that something unplanned is happening. I looked up and saw Henry Reed, the conservative, the proper, the A student,
turn his back to the audience and turn to us (the proud graduating class of 1940) and
sing, nearly speaking.

> *Lift ev'ry voice and sing*
> *Till earth and heaven ring*
> *Ring with the harmonies of Liberty . . .*

It was the poem written by James Weldon Johnson. It was the music composed
by J. Rosamond Johnson. It was the Negro National Anthem. Out of habit we were
singing it.

55   Our mothers and fathers stood in the dark hall and joined the hymn of encouragement. A kindergarten teacher led the small children onto the stage and the buttercups and daisies and bunny rabbits marked time and tried to follow:

> *Stoney the road we trod*
> *Bitter the chastening rod*
> *Felt in the days when hope, unborn, had died.*
> *Yet with a steady beat*
> *Have not our weary feet*
> *Come to the place for which our fathers sighed?*

56   Every child I knew had learned that song with his ABC's and along with "Jesus Loves Me This I Know." But I personally had never heard it before. Never heard the words, despite the thousands of times I had sung them. Never thought they had anything to do with me.

57   On the other hand, the words of Patrick Henry had made such an impression on me that I had been able to stretch myself tall and trembling and say, "I know not what course others may take, but as for me, give me liberty or give me death."

58   And now I heard, really for the first time:

> *We have come over a way that with tears has been watered,*
> *We have come, treading our path through the blood of the slaughtered.*

While echoes of the song shivered in the air, Henry Reed bowed his head, said "Thank you," and returned to his place in the line. The tears that slipped down many faces were not wiped away in shame.

59   We were on top again. As always, again. We survived. The depths had been icy and dark, but now a bright sun spoke to our souls. I was no longer simply a member of the proud graduating class of 1940; I was a proud member of the wonderful, beautiful Negro race.

60   Oh, Black known and unknown poets, how often have your auctioned pains sustained us? Who will compute the lonely nights made less lonely by your songs, or the empty pots made less tragic by your tales?

61   If we were a people much given to revealing secrets, we might raise monuments and sacrifice to the memories of our poets, but slavery cured us of that weakness. It may be enough, however, to have it said that we survive in exact relationship to the dedication of our poets (include preachers, musicians, and blues singers).

■ **TOPICAL CONSIDERATIONS**

1. What signs does Angelou give that reveal graduation to be an important occasion for the children in Stamps? Why do you think it was so important, not only to the children and parents but also to the community?
2. Is there any particular reason why the principal should allude to Booker T. Washington just prior to Mr. Donleavy's speech? How does the audience's

response to his speech reflect the black leader's own feelings about how blacks should act toward white people?

3. Angelou appears to have been particularly sensitive to what was happening during the graduation ceremony. What first prompted her to suspect that something was amiss? How does the atmosphere change as Mr. Donleavy's speech progresses? What specifically does he say to cause the change?

4. What does Angelou resent most about Donleavy's remarks? Are his assumptions about the future aspirations of the Lafayette County Training School graduates justified? What clues do we have about the quality of education at Angelou's school that might suggest otherwise? Note Angelou's frequent historical and literary allusions.

5. The Negro National Anthem was not sung at the usual place in the program. Why does its postponement turn out to be a blessing? What effect does it have on Angelou?

6. If Dick Gregory had been attending Angelou's graduation as an adult, he no doubt would have been singing as loudly as the next person. Why? How might graduation have been different if he had been the guest speaker instead of Mr. Donleavy? What might Gregory have said?

7. How is this graduation a "commencement" for Angelou?

■ RHETORICAL CONSIDERATIONS

1. Look closely at Angelou's first paragraph. What specific word choices does she use to suggest how important graduation is for children and teachers? How do these words contribute to the development of the essay?

2. How would you describe Angelou's point of view? Does she exaggerate the importance of this event? Or do you think her account is fairly accurate? How might the narrative have been different if told by Bailey (Angelou's older brother)? By the minister? By Mr. Donleavy?

3. In paragraph 36, Angelou remarks that "Amens and Yes, sir's began to fall around the room like rain through a ragged umbrella." What does this suggest about the atmosphere in the room during Mr. Donleavy's speech? What other figurative language does Angelou use?

4. Writers strive to make their material interesting by using specific, concrete details. How successful is Angelou in doing this? Cite specific examples to prove your point.

■ WRITING ASSIGNMENTS

1. If Maya Angelou were asked to be a guest speaker at Lafayette County Training School today, what do you think she would say? Write her speech. Imitate her frequent allusions to important historical events and literary works.

2. In an essay, describe the graduation ceremonies at Lafayette County Training School from the minister's point of view, from Bailey's, and from Mr. Donleavy's.

3. Write an essay about your own graduation. Describe how you, your classmates, the school, and the community prepared for the event. Use figurative language and other vivid word pictures to re-create the atmosphere of the graduation hall during the ceremony.

4. Maya Angelou concludes, "It may be enough, however, to have it said that we survive in exact relationship to the dedication of our poets (include preachers, musicians, and blues singers)." Write a research paper in which you compare the influence of black poets (include preachers, musicians, and blues singers) from one earlier period (e.g., the Harlem Renaissance or the Charlie Parker days or the Martin Luther King era) to black poets of the 1990s.

Salvation	
Langston Hughes	

Langston Hughes (1902–1967) was a remarkably prolific and celebrated writer. In addition to his autobiography, *The Big Sea* (1940), Hughes published seventeen books of poetry, two novels, seven short story collections, and twenty-six plays. He also wrote a column for the *New York Post*. Much of his life was devoted to the promotion of black art, music, and history. In the essay below, Hughes looks back to a dramatic event that took place when he was twelve—an event that would forever leave its mark on him. The essay, taken from his autobiography, is a fine example of how a writer's control of language and detail can re-create the point of view of a child.

1   I was saved from sin when I was going on thirteen. But not really saved. It happened like this. There was a big revival at my Auntie Reed's church. Every night for weeks there had been much preaching, singing, praying, and shouting, and some very hardened sinners had been brought to Christ, and the membership of the church had grown by leaps and bounds. Then just before the revival ended, they held a special meeting for children, "to bring the young lambs to the fold." My aunt spoke of it for days ahead. That night I was escorted to the front row and placed on the mourners' bench with all the other young sinners, who had not yet been brought to Jesus.

2   My aunt told me that when you were saved you saw a light, and something happened to you inside! And Jesus came into your life! And God was with you from then on! She said you could see and hear and feel Jesus in your soul. I believed her. I have heard a great many old people say the same thing and it seemed to me they ought to know. So I sat there calmly in the hot, crowded church, waiting for Jesus to come to me.

3   The preacher preached a wonderful rhythmical sermon, all moans and shouts and lonely cries and dire pictures of hell, and then he sang a song about the ninety and nine safe in the fold, but one little lamb was left out in the cold. Then he said: "Won't you come? Won't you come to Jesus? Young lambs, won't you come?" And he held out his arms to all us young sinners there on the mourners' bench. And the little girls cried. And some of them jumped up and went to Jesus right away. But most of us just sat there.

4   A great many old people came and knelt around us and prayed, old women with jet-black faces and braided hair, old men with work-gnarled hands. And the church sang a song about the lower lights are burning, some poor sinners to be saved. And the whole building rocked with prayer and song.

5   Still I kept waiting to *see* Jesus.

6   Finally all the young people had gone to the altar and were saved, but one boy and me. He was a rounder's son named Westley. Westley and I were surrounded by sisters and deacons praying. It was very hot in the church, and getting late now. Finally Westley said to me in a whisper: "God damn! I'm tired o'sitting here. Let's get up and be saved." So he got up and was saved.

7   Then I was left all alone on the mourners' bench. My aunt came and knelt at my knees and cried, while prayers and songs swirled all around me in the little church. The whole congregation prayed for me alone, in a mighty wail of moans and voices. And I kept waiting serenely for Jesus, waiting, waiting—but he didn't come. I wanted to see him, but nothing happened to me. Nothing! I wanted something to happen to me, but nothing happened.

8   I heard the songs and the minister saying: "Why don't you come? My dear child, why don't you come to Jesus? Jesus is waiting for you. He wants you. Why don't you come? Sister Reed, what is this child's name?"

9   "Langston," my aunt sobbed.

10   "Langston, why don't you come? Why don't you come and be saved? Oh, Lamb of God! Why don't you come?"

11   Now it was really getting late. I began to be ashamed of myself, holding everything up so long. I began to wonder what God thought about Westley, who certainly hadn't seen Jesus either, but who was now sitting proudly on the platform, swinging his knickerbockered legs and grinning down at me, surrounded by deacons and old women on their knees praying. God had not struck Westley dead for taking his name in vain or for lying in the temple. So I decided that maybe to save further trouble, I'd better lie, too, and say that Jesus had come, and get up and be saved.

12   So I got up.

13   Suddenly the whole room broke into a sea of shouting, as they saw me rise. Waves of rejoicing swept the place. Women leaped in the air. My aunt threw her arms around me. The minister took me by the hand and led me to the platform.

14   When things quieted down, in a hushed silence, punctuated by a few ecstatic "Amens," all the new young lambs were blessed in the name of God. Then joyous singing filled the room.

15   That night, for the last time in my life but one—for I was a big boy twelve years old—I cried. I cried, in bed alone, and couldn't stop. I buried my head under the

quilts, but my aunt heard me. She woke up and told my uncle I was crying because the Holy Ghost had come into my life, and because I had seen Jesus. But I was really crying because I couldn't bear to tell her that I had lied, that I had deceived everybody in the church, that I hadn't seen Jesus, and that now I didn't believe there was a Jesus any more, since he didn't come to help me.

■ TOPICAL CONSIDERATIONS

1. Why does Hughes say in the first sentence that he was "saved from sin" then, in the second sentence, "But not really saved"?
2. Young Hughes does not get up until the very end. What finally moves him to rise up and be saved? How do his motives compare or contrast with those of Westley's?
3. What reasons does Hughes offer for his crying at the end? How does it compare with his aunt's explanation? What has young Hughes learned from his experience?
4. If you were Hughes's aunt or uncle and were aware of his plight, how might you have comforted young Langston? What words of consolation or explanation would you have offered him?
5. How does Hughes's experience underscore the problems inherent in some people's expectations of religion?

■ RHETORICAL CONSIDERATIONS

1. Hughes chose to re-create the scene of his actual "salvation" like a short story, rather than simply tell what happened in an expository format. Why do you think he chose this format? How effective do you think his efforts were to recapture the episode?
2. Comment on how effective Hughes was in re-creating the scene in the church. Consider his use of descriptive details.
3. Hughes recalls the story of his "salvation" as an adult. How does Hughes's language help create a 12-year-old's point of view? Find passages where the adult author's attitude toward the experience comes through. How would you describe that attitude?

■ WRITING ASSIGNMENTS

1. Have you ever had a religious experience? If so, try to describe the circumstances and the experience as best you can.
2. Have you ever been compelled by group pressure to do something you didn't believe in? If so, describe the experience.

3. Write a paper in which you explore your own religious beliefs. Do you believe in a supreme being and find evidence of such in the natural world? Do you not believe in a supreme being? In either case, state the reasons behind your stand.

The Eye of the Beholder
Grace Suh

The notion that cosmetics enhance one's appearances is prone to exaggeration. For example, it is said that a touch of lipstick can transform plain to pretty or a blush of rouge make the ordinary lovely. In this piece Grace Suh describes her visit to a makeup counter in search of the transformation promised by the "priestesses of beauty." But after the careful and comprehensive application of ointments, blush, and gloss, the face that greeted Ms. Suh in the mirror was one she neither recognized nor liked. The adage that "beauty lies in the eye of the beholder" resonated with new meaning for her.

Grace Elaine Suh was born in Seoul, Korea, and reared in Wisconsin and Chicago. She lives in New York City and works in academic publishing by day and as a poetry editor of the *Asian Pacific American Journal* by night.

1 Several summers ago, on one of those endless August evenings when the sun hangs suspended just above the horizon, I made up my mind to become beautiful.

2 It happened as I walked by one of those mirrored glass-clad office towers, and caught a glimpse of my reflection out of the corner of my eye. The glass on this particular building was green, which might have accounted for the sickly tone of my complexion, but there was no explaining away the limp, ragged hair, the dark circles under my eyes, the facial blemishes, the shapeless, wrinkled clothes. The overall effect—the whole being greater than the sum of its parts—was one of stark ugliness.

3 I'd come home from college having renounced bourgeois suburban values, like hygiene and grooming. Now, home for the summer, I washed my hair and changed clothes only when I felt like it, and spent most of my time sitting on the lawn eating mini rice cakes and Snickers and reading dogeared back issues of *National Geographic.*

4 But that painfully epiphanous day, standing there on the hot sidewalk, I suddenly understood what my mother had been gently hinting these past months: I was no longer just plain, no longer merely unattractive. No, I had broken the Unsightliness Barrier. I was now UGLY, and aggressively so.

5 And so, in an unusual exertion of will, I resolved to fight back against the forces of entropy. I envisioned it as reclamation work, like scything down a lawn that has grown into meadow, or restoring a damaged fresco. For the first time in ages, I felt elated and hopeful. I nearly sprinted into the nearby Nieman Marcus. As I entered the cool, hushed,

dimly lit first floor and saw the gleaming counters lined with vials of magical balm, the priestesses of beauty in their sacred smocks, and the glossy photographic icons of the goddesses themselves—Paulina, Linda, Cindy, Vendella—in a wild, reckless burst of inspiration I thought to myself, Heck, why just okay? Why not BEAUTIFUL?

6   At the Estée Lauder counter, I spied a polished, middle-aged woman whom I hoped might be less imperious than the aloof amazons at the Chanel counter.

7   "Could I help you?" the woman (I thought of her as "Estée") asked.

8   "Yes," I blurted. "I look terrible. I need a complete makeover—skin, face, everything."

9   After a wordless scrutiny of my face, she motioned me to sit down and began. She cleansed my skin with a bright blue mud masque and clear, tingling astringent and then applied a film of moisturizer, working extra amounts into the rough patches. Under the soft pressure of her fingers, I began to relax. From my perch, I happily took in the dizzying, colorful swirl of beautiful women and products all around me. I breathed in the billows of perfume that wafted through the air. I whispered the names of products under my breath like a healing mantra: cooling eye gel, gentle exfoliant, night time neck area reenergizer, moisture recharging intensifier, ultra-hydrating complex, emulsifying immunage. I felt immersed in femininity, intoxicated by beauty.

10   I was flooded with gratitude at the patience and determination with which Estée toiled away at my face, painting on swaths of lip gloss, blush, and foundation. She was not working in vain, I vowed, as I sucked in my cheeks on her command. I would buy all these products. I would use them every day. I studied her gleaming, polished features—her lacquered nails, the glittering mosaic of her eyeshadow, the complex red shimmer of her mouth, her flawless, dewy skin—and tried to imagine myself as impeccably groomed as she.

11   Estée's voice interrupted my reverie, telling me to blot my lips. I stuck the tissue into my mouth and clamped down, watching myself in the mirror. My skin was a blankly even shade of pale, my cheeks and lips glaringly bright in contrast. My face had a strange plastic sheen, like a mannequin's. I grimaced as Estée applied the second lipstick coat: Was this right? Didn't I look kind of—fake? But she smiled back at me, clearly pleased with her work. I was ashamed of myself: Well, what did I expect? It wasn't like she had anything great to start with.

12   "Now," she announced, "Time for the biggie—Eyes."

13   "Oh. Well, actually, I want to look good and everything, but, I mean, I'm sure you could tell, I'm not really into a complicated beauty routine . . . " My voice faded into a faint giggle.

14   "So?" Estée snapped.

15   "Sooo . . . " I tried again, "I've never really used eye makeup, except, you know, for a little mascara sometimes, and I don't really feel comfortable—"

16   Estée was firm. "Well, the fact is that the eyes are the windows of the face. They're the focal point. An eye routine doesn't have to be complicated, but it's important to emphasize the eyes with some color, or they'll look washed out."

17   I certainly didn't want that. I leaned back again in my chair and closed my eyes.

18 Estée explained as she went: "I'm covering your lids with this champagne color. It's a real versatile base, 'cause it goes with almost any other color you put on top of it." I felt the velvety pad of the applicator sweep over my lids in a soothing rhythm.

19 "Now, being an Oriental, you don't have a lid fold, so I'm going to draw one with this charcoal shadow. Then, I fill in below the line with a lighter charcoal color with a bit of blue in it—frosted midnight—and then above it, on the outsides of your lids, I'm going to apply this plum color. There. Hold on a minute . . . Okay. Open up."

20 I stared at the face in the mirror, at my eyes. The drawn-on fold and dark, heavy shadows distorted and reproportioned my whole face. Not one of the features in the mirror was recognizable, not the waxy white skin or the redrawn crimson lips or the sharp, deep cheekbones, and especially, not the eyes. I felt negated; I had been blotted out and another face drawn in my place. I looked up at Estée, and in that moment I hated her. "I look terrible," I said.

21 Her back stiffened. "What do you mean?" she demanded.

22 "Hideous. I don't even look human. Look at my eyes. You can't even see me!" My voice was hoarse.

23 She looked. After a moment, she straightened up again, "Well, I'll admit, the eye shadow doesn't look great." She began to put away the pencils and brushes, "But at least now you have an eyelid."

24 I told myself that she was a pathetic, middle-aged woman with a boring job and a meaningless life. I had my whole life before me. All she had was the newest Richard Chamberlain miniseries.

25 But it didn't matter. The fact of the matter was that she was pretty, and I was not. Her blue eyes were recessed in an intricate pattern of folds and hollows. Mine bulged out.

26 I bought the skincare system and the foundation and the blush and the lip liner pencil and the lipstick and the primer and the eyeliner and the eyeshadows—all four colors. The stuff filled a bag the size of a shoebox. It cost a lot. Estée handed me my receipt with a flourish, and I told her, "Thank you."

27 In the mezzanine level washroom, I set my bag down on the counter and scrubbed my face with water and slimy pink soap from the dispenser. I splashed my face with cold water until it felt tight, and dried my raw skin with brown paper towels that scratched.

28 As the sun sank into the Chicago skyline, I boarded the Burlington Northern Commuter for home and found a seat in the corner. I set the shopping bag down beside me, and heaped its gilt boxes and frosted glass bottles into my lap. Looking out the window, I saw that night had fallen. Instead of trees and backyard fences I saw my profile—the same reflection, I realized, that I'd seen hours ago in the side of the green glass office building. I did have eyelids, of course. Just not a fold. I wasn't pretty. But I was familiar and comforting. I was myself.

29 The next stop was mine. I arranged the things carefully back in the rectangular bag, large bottles of toner and moisturizer first, then the short cylinders of masque and scrub and powder, small bottles of foundation and primer, the little logs of pencils and lipstick, then the flat boxed compacts of blush and eyeshadow. The packages fit around each other cleverly, like pieces in a puzzle. The conductor called out, "Fairview

Avenue," and I stood up. Hurrying down the aisle, I looked back once at the neatly packed bag on the seat behind me, and jumped out just as the doors were closing shut.

■ TOPICAL CONSIDERATIONS

1. In one sentence, summarize what you think is the theme of Suh's essay.
2. What experience made Suh decide to become "beautiful"? In this decision, what image of herself was she giving up? How does she envision becoming beautiful? Can you identify with her experience here? Have you ever decided to remake your image? If so, explain your motives and what you aspired to.
3. Why does Suh trust the middle-aged woman from the Estée Lauder counter? What goes through her imagination as she undergoes the beauty treatment? Can you relate to her experience in the beauty chair?
4. Explain Suh's reaction when she looks at her made-up face in the mirror? How does the Estée Lauder beautician react? What negative conclusion does Suh draw about her own looks? Have you ever had a similar experience at a cosmetics counter or hair salon?
5. Toward the end of the makeover, the beautician applies makeup to Suh's eyelids to make them appear more Western. What words does the beautician use that insult Suh's sense of self and cultural identity? How does Suh respond? Do you think Suh gets her revenge? What would you have done?
6. Explain Suh's action upon leaving the salon with her makeup kit? What does Suh finally realize about herself? How is the ending a sign of her transformation?
7. Consider Maya Angelou's "Graduation" and the indifferent white official who makes her and her community feel unrecognized and undervalued. Where in her essay does Suh explore a similar theme? In the end, what does Suh do to recapture her sense of self-worth? What does Angelou's community do to express their pride?

■ RHETORICAL CONSIDERATIONS

1. Consider the appropriateness of the title of Suh's essay. Do you recognize the allusion? Can you explain its meaning? How does the title forecast the issues Suh addresses in the essay?
2. How would you describe the author's voice in the essay? What does this voice reveal about the author as a person? Find a paragraph that demonstrates the tone of her voice. How well does such a tone add to the persuasiveness of the author's argument?
3. Suh uses striking, vivid language in this essay. What particular words and phrases capture her views of her own appearance? Her views of the beautician? What might be the strategy in using such strong visual language? Was it effective for you?
4. Without using the word "racist" Suh portrays someone who has had a limited experience with people of other races and cultures. Find specific pas-

sages where Suh captures the counter-worker's prejudices. Are these convincing to you? Do they work well to enhance the essay's messages? Explain.

5. Find examples of irony in the essay.

■ WRITING ASSIGNMENTS

1. How do you feel about your looks? Are you satisfied? What, if any, changes have you made? What, if any, changes would you make? Explain your answers. Do you feel social pressure to look any particular way?

2. Powerlessness is a universal theme when someone else takes charge, however briefly, of our bodies or appearance. Both men and women have felt it strongly, even if they are members of the dominant culture. Explore your own feelings of powerlessness when you've had to undergo a physical examination, a hair cut, physical conditioning, and so on. What messages about your culture, your body, or your appearance was the person in charge conveying to you? In an essay, explore this theme using Suh's techniques of description and dialog.

3. In her essay "The Beauty Myth" (Chapter 6), Naomi Wolf writes (page 241) "The beauty myth tells a story: The quality called 'beauty' objectively and universally exists. Women must want to embody it and men must want to possess women who embody it." Do you think Grace Suh would agree with this definition? Grace Suh does not mention men's views of beauty in her essay, but Naomi Wolf does. What statement about beauty and culture is Suh making by focusing on women's views of beauty instead of men's? Explain your answers in an essay.

4. More Asian writers are exploring themes of identity in poetry, non-fiction, and fiction. Research the writing of David Mura, a Japanese American who wrote *Turning Japanese: Memoirs of a Sansei,* a collection of essays in which he comes to grips with both his American and his Japanese identities. In an essay, explore these questions: What does Mura say about the expectations Americans have of him as a Japanese-American? When he visits Japan, what do the Japanese expect of him as an American?

The Ambivalence of Abortion

Linda Bird Francke

Abortion is one of the most controversial issues in our society. At the heart of all the moral, political, legal, and religious debates is the very definition of life itself. Does it begin at conception, or not? Does a fetus have human status and rights, or not? Science and the courts have not yet resolved these questions, and the issue is further complicated by the demands for a woman's right not to give birth to unwanted children. The author of the piece below powerfully dramatizes this fundamental conflict—a conflict between heart and mind. Francke tells how her strong prochoice convictions suddenly came into question with her own conscience, when faced with her own unwanted pregnancy. Francke, who is a journalist and biographer, collaborated with Rosalynn Carter on *First Lady from Plains* (1984) and with Geraldine Ferraro on her autobiography, *Ferraro* (1986). Her latest collaboration is a work on Madame Jihan Sidat. Francke is also the author of *Growing up Divorced: Children of the Eighties* (1983). This article first appeared in *The New York Times* in 1976.

1   We were sitting in a bar on Lexington Avenue when I told my husband I was pregnant. It is not a memory I like to dwell on. Instead of the champagne and hope which had heralded the impending births of the first, second and third child, the news of this one was greeted with shocked silence and Scotch. "Jesus," my husband kept saying to himself, stirring the ice cubes around and around, "Oh, Jesus."

2   Oh, how we tried to rationalize it that night as the starting time for the movie came and went. My husband talked about his plans for a career change in the next year, to stem the staleness that fourteen years with the same investment-banking firm had brought him. A new baby would preclude that option.

3   The timing wasn't right for me either. Having juggled pregnancies and child care with what freelance jobs I could fit in between feedings, I had just taken on a full-time job. A new baby would put me right back in the nursery just when our youngest child was finally school age. It was time for *us,* we tried to rationalize. There just wasn't room in our lives now for another baby. We both agreed. And agreed. And agreed.

4   How very considerate they are at the Women's Services, known formally as the Center for Reproductive and Sexual Health. Yes, indeed, I could have an abortion that very Saturday morning and be out in time to drive to the country that afternoon. Bring a first morning urine specimen, a sanitary belt and napkins, a money order or $125 cash—and a friend.

5   My friend turned out to be my husband, standing awkwardly and ill at ease as men always do in places that are exclusively for women, as I checked in at nine A.M. Other men hovered around just as anxiously, knowing they had to be there, wishing they weren't. No one spoke to each other. When I would be cycled out of there four hours later, the same men would be slumped in their same seats, locked downcast in their cells of embarrassment.

6   The Saturday morning women's group was more dispirited than the men in the waiting room. There were around fifteen of us, a mixture of races, ages and backgrounds. Three didn't speak English at all and a fourth, a pregnant Puerto Rican girl around eighteen, translated for them.

7   There were six black women and a hodgepodge of whites, among them a T-shirted teenager who kept leaving the room to throw up and a puzzled middle-aged woman from Queens with three grown children.

8   "What form of birth control were you using?" the volunteer asked each one of us. The answer was inevitably "none." She then went on to describe the various forms of birth control available at the clinic, and offered them to each of us.

9   The youngest Puerto Rican girl was asked through the interpreter which she'd like to use: the loop, diaphragm, or pill. She shook her head "no" three times. "You don't want to come back here again, do you?" the volunteer pressed. The girl's head was so low her chin rested on her breastbone. "*Sí,*" she whispered.

10   We had been there two hours by that time, filling out endless forms, giving blood and urine, receiving lectures. But unlike any other group of women I've been in, we didn't talk. Our common denominator, the one which usually floods across language and economic barriers into familiarity, today was one of shame. We were losing life that day, not giving it.

11   The group kept getting cut back to smaller, more workable units, and finally I was put in a small waiting room with just two other women. We changed into paper bathrobes and paper slippers, and we rustled whenever we moved. One of the women in my room was shivering and an aide brought her a blanket.

12   "What's the matter?" the aide asked her. "I'm scared," the woman said. "How much will it hurt?" The aide smiled. "Oh, nothing worse than a couple of bad cramps," she said. "This afternoon you'll be dancing a jig."

13   I began to panic. Suddenly the rhetoric, the abortion marches I'd walked in, the telegrams sent to Albany to counteract the Friends of the Fetus, the Zero Population Growth buttons I'd worn, peeled away, and I was all alone with my microscopic baby. There were just the two of us there, and soon, because it was more convenient for me and my husband, there would be one again.

14   How could it be that I, who am so neurotic about life that I step over bugs rather than on them, who spend hours planting flowers and vegetables in the spring even though we rent out the house and never see them, who make sure the children are vaccinated and inoculated and filled with vitamin C, could so arbitrarily decide that this life shouldn't be?

15   "It's not a life," my husband had argued, more to convince himself than me. "It's a bunch of cells smaller than my fingernail."

16   But any woman who has had children knows that certain feeling in her taut, swollen breasts, and the slight but constant ache in her uterus that signals the arrival of a life. Though I would march myself into blisters for a woman's right to exercise the option of motherhood, I discovered there in the waiting room that I was not the modern woman I thought I was.

17   When my name was called, my body felt so heavy the nurse had to help me into the examining room. I waited for my husband to burst through the door and yell "stop," but of course he didn't. I concentrated on three black spots in the acoustic ceiling until they grew in size to the shape of saucers, while the doctor swabbed my insides with antiseptic.

18   "You're going to feel a burning sensation now," he said, injecting Novocain into the neck of the womb. The pain was swift and severe, and I twisted to get away from him. He was hurting my baby, I reasoned, and the black saucers quivered in the air. "Stop," I cried. "Please stop." He shook his head, busy with his equipment. "It's too late to stop now," he said. "It'll just take a few more seconds."

19   What good sports we women are. And how obedient. Physically the pain passed even before the hum of the machine signaled that the vacuuming of my uterus was completed, my baby sucked up like ashes after a cocktail party. Ten minutes start to finish. And I was back on the arm of the nurse.

20   There were twelve beds in the recovery room. Each one had a gaily flowered draw sheet and a soft green or blue thermal blanket. It was all very feminine. Lying on these beds for an hour or more were the shocked victims of their sex, their full wombs now stripped clean, their futures less encumbered.

21   It was very quiet in that room. The only voice was that of the nurse, locating the new women who had just come in so she could monitor their blood pressure, and checking out the recovered women who were free to leave.

22   Juice was being passed about, and I found myself sipping a Dixie cup of Hawaiian Punch. An older woman with tightly curled bleached hair was just getting up from the next bed. "That was no goddamn snap," she said, resting before putting on her miniskirt and high white boots. Other women came and went, some walking out as dazed as they had entered, others with a bounce that signaled they were going right back to Bloomingdale's.

23   Finally then, it was time for me to leave. I checked out, making an appointment to return in two weeks for an IUD insertion. My husband was slumped in the waiting room, clutching a single yellow rose wrapped in a wet paper towel and stuffed into a Baggie.

24   We didn't talk the whole way home, but just held hands very tightly. At home there were more yellow roses and a tray in bed for me and the children's curiosity to divert.

25   It had certainly been a successful operation. I didn't bleed at all for two days just as they had predicted, and then I bled only moderately for another four days. Within a week my breasts had subsided and the tenderness vanished, and my body felt mine again instead of the eggshell it becomes when it's protecting someone else.

26   My husband and I are back to planning our summer vacation and his career switch.

27   And it certainly does make more sense not to be having a baby right now—we say that to each other all the time. But I have this ghost now. A very little ghost that only appears when I'm seeing something beautiful, like the full moon on the ocean last weekend. And the baby waves at me. And I wave at the baby. "Of course, we have room," I cry to the ghost. "Of course, we do."

■ TOPICAL CONSIDERATIONS

1. What are the reasons the author and her husband do not want another child?
2. How does Francke describe the state of the men in the waiting room of the abortion clinic? What feelings do they seem to share?
3. According to Francke, what "common denominator" links the women at the clinic?
4. In paragraph 13, Francke says she suddenly panicked. Why did she?
5. What had been Francke's political stand on the abortion issue before her visit to the clinic? Do you think she has had a change of heart since? Explain your reasons for your answer.
6. In paragraph 16, Francke admits that she "was not the modern woman" she had thought she was. What does she mean by this statement? Why the term "modern woman"?
7. In paragraph 17, Francke says that she waited for her husband to burst through the door of the operating room and yell "stop." What does this say about what was going on in Francke's mind? What does it say about her own strength of will? Do you think this is another confession that she is not the "modern woman" she thought she was but, rather, one who hopes to be rescued from a bad situation by a man? Or is this a momentary fantasy that goes beyond sex roles?
8. Francke says that the physical pain of the operation was "swift and severe." But the mental pain, though also severe, is not so swift in passing. What evidence is there in the essay that Francke's mental anguish persisted after the operation?

■ RHETORICAL CONSIDERATIONS

1. What does *ambivalence* mean? How does the author demonstrate ambivalence in the first paragraph? Where in the essay does she actually discuss her ambivalence rather than simply dramatize it?
2. Explain the rhetorical effect of the repetition in paragraph 3: "We both agreed. And agreed. And agreed." Where else do you find such repetition? Explain its effect, too.
3. This is a highly emotional and moving essay. Does the author convey her emotional trauma by becoming overly emotional or sentimental in the piece? If you think so, cite examples. If you think not, how does she avoid being sentimental?
4. What is the effect of telling us that the Women's Services is formally known as the Center for Reproductive and Sexual Health? What does the name difference suggest about the clinic's self-perception? About the clinic's relationship to the community?
5. Discuss the matter-of-fact tone of paragraph 4. How is Francke's own emotional anxiety sustained by the seemingly neutral tone? Is her tone ironic? Explain your answers.

6. Francke says that the women at the abortion clinic were a mixture of ages, races, and social strata. How would you describe Francke's attitude toward these other women? What is her feeling toward the youngest girl?

7. At the end of paragraph 12, the aide with a smile tells one scared woman, "This afternoon you'll be dancing a jig." What is the effect of the observation of the aide's manner and words? How does it contrast with what is going on inside the author?

8. Discuss the effect of the first two lines of paragraph 19: "What good sports we women are. And how obedient."

9. Why would Francke mention the seemingly minor detail of her husband "clutching a single yellow rose wrapped in a wet paper towel and stuffed into a Baggie" (paragraph 23)? Does this detail have a higher, symbolic function in the essay?

10. Throughout the essay, Francke writes in the past tense. Why did she switch to the present tense in the last two paragraphs? To what effect?

■ WRITING ASSIGNMENTS

1. Abortion is one of our society's most controversial issues, because what is being debated hinges on the definition of life itself—whether life begins at conception or at birth. Write an essay stating your own feelings about when life begins and about the abortion issue. In your essay, also discuss whether modern science has helped or complicated the problem of determining when life occurs.

2. Write a political speech defending a woman's right to have a legal abortion.

3. Write a political speech against the legalization of abortion.

4. Linda Bird Francke's essay is about her ambivalence on a particularly sensitive social issue. Write a paper in which you face your own ambivalence about some social issue. Like Francke, consider both sides and explain your ambivalence. You might want to consider some of the other social issues talked about in this book—capital punishment, legalization of drugs, gun control, and so on.

5. None of the women at Francke's abortion clinic had used any birth control measures. Write an essay in which you argue for or against compulsory sex education programs in elementary schools. In your essay, be sure to state your stand clearly and give your reasons behind it.

6. Francke's essay is a powerful piece, not just because the issue is highly controversial but because she was caught up in an emotional tug-of-war between strong political convictions and an intense personal experience. If you have ever been caught up in such a conflict between ideals and real experience, write a first-person account describing it, and explore any ambivalence or change of heart you might have experienced as a result. (If you have been a victim of a crime, for example, you might want to consider your attitudes toward criminals and punishment before and after the event.)

Why I Quit Practicing Law

Sam Benson

We often view our professions as a means to cultivate our skills, to achieve personal fulfillment and, possibly, to contribute to the greater good of society. In this essay, Sam Benson, who was a practicing attorney, explains he why quit the practice: He reached a point where he no longer found ethical or moral underpinnings in the legal profession. It had become so adversarial that justice lost its significance. Benson is currently writing a book about why he quit the law. This piece first appeared in *Newsweek* in November 1991.

1   One day two summers ago I sat and looked out the window of my office at the fancy landscaping and the immaculately kept brick driveway and I suddenly knew I was going to quit my job. The next morning I told one of the firm's partners, an old friend, that I did not want to practice law anymore. I will never forget the overwhelming sense of relief I felt as soon as the words were out. Now, many months later, I am astounded that I was able to practice law for more than two years of my life. It was not any single event that pushed me over the edge. It was an uneasiness, an uncomfortableness that was always there for me. I was tired of the deceit. I was tired of the chicanery. But most of all, I was tired of the misery my job caused other people.

2   In the United States, we have what is known as an adversarial system of law. This means that attorneys in private practice are hired to oppose somebody or some entity with all the power and vigor that the system gives them. The code of ethics states that an attorney must zealously represent his or her client. This is where the concept of the attorney as a "hired gun" originates. In practice this creates a warlike atmosphere for attorneys in which they are pressured by clients to win at any cost and by any means available. And, as we found out during Desert Storm, truth is often the first casualty of war.

3   In this warlike setting, cooperation is often seen as a sign of weakness. Many attorneys believe that "zealously representing their clients" means pushing all rules of ethics and decency to the limit. The sad thing is, they may be right. A nice guy does not usually make a good attorney in the adversarial system.

4   The old warring axiom that "the best defense is a good offense" is usually the battle cry for zealous lawyers. An attorney launches his or her offense by using "discovery" as a weapon. During litigation, both sides are allowed to "discover" as much as they can about the other side's case prior to trial. This is done with oral depositions (transcribed testimony in a formal setting), detailed interrogatories (written questions) and requests for documents and other records calculated to lead to relevant evidence. While this all sounds fine and dandy, in reality the discovery process is often used to intimidate, harass and cost an opponent time and attorneys' fees in addition to finding facts. In many cases, the winner is the last party still financially able to pay the attorney.

5   Justice is an insignificant concept in today's legal system. Attorneys who specialize in civil litigation—the personal-injury cases, contract disputes, malpractice cases etc. that are the bread and butter of most practices—are simply more interested in winning cases than solving disputes by finding a fair solution. When people pay an attorney $250 an hour they do not want compromise: they want their attorney to do battle with all guns blazing. The theory is that with the two sides battling it out tooth and nail, the deserving party will prevail. The reality is that the side that strikes hardest and fastest is often likely to prevail regardless of the relative merits of their cases.

6   This makes most lawsuits entirely passionless adventures, undertaken with little or no conviction or principles. To be successful you either have to make winning an imperative with a life of its own, or you learn to rationalize by ignoring the detrimental facts of your case while accentuating the helpful ones until you begin to believe your own position. By using the adversarial system, we have created a profession in this country that by its very nature encourages being disagreeable, pushy and sometimes even dishonest to be successful. Then we turn around and hate attorneys for being disagreeable, pushy and dishonest.

7   *Cutting Corners:*   There are attorneys who do their best to balance these inherent conflicts without sacrificing their integrity. My point is that the adversarial system makes it inherently difficult to do so. Those who act ethically often put themselves at a competitive disadvantage. Obviously, this is a very difficult situation to explain to a frustrated client.

8   It is not hard to imagine in this atmosphere how easy it is for attorneys to start cutting corners. In fact, it has been suggested by at least one legal scholar that lying and deception in the legal profession are serious and pervasive problems. "For years we have 'winked, blinked, and nodded' at blatant if not outrageous lying and deception in pleading, negotiating, investigating, testifying, and bargaining. In almost every aspect of our professional practice we have come to accept, in fact to expect, a certain amount of lying and deception . . . ," wrote Richard K. Burke, professor of law at the University of Arkansas at Little Rock, in a 1984 law-review article. "Not only our code of ethics, but also many of our rules of evidence and procedure frustrate and inhibit truthtelling and truthfinding and are largely responsible for the wholesale public condemnation that plagues us."

9   At the present time, I know that there are assaults on these problems such as revisions in the code of ethics and the use of mediation and arbitration to settle disputes outside the courtroom. I am simply stating my perception that there are some built-in conflicts in the "adversarial system" that are going to make real reform very difficult. As long as we have an adversarial system we must expect attorneys to in fact be adversarial and zealously represent their clients. However, attorneys cannot expect the public to love them while they are acting in that role. If the legal profession wants to change its image, it needs to get serious about solving problems rather than justifying, exacerbating and inflaming problems just to win a case. To do this would involve a total overhaul of the legal system, not just a new paint job. I doubt that this is likely to occur anytime soon.

■ TOPICAL CONSIDERATIONS

1. What reason does the author give for leaving his law practice? Were you surprised by Benson's relief when he decided to leave a well-paying, highly respected profession? Can you think of other respected professions that are losing their popularity? If so, what reasons can you offer for the decline? Any that overlap with Benson's?

2. What is the "adversarial system of law"? Are you familiar with legal systems in other countries? If so, do you think any other system works better than that in the United States? Explain your answer.

3. What is Benson's critique of our justice system? In paragraph 5, specifically, what does he mean by the claim that "justice is an insignificant concept in today's legal system"?

4. Benson says that there are some very clear consequences for lawyers who strive to maintain their integrity. What are these consequences? Do you see similar conflicts in other professions?

5. In paragraph 8, Benson quotes law professor Richard K. Burke: "Not only our code of ethics, but also many of our rules of evidence and procedure frustrate and inhibit truthtelling and truthfinding and are largely responsible for the wholesale public condemnation that plagues us." What does Burke mean here? From your experience, does his claim about "public condemnation" ring true?

6. What is Benson's conclusion? Is he optimistic or pessimistic? After reading this essay, would you consider the legal profession?

■ RHETORICAL CONSIDERATIONS

1. Consider Benson's first paragraph. What word choices reveal his attitude about the legal profession?

2. Benson uses figurative language in many places to emphasize his points. Cite a few examples and explain Benson's intention behind them.

3. How would you describe the author's tone in his essay?

4. This essay is a highly reasoned explanation of why the author decided to leave the legal profession. Do you think his argument is well structured? Did you find it convincing? Explain your answers.

■ WRITING ASSIGNMENTS

1. Did you ever undertake a course of study or a project that you had to abandon because of ethical or moral reservations? If so, explore your experience in an essay.

2. Write an essay in which you defend the adversarial style of justice.

3. Using your library and, if possible, personal experience abroad, write a defense of another judicial system—say, that in Great Britain, Europe, or else-

where. Be sure to specify the features that distinguish it from our own adversarial system.

4. Research other critiques of the American justice system and compare them to Benson's in an essay. For example, Sister Helen Prejean's book, *Dead Man Walking,* details some hazards of our system particularly regarding the death penalty. What is Prejean's critique of the American justice system? Do you think she would agree with Benson?

A Clack of Tiny Sparks: Remembrance of a Gay Boyhood

Bernard Cooper

Discovery is the essence of adolescence. And discovery of one's sexual identity is a major task of that age. But what happens when a young man is on the brink of discovering that he is gay? On the brink of acknowledging a homosexual identity that the larger culture devalues, denies, and often even denigrates? In this personal memoir of his high-school years, Bernard Cooper captures his inexplicable attraction to an amicable and handsome male classmate, Grady. And he writes of the fear and confusion he feels trying to reconcile these feelings amidst a high-school culture that ritualizes make-out parties and decries "fags."

Cooper has been a creative writing instructor at the Otis/Parsons Institute of Art and Design and at Southern California Institute of Architecture both in Los Angeles. A collection of essays, *Maps to Anywhere,* was published in 1990; and his first novel *A Year of Rhymes* appeared in 1993. This piece was first published in *Harper's* in January 1991.

1 Theresa Sanchez sat behind me in ninth-grade algebra. When Mr. Hubbley faced the blackboard, I'd turn around to see what she was reading; each week a new book was wedged inside her copy of *Today's Equations.* The deception worked; from Mr. Hubbley's point of view, Theresa was engrossed in the value of $X,$ but I knew otherwise. One week she perused *The Wisdom of the Orient,* and I could tell from Theresa's contemplative expression that the book contained exotic thoughts, guidelines handed down from high. Another week it was a paperback novel whose title, *Let Me Live My Life,* appeared in bold print atop every page, and whose cover, a gauzy photograph of a woman biting a strand of pearls, head thrown back in an attitude of ecstasy, confirmed my suspicion that Theresa Sanchez was mature beyond her years. She was the tallest girl in school. Her bouffant hairdo, streaked with blond, was higher than the flaccid bouffants of other girls. Her smooth skin, plucked eyebrows, and painted fingernails suggested hours of pampering, a worldly and sensual vanity that placed her within the domain of adults. Smiling dimly, steeped in daydreams, Theresa moved through the crowded halls with a languid, self-satisfied indifference to those around her. "You are merely children," her posture seemed to

say. "I can't be bothered." The week Theresa hid *101 Ways to Cook Hamburger* behind her algebra book, I could stand it no longer and, after the bell rang, ventured a question.

2   "Because I'm having a dinner party," said Theresa. "Just a couple of intimate friends."

3   No fourteen-year-old I knew had ever given a dinner party, let alone used the word "intimate" in conversation. "Don't you have a mother?" I asked.

4   Theresa sighed a weary sigh, suffered my strange inquiry. "Don't be so naive," she said. "Everyone has a mother." She waved her hand to indicate the brick school buildings outside the window. "A higher education should have taught you that." Theresa draped an angora sweater over her shoulders, scooped her books from the graffiti-covered desk, and just as she was about to walk away, she turned and asked me, "Are you a fag?"

5   There wasn't the slightest hint of rancor or condescension in her voice. The tone was direct, casual. Still I was stunned, giving a sidelong glance to make sure no one had heard. "No," I said. Blurted really, with too much defensiveness, too much transparent fear in my response. Octaves lower than usual, I tried a "Why?"

6   Theresa shrugged. "Oh, I don't know. I have lots of friends who are fags. You remind me of them." Seeing me bristle, Theresa added, "It was just a guess." I watched her erect, angora back as she sauntered out the classroom door.

7   She had made an incisive and timely guess. Only days before, I'd invited Grady Rogers to my house after school to go swimming. The instant Grady shot from the pool, shaking water from his orange hair, freckled shoulders shining, my attraction to members of my own sex became a matter I could no longer suppress or rationalize. Sturdy and boisterous and gap-toothed, Grady was an inveterate backslapper, a formidable arm wrestler, a wizard at basketball. Grady was a boy at home in his body.

8   My body was a marvel I hadn't gotten used to; my arms and legs would sometimes act of their own accord, knocking over a glass at dinner or flinching at an oncoming pitch. I was never singled out as a sissy, but I could have been just as easily as Bobby Keagan, a gentle, intelligent, and introverted boy reviled by my classmates. And although I had always been aware of a tacit rapport with Bobby, a suspicion that I might find with him a rich friendship, I stayed away. Instead, I emulated Grady in the belief that being seen with him, being like him, would somehow vanquish my self-doubt, would make me normal by association.

9   Apart from his athletic prowess, Grady had been gifted with all the trappings of what I imagined to be a charmed life: a fastidious, aproned mother who radiated calm, maternal concern; a ruddy, stoic father with a knack for home repairs. Even the Rogerses' small suburban house in Hollywood, with its spindly Colonial furniture and chintz curtains, was a testament to normalcy.

10   Grady and his family bore little resemblance to my clan of Eastern European Jews, a dark and vociferous people who ate with abandon—matzo and halvah and gefilte fish; foods the goyim couldn't pronounce—who cajoled one another during endless games of canasta, making the simplest remark about the weather into a lengthy philosophical discourse on the sun and the seasons and the passage of time.

My mother was a chain-smoker, a dervish in a frowsy housedress. She showed her love in the most peculiar and obsessive ways, like spending hours extracting every seed from a watermelon before she served it in perfectly bite-sized, geometric pieces. Preoccupied and perpetually frantic, my mother succumbed to bouts of absentmindedness so profound she'd forget what she was saying midsentence, smile and blush and walk away. A divorce attorney, my father wore roomy, iridescent suits, and the intricacies, the deceits inherent in his profession, had the effect of making him forever tense and vigilant. He was "all wound up," as my mother put it. But when he relaxed, his laughter was explosive, his disposition prankish: "Walk this way," a waitress would say, leading us to our table, and my father would mimic the way she walked, arms akimbo, hips liquid, while my mother and I were wracked with laughter. Buoyant or brooding, my parents' moods were unpredictable, and in a household fraught with extravagant emotion it was odd and awful to keep my longing secret.

11   One day I made the mistake of asking my mother what a "fag" was. I knew exactly what Theresa had meant but hoped against hope it was not what I thought; maybe "fag" was some French word, a harmless term like "naive." My mother turned from the stove, flew at me, and grabbed me by the shoulders. "Did someone call you that?" she cried.

12   "Not me," I said. "Bobby Keagan."

13   "Oh," she said, loosening her grip. She was visibly relieved. And didn't answer. The answer was unthinkable.

14   For weeks after, I shook with the reverberations from that afternoon in the kitchen with my mother, pained by the memory of her shocked expression and, most of all, her silence. My longing was wrong in the eyes of my mother, whose hazel eyes were the eyes of the world, and if that longing continued unchecked, the unwieldy shape of my fate would be cast, and I'd be subjected to a lifetime of scorn.

15   During the remainder of the semester, I became the scientist of my own desire, plotting ways to change my yearning for boys into a yearning for girls. I had enough evidence to believe that any habit, regardless of how compulsive, how deeply ingrained, could be broken once and for all: The plastic cigarette my mother purchased at the Thrifty pharmacy—one end was red to approximate an ember, the other tan like a filtered tip—was designed to wean her from the real thing. To change a behavior required self-analysis, cold resolve, and the substitution of one thing for another: plastic, say, for tobacco. Could I also find a substitute for Grady? What I needed to do, I figured, was kiss a girl and learn to like it.

16   This conclusion was affirmed one Sunday morning when my father, seeing me wrinkle my nose at the pink slabs of lox he layered on a bagel, tried to convince me of its salty appeal. "You should try some," he said. "You don't know what you're missing."

17   "It's loaded with protein," added my mother, slapping a platter of sliced onions onto the dinette table. She hovered above us, cinching her housedress, eyes wet from onion fumes, the mock cigarette dangling from her lips.

18   My father sat there chomping with gusto, emitting a couple of hearty grunts to dramatize his satisfaction. And still I was not convinced. After a loud and labored swallow, he told me I may not be fond of lox today, but sooner or later I'd learn to like it. One's tastes, he assured me, are destined to change.

19   "Live," shouted my mother over the rumble of the Mixmaster. "Expand your horizons. Try new things." And the room grew fragrant with the batter of a spice cake.

20   The opportunity to put their advice into practice, and try out my plan to adapt to girls, came the following week when Debbie Coburn, a member of Mr. Hubbley's algebra class, invited me to a party. She cornered me in the hall, furtive as a spy, telling me her parents would be gone for the evening and slipping into my palm a wrinkled sheet of notebook paper. On it were her address and telephone number, the lavender ink in a tidy cursive. "Wear cologne," she advised, wary eyes darting back and forth. "It's a make-out party. Anything can happen."

21   The Santa Ana wind blew relentlessly the night of Debbie's party, careening down the slopes of the Hollywood hills, shaking the road signs and stoplights in its path. As I walked down Beachwood Avenue, trees thrashed, surrendered their leaves, and carob pods bombarded the pavement. The sky was a deep but luminous blue, the air hot, abrasive, electric. I had to squint in order to check the number of the Coburns' apartment, a three-story building with glitter embedded in its stucco walls. Above the honeycombed balconies was a sign that read BEACHWOOD TERRACE in lavender script resembling Debbie's.

22   From down the hall, I could hear the plaintive strains of Little Anthony's "I Think I'm Going Out of My Head." Debbie answered the door bedecked in an Empire dress, the bodice blue and orange polka dots, the rest a sheath of black and white stripes. "Op art," proclaimed Debbie. She turned in a circle, then proudly announced that she'd rolled her hair in orange juice cans. She patted the huge unmoving curls and dragged me inside. Reflections from the swimming pool in the courtyard, its surface ruffled by wind, shuddered over the ceiling and walls. A dozen of my classmates were seated on the sofa or huddled together in corners, their whispers full of excited imminence, their bodies barely discernible in the dim light. Drapes flanking the sliding glass doors bowed out with every gust of wind, and it seemed that the room might lurch from its foundations and sail with its cargo of silhouettes into the hot October night.

23   Grady was the last to arrive. He tossed a six-pack of beer into Debbie's arms, barreled toward me, and slapped my back. His hair was slicked back with Vitalis, lacquered furrows left by the comb. The wind hadn't shifted a single hair. "Ya ready?" he asked, flashing the gap between his front teeth and leering into the darkened room. "You bet," I lied.

24   Once the beers had been passed around, Debbie provoked everyone's attention by flicking on the overhead light. "Okay," she called. "Find a partner." This was the blunt command of a hostess determined to have her guests aroused in an orderly fashion. Everyone blinked, shuffled about, and grabbed a member of the opposite sex. Sheila Garabedian landed beside me—entirely at random, though I wanted to

believe she was driven by passion—her timid smile giving way to plain fear as the light went out. Nothing for a moment but the heave of the wind and the distant banter of dogs. I caught a whiff of Sheila's perfume, tangy and sweet as Hawaiian Punch. I probed her face with my own, grazing the small scallop of an ear, a velvety temple, and though Sheila's trembling made me want to stop, I persisted with my mission until I found her lips, tightly sealed as a private letter. I held my mouth over hers and gathered her shoulders closer, resigned to the possibility that, no matter how long we stood there, Sheila would be too scared to kiss me back. Still, she exhaled through her nose, and I listened to the squeak of every breath as though it were a sigh of inordinate pleasure. Diving within myself, I monitored my heartbeat and respiration, trying to will stimulation into being, and all the while an image intruded, an image of Grady erupting from our pool, rivulets of water sliding down his chest. "Change," shouted Debbie, switching on the light. Sheila thanked me, pulled away, and continued her routine of gracious terror with every boy throughout the evening. It didn't matter whom I held—Margaret Sims, Betty Vernon, Elizabeth Lee—my experiment was a failure; I continued to picture Grady's wet chest, and Debbie would bellow "change" with such fervor, it could have been my own voice, my own incessant reprimand.

25   Our hostess commandeered the light switch for nearly half an hour. Whenever the light came on, I watched Grady pivot his head toward the newest prospect, his eyebrows arched in expectation, his neck blooming with hickeys, his hair, at last, in disarray. All that shuffling across the carpet charged everyone's arms and lips with static, and eventually, between low moans and soft osculations, I could hear the clack of tiny sparks and see them flare here and there in the dark like meager, short-lived stars.

26   I saw Theresa, sultry and aloof as ever, read three more books—*North American Reptiles, Bonjour Tristesse,* and *MGM: A Pictorial History*—before she vanished early in December. Rumors of her fate abounded. Debbie Coburn swore that Theresa had been "knocked up" by an older man, a traffic cop, she thought, or a grocer. Nearly quivering with relish, Debbie told me and Grady about the home for unwed mothers in the San Fernando Valley, a compound teeming with pregnant girls who had nothing to do but touch their stomachs and contemplate their mistake. Even Bobby Keagan, who took Theresa's place behind me in algebra, had a theory regarding her disappearance colored by his own wish for escape; he imagined that Theresa, disillusioned with society, booked passage to a tropical island, there to live out the rest of her days without restrictions or ridicule. "No wonder she flunked out of school," I overheard Mr. Hubbley tell a fellow teacher one afternoon. "Her head was always in a book."

27   Along with Theresa went my secret, or at least the dread that she might divulge it, and I felt, for a while, exempt from suspicion. I was, however, to run across Theresa one last time. It happened during a period of torrential rain that, according to reports on the six o'clock news, washed houses from the hillsides and flooded the downtown streets. The halls of Joseph Le Conte Junior High were festooned with Christmas decorations: crepe-paper garlands, wreaths studded with plastic berries,

and one requisite Star of David twirling above the attendance desk. In Arts and Crafts, our teacher, Gerald (he was the only teacher who allowed us—*required* us— to call him by his first name), handed out blocks of balsa wood and instructed us to carve them into bugs. We would paint eyes and antennae with tempera and hang them on a Christmas tree he'd made the previous night. "Voilà," he crooned, unveiling his creation from a burlap sack. Before us sat a tortured scrub, a wardrobe-worth of wire hangers that were bent like branches and soldered together. Gerald credited his inspiration to a Charles Addams cartoon he's seen in which Morticia, grimly preparing for the holidays, hangs vampire bats on a withered pine. "All that red and green," said Gerald. "So predictable. So *boring.*"

28   As I chiseled a beetle and listened to rain pummel the earth, Gerald handed me an envelope and asked me to take it to Mr. Kendrick, the drama teacher. I would have thought nothing of his request if I hadn't seen Theresa on my way down the hall. She was cleaning out her locker, blithely dropping the sum of its contents—pens and textbooks and mimeographs—into a trash can. "Have a nice life," she sang as I passed. I mustered the courage to ask her what had happened. We stood alone in the silent hall, the reflections of wreaths and garlands submerged in brown linoleum.

29   "I transferred to another school. They don't have grades or bells, and you get to study whatever you want." Theresa was quick to sense my incredulity. "Honest," she said. "The school is progressive." She gazed into a glass cabinet that held the trophies of track meets and intramural spelling bees. "God," she sighed, "this place is so . . . barbaric." I was still trying to decide whether or not to believe her story when she asked me where I was headed. "Dear," she said, her exclamation pooling in the silence, "that's no ordinary note, if you catch my drift." The envelope was blank and white; I looked up at Theresa, baffled. "Don't be so naive," she muttered, tossing an empty bottle of nail polish into the trash can. It struck bottom with a resolute thud. "Well," she said, closing her locker and breathing deeply, "bon voyage." Theresa swept through the double doors and in seconds her figure was obscured by rain.

30   As I walked toward Mr. Kendrick's room, I could feel Theresa's insinuation burrow in. I stood for a moment and watched Mr. Kendrick through the pane in the door. He paced intently in front of the class, handsome in his shirt and tie, reading from a thick book. Chalked on the blackboard behind him was THE ODYSSEY BY HOMER. I have no recollection of how Mr. Kendrick reacted to the note, whether he accepted it with pleasure or embarrassment, slipped it into his desk drawer or the pocket of his shirt. I have scavenged that day in retrospect, trying to see Mr. Kendrick's expression, wondering if he acknowledged me in any way as his liaison. All I recall is the sight of his mime through a pane of glass, a lone man mouthing an epic, his gestures ardent in empty air.

31   Had I delivered a declaration of love? I was haunted by the need to know. In fantasy, a kettle shot steam, the glue released its grip, and I read the letter with impunity. But how would such a letter begin? Did the common endearments apply? This was a message between two men, a message for which I had no precedent, and when I tried to envision the contents, apart from a hasty, impassioned scrawl, my imagination faltered.

32   Once or twice I witnessed Gerald and Mr. Kendrick walk together into the faculty lounge or say hello at the water fountain, but there was nothing especially clan-

destine or flirtatious in their manner. Besides, no matter how acute my scrutiny, I wasn't sure, short of a kiss, exactly what to look for—what semaphore of gesture, what encoded word. I suspected there were signs, covert signs that would give them away, just as I'd unwittingly given myself away to Theresa.

33   In the school library, a *Webster's* unabridged dictionary lay on a wooden podium, and I padded toward it with apprehension; along with clues to the bond between my teachers, I risked discovering information that might incriminate me as well. I had decided to consult the dictionary during lunch period, when most of the students would be on the playground. I clutched my notebook, moving in such a way as to appear both studious and nonchalant, actually believing that, unless I took precautions, someone would see me and guess what I was up to. The closer I came to the podium, the more obvious, I thought, was my endeavor; I felt like the model of The Visible Man in our science class, my heart's undulations, my overwrought nerves legible through transparent skin. A couple of kids riffled through the card catalogue. The librarian, a skinny woman whose perpetual whisper and rubber-soled shoes caused her to drift through the room like a phantom, didn't seem to register my presence. Though I'd looked up dozens of words before, the pages felt strange beneath my fingers. *Homer* was the first word I saw. *Hominid. Homogenize.* I feigned interest and skirted other words before I found the word I was after. Under the heading HO·MO·SEX·U·AL was the terse definition: *adj. Pertaining to, characteristic of, or exhibiting homosexuality.—n. A homosexual person.* I read the definition again and again, hoping the words would yield more than they could. I shut the dictionary, swallowed hard, and, none the wiser, hurried away.

34   As for Gerald and Mr. Kendrick, I never discovered evidence to prove or dispute Theresa's claim. By the following summer, however, I had overheard from my peers a confounding amount about homosexuals: They wore green on Thursday, couldn't whistle, hypnotized boys with a piercing glance. To this lore, Grady added a surefire test to ferret them out.

35   "A test?" I said.

36   "You ask a guy to look at his fingernails, and if he looks at them like this"— Grady closed his fingers into a fist and examined his nails with manly detachment— "then he's okay. But if he does this"—he held out his hands at arm's length, splayed his fingers, and coyly cocked his head—"you'd better watch out." Once he'd completed his demonstration, Grady peeled off his shirt and plunged into our pool. I dove in after. It was early June, the sky immense, glassy, placid. My father was cooking spareribs on the barbecue, an artist with a basting brush. His apron bore the caricature of a frazzled French chef. Mother curled on a chaise longue, plumes of smoke wafting from her nostrils. In a stupor of contentment she took another drag, closed her eyes, and arched her face toward the sun.

37   Grady dog-paddled through the deep end, spouting a fountain of chlorinated water. Despite shame and confusion, my longing for him hadn't diminished; it continued to thrive without air and light, like a luminous fish in the dregs of the sea. In the name of play, I swam up behind him, encircled his shoulders, astonished by his taut flesh. The two of us flailed, pretended to drown. Beneath the heavy press of water, Grady's orange hair wavered, a flame that couldn't be doused.

38   I've lived with a man for seven years. Some nights, when I'm half-asleep and the room is suffused with blue light, I reach out to touch the expanse of his back, and it seems as if my fingers sink into his skin, and I feel the pleasure a diver feels the instant he enters a body of water.

39   I have few regrets. But one is that I hadn't said to Theresa, "Of course I'm a fag." Maybe I'd have met her friends. Or become friends with her. Imagine the meals we might have concocted: hamburger Stroganoff, Swedish meatballs in a sweet translucent sauce, steaming slabs of Salisbury steak.

■ TOPICAL CONSIDERATIONS

1. Like Dick Gregory, Bernard Cooper's memoir is set in school, and involves a crush on a classmate that causes him confusion and discomfort. How does this relationship compare to Gregory's crush on Helene Tucker? How are both crushes complicated by social and cultural barriers? Cite specific passages and scenes as evidence.

2. Theresa Sanchez appears at the beginning and end of Cooper's essay. How does the author characterize her? Why is she so important in his life? What does she help Cooper come to understand about himself?

3. What made it difficult for Cooper to admit to his family that he was gay? Cite evidence from the essay to support your answer. Can you in any way identify with Cooper's difficulty here? Why is it so hard to talk about our sexual lives with parents or family? Why is their judgment so significant?

4. How did the author at first view his attraction to men? What did he do about his feelings? What caused him to take such an approach? Why did this approach fail? Do you think forcing yourself to forget about loving another person works? Explain your answer.

5. How did Cooper learn about a gay relationship at his school? What was his response to it? What is behind the author's purpose in including this discovery in the essay?

6. According to Cooper's classmates, what were some characteristics of gay men? What was Cooper's response to these beliefs? How did it make him feel about himself? What are the common stereotypes about gay people? Do you think these stereotypes ring true? What cultural or societal factors account for such stereotypes?

■ RHETORICAL CONSIDERATIONS

1. Consider the ending of the essay. What do you know about the author? How does the ending work in resolving the issues of identity the author has introduced? Why did the author choose this particular ending?

2. Consider Cooper's final description of Grady (paragraph 36). What major theme is the author expressing in this passage? Comment upon the visual imagery. Comment also on the tone of Cooper's language.

3. What is the significance of Cooper's title? Locating the image in the narrative, explain how it works. How does "a clack of tiny sparks" metaphorically represent Cooper's gay boyhood?

■ WRITING ASSIGNMENTS

1. Imagine a scene between Cooper and his parents, in which he tells them of his gay feelings. Based on what Cooper has projected of their characters, how would they respond? How would Cooper approach the topic with them? Write a scene using dialogue and descriptive details.
2. Imagine that you are a friend of Cooper's and that you know his secret. What would you tell him about being gay? about friendship? Would you encourage him? Would you be afraid of the friendship? Write an essay in the form of a letter in which you explore your honest feelings about a friendship with Cooper.
3. Authors Randy Shilts (*The Band Played On*) and Paul Monette (*Becoming a Man*) have written about what it is like to be a gay man in these times. If possible, research their books and write an essay exploring the problems gay men have in coming out to their families, friends, or co-workers. What prejudices do they encounter? How do these authors counter that prejudice? How has the impact of AIDS affected these authors' lives and how others view them?

Our first relationships and, perhaps, our most important are those with the people in our family—our mothers and fathers, siblings, grandparents, and others. It is in the family context where we develop as people and social beings, where we become who and what we are, and where we learn about love. Each of the essays in this chapter will explore some aspect of family identity and love. And each invites you to recollect some early family experience that helped define the person you are today.

In the opening piece "In Search of Our Mothers' Gardens," Alice Walker pays homage to her own mother as well as to the generation of nameless black women whose spirit of creativity managed to survive centuries of misery and degradation. A different sort of homage is paid by Chester Higgins, Jr. in "A Father's Rite." In the shadows of an ancient Egyptian tomb, Higgins performs a ceremony with his 20-year-old son—a ceremony that serves to bond the boy to his African ancestors and to his father.

Randall Williams was born in poverty and raised in its humiliation. Nonetheless, in "Daddy Tucked the Blanket," the author recalls his parents' love—a devotion so intense that it transcended the jagged edge of destitution.

In the next essay, "My Brother, My Self," the familiar ABC News commentator, Dick Schaap, examines the great similarities and even greater differences shared by siblings. Following that is "My Grandmother, the Bag Lady," which is Patsy Neal's tribute to her grandmother. It is also a poignant and loving portrait of an elderly woman who has lost so much of her world and her memory of it.

The family is the most basic of society's institutions. It is also the most vulnerable. With the soaring divorce rate, the very structure of the American family is being reshaped. The final piece examines divorce and its fallout. However, as suggested by the title, "Older Children and Divorce," author Barbara Cain approaches the subject from a slant not often taken: the effects of family breakup on college-age children.

In Search of Our Mothers' Gardens
Alice Walker

Alice Walker is an eminent writer who has chronicled the black experience in novels such as *The Color Purple* (1982)—winner of both the Pulitzer Prize and the American Book Award—and *The Temple of My Familiar* (1989). She has written collections of poems, short stories, and essays including *Living by the Word: Selected Writings (1973–1987)* (1988) and *Her Blue Body Everything We Know: Earthling Poems 1965–1990* (1991). Her latest novel is *Possessing the Secret of Joy* (1992). In the piece below, Ms. Walker seeks to understand how the creativity of black women has survived despite centuries of degradation and misery. With some bitterness she reflects on the shunted lives of black women who never had the freedom or license to be the poets, novelists, and artists they might have been. Yet Walker credits these countless unknown with nurturing and passing on the creative spirit. This discovery is made when Walker remembers her own mother's garden and recognizes it as the place where she cultivated the seed of creativity—her legacy to her daughter.

> *I described her own nature and temperament. Told how they needed a larger life for their expression. . . . I pointed out that in lieu of proper channels, her emotions had overflowed into paths that dissipated them. I talked, beautifully I thought, about an art that would be born, an art that would open the way for women the likes of her. I asked her to hope, and build up an inner life against the coming of that day. . . . I sang, with a strange quiver in my voice, a promise song.*
>
> JEAN TOOMER, "AVEY," *Cane*

The poet speaking to a prostitute who falls asleep while he's talking—

1   When the poet Jean Toomer walked through the South in the early twenties, he discovered a curious thing: black women whose spirituality was so intense, so deep, so *unconscious,* that they were themselves unaware of the richness they held. They stumbled blindly through their lives: creatures so abused and mutilated in body, so dimmed and confused by pain, that they considered themselves unworthy even of hope. In the selfless abstractions their bodies became to the men who used them, they became more than "sexual objects," more even than mere women: they became "Saints." Instead of being perceived as whole persons, their bodies became shrines: what was thought to be their minds became temples suitable for worship. These crazy Saints stared out at the world, wildly, like lunatics— or quietly, like suicides; and the "God" that was in their gaze was as mute as a great stone.

2   Who were these Saints? These crazy, loony, pitiful women?

3   Some of them, without a doubt, were our mothers and grandmothers.

4   In the still heat of the post-Reconstruction South, this is how they seemed to Jean Toomer: exquisite butterflies trapped in an evil honey, toiling away their lives in an era, a century, that did not acknowledge them, except as "the *mule* of the world." They dreamed dreams that no one knew—not even themselves, in any coherent fashion—and saw visions no one could understand. They wandered or sat about the countryside crooning lullabies to ghosts, and drawing the mother of Christ in charcoal on courthouse walls.

5   They forced their minds to desert their bodies and their striving spirits sought to rise, like frail whirlwinds from the hard red clay. And when those frail whirlwinds fell, in scattered particles, upon the ground, no one mourned. Instead, men lit candles to celebrate the emptiness that remained, as people do who enter a beautiful but vacant space to resurrect a God.

6   Our mothers and grandmothers, some of them: moving to music not yet written. And they waited.

7   They waited for a day when the unknown thing that was in them would be made known; but guessed, somehow in their darkness, that on the day of their revelation they would be long dead. Therefore to Toomer they walked, and even ran, in slow motion. For they were going nowhere immediate, and the future was not yet within their grasp. And men took our mothers and grandmothers, "but got no pleasure from it." So complex was their passion and their calm.

8   To Toomer, they lay vacant and fallow as autumn fields, with harvest time never in sight: and he saw them enter loveless marriages, without joy; and become prostitutes, without resistance; and become mothers of children, without fulfillment.

9   For these grandmothers and mothers of ours were not Saints, but artists; driven to a numb and bleeding madness by the springs of creativity in them for which there was no release. They were Creators, who lived lives of spiritual waste, because they were so rich in spirituality—which is the basis of Art—that the strain of enduring their unused and unwanted talent drove them insane. Throwing away this spirituality was their pathetic attempt to lighten the soul to a weight their work-worn, sexually abused bodies could bear.

10   What did it mean for a black woman to be an artist in our grandmothers' time? In our great-grandmothers' day? It is a question with an answer cruel enough to stop the blood.

11   Did you have a genius of a great-great-grandmother who died under some ignorant and depraved white overseer's lash? Or was she required to bake biscuits for a lazy backwater tramp, when she cried out in her soul to paint watercolors of sunsets, or the rain falling on the green and peaceful pasturelands? Or was her body broken and forced to bear children (who were more often than not sold away from her)— eight, ten, fifteen, twenty children—when her one joy was the thought of modeling heroic figures of rebellion, in stone or clay?

12   How was the creativity of the black woman kept alive, year after year and century after century, when for most of the years black people have been in America, it was a punishable crime for a black person to read or write? And the freedom to paint, to sculpt, to expand the mind with action did not exist. Consider, if you can bear to imagine it, what might have been the result if singing, too, had been forbidden by law. Listen to the voices of Bessie Smith, Billie Holiday, Nina Simone, Roberta Flack, and Aretha Franklin, among others, and imagine those voices muzzled for life. Then you may begin to comprehend the lives of our "crazy," "Sainted" mothers and grandmothers. The agony of the lives of women who might have been Poets, Novelists, Essayists, and Short-Story Writers (over a period of centuries), who died with their real gifts stifled within them.

13   And, if this were the end of the story, we would have cause to cry out in my paraphrase of Okot p'Bitek's great poem:

> *O, my clanswomen*
> *Let us all cry together!*
> *Come,*
> *Let us mourn the death of our mother,*

The death of a Queen
The ash that was produced
By a great fire!
O, this homestead is utterly dead
Close the gates
With lacari *thorns,*
For our mother
The creator of the Stool is lost!
And all the young women
Have perished in the wilderness!

14 But this is not the end of the story, for all the young women—our mothers and grandmothers, *ourselves*—have not perished in the wilderness. And if we ask ourselves why, and search for and find the answer, we will know beyond all efforts to erase it from our minds, just exactly who, and of what, we black American women are.

15 One example, perhaps the most pathetic, most misunderstood one, can provide a backdrop for our mothers' work: Phillis Wheatley, a slave in the 1700s.

16 Virginia Woolf, in her book *A Room of One's Own,* wrote that in order for a woman to write fiction she must have two things, certainly: a room of her own (with key and lock) and enough money to support herself.

17 What then are we to make of Phillis Wheatley, a slave, who owned not even herself? This sickly, frail black girl who required a servant of her own at times—her health was so precarious—and who, had she been white, would have been easily considered the intellectual superior of all the women and most of the men in the society of her day.

18 Virginia Woolf wrote further, speaking of course not of our Phillis, that "any woman born with a great gift in the sixteenth century [insert "eighteenth century," insert "black woman," insert "born or made a slave"] would certainly have gone crazed, shot herself, or ended her days in some lonely cottage outside the village, half witch, half wizard [insert "Saint"], feared and mocked at. For it needs little skill and psychology to be sure that a highly gifted girl who had tried to use her gift for poetry would have been so thwarted and hindered by contrary instincts [add "chains, guns, the lash, the ownership of one's body by someone else, submission to an alien religion"], that she must have lost her health and sanity to a certainty."

19 The key words, as they relate to Phillis, are "contrary instincts." For when we read the poetry of Phillis Wheatley—as when we read the novels of Nella Larsen or the oddly false-sounding autobiography of that freest of all black women writers, Zora Hurston—evidence of "contrary instincts" is everywhere. Her loyalties were completely divided, as was, without question, her mind.

20 But how could this be otherwise? Captured at seven, a slave of wealthy, doting whites who instilled in her the "savagery" of the African they "rescued" her from . . . one wonders if she was even able to remember her homeland as she had known it, or as it really was.

21   Yet, because she did try to use her gift for poetry in a world that made her a slave, she was "so thwarted and hindered by . . . contrary instincts, that she . . . lost her health. . . ." In the last years of her brief life, burdened not only with the need to express her gift but also with a penniless, friendless "freedom" and several small children for whom she was forced to do strenuous work to feed, she lost her health, certainly. Suffering from malnutrition and neglect and who knows what mental agonies, Phillis Wheatley died.

22   So torn by "contrary instincts" was black, kidnapped, enslaved Phillis that her description of "the Goddess"—as she poetically called the Liberty she did not have—is ironically, cruelly humorous. And, in fact, has held Phillis up to ridicule for more than a century. It is usually read prior to hanging Phillis's memory as that of a fool. She wrote:

> *The Goddess comes, she moves divinely fair,*
> *Olive and laurel binds her golden hair.*
> *Wherever shines this native of the skies,*
> *Unnumber'd charms and recent graces rise.* [My italics]

23   It is obvious that Phillis, the slave, combed the "Goddess's" hair every morning; prior, perhaps, to bringing in the milk, or fixing her mistress's lunch. She took her imagery from the one thing she saw elevated above all others.

24   With the benefit of hindsight we ask, "How could she?"

25   But at last, Phillis, we understand. No more snickering when your stiff, struggling, ambivalent lines are forced on us. We know now that you were not an idiot or a traitor; only a sickly little black girl, snatched from your home and country and made a slave; a woman who still struggled to sing the song that was your gift, although in a land of barbarians who praised you for your bewildered tongue. It is not so much what you sang, as that you kept alive, in so many of our ancestors, *the notion of song.*

26   Black women are called, in the folklore that so aptly identifies one's status in society, "the *mule* of the world," because we have been handed the burdens that everyone else—*everyone* else—refused to carry. We have also been called "Matriarchs," "Superwomen," and "Mean and Evil Bitches." Not to mention "Castraters" and "Sapphire's Mama." When we have pleaded for understanding, our character has been distorted; when we have asked for simple caring, we have been handed empty inspirational appellations, then stuck in the farthest corner. When we have asked for love, we have been given children. In short, even our plainer gifts, our labors of fidelity and love, have been knocked down our throats. To be an artist and a black woman, even today, lowers our status in many respects, rather than raises it: and yet, artists we will be.

27   Therefore we must fearlessly pull out of ourselves and look at and identify with our lives the living creativity some of our great-grandmothers were not allowed to know. I stress *some* of them because it is well known that the majority of our great-grandmothers knew, even without "knowing" it, the reality of their spirituality, even

if they didn't recognize it beyond what happened in the singing at church—and they never had any intention of giving it up.

28   How they did it—those millions of black women who were not Phillis Wheatley, or Lucy Terry or Frances Harper or Zora Hurston or Nella Larsen or Bessie Smith; or Elizabeth Catlett, or Katherine Dunham, either—brings me to the title of this essay, "In Search of Our Mothers' Gardens," which is a personal account that is yet shared, in its theme and its meaning, by all of us. I found, while thinking about the far-reaching world of the creative black woman, that often the truest answer to a question that really matters can be found very close.

29   In the late 1920s my mother ran away from home to marry my father. Marriage, if not running away, was expected of seventeen-year-old girls. By the time she was twenty, she had two children and was pregnant with a third. Five children later, I was born. And this is how I came to know my mother: she seemed a large, soft, loving-eyed woman who was rarely impatient in our home. Her quick, violent temper was on view only a few times a year, when she battled with the white landlord who had the misfortune to suggest to her that her children did not need to go to school.

30   She made all the clothes we wore, even my brothers' overalls. She made all the towels and sheets we used. She spent the summers canning vegetables and fruits. She spent the winter evenings making quilts enough to cover all our beds.

31   During the "working" day, she labored beside—not behind—my father in the fields. Her day began before sunup, and did not end until late at night. There was never a moment for her to sit down, undisturbed, to unravel her own private thoughts; never a time free from interruption—by work or the noisy inquiries of her many children. And yet, it is to my mother—and all our mothers who were not famous—that I went in search of the secret of what has fed that muzzled and often mutilated, but vibrant, creative spirit that the black woman has inherited, and that pops out in wild and unlikely places to this day.

32   But when, you will ask, did my overworked mother have time to know or care about feeding the creative spirit?

33   The answer is so simple that many of us have spent years discovering it. We have constantly looked high, when we should have looked high—and low.

34   For example: in the Smithsonian Institution in Washington, D.C., there hangs a quilt unlike any other in the world. In fanciful, inspired, and yet simple and identifiable figures, it portrays the story of the Crucifixion. It is considered rare, beyond price. Though it follows no known pattern of quilt-making, and though it is made of bits and pieces of worthless rags, it is obviously the work of a person of powerful imagination and deep spiritual feeling. Below this quilt I saw a note that says it was made by "an anonymous Black woman in Alabama, a hundred years ago."

35   If we could locate this "anonymous" black woman from Alabama, she would turn out to be one of our grandmothers—an artist who left her mark in the only

materials she could afford, and in the only medium her position in society allowed her to use.

36   As Virginia Woolf wrote further, in *A Room of One's Own:*

> Yet genius of a sort must have existed among women as it must have existed among the working class. [Change this to "slaves" and "the wives and daughters of sharecroppers."] Now and again an Emily Brontë or a Robert Burns [change this to "a Zora Hurston or a Richard Wright"] blazes out and proves its presence. But certainly it never got itself on to paper. When, however, one reads of a witch being ducked, of a woman possessed by devils [or "Sainthood"], of a wise woman selling herbs [our root workers], or even a very remarkable man who had a mother, then I think we are on the track of a lost novelist, a suppressed poet, of some mute and inglorious Jane Austen. . . . Indeed, I would venture to guess that Anon, who wrote so many poems without signing them, was often a woman. . . .

37   And so our mothers and grandmothers have, more often than not anonymously, handed on the creative spark, the seed of the flower they themselves never hoped to see: or like a sealed letter they could not plainly read.

38   And so it is, certainly, with my own mother. Unlike "Ma" Rainey's songs, which retained their creator's name even while blasting forth from Bessie Smith's mouth, no song or poem will bear my mother's name. Yet so many of the stories that I write, that we all write, are my mother's stories. Only recently did I fully realize this: that through years of listening to my mother's stories of her life, I have absorbed not only the stories themselves, but something of the manner in which she spoke, something of the urgency that involves the knowledge that her stories—like her life—must be recorded. It is probably for this reason that so much of what I have written is about characters whose counterparts in real life are so much older than I am.

39   But the telling of these stories, which came from my mother's lips as naturally as breathing, was not the only way my mother showed herself as an artist. For stories, too, were subject to being distracted, to dying without conclusion. Dinners must be started, and cotton must be gathered before the big rains. The artist that was and is my mother showed itself to me only after many years. This is what I finally noticed:

40   Like Mem, a character in *The Third Life of Grange Copeland,* my mother adorned with flowers whatever shabby house we were forced to live in. And not just your typical straggly country stand of zinnias, either. She planted ambitious gardens—and still does—with over fifty different varieties of plants that bloom profusely from early March until late November. Before she left home for the fields, she watered her flowers, chopped up the grass, and laid out new beds. When she returned from the fields she might divide clumps of bulbs, dig a cold pit, uproot and replant roses, or prune branches from her taller bushes or trees—until night came and it was too dark to see.

41   Whatever she planted grew as if by magic, and her fame as a grower of flowers spread over three counties. Because of her creativity with her flowers, even my memories of poverty are seen through a screen of blooms—sunflowers, petunias, roses, dahlias, forsythia, spirea, delphiniums, verbena . . . and on and on.

42   And I remember people coming to my mother's yard to be given cuttings from her flowers; I hear again the praise showered on her because whatever rocky soil she landed on, she turned into a garden. A garden so brilliant with colors, so original in its design, so magnificent with life and creativity, that to this day people drive by our house in Georgia—perfect strangers and imperfect strangers—and ask to stand or walk among my mother's art.

43   I notice that it is only when my mother is working in her flowers that she is radiant, almost to the point of being invisible—except as Creator: hand and eye. She is involved in work her soul must have. Ordering the universe in the image of her personal conception of Beauty.

44   Her face, as she prepares the Art that is her gift, is a legacy of respect she leaves to me, for all that illuminates and cherishes life. She has handed down respect for the possibilities—and the will to grasp them.

45   For her, so hindered and intruded upon in so many ways, being an artist has still been a daily part of her life. This ability to hold on, even in very simple ways, is work black women have done for a very long time.

46   This poem is not enough, but it is something, for the woman who literally covered the holes in our walls with sunflowers:

They were women then
My mama's generation
Husky of voice—Stout of
Step
With fists as well as
Hands
How they battered down
Doors
And ironed
Starched white
Shirts
How they led
Armies
Headragged Generals
Across mined
Fields
Booby-trapped
Kitchens
To discover books
Desks
A place for us
How they knew what we
Must *know*
Without knowing a page
Of it
Themselves.

47   Guided by my heritage of a love of beauty and a respect for strength—in search of my mother's garden, I found my own.

48   And perhaps in Africa over two hundred years ago, there was just such a mother; perhaps she painted vivid and daring decorations in oranges and yellows and greens on the walls of her hut; perhaps she sang—in a voice like Roberta Flack's—*sweetly* over the compounds of her village; perhaps she wove the most stunning mats or told the most ingenious stories of all the village storytellers. Perhaps she was herself a poet—though only her daughter's name is signed to the poems that we know.

49   Perhaps Phillis Wheatley's mother was also an artist.

50   Perhaps in more than Phillis Wheatley's biological life is her mother's signature made clear.

■ TOPICAL CONSIDERATIONS

1. Alice Walker speaks of women who were what poet Jean Toomer called "Saints." Who were these women and why were they referred to as "Saints"?
2. Then Walker refutes Toomer's epithet and calls the black women of the past "Creators," "Artists." In what ways were they "Creators"? "Artists"?
3. Explain how black American women like Phillis Wheatley managed to use their creativity under such adverse conditions.
4. What is the meaning of the title and why does the author say she uses it?
5. In what ways did the author's mother hand "on the creative spark, the seed of the flower they themselves never hoped to see" (paragraph 37)?
6. What does the author mean when she says, "Guided by my heritage of a love of beauty and a respect for strength—in search of my mother's garden, I found my own" (paragraph 47)?

■ RHETORICAL CONSIDERATIONS

1. Walker uses strong emotional language to depict the way in which black women were abused. She also uses lyrical language, describing these women as "exquisite butterflies trapped in an evil honey" (paragraph 4). Select an example of Walker's emotional language and explain why it is or is not effective.
2. Walker begins the essay with a quotation from *Cane* by Jean Toomer. Do you think the passage sets the tone for the essay? Do you think this excerpt by a black male is effective?
3. The author takes editorial license when she uses Virginia Woolf's *A Room of One's Own*. Do you think her editorial insertions in Woolf's quotation are effective? What points do these insertions make?

4. Walker next uses a quotation from Phillis Wheatley's poem describing the "Goddess," Freedom. Relate this example to the use of the Woolf quotation. Is there any irony there?

5. In paragraph 26, the author puts herself into the essay when she says, "we have been handed the burdens that everyone else—*everyone* else—refused to carry." This paragraph shows the strong feelings Walker herself has toward the way she and other black women have been treated. Explain the change in tone from this paragraph to the next one.

6. Toward the end of the essay Walker returns to Woolf and again uses editorial insertions. For what purpose does she use them this time?

■ WRITING ASSIGNMENTS

1. Select a parent or grandparent to describe. Was there a special talent or creativity that person possessed? Write an essay in search of your relative's "garden" and see where it leads you.

2. Consider the roles of race and gender in this essay. If you feel that any of your relatives had their creativity stifled because of their ethnic background or gender, describe the experience in an essay.

3. Write a letter to Alice Walker telling her what language, emotions, or points in her essay moved you in a positive or negative way. Try to be as specific as possible.

4. Interview a relative or an older friend. Ask them to describe a talent that they would have liked to cultivate if their lives had been different. If they did cultivate a talent, have them describe it. Present the information you have gathered in an essay called "[Name]'s Garden."

5. Consider the legacy you will leave your children or grandchildren. Write an essay from the point of view of your child or grandchild, describing your "garden."

A Father's Rite

Chester Higgins, Jr.

What is the role of a father? What might he pass on to his son: his wealth, special skills, knowledge about the world, a love of nature, or a pride in self? In this piece a black man gives his 20-year-old son a special gift when they travel to Egypt and Ethiopia, lands holding the heritage of black people. Amidst the ancient tombs of the Pharaohs in the Valley of the Kings, Chester Higgins, Jr. reenacts a quiet ceremony connecting his son with the greatness of his African ancestry while exhorting him to pursue his destiny.

Chester Higgins, Jr. is a staff photographer with *The New York Times*. He has traveled the world photographing people of African descent for his book *Feeling the Spirit: The Family of Africa* (1994).

1   I took my son to Africa this year. For three weeks my 20-year-old son and I explored the past and present of our people in Egypt and Ethiopia. I wanted him to see what I regard as the land of his heritage; I wanted him to experience the ecstasy I felt on my first visit to Africa when I was in my 20's.

2   I had envisioned a kind of rite of passage for my son; what transpired between us became a turning point—in our relationship, for me as his father and I hope for him as well.

3   Being a father seems to require skills never taught to me. Throughout my son's 20 years and my daughter's 22 years, I have often felt as if I were in a boat slipping along the water in a dark night without a lamp or a lighthouse to guide me. I felt like an impostor. I was reared by my stepfather, a distant man, and at 19 I sought out my biological father, whom I had never known. Those experiences made me determined to take the role of a father seriously.

4   When my son was 9 years old and my daughter was 11, their mother and I divorced, and it nearly sank the already adrift boat. With divorce often comes anger, a welter of conflicting feelings and much pain for everybody. New York State court-restricted visitations for a father can reduce his relationship with his children to that of an uncle. Having been deprived of my own father, I was determined to maintain as much contact with my children as the law would allow.

5   For my 15th trip to Africa, in July, to photograph the reinterment of His Majesty Haile Selassie on what would have been his 100th birthday, I decided to ask my son, Damani, to come along as my assistant. Damani, who has dreadlocked his hair, shares my love of His Majesty and of reggae, the music of the Rastafarians who worship Selassie. I added to our itinerary a stopover in Egypt so that my son could also see the pyramids, temples and tombs of our ancestors.

6   Haile Selassie's reinterment was postponed by the new Ethiopian regime about two weeks before we were to arrive. Though deeply disappointed, neither Damani nor I considered canceling our trip, nor did the thousands of Rastafarians who annually gather for Selassie's birthday. While we were in Ethiopia, my son in his dreadlocks blended into the population; his enthusiasm for this venerable African country warmed my heart. On a four-day trip to visit the ancient sacred city of Lalibala, where, in the 12th century, churches were hewn out of the surrounding mountains, I had a dream. In my dream, I saw two men, one older and one younger, facing one another against a background of temples and pyramids. The father was speaking as he anointed the head of his son.

7   I became enamored of the possibility of enacting a ceremony with my son in Africa. For the next six days I privately wondered what words to use in such a ceremony. Gradually the words came to me. By the time we arrived in Cairo, I was ready. I told my son that there was a ceremony I wanted to perform with him in the tombs

at Luxor, Egypt. His eyes shone with anticipation. But I wondered if he would still be receptive after my next statement. In the dream I remembered that the son was anointed, as it were, with a dry substance. I took this to mean that powder rather than oil was used. But what powder? I ruled out ground herbs and flowers, and finally settled on sand. Sand represents the Sahara, and sand also contains the remains of the ancient people of Pharaonic Egypt. That made metaphysical sense to me, but in the real world, young adults or almost anybody for that matter, are disinclined to have sand poured on their hair.

8 "I will need sand to anoint your head," I told my son.

9 "Sand?" he asked, hesitantly. "How much?"

10 "Just a little; you can put some in a film canister," I said hastily. We both knew a 35-millimeter film canister wouldn't hold much sand. "Take the canister and find sand you feel special about and I'll use that."

11 Once he was in control of the amount of sand and where it would come from, he decided to take some from the desert in the shadow of the pyramids in Cairo. Days later, when we reached Luxor, he collected more from around the remains of the Temple of Karnak—one of the largest, oldest stone temples in the world.

12 The next afternoon we sailed across the Nile to Thebes and to the Valley of the Kings, a basin formed by towering mountains. From the heavenly perch of the ancient Egyptian gods, the valley resembles a huge bowl to which there is one narrow entrance, flanked by more tall peaks. The tombs of the Pharaohs are hewn into the lower part of the mountains that form the basin. Inside each tomb, 12-foot-square passageways lead down several thousand feet into the solid rock. The scene that greets modern-day visitors to these sacred chambers is astonishing: Ornately painted walls reveal images of animals, people and scenes that were part of the real and imaginary lives of Pharaonic Egyptians. It was here, inside one of the tombs of an 18th Dynasty Pharaoh, that I chose to perform the ceremony revealed to me in my dream in Ethiopia.

13 In front of an enormous wall painting of Osiris, the god of resurrection, my son and I faced each other. I poured the sand he had collected into the palm of my left hand, and with my right, I anointed the top of his head with this sand. Looking into his eyes, I said:

14 "I, your father, anoint the crown of your head with the soil of Africa. This piece of earth is a symbol of the lives of your ancestors. It is a bonding of their lives to yours. Like your father, you, too, are African. We are Africans not because we were born in Africa, but because Africa was born in us. Look around you and behold us in our greatness. Greatness is an African possibility; you can make it yours. Just as the great ones before you have, by their deeds, placed their names on history, so can you by your deeds place your name on tomorrow . . . So here, in the company of those great ones who have waited patiently for your visit—you are loved, you are encouraged. Our faces shine toward yours. Go forward; may you live long, may you prosper and have health."

15 We hugged each other, enjoying the specialness of the moment. Leaving him alone inside the tomb to meditate, I walked back toward the light and waited for him outside on the valley floor.

16   Here in the land of our ancient fathers, in the tomb of one of the great fathers of the ancient Egyptian empire, my perception of what it means to be a father was unalterably expanded and enhanced.

■ TOPICAL CONSIDERATIONS

1. Consider Higgins's personal experience with fathers and fatherhood (paragraphs 3–4). What characterizes the fathers in his family? How did his childhood experience shape Higgins's own attitude toward parenting?
2. In what ways is Damani like his father? Why do you think these similarities are important to Higgins?
3. Analyze the sacred places and practices described in this essay. How do the Rastafarians, the sacred city of Lalibala, and the Temple of Karnak inspire the "father's rite" of the title?
4. Look back over the essay, especially at the words Higgins uses to describe the ceremony with his son (paragraph 14). In what ways is "Africa" more than simply a geographical place to Higgins?
5. Consider the sense of the past created in the words of the ritual. Where else in the essay does Higgins refer to the African past? Why do you think the past is so important to Higgins here?
6. Higgins claims that on this trip his "perception of what it means to be a father was unalterably expanded and enhanced" (paragraph 16). What new perception of fatherhood do the words of the ceremony suggest? Why do you think Higgins and his son had to travel to Africa to discover this new perception?

■ RHETORICAL CONSIDERATIONS

1. What especially vivid images does Higgins, a photographer by profession, create in this essay? Analyze the emotional effect of the visual images you found most powerful.
2. Consider the symbolic importance of the sand used in the ritual, comparing it to other images of earth in the essay.
3. Analyze the thematic significance of the Valley of the Kings. What about this place makes it particularly appropriate for performing the "father's rite" of the title?
4. This essay first appeared in a weekly column entitled "About Men." Do you think men are its main audience? If you are a woman, did you feel put off by this argument in any way?
5. In paragraph 7, Higgins tells us he has arrived at the words for the ceremony, but we only actually hear them in paragraph 14. Why does he do this? How did the delay affect you as a reader?

■ WRITING ASSIGNMENTS

1. Describe a personal ritual performed between you and one or more members of your family. The ritual should represent some important aspect of your relationship. If you cannot think of one, try to create such a ritual. What might it be, and what might be its significance?
2. Find in the library at least three descriptions or photographs of the Valley of the Kings and the Temple of Karnak. Using these as a basis for comparison, write an analysis which explains how Higgins's description is also a subjective interpretation of the Temple.
3. Assuming the role of Higgins's daughter, write a letter telling your "father" how you feel about "A Father's Rite."
4. Describe a place that has great significance to you without explicitly stating its meaning; instead, use adjectives, similes, and metaphors to make your reader appreciate the specialness of the place.
5. Using your library resources, write a research paper on the importance of Haile Selassie to the Rastafarian religion.

Daddy Tucked the Blanket
Randall Williams

In this autobiographical account of a young man who grew up in poverty, Randall Williams illustrates the physical and emotional conditions of growing up poor. He also shows how the environment of poverty—the deprivation and humiliation—can destroy a family. Williams is a journalist living in Alabama. This article first appeared in *The New York Times* in 1975.

1 About the time I turned 16, my folks began to wonder why I didn't stay home any more. I always had an excuse for them, but what I didn't say was that I had found my freedom and I was getting out.

2 I went through four years of high school in semirural Alabama and became active in clubs and sports; I made a lot of friends and became a regular guy, if you know what I mean. But one thing was irregular about me: I managed those four years without ever having a friend visit at my house.

3 I was ashamed of where I lived. I had been ashamed for as long as I had been conscious of class.

4 We had a big family. There were several of us sleeping in one room, but that's not so bad if you get along, and we always did. As you get older, though, it gets worse.

5 Being poor is a humiliating experience for a young person trying hard to be accepted. Even now—several years removed—it is hard to talk about. And I resent the weakness of these words to make you feel what it was really like.

6 We lived in a lot of old houses. We moved a lot because we were always looking for something just a little better than what we had. You have to understand that my folks worked harder than most people. My mother was always at home, but for her that was a full-time job—and no fun, either. But my father worked his head off from the time I can remember in construction and shops. It was hard, physical work.

7 I tell you this to show that we weren't shiftless. No matter how much money Daddy made, we never made much progress up the social ladder. I got out thanks to a college scholarship and because I was a little more articulate than the average.

8 I have seen my Daddy wrap copper wire through the soles of his boots to keep them together in the wintertime. He couldn't buy new boots because he had used the money for food and shoes for us. We lived like hell, but we went to school well-clothed and with a full stomach.

9 It really is hell to live in a house that was in bad shape 10 years before you moved in. And a big family puts a lot of wear and tear on a new house, too, so you can imagine how one goes downhill if it is teetering when you move in. But we lived in houses that were sweltering in summer and freezing in winter. I woke up every morning for a year and a half with plaster on my face where it had fallen out of the ceiling during the night.

10 This wasn't during the Depression; this was in the late 60's and early 70's.

11 When we boys got old enough to learn trades in school, we would try to fix up the old houses we lived in. But have you ever tried to paint a wall that crumbled when the roller went across it? And bright paint emphasized the holes in the wall. You end up more frustrated than when you began, especially when you know that at best you might come up with only enough money to improve one of the six rooms in the house. And we might move out soon after, anyway.

12 The same goes for keeping a house like that clean. If you have a house full of kids and the house is deteriorating, you'll never keep it clean. Daddy used to yell at Mama about that, but she couldn't do anything. I think Daddy knew it inside, but he had to have an outlet for his rage somewhere, and at least yelling isn't as bad as hitting, which they never did to each other.

13 But you have a kitchen which has no counter space and no hot water, and you will have dirty dishes stacked up. That sounds like an excuse, but try it. You'll go mad from the sheer sense of futility. It's the same thing in a house with no closets. You can't keep clothes clean and rooms in order if they have to be stacked up with things.

14 Living in a bad house is generally worse on girls. For one thing, they traditionally help their mother with the housework. We boys could get outside and work in the field or cut wood or even play ball and forget about living conditions. The sky was still pretty.

15   But the girls got the pressure, and as they got older it became worse. Would they accept dates knowing they had to "receive" the young man in a dirty hallway with broken windows, peeling wallpaper and a cracked ceiling? You have to live it to understand it, but it creates a shame which drives the soul of a young person inward.

16   I'm thankful none of us ever blamed our parents for this, because it would have crippled our relationships. As it worked out, only the relationship between our parents was damaged. And I think the harshness which they expressed to each other was just an outlet to get rid of their anger at the trap their lives were in. It ruined their marriage because they had no one to yell at but each other. I knew other families where the kids got the abuse, but we were too much loved for that.

17   Once I was about 16 and Mama and Daddy had had a particularly violent argument about the washing machine, which had broken down. Daddy was on the back porch—that's where the only water faucet was—trying to fix it and Mama had a washtub out there washing school clothes for the next day and they were screaming at each other.

18   Later that night everyone was in bed and I heard Daddy get up from the couch where he was reading. I looked out from my bed across the hall into their room. He was standing right over Mama and she was already asleep. He pulled the blanket up and tucked it around her shoulders and just stood there and tears were dropping off his cheeks and I thought I could faintly hear them splashing against the linoleum rug.

19   Now they're divorced.

20   I had courses in college where housing was discussed, but the sociologists never put enough emphasis on the impact living in substandard housing has on a person's psyche. Especially children's.

21   Small children have a hard time understanding poverty. They want the same things children from more affluent families have. They want the same things they see advertised on television, and they don't understand why they can't have them.

22   Other children can be incredibly cruel. I was in elementary school in Georgia— and this is interesting because it is the only thing I remember about that particular school—when I was about eight or nine.

23   After Christmas vacation had ended, my teacher made each student describe all his or her Christmas presents. I became more and more uncomfortable as the privilege passed around the room toward me. Other children were reciting the names of the dolls they had been given, the kinds of bicycles and the grandeur of their games and toys. Some had lists which seemed to go on and on for hours.

24   It took me only a few seconds to tell the class that I had gotten for Christmas a belt and a pair of gloves. And then I was laughed at—because I cried—by a roomful of children and a teacher. I never forgave them, and that night I made my mother cry when I told her about it.

25   In retrospect, I am grateful for that moment, but I remember wanting to die at the time.

■ TOPICAL CONSIDERATIONS

1. Why, after he had turned 16, did Williams not stay home any more?
2. What were some of the conditions of the houses Williams and his family lived in? Why was it so hard to keep those houses neat and clean?
3. How does he characterize his parents? Why, according to the author, did the Williams family never make much "progress up the social ladder"?
4. According to Williams, what was the main reason his parents' marriage fell apart?
5. How do you interpret the last sentence in the essay? Why would Williams be "grateful for that moment"?

■ RHETORICAL CONSIDERATIONS

1. Where exactly does Williams make his thesis statement?
2. How does the author illustrate the impoverished conditions of his family life?
3. How does Williams illustrate how poverty helped ruin his parents' marriage?
4. Cite some descriptive details Williams employs. Do you think he could have used more?
5. The author's style of writing is quite direct and simple. How is this style created? Consider his sentence length and structure, his vocabulary and expressions, and the length of most of his paragraphs.
6. Why do you think Williams chose the title he did for this essay? Where in the essay does it have particular meaning?
7. Did you find this essay sentimental in places? If so, where? Did you think there were places where Williams consciously avoided being overly emotional or sentimental?

■ WRITING ASSIGNMENTS

1. We have all seen evidence of poverty; many of us have lived in poverty. Write an essay in which you show through specific illustrations poverty as you have experienced or seen it in your neighborhood or city or state, or some place you have visited.
2. Williams talks about how poverty adversely affected his parents. Write an essay in which you describe through illustration how certain conditions affected your parents' relationship. You might choose to talk about how the economic status of your family affected them. Or you might focus on sickness in the family, education, religion, love, children, and so on.
3. Williams selects from his past a few key instances that characterize the relationship between his mother and father. Write an essay in which you recall a few telling moments that help characterize the relationship between your parents.

| My Brother, My Self |
| Dick Schaap |

The words, "I do not really know my brother," make a startling opening sentence for a tribute from one sibling to another. And when Schaap goes on to elaborate the striking contrast between his own professional aspirations, political commitment, and journalistic focus and those of his brother, it seems even less likely that the brothers will be close. Yet the author finds that it is precisely these differences that make the brotherly bond so strong.

Dick Schaap worked as a sports editor, general editor and senior editor for *Newsweek* before he moved to WNBC-TV in New York as a sportscaster. Today he is a sports reporter for ABC News. He is the author of several books on sports figures including a biography of Mickey Mantle. The essay here first appeared in *Ms.* magazine, in September 1986.

1   I do not really know my brother. I do not see him often or speak to him regularly, even though we live in the same city and we both make our living with words. We both consider ourselves to be, above all else, journalists, and yet, professionally, our paths almost never cross, and we rarely turn to each other for either advice or criticism. We are not close, not in any customary sense of the word, and yet I love him very much and admire him immensely and, even though I hardly ever read his writings, I take fierce pride in almost everything he does. I do not think this is because we sprang from the same womb, and share genes and memories. I think it is more because he is the me I once wanted to be, the me I might have been, the me I'll never be.

2   I work for ABC. My brother works against the CIA. I write, mostly, to entertain, to make people smile, perhaps even laugh. My brother writes, mostly, to incite, to make people angry, perhaps even act. I am a correspondent for ABC News, specializing, until recently, in sports. My brother is one of the three editors of the *Covert Action Information Bulletin*. I cover the American League. He covers American imperialism. I go to the Super Bowl and the Boston Marathon. He goes to Cuba and Nicaragua. Our philosophical interests coincide only occasionally. I agree with his Cuban friends that the D.H., the designated hitter in baseball, is a dreadful idea, a sure sign of decadent capitalism. I sometimes get tickets for his Cuban friends to go see baseball games in New York. They are just like capitalists. They prefer free tickets. They also love *those* Yankees.

3   I am what is called, not always with scorn, a television personality. My brother is a radical, a full-time, grown-up radical, a rare breed, a writer and an editor and a publisher. People who watch me on television, and see him in print, know that we are very different. We always were.

4   We both went to Cornell University, consecutively, not concurrently, but while I attended the New York State School of Industrial and Labor Relations, which was sometimes called the Little Kremlin, and served as editor in chief of the Cornell *Daily Sun,* which was sometimes called the upstate *Daily Worker,* my brother, five

years younger than I, was a disc jockey on the campus radio station and the social chairman of his fraternity.

5   I was, probably, the more *committed,* the more *concerned* undergraduate, but even then, I suffered from a form of cultural schizophrenia. I covered Averell Harriman's gubernatorial campaign and I covered football games. I wrote editorials resisting the lingering McCarthyism of the mid-1950s, and I played lacrosse against Jimmy Brown.

6   In the early to mid-1960s, I abandoned sports entirely, became senior editor of *Newsweek* and city editor of the New York *Herald Tribune,* wrote books on drug addiction and Robert Kennedy. Then, in 1966, the *Tribune* died, and the following year I collaborated with a football player named Jerry Kramer on a book called *Instant Replay,* which spent 29 weeks on the New York *Times* best-seller list, changed the publishing industry's perception of sports books, and changed my life. I wrote nine sports books in the next two years and, ever since, have never completely escaped from sports. If the *Tribune* had survived, I'd probably still be in the newspaper business, as writer or editor, far from sports, except as an occasional diversion.

7   Bill went from Cornell to law school at the University of Chicago, married a wealthy young woman from Cleveland, joined a prestigious Wall Street law firm, bought a town house in Greenwich Village. He might have grown up comfortably liberal if he hadn't been assigned to a case in which his co-counsel were the Lubells, Jon and David, twin radicals, graduates of the labor school at Cornell and the law school at Harvard, who, along with his second wife, converted Bill to causes both celebrated and little known.

8   He was, of course, already predisposed. He hadn't spent all his time in college shooting pool and playing bridge. At Cornell he demonstrated against the university administration; at law school, he helped in the defense of Lenny Bruce.

9   In the late 1960s and into the 1970s, while I paddled more or less up the mainstream, my brother became involved with Mark Rudd and the Chicago Seven, Bill Kunstler and the National Lawyers Guild, Ramsey Clark and Abbie Hoffman and Huey Newton and the Attica rebellion. One of the leaders of the Attica rebellion was a Muslim inmate named Brother Richard, and Bill brought us together, to plot the writing of a book, mostly, I think, so that he could say, "Brother Richard, I'd like you to meet my brother, Richard."

10   Through most of our adult lives, I have been the more visible of the Schaap brothers, and Bill has frequently had to put up with, "Aren't you Dick Schaap's brother?" Arthur Ashe, as I recall, was the first person in my world to ask me, "Aren't you Bill Schaap's brother?" The tide may be turning. One of the film editors at ABC, the house radical, considers *Covert Action* and *Mother Jones,* for which my brother has also written, among the few honest publications in America and considers my brother one of the few true journalists. I am gilded by association.

11   Not everyone chooses to associate Bill and me. A few years ago, on one of NBC's many incarnations of a television newsmagazine, Chris Wallace narrated a profile of my brother and his wife, a portrait of two radicals. The program was produced by a good friend, a former student of mine, and when I next saw him, I told him I thought it was a very fair report. "But, journalistically," I said, "I thought you

should have said that Bill is my brother, and that his wife is the daughter of a former Nebraska football player. It would have given some insight into their roots."

12   "Not on your life," said my friend the producer, protectively.

13   I do not think I have to be protected from my brother, and his beliefs. Even if I do not share all the specifics of his feelings, I haven't lost all my liberalism, all my idealism. I love him for being the one who stands up, who speaks out, who tilts at dangerous windmills. I worry about him when he disappears into Bulgaria or Algeria or Okinawa for weeks at a time. I admire his lifestyle, barnstorming the world, supported largely by grants from foundations and by gifts from that very conflicted corner of the population, the affluent left. Bill certainly doesn't make a lot of money, but he has fun fomenting unrest.

14   No one has ever asked me to denounce my brother, which is, essentially, what my former employer, *Newsweek,* once asked my former associate, John Lardner, to do to his. When John's brother, Ring, Jr., was blacklisted and imprisoned, a victim of McCarthyism, *Newsweek* asked John, who wrote a magnificently literate sports column, to put a note in his column saying that it was his brother, not he, who was the Commie and that he did not share his brother's views. John said he would be willing to write a note saying that Ring Lardner, Jr., was his brother. Period.

15   Writing brothers are not uncommon. I have encountered several and can detect no predictable pattern. I worked with Red and Art Smith at the New York *Herald Tribune,* and one was revered and famous, and the other was merely a capable wordsmith. I also worked with Tom O'Hara, the brother of novelist John, at the *Tribune,* and Tom, ironically, hated to write a simple straightforward sentence. He did emulate his brother in one way. He wore John's old clothes, his Princeton hand-me-downs. In the 1960s, Tom was one of the best-dressed men of the 1950s. He was a good reporter, and a sweet, lovable man whom I never heard say anything but the kindest words about John O'Hara as writer and brother.

16   More recently, I've known the Vecsey brothers, George and Peter, both sports columnists, one in the New York *Times,* the other, continents away, in the New York *Post.* To judge by their prose, and their personas, they are no more brothers than, say, Nate and Strom Thurmond. George is the saint, gentle, compassionate, intellectual; Peter the sinner, blunt, harsh, street-smart. And then, of course, there are the Simons, Neil and Danny. The elder, Danny, broke in the playwright, Neil, trained him, guided him, then watched him soar. Danny tells the story of Neil buying an apartment in Los Angeles for their mother. Soon after she moved in, she invited Danny to visit. When he arrived, she was sitting by the pool with a group of women. "Girls," she said, as Danny approached, "I'd like you to meet my son's brother." Once, when I was doing a story for ABC's "20/20" about Neil, I mentioned to Danny that several people, including George Burns and Carl Reiner, had compared Neil, in awesome productivity, to Shakespeare. "When I think of Neil," Danny said, "I don't think of Shakespeare. I think of Shakespeare's brother. Do you know that after Shakespeare wrote his twelfth hit, his brother threw himself into a moat?"

17   I am jealous of my brother, too; jealous of his commitment, jealous of the potential importance of the work he does, jealous of the time he finds to study the English language, to read Eric Partridge and, politics aside, William Safire. Bill objects to

Safire putting politics into his language columns, but, I tell him, it's only fair. After all, Bill puts language into his political columns.

18   Politics does keep intruding into our relationship. A few years ago, we went out to dinner at an Italian restaurant in Manhattan, and during the course of the evening, Clay Felker, Edward Jay Epstein, and Arnaud de Borchgrave, three journalists with links, past or present, direct or indirect, to the CIA, stopped to say hello to me. "Don't ever tell any of my friends that those three stopped at my table," my brother begged me.

19   We have a sister, too, Nancy, though neither of us relates to her as well as we do to each other, which is unfortunate because she, more than either of us, tries to keep the family together. My rationale is that I am 10 years older than she, and when I moved out of the house, more or less for good, at the age of 16, she was only six, and we had very little in common. I blame the lack of strong attachment on the difference in age, rather than gender, and I think I am right. I am not positive. My sister and I have gotten closer in the past few years—thanks largely to the urging of my wife—but we still do not have the bond that exists unsolicited and, until now, unspoken, between my brother and me.

20   Bill and I share a bizarre sense of humor. When our father died—a man we both loved and respected, a man whose dreams we only sensed because he held so much inside—we went together to make the funeral arrangements. The director of the funeral parlor was Mr. Lazarus, and without a word, without even a glance, every conceivable pun and joke about rising from the dead raced, uninvited, into my head and my brother's. We kept proper faces until we went outside, and then, in the car, we looked at each other and broke into laughter. We'd like to think that our father would have laughed, too, and that he would have smiled at the love we felt, at that strange moment, for each other.

■ TOPICAL CONSIDERATIONS

1. Consider the relationship between the Schaap brothers described in paragraph 1. How is this relationship odd or unusual? In your experience, how do relations between brothers differ from relations among sisters, or between parents and children? What are the most important differences between the intimacy you have with friends and with family members? What kinds of topics can you discuss with one group and not the other?

2. Dick Schaap tells us that "People who watch me on television, and see [Bill Schaap] in print, know that we are very different. We always were" (paragraph 3). How were Schaap and his brother different when they were in and college and in their twenties (paragraphs 4–9)? How do they differ now?

3. In a recent encyclopedia, almanac, or dictionary of American biography, look up the names of people and causes cited in the article that Bill Schaap became involved with in the 1960s and 1970s (paragraph 9). What do these past associations tell you about Bill Schaap's political convictions?

4. Is Dick Schaap serious when he says, in paragraph 18, "Politics does keep intruding into our relationship"? Does Dick Schaap think he and his brother are divided by their political beliefs? From what you've read here, do you think they are?
5. Consider the long list of other "writing brothers" Schaap describes in paragraphs 14 to 16. How do these relationships further your understanding of the Schaaps?

■ RHETORICAL CONSIDERATIONS

1. Analyze the sentence construction Schaap uses in paragraph 2. What is the relationship here between the style—the way Schaap writes—and the substance—what he says?
2. Schaap refers many times in his essay to current events. As a reader, how did you respond to all the names, places, incidents and dates cited in this essay? Reflect on the impression created by these constant topical references; how do they influence your sense of Schaap and his brother?
3. Dick Schaap says that the bond between him and his brother "exists unsolicited and, until now, unspoken . . . " (paragraph 19). What does this statement suggest is Schaap's purpose in writing this essay? What does this purpose confirm about the nature of the Schaap brothers' relationship?
4. In what ways does the anecdote relating to the funeral of Schaap's father (paragraph 20) differ from the incidents recounted in the rest of the essay? Why do you suppose Schaap chose to end with this story?

■ WRITING ASSIGNMENTS

1. Write an essay directed to a third person (perhaps another family member) comparing yourself to a brother or sister.
2. Using the biographical information within the article as a research guide, find in the library one article each by Dick Schaap and Bill Schaap. Write an essay comparing the style of the two.
3. Find one of Dick Schaap's sports columns in the library; write an essay comparing the style of that column with "My Brother, My Self."
4. Write an essay describing the effect blacklisting had on the family of a targeted man or woman. In order to complete research for this project you will need to familiarize yourself with McCarthyism, the House Un-American Activities Committee, and the practice of blacklisting in America during the 1950s.

My Grandmother, the Bag Lady

Patsy Neal

What follows is a touching portrait of an elderly woman, the author's grandmother, whose world has shrunken away to the contents of a paper bag. Not one of the pathetic homeless who roam big-city streets, this "bag lady" lives comfortably in a nursing home with around-the-clock attendants and a family who cares and visits her regularly. Yet she shares with the homeless the loss of possessions, place, and independence. Neal is Wellness Coordinator at Memorial Mission Hospital in Asheville, North Carolina. This article first appeared in the "My Turn" column in *Newsweek* in 1985.

1   Almost all of us have seen pictures of old, homeless ladies, moving about the streets of big cities with everything they own stuffed into a bag or a paper sack.

2   My grandmother is 89 years old, and a few weeks ago I realized with a jolt that she, too, had become one of them. Before I go any further, I had best explain that I did not see my grandmother's picture on TV. I discovered her plight during a face-to-face visit at my mother's house—in a beautiful, comfortable, safe, middle-class environment with good china on the table and turkey and chicken on the stove.

3   My grandmother's condition saddened me beyond words, for an 89-year-old should not have to carry around everything she owns in a bag. It's enough to be 89, without the added burden of packing the last fragments of your existence into a space big enough to accommodate only the minutest of treasures.

4   Becoming a bag lady was not something that happened to her overnight. My grandmother has been in a nursing home these last several years; at first going back to her own home for short visits, then less frequently as she became older and less mobile.

5   No matter how short these visits were, her greatest pleasure came from walking slowly around her home, touching every item lovingly and spending hours browsing through drawers and closets. Then, I did not understand her need to search out all her belongings.

6   As she spent longer days and months at the nursing home, I could not help noticing other things. She began to hide her possessions under the mattress, in her closet, under the cushion of her chair, in every conceivable, reachable space. And she began to think that people were "stealing" from her.

7   *Unsteady:*   When a walker became necessary, my mother took the time to make a bag that could be attached to it, so that my grandmother could carry things around while keeping her hands on the walker. I had not paid much attention to this bag until we went to the nursing home to take her home with us for our traditional Christmas Eve sharing of gifts.

8   As we left, my grandmother took her long, unsteady walk down the hallway, balancing herself with her walker, laboriously moving it ahead, one step at a time, until finally we were at the car outside. Once she was safely seated, I picked up her walker

to put it in the back. I could barely lift it. Then I noticed that the bag attached to it was bulging. Something clicked, but it still wasn't complete enough to grasp.

9   At home in my mother's house, I was asked to get some photographs from my grandmother's purse. Lifting her pocketbook, I was surprised again at the weight and bulk. I watched as my mother pulled out an alarm clock, a flashlight, a small radio, thread, needles, pieces of sewing, a book and other items that seemed to have no reason for being in a pocketbook.

10   I looked at my grandmother, sitting bent over in her chair, rummaging through the bag on the walker, slowly pulling out one item and then another, and lovingly putting it back. I looked down at her purse with all its disconnected contents and remembered her visits to her home, rummaging through drawers and through closets.

11   "Oh, Lord," I thought with sudden insight. "That walker and that purse are her home now."

12   I began to understand that over the years my grandmother's space for living had diminished like melting butter—from endless fields and miles of freedom as a child and young mother to, with age, the constrictions of a house, then a small room in a nursing home and finally to the tightly clutched handbag and the bag on her walker.

13   When the family sent her to a nursing home, it was the toughest decision it had ever had to make. We all thought she would be secure there; we would no longer have to worry about whether she had taken her medicine, or left her stove on, or was alone at night.

14   But we hadn't fully understood her needs. Security for my grandmother was not in the warm room at the nursing home, with 24-hour attendants to keep her safe and well fed, nor in the family who visited and took her to visit in their homes. In her mind her security was tied to those things she could call her own—and over the years those possessions had dwindled away like sand dropping through an hourglass: first her car, sold when her eyes became bad and she couldn't drive; then some furnishings she didn't really need. Later it was the dogs she had trouble taking care of. And finally it would be her home when it became evident that she could never leave the nursing home again. But as her space and mobility dwindled, so did her control over her life.

15   *Dignity:*   I looked at my grandmother again, sitting so alone before me, hair totally gray, limbs and joints swollen by arthritis, at the hearing aid that could no longer help her hear, and the glasses too thick but so inadequate in helping her to see . . . and yet there was such dignity about her. A dignity I could not understand.

16   The next day, after my grandmother had been taken back to the nursing home and my mother was picking up in her room, she found a small scrap of paper my grandmother had scribbled these words on:

17   "It is 1:30 tonight and I had to get up and go to the bathroom. I cannot go back to sleep. But I looked in on Margaret and she is sleeping *so* good, and Patsy is sleeping too."

18   With that note, I finally understood, and my 89-year-old bag-lady grandmother changed from an almost helpless invalid to a courageous, caring individual still very much in control of her environment.

19   What intense loneliness she must have felt as she scribbled that small note on that small piece of paper with the small bag on her walker and her small purse next to her. Yet she chose to experience it alone rather than wake either of us from much-needed sleep. Out of her own great need, she chose to meet our needs.

20   As I held that tiny note, and cried inside, I wondered if she dreamed of younger years and more treasured possessions and a bigger world when she went back to sleep that night. I certainly hoped so.

■ TOPICAL CONSIDERATIONS

1. Describe how Neal's 89-year-old grandmother became a bag lady.
2. The grandmother's family sent her to a nursing home to provide security. How did the family's definition of security differ from the grandmother's? How, paradoxically, did the nursing home erode the woman's sense of security?
3. What does the grandmother's note reveal to the author?
4. Although she is feeble and infirm, control is still a major issue for Neal's grandmother. In what ways does she manifest control over her life?

■ RHETORICAL CONSIDERATIONS

1. How does the labeling of a grandmother as a bag lady capture the reader's attention?
2. What similes does the author use to describe the gradual diminishing of her grandmother's world and possessions? Are they effective? Are they original? Try to supply some of your own, if you can.
3. Did you find the concluding paragraph of the essay sentimental, that is, a deliberate ploy of the author to evoke emotion from the reader?

■ WRITING ASSIGNMENTS

1. In this essay, seemingly minor events give great insight into the grandmother's character. Write a brief character sketch, in which a seemingly insignificant event (or events) lends insight into the character of someone you know.
2. Write a portrait of someone in your neighborhood, community, or school, who for whatever reasons, does not seem to adjust. Use specific details about the person's behavior and dialogue to capture the individual.

	Older Children and Divorce
	Barbara S. Cain

Most studies examining the effect of divorce focus on young children living at home. Unfortunately, the impact of midlife divorce on college-age children has been a neglected topic. Barbara S. Cain, the author of this article and a clinical supervisor at the Psychological Clinic at the University of Michigan, narrows this gap in research and, at the same time, dispels the myth that older children are less vulnerable to the trauma of divorce. Having interviewed fifty college students between the ages of 18 and 20, Cain discovered recurrent themes and reactions to divorce. In the following essay, which originally appeared in *The New York Times* Magazine in February 1990, these interviews come to life as students recall the shock, disbelief, and profound sense of loss they experienced when their parents announced their separation. While shedding new light on the fallout of divorce for the older child, this piece is also compelling reading for anyone touched by family breakup.

1 They were more sanguine about Laura. She was, after all, in college and on the far side of growing up. They said she had loosened her tether to the family and was no longer hostage to the twists of their fate. They allowed that she would be shaken for a time by their divorce, but insisted that before long she would find her balance and regain her stride. Her younger brothers, on the other hand, were a constant source of nagging concern. At home and in the eye of the storm, they were in closer range and at higher risk. But Laura, they said, was less vulnerable. Not to worry, Laura would be fine.

2 So go the prevailing attitudes toward college-age children of a midlife divorce. Moreover, these assumptions appear to be shared by social scientists and cultural tribunes who have rigorously investigated the impact of divorce on younger children but have, nevertheless, overlooked the plight of a college-age population, even though statistics show increased incidence of divorce during midlife, thereby involving greater numbers of young adult offspring.

3 In an effort to narrow this gap in the literature, a study was launched in 1984 at the University of California at San Diego and the University of Michigan at Ann Arbor—in which 50 college students between the ages of 18 and 26 were interviewed by this writer, who reported the findings in the journal *Psychiatry* in May 1989. There were obvious differences among the students, their families and each individual divorce process, but recurrent themes and threads of discourse wove themselves within and across the interviews with striking regularity.

4 Perhaps most consistent among them were the students' initial reactions to news of their parents' divorce. All but three in the study recalled an immediate state of shock followed by a lingering sense of disbelief. Even those who grew up amid a turbulent marriage were incredulous when a separation was announced.

5 "I shouldn't have been surprised," a 20-year-old woman reflected. "I used to hear them argue night after night. I used to hear Mom cry and Dad take off in the

car. I used to lie awake until he came back, but he always did come back, so I just assumed they would carry on like that for the rest of their lives."

6   Others who had observed their parents slowly disengage solaced themselves with the belief that though a marriage of more than two decades might inevitably lose its luster it would not necessarily lose its life. "Sure, I noticed them drift apart," a 21-year-old woman remarked. "But then I surveyed the marriages in our neighborhood, and nobody was exactly hearing violins, so I relaxed and told myself that Mom and Dad were like every other couple who had spent half their lives in one relationship."

7   An unexpected finding was that more than half the youngsters surveyed had glorified the marriage preceding its breach, claiming theirs was "the all-American family," their parents were "the ideal couple"—and "the envy of everyone they knew."

8   "I mean I wasn't exactly naïve about divorce," a 19-year-old woman explained. "Half my friends grew up with a single parent, but my Mom and Dad were considered Mr. and Mrs. Perfect Couple. So when they split up, all our friends were just as freaked out as I was."

9   When the veil of denial began to lift and reality took hold, these young adults experienced a profound sense of loss. They felt bereft of the family of childhood, the one in the photo album, the one whose members shared the same history, the same humor, the same address. Many described in graphic detail the wrenching pain when the family house was sold, when the furniture was divided and delivered to two separate addresses, neither of which "would ever be home."

10   "Nothing really sank in," explained a 20-year-old man, "until I watched the movers denude the house I lived in for most of my life. And then I sat on the bare floor and stared at the marks on the wall which outlined the places where our furniture used to be. And I cried until I couldn't see those borders anymore." Clearly the dismantling of the family house symbolized in stark relief the final dismantling of the family itself.

11   As each parent began living with new partners, the young adults surveyed said that they felt estranged from the resented interloper and displaced by the new mate's younger (often live-in) children. Others felt virtually evicted from the parents' new homes, which simply could not accommodate two sets of children during overlapping visits.

12   "When neither Mom nor Dad had room for me during spring break," a 19-year-old man recalled, "it finally hit me that I no longer had a home to go back to and, like it or not, I'd better get my act together because it was, 'Welcome to the adult world, kid, you're now completely on your own.'"

13   Because the divorce represented the first sobering crisis in their young adult lives, many in the study believed it marked the end of an era of trust and ushered in a new apprehension about life's unforeseen calamities. They reported an unprecedented preoccupation with death, disease and crippling disabilities. They became self-described cynics, and began scanning relationships for subterfuge. "I used to believe what people said," a 22-year-old woman recalled. "I used to trust my roommates. I used to trust my boyfriends, and now I know I also used to be certifiably 'judgment impaired.'"

14   Striking among this age group was the way in which harsh moral opprobrium became the conduit through which anger toward parents was expressed. Pejoratives like irresponsible, self-indulgent and hypocritical punctuated the interviews.

15   "You accept as an article of faith that your parents will stay together until they die," explained a thoughtful 20-year-old woman, "and then they pull the rug out from under you and you want to scream out" and ask, "How can you break the very rules you yourselves wrote?"

16   Many described being gripped by an unforgiving fury toward parents who they felt had deprived them of a home, a family and that inseparable parental pair they assumed would always be there, together, at birthdays, holidays and vacations at home. Furthermore, they viewed these losses to have been preventable, hence they deeply resented learning of the decision when it was a fait accompli. And they upbraided their parents for excluding them from a process they might have otherwise reversed.

17   "Why didn't they tell me they were having trouble?" one young woman asked in barely muted exasperation. "If I had known, I would have helped them find a marriage counselor. If they were unhappy then why didn't they do something about it? My dad spent more time fixing his car than he ever did his marriage."

18   Most in the study blamed the parent who initiated the break and relentlessly hectored that parent for explanations. "Every day I'd ask my mother 'Why,'" one young woman recalled, "and no answer ever made sense. They all sounded so feeble, and so absolutely wrong."

19   The young adults surveyed were most staggered by the apparent moral reversals in their parents' behavior. In stunned disbelief, a 20-year-old woman discovered her "buttoned up, Bible-carrying" mother in bed with a man two years older than her son. Another student witnessed his ambitious, seemingly conscience-ridden father walk away from his family and his lucrative law firm for destinations unknown. As though looking through lenses badly out of focus, many gazed upon parents they no longer recognized and struggled over which image was false, which authentic.

20   "Was the old Mom just hiding under the real one that was coming out now?" a 21-year-old man wondered. "Was that tender, loving person all a lie? Was I just not seeing what I didn't want to see? And if that's true, then how am I supposed to trust what I think I see now?"

21   Upon observing their mothers' unbridled sexuality, several young women withdrew from romantic relationships, retreated to solitary study, became abstemious and, in Anna Freud's words, declared war on the pursuit of pleasure.

22   In sharp contrast, others plunged into hedonism, flaunting their indulgences, daring their parents to forbid activity that mirrored their own. A 20-year-old woman launched a series of sexual liaisons with older married men. A 19-year-old moved in with a graduate student after knowing him for 10 days. And a 22-year-old male dropped out of school to deal in drugs.

23   In response to their parents' apparent moral inversion, a small subgroup temporarily took refuge in a protective nihilism, reasoning that illusions that never form are illusions that never shatter. "Since their breakup I don't pin my hopes on anything anymore," a disenchanted young man declared. "And I no longer have a secret

dream. What will be will be. Since I can't change any of that, why even try and why even care?"

24   At variance with the familiar loyalty conflict observed in younger children of divorce, most young adults considered one parent worthy of blame, the other worthy of compassion. Several openly stated they were sorely tempted to sever ties permanently with the parent who initiated the break. And when asked, "What would you advise someone your age whose parents were divorcing?" many answered, "Do not write one parent off totally, even though you might be tempted to at the time of the split."

25   Several said they feigned an affectionate tie to the rejected parent simply because of financial need. "Between you and me," a spunky 19-year-old man confessed, "I can't wait till I'm self-supporting, so then I won't have to humor my father with a phony song and dance every time my tuition is due." And a number reported that their overt condemnation of their father cost them a long-enjoyed relationship with paternal grandparents as battle lines between "his" and "her" side of the family were drawn.

26   Despite their censoriousness and ascriptions of blame, these young adults staunchly insisted that each parent honor their attempted neutrality. "I refused to let my Mom put down my Dad," one 23-year-old man declared emphatically, "and I artfully dodged every invitation to spy on one and report to the other."

27   Remarks such as these suggest that, whatever else, these college-age youngsters are better able than younger children to remove themselves from the internecine warfare and resist colluding with the parent "spurned" in excoriating the parent blamed.

28   In sharp contrast to younger children of divorce who frequently hold themselves responsible for the separation, the young adults surveyed did not reveal even the slightest traces of guilt or blame. Though most were certain they had not caused their parents' divorce, several lamented having failed to prevent it. A 19-year-old woman believed that had she managed her mother's domestic chores more effectively, her mother would not have ended her marriage in favor of her career. And a 21-year-old woman chided herself for not noticing her parents' estrangement: "Sometimes I still wonder if I had paid more attention to *them,* maybe we would all still be *us.*"

29   And because each youngster in the study was living away from home at the time of the separation, many believed that their parents had literally "stayed together for the sake of the children." Indeed, several parents did not disabuse their children of this notion. When a 20-year-old man accused his father of being foolishly headstrong in abruptly ending his 25-year marriage, his father informed him that he had wanted to end his marriage for more than 20 years but had waited until his son was grown and gone.

30   Three in the study proudly announced that they were responsible for their parents' separations and celebrated the fact that they urged upon their mothers a much overdue separation from chronically abusive alcoholic fathers. "Do I feel responsible for my parents splitting? You bet I do," one 24-year-old man trumpeted. "And my only regret is not pushing for it sooner."

31   With few exceptions, the young adults surveyed described an unremitting concern for their single parents, particularly the one who opposed the break. They
dropped courses, cut classes, extended weekends away from school in an effort to
bolster the spirit of the parent at home. "I flew home so often," one young man
mused, "I was awarded three free tickets in less than one year."

32   In striking role reversals, these youngsters disavowed their own wish for support
and ministered to their parents instead. They nurtured mothers who cried in their
arms, they discouraged fathers from reckless decisions, they variously counseled,
succored, reassured and advised. And many reported they were unable to resume the
natural rhythms of their lives until their parents were clearly back on track.

33   "I was nervous most of the time I wasn't with my Mom," a 20-year-old man explained. ". . . I called her constantly and went home as often as I could. . . . Deep
down, I was worried she'd take her own life or accidentally smash the car as she was
thinking about Dad or money or being too old and too fat to start over again."

34   These young adults also assumed the role of proxies. "After the split, I felt I was
wearing a thousand hats," a 19-year-old woman recalled. "In one day I could be a
college student, my mother's therapist, my dad's escort and my brother's mother.
Small wonder I was a little ditzy that year."

35   After their parents had parted, some of those surveyed recalled allowing themselves to return to a recently relinquished parent-child relationship in which they
"tolerated" parental overprotection from the "spurned" partner. They no longer
balked at queries about eating habits and dating behavior. "If Mom's happier treating
me like a kid, I'm willing to be that for her," a 20-year-old man admitted. "She just
lost her husband, the least I can do is let her have her kid." Others described a quasi-
symbiotic relationship with one or the other parent in which both parent and child
were by turns both host and parasite.

36   Though many felt compelled to rescue their parents, several baldly stated that they
deeply resented the "hysterical calls in the middle of the night," the incessant rumina-
tions about "the same old stuff." It is noteworthy, however, that those who were enraged
by parental pleas and demands felt, nonetheless, obliged to leave school at times and
comfort the beleaguered parent at home. As a young woman stated succinctly, "If I
stayed at school, I was worried about my Mom; if I went home I was worried about me."

37   Perhaps the most uniform finding in this study was the radically altered attitudes toward love and marriage held by many following their parents' divorce.

38   When a young woman's parents separated soon after their 20th anniversary, she
created her own theory of marriage: "People marry in order to have children, and
parenthood is what holds a marriage together. When children are grown and gone,
marriage no longer has a reason for being and couples will then drift apart and the
marriage will slowly die. If couples stay together even after their last child leaves
home, then they are truly in love and they are the lucky few."

39   Several categorically forswore marriage, vowing to spare themselves and their
unborn children the pain and dislocation they had recently endured. Others allowed
for a long-term live-in relationship but pledged to forestall indefinitely a legally
binding commitment. A disenchanted young man spoke for many: "Since their divorce, I'm gun-shy about love and spastic about marriage. To me, getting married is

like walking over a minefield, you know it's going to explode . . . you just don't know when!"

40   Those who were already involved in longstanding romances felt their parents' divorce cast a long shadow on their own relationship. As a 20-year-old woman explained: "You become super alert to everything your boyfriend does. You suddenly notice his wandering eye as you walk together across campus. You start resenting it when he yawns or fidgets or looks at his watch while you're talking. And you spend a whole lot of time holding your breath braced for the moment when he hits you with, 'I mean I really like you, but I really need more space.'"

41   Some young women withdrew from boyfriends they suddenly suspected as being unfaithful, indifferent or increasingly remote. Others demanded premature commitments or promises thereof. And many abruptly aborted solid relationships in an effort to actively master what they believed they might otherwise helplessly endure.

42   With rare exception, most in the study feared they were destined to repeat their parents' mistakes, a concern frequently reinforced by the parents themselves. "You're attracted to the same kind of charming Don Juan who did me in," one mother admonished. "Beware of the womanizer just like your father or you'll be dumped in your 40's, just like me." Many of the youngsters deeply resented these apocalyptic, cautionary tales. Others felt burdened by having to wrestle with the ghosts of their parents' past. "Most people meet, fall in love and marry," a 21-year-old lamented, "but I have to find someone who convinces my mother he's not my father and then he has to fit the job description of a saint."

43   Whereas most felt fated to repeat their parents' past, many were determined to avoid the perils their parents did not. Many pledged never to let feelings fester until "they explode in everybody's face." They planned a "playmate relationship" in order to avoid the pallor of their parents' middle years. In an effort to revise their parents' history, some feared they would submit a potential partner to such dissecting scrutiny no mortal would qualify, and marriage would be forever postponed.

44   Nevertheless, when asked at the close of their interviews, "Where do you see yourself 10 years from now?" many of those who earlier had denounced marriage stated unhesitatingly that they would in all probability "be married with kids and a house of my own."

45   Not every divorce was emotionally wrenching. It was least disruptive when the parents' decision was mutual and their initial rancor was relatively shortlived. Youngsters fared best when their attachment to each parent was honored by the other, when their quest for neutrality was respected and when their relationship with each parent remained virtually unmarred. Few were so fortunate, however.

46   Friendship and religion were great comforts for many, but the majority said that soul-baring marathons with siblings clearly offered the greatest amount of comfort with the least amount of shame.

47   "I couldn't have made it without my sister," one college junior recalled. "Talking to friends was like going public, but with my sister it was safe, it was private, and a lifeline for us both."

48   Whether or not the profound sense of loss, the disillusionment, the revised attitudes toward love and marriage remain an enduring legacy of parental divorce for college-age youngsters, only future studies can determine. It should be noted, however, that most of these youngsters unsuccessfully disguised a deep and abiding wish to marry, to have children and to recapture the family of childhood—the one in the picture frame, animated, intertwined and inseparable.

■ TOPICAL CONSIDERATIONS

1. Why does the author think this study was necessary? Do you agree with the author's concern for college-age children of divorce? Why or why not?
2. The study indicates that many respondents expected their parents to drift apart. Do you think that most college-age students expect their parents to drift apart after 20 years of marriage? Why or why not?
3. The author mentions the shock by college students at the apparent "moral reversals in their parents' behavior" (paragraph 19). She goes on to describe the students' reactions to this behavior. What three responses were most common? What would be your reaction? Explain your answer.
4. The author discovered two important contrasts in comparing college-age to younger children of divorce. Describe one difference and explain why you think that difference showed up in the study.
5. In the report, the author describes how many young adults indicated that they ministered to their parents and neglected their own concerns. Would you respond in the same way if one or both of your parents needed your help to get "back on track" (paragraph 32)?

■ RHETORICAL CONSIDERATIONS

1. What is the function of the opening paragraph? How does it prepare the reader for the second paragraph?
2. Interspersed throughout this essay are words like "moral opprobrium," "pejorative," "fait accompli," "abstemious," "internecine," and "excoriating." Do you think such words fit the tone and style of this essay? Did the language prevent you from focusing on the report? If you found any unfamiliar words, did you look them up in the dictionary? Did the language enhance the essay? Explain using an example.
3. In paragraph 9, the author mentions "the family of childhood." This phrase is repeated at the end of the essay. Why does the author repeat it?
4. Cain uses quotations from interviews with college-age children of divorce in this essay. She mixes these quotations with the results of the report. Is this strategy effective or not? Why?
5. The author reports the feelings of young adults when their family house was sold. She says, "The dismantling of the house symbolized in stark relief the final dismantling of the family itself." Explain the ways in which the family house itself represents the family itself.

■ **WRITING ASSIGNMENTS**

1. Imagine that you write an advice column for colleagues in the school paper. Respond to a letter from a fellow student who wants to know how to deal with his parents' divorce.

2. Imagine that it is 20 years from now. Report on whether the profound sense of loss, disillusionment, and "revised attitudes toward love and marriage remain an enduring legacy of parental divorce for college-age youngsters" (paragraph 48).

3. As a college-age child of divorce, write a letter to Barbara S. Cain in which you tell her why you agree or disagree with the results of her study.

4. Did your parents divorce? If so, write a personal account of how the divorce affected you.

5. Do you know parents who have divorced? If so, how would they respond to this essay? You may write a response as if you were the divorced parents of a college-age student.

·3·
Changing Times

O urs is the Fast-forward Age. An era of dizzying social and cultural changes. So caught up in the momentum, we can barely stand back to examine what we've made of ourselves. Yet when we do, we may not like what we see. The essays in this chapter take a hard look at contemporary American society in flux—at its values and its costs.

The overview piece we open with is a provocative letter by a college student to his parents' generation. In "The Terrible Twenties," Daniel Smith-Rowsey complains that the future of today's 20-year-olds is bleak because the past generation had consumed too much and given too little. What chance, he asks, do young people have in a society whose preference is pop culture to education, whose selfishness and mall-culture indulgence reduced "us all to 12-year-olds who want everything *now*."

In the next piece, "As Busy As We Wanna Be," Deborah Baldwin examines the time crunch created by our workaday world. "The go-go '80s may be gone," but the 1990s, she argues, is life in a "caffeinated jungle" where we are driven by the belief that there just isn't enough time to get done everything we want. One wonders if we really want to return to the simple life.

During the 1980s much of America looked up and saw only endless blue sky. As never before, the good life was upon us. As never before, our culture defined itself in terms of what we owned. But while Wall Street and Main Street enjoyed a feeding frenzy, others went hungry in body and spirit. The penalties for the imbalance are the focus of the next essay. In "A Child of Crack," Michele Norris offers a graphic picture of a 6-year-old boy growing up in a crack house apartment in the shadow of the nation's capitol.

Our popular media projects a culture obsessed with sexuality. Racy movies, naughty TV sitcoms, fleshy commercials, and the soft porn of MTV videos bear the message that sex and fun are what adolescence is all about. It's no wonder that to-day's generation of young people are sexually more active than their predecessors. It's no wonder that more schools, churches, and synagogues offer courses in sex education. But as Ellen Hopkins sees it, sex education doesn't work. In "Sex Is for Adults," she argues that while today's kids are more knowledgeable about sex, they are not more responsible. In this age of AIDS, that can be deadly.

Surviving in today's society is also the topic of "On Kids and Slasher Movies." Here, Michael Ventura speculates on young people's attraction to Hollywood psycho-killers. His concern is not that slasher movies may lead to violence, but whether we have created a world where kids need heavy doses of horror to deal with everyday life.

The next essay, "Stolen Promise," expresses the profound frustration of a black American mother, Patricia Raybon, who laments that there are too few good black men around to date her daughter. Either they have dropped out of college or are in jail or, worse, they're dead—victims of senseless street warfare plaguing our cities.

The next piece turns to the streets of suburban America. In "Houses and Streets, but No Neighborhood," Alan Lupo laments that "something has stolen the people." When he was a kid, the streets were bustling with activity—hide'n' seek, tag, cops and robbers, jump rope, stickball. People sat on porches talking, radios blared, kids played to sundown. But not today, he says. The modern world has shut us inside.

In our final selection, intended for comic relief, humorist Dave Barry exults in the newfound joys of tooling down the information highway. In "You Have to Be a Real Stud Hombre Cybermuffin to Handle 'Windows,'" Barry describes the power and freedom of working out on his new computer: of hours spent trying to decipher the software, linking onto Internet, exchanging messages with others. In short, of being "a happy nerd in cyberspace."

The Terrible Twenties

Daniel Smith-Rowsey

Like most of you reading this essay, Daniel Smith-Rowsey is from the "twentysomething" generation. And like most of you, he was brought up in a culture of MTV, Nintendo, latchkey freedom, cellular phones, BMWs, and sprawling malls. But as adulthood weighs in on him, he questions the values and resources he and his indulged generation inherited from their parents. "You never taught us to be smart—you only taught us to be young." With skyrocketing costs and unemployment and a college degree that no longer guarantees a good job, he wonders if today's twentysomethings have the wherewithall to survive a future rushing down on them. At the time he wrote this article, Smith-Rowsey was a senior majoring in politics and film-making at the University of California, Santa Cruz. This article first appeared in *Newsweek* in June 1991.

1 Sometimes I wonder what it would be like to have been 20, my age, in the '60s. Back when you could grow up, count on a career and maybe think about buying a house. When one person could expect to be the wage earner for a household.

2 In the space of one generation those dreams have died. The cost of living has skyrocketed, unemployment has gone up, going to college doesn't guarantee you can get a good job. And no one seems to care. Maybe it's because the only people my age you older people have heard from are those who *do* make a lot of money: investment bankers, athletes, musicians, actors. But more and more of us twentysomethings are underachievers who loaf around the house until well past our college years.

3 This is an open letter to the baby boomers from the *next* generation. I think it's time we did a little hitting back. Aside from the wealthy, none of you ever told your children, "Someday this will all be yours," and you're the first middle class to fail that way. Did you think we wouldn't care? Thanks a lot. But the real danger lies in the way we've been taught to deal with failure: gloss over and pretend the prob-

lem doesn't exist. It's evidence you never taught us to be smart—you only taught us to be young.

4   We are the stupidest generation in American history, we 20-year-olds. You already know that. We really do get lower SAT scores than our parents. Our knowledge of geography is pathetic, as is our ability with foreign languages and even basic math. We don't read books like you did. We care only about image. We love fads. Talk to college professors, and they'll tell you they don't get intelligent responses like they used to, when you were in school. We're perfectly mush-headed.

5   You did this to us. You prized your youth so much you made sure ours would be carefree. It's not that you didn't love us; you loved us so much you pushed us to follow your idea of what you were—or would like to have been—instead of teaching us to be responsible. After legitimizing youthful rebellion you never let us have our own innocence—perhaps because Vietnam and Watergate shattered yours. That's why we're already mature enough to understand and worry about racism, the environment, abortion, the homeless, nuclear policy. But we also were fed on the video culture you created to idealize your own irresponsible days of youth. Your slim-and-trim MTV bimbos, fleshy beer commercials and racy TV shows presented adolescence as a time only for fun and sex. Why should we be expected to work at learning anything?

6   Not that we're not smart—in some ways. We're street smart, David Letterman clever, whizzes at Nintendo. We can name more beers than presidents. Pop culture is, to us, more attractive than education.

7   I really don't think we can do this dance much longer. Not a single industrialized country has survived since 1945 without a major re-evaluation of its identity except ours. That's what you thought you were doing in the '60s, but soon you gave way to chasing the dreams of the Donald Trump–Michael Milken get-rich-quick ethos—and all you had left for us was a bankrupt economy. The latchkey lifestyle you gave us in the name of your own "freedom" has made us a generation with missing parents and broken homes. And what about the gays and blacks and Hispanics and Asians and women who you pretended to care so much about, and then forgot? It's not that I'm angry at you for selling out to the system. It's that there won't be a system. It's that there won't be a system for *me* to sell out to, if I want to. The money isn't there anymore because you spent it all.

8   To be honest, I can't blame you for all that's happened. The pre-eminence of new technologies and the turn toward cutthroat capitalism over the past two decades would have happened with or without the peculiarities of your generation. If I had been born in the '50s, I too would have been angry at racism and the war in Vietnam. But that's not the same thing as allowing the system to unravel out of my own greed. Don't say you didn't start the fire of selfishness and indulgence, building it up until every need or desire was immediately appeased. Cable TV, BMWs, cellular phones, the whole mall culture has reduced us all to 12-year-olds who want everything *now.* I'm not in love with everything your parents did, but at least they gave you a chance. As Billy Joel said, "Every child had a pretty good shot to get at least as far as their old man got." For most of us, all we've been left with are the erotic fantasies, aggressive tendencies and evanescent

funds of youth. Pretty soon we won't have youth *or* money, and that's when we may get a little angry.

9   Or maybe we won't. Perhaps you really have created a nation of mush-heads who will always prefer style over substance, conservative politics and reading lessons. If that's so, the culture can survive, as it seems to be doing with the bright smile of optimism breaking through the clouds of decaying American institutions. And then you really will be the last modern smart generation because our kids will be even dumber, poorer and more violent than us. You guys will be like the old mule at the end of Orwell's "Animal Farm," thinking about how great things used to be when you were kids. You will differ from your own parents in that you will have missed your chance to change the world and robbed us of the skills and money to do it ourselves. If there's any part of you left that still loves us enough to help us, we could really use it. And it's not just your last chance. It's our only one.

■ TOPICAL CONSIDERATIONS

1. In paragraph 8, Smith-Rowsey writes, "For most of us, all we've been left with are the erotic fantasies, aggressive tendencies and evanescent funds of youth." In the context of the essay, how does he substantiate this claim? As a member of the "twentysomething" generation, do you agree with this claim?

2. In paragraph 4, the author says, "We are the stupidest generation in American history, we 20-year-olds." On what does he base his assessment? Does his claim offend you? On what points do you agree or disagree with him?

3. In paragraph 6, Smith-Rowsey states, "Pop culture is, to us, more attractive than education." Is he indicting 1990s youth or explaining a universal experience felt by 20-year-olds for generations? Do you find pop culture more attractive than education? Has your parents' generation influenced your preference?

4. According to Smith-Rowsey in paragraph 7, how have the civil rights and equal rights movements survived? How does the author feel about social causes? Do you believe that youth today are apathetic to social causes or that there has been a resurgence in political activism?

5. How does the essay prove or disprove the Billy Joel line, "Every child had a pretty good shot to get at least as far as their old man got"? Considering America today, do you think you can achieve what your parents did?

6. According to Smith-Rowsey, what products and technological advancements has the younger generation gained from the older generation? Are all of Smith-Rowsey's examples negative? What products and advancements from his parents' generation can you think of to present a more balanced picture?

■ RHETORICAL CONSIDERATIONS

1. This essay is written as an open letter. To whom is the letter addressed? How are first person and second person used in the essay? Do you as a reader feel part of Smith-Rowsey's "twentysomethings"?

2. In paragraph 7, what does the word "latchkey" connote? What other allusions or terms in the essay are products of 1980s and 1990s culture? What do these products say about American culture? Add your own list of 1990s vocabulary words that reveal contemporary American philosophy.

3. Does Smith-Rowsey's lead grab you? Why or why not? As a member of the twentysomethings, have you wondered about the same things he has?

4. Characterize the tone of the essay. Do you think it captures the attitude of your generation? Would you have written the essay from a different approach?

■ WRITING ASSIGNMENTS

1. Billy Joel is part of the older generation whose creed was, "Every child had a pretty good shot to get at least as far as their old man got." Consider songwriters and singers of your generation. Write a paper that explains the 1990s creed using lyrics from at least three different songs.

2. Smith-Rowsey writes (paragraph 9), "And then you really will be the last modern smart generation because our kids will be even dumber, poorer and more violent than us." Write a paper that shows how we can turn future generations around and begin to create a smarter, more peaceful society. Consider our current technological, environmental, and global-political knowledge.

3. Do you think Smith-Rowsey has fairly characterized your generation and that of your parents? If not, write a rebuttal to him. In it, try to render a more positive portrayal of the twentysomething generation and the influences that have molded it.

As Busy As We Wanna Be

Deborah Baldwin

Are you out of breath? Did you spend today racing from one class to another? Trying to sandwich your job between a string of errands and a workout at the gym or health club? Did you miss a coffee date with a friend and discover, too late, that the dry cleaner closed early today? If this scenario is familiar to you, perhaps you are a victim of what Deborah Baldwin describes as "the Great American Time Crunch," a syndrome in which there is never enough time to get everything done. While painting a comical picture of a nation in a rush, Ms. Baldwin provides a serious analysis of some of the national cultural values that fuel this obsession with productivity.

Deborah Baldwin is former editor of *Common Cause* Magazine and has written for numerous publications including the *Utne Reader,* which first published this piece in 1994.

1   The gleaming escalators that whisk passengers to and from Washington's high-speed subway never seem to move fast enough for some people. So by unspoken rule, the moving steps have been divided down the middle: On the left is the passing lane. Pause in the passing lane on one of the escalators at, say, the Dupont Circle station, a beehive of white-collar activity ringed by no fewer than five espresso stands, and risk the uncomfortable sensation of some lawyer's briefcase bumping the back of your knees.

2   The go-go '80s may be gone, but not the Great American Time Crunch, which is fueled by the perception that there's never enough time to get everything done and, no matter how fast you move, someone—or something—is bound to get there faster. To survive in this caffeinated jungle, we surround ourselves with *objets de temps*— everything from digital watches that beep on the hour to bulging Filofaxes that master our days. We buy computers that measure time in nanoseconds, cars that leap from zero to 60, kitchen equipment able to reduce a head of cabbage to slaw in less time than it takes to clean up afterward.

3   It may all sound like a losing battle, but here's a little secret from one of the nation's leading experts on time use: With some key exceptions (most notably parents of young children), Americans generally have more free time today than they had 30 years ago—about five hours more a week, to be exact. We're doing less housework, having fewer children, and retiring earlier than previous generations. Many of us are busy, says University of Maryland sociologist John P. Robinson, who heads the Americans' Use of Time Project, *because we want to be.*

4   Here's another thought: We could return to simpler times. But who would want to?

5   The fact is, most of us are addicted, as Joni Mitchell once put it, to "the crazies you get from too much choice." As we jump from activity to activity, many of us also are dabbling in a rich stew of options, identities, ways of life. Yes, it is possible these days to be a parent, hold down a demanding job, participate in political activities, cultivate an interest in folk art, take up Brazilian cooking, do some traveling, and, in your spare time, carry on a romance with your partner. Or at least it's fun to try.

6   The busier our schedules, the more important we feel and the easier it is to back out of things we secretly don't want to do, like reading Proust or volunteering at the shelter for the homeless. Yet paradoxically, the more we cram into our lives, the less we feel in control.

7   My mother likes to refer to a wise and purposeful Catholic saint who, when asked what he would do if he knew he had only a few days left on earth, replied: "Just what I'm doing now."

8   This radical notion, which implies that one should think about what is important and set about doing it, bears special meaning for those of us who would be more apt to answer "travel to Bali" or "order everything on the menu at the Four Seasons." What matters in life is not some fantasy of what it would be like to cover a lot of ground and "have" a lot of experiences, as if they could be tagged and stored in a footlocker, but rather the quality of how we choose to live right now.

9   The problem is not only figuring out what that life might be and how to attain it but also shedding our other possible lives. Thanks in part to the expanding horizons we're exposed to in the media, most of us have a hard time letting go of the multiple fan-

tasies we hold about our future—moving to Paris to join the café society but also knowing the satisfaction of watching seasons change on a Wyoming ranch. Maybe an epiphany one day will lead us to adopt a quiet life that, say, incorporates caring for others while caring for the land—a kind of Wendell Berry meets Dorothy Day vision that will finally pull us away from the distractions of interesting co-workers, new clothes, and cable TV. But until then, we find pleasure in moving through our days as if we were in a supermarket, pulling items from the shelves in a dozen different aisles.

10   Contrast the sense of everyday well-being expressed by my mother's favorite saint with the barely controlled chaos that characterizes the average two-income household, circa 1994. Rather than rise with the sun and seek transcendence in our herb gardens like medieval monks, we drive to work, put in eight hours, race home, get some exercise, pick up a newspaper, quiz the kids, play the piano, make dinner, take in a movie, turn out for the zoning meeting, learn a second language, write in our journals, squeeze in a few calls to old friends, and pick up a novel before finally passing out.

11   With so much to choose from, no wonder many of us think we can keep doing a little bit of everything, and somehow the important stuff will take care of itself. And small wonder our powers of concentration are so faint we need written instructions to remember to feed the cat. It was hard to know whether to laugh or applaud when a *Saturday Night Live* send-up advertised an Apple computer that had been crossed with one of those pads of yellow stickums to create the perfect product for today's forgetful, tech-loving consumer: a 3-inch by 3-inch computer notebook that allows users to edit their reminders and stick them to any surface.

12   We tend to value machines that speed the way, even if they don't ease the load. We're even willing to pay for the opportunity to do two things at once: Witness the rise of cellular phones, audio books, and National Public Radio—which all allow commuters to soak up useful information while they're locked in traffic or stranded at bus stops.

13   We measure meaning with productivity; maybe that's one reason Americans don't demand more vacation time (we average about half that of Europeans) and speak hopefully about the 12-month school year. It certainly helps explain why professionals who could afford to work fewer hours hesitate to let go of their manic schedules; they fear their co-workers will take them less seriously if they work part time, and maybe take their jobs.

14   "We're living in a culture of work," says University of Iowa labor historian Benjamin K. Hunnicutt, who co-edits *The Newsletter of the Society for the Reduction of Human Labor* ($25/yr., 1610 E. College St., Iowa City, IA 52245). He bemoans the loss of downtime when people could nurture heart and soul—"the things we think of as human."

15   During the early 19th century, the drive was toward fewer work hours, not more. "Workers adopted the American Revolutionary vision of liberty and applied it to their own lives," Hunnicutt wrote in a 1990 essay. The drive to reduce the number of hours spent on the job ended during the Great Depression, Hunnicutt maintains. In 1932 both political parties endorsed the notion of a 30-hour workweek as a way of spreading jobs around, a reform supported by President Franklin D. Roosevelt until

pressure from big business forced him to back down. After that, New Deal programs abandoned shortening the workweek.

16   More than 50 years later, for the first time in decades, organized labor is once again looking at the possibility of creating jobs by reducing the workweek. "There's no question that the long-term salvation of work lies in reducing working hours," AFL-CIO secretary-treasurer Thomas R. Donahue said in October. Unfortunately, the cost of health insurance and other benefits compels many employers to do just the opposite, reducing the number of employees and creating more overtime for those who remain on the job.

17   Whether we're working overtime or punching out early, Americans historically have viewed an active life as morally superior—perhaps one reason so many of us pretend not to like TV. Indeed, writes Cecelia Tichi in her book *Electronic Hearth: Creating an American Television Culture,* a tradition of busy-ness is ingrained in American myth. She points to a series of profiles in *Life* magazine following World War II that celebrated busy Americans in history. Thomas Jefferson was portrayed as architect, inventor, statesman, and farmer, and Henry David Thoreau, that embodiment of voluntary simplicity, was described as "an industrious writer even at Walden Pond," a man who "may have talked about leisure more than [he] enjoyed it." Women's magazines of the postwar era, in cahoots with the advertising industry, flogged a form of household hyperactivity for women, many of whom had worked during the war but came home to new appliances and the expectation that kitchen floors should be clean enough to eat upon. As Tichi sees it, the powers behind television had to work hard to reconcile America's love affair with busy-ness and the image of pausing in one's round of household duties long enough to watch a soap opera, never mind lolling in a La-Z-Boy with a TV dinner.

18   The strategy seems to have worked. Time-use chronicler John Robinson says an astounding 40 percent of the average American's free time dissipates in front of the tube. This may account for some of the discrepancies between Robinson's assertion that we have more free time than a generation ago and most people's feeling that they have less. We may notice less of a chance for reading, visiting, and preparing meals because television absorbs more of our time.

19   Marked increases in both women working away from home and longer and longer commuting distances also contribute to the feeling that time is running out. Pointing to various trends, including the twin pressures on women to work both at home and away from it, Harvard economist Juliet Schor challenges Robinson's assertion that leisure time is on the rise. Her 1991 best-seller, *The Overworked American: The Unexpected Decline of Leisure,* maintains that Americans are trapped in a work-and-spend cycle with less free time than ever.

20   And if Robinson believes work hours began to ease up a little bit in the 1960s and '70s, in part because Americans began to use work hours to take care of miscellaneous personal business, Hunnicutt has a different take. "Instead of viewing progress as a means of transcending work, Americans now view work as an end in itself—the more of it the better," he asserted in his 1990 essay. For some, he believes, it may even have replaced religion.

21   Part of this is related to cultural traditions that stress independence, perseverance, and hard work, even at the expense of family and neighbors. Ours is a restless
nation, constantly in search of the next opportunity. After six years in one house, the
average American feels like a hermit crab anxious to shed its shell and move into
something new, preferably in a different neighborhood. Hunnicutt also believes
America underwent a sea change during the Depression, which instilled the notion
that, as he puts it, "there is nothing better than work." Part of the blame, he says,
goes not only to politics but also to the collapse of local community.

22   For many Americans, the work ethic spills over from job to leisure hours as we
set out to achieve results in our "spare" time. This goal-oriented approach to fun is
reflected in brisk sales of mile-clocking treadmills and serious sneakers: According
to research cited by Witold Rybczynski, author of *Waiting for the Weekend,* in 1989
alone consumers sank more than $13 billion into sports clothing—the equivalent of
a billion hours of work. Aside from underscoring the significance we attach to weekend activities, having different costumes for different activities contributes to today's
postmodern sensibilities: With each change of clothing—from spandex, which
showcases the muscles, to natural fibers, which establish social standing—we can
try on something new.

23   The zeitgeist-savvy fashion industry, realizing that women enjoy dabbling in
different decades as well as identities, is providing Victorian boots to go with
crushed-velvet '70s waif-wear this year—assuming the fashion-conscious aren't still
stuck in an '80s-induced, '50s-nostalgic blue-jeans fantasy involving a latter-day
Marilyn Monroe and a bunch of cowboys.

24   If busy-ness exhausts us, it also fills our multiple lives with multiple purposes.
In a quintessentially American way, being busy conveys self-worth, even status.
Fitness classes and personal grooming—two major time consumers—complement
the great American desire to improve ourselves, and shopping takes care of a powerful cultural urge to consume.

25   But in talking to pollsters or commenting in diaries kept for Robinson's time-use
studies, Americans don't confess a desire to spend more time in the gym, at the mall,
or in front of the TV. They say they wish they had more time to socialize with friends
and family. A Gallup Poll cited by Juliet Schor found that, when respondents were
asked what was most important to them, they ranked family life and betterment of
society above "having a nice home, car, and other belongings."

26   Robinson is probably right in suggesting that what people do is more important than what they say. But sometimes people express a longing long before
they act on it. For years, for example, I've been paying lip service to the idea of
one day becoming more active in the community, even if it extends only to the
end of the block where we live in Washington, D.C., or the public school my
daughter attends. But now I find the challenge is to learn new habits, not so
easy an undertaking for an office worker with a short attention span and a frontier spirit. It takes some unstructured time, after all, to chat with neighbors in
a leisurely way over the back fence. And looking up relatives, in its own way, can
be a chore. Plunging into school politics or community organizations means

learning to be patient when they eat up valuable time—sometimes in the most inefficient way.

27   And working with a community is different from striving alone at the computer or on the job—something I learned the hard way recently after volunteering to help organize a potluck dinner for the parents of 300 seventh graders at my daughter's new school. Asking people to RSVP and bring a covered dish was no big deal; what I didn't know was how important it is to involve other parents, not to mention the PTA and the principal, in a project that could build bonds in the months ahead, as the local public schools continue their struggle to survive in a budget-starved city. I was so anxious to "do a good job" I had all the paper plates in the garbage before people had a chance to mix, and everyone went home early.

28   One reason people gravitate toward volunteer work, whether it's tutoring, serving on the PTA, organizing activities at church or school, or working in a soup kitchen, is that it can offer surprising personal rewards, as profound as they are hard to articulate. This is the gist of *The Call of Service: A Witness to Idealism,* a new book by Robert Coles that explores the human need to serve others. Coles doesn't get into the issue of how people value and use their time, although implicit in his life and his work is the notion that there can be no higher calling than donating time to others.

29   Many of us haven't quite reached that stage of enlightenment; perhaps we must first pass through a post-'80s period of forsaking materialism for a less tangible, but no less driving, desire to possess time and to wring from it a dozen different experiences—from reading Jane Austen to rafting down the Colorado. Some of this is dilettantism, of course. But it can also reflect a kind of reverence, however perverse, for the fact that we pass this way but once.

■ TOPICAL CONSIDERATIONS

1. Baldwin introduces the idea of the "Great American Time Crunch." Do you feel the effects of such a crunch in your daily life? In your opinion, if time were managed differently could we effectively slow it down?

2. Baldwin attributes our desire for "fuller" lives to the "expanding horizons we're exposed to in the media" (paragraph 9). How would you define these expanding horizons? How might your view of lifestyle options be different without this media presence? In your opinion, what role does the media play in shaping what we want to "get" out of life?

3. In paragraph 11, Baldwin exclaims, "small wonder our powers of concentration are so faint we need written instructions to remember to feed the cat." Do you believe there is a link between the ever-expanding "options" available to the average U.S. citizen and reduced levels of concentration? Does the media play a part in this phenomenon? How do you experience this in your own daily life?

4. "We measure meaning with productivity" (paragraph 13). What do you take this statement to mean, and how does it affect our understanding and man-

agement of time? Do you feel the pressure to "produce" as a part of your daily life? In your opinion, what might alternative measures of "meaning" be, and how would they affect our lives?

5. From the Depression on, Baldwin notes, the goal has generally been to reduce the number of working hours. And, yet, professionals today seem trapped in a "work-and-spend cycle with less free time than ever" (paragraph 19). To what can this increased work activity be attributed? Do you find that you or members of your family are overworked? How might we think about changing this situation?

6. Do you agree with Baldwin's statement in paragraph 17 that "Americans historically have viewed an active life as morally superior"? What does being busy have to do with morality or self-worth? Explain with some specific examples.

7. Baldwin concludes by noting that the challenge in time management isn't so much to squeeze more time and activity out of one's schedule but to "learn new habits." How might you change your habits in order to maximize your time while minimizing the sense that "there isn't enough time"?

8. Baldwin wonders if we really want to return to "the simple life." What is your perception of "the simple life"? When and how were times simpler in this country, and how might this be preferable to the present state of affairs? Would you personally like to return to a more simple way of living? Why or why not?

■ RHETORICAL CONSIDERATIONS

1. How does the image of the escalator work in Baldwin's introduction? Why do you suppose she chose this image to begin her piece?

2. Baldwin uses spatial breaks in her essay as a device to order the large amounts of information she is working with. As a reader, do you find this technique useful in clarifying the material? Examine particular places in the essay where you are aware of Baldwin's organizational mechanisms, analyzing their effectiveness.

3. Consider Baldwin's use of the words *us, our,* and *we.* How does this point of view affect your reception of the essay? What is the effect of the change in perspective in paragraphs 26 and 27 to the first-person?

4. Baldwin's essay is packed with details and authoritative evidence to support her argument. Find two examples of details and two examples of authoritative sources used as evidence. Then try to determine their effectiveness in the essay. In what situations does Baldwin use specific details to support her argument, and when does she choose quotations from experts?

■ WRITING ASSIGNMENTS

1. Baldwin says that "Americans generally have more free time today than they had 30 years ago" (paragraph 3); and, yet, it seems, our lives are more crammed than ever, making us feel without control. Write a paper in which you explore how you maintain a sense of control over your time. How do

you manage the chaos of a full schedule while still setting aside time for friends, family, and yourself?

2. Are there any activities that you don't have time for but wish you had? What are these activities, and how might you go about changing your daily habits in order to accommodate them? In your paper explain why you are interested in these activities—that is, for personal or social fulfillment, education, increased productivity, health, or some other reason?

3. Write a scenario that envisions life in America in the year 2050. Take the perspective of a college student. Describe the makeup of this person's daily life. What sorts of changes do you envision in the workplace, at home, and in leisure time? What about people's ability to communicate? the role of the media? How does this future U.S. citizen manage his or her time? Do people look back nostalgically at the 1990s as a "simpler" time?

4. Ask your school librarian to help you find a narrative account of life in another time period in the United States—for example, during colonial times, the frontier era, the age of industrialization. After reading relevant portions of this narrative, try to determine how time might have been perceived and managed differently, taking into account such things as levels of technology, modes of communication and transportation, cultural demands such as marriage and family structure, and more. From your research, how did people seem to manage time back then? Did they organize their culture around priorities of leisure and rest time, or work?

A Child of Crack

Michele L. Norris

It has been said that the children of poverty are the most maligned and most deprived subclass in America. They are also the most vulnerable to the violence that plagues inner-city neighborhoods. The essay below is a dramatic and disturbing portrait of 6-year-old Dooney Waters who was raised in an inner-city apartment where his mother conducted a steady trade in crack cocaine. Sadly, the destructive impact of drugs and drug money illustrated here is a story played out in the daily lives of thousands of children throughout the country. "A Child of Crack" is an excerpt from the 1989 *Washington Post* series on Dooney Waters by reporter Michele L. Norris—a series that won Ms. Norris several awards for journalism.

1   Dooney Waters, a thickset six-year-old missing two front teeth, sat hunched over a notebook, drawing a family portrait.

2   First he sketched a stick-figure woman smoking a pipe twice her size. A coil of smoke rose from the pipe, which held a white square he called a "rock." Above that, he drew a picture of himself, another stick figure with tears falling from its face.

3   "Drugs have wrecked my mother," Dooney said as he doodled. "Drugs have wrecked a lot of mothers and fathers and children and babies. If I don't be careful, drugs are going to wreck me too."

4   His was a graphic rendering of the life of a child growing up in what police and social workers have identified as a crack house, an apartment in Washington Heights, a federally subsidized complex in Landover, Maryland, where people congregated to buy and use drugs. Dooney's life was punctuated by days when he hid behind his bed to eat sandwiches sent by teachers who knew he would get nothing else. Nights when Dooney wet his bed because people were "yelling and doing drugs and stuff." And weeks in which he barely saw his thirty-two-year-old mother, who spent most of her time searching for drugs.

5   Addie Lorraine Waters, who described herself as a "slave to cocaine," said she let drug dealers use her apartment in exchange for the steady support of her habit. The arrangement turned Dooney's home into a modern-day opium den where pipes, spoons, and needles were in supply like ketchup and mustard at a fast-food restaurant. . . .

6   Addie's apartment was on Capital View Drive, site of more than a dozen slayings last year. Yet, the locks were removed from the front door to allow an unyielding tide of addicts and dealers to flow in and out. Children, particularly toddlers, often peered inside to ask: "Is my mommy here?"

7   While he was living in the crack house, Dooney was burned when a woman tossed boiling water at his mother's face in a drug dispute, and his right palm was singed when his thirteen-year-old half brother handed him a soft drink can that had been used to heat crack cocaine on the stove.

8   Teachers say that Dooney often begged to be taken to their homes, once asking if he could stay overnight in his classroom. "I'll sleep on the floor," Dooney told an instructor in Greenbelt Center Elementary School's after-school counseling and tutorial program. "Please don't make me go home. I don't want to go back there."

9   Dooney was painfully shy or exhaustively outgoing, depending largely on whether he was at home or in school—the one place where he could relax. In class, he played practical jokes on friends and passed out kisses and hugs to teachers. But his mood darkened when he boarded a bus for home.

10   The violence that surrounded Dooney at home was, in most cases, a byproduct of the bustling drug trade. Washington Heights was host to one of the largest open-air drug markets in Prince George's County, Maryland, until a series of police raids last winter drove the problem indoors.

11   On Saturday, April 29, Dooney was sitting in the living room near his mother when a fifteen-year-old drug dealer burst in and tossed a pan of boiling water, a weapon that anybody with a stove could afford. Dooney, his mother, and two neighbors recalled that the dealer then plopped down on a sofa and watched as Dooney's weeping mother soothed the burns on her shoulder and neck. Dooney also was at home when another adolescent enforcer leaned through an open window on Sunday, May 14 and pitched a blend of bleach and boiling water in the face of nineteen-year-old Clifford E. Bernard, a regular in the apartment, for ignoring a $150 debt.

12   "People around here don't play when you owe them money," said Sherry Brown, twenty-five, a friend of Addie Waters who frequented the apartment. Brown said she smokes crack every day and has given birth to two crack-addicted babies in the past three years. "These young boys around here will burn you in a minute if you so much as look at them the wrong way," she said. "I'm telling you sure as I'm sitting here, crack has made people crazy."

13   Almost everyone was welcome at "Addie's place." Her patrons included some unlikely characters, but as one said, "Addie don't turn nobody away." Not the fifteen-year-old who in May burned her furniture and clothing intentionally with a miniature blow torch. Not even the twenty-one-year-old man who "accidentally" shot her thirteen-year-old son, Frank Russell West, five inches above the heart last Dec. 16. Police ascribed the shooting to a "drug deal gone bad."

14   Dooney was sleeping when Russell, shot in the left shoulder, stumbled back into the apartment. Dooney will not talk about the night his half brother was shot except to say, "Russell was shot 'cause of drugs."

15   Waters did not press charges against Edward "June" Powell, the man police charged with shooting Russell. Powell, whose trial has been continued because he did not have an attorney, is out on bail. "He didn't mean to do it," said Waters, who referred to Powell as a close friend of the family. "It was an accident. He meant to kill someone else.". . .

16   Dooney's mother and others who congregated in her apartment were bound by a common desperation for drugs. The majority, in their late twenties or early thirties, described themselves as "recreational" drug users until they tried the highly addictive crack. Many said they had swapped welfare checks, food stamps, furniture, and sexual favors to support their craving for crack. They had lost jobs, spouses, homes, and self-respect. Nearly all were in danger of losing children, too.

17   The Prince George's County Department of Social Services was investigating charges of parental neglect against many of the people who frequented Water's apartment. But they rarely took the county's investigations seriously. Some would joke about timid caseworkers who were too "yellow" to visit Washington Heights or would pass around letters in which officials threatened to remove children from their custody. The problem, as in Dooney's case, was that the county's threats lacked teeth. Caseworkers were usually so overloaded that they rarely had time to bring cases to court, even after they had corroborated charges of abuse and neglect.

18   Prince George's County police said they knew about Water's operation but never found enough drugs in the apartment to charge her or others. "The problem is that drugs don't last long up there," said Officer Alex Bailey, who patrols the Washington Heights neighborhood. "They use them up as soon as they arrive."

19   Such explanations seemed lost on Dooney.

20   "Everybody knows about the drugs at my house," he said with a matter-of-fact tone not common to a first-grader. "The police know, too, but they don't do nothing about it. Don't nobody do nothing about it," he said.

21   Police did raid Dooney's apartment on Saturday, May 13, after they were called there by a neighbor who complained about noise. "They were looking for the drugs,"

Dooney said two days later, as his eyes grew full of tears. "They took all the clothes out of my mother's closets. They threw it all on my mother. They called my mother names."

22   Dooney also said he was afraid of the police, and when asked why, he inquired, "How do you spell the word 'shoot'?" Supplied with a notebook and pen, he wrote the word slowly in large, shaky letters and then repeatedly punched the pen into the paper to form a circle of black marks. Pausing a minute, he drew a person holding a pipe, a smiling face atop a body with a circle in her belly. "That's my mother." Dooney said, pointing to the figure's face. He moved his finger toward the circle. "And that's a bullet hole."

23   Around the apartment, Dooney was constantly on guard, watchful for signs of a ruckus or a raid. "Don't stand too close," he told a visitor standing near the front door, warning that the lockless door was often kicked open.

24   Since kindergarten, Dooney has pulled himself out of bed almost every school morning without the help of adults or alarm clocks, said his mother, who boasted about his independence. Asked how he got himself up in the morning, Dooney tapped a finger to his forehead and said, "My brain wakes me up. I get up when it gets light outside."

25   Dooney rarely bathed or brushed his hair before he went to school while he was living with his mother. The bathroom was inoperable during the period that a *Washington Post* reporter and photographer regularly visited. The toilet overflowed with human waste. Stagnant water stood in the bathtub. There was no soap, no shampoo, no toilet paper or toothpaste.

26   When Dooney did wash, he used a yellow dishpan that doubled as a washtub for rinsing out his clothes. Without a working toilet in the apartment, Dooney went across the hall when he needed to use the bathroom. If he couldn't wait, or if the neighbors weren't home, Dooney went outside in the bushes or urinated in the bathtub. He reasoned that this was the root of his bed-wetting. "I didn't want to get up to go to the bathroom, and now I pee in my bed every night," he said. . . .

27   Dooney's mother moved to Washington Heights in 1977, a time when the complex advertised "luxury apartments." During Dooney's preschool years, Waters says, the complex was "a nice, clean place full of working class folks." Even then, marijuana, speed, powder cocaine, and other drugs circulated through the community.

28   But the introduction of crack swept in a new era. Nothing before it had spawned so rapid and so wrenching an addiction.

29   Not all Washington Heights residents are involved in the drug trade. Many families take pains to shield themselves and their children from drugs and violence. But the vast numbers that started using crack tell similar tales about addictions that rapidly exceeded their incomes.

30   Three years ago, Dooney's father worked as an electrician's apprentice. His mother was a typist for the Prince George's County Board of Education and took night courses in interior design at a nearby community college.

31   "We had two incomes, two kids, all the things that you dream about in a marriage," Waters said. "There was always food in the refrigerator and money in the bank. We did drugs then, but only at night and on weekends."

32   Dooney's parents were introduced to crack shortly after their separation, and their drug use became less recreational. Dooney's father said he became a small-time drug dealer to support his crack habit and spent six months in jail in 1988 for selling drugs. Dooney's mother said she traded away most of the family belongings—and all of her sons' toys—to buy drugs.

33   Waters, who has no criminal record, said she lost her job with the Armed Forces Benefit and Relief Association in the District of Columbia a few months after she was hired last year because she kept falling asleep on the job after smoking crack all night. With an abundance of time and a circle of drug-addicted neighbors, Waters's occasional crack use became an insatiable ache. She said she began selling crack to support her mounting habit by buying one large rock, smoking some, and selling the rest at a profit. By her account, the addiction quickly outgrew her drug-dealing income, and she began to let people smoke or sell drugs in her apartment on the condition that they shared their bounty with her.

34   At that point, Dooney's apartment became a crack house. "All of a sudden, they just set up shop," his mother said. "I told people never to keep more than $100 worth in my house. Smoking is one thing but for the police to walk up in your house and have people selling, that's two charges."

35   The children's lives declined in step with their parents. Dooney's thirteen-year-old half brother dropped out of the seventh grade last fall and has been arrested six times in two years on charges ranging from jumping trains to stealing cars.

36   Both of Waters's sons begged her to seek help. In the last three years, addiction had whittled her body from a size 16 to a size 5. Her eyes were sunken, underlined by tufts of purplish skin. Her complexion, which she said was once "the envy" of her three sisters, was lifeless, almost like vinyl.

37   Pictures in a blue photo album she kept in her living room show a more attractive Addie L. Waters—a buxom woman with radiant eyes, bright red lipstick, and a voluminous hairdo. Dooney paged through the photo album one afternoon and said, "My mother used to be pretty."

38   Dooney comes from a family with a legacy of addiction. His mother said she bought her first bag of drugs, a $5 sack of marijuana, from her alcoholic father in the late seventies. Dooney's father said he started smoking marijuana in high school and moved on to using PCP, speed, and powder cocaine.

39   Dooney's father says he smoked his first hit of crack about two years ago, when a girlfriend encouraged him to try the drug. Dooney's mother also tried crack for the first time with a lover, a boyfriend who said it "was the best high around."

40   When she first started smoking crack, Waters said, she would lock herself in the bathroom to hide from her two sons. The charade didn't last long. One evening Russell threw open the bathroom door and discovered his mother with a plastic pipe in her mouth.

41   "I tried to hide it and he saw me," says Waters, who went on to describe how Russell, then in the fifth grade, slapped her several times and flushed the drugs down the toilet. "By him seeing me, it really affected me," Waters says. "I left it alone for about an hour."

42   Eventually she says, Russell's reactions became less extreme, and he got involved with the drug trade himself by selling soap chips on the street to unsuspecting buyers.

43   In early interviews, Waters called herself a good parent, a claim her two sons disputed. During the two months a reporter and photographer visited the apartment. Waters never checked Dooney's homework after school and in interviews couldn't remember his teachers' names.

44   Over time, Waters backed away from her earlier descriptions of herself. "I can't be the kind of mother I should be when I'm smoking crack," she said. "If I could do it all over again I would not do drugs."

45   Waters will take the blame for Russell, but she maintained that it would not be her fault if Dooney started using or selling drugs.

46   "If he does, it won't be because of me," Waters said. "I learned with Russell so I tell [Dooney] not to smoke or sell drugs. It's my fault that I'm doing it but I think [Dooney] knows better. I tell him all the time that he don't want to live like me."

47   Waters said that Dooney had seen her smoke crack "hundreds" of times. "He would always tell me, 'Mommy, say no to drugs' and I would say, 'Okay, baby.'" She eventually stopped trying to hide her crack habit from Dooney.

48   Crack became such a part of Dooney's life that he could list the steps for cooking it before he could tie his shoelaces. Perhaps that's why he sometimes scoffed at school programs designed to teach pupils to "just say no" to drugs.

49   "The Drug Avengers ain't real," he said, referring to an educational cartoon in which a band of superheroes prevents children from buying and using drugs. "They couldn't stop my mother from doing drugs."

50   "You have to ask yourself, 'What am I telling a child when I say to him that drugs are bad and yet everyone he knows is using drugs regularly?'" says John Van Schoonhoven, principal of Greenbelt Center. "It worries me that perhaps we aren't reaching these children and teaching them that they don't have to get involved with drugs, even though almost everyone they know already has." . . .

51   To help Dooney and others like him, teachers are being called on increasingly to attend to physical and emotional needs that are ignored in the pupils' homes.

52   "You do more parenting than teaching nowadays," says Wendy Geagan, an instructional aide who tutors children with learning problems at Greenbelt Center. "It's all so different now. We have always had to help children with their problems, but these kids want to be held. They want to be mothered. They need affection. They need their emotions soothed." . . .

53   Dooney's teachers began to suspect that his mother had a drug problem shortly after he entered kindergarten.

54   "It was rather sudden," said Janet Pelkey, Dooney's kindergarten teacher. "He wasn't bathed. He became very angry and started striking out. He started gobbling

down food whenever he got it, even candy and snacks in the classroom. It was obvious that something was going on at home."

55   School officials said they could not reach Dooney's mother by phone and no one answered the door during several home visits. The school-community link is difficult to maintain for many pupils from Washington Heights because they are bused to the school for desegregation purposes. Many families in Washington Heights do not own cars, making it difficult to visit a school that took three bus transfers to reach. Conversely, teachers say they are afraid to visit Washington Heights, particularly during the winter, when daylight is scarce. So teachers had little or no contact with the parents of pupils with the most turbulent home lives.

56   Concerned about his emotional problems, Dooney's kindergarten teacher placed him in the "transitional first grade," a class for students with academic problems that set them a few steps behind other children their age.

57   Dooney's condition worsened when he entered first grade last September, teachers said. He was given to fits of screaming and crying and came to school wearing torn and filthy clothes. "It was almost like he was shellshocked when he came to school . . . ," Field said. "He is such a sad little boy. He walks around with his head down and he's always sucking his little thumb."

58   "When I discovered what he was going through at home, I thought, 'My goodness, it's amazing that he even gets to school,'" Field said.

59   His mood swung like a pendulum. "Sometimes he comes in and he is just starving for affection," said Susan Bennett, an instructional assistant. "He clings to his teacher like he is afraid to let go. . . . Or sometimes when he comes to school he is angry. You brush by him and he is ready to attack."

60   Dooney entered first grade lacking several basic skills children normally master before leaving kindergarten. Teachers say he had a difficult time distinguishing among colors and could not count past ten. But Dooney's academic skills improved in classes that provided special equipment and individual tutoring. By the end of the year, his test scores put him in line with others his age, though he still had trouble tying his shoes and telling time.

61   Acting on the advice of teachers, the Prince George's County Department of Child Protective Services investigated Dooney's mother in April 1988.

62   "Based on the provided investigative information, the allegations of neglect have been indicated," child protective services worker Conchita A. Woods wrote in a letter to Waters dated April 24, 1989, a year after the investigation began. But a caseworker said that it would be "months, maybe even years" before they could seek to remove Dooney from his mother's custody.

63   Russell Brown, the investigator, said he had about twenty cases on his desk just like Waters's.

64   "We have a lot of cases that are much worse than that," Brown said. "There's probably not a whole lot I can do" for Dooney. Brown said that he does not have time to go through the arduous process of taking a child from a parent unless there is imminent danger.

65   "It's up to you guys to help this little boy because we just don't have the manpower to do it," Brown told Dooney's teachers over lunch on April 27. . . .

66   At the principal's urging, Prince George's school and government officials created a pilot after-school program that offers tutoring, counseling, and drug education for students at Greenbelt Center. Equally important, it shields them from neighborhood violence for a few extra hours. Although its primary function is to help children with drug-related trauma, the program also provides academic enrichment and free day care for other students. From 3:00 to 6:30 P.M., children get help with homework, counseling, playtime, and a snack—the last meal of the day for many of them.

67   School officials around the country say such programs may be the vanguard of school reform as more children enter schools with a crush of physical and emotional problems that detract from standard academic work.

68   "It's become apparent that schools cannot do all that they are supposed to be doing in a six-hour day," says Nancy Kochuk, a spokeswoman for the National Education Association. "The schools are basically set up as an industrial model. It's like a factory line. That doesn't seem to serve our society very well anymore when we are dealing with children with such intense and overwhelming problems." . . .

69   Last spring Dooney said he hated drugs and what they have done to his life. Yet he seemed to view the drug trade as an inevitable calling in the way that some children look at the steel mills and coal mines in which their forebears worked.

70   Asked if he would sell or use drugs when he grows up, Dooney shook his head violently and wrinkled his nose in disgust. But the expression faded, and Dooney looked at the floor: "I don't want to sell drugs, but I will probably have to."

■ **TOPICAL CONSIDERATIONS**

1. Describe Addie and Dooney Waters's apartment. How is it a perversion of the typical middle-class American home? How do you think growing up in such conditions would have affected your intellectual and moral development?

2. What specific instances of violence has Dooney already witnessed? What is particularly shocking about the nature of these experiences? Has this essay exposed a kind of violence you never imagined existed? If so, has this exposure changed your attitudes at all?

3. Explain the bureaucratic problems exposed in paragraph 17 when Norris introduces Prince George's County Department of Social Services. Do the problems described occur in your community? If so, is there a need for national change with respect to social services departments?

4. What is the socioeconomic history of the Washington Heights apartment complex? How had it changed so drastically? Are you aware of similar apartment complexes that have suffered such ruin? Do you think cities should cease funding for housing projects in high-risk areas?

5. According to Dooney Waters how effective has been the "Just Say No" to drugs campaign? Do you agree or disagree with is precocious assessment? Has the program been effective in your community? Do you believe the campaign is geared toward people of all classes?

6. Explain the role of public schools and their teachers in Dooney Waters's case. Public school systems today receive much criticism and little praise. If you attended public school, how did the system treat you?

■ RHETORICAL CONSIDERATIONS

1. Explain the analogy in paragraph 5: "The arrangement turned Dooney's home into a modern-day opium den where pipes, spoons, and needles were in supply like ketchup and mustard at a fast-food restaurant." How apt and effective is the comparison?
2. To what degree is the essay journalistically responsible? Did Norris thoroughly research her subject, or do you find gaps in her evidence?
3. Analyze the power of the introduction. How exactly does Norris capture your interest? Explain the contradictions and ironies.
4. Consider Dooney's language. Where does his speech belie his 6 years of age? Use specific examples. How does Dooney's speech compare to that of a 6-year-old white child from a two-parent middle-class family that cares about education?
5. Comment on the conclusion of the essay. Is it effective? Did it move you? Use evidence from the essay to determine whether the ending is logical, consistent, or contrived.

■ WRITING ASSIGNMENTS

1. Assume the perspective of a child psychologist. Write a paper that explains Dooney's behavior, appearance, and belief that he will one day sell drugs. Determine what has caused his pain. Decide whether or not he can escape the crack world. Consider issues of race and class.
2. Explore the implications of the essay's title, "A Child of Crack." How is Dooney a child of crack? And how are Sherry Brown's children (paragraph 12) also crack babies? Using the other relevant essays in this chapter, show how children are the victims of society's decay.
3. What antidrug measures are being taken in your community? Which seem the most effective? Write a paper in which you discuss the kinds of measures you would take. Consider federal and local government, school systems, parents, civic leaders, the law, and private citizens.

	Sex Is for Adults
	Ellen Hopkins

For young people today, there are too many high risks attendant with sexual activity. The price of unprotected sex ranges from pregnancy, to venereal disease, to AIDS. Two responses to these threats include sex education and abstinence. In the piece below, Ellen Hopkins, a feminist and a liberal, argues in support of advocating abstinence for a simple and practical reason: She thinks it works. This essay first appeared in *The New York Times,* in December 1992.

1 Remember how drunken driving used to be kind of funny? Or if not funny, inevitable, especially for the young. When I was in high school (I'm 35) only losers worried about the alcoholic consumption of the person behind the wheel. Fourteen years later, when my sister made her way through the same suburban high school, designated drivers had become the norm and only losers swerved off into the night.

2 I was reminded of this remarkable evolution in attitude when I began to explore the idea that teaching abstinence to teen-agers need not be the province of right-wing crazies. Could it be that teen-age sex is no more inevitable than we once thought teen-age drunken driving? Is it possible to make a liberal, feminist argument for pushing abstinence in the schools? I believe it is.

3 The argument goes like this:

4 *Sex education doesn't work.*

5 There are lots of nice things to be said for sex education. It makes kids more knowledgeable, more tolerant and maybe even more skillful lovers. But it does not do the one thing we all wish it would: make them more responsible.

6 In a landmark study of 10 exemplary programs published by the Centers for Disease Control in 1984, no evidence was found that knowledge influenced teen-agers' behavior significantly. Supporters of sex education point to studies that show that educated teen-agers are slightly more likely to use birth control. Opponents point to studies that show they are slightly more likely to have sex at a younger age. No one points to the many studies that compare the pregnancy rates of the educated and the ignorant: depressingly similar.

7 *Even if sex education worked, birth control doesn't.*

8 At least it doesn't work often enough. The Alan Guttmacher Institute, a research organization that specializes in reproductive health, estimates that up to 36 percent of women in their early 20's will get pregnant while relying on male use of condoms in the first year; and with the supposedly foolproof pill, up to 18 percent of teen-age girls get pregnant in the first year. (The more effective and more expensive contraceptive Norplant is not widely available to young women.) If you project these failure rates a few years ahead, unintended pregnancy begins to look uncomfortably close to an inevitability.

9 *So let's follow one sexually active teen-ager who does just what she's statistically likely to do. Her options are bleak.*

10 If she wants an abortion, good luck to her if she's poor, under 18 or doesn't live near a big city. The simplest abortion costs about $300. Only 12 states have no laws requiring parental consent or notification for minors seeking an abortion. And 83 percent of America's countries don't even have an abortion provider.

11 What if our teen-ager chose to have the baby and give it up for adoption? While there's a dearth of solid follow-up research on birth mothers, surrendering the flesh of your flesh is obviously wrenching. Suppose our teenager keeps the baby. She may be ruining her life. Only 50 percent of women who have their first child at 17 or younger will have graduated from high school by the age of 30. And many of those who do have merely gotten a General Education Development degree, which is of such dubious worth that the Army no longer accepts recruits with it.

12 *Even a ruined life may be better than a life cut short by AIDS.*

13 If condoms—or young condom users—are so unreliable that up to 36 percent of young women get pregnant in a single year of use, what does that say about our teen-ager's chances of being exposed to H.I.V. as she "protects" herself with a latex sheath?

14 *Our teen-ager, though, leads a charmed life. Or so she thinks. Even if she doesn't get pregnant and none of her boyfriends is H.I.V. positive, she still puts herself at substantial risk for later infertility.*

15 More than 12 million episodes of sexually transmitted diseases occur each year in the United States, and two-thirds of those afflicted are under 25. Most such diseases can damage the female and male reproductive systems. Infectious-disease experts estimate that after just one episode of pelvic inflammatory disease (a common result of contracting a sexually transmitted disease), 35 percent of women become infertile. After three episodes, the odds of becoming infertile soar to more than 75 percent. Many infertility specialists believe that one of the prime causes for today's high infertility rate is that so many baby boomers had sex early and with multiple partners.

16 *Current recommendations for "safer" sex are unrealistic.*

17 Our teen-ager knows that before going to bed with someone, she and the guy are supposed to exchange detailed sexual histories. Tandem AIDS tests are next, and if both can forge a monogamy pact, they will use condoms (and a more reliable form of birth control like the pill) for six months and then get tested again.

18 Does our teen-ager hammer out these elaborate social contracts every time Cupid calls? Of course not. I had always assumed that abstinence lessons were synonymous with Sex Respect, the religious right's curriculum that uses fear to pressure kids to avoid all sexual activity—including necking—until marriage. While supporters claim success, their evaluation techniques are problematic. Plus, imagine those poor kids having to chant silly Sex Respect slogans ("control your urgin', be a virgin" is my favorite).

19 But studies of a program in Atlanta's public schools suggest that promoting abstinence can be done intelligently and effectively. Eighth graders are taught by peer counselors (popular, reasonably chaste kids from the upper grades—kids who look

like they *could* have sex if they wanted it). Their message is simple: Sex is for grown-ups. Weirdly, it works. By the end of eighth grade, girls who weren't in the program were as much as 15 times more likely to have begun having sex as those who were.

20   While the program in Atlanta is backed up by contraceptive counseling, kids who choose to have sex are erratic birth-control users and just as likely to get pregnant as sexually active kids who aren't in the program.

21   In other words, sex is for grown-ups. I feel strange writing this. Then I remember my first heady experimentations (at a relatively geriatric age) and contrast them with those of a 16-year-old girl who recently visited Planned Parenthood in Westchester County. Three boys were with her, their relationship to her unclear. On the admittance form, the girl wrote that she wasn't in a relationship and had been sexually active for some time. An exam proved her pregnant. Her entire being was joyless.

22   I once thought I'd tell my young son that anything goes—so long as he used condoms. Now I'm not so sure. Not only do I want my son to live, I don't want him to miss out on longing—longing for what he isn't yet ready to have.

■ TOPICAL CONSIDERATIONS

1. Hopkins argues that despite prevailing thought, teenage sex is not "inevitable," meaning, it can be controlled through education. What is your position on this issue? Do you believe there is a problem with teenagers having sex? If so, can it be solved in the classroom? Explain your answer.
2. In paragraph 2, Hopkins identifies two groups invested in the debate over teenage abstinence: "right-wing crazies" and "liberal feminists." How would you define these two groups, and what is your understanding of their positions on the issue?
3. What is your experience with sex education? Did your high school require sex education classes? How were they run, and how useful were they for you? Did they emphasize knowledge of sex and sexuality, or was the focus on responsibility, health issues, and abstinence?
4. What is your experience with AIDS education? If you went to a school that sponsored an AIDS education program, was this program part of a more general sex education program? In either case, do you think AIDS education works? Explain.
5. Given the statistics provided by Hopkins, do you believe in the idea of "safe"—or even "safer"—sex? Could it be that in the time of AIDS this concept is invalid? Explain your answer.
6. In your opinion, can abstinence be "taught" to teenagers? Or is sexual abstinence or activity a matter of choice, circumstance, or experience having little or nothing to do with educational programs? Explain.
7. In terms of abstinence education, Hopkins comes to the conclusion that "sex is for grown-ups." Do you agree with this statement? Is this a valid reason for abstention from sexual activity? Explain your answer.

8. *The New York Times* reports that in the past 30 years the divorce rate has tripled, as has the percentage of children living in single-parent families. Do you see a relationship between the breakdown of the traditional two-parent family and the cycle of teenage sex and pregnancy? Explain.

■ RHETORICAL CONSIDERATIONS

1. Hopkins opens her piece with a comparison between teenage sex and drunk driving, noting that drunk driving—once thought to be uncontrollable and inevitable—is now the exception rather than the rule in teenage behavior. Is this an effective analogy? Why or why not?
2. In paragraph 2, Hopkins makes a distinction between "right-wing crazies" and "liberal feminists," positioning herself in the latter category. How does this distinction work throughout the piece? In your opinion, does her use of such categories strengthen her argument? Why or why not?
3. Why do you suppose Hopkins chose to italicize certain passages in this essay? How do these passages "work" in terms of the overall argument? Is this an effective rhetorical technique? Why or why not?
4. What kind of evidence does Hopkins provide in support of her argument? Do you find this evidence to be effective and persuasive? Explain.
5. In her conclusion, Hopkins moves away from statistics to "real people" affected by the problem of teenage sex: a 16-year-old pregnant girl visiting Planned Parenthood and Hopkins's own son. How do these personal references work in a piece dominated by statistics? Why do you suppose Hopkins chose to place them in her conclusion?

■ WRITING ASSIGNMENTS

1. Write an essay responding to Hopkins's position here. Be careful to make clear your argument and to provide supporting evidence—statistical, personal, or anecdotal. Your school's health center might be a good place to obtain information regarding teenage pregnancy, sexually transmitted disease, and AIDS.
2. Hopkins advocates the development of abstinence education programs in the schools based upon the assertion that "sex is for grown-ups." She also cites programs by other groups using Sex Respect slogans, among other tactics, to "scare" kids away from all sexual activity before marriage. Imagine that you are an educator in charge of developing either a sex education or an abstinence education program. Write a description of your approach to this project: What tools would you use? What would the emphasis of your program be? and how would you structure it? Be sure to provide a rationale for your program, supporting your belief in its effectiveness.
3. Do you consider rising teenage sexual activity to be a result of the "changing times" of this country? Consider how the breakdown of the traditional

two-parent family, increased sex and violence on television, growing drug use, and the AIDS epidemic have affected teenage sexual activity and the risks? Write an essay in which you explore how some of these phenomena relate to teenage sexual activity and its consequences.

4. Many current studies cite teenagers and young adults as the group with the fastest growing rate of infection by HIV. Forming groups of 4 to 5 students, collaborate on strategies for AIDS education both in and outside the classroom. After conceptualizing your strategies, write a collaborative proposal to either your campus health center or a local AIDS action organization outlining your ideas for effective AIDS education campaigns targeting young people.

On Kids and Slasher Movies

Michael Ventura

One day Michael Ventura spotted a 10-year-old boy buying a Halloween costume in Woolworth's. The package consisted of a lifelike rubber meat cleaver and the faceless mask from one of the many horror movies. What got to him was not so much the maniac-killer getup as the boy's eagerness to make believe. In the narrative below, the author wonders what the little scene says about us and the world we have made for our kids. Michael Ventura is a freelance writer living in Los Angeles. This article first appeared in the *L.A. Weekly* in November 1989.

1   It's a simple thing, really. I shouldn't take it so seriously, I realize that. For it was only a child, a boy of about 10, buying a toy. For Halloween. This was the toy:

2   A sinister white mask and a quite convincing little rubber meat cleaver. Packaged together in cellophane. It's the "costume" of a maniac killer from one of the slasher movies. The boy wants to play at being a faceless, unstoppable murderer of innocent people (mostly women). At this moment, in this Woolworth's, that's this boy's idea of fun.

3   Understand that I didn't stand there and decide intellectually that this simple and small event is, when all is said and done, the worst thing I've seen. My body decided. My intestines, my knees, my chest. It was only later that I tried to think about it.

4   This boy's eagerness to "play" maniac killer is an event worse than the Bomb, worse even than Auschwitz. Reduced to its simplest terms, the bomb is a fetish, an object of worship—like other objects of worship before it, it is used as an excuse for arranging the world in a certain fashion, allocating resources, assigning powers. It is insane, but in many ways it is an extension of familiar, even

honored, insanities. As for the Nazi camps: The people being murdered knew, as they were being murdered, *that* they were being murdered; the murderers knew they were murdering; and, when the world finally knew, the camps became the measure of ultimate human evil. A crime to scar us all, and our descendants, forever.

5   There is nothing so clear in the Woolworth's scene. The boy is certainly not committing a crime. The toy's merchandisers are within their rights. To legislate against them would be to endanger most of our freedoms. The mother buying the toy is perhaps making a mistake, perhaps not. Without knowing the boy, and knowing him well, who's to be certain that it isn't better for him to engage in, rather than re-press, such play? The mother did not put the desire for the toy in him. Three thousand years of Judeo-Christian culture did that. Nor has the mother the power to take that desire from him. Nobody has that power. If he can want the toy at all, then it al-most doesn't matter whether the toy exists or not. Doesn't the boy's need for such play exist with or without the toy?

6   Nor would I be too quick to blame the boy's desire on television and slasher films. The Nazis who crewed the camps and the scientists who built the bomb did not need television and slasher films to school them in horror. In fact, the worst atrocities from the pharaohs to Vietnam were committed quite ably before the first slasher film was made. Keeping your child away from TV may make *you* feel better, but can any child be protected from the total weight of Western history?

7   In a world shorn of order, stripped of traditions, molting every decade, every year, a dancing, varicolored snake of a century—pointless violence is evident everywhere, on every level. Professional soldiers are statistically safer than urban women; senseless destruction is visited on trees and on the ozone and on every species of life. No one feels safe anywhere. This has become the very meaning of the 20th century.

8   So I am in a Woolworth's one day and I feel a sort of final horror as I watch a boy buy a psycho-killer toy so that he can pretend he's an unstoppable maniacal murderer. What is so horrible is that this boy is doing this instinctively, for his very survival. In order to live, in order not to go mad, this boy is acclimating himself to the idea of the killer-maniac, because killer-maniac energy is so present in his world. He's trying to inoculate himself through play, as all children have, every-where, in every era. He thus lets a little bit of the energy into him—that's how inoculations work. Too little, and he is too afraid of the world—it's too terrifying to feel powerless amid the maniacal that's taken for granted around him; to feel any power at all he needs a bit of it inside him. But if he takes in too much, he could be swamped.

9   How horrible that he is forced to such a choice. You'd think it would be enough to stop the world in its tracks. And what can we do for him? Struggle for a different world, yes, but that won't change what's already happened to him. What can we do for that boy except be on his side, stand by his choice, and pray for the play of his struggling soul?

■ TOPICAL CONSIDERATIONS

1. According to the author, what does the boy's choice of costume say about today's society? In light of your own costume choices as a kid, what do you think has gone into the child's choice? Does he really long for the power of a maniacal killer, or is he simply following a fad?

2. According to the author, what is attractive about "being a faceless, unstoppable murderer of innocent people (mostly women)" (paragraph 2)? Do you agree with Ventura's theory, or do you think his assessment of the contemporary world is unfair?

3. According to Ventura, is there a direct connection between slasher movies and kids' violence? What is your opinion of slasher movies? Do you think young people are too hooked on them? Do you think they have any socially redeeming values? Do you think they are damaging to young viewers? Could movie violence inspire violence in children? Explain your answer.

4. Ventura says in paragraph 3 that his "body decided" that the boy's purchase was "the worst thing" he had seen some time before his mind caught up. How does that distinction make his reaction seem more significant? Can you recall ever feeling horror before you thought about it?

5. Explain Ventura's assertion in paragraph 4 that the bomb is "used as an excuse for arranging the world in a certain fashion." What alternatives to the bomb do we have for rearranging the world? What or who do you think will determine the arrangement of the world in the next century?

6. How would Smith-Rowsey react to this essay? What would he think was the source for a child's wanting to be an "unstoppable murderer"?

■ RHETORICAL CONSIDERATIONS

1. How well does the essay's title forecast Ventura's discussion and his moral stand?

2. Look up the definition of *fetish*. Explain the metaphor of the bomb as a fetish object in paragraph 4. Which definition of *fetish* is most applicable?

3. In the last paragraph Ventura appeals to the reader. What does he expect from the reader? Is this strategy effective? How are you affected by the essay? Does it call you to action against the "pointless violence" that is everywhere?

4. In paragraph 7, how is the twentieth century like a snake? Do you agree with this comparison? Choose an animal and develop a metaphor that describes your own lifetime.

5. What does Ventura mean in paragraph 5 by "Three thousand years of Judeo-Christian culture did that"? How is this statement ironic?

■ WRITING ASSIGNMENTS

1. Do you think that particularly gruesome, violent, or offensive Halloween costumes should be banned from the market? Are there limits of propriety?

Write a paper in which you explore these questions, taking into account the First Amendment rights to freedom of expression.

2. Ventura writes in paragraph 6, "Keeping your child away from TV may make *you* feel better, but can any child be protected from the total weight of Western history?" Does this statement negate the cause of parents against violence on TV? Can children be spared the violence of our world? Should they, and to what age? Write a paper in which you explore these questions.

3. Who are the usual victims in slasher films? What do they have in common? How are their death's portrayed? Select some slasher movies you have seen, then write a paper in which you explore these questions and how such films relate to young adults. What moral messages do the movies project?

	Stolen Promise
	Patricia Raybon

In this piece a black mother dreams of her daughter's wedding replete with "romance and Champagne and sugary cake." But she fears that the forces of poverty, drugs, and inner city violence are destroying the young black men integral to traditional courtship and marriage. "All the men are gone," she laments. "Gone to jail. Gone to drugs. Gone to graves." Thus, a mother's dream becomes a nightmare, as urban violence claims young black men and steals the dreams of black daughters.

Patricia Raybon is an associate professor at the University of Colorado School of Journalism and Mass Communication in Boulder. This essay first appeared in *The New York Times* in May 1992.

1 It is cruel, like a bad joke. Spring has come, and soon the season of love and weddings will enter nicely in—but not for my daughter.

2 She is smart and beautiful. But she is black.

3 And all the men are gone.

4 Gone to jail. Gone to drugs. Gone to graves.

5 I exaggerate, I suppose, but I am a mother. I know about logic. But I dream of the unlikely. Of romance and Champagne and sugary cake. Of bouquets and white dresses and silky veils. Instead I get the evening news and the morning papers, and the reports have not been good: more black men in jail than in college. More dropping out of some schools than dropping in. Hundreds killed on mean streets every year. It is a war, but nobody with power is fighting it. It is the news, but no one with clout will explain it.

6 I put down the papers and telephone my daughter, for a chat that ends with a question I shouldn't ask.

7   "So do you have a date this weekend?" My daughter, listening 2,500 miles away at an all-black university in Atlanta, answers first with a pause.

8   "A date?" she finally says. "Mom, with *who?*"

9   I clear my throat, primed for the logic I want to believe. Surely, I say, there are some nice young men on the campus.

10   "Mom," she says with a voice all mothers know. "We're talking supply and demand here, and the supply is low." She knows the numbers. "Seven to one, Mom. That's the ratio of women to men on this campus. Bad odds," she tells me.

11   So bad I want to blame somebody. Or better, I want somebody to fix it—to take away the bad juju stealing the virility and pride and promise from black American life and leaving in its place crowded jail cells and dead boys and too many girls without husbands or Saturday night dates.

12   I want somebody to fix the look on the face of a friend whose daughter is getting married—to a man the girl would not have chosen in the past. "Too few black men to choose from," my friend explains, tapping a truth I can't deny.

13   The inner city's chaos and the neglect that causes it aren't somebody else's problems, they're mine. And I am surprised. Stupidly so. Have I been blind? Dumb? Indifferent? No, but I live a comfortable life. Privilege and advantage have blessed three generations of my family, and I will admit this: Comfort is a dangerous drug. It dulls one's sense of the scope of disarray in America. It makes the 6 o'clock news seem like another world—certainly not a threat to one's own—certainly not a worry for us in the charmed circle: handsome, vibrant people living our rewarding, productive lives and rearing our beautiful, talented children.

14   But no woman is an island. What pulls at one tugs at another. It is a circle unbroken. When mother after mother bury their sons, daughters remain to shoulder the grief. Daughters, like my own, whose phones rarely ring, whose friends are now rivals, whose quiet weekends force them to wonder where the boys are.

15   The boys are all gone. Far too many of them anyway.

16   Pain has caught up with them and turned them against one another and even against themselves. They live lives of danger, lives too cheap and too quick for the leisure and tenderness of romance and dreams and hope.

17   Too hazardous to look at a pretty girl like mine and want to make a long life together, because what's life? A struggle, unfair, a stacked deck with the other guy holding all the aces.

18   That is frustration talking, because it conjures up nagging demons I try to resist: envy when somebody else's daughter meets a wonderful boy and falls in love. Fear that my own "educated" girl will have to "marry down." And shame for thinking it. Anger when accomplished black men choose white women for their wives. Rage that history and indifference have let segments of black America unhinge and implode. Hate for forces that allow it.

19   These are "race" feelings, of course, so they churn up from some unfathomable well that holds hurts and hidden memories. Mix in romance. The feelings and images get hot and combustible. One floats out of nowhere: my father, now dead, is sitting at our kitchen table at the "new" house in the suburbs—not the "old" house in

the city—and he is shyly and painfully spelling out a new and curious rule: no daughter of his will be allowed to date white boys.

20   "Yes?" I say, waiting for more. To live near them and attend their schools and take advantage of the opportunities that their neighborhoods provide is one thing. To go on dates with them, not to mention marry them, is something else again—and it is forbidden. "Yes," I say.

21   Not bigotry, but deep pain and long history—and the chance, innocent phone call from a white male schoolmate—give birth to this American moment: a father's feverish dictate against race and sex and all that the combination can mean.

22   But during that summer, his anxiousness seems over-wrought, and his rule—replete with his pain—doesn't matter much anyway.

23   Because handsome *black* suitors are around every corner, on every dance floor, across every crowded room.

24   Brown, beautiful, smart young men with "possibility" still part of their vocabulary—they are everywhere, and they pursue black womanhood as moths chase down flame.

25   Something hopeful and lovely propels them to our doorsteps, where they offer flowers and candy and marriage and happiness ever after. And it is magic. We are alive and desirable, and their boldness, their *maleness*—in their soft white shirts and creased trousers and heady after-shave scents and Saturday-night haircuts—prove it.

26   That was then.

27   This is now:

28   My porch is empty. Rarely is it graced by the footfall of brave and earnest young men seeking the company of someone to watch over and love.

29   Last month in Denver, where I live, three young black men were gunned down for something to do with anger and macho and maybe crack cocaine—fuzzy reasons for dying, little consolation when a coffin lid closes for good.

30   On the evening news, I recognize the mother of one of the dead boys. She went to my junior high school many years ago. She was a high flame then, a bright spirit with dancing eyes and frosted lipstick and laughter and sass. But the pretty girl I remember is now a grieving mother, chanting the litany for our sad season. "A senseless act," she says. Nobody argues that she is wrong.

31   In another time, her son might have met my daughter and danced off with her into the night—their laughter following them in the dark like a sweet essence, a prelude to all the things that they could be, a melody they could call their song, through these long, dark years of death without meaning and dying without love.

32   A mother's dream is a hopeful thing. One day perhaps it won't be folly.

■ **TOPICAL CONSIDERATIONS**

1. In paragraph 5, Raybon says of her problem "It is a war, but nobody with power is fighting it." What are the problem's warlike characteristics? And what does she mean by stating that nobody with power is fighting it? Have you had experience with the war to which Raybon refers?

2. In paragraph 13, Raybon notes that "comfort is a dangerous drug." In the context of her argument, how do you understand this statement? How do you feel about it in terms of your own life? Do you agree with her? Why or why not?

3. Why, according to Raybon, do many young black men live lives too cheap and too quick for the leisure and tenderness of romance and dreams and hope" (paragraph 16).

4. In paragraph 18, Raybon fears that her own "'educated' girl will have to 'marry down.'" What does she mean by this? Can you empathize with Raybon here? Explain. Think of other ways people can "marry down." What cultural prescriptions are operating here? Do you feel compelled to follow these prescriptions? Explain.

5. Raybon describes her father's intolerance of interracial dating, attributing this feeling not to bigotry but to "deep pain and long history" (paragraphs 19–21). What might be the "long history" to which she refers? In your opinion, are interracial relationships or marriages any more acceptable today on either side than they have been in the past? Explain.

6. In paragraph 18, Raybon reveals a progression of feelings ranging from "frustration" to "hate," after referring to them as "race" feelings. Would you say she is confessing to bigotry? If so, explain. If not, what is she referring to?

■ RHETORICAL CONSIDERATIONS

1. How does Raybon's position as a "mother" influence your reception of her argument? How does this choice of perspective (a mother's point-of-view) affect the information contained in the article, and the angle from which that information is presented?

2. Paragraphs 2–4, 15, 26, and 27 contain only 1 to 3 short sentences each. Why do you suppose Raybon makes such short cuts for her paragraphs? How do these help convey the information contained in them? Would you say this is an effective rhetorical strategy for this piece? Explain.

3. At the heart of the problem, Raybon cites power imbalances (paragraph 5) and inner-city chaos (paragraph 13). Do you feel she provides enough background evidence to support her argument? Or do you think her reliance on reader familiarity is sufficient? Explain.

4. Raybon uses direct dialogue (from her daughter and from a friend) in her essay. Is this usage a more effective rhetorical strategy than presenting the information in summary form? Why or why not?

5. Patricia Raybon's complaint infers some deep and complex social issues. How does the style of her essay relate to its political content? Does the style "reflect" that content? How does it affect reader perception of the essay?

■ WRITING ASSIGNMENTS

1. Consider your own dreams and hopes for the future, in terms of relationships, career, and so on. In a paper explain what they are, then explore any

social, economic, or cultural issues or events that might have an effect—either positive or negative—on those dreams for the future.

2. Choose one aspect of the racial history of the United States—anything from slavery to civil rights to the contemporary urban "war" described by Raybon—and conduct research on that issue. Write an essay in which you first summarize the relevant events, then speculate upon the effect of your historical "moment" on race relations in this country. What does your research reveal about the race "feelings" cited by Raybon in paragraph 18? Be clear about your position and perspective when working on your analysis.

3. One thing lacking from Raybon's piece is the voice of her daughter. Choose an issue in your life with which your parents are deeply concerned or involved. Taking into account differences in perception between parent and child, write two narratives: the first relating the issue from your parents' point of view, the second from your point of view. Finally, write a paragraph considering the ways in which stories are told, and how the perspective of the narrator can change the reader's understanding of the story or issue.

Houses and Streets, but No Neighborhood

Alan Lupo

In this nostalgic and reflective piece, Alan Lupo describes the neighborhoods that no longer exist by evoking images of what once was. As Lupo walks down his strangely quiet and deserted street on a warm summer evening, he remembers the children's games, the muted radio broadcasts, the overheard conversations on porches that once characterized hot midsummer nights in neighborhood days gone by. He can explain this emptiness only by concluding that "somebody has stolen the people." And he makes us wonder if the technological innovations that afford us so much convenience and privacy are worth the price we paid.

Alan Lupo is a columnist for the *Boston Globe* where this article first appeared in July 1994. Lupo is also the author of *Liberty's Chosen Home* (1988).

1 Somebody has stolen the people. In trying to lower his blood pressure and keep down to his "old fat weight," as opposed to his "new fat weight," the man takes long walks at least once a day in the good weather. He walks fast, but not so fast that he does not notice that there is less to notice than there used to be.

2 He takes in whatever he can. He looks for kids playing on the street or adults sitting on the front steps. He listens for the sounds of conversation or of broadcasting coming through the screens. He sniffs for the odors of familiar foods.

3   The attempts rarely bear fruit. His senses have not dulled that much over the years, he knows. That's not it. No, somebody clearly has stolen the people.

4   In the time of his parents, in his own time and even in that of his own kids, the streets were full of activity. Even in the 1950s, when the abominable television sets sucked parents off the streets, the kids, at least, stayed out, hung out, played out until they couldn't run another foot.

5   Hide 'n seek. Relievo. Tag. Cops and robbers. Robin Hood. Pirates. Jump rope. Jacks. Baseball against the stairs. Outlaws. Red Rover. Stickball. Punch ball. Box ball. Pickup games of baseball. Hoops. Irritating members of the opposite sex. Games. All the time, games. Scores of games. Old games that had stood the test of decades. New games born of Saturday matinees.

6   They'd play through the last sliver of light on the western horizon and then some, their ranks diminishing one by one as windows were raised one by one, and mothers called for their offspring one by one, and offspring complained to no avail one by one, and dejectedly—and slowly—walked back to their apartments, one by one.

7   But even as the darkness settled in, the streets were not still. Voices of adults, both the in-person sort and the on-the-radio variety, filtered through the screens and dropped lightly, like pollen, on the dark street below, so that kids went to sleep with the reassuring soundtrack of familiar voices.

8   The other night, he noticed, the light remained until about 8:40 P.M. He heard no cries for children to come home. He had seen few kids when it was light.

9   Even the houses now are often dark, or dark but for a room or two. Shades are drawn almost to the bottoms of windows. In the 2 inches or so of opening, he could see the color images on the television screen.

10   He doesn't hear pianos being played in apartments anymore. He does not hear the ballgame on the radio. Once in a while, he spots some adults on a porch here or there, but most are inside, away from their neighbors.

11   His druggist shakes his head affirmatively. Ah yes, true enough. "What gets me," Lloyd Lyons says, "is when you go past a ball field, and it's empty. Years ago, you couldn't find a spot on a ball field. Now? Nobody."

12   Somebody has stolen us off the streets. Something, really. Television first did it, wiped the streets clear of people, young and old, until the young quickly got bored and returned to play, albeit with less adult supervision.

13   Then there was the suburban boom, where a kid could grow up in a cul-de-sac and never know the joys of hanging around a corner in front of a store, just a store, owned by somebody local, not a franchise of some chain operation in a look-alike mall. Just a store, where the guy sold candy, a few toys, newspapers, bulkie rolls, some milk and maybe took numbers on the side and who either came out to join you hanging around or shooed you away so that you could curse and return another day.

14   And then came the high-tech games, the stuff you could play on television screens or on computers. Everybody into the house. Maybe lock the doors. Draw down the shades. Air-condition those rooms. Install a pool, if you can; forget the local beach. We are the new Americans. We isolate ourselves.

15 Get a special card for a cash machine. Don't bother to talk to a bank teller. That's another human. Don't hire a secretary or a phone operator. Get a machine. We humans are to be avoided at all costs.

16 Oh, there are organized functions, associations, affiliations and such. There are, in some places, annual neighborhood nights out, or lights-on, or whatever—a symbolic, once-a-year revolt against real or imagined street crime.

17 But organized fun cannot replace what comes naturally, except that conversation, and hanging around, and playing on the street, and sitting on the stoop and having a cold one, and tinkling the piano keys, and even singing a song with your friends so loud that it embarrasses your kids; except that all of that doesn't come naturally anymore in too many places that we used to call neighborhoods.

18 Call the cops. Get a large milk carton or post office poster, big enough for many pictures. Somebody, something has stolen the people.

■ TOPICAL CONSIDERATIONS

1. Lupo remembers a time when kids played games in the neighborhood before dinner and parents gathered on the stoop until dark, sharing stories and conversation. How do you remember your own neighborhood? Does it bear any resemblance to Lupo's description of this earlier time?

2. What factors does Lupo say are responsible for the changes he laments? What is your perspective on these issues?

3. Lupo is critical of the increasing homogeneity of franchises, chains, and malls marking American culture. What is your sense of the mall phenomenon? Do you agree that American culture has become "look-alike," that individualism has been lost to mass-produced consumer goods and malls?

4. "We are the new Americans. We isolate ourselves." In your opinion, is this conclusion true? Do you feel that it has somehow become desirable to maintain less contact with neighbors? Explain. What is the difference between "organized" fun and the "natural" associations Lupo feels were lost with the traditional neighborhood?

■ RHETORICAL CONSIDERATIONS

1. Lupo's essay distinguishes between the physical neighborhood—a series of houses and streets making up a community—and deeper implications of the term evoking images and feelings of warmth, sharing, and solidarity. How does Lupo make that distinction understood throughout the essay?

2. Lupo opens his piece by stating that "somebody has stolen the people," later modifying this statement, concluding that "something" has stolen the people. Why this switch in naming factors responsible for the decline of the traditional neighborhood? It is conceivable that *somebody* is responsible for this phenomenon? or *something?* How does this metaphor work?

3. Who is the narrator of this essay? Do you think this narrative device is an effective one? Why or why not?

■ **WRITING ASSIGNMENTS**

1. Write an essay in which you explore your understanding of the words *neighborhood* and *community*. Do they carry implications deeper than just houses and streets grouped together? If so, what are these implications?
2. Interview four or five fellow students about their backgrounds. Try to get a large cross section of people—from the city, the suburbs, or from rural locations. Record how their experiences differed one from the other: Did they feel a sense of community as Lupo understands it? What did they do for fun and entertainment? Were there organized community groups and outings, or was there more spontaneity? Write a report of your findings, drawing any conclusions you can about contemporary "neighborhoods" in relation to Lupo's article.
3. Write a narrative essay describing the neighborhood you grew up in. Include telling details and anecdotes, bringing the houses and streets of your neighborhood to life and giving your reader a sense of what the word *neighborhood* means to you.

You Have to Be a Real Stud Hombre Cybermuffin to Handle "Windows"
Dave Barry

Synonymous with the word computer are speed, efficiency, and ease of operation. Tongue-in-cheek Dave Barry extols these virtues only to reveal that for him they simply don't exist.

Dave Barry has been described as "America's most preposterous newspaper columnist," a man "incapable of not being funny." He is the author of ten books and is a Pulitzer Prize–winning humorist whose *Miami Herald* column is syndicated in more than 200 publications. His books include *Babies and Other Hazards of Sex* (1984), *Dave Barry's Greatest Hits* (1989) and most recently *Dave Barry's Guide to Guys* (1995). The CBS sitcom "Dave's World" is based on Mr. Barry. This essay first appeared in his column in 1994.

1 People often say to me: "Dave, as a professional columnist, you have a job that requires you to process large quantities of information on a timely basis. Why don't you get a real haircut?"

2 What these people are REALLY asking, of course, is: How am I able to produce columns with such a high degree of accuracy, day in and day out, 54 weeks per year?

3   The answer is: I use a computer. This enables me to be highly efficient. Suppose, for example, that I need to fill up column space by writing BOOGER BOOGER BOOGER BOOGER BOOGER. To accomplish this in the old precomputer days, I would have had to type "BOOGER" five times manually. But now all I have to do is type it once, then simply hold the left-hand "mouse" button down while "dragging" the "mouse" so that the "cursor" moves over the text that I wish to "select" then release the left-hand "mouse" button and position the "cursor" over the "Edit" heading on the "menu bar"; then click the left-hand "mouse" button; then move the "cursor" to the point where I wish to insert the "selected" text, then click the left-hand "mouse" button; then position the "cursor" over the "Edit" heading on the "menu bar" again; then click the left-hand "mouse" button to reveal the "edit menu"; then position the "cursor" over the "Paste" command; then click the left-hand "mouse" button four times; and then, as the French say, "voilà!" (Literally, "My hand hurts!")

4   If you need this kind of efficiency in your life, you should get a computer. I recommend the kind I have, which is a "DOS" computer ("DOS" is an acronym, meaning "ROM"). The other major kind of computer is the "Apple," which I do not recommend, because it is a wuss-o-rama New-Age computer that you basically just plug in and use. This means you don't get to participate in the most entertaining aspect of computer-owing which is trying to get the computer to work. This is where "DOS" really shines. It is way beyond normal human comprehension.

5   It was invented by Bill Gates. He is now one of the wealthiest individuals on Earth—wealthier than Queen Elizabeth; wealthier even than some people who fix car transmissions—and do you want to know why? Because he's the only person in the world who understands "DOS." Every day he gets frantic phone calls like this:

6 BUSINESS EXECUTIVE: Our entire worldwide corporate accounting system is paralyzed, and no matter what we type into the computer, it replies, "WHO WANTS TO KNOW? (signed) 'DOS.'"

7 BILL GATES: Ha-ha! I mean, sounds pretty serious.

8 BUSINESS EXECUTIVE: We'll give you $17 million to tell us how to fix it.

9 BILL GATES: OK. Press the "NUM LOCK" key.

10 BUSINESS EXECUTIVE: So THAT's what that thing does! Thanks! The check is on the way!

11   My current computer, in addition to "DOS," has "Windows," which is another invention of Bill Gates, designed as a security measure to thwart those users who are somehow able to get past "DOS." You have to be a real stud hombre cybermuffin to handle "Windows." I have spent countless hours trying to get my computer to perform even the most basic data-processing functions, such as letting me play "F-117A Stealth Fighter" on it. I have personally, with my bare hands, changed my "WIN.INI" and "CONFIG.SYS" settings. This may not mean much to you, but trust me, it is a major data-processing accomplishment. Albert Einstein died without ever doing it. ("WAIT a minute!" were his last words. "It erased my equation! It was 'E' equals something!")

12   I am not the only person who uses his computer mainly for the purpose of diddling with his computer. There are millions of others. I know this, because I encounter them on the Internet, which is a giant international network of intelligent, informed computer enthusiasts, by which I mean, "people without lives." We don't care. We have each other, on the Internet. "Geek pride," that is our motto. While you are destroying your mind watching the worthless, brain-rotting drivel on TV ("Dave's World," Monday nights, CBS, check your local listings), we on the Internet are exchanging, freely and openly, the most uninhibited, intimate and—yes—shocking details about our "CONFIG.SYS" settings.

13   You would not believe how wrought up we get about this type of thing, on the Internet. I regularly connect with a computer group that has a heated debate going on about—I am not making this up—the timing of Hewlett-Packard's decision to upgrade from a 386 to a 486 microprocessor in its Omnibook computer. This has aroused enormous passion. People—some of them from other continents—are sending snide, angry, sometimes furious messages to each other. I'm sure that some participants, even as we speak, are trying to figure out if there is a way to alter their CONFIG.SYS settings so that they can electronically punch their opponents in the mouth. This debate has been raging, soap-opera-like, for months now, and I have become addicted to it. I tune in every day to see what the leading characters are saying. You probably think this is weird, but I don't care. I am a happy nerd in cyberspace, where nobody can see my haircut.

■ TOPICAL CONSIDERATIONS

1. Barry describes the incredible efficiency and simultaneously infuriating inefficiency of his computer. Where do you fall in the computer shuffle? Do you use one? If so, what kind of efficiency does it provide your daily life? Does your computer ever get you frustrated or make you wish you weren't so dependent upon it?

2. In your own lifetime, consider how the computer phenomenon has changed the quality of life. Has the infiltration of computers into everyday living been a positive thing in general? Can you think of any negative effects of mass computer dependence?

3. In paragraph 12, Barry humorously cites the enormous Internet of computer enthusiasts. Do you have any experience with the Internet? How might such a global form of communication affect life as we know it, for better and for worse?

4. Compare Barry's description of computer pitfalls with Deborah Baldwin's discussion, in "As Busy As We Wanna Be," of technological changes in the name of saving time. How do you suppose Baldwin would respond to Barry's description of the effect of computers on the workplace?

5. In his article, "Houses and Streets, but No Neighborhood," Alan Lupo cites (paragraph 14) the "high-tech games, the stuff you could play on television screens or on computers" as contributing to decreasing neighbor-

hood and community life. Given Barry's description of life on the Internet, how do you think he would respond to Lupo's complaint? How do you feel about the relationship between technology—media, computers, and so forth—and declining community? Do these issues have any effect on your lifestyle?

■ RHETORICAL CONSIDERATIONS

1. Barry is a professional humorist. Aside from making his readers laugh, does he strike a deeper chord here? Is there more in this essay than simply a humorous send-up of computer use? What, in other words, do you come away with as a reader beside some laughs?
2. One way Barry creates his humorous effects is through irony. Try to pinpoint some examples of irony here. How do they work? How does the irony allow Barry to make some funny though meaningful points?
3. How would you characterize Barry's attitude toward computers?
4. What is the relationship between Barry's title and his essay? Is the title effective? Why or why not?
5. Barry's essay flows in and out of the first and second persons. Why do you suppose he chose this rhetorical device?

■ WRITING ASSIGNMENTS

1. A major thrust of Dave Barry's humor is self-deprecation—that is, making fun of himself. Try writing some self-deprecating humor of your own by describing some aspect of contemporary life. As Barry does, use exaggeration, irony, overstatement, understatement, surprise, and other humorous strategies.
2. Consider ways in which computers have changed either your own life, or the work life of this country in general. Then write an essay in either the first or third person exploring your perspective on positive and negative aspects of computers.

Consumer Culture

Since the 1920s technological advances, rising capital, and cheaper goods have conspired to make America the world's most affluent society—and the most consumptive. In fact, consumption is the central dynamo driving the American way of life and forging its social values. In this chapter we will explore how the giddiness to consume has affected our sense of well-being and our values.

We open with a historical view of American consumerism. In "Work and Spend," economist Juliet B. Schor argues that consumerism is not a natural trait of human nature but a product of capitalism, which for the last 70 years has conditioned people to pursue an endless quest for material wealth.

The next piece addresses the double messages we get every day from our consumer culture: *Go spend your money on what you want,* and *save a buck for when you really need it.* As Barbara Ehrenreich explains it in "Spend and Save," the first message, the "permissive" one, is the inescapable by-product of advertising. The second, "puritanical" message arises from the core American values of hard work and deferred gratification. What bothers Ehrenreich is not the economic paradox in such messages but their psychological consequences on the consumer.

Perhaps the greatest monument to our consumer culture is the shopping mall. Self-contained, enclosed from the outside world, and carefully regulated, the American mall has become *the* gathering place. Just as the malls have replaced parks for families to spend their leisure time, they have bumped the local malt shop and diner for teenagers to meet. So observes William Glaberson in the next essay, "Mall Rats," where he records some of the rites of passage of kids—flirting with each other, trendy looks, and sometimes jail.

The next essay takes a very small incident and raises some large and troubling questions about how consumer mentality has reduced the basic values of honesty and kindness to commodities. In "Money for Morality," Mary Arguelles wonders why virtue isn't its own reward anymore or why simple pleasures require a purchase.

No article of clothing is more synonymous with America than blue jeans. They span all ages, all social classes, and all continents—and nearly 150 years. The next article, "The Ends Justify the Jeans," by Stuart Ewen and Elizabeth Ewen, is a brief review of how this American staple has gone beyond mere function or fashion to become an ideological symbol of Western democracy.

As a consumer, you probably have had the experience of calling some large impersonal company with a complaint. Either you got an automatic answering system that kept you on hold forever, or you connected with a bored, rude voice in "Customer Service" who made you wish you hadn't called. You know the experience, right? So does humorist Dave Barry who hits a few nerves while sparking some laughs in "The Customer's Always Right."

	Work and Spend
	Juliet B. Schor

Juliet B. Schor is a professor of economics at Harvard University and author of *The Overworked American: The Unexpected Decline of Leisure* (1992), from which this essay comes. In her book, she argues that working hours in the United States have increased substantially over the last 20 years—by about 160 hours or one month per year. The result is less leisure time to enjoy ourselves and, thus, a decline in our standard of living. This is true of men and women, from corporate executives to hamburger flippers. As she explains in this excerpt, the prime culprit is the capitalist system, which has spawned a "consumerist treadmill and long-hour jobs" that have in turn created a cycle of work and spend.

1 [M]aterialism (and its attendant discontent) is taken for granted. It is widely believed that our unceasing quest for material goods is part of the basic makeup of human beings. According to the folklore, we may not like it, but there's little we can do about it.

2 Despite its popularity, this view of human nature is wrong. While human beings may have innate desires to strive toward something, there is nothing preordained about material goods. There are numerous examples of societies in which *things* have played a highly circumscribed role. In medieval Europe, there was relatively little acquisitiveness. The common people, whose lives were surely precarious by contemporary standards, showed strong preferences for leisure rather than money. In the nineteenth- and early twentieth-century United States, there is also considerable evidence that many working people exhibited a restricted appetite for material goods. Numerous examples of societies where consumption is relatively unimportant can be found in the anthropological and historical literature.[1]

3 Consumerism is not an ahistorical trait of human nature, but a specific production of capitalism. With the development of the market system, consumerism "spilled over," for the first time, beyond the charmed circles of the rich. The growth of the middle class created a large group of potential buyers and the possibility that mass culture could be oriented around material goods. This process can be seen not only in historical experiences but is now going on in places such as Brazil and India, where the growth of large middle classes have contributed to rampant consumerism and the breakdown of longstanding values.[2]

4 In the United States, the watershed was the 1920s—the point at which the "psychology of scarcity" gave way to the "psychology of abundance." This was a crucial period for the development of modern materialist culture. Thrift and sobriety were out; waste and excess were in. The nation grew giddy with its exploding wealth. Consumerism blossomed—both as a social ideology and in terms of high rates of real spending. In the midst of all this buying, we can discern the origins of modern consumer discontent.

5   This was the decade during which the American dream, or what was then called "the American standard of living," captured the nation's imagination. But it was always something of a mirage. The historian Winifred Wandersee explains:

> It is doubtful that the average American could have described the precise meaning of the term "American standard of living," but nearly everyone agreed that it was attainable, highly desirable, and far superior to that of any other nation. Its nature varied according to social class and regional differences, but no matter where a family stood socially and financially, it was certain to have aspirations set beyond that stance. This was the great paradox posed by the material prosperity of the twentieth century: prosperity was conspicuously present, but it was always just out of reach, for nearly every family defined its standard of living in terms of an income that it hoped to achieve rather than the reality of the paycheck.[3]

The phenomenon of yearning for more is evident in studies of household consumption. In a 1928 study of Yale University faculty members, the bottom category (childless couples with incomes of $2,000) reported that their situation was "life at the cheapest and barest with nothing left over for the emergencies of sickness and childbirth." Yet an income of $2,000 a year put them above 60 percent of all American families. Those at the $5,000 level (the top 10 percent of the income distribution) reported that they "achieve nothing better than 'hand to mouth living.'" At $6,000, "the family containing young children can barely break even." Yet these were the top few percent of all Americans. Even those making $12,000—a fantastic sum in 1928—complained about items they could not afford. A 1922 Berkeley study revealed similar sentiments of discontent—despite the facts that all the families studies had telephones, virtually all had purchased life insurance, two-thirds owned their own homes and took vacations, over half had motor cars, and nearly every family spent at least a little money on servants or housecleaning help.[4]

6   The discontent expressed by many Americans was fostered—and to a certain extent even created—by manufacturers. Business embarked on the path of the "hard sell." The explosion of consumer credit made the task easier, as automobiles, radios, electric refrigerators, washing machines—even jewelry and foreign travel—were bought on the installment plan. By the end of the 1920s, 60 percent of cars, radios, and furniture were being purchased on "time."[5] The ability to buy without actually having money helped foster a climate of instant gratification, expanding expectations, and, ultimately, materialism.

7   The 1920s was also the decade of advertising. The admen went wild: everything from walnuts to household coal was being individually branded and nationally advertised. Of course, ads had been around for a long time. But something new was afoot, in terms of both scale and strategy. For the first time, business began to use advertising as a psychological weapon against consumers. "Scare copy" was invented. Without Listerine, Postum, or a Buick, the consumer would be left a spinster, fall victim to a crippling disease, or be passed over for a promotion. Ads developed an association between the product and one's very identity. Eventually they came to promise everything and anything—from self-esteem, to status, friendship, and love.[6]

8   The psychological approach responded to the economic dilemma business faced. Americans in the middle classes and above (to whom virtually all advertising was targeted) were no longer buying to satisfy basic needs—such as food, clothing and shelter. These had been met. Advertisers had to persuade consumers to acquire things they most certainly did not need. In the words of John Kenneth Galbraith, production would have to "create the wants it seeks to satisfy." This is exactly what manufacturers tried to do. The normally staid AT&T attempted to transform the utilitarian telephone into a luxury, urging families to buy "all the telephone facilities that they can conveniently use, rather than the smallest amount they can get along with." One ad campaign targeted fifteen phones as the style for an affluent home. In product after product, companies introduced designer colors, styles, even scents. The maid's uniform had to match the room decor, flatware was color-coordinated, and Kodak cameras came in five bird-inspired tints—Sea Gull, Cockatoo, Redbreast, Bluebird, and Jenny Wren.[7]

9   Business clearly understood the nature of the problem. It even had a name—"needs saturation." Would-be sellers complained of buyers' strike and organized a "Prosperity Bureau," urging people to "Buy Now." According to historian Frederick Lewis Allen: "Business had learned as never before the importance of the ultimate consumer. Unless he could be persuaded to buy and buy lavishly, the whole stream of six-cylinder cars, super helerodynes, cigarettes, rouge compacts, and electric ice boxes would be dammed up at its outlets."[8]

10   But would the consumer be equal to her task as "the savior of private enterprise"? The general director of General Motors' Research Labs, Charles Kettering, stated the matter baldly: business needs to create a "dissatisfied consumer"; its mission is "the organized creation of dissatisfaction." Kettering led the way by introducing annual model changes for GM cars—planned obsolescence designed to make the consumer discontented with what he or she already had. Other companies followed GM's lead. In the words of advertising historian Roland Marchand, success now depended on "the nurture of qualities like wastefulness, self-indulgence, and artificial obsolescence." The admen and the businessmen had to instill what Marchand has called the "consumption ethic," or what Benjamin Hunnicutt termed "the new economic gospel of consumption."[9]

11   The campaign to create new and unlimited wants did not go unchallenged. Trade unionists and social reformers understood the long-term consequences of consumerism for most Americans: it would keep them imprisoned in capitalism's "squirrel cage." The consumption of luxuries necessitated long hours. Materialism would provide no relief from the tedium, the stultification, the alienation, and the health hazards of modern work; its rewards came outside the workplace. There was no mystery about these choices: business was explicit in its hostility to increases in free time, preferring consumption as the *alternative* to taking economic progress in the form of leisure. In effect, business offered up the cycle of work-and-spend. In response, many trade unionists rejected what they regarded as a Faustian bargain of time for money: "Workers have declared that their lives are not to be bartered at any price, that no wage, no matter how high can induce them to sell their birthright. [The worker] is not the slave of fifty years ago. . . . he [*sic*] reads . . . goes to the

theater . . . [*and*] has established his own libraries, his own educational institutions. . . . And he wants time, time, time, for all these things."[10]

12   Progressive reformers raised ethical and religious objections to the cycle of work-and-spend. Monsignor John A. Ryan, a prominent Catholic spokesman, articulated a common view:

> One of the most baneful assumptions of our materialistic industrial society is that all men should spend at least one-third of the twenty-four hour day in some productive occupation. . . . If men still have leisure [after needs are satisfied], new luxuries must be invented to keep them busy and new wants must be stimulated . . . to take the luxuries off the market and keep the industries going. Of course, the true and rational doctrine is that when men have produced sufficient necessaries and reasonable comforts and conveniences to supply all the population, they should spend what time is left in the cultivation of their intellects and wills, in the pursuit of the higher life.[11]

The debates of the 1920s clearly laid out the options available to the nation. On the one hand, the path advocated by labor and social reformers: take productivity growth in the form of increases in free time, rather than the expansion of output; limit private consumption, discourage luxuries, and emphasize public goods such as education and culture. On the other hand, the plan of business: maintain current working hours and aim for maximal economic growth. This implied the encouragement of "discretionary" consumption, the expansion of new industries, and a culture of unlimited desires. Production would come to "fill a void that it has itself created."[12]

13   It is not difficult to see which alternative was adopted. Between 1920 and the present, the bulk of productivity advance has been channeled into the growth of consumption. Economist John Owen has found that between 1920 and 1977, the amount of labor supplied over the average American's lifetime fell by only 10 percent; and since 1950, there has even been a slight increase.[13] The attitude of businessmen was crucial to this outcome. As employers, they had strong reasons for preferring long hours. As sellers, they craved vigorous consumption to create markets for their products. Labor proved to be no match for the economic and political power of business.

14   Finally, we should not underestimate the appeal of consumption itself. The working classes and the poor, particularly those migrating from Europe or the rural United States, grew up in conditions of material deprivation. The array of products available in urban America was profoundly alluring, at times mesmerizing. For the middle classes, consumption held its own satisfactions. Designer towels or the latest GM model created a sense of privilege, superiority, and well-being. A Steinway "made life worth living." Once the Depression hit, it reinforced these tendencies. One of its legacies was a long-lasting emphasis on finding security in the form of material success.[14]

THE PITFALLS OF CONSUMERISM

15 The consumerism that took root in the 1920s was premised on the idea of *dis*satisfaction. As much as one has, it is never enough. The implicit mentality is that the next purchase will yield happiness, and then the next. In the words of the baby-boom

writer, Katy Butler, it was the new couch, the quieter street, and the vacation cottage. Yet happiness turned out to be elusive. Today's luxuries became tomorrow's necessities, no longer appreciated. When the Joneses also got a new couch or a second home, these acquisitions were no longer quite as satisfying. Consumerism turned out to be full of pitfalls—a vicious pattern of wanting and spending which failed to deliver on its promises.

16 The inability of the consumerist lifestyle to create durable satisfaction can be seen in the syndrome of "keeping up with the Joneses." This competition is based on the fact that it is not the absolute level of consumption that matters, but how much one consumes relative to one's peers. The great English economist John Maynard Keynes made this distinction over fifty years ago: "[Needs] fall into two classes— those which are absolute in the sense that we feel them whatever the situation of our fellow human beings may be, and those which are relative only in that their satisfaction lifts us above, makes us feel superior to, our fellows." Since then, economists have invented a variety of terms for "keeping up with the Joneses": "relative income or consumption," "positional goods," or "local status." A brand-new Toyota Corolla may be a luxury and a status symbol in a lower-middle-class town, but it appears paltry next to the BMWs and Mercedes that fill the driveways of the fancy suburb. A 10-percent raise sounds great until you find that your co-workers all got 12 percent. The cellular phone, fur coat, or _____ (fill in the blank) gives a lot of satisfaction only before everyone else has one. In the words of one 1980s investment banker: "You tend to live up to your income level. You see it in relation to the people of your category. They're living in a certain way and you want to live in that way. You keep up with other people of your situation who have also leveraged themselves."[15]

17 Over time, keeping up with the Joneses becomes a real trap—because the Joneses also keep up with you. If everyone's income goes up by 10 percent, then relative positions don't change at all. No satisfaction is gained. The more of our happiness we derive from comparisons with others, the less additional welfare we get from general increases in income—which is probably why happiness has failed to keep pace with economic growth. This dynamic may be only partly conscious. We may not even be aware that we are competing with the Joneses, or experience it as a competition. It may be as simple as the fact that exposure to their latest "lifestyle upgrade" plants the seed in our own mind that we must have it, too—whether it be a European vacation, this year's fashion statement, or piano lessons for the children.

18 In the choice between income and leisure, the quest for relative standing has biased us toward income. That's because status comparisons have been mostly around commodities—cars, clothing, houses, even second houses. If Mrs. Jones works long hours, she will be able to buy the second home, the designer dresses, or the fancier car. If her neighbor Mrs. Smith opts for more free time instead, her two-car garage and walk-in closet will be half empty. As long as the competition is more oriented to visible commodities, the tendency will be for both women to prefer income to time off. But once they both spend the income, they're back to where they started. Neither is *relatively* better off. If free time is less of a "relative" good than other commodities, then true welfare could be gained by having more of it, and worrying less about what the Joneses are buying.

19   It's not easy to get off the income treadmill and into a new, more leisured life-style. Mrs. Smith won't do it on her own, because it'll set her back in comparison to Mrs. Jones. And Mrs. Jones is just like Mrs. Smith. They are trapped in a classic Prisoner's Dilemma: both would be better off with more free time; but without coop-eration, they will stick to the long hours, high consumption choice.[16] We also know their employers won't initiate a shift to more leisure, because they prefer employees to work long hours.

20   A second vicious cycle arises from the fact that the satisfactions gained from consumption are often short-lived. For many, consumption can be habit forming. Like drug addicts who develop a tolerance, consumers need additional hits to main-tain any given level of satisfaction.[17] The switch from black and white to color tele-vision was a real improvement when it occurred. But soon viewers became habitu-ated to color. Going back to black and white would have reduced well-being, but having color may not have yielded a permanently higher level of satisfaction. Telephones are another example. Rotary dialing was a major improvement. Then came touch-tone, which made us impatient with rotaries. Now numbers are pre-programmed and some people begin to find any dialing a chore.

21   Our lives are filled with goods to which we have become so habituated that we take them for granted. Indoor plumbing was once a great luxury—and still is in much of the world. Now it is so ingrained in our life style that we don't give it a sec-ond thought. The same holds true for all but the newest household appliances—stoves, refrigerators, and vacuum cleaners are just part of the landscape. We may pay great attention to the kind of automobile we drive, but the fact of having a car is something adults grew accustomed to long ago.

22   The process of habituation can be seen as people pass through life stages—for example, in the transition from student life to a first job. The graduate student makes $15,000 a year. He has hand-me-down furniture, eats at cheap restaurants, and, when traveling long distances, finds a place in someone else's car. After graduation, he gets a job and makes twice as much money. At first, everything seems luxurious. He rents a bigger apartment (with no roommates), buys his own car, and steps up a notch in restaurant quality. His former restaurant haunts now seem unappetizing. Hitching a ride becomes too inconvenient. As he accumulates possessions, the large apartment starts to shrink. In not too many years, he has become habituated to twice as much income and is spending the entire $30,000. It was once a princely sum, which made him feel rich. Now he feels it just covers a basic standard of living, without much left over for luxuries. He may not even feel any better off. Yet to go back to $15,000 would be painful.

23   Over time, further increases in income set in motion another round of the same. He becomes dissatisfied with renting and "needs" to buy a home. Travel by car takes too long, so he switches to airplanes. His tastes become more discriminating, and the average price of a restaurant meal slowly creeps upward. Something like this process is why Americans making $70,000 a year end up feeling stretched and discontented.[18]

24   Of course, part of this is a life-cycle process. As our young man grows older, possessions like cars and houses become more important. But there's more to it than

aging. Like millions of other American consumers, he is becoming addicted to the accoutrements of affluence. This may well be why the doubling of per-capita income has not made us twice as well off. In the words of psychologist Paul Wachtel, we have become an "asymptote culture . . . in which the contribution of material goods to life satisfaction has reached a point of diminishing returns. . . . Each individual item seems to us to bring an increase in happiness or satisfaction. But the individual increments melt like cotton candy when you try to add them up."[19]

25   These are not new ideas. Economists such as James Duesenberry, Edward Schumacher, Fred Hirsch, Tibor Scitovsky, Robert Frank, and Richard Easterlin have explored these themes. Psychologists have also addressed them, providing strong support for the kinds of conclusions I have drawn. My purpose is to add a dimension to this analysis of consumption which has heretofore been neglected—its connection to the incentive structures operating in labor markets. The consumption traps I have described are just the flip side of the bias toward long hours embedded in the production system. We are not merely caught in a pattern of spend-and-spend—the problem identified by many critics of consumer culture. The whole story is that we work, and spend, and work and spend some more.

■ NOTES

1. On the United States, see Herbert Gutman, *Work, Culture and Society in Industrializing America* (New York: Vintage, 1977). See also the discussion of the 1925 Consumer League of New York study in Benjamin Hunnicutt, *Work Without End: Abandoning Shorter Hours for the Right to Work* (Philadelphia: Temple University Press, 1988), 68–69, where respondents displayed strong preferences for leisure.

   On the anthropological evidence, see Marshall Sahlins, *Stone Age Economics* (New York: Aldine, 1972).

2. See Neil McKendrick, John Brewer, and J. H. Plumb, *The Birth of a Consumer Society: The Commercialization of Eighteenth-Century England* (London: Europa Publications, 1982); and Arjun Appadurai, "Technology and the Reproduction of Values in Rural Western India," in Frédérique Apffel-Marglin and Stephen A. Marglin, eds., *Dominating Knowledge: Development, Culture, and Resistance* (Oxford: Clarendon Press, 1990), 185–216.

3. Winifred D. Wandersee, *Women's Work and Family Values, 1920–1940* (Cambridge, Mass.: Harvard University Press, 1981), 7–8.

4. On the Yale study, see ibid., 10, table 1.1, and 21–22.

   On the Berkeley study, see Jessica Peixotto, *Getting and Spending at the Professional Standard of Living* (New York: Macmillan, 1927). Data from chapter 6.

5. Roland Marchand, *Advertising the American Dream: Making Way for Modernity* (Berkeley: University of California Press, 1985), 4, 5.

6. Ibid.

7. John Kenneth Galbraith, *The Affluent Society,* 4th ed. (Boston: Houghton Mifflin, 1984), 127. Marchand, *Advertising the American Dream,* chap. 5.

8. Hunnicutt, *Work Without End,* 38.
   Allen quoted in ibid., 45.
9. The "savior" phrase is Thomas Cochran's, cited in Hunnicutt, *Work Without End,* 44.
   Charles F. Kettering, "Keep the Consumer Dissatisfied," *Nation's Business,* January 1929; "organized creation," Marchand, *Advertising the American Dream,* 156.
   Marchand, *Advertising the American Dream,* 158, and Hunnicutt, *Work Without End,* chap. 2.
10. From an ILGWU pamphlet cited in Hunnicutt, *Work Without End,* 75.
11. Ibid., 94.
12. Galbraith, *Affluent Society,* 127.
13. This conclusion is from John Owen, *Working Lives: The American Work Force Since 1920* (Lexington, Mass.: Lexington Books, 1986), 23.
14. On "mesmerization," see Stuart Ewen and Elizabeth Ewen, *Channels of Desire: Mass Images and the Shaping of American Consciousness* (New York: McGraw-Hill, 1982).
   From a Steinway ad cited in Marchand, *Advertising the American Dream,* 142.
15. John Maynard Keynes, "Economic Possibilities for Our Grandchildren," in *Essays in Persuasion* (New York: Harcourt, Brace, 1932), 365.
   The classic statement of the importance of relative consumption was made in 1949 by Harvard economist James Duesenberry in *Income, Saving and the Theory of Consumer Behavior* (Cambridge, Mass.: Harvard University Press, 1949). Unfortunately, the ideas put forward in this pioneering work have not been adequately tested and pursued. For further discussion of these issues, in addition to Duesenberry, see the works of Tibor Scitovsky, Richard Easterlin, Fred Hirsch, and Robert Frank.
   Investment banker from Brooke Kroeger, "Feeling Poor," p. 8.
16. In a Prisoner's Dilemma, both partners would be made better off if they cooperated, but failure to do so leads both to be worse off. This point has been made by Robert H. Frank in *Choosing the Right Pond* (New York: Oxford University Press, 1985), 133–35.
17. Galbraith calls this "the dependence effect"; Scitovsky, the difference between "pleasure" (what one gets at first) and "comfort" (the sensation after habituation).
18. This passage from Jonathan Freedman, the author of a book on happiness, describes the syndrome: "As a student, I lived on what now seems no money at all, but I lived in a style which seemed perfectly fine . . . As my income has grown since then, I have spent more . . . but it has always seemed to be just about the same amount of money and bought just about the same things. The major change is that I have spent more on everything, and I consider buying more expensive items. None of this has had an appreciable effect on my life or on my feelings of happiness or satisfaction. I imagine that if I earned five times as much, the same would be true—at least it would once I got used to the extra money. This is not to say that I would turn down a

raise—quite the contrary. But after a while everything would settle down, the extra money would no longer be 'extra,' and my life would be the same as before." From *Happy People* (New York: Harcourt, Brace, Jovanovich, 1978), 140.

19. Paul Wachtel, *The Poverty of Affluence: A Psychological Portrait of the American Way of Life* (Philadelphia: New Society Publishers, 1989), 39.

■ TOPICAL CONSIDERATIONS

1. In the first paragraph of this essay, Schor refutes the common knowledge that desire for material goods is a natural human process. What influences you to want a new car, new clothes, and other material goods?

2. Does Schor's evidence, beginning in paragraph 2 and continuing through paragraph 11, convince you that consumerism has produced discontent in middle-class and lower-class Americans? Which of her examples are most convincing?

3. According to Schor, which two groups challenged the rise of consumerism in the 1920s? Which side won the debate? Where do you think each of these groups would stand today on the conflict between consumerism and leisure time?

4. Schor argues throughout her essay that consumerism is based on the idea of dissatisfaction with what one has. If buying more things can make you happy, why are some rich people discontented with their lives, according to Schor? Would you be happier if you were rich? Why or why not?

5. In paragraph 16, the author quotes the great English economist John Maynard Keynes on the notion that there is a difference between absolute needs and relative needs. How does this thesis apply to "keeping up with the Joneses" (paragraph 17)? What relevance has Keynes's work to this essay?

6. Paragraphs 18 and 19 introduce two fictional women, Mrs. Jones and Mrs. Smith, who illustrate the problems of "keeping up with the Joneses." Describe people you know who fall into this category. Have you had the same experiences?

7. Would readers from other cultures and ethnic groups respond to this article any differently than middle-class Americans? How would Native Americans or New Age individuals view consumerism in contemporary culture?

■ RHETORICAL CONSIDERATIONS

1. How does the author structure her argument in this essay? Is it an inductive or deductive argument? Where does her major claim appear?

2. How would you describe the tone of this essay? Do you find it difficult to follow? Why or why not?

3. Schor includes words such as "super heterodynes" (paragraph 9) and "asymptote" (paragraph 24), which she does not define. If you do not know the meanings of these words, look them up in an encyclopedia or dictionary and explain how they are used in this context. Did you wish the author had defined these terms?

4. Throughout this essay the author gives only her side of the argument that business has fostered unbridled consumerism over leisure time. She does not include any negative evidence from labor and religious groups—that labor is more interested in workers' rights than economic expansion, and that religious organizations try to keep people in their place. Could these omissions weaken her argument? Why or why not?

5. In the first line of paragraph 10, Schor uses the pronoun *her* when referring to the general consumer, instead of the generic *him*. In paragraphs 18 and 19 she calls her characters, *Mrs*. Jones and *Mrs*. Smith, instead of the more usual title, *Mr*. How does this usage appeal to you? Have you noticed this trend toward gender balance in other publications?

■ WRITING ASSIGNMENTS

1. In paragraphs 22 through 24 Schor gives an example of the "process of habituation" in the life of a graduate student. Write a story about this graduate student, or someone else going through this process of becoming "addicted to the accoutrements of affluence." Flesh out your character's life with descriptions of each stage in his or her life.

2. Write an essay on advertising in the 1990s, incorporating examples of "advertising as a psychological weapon against consumers." Find current ads from magazines, such as those mentioned in paragraph 7, that appeal to consumers' psychological needs. Discuss what the advertisers are trying to do in these ads.

3. If you disagree with specific sections of Schor's essay, write a rebuttal to these arguments, giving your own opinions. Back up your ideas with solid evidence.

Spend and Save

Barbara Ehrenreich

In the previous essay, Juliet Schor argued that we American consumers fail to find happiness in our endless consumption. Paradoxically, she says that the ever-increasing material choices simply accelerate our rat-race efforts toward impossible fulfillment. In the essay below, Barbara Ehrenreich examines a different kind of consumer choice paradox. Every day, she says, we are bombarded with two contradictory sets of messages—one that says Go for it! the other that says Don't!

Barbara Ehrenreich is a widely published writer. She is the author of *The Worst Years of Our Lives: Irreverent Notes of the Middle Class* and *Fear of Falling: The Inner Life of the Middle Class.* This article is an excerpt from an address at the 1992 Family Therapy Networker Symposium.

1 A week or so ago, a billboard appeared a few blocks from my home. It shows a giant dollar bill, so I thought it was going to be something about "buying American," but when I got close enough to see the writing, it said, "Buck the recession, spend a buck." On what? It didn't say. Just get out there and buy. I found this deeply confusing. Wasn't our problem—only 10 minutes ago, historically speaking—that we didn't save enough? (It certainly is *my* problem!) What are we supposed to do? Spend? Save? Spend *and* save?

2 Here's another example that may be familiar to many of you: If I don't pay my credit card bill on time, I get one of those really cold, nasty messages from American Express, or whoever, saying, "You miserable wretch, pay up or die." As soon as I send in the check, another letter comes back saying, in fawning tones, "Ms. Ehrenreich, you are one of our most valued customers. How would you like us to increase your credit limit by $2,000?" Well, which am I: valued customer or miserable wretch?

3 The paradox is that we get two sets of messages coming at us every day. One is the "permissive" message, saying, "Buy, spend, get it now, indulge yourself," because your wants are also your needs—and you have plenty of needs that you don't even know about because our consumer culture hasn't told you about them yet! The other we could call, for lack of a better word, a "puritanical" message, which says, "Work hard, save, defer gratification, curb your impulses." What are the psychological and social consequences of getting such totally contradictory messages all the time? I think this is what you would call "cognitive dissonance," and the psychological consequence is a pervasive anxiety, upon which the political right has been very adept at mobilizing and building.

4 The puritanical message comes to us from a variety of sources: from school, from church, often from parents, and every so often from political figures when they refer to "traditional values." Hard work, family loyalty, the capacity to defer gratification—these are supposed to be core, American values, the traits that made our country great and so forth.

5 But the permissive message, as I said, comes to us chiefly in the form of advertising, which is a force to which family therapists should perhaps devote more attention. Advertising is inescapable; it is fed to us in dozens of forms and in more and more settings:

- —on TV, in movie theaters, in movies themselves (*Die Hard 2* contained 19 paid ads for products featured in it; *Pretty Woman* was, in a way, one long discourse on the joys of shopping);
- —in the print media (including in the "advertorials," or ads disguised as articles, which are so common in the fashion magazines);
- —over the phone; and there is advertising now even in the schools (through Channel One, which brings kids 12 minutes of news plus two minutes of commercials for, for example, Burger King—during school time).

6 Someone has calculated that by the time an American reaches the age of 40, he or she has been exposed to one million ads. Another estimate is that we have encountered more than 600,000 ads by the time we reach the age of only 18. Now, of course, we don't remember what exactly they said or even what the product was, but the underlying message gets through: That you deserve the best, that you should have it now, and that it's *alright* to indulge yourself—now—because this is a Michelob moment, or because you *prefer* those silky Hanes pantyhose, or because you *deserve* the greater control, sex appeal, or adventure you are going to get from a BMW or Flex shampoo or Merit cigarettes.

7 One of the best—in fact one of the only—books dealing with this paradox was written by Daniel Bell, who pointed out, in 1979, that our consumer-based economy makes two absolutely contradictory psychological demands on its members. On the one hand, you need the "puritanical" values to ensure that people will be good workers and lead orderly, law-abiding lives. On the other hand, you need the "permissive" messages to get people to be good consumers. Bell was disturbed about the permissive side, but acknowledged that "without the hedonism stimulated by mass consumption, the very structure of [our] business enterprises would collapse."

8 The interesting question, which Bell did not explore, has to do with the psychological consequences of the double message we are taking in all the time. In old-fashioned, Freudian terms, the puritanical, or "traditional values," theme is addressed to the superego and demands a personality with a strong enough superego to keep the individual doing unpleasant work at inadequate wages, or to stay in an unhappy marriage, and, in general, to play by the rules.

9 The permissive message, on the other hand, is addressed to the id and tends to endorse a very different kind of personality—one that is childlike, self-centered, impulsive, has a short attention span and is unwilling to defer gratification because even the most transient desires are experienced as genuine needs. As an illustration, I can't resist citing one of my favorite ads of all time, a 1975 ad from the magazine *Psychology Today*. The caption says, in boldface, "I love me. I'm just a good friend to myself. And I like to do what makes me feel good. Me, myself and I used to sit around, putting things off till tomorrow. Tomorrow we'll buy new ski equipment,

and look at new compact cars, and pick up that new camera . . . [But now] I live my dreams today, not tomorrow."

10   So what happens to us as we take in these contradictory messages, as we are, in fact, torn between the contradictory personality types that our society seems to require of us? As I argued in my book, *Fear of Falling,* the result is anxiety, fear, a nameless dread. We want more things, we want to indulge ourselves, and not just because advertising tells us to—who wouldn't want that scuba equipment?

11   But at the same time, a little voice inside us echoes all those puritanical messages and says, "Watch out, don't get sucked in, you'll get into debt—worse still, you'll lose your edge, you'll get soft, you won't be able to make it anymore."

12   In the 1980s, this anxiety was often expressed in Cold War terms. The fear was that we Americans were being softened—that was the word they used—by our affluence and consumer culture, while the Russians, who didn't have TVs or toaster ovens, were supposedly still tough and hard and smart. Johnny couldn't read, but—as another book title from the '50s informed us—Ivan could.

13   But even without Cold War propaganda to reinforce it, the fear of being sucked in and dragged down by the consumer culture is real: American Express is not friendly when you can't pay your bills. And we all know that the path of self-indulgence and consumerism leads pretty quickly to financial ruin—for most of us, anyway—and that, in American society, there isn't much of a safety net to catch you if you fall.

■ TOPICAL CONSIDERATIONS

1. Describe what Ehrenreich calls the "puritanical" and "permissive" messages of consumer culture. Where do these messages come from, according to this essay? When and where have you felt the influence of the "puritanical" message in your own life? At what times have you lived according to the dictates of the "permissive" message?

2. Ehrenreich claims that "the underlying message" of advertising is "that you deserve the best, that you should have it now, and that it's alright to indulge yourself. . . " (paragraph 6). Do you agree that this concept underlies all advertisements? Consider the products Ehrenreich uses as examples in this paragraph. What other goods and services might not sell with the "indulge yourself" message? (You may consider some of the ads reproduced at the end of this chapter.) To what other values and beliefs do advertisers typically appeal?

3. Ehrenreich's essay first appeared in the *Family Therapy Networker.* Why would this essay be of interest to mental health professionals? What main point does Ehrenreich want to get across to this particular readership?

4. Explain the Freudian terms *id* and *superego* that Ehrenreich refers to in paragraphs 8 and 9. How do these concepts relate to her argument?

5. How did the Cold War increase the power of the "puritanical" message in the 1980s, according to paragraph 12? Evaluate the logic and supporting

evidence offered here. What do you know about the 1980s that might challenge Ehrenreich's description of this decade?

■ RHETORICAL CONSIDERATIONS

1. How effectively do the first two paragraphs draw the reader into Ehrenreich's argument? How accurately do they predict the argument to come? Consider both content and tone.
2. Ehrenreich labels the "save" message of American culture as puritanical, "for lack of a better word" (paragraph 3); she labels the "spend" message as permissive. What effect do these labels have on your understanding of the two concepts? What are the connotations of the word *puritanical?* of the word *permissive?* What other words might Ehrenreich have used to create a slightly different impression?
3. What evidence does Ehrenreich use to support the claim that "the puritanical message comes to us . . . from school, from church, often from parents. . . " (paragraph 4)? Do you agree that these places are the source of the conservative, "save" message? In your experience, what other kinds of values of families, churches, and schools promote?
4. How does Ehrenreich support her theory that "cognitive dissonance" (paragraph 3) is created by the "spend and save" messages? To what extent do you agree that the two messages create psychic distress? What, if anything, do you find dubious about her theory of cognitive dissonance?
5. How effective did you find Ehrenreich's use of Daniel Bell as an outside authority? Analyze the relationship between the theories of Ehrenreich and Bell. Why is Ehrenreich so impressed with Bell?

■ WRITING ASSIGNMENTS

1. Compare Ehrenreich's essay to Juliet B. Schor's "Work and Spend." Examine particularly the kinds of evidence marshaled by these two writers and their use of secondary authorities. Which essay do you find more convincing, and why?
2. Write a letter to a major manufacturer suggesting how they might capitalize on the contradictory "spend and save" cultural messages in advertising their particular product.
3. Apply Ehrenreich's theory to a friend or relative who you think has been unduly influenced by the "permissive" or the "puritanical" message. Choose someone who has either damaged their financial future through overindulgence or whose whole life seems hostage to a kind of dreary, and unwarranted, economic self-denial. In a paper, describe how that person's life has been so influenced.

	# Mall Rats
	William Glaberson

According to Barbara Ehrenreich's article, we will be exposed to 600,000 ads by the time we reach 18 years of age. With so powerful a force working on us, it comes as no surprise that the local shopping mall has become the modern Mecca for today's adolescents. Over a period of several weeks William Glaberson visited some malls and observed the patterns of behavior of these "mall rats"—kids who like lemmings flock there regularly whether to buy or not. It's what they do to keep trendy; it's what they do when there's nothing to do. This article first appeared in *The New York Times* in April 1993.

1   It was Friday night at the mall. Christine Tako, 18 years old, with her straight brown hair falling down over her shoulders, was not sure whether to let the boy with the blue eyes know how much she liked him.

2   The teen-agers were gathering in little groups in the food court near Time Out Amusement, the video arcade that serves as headquarters for what regulars at the Danbury Fair Mall—and malls everywhere—call mall rats, the adolescents who seem to live to go to the mall.

3   Christine Tako kept wavering. She could get hurt again, the way she had in her last mall romance. But, then, there were those blue eyes.

4   She was sure about one thing, though. He would show up sooner or later.

5   "Everybody's a mall rat to an extent," she said. "It's something to do when there is nothing else to do. And there is nothing else to do."

6   Once, it was the malt shop or the diner. These days across the New York region, the mall is the teen-age clubhouse. Sometimes by the hundreds, adolescents meet, mill about, issue dares and join in that ancient teen-age conviction that there is nothing else to do.

SHARING "A BORING EMPTINESS"

7   Some say their time in the shadows of the mall's neon lights leaves them with a hollowness that is deeper than that of former teen-age pastimes. You sit with someone you know and you wait for something to happen, said Brian Fuda, a slight high school graduate with a mustache of fine brown hairs, who dreams of becoming an actor. "You don't become great friends," he said. "You both share that boring emptiness."

8   But if there is a special starkness in the lives of the mall's teen-agers, it is a backdrop to all the usual themes of adolescence. The food court has seen its loves and heartbreaks. It has become the venue for timeless experiments: drugs and liquor can be had for a price.

9   Cars in the mall parking garage are as popular for intimate moments as they have always been. And shoplifting can be a badge of honor for those in search of a rebellious image.

10   Here in Danbury, the tough and the timid come from quiet nearby towns like Brookfield, Bethel and Redding and from comfortable suburbs in Putnam County and northern Westchester, just over the border in New York State. "If you're not here, you're just drawn here," Brian Fuda said.

11   There are the teen-agers flirting with different identities. Nose rings and beepers constitute current chic.

12   There are the picture-perfect suburban youths who seem to have just outfitted at The Gap downstairs and who watch the rougher ones warily.

MALL RAT PACK

13   And then there are the ones whose dress shows their pride in being called mall rats, like Chris Roman, 21, whose hair makes a statement and whose black leather jacket, he said, he bought with a stolen credit card.

14   The afternoon before Christine Tako's night of decision, Chris Roman, known to all the mall rats as Scooby, had been sitting at that same table. He described what he called the dark side of the mall-rat world. His black hair was shoulder length but a three-inch-wide band of white skin showed above his ears where he had shaved it with a straight razor to provide a threatening "heavy metal" look.

15   "I've been smoking pot since I was 12," he said. "I've been drinking since I was 9. I've been hanging out at the mall since it opened." He was 16 then.

16   The nickname came from the inebriated position he was in when he passed out at a party in his early teens, he said. He was entangled with his host's family's dog, and the situation, for some reason, reminded everyone of Scooby Doo, the television cartoon canine.

17   That, Scooby said, was before he was jailed for car theft and before he was arrested for smoking marijuana in the parking garage. It was back, he said, before the time when he and some of the other mall rats ran what he called a "black market" in shoplifted items at the mall.

FONZI OF THE FOOD COURT

18   Scooby's tales and his studied ability to strike a match for his Newport Light cigarettes on the smooth-as-glass surface of the food-court tables have given him a measure of Danbury Fair notoriety. Some say he is the Fonzi of the food court, their symbol of what it is to be a mall rat.

19   "Scoob's one of a kind," said Michelle Sell, 17, who had dated Scooby. She seemed proud that her inauguration into mall-rat society had included a fling with the famous rat.

20   There were, she said, few rites. Like hundreds of other teen-agers here every year, she got a part-time job in one of the shops that survive on hourly wage labor. Soon, she said, the mall made its bid even for her free time.

21   "When I'm off, I'm at home saying, 'Cool, I have a day off,'" the round-faced teen-ager said. "I'll be watching TV and my friends call me up and say, 'Michelle,

Come and hang out.' And I say, 'Where are you?' And they say, 'I'm at the mall,' And I say, 'Oh, O.K.' So after a while, I just became a mall rat."

22 Scooby said he has had a string of such girlfriends from the mall-rat ranks. At the table that Thursday, Jesse Amila, another young Danbury resident, said that he rarely misses a day outside Time Out and that some of the newcomers are drawn to veteran rats because they think they have status.

23 "We do have status," Scooby answered without a smile. "We own the mall. 'Cause we know so many people—so many mall rats come around. The more people you know, the more status you have."

24 A few days after that conversation, Scooby disappeared from his table outside Time Out. Instantly, it seemed, the mall regulars knew where he was. "When he's not in jail, he's here," said Richard N. DeMerell, one of the mall's security officers. This time, the charges had to do with credit-card theft.

25 "I kind of miss him," said Chris Sullivan, another regular, known as Sully around the food court.

26 He is a handsome 20-year-old who is never without his red baseball cap. He says he is an alcoholic, and he often comes to the mall drunk. Some of the food-court regulars say they surreptitiously add alcohol to their soft-drink cups. Sully's problems with liquor, he said, have contributed to his having been jailed 13 times.

27 He and Scooby, Sully said, have a lot in common. Scooby's father is a Danbury detective. Sully's is a Fairfield County deputy sheriff.

28 Quietly, some of the regulars said Scooby and his crew give the other loiterers a bad name. Jon Bourque, who graduated from Danbury High School last year, said he did not like the name mall rat and resented the suggestion that Scooby was the leader. "Not even close," he insisted.

29 "I don't think there is a mall-rat king," he said. And then he pointed out that he believed he had logged as many hours as anyone outside Time Out. "I'm here every day of the week all day," he said.

30 At her table in the food court that Friday before Scooby was arrested, Christine Tako, made a face at the mention of the full-timers in the food court. Rats like Scooby, she said, are friends. But not her type.

31 She started coming to the mall after her family moved to this corner of Connecticut in search of safety. They moved from Riverdale in the Bronx for her last year of high school after someone she had never seen before fired a shot in her direction as she walked home from school.

FAITHLESS SUITOR

32 Her parents wanted to protect her. But there are some hurts, she learned at the mall, for which there is no protection.

33 Last year, in the Friday night crowd of teen-agers, she met a boy from Brookfield who always wore suits. Not your typical mall rat, she said. For a month and a half, she said, they were together.

34   And then, as sometimes happens, there was a new group of teen-agers from a high school a few miles into New York State who started to show up and tried to break in to the Connecticut cliques. "They wanted to be a part of it," she said.

35   One of them, a wiry 14-year-old girl with black hair, seemed to want very badly to be a part of it. Before long, there was talk about her among the teen-agers and how she would do anything to be part of the group. And then one night, when Christine Tako was late for the mall, she said, everyone noticed how the boy in the suit and then the wiry girl slipped away to the mall parking garage.

36   "People see two people walking out," she said, "and they go to the car and the car doesn't go anywhere. And then they come in."

37   By the time she got to the mall that night, the news was all over the food court. "I walked into the mall," she said, "and everybody looked at me because they knew. And once that happened, I knew everybody knew. It's an odd feeling. Everybody knows what's going on and either they tell you or they don't and it separates you from everybody."

38   At the table in the food court that Friday night, she remembered that she didn't cry until she got home the night she lost the boy in the suit.

39   And then she took a deep breath and said her best friend from Danbury High School, who scoops out ice cream at the mall's Häagen Dazs shop, had warned her that the boy with the blue eyes was the same kind. "He could ignore me or push me away," she said.

40   By then, there were more teen-agers filling up the tables in the food court. Someone called to her from over near Time Out Amusement and she stood up. But just at that moment Christine Tako said, she had decided. "I think I like him enough so I'll just go for it, I guess," she said.

41   It was Friday night at the mall. And she disappeared into the crowd.

■ TOPICAL CONSIDERATIONS

1. How does Glaberson's description of mall culture compare with your own experience? Have you encountered similar social patterns in malls? In other places?

2. Consider how the physical surroundings of the mall affect adolescent behavior. Does Glaberson agree with the teenagers who claim mall culture "leaves them with a hollowness that is deeper than that of former teen-age pastimes" (paragraph 7)? Do you agree with this statement?

3. Consider Christine Tako's parents' decision to move to suburbia to protect their daughter (paragraph 31). Is Christine safer at the mall than on the streets of Riverdale? What kind of dangers does Christine encounter at the mall?

4. "Scooby" has his hair cut to achieve a "threatening 'heavy metal'" look (paragraph 14). How threatening is he? What was impressive about Scooby? What, if anything, did you find unappealing about him?

5. What does Jon Bourque inadvertently reveal about himself in his assessment of Scooby (paragraphs 28–29)? What about the apparent tension between these two is familiar to you from your own experience as a teenager?

■ RHETORICAL CONSIDERATIONS

1. Glaberson calls one of the evenings he spends at the mall "Christine Tako's night of decision" (paragraph 14). What is Glaberson's tone here? What other words or phrases create a similar tone?
2. Explain how the example of Christine Tako helps shape Glaberson's message. How does Glaberson use her in presenting his material? How differently would the essay read without her?
3. The characters at the mall include "Scooby" (paragraph 13), "the boy in the suit" (paragraph 35), "the boy with the blue eyes" (paragraph 1), and "the wiry girl" (paragraph 35). What effect does Glaberson's use of nicknames or descriptions instead of proper names have on your sense of the teenagers at the mall? How do they seem different from the people who are named?
4. Analyze the speech patterns of Michelle Sell in paragraph 21. What makes her sound like a teenager? Why do you suppose Glaberson made the editorial decision to repeat so much of Michelle's own words here?

■ WRITING ASSIGNMENTS

1. Spend one or two nights at a local teenage hangout. Write an account of your observations that makes a point about the nature of teenage rituals.
2. Write a character sketch of a friend or family member, conveying their personality, eccentricities, strengths and weaknesses, as well as likes and dislikes solely through descriptions of their clothing and activities. Your sketch should quote them several times, capturing their characteristic speech patterns.
3. At a local mall, interview security guards, shop owners, and the managers of food concessions to determine the impact of so-called mall rats on mall life. What hostility do you find toward these teenagers? In what ways are teenagers welcomed as a vibrant part of the mall's economic life?
4. Using library resources, write a paper about the development of shopping malls in America in the 1970s, 1980s, and 1990s. Consider the origins of malls, patterns of geographical distribution, and the economic impact malls have had on traditional downtown shopping areas.

	Money for Morality
	Mary Arguelles

In the consumer culture, where the bottom line is money, what happens to some basic old-fashioned values such as honesty and kindness? That's the question Mary Arguelles asks after pondering a newspaper story about a little boy who returned some found money. What bothers her is that some people were not happy with the token reward for the boy's good deed. They wanted more.

Ms. Arguelles is a freelance writer whose articles have appeared in *New Mother, Baby Talk,* and *Reader's Digest.* She is the producer and host of "Twigs," a local parenting education program in Reading, Pennsylvania. This essay first appeared in *Newsweek* magazine's "My Turn" column in October 1991.

1   I recently read a newspaper article about an 8-year-old boy who found an envelope containing more than $600 and returned it to the bank whose name appeared on the envelope. The bank traced the money to its rightful owner and returned it to him. God's in his heaven and all's right with the world. Right? Wrong.

2   As a reward, the man who lost the money gave the boy $3. Not a lot, but a token of his appreciation nonetheless and not mandatory. After all, returning money should not be considered extraordinary. A simple "thank you" is adequate. But some of the teachers at the boy's school felt a reward was not only appropriate, but required. Outraged at the apparent stinginess of the person who lost the cash, these teachers took up a collection for the boy. About a week or so later, they presented the good Samaritan with a $150 savings bond, explaining they felt his honesty should be recognized. Evidently the virtues of honesty and kindness have become commodities that, like everything else, have succumbed to inflation. I can't help but wonder what dollar amount these teachers would have deemed a sufficient reward. Certainly they didn't expect the individual who lost the money to give the child $150. Would $25 have been respectable? How about $10? Suppose that lost money had to cover mortgage, utilities and food for the week. In light of that, perhaps $3 was generous. A reward is a gift; any gift should at least be met with the presumption of genuine gratitude on the part of the giver.

3   What does this episode say about our society? It seems the role models our children look up to these days—in this case, teachers—are more confused and misguided about values than their young charges. A young boy, obviously well guided by his parents, finds money that does not belong to him and he returns it. He did the right thing. Yet doing the right thing seems to be insufficient motivation for action in our materialistic world. The legacy of the '80s has left us with the ubiquitous question: what's in it for me? The promise of the golden rule—that someone might do a good turn for you—has become worthless collateral for the social interactions of the mercenary and fast-paced '90s. It is in fact this fast pace that is, in part, a source of the problem. Modern communication has catapulted us into an instant world.

Television makes history of events before any of us has even had a chance to absorb them in the first place. An ad for major-league baseball entices viewers with the reassurance that "the memories are waiting"; an event that has yet to occur has already been packaged as the past. With the world racing by us, we have no patience for a rain check on good deeds.

4   Misplaced virtues are running rampant through our culture. I don't know how many times my 13-year-old son has told me about classmates who received $10 for each A they receive on their report cards—hinting that I should do the same for him should he ever receive an A (or maybe he was working on $5 for a B). Whenever he approaches me on this subject, I give him the same reply: "Doing well is its own reward. The A just confirms that." In other words, forget it! This is not to say that I would never praise my son for doing well in school. But my praise is not meant to reward or elicit future achievements, but rather to express my genuine delight in the satisfaction he feels at having done his best. Throwing $10 at that sends out the message that the feeling alone isn't good enough.

5   ***Kowtowing to ice cream:***   As a society, we seem to be losing a grip on our internal control—the ethical thermostat that guides our actions and feelings toward ourselves, others, and the world around us. Instead, we rely on external "stuff" as a measure of our worth. We pass this message to our children. We offer them money for honesty and good grades. Pizza is given as a reward for reading. In fact, in one national reading program, a pizza party awaits the entire class if each child reads a certain amount of books within a four-month period. We call these things incentives, telling ourselves that if we can just reel them in and get them hooked, then the built-in rewards will follow. I recently saw a television program where unmarried, teenaged mothers were featured as the participants in a parenting program that offers a $10 a week "incentive" if these young women don't get pregnant again. Isn't the daily struggle of being a single, teenaged mother enough of a deterrent? No, it isn't, because we as a society won't allow it to be. Nothing is permitted to succeed or fail on its own merits anymore.

6   I remember when I was pregnant with my son I read countless child-care books that offered the same advice: don't bribe your child with ice cream to get him to eat spinach; it makes the spinach look bad. While some may say spinach doesn't need any help looking bad, I submit it's from years of kowtowing to ice cream. Similarly, our moral taste buds have been dulled by an endless onslaught of artificial sweeteners. A steady diet of candy bars and banana splits makes an ordinary apple or orange seem sour. So too does an endless parade of incentives make us incapable of feeling a genuine sense of inner peace (or inner turmoil).

7   The simple virtues of honesty, kindness and integrity suffer from an image problem and are in desperate need of a makeover. One way to do this is by example. If my son sees me feeling happy after I've helped out a friend, then he may do likewise. If my daughter sees me spending a rainy afternoon curled up with a book instead of spending money at the mall, she may get the message that there are some simple pleasures that don't require a purchase. I fear that in our so-called upwardly mobile world we are on a downward spiral toward moral bankruptcy. Like

pre–World War II Germany, where the basket holding the money was more valuable than the money itself, we too may render ourselves internally worthless while desperately clinging to a shell of appearances.

■ TOPICAL CONSIDERATIONS

1. How did you first respond to the story of the boy who was rewarded $3 for returning $600 in cash? Did you, like the boy's teachers, think the reward was too stingy? If so, in what ways does Arguelles revise your thinking?
2. What do you think about the practice of rewarding scholastic performance with money or prizes? If you have ever been offered such incentives, what were the positive and negative effects of these rewards?
3. Evaluate the parallel Arguelles makes between the teachers' reward to the 8-year-old "good Samaritan" and parents who pay "$10 for each A" on a report card. How is the act of returning $600 untouched different from the achievement of a good grade? How is it similar?
4. What is "the golden rule" (paragraph 3)? How, in Arguelles's estimation, has the fast pace of today's world rendered the "promise of the golden rule" worthless?
5. Arguelles believes that "misplaced virtues are running rampant through our culture" (paragraph 4). What specific virtues does Arguelles praise in this essay? What virtues does she seem implicitly to hold in her discussion of the 8-year-old boy (paragraph 2), money for grades (paragraph 4), the national reading program (paragraph 5), the parenting program (paragraph 5), or other examples?

■ RHETORICAL CONSIDERATIONS

1. How is the idea of the "ethical thermostat" (paragraph 5) central to Arguelles's thesis in this essay? What is a *thermostat?* How does Arguelles use this image to illustrate her argument?
2. Consider the analogy between food and morality Arguelles constructs in paragraph 6. Logically, how does she relate the spinach-ice cream dilemma to the use of incentives? How effective is this analogy in supporting Arguelles's point? In what ways does it seem strained or unconvincing?
3. What kind of evidence does Arguelles use to suggest the existence of a morality crisis in our culture? To what extent do you agree with her that certain virtues currently "suffer from an image problem" (paragraph 7)? What other evidence might Arguelles have used to strengthen her argument on this point?
4. Consider the author's tone. Does she ever sound argumentative, sanctimonious, or self-righteous? Is her tone appropriate for the subject matter? Did you find any of her discussion humorous? What other adjectives would you

use to describe the narrative voice here? Does her tone remain the same throughout the essay, or does it modulate?

5. How in this essay does Arguelles increase her credibility as a moral arbiter? Were you willing to grant her authority on questions of right and wrong? Why or why not?

■ **WRITING ASSIGNMENTS**

1. Write a letter to Arguelles defending the teachers who took up a collection for the 8-year-old "good Samaritan" (paragraph 2).

2. Interview students, parents, and teachers to determine how widespread the practice of rewarding good academic performance with money is in your own school. Ask questions that will both encourage truthful answers and help you understand possible motivations for this practice; supplement your field research with library material. Then write a paper assessing the effect of monetary rewards for academic performance among your peers.

3. Consider Arguelles's essay in light of Barbara Ehrenreich's theory of the puritanical message of American society. To what extent is Arguelles's attitude *puritanical* in the sense that Ehrenreich defined the term in "Spend and Save"?

	The Ends Justify the Jeans
	Stuart Ewen and Elizabeth Ewen

Perhaps no other item from our consumer culture has been infused with so much history and meaning as blue jeans. A simple pair of pants has linked nineteenth century gold miners to nonconformist youths of the 1950s and to high fashion models of today. In this article, Stuart Ewen and Elizabeth Ewen examine the development of this sturdy all-American symbol and its rich connections to matters of class, gender, self-image, and social rebellion.

Stuart Ewen is professor of media studies at Hunter College and professor of sociology at the Graduate Center, CUNY. Elizabeth Ewen is professor of American studies at SUNY. They are the authors of *Channels of Desire: Mass Images and the Shaping of American Consciousness* (1992) from which this essay was taken.

Have we worked out our democracy further in regard to clothes than anything else?

—JANE ADDAMS (1902)

1   July 14, 1980. Bastille Day. On Broadway, at Seventy-second, a bus rattles to its stop. Above, a blur of color—bright red, orange, shocking saffron, lavender blue, marine, livid, purplescent, raven—invades the corridor of vision. Looking up, we see a poster ad that, running along the entire roof of the bus, offers an outrageous display: an assembly line of female backsides, pressed emphatically into their designer jeans. On the right hip pocket of each, the signature of an heiress.

2   We see the figures from waist to midthigh, yet we *know* they are women. We have seen it before. These buttocks greet us from a rakish angle, a posture widely cultivated in women from time to time, in place to place. What was termed in nineteenth-century America the *Grecian bend.* The bustle. Foot-bound women of China. Corsets. High heels. Hobble skirts. Here it is, women hobbled in the finery of freedom.

3   The bus moves along. Pinned to its rear, we see its final reminder: "The *Ends* Justify the Jeans . . . Gloria Vanderbilt for Murjani." Today's freedom is molded and taut. An animal in perpetual heat. Individuals are identical, but come in colors. Over *this* rainbow lies the promise of perpetual pleasure.

4   Calvin Klein makes a similar promise. These jeans are blue; their double-stitched seams mottled by the *image* of wear. But there all evidence of toil evaporates. The shirt—white, casual, rolled at the sleeves—is satin. His model stands locked at the knees, flexed in a paroxysm of ecstasy. She too assumes the Grecian bend; a moment of submission, captured for you, by a pair of pants. She purrs; she growls—restrained by the cloth, caressed by the seams. Calvin Klein has done this for her. He will do it for you.

5   Bon Jour Jeans are "built to look like you're moving even when you're idle." The Protestant ethic creeps in. Ben Franklin would have loved it.

6   A simple pair of pants is infused with a multiplicity of meanings. In the 1850s, denims were the unemotional, durable garb of miners and others among a newly mobile work force that came to California in the aftermath of the gold strike. Seams were riveted to make them hold, a technology borrowed from the construction of horse blankets.[1] Cloth for beasts of burden was translated to the needs of men of burden. These were the clothes of hard-laboring people. Loose and ill-fitting, these pants were mass-produced for men separated from their homes and from the clothing those homes had customarily produced. These pants held little promise for the men who wore them, save the promise that they would be ready for the next day's labors.

7   For others during the same decade, horse blankets were hardly enough. In the court of Empress Eugénie, "the dress worn by a fashionable lady in attendance contained 1,100 yards of material used in the construction of flounces and worked into tucks, folds and various trimmings."[2] American women of means were also wrapped in an abundance of cloth. While such makers of overalls as Levi Strauss and John H. Browning worried over how many men could be fitted into a given yardage of cloth, for women of wealth the concern was with how many yards of cloth could be pleasingly draped upon a given individual. This was the mark of prosperity: to wear enough material on one's back to clothe many of a more common caste.

8   "Three-flounce skirts were commonly seen" on women of property:

> Full sleeves were split in front revealing the white sleeves of the soft blouse under-neath. . . . The skirt and bodice were often separate because of the immense weight of the full skirt with the stiffly boned point of the bodice coming over the fullness to flatten it. . . . Braid trims the skirt flounces; split sleeves, and bodice. It covers the curved bodice side-front and dropped-shoulder armhole seams too. Wide grosgrain ribbon sashes, caught up in poufs, decorate the skirt. Sometimes flowers were added to them.[3]

9   While merchant burghers in America were not as fancily dressed as were the women of their estate, neither did they wear horse blankets. Box coats, edges "trimmed with dark braid accenting the lapels and cuffs," provided a sporty proto-type for today's "business suit." For those more tied to an elegant past, the "double-breasted coat has a fitted bodice and flared skirt with a split. . . . This man wears a black satin vest with a collar and a black cravat on his high shirt collar."[4] The display of cloth was the mark of substance and, most certainly, profit.

10   In the 1850s, the *fashionable* rich could not imagine themselves wearing the dungaree pants of proletarians and "peasants."[5] Neither could working-class people realistically imagine themselves in the finery of wealth and power. The only fashion link between them—subtle at best—was the austere, coal-black stovepipe hat of capitalist wealth, symbolizing the factory smokestacks that brought profit to one, toil to the other. Blue jeans wore the signature of deprivation and sweat.

11   Success in that world required a dramatic change of clothes. In Horatio Alger's *Ragged Dick* (1866), it is a neat gray suit of clothes, a gift from a fortuitous benefac-tor, that signals Dick's impending metamorphosis from a ragged bootblack to "Richard Hunter, Esq.," a gentleman of substance:

> When Dick was dressed in his new attire, with his face and hands clean, and his hair brushed, it was difficult to imagine that he was the same boy. . . . He now looked quite handsome, and might readily have been taken for a young gentleman, except that his hands were red and grimy.[6]

12   Years later, the clothing of nineteenth-century laborers would assume new and different meanings. Functional beginnings became increasingly obscure within un-folding imagery. In the movies, the range hands of the early cattle industry were re-born as icons of a noble, rural simplicity; rugged individualism; primal morality and law. Blue jeans were conspicuous within the moral landscape of media Americana. On the screen these pants taunted the imaginations of city folk as emblems of a simpler and uncorrupted life. While laborers would continue to wear them at work, now the well-heeled might don a pair—a symbolic escape from the regimen of the marketplace, at home or in the garden. Democracy in action!

13   In the fifties, blue denim became part of a statement, a rejection of postwar sub-urban society and of the tyrannies of the fashion-conscious consumerism that gave that society its definition. In James Dean's *Rebel without a Cause,* or Marlon Brando's *Wild One,* dungarees provided a channel of contempt toward the empty and conformist quietude of cold-war suburbia, and for the "rural idiocy" of small-town life. The affirmative images of American consumer capitalism were under cultural siege. What had been a piece of Americana—blue jeans—became a rejec-

tion of Americana. These images found a responsive audience among those for whom gray flannel suits and crinoline shirtwaist dresses had been elevated as ideals of the age. In blue jeans, men and boys found relief from the priorities of the business world. Women and girls found relief from the Grecian bend. Even some suburban gardeners slipped into their Levis for their moments of casual comfort, for a nap on the porch.

14   By the mid-sixties, blue jeans were part of an essential ensemble within an emerging commitment to social struggle. In the Deep South, where tenant farmers and sharecroppers, grandchildren of slaves, continued to wear denim in its mid-nineteenth-century sense, they were joined by college student activists—black and white—in a battle to overturn the deeply embedded centuries of segregation and race hatred. Blue denim—pants, jackets, overalls—became a sacred bond between them. The garb of toil was sanctified by the dignity of struggle. The blue *image* moved north with the song:

> *We've been 'buked, and we've been scorned.*
> *We've been talked about, sure as you're born.*
> *But we'll never turn back.*
> *No we'll never turn back.*
> *Until we've all been freed,*
> *And we've got e-qual-i-ty.*

15   In the student rebellion and the antiwar movement that followed, blue jeans and work shirts provided a counterpoint to the uniforms of the dominant culture, whether fatigue green in Southeast Asia, or police blue in Chicago, or gray flannel on Madison Avenue. Denim provided an antifashion, an antiuniform.

16   With the rekindling of a long-dormant feminism in the late 1960s, the political configurations of dress became increasingly explicit. Rejecting the sex roles of convention, blue jeans were a feminist weapon against restrictive fashion, sexual objectification, passive femininity. This was the cloth of action, a challenge to the social fabric of sexuality. The cloth of labor became the emblem of liberation.

17   If blue jeans were renegade in the 1960s and early 1970s, by the 1980s they had become the mainstay of fashion—available in a variety of colors, textures, fabrics, and fit. These simple pants have made the long trek "from workers' garb to counter culture revolt to status symbol." According to a newspaper article:

> As American families back away from having their used-to-be requisite 2.3 children, they're snapping up jeans at a rate of 2.3 pair per person *per year.* That's 16 pairs of jeans bought per second, or 50,000 pairs per hour. Annually, that adds up a cool $5 billion industry figure.[7]

18   On television, in magazine advertising, on the sides of buildings and buses, jeans and backsides call out to us. Their humble past is obscured in the imagery. In ads, "horse blankets" are infused with "a surrealistic, new-wave flavor." Functional roots are rendered aesthetic; corporate sources are hidden. Dan Carroll, advertising director for Bon Jour Jeans, explains his task simply. "We try to stay away from commercial-looking ads. . . . We try to make advertising artistic."[8] The exploitative

labor system that underwrites these fantasies of freedom in capitalist America is nowhere in evidence. The image is seductive; the name is French; the signature is personal; the cotton is American; the weavers and dyers and cutters and sewers and finishers toil in the sweatshops of Hong Kong.[9]

19   The contradiction between promise and production resides in the image of itself. Jeans are the facsimile of freedom, brought to us by models who are tucked—painfully—into a skintight fit. They are the universal symbol of individualism and Western democracy; mass-produced clothing of workers, embellished by the imprimatur of Paris, the home of *haute couture* since the time of Louis XIV. They are the vestments of liberated women, cut to impose the postures of Victorianism: corsets with the *look* of freedom and motion.

20   Their allure is compelling. A student writes to the Soviet youth newspaper, *Komsomolskaya Pravda*. He explains that when he went to a dance wearing the clothing available in the Russian stores, "Nothing happened." He continues:

> The next night I dressed entirely in foreign clothes and brought some Western records with me as well. You should see what happened. Invitations and telephone numbers came raining down on me. Now I have jeans, good suits, records and all that sort of junk. I have plenty of friends who can get me anything I want. I have gone into businesses, but now I dictate my own conditions.[10]

21   The ideological attraction is international in scope; fashion is the "bounty" of capitalist culture. Growing up in the cold war of the fifties, fashion was the dividing line between friends and enemies. Russians and Chinese could be known by the uniformity of their dress; Americans were brightly packaged.

22   In blue jeans, the most functional and least ritualistic of clothes, fashion reveals itself as a complex world of history, promise, and change; as a capturing of continual "truths." Opposite worlds collide violently and then mesh in fashion. Social conflict and contradiction are displayed . . . and diffused. Resistance and conformity coexist within "the mirror of fashion."

23   What are we to make of all this? Do we dismiss it as a meaningless frivolity, irrelevant and immaterial? Paul Nystrom, a writer on fashion and economics in the 1920s and 1930s, and a father of modern mass-merchandising techniques, contended that it was "foolish and shallow-minded people" who refused to take fashion seriously. "The wiser ones," he said, "have tried to find explanations and to understand."[11] Yet looking at fashions, in and of themselves, provides explanations that often defy understanding. Our ability to interpret a specific fashion—the current one of jeans, for example—shows us that as we try to make sense of it, our confusion intensifies. It is a fashion whose very essence is contradiction and confusion.

24   To pursue the goal of understanding is to move beyond the artifact of cloth itself, toward the more general phenomenon of fashion and the world in which it has risen to prominence. It is a piece in the political discourse of consent, and of revolution. It is a keystone in the shifting architectures of class, sexuality, national identity. Fashion is situated within the framework of industrial development; it interacts with the rise of consumer capitalism and mass-media imagery. It is a way in which people identify themselves as individuals and collectively.

25   What events, what developments, what forces proceeded to make *fashion* a more considerable concern than *function* among increasing numbers of people? In what ways have fashion and sexuality coincided, particularly in the context of palpable transformations in the structure, ceremony, and economy of family life? How does fashion provide a social language that infuses the historic emergence of women's liberation?

26   Exploring the role of fashion within the social and political configuration of industrial America helps to reveal the parameters and possibilities, the fantasies of freedom, the industrial democracy of American capitalism. Blue jeans alone suggest that politics and fashion may be the warp and woof of American culture in an era of mass production and mass merchandising. The ultimate question is whether the incorporation of images of rebellion into mass-produced fashions has been a meaningful component of social change.

■ NOTES

1. A fairly detailed description of the rise of the blue jean may be found in Ed Cray, *LEVI's,* Boston, 1978.
2. Paul H. Nystrom, *Economics of Fashion.* New York, 1928, p. 278.
3. Estelle Ansley Worrell, *American Costume: 1840–1920.* Harrisburg, Pennsylvania, 1979, p. 38.
4. *Ibid.,* pp. 28–29.
5. The term "dungaree," although it sounds as though it may derive from a close proximity to dung, is, instead, of Hindi origin; a reference to a rough cotton fabric imported from India, commonly worn by sailors.
6. Horatio Alger, Jr., *Ragged Dick and Mark, The Match Boy.* Reprinted New York, 1962, p. 58.
7. Amy Pagnozzi, "Jeans: No Stone Unturned in Fight to Cover the Rear." *New York Post,* July 15, 1980.
8. William Thomas, "The Jeans of Summer." *Back Stage,* July 18, 1980, p. 1.
9. *Ibid.*
10. Craig Whitney, "Moscow Bracing for Big Influx of Western Influences." *New York Times,* July 3, 1980.
11. Paul H. Nystrom, *Fashion Merchandising.* New York, 1932, p. 31.

■ TOPICAL CONSIDERATIONS

1. What is the "promise" of designer jeans (paragraph 3)? In what sense does fashion always make promises to its buyers, according to the Ewens' article?
2. What was the different promise clothes held for the "fashionable rich" and the "proletarians" of the 1850s (paragraphs 6–10)?
3. Explain how blue jeans in the twentieth century symbolically bridged gaps between members of the American public—city and country dwellers, rebels and conformists, Northerners and Southerners, rich and poor. Do the Ewens believe that "the incorporation of images of rebellion into mass-

produced fashions has been a meaningful component of social change" (paragraph 26)?

4. Describe the appeal of blue jeans to the feminist movement of the 1960s. What movement goals did the jeans symbolize? What different appeal did designer jeans have for women in the 1980s?

5. What do the Ewens mean by "the contradiction between promise and production" (paragraph 19)?

6. What is the Ewens' thesis? Are jeans the true subject of their essay, or do they symbolize other issues about which the Ewens want to comment?

■ RHETORICAL CONSIDERATIONS

1. The last five paragraphs of the Ewens' essay make a series of detailed arguments about the cultural importance of fashion. Why do you think the Ewens delayed making these arguments until the end of the essay? What do they gain by this organization; in what way does it weaken the effectiveness of their essay?

2. Consider the Ewens' use of the bus anecdote in the opening paragraphs. How, stylistically, do the Ewens involve readers dramatically in this incident? How accurately do these paragraphs set up the argument to follow?

3. Why do the Ewens use so many short, declarative, even verbless sentences in paragraph 2? How does this style contribute to the point the Ewens want to make in this paragraph?

4. Why do the Ewens include the reference to Horatio Alger in paragraph 11? How does the Alger reference comment on the paragraphs that precede and follow it?

5. Consider the way the Ewens use secondary authorities in paragraphs 7 through 9. What function do outside authorities have in their arguments in these paragraphs?

■ WRITING ASSIGNMENTS

1. Would you like to own Calvin Klein, Gloria Vanderbilt, or Bon Jour jeans? Explain why or why not. Describe the sort of environment in which you imagine yourself wearing these jeans. How does that environment differ from where you might wear Levis or Lees?

2. Write an essay evaluating the importance of the epigram by Jane Addams. Who is Addams? How is the idea of democracy important in this essay? Be sure to consider the way in which blue jeans become "the universal symbol of individualism and Western democracy" (paragraph 19) in the twentieth century.

3. Write an essay on the evolution of a particular fashion (such as hats and gloves for women, men's top hats, bikinis, or miniskirts), analyzing the cultural significance of this changing fashion.

4. Analyze the image of America projected by *Rebel Without a Cause, The Wild One,* or an early cowboy movie. How do these movie images represent "democracy in action" (paragraph 12)?

The Customer's Always Right
Dave Barry

The title of this essay hearkens to a time when consumers got respect and satisfaction from merchants. If we had a complaint, someone was right there to turn things around. But as Dave Barry reminds us, our modern consumer world has become rather indifferent. Instead of friendly cooperation, we get either an automatic answering system or somebody in "Customer Service" who hates us.

    Dave Barry has been described as "America's most preposterous newspaper columnist," a man "incapable of not being funny." He is the author of ten books and is a Pulitzer Prize–winning humorist whose *Miami Herald* column is syndicated in more than 200 publications. His books include *Babies and Other Hazards of Sex* (1984), *Dave Barry's Greatest Hits* (1989), and most recently *Dave Barry's Guide to Guys* (1995). The CBS sitcom "Dave's World" is based on Mr. Barry. This essay first appeared in his column in 1994.

1 If you're a typical consumer—defined as "a consumer whose mail consists mainly of offers for credit cards that he or she already has"—chances are sooner or later you're going to have a dispute with a large company. You're going to call the company up, and you're going to wind up speaking with people in a department with a friendly name such as "Customer Service." These people hate you.

2 I don't mean they hate you PERSONALLY. They hate the public in general, because the public is forever calling them up to complain.

3 I know whereof I speak. I used to be—I am not proud of this—a newspaper editor. This was at a paper in West Chester, Pa., called—I am not proud of this, either—the "Daily Local News." We came out daily, and we specialized in local news. For example, if Richard M. Nixon resigned the presidency, we'd send reporters out to the shopping mall to badger randomly selected shoppers into having an opinion about this, and our big headline would be, LOCAL RESIDENTS REACT TO NIXON RESIGNATION. As though they really were reacting to it, as opposed to trying to find the right color bedsheets. This is basically how we handled all news (LOCAL RESIDENTS REACT TO DISCOVERY THAT CLAMS MATE FOR LIFE).

4 So one spring day I made the editorial decision to put a photograph of some local ducks on the front page. At least I thought they were ducks, and that's what I

called them in the caption. But it turns out that they were geese. I know this because a WHOLE lot of irate members of the public called to tell me so. They never called about, say, the quality of the schools, but they were RABID about the duck vs. goose issue. It was almost as bad as when we left out the horoscope.

5   I tried explaining to the callers that, hey, basically a goose is just a big duck, but this did not placate them. Some of them demanded that we publish a correction (For whom? The geese?), and by the end of the day I was convinced that the public consisted entirely of raging idiots. (This is the fundamental underlying assumption of journalism.)

6   This is what people who answer the phone at, for example, the electric company, go through every day. I don't mean that they get calls about incorrectly captioned goose photographs, although this would not surprise me. I mean that they get an endless stream of calls from people who are furious that their electricity got turned off just because they failed to pay their bill for 297 consecutive months, or people asking questions like is it OK to operate a microwave oven in the bathtub.

7   So let's say that you have a genuine problem with your electric bill. The people in "Customer Service" have no way of knowing that you're an intelligent, rational person. They're going to lump you in with the whining non-rocket-scientist public. As far as they're concerned, the relevant facts, in any dispute between you and them, are these:

1. They have a bunch of electricity.
2. You need it.
3. So shut up.

8   This is why, more and more, the people in "Customer Service" won't even talk to you. They prefer to let you interface with the convenient Automated Answering System until such time as you die of old age (". . . if your FIRST name has more than eight letters, and your LAST name begins with 'H' through 'L' press 251 NOW. If your first name has LESS than eight letters, and your last name contains at least two 'E's, press 252 NOW. If your. . . ").

9   So is there any way that you, the lowly consumer, can gain the serious attention of a large and powerful business? I am pleased to report that there IS a way, which I found out about thanks to alert reader Jim Ganz Jr., who sent me an Associated Press news report from Russia. According to this report, a Russian electric company got into a billing dispute with a customer and cut off the customer's electricity. This customer, however, happened to be a Russian army arsenal. So the commander ordered a tank to drive over to the electric company's office and aim its gun at the windows. The electricity was turned right back on.

10   On behalf of consumers everywhere, I want to kiss this arsenal commander on the lips. I mean, what a GREAT concept. Imagine, as a consumer, how much more seriously your complaint would be taken if you were complaining from inside an armored vehicle capable of reducing the entire "Customer Service" department to tiny smoking shards. What I am saying is: Forget the Automated Answering System. Get a tank.

11   Perhaps you are thinking: "But a tank costs several million dollars, not including floor mats. I don't have that kind of money."

12   Don't be silly. You're a consumer, right? You have credit cards, right?

13   Perhaps you are thinking: "Yes, but how am I going to pay the credit-card company?"

14   Don't be silly. You have a tank, right?

■ TOPICAL CONSIDERATIONS

1. What in Barry's essay struck a chord with your own experience as a consumer? How accurate, for example, is his account of "the convenient Automated Answering System" (paragraph 8)? What other frustrating consumer experiences have you had?

2. When have you ever felt that "the public consisted entirely of raging idiots" (paragraph 5)? In your experience, to what extent are customer service representatives justified in disliking the anonymous public?

3. Consider the "duck vs. goose" incident (paragraphs 4–5). Why does Barry include this story? What is most ridiculous about "the public" here; what is absurd about Barry's own behavior? Why is this story so funny?

4. Why does Barry tell his readers so much about the "Daily Local News" in paragraph 3? What does the information in this paragraph tell you about Barry's attitude toward journalism? About his attitude toward customer service in general?

5. What is so appealing about Barry's account of the Russian "billing dispute" (paragraphs 9–10)? Who is in the right in this controversy? Consider the Russian army: What associations do you have with that institution that makes its use in this article particularly amusing or significant?

6. What is Barry's main point about disputes between customers and those who serve them? To what extent is the anonymous public made up "entirely of raging idiots" (paragraph 5)? To what extent are customer service personnel at fault for despising "the public in general" (paragraph 2)?

■ RHETORICAL CONSIDERATIONS

1. Analyze the tone of the title: "The Customer's Always Right." In what contexts have you heard this cliché before? What does it insinuate about the "the customer"? How well does the title fit Barry's essay?

2. Why do you think Barry capitalizes some words and not others? How does capitalization affect your sense of the narrator?

3. Consider the effect Barry's organization has on the message of his essay. In which paragraphs does Barry seem to side with the consumer? When does he appear to support the opinions of customer service representatives? What is the overall effect of his switching sides?

4. Evaluate the essay's ending. What is satisfying or appropriate about the last four paragraphs? What's funny about them? How does this ending tie together earlier parts of the essay?

■ WRITING ASSIGNMENTS

1. Write a letter to a large company requesting they fix a problem you have had with their product or services. Use all your argumentative powers, including humor, to convince them to comply with your demands.
2. Write a response to your letter in the assignment above. Try to create the impersonal bureaucratic tone and logic that Barry assails here. Have some fun here.
3. Research the use of "Automated Answering Systems" in large companies. In addition to library research, you should contact several firms by phone, requesting information about the financial benefits of such services.

·5·

Advertising

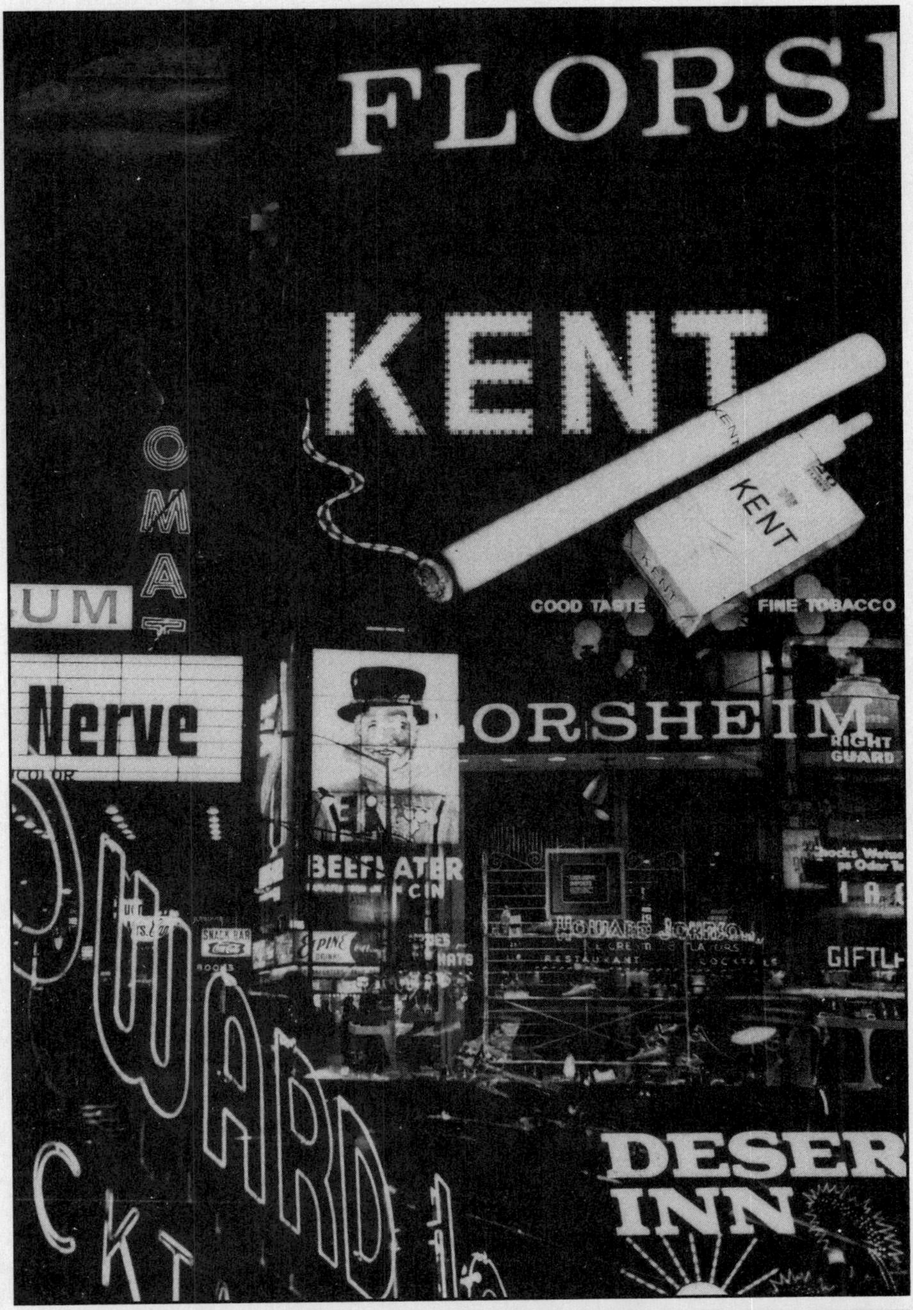

Most of us are so accustomed to the incessant roar of advertising that we hear it without listening, we see it without looking. But if we stop to examine how it works, we may be amazed at just how powerful and complex a psychological force advertising is. In this chapter we examine how a simple page in a magazine or a fifteen-second TV spot feeds our fantasies and fears with the sole intention of separating us from our money.

While critics of advertising don't call for its elimination, they do ask for more honest, straightforward, and responsible advertising. And less of it. And that is what Deborah Baldwin complains about in "The Hard Sell"—the mind-numbing flood of commerce that fills our day and narrows our worth to purchasing power alone. But not all people see advertising as insidious, manipulative overkill. Michael Schudson, for one, comes to the defense of advertising. In "Delectable Materialism," he argues that our abnormal craving to buy, buy, buy is not the result of advertising but, rather, our basic desire to own things.

Our next piece looks at some recent trends in advertising—the kind of no-pain, no-gain slant in selling. Ever since the health-and-wellness consciousness of the American populace was raised, advertisers have redefined eating, drinking, and fun. So laments George Felton in his amusing and insightful piece, "The Selling of Pain: We Writhe, Therefore We Are."

Each of the final three essays was written by a professional advertiser and, thus, they provide some inside views of the craft. "A Word from Our Sponsor" is a confession of one-time copywriter Patricia Volk. Talking frankly about the craft of charging language to sell, she admits that there is only one rule in writing ads: "There are no rules." Charles O'Neill, also an ad writer, agrees that the language of advertising can charm the consumer. However as powerful as the language is, he argues, no ad forces consumers to lay their money down. In fact, O'Neill praises the craft and the craftiness that have gone into some familiar commercials and print ads. The title of Carol Moog's essay makes clear the focus of our final selection here. "Sex, Sin, and Suggestion" takes a hard and close look at some sexy images that forge a short circuit from our psyches to our wallets.

We end this chapter with nine recently published magazine ads each followed by a set of questions to help you analyze how ads work their appeal on us. Our hope is that by inviting you to apply a critical eye, some of the power of advertising might be unraveled and dispelled.

	The Hard Sell
	Deborah Baldwin

Imagine our world without ads. If Deborah Baldwin's vision is accurate, it would be a world of reduced clutter, clamour, and anxiety. In this piece, Baldwin catalogues the innumerable ways advertising intrudes and, more dangerously, seamlessly blends into daily life through television, corporate sponsorships, sports events, museum exhibits, print media, and even school programs. What concerns her is not so much the "ad-saturation" per se, but how all the advertising has turned America into a consumption-crazy culture. She makes a strong argument that the line between citizen and consumer has nearly vanished.

  Baldwin is former editor of *Common Cause* Magazine, in which this essay in longer form first appeared in 1991.

1 Consider a day in the life of the semi-fictional American household—let's call them the Urbanes.

2 The Urbane family awakens to the strains of National Public Radio—"non-commercial" radio brought to us this morning by "REI, Recreational Equipment Inc., Providing Outdoor Gear and Clothing." Mom grabs her Liz Claiborne signature purse, stuffs her Fila sweats into a Bloomies shopping bag and heads downstairs. Let's eat! Pass the Teenage Mutant Ninja Turtle cereal to the kids. Front page of the newspaper looks grim, but not the ad for Petites Week at Macy's or the article by the 15-Minute Gourmet on the back of the Safeway ad in yesterday's Food section.

3 Snatches of conversation about world affairs emanate from *Good Morning America* between plugs for Tylenol and Toyota. Dad reminds the kids to take their Flintstone vitamins. And for the third time, put on your Reeboks! They pile into the car with the She-Ra lunchboxes and Lands' End backpacks, drive past the bus-stop billboard advertising those bright Benetton clothes, turn on the oldies station and sing along with the Connie Francis remake that's now an ad for the local mall—"Where the Stores Are."

4 Five o'clock and time to go home! The country music station is playing a song from Barbara Mandrell's album "No Nonsense"—as in No Nonsense Pantyhose, which the singer is under contract to promote. Flipping through the mail, Mom finds three fund-raising appeals, a glossy from Hecht's department store announcing unbelievable sales, four catalogs, and a *New Yorker* with an attractive 10-page spread on the glories of the Caribbean, which turns out to be not colorized John McPhee but a paid "advertorial."

5 After the Urbanes wrest their kids away from the TV, they tuck them into their Little Mermaid sheets and catch the tail end of *Washington Week in Review*, made possible by a generous grant from Ford Motor Co., whose high-powered Crown Victoria sedan fills the screen. Checking the time on tomorrow's theater tickets, they notice a plug for USAir. Dad spends a few absorbing moments with the J. Crew

catalog, then admires the way car ads during the 11 o'clock news are always photographed on empty mountaintops.

6   Bedtime already?

7   Welcome to Real Life, circa 1991. While our forefathers and mothers rose with the sun to labor in the fields, we rise with the radio and TV, immersed every waking hour in non-stop nudges from corporate America to Just Say Yes.

8   Round-the-clock commercialism has crept up on us, evolving from 19th-century pitches for products like Lydia Pinkham's medicinal pick-me-up into a sophisticated art form that pops up everywhere we are—from the brand-name labels that turn consumers into walking billboards to the corporate-sponsored informational posters that hang in classrooms.

9   Few things, it seems, are sacred: *Advertising Age* says there's a firm that sells space at the bottom of golf cups, reasoning that nothing concentrates the mind amid all that green like a word from a sponsor. Some advertisers have been known to put their messages in public restrooms—one of the few places most people think of as a commercial-free zone.

10   Despite such incursions, many people might nonetheless wonder: With all the problems besetting the world, why lie awake at night worrying about commercialism? Besides, what can one person do to beat back the media equivalent of a 20-foot snowstorm?

11   Enter the brave little Center for the Study of Commercialism. Just over a year old, it is headed by nutrition activist Michael Jacobson of the Center for Science in the Public Interest. Jacobson hopes to do the same thing to ad glut that he has done to greasy food: make the public realize that too much of this stuff can make a person sick.

12   Armed with a board of advisers whose professional lives are dedicated to the study of the consumer culture, the Washington-based center wants to raise awareness of commercialism's costs and counteract the gimmees with a vision of a "less selfish, more civic-minded" lifestyle. As Jacobson and cofounder Ronald Collins wrote in one manifesto, "Omnipresent commercialism is wrecking America. Our cultural resources are dwindling. Value alternatives beyond those of the marketplace are disappearing. The very idea of *citizen* has become synonymous with *consumer*."

13   Fighting commercialism, of course, is like wrestling your way out of a spider web. Indeed the commercial and non-commercial often blend together so seamlessly, says critic Mark Crispin Miller, an adviser to the center and author of *Boxed In: The Culture of TV,* that life can be lived as "a theme park experience."

14   He points to the way the war in the Persian Gulf was turned into a spectacle—partly thanks to the networks' presentation of this dramatic conflict in the best mini-series tradition. While advertisers initially were reluctant to sponsor war footage, before long they rushed to associate their products with patriotic good feelings, donating goods to the troops and incorporating the red white and blue in their ad campaigns.

15   Miller sees sharp parallels between the way the war was presented to the public and the way the 1988 presidential campaign unfolded on TV. Both involved simplistic plots, with beginnings, middles, and ends, and both made heavy use of emotional images and sound bites.

16   Sort of like ads.

17   Advertising has long oiled the machinery of our economy and probably always will. All told, corporations spent an unbelievable $130 billion on it last year—the equivalent of $6 a week for every man, woman, and child in the United States, according to the *Wall Street Journal.* That's 50 percent more per capita than is spent in any other nation. Essayist Pico Iyer once calculated that by age 40 we've seen one million ads, with incalculable effects on the way we view the world—never mind our capacity to absorb information of a more profound nature. And conventional ads are only the flotsam in the flood tide: Every day the average American is bombarded by hundreds of marketing messages, many of them adroitly woven into the content of the print and electronic media we depend on for information and entertainment.

18   The post office delivered 63 billion pieces of junk mail last year, much of it aimed at selling something. Product manufacturers stuck ads on videotapes and in movie theaters, and they spent millions to plant their products in Hollywood movies. Automatic dialing systems delivered canned messages at a rate of seven million a day, according to a congressional study, and that's nothing—coming soon to a store near you will be grocery carts outfitted with TV monitors that sense which aisle you're strolling down and advertise the relevant name-brand products.

19   The big brains on Madison Avenue are coming up with such innovations at a time when the public suffers, in the words of the *Wall Street Journal,* from "ad nauseam." The ads on TV come so thick that many advertisers overcompensate, stepping up the volume and intensity in order to be heard over the clutter. Or they act as seductively entertaining as the sitcoms and melodramas they make possible. Try zapping through the Taster's Choice campaign that basically consists of 45-second episodes from an ongoing soap opera, complete with romantic leads.

20   "It's no longer enough to show the product and tell what's good about it," says one marketing executive at a personal-care products company that is among the nation's top advertisers. "You have to be as entertaining as the regular programs."

21   Ads once celebrated the pleasures of society and the senses, says Miller, but today they're more likely to celebrate personal empowerment. Kids' candy ads, for example, used to suggest that having some would make you popular. Now such ads are more likely to revolve around the "story" of having it when someone else wants it.

22   Some of the most sophisticated ads—the so-called postmodernist genre—poke fun at the art form itself, which becomes a kind of shared joke. But this appealing self-parody doesn't mean audiences are so savvy that they know they're being manipulated. "Everybody's sophisticated," Miller says, "in a superficial kind of way. But a kind of knowingness, the fact of growing up with TV, does not imbue you with an understanding of how images work." And even when a specific ad fails to sell a certain product, adds Pat Aufderheide, a communications professor at American

University who writes about popular culture for *In These Times,* it contributes to the ceaseless message that "you can solve life problems with commodities."

23   Corporations use various strategies to reach the various segments of the market. To move the consumer spirit of opinion leaders, they buy time on public broadcasting, where $250,000 will yield two mentions on National Public Radio six days a week for a year. Private art galleries and museums have become so dependent on corporate money in recent years they hardly mind when it comes with name-brand banners and posters attached.

24   To reach middle America, advertisers are turning to cable TV, which has greatly eroded the networks' hegemony because it divides the market into easily targeted segments. Low-cost time during sports events on cable, for example, is a big draw for the makers of shaving cream.

25   When companies aren't hawking their goods during halftime, they're hanging their logos everywhere the eye or camera can see, plugging beer and cigarettes to armchair athletes with no apparent irony. Sports sponsorship is a booming business, reports the *Wall Street Journal,* with 4,200 companies pouring nearly $3 billion into special events ranging from the Olympics to the Virginia Slims tennis tournament. Nike invested $7 million last year on basketball-related promotional efforts alone, including contracts with college coaches to put their teams in name-brand hightops, a *Washington Post* investigation revealed.

26   One of the fastest growing target audiences is America's youth. Companies spent about $500 million last year to reach children age 2 to 12—five times what they spent in the early '80s—according to James McNeal, a marketing professor at Texas A&M University.

27   As many beleaguered parents may suspect, advertisers are drawn to children because children have more influence over the household pocketbook than ever before. According to Consumers Union, children age 4 to 12 spend $8 billion annually and indirectly influence household expenditures of a $1 billion *a week.* Bombarded by slick ads for fast-food joints, junky breakfast cereals, and—a recent phenomenon—shoes and clothes, children have learned to speak up at the mall.

28   Corporations long ago infiltrated the schools, emblazoning their logos on educational materials and offering rewards like free computers and pizza in exchange for brand-name recognition among the next generation of consumers. Whittle Communications, which is credited with some of the most innovative marketing practices of the '80s, beams Channel One, a 12-minute TV news show that includes two minutes of ads, free to more than 8,900 high schools. To sweeten the deal, Whittle gives the schools satellite dishes, VCRs, and TVs as well; all the teachers have to do is round up the kids to watch the spots for Burger King, etc.

29   Unfortunately, many of us aren't even aware of the extent to which we are immersed in messages that say "buy, buy, buy," says George Gerbner, former dean of the Annenberg School for Communication and a member of the commercialism study center's board of advisers. "It's like saying, 'Is the average fish aware it's swimming in salt water?'" The average consumer literally can't imagine life without commercials, not to mention life without the many possessions commercials so effectively sell.

30 "My interest is the kind of culture we have created and in which our children are being raised," says Gerbner, a longtime critic of commercial TV who is trying to launch what he calls a cultural environment movement. "The mainstream of our culture is television, which is on an average of seven hours a day. It's not a product of the home, family, community, or even the native country for some, but transnational corporations with something to sell." He adds ominously, "Entertainment is the main source of information for most people . . . and whoever tells all the stories will guide what we think and do as a civilization."

31 If Gerbner seems most concerned about the impact of commercialism on the littlest consumers, it's because preschoolers spend more time watching TV than doing anything else except sleeping and are perceived as especially vulnerable to Madison Avenue's unsavory ways. As Neil Postman, an adviser to the center, argues in his book *The Disappearance of Childhood,* TV reduces literacy and distorts the learning process. Children also age quickly from exposure to violence, ineptitude, and other adult themes on TV.

32 If the ceaseless barrage of hyped-up, MTV-style plugs for toys and junk food during Saturday-morning cartoon shows strikes adults as manipulative and almost cynically deceptive, so are the ads targeted at the rest of society. "The thing I hear most often is, 'I don't even look at ads, I don't pay any attention to them,'" Jean Kilbourne, a lecturer and adviser to the center, said in her film *Killing Us Softly: Advertising's Image of Women.* Yet "advertising is one of the most powerful socializing forces in the culture. And the effects are as inescapable as the effects of pollution in the air. . . . Ads sell more than products. They sell images, values, goals, concepts of who we are and who we should be. . . . They shape our attitudes, and our attitudes shape our behavior."

33 When we aren't buying self-images, we are "turning time into entertainment and connecting entertainment to buying," says Tom Engelhardt, who writes about advertising and children's TV. Tackling kidvid alone won't do much as long as kids keep getting the message that buying stuff is the ultimate fun. Adds Engelhardt, a father himself, "You can barely head into a museum without stumbling into seven gift shops. . . . Take the family on a visit to a historic site, and everything boils down to, yes or no, do we buy the Liberty Bell earrings?"

34 Once upon a time, Pat Aufderheide observes, children and adults alike could seek refuge from the commercial world at school—not to mention at home. Now the average busy household is itself a target of new products—such as kids' microwavable TV dinners—emanating from the outside world. The only sanctuary left, she says, is inside a church.

35 What's got the critics upset is not just marketing's encouragement of the human urge to own, which has done so much damage to the environment and eaten away so thoroughly at our sense of values. It's the changing nature of commercialism, its gradual intrusion into the privacy of our homes, the fabric of our cultural lives, and the sanctity of our public places.

36 The corporate invasion is taking place at a time when public institutions are particularly vulnerable to economic pressure—one legacy of the Reagan era, when taxes declined and so did the resources available for public libraries, schools, muse-

ums, and other institutions. Robbed of government support, these institutions "now have to appreciate the crumbs they get from corporations," says the Center for the Study of Commercialism's Michael Jacobson. "Instead of giving these companies tax deductions for their contributions," he adds, "the government ought to raise corporate income taxes."

37   That seems unlikely, given the tax-loathing politics of the '90s. Indeed, one element of President Bush's ballyhooed education initiative would be greater corporate involvement in the classroom, not less. This is the same administration, incidentally, that asked the Beer Institute to sponsor a safe-driving campaign for the National Highway Traffic Safety Administration.

38   Because corporate America feels strapped—thanks partly to the merger mania of the '80s—it is becoming more demanding of the media. In the magazine world, advertisers have become shameless in seeking special treatment from editors, a practice that has long plagued women's magazines. "It's not just a matter of individual advertisers influencing editorial content," says a former *Self* magazine editor. "The whole point of the magazine is to promote products, so the advertiser doesn't even have to ask." Once unique to beauty and fashion rags, this concept is spreading throughout the magazine world.

39   Moviemakers have long been open to the notion of incorporating paid ads into their works, but in the '80s the practice became institutionalized, says Mark Crispin Miller, as professional brokers set up business in Hollywood to negotiate ever more lucrative deals. According to one tally, the creative minds behind *Die Hard 2* found room for 19 paid ads. When one company, Black & Decker, discovered "its" scene on the cutting room floor, it sued for $150,000.

40   Feeding into the product placement phenomenon is the sheer cost of producing movie blockbusters, TV series, new magazines, and even books. While the practice is hardly commonplace—at least not yet—the *New York Times* uncovered one instance of literary encroachment in a novel featuring a Maserati whose "V-6 engine had two turbochargers, 185 horsepower, and got up to 60 in under seven seconds." Turns out the author had cut a deal with Maserati that landed her $15,000 worth of book promotion in exchange for the mention. The publisher meanwhile was thrilled to have the help.

41   So symbiotic are commercial and creative interests that well-known actors, producers, and filmmakers frequently "cross over," lending their talents to Madison Avenue and further blurring the line between merchandising and the arts.

42   In his book *Boxed In,* Miller quotes Bill Cosby as saying his popularity stems not from his role as the quintessential TV dad, but from his appealing ads for Jell-O and the like. Thirty-second commercials, he confided, "can cause people to love you and see more of you than in a full 30-minute show." Along with sheer entertainment, there's an intensity in these spots, a one-on-one connection that few can resist. Such intimacy helps explain why kids not only stick around when the commercials come on during those tiresome Saturday-morning cartoon shows, but pay special attention. "Don't turn it down!" my 9-year-old daughter exclaimed when I wandered by the TV during one particularly colorful, fast-cut spot. "This is the best part!"

■ TOPICAL CONSIDERATIONS

1. In a single sentence summarize the message about advertising that Deborah Baldwin wants her readers to get from this essay? Who is the audience for whom she writes? Do you consider yourself part of that audience?
2. According to the author, what are the differences between today's ads and ads from earlier periods? How do these differences affect our roles as consumers and our self-image? Is it possible to solve the problems in our lives by buying products as ads suggest?
3. How do corporations advertise on public broadcasting networks and in private art galleries and museums? Do you think private companies should sponsor sporting events such as women's tennis tournaments and the Olympics? Do you think such sponsorship compromises the integrity of an art exhibit or a sporting event?
4. How do you feel about ad-saturation in your daily life? Do you enjoy ads, hate them, or simply ignore them? Do you agree with Jean Kilbourne that "the effects [of ads] are as inescapable as the effects of pollution in the air" (paragraph 32)?
5. What is the Center for the Study of Commercialism? What key criticisms of the ad industry do the members of the center's advisory board make? Do you agree or disagree with their observations? Have their comments made you more aware of the high presence of advertising in your daily life?
6. What are some similarities between commercial ads and political ads? Analyze some of the political ads from the 1992 presidential campaign or more recent campaigns and show how these ads resemble product ads.
7. How, according to Baldwin, do advertisements influence the very young in our society? Do you see this as a problem? Do you agree or disagree with George Gerbner that children are very vulnerable to "Madison Avenue's unsavory ways" (paragraph 31)?

■ RHETORICAL CONSIDERATIONS

1. Why does Baldwin begin her article with a description of a day in the life of the Urbane family? What does she mean by a "semi-fictional" American household? Do you find her description accurate and amusing, or do you find it offensive?
2. What does "advertorial" mean (paragraph 4)? Which two words are contained in this neologism, coined by *The New Yorker?* How does this word incorporate a basic message of the essay?
3. Where do you find the thesis statement in this essay? Which parts of the essay most strongly support the thesis? Were there sections of the essay that drifted from the main point? If so, where exactly were they?
4. Give two examples of words with negative connotations used to describe how the administrations of Presidents Reagan and Bush fostered greater

corporate involvement in schools, libraries, and museums. How do these expressions project Baldwin's opinion of the administrations' treatment of these institutions?

5. How does the author use humor throughout the article to engage the reader? Point out specific examples, in addition to the opening six paragraphs, that a general audience would find amusing.

■ WRITING ASSIGNMENTS

1. Listen to your local public radio station or watch your local public TV channel, or both and identify the sponsors who fund various programs. How are these sponsors described on public broadcasting? Write an essay in which you argue that public broadcasting sponsorships are sneaky forms of advertisements.

2. In the periodical section of your library find editions of a popular magazine such as *Life* or *Time* published 20 and 10 years ago. Choose a product that is still being advertised and compare the ads with current ads for the same product from the same publication if possible. Write an essay discussing how the ads have changed over the years. To which personal desires do the ads cater?

3. Rent a video of a current movie and watch it to see how many products are clearly identified during the movie. Write an essay in which you discuss the obvious commercialism in this movie.

4. Has reading this essay heightened your awareness about current marketing procedures? Write a paper discussing how you intend to respond to commercialism in your daily life if you have become sensitized to its insidiousness. Give examples from your own experiences.

5. Make a list of some of the ads you are exposed to in a single day. Then write your own funny account of your typical ad-saturated day.

	Delectable Materialism
	Michael Schudson

How big a role does advertising play in your life? Have ads really transformed you into an insatiable consumer as Deborah Baldwin claims—someone incapable of discriminating between mindless desire and legitimate needs? Michael Schudson thinks not. In this piece, he disputes those social critics who attribute near magical power to advertising. Instead, he challenges the reader to take the unusual view that it's not advertising that creates our acquisition frenzy but our natural love of material things that make life comfortable and convenient.

Schudson is a professor of sociology and chair of the communications department at the University of California, San Diego. He is the author of *Advertising, The Uneasy Persuasion* and numerous articles on advertising and the media. This piece originally appeared in The *American Prospect*, Spring 1991.

1 Contemporary social critics may imagine their ringing critiques of consumer culture to be deeply radical and subversive, but they are generally only new versions of a critique that goes back a long way in American culture. And confused versions, at that. Take, for example, criticism of advertising, often attacked as the most egregious emblem of materialism, even as its cause. In fact, America was materialist, consumerist, and enterprising, as Alexis de Tocqueville observed in the 1830s, long before advertising held much visibility or importance in American cultural life. Yet advertising is looked on today as the chief symbol, if not the chief engine, of consumer culture.

2 As the chief symbol of consumer culture, advertising has also been a chief subject of analysis for social critics looking for the hidden springs of American life. David Potter, a widely respected American historian, got it wrong 40 years ago in his classic study of consumer culture, *People of Plenty* (1954), and much American thinking about advertising and culture has yet to recover from the error he expressed more directly and clearly than anyone else. Potter held that a society that moves from a producer orientation to a consumer orientation must develop a culture to correspond to it. Advertising responds to "the need to stimulate desire for the goods which an abundant economy has to offer and which a scarcity economy would never have produced."

3 For Potter, advertising was one of a very few institutions that could "properly be called instruments of social control." And what is an institution of social control? It is one that guides a person "by conceiving of him in a distinctive way and encouraging him to conform as far as possible to the concept." Potter used as examples the church, which conceives of a person as having an immortal soul; the schools, conceiving of the person as a reasonable creature; and the free-enterprise economy, conceiving of the person as a useful producer. Advertising, in contrast, "conceives of man as a consumer."

4 The trouble with Potter's argument is that advertising is not at all like church, school, and workplace, the institutions he listed as archetypal institutions of social control. Having recently watched my 5-year-old go off to kindergarten, I have no illusion that the kind of control advertising exercises is half as determinative, controlling, influential, or potentially as destructive as that exerted by the institution of schooling. Even if children were to spend as much time watching commercial television as they spend in school (and they do not—television is turned on in the average American household seven hours a day but no individual member of the family watches it for that length of time), they can exercise freedoms in front of the television that they instantly lose in the classroom. In front of the television, they can come and go as they like; they can choose to attend or not to attend without fear of the punishing glance, voice, or raised eyebrows of the advertiser responding imme-

diately to their inattention. In short, the television advertisement can offer no social punishment, no social reward, no social reference group.

5 Potter, like many others, failed to distinguish the social control exercised by schools and churches from the cultural influence exercised by the mass media. A cultural or symbolic medium, like advertising, does not necessarily have a social dimension. Or, to put it another way, the social aspects of consumption do not depend on advertising. For example, when we feel good and think we look smart wearing a cashmere coat, we may be reflecting some influence of advertising. But we are just as likely reflecting the practices of other people in the social set to which we belong or aspire. Owning a book rather than borrowing it, or owning a washer and dryer rather then using the neighborhood Laundromat, gives a pleasure of possession, convenience, and independence that ads for Stephen King blockbusters or laundry detergents have no part in. If the things we buy did not satisfy or seduce, the images conjured up by advertising would ordinarily fade. The consumer culture is sustained socially not by manufactured images but by the goods themselves as they are used.

6 Potter's analysis seems to suggest, as did other analyses of the 1950s that still guide our thought on this matter, that people need to be instructed in the emotions as well as the arts of consumption. People have to learn to desire more goods. That was the argument made by liberals like Potter and John Kenneth Galbraith and by social critic Vance Packard. It was the point argued by Marxists and taken up later by Stuart Ewen (see Ewen's "Our all-consuming quest for style," *Utne Reader,* Sept./Oct. 1989, p. 81). It is also a notion pushed by the people responsible for selling propaganda to business—that is, by advertising agencies themselves.

7 Curiously, both the critics of advertising and its advocates seem to share the peculiar premise that material goods require force feeding. But is consuming so unpleasant? Is wanting more so unnatural? Is aping the neighbors or seeking to be fashionable so unheard of that a multi-billion-dollar enterprise is required to coax us into it? Is desire for possessions so rare? Is pleasure in goods so unusual a joy?

8 I do not claim that wanting more is universal. But I do claim that in America no multi-billion-dollar industry was needed to make people want more and more or to breed in them a dissatisfaction that they could quell only in the marketplace.

9 Just as the longing for more has deep roots in American culture, so does criticism of consumer culture have deep roots in America. Indeed, criticism of what today we call consumer culture originated with the Quakers, the Puritans, and others before anything very closely resembling consumer culture had emerged—certainly before advertising as the central institutional expression of abundance took root.

10 Advertising at times seems to be consumer culture materialism at its worst, the sizzle without the steak, the idolatry of goods divorced from the utility and enjoyment goods provide, but even this is too simple a view. It recognizes neither the aesthetic appeal of some advertising that touches us nor the plain wrapping, anti-magical character of most advertising. The most common advertising is, in a sense, Quaker itself—it points to price and so helps keep in mind economy as a chief criterion in buying. Or it is Puritan—recommending a product not because it provides

moral or social or theological salvation but because it serves certain banal purposes well. It cleans your sink. It gets you to New York in time for your business meeting. It provides high-fidelity sound recording.

11   True, advertising is rarely republican—it does not focus on the needs of public life. And it often takes a stance toward the public life that may not be healthy. If views of the person and the society can be ranged along a continuum between those that emphasize the moral embeddedness of the individual in a community and those that emphasize the isolation of the autonomous individual, then advertising typically falls near the latter end of the continuum.

12   Advertising offers and is expressive of an ideology of choice. It unifies us around a belief in difference, variety, abundance, pluralism, choice, democracy. Consumer culture and advertising, along with elections, are the most important institutions that promote the American ideology of choice.

13   In the past generation, people have listened to one set of voices from the East and have borrowed notions of a simple life, a life of self-discipline and self-denial, from Buddhist traditions of Asia. Now we are listening to a different set of voices from a different East—the voices of East Berlin, Hungary, and Russia, with their unashamed emulation of economic abundance. Eastern European nations, as symbol and substance of their legitimacy on a world stage, are seeking to partake in the kind of consumer affluence the West has enjoyed for two generations.

14   This should stir us to question our harsh criticisms of consumer culture. At the same time, we have growing concerns about environmental and ecological catastrophe and the distribution of consumption not only among rich and poor within a society but among rich and poor nations within a world system. We should not learn the lessons of Eastern Europe so well as to deny ourselves the right to criticize consumerism. But it must be a new critique. Freeing ourselves from biblical or Marxist moralisms and recognizing a certain dignity and rationality in the desire for material goods, we should seek to reconstruct an understanding of our moral and political view of consumption that we and others can live with.

■ TOPICAL CONSIDERATIONS

1. In what ways does Michael Schudson disagree with Deborah Baldwin's contention that advertising invades all facets of our lives, including our institutions and homes? (See paragraphs 9, 23, and 28 of Baldwin's article.) Which author do you agree with regarding the influence of advertising on the American public?
2. Schudson argues that advertising is not as important an influence on children's lives as their schooling. What reasons does he give to support his viewpoint? Do you agree with him?
3. Schudson concurs with Baldwin's statement that the average American family has its TV running seven hours a day. At what point does Schudson contradict Baldwin's comments about TV viewing? From your own TV-watching experience, who seems closer to the truth?

4. Do you buy products because you have seen them advertised? Because your friends have them? For other reasons? What are those other reasons? How would Baldwin respond to your reasons?

5. Do you think Schudson proves his contention that most advertising can be considered Puritan or Quaker? Give reasons from paragraph 10 to support your answer.

6. How would Eastern European refugees fleeing from ethnic wars react to Schudson's argument that the newly formed Eastern European nations should continue to emulate the West's consumerism? Would you give countries emerging from communist rule the same advice? Why or why not?

7. In paragraph 6, Schudson states the argument of liberals concerning consumerism: "People have to learn to desire more goods." However, Schudson refutes this argument in the following paragraphs. Do you agree with Schudson or the liberals? Why?

■ RHETORICAL CONSIDERATIONS

1. What argumentative technique or strategy does Schudson use to refute the arguments of John Kenneth Galbraith, Vance Packard, and Stuart Ewen? Is this an effective tactic?

2. What is the author's purpose in using so many questions in paragraph 7? How does he expect the reader to respond to these questions? Did you respond in the desired manner?

3. Does Schudson give enough evidence to support his criticism of the authorities he quotes? Which points are unsubstantiated?

4. Schudson and Baldwin each offer a personal experience regarding the influence of ads in our lives. What is the personal experience in each piece? Do these anecdotes influence you to side with either of them?

5. What do the arguments presented by Schudson and Baldwin reveal about their political leanings? Would you label them "liberal" or "conservative"? What evidence do you have for your choices?

■ WRITING ASSIGNMENTS

1. Take sides with either Deborah Baldwin or Michael Schudson and show how one author's argument is superior to the other's. Refer to the points that are contradictory in the articles. Resolve these contradictions according to the evidence in the essay you favor. Prove that one argument is more logical than the other by providing examples and evidence from your choice.

2. Make a one-week survey of your friends or family members to see how many hours a day their TV sets are on. Have them log the actual hours watched. In a paper, try to determine the influence that TV has on its viewers. With which author's (Schudson or Baldwin) assessment do you tend to agree?

3. Write a paper agreeing or disagreeing with Schudson's contention in paragraph 12: "Consumer culture and advertising, along with elections, are the most important institutions that promote the American ideology of choice." Give examples from each institution to support your argument.
4. Write a letter to parents in which you try to persuade them that TV watching is harmless to children. If necessary, use evidence from Schudson's article for support.

The Selling of Pain: We Writhe, Therefore We Are

George Felton

A point common to all the essays in this chapter is that advertising reflects the values and motivations of the consumer world. It sells products by selling us hopes and dreams and the images we aspire to. In the 1980s, a dominant advertising theme was "having it all"; beer, soap, and automobiles were promoted with images of material wealth and glamour. But as George Felton points out, ads of the 1990s have taken a different twist: They're "selling the virtue of self-denial." Here Felton demonstrates how pain and deprivation have been the appeal from bottled water to BMWs.

George Felton is an associate professor of English at the Columbus College of Art & Design in Ohio, where he teaches writing and copywriting. He has published essays in, among others, *Newsweek, The New York Times*, and *Advertising Age*. He is the author of a textbook, *Advertising: Concept and Copy*, published in 1994 by Prentice Hall. This essay originally appeared in the *Miami Herald*. It has been expended and updated by the author especially for the present edition of this text.

1 Advertising is a funny thing. We tell it our dreams, we tell it what to say, but after a while it learns the message so well, it starts telling us. What are we being told now? Simply this: Not only can we extend our life span, we are required to. The trend started when Nike, assuming responsibility for our physical, and by implication spiritual, health, issued our marching orders with the admonitions of its campaign "Just Do It." Bold type and bold people looked up from the page or from their workouts and scolded us for being our usual, sloppy selves. "Just Do It," we were warned, and as one of the players added, "And it wouldn't hurt to stop eating like a pig, either." Ouch. Yes, ma'am.

2 We asked for this, of course. Ever since the first jogger spurted out the back door, we've been headed on a course past simple health and toward self-denial, asceticism, pain-as-pleasure. "Let's live forever," we now say with no particular joy, and advertising couldn't agree more. In this Era of Healthism, any marketer with his finger in the wind knows that Nike need not be alone in selling the virtue of self-denial. "No Pain, No Gain" can now sell much more than workout gear.

3   Take food, for instance. Advertising has taught us that eating isn't fun anymore, not if we do it right. Breakfast has become the day's first moral test—will we or won't we do the right thing? Quaker Oats' pretty boy is not the smiling Quaker of the package but the noticeably unsmiling actor Wilford Brimley, who admonishes us to eat oatmeal, not because it tastes good, but because "it's the right thing to do." Casting a baleful eye upon us, he says, "First thing tomorrow morning, do something that brings down your cholesterol." We have our orders. Breakfast has been redefined as work: Out of bed and on the job.

4   The cereal aisle at the grocery store now presents us with one trail mix after another designed for the long march through our large intestines, each another grainy way to combat cancer, cholesterol, our own weak desire for pleasure. I now walk down the aisle trying, not to satisfy my hunger, but to represent my colon. What would *it* like? What does *it* need?, I wonder. "Bran!" the shelves shout back, a recent Ralston cereal, Bran News, lecturing me with its pun about what news is good in food. Even Cheerios has come to see its own name as deeply ironic, no longer a smiling matter. A recent ad's headline straightens the minds of those of us inclined to play with our food: "The O stands for oat bran."

5   Adland has redefined eating as an exercise in careful body management, a study in the replenishment of necessary ingredients, a kind of nutrient workout. Mazola corn oil and margarine appear in ads next to workout gear with the headline: "Standard equipment in the fight against heart disease." America's Dairy Farmers now invite us to go to the grocery store, not for anything as sensuous as milk or cheese, but for something called "Dairy Calcium," which, of course, is "calcium the way nature intended." Even orange juice, God's original health drink, has acquired an inferiority complex and now comes in a calcium-injected version, "as much calcium as milk," one carton announces with relief. Careful ingestion can even include things we didn't think *were* food: Tums and Rolaids antacids, for example, are now marketed as a good source of—we could have guessed this—calcium.

6   But in the war against turpitude, food not only giveth, it taketh away. We now buy whole categories of food solely for what they *don't* have: no caffeine, no sugar, no salt, no fat, no calories, no artificial coloring or flavoring. Drinking an unmodified, high-octane pop, for instance, has become such a blowout of self-restraint that if we want to have our pop and drink it too, we must make it hurt a little. We now stand in the soda aisle reading our way through the brightly lettered, increasingly annotated cans, asking ourselves, "How much can I do without today?" Frequently, the less the pop contains, the more expensive it is, which of course makes us feel even better since it hurts even more. What, after all, are Perrier, Evian, and the other expensive bottled waters but the right to buy the ultimate non-pop? We can tame our slutty taste buds and drive our thirst all the way back to its minimal satisfaction: water itself.

7   Nothingness of various sorts has, in fact, become a potent sales category. Once again Nike may have shown other advertisers the way with its Nike Air idea, shoes whose sales differential was literally nothing: a hole of air in the heel, which featured a see-through window on its side so we could prove to ourselves, by golly, there *was* nothing in there. Everywhere we look, once color-rich products have grown translucent, transparent. Mascara now comes in an invisible version; its

beauty is that no one knows the wearer has any on. Pepsi created a clear cola, Crystal Pepsi; Coors markets the beer substitute Zima, a clear liquid in a clear beer bottle. We can buy clear toothpastes, clear deodorants, clear mouthwashes, clear soaps (interestingly, all of them cleansers with which to scrub our gluttonous selves). Visually less has become psychologically more. We'll downsize our desires and curb our destructive appetites, we tell ourselves, and we'll start with color.

8   Can we extend self-denial to romance? Certainly. After all, if we're going to live forever, it may be best to sidestep passion, with its volcanic eruptions and slippery slopes, its short life span. Thus Calvin Klein presents cologne's answer to our prayers: Eternity. The campaign's black and white print ads (they're almost gray, the absence not only of color but of contrast) feature WASP lookalikes, sometimes in whole families strolling down beaches, sometimes in various clusters lying on the sand, gazing mutely off the page. The campaign is often seen as a safe-sex euphemism, an offbeat approach to a product usually sold with more heat, and so it is. But from the name itself in elongated type to the visual suggestion that we aren't looking at different people so much as at several versions of the *same* person, Eternity aligns itself with fantasies of prolonged life. By wearing cologne, we can, if not literally become our progeny, at least stay on their minds—apparently for generations. Even the TV spots sell, not passion, but the philosophical psychobabble of two lovers who don't touch, instead merely muse about what it might mean *to* touch. Let the oceans crash, these ads seem to say, we just like to watch.

9   This idea of equating denial with fulfillment extends to women's fashion models. Thin has always been desirable, but lately, looking at fashion ads, we can't tell if we're facing the misery of third world starvation or an eminently desirable personal physique. The waif look is in. Its most celebrated embodiment is supermodel Kate Moss, who, whether wearing underwear for Calvin Klein or a pained expression and nothing else for Obsession cologne, looks exactly like an anorexic 12-year-old. Her hollowed-out eyes, too-big ears, and emaciated boy-body all have acquired a chic sexuality, the sexuality of repression and self-denial. You have to hurt yourself to look like she does. Kate and her starve-alikes are the undernourished underbelly of the fitness phenomenon: If you can't be obsessively fit, we are told, then be obsessively emaciated. One way or another, make it hurt.

10   Since romance, passion, and sex aren't fun, why should anything else be? Everywhere, Healthism's central advertising strategy is to redefine products away from fun and toward functionalism. Take shoes for instance. Forget stylish, sexy, chic—forget all that. A recent Rockport campaign headlined itself: "Shoes that help you live longer," and the copy explained that shoes are really well-engineered things we stick on our feet for fitness walking. Similarly, we see watches sold, not as jewelry nor as fashion, but as ways to time our workout. Listerine mouth rinse, which could promise to make us more kissable, opts for health maintenance instead; an ad asks us to "Pick one: Gingivitis or Listerine." Even gum chewing need not be idle amusement. Trident tells us it's really a fighter in the war for healthy teeth: "An ounce of prevention" one ad claims. "Toothpaste should come in as many flavors," says another. In the war against sloth and decay, no product is unarmed, no moment without its purpose.

11   And our purpose, more and more ads tell us, is to sweat, to train relentlessly, to exist in endless, energetic motion. As an Avia shoewear headline succinctly puts it, "Life is a workout." If so, then almost any product qualifies as workout gear: "Genuine Jockey. It's not underwear. It's equipment," and the copy adds, "radical exertion calls for revolutionary underwear." Why buy sunglasses? Because we can "live ten times harder than ordinary mortals with Ray-Ban DiamondHard scratch-resistant lenses," that's why. How should men smell? Like they've been busy: Alongside photos of men skiing, swimming, pole vaulting, marathoning, and basketballing, Ralph Lauren now presents "Polo Sport, the fitness fragrance." Even Vaseline lipstick and skin care products are training tools. A recent promotion asserts that they're tough-enough-to-climb-mountains-with and is sponsoring the first climb by a woman up Mount Everest in something called the Vaseline Research '94 Expedition.

12   Obsessive-compulsive behavior has become *de rigueur.* BMW seems pleased that "the new M3 isn't just built for car fanatics. It's built by them." And rather than idealize the car, the slogan for Lexus celebrates "the relentless pursuit of perfection." Evian natural spring water puts life's purpose on the head of a pin: "Another day. Another chance to feel healthy." A second ad in the series shows us a young woman bicycler draining a bottle in midride—through what appears to be impassable terrain high in the Rockies—and entitles the moment, "Revival of the fittest."

13   Looking at this lithe young woman of the Evian ad, I sense that she's never coming down, never stopping, never arriving. She is simply refueling. Her trek—and ours—has become metaphorical: the constant pursuit, through spectacular but painful terrain, of a goal never articulated. We are meant to exist like this, whirling round and round, elegant gerbils in elegant cages. Advertising once sold us products as rewards, ways to put our feet up and congratulate ourselves (McDonald's "you deserve a break today," American Express's "membership has its privileges," Virginia Slims' "you've come a long way, baby"). But now products are things we splash on, strap on, or pour down in midstroke.

14   More than means to an end, Healthism's rigor has become an end unto itself, a psychological destination: We hurt, therefore we are. This pain-as-pleasure motif of recent advertising could signal a new national restraint, a cultural move away from self-gratification and toward control, the awareness of limits, the virtue of a Just Say No trek to self-actualization. However, it might simply be good old-fashioned Hedonism's greatest idea: Through denial we can live forever and thus have everything.

15   There is, after all, nothing stronger than the Healthism promise. It's better than sex, it's better than money, it's even better than love, not least because it makes all these more possible with the extra time we'll have. In an era so health conscious that we apologize for not knowing our cholesterol count, what can be stronger than the me-too-ism of longer life? Much of this advertising is aimed at the late-thirties and early-forties crowd, the Boomers, who overdid things in the 1960s and may be overdoing them again. Self-indulgence could be masquerading as asceticism. The temper of our times, Healthism first, is really an inverted hippie principle via William Blake: "The road of excess leads to the palace of wisdom." And the endorphin gobblers, straining in their Gore-Tex, couldn't agree more.

■ TOPICAL CONSIDERATIONS

1. What is Felton's basic argument about "healthism" in advertising? Do you agree with him?
2. In his opening, Felton says that advertising reflects our dreams and desires so well that soon "it starts telling us." In your opinion, does advertising reflect our values and concerns? Or does it shape and form them, controlling our consciousness as well as our consumption? Explain.
3. Felton claims that we are "headed on a course past simple health and toward self-denial, asceticism, pain-as-pleasure" (paragraph 2). Where do you draw the line between simple health and self-denial? How do you experience healthism in your own life; and is there a relationship between your experience and the media barrage of pain-as-pleasure?
4. How do your spending choices reflect the phenomenon of healthism as described by Felton? Do you pay attention to product lures such as "no cholesterol," "low sodium," or "fat free"? Do you buy clothes and shoes designed for maximum workout potential?
5. In paragraph 9, Felton continues his discussion of "denial as fulfillment," describing superwaif models like Kate Moss as the "undernourished underbelly of the fitness phenomenon," and accusing them of glorifying emaciation and pain. What's your position in the body image debate? How much credit do you give fashion models and advertising campaigns in influencing people's desired body image? Do you feel that these campaigns can be dangerous in any way? Explain your answer.

■ RHETORICAL CONSIDERATIONS

1. What is Felton's attitude toward contemporary ad campaigns touting healthism? What about his attitude toward the general public in their relation to this advertising trend? How does this attitude come through in his style?
2. Felton creates the word *healthism* to label the advertising phenomenon he describes. Do you think this is an apt label? Does it cause any confusion as to what exactly it is meant to describe? Explain your reasoning.
3. Felton describes both the copy and the visual images of particular ads to support his argument. Are they vivid enough to be persuasive as evidence? Did you notice any slanted language in these descriptions? Cite specific examples to support your answer.

■ WRITING ASSIGNMENTS

1. Find three or four print ads that rely upon "healthism" in their visuals or their copy. Write an essay in which you describe the ads in detail for your reader, drawing conclusions either in support of or against Felton's argument about the problems of pain-as-pleasure advertising.

2. In paragraph 13, Felton notes that "advertising once sold us products as rewards, ways to put our feet up and congratulate ourselves. . . . But now products are things we splash on, strap on, or pour down in midstroke." Write an essay in which you consider past or present advertising strategies other than healthism. How do you respond to these other trend-based ads? Do you see any problems with these other kinds of ads? Be sure to describe the ads and trends in detail, providing enough evidence for your reader to follow your argument.

3. In his essay, "The Language of Advertising," Charles O'Neill says that "advertising mirrors the fears, quirks, and aspirations of the society that creates it." Write an essay in which you select and analyze an advertising trend, examining how that trend reflects life in the nineties.

4. Find two or three ads that make health benefits claims (Felton cites several). Then interview one or two doctors, nurses, or nutritionists at your campus health center, asking their opinion of the validity of the ad's claims and the product's health benefit. Write a brief report of your findings, concluding with speculations about the strategy behind the ad campaign in terms of consumer response to healthism.

A Word from Our Sponsor

Patricia Volk

The following piece, which originally appeared in the "On Language" column of *The New York Times Magazine*, was written by a professional advertising copywriter. However, Patricia Volk is anything but defensive of the practices of her profession. While demonstrating some of the jargon of the trade, Volk confesses that the language of advertising is a language "without rules," a language with "little to protect it." Ad people, she explains, will stop at nothing to make a product that the world neither wants nor needs sound wonderful. Besides being a copywriter, Patricia Volk is author of the award-winning short-story collection *The Yellow Banana and Other Stories* (1985) and the novel *White Light* (1987).

1 Linguistically speaking (and that's still the preferred way), there is only one rule in advertising: There are no rules. "We try harder," lacks parallelism. "Nobody doesn't like Sara Lee," is a double negative. And "Modess. Because. . . ." Because . . . why? My friends didn't know. My mother wouldn't tell. My sister said, like Mount Everest, because it was there. The word "creme" on a product means there's no cream in it. "Virtually," as in "Virtually all our cars are tested," means in essence, not in fact. Even a casual "Let's have lunch," said in passing on Mad Ave. means "Definitely, let's not."

2 Language without rules has little to protect it. Some of the most familiar lines would disappear like ring-around-the-collar if you put a mere "Says who?" after them. "Coke is it." Says who? "Sony. The one and only." Oh, yeah?

3   Still, one word in advertising has virtually limitless power. It gives "permission to believe." It inspires hope. It is probably (disclaimer) the oldest word in advertising.

4   What "new" lacks in newness, it makes up for in motivation. Unfortunately, new gets old fast. Legally, it's usable for only six months after a product is introduced. As in, say, "Introducing New Grippies. The candy that sticks to "the woof of your mouf."

5   Once Grippies are six months old, unlike newlyweds, who get a year, and the New Testament which has gotten away with it for who knows how long, Grippies are reduced to just plain Grippies. That's when you improve them and say "Introducing New Improved Grippies." Now they really stick like cwazy to that woof.

6   Had you named your product "New" to start with, as in "New Soap. The soap that cleans like new," you'd never have to worry about your product sounding old. Introduced as "New New Soap," six months down the road it segues into "New Improved New Soap." Or you could avoid the six-month thing entirely and just call it "The Revolutionary New Soap" from day one.

PITCHING GLUE

7 How do you get the Grippies account in the first place? You "pitch" it in a flurry of work called a "push." A creative team works weekends and sleeps in the office. It's intense.

8   A successful pitch winds up in a "win," and you've "landed" the account. By the end of the week, everyone in the agency has a free box of Grippes and work begins. This is the "honeymoon period."

9   Everybody loves everybody else. You take the factory tour. You eat Grippies till your molars roll. And you attend "focus groups," i.e., meetings between researchers and preselected members of your "target audience," the people you hope will love Grippies.

10   You sit behind a two-way mirror and watch people eat Grippies. You take notes. You start hating the man who scratches the exposed area of his leg between the top of his sock and the bottom of his pants. "Look! He's doing it! He's doing it *again!*" And what you learn in the focus group, you use to build "share," which is the percentage of the population using your *kind* of product that buys yours in particular.

11   It gives you some idea of how large this country is when you realize that if you can raise Forever Glue's .01 share of market (one person per thousand) to .03, Forever Glue will be a dazzling success. So you do the "Nothing lasts like Forever" campaign, complete with "The Big Idea." You find a small town in a depressed area upstate and glue it back together. Brick by brick, clapboard by clapboard, you actually (favorite ad word) glue a town together and restore it in a classic "demo" with "product as hero." You get a corner office and a Tizio lamp.

12   Forever is stickier. Grippies are grippier. But what if your product is "parity," a "me-tooer"? What if it has no "unique selling point" or "exclusivity"? What if the world is not waiting for Mega-Bran, the cereal that tastes like Styrofoam pellets and gets soggy in the bowl?

13 Some folks "make it sing." It's what everybody thinks people in advertising do anyway, as in, "Oh, you're in advertising! You must write jingles!" So you write new words to Bon Jovi's "Never Say Good-bye," only the client doesn't want to spend $2 million for the rights. So you check out the P.D.'s, public domain songs, songs with lapsed copyrights that are at least 75 years old. You just have to hope the Mega-Bran lyrics work to the tune of "Ach, the Moon Climbs High," "Jim Crack Corn," or "Whoopee Ti Yi Yo—Git Along Little Dogies."

14 At last the new Mega-Bran campaign is ready to crawl through all the "loops" in the "approval cycle," from your client's kids to the network's lawyers. Everybody "signs off" on it.

15 In "pretest," you get "rich verbatims"—a lot of people who remember everything about your commercial. You go for it. You shoot a finished "spot." You spend $250,000 on production, "net net," and $3 million on network and uh-oh, nobody buys the bran. Your commercial has failed to generate "trial" and "brand awareness." It's the Edsel of brans.

16 Quick, you do another "execution," a celebrity endorsement using someone with a high "Q" (familiarity and popularity) score. (Bill Cosby has the highest.) You try "image advertising," which says almost nothing, but leaves the viewer feeling good about your product. (Soft drinks do it all the time.)

17 Still, no one remembers Mega-Bran. It's a case of "vampire video"—what people saw in your ad was so strong that it sucked the blood out of your message. The account becomes "shaky." "Doomers and gloomers" worry all over your carpet. They "bail." Bailers are people in a room who sniff out with whom the power lies; whatever that person says, the bailer agrees. The fastest bailer I ever knew was an account man who told me every time he was asked his opinion, he saw his mortgage float in front of his eyes.

18 The account goes from shaky to the ICU. Then it's "out the door." There is no funeral, no period of mourning because every loss presents an opportunity, a chance to roll up your sleeves, grease up your elbow and pitch again.

BODY PARTS

19 Clients like to find "niches" for their products. A niche is a special place no other product can fit. Sometimes you find the niche before you find the product and then you have to find a product to fill the niche you found.

20 Body parts are always good, though by now almost everything has been spoken for. There are still the navel and the philtrum. If you can do "exploratories" and with a little prodding make consumers aware that their philtrums sweat too much, smell funny or have unwanted hair, you're in business. You create a new form of consumer anxiety and cure it in a single stroke. You launch "Creme de Philtrum," with no cream in it, and have "preemptiveness." You're hot.

21 You don't have to go to school to write great copy. The best writers I know wrap fish in the Elements of Style. Schools say they can teach it, but you either have it or you don't. It's like perfect pitch, good gums, or being able to sit on the floor with your ankles around your neck. They use language to convince, persuade, and, at its

best, educate. They twist and twiddle words and understand their power. They make people do things they hadn't thought of doing before. They make them change.

22   One of the best writers ever had a great line: "The only thing we have to fear is fear itself." It led a whole country out of Depression. Imagine what he could have done with detergent.

■ TOPICAL CONSIDERATIONS

1. How is the language of advertising a language "without rules"? Can you think of some current ads that illustrate this claim? What rules of grammar or meaning are being broken?
2. According to Volk, the advertiser's word "inspires hope" (paragraph 3). Do you agree? How do claims of "newness" appeal to the consumer? Have you ever been seduced into buying a product because it's "new" or "improved"? Can you think of any other potent "hope" words?
3. How does the author, who is an advertising copywriter, characterize her profession? Would you want to be an ad writer? Why or why not?
4. What strategies do ad writers resort to if their "product is 'parity,'" if it has no "'unique selling point'"?
5. What special power of advertising does Volk's hypothetical "Creme de Philtrum" illustrate (paragraph 20)? Can you think of any real products that this might describe?
6. Why does Volk say, "You don't have to go to school to write great copy" (paragraph 21)?

■ RHETORICAL CONSIDERATIONS

1. Volk says that the language of advertising has no rules. How well does she illustrate this assertion in her essay? Can you think of other examples?
2. How would you characterize Volk's attitude toward advertising claims?
3. Throughout the essay, Volk resorts to ad industry jargon highlighted in quotation marks. What would you say her purpose is here? How do you evaluate her attitude toward the jargon? What do you think of some of the expressions? Any strike you as particularly amusing?
4. Explain the effectiveness of the final paragraph. What point is being made? How does the paragraph summarize the theme of the essay? How consistent is her tone here with the rest of the piece?

■ WRITING ASSIGNMENTS

1. Can you think of any ads whose claims particularly irritate you? Which ones? And what bothers you about them?
2. Volk says in paragraph 3 that there is "limitless power" in the words of advertising because what is being sold is hope. Select a familiar ad and write a paper analyzing how its language—verbal and visual—inspires hope.

3. Has this essay in any way changed your attitude toward advertising? Has it sensitized you to the power of advertising language? Has it made you more wary of the claims in ads? Discuss the article's effect on you in an essay.

4. Would you like to be a professional copywriter? In an essay explain why you would or would not want to write ad copy for a living.

The Language of Advertising

Charles A. O'Neill

Taking the minority opinion is advertising executive Charles A. O'Neill, who disputes the criticism of advertising language by Patricia Volk and others. While admitting to some of the craftiness of his profession, O'Neill defends the huckster's language—both verbal and visual—against claims that it distorts reality. Examining some familiar television commercials and print ads, he explains why the language may be seductive but far from brainwashing.

This essay, originally written for the first edition of this text, has been updated for this edition. Charles O'Neill is Senior Vice President of Marketing for Colonial Investments Services in Boston.

1   The cosmopolitan figure on the billboard looks like a rock singer, perhaps photographed on a break in a music videotaping session. He is poised, confident; as he leans against a railing, a view of the night-time city behind him, the personal geometry is just right. He wears a white suit, dark shirt, no tie. He sports a small red flower in his lapel. He holds a cigarette in his left hand. His attitude is distinctly confident, urban: "I own this city." His wry smile and full lips are vaguely familiar.

2   Think. You've seen him before, carefully posed on the pages of magazines, on posters and matchbooks, sitting astride a motorcycle or playing in a band. Mick Jagger? Bill Wyman? No. He is truly a different sort of animal; more precisely, he is a camel, a cartoon camel, and his name is Old Joe. Next to him on the billboard is one sentence: "Smoke New Camel Lights."

3   At first glance, this combination of artwork and text does not appear to be unusual. What is different about Camel's ad campaign is that it has spawned debates on newspaper editorial pages and has triggered organized protest. Old Joe, imported to these shores in the late 1980s, after a successful test run in Europe, has been declared by some an unwelcome visitor—an intruder whose very charm and decidedly cool style is seducing the nation's youth into a deadly habit that results in 400,000 deaths by lung cancer every year. Those who want to eliminate Joe—send him back to obscurity amid the pyramids, as it were—have a simple argument: "Everyone knows smoking is bad for the health. You're using a cartoon to sell cigarettes to our

children. The public interest is more important than your right to free speech. And it's in the public interest for us to protect our children from your unhealthy, dangerous product." Those who support Old Joe—principally his "colleagues" at R. J. Reynolds—argue that their constitutionally affirmed right to free speech extends to advertisements about their product. Given the opportunity, they would likely add: "Is smoking unhealthy? Driving is dangerous, too. Where will the "advertising censors" draw the line? We feel people should make their own decisions about smoking. We've chosen to use a cartoon character in our ads only because it is noticeable and effective."

4   The obvious topic of the debate is cigarette advertising, but beneath the surface it signals something more interesting and broad based: the rather uncomfortable, tentative acceptance of advertising in our society. We recognize the value of advertising, but on some level we can't quite fully reconcile ourselves to it. At best, we view it as distracting, something wedged into 30- or 60-second spaces between scenes in a TV special. At worst, we view it as dangerous to our health and culture.

5   How does advertising work? Why is it so powerful? What thoughtful cases can be made for and against the advertising business, circa 1995? In order to begin to understand advertising, you must accept that it is not about truth, virtue, love, or positive social values. It is about money. Ads play a role in moving customers through the sales process. This process begins with an effort to build awareness of a product, typically achieved by tactics designed to break through the clutter of competitive messages. By presenting a description of product benefits, ads convince the customer to buy the product. Once prospects have become purchasers, advertising is used to sustain brand loyalty, reminding customers of all the good reasons for their original decision to buy.

6   But all of this detail does not sufficiently explain the ultimate, unique power of advertising. Whatever the product or creative strategy, advertisements derive their power from a purposeful, directed combination of images. Images can take the form of words, sounds, or visuals, used individually or together. The combination of images is the language of advertising, a language unlike any other.

7   Everyone who grows up in the Western World soon learns that advertising language is different from other languages. Most children would be unable to explain how such lines as "With Nice 'n Easy, it's color so natural, the closer he gets the better you look!" (the famous ad for Clairol's Nice 'n Easy hair coloring) differed from ordinary language, but they would be able to tell you, "It sounds like an ad." Whether printed on a page, blended with music on the radio, or whispered on the sound track of a television commercial, advertising language is "different."

8   Over the years, the texture of advertising language has frequently changed. Styles and creative concepts come and go. But there are at least four distinct, general characteristics of the language of advertising that make it different from other languages. Taken together, they lend advertising its persuasive power:

1. The language of advertising is edited and purposeful.
2. The language of advertising is rich and arresting; it is specifically intended to attract and hold our attention.

3. The language of advertising involves us; in effect, *we* complete the message.

4. The language of advertising is a simple language; it holds no secrets from us.

EDITED AND PURPOSEFUL

9 In his book, *Future Shock,* Alvin Toffler describes various types of messages we receive from the world around us each day. As he sees it, there is a difference between normal "coded" messages and "engineered" messages. Much of normal, human experience is "uncoded"; it is merely sensory. For example, Toffler describes a man walking down a street. Toffler notes that the man's sensory perceptions of this experience may form a mental image, but the message is not "designed by anyone to communicate anything, and the man's understanding of it does not depend directly on a social code—a set of agreed-upon signs and definitions."[1] In contrast, Toffler describes a talk show conversation as "coded"; the speakers' ability to exchange information with their host, and our ability to understand it, depend upon social conventions.

10 The language of advertising is coded. It is also a language of finely engineered, ruthlessly purposeful messages. By Toffler's calculation, the average adult American is assaulted by at least 560 advertising messages a day.[2] Not one of these messages would reach us, to attract and hold our attention, if it were completely unstructured. Advertising messages have a clear purpose; they are intended to trigger a specific response.

RICH AND ARRESTING

11 Advertisements—no matter how carefully "engineered" and packed with information—cannot succeed unless they capture our attention in the first place. Of the hundreds of advertising messages in store for us each day, very few (Toffler estimates seventy-six) will actually obtain our conscious attention.[3] The rest are screened out. The people who design and write ads know about this screening process; they anticipate and accept it as a basic premise of their business. They expend a great deal of energy to improve the odds that their ads will make it past the defenses and distractions that surround us.

12 The classic, all-time favorite device used to breach the barrier is sex. The desire to be sexually attractive to others is an ancient instinct, and few drives are more powerful. In a magazine ad for Ultima II, a line of cosmetics, retailer Jordan Marsh invites readers to "find everything you need for the sexxxxiest look around. . . ." The ad goes on to offer other "Sexxxy goodies," including "Lipsexxxxy lip color, naked eye color . . . Sunsexxxy liquid bronzer." No one will accuse Ultima's marketing tacticians of subtlety. In fact, this ad is a current example of an approach that is as old as advertising.

13 After countless years of using images of women in various stages of undress to sell products, ads are now displaying men's bodies as well. A magazine ad for Brut,

a men's cologne, declares in bold letters, "MEN ARE BACK," while in the background a muscular, shirtless young man is shown wrapping his hands in tape in preparation for boxing.

14   Whether it takes one approach or another, every successful advertisement uses a creative strategy based on an idea that will attract and hold the attention of the targeted consumer audience. The strategy may include strong creative execution, repetition for sheer impact, or a straightforward presentation of product features and customer benefits. Many ads use humor or simply a play on words:

"Reeboks let U B U"   (Reebok)

"My chickens eat better than you do."   (Perdue Chickens)

"Introducing the ultimate concept in air   (Emery Air Freight)
      freight. Men that fly."

"Look deep into our ryes."   (Wigler's bakery products)

"Me. 4 U."   (The State of Maine)

"If gas pains persist, try Volkswagen,"   (Volkswagen)

Even if the text contains no incongruity and does not rely on a pun for its impact, every effective ad needs a creative strategy based on some striking concept or idea. In fact, the concept and execution are often so good that many successful ads entertain while they sell.

15   Consider, for example, the campaigns created for Federal Express. A campaign was developed to position Federal Express as the company that would deliver packages, not just "overnight," but "by 10:30 A.M." the next day. The plight of the junior executive in "Presentation," one TV ad in the campaign, is stretched for dramatic purposes, but it is, nonetheless, all too real: The young executive, who is presumably trying to climb his way up the corporate ladder, is shown calling another parcel delivery service and all but begging for assurance that he will have his slides in hand by 10:30 the next morning. "No slides, no presentation," he pleads. Only a viewer with a heart of stone can watch without feeling sympathetic as the next morning our junior executive struggles to make his presentation *sans* slides. He is so lost without them that he is reduced to using his hands to perform imitations of birds and animals in shadows on the movie screen. What does the junior executive *viewer* think when he or she sees the ad?

1. Federal Express guarantees to deliver packages "absolutely, positively overnight."
2. Federal Express packages arrive early in the day.
3. What happened to that fellow in the commercial will absolutely not happen to me, now that I know what package delivery service to call.

16   A sound, creative strategy supporting an innovative service idea sold Federal Express. But the quality and objective "value" of execution doesn't matter. A magazine ad for Merit Ultra Lights (August 1990) made use of one word in its headline:

"Yo!" This was, one hopes, not the single most powerful creative idea generated by the agency's creative team that particular month—but it probably sold cigarettes.

17   Soft-drink and fast-food companies often take another approach. "Slice of life" ads (so-called because they purport to show people in "real life" situations) created to sell Coke or Pepsi have often placed their characters in Fourth-of-July parades or other family events. The archetypical version of this approach is filled-to-overflowing with babies frolicking with puppies in the sunlit foreground while their youthful parents play touch football. On the porch, Grandma and Pops are seen quietly smiling and apparently getting ready for all of this affection to transform itself into an astonishing climax of warmth, harmony, and joy. Beneath the veneer, these ads work through sheer repetition: How-many-times-can-you-spot-the-logo-in-this-commercial?

18   More subtly, these ads are designed to seduce us into feeling that if we drink the right combination of sugar, preservatives, caramel coloring, and a few secret ingredients—known only to a select group of the company's most trusted employees—we'll fulfill our yearning for a world where young folks and old folks live together in perfect bliss.

19   If you don't buy this version of the American Dream, search long enough and you are sure to find an ad designed to sell you what it takes to gain prestige within whatever posse you do happen to run with. As reported by the *Boston Globe* (March 1992) "the malt liquor industry relies heavily on rap stars in delivering its message to inner-city youths, while Black Death Vodka, which features a top-hatted skull and a coffin on its label, has been using Guns N' Roses guitarist Slash to endorse the product in magazine advertising." A malt liquor company reportedly promotes its 40-ounce size with rapper King T singing, "I usually drink it when I'm just out clowning, me and the home boys, you know, be like downing it . . . I grab me a 40 when I want to act a fool."

20   Ads do not emerge like Botticelli's Venus from the sea, flawless and fully grown. This happens, but rarely. Most often, the creative strategy is developed only after extensive research. "Who will be interested in our product? How old are they? Where do they live? How much money do they earn? What problem will our product solve?" Answers to these questions provide the foundation on which the creative strategy is built. The creative people in the advertising business are well aware that consumers do not watch television or read magazines in order to see ads. Ads have to earn the right to be seen, read, and heard.

INVOLVING

21 We have seen that the language of advertising is carefully engineered; we have discovered a few of the devices it uses to get our attention. R. J. Reynolds has us identifying with Old Joe in one of his many uptown poses. Coke and Pepsi have caught our eye with visions of peace, love, or Ray Charles crooning, yes folks, "Uh Huh"—with the full and enthusiastic endorsement of the swaying female singers. Now that they have our attention, advertisers present information intended to show us that their product fills a need and differs from the competition. It is the copywriter's responsibility to express such product differences and to exploit and intensify them.

22   When product differences do not exist, the writer must glamorize the superficial differences—for example, differences in packaging. As long as the ad is trying to get our attention, the "action" is mostly in the ad itself, in the words and visual images. But as we read an ad or watch it on television, we become more deeply involved. The action starts to take place in us. Our imagination is set in motion, and our individual fears and aspirations, our little quirks and insecurities, superimpose themselves on that tightly engineered, attractively packaged message.

23   Consider, once again, the running battle among the low-calorie soft drinks. The cola wars have spawned many "look-alike" advertisements, because the product features and consumer benefits are generic, applying to all products in the category. Substitute one cola brand name for another, and the messages are often identical, right down to the way the cans are photographed in the closing sequence. This strategy relies upon mass saturation and exposure for impact.

24   In recent years, some companies have set themselves apart from their competitors by making use of bold, even disturbing, themes and images. In its controversial ad campaign, Benetton has tried to draw attention to its clothing line in unusual ways. One magazine ad displays a photograph of a father comforting his son who is dying of AIDS while other family members huddle nearby. The company's clothing may or may not be truly different from competitors' products, but the image surely is different—that of a company that focuses on social issues.

25   Is Benetton committing an outrageously immoral act by exploiting people who suffer from a horrible disease? Or is this company brilliantly drawing attention to itself while reminding a largely complacent consumer population that the scourge of AIDS needs to be arrested.

26   Benetton's campaign has made use of other, equally provocative images. Like the ad described above, other themes are intended to provoke controversy. But Benetton is far from the first company whose marketing efforts are subject to the charge of exploitation. In fact, on one level, all advertising is about exploitation: the systematic, deliberate identification of our needs and wants, followed by the delivery of a carefully constructed promise that we will find fulfillment or satisfaction by purchasing Brand X.

27   Symbols offer an important tool for involving consumers in advertisements. Symbols have become important elements in the language of advertising, not so much because they carry meanings of their own, but because we bring a meaning to them: We charge them with significance. Symbols are efficient, compact vehicles for the communication of an advertising message. One noteworthy example is provided by the campaign begun in 1978 by Somerset Importers for Johnnie Walker Red Scotch. Sales of Johnnie Walker Red had been trailing sales of Johnnie Walker Black, and Somerset Importers needed to position Red as a fine product in its own right. Their agency produced ads that made heavy use of the color red. One magazine ad, often printed as a two-page spread, is dominated by a close-up photo of red autumn leaves. At lower right, the copy reads, "When their work is done, even the leaves turn to Red." Another ad—also suitably dominated by a photograph in the appropriate color—reads: "When it's time to quiet down at the end of the day, even a fire turns to Red." Red. Warm. Experienced. Seductive. A perfect symbol to use in a liquor advertisement.

28   As we have seen, advertisers make use of a great variety of techniques and devices to engage us in the delivery of their messages. Some are subtle, making use of

warm, entertaining, or comforting images or symbols. Others, like Black Death Vodka, are about as subtle as a recording of MTV's Generation X alter egos, "Beavis and Butt-head," played in fast-forward mode. Another common device used to engage our attention is old but still effective: the use of famous or notorious personalities as product spokespeople or models. Advertising writers did not invent the normal, human tendency to admire or otherwise identify ourselves with famous people. Once we have seen a famous person in an ad, we associate the product with the person. "Joe DiMagio is a good guy. He likes Mr. Coffee. Therefore, I'll add this to my shopping list." "Guns 'N Roses totally rule my world and Slash is the only reason I, like, live and all, so I will definitely make the scene with a bottle of Black Death stuck into the waistband of my four-sizes-too-large black sweat pants with 'Charlie Don't Surf' embroidered on the back pocket." The logic is faulty, but we fall for it just the same. The creators of testimonial ads did not create our interest in famous personalities; they merely recognize our inclinations and exploit them.

29   Advertising works, not because Joe DiMagio is a coffee expert or Slash has discriminating taste, but because we participate in it; in fact, we charge ads with most of their power.

A SIMPLE LANGUAGE

30 Advertising language differs from other types of language in another important respect; it is a simple language. To determine how the copy of a typical advertisement rates on a "simplicity index" in comparison with text in a magazine article, for example, try this exercise: Clip a typical story from the publication you read most frequently. Calculate the number of words in an average sentence. Count the number of words of three or more syllables in a typical 100-word passage, omitting words that are capitalized, combinations of two simple words, or verb forms made into three-syllable words by the addition of *-ed* or *-es*. Add the two figures (the average number of words per sentence and the number of three-syllable words per 100 words), then multiply the result by .4. According to Robert Gunning, if the resulting number is seven, there is a good chance that you are reading *True Confessions*.[4] He developed this formula, the "Fog Index," to determine the comparative ease with which any given piece of written communication can be read. Here is the complete text of a typical cigarette advertisement:

> I demand two things from my cigarette. I want a cigarette with low tar and nicotine. But, I also want taste. That's why I smoke Winston Lights. I get a lighter cigarette, but I still get a real taste. And real pleasure. Only one cigarette gives me that: Winston Lights.

The average sentence in this ad runs seven words. *Cigarette* and *nicotine* are three-syllable words, with *cigarette* appearing four times; *nicotine,* once. Considering *that's* as two words, the ad is exactly fifty words long, so the average number of three-syllable words per 100 is ten.

7 words per sentence
+10 three-syllable words/100
17
×.4
6.8 Fog Index

31   According to Gunning's scale, this particular ad is written at about the seventh grade level, comparable to most of the ads found in mass circulation magazines.[5] It's about as sophisticated as *True Confessions,* that is, harder to read than a comic book, but easier than *Ladies Home Journal.* Of course, the Fog Index cannot evaluate the visual aspect of an ad—another component of advertising language. The headline, "I demand two things from my cigarette," works with the picture (that of an attractive woman) to arouse consumer interest. The text reinforces the image. Old Joe's simple plea, "Try New Camel Lights," is too short to move the needle on the Fog Index meter, but in every respect it represents perhaps the simplest language possible, a not-distant cousin of Merit Ultra Lights' groundbreaking and succinct utterance, "Yo!"

32   Why do advertisers generally favor simple language? The answer lies with the consumer. Consider Toffler's speculation that the average American adult is subject to some 560 advertising or commercial messages each day. As a practical matter, we would not notice many of these messages if length—or even eloquence— were counted among their virtues. Today's consumer cannot, and does not, take the time to focus on anything for long, much less blatant advertising messages. With the advent of new media and an accelerating volume of product offerings, the message count today must be at least two to three times greater than it was in 1970 when Toffler published the first edition of his seminal book. In effect, Toffler's "future" is here now, and it is perhaps more "shocking" than he could have foreseen at the time. Every aspect of modern life runs at an accelerated pace. Overnight mail has moved in less than ten years from a novelty to a common business necessity. Voice mail, cellular phones, E mail, Internet, Prodigy—the human world is always awake, always switched on, and hungry for more information, now. Time generally, and TV-commercial time in particular, is now dissected into increasingly smaller segments. Fifteen-second commercials are no longer unusual, and in that one-quarter minute, the advertiser is best advised to make every one-quarter second count.

33   Toffler views the evolution toward shorter language as a natural progression: three-syllable words are simply harder to read than one- or two-syllable words. Simple ideas are more readily transferred from one person to another than complex ideas. Therefore, advertising copy uses increasingly simpler language, as does society at large. In *Future Shock,* Toffler speculates:

> If the [English] language had the same number of words in Shakespeare's time as it does today, at least 200,000 words—perhaps several times that many—have dropped out and been replaced in the intervening four centuries. The high turnover rate reflects changes in things, processes, and qualities in the environment from the world of consumer products and technology.[6]

It is no accident that the first terms Toffler uses to illustrate his point ("fastback," "wash-and-wear," and "flashcube") were invented not by engineers, or journalists, but by advertising copywriters.

34 Advertising language is simple language; in the ad's engineering process, difficult words or images—which in other forms of communication may be used to lend color or fine shades of meaning—are edited out and replaced by simple words or images not open to misinterpretation. You don't have to ask whether Old Joe likes his Camels or whether King T likes to "grab a 40" when he wants to "act a fool."

WHO IS RESPONSIBLE?

35 Some critics view the advertising business as a cranky, unwelcomed child of the free enterprise system—a noisy, whining, brash kid who must somehow be kept in line, but can't just yet be thrown out of the house. In reality, advertising mirrors the fears, quirks, and aspirations of the society that creates it (and is, in turn, sold by it). This factor alone exposes advertising to parody and ridicule. The overall level of acceptance and respect for advertising is also influenced by the varied quality of the ads themselves. Some ads, including a few of the examples cited here, seem deliberately designed to provoke controversy. For example, it is easy—as some critics have charged—to conclude that Benetton's focus on social issues is merely a cynical effort to attract attention and obtain editorial coverage. But critics miss the point. If an ad stimulates controversy, so what? This is smart marketing—a successful effort to make the advertising dollar work harder.

36 In his book, *Strictly Speaking,* journalist Edwin Newman poses the question, "Will America be the death of English?" Newman's "mature, well thought out judgment" is that it will. As evidence, he cites a number of examples of fuzzy thinking and careless use of the language, not just by advertisers, but by many people in public life, including politicians and journalists:

> The federal government has adopted the comic strip character Snoopy as a symbol and showed us Snoopy on top of his doghouse, flat on his back, with a balloon coming out of his mouth, containing the words, "I believe in conserving energy," while below there was this exhortation: savEnergy. An entire letter e at the end was saved. In addition, an entire space was saved.
> . . . Spelling has been assaulted by Duz, E-Z Off, Fantastik, Kool, Kleen . . . and by products that make you briter, so that you will not be left hi and dri at a parti, but made welkom. . . . Under this pressure, adjectives become adverbs; nouns become adjectives; prepositions disappear, compounds abound.[7]

In this passage, Newman represents three of the charges most often levied against advertising:

1. Advertising debases English.
2. Advertising downgrades the intelligence of the public.

3. Advertising warps our vision of reality, implanting in us groundless fears and insecurities. (He cites, as examples of these groundless fears, "tattletale gray," "denture breath," "morning mouth," "unsightly bulge," and "ring around the collar.")

Other charges have been made from time to time. They include:

1. Advertising sells daydreams—distracting, purposeless visions of lifestyles beyond the reach of most of the people who are most exposed to advertising.
2. Advertising feeds on human weaknesses and exaggerates the importance of material things, encouraging "impure" emotions and vanities.
3. Advertising encourages unhealthy habits.
4. Advertising perpetuates racial and sexual stereotypes.

37   What can be said in advertising's defense? Advertising is only a reflection of society; slaying the messenger would not alter the fact—if it is a fact—that "America will be the death of English." A case can be made for the concept that advertising language is an acceptable stimulus for the natural evolution of language. Is "proper English" the language most Americans actually speak and write, or is it the language we are told we should speak and write?

38   What about the charge that advertising debases the intelligence of the public? Those who support this particular criticism would do well to ask themselves another question: Exactly how intelligent is the public? Sadly, evidence abounds that "the public" at large is not particularly intelligent, after all. Johnny can't read. Susie can't write. And the entire family spends the night in front of the television, channel surfing for the latest "SWAT Team Kicks Butt/Sexy Teen Transvestite Marries Own Half Brother" media fest.

39   Ads are effective because they sell products. They would not succeed if they did not reflect the values and motivations of the real world. Ads for Black Death Vodka, for example, may stimulate preference for this brand among certain buyers, but Slash can hardly be blamed for young men's interest in high-octane beverages.

40   Our discussion of advertising would not be complete without acknowledging that it both reflects and shapes our perception of reality. Consider several brand names and the impressions they create: Ivory Snow is pure; Edsel was a failure; Federal Express won't let you down. These attributes may well be correct, but our sense of what these brand names mean has as much to do with marketing communications as it does with objective "fact."

41   Advertising shapes our view of reality as surely as architecture shapes our impression of a city. Good, responsible advertising can serve as a positive influence for change while generating profits. Of course, the problem is that the obverse is also true: Advertising, like any form of mass communication, can be a force for both "good" and "bad." It can just as readily reinforce or encourage irresponsible sexual behavior, ageism, sexism, ethnocentrism, racism, homophobia, heterophobia—you name it—as it can encourage support for democracy, diversity, and important social causes. People living in society create advertising. Human society isn't perfect; neither is its image as reflected in advertising.

42   Perhaps much of the fault lies with the public for accepting advertising so readily. S. I. Hayakawa finds "the uncritical response to the incantations of advertising . . . a serious symptom of a widespread evaluation disorder." He does not find it "beyond the bounds of possibility" that "today's suckers for national advertising will be tomorrow's suckers for the master political propagandist who will, by playing up the 'Jewish menace,' in the same way as national advertisers play up the 'pink toothbrush menace,' and by promising us national glory and prosperity, sell fascism in America."[8]

43   Fascism in America is fortunately a far cry from Joe Camel, but the point is well taken. In the end, advertising simply attempts to change behavior. Like any form of communication, it can be used for positive social purposes, neutral commercial purposes, or for the most pernicious kind of paranoid propaganda. Do advertisements sell distracting, purposeless visions? Occasionally. But perhaps such visions are necessary components of the process through which our society changes and improves.

44   Old Joe's days as Camel's spokesman appear to be numbered. His very success in reaching new smokers may prove to be the source of his undoing. But standing nearby and waiting to take his place is another campaign; another character, real or imagined; another product for sale. Perhaps, by learning how advertising works, we can become better equipped to sort out content from hype, product values from emotions, and salesmanship from propaganda.

■ NOTES

1. Alvin Toffler, *Future Shock* (New York: Random House, 1970), p. 146.
2. Ibid., p. 149
3. Ibid.
4. Curtis D. MacDougall, *Interpretive Reporting* (New York: Macmillan, 1968), p. 94
5. Ibid., p. 95
6. Toffler, *Future Shock,* p. 151.
7. Edwin Newman, *Strictly Speaking* (Indianapolis: Bobs-Merrill, 1974), p. 13.
8. S. I. Hayakawa, *Language in Thought and Action* (New York: Harcourt, Brace, 1990), p. 235.

■ TOPICAL CONSIDERATIONS

1. O'Neill opens his essay on a discussion of the controversial figure of Joe Camel. What are your views on the Joe Camel controversy? Do you think such ads target young people and, thus, should be outlawed? Why or why not?

2. Are you familiar with the Benetton AIDS patient ad O'Neill mentions here? If so, do you view it as an attempt to raise social awareness or as simple exploitation?

3. Do you think it is ethical for advertisers to create a sense of product difference when there really isn't any? Consider ads for gasoline, beer, and instant coffee.
4. In the last section of the essay, O'Neill anticipates potential objections to his defense of advertising. What are some of these objections? What does he say in defense of advertising? Which set of arguments do you find stronger?
5. O'Neill describes several ways in which the language of advertising differs from other kinds of language. Briefly list the ways he mentions. Can you think of any other characteristics of advertising language that set it apart?
6. What is "proper English," as contrasted with colloquial or substandard? Do you use proper English in your written course work and in your own correspondence? What do you think about using proper English in advertising?
7. O'Neill asserts that "symbols are efficient, compact vehicles for the communication of an advertising message" (paragraph 27). Can you think of some specific symbols from the advertising world that you associate with your own life? Are they effective symbols for selling?
8. In paragraph 28, O'Neill claims that celebrity endorsement of a product is "faulty" logic? Explain what he means. Why do people buy products sold by famous people?

■ RHETORICAL CONSIDERATIONS

1. How effective do you think O'Neill's introductory paragraphs are? How well does he hook the reader? What particular audience might he be appealing to early on? What attitude toward advertising is established in the introduction?
2. O'Neill is an advertising professional. Does his writing style reflect the advertising techniques he describes? Cite examples to support your answer.
3. Describe the author's point of view about advertising. Does he ever tell us how he feels? Does his style indicate his attitude?

■ WRITING ASSIGNMENTS

1. Obtain a current issue of each of the following publications: *The New Yorker, Time, GQ, Vogue,* and *People.* Choose one article from each periodical and calculate its Fog Index according to the technique described in paragraph 30. Choose one ad from each periodical and figure out its Fog Index. What different reading levels do you find among the publications? What do you know about the readers of these periodicals from your survey of the reading difficulty of the articles? Write a paper with your findings.
2. Clip three ads for products that use sex as a selling device, yet have no sexual connotations whatsoever. Explain how sex helps sell the products. Do you consider these ads demeaning to women or men?

3. The author believes that advertising language mirrors the fears, quirks, and aspirations of the society that creates it. Do you agree or disagree with this statement? Explain in a brief essay.

4. Choose a brand-name product you use regularly and one of its competitors—one whose differences are negligible, if they exist at all. Examine some advertisements for each brand. Write a short paper explaining what really makes you prefer your brand.

5. O'Neill says that advertising "can be used for positive social purposes, neutral commercial purposes, or for the most pernicious kind of paranoid propaganda" (paragraph 43). Write a research paper in which you undertake an analysis of actual propaganda. (Consulting your library, look at propaganda from Nazi Germany or from this country during the Cold War.) How are they different? How are they the same?

Sex, Sin, and Suggestion

Carol Moog

Does sex in advertising sell? Does sex in advertising attract attention? Does sex in advertising influence people? What are we really buying—a product or a compelling image of ourselves? The essay below answers these questions and raises many others. Drawing on her training as a psychologist, Dr. Carol Moog guides us through several recent print ads and campaigns pointing out the subtle and not-so-subtle symbols that shape our psyches and consumer behavior. Carol Moog is a clinical psychologist and advertising consultant. She has taught at the Charles Morris Price School of Advertising and Journalism. Her articles have appeared in *Advertising Age, Art Direction, Adweek,* and other publications. This essay was excerpted from Ms. Moog's book, *Are They Selling Her Lips?* (1990)

1 Sex *is* rampant in advertising. And no other type of psychological imagery hits people closer to where they really live. Advertisers didn't create the need for men and women to feel sexually viable, and advertisers didn't create the insecurities people have about being able to love. These are core issues in human development that cut right through to the heart of self-esteem, where people are most vulnerable. And advertisers, because they're in the business of making money, have long dangled the lure of enhanced sexuality to motivate consumers to buy.

2 Does sex in advertising sell? Sometimes.

3 Does sex in advertising attract attention? Yes. Does sex in advertising influence people? Yes. And vice versa.

4 Some of the most pervasive, and persuasive, sexual imagery in advertising is more symbolic than blatant, although the connotations are often far from subtle. The

ad for Chanel lipstick by Doyle Dane Bernbach (Milan) shows a woman with her upturned, open mouth grasping a tube of the product between her teeth. The red lipstick is fully extended, her eyes are closed, and her face shows pleasure. The image is visually arresting, clearly evocative of fellatio, and symbolically links the cosmetic with the promise of sexual allure.

5   What Chanel is selling here isn't simply lipstick; the imagery sends a message to the unconscious, granting permission to fulfill sexual wishes and points the way to an attractor that can facilitate the encounter. But she's also thumbing her nose—symbolically sticking her tongue out—at conventional refinement. She's playful, arrogant, and Chanel uses that message (intentionally or not) as a way of poking fun at its own reserved image.

6   Seagram's Extra Dry Gin ad, created by Ogilvy & Mather, is on a direct line to the male unconscious with its imagery. Dominating the center of the page is a huge Spanish olive, its nearly neon-red pimiento pushing out at the viewer as it is engulfed by a clear, viscous liquid. Presumably, the fluid is Seagram's Extra Dry Gin, an elixir that, the headline claims, can "Arouse an Olive." Metaphorically speaking, this is a very sexy imperative and a very sexy product benefit. The archetypal shape, signifying the female, which has endured since the Paleolithic Era, is round. À la olive. And this one, with its bulging scarlet center, is suggestive both of a tumescent clitoris or nipple—and essentially of a woman in a state of arousal. The invitation "Arouse an Olive," written in a classic masculine typeface, is psychologically directed to men, and delivers a message that promises, and then visually delivers, a sexual seduction, complete with a climactic outpouring of liquid.

7   Psychological analysis aside, it's gut-level obvious what the advertiser's up to here. "Arouse" is not a word generally applied to an olive.

8   The sexual message Seagram's Extra Dry Gin symbolizes in its "Olive" ad is sent, but more overtly, in a different ad for the same product. In the upper right is a picture of an upright bottle (male) overlapping the rounded edge of an orange (female)—a graphic echo of the lower-right image of a couple in heated embrace. As if there could be any doubt about the advertiser's imbuing Seagram's Gin with aphrodisiac powers, the copy reads like a litany of praises for the product's capabilities, which ends with the line, positioned as being spoken by the lovers, "They also say it could turn a 'maybe' into . . . 'again.'" Interpreted at its most basic level, the ad's message about the link between the product and sexuality would appear to be "Get her drunk and get her in bed."

9   It's easier for consumers to dismiss the transparent seduction of the "Maybe" Seagram's ad than the symbolic, indirect sexual message of the "Arouse" piece. Symbolic communications bypass the layers of logic and cultural appropriateness and head straight for the unconscious, which is then free to find an equivalence between what is symbolized, in this case sexual arousal, and the brand, Seagram's Extra Dry Gin.

10   . . . The pressures to be sexy, stay sexy, and get sexier are enormous. We are a driven culture, and the fuel firing the more-is-always-better machine is internal as well as external. Madison Avenue's *pressure* to measure up is only matched in intensity by the level of *need* to measure up that people bring to the relationship. And that need boils down to the need to love and be loved.

11   People who are secure enough to develop an enduring, mutual, affectionate relationship with another person have accomplished an extraordinarily difficult psychological task. Too often, people get stuck in their insecurities; in their desperate determination not to expose their insecurities, they frantically try to fill up a sense of emptiness with cultural facsimiles of love. And the culture—with advertisers ranking right up there, our sergeant-at-arms of imagery—holds up an endless array of tempting surrogates in designer packaging: popularity, prestige, glamour, sexiness.

12   What's vicious about this particular cycle is that the more people try to fill themselves up by propping up the *outside,* the more terrified they are about exposing who they really are on the *inside.* The discrepancy becomes too great, and the investment in the decoy self becomes too high to risk losing whatever security it does provide. Probably the single biggest barrier to love is the fear of psychological exposure, of being found out and found lacking. When advertisers link products with sexuality, they lock in with people's deepest fears of being unlovable; they offer their products and images as the tickets to love, when what they're really providing are more masks for people to hide behind. . . .

13   Cheesy sexual-power games are recurrent themes in [a] long-standing cigarette campaign. Newport, a product of Lorillard, Inc., has been successfully profiting from associating cigarettes with themes of sexual dominance and submission for a decade. Targeted to a young market, the campaign's slogan is "Alive with pleasure!" What Newport's imagery suggests, in ad after ad, is that its smokers will become *sexually* alive with pleasure. The gist of the campaign is that if it feels good, do it, an insidiously shrewd strategy for a product that invites people to sell their birthrights to health for a bowl of momentary pleasure.

14   In one vivid example of the ravishing sexual adventures young singles *could* have if they started smoking Newports, two men are carrying a long pole between them from which is hanging, in deer-bounty fashion, their female prey. All three are having a great time as her head hangs down exactly at one man's crotch level, while her up-ended legs expose her rear to the opposite man—at just about the right level for a soft-porn ménage à trois. Just as the primary acceptable justification today's smokers can feed themselves is simply that they *like* to smoke, sexual entanglements like the merry threesomes are justified as worthy of pursuit as long as they're fun. As Newport puts it in the ad's closing tag line, "After all, if smoking isn't a pleasure, why bother?"

15   There's nothing wrong with a fun fantasy, except that while the sexy scene can remain solely in consumers' imaginations, smoking and its medical sequelae are very real indeed. The advertiser's imagery isn't intended to get consumers to *fantasize* about Newports, it's designed to get consumers to *smoke* Newports. All the persuasive copy and visuals going into pushing the *pleasure* of Newports are just as busy pushing the pleasure of sexuality, a human drive that needs no advertising support. The unconscious doesn't separate the product from the passion, and sexual *expectations* get sold just as hard as the brand.

16   Men in this culture feel just as pressured to exude sexual prowess and proficiency as women, and advertisers provide steady, compelling reinforcement of these expectations. There is no dearth of ads offering men groaning boards heaped with

tasty images of available young women, designed to whet their appetites for associated consumer goods. But does it work? Does sex sell?

17 Women perceive romantic imagery and even symbolic metaphors (like the Chanel ad) as sexy; to men, nudity means sexiness. While women can look at ads with considerable sexual content and still remember what brand is being promoted, when men are faced with overtly sexual imagery, they can't remember *anything*—often they can't even describe what was in the ad, let alone name the product! Sexy ads *do* rivet a man's attention, but the intellectual circuits can get overloaded fast and, at that point, all that gets marketed is food for fantasies. And that's no cause for a bottom-line celebration. If their consumer target can't ask for it by name, the advertiser has just squandered a bundle. For men in this culture trying to grow up, to move from sexual preoccupations into committed relationships, advertisers' sexual preoccupations help keep them stuck in the crippling quicksand of adolescence. And that's no cause for psychological celebration. . . .

18 In the world of primitive cultures, New Guinea tribesmen attach foot-long tubes to their penises. In the world of civilized advertisers, Pierre Cardin man's cologne, shaped unmistakably like a phallus, is shown in an ad as a dominance display object of a superior male who is admired by his subordinates: "You wear it well."

19 In this case, hyperphallic packaging combines with power-message advertising. The guy is visibly a big player. (Comfortable in a tux.) Hardworking, smart, suave. (Reading his speech? Briefing himself for a diplomatic reception? Preparing for tomorrow's contest with Manly Power in a Man's World?) He has nouveaux tastes. (Checker-patterned linoleum—*very* classy.) Could be married or single. (The ring finger is neatly concealed.) Nothing particularly effeminate, but no women to be seen either.

20 And that's important, because this phallic-shaped bottle of men's perfume should hit two markets, straight and gay, if all goes well. The phallic symbol, for anyone for whom it resonates, stands up and says precisely what it is without any embarrassment about what it's doing. If the straight male prefers to ignore the blatant hard-on in the foreground, the ad gives him permission to do so. If the gay male responds to the obvious suggestiveness, that's okay too. It's a clever male-manipulation ad, not least of all because it allows both markets to get their own messages without catering to either specifically.

21 Guess Jeans is one of those advertisers with a huge stake in the attraction of some women to the sadomasochistic side of sexuality, and the women it's after are young. Until quite recently, the campaign featured highly provocative black-and-white photos of porcelain-skinned girls in a string of seemingly endless encounters with salacious older men, labeled only by the scribbled red-lipsticked script "Georges Marciano" or "Guess Jeans."

22 Some of the more notorious scenes in Guess ads along the way include an aging Mafioso-type wearing sunglasses, in postures of sexual dominance toward young, semibuttoned women with apathetic expressions. One has us facing the kneeling rear of a woman looking up at the crotch of a man standing above her, arms folded expectantly. Although she *is* wearing a Guess jeans jacket, what is actually being advertised here? In most of the Guess ads, the advertiser's product is simply a prop for the center-stage interplay between the fragile, loosened-clothing, exposed vulnera-

bility of a nubile female and a possessive, unsavory Daddy-like male, as we see in one of the car scenes. Evocative of Louis Malle's 1978 film *Pretty Baby,* or Elia Kazan's earlier *Baby Doll* (1956), Guess is associating an edge of danger with its brand name, a strategy that plays directly on the urgency and ambivalence of adolescents' sexual impulses. Much of the time, the Guess girls look like runaways photographed in distasteful situations their mothers would never approve of.

23   Irresponsible? Guess jeans sell. The advertiser has gone to whatever lengths it takes to get noticed by its market and has been handsomely rewarded by the public. Some teenagers, like my daughter Julie's friend Alison, buy Guess jeans because "they're comfortable." But for others, the imagery does more than persuade them to wear the brand; the broader effects of this kind of advertising fall outside of the narrow realm of marketing and into the larger universe of moral issues. The psychological messages sent by Guess imagery strongly imply that girls can use their sexuality to free themselves from parental constraints. The ads create the illusion that being possessed by a powerful, older man can be a glamorous identity for a confused, angry adolescent. Being used sexually, or running away, isn't portrayed as being either self-destructive or hostile; it's presented as a daring walk on the rebel side of the tracks. The perfect counter to the ruling party of adults. The latest from Guess? Young women are still often portrayed as sexually submissive and dominated in ads, but now the man strong-arming her from behind while she straddles him and his motorcycle is as young as she.

24   In Revlon's internally produced ad for its Trouble fragrance, the psychological message isn't one of female submission, but rather one of equality between the sexes—both are equally ignorant. In plunging black décolletage, she smiles dreamily, conspiratorially, at her audience. The object of her designs leans on a bar in the shadows, wearing black, a fashionably decadent stubble, and slightly narrowed eyes. The headline titles this scene "He's Trouble, But He's Finally Met His Match." What qualities does she bring to this sexual showdown? If she's sufficiently doused herself with Trouble, she's unhinged whatever mental apparatus might have stopped her from stepping into a story designed to come to a ruinous end. With Revlon's help, she'll match him in destructiveness. Trouble, the imagery tells consumers, can loosen the bothersome intellectual controls that so often interfere with romantic meetings at bars. As the copy explains, Trouble is "The fragrance for those times when your better judgment is better off ignored. After all, a little Trouble keeps life interesting."

25   How can all these images of sexual entanglings be going on today? Hasn't anyone told advertisers about AIDS? Over the years, I've frequently had the opportunity of being asked to comment on trends in advertising. The effect of the AIDS tragedy on the culture has been one of the year's hottest topics. Often, conclusions come to me masquerading as questions such as: What do you think about the new trend in advertising toward love and romance? What I think is that, given the sheer magnitude of print and broadcast messages, advertising "trends" are more often created by the media feeding off its own perceptions than reflecting a true groundswell of change in the industry.

26   While it is true that some advertisers have modified their explicitly young-and-sexual imagery to better reach maturing baby boomers engaged in long-term, committed romantic relationships, these instances can easily be counter-balanced by examples of advertisers calling for attention on the same old hormone hotline. There is little doubt that a combination of AIDS and aging has intensified the desire of people in our culture for lasting, substantive relationships, where two people fall in love and grow old together. Hollywood has jumped on this bandwagon and produced rashes of films, such as *Baby Boom, Three Men and a Baby, For Keeps,* and *She's Having a Baby*—that not only deemphasize the joys of promiscuity, but elevate to near-mythic wonder the pleasures of child rearing. These movies reflect a natural consequence of the inevitable winding down of the prolonged adolescence of the sixties. Again, while there are some noticeable recent changes in the culture's images of relationships, I believe that these do not eclipse the emphasis on sexuality that has been so pervasive in the media; instead, they provide some balance in a cultural marketing mix long skewed toward the sexual sell. . . .

27   One psychological development cropping up increasingly in ad imagery has little to do with romance in the traditional, interpersonal sense of the word. Some people find it safer to relate simply to themselves—and the monstrosity of AIDS looms as a conveniently unassailable reason to stay isolated. The myth of Narcissus lives.

28   Handsome Narcissus was extraordinarily enamored of his beauty. Although young maidens loved him, he paid no attention to any of them. Echo, a lovely nymph, was so pained by his coldness that she faded away, leaving only her voice, hopelessly repeating the last syllables of words it heard. The gods, angry at Narcissus because Echo was their favorite, punished him by making him fall in love with his own reflection in a pool. Despairing because he could never possess what he loved, he killed himself with a knife. The narcissus flower grew from the drops of his blood.

29   Calvin Klein's ad for Calvin Klein fragrance for men is a perfect contemporary rendition of the classical myth of Narcissus. Shot in black-and-white, sleekly oblong, the product has the form of a brick bullion—the same kind of gold that gilds the frame of the mirror in the photo—a mirror into which the transfixed, mesmerized face of a man enraptured by his own image is staring. He looks as if he could stay there forever. Clearly, this is the face of a man in love—and he only has eyes for himself. Homoerotic undertones aside, this is what narcissistic self-absorption is all about. Psychologically, it's a dead-end street.

30   At the root of this kind of narcissism are feelings of worthlessness, the inability to live up to unattainable expectations coupled with an insatiable need to extract admiration from others. Legions of advertisers use imagery that is ostensibly designed to be sexually provocative but that actually sets up a self-perpetuating cycle of narcissistic needs.

31   People in desperate need of validation from others are caught in a media avalanche of narcissistic images of people who essentially feel empty and unlovable beneath their grandiose postures. The sole purpose of these images is to persuade people that the way to achieve the sexual and personal power reflected by a commer-

cial model is to buy the associated product. Consumers buy the product unconsciously hoping that they will win the admiration they covet, but since they're still trying to measure up to somebody else's expectations, they feel just as empty as ever on the inside. The process continues to fuel the quest for approval, which, in turn, fuels the sales of products selling a promise of narcissistic gratification. . . .

32   *Harper's Bazaar* uses narcissistic self-absorption to interest female consumers in buying the magazine. The campaign, using no copy at all, focuses on pictures of women so locked into reading a copy of *Bazaar* that they are completely oblivious to the activities of the man, however unusual, in the same room. In one, a nude man is shown in the shower, vainly kissing the glass door—talk about protection!—to get the attention of a young woman in pearls and cocktail dress, engrossed in reading the magazine. The campaign, created by Margeotes-Fertitta & Weiss, Inc., is intended to be provocative, startling, slick, alienated, and ironic. But what is most arresting to me about the imagery is the level of narcissism and distance displayed by the women. The men might as well be pieces of furniture for all the interest they stir.

33   Even perfume advertising, which, given the nature of the product's intrinsic sensuality, has appropriately featured traditional imagery suggestive of romantic or sexually charged interludes, abounds with examples of pure self-indulgence and smug egocentricity rather than relationships. Elizabeth Arden is the sublicenser of Fendi perfume, and its advertising is dominated by a luminous photograph of a beautiful woman, eyes closed in the passion of the moment, kissing the marble lips of a sculptured male bust. No risk of messy intimate exposure with this packaged smell. The message is resoundingly clear on the subject of emotional closeness: Don't do it. Stick with statues and cozy up to a healthy hunk of alabaster and you won't get hurt. Here, any sexuality resides exclusively on Fantasy Island, an island inhabited by the very embodiment of a nonthreatening male with no needs of his own: a Roman statue. . . .

34   Although Calvin Klein Cosmetic Corporation's use of sexual imagery in advertising, from the earlier Obsession through the more recent Eternity brands of fragrances, appears, on the surface, to have moved from uncommitted, self-centered couplings toward visions of mature, mutual relationships, underneath the seemingly disparate images runs a common thread that sends a consistent message to the public. Despite Calvin Klein's assiduous efforts to package the personalities of Obsession and Eternity differently, the advertiser's family album of brands is still filled with people who appear incapable of having a relationship with a person separate from themselves.

35   Consider Calvin Klein's Obsession perfume. When its ménage-à-many ads first broke, the intentionally scandalous, enormously successful campaign was met with a combination of titillation and outrage, depending on how well the imagery fit into the sexual fantasies of the viewer. Grainy, chiaroscuro nudes of all genders, sensuously coupled in all configurations, formed the backdrop for the print ads; commercials ended with a man's voice achingly murmuring, "Ah! The smell of it!" The use of the word "smell," with its primitive biological connotations, rather than the more usual "scent" or "fragrance," cued even more basic sexuality for Obsession, creating a brand personality built on the free expression of basic human lust.

36   Obsession's smell is strongly musky, a scent categorized by perfumers as "animalic" because of its organic source, and is quite recognizable on the wearer. I am regularly struck by the range of women I pass during a day whose choice of perfume message to send is Obsession's. Many are far from young, and far from the media-based definition of sexy, but they're doused with a scent-image that reveals their underlying fantasies of themselves—fantasies nourished by advertising.

37   Not long ago, I was in a Saks Fifth Avenue and an unmistakable current of Obsession wafted by, trailed by an energetic, pink-haired, cosmetic-laden matron with hat and gloves. While it is true that, demographically, women of her age tend to wear heavier fragrances, that's not the whole show. Perfume advertising is all image—that's what drives the product category. At some level, here was a woman with a fantasy of herself as a femme fatale—a lascivious consort—in secret longing.

38   After the mating-hydra approach to selling Obsession, a shift occurs in the brand's advertising imagery. What do we have next? A bunch of naked people who studiously avoid contact of any kind with each other. In one ad for Obsession, four muscular men and two well-toned women organize their oiled, nude bodies into approximate pairs—not all of which include one member of the opposite sex—on and about a tall, aggressively angled white obelisk. Any sign of emotion, let alone sexual passion, has been eradicated. The people are turned stiffly away from each other, posturing states of grand boredom—noses hoisted in the air as if listening to a private muse. These people have no more feelings or thoughts going on than the phallic prop they surround. What's being sold here is an elaborate image of self-control through psychological detachment. It's as if only two poles of the erotic continuum can be conceptualized by Obsession's advertiser—unbounded promiscuity or asexual androidism. The real obsession is again with the self, which is certainly one way of pulling back from messy, possibly even disease-carrying, relationships, with no expectations of closeness that counts. That's a fairly discouraging cultural mirror.

39   Calvin Klein's Eternity, the advertiser's latest fragrance entry, uses advertising that creates the impression that the image of this product is radically different from the type of flagrant sexual displays associated with Obsession—and they are, but only on the surface. In one of the introductory print ads, a married couple, ring glinting in evidence, rest against one another, beneath the word "Eternity," written in classic typeface; in others, the couple are joined by their children in tranquil settings. Squeakily wholesome commitment and tender romance look like the new name of the game, until the characters play out a bizarre view of what their relationship might really be about in Eternity's *television* campaign.

40   In Eternity's series of surrealistic, technically superb spots, a man and woman voice their fears of being engulfed and consumed by the fervor of their cravings for each other. Speaking in the hollow, hurried flatness of an Ingmar Bergman film, the lovers engage in ardent psychological jargon about the frightening nature of their hopelessly enmeshed relationship. They say things like "We haven't hurt each other yet, but we soon will. . . ."; "Help me destroy me—become me until there's nothing left but you. . . ."; "I destroy everything I love. . . ."; "I don't know where I end and you begin . . . would you still love me if I were a woman?"; and the familiar narcissistic refrain, "When I look at you, I feel like I'm looking in a mirror."

41   This isn't love, and it isn't romance; this is an *obsession,* an addiction. With this type of psychological message, the advertiser's imagery may be moving away from multiple naked sex partners, but the model of narcissistic self-involvement is just as entrenched as ever. The romantic potential of these ads is mired in the fears of the emotional risks of closeness, fears that are often rooted in a poorly defined self-identity. For the commercials' heroes, spending an eternity together—Eternity's promise—would be tantamount to a hereafter in Sartre's *No Exit.*

42   Advertisers aren't the cause of people's problems with true intimacy, but neither are they the passive, neutral reflectors of how our society views relationships. In their frenzied bids for attention, advertisers frequently wave sexual imagery at consumers, hoping to be remembered. Some are; many are not. But what does get set in the collective memory of the culture are portraits of stunted sexual development, portraits of sexual-status displays, narcissistic glorification, and crude innuendo, portraits that are sold along with products pledging to help consumers put themselves in the power positions promoted by the advertiser as enviable.

43   Because these portraits reflect essentially insecure identities, the images promoted point the way toward more, rather than less, emotional emptiness. When Madison Avenue's idea of a loving relationship includes mutual self-destruction, the measuring-up game can become downright crippling. Ideally, relationships are strongest when both partners play with a full deck, with a sense of security and solid identity. Barring that, it's a safe bet to play with fewer cards than to borrow advertisers' pictures and try to build a winning hand from them.

■ TOPICAL CONSIDERATIONS

1. Why, according to the author, is sexual imagery used so extensively in advertising?

2. Why are ads with symbolic or indirect sexual messages, such as the Seagram's "Arouse an Olive" (paragraphs 6–7), more effective than ads with more straightforward and transparent messages, such as the Seagram's "Maybe" ad (paragraph 8)?

3. How is the theme of dominance-and-submission used to sell cigarettes? Include an explanation of the connection established between sexual passion and smoking cigarettes. Can you think of other products that are advertised using this approach? Will your awareness of this theme change your attitude toward the products being advertised?

4. According to this piece, do men and women react differently to sexual imagery in advertisements? Do you agree, or do you feel Moog's analysis reflects commonly held stereotypes about men and women?

5. Describe the kinds of images commonly found in Guess Jeans' ads. Do you agree that the "psychological messages sent by Guess imagery strongly imply that" girls can use their sexuality to free themselves from parental constraints" (paragraph 23)? Based on your personal experiences, can you

make any generalizations about the kinds of people who are attracted to, turned off by, or indifferent to these ads?

6. Do you feel that ads such as that for Trouble are irresponsible in the age of AIDS? Explain your answer.

7. How does the myth of Narcissus live on in advertising? Why does Moog say of this narcissistic self-absorption, "Psychologically, it's a dead-end street" (paragraph 29).

8. Do you feel advertisers should avoid sexual imagery that may promote psychologically undesirable themes (i.e., narcissism, alienation, domination, and submission)? Or should they feel free to incorporate any themes that the culture will tolerate to sell products?

9. According to Moog, what kind of impact does the sexual sell have on one's emotional development? Do you agree or disagree?

■ RHETORICAL CONSIDERATIONS

1. We could not reproduce the various visuals for the ads Moog discusses. However, are her descriptions vivid enough for you? Are they persuasive and engaging?

2. Ms. Moog is a clinical psychologist and an advertising consultant. Does her expertise in these fields come through in this essay? Cite some examples as evidence.

3. Since Ms. Moog is an ad consultant the reader may question her objectivity. Does her professional connection with the advertising world seem to compromise her analysis of the way sex is used in ads? In other words, does she act as an apologist for advertising?

4. Are there instances in the essay where you feel Moog reads things into ads that were not there? Explain your answer with examples.

■ WRITING ASSIGNMENTS

1. In paragraph 25, Moog asks, "How can all these images of sexual entanglings be going on today? Hasn't anyone told advertisers about AIDS?" Write an essay expressing your feelings about the use of sexual imagery to sell in an age when the consequences of a sexual alliance can be deadly.

2. Interview some acquaintances to determine what they think of particular ads using the kind of sexual imagery described here. Write an essay giving an overview of their reactions. In your conclusion try to determine whether Moog's concern about psychological messages were warranted or not.

3. Write an essay defending the sexual sell. You might take as your slant the fact that advertisers are in business to make money not regulate morality.

4. Peruse a current magazine and select three or four ads that use symbolic sexual imagery to sell a product. As Moog does, analyze the imagery, the psychological message, and the potential impact on the viewer of the ad.

5. In paragraph 37, Moog describes a "matron with hat and gloves" wearing Obsession, an "animalic" scent. Moog finds this an incompatible combination. Write an essay describing someone who has purchased a product whose ad image does not fit the person. What conclusions can you make about the power of the ads and what might have motivated the purchaser?

Sample Ads and Study Questions

Here, we reproduced nine recently published magazine ads—familiar pitches for clothes, handbags, cereal, computers, beer, soft drinks, and drug prevention. The ads are as diversified in their products as in their selling strategies. Some are nearly all graphics with no hard-sell copy, whereas others are informative, even chatty. To demonstrate the wide variety in advertising strategies and styles, three of the ads are for different kinds of nonalcoholic beverages. Accompanying each of the ads is a set of questions to assist you in analyzing how the ads work their appeal on us—how they, subtly and not-so-subtly, try to convince us that their product is worth our money.

■ RALPH LAUREN

1. As Charles O'Neil pointed out in his essay, "The Language of Advertising" (p. 180), image is everything. Much of an ad's appeal depends upon the consumer's identification with the image projected. Consider the overall image that is projected by this ad. Take into account the model, how she is dressed, her hair, the setting, furniture and layout.

2. This ad originally appeared in black and white. Why black and white rather than color? What might have been the reasoning of the ad designers?

3. What might have been the reason for photographing the model from behind rather than from in front? What's the effect of not showing her face? How would the ad have been affected were the model staring at the camera?

4. Do you find this ad appealing? Why or why not? Does it make you consider Ralph Lauren products?

5. List five adjectives that best describe the model in this ad. What kind of appeal, if any, does the model have? In your estimation, how well does her image project Ralph Lauren product?

6. In her essay "Spend and Save" (Chapter 4, page 134), Barbara Ehrenreich claims that our consumer culture creates two conflicting messages—one "permissive" ("You deserve the best, that you should have it now, and that it's all right to indulge yourself"), the other "puritanical" ("Work hard, save, defer gratification, curb your impulses"). Do you see either of these messages in this ad? If so, explain how it is projected. If not, what message is projected?

7. Except for the name, there is no text in this ad. What takes the place of text? What would you say are the Ralph Lauren products this ad is selling? Would the ad have been more effective if copy described why Ralph Lauren products were superior to other brands? How important is label recognition?

{ Norman Rockwell's granddaughter,
Abigail Rockwell, with her Coach Duffle Sac. }

COACH
AN AMERICAN LEGACY

Abigail Rockwell, an actress and weekend watercolorist, lives in California. She's seen here with her Coach Duffle Sac,
No. 9085, $228. The Duffle Sac combines both function and style, and is handcrafted of full-grain leather which develops a rich patina overtime.
To order, or for a complimentary catalogue, call 800 262-2411. Also available at Coach stores.

■ COACH

1. Though we cannot reproduce it here, the original ad appeared in a sepia tone, and the Coach bag in tones of reddish brown. Why the sepia tones rather than black and white or color? What is the "message" of sepia? How does that message help sell Coach bags?

2. For the last few years, Coach has run ads featuring offspring of famous American personages such as John Wayne's son, ... and George Washington's five times removed great granddaughter. How does Norman Rockwell's granddaughter fit this roster? How is the Rockwell name enlisted to sell leather handbags? What's the point?

3. Both Ralph Lauren and Coach make use of female models to sell their products. Compare the different images of women that are projected here. Would the same woman attracted to the Ralph Lauren ad be attracted to this Coach ad? Why or why not?

4. The copy in the fine print at the bottom reads: "Abigail Rockwell, an actress and weekend watercolorist, lives in California." How would the impact of this ad be affected were Abigail Rockwell featured, say, as a "weekend tennis player" rather than a "weekend watercolorist" and shown on a tennis court instead of her studio? Or if she were shown posed during rehearsal for a play or movie?

5. The next line of copy reads: "She's seen here with her Coach Duffle Sac, No. 9085, $228. The Duffle Sac combines both function and style. . . " How does "function and style" fit the image of the bag pictured? How does it fit the image of Abigail Rockwell? How might a bag "handcrafted of full-grain leather which develops a rich patina over time" appeal to Ms. Rockwell?

6. As has already been pointed out, the image projected by an ad is critical. What image is projected by Abigail Rockwell here? Consider her pose, expression, appearance, and setting. Also, consider her outfit—the open collar shirt with rolled-up sleeves, the buttoned vest, loose pants with rolled up cuffs, the socks and shoes. Consider also the uncluttered studio, and the large bank of windows and the city setting beyond. In short, how do all of these elements help promote the Coach Duffle Sac?

7. Considering the various aspects of the image projected, and the $228 price tag, characterize the kind of consumer this ad is appealing to.

■ KELLOGGS: "DON'T LET ME GO YET, DAD!"

1. The headline of this ad—the words with the biggest print—reads, "Don't let me go yet, Dad!" What different messages does this statement convey? How do these messages appeal to our emotions? How do these messages help promote Kellogg's Corn Flakes?

2. The use of consumer testimonial is common in advertising. What is the strategy behind making all the copy of this ad a testimonial by a father? How does it help promote the product? In your answer, consider the image of the father. What kind of a man does he seem? Does he strike you as fatherly? How effectively does his image—expression, stance, clothing, general appearance—work with the copy?

3. Would the impact of this ad be affected if the models were not smiling? if the father were standing up behind his son and not touching him? if the father were dressed more formally or less formally? if the father were replaced by the mother (and copy adjusted accordingly)?

4. Consider the bike that the boy is sitting on. What are the subtle messages in the fact that the bike has hand brakes and a rubber bumper across the handlebar bridge? How would the impact of the ad be affected were these features not in the photo? Or if the boy were on a skateboard or roller skates?

5. As best you can, draw up a profile of the consumers this ad is meant to appeal to. Consider in your description the following: socio-economic class, lifestyle, age group, gender, background, and so forth.

6. Notice that "cholesterol free," "fat free" and "low in sugar" are set off in emboldened italics. What is the strategy behind this emphasis? What aspect of Kellogg's Corn Flakes is being promoted here? Can you think of any other cereals that are fat free or low in sugar? Can you think of any cereals that contain cholesterol? If so, name them. If not, is Kellogg's claim here warranted? Explain.

7. Does this ad make you consider purchasing the product? Why or why not?

What's on your PowerBook?

**Martina
Navratilova
Tennis Player**

Game plans
Scouting reports
Vegetarian restaurants
around the world
Chess game
Bridge game
Golf for my coach
Craig Kardon
Fax/modem
Chiropractors and
osteopaths
around the world
Homeopathic doctors
List of favorite hotels
Travel itinerary
Dog and horse photos
Alarm clock
Vet records
Microsoft Word
Adobe Photoshop
Prodigy
March on
Washington speech
Catalog of my dreams
Tennis diary
Personal diary
Tournament schedule

**Art Monk
Wide Receiver**

List of favorite stadiums
Season schedule
and itinerary
Player roster
WordPerfect
Locations of
good bass lakes
List of the biggest fish
I've caught
Strength and
conditioning program
Corel Draw
Season diet
Off-season diet
QuarkXPress
Favorite lasagna recipes
List of restaurants
in New Orleans
Game plan
Appointment book
Competitors' weaknesses
Home phone numbers
of league players
Aldus FreeHand
Layouts
QuickTime movie
of opposing defensive
backs' moves
Aldus PageMaker

© 1994 Apple Computer, Inc. All rights reserved.

■ APPLE: "WHAT'S ON YOUR POWERBOOK?"

1. Celebrity endorsement is a powerful strategy in selling products. Are Martina Navratilova and Art Monk a good pair to promote Apple products? Explain. Was it necessary to identify Navratilova or Monk by their professions? Did you recognize them at first glance?

2. How do the lists, left and right of the photograph, seem to fit Martina Navratilova and Art Monk? Explain in detail, drawing from particular details in their projected images. Do any items not seem to fit the personalities? If so, which? Which are interchangeable? Which seem not to be so?

3. In his essay "The Language of Advertising," Charles O'Neill made the point that much of an ad's appeal depends upon the consumer's identification with the image projected. Even though the two figures in this ad are famous, consider the images projected by their respective attire? their facial expressions? their body poses? their ages, genders, and races? their general appearances? How do these images work to promote Apple products? How would the ad's message and impact be affected were Navratilova dressed in tennis attire? Monk in his football uniform?

4. Consider the positioning of the PowerBooks in the photo. How would the impact of the ad be affected were Art Monk holding his machine down as is Navratilova? Or if the positions were reverse—Monk's machine was down and Navratilova's was up?

5. Consider the setting and angle of this photograph. Is there a message in the facts that it was shot outside and with a background of only clouded sky? How would the ad's impact be affected were the shot not taken from ground level—say, from eye level with the models?

6. Sometimes celebrity endorsement is not enough to sell a product. Consumer need is highly significant. Consider how the advertisers address the needs of potential buyers. As best you can, try to describe the range of needs addressed in this ad. Can you think of any prospective buyer of a PowerBook whose needs are not covered? Explain your answer.

7. Draw up a profile of the kinds of consumers this ad targets. Consider in your answer the following: age group, socioeconomic class, educational background, gender, lifestyle, interests, hobbies, and so forth. Do you fall into the target audience? Explain your answers.

8. Consider the effectiveness of the headline: "What's on your PowerBook?" Do you find it catchy? Why or why not? Does it make you want to read the finer print copy?

Which one makes a beer taste great?

☐ Blondes in bikinis
☐ Sports stars
☐ Catchy jingles
☐ Snow-capped mountains

Just being the best is enough.

■ HEINEKEN. JUST BEING THE BEST IS ENOUGH.

1. How does this ad satirize beer ads in general? What particular beer ads are being made fun of? Can you think of specific brands?
2. What is the implied message behind the question: "Which one makes a beer taste great?" What point is being made about such ads?
3. What is the message in the claim, "Just being the best is enough"? How does it work in this ad? What assumptions do the advertisers make about the audience for this ad?
4. Comment on the minimalist style of this ad. Do you find it appealing? disaffecting? silly? desperate? clever? Something else? Explain your answer.
5. Taking the role of the ad agency, explain the strategy behind this ad to the Heineken people. Consider the different print styles, the use of white space, the small color photograph of a full glass and a bottle of Heineken. Explain the rationale behind the use of check boxes in the ad.

■ **PEPSI: "GIVE UP MY PEPSI? DON'T EVEN THINK ABOUT IT."**

1. What first caught your eye in this ad? The visuals? the copy? the white space? the models? Explain.
2. Celebrity endorsement is common in ads. Did you recognize basketball pro, Shaquille O'Neill? Would most people? Do you think he should have been named as were Martina Navratilova and Art Monk in the Apple PowerBook ad? Why or why not?
3. The recent Pepsi slogan and trademark is "BE YOUNG HAVE FUN DRINK PEPSI." There are three directives here. Explain the specific messages here? What fantasies and/or anxieties are played upon? Are you familiar with any of the past "Pepsi Generation" ad campaigns? If so, how does this ad continue the dominant theme(s)?
4. Consider the actual typeface and layout of the Pepsi slogan cited in question 3. Why the bold all-capital letters? And what are the effects of the ragged-edged black background, the slight slant of the slogan, and its placement in the lower right-hand corner? How does the overall visual effect of this slogan contribute to the ad?
5. Both, the subsequent Sprite ad and this one end with trademark imperatives: "OBey Your Thirst" and "BE YOUNG HAVE FUN DRINK PEPSI." Explain the strategies here. Why the bold, terse directives? What effect is intended?
6. What do you make of the copy attributed to the little boy? What's the message? What do you make of Shaquille O'Neill's expression? What might be his thoughts or response? Explain the effectiveness of the interlude between the boy and O'Neill. How does it help promote Pepsi? Does it make you want to have a Pepsi? or prefer it to, say, Coke, Sprite or some other soft drink? Explain.

You're a woman

of the 90's

Bold, self-assured and empowered.

Climbing the ladder of success at work

and the StairMaster™ at the gym.

You're socially aware and politically correct.

But you probably know all this already

because every ad and magazine

has told you a zillion times.

NO wonder you're thirsty.

Cool, Crisp, Clear.

OBey Your Thirst.

©1994 The Coca-Cola Company. "diet Sprite" and "Obey Your Thirst" are trademarks of The Coca-Cola Company. StairMaster is a trademark of StairMaster Sports/Medical Products, Inc.

■ DIET SPRITE: "YOU'RE A WOMAN OF THE 90'S."

1. What catches your eye first in this ad? The type? the photograph of the woman standing on the world? or the photo of the Sprite can? Does your eye travel from one image to another?

2. Carefully examine the type used and the decision behind its use. List all the ways it is irregular, distorted or unconventional. Is its overall effect jarring? playful? disturbing? lively? Explain your answer.

3. Now consider how the particular type fits—or fails to fit—the message. For instance, look at the line, "Bold, self-assured and empowered." Does the print style fit the message of the words, or is there an inherent contradiction between them? What about the line, "You're socially aware and politically correct." What might be the ad designer's strategy here?

4. The ad exclaims, "No wonder you're thirsty." What is the stated reason for the thirst? What might be an underlying and less obvious reason for the thirst?

5. Sketch a profile of the type of woman this ad is directed to. Consider interests, political leanings, temperament, lifestyle, age, socioeconomic class.

6. Patricia Volk and Charles O'Neill argued that all advertising plays on hopes and fears. What particular hopes or fears, or both does Sprite play on here?

7. Is the person to whom this ad is addressed a "liberated" woman? Why or why not?

8. Note the final line of the copy: "Obey Your Thirst." Explain the use of the imperative. Why is this final directive so terse? What is the intended effect on the reader?

9. Examine the photograph of the woman on the world (the original was shot in a green tint as was the can.) What kind of image does this illustration evoke? Who might the woman be or represent? What is she looking at? Explain the rays of light in the background. Why is she wearing a long dress instead of something shorter or pants? Why is she holding a can of Sprite? Do you like the image? What is its tone? Is it effective?

10. Notice the soft edge of the photograph's border. And the soft edges of some of the type. Are there any hard edges anywhere in the ad? Explain the significance of the use of hard and soft edges.

11. Why are ice cubes prominent in the glass of Sprite? What would be the effect were the glass empty?

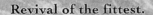

Revival of the fittest.

Proper hydration is *essential* for peak performance.

But if you wait for your body's *thirst mechanism* to tell you when and how much extra water to drink, *you risk dehydration.*

A fairly *reliable solution?*

First, drink 8 ounces of water 30 minutes before exercising.

And *again* 15 minutes before exercising. And once *again* for every 20 minutes of exercise.

And *(this is important)* keep drinking *after* you stop exercising.

Why should those 8-ounce glasses be filled with Evian®?

After a 15-year *journey* deep within the French Alps, Evian emerges *as it has for centuries,* enriched by the mountains. Pure and balanced. A gift.

From our peaks to yours.

evian
natural spring water
IMPORTED • NON CARBONATED

©1995 Evian Waters of France

■ EVIAN: "REVIVAL OF THE FITTEST."

1. Consider this ad's catch phrase, "Revival of the fittest." Explain the intended pun. How does it work to catch your attention? How does it fit the message of the ad? How does it promote Evian? Is it appealing to you personally? Explain why.

2. How does this ad reflect the recent trend in "healthism" as discussed by George Felton in "The Selling of Pain: We Writhe, Therefore We Are"? Find specific wording or layout features that push the virtues of self-denial and pain. How does this ad reflect Barbara Ehrenreich's views of our consumer culture (see "Spend and Save," Chapter 4, page 134)?

3. Charles O'Neill ("The Language of Advertising") made the point that some products are nearly indistinguishable from each other (such as gasoline), which is why advertisers try to distinguish their product by association. Some would argue that spring water is spring water is spring water. How do the ad makers here try to distinguish Evian from all the competition?

4. Go through the copy in this ad looking for examples of "doublespeak"—that is, inflated language that gives importance to the insignificant. Find any? If so what are they?

5. Consider the strategy behind the decision to italicize certain words in the copy. What do these words have in common.

6. It's been said by several critics of advertising that it appeals either to our fantasies or fears. What fantasies does this ad appeal to? What fears? How does Evian address each?

7. What would you say is the target audience for this ad—age group, gender, socioeconomic level, lifestyle? Explain by citing specific parts of the ad. Consider the image projected by the model, what she is doing, her attire, where she is located, and so forth. How would the ad's impact be affected were the model smiling at the camera with the Evian bottle in her hand?

8. Evian, Ralph Lauren, and Coach ads make use of single female models. Consider the different images of women that are projected in these ads. Would the Evian model be attracted to the Ralph Lauren ad? the Coach ad? Explain your answers. Would the Ralph Lauren model be attracted to either the Coach or Evian ads? Explain.

9. Consider the fact that here, as in other ads, sentence fragments are used instead of full sentences. Why is that? What is the strategy?

10. Charles O'Neill claims that the language of advertising is a simple language. Does that seem accurate given the copy here? Consider the vocabulary, grammar, sentence length, and structure. Calculate the Fog Index for this ad. (Consult O'Neill's essay, "The Language of Advertising" for instructions.) At what reading level was this ad written?

11. Reread the copy. What stance and tone does the ad take?

VANESSA WAS IN A FATAL CAR ACCIDENT LAST NIGHT. ONLY SHE DOESN'T KNOW IT YET.

Every year, thousands of young people die in car accidents caused by drugs and alcohol. But now you can wreck your life without hitting the gas pedal. The number of reported AIDS cases among teenagers has increased by 96% in the last two years. If you get high and forget, even for a moment, how risky sex can be, you're putting your life on the line. Call 1-800-662-HELP for help and information. **AIDS. ANOTHER WAY DRUGS CAN KILL.**

Photo by Ken Nahoum

National Institute on Drug Abuse. U.S. Department of Health & Human Services.

■ "AIDS. ANOTHER WAY DRUGS CAN KILL."

1. How does the photograph in this ad capture your attention? What assumption did you initially make about the subject matter of the ad? What components of the visuals reinforced this interpretation? (The original photograph is black and white.)

2. Considering your response to question 1, how is shock or surprise used in this ad? Is this an effective strategy? Does the shock value reinforce the message of the ad?

3. Although much of this ad consists of a photograph, there is some copy, set in three different sizes of print. In the largest type and at the top is the line, "Vanessa was in a fatal car accident last night. Only she doesn't know it yet." What is the strategy behind the placement of this line and behind the use of the largest type? What is the first message this line conveys to you? Did you sense a subtle, more ominous message in the wording at first glance?

4. The middle-sized print is at the bottom: "AIDS. Another way drugs can kill." What is the strategy of placing it at the bottom and in the next largest size type? What is the subtle strategy of printing it in the same style of type as the first two lines of the ad?

5. Consider how the wording in the smallest of the three print sizes continues to develop the message of the ad. Is its affect emotional, factual, or a blend of the two?

6. Consider the brevity of the text in the small print. What, if any, assumptions about the readers' knowledge of the transmission of AIDS are made? Does this broaden or limit the ad's audience? Is this a strength or weakness of the ad?

7. Describe fully the audience to whom this ad is addressed. Consider not only the text but also the visual image: the appearance of the models, the setting, what they're doing.

The feminist movement was reborn, some thirty years ago, out of the recognition that women lacked the access to power and opportunity enjoyed by men. Over the decades much has been accomplished for women in areas of equal pay, reproductive rights, and child care. Likewise, traditional roles of both women and men at home, in the workplace, and in society have been challenged and, to some extent, altered. The essays in this chapter explore the struggles and triumphs of men and women in the last decade of the twentieth century as they continue to redefine who they are.

Our opening piece, "Masculine/Feminine," is the lament of Prudence Mackintosh who went out of her way to raise her sons in a nonviolent, nonsexist environment. In her home, toy guns were replaced by dolls, dads and moms did dishes, and it was okay for boys to cry. Despite all her efforts at consciousness-raising, the forces of nature and culture, alas, conspired to demonstrate that boys will be boys.

Next, Deborah Tannen examines the ways women are "marked" in American culture. From the way they do their hair, the shoes they wear, the decision to wear makeup or not, the title they take (Miss, Ms., or Mrs.) messages go out. In fact, a woman can't get dressed in the morning without "inviting interpretations of her character," Tannen says. But for American men there are fewer options and, thus, greater freedom from being marked.

Because of the feminist movement begun in the 1960s, today's women have a greater range of choices on the job market than the forced accommodations of the past. From medical schools to welding unions, many of the old barriers are down and the old stereotypes have been trampled. But not all women celebrate the hard-won victories. To Kay Ebeling the feminist movement has backfired on women. In "The Failure of Feminism" she complains that a woman "can't live the true feminist life unless she denies her child-bearing biology." Linking the movement to unrealistic demands and expectations, Ebeling condemns feminism for creating a caste of overworked women abandoned by men free to live the good life.

The next essay exposes what the author sees as a "violent backlash against feminism"—a dark and punishing conspiracy to keep women from power. In "The Beauty Myth," Naomi Wolf contends that our male-dominated mass culture has put such a premium on female beauty that it has created in women a cult of self-contempt, physical obsession, and terror.

In the wake of the feminist movement, interest in men's issues has exploded. More and more colleges offer courses in men's studies; male-bonding wilderness-retreats have become big business; and books on the male psyche and the mythic dimensions of masculinity have appeared regularly on bestsellers lists over the last ten years. In fact, some say that the 1990s might just turn out to be the decade of the Men's movement. Driving the movement is a variety of forces: women's criticism of men's shortcomings as husbands, fathers, and lovers; the debilitating pressures of the economy; and men's confusion over what it means to be a man today.

The next three essays address what it means to be a man in the 1990s. In "Why Men Are the Way They Are," psychologist Warren Farrell examines the roots of men's anxiety about themselves. Just as women in our culture are unfairly valued for their beauty, men, he argues, are valued for their earning potential—even by successful women. Next, Sam Allis examines "postfeminist males" who are confused and angry over the limited range of roles they are granted today, when compared with the new options women have won. Is macho outdated? Is the "sensitive" male the solution? Will beating tom-toms at wilderness retreats make men feel more like men? Can the "Daddy Track" be part of corporate life? In "What Do Men Really Want?" Allis paints a turbulent picture of 1990s men desperately seeking manhood.

We close the chapter on an amusing and thoughtful anecdote of a man whose sense of his own manhood is tested at a critical moment. As Bill Persky explains in "Conan and Me," it comes in the wee hours of the morning when he is wakened by the sounds of a burglar in his apartment. The struggle with the intruder in his bedroom sets off an even greater conflict inside him—a conflict between his traditional macho-male ideal and his mom.

Masculine/Feminine

Prudence Mackintosh

Prudence Mackintosh, a freelance writer, is the author of a very funny book, *Thundering Sneakers* (1981) from which this essay was taken. She is also the mother of three boys, whom she intended to raise free of sex-role differences and cultural stereotyping. She gave them dolls to play with rather than guns and taught them that Mom and Dad shared household chores. As she has sadly learned, however, there is "more to this sex-role learning than the home environment can handle," including powerful forces of culture and, perhaps, nature.

1 I had every intention to raise liberated, nonviolent sons whose aggressive tendencies would be mollified by a sensitivity and compassion that psychologists claim were denied their father's generation.

2 I did not buy guns or war toys (although Grandmother did). My boys even had a secondhand baby doll until the garage sale last summer. I did buy Marlo Thomas' *Free to Be You and Me* record, a collection of nonsexist songs, stories, and poems, and I told them time and time again that it was okay to cry and be scared sometimes. I overruled their father and insisted that first grade was much too early for organized competitive soccer leagues. They know that moms *and dads* do dishes and diapers. And although they use it primarily for the convenient bathroom between the alley and the sandpile, my boys know that the storeroom is now mother's office. In such an environment, surely they would grow up free of sex-role stereotypes. At the very least wouldn't they pick up their own socks?

3   My friends with daughters were even more zealous. They named their daughters strong, cool unisex names like Blakeney, Brett, Brook, Lindsay, and Blair, names that lent themselves to corporate letterheads, not Tupperware party invitations. These moms looked on Barbie with disdain and bought trucks and science kits. They shunned frilly dresses for overalls. They subscribed to Feminist Press and read stories called "My Mother the Mail Carrier" instead of "Sleeping Beauty." At the swimming pool one afternoon, I watched a particularly fervent young mother, ironically clad in a string bikini, encourage her daughter. "You're so strong, Blake! Kick hard, so you'll be the strongest kid in this pool." When my boys splashed water in Blakeney's eyes and she ran whimpering to her mother, this mom exhorted, "You go back in that pool and shake your fist like this and say, 'You do that again and I'll bust your lights out.'" A new generation of little girls, assertive and ambitious, taking a backseat to no one?

4   It's a little early to assess the results of our efforts, but when my seven-year-old son, Jack, comes home singing—to the tune of *"Frère Jacques"*—"Farrah Fawcett, Farrah Fawcett, I love you" and five minutes later asks Drew, his five-year-old brother, if he'd like his nose to be a blood fountain, either we're backsliding or there's more to this sex-role learning than the home environment can handle.

5   I'm hearing similar laments from mothers of daughters. "She used to tell everyone that she was going to grow up to be a lawyer just like Daddy," said one, "but she's hedging on that ambition ever since she learned that no one wears a blue fairy tutu in the courtroom." Another mother with two sons, a daughter, and a very successful career notes that, with no special encouragement, only her daughter keeps her room neat and loves to set the table and ceremoniously seat her parents. At a Little League game during the summer, fearful that this same young daughter might be absorbing the stereotype "boys play while girls watch," her parents readily assured her that she too could participate when she was eight years old. "Oh," she exclaimed with obvious delight, "I didn't know they had cheerleaders."

6   How does it happen? I have my own theories, but decided to do a little reading to see if any of the "experts" agreed with me. I was also curious to find out what remedies they recommended. The books I read propose that sex roles are culturally induced. In simplistic terms, rid the schools, their friends, and the television of sexism, and your daughters will dump their dolls and head straight for the boardroom while your sons contemplate nursing careers. *Undoing Sex Stereotypes* by Marcia Guttentag and Helen Bray is an interesting study of efforts to overcome sexism in the classroom. After reading it, I visited my son's very traditional school and found it guilty of unabashedly perpetrating the myths that feminists abhor. Remember separate water fountains? And how, even if the line was shorter, no boy would be caught dead drinking from the girls' fountain and vice versa? That still happens. "You wouldn't want me to get cooties, would you, Mom?" my son says, defending the practice. What did I expect in a school where the principal still addresses his faculty, who range in age from 23 to 75, as "girls"?

7   Nevertheless, having been a schoolteacher myself, I am skeptical of neatly programmed nonsexist curriculum packets like Guttentag and Bray's. But if you can wade through the jargon ("people of the opposite sex hereafter referred to as

POTOS"), some of the observations and exercises are certainly thought-provoking and revealing. In one exercise fifth-grade students were asked to list adjectives appropriate to describe women. The struggle some of the children had in shifting their attitudes about traditional male roles is illustrated in this paragraph written by a fifth-grade girl who was asked to write a story about a man using the adjectives she had listed to describe women:

> Once there was a boy who all his life was very *gentle.* He never hit anyone or started a fight and when some of his friends were not feeling well, he was *loving* and *kind* to them. When he got older he never changed. People started not liking him because he was *weak, petite,* and he wasn't like any of the other men—not strong or tough. Most of his life he sat alone thinking about why no one liked him. Then one day he went out and tried to act like the other men. He joined a baseball team, but he was no good, he always got out. Then he decided to join the hockey team. He couldn't play good. He kept on breaking all the rules. So he quit the team and joined the soccer team. These men were *understanding* to him. He was really good at soccer, and was the best on the team. That year they won the championship and the rest of his life he was happy.*

8   After reading this paragraph it occurred to me that this little girl's self-esteem and subsequent role in life would be enhanced by a teacher who spent less time on "nonsexist intervention projects" and more time on writing skills. But that, of course, is not what the study was meant to reveal.

9   The junior high curriculum suggested by *Undoing Sex Stereotypes* has some laudable consciousness-raising goals. For example, in teaching units called "Women's Roles in American History" and "The Socialization of Women and the Image of Women in the Media" teenagers are encouraged to critically examine television commercials, soap operas, and comic books. But am I a traitor to the cause if I object when the authors in another unit use *Romeo and Juliet* as a study of the status of women? Something is rotten in Verona when we have to consider Juliet's career possibilities and her problems with self-actualization. The conclusions of this project were lost on me; I quit reading when the author began to talk about ninth-graders who were "cognitively at a formal operational level." I don't even know what my "external sociopsychological situation" is. However, I think I did understand some of the conclusions reached by the kids:

> "Girls are smart."
> "If a woman ran a forklift where my father works, there would be a walkout."
> "Men cannot be pom-pom girls."

10   Eminently more readable, considering that both authors are educators of educators, is *How to Raise Independent and Professional Successful Daughters,* by Drs. Rita and Kenneth Dunn. The underlying and, I think, questionable assumption in this book is that little boys have been reared correctly all along. Without direct parental intervention, according to the Dunns, daughters tend to absorb and reflect society's values. The Dunns

---

*From *Undoing Sex Stereotypes* by Marcia Guttentag and Helen Bray © 1976 McGraw-Hill, Inc. Used with permission of McGraw-Hill Book Co.

paint a dark picture indeed for the parents who fail to channel their daughters toward professional success. The woman who remains at home with children while her husband is involved in the "real world" with an "absorbing and demanding day-to-day commitment that brings him into contact with new ideas, jobs, and people (attractive self-actualized females)" is sure to experience lowered IQ, according to the Dunns. They go on to predict the husband's inevitable affair and the subsequent divorce, which leaves the wife emotionally depressed and probably financially dependent on her parents.

11   Now I'm all for women developing competency and self-reliance, but the Dunns' glorification of the professional is excessive. Anyone who has worked longer than a year knows that eventually any job loses most of its glamour. And the world is no less "real" at home. For that matter, mothers at home may be more "real" than bankers or lawyers. How is a corporate tax problem more real than my counseling with the maid whose boyfriend shot her in the leg? How can reading a balance sheet compare with comforting a five-year-old who holds his limp cat and wants to know why we have to lose the things we love? And on the contrary, it is my husband, the professional, who complains of lowered IQ. Though we wooed to Faulkner, my former ace English major turned trial lawyer now has time for only an occasional *Falconer* or Peter Benchley thriller. Certainly there is value in raising daughters to be financially self-supporting, but there is not much wisdom in teaching a daughter that she must achieve professional success or her marriage probably won't last.

12   In a chapter called "What to Do from Birth to Two," the authors instruct parents to introduce dolls only if they represent adult figures or groups of figures. "Try not to give her her own 'baby.' A baby doll is acceptable only for dramatizing the familiar episodes she has actually experienced, like a visit to the doctor." If some unthinking person should give your daughter a baby doll, and she likes it, the Dunns recommend that you permit her to keep it without exhibiting any negative feelings, "but do not lapse into cuddling it or encouraging her to do so. Treat it as any other object and direct attention to other more beneficial toys." I wonder if the Dunns read an article by Anne Roiphe called "Can You have Everything and Still Want Babies?" which appeared in *Vogue* a couple of years ago. Ms. Roiphe was deploring the extremes to which our liberation has brought us. "It is nice to have beautiful feet, it may be desirable to have small feet, but it is painful and abusive to bind feet. It is also a good thing for women to have independence, freedom and choice, movement, and opportunity; but I'm not so sure that the current push against mothering will not be another kind of binding of the soul. . . . As women we have thought so little of ourselves that when the troops came to liberate us we rushed into the streets leaving our most valuable attributes behind as if they belonged to the enemy."

13   The Dunns book is thorough, taking parents step-by-step through the elementary years and on to high school. Had I been raising daughters, however, I think I would have flunked out in the chapter "What to Do from Age Two to Five." In discussing development of vocabulary, the Doctors Dunn prohibit the use of nonsensical words for bodily functions. I'm sorry, Doctors, but I've experimented with this precise terminology and discovered that the child who yells "I have to defecate, Mom" across four grocery aisles is likely to be left in the store. A family without a few poo-poo jokes is no family at all.

14   These educators don't help me much in my efforts to liberate my sons. And although I think little girls are getting a better deal with better athletic training and broader options, I believe we're kidding ourselves if we think we can raise our sons and daughters alike. Certain inborn traits seem to be immune to parental and cultural tampering. How can I explain why a little girl baby sits on a quilt in the park thoughtfully examining a blade of grass, while my baby William uproots grass by handfuls and eats it? Why does a mother of very bright and active daughters confide that until she went camping with another family of boys, she feared that my sons had a hyperactivity problem? I'm sure there are plenty of rowdy, noisy little girls, but I'm not just talking about rowdiness and noise. I'm talking about some sort of primal physicalness that causes the walls of my house to pulsate on rainy days. I'm talking about something inexplicable that makes my sons fall into a mad, scrambling, pull-your-ears-off-kick-your-teeth-in heap just before bedtime, when they're not even mad at each other. I mean something that causes them to climb the doorjamb with honey and peanut butter on their hands while giving me a synopsis of *Star Wars* that contains only five intelligible words: "And this this guy, he 'pssshhhhhhh.' And then this thing went 'vrongggggg.' But this little guy said, 'Nong-neee-nonh-nee.'" When Jack and Drew are not kicking a soccer ball or each other, they are kicking the chair legs, the cat, the baby's silver rattle, and, inadvertently, Baby William himself, whom they have affectionately dubbed "Tough Eddy." Staying put in a chair for the duration of a one-course meal is torturous for these boys. They compensate by never quite putting both feet under the table. They sit with one leg doubled under them while the other leg extends to one side. The upper half of the body appears committed to the task at hand—eating—but the lower extremities are poised to lunge should a more compelling distraction present itself. From this position, I have observed, one brother can trip a haughty dessert-eating sibling who is flaunting the fact he ate all his "sweaty little pease." Although we have civilized them to the point that they dutifully mumble, "May I be excused, please?" their abrupt departure from the table invariably overturns at least one chair or whatever milk remains. This sort of constant motion just doesn't lend itself to lessons in thoughtfulness and gentleness.

15   Despite my encouragement, my sons refuse to invite little girls to play anymore. Occasionally friends leave their small daughters with us while they run errands. I am always curious to see what these females will find of interest in my sons' roomful of Tonka trucks and soccer balls. One morning the boys suggested that the girls join them in playing Emergency with the big red fire trucks and ambulance. The girls were delighted and immediately designated the ambulance as theirs. The point of Emergency, as I have seen it played countless times with a gang of little boys, is to make as much noise with the siren as possible and to crash the trucks into each other or into the leg of a living-room chair before you reach your destination.

16   The girls had other ideas. I realized why they had selected the ambulance. It contained three dolls: a driver, a nurse, and sick man on the stretcher. My boys have used that ambulance many times, but the dolls were always secondary to the death-defying race with the fire trucks; they were usually just thrown in the back of the van as an afterthought. The girls took the dolls out, stripped and re-dressed them tenderly, and made sure that they were seated in their appropriate places for the first rescue. Once the fire truck had been lifted off the man's leg, the girls required a box of Band-Aids and spent the next half hour making a bed for the patient and reassuring him that he was going to be all right. These little girls and my sons had seen the same NBC *Emergency* series, but the girls had apparently picked up on the show's nurturing aspects, while Jack and Drew were interested only in the equipment, the fast driving, and the sirens. . . .

17   Of course, I want my sons to grow up knowing that what's inside a woman's head is more important than her appearance, but I'm sure they're getting mixed signals when I delay our departure for the swimming pool to put on lipstick. I also wonder what they make of their father, whose favorite aphorism is "beautiful women rule the world." I suppose what we want for these sons and the women they may marry someday is a sensitivity that enables them to be both flexible and at ease with their respective roles, so that marriage contracts are unnecessary. When my sons bring me the heads of two purple irises from the neighbor's yard and ask, "Are you really the most beautiful mama in the whole world like Daddy says, and did everyone want to marry you?" do you blame me if I keep on waffling?

■ TOPICAL CONSIDERATIONS

1. Mackintosh discusses what raising a family has taught her about the differences in the way boys and girls behave. She includes a number of amusing illustrations. What are some of these examples? Do the scenes she describes sound like any you've experienced in your own home?

2. Reread Mackintosh's description (paragraph 15) of how her sons and their little girl visitors played *Emergency.* What is significant about this illustration? Do you think its implications are always true? For example, do nurturing qualities belong exclusively to girls? Is aggressiveness typical only of boys? Give examples to support your answer.

3. What do you think of the efforts Mackintosh and her friends have made to keep their children from assuming stereotypical sex roles? Would you raise your children the same way or differently? Explain your answer.

4. Mackintosh's essay encourages a healthy acceptance of the fact that boys and girls act differently when they are growing up and that these differences are inherent. Can you also think of some qualities or traits that boys and girls have in common? Or some that could be expressed by either?

5. Mackintosh implies that boys don't need to be encouraged to be nurses, just to avoid stereotypical sex roles. Is it necessarily true, though, that a man wouldn't want to be a nurse? Or a secretary? Or a kindergarten teacher? Or that he wouldn't have a natural aptitude for these careers? Is Mackintosh implying that a woman naturally wouldn't want to be a lawyer? Would you agree if this were the assumption? Give reasons for your answer.

■ RHETORICAL CONSIDERATIONS

1. Where does Mackintosh state her thesis? Is it implicit or explicit?

2. What is the primary rhetorical strategy Mackintosh uses to develop her essay? Cite individual passages to substantiate your answer.

3. Find five sentences that demonstrate Mackintosh's use of concrete detail. Revise the sentences by replacing these specifics with generalities. Read the two versions aloud. What is the difference in effect?

4. Examine Mackintosh's first and last paragraphs. Explain how the last paragraph ties in with the first to unify the essay and bring it to a conclusive finish.

■ **WRITING ASSIGNMENTS**

1. What was it like growing up in your home? Were you encouraged to assume a stereotypical sex role? Or did your parents try to avoid this? In an essay, discuss these questions.

2. Identify a career that tends to be either male-oriented or female-oriented. Write an essay in which you discuss why this is true. Analyze whether you think it should or will continue to be this way.

■	**Wears Jump Suit. Sensible Shoes. Uses Husband's Last Name**
	Deborah Tannen

The next time you're in class take note of the different clothing styles of your male classmates. Then note the different styles worn by the females. Chances are there is a much greater range in how the women dress than the men. There are also more "markers" in women's style— and more messages being sent. According to Deborah Tannen, women are disproportionately "marked" beings in our society. How they do their hair, what kinds of clothes or shoes they wear, the makeup they wear—or don't wear; these actions all signal certain messages. Messages that will be judged. By comparison, men have fewer options and, thus, are free to remain unmarked.

Deborah Tannen is a professor of linguistics at Georgetown University and the author of eleven books including the bestseller *You Just Don't Understand: Women and Men in Conversation* (1990). This essay originally appeared in *The New York Times Magazine* in June 1993.

1   Some years ago I was at a small working conference of four women and eight men. Instead of concentrating on the discussion I found myself looking at the three other women at the table, thinking how each had a different style and how each style was coherent.

2   One woman had dark brown hair in a classic style, a cross between Cleopatra and Plain Jane. The severity of her straight hair was softened by wavy bangs and ends that turned under. Because she was beautiful, the effect was more Cleopatra than plain.

3   The second woman was older, full of dignity and composure. Her hair was cut in a fashionable style that left her with only one eye, thanks to a side part that let a curtain of hair fall across half her face. As she looked down to read her prepared paper, the hair robbed her of bifocal vision and created a barrier between her and the listeners.

4   The third woman's hair was wild, a frosted blond avalanche falling over and beyond her shoulders. When she spoke she frequently tossed her head, calling attention to her hair and away from her lecture.

5   Then there was makeup. The first woman wore facial cover that made her skin smooth and pale, a black line under each eye and mascara that darkened already dark lashes. The second wore only a light gloss on her lips and a hint of shadow on her eyes. The third had blue bands under her eyes, dark blue shadow, mascara, bright red lipstick and rouge; her fingernails flashed red.

6   I considered the clothes each woman had worn during the three days of the conference: In the first case, man-tailored suits in primary colors with solid-color blouses. In the second, casual but stylish black T-shirts, a floppy collarless jacket and baggy slacks or a skirt in neutral colors. The third wore a sexy jump suit; tight sleeveless jersey and tight yellow slacks; a dress with gaping armholes and an indulged tendency to fall off one shoulder.

7   Shoes? No. 1 wore string sandals with medium heels; No. 2, sensible, comfortable walking shoes; No. 3, pumps with spike heels. You can fill in the jewelry, scarves, shawls, sweaters—or lack of them.

8   As I amused myself finding coherence in these styles, I suddenly wondered why I was scrutinizing only the women. I scanned the eight men at the table. And then I knew why I wasn't studying them. The men's styles were unmarked.

9   The term "marked" is a staple of linguistic theory. It refers to the way language alters the base meaning of a word by adding a linguistic particle that has no meaning on its own. The unmarked form of a word carries the meaning that goes without saying—what you think of when you're not thinking anything special.

10   The unmarked tense of verbs in English is the present—for example, *visit*. To indicate past, you mark the verb by adding *ed* to yield *visited*. For future, you add a word: *will visit*. Nouns are presumed to be singular until marked for plural, typically by adding *s* or *es*, so *visit* becomes *visits* and *dish* becomes *dishes*.

11   The unmarked forms of most English words also convey "male." Being male is the unmarked case. Endings like *ess* and *ette* mark words as "female." Unfortunately, they also tend to mark them for frivolousness. Would you feel safe entrusting your life to a doctorette? Alfre Woodard, who was an Oscar nominee for best supporting actress, says she identifies herself as an actor because "actresses worry about eyelashes and cellulite, and women who are actors worry about the characters we are playing." Gender markers pick up extra meanings that reflect common associations with the female gender: not quite serious, often sexual.

12   Each of the women at the conference had to make decisions about hair, clothing, makeup and accessories, and each decision carried meaning. Every style available to us was marked. The men in our group had made decisions, too, but the range from

which they chose was incomparably narrower. Men can choose styles that are marked, but they don't have to, and in this group none did. Unlike the women, they had the option of being unmarked.

13   Take the men's hair styles. There was no marine crew cut or oily longish hair falling into eyes, no asymmetrical, two-tiered construction to swirl over a bald top. One man was unabashedly bald; the others had hair of standard length, parted on one side, in natural shades of brown or gray or graying. Their hair obstructed no views, left little to toss or push back or run fingers through and, consequently, needed and attracted no attention. A few men had beards. In a business setting, beards might be marked. In this academic gathering, they weren't.

14   There could have been a cowboy shirt with string tie or a three-piece suit or a necklaced hippie in jeans. But there wasn't. All eight men wore brown or blue slacks and nondescript shirts of light colors. No man wore sandals or boots; their shoes were dark, closed, comfortable and flat. In short, unmarked.

15   Although no man wore makeup, you couldn't say the men didn't wear makeup in the sense that you could say a woman didn't wear makeup. For men, no makeup is unmarked.

16   I asked myself what style we women could have adopted that would have been unmarked, like the men's. The answer was none. There is no unmarked woman.

17   There is no woman's hair style that can be called standard, that says nothing about her. The range of women's hair styles is staggering, but a woman whose hair has no particular style is perceived as not caring about how she looks, which can disqualify her for many positions, and will subtly diminish her as a person in the eyes of some.

18   Women must choose between attractive shoes and comfortable shoes. When our group made an unexpected trek, the woman who wore flat, laced shoes arrived first. Last to arrive was the woman in spike heels, shoes in hand and a handful of men around her.

19   If a woman's clothing is tight or revealing (in other words, sexy), it sends a message—an intended one of wanting to be attractive, but also a possibly unintended one of availability. If her clothes are not sexy, that too sends a message, lent meaning by the knowledge that they could have been. There are thousands of cosmetic products from which women can choose and myriad ways of applying them. Yet no makeup at all is anything but unmarked. Some men see it as a hostile refusal to please them.

20   Women can't even fill out a form without telling stories about themselves. Most forms give four titles to choose from. "Mr." carries no meaning other than that the respondent is male. But a woman who checks "Mrs." or "Miss" communicates not only whether she has been married but also whether she has conservative tastes in forms of address—and probably other conservative values as well. Checking "Ms." declines to let on about marriage (checking "Mr." declines nothing since nothing was asked), but it also marks her as either liberated or rebellious, depending on the observer's attitudes and assumptions.

21   I sometimes try to duck these variously marked choices by giving my title as "Dr."—and in so doing risk marking myself as either uppity (hence sarcastic re-

sponses like "Excuse *me!*") or an overachiever (hence reactions of congratulatory surprise like "Good for you!").

22   All married women's surnames are marked. If a woman takes her husband's name, she announces to the world that she is married and has traditional values. To some it will indicate that she is less herself, more identified by her husband's identity. If she does not take her husband's name, this too is marked, seen as worthy of comment: she has *done* something; she has "kept her own name." A man is never said to have "kept his own name" because it never occurs to anyone that he might have given it up. For him using his own name is unmarked.

23   A married woman who wants to have her cake and eat it too may use her surname plus his, with or without a hyphen. But this too announces her marital status and often results in a tongue-tying string. In a list (Harvey O'Donovan, Jonathan Feldman, Stephanie Woodbury McGillicutty), the woman's multiple name stands out. It is marked.

24   I have never been inclined toward biological explanations of gender differences in language, but I was intrigued to see Ralph Fasold bring biological phenomena to bear on the question of linguistic marking in his book "The Sociolinguistics of Language." Fasold stresses that language and culture are particularly unfair in treating women as the marked case because biologically it is the male that is marked. While two X chromosomes make a female, two Y chromosomes make nothing. Like the linguistic markers *s, es* or *ess,* the Y chromosome doesn't "mean" anything unless it is attached to a root form—an X chromosome.

25   Developing this idea elsewhere, Fasold points out that girls are born with fully female bodies, while boys are born with modified female bodies. He invites men who doubt this to lift up their shirts and contemplate why they have nipples.

26   In his book, Fasold notes "a wide range of facts which demonstrates that female is the unmarked sex." For example, he observes that there are a few species that produce only females, like the whiptail lizard. Thanks to parthenogenesis, they have no trouble having as many daughters as they like. There are no species, however, that produce only males. This is no surprise, since any such species would become extinct in its first generation.

27   Fasold is also intrigued by species that produce individuals not involved in reproduction, like honeybees and leaf-cutter ants. Reproduction is handled by the queen and a relatively few males; the workers are sterile females. "Since they do not reproduce," Fasold says, "there is no reason for them to be one sex or the other, so they default, so to speak, to female."

28   Fasold ends his discussion of these matters by pointing out that if language reflected biology, grammar books would direct us to use "she" to include males and females and "he" only for specifically male referents. But they don't. They tell us that "he" means "he or she," and that "she" is used only if the referent is specifically female. This use of "he" as the sex-indefinite pronoun is an innovation introduced into English by grammarians in the 18th and 19th centuries, according to Peter Mühlhäusler and Rom Harré in "Pronouns and People." From at least about 1500,

the correct sex-indefinite pronoun was "they," as it still is in casual spoken English. In other words, the female was declared by grammarians to be the marked case.

29   Writing this article may mark me not as a writer, not as a linguist, not as an analyst of human behavior, but as a feminist—which will have positive or negative, but in any case powerful, connotations for readers. Yet I doubt that anyone reading Ralph Fasold's book would put that label on him.

30   I discovered the markedness inherent in the very topic of gender after writing a book on differences in conversational style based on geographical region, ethnicity, class, age and gender. When I was interviewed, the vast majority of journalists wanted to talk about the differences between women and men. While I thought I was simply describing what I observed—something I had learned to do as a researcher— merely mentioning women and men marked me as a feminist for some.

31   When I wrote a book devoted to gender differences in ways of speaking, I sent the manuscript to five male colleagues, asking them to alert me to any interpretation, phrasing or wording that might seem unfairly negative toward men. Even so, when the book came out, I encountered responses like that of the television talk show host who, after interviewing me, turned to the audience and asked if they thought I was male-bashing.

32   Leaping upon a poor fellow who affably nodded in agreement, she made him stand and asked, "Did what she said accurately describe you?" "Oh, yes," he answered. "That's me exactly." 'And what she said about women—does that sound like your wife?" "Oh yes," he responded. "That's her exactly." "Then why do you think she's male-bashing?" He answered, with disarming honesty, "Because she's a woman and she's saying things about men."

33   To say anything about women and men without marking oneself as either feminist or anti-feminist, male-basher or apologist for men seems as impossible for a woman as trying to get dressed in the morning without inviting interpretations of her character.

34   Sitting at the conference table musing on these matters, I felt sad to think that we women didn't have the freedom to be unmarked that the men sitting next to us had. Some days you just want to get dressed and go about your business. But if you're a woman, you can't, because there is no unmarked woman.

■ TOPICAL CONSIDERATIONS

1. In paragraphs 1 through 7, Tannen describes the styles of three different women, noting that each style was "coherent." At the end of paragraph 7, based upon the information provided by Tannen, what kinds of generalizations might you make about the three different women described? In your opinion, are such generalizations useful in thinking about your "impressions" of people? Explain.

2. According to Tannen, women's style choices are all marked in some way, whereas men have the option of "unmarked" styles. What does she mean by marked and unmarked styles? Do you experience the same difficulties with marking in your life? Explain.

3. According to Tannen, how might a woman's style choices affect her employment opportunities? Is the same true for men? How do you, regardless of your gender, make choices about your own appearance? What do these choices have to do with employment and other opportunities you might be interested in?

4. In paragraph 24, Tannen states that she has "never been inclined toward biological explanations of gender differences in language." Based on the information in Tannen's article, what is your understanding of such "biological" explanations? Do you buy into them as relevant to the issues of gender marking in language or fashion? Why or why not?

5. According to Tannen, what is the relationship between the marking of females linguistically and the marking of female style choices? In your opinion, what kind of effect does this marking have upon men and women in their daily lives?

6. Regarding her work on gender differences in language, Tannen says, "While I thought I was simply describing what I observed . . . merely mentioning women and men marked me as a feminist for some" (paragraph 30). What is Tannen's complaint about being labeled as such? From this sample of her work, would you describe Tannen as a feminist? Why or why not?

■ RHETORICAL CONSIDERATIONS

1. In her introduction (paragraphs 1–7), Tannen describes in detail the appearance of three women at a recent conference. What is Tannen's strategy in these paragraphs? In your opinion, is this an effective introduction to the piece? Explain.

2. Tannen's essay links gendered marking in terms of style with marking in linguistic theory. Reread the article, circling passages that serve as transitions or direct connections between these two ideas. Overall, has Tannen made smooth connections here? How so?

3. Is Tannen's use of the first-person perspective effective in this essay? Why or why not? What is the effect of her shift to the third person in certain parts of her essay?

4. What kind of evidence does Tannen provide for her argument that females are the "marked" case in contemporary culture? Has she provided enough evidence to convince you as a reader? Why or why not?

■ WRITING ASSIGNMENTS

1. Write a detailed first-person description of the dress of women and men in a given situation—for example, your classroom, your table at dinner, your dormitory or apartment building. Draw conclusions that either support or refute Tannen's idea of gender marking in terms of fashion.

2. Write an essay in which you compare Tannen's basic argument here with Naomi Wolf's in "The Beauty Myth." What do these two arguments have in

common? How do they differ? Conclude your piece with a personal response to each argument.

3. Imagine a society where neither men nor women were "marked" with regard to appearance. What would men and women look like? What would they wear? How would this "unmarked" society differ from the one we currently inhabit? In creating this new world, think of all the consequences of removing markings according to gender—socially, politically, economically, culturally. Be as creative as you can!

4. With three or four other classmates, conduct an examination of sources in popular culture of "marked" fashion choices. You might explore television, magazines, films, and advertisements for their fashion content. Then write a collaborative essay discussing the role of the media in the phenomenon of marking described by Tannen, including a consensus of your positions on the issue. Does the media play a positive role in the development of fashion trends? How does this role affect gender relationships and the marking of women, or both men? Your writing project might be supplemented with visuals illustrating your arguments.

<table>
<tr><td></td><td>

The Failure of Feminism

Kay Ebeling
</td></tr>
</table>

Like so many women, Kay Ebeling joined the feminist revolution when she was younger. Unlike most, Ebeling has little praise for what the feminist movement has accomplished in the past thirty years. While others celebrate women's hard-won victories in education, employment, and reproduction, the author of this provocative essay calls feminism "The Great Experiment That Failed." Given the biological reality that women have babies and men don't, Ebeling says that all the movement has produced is "frenzied and overworked women dropping kids off at daycare centers." Only men have been liberated by feminism. A single mother, Ebeling is a freelance writer from Humboldt County, California. This tough and spirited essay first appeared in *Newsweek* in November 1990.

1 The other day I had the world's fastest blind date. A Yuppie from Eureka penciled me in for 50 minutes on a Friday and met me at a watering hole in the rural northern California town of Arcata. He breezed in, threw his jammed daily planner on the table and shot questions at me, watching my reactions as if it were a job interview. He eyed how much I drank. Then he breezed out to his next appointment. He had given us 50 minutes to size each other up and see if there was any chance for romance. His exit was so fast that as we left he let the door slam back in my face. It was an interesting slam.

2 Most of our 50-minute conversation had covered the changing state of male-female relationships. My blind date was 40 years old, from the Experimental

Generation. He is "actively pursuing new ways for men and women to interact now that old traditions no longer exist." That's a real quote. He really did say that, when I asked him what he liked to do. This was a man who'd read Ms. Magazine and believed every word of it. He'd been single for 16 years but had lived with a few women during that time. He was off that evening for a ski weekend, meeting someone who was paying her own way for the trip.

3   I too am from the Experimental Generation, but I couldn't even pay for my own drink. To me, feminism has backfired against women. In 1973 I left what could have been a perfectly good marriage, taking with me a child in diapers, a 10-year-old Plymouth and Volume 1, Number One of Ms. Magazine. I was convinced I could make it on my own. In the last 15 years my ex has married or lived with a succession of women. As he gets older, his women stay in their 20s. Meanwhile, I've stayed unattached. He drives a BMW. I ride buses.

4   Today I see feminism as the Great Experiment That Failed, and women in my generation, its perpetrators, are the casualties. Many of us, myself included, are saddled with raising children alone. The resulting poverty makes us experts at cornmeal recipes and ways to find free recreation on weekends. At the same time, single men from our generation amass fortunes in CDs and real-estate ventures so they can breeze off on ski weekends. Feminism freed men, not women. Now men are spared the nuisance of a wife and family to support. After childbirth, if his wife's waist doesn't return to 20 inches, the husband can go out and get a more petite woman. It's far more difficult for the wife, now tied down with a baby, to find a new man. My blind date that Friday waved goodbye as he drove off in his RV. I walked home and paid the sitter with laundry quarters.

5   The main message of feminism was: woman, you don't need a man; remember, those of you around 40, the phrase: "A woman without a man is like a fish without a bicycle?" That joke circulated through "consciousness raising" groups across the country in the '70s. It was a philosophy that made divorce and cohabitation casual and routine. Feminism made women disposable. So today a lot of females are around 40 and single with a couple of kids to raise on their own. Child-support payments might pay for a few pairs of shoes, but in general, feminism gave men all the financial and personal advantages over women.

6   What's worse, we asked for it. Many women decided: you don't need a family structure to raise your children. We packed them off to day-care centers where they could get their nurturing from professionals. Then we put on our suits and ties, packed our briefcases and took off on this Great Experiment, convinced that there was no difference between ourselves and the guys in the other offices.

7   *'Biological Thing':* How wrong we were. Because like it or not, women have babies. It's this biological thing that's just there, these organs we're born with. The truth is, a woman can't live the true feminist life unless she denies her childbearing biology. She has to live on the pill, or have her tubes tied at an early age. Then she can keep up with the guys with an uninterrupted career and then, when she's 30, she'll be paying her own way on ski weekends too.

8   The reality of feminism is a lot of frenzied and overworked women dropping kids off at day-care centers. If the child is sick, they just send along some children's Tylenol and then rush off to underpaid jobs that they don't even like. Two of my working-mother friends told me they were mopping floors and folding laundry after midnight last week. They live on five hours of sleep, and it shows in their faces. And they've got husbands! I'm not advocating that women retrogress to the brainless housewives of the '50s who spent afternoons baking macaroni sculptures and keeping Betty Crocker files. Post–World War II women were the first to be left with a lot of free time, and they weren't too creative in filling it. Perhaps feminism was a reaction to that Brainless Betty, and in that respect, feminism has served a purpose.

9   Women should get educations so they can be brainy in the way they raise their children. Women can start small businesses, do consulting, write freelance out of the home. But women don't belong in 12-hour-a-day executive office positions, and I can't figure out today what ever made us think we would want to be there in the first place. As long as that biology is there, women can't compete equally with men. A ratio cannot be made using disproportionate parts. Women and men are not equal, we're different. The economy might even improve if women came home, opening up jobs for unemployed men, who could then support a wife and children, the way it was, pre-feminism.

10   Sometimes on Saturday nights I'll get dressed up and go out club-hopping or to the theater, but the sight of all those other women my age, dressed a little too young, made up to hide encroaching wrinkles, looking hopefully into the crowds, usually depresses me. I end up coming home, to spend my Saturday night with my daughter asleep in her room nearby. At least the NBC Saturday-night lineup is geared demographically to women at home alone.

■ TOPICAL CONSIDERATIONS

1. What are the main objections Ebeling makes about the impact of feminism on her life? Do you have any objections about the impact of feminism on your own life? Discuss.

2. What does the "Experimental Generation" value according to Ebeling? Does she also value these ideas? Do you? Why or why not?

3. What attitude does the "Yuppie from Eureka" have that Ebeling objects to? Would you have objected? Why or why not?

4. How does Ebeling use the fact that "like it or not, women have babies" to further argue that feminism has failed women? Do you agree with her? Why or why not?

5. What solutions to the failure of feminism does Ebeling offer? What other solutions can you think of that might help Ebeling's situation?

6. How do the arguments presented here affect your thinking about divorce? Explain your answer in detail.

■ **RHETORICAL CONSIDERATIONS**

1. Ebeling begins and ends her essay with anecdotes about dating. How does this framing device serve her argument?
2. Throughout the essay, Ebeling uses short, terse sentences ("He drives a BMW. I ride buses." "How wrong we were.") to drive home her points. How effective is this device for you as a reader?
3. Look at the words that Ebeling capitalizes in her article. How does this naming device serve her argument?

■ **WRITING ASSIGNMENTS**

1. Write an essay in which you explain your own views about the failure or success of feminism. Use examples from the lives of people you know to support your argument.
2. Research the laws in your state that explain the legal responsibilities of fathers and mothers. Write a detailed letter to your congressman or congresswoman explaining how you feel about the fairness of these laws. Suggest any changes that you think should be made in these laws. (By law, your congressional representative must answer your letter.)
3. Ebeling's essay explores some of the painful results of a society that increasingly values individuality over social responsibility. Write an essay in which you explore the conflict between individual rights and social responsibility in your own life. How, and in what ways, do you establish your individuality? What social responsibilities do you have? Which of these takes up more of your time and why?

The Beauty Myth
Naomi Wolf

"Mirror, mirror on the wall, who's the fairest of them all?" If Naomi Wolf is correct, this is a question women don't leave behind in childhood but continue to ask themselves all their lives. But why is that so nearly three decades after the birth of the women's movement that supposedly raised consciousness and won women rights? In her controversial book *The Beauty Myth* (1991) from which this essay was taken, Ms. Wolf passionately argues that women are in a "violent backlash against feminism that uses images of female beauty as a political weapon against women's advancement." Whether or not one agrees with the wide-ranging implications put forth here, Wolf raises some disturbing issues about women and appearances. Her most recent book is *Fire With Fire* (1994).

1   At last, after a long silence, women took to the streets. In the two decades of radical action that followed the rebirth of feminism in the early 1970s, Western women gained legal and reproductive rights, pursued higher education, entered the trades and the professions, and overturned ancient and revered beliefs about their social role. A generation on, do women feel free?

2   The affluent, educated, liberated women of the First World, who can enjoy freedoms unavailable to any women ever before, do not feel as free as they want to. And they can no longer restrict to the subconscious their sense that this lack of freedom has something to do with apparently frivolous issues, things that really should not matter. Many are ashamed to admit that such trivial concerns—to do with physical appearance, bodies, faces, hair, clothes—matter so much. But in spite of shame, guilt, and denial, more and more women are wondering if it isn't that they are entirely neurotic and alone but rather that something important is indeed at stake that has to do with the relationship between female liberation and female beauty.

3   The more legal and material hindrances women have broken through, the more strictly and heavily and cruelly images of female beauty have come to weigh upon us. Many women sense that women's collective progress has stalled; compared with the heady momentum of earlier days, there is a dispiriting climate of confusion, division, cynicism, and above all, exhaustion. After years of much struggle and little recognition, many older women feel burned out; after years of taking its light for granted, many younger women show little interest in touching new fire to the torch.

4   During the past decade, women breached the power structure; meanwhile, eating disorders rose exponentially and cosmetic surgery became the fastest-growing medical specialty. During the past five years, consumer spending doubled, pornography became the main media category, ahead of legitimate films and records combined, and thirty-three thousand American women told researchers that they would rather lose ten to fifteen pounds than achieve any other goal. More women have more money and power and scope and legal recognition than we have ever had before; but in terms of how we feel about ourselves *physically,* we may actually be worse off than our unliberated grandmothers. Recent research consistently shows that inside the majority of the West's controlled, attractive, successful working women, there is a secret "underlife" poisoning our freedom; infused with notions of beauty, it is a dark vein of self-hatred, physical obsessions, terror of aging, and dread of lost control.

5   It is no accident that so many potentially powerful women feel this way. We are in the midst of a violent backlash against feminism that uses images of female beauty as a political weapon against women's advancement: the beauty myth. It is the modern version of a social reflex that has been in force since the Industrial Revolution. As women released themselves from the feminine mystique of domesticity, the beauty myth took over its lost ground, expanding as it waned to carry on its work of social control.

6   The contemporary backlash is so violent because the ideology of beauty is the last one remaining of the old feminine ideologies that still has the power to control those women whom second wave feminism would have otherwise made relatively uncontrollable: It has grown stronger to take over the work of social coercion that

myths about motherhood, domesticity, chastity, and passivity, no longer can manage. It is seeking right now to undo psychologically and covertly all the good things that feminism did for women materially and overtly.

7   This counterforce is operating to checkmate the inheritance of feminism on every level in the lives of Western women. Feminism gave us laws against job discrimination based on gender; immediately case law evolved in Britain and the United States that institutionalized job discrimination based on women's appearances. Patriarchal religion declined; new religious dogma, using some of the mind-altering techniques of older cults and sects, arose around age and weight to functionally supplant traditional ritual. Feminists, inspired by Friedan, broke the stranglehold on the women's popular press of advertisers for household products, who were promoting the feminine mystique; at once, the diet and skin care industries became the new cultural censors of women's intellectual space, and because of their pressure, the gaunt, youthful model supplanted the happy housewife as the arbiter of successful womanhood. The sexual revolution promoted the discovery of female sexuality; "beauty pornography"—which for the first time in women's history artificially links a commodified "beauty" directly and explicitly to sexuality—invaded the mainstream to undermine women's new and vulnerable sense of sexual self-worth. Reproductive rights gave Western women control over our own bodies; the weight of fashion models plummeted to 23 percent below that of ordinary women, eating disorders rose exponentially, and a mass neurosis was promoted that used food and weight to strip women of that sense of control. Women insisted on politicizing health; new technologies of invasive, potentially deadly "cosmetic" surgeries developed apace to re-exert old forms of medical control of women.

8   Every generation since about 1830 has had to fight its version of the beauty myth. "It is very little to me," said the suffragist Lucy Stone in 1855, "to have the right to vote, to own property, etcetera, if I may not keep my body, and its uses, in my absolute right." Eighty years later, after women had won the vote, and the first wave of the organized women's movement had subsided, Virginia Woolf wrote that it would still be decades before women could tell the truth about their bodies. In 1962, Betty Friedan quoted a young woman trapped in the Feminine Mystique: "Lately, I look in the mirror, and I'm so afraid I'm going to look like my mother." Eight years after that, heralding the cataclysmic second wave of feminism, Germaine Greer described "the Stereotype": "To her belongs all that is beautiful, even the very word beauty itself . . . she is a doll . . . I'm sick of the masquerade." In spite of the great revolution of the second wave, we are not exempt. Now we can look out over ruined barricades: A revolution has come upon us and changed everything in its path, enough time has passed since then for babies to have grown into women, but there still remains a final right not fully claimed.

9   The beauty myth tells a story: The quality called "beauty" objectively and universally exists. Women must want to embody it and men must want to possess who embody it. This embodiment is an imperative for women and not for men, which situation is necessary and natural because it is biological, sexual, and evolutionary: Strong men battle for beautiful women, and beautiful women are more

reproductively successful. Women's beauty must correlate to their fertility, and since this system is based on sexual selection, it is inevitable and changeless.

10 None of this is true. "Beauty" is a currency system like the gold standard. Like any economy, it is determined by politics, and in the modern age in the West it is the last, best belief system that keeps male dominance intact. In assigning value to women in a vertical hierarchy according to a culturally imposed physical standard, it is an expression of power relations in which women must unnaturally compete for resources that men have appropriated for themselves.

11 "Beauty" is not universal or changeless, though the West pretends that all ideals of female beauty stem from one Platonic Ideal Woman; the Maori admire a fat vulva, and the Padung, droopy breast. Nor is "beauty" a function of evolution: Its ideals change at a pace far more rapid than that of the evolution of species, and Charles Darwin was himself unconvinced by his own explanation that "beauty" resulted from a "sexual selection" that deviated from the rule of natural selection; for women to compete with women through "beauty" is a reversal of the way in which natural selection affects all other mammals. Anthropology has overturned the notion that females must be "beautiful" to be selected to mate: Evelyn Reed, Elaine Morgan, and others have dismissed sociobiological assertions of innate male polygamy and female monogamy. Female higher primates are the sexual initiators; not only do they seek out and enjoy sex with many partners, but "every nonpregnant female takes her turn at being the most desirable of all her troop. And that cycle keeps turning as long as she lives." The inflamed pink sexual organs of primates are often cited by male sociobiologists as analogous to human arrangements relating to female "beauty," when in fact that is a universal, nonhierarchical female primate characteristic.

12 Nor has the beauty myth always been this way. Though the pairing of the older rich men with young, "beautiful" women is taken to be somehow inevitable, in the matriarchal Goddess religions that dominated the Mediterranean from about 25,000 B.C.E. to about 700 B.C.E., the situation was reversed: "In every culture, the Goddess has many lovers. . . . The clear pattern is of an older woman with a beautiful but expendable youth—Ishtar and Tammuz, Venus and Adonis, Cybele and Attis, Isis and Osiris . . . their only function the service of the divine 'womb.'" Nor is it something only women do and only men watch: Among the Nigerian Wodaabes, the women hold economic power and the tribe is obsessed with male beauty; Wodaabe men spend hours together in elaborate makeup sessions, and compete—provocatively painted and dressed, with swaying hips and seductive expressions—in beauty contests judged by women. There is no legitimate historical or biological justification for the beauty myth; what it is doing to women today is a result of nothing more exalted than the need of today's power structure, economy, and culture to mount a counteroffensive against women.

13 If the beauty myth is not based on evolution, sex, gender, aesthetics, or God, on what is it based? It claims to be about intimacy and sex and life, a celebration of women. It is actually composed of emotional distance, politics, finance, and sexual repression. The beauty myth is not about women at all. It is about men's institutions and institutional power.

14   The qualities that a given period calls beautiful in women are merely symbols of the female behavior that that period considers desirable: *The beauty myth is always actually prescribing behavior and not appearance.* Competition between women has been made part of the myth so that women will be divided from one another. Youth and (until recently) virginity have been "beautiful" in women since they stand for experiential and sexual ignorance. Aging in women is "unbeautiful" since women grow more powerful with time, and since the links between generations of women must always be newly broken: Older women fear young ones, young women fear old, and the beauty myth truncates for all the female life span. Most urgently, women's identity must be premised upon our "beauty" so that we will remain vulnerable to outside approval, carrying the vital sensitive organ of self-esteem exposed to the air.

15   Though there has, of course, been a beauty myth in some form for as long as there has been patriarchy, the beauty myth in its modern form is a fairly recent invention. The myth flourishes when material constraints on women are dangerously loosened. Before the Industrial Revolution, the average woman could not have had the same feelings about "beauty" that modern women do who experience the myth as continual comparison to a mass-disseminated physical ideal. Before the development of technologies of mass production—daguerrotypes, photographs, etc.—an ordinary woman was exposed to few such images outside the Church. Since the family was a productive unit and women's work complemented men's, the value of women who were not aristocrats or prostitutes lay in their work skills, economic shrewdness, physical strength, and fertility. Physical attraction, obviously, played its part; but "beauty" as we understand it was not, for ordinary women, a serious issue in the marriage marketplace. The beauty myth in its modern form gained ground after the upheavals of industrialization, as the work unit of the family was destroyed, and urbanization and the emerging factory system demanded what social engineers of the time termed the "separate sphere" of domesticity, which supported the new labor category of the "breadwinner" who left home for the workplace during the day. The middle class expanded, the standards of living and of literacy rose, the size of families shrank; a new class of literate, idle women developed, on whose submission to enforced domesticity the evolving system of industrial capitalism depended. Most of our assumptions about the way women have always thought about "beauty" date from no earlier than the 1830s, when the cult of domesticity was first consolidated and the beauty index invented.

16   For the first time new technologies could reproduce—in fashion plates, daguerreotypes, tintypes, and rotogravures—images of how women should look. In the 1840s the first nude photographs of prostitutes were taken; advertisements using images of "beautiful" women first appeared in mid-century. Copies of classical artworks, postcards of society beauties and royal mistresses, Currier and Ives prints, and porcelain figurines flooded the separate sphere to which middle-class women were confined.

17   Since the Industrial Revolution, middle-class Western women have been controlled by ideals and stereotypes as much as by material constraints. This situation, unique to this group, means that analyses that trace "cultural conspiracies" are

uniquely plausible in relation to them. The rise of the beauty myth was just one of several emerging social fictions that masqueraded as natural components of the feminine sphere, the better to enclose those women inside it. Other such fictions arose contemporaneously: a version of childhood that required continual maternal supervision; a concept of female biology that required middle-class women to act out the roles of hysterics and hypochondriacs; a conviction that respectable women were sexually anesthetic; and a definition of women's work that occupied them with repetitive, time-consuming, and painstaking tasks such as needlepoint and lacemaking. All such Victorian inventions as these served a double function—that is, though they were encouraged as a means to expend female energy and intelligence in harmless ways, women often used them to express genuine creativity and passion.

18   But in spite of middle-class women's creativity with fashion and embroidery and child rearing, and, a century later, with the role of the suburban housewife that devolved from these social fictions, the fictions' main purpose was served: During a century and a half of unprecedented feminist agitation, they effectively counteracted middle-class women's dangerous new leisure, literacy, and relative freedom from material constraints.

19   Though these time- and mind-consuming fictions about women's natural role adapted themselves to resurface in the postwar Feminine Mystique, when the second wave of the women's movement took apart what women's magazines had portrayed as the "romance," "science," and "adventure" of homemaking and suburban family life, they temporarily failed. The cloying domestic fiction of "togetherness" lost its meaning and middle-class women walked out of their front doors in masses.

20   So the fictions simply transformed themselves once more: Since the women's movement had successfully taken apart most other necessary fictions of femininity, all the work of social control once spread out over the whole network of these fictions had to be reassigned to the only strand left intact, which action consequently strengthened it a hundredfold. This reimposed onto liberated women's faces and bodies all the limitations, taboos, and punishments of the repressive laws, religious injunctions and reproductive enslavement that no longer carried sufficient force. Inexhaustible but ephemeral beauty work took over from inexhaustible but ephemeral housework. As the economy, law, religion, sexual mores, education, and culture were forcibly opened up to include women more fairly, a private reality colonized female consciousness. By using ideas about "beauty," it reconstructed an alternative female world with its own laws, economy, religion, sexuality, education, and culture, each element as repressive as any that had gone before.

21   Since middle-class Western women can best be weakened psychologically now that we are stronger materially, the beauty myth, as it has resurfaced in the last generation, has had to draw on more technological sophistication and reactionary fervor than ever before. The modern arsenal of the myth is a dissemination of millions of images of the current ideal; although this barrage is generally seen as a collective sexual fantasy, there is in fact little that is sexual about it. It is summoned out of political fear on the part of male-dominated institutions threatened by women's freedom, and it exploits female guilt and apprehension about our own liberation—latent fears that we might be going too far. This frantic aggregation of imagery is a collec-

tive reactionary hallucination willed into being by both men and women stunned and disoriented by the rapidity with which gender relations have been transformed: a bulwark of reassurance against the flood of change. The mass depiction of the modern woman as a "beauty" is a contradiction: Where modern women are growing, moving, and expressing their individuality, as the myth has it, "beauty" is by definition inert, timeless, and generic. That this hallucination is necessary and deliberate is evident in the way "beauty" so directly contradicts women's real situation.

22 And the unconscious hallucination grows ever more influential and pervasive because of what is now conscious market manipulation: powerful industries—the $33-billion-a-year diet industry, the $20-billion cosmetics industry, the $300-million cosmetic surgery industry, and the $7-billion pornography industry—have arisen from the capital made out of unconscious anxieties, and are in turn able, through their influence on mass culture, to use, stimulate, and reinforce the hallucination in a rising economic spiral.

23 This is not a conspiracy theory; it doesn't have to be. Societies tell themselves necessary fictions in the same way that individuals and families do. Henrik Ibsen called them "vital lies," and psychologist Daniel Goleman describes them working the same way on the social level that they do within families: "The collusion is maintained by directing attention away from the fearsome fact, or by repackaging its meaning in an acceptable format." The costs of these social blind spots, he writes, are destructive communal illusions. Possibilities for women have become so open-ended that they threaten to destabilize the institutions on which a male-dominated culture has depended, and a collective panic reaction on the part of both sexes has forced a demand for counterimages.

24 The resulting hallucination materializes, for women, as something all too real. No longer just an idea, it becomes three-dimensional, incorporating within itself how women live and how they do not live: It becomes the Iron Maiden. The original Iron Maiden was a medieval German instrument of torture, a body-shaped casket painted with the limbs and features of a lovely, smiling young woman. The unlucky victim was slowly enclosed inside her; the lid fell shut to immobilize the victim, who died either of starvation or, less cruelly, of the metal spikes embedded in her interior. The modern hallucination in which women are trapped or trap themselves is similarly rigid, cruel, and euphemistically painted. Contemporary culture directs attention to imagery of the Iron Maiden, while censoring real women's faces and bodies.

25 Why does the social order feel the need to defend itself by evading the fact of real women, our faces and voices and bodies, and reducing the meaning of women to these formulaic and endlessly reproduced "beautiful" images? Though unconscious personal anxieties can be a powerful force in the creation of a vital lie, economic necessity practically guarantees it. An economy that depends on slavery needs to promote images of slaves that "justify" the institution of slavery. Western economies are absolutely dependent now on the continued underpayment of women. An ideology that makes women feel "worthless" was urgently needed to counteract the way feminism had begun to make us feel worth more. This does not require a conspiracy; merely an atmosphere. The contemporary economy depends right now on the representation of women within the beauty myth. Economist John Kenneth Galbraith of-

fers an economic explanation for "the persistence of the view of homemaking as a 'higher calling'": the concept of women as naturally trapped within the Feminine Mystique, he feels, "has been forced on us by popular sociology, by magazines, and by fiction to disguise the fact that woman in her role of consumer has been essential to the development of our industrial society. . . . Behavior that is essential for economic reasons is transformed into a social virtue." As soon as a woman's primary social value could no longer be defined as the attainment of virtuous domesticity, the beauty myth redefined it as the attainment of virtuous beauty. It did so to substitute both a new consumer imperative and a new justification for economic unfairness in the workplace where the old ones had lost their hold over newly liberated women.

26   Another hallucination arose to accompany that of the Iron Maiden: The caricature of the Ugly Feminist was resurrected to dog the steps of the women's movement. The caricature is unoriginal; it was coined to ridicule the feminists of the nineteenth century. Lucy Stone herself, whom supporters saw as "a prototype of womanly grace . . . fresh and fair as the morning," was derided by detractors with "the usual report" about Victorian feminists: "a big masculine woman, wearing boots, smoking a cigar, swearing like a trooper." As Betty Friedan put it presciently in 1960, even before the savage revamping of that old caricature: "The unpleasant image of feminists today resembles less the feminists themselves than the image fostered by the interests who so bitterly opposed the vote for women in state after state." Thirty years on, her conclusion is more true than ever: That resurrected caricature, which sought to punish women for their public acts by going after their private sense of self, became the paradigm for new limits placed on aspiring women everywhere. After the success of the women's movement's second wave, the beauty myth was perfected to checkmate power at every level in individual women's lives. The modern neuroses of life in the female body spread to woman after woman at epidemic rates. The myth is undermining—slowly, imperceptibly, without our being aware of the real forces of erosion—the ground women have gained through long, hard, honorable struggle.

27   The beauty myth of the present is more insidious than any mystique of femininity yet: A century ago, Nora slammed the door of the doll's house; a generation ago, women turned their backs on the consumer heaven of the isolated multiapplianced home; but where women are trapped today, there is no door to slam. The contemporary ravages of the beauty backlash are destroying women physically and depleting us psychologically. If we are to free ourselves from the dead weight that has once again been made out of femaleness, it is not ballots or lobbyists or placards that women will need first; it is a new way to see.

■ TOPICAL CONSIDERATIONS

1. Describe in your own words the beauty myth that Wolf is talking about. What, according to Wolf, is the purpose of this beauty myth?
2. In paragraph 3, Wolf states that "the more legal and material hindrances women have broken through, the more strictly and heavily and cruelly im-

ages of female beauty have come to weigh upon us." What examples from today's society can you think of that support this statement?

3. How does the beauty myth work to control women?

4. In paragraph 11, Wolf asserts that the *ideals* of the beauty myth, what is called beautiful, change very rapidly. Can you think of how the concept of female beauty has changed in just your lifetime? What used to be valued as beautiful that no longer is? What is considered beautiful today that would have been ignored ten years ago?

5. What does Wolf mean in paragraph 13 when she writes that "the beauty myth is not about women at all. It is about men's institutions and institutional power"?

6. In paragraph 14, Wolf states that "the qualities that a given period calls beautiful in women are merely symbols of the female behavior that the period considers desirable." What are the qualities of a woman that we call beautiful today? What female behaviors do you think these qualities are symbolizing?

7. What role does the "development of technologies of mass production" (paragraph 15) play in the promotion of the beauty myth?

8. In paragraph 17, Wolf mentions other "social fictions" that were meant to keep women in the domestic sphere during the Industrial Revolution. Which of these are still true today? What modern-day social fictions can you think of that work with the beauty myth to keep women out of positions of power in society?

9. What aspects of the beauty myth does your mother and other women of her generation adhere to?

10. Do you know women who are obsessed with beauty? Describe their efforts to be beautiful. What do you think they are hoping to gain with their beauty?

11. In paragraphs 21 to 23, Wolf explains why *women* as well as men feel the need to promote the beauty myth as well as participate in it. What reasons does she give? Can you think of any other reasons why women would want to promote the beauty myth?

12. Put into your own words an answer to the question Wolf poses at the beginning of paragraph 25—"Why does the social order feel the need to defend itself by evading the fact of real women, our faces and voices and bodies, and reducing the meaning of women to these formulaic and endlessly reproduced 'beautiful' images?"

13. Wolf contends that "woman in her role of consumer has been essential to the development of our industrial society" (paragraph 25). Do you think that women do more of the buying in today's society than men do? What makes you think this?

14. When Wolf states in paragraph 25 that "behavior that is essential for economic reasons is transformed into a social virtue," she is explaining how the virtues a society values are actually myths or fictions created to make the society run more smoothly. In addition to the beauty myth, can you think of

other myths or fictions our society promotes to make things run more smoothly? What, for instance, might be some myths about men's behavior?

■ RHETORICAL CONSIDERATIONS

1. It is not until paragraph 5 that Wolf states the thesis of her article—"We are in the midst of a violent backlash against feminism that uses images of female beauty as a political weapon against women's advancement: the beauty myth." Look at all of the other information that Wolf gives before she gives us her thesis statement. Why do you suppose such a controversial thesis would need to be introduced in this way?
2. Paragraphs 4 and 7 both are catalogs of contrasting facts about women's accomplishments versus the beauty myth. How effective is this contrasting catalog for you? Add some other contrasting facts to the ones Wolf lays out.
3. If you had to change the title of this article to reflect how Wolf feels about the beauty myth, what would you change it to? Do you think this would have been a more or less effective title for this article than the one Wolf used?
4. How does Wolf use the metaphor of the Iron Maiden to support her thesis?
5. What does it mean to *colonize* something? What does Wolf mean when she says in paragraph 20 that "a private reality colonized female consciousness"? Is Wolf using this term in a positive or a negative sense?

■ WRITING ASSIGNMENTS

1. Compare the articles by Mackintosh and Wolf to see what each one says about where gender role stereotyping comes from. Write an essay that explores some of the possible aspects of society that help to shape our concepts of gender roles. Be sure to include your own observations in this essay.
2. In her article, Wolf states that advancements in the media have helped to promote the beauty myth. What other myths or social fictions have benefitted from advances in the media? Write an essay that explores the role that the media plays in keeping society's myths and fictions valued and believable.
3. Wolf notes in paragraph 20 that "the women's movement had successfully taken apart most other necessary fictions of femininity." What, in addition to the beauty myth, are some other "necessary fictions of femininity"? If there were another feminist movement today, what aspects of social control would feminist seek to do away with?
4. Toys and games are some of the earliest "socializing" devices females interact with. How do toys and games help to support the beauty myth? Choose some toys and games that are popular with little girls today and analyze what behavior these items are seeking to promote in little girls.
5. Think about some of your favorite musical groups and songs. Are they promoting the beauty myth in any way? Write an essay that focuses on one musical group or a small number of songs and explain to what extent these are promoting the beauty myth.

	Why Men Are the Way They Are
	Warren Farrell

"With all the focus on discrimination against women, few understand the sexism directed against men." Such is the claim of author Warren Farrell who examines the roots of men's anxiety about themselves in this essay. Farrell's focus is on men's unequal responsibility to succeed in the workplace, to prove their worth by making money, to be, as the author puts it, "a wallet." Warren Farrell is a psychologist and author of the 1986 bestseller, *Why Men Are the Way They Are*. This article first appeared in *Family Therapy Network* in the 1988 November/December issue.

1 For thousands of years, marriages were about economic security and survival. Let's call this Stage I in our culture's conception of marriage. Beginning in the 1950s, marriages became focused on personal fulfillment and we entered into the era of the Stage II relationship. In Stage II, love was redefined to include listening to each other, joint parenting, sexual fulfillment, and shared decision-making. As a result, many traditional marriages consummated in Stage I failed under the new Stage II expectations. Thus we had the great surge of divorces beginning in the '60s.

2 The increasing incidence of divorce altered the fundamental relationship between women, men, and the workplace. Before divorce became common, most women's income came from men, so discrimination in favor of a woman's husband benefited her. But, as the divorce rate mushroomed, the same discrimination often hurt her. Before divorce became a common expectation, we had two types of inequality—women's experience of unequal rights in the workplace and men's experience of unequal responsibility for succeeding in the workplace. To find a woman to love him, a man had to "make his mark" in the world. As women increasingly had to provide for themselves economically, we confined our examination of inequality between the sexes to inequality in the workplace. What was ignored was the effect of inequality in the homeplace. Also ignored was a man's feeling that no woman would love him if he volunteered to be a full-time househusband instead of a full-time provider. As a result, we falsely assumed that the experience of inequality was confined to women.

3 Because divorces led to a change in the pressures on women (should she *become* a doctor, marry a doctor, or have a career and marry a doctor?), that change became "news" and her new juggling act got attention in the media. Because the underlying pressures on men did not change (women still married men who earned more than they did), the pressure on men to succeed did not change, and, therefore, received no attention. With all the focus on discrimination against women, few understood the sexism directed against men.

4 The feminist perspective on relationships has become like fluoride in water—we drink it without being aware of its presence. The complaints about men, the idea that "men are jerks," have become so integrated into our unconscious that even ad-

vertisers have caught on. After analyzing 1,000 commercials in 1987, researcher Fred Hayward found that when an ad called for a negative portrayal in a male-female interaction, an astonishing 100 percent of the time the "bad guy" was the man.

5   This anti-male bias isn't confined to TV commercials. A sampling of the cards in the "Love and Friendship" section of a greeting card store revealed these gems:

> "If they can send one man to the moon, why can't they send them all?"
> "When you unzip a man's pants . . . his brains fall out."
> "If we can make penicillin out of moldy cheese . . . maybe we can make men out of the low-lifes in this town."

6   A visit to the bookstore turns up titles like *No Good Men*. Imagine *No Good Women* or *No Good Jews*. And what do the following titles have in common? *Men Who Can't Love; Men Who Hate Women and the Women Who Love Them; Smart Women/Foolish Choices; Successful Women, Angry Men; Peter Pan Syndrome.*

7   Feminism-as-fluoride has left us acknowledging the working mother ("Superwoman") without even being aware of the working father. It is by now well recognized that, even among men who do more housework or more childcare than their wives, almost never does the man truly share the 24-hour-a-day psychological responsibility of ministering to everyone's needs, egos, and schedules.

8   But it is not so widely recognized that, despite the impact feminism has had on the contemporary family, almost every father still retains 24-hour-a-day psychological responsibility for the family's financial well-being. Even women who earn more than their husbands tell me that they know their husbands would support their decision to earn as much or as little as they wish. If a woman marries a successful man, then she knows she will have an option to work or not, but not an obligation. Almost all men see bringing home a healthy salary as an obligation, not an option.

9   A woman today has three options.

Option 1: Full-time career.
Option 2: Full-time family.
Option 3: Some combination of career and family.

10   A man sees himself as having three "slightly different" options:

Option 1: Work full time.
Option 2: Work full time.
Option 3: Work full time.

11   The U.S. Bureau of the Census explains that full-time working males work an average of eight hours more per week on their jobs than full-time working females.

12   Since many women now earn substantial incomes, doesn't this relieve the pressure on men to be a wallet? No. Why? Because successful women do exactly what less-successful women do—"marry up," that is, marry a man whose income is greater than her own. According to statistics, if a woman cannot marry up or marry someone with a high wage-earning potential, she does not marry at all. Therefore, a man often reflexively backs away from a woman he's attracted to when he discovers

she's more successful than he is because he senses he's only setting himself up for rejection. Ultimately, she'll dump him for a more successful man. She may sleep with him, or live with him, but not marry him unless she spots "potential." Thus, of top female executives, 85 percent don't get married; the remaining 15 percent almost all marry up. Even successful women have not relaxed the pressure on men to succeed.

13   Ask a girl in junior high or high school about the boy whom she would "absolutely love" to ask her out to the prom and chances are almost 100 percent that she would tell you her fantasy boy is *both* good-looking *and* successful (a jock or student leader, or someone who "has potential"). Ask a boy whom he would absolutely love to ask out to the prom and chances are almost 100 percent his fantasy girl is good-looking. Only about 25 percent will also be interested in a girl's "strong career potential" (or her being a top female jock). His invisible curriculum, then, taught him that being good-looking is not enough to attract a good-looking girl—he must be successful *in addition* to being good-looking. This was his experience of inequality: "Good-looking boy does not equal good-looking girl." Why are boys willing to consider themselves unequal to girls' attention until they hit their heads against 21 other boys on a football field?

14   In part, the answer is because boys are addicted. In all cultures, boys are addicted to the images of beautiful women. And in American culture this is enormously magnified. Boys are exposed to the images of beautiful women about 10 million times per year via television, billboards, magazines, etc. In the process, the naturally beautiful girl becomes a *genetic celebrity*. Boys become addicted to the image of the quasi-anorexic female. To be the equal of this genetic celebrity, the adolescent boy must become an *earned celebrity* (by performing, paying on dates, etc.). Until he is an earned celebrity, he feels like a groupie trying to get a celebrity's attention.

15   Is there an invisible curriculum for girls and boys growing up? Yes. For girls, "If you want to have your choice among boys, you had better be beautiful." For boys, it's "You had better be handsome *and* successful." If a boy wants a romantic relationship with a girl he must not only be successful and perform, he must pay and pursue—risk sexual rejection. Girls think of the three Ps—performing, paying, and pursuing—as male power. Boys see the three Ps as what they must do to earn their way to female love and sexuality. They see these not as power, but as compensations for powerlessness. This is the adolescent male's experience of inequality.

■ **TOPICAL CONSIDERATIONS**

1. What arguments does Farrell present to prove that the increase in the number of divorces has "altered the fundamental relationship between women, men, and the workplace" (paragraph 2)? Do you agree with his points? Why or why not?

2. How do Farrell's views on the effects of divorce on men and women compare with Ebeling's? How do you account for the differences in these two viewpoints?

3. Do you agree or disagree with Farrell when he writes in paragraph 4 that "complaints about men, the idea that 'men are jerks,' have become so integrated into our unconscious that even advertisers have caught on"? Describe some recent advertisements that support your stance.

4. What are the differences between men's and women's options, according to Farrell? Looking back over your own experience and the experiences of people you know, does what Farrell says ring true to you? How so? If not, where does your experience differ?

5. In paragraph 13, Farrell claims that junior-high and high-school girls' "fantasy boy" is "*both* good-looking *and* successful" while boys' "fantasy girl" is simply "good-looking." From your experience, is this claim true? Have you ever been dated because of your looks and/or "earned celebrity"?

6. What do you think Farrell hoped his readers would learn from this article? How do you think he wants them to respond? On what do you base your answers? Has this article made you more aware of the unfair pressures our culture puts on males and females? Explain.

■ RHETORICAL CONSIDERATIONS

1. What are the strengths and weaknesses of Farrell's use of statistics in his article?

2. Look at the language Farrell uses to talk about feminism. How would you describe his attitude toward feminism? Is he angry? Dismissive? Supportive? Use his language to support your answer.

3. How would you describe Farrell's voice in this article? What sense do you get of Farrell as an individual? Use passages from the article to support your answers.

■ WRITING ASSIGNMENTS

1. Write a conversation between Farrell and Ebeling about the relationship between women, men, and the workplace. In this conversation, be sure to write about the points that these authors agree upon, as well as the points where they differ. As a conclusion, have Farrell and Ebeling decide to write an article they both would agree upon. What would this article be about?

2. This article as well as the next article by Allis both talk about the difficulties of being male today. Have these pieces sensitized you to issues you've never really considered before? If so, do you think you now regard male roles in a different light? Enough as to consider changing your behavior? If so, write a

paper explaining how you have been affected by the arguments presented in these three articles, and how your thinking/behavior might be affected.

3. Conduct a survey of both men and women in your age group, asking them to list at least five qualities of an ideal mate. What seem to be predominant qualities that both sexes want in a mate? Do the statistics you have gathered break down along gender lines, as Farrell suggests? What do men want? What do women want? Write an essay that summarizes the findings of your survey and then goes on to make some conclusions about the gender role expectations of the group you have surveyed.

4. There are many other aspects of our culture that contribute to our definitions of what it means to be female or male. How do rock music, advertising, and movies contribute to stereotypes of females as sex objects and men as success objects? Write an essay that explores how these three aspects of our culture (or any others you may wish to include) shape our notions of gender.

What Do Men Really Want?

Sam Allis

Might the 1990s turn out to be the decade of the Men's movement? Some say the time is right. Angered by the incessant criticism of their inadequacies as lovers, husbands, and fathers, exhausted by the demands of the workplace, and confused over what it means to be a man today, many men seek new roles and identities. In this piece, Sam Allis, a Time *magazine correspondent, lets us eavesdrop on men struggling with a need to define themselves the way women did about thirty years ago. This essay first appeared in* Time *in 1990.*

1 Freud, like everyone else, forgot to ask the second question: What do *men* really want? His omission may reflect the male fascination with the enigma of woman over the mystery of man. She owns the center of his imagination, while the fate of man works the margins. Perhaps this is why so many men have taken the Mafia oath of silence about their hopes and fears. Strong and silent remain de rigueur.

2 But in the wake of the feminist movement, some men are beginning to pipe up. In the intimacy of locker rooms and the glare of large men's groups, they are spilling their bile at the incessant criticism, much of it justified, from women about their inadequacies as husbands, lovers, fathers. They are airing their frustration with the limited roles they face today, compared with the multiple options that women seem to have won. Above all, they are groping to redefine themselves on their own terms instead of on the performance standards set by their wives or bosses or family

ghosts. "We've heard all the criticism," says New York City–based television producer Tom Seligson. "Now we'll make our own decisions."

3   In many quarters there is anger. "The American man wants his manhood back. Period," snaps John Wheeler, a Washington environmentalist and former chairman of the Vietnam Veterans Memorial Fund. "New York feminists [a generic term in his lexicon] have been busy castrating American males. They poured this country's testosterone out the window in the 1960s. The men in this country have lost their boldness. To raise your voice these days is a worse offense than urinating in the subway."

4   Even more prevalent is exhaustion. "The American man wants to stop running; he wants a few moments of peace," says poet Robert Bly, one of the gurus of the nascent men's movement in the U.S. "He has a tremendous longing to get down to his own depths. Beneath the turbulence of his daily life is a beautiful crystalline infrastructure"—a kind of male bedrock.

5   Finally, there is profound confusion over what it means to be a man today. Men have faced warping changes in role models since the women's movement drove the strong, stoic John Wayne–type into the sunset. Replacing him was a new hero: the hollow-chested, sensitive, New Age man who bawls at Kodak commercials and handles a diaper the way Magic Johnson does a basketball. Enter Alan Alda.

6   But he, too, is quickly becoming outdated. As we begin the '90s, the zeitgeist has changed again. Now the sensitive male is a wimp and an object of derision to boot. In her song *Sensitive New Age Guys,* singer Christine Lavin lampoons, "Who carries the baby on his back? Who thinks Shirley MacLaine is on the inside track?" Now it's goodbye, Alan Alda; hello, Mel Gibson, with your sensitive eyes and your lethal weapon. Hi there, Arnold Schwarzenegger, the devoted family man with terrific triceps. The new surge of tempered macho is everywhere. Even the male dummies in store windows are getting tougher. Pucci Manikins is producing a more muscular model for the new decade that stands 6 ft. 2 in. instead of 6 ft. and has a 42-in. chest instead of its previous 40.

7   What's going on here? Are we looking at a backlash against the pounding men have taken? To some degree, yes. But it's more complicated than that. "The sensitive man was overplayed," explains Seattle-based lecturer Michael Meade, a colleague of Bly's in the men's movement. "There is no one quality intriguing enough to make a person interesting for a long time." More important, argues Warren Farrell, author of the 1986 best seller *Why Men Are the Way They Are,* women liked Alan Alda not because he epitomized the sensitive man but because he was a multimillionaire superstar success who also happened to be sensitive. In short, he met all their performance needs before sensitivity ever entered the picture. "We have never worshiped the soft man," says Farrell. "If Mel Gibson were a nursery school teacher, women wouldn't want him. Can you imagine a cover of TIME featuring a sensitive musician who drives a cab on the side?"

8   The women's movement sensitized many men to the problems women face in society and made them examine their own feelings in new ways. But it did not substantially alter what society expects of men. "Nothing fundamental has changed," says Farrell. Except that both John Wayne and Alan Alda have been discarded on the same cultural garbage heap. "First I learned that an erect cock was politically incorrect," complains producer Seligson. "Now it's wrong not to have one."

9　　As always, men are defined by their performance in the workplace. If women don't like their jobs, they can, at least in theory, maintain legitimacy by going home and raising children. Men have no such alternative. "The options are dismal," says Meade. "You can drop out, which is an abdication of power, or take the whole cloth and lose your soul." If women have suffered from being sex objects, men have suffered as success objects, judged by the amount of money they bring home. As one young career woman in Boston puts it, "I don't want a Type A. I want an A-plus." Chilling words that make Farrell wonder, "Why do we need to earn more than you to be considered worthy of you?"

10　　This imbalance can be brutal for a man whose wife tries life in the corporate world, discovers as men did decades ago that it is no day at the beach, and heads for home, leaving him the sole breadwinner. "We're seeing more of this 'You guys can have it back. It's been real,'" observes Kyle Pruett, a psychiatrist at the Yale Child Studies Center. "I have never seen a case where it has not increased anxiety for the man."

11　　There has been a lot of cocktail-party talk about the need for a brave, sensitive man who will stand up to the corporate barons and take time off to watch his son play Peter Pan in his school play, the fast track be damned. This sentiment showed up in a 1989 poll, conducted by Robert Half International, in which about 45% of men surveyed said they would refuse a promotion rather than miss time at home. But when it comes to trading income for "quality time," how many fathers will actually be there at the grade-school curtain call?

12　　"Is there a Daddy Track? No," says Edward Zigler, a Yale psychologist. "The message is that if a man takes paternity leave, he's a very strange person who is not committed to the corporation. It's very bleak." Says Felice Schwartz, who explored the notion of a Mommy Track in a 1989 article in the *Harvard Business Review:* "There isn't any forgiveness yet of a man who doesn't really give his all." So today's working stiff really enjoys no more meaningful options than did his father, the pathetic guy in the gray flannel suit who was pilloried as a professional hamster and an emotional cripple. You're still either a master of the universe or a wimp. It is the cognitive dissonance between the desire for change and the absence of ways to achieve it that has reduced most men who even think about the subject to tapioca.

13　　Robert Rackleff, 47, is one of the rare men who have stepped off the corporate treadmill. Five years ago, after the birth of their third child, Rackleff and his wife Jo-Ellen fled New York City, where he was a well-paid corporate speechwriter and she a radio-show producer. They moved to his native Florida, where Rackleff earns a less lavish living as a free-lance writer and helps his wife raise the kids. The drop in income, he acknowledges, "was scary. It put more pressure on me, but I wanted to spend more time with my children." Rackleff feels happy with his choice, but isolated. "I know only one other guy who left the fast track to be with his kids," he says. "Men just aren't doing it. I can still call up most of them at 8 P.M. and know they will be in the office."

14　　Men have been bombarded with recipes to ripen their personal lives, if not their professional ones. They are now Lamaze-class regulars and can be found in the delivery room for the cosmic event instead of pacing the waiting-room floor. They have been instructed to bond with children, wives, colleagues and anyone else they can find. Exactly how remains unclear. Self-help books, like Twinkies, give brief highs and do not begin to address the uneven changes in their lives over the past 20 years. "Men aren't any happier in the '90s than they were in the '50s," observes Yale psychiatrist Pruett, "but their inner lives tend to be more complex. They are interested in feeling less isolated. They are stunned to find out how rich human relationships are."

15   Unfortunately, the men who attempt to explore those riches with the women in their lives often discover that their efforts are not entirely welcome. The same women who complain about male reticence can grow uncomfortable when male secrets and insecurities spill out. Says Rackleff: "I think a lot of women who want a husband to be a typical hardworking breadwinner are scared when he talks about being a sensitive father. I get cynical about that."

16   One might be equally cynical about men opening up to other men. Atlanta psychologist Augustus Napier tells of two doctors whose lockers were next to each other in the surgical dressing room of a hospital. For years they talked about sports, money and other safe "male" subjects. Then one of them learned that the other had tried to commit suicide—and had never so much as mentioned the attempt to him. So much for male bonding.

17   How can men break out of the gender stereotypes? Clearly, there is a need for some male consciousness raising, yet men have nothing to rival the giant grass-roots movement that began razing female stereotypes 25 years ago. There is no male equivalent for the National Organization for Women or *Ms.* magazine. No role models, other than the usual megabillionaire success objects.

18   A minute percentage of American males are involved in the handful of organizations whose membership ranges from men who support the feminist movement to angry divorcés meeting to swap gripes about alimony and child-custody battles. There is also a group of mostly well-educated, middle-class men who sporadically participate in a kind of male spiritual quest. Anywhere from Maine to Minnesota, at male-only weekend retreats, they earnestly search for some shard of ancient masculinity culled from their souls by the Industrial Revolution. At these so-called warrior weekends, participants wrestle, beat drums and hold workshops on everything from ecology to divorce and incest. They embrace, and yes, they do cry and confide things they would never dream of saying to their wives and girlfriends. They act out emotions in a safe haven where no one will laugh at them.

19   At one drumming session in the municipal-arts center of a Boston suburb, about 50 men sit in a huge circle beating on everything from tom-toms to cowbells and sticks. Their ages range from the 20s to the 60s. A participant has brought his young son with him. Drummers nod as newcomers appear, sit down and start pounding away. Before long, a strong primal beat emerges that somehow transcends the weirdness of it all. Some men close their eyes and play in a trance. Others rise and dance around the middle of the group, chanting as they move.

20   One shudders to think what *Saturday Night Live* would do with these scenes. But there is no smirking among the participants. "When is the last time you danced with another man?" asks Paul, a family man who drove two hours from Connecticut

to be there. "It tells you how many walls there are still out there for us." Los Angeles writer Michael Ventura, who has written extensively about men's issues, acknowledges the obvious: much of this seems pretty bizarre. "Some of it may look silly," he says. "But if you're afraid of looking silly, everything stops right there. In our society, men have to be contained and sure of themselves. Well, f——— that. That's not the way we feel." The goal, continues Ventura, is to rediscover the mystery of man, a creature capable of strength, spontaneity and adventure. "The male mystery is the part of us that wants to explore, that isn't afraid of the dark, that lights a fire and dances around it."

21   One thing is clear: men need the support of other men to change, which is why activities like drumming aren't as dumb as they may look. Even though no words are exchanged, the men at these sessions get something from other men that they earnestly need: understanding and acceptance. "The solitude of men is the most difficult single thing to change," says Napier. These retreats provide cover for some spiritual reconnaissance too risky to attempt in the company of women. "It's like crying," says Michael Meade. "Men are afraid that if they start, they'll cry forever."

22   Does the search for a lineal sense of masculinity have any relevance to such thorny modern dilemmas as how to balance work and family or how to talk to women? Perhaps. Men have to feel comfortable with themselves before they can successfully confront such issues. This grounding is also critical for riding out the changes in pop culture and ideals. John Wayne and Alan Alda, like violence and passivity, reflect holes in a core that needs fixing. But men can get grounded in many ways, and male retreats provide just one stylized option, though not one necessarily destined to attract most American men.

23   What do men really want? To define themselves on their own terms, just as women began to do a couple of decades ago. "Would a women's group ask men if it was O.K. to feel a certain way?" asks Jerry Johnson, host of the San Francisco–based KCBS radio talk show *Man to Man*. "No way. We're still looking for approval from women for changes, and we need to get it from the male camp."

24   That's the point. And it does not have to come at women's expense. "It is stupid to conclude that the empowerment of women means the disempowerment of men," says Robert Moore, a psychoanalyst at the C. G. Jung Institute in Chicago. "Men must also feel good about being male." Men would do well, in fact, to invite women into their lives to participate in these changes. It's no fun to face them alone. But if women can't or won't, men must act on their own and damn the torpedoes. No pain, no gain.

■ TOPICAL CONSIDERATIONS

1. According to the author, what changes have taken place in the role models men look up to? What has caused these changes? Do Allis's claims here jive with your own observations. How or how not?

2. How, according to Allis, have men reacted to these changing role models? How do you feel about these changing definitions of what it means to be a male in our society?

3. Who are some of the male role models you admire today? What traits do they have that are admirable? What traits do these men have in common? What can you generalize about the traits of the "90's" male?

4. Do you agree or disagree with Allis when he says in paragraph 9 that "men are defined by their performance in the workplace"? Why or why not?

5. How do you feel about Allis's comment in paragraph 11 about "trading income for 'quality time'"? Do you think that it is easier for women to do this than men? Do you think women *should* do this more often than men do? Explain your answers.

6. What does Allis mention as possible remedies to the dilemma of shifting definitions of what it means to be a male? What other solutions can you suggest?

7. In paragraph 2, Allis states that men are "airing their frustration with the limited roles they face today, compared with the multiple options that women seem to have won." Do you think that men's opportunities today are *more* limited than women's opportunities or *less* limited? Give examples to support your answer.

8. In paragraph 2, Allis contends that women have won "multiple options" as a result of the women's movement. What, in your opinion, have women won as a result of the women's movement? Which of these opportunities might men benefit from?

■ RHETORICAL CONSIDERATIONS

1. Look at the figurative language Allis uses in paragraphs 5 and 6 to describe different types of men. Do you think Allis accurately and fairly describes each type of man, or does his language suggest that he has a preference for some types over others?

2. Compare the tone of this essay to the tone Ebeling uses in her article. How are they the same? How are they different? What accounts for these similarities and/or differences?

3. How is the information in this essay organized? Do you think this organization is effective? Why or why not?

■ WRITING ASSIGNMENTS

1. Write an essay explaining what you think men really want. Draw from the men you know, as well as the information in Allis's article to flesh out your essay.

2. Gather together all of the solutions the class suggested for question 6 in Topical Considerations. Write an essay about solutions to the male

dilemma, using the class's information as well as your own. Think about what would be the best combination of actions to help resolve this dilemma.

3. Allis, Farrell, and Ebeling all write about the difficulties of working for a living and raising a family at the same time. Write an essay that summarizes their various points of view about these difficulties. Then go on to explain your own views on this. Propose some solutions you think might ease at least some of the difficulties you talk about.

4. Ebeling uses examples from her own experience to support the points she is making in her article. Farrell and Allis use examples from the general society to support the points they are making. Which do you prefer to use when you write? Do you think that any essay would benefit from examples of personal experience being placed in it, or are there some kinds of writing that need to remain more formal? Explore this issue by thinking back over papers you have written and the uses you have made in these of personal experiences and of examples from more general society.

Conan and Me

Bill Persky

Sam Allis, in the previous essay, made the observation that the strong, stoic traditional ideal of masculinity has of late given way to a "tempered macho." That is, a man of strength and sensitivity—or, Arnold Schwarzenegger with feelings. What follows is an amusing but telling anecdote about such a man whose ideal of himself comes to the rescue at a dangerous moment. Mr. Persky's reflections on his behavior one fated night celebrate not just traditional male behavior but, ultimately, trust in oneself.

Bill Persky has been writing, directing and producing television shows for the last four decades. He is the winner of five Emmy awards. With Sam Danoff, he wrote and produced "The Dick Van Dyke Show," "That Girl," and "Kate & Allie," among others. His considerable talent for eliciting dramatic meaning from an incident is evident in this essay which originally appeared in *Esquire* magazine in May 1989.

1 Carl Reiner once said that he didn't believe Englishmen really had accents, they just all got together and agreed to talk that way to make the rest of us feel bad. The act was probably rooted in feelings of inadequacy dating back to their origin as druids who were still running around painted blue long after everyone else had moved on to cooked food and world conquest. Carl believed that if, at three in the morning, you crept into a room where an Englishman was sleeping and shouted "*Fire!*" he would wake in panic and say, "*Fire! Let's get the hell out of here!*" with no accent whatsoever.

2   Though I would gladly lose my New York accent under any circumstance, I have some images of myself that I'd like to think are real. And I have wondered how they would hold up if Carl crept into my room some night and sounded the alarm. I know who I would *like* to be in that rude awakening: I'd grab the kids and the cat and lead everyone in the building to safety, all with the calm, clear voice that I've already selected from several I've tried out in the shower. But I've always known that if that moment came, no matter what I may have hoped or planned, there would be only me, the real me, the one I doubt, question, and hide from the world and, with less success, from myself.

3   My moment came one morning last summer. It wasn't 3:00 A.M. but sometime after 5:00, and it wasn't Carl's shout of "Fire!" but the muffled thumping of a man climbing through my bedroom window. Instantly I found out who I was: an unlikely combination of Arnold Schwarzenegger and my mother.

4   I am still not sure who was the most effective as I leapt naked from my bed, grabbing the first weapon at hand, my pillow, and went on the attack, screaming, "*Get out! Get out!*" in a high-pitched voice. I resented my mother speaking for me at a time like that, and I consciously tried to get into a lower register, but it was her moment, and I couldn't take it away from her.

5   Schwarzenegger was doing a lot better, and I was pleased with him. He was actually engaged in hand-to-hand combat with an intruder who was three-quarters of the way into my room. The window opened only a foot and a half, being held in place by a dowel I had inserted between the top and the frame to prevent anyone from climbing in. I made a note to get a longer pole if I lived.

6   The struggle raged as my burglar (we'd known each other long enough at this point for some familiarity) was pushing against a flower box to come the rest of the way in, and I was pushing and swinging my pillow to get him out. I needed a more formidable weapon. Actually, it was right there on the night table, but in my initial panic I had missed it—*The Bonfire of the Vanities*. Hitting him with that would have done major damage *and* made some kind of social comment.

7   Since the narrow opening was preventing either of us from making any headway, we were at a stalemate. My warrior self suddenly perceived with Zen clarity that if I removed the pole, I could open the window fully and my chances of getting him all the way out would improve. The thought that it would improve his chance of getting all the way in didn't occur to me. That's the trouble with Zen, it's so self-involved. I emitted a fierce yell borrowed from a sushi chef and yanked the pole free. Suddenly the tide of battle turned in my favor, as he was now up against a naked maniac with a pole instead of a pillow, and my mother switched from "Get out! Get out!" to a more macho "*You son of a bitch!*"

8   The combination must have been awesome, because he started to plead in what I am sure was his mother's voice, "*Don't hurt me! Don't hurt me!*" Don't hurt him? The thought never entered my mind, but as long as he brought it up, I considered it as an option. I could use the new upper-body strength I'd developed at the Vertical Club to knock him senseless. Originally I'd planned on using it to improve my serve. The struggle intensified until somehow his mother and my mother got to talking, as mothers will, and "Don't hurt me, Don't hurt me" seemed like a good idea all around. So I gave him a

shove that wasn't needed to get him out and covered his escape over the wall with a hail of four-letter words, finally finding the voice I'd practice for the occasion.

9   I closed and locked the window, drew the drapes, and stood waiting. I wasn't sure for what, probably to go into shock or some other reaction that comes when danger is past. This was only the second real fight I ever had. The first was fifty years ago in the third grade when Jerry Matz challenged me to meet him after school for reasons I can't for the life of me recall, but I think it was about who was going to marry Nina Yanoff. What I do remember is that I was nauseated all day and cried throughout the fight and even after I had won. Now here I was, not crying, not even breathing hard. I settled for calling the police. I felt it was the responsible thing to do, and I was dying to tell somebody.

10   My burglar and I are now just another crime statistic along with the other apartment on Sixty-second Street that was burglarized that night while the occupants slept. The police are sure it was my burglar after he left me, so apparently our encounter had little impact on his life. But it's had a very profound effect on mine. I've made the obvious adjustments of sleeping in shorts, keeping the fireplace poker next to my bed, and getting bars for the windows. (That information is for my mother, whom I never told about the incident but who will probably read this, and I wouldn't want her to worry.)

11   On a less obvious but more meaningful level, the incident has changed the way I see myself in Carl's hypothesis. At the core I am tougher and braver than I knew. Even with the high-pitched voice, I really like the guy I turned out to be. I'd like to be that guy more often, and I think I know why I'm not. It isn't a question of courage but *clarity,* and the freedom that comes when you know you're right. In our daily lives things are never as clear-cut as someone coming through our bedroom window. They're vague or oblique, and our first instinct waits as we filter through too much information and conditioning. We lose that initial impulse that's pure us.

12   My burglar probably had a lousy childhood and was from a deprived racial or economic group. He might have been a terrific kid with all kinds of potential who never had a chance. In retrospect he might have been the real victim. But that night he was coming through my bedroom window, and one thing was crystal clear—he didn't belong there. So I was free to act as who I really am. It was a great feeling, one I would like to hold on to, trust, and go with. Every day there are less obvious intruders coming through the windows of my spirit and my soul, and they don't belong there either. So let them beware: Arnold and my mother are waiting.

■ **TOPICAL CONSIDERATIONS**

    1. Explain what Carl Reiner meant when he said that he "didn't believe Englishmen really had accents, they just all got together and agreed to talk that way to make the rest of us feel bad." How might a British accent make an American feel bad about him- or herself? Do you have different responses to different kinds of accents? If so, do these responses reflect feelings you might have about yourself? Explain.

2. In paragraph 2, Persky says that if ever faced with an urgent situation "there would be only me, the real me, the one I doubt, question, and hide from the world and, with less success, from myself." What does this statement say about the kinds of behavior Persky attributes to "men" in dangerous situations? What kinds of demands and expectations are placed upon men by society? How are these expectations reinforced? Do these expectations—as well as those placed upon women—create the need for people to hide their real selves from the world? Explain.

3. When Persky describes his initial response to an intruder he calls himself "an unlikely combination of Arnold Schwarzenegger and my [Persky's] mother." What do you take these two referents, in combination, to signify about Persky? How does Persky's choice of models here correspond to the stereotypes he is exposing in the piece?

4. In her essay "Masculine/Feminine," Prudence Mackintosh considers the question of whether sex-role differences are biological and essential or culturally induced. Compare her conclusions with Persky's here. On which side of the debate do these authors fall? Are their positions compatible at all? Do you believe that sex-role differences are determined biologically or culturally? Explain.

■ RHETORICAL CONSIDERATIONS

1. How effective is the opening Reiner quote? In what way does this introductory paragraph set up the tone and content of the rest of the piece? Explain.

2. From the information provided, what do you know about the narrator? Is he reliable—one with whom you find yourself identifying? If so, point to specific places where you feel Persky has made his narrator particularly accessible. Do you feel that the perspective from which the essay is narrated is in keeping with the content of the piece? Explain.

3. Part of the point of this essay is that men are culturally conditioned to act in ways corresponding to sex-role stereotypes. What kind of clues—in the form of cultural artifacts—does Persky drop regarding his own cultural conditioning? What function do these clues have on reader response to Persky's argument?

4. Reread Persky's concluding paragraph. How would you summarize this conclusion in relation to the main thrust of the argument? In your opinion, does it work effectively to close the piece? Explain.

■ WRITING ASSIGNMENTS

1. Write an essay in which you consider your own sense of cultural conditioning. How do you feel your behavior has been conditioned by sex-role expectations? Is there a gap between the "real" you and the affectations you take on as a means of survival in contemporary culture?

2. Write a first-person narrative of a situation where your actions were based upon the demands of sex-role conditioning—or a situation in which you were able to shed your cultural conditioning, as Persky did when confronted by an intruder.
3. Conduct interviews with at least five other students regarding the force of sex-role conditioning. You might ask them what role such conditioning plays in their lives and what are its sources in popular culture; also, what are their feelings as to the pros and cons derived from such conditioning? Then write a report of your findings.
4. Write an essay in which you explore the terms *masculine* and *feminine*. You might undertake library research as to the origins of the words—their derivations and original connotations—or research their changing implications over the years (the word masculine had a meaning in 1600 very different from that of today—see Sam Allis's preceding piece, "What Do Men Really Want?").

Multicultural America

America is a union predicated on like-minded moral values, political and economic self-interest, and a common tongue. But lest we forget, America is also a nation of immigrants—people of different races, ethnic identities, religions, and languages. It is a nation whose motto *e pluribus unum* ("one out of many") bespeaks the pride in its multicultural heritage.

We have divided the essays in this chapter into two groups: Ethnic Identity and Taking a Stand. The five essays in the first group are accounts of personal experiences written by individuals with different ethnic and racial identities—people who when caught between two cultures, have experienced prejudice, social conflicts, and a search for roots. The chapter's final five essays, the second group, are arguments centered around cultural conflicts arising out of the growing diversity of American society.

Our opening piece, "Getting to Know About You and Me," clearly illustrates the dangerous kind of ignorance that many people suffer when it comes to other people's religions. Although she was with 20 other scholarship students representing eight different religions, Chana Schoenberger was astounded to learn that the only Jews some people knew were those from the Bible.

The next selection examines how some Hispanic-Americans—the fastest growing minority in America today—deal with the pressures of assimilation. In "Your Parents Must Be Very Proud," Richard Rodriguez makes it clear that he yearned for Americanization. Embarrassed by his poor command of English when he first entered school, he tells of how he quickly grasped onto opportunities his parents never had as Mexican immigrants—opportunities that would later distance him from his heritage.

The next essay is a subdued protest against the stereotype that casts all black men as villains. Brent Staples captures the pain and isolation he has endured since first discovering, at "the ripe old age of twenty-two," that his mere presence in public places can arouse fear and suspicion in others.

For Asian-Americans, the problems of being a minority are no different from those other ethnic, people experience as we see in the subsequent essay. "To Be an All-American Girl" is the powerful memoir of Elizabeth Wong who made every effort to deny her Chinese roots. While her family insisted that she go to Chinese school, Wong was too caught up in assimilating the greater culture, at a cost she would only comprehend years later.

Lots of people, black and white, had trouble with Itabari Njeri's name. Some couldn't pronounce it. Others wanted to know what her *real* name was. Others still were disappointed to learn that behind the exotic name was just another "home-town Negro" from Brooklyn who refused to go by her "slave name." In "What's in a Name?" Njeri examines the significance of racial labels and names in the context of African-Americans whose real names nobody knows.

By the next century, one-third of our nation will be made up of people of color. In many states, African-Americans, Hispanic-Americans, Asian-Americans and Native Americans will comprise the majority of the population. In the next essay, "America: The Multinational Society," Ishmael Reed surveys the rapidly changing complexion of the contemporary American landscape. Instead of fearing the changes, he argues, we should embrace them as they can only make us stronger as a nation.

Although America has been a multiethnic and multiracial society since its founding, it was not until the last three decades that different groups of Americans began to reassert their ethnic and racial identity. In their search for roots African-Americans and Native Americans, Latinos, and Latvians alike have looked with pride to their heritage to distinguish themselves from the mainstream. But to some people the emphasis on racial and ethnic identification is excessive, even dangerous. In "The Cult of Ethnicity, Good and Bad," the respected historian Arthur M. Schlesinger, Jr. argues that ethnic and racial separatism in America has been pushed too far.

According to some critics of multiculturalism all the celebration of differentness has created a heightened sensitivity to offense. In the essay, "Come, Let Me Offend You," Eve Drobot argues that it is difficult to make conversation nowadays without saying something that's politically incorrect, that doesn't hurt the feelings of some "special interest" group—whether Muslim, Jew, Christian, or vegetarian. As a result, simple conversation has become stifled.

The essay, "Why I Dread Black History Month," is a complaint against one of the consequences of cultural separatism in multicultural America. As suggested by the title, Wayne M. Joseph does not celebrate his heritage with the rest of the black community every February. On the contrary, to Joseph, Black History Month is "a thriving monument to tokenism." Black contributions to American history, he argues, are too vast and varied to be squeezed into a four-week celebration. Furthermore, black history is not separate from American history. It is American history.

The final piece, "Race Matters," is a call to "invigorate the common good" in American society. Putting into perspective the problems of race, prominent scholar and author, Cornel West, argues that blacks are not "a problem people" as is traditionally viewed by liberals and conservatives alike but fellow citizens with problems. And as long as we deny our commonalities and allow racial injustice and double standards to persist, the problems will continue to fester. Pointing to the 1992 Los Angeles riots and the Rodney King case, West maintains that we must as a nation put an end to racial hierarchy and concern ourselves with ensuring access to basic social goods—housing, jobs, education, and health care—for all people. Or, as a nation, we are doomed.

Getting to Know About You and Me

Chana Schoenberger

By definition, stereotypes are erroneous assumptions about individuals based on their race, ethnic descent, religion, social class, gender, physical appearance, and so forth. Forged by ignorance and fear, stereotypes damningly reduce whole groups of people to certain ascribed characteristics so as to justify their presumed faults. Jews are materialistic, blacks are lazy, Latins are hot-tempered, Asians are mysterious, Native Americans are stoical, French are oversexed, Irish are drunks. Not only are such caricatures simplistic impositions on others, they restrict and distort our expectations of the victims. The first essay in this chapter is a young woman's account of religious ignorance in action. As Chana Schoenberger explains, even the smartest students in a summer scholarship program thought Jews still practiced animal sacrifice.

This essay first appeared in *Newsweek* (September 1993) when Chana Schoenberger was a high-school student in Bethesda, Maryland.

1   As a religious holiday approaches, students at my high school who will be celebrating the holiday prepare a presentation on it for an assembly. The Diversity Committee, which sponsors the assemblies to increase religious awareness, asked me last spring if I would help with the presentation on Passover, the Jewish holiday that commemorates the Exodus from Egypt. I was too busy with other things, and I never got around to helping. I didn't realize then how important those presentations really are, or I definitely would have done something.

2   This summer I was one of 20 teens who spent five weeks at the University of Wisconsin at Superior studying acid rain with a National Science Foundation Young Scholars program. With such a small group in such a small town, we soon became close friends and had a good deal of fun together. We learned about the science of acid rain, went on field trips, found the best and cheapest restaurants in Superior and ate in them frequently to escape the lousy cafeteria food. We were a happy, bonded group.

3   Represented among us were eight religions: Jewish, Roman Catholic, Muslim, Hindu, Methodist, Mormon, Jehovah's Witness and Lutheran. It was amazing, given the variety of backgrounds, to see the ignorance of some of the smartest young scholars on the subject of other religions.

4   On the first day, one girl mentioned that she had nine brothers and sisters. "Oh, are you Mormon?" asked another girl, who I knew was a Mormon herself. The first girl, shocked, replied, "No, I dress normal!" She thought Mormon was the same as Mennonite, and the only thing she knew about either religion was that Mennonites don't, in her opinion, "dress normal."

5   My friends, ever curious about Judaism, asked me about everything from our basic theology to food preferences. "How come, if Jesus was a Jew, Jews aren't Christian?" my Catholic roommate asked me in all seriousness. Brought up in a

small Wisconsin town, she had never met a Jew before, nor had she met people from most of the other "strange" religions (anything but Catholic or mainstream Protestant). Many of the other kids were the same way.

6   "Do you all still practice animal sacrifices?" a girl from a small town in Minnesota asked me once. I said no, laughed, and pointed out that this was the 20th century, but she had been absolutely serious. The only Jews she knew were the ones from the Bible.

7   Nobody was deliberately rude or anti-Semitic, but I got the feeling that I was representing the entire Jewish people through my actions. I realized that many of my friends would go back to their small towns thinking that all Jews liked Dairy Queen Blizzards and grilled cheese sandwiches. After all, that was true of all the Jews they knew (in most cases, me and the only other Jewish young scholar, period).

8   The most awful thing for me, however, was not the benign ignorance of my friends. Our biology professor had taken us on a field trip to the EPA field site where he worked, and he was telling us about the project he was working on. He said that they had to make sure the EPA got its money's worth from the study—he "wouldn't want them to get Jewed."

9   I was astounded. The professor had a doctorate, various other degrees and seemed to be a very intelligent man. He apparently had no idea that he had just made an anti-Semitic remark. The other Jewish girl in the group and I debated whether or not to say something to him about it, and although we agreed we would, neither of us ever did. Personally, it made me feel uncomfortable. For a high-school student to tell a professor who taught her class that he was a bigot seemed out of place to me, even if he was one.

10   What scares me about that experience, in fact about my whole visit to Wisconsin, was that I never met a really vicious anti-Semite or a malignantly preju- diced person. Many of the people I met had been brought up to think that Jews (or Mormons or any other religion that's not mainstream Christian) were different and that difference was not good.

11   Difference, in America, is supposed to be good. We are expected—at least, I always thought we were expected—to respect each other's traditions. Respect re- quires some knowledge about people's backgrounds. Singing Christmas carols as a kid in school did not make me Christian, but it taught me to appreciate beauti- ful music and someone else's holiday. It's not necessary or desirable for all ethnic groups in America to assimilate into one traditionless mass. Rather, we all need to learn about other cultures so that we can understand one another and not feel threat- ened by others.

12   In the little multicultural universe that I live in, it's safe not to worry about ex- plaining the story of Passover because if people don't hear it from me, they'll hear it some other way. Now I realize that's not true everywhere.

13   Ignorance was the problem I faced this summer. By itself, ignorance is not always a problem, but it leads to misunderstandings, prejudice and hatred. Many of today's problems involve hatred. If there weren't so much ignorance about other people's backgrounds, would people still hate each other as badly as they do now? Maybe so, but at least that hatred would be based on facts and not flawed beliefs.

14   I'm not back at school, and I plan to apply for the Diversity Committee. I'm going to get up and tell the whole school about my religion and the tradition I'm proud of. I see now how important it is to celebrate your heritage and to educate others about it. I can no longer take for granted that everyone knows about my religion, or that I know about theirs. People who are suspicious when they find out I'm Jewish usually don't know much about Judaism. I would much prefer them to hate or distrust me because of something I've done, instead of them hating me on the basis of prejudice.

■ TOPICAL CONSIDERATIONS

1. What kinds of misconceptions did Schoenberger's friends at the National Science Foundation Young Scholars program have about people of different religions? Did you find yourself laughing at any of the mistakes they made? Do the questions they ask seem to be determined by the religion of the person asking the question?

2. How did members of the eight religious groups respond to each other's questions? That is, were they tolerant, intolerant, sarcastic, belligerent, or other? Have you ever asked, or responded to, a question about religion (or race, or ethnicity, or nationality)? If so, what kinds of feelings did you have about the question or the response?

3. Why is Schoenberger so shocked at her professor's statement that he didn't want the EPA "to get Jewed"? Why is this statement different from the kinds of discussions she has had with other young scholars?

4. Do all Jews like Dairy Queen Blizzards and grilled cheese sandwiches? If not, why does Schoenberger seem concerned that her friends from the program will believe this statement? Is she worried about something more than food here? Have you ever been in a situation where your own unique qualities have been taken to mean something about a group of people?

5. Where does Schoenberger finally explain the issue she raised in paragraph 1, about the importance of her high school's presentation of the Passover celebration? Why does she say it is important? What good does she think it will do?

■ RHETORICAL CONSIDERATIONS

1. Why does Schoenberger move from innocuous, silly comments at the beginning of her article to more serious problems? How does this strategy shape her characterizations of friends and her biology professor? How does this strategy affect the way audiences are likely to respond to the article?

2. Schoenberger says little about religious observances or beliefs—how people worship, or what they believe. Why does she say so little about religious practices, and so much about peripheral, cultural stereotypes (dress, number

of children, attitudes toward money)? How would her article have been different if she had focused on, say, the meaning of the Passover Seder and other Jewish observances?

3. Why does Schoenberger spend so much time emphasizing the intelligence of her friends in the Young Scholars program? How would this article have been different if she had been describing, say, a group of young people on parole for minor offenses, or students in a remedial class, or honor-roll nerds?

4. Do you think Schoenberger's article has a thesis? Or is it a personal experience narrative without a thesis? What do you think the thesis, or the purpose for this narrative, is? Why do you think Schoenberger does not state it forthrightly?

■ WRITING ASSIGNMENTS

1. Imagine that someone from an entirely different country (or even a different planet) has come to your classroom to study Americans. This visitor will base his or her entire set of impressions on the information and observations possible in only one class session. What kind of an idea do you think the visitor would have of Americans? Do you think the visitor might get any misimpressions? In a paper, capture this visitor's impressions.

2. Using your telephone directory, and your school's resources (such as spiritual counseling, worship or support groups for students of a specific religion, chaplaincy, religious studies faculty member), identify a local meeting or worship service of a group to which you do not belong, but at which you would be welcome. This might be a mass, a Passover Seder, or a study group. Write a report on your visit. What did you find familiar? What was new and different to you?

3. Choose a religion about which you know very little. Before you begin the assignment, write a list of things you know about people who practice this religion, and about the beliefs they hold. Then, using your school's library resources, find as complete a description as possible about practices and beliefs. If possible, try to find members of the religious group you can interview. Compare your findings to your original list. What were you able to confirm? What turned out to be false or incomplete?

4. Using your library's resources, locate some contemporary discussions of how and why study of the Holocaust—the extermination of 6 million Jews under Nazi rule in Germany during the second World War—must be continued. You may wish to focus on historical scholarship, the creation of museums and monuments or even on allegations raised in the last few years that the Holocaust never really happened. What role does anti-Semitism play in contemporary discussions?

Your Parents Must Be Very Proud

Richard Rodriguez

Although he was born and raised in California, Richard Rodriguez knew almost no English when he entered grade school. His parents were Mexican immigrants who spoke Spanish almost exclusively at home. Linguistically handicapped, he entered grammar school and the English-speaking world. Yearning for total assimilation in the dominant culture, Rodriguez flourished as a student in the American system. And he made his parents very proud. But, as he explains in the poignant memoir below, that personal success came at a cost to the cultural identity and the closeness he once shared with his family. Richard Rodriguez, who holds degrees from Stanford, Columbia, and the University of California at Berkeley, is an editor at Pacific News Service in San Francisco. In addition to teaching college English, Rodriguez has written several articles for the Saturday Review, American Scholar, Change, and other magazines. This essay was taken from his autobiography, Hunger of Memory (1982). His latest book is Mexico's Children (1992).

1   "Your parents must be very proud of you." People began to say that to me about the time I was in sixth grade. To answer affirmatively, I'd smile. Shyly I'd smile, never betraying my sense of the irony: I was not proud of my mother and father. I was embarrassed by their lack of education. It was not that I ever thought they were stupid, though stupidly I took for granted their enormous native intelligence. Simply, what mattered to me was that they were not like my teachers.

2   But, "Why didn't you tell us about the award?" my mother demanded, her frown weakened by pride. At the grammar school ceremony several weeks after, her eyes were brighter than the trophy I'd won. Pushing back the hair from my forehead, she whispered that I had "shown" the *gringos*. A few minutes later, I heard my father speak to my teacher and felt ashamed of his labored, accented words. Then guilty for the shame. I felt such contrary feelings. (There is no simple roadmap through the heart of the scholarship boy.) My teacher was so soft-spoken and her words were edged sharp and clean. I admired her until it seemed to me that she spoke too carefully. Sensing that she was condescending to them, I became nervous. Resentful. Protective. I tried to move my parents away. "You both must be very proud of Richard," the nun said. They responded quickly. (They were proud.) "We are proud of all our children." Then this afterthought: "They sure didn't get their brains from us." They all laughed. I smiled.

3   Tightening the irony into a knot was the knowledge that my parents were always behind me. They made success possible. They evened the path. They sent their children to parochial schools because the nuns "teach better." They paid a tuition they couldn't afford. They spoke English to us.

4   For their children my parents wanted chances they never had—an easier way. It saddened my mother to learn that some relatives forced their children to start working right after high school. To *her* children she would say, "Get all the education you

can." In schooling she recognized the key to job advancement. And with the remark she remembered her past.

5   As a girl new to America my mother had been awarded a high school diploma by teachers too careless or busy to notice that she hardly spoke English. On her own, she determined to learn how to type. That skill got her jobs typing envelopes in letter shops, and it encouraged in her an optimism about the possibility of advancement. (Each morning when her sisters put on uniforms, she chose a bright-colored dress.) The years of young womanhood passed, and her typing speed increased. She also became an excellent speller of words she mispronounced. "And I've never been to college," she'd say, smiling, when her children asked her to spell words they were too lazy to look up in a dictionary.

6   Typing, however, was dead-end work. Finally frustrating. When her youngest child started high school, my mother got a full-time office job once again. (Her pay-check combined with my father's to make us—in fact—what we had already become in our imagination of ourselves—middle class.) She worked then for the (California) state government in numbered civil service positions secured by examinations. The old ambition of her youth was rekindled. During the lunch hour, she consulted bulletin boards for announcements of openings. One day she saw mention of something called an "anti-poverty agency." A typing job. A glamorous job, part of the governor's staff. "A knowledge of Spanish required." Without hesitation she applied and became nervous only when the job was suddenly hers.

7   "Everyone comes to work all dressed up," she reported at night. And didn't need to say more than that her co-workers wouldn't let her answer the phones. She was only a typist, after all, albeit a very fast typist. And an excellent speller. One morning there was a letter to be sent to a Washington cabinet officer. On the dictating tape, a voice referred to urban guerrillas. My mother typed (the wrong word, correctly): "gorillas." The mistake horrified the anti-poverty bureaucrats who shortly after arranged to have her returned to her previous position. She would go no further. So she willed her ambition to her children. "Get all the education you can; with an education you can do anything." (With a good education *she* could have done anything.)

8   When I was in high school, I admitted to my mother that I planned to become a teacher someday. That seemed to please her. But I never tried to explain that it was not the occupation of teaching I yearned for as much as it was something more elusive: I wanted to *be* like my teachers, to possess their knowledge, to assume their authority, their confidence, even to assume a teacher's persona.

9   In contrast to my mother, my father never verbally encouraged his children's academic success. Nor did he often praise us. My mother had to remind him to "say something" to one of his children who scored some academic success. But whereas my mother saw in education the opportunity for job advancement, my father recognized that education provided an even more startling possibility: It could enable a person to escape from a life of mere labor.

10   In Mexico, orphaned when he was eight, my father left school to work as an "apprentice" for an uncle. Twelve years later, he left Mexico in frustration and arrived in America. He had great expectations then of becoming an engineer. ("Work for my hands and my head.") He knew a Catholic priest who promised to get him money

enough to study full time for a high school diploma. But the promises came to nothing. Instead there was a dark succession of warehouse, cannery, and factory jobs. After work he went to night school along with my mother. A year, two passed. Nothing much changed, except that fatigue worked its way into the bone; then everything changed. He didn't talk anymore of becoming an engineer. He stayed outside on the steps of the school while my mother went inside to learn typing and shorthand.

11   By the time I was born, my father worked at "clean" jobs. For a time he was a janitor at a fancy department store. ("Easy work; the machines do it all.") Later he became a dental technician. ("Simple.") But by then he was pessimistic about the ultimate meaning of work and the possibility of ever escaping its claims. In some of my earliest memories of him, my father already seems aged by fatigue. (He has never really grown old like my mother.) From boyhood to manhood, I have remembered him in a single image: seated, asleep on the sofa, his head thrown back in a hideous corpselike grin, the evening newspaper spread out before him. "But look at all you've accomplished," his best friend said to him once. My father said nothing. Only smiled.

12   It was my father who laughed when I claimed to be tired by reading and writing. It was he who teased me for having soft hands. (He seemed to sense that some great achievement of leisure was implied by my papers and books.) It was my father who became angry while watching on television some woman at the Miss America contest tell the announcer that she was going to college. ("Majoring in fine arts.") "College!" he snarled. He despised the trivialization of higher education, the inflated grades and cheapened diplomas, the half education that so often passed as mass education in my generation.

13   It was my father again who wondered why I didn't display my awards on the wall of my bedroom. He said he liked to go to doctors' offices and see their certificates and degrees on the wall. ("Nice.") My citations from school got left in closets at home. The gleaming figure astride one of my trophies was broken, wingless, after hitting the ground. My medals were placed in a jar of loose change. And when I lost my high school diploma, my father found it as it was about to be thrown out with the trash. Without telling me, he put it away with his own things for safekeeping.

14   These memories slammed together at the instant of hearing that refrain familiar to all scholarship students: "Your parents must be very proud. . . ." Yes, my parents were proud. I knew it. But my parents regarded my progress with more than mere pride. They endured my early precocious behavior—but with what private anger and humiliation? As their children got older and would come home to challenge ideas both of them held, they argued before submitting to the force of logic or superior factual evidence with the disclaimer. "It's what we were taught in our time to believe." These discussions ended abruptly, though my mother remembered them on other occasions when she complained that our "big ideas" were going to our heads. More acute was her complaint that the family wasn't close anymore, like some others she knew. Why weren't we close, "more in the Mexican style"? Everyone is so private, she added. And she mimicked the yes and no answers she got in reply to her questions. Why didn't we talk more? (My father never asked.) I never said.

15   I was the first in my family who asked to leave home when it came time to go to college. I had been admitted to Stanford, one hundred miles away. My departure would only make physically apparent the separation that had occurred long before. But it was going too far. In the months preceding my leaving, I heard the question my mother never asked except indirectly. In the hot kitchen, tired at the end of her workday, she demanded to know, "Why aren't the colleges here in Sacramento good enough for you? They are for your brother and sister." In the middle of a car ride, not turning to face me, she wondered, "Why do you need to go so far away?" Late at night, ironing, she said with disgust, "Why do you have to put us through this big expense? You know your scholarship will never cover it all." But when September came there was a rush to get everything ready. In a bedroom that last night I packed the big brown valise, and my mother sat nearby sewing initials onto the clothes I would take. And she said no more about my leaving.

16   Months later, two weeks of Christmas vacation: The first hours home were the hardest. ("What's new?") My parents and I sat in the kitchen for a conversation. (But, lacking the same words to develop our sentences and to shape our interests, what was there to say? What could I tell them of the term paper I had just finished on the "universality of Shakespeare's appeal"?) I mentioned only small, obvious things: my dormitory life; weekend trips I had taken; random events. They responded with news of their own. (One was almost grateful for a family crisis about which there was much to discuss.) We tried to make our conversation seem like more than an interview.

■ TOPICAL CONSIDERATIONS

1. Summarize Rodriguez's conflicting feelings in the essay. When have you felt a similar conflict? With family? Friends?
2. Compare the parents in the Rodriguez essay to those in the Elizabeth Wong piece that follows later in this chapter. Are their similarities cross-cultural?
3. Education has several meanings in the essay. Compare the author's view of education to his mother's and his father's. Which view do you most agree with?
4. The author's mother complains in paragraph 14 "that the family wasn't close anymore." What has broken the family apart? What role does culture play in this?

■ RHETORICAL CONSIDERATIONS

1. Rodriguez admits in paragraph 1, "I was not proud of my mother and father." Though he never states that he becomes proud of his parents, what phrases, if any, imply that as he grew older, he changed his mind?
2. Explain the metaphor in paragraph 2: "There is no simple roadmap through the heart of the scholarship boy."

3. The subject of Rodriguez's freshman English paper was the "universality of Shakespeare's appeal." Consider the author's relationship with his parents. What is ironic about his paper topic?

4. The beginning of paragraph 3 states, "Tightening the irony into a knot was the knowledge that my parents were always behind me." Link this statement to the essay's title and fully explain the irony that pervades the essay.

5. What do "soft hands" (paragraph 12), "high school diploma" (paragraph 10) mean to the author's father? How do these reflect the fact that the author's "father never verbally encouraged his children's academic success" (paragraph 9)?

6. Comment on the conclusion of the essay. Is it climactic? True to life? Effective?

■ WRITING ASSIGNMENTS

1. Rodriguez in paragraph 5 writes, "As a girl new to America my mother had been awarded a high school diploma by teachers too careless or busy to notice that she hardly spoke English." Do you believe that language is power? Consider the Rodriguez essay and, perhaps, Elizabeth Wong's essay. Write a paper that develops your own view of the power of language in light of these two authors.

2. Several of the essays in this chapter are written from first-person retrospective. Much of what the authors have learned from looking back on their childhoods is concealed in subtle endings and implied hurts. Write a paper that traces this narrative perspective in three essays. Discuss the effectiveness of this approach and explain any weaknesses this point of view has.

3. Considering your own race, class, and ethnicity, write a first-person retrospective of your own. In your essay, tell what particular endings and hurts you have felt and what lessons you have learned from them.

4. In paragraph 12, Rodriguez says of his father, "He despised the trivialization of higher education, the inflated grades and cheapened diplomas, the half education that so often passed as mass education in my generation." Is this a fair assessment of education in the United States as you've experienced it? Write a paper in which you compare the father's viewpoint of education to your own. Consider socioeconomic backgrounds.

5. Professional literature in education has, in the last few decades, included discussions about the ways that a college education can drive a wedge between parents and children, or can distance graduates from their community of origin. Using your library's news resources and professional journal literature, discuss this phenomenon among students who are the first generation in their family to attend college; minority students; or students who identify themselves as working class. You may also want to ask your school's academic advising counselor, or school of education faculty, for additional insights or leads.

<table>
<tr><td>

Black Men and Public Space

</td></tr>
<tr><td>

Brent Staples

</td></tr>
</table>

Brent Staples, born in Chester, Pennsylvania, in 1951, is an editor at the *New York Times*. In the piece below, Staples tells of a shocking realization he had at the age of 22: that because he was a black male, he could "alter public space in ugly ways." Forever a suspect, Staples describes the alienation and danger he suffers from such a perception—a perception he has learned to deal with. This essay appeared in *Harper's* in December 1987.

1   My first victim was a woman—white, well dressed, probably in her early twenties. I came upon her late one evening on a deserted street in Hyde Park, a relatively affluent neighborhood in an otherwise mean, impoverished section of Chicago. As I swung onto the avenue behind her, there seemed to be a discreet, uninflammatory distance between us. Not so. She cast back a worried glance. To her, the youngish black man—a broad six feet two inches with a beard and billowing hair, both hands shoved into the pockets of a bulky military jacket—seemed menacingly close. After a few more quick glimpses, she picked up her pace and was soon running in earnest. Within seconds she disappeared into a cross street.

2   That was more than a decade ago, I was twenty-two years old, a graduate student newly arrived at the University of Chicago. It was in the echo of that terrified woman's footfalls that I first began to know the unwieldy inheritance I'd come into—the ability to alter public space in ugly ways. It was clear that she thought of herself the quarry of a mugger, a rapist, or worse. Suffering a bout of insomnia, however, I was stalking sleep, not defenseless wayfarers. As a softy who is scarcely able to take a knife to a raw chicken—let alone hold one to a person's throat—I was surprised, embarrassed, and dismayed all at once. Her flight made me feel like an accomplice in tyranny. It also made it clear that I was indistinguishable from the muggers who occasionally seeped into the area from the surrounding ghetto. That first encounter, and those that followed, signified that a vast, unnerving gulf lay between nighttime pedestrians—particularly women—and me. And I soon gathered that being perceived as dangerous is a hazard in itself. I only needed to turn a corner into a dicey situation, or crowd some frightened, armed person in a foyer somewhere, or make an errant move after being pulled over by a policeman. Where fear and weapons meet—and they often do in urban America—there is always the possibility of death.

3   In that first year, my first away from my hometown, I was to become thoroughly familiar with the language of fear. At dark, shadowy intersections, I could cross in front of a car stopped at a traffic light and elicit the *thunk, thunk, thunk, thunk* of the driver—black, white, male, or female—hammering down the door locks. On less traveled streets after dark, I grew accustomed to but never comfortable with people crossing to the other side of the street rather than pass me. Then there were the standard unpleasantries with policemen, doormen, bouncers, cab-

drivers, and others whose business it is to screen out troublesome individuals *before* there is any nastiness.

4   I moved to New York nearly two years ago and I have remained an avid night walker. In central Manhattan, the near-constant crowd cover minimizes tense one-on-one street encounters. Elsewhere—in SoHo, for example, where sidewalks are narrow and tightly spaced buildings shut out the sky—things can get very taut indeed.

5   After dark, on the warrenlike streets of Brooklyn where I live, I often see women who fear the worst from me. They seem to have set their faces on neutral, and with their purse straps strung across their chests bandolier-style, they forge ahead as though bracing themselves against being tackled. I understand, of course, that the danger they perceive is not a hallucination. Women are particularly vulnerable to street violence, and young black males are drastically overrepresented among the perpetrators of that violence. Yet these truths are no solace against the kind of alienation that comes of being ever the suspect, a fearsome entity with whom pedestrians avoid making eye contact.

6   It is not altogether clear to me how I reached the ripe old age of twenty-two without being conscious of the lethality nighttime pedestrians attributed to me. Perhaps it was because in Chester, Pennsylvania, the small, angry industrial town where I came of age in the 1960s, I was scarcely noticeable against a backdrop of gang warfare, street knifings, and murders. I grew up one of the good boys, had perhaps a half-dozen fistfights. In retrospect, my shyness of combat has clear sources.

7   As a boy, I saw countless tough guys locked away; I have since buried several, too. They were babies, really—a teenage cousin, a brother of twenty-two, a childhood friend in his mid-twenties—all gone down in episodes of bravado played out in the streets. I came to doubt the virtues of intimidation early on. I chose, perhaps unconsciously, to remain a shadow—timid, but a survivor.

8   The fearsomeness mistakenly attributed to me in public places often has a perilous flavor. The most frightening of these confusions occurred in the late 1970s and early 1980s, when I worked as a journalist in Chicago. One day, rushing into the office of a magazine I was writing for with a deadline story in hand, I was mistaken for a burglar. The office manager called security and, with an ad hoc posse, pursued me through the labyrinthine halls, nearly to my editor's door. I had no way of proving who I was. I could only move briskly toward the company of someone who knew me.

9   Another time I was on assignment for a local paper and killing time before an interview. I entered a jewelry store on the city's affluent Near North Side. The proprietor excused herself and returned with an enormous red Doberman pinscher straining at the end of a leash. She stood, the dog extended toward me, silent to my questions, her eyes bulging nearly out of her head. I took a cursory look around, nodded, and bade her good night.

10   Relatively speaking, however, I never fared as badly as another black male journalist. He went to nearby Waukegan, Illinois, a couple of summers ago to work on a story about a murderer who was born there. Mistaking the reporter for the killer, police officers hauled him from his car at gunpoint and but for his press credentials

would probably have tried to book him. Such episodes are not uncommon. Black men trade tales like this all the time.

11   Over the years, I learned to smother the rage I felt at so often being taken for a criminal. Not to do so would surely have led to madness. I now take precautions to make myself less threatening. I move about with care, particularly late in the evening. I give a wide berth to nervous people on subway platforms during the wee hours, particularly when I have exchanged business clothes for jeans. If I happen to be entering a building behind some people who appear skittish, I may walk by, letting them clear the lobby before I return, so as not to seem to be following them. I have been calm and extremely congenial on those rare occasions when I've been pulled over by the police.

12   And on late-evening constitutionals I employ what has proved to be an excellent tension-reducing measure: I whistle melodies from Beethoven and Vivaldi and the more popular classical composers. Even steely New Yorkers hunching toward nighttime destinations seem to relax, and occasionally they even join in the tune. Virtually everybody seems to sense that a mugger wouldn't be warbling bright, sunny selections from Vivaldi's *Four Seasons*. It is my equivalent of the cowbell that hikers wear when they know they are in bear country.

■ TOPICAL CONSIDERATIONS

1. What did Staples's episode with the fleeing woman in Hyde Park make him realize? How did it make him feel?
2. Staples learns that his being a black male is perceived as a danger to others. How could this perception be a hazard to him? How has this perception actually been hazardous to him?
3. How does Staples's personal background explain his unawareness of the threat he posed to nighttime pedestrians?
4. How does Staples explain the submergence of his rage at being "taken for a criminal"?
5. What are some of the ways Staples has tried to mitigate the threat he poses to other night pedestrians? If you were Staples, would you resort to these strategies or not bother at all?
6. Does Staples describe attitudes and fears to which you can relate?

■ RHETORICAL CONSIDERATIONS

1. Comment on the effectiveness of the opening sentence of this essay. Why does Staples use the word "victim"? What is the woman a victim of?
2. Why does Staples choose to describe himself in the first paragraph?
3. Do you find any examples of humor in the essay? If so, do you think this humor adds to or detracts from the seriousness of the subject?

■ WRITING ASSIGNMENTS

1. Have you ever felt threatened by a person or persons on a street at night? Write a paper in which you describe the experience and the threat you felt.

2. Have you ever been aware of the threat you might have posed to strangers in public places? If so, describe how you might have been perceived in such circumstances.

3. If you were Staples, how would you feel knowing that you were perceived as dangerous? Could you imagine yourself going through the measures he does, just to make those around you feel at ease? Write out your thoughts in an essay.

4. Choose an African-American man who has recently been charged with criminal misconduct—for example, O.J. Simpson. Research discussions of the trial or public proceedings in news sources drawn from both mainstream and African-America media sources. What differences do you find in the descriptions offered about the man who has been accused? What, if any, protests were raised about the way his identity as a black man influenced public discussion and legal decisions? What do you think Staples would say about this portrayal, based on his experiences?

	# To Be an All-American Girl
	Elizabeth Wong

Like Richard Rodriguez, Elizabeth Wong experienced a cultural conflict with her immigrant parents. Like Rodriguez, her native tongue was a source of embarrassment for her. And like Rodriguez, she was too caught up with becoming all-American. The essay below briefly chronicles Ms. Wong's rejection of all things Chinese in her campaign to redefine herself—a success she seems to celebrate until the very last line. This essay first appeared in the *Los Angeles Times* in 1989.

1 It's still there, the Chinese school on Yale Street where my brother and I used to go. Despite the new coat of paint and the high wire fence, the school I knew 10 years ago remains remarkably, stoically the same.

2   Every day at 5 P.M., instead of playing with our fourth- and fifth-grade friends or sneaking out to the empty lot to hunt ghosts and animal bones, my brother and I had to go to Chinese school. No amount of kicking, screaming, or pleading could dissuade my mother, who was solidly determined to have us learn the language of our heritage.

3   Forcibly, she walked us the seven long, hilly blocks from our home to school, depositing our defiant tearful faces before the stern principal. My only memory of

him is that he swayed on his heels like a palm tree, and he always clasped his impatience twitching hands behind his back. I recognized him as a repressed maniacal child killer, and knew that if we ever saw his hands we'd be in big trouble.

4 We all sat in little chairs in an empty auditorium. The room smelled like Chinese medicine, an imported faraway mustiness. Like ancient mothballs or dirty closets. I hated that smell. I favored crisp new scents. Like the soft French perfume that my American teacher wore in public school.

5 There was a stage far to the right, flanked by an American flag and the flag of the Nationalist Republic of China, which was also red, white and blue but not as pretty.

6 Although the emphasis at the school was mainly language—speaking, reading, writing—the lessons always began with an exercise in politeness. With the entrance of the teacher, the best student would tap a bell and everyone would get up, kowtow, and chant, "Sing san ho," the phonetic for "How are you, teacher?"

7 Being ten years old, I had better things to learn than ideographs copied painstakingly in lines that ran right to left from the tip of a *moc but,* a real ink pen that had to be held in an awkward way if blotches were to be avoided. After all, I could do the multiplication tables, name the satellites of Mars, and write reports on "Little Women" and "Black Beauty." Nancy Drew, my favorite book heroine, never spoke Chinese.

8 The language was a source of embarrassment. More times than not, I had tried to disassociate myself from the nagging loud voice that followed me wherever I wandered in the nearby American supermarket outside Chinatown. The voice belonged to my grandmother, a fragile woman in her seventies who could outshout the best of the street vendors. Her humor was raunchy, her Chinese rhythmless, patternless. It was quick, it was loud, it was unbeautiful. It was not like the quiet, lilting romance of French or the gentle refinement of the American South. Chinese sounded pedestrian. Public.

9 In Chinatown, the comings and goings of hundreds of Chinese on their daily tasks sounded chaotic and frenzied. I did not want to be thought of as mad, as talking gibberish. When I spoke English, people nodded at me, smiled sweetly, said encouraging words. Even the people in my culture would cluck and say that I'd do well in life. "My, doesn't she move her lips fast," they would say, meaning that I'd be able to keep up with the world outside Chinatown.

10 My brother was even more fanatical than I about speaking English. He was especially hard on my mother, criticizing her, often cruelly, for her pidgin speech— smatterings of Chinese scattered like chop suey in her conversation. "It's not 'What it is,' Mom," he'd say in exasperation. "It's 'What *is* it, what *is* it, what *is* it!" Sometimes Mom might leave out an occasional "the" or "a," or perhaps a verb of being. He would stop her in midsentence: "Say it again, Mom. Say it right." When he tripped over his own tongue, he'd blame it on her: "See, Mom, it's all your fault. You set a bad example."

11 What infuriated my mother most was when my brother cornered her on her consonants, especially "r." My father had played a cruel joke on Mom by assigning her an American name that her tongue wouldn't allow her to say. No matter how hard she tried, "Ruth" always ended up "Luth" or "Roof."

12   After two years of writing with a *moc but* and reciting words with multiples of meanings, I finally was granted a cultural divorce. I was permitted to stop Chinese school.

13   I thought of myself as multicultural. I preferred tacos to egg rolls; I enjoyed Cinco de Mayo more than Chinese New Year.

14   At last, I was one of you; I wasn't one of them.

15   Sadly, I still am.

■ **TOPICAL CONSIDERATIONS**

1. This essay is written from a first-person retrospective viewpoint. What has Elizabeth Wong learned between the time she went to Chinese school and now?

2. What does language represent in the essay? Use specific passages in the essay to describe what language means to Wong, her brother, and her mother. Compare learning English to speaking Chinese to listening to French.

3. Much has been written in child psychology about the Maternal Voice and the comfort it brings. Elizabeth Wong describes the Grandmaternal Voice; but it is not comforting. How variously does Wong describe her grandmother's voice? What might it represent for the author?

4. The author writes that she hated the smell of "ancient mothballs or dirty closets," and she "favored new scents" (paragraph 4). How does her preference for *new scents* reflect the theme of the essay?

5. What does the author mean by "the phonetic for 'How are you, teacher?'" (paragraph 6)? How does this reflect the distance between the American and Chinese culture?

6. In paragraph 9, Wong writes, "Even the people in my culture would cluck and say that I'd do well in life." What is Wong's definition of *culture* in this statement and throughout the essay? Compare Wong's definition of culture to your own.

7. Are Wong's feelings toward Chinese school specific to Chinese-Americans? If not, what is universal about her feelings? Can you relate to her?

8. Discuss the theme of rejection in the essay. Take into consideration not just Elizabeth Wong's attitudes, but those of her father and brother.

■ **RHETORICAL CONSIDERATIONS**

1. At what point in the essay do we know how Elizabeth Wong really feels about her experience at Chinese school? Does this make the essay more effective?

2. What connotation do "pedestrian" and "public" have in paragraph 8? Explain.

3. In paragraph 10, Wong's brother corrects his mother, "It's not 'What it is,' Mom." Why is correct grammar so important to Elizabeth and her brother? Do you feel correct grammar is as important as the Wong's consider it to be?

4. Wong writes in paragraph 12, "I finally was granted a cultural divorce." Consider the literal meaning of divorce. What is the full implication of her statement?

5. Explain the simile in paragraph 10: "for her pidgin speech—smatterings of Chinese scattered like chop suey in her conversation."

■ WRITING ASSIGNMENTS

1. Wong in paragraph 13 writes, "I thought of myself as multicultural. I preferred tacos to egg rolls." Ishmael Reed describes our nation as a "cultural bouillabaisse." Think about your own multicultural experience in America. How much of it is rooted in food? Write a paper discussing the effect food has on cultural awareness.

2. Wong finishes her essay, "Sadly, I still am." Although she has Asian features, she feels completely American. Write a paper discussing one's social environment versus cultural heritage. Consider Wong's and Rodriguez's essays and your own experiences.

3. Write a paper discussing how the language barrier affects parent-child relationships. Consider how a parent's learning English as a second language might be a source of embarrassment for a child. If you have had any such experiences because of your own race or ethnicity, try to capture them in a paper.

4. Write a report on a special school in your community for an ethnic group of which you are not a member—for example, Chinese school, Hebrew school, an African-American academy, or any organization that instructs young people at least once a week. Use your school's minority affairs office, yellow pages, or community resources to identify the school; interview staff, parents, and pupils as available; and use your library's news resources, especially minority-community media, to find opinion and commentary on the mission and curriculum of similar schools.

What's in a Name?

Itabari Njeri

The author of this essay is a black woman born and raised in America. Early in her adult life she decided to change what she calls her "slave name" to Itabari Njeri. In this essay she explains why she adopted her African name, and how doing so changed her life. But her essay is more than an account of one woman's search for racial identity. It is an exploration of the importance of names, especially for black Americans whose ancestors were pulled from their homeland culture and forced into bondage under names slavemasters gave them.

Itabari Njeri is a distinguished journalist and winner of the 1990 American Book Award for her memoir, *Every Good-bye Ain't Gone*. Her essays on race and identity in an increasingly multicultural America have appeared in numerous newspapers. From 1986 to 1992 she was a staff writer for *Los Angeles Times Magazine* where this essay first appeared. Her latest book is *The Last Plantation*, (1995), an exploration of discrimination and identity in minority communities.

1 The decade was about to end when I started my first newspaper job. The seventies might have been the disco generation for some, but it was a continuation of the Black Power, post-civil rights era for me. Of course in some parts of America it was still the pre–civil rights era. And that was the part of America I wanted to explore. As a good reporter I needed a sense of the whole country, not just the provincial Northeast Corridor in which I was raised.

2 I headed for Greenville ("Pearl of the Piedmont"), South Carolina.

3 "*Wheeere,*" some people snarled, their nostrils twitching, their mouths twisted so their top lips went slightly to the right, the bottom ones way down and to the left, "did you get *that* name from?"

4 Itabiddy, Etabeedy. Etabeeree. Eat a berry. Mata Hari. Theda Bara. And one secretary in the office of the Greenville Urban League told her employer: "It's Ms. Idi Amin."

5 Then, and now, there are a whole bunch of people who greet me with: "Hi, Ita." They think "Bari" is my last name. Even when they don't, they still want to call me "Ita." When I tell them my first name is Itabari, they say, "Well, what do people call you for short?"

6 "They don't call me anything for short," I say. "The name is Itabari."

7 Sophisticated white people, upon hearing my name, approach me as would a cultural anthropologist finding a piece of exotica right in his own living room. This happens a lot, still, at cocktail parties.

8 "Oh, what an unusual and beautiful name. Where are you from?"

9 "Brooklyn," I say. I can see the disappointment in their eyes. Just another home-grown Negro.

10 Then there are other white people who, having heard my decidedly northeastern accent, will simply say, "What a lovely name," and smile knowingly, indicating that they saw Roots and understand.

11   Then there are others, black and white, who for different reasons take me through this number:

12   "What's your *real* name?"

13   "Itabari Njeri is my real, legal name," I explain.

14   "Okay, what's your original name?" they ask, often with eyes rolling, exasperation in their voices.

15   After Malcolm X, Muhammad Ali, Kareem Abdul-Jabbar, Ntozake Shange, and Kunta Kinte, who, I ask, should be exasperated by this question-and-answer game?

16   Nevertheless, I explain, "Because of slavery, black people in the Western world don't usually know their original names. What you really want to know is what my slave name was."

17   Now this is where things get tense. Four hundred years of bitter history, culture, and politics between blacks and whites in America is evoked by this one term, "slave name."

18   Some white people wince when they hear the phrase, pained and embarrassed by this reminder of their ancestors' inhumanity. Further, they quickly scrutinize me and conclude that mine was a post–Emancipation Proclamation birth. "You were never a slave."

19   I used to be reluctant to tell people my slave name unless I surmised that they wouldn't impose their cultural values on me and refuse to use my African name. I don't care anymore. When I changed my name, I changed my life, and I've been Itabari for more years now than I was Jill. Nonetheless, people will say: "Well, that's your *real* name, you were born in America and that's what I am going to call you." My mother tried a variation of this on me when I legalized my traditional African name. I respectfully made it clear to her that I would not tolerate it. Her behavior, and subsequently her attitude, changed.

20   But many black folks remain just as skeptical of my name as my mother was.

21   "You're one of those black people who changed their name, huh," they are likely to begin. "Well, I still got the old slave master's Irish name," said one man named O'Hare at a party. This man's defensive tone was a reaction to what I call the "blacker than thou" syndrome perpetrated by many black nationalists in the sixties and seventies. Those who reclaimed their African names made blacks who didn't do the same thing feel like Uncle Toms.

22   These so-called Uncle Toms couldn't figure out why they should use an African name when they didn't know a thing about Africa. Besides, many of them were proud of their names, no matter how they had come by them. And it should be noted that after the Emancipation Proclamation in 1863, four million black people changed their names, adopting surnames such as Freeman, Freedman, and Liberty. They eagerly gave up names that slave masters had imposed upon them as a way of identifying their human chattel.

23   Besides names that indicated their newly won freedom, blacks chose common English names such as Jones, Scott, and Johnson. English was their language. America was their home, and they wanted names that would allow them to assimilate as easily as possible.

24   Of course, many of our European surnames belong to us by birth-right. We are the legal as well as "illegitimate" heirs to the names Jefferson, Franklin, Washington, et al., and in my own family, Lord.

25   Still, I consider most of these names to be by-products of slavery, if not actual slave names. Had we not been enslaved, we would not have been cut off from our culture, lost our indigenous languages, and been compelled to use European names.

26   The loss of our African culture is a tragic fact of history, and the conflict it poses is a profound one that has divided blacks many times since Emancipation: do we accept the loss and assimilate totally or do we try to reclaim our culture and synthesize it with our present reality?

27   A new generation of black people in America is reexamining the issues raised by the cultural nationalists and Pan-Africanists of the sixties and seventies: what are the cultural images that appropriately convey the "new" black aesthetic in literature and art?

28   The young Afro-American novelist Trey Ellis has asserted that the "New Black Aesthetic shamelessly borrows and reassembles across both race and class lines." It is not afraid to embrace the full implications of our hundreds of years in the New World. We are a new people who need not be tied to externally imposed or self-inflicted cultural parochialism. Had I understood that as a teenager, I might still be singing today.

29   Even the fundamental issue of identity and nomenclature, raised by Baraka and others twenty years ago, is back on the agenda: are we to call ourselves blacks or African-Americans?

30   In reality, it's an old debate. "Only with the founding of the American Colonization Society in 1816 did blacks recoil from using the term African in referring to themselves and their institutions," the noted historian and author Sterling Stuckey pointed out in an interview with me. They feared that using the term "African" would fuel white efforts to send them back to Africa. But they felt no white person had the right to send them back when they had slaved to build America.

31   Many black institutions retained their African identification, most notably the African Methodist Episcopal Church. Changes in black self-identification in America have come in cycles, usually reflecting the larger dynamics of domestic and international politics.

32   The period after World War II, said Stuckey, "culminating in the Cold War years of Roy Wilkins's leadership of the NAACP," was a time of "frenzied integrationism." And there was "no respectable black leader on the scene evincing any sort of interest in Africa—neither the NAACP or the Urban League."

33   This, he said, "was an example of historical discontinuity, the likes of which we, as a people, had not seen before." Prior to that, for more than a century and a half, black leaders were Pan-Africanists, including Frederick Douglass. "He recognized," said Stuckey, "that Africa was important and that somehow one had to redeem the motherland in order to be genuinely respected in the New World."

34   The Reverend Jesse Jackson has, of course, placed on the national agenda the importance of blacks in America restoring their cultural, historical, and political links with Africa.

35 But what does it really mean to be called an African-American?

36 "Black" can be viewed as a more encompassing term, referring to all people of African descent. "Afro-American" and "African-American" refer to a specific ethnic group. I use the terms interchangeably, depending on the context and the point I want to emphasize.

37 But I wonder: as the twenty-first century breathes down our necks—prodding us to wake up to the expanding mélange of ethnic groups immigrating in record numbers to the United States, inevitably intermarrying, and to realize the eventual reshaping of the nation's political imperatives in a newly multicultural society—will the term "African-American" be as much of a racial and cultural obfuscation as the term "black"? In other words, will we be the only people, in a society moving toward cultural pluralism, viewed to have no history and no culture? Will we just be a color with a new name: African-American?

38 Or will the term be—as I think it should—an ethnic label describing people with a shared culture who descended from Africans, were transformed in (as well as transformed) America, and are genetically intertwined with myriad other groups in the United States?

39 Such a definition reflects the historical reality and distances us from the fallacious, unscientific concept of separate races when there is only one: *Homo sapiens.*

40 But to comprehend what should be an obvious definition requires knowledge and a willingness to accept history.

41 When James Baldwin wrote *Nobody Knows My Name,* the title was a metaphor—at the deepest level of the collective African-American psyche—for the blighting of black history and culture before the nadir of slavery and since.

42 The eradication or distortion of our place in world history and culture is most obvious in the popular media. Liz Taylor—and, for an earlier generation, Claudette Colbert—still represent what Cleopatra—a woman of color in a multiethnic society, dominated at various times by blacks—looks like.

43 And in American homes, thanks to reruns and cable, a new generation of black kids grow up believing that a simpleton shouting "Dy-no-mite!" is a genuine reflection of Afro-American culture, rather than a white Hollywood writer's stereotype.

44 More recently, *Coming to America,* starring Eddie Murphy as an African prince seeking a bride in the United States, depicted traditional African dancers in what amounted to a Las Vegas stage show, totally distorting the nature and beauty of real African dance. But with every burlesque-style pelvic thrust on the screen, I saw blacks in the audience burst into applause. They think that's African culture, too.

45 And what do Africans know of us, since blacks don't control the organs of communication that disseminate information about us?

46 "No!" screamed the mother of a Kenyan man when he announced his engagement to an African-American woman who was a friend of mine. The mother said marry a European, marry a white American. But please, not one of those low-down, ignorant, drug-dealing, murderous black people she had seen in American movies. Ultimately, the mother prevailed.

47 In Tanzania, the travel agent looked at me indignantly. "Njeri, that's Kikuyu. What are you doing with an African name?" he demanded.

48   I'd been in Dar es Salaam about a month and had learned that Africans assess in a glance the ethnic origins of the people they meet.

49   Without a greeting, strangers on the street in Tanzania's capital would comment, "Oh, you're an Afro-American or West Indian."

50   "Both."

51   "I knew it," they'd respond, sometimes politely, sometimes not.

52   Or, people I got to know while in Africa would mention, "I know another half-caste like you." Then they would call in the "mixed-race" person and say, "Please meet Itabari Njeri." The darker-complected African, presumably of unmixed ancestry, would then smile and stare at us like we were animals in the zoo.

53   Of course, this "half-caste" (which I suppose is a term preferable to "mulatto," which I hate, and which every person who understands its derogatory meaning— "mule"—should never use) was usually the product of a mixed marriage, not generations of ethnic intermingling. And it was clear from most "half-castes" I met that they did not like being compared to so mongrelized and stigmatized a group as Afro-Americans.

54   I had minored in African studies in college, worked for years with Africans in the United States, and had no romantic illusions as to how I would be received in the motherland. I wasn't going back to find my roots. The only thing that shocked me in Tanzania was being called, with great disdain, a "white woman" by an African waiter. Even if the rest of the world didn't follow the practice, I then assumed everyone understood that any known or perceptible degree of African ancestry made one "black" in America by law and social custom.

55   But I was pleasantly surprised by the telephone call I received two minutes after I walked into my Dar es Salaam hotel room. It was the hotel operator. "Sister, welcome to Tanzania. . . . Please tell everyone in Harlem hello for us." The year was 1978, and people in Tanzania were wearing half-foot-high platform shoes and dancing to James Brown wherever I went.

56   Shortly before I left, I stood on a hill surrounded by a field of endless flowers in Arusha, near the border of Tanzania and Kenya. A toothless woman with a wide smile, a staff in her hand, and two young girls at her side, came toward me on a winding path. I spoke to her in fractured Swahili and she to me in broken English.

57   "I know you," she said smiling. "Wa-Negro." "Wa" is a prefix in Bantu languages meaning people. "You are from the lost tribe," she told me. "Welcome," she said, touching me, then walked down a hill that lay in the shadow of Mount Kilimanjaro.

58   I never told her my name, but when I told other Africans, they'd say: "*Emmmm* Itabari. Too long. How about I just call you Ita."

■ **TOPICAL CONSIDERATIONS**

1. Have you ever changed your name, or would you consider doing so? Do you know someone who has? What reasons or circumstances do you think appropriate or inappropriate for such a change? What kinds of names do you think appropriate or inappropriate?

2. What kinds of questions do people ask when they find out Njeri's name in paragraphs 3 through 21? What do their reactions or questions reveal about

the kind of person asking the question? What kind of response do you think Njeri would find preferable?

3. Why does Njeri observe that English-language names such as Jones, Scott and Johnson are by-products of slavery? What history does she offer to support her contention? Do you agree with this opinion?

4. Does Njeri prefer to be called black, Negro, Afro-American, African-American, or something else? What questions of importance to Njeri lie behind this decision? What does Njeri say about the differences in regarding people so designated as a color, a race, or an ethnic group? Do you agree? Explain your own views.

5. What kinds of misconceptions about her name or her sense of ethnic identity as an African-American does Njeri find in Africa? Do any of the reactions surprise or annoy her? Why? Were you surprised at any of the responses?

■ RHETORICAL CONSIDERATIONS

1. Although Njeri provides a number of good reasons for taking an African name, she never does say why or how she chose hers. Why do you think she doesn't focus on the history of her own, personal decision? How does this decision help shape the main idea of her essay?

2. Where does Njeri state her thesis? If you could locate one sentence that captures the main idea of the essay, what would this idea be? How closely related to the discussion about names and naming is her thesis? How effective a strategy do you think it is?

3. Name some of the ways that personal names and the name for a people are similar. What kinds of objections have you heard voiced against personal or group name changes? How does Njeri's strategy of pairing these two kinds of names strengthen her discussion against possible objections against either one?

4. Why do you think Njeri makes no statements about the problems other ethnic groups or races have in naming themselves? Why does she focus solely on issues related to African-American identity and heritage? How does her discussion of her experiences in Africa (paragraph 45–58) help explain her reason?

5. What is the effect of placing the name-shortening anecdote in Africa as the final paragraph? How does its placement relate to the form of the article and to the theme of the article? Do you think this is an effective way for Njeri to end the piece?

■ WRITING ASSIGNMENTS

1. If you could change your name to anything, what would it be? Or if you wouldn't change your name, why not? Do you prefer a nickname to your given name (or your given name to a nickname that people insist on using)?

Write a personal essay in which you reflect on the history of your own name, if you know it, and defending your decision to change or not to change it.

2. Compare and contrast the attitude of Njeri and her mother with that of Elizabeth Wong and her mother in "To Be an All-American Girl." What is the same about each daughter's wishes to be part of a specific culture? What is different? How are the mothers' responses similar? How are they different? Can you think of any reasons for these similarities or differences?

3. Using your library's encyclopedias and international news sources for the past half a century, research the Kikuyu people of Kenya. Pay special attention to the Kikuyu tribe's role in struggles as the modern-day African nation of Kenya gained its independence. Do you find any possible reasons that Njeri might have taken a Kikuyu name?

4. Using your library's resources on African-Americans, research the decisions of Malcolm X, Muhammad Ali, Kareem Abdul-Jabbar, and Ntozake Shange to change their names. (These names are all listed in paragraph 15 along with a fifth name, Kunte Kinte, which is the name of a fictional character created by Arthur Haley in his novel *Roots*.) What was the "slave name" of each individual? What reasons does each one give for changing his or her name? What responses did each experience?

TAKING A STAND

America: The Multinational Society

Ishmael Reed

In this essay, Ishmael Reed looks at the constant reminders of how once distinctly foreign cultural styles have now become part of the American landscape. Ishmael Reed is regarded as one of the most provocative and thoughtful black satirists writing today. He is the author of several novels, plays, books of poetry, and essay collections. He has taught at Harvard, Yale, Dartmouth, and the University of California at Berkeley. The essay below was taken from his latest collection, *Writin' Is Fightin'* (1990).

At the annual Lower East Side Jewish Festival yesterday, a Chinese woman ate a pizza slice in front of Ty Thuan Duc's Vietnamese grocery store. Beside her a Spanish-speaking family patronized a cart with two signs: "Italian Ices" and "Kosher by Rabbi Alper." And after the pastrami ran out, everybody ate knishes.

New York Times, 23 JUNE 1983

1 On the day before Memorial Day, 1983, a poet called me to describe a city he had just visited. He said that one section included mosques, built by the Islamic people who dwelled there. Attending his reading, he said, were large numbers of Hispanic people, forty thousand of whom lived in the same city. He was not talking about a fabled city located in some mysterious region of the world. The city he'd visited was Detroit.

2 A few months before, as I was leaving Houston, Texas, I heard it announced on the radio that Texas's largest minority was Mexican-American, and though a foundation recently issued a report critical of bilingual education, the taped voice used to guide the passengers on the air trams connecting terminals in Dallas Airport is in both Spanish and English. If the trend continues, a day will come when it will be difficult to travel through some sections of the country without hearing commands in both English and Spanish; after all, for some western states, Spanish was the first written language and the Spanish style lives on in the western way of life.

3 Shortly after my Texas trip, I sat in an auditorium located on the campus of the University of Wisconsin at Milwaukee as a Yale professor—whose original work on the influence of African cultures upon those of the Americas has led to his ostracism from some monocultural intellectual circles—walked up and down the aisle, like an old-time southern evangelist, dancing and drumming the top of the lectern, illustrating his points before some serious Afro-American intellectuals and artists who cheered and applauded his performance and his mastery of information. The professor was "white." After his lecture, he joined a group of Milwaukeeans in a conversation. All of the participants spoke Yoruban, though only the professor had ever traveled to Africa.

4 One of the artists told me that his paintings, which included African and Afro-American mythological symbols and imagery, were hanging in the local McDonald's restaurant. The next day I went to McDonald's and snapped pictures of smiling youngsters eating hamburgers below paintings that could grace the walls of any of the country's leading museums. The manager of the local McDonald's said, "I don't know what you boys are doing, but I like it," as he commissioned the local painters to exhibit in his restaurant.

5 Such blurring of cultural styles occurs in everyday life in the United States to a greater extent than anyone can imagine and is probably more prevalent than the sensational conflict between people of different backgrounds that is played up and often encouraged by the media. The result is what the Yale professor, Robert Thompson, referred to as a cultural bouillabaisse, yet members of the nation's present educational and cultural Elect still cling to the notion that the United States belongs to some vaguely defined entity they refer to as "Western civilization," by which they mean, presumably, a civilization created by the people of Europe, as if Europe can be viewed in monolithic terms. Is Beethoven's Ninth Symphony, which includes Turkish marches, a part of Western civilization, or the late nineteenth- and twentieth-century French paintings, whose creators were influenced by Japanese art? And what of the cubists, through whom the influence of African art changed modern painting, or the surrealists, who were so impressed with the art of the Pacific

Northwest Indians that, in their map of North America, Alaska dwarfs the lower forty-eight in size?

6 Are the Russians, who are often criticized for their adoption of "Western" ways by Tsarist dissidents in exile, members of Western civilization? And what of the millions of Europeans who have black African and Asian ancestry, black Africans having occupied several countries for hundreds of years? Are these "Europeans" members of Western civilization, or the Hungarians, who originated across the Urals in a place called Greater Hungary, or the Irish, who came from the Iberian Peninsula?

7 Even the notion that North America is part of Western civilization because our "system of government" is derived from Europe is being challenged by Native American historians who say that the founding fathers, Benjamin Franklin especially, were actually influenced by the system of government that had been adopted by the Iroquois hundreds of years prior to the arrival of large numbers of Europeans.

8 Western civilization, then, becomes another confusing category like Third World, or Judeo-Christian culture, as man attempts to impose his small-screen view of political and cultural reality upon a complex world. Our most publicized novelist recently said that Western civilization was the greatest achievement of mankind, an attitude that flourishes on the street level as scribbles in public restrooms: "White Power," "Niggers and Spic Suck," or "Hitler was a prophet," the latter being the most telling, for wasn't Adolf Hitler the archetypal monoculturalist who, in his pigheaded arrogance, believed that one way and one blood was so pure that it had to be protected from alien strains at all costs? Where did such an attitude, which has caused so much misery and depression in our national life, which has tainted even our noblest achievements, begin? An attitude that caused the incarceration of Japanese-American citizens during World War II, the persecution of Chicanos and Chinese-Americans, the near-extermination of the Indians, and the murder and lynchings of thousands of Afro-Americans.

9 Virtuous, hardworking, pious, even though they occasionally would wander off after some fancy clothes, or rendezvous in the woods with the town prostitute, the Puritans are idealized in our schoolbooks as "a hardy band" of no-nonsense patriarchs whose discipline razed the forest and brought order to the New World (a term that annoys Native American historians). Industrious, responsible, it was their "Yankee ingenuity" and practicality that created the work ethic. They were simple folk who produced a number of good poets, and they set the tone for the American writing style, of lean and spare lines, long before Hemingway. They worshiped in churches whose colors blended in with the New England snow, churches with simple structures and ornate lecterns.

10 The Puritans were a daring lot, but they had a mean streak. They hated the theater and banned Christmas. They punished people in a cruel and inhuman manner. They killed children who disobeyed their parents. When they came in contact with those whom they considered heathens or aliens, they behaved in such a bizarre and irrational manner that this chapter in the American history comes down to us as a late-movie horror film. They exterminated the Indians, who taught them how to survive in a world unknown to them, and their encounter with the calypso culture of

Barbados resulted in what the tourist guide in Salem's Witches' House refers to as the Witchcraft Hysteria.

11   The Puritan legacy of hard work and meticulous accounting led to the establishment of a great industrial society; it is no wonder that the American industrial revolution began in Lowell, Massachusetts, but there was the other side, the strange and paranoid attitudes toward those different from the Elect.

12   The cultural attitudes of that early Elect continue to be voiced in everyday life in the United States: the president of a distinguished university, writing a letter to the *Times,* belittling the study of African civilizations; the television network that promoted its show on the Vatican art with the boast that this art represented "the finest achievements of the human spirit." A modern up-tempo state of complex rhythms that depends upon contacts with an international community can no longer behave as if it dwelled in a "Zion Wilderness" surrounded by beasts and pagans.

13   When I heard a schoolteacher warn the other night about the invasion of the American educational system by foreign curriculums, I wanted to yell at the television set, "Lady, they're already here." It has already begun because the world is here. The world has been arriving at these shores for at least ten thousand years from Europe, Africa, and Asia. In the late nineteenth and early twentieth centuries, large numbers of Europeans arrived, adding their cultures to those of the European, African, and Asian settlers who were already here, and recently millions have been entering the country from South America and the Caribbean, making Yale Professor Bob Thompson's bouillabaisse richer and thicker.

14   One of our most visionary politicians said that he envisioned a time when the United States could become the brain of the world, by which he meant the repository of all of the latest advanced information systems. I thought of that remark when an enterprising poet friend of mine called to say that he had just sold a poem to a computer magazine and that the editors were delighted to get it because they didn't carry fiction or poetry. Is that the kind of world we desire? A humdrum homogeneous world of all brains and no heart, no fiction, no poetry; a world of robots with human attendants bereft of imagination, of culture? Or does North America deserve a more exciting destiny? To become a place where the cultures of the world crisscross. This is possible because the United States is unique in the world: The world is here.

■ TOPICAL CONSIDERATIONS

1. What would you say is the basic point of Reed's essay? Where does he make his thesis statement? Does the essay prove this thesis? Do you agree with Reed's assessment of America as a multicultural environment?

2. Consider Yale professor Robert Thompson's term "cultural bouillabaisse" (paragraph 5). Why does Reed favor this term over the familiar label, "melting pot," or "Western civilization"?

3. In paragraph 5, Reed discusses various influences on "Western" art. How, according to the author, does art blur cultural lines? Did his examples open your eyes to the narrowness of the label "Western culture"?

4. Explain the term "monoculturalist" in paragraph 8. How according to Reed has this philosophy affected America? Do you think monoculturalism is prevalent in your immediate environment? How about when you were growing up?
5. Consider the "street level scribbles" in paragraph 8. Thinking of this graffiti as actual text, try to determine what kind of power it has?
6. Comment on Reed's revisionist description of the founding of America (paragraph 9). What is his point here? How does it add to the theme of the essay? Have you ever been exposed to this side of the Puritans before? If not, how does it make you regard your early "schoolbook" concept of America's founding?
7. Reed writes in his final paragraph, "Or does North America deserve a more exciting destiny?" What kind of destiny does Reed envision?

■ RHETORICAL CONSIDERATIONS

1. What does "the Elect" (with a capital *E*) mean in paragraph 11?
2. The essay is written in first person. Do you consider the narrator an authority on this subject? If so, how are you convinced of his expertise?
3. Does this essay convince you that "the world is here"? Explain where the essay is most effective and where it is lacking.
4. Consider the number of different locales Reed mentions throughout his essay. What is the rhetorical purpose of including the names of all these places?

■ WRITING ASSIGNMENTS

1. Reed writes (in paragraph 10) of the Puritans, "When they came in contact with those whom they considered heathens or aliens, they behaved in such a bizarre and irrational manner that this chapter in the American history comes down to us as a late-movie horror film." Investigate some facet of early American history that is like a horror movie. Perhaps look at captivity narratives, letters, diaries, and the like that present new information to you. Juxtapose your findings with a standard "factual" account in a history textbook. Write a paper that focuses on a single event and compare the two accounts. Try to decide where the truth lies.
2. Explore the idea of a "Cultural bouillabaisse." Does America as the Melting Pot accept non-Western people as an ingredient, or is ours a discriminating bouillabaisse?
3. In the final paragraph, Reed asks if Americans desire "a humdrum homogeneous world of all brains and no heart, no fiction, no poetry; a world of robots with human attendants bereft of imagination, of culture? Or does North America deserve a more exciting destiny?" Write a paper in which you construct America's destiny. Include Reed's argument for multiculturalism and predict the route America has taken.

4. How does Reed's vision of a "Multinational Society" compare to popular culture's picture of America? Consider Spike Lee's *Do the Right Thing* and *Jungle Fever*, John Singleton's *Boyz 'N the Hood*, Public Enemy, and other segments of the media that address these issues.

5. Write a letter to Ishmael Reed telling him what you think of his essay—whether or not he was convincing; whether or not the essay made you more aware of the true makeup of our society, its history, and destiny. Also comment on the effectiveness of his writing.

6. Some of Reed's statements about influences on American culture probably surprised you. Choose one statement that piques your interest and report on these influences. Be sure your topic is adequately narrow to examine scholarly journal literature in history, art, ethnomusicology, or political science, depending on your choice. Some examples to get you started: African origins of contemporary "rock 'n' roll" music; Benjamin Franklin's adaptation of the Iroquois system of government; African motifs in cubist art, or Pacific Northwest native peoples' influences on surrealism; or misunderstandings about the Barbadian woman Tituba in the Salem witchcraft trials.

The Cult of Ethnicity, Good and Bad

Arthur M. Schlesinger, Jr.

While Ishmael Reed celebrates the emerging signs of America's multicultural society, the noted historian Arthur M. Schlesinger, Jr. warns of dangerous divisiveness. What concerns him are those proponents of multiculturalism who reject historic American purposes of assimilation and integration and who promote ethnic separatism at the expense of the idea of a common culture and common national identity. Pushed too far, the "cult of ethnicity" can create separate ethnic and racial groups whose differences and hostilities would be intensified.

In 1994, Arthur Schlesinger retired after 28 years as professor at the City University of New York Graduate School. He is the author of 14 books, including *The Age of Jackson* (1948) and *A Thousand Days: John F. Kennedy in the White House* (1966), each of which won a Pulitzer Prize, and *The Imperial Presidency: Robert Kennedy and His Times* (1978). In 1960, Professor Schlesinger became special assistant to President Kennedy and served as an informal adviser to Robert Kennedy and Senator Edward M. Kennedy. In 1992, he published the controversial book, *The Disunity of America*, which argues against contemporary multiculturalism for its promotion of separatism. This article, which forecast that book, first appeared in *Time* magazine in 1991.

1   The history of the world has been in great part the history of the mixing of peoples. Modern communication and transport accelerate mass migrations from one continent to another. Ethnic and racial diversity is more than ever a salient fact of the age.

2   But what happens when people of different origins, speaking different languages and professing different religions, inhabit the same locality and live under the same political sovereignty? Ethnic and racial conflict—far more than ideological conflict—is the explosive problem of our times.

3   On every side today ethnicity is breaking up nations. The Soviet Union, India, Yugoslavia, Ethiopia are all in crisis. Ethnic tensions disturb and divide Sri Lanka, Burma, Indonesia, Iraq, Cyprus, Nigeria, Angola, Lebanon, Guyana, Trinidad—you name it. Even nations as stable and civilized as Britain and France, Belgium and Spain, face growing ethnic troubles. Is there any large multiethnic state that can be made to work?

4   The answer to that question has been, until recently, the United States. "No other nation," Margaret Thatcher* has said, "has so successfully combined people of different races and nations within a single culture." How have Americans succeeded in pulling off this almost unprecedented trick?

5   We have always been a multiethnic country. Hector St. John de Crèvecoeur, who came from France in the eighteenth century, marveled at the astonishing diversity of the settlers—"a mixture of English, Scotch, Irish, French, Dutch, Germans, and Swedes . . . this promiscuous breed." He propounded a famous question: "What then is the American, this new man?" And he gave a famous answer: "Here individuals of all nations are melted into a new race of men." *E pluribus unum.*

6   The United States escaped the divisiveness of a multiethnic society by a brilliant solution: the creation of a brand-new national identity. The point of America was not to preserve old cultures but to forge a new, *American* culture. "By an intermixture with our people," President George Washington told Vice President John Adams, immigrants will "get assimilated to our customs, measures and laws: in a word, soon become one people." This was the ideal that a century later Israel Zangwill crystallized in the title of his popular 1908 play *The Melting Pot.* And no institution was more potent in molding Crèvecoeur's "promiscuous breed" into Washington's "one people" than the American public school.

7   The new American nationality was inescapably English in language, ideas, and institutions. The pot did not melt everybody, not even all the white immigrants; deeply bred racism put black Americans, yellow Americans, red Americans, and brown Americans well outside the pale. Still, the infusion of other stocks, even of nonwhite stocks, and the experience of the New World reconfigured the British legacy and made the United States, as we all know, a very different country from Britain.

8   In the twentieth century, new immigration laws altered the composition of the American people, and a cult of ethnicity erupted both among non-Anglo whites and among nonwhite minorities. This had many healthy consequences. The American culture at last began to give shamefully overdue recognition to the achievements of groups subordinated and spurned during the high noon of Anglo dominance, and it began to acknowledge the great swirling world beyond Europe. Americans acquired a more complex and invigorating sense of their world—and of themselves.

---

*Thatcher (born 1925) was Britain's prime minister 1979–1990.—Ed.

9   But, pressed too far, the cult of ethnicity has unhealthy consequences. It gives rise, for example, to the conception of the United States as a nation composed not of individuals making their own choices but of inviolable ethnic and racial groups. It rejects the historic American goals of assimilation and integration. And, in an excess of zeal, well-intentioned people seek to transform our system of education from a means of creating "one people" into a means of promoting, celebrating, and perpetuating separate ethnic origins and identities. The balance is shifting from *unum* to *pluribus.*

10   That is the issue that lies behind the hullabaloo over "multiculturalism" and "political correctness," the attack on the "Eurocentric" curriculum and the rise of the notion that history and literature should be taught not as disciplines but as therapies whose function is to raise minority self-esteem. Group separatism crystallizes the differences, magnifies tensions, intensifies hostilities. Europe—the unique source of the liberating ideas of democracy, civil liberties, and human rights—is portrayed as the root of all evil, and non-European cultures, their own many crimes deleted, are presented as the means of redemption.

11   I don't want to sound apocalyptic about these developments. Education is always in ferment, and a good thing too. The situation in our universities, I am confident, will soon right itself. But the impact of separatist pressures on our public schools is more troubling. If a Kleagle of the Ku Klux Klan wanted to use the schools to disable and handicap black Americans, he could hardly come up with anything more effective than the "Afrocentric" curriculum. And if separatist tendencies go unchecked, the result can only be the fragmentation, resegregation, and tribalization of American life.

12   I remain optimistic. My impression is that the historic forces driving toward "one people" have not lost their power. The eruption of ethnicity is, I believe, a rather superficial enthusiasm stirred by romantic ideologues on the one hand and by unscrupulous con men on the other: self-appointed spokesmen whose claim to represent their minority groups is carelessly accepted by the media. Most American-born members of minority groups, white or nonwhite, see themselves primarily as Americans rather than primarily as members of one or another ethnic group. A notable indicator today is the rate of inter-marriage across ethnic lines, across religion lines, even (increasingly) across racial lines. "We Americans," said Theodore Roosevelt, "are children of the crucible."

13   The growing diversity of the American population makes the quest for unifying ideals and a common culture all the more urgent. In a world savagely rent by ethnic and racial antagonisms, the United States must continue as an example of how a highly differentiated society holds itself together.

■ TOPICAL CONSIDERATIONS

1. See if you can write a definition for each of Schlesinger's three key terms, as he uses them in the first four paragraphs of his article: *race, ethnicity, diversity.* Does he make a distinction between ethnicity and race?
2. What does Schlesinger say are the "causes" of ethnic and racial diversity?

3. Schlesinger says at the beginning of paragraph 5 that the United States has always been "a multiethnic country." What historical sources does he use to support his statement? How does he more narrowly define this term when he focuses on integration into a single, unified society? Why does he believe the specific kind of multiethnic country he promotes is best?

4. What is the "cult of ethnicity" according to Schlesinger—and why does he use the term *cult?* When did it begin, and in response to what kinds of circumstances? What was good about it? Why have we taken it too far today? Do you agree with his views? Explain your answer.

5. According to Schlesinger, what role does education play in creating a unified, national American identity? How does he say the role of education has changed in recent years? What distinction does he make between the roles of public schools (through high school), and colleges and universities?

6. In your experience, are people from minority groups the only ones who receive or benefit from education that celebrates and tries to preserve distinctive ethnic characteristics? For example, has it been your experience that only African-American students learn about black history? If so, do you think that such an education promotes the kind of fragmentation that Schlesinger fears?

7. According to Schlesinger, would "Americans" (U.S. citizens) be considered an ethnic group? Can everyone be considered part of an ethnic group, or do some people lack ethnicity? Why or why not? What is your opinion?

■ RHETORICAL CONSIDERATIONS

1. Schlesinger breaks his article into three distinct parts: paragraphs 1 through 4; 5 through 8; and 9 through 13. Briefly summarize the main idea in each section, and the contribution of each to the overall argument. Where does he place his thesis? Why do you think he uses this strategy?

2. Do you think that Schlesinger depends too much on generalizations? Did any parts of his argument seem vague or any statements about history seem vague to you? What information did you wish he had supplied? Why do you think Schlesinger doesn't provide more specific discussion of, say, the crises and tensions in countries he lists in paragraph 3? What assumptions does he make about his audience?

3. What does Schlesinger mean when he claims that we are a "multiethnic country"? How do you think that his definition of multiethnic would be different from Ishmael Reed's use of the term in his article "America: The Multinational Society"? On what points do you think the two authors would disagree?

■ WRITING ASSIGNMENTS

1. Write an essay discussing your own family's sense of ethnic or racial identity. Did your parents, or their parents, or anyone in your family history that you know of, come from another country or ethnic origin? What generations

of your family have assimilated? Has assimilation created any tensions among family members? Do you wish that you knew more about their original culture—or do you prefer feeling assimilated with the larger national American culture?

2. Drawing on the other essays throughout this textbook that deal with race and ethnicity, write an essay supporting or refuting the first sentence of Schlesinger's sixth paragraph: "The United States escaped the divisiveness of a multiethnic society by a brilliant solution: the creation of a brand-new national identity." Do the other authors you have read in this textbook agree that the United States in fact does have a single national identity? Why or why not? If not, do they think that a single national identity is a desirable goal?

3. Using your library's resources, look up some of the recent debates and discussion on Afrocentricity. What does this term mean? Does every author who writes about it have the same meaning in mind—and if not, what are the differences? What do promoters of this idea in education have to say about it? What do those who disagree say?

4. Using your library's news resources, identify and research ethnic conflicts in another part of the world. You may use the list Schlesinger provides in paragraph 3, or you may wish to follow more recent current events. What are the effects of ethnic conflict? When does ethnic conflict become an international problem, worthy of the attention of the United Nations or some other international mediating body, and when is it considered a "private" conflict in which other nations should not intervene?

Come, Let Me Offend You

Eve Drobot

Separatism is also the issue at the heart of Eve Drobot's argument. While she condemns racist jokes, the downside of multiculturalism and political correctness, she says, is that we have become too afraid of hurting one another's feelings. Everybody these days, she complains, is a minority, everybody has an agenda, everybody wears their sensitivities on their sleeves.

Eve Drobot is a columnist for The *Globe and Mail* in Toronto. She is the author of five books and is a freelance writer and television interviewer.

1 Can we talk? It is becoming increasingly difficult, because I never know when I'm inadvertently going to offend you. Here I go, raving about the divine veal piccata I had at that hot new trattoria, and you're gritting your teeth and about to pop a blood vessel because you haven't had a chance to inform me that you are a raging vegetarian who spends his weekends stuffing envelopes for People for Ethical Treatment of Animals.

2   I mean, how can we ever talk if you've always got an agenda I have no way of knowing about? There we are at a party discussing censorship—at least, I think we're discussing censorship—when you bring everything to a grinding halt by announcing you're a Muslim who believes the *fatwa* against Salman Rushdie is entirely justified. Or, God forbid, I tell a good, old-fashioned heterosexual joke and you stare at me straight-faced and explain you are a lesbian female separatist.

3   Everywhere I turn, it seems that certain things are no longer deemed appropriate conversation. We are awash in earnestness, afraid to open our mouths because we never know when our words are going to hurt somebody's feelings.

4   I can understand—even applaud—the taboos on racist and sexist jokes (unless we've established a priori that we're both feminists, in which case, have you heard the one about the man who was so dumb that . . .). But is there anything left to have an opinion on these days besides the weather? Oh, but now you tell me you're an environmentalist, and I have no right to complain about the rain because the atmosphere has been raped by pollution, and if I've used so much as one squirt of hair spray in my life it's probably all my fault anyway. Pardon me.

5   You see, it has become simply impossible for us to speak to one another as long as you insist on wearing your special interests and sensitivities on your sleeve.

6   Now, wait a minute. *There's* a concept. Why don't you wear your agenda on your sleeve, literally? We could develop an entire iconography of sensibilities. Pins, badges, what have you—I'm open to suggestions. Devout Christians wear crosses around their necks; some Jews display a Star of David or Hebrew letters on a chain. We could carry this idea further.

7   Let's start with a classic and work from there. Take a pink triangle (for gay) and add sequins if you're a drag queen. If you're a male bisexual, how about a pink triangle bisected by the biological symbol for female? Or, if you're a female bisexual, a pink triangle bisected by the biological symbol for male?

8   Are you sensitive about being a single mother? Let the world know by displaying Dan Quayle's face with a red slash through it.

9   We could issue broccoli stickpins to vegetarians, bunny heads in profile to animal-rights activists. A pentacle for practicing witches, a golden calf for ardent pagans. A baby basket in front of a door if you were adopted. A child with a suitcase if your parents were immigrants. An ear if someone in your family is deaf, an ear and a musical note if someone in your family is tone-deaf. The possibilities are endless: define your sore point and design an insignia. Wear it proudly, if not defiantly.

10   ***Stamps and stickers:***   And let's not stop with badges. How about making little stamps or stickers to affix to anything you write? Let's say you write a letter to the editor protesting the fatuousness of this article. Append your offended affiliation visually to the letter, thereby ensuring that your opinion will be judged not on the merit of your argument but on the merit of your minority-group adherence.

11   This sort of symbolic shorthand would certainly have helped get a fellow I know out of a fix he recently found himself in. A major publishing house asked him to select some poems to include in an anthology. Silly liberal-minded fool

that he is, he simply chose poems he thought were good. His selections were returned to him for further clarification. Could he please let the publisher know which poems were written by gays, third-generation Americans, Native Americans, refugees, Young Republicans and those who use wheelchairs? When he had supplied the appropriate designation for each entry, then—and only then—could the publisher know that the editor had made the demographically representative choices.

12   Now, I realize I am probably dating myself, or setting myself up as a total Pollyanna, but wasn't there a time when the goal was *not* to notice the things that set us apart? Weren't we once working toward a perfect world, where we would see past color, race, creed, gender, ethnic background and physical limitations, straight through to talent and ability? What ever happened to that idea?

13   I can't pinpoint exactly where it went off the rails, but there must definitely have been a moment in time when somebody figured out there was more to be gained by being indignant than by being right.

14   You see, we can't talk, we can't think, we can't presume to judge unless we have all the pertinent information. And the most pertinent information these days is: whom does this offend?

15   Labeling yourself by your narrowest interests has become quite the rage during the past few years. I'm just surprised that no one has thought of taking this trend one logical step further and making those labels outwardly visible. Who knows? There might even be money to be made.

16   I wish I could take credit for this clever badge idea, but unfortunately, I can't. Some insane fellow with a ridiculous mustache came up with it more than 50 years ago. He wanted homosexuals to wear those pink triangles, Jews to wear yellow Stars of David, and so on. His motives weren't as pure as mine, I grant you. He wanted to kill people. I merely want to avoid hurting their feelings.

■ TOPICAL CONSIDERATIONS

1. What kinds of discussion topics or jokes does Drobot mention in paragraphs 1 through 4 that might offend someone? Do you think she's discussing responses she's actually experienced? What suggests they're exaggerations? Have you ever felt offended, or found out later that you've inadvertently offended someone?

2. What does "wearing your special interests . . . on your sleeve" (paragraph 5) mean? Where does the expression come from? How does Drobot suggest we take it literally?

3. If you're a member of any of the groups for whom Drobot has a suggestion, do you like her choice of icons? How many of these little icons would you need to wear to make a complete statement about your identity?

4. How would pins, badges, or stickers have aided Drobot's friend, the editor who was asked to assemble a selection of poetry for an anthology? What does Drobot say is wrong with this approach to identifying ourselves and our special interests or affiliations?

5. Does Drobot think that it's okay to insult people, deliberately or otherwise? Do you think that she would condone prejudice or discrimination toward people based on who they are or what they believe?

6. Do you think Drobot's protest over political correctness is not strong enough, just about right, or excessive? Explain your answer.

■ RHETORICAL CONSIDERATIONS

1. Look again at the first few paragraphs of this article, at the kinds of people Drobot says might be insulted. What unifying principles or ideas behind this selection can you find? Why did she choose this list for extended discussion, rather than, say, Young Republicans, adoptees, or people whose families are tone deaf?

2. What effect does Drobot's mention of the incomplete joke "about the man who was so dumb" have on her argument? What point does she seem to be making here? Does this exception to the rule just muddy the points she's trying to make?

3. In your opinion, is it possible to create a "perfect world" like the one Drobot describes in paragraph 12? Since Americans live in a diverse country, do you think the problem she describes will ever go away? Why do you think Drobot refers to this ideal world at this point in her article?

4. What is the effect of Drobot's final paragraph, in which she calls attention to Hitler's plan to identify people in order to kill them more efficiently? Why does Drobot end her article on such a serious note? What strengths or weaknesses in earlier parts of her argument does this mention highlight?

5. Try to determine the different ways Drobot creates the conversational tone of this article. From the title onward, consider the word choice, specific phrases, and devices she uses. How effective is this style in her argument?

■ WRITING ASSIGNMENTS

1. Take Eve Drobot up on her suggestion, in paragraph 10, that you "write a letter to the editor protesting the fatuousness of this article." Make sure that you describe exactly which minority groups you belong to (with an appropriate symbol for each group), and why your sensibilities are offended.

2. How do you think that Eve Drobot would respond to Arthur Schlesinger's article "The Cult of Ethnicity, Good and Bad"? What similarities and differences do you find between Drobot's special interest groups and the "inviolable ethnic and racial groups" that Schlesinger deplores? How do you think Schlesinger would respond to the problems that the poetry editor in Drobot's article faced?

3. Skim several weeks' worth of op-ed (opinions and editorials, which usually include letters to the editor) sections in a local newspaper, even in your school's newspaper. What kinds of insults do people seem to be complaining about right now? Have there been exchanges of several sets of letters on one

particular issue? What insults are arousing people's anger? What do you think Drobot would say to these writers?

4. Using professional journals in education and literature, explore some of the issues that the poetry anthology publisher and editor in Drobot's article faced. What are the arguments for and against diversity in anthologies? What practices are publishers currently following? If you were the publisher, how would you go about creating the "perfect world's poetry anthology"? What standards would you use to judge what to include and what to exclude?

Why I Dread Black History Month

Wayne M. Joseph

Wayne M. Joseph is the principal of Lorbeer Middle School in Diamond Bar, California. Although black teachers and other members of the African-American community celebrate February as Black History Month, Joseph laments the tokenism. "'Black' history *is* American history," he argues, not something separate. This article first appeared in the "My Turn" column of *Newsweek* in February 1994.

1 Every year when the month of February approaches, I'm overcome with a feeling of dread. February is hailed as Black History Month, a national observance that is celebrated neither at the school in which I am the principal nor in my own home. This may come as a surprise to the even casual observer, since I am black. In my humble estimation Black History Month is a thriving monument to tokenism which, ironically, has been wholeheartedly embraced and endorsed by the black community.

2 For at least 28 days we are bombarded by the media with reminders of great black Americans. Teachers across America dust off last year's lesson plans and speak of African kings and queens. Dr. Martin Luther King's "I Have A Dream" speech is played repeatedly and there are festivities where people wear traditional African garb and may even speak a few words of Swahili.

3 So, you might ask, what is wrong with this?

4 Black contribution to American history is so rich and varied that attempting to confine the discussion and investigation to four weeks a year tends to trivialize the momentous impact that blacks have had on American society.

5 There is also a tendency to somehow feel that "black" history is separate from "American" history. "Black" history *is* American history—they are not mutually exclusive. The struggles of black people in America strike at the core of our country's past and its development. One cannot, for instance, hope to thoroughly

study the factors leading to the Civil War or Reconstruction without investigating the issue of slavery and the emancipation of those slaves. American music and dance has little significance without the recognition of black influences. Spirituals, jazz and the blues are a vital and important part of American culture. To speak of the experience of black people in America (as some are inclined to do during the month of February) as independent of the American social, political and economic forces at work in our country is a misreading of history at best and a flagrant attempt to rewrite it at worst.

6   Of course very few people will be courageous enough during February to say that it's irrelevant whether or not Cleopatra and Jesus were black, since their experiences have not the slightest kinship with those of black Americans.

7   It is not very difficult to understand why the distant (usually African) past is used as a way to give blacks a sense of cultural identity. In the final analysis, however, it's a hollow attempt to fill a vacuum that was created by the institution of slavery. It is widely acknowledged that one of the more insidious aspects of American slavery was that Africans of different cultures and languages were stripped of their cultural base and were forced to learn the enslaver's tongue to survive. Unlike the German, Italian and Jewish immigrants who came to this country with their own languages, religions and customs, Africans of different backgrounds were compelled to eschew their own roots in order to survive on American soil.

8   *Slavery and segregation:* Instead of African kings and queens who never set foot in America, it is the black people who survived the infamous "middle passage" and endured slavery who should be heralded as "kings" and "queens" for their courage and perseverance. After slavery, there were scores of blacks who endured beatings, lynchings and daily degradations indigenous to the system of discrimination in both the North and the South; yet these paragons of endurance are seldom lauded. It's as if the words "slavery" and "segregation" are to be mentioned only fleetingly during February. We should look to our own grandfathers and grandmothers to find examples of real heroism. Unfortunately, the significance of these black men and women as well as the traditional black icons—Dr. King, Malcolm X, Jackie Robinson, et al.—are lost in a month in which people are studied in isolation instead of within the historical context that produced them.

9   Black parents must try to instill in children a sense of their own history. This should include a sense of family—the accomplishments of parents, grandparents and ancestors has more relevance than some historical figure whose only connection to the child is skin color. We in the schools are often expected to fill the gaps that parents have neglected in their child's development; but for every child a knowledge of identity and self-worth must come from home to be meaningful and long-lasting. For the black child, a monthlong emphasis on black culture will never fill that void.

10   There will be those, I'm sure, who will say that I should feel pleased that black people are recognized one month out of the year, knowing the difficulty black Americans have historically encountered validating their accomplishments. But

being black does not entitle one to more or less recognition based solely on heritage. In a multicultural society, there is a need to celebrate our cultural differences as well as our commonalities as human beings. No one group has a monopoly on this need.

11   One month out of every year, Americans are "given permission" to commemorate the achievements of black people. This rather condescending view fails to acknowledge that a people and a country's past should be nurtured and revered; instead, at this time, the past of black Americans is handled in an expedient and cavalier fashion denigrating the very people it seeks to honor.

12   February is here again, and I'll be approached by a black student or parent inquiring as to what the school is doing to celebrate Black History Month. My answer, as always, will be that my teachers and I celebrate the contributions of *all* Americans *every* month of the school year.

■ TOPICAL CONSIDERATIONS

1. According to Joseph, what is Black History Month? What Black History Month events, if any, have you participated in? How well do you feel your schools have commemorated black Americans in February?
2. Joseph lists three things he finds wrong with Black History Month in paragraphs 4 through 8. What are they?
3. Why does Joseph suggest that one important alternative to Black History Month would be to have children learn about their own family's history? Do you agree? How important is your own family's history to your sense of "identity and self-worth"? Do you think that your family history is more or less important than the history of your ethnicity or group heritage?
4. Based on information in paragraph 10, what do you think Joseph would say about celebrating "Black Firsts"—the first African-American woman to become a licensed pilot, the first African-American man to sit on the Supreme Court, and so on? What basis does he offer for his opinion?
5. In paragraphs 11 and 12, why does Joseph say that a one-month celebration of the achievements of African-Americans is inappropriate? What does he suggest instead? Do you think his idea is a satisfactory solution to the problem of making sure that black people's contributions to American history are not overlooked?

■ RHETORICAL CONSIDERATIONS

1. Consider how Joseph projects his feelings about Black History Month's proceedings in the first two paragraphs. What words, figures of speech, or phrases does he use to communicate his tone here?
2. In paragraph 5, Joseph says Black history and American history are so intertwined that one cannot be discussed without the other. Why do his examples

show only how distorted mainstream American history is without black history, rather than how distorted black history is without the rest of American history? Why does Joseph choose this emphasis? How does it help (or hinder) his argument?

3. How important are Joseph's alternative suggestions to Black History Month? How do they support his argument that the event as it presently stands should be abolished? That is, how would the effect of the article be different if it were to end with paragraph 7?

4. Why does Joseph use the passive voice when he writes in paragraph 11 that each month "Americans are 'given permission' to commemorate the achievements of black people"? Who (hidden in the passive structure) exactly *gives* this permission? What is the effect of the passive here? What does it contribute to his argument?

5. Why does Joseph refer to "multicultural society" only once in paragraph 10, and refer briefly in paragraph 12 to "the contributions of *all* Americans"? Do you think these brief references are gratuitous? If not, how do they support Joseph's argument?

■ WRITING ASSIGNMENTS

1. Write a personal essay in which you discuss the effect (or lack of effect) of Black History Month in your life. Have you enjoyed or benefited from programs and cultural offerings? Have you missed the opportunity to attend any events? Have you been inspired? bored? learned anything useful? In light of your own experiences, what do you think of Joseph's suggestions that children learn about their own families, and that the achievements of all groups be taught and celebrated at all times?

2. Contact your school's African-American student group, support services, or academic program—or whatever organization on campus is responsible for putting together your school's Black History Month activities. What events are planned for this coming year (or have already taken place)? How far in advance did bookings have to be made for special lectures, performances, or other high-profile events? How did the budget for these events compare to funding for other cultural events sponsored by your school? Has attendance at these events been satisfactory in past years, or do organizers see a need to publicize events more widely?

3. Using your library's resources in history, look up the reason and explanations offered by Carter G. Woodson in the 1920s for founding Negro History Week (as it was then called). If possible, review the responses and discussions from that era in journals published by and for African-Americans. How true to its original aims has this February celebration remained? What do you think Joseph would say to Woodson, if he had the opportunity?

4. Compare Joseph's sense of the importance of education in this article with that of Arthur M. Schlesinger, Jr., in "The Cult of Ethnicity, Good and Bad."

What assumptions does each author make about the role of education in shaping Americans' sense of who they are and what they have accomplished? What qualities does each author find desirable to teach children? Why do they focus on education, rather than on media or fine arts?

Race Matters
Cornel West

We close with an appeal for a meaningful discussion of race by one of America's eminent black scholars. Cornel West, who is a professor of religion at Princeton University and director of its Afro-American Studies Program, agrees with Ishmael Reed that America is emerging as a truly multicultural society. He also agrees with Arthur M. Schlesinger, Jr. that Afrocentrism is "misguided" because it perceives race in ways too narrow and divisive. However, he sees a tired and dangerous double standard still operating when it comes to race. "White America," he says, "has been historically weak-willed in ensuring racial justice and has continued to resist fully accepting the humanity of blacks." Pointing to the 1992 Los Angeles riots, he calls for some fundamental changes in the way we view black Americans. And toward the end of creating a "genuine multiracial democracy," West proposes some major steps for reconstituting social equality.

Cornel West is the author of several books including *The American Evasion of Philosophy: A Genealogy of Pragmatism* (1989), *The Ethical Dimensions of Marxist Thought* (1991), *Breaking Bread: Insurgent Black Intellectual Life* (1991), and his best-selling *Race Matters* (1993), from which this essay comes.

Since the beginning of the nation, white Americans have suffered from a deep inner uncertainty as to who they really are. One of the ways that has been used to simplify the answer has been to seize upon the presence of black Americans and use them as a marker, a symbol of limits, a metaphor for the "outsider." Many whites could look at the social position of blacks and feel that color formed an easy and reliable gauge for determining to what extent one was or was not American. Perhaps that is why one of the first epithets that many European immigrants learned when they got off the boat was the term "nigger"—it made them feel instantly American. But this is tricky magic. Despite his racial difference and social status, something indisputably American about Negroes not only raised doubts about the white man's value system but aroused the troubling suspicion that whatever else the true American is, he is also somehow black.

RALPH ELLISON, What America Would Be Like Without Blacks (1970)

1 What happened in Los Angeles in April of 1992 was neither a race riot nor a class rebellion. Rather, this monumental upheaval was a multiracial, trans-class, and largely male display of justified social rage. For all its ugly, xenophobic resentment, its air of adolescent carnival, and its downright barbaric behavior, it signified the sense of powerlessness in American society. Glib attempts to reduce its meaning to the pathologies of the black underclass, the criminal actions of hoodlums, or the political revolt of the oppressed urban masses miss the mark. Of those arrested, only 36 percent were black, more than a third had full-time jobs, and most claimed to shun political affiliation. What we witnessed in Los Angeles was the consequence of a lethal linkage of economic decline, cultural decay, and political lethargy in American life. Race was the visible catalyst, not the underlying cause.

2 The meaning of the earthshaking events in Los Angeles is difficult to grasp because most of us remain trapped in the narrow framework of the dominant liberal and conservative views of race in America, which with its worn-out vocabulary leaves us intellectually debilitated, morally disempowered, and personally depressed. The astonishing disappearance of the event from public dialogue is testimony to just how painful and distressing a serious engagement with race is. Our truncated public discussions of race suppress the best of who and what we are as a people because they fail to confront the complexity of the issue in a candid and critical manner. The predictable pitting of liberals against conservatives, Great Society Democrats against self-help Republicans, reinforces intellectual parochialism and political paralysis.

3 The liberal notion that more government programs can solve racial problems is simplistic—precisely because it focuses *solely* on the economic dimension. And the conservative idea that what is needed is a change in the moral behavior of poor black urban dwellers (especially poor black men, who, they say, should stay married, support their children, and stop committing so much crime) highlights immoral actions while ignoring public responsibility for the immoral circumstances that haunt our fellow citizens.

4 The common denominator of these views of race is that each still sees black people as a "problem people," in the words of Dorothy I. Height, president of the National Council of Negro Women, rather than as fellow American citizens with problems. Her words echo the poignant "unasked question" of W. E. B. Du Bois, who, in *The Souls of Black Folk* (1903), wrote:

> They approach me in a half-hesitant sort of way, eye me curiously or compassionately, and then instead of saying directly, How does it feel to be a problem? they say, I know an excellent colored man in my town. . . . Do not these Southern outrages make your blood boil? At these I smile, or am interested, or reduce the boiling to a simmer, as the occasion may require. To the real question, How does it feel to be a problem? I answer seldom a word.

Nearly a century later, we confine discussions about race in America to the "problems" black people pose for whites rather than consider what this way of viewing black people reveals about us as a nation.

5   This paralyzing framework encourages liberals to relieve their guilty consciences by supporting public funds directed as "the problems"; but at the same time, reluctant to exercise principled criticism of black people, liberals deny them the freedom to err. Similarly, conservatives blame the "problems" on black people themselves—and thereby render black social misery invisible or unworthy of public attention.

6   Hence, for liberals, black people are to be "included" and "integrated" into "our" society and culture, while for conservatives they are to be "well behaved" and "worthy of acceptance" by "our" way of life. Both fail to see that the presence and predicaments of black people are neither additions to nor defections from American life, but rather *constitutive elements of that life.*

7   To engage in a serious discussion of race in America, we must begin not with the problems of black people but with the flaws of American society—flaws rooted in historic inequalities and longstanding cultural stereotypes. How we set up the terms for discussing racial issues shapes our perception and response to these issues. As long as black people are viewed as a "them," the burden falls on blacks to do all the "cultural" and "moral" work necessary for healthy race relations. The implication is that only certain Americans can define what it means to be American—and the rest must simply "fit in."

8   The emergence of strong black-nationalist sentiments among blacks, especially among young people, is a revolt against this sense of having to "fit in." The variety of black-nationalist ideologies, from the moderate views of Supreme Court Justice Clarence Thomas in his youth to those of Louis Farrakhan today, rest upon a fundamental truth: white America has been historically weak-willed in ensuring racial justice and has continued to resist fully accepting the humanity of blacks. As long as double standards and differential treatment abound—as long as the rap performer Ice-T is harshly condemned while former Los Angeles Police Chief Daryl F. Gates's antiblack comments are received in polite silence, as long as Dr. Leonard Jeffries's anti-Semitic statements are met with vitriolic outrage while presidential candidate Patrick J. Buchanan's anti-Semitism receives a genteel response—black nationalisms will thrive.

9   Afrocentrism, a contemporary species of black nationalism, is a gallant yet misguided attempt to define an African identity in a white society perceived to be hostile. It is gallant because it puts black doings and sufferings, not white anxieties and fears, at the center of discussion. It is misguided because—out of fear of cultural hybridization and through silence on the issue of class, retrograde views on black women, gay men, and lesbians, and a reluctance to link race to the common good—it reinforces the narrow discussions about race.

10   To establish a new framework, we need to begin with a frank acknowledgment of the basic humanness and Americanness of each of us. And we must acknowledge that as a people—*E Pluribus Unum*—we are on a slippery slope toward economic strife, social turmoil, and cultural chaos. If we go down, we go down together. The Los Angeles upheaval forced us to see not only that we are not connected in ways we would like to be but also, in a more profound sense, that this failure to connect

binds us even more tightly together. The paradox of race in America is that our common destiny is more pronounced and imperiled precisely when our divisions are deeper. The Civil War and its legacy speak loudly here. And our divisions are growing deeper. Today, eighty-six percent of white suburban Americans live in neighborhoods that are less than 1 percent black, meaning that the prospects for the country depend largely on how its cities fare in the hands of a suburban electorate. There is no escape from our interracial interdependence, yet enforced racial hierarchy dooms us as a nation to collective paranoia and hysteria—the unmaking of any democratic order.

11   The verdict in the Rodney King case which sparked the incidents in Los Angeles was perceived to be wrong by the vast majority of Americans. But whites have often failed to acknowledge the widespread mistreatment of black people, especially black men, by law enforcement agencies, which helped ignite the spark. The verdict was merely the occasion for deep-seated rage to come to the surface. This rage is fed by the "silent" depression ravaging the country—in which real weekly wages of all American workers since 1973 have declined nearly 20 percent, while at the same time wealth has been upwardly distributed.

12   The exodus of stable industrial jobs from urban centers to cheaper labor markets here and abroad, housing policies that have created "chocolate cities and vanilla suburbs" (to use the popular musical artist George Clinton's memorable phrase), white fear of black crime, and the urban influx of poor Spanish-speaking and Asian immigrants—all have helped erode the tax base of American cities just as the federal government has cut its supports and programs. The result is unemployment, hunger, homelessness, and sickness for millions.

13   And a pervasive spiritual impoverishment grows. The collapse of meaning in life—the eclipse of hope and absence of love of self and others, the breakdown of family and neighborhood bonds—leads to the social deracination and cultural denudement of urban dwellers, especially children. We have created rootless, dangling people with little link to the supportive networks—family, friends, school—that sustain some sense of purpose in life. We have witnessed the collapse of the spiritual communities that in the past helped Americans face despair, disease, and death and that transmit through the generations dignity and decency, excellence and elegance.

14   The result is lives of what we might call "random nows," of fortuitous and fleeting moments preoccupied with "getting over"—with acquiring pleasure, property, and power by any means necessary. (This is not what Malcolm X meant by this famous phrase.) Post-modern culture is more and more a market culture dominated by gangster mentalities and self-destructive wantonness. This culture engulfs all of us—yet its impact on the disadvantaged is devastating, resulting in extreme violence in everyday life. Sexual violence against women and homicidal assaults by young black men on one another are only the most obvious signs of this empty quest for pleasure, property, and power.

15   Last, this rage is fueled by a political atmosphere in which images, not ideas, dominate, where politicians spend more time raising money than debating issues. The functions of parties have been displaced by public polls, and politicians behave less as thermostats that determine the climate of opinion than as thermometers regis-

tering the public mood. American politics has been rocked by an unleashing of greed among opportunistic public officials—who have followed the lead of their counterparts in the private sphere, where, as of 1989, 1 percent of the population owned 37 percent of the wealth and 10 percent of the population owned 86 percent of the wealth—leading to a profound cynicism and pessimism among the citizenry.

16 And given the way in which the Republican Party since 1968 has appealed to popular xenophobic images—playing the black, female, and homophobic cards to realign the electorate along race, sex, and sexual-orientation lines—it is no surprise that the notion that we are all part of one garment of destiny is discredited. Appeals to special interests rather than to public interests reinforce this polarization. The Los Angeles upheaval was an expression of utter fragmentation by a powerless citizenry that includes not just the poor but all of us.

17 What is to be done? How do we capture a new spirit and vision to meet the challenges of the post-industrial city, post-modern culture, and post-party politics?

18 First, we must admit that the most valuable sources for help, hope, and power consist of ourselves and our common history. As in the ages of Lincoln, Roosevelt, and King, we must look to new frameworks and languages to understand our multi-layered crisis and overcome our deep malaise.

19 Second, we must focus our attention on the public square—the common good that undergirds our national and global destinies. The vitality of any public square ultimately depends on how much we *care* about the quality of our lives together. The neglect of our public infrastructure, for example—our water and sewage systems, bridges, tunnels, highways, subways, and streets—reflects not only our myopic economic policies, which impede productivity, but also the low priority we place on our common life.

20 The tragic plight of our children clearly reveals our deep disregard for public well-being. About one out of every five children in this country lives in poverty, including one out of every two black children and two out of every five Hispanic children. Most of our children—neglected by overburdened parents and bombarded by the market values of profit-hungry corporations—are ill-equipped to live lives of spiritual and cultural quality. Faced with these facts, how do we expect ever to constitute a vibrant society?

21 One essential step is some form of large-scale public intervention to ensure access to basic social goods—housing, food, health care, education, child care, and jobs. We must invigorate the common good with a mixture of government, business, and labor that does not follow any existing blueprint. After a period in which the private sphere has been sacralized and the public square gutted, the temptation is to make a fetish of the public square. We need to resist such dogmatic swings.

22 Last, the major challenge is to meet the need to generate new leadership. The paucity of courageous leaders—so apparent in the response to the events in Los Angeles—requires that we look beyond the same elites and voices that recycle the older frameworks. We need leaders—neither saints nor sparkling television personalities—who can situate themselves within a larger historical narrative of this country and our world, who can grasp the complex dynamics of our peoplehood and imagine a future grounded in the best of our past, yet who are attuned to the fright-

ening obstacles that now perplex us. Our ideals of freedom, democracy, and equality must be invoked to invigorate all of us, especially the landless, propertyless, and luckless. Only a visionary leadership that can motivate "the better angels of our nature," as Lincoln said, and activate possibilities for a freer, more efficient, and stable America—only that leadership deserves cultivation and support.

23   This new leadership must be grounded in grass-roots organizing that highlights democratic accountability. Whoever *our* leaders will be as we approach the twenty-first century, their challenge will be to help Americans determine whether a genuine multiracial democracy can be created and sustained in an era of global economy and a moment of xenophobic frenzy.

24   Let us hope and pray that the vast intelligence, imagination, humor, and courage of Americans will not fail us. Either we learn a new language of empathy and compassion, or the fire this time will consume us all.

■ TOPICAL CONSIDERATIONS

1. According to West's first two paragraphs, what was the meaning or reason for the Los Angeles riots in April 1992, following the return of the verdict in the first trial against L.A. police officers for beating Rodney King? What does West say the riots did *not* mean? What evidence does he supply for his interpretation?

2. In paragraphs 3 through 6, West dismisses both the liberal and the conservative approaches to solving racial problems. What views does he say are typical of each position? Why does each one fail according to West?

3. West says that both liberals and conservatives treat black people as "problems." What does he mean by this statement? How does each group differ in its solution to the "problem"? Have you ever been "a problem," rather than a human being?

4. What is black nationalism, according to West's discussion in paragraphs 8 through 9? How does it try to respond to the shortcomings of liberal and conservative solutions to "the problem"? Under what conditions does it thrive? How does black nationalism fail to resolve America's racial problems?

5. In paragraph 10, West calls for a "new framework" for American identity, a working coalition that acknowledges and benefits everyone in the nation, of every heritage or background. What does he have to say from here through paragraph 16 about the following problems that need to be resolved: (a) economics; (b) class, and geographic mobility; and (c) political structures?

6. In paragraphs 10 through 16, West also talks about spiritual decay and cultural decay which either have been caused by or are symptoms of the three concerns mentioned in question 4. How does West believe the quality and integrity of life has deteriorated for all Americans?

7. In paragraphs 17 through 23, West offers some solutions to the problems he has outlined. What does he mean by the "public square"? Where does this metaphor come from? What meanings does West attach to it?

8. What kinds of leaders does West call for? How does his description of the new kind of leader in paragraphs 22 and 23 remedy some of the problems he has outlined in paragraphs 15 and 16? How easy do you think it will be to locate or put such individuals into power?

■ RHETORICAL CONSIDERATIONS

1. West does not introduce the thesis or the central question of his essay until paragraph 17. Why do you think he places his discussions of the riots, the failings of liberals and conservatives, the critiques of black nationalism, and the litany of America's woes prior to this central question? What effect does this structure have? How does each section lead up to his main idea?

2. Why does West begin his article with the epigraph from Ralph Ellison's essay? What do you think of the length of this passage? Why doesn't West discuss it directly in his article? How are content and theme related to West's own ideas?

3. West uses personification (attributing human qualities to abstract nouns, or to institutional groups, which are incapable of embodying those qualities)—for example, the Civil War and its legacy "speak loudly" in paragraph 10. What other examples does he use throughout the article? Do you find a pattern to such personification here? What effect do these figures of speech have?

4. In the first sentence of paragraph 6, West uses quotes, but not to mean that he's citing another source. How does he use quote marks here? Is his use of punctuation excessive? What ideas in his argument do the quote marks reinforce? Can you rewrite the sentence to retain the same meaning without quote marks? How does the effect of your rewrite differ from the original?

5. How hopeful would you characterize Cornel West's attitude in this essay? That is, how optimistic is he that Americans will resolve the problems he has outlined? In your opinion, how realistic are the solutions he offers?

6. In his preface to the book in which this essay appears, West uses as an epigraph a quote from a 1963 James Baldwin essay. In this passage, Baldwin has called for changes in race matters; he concludes "If we do not now dare everything, the fulfillment of that prophecy, recreated from the Bible in song by a slave, is upon us: GOD GAVE NOAH THE RAINBOW SIGN, NO MORE WATER, THE FIRE NEXT TIME!" What effect does West's echo of Baldwin at the end of his essay create?

■ WRITING ASSIGNMENTS

1. Write a personal experience essay in which you describe your personal response to the L.A. riots in April 1992. You may want to include your responses to the Rodney King beating, and to the second trial of the police

officers after the riots. How aware were you of these events? Did you notice any changes or responses in your community? What did you personally think about the riots at the time? Have your opinions and feelings changed at all?

2. Cornel West in this article, Ishmael Reed in "America: The Multinational Society," and Arthur M. Schlesinger, Jr. in "The Cult of Ethnicity," all begin from the same basic problem: America lacks national unity, and that lack has something to do with multicultural diversity. How does each author define the problem? What differences and similarities does each have with the other two? On what points might all agree?

3. Select one pair of the African-American and white newsmakers West lists in paragraph 8, that is, Ice-T and Daryl Gates, or Leonard Jeffries and Patrick Buchanan. Then, using recent news resources, find out what has each man said or done to have earned him notoriety? What was the public response to each one? Why does West say that a double standard was applied based on race?

4. Choose one contemporary reform issue which you think West would approve of, based on his discussions about a new framework and new spirit for public governance in paragraphs 17 through 24. For example, you might use health-care reform, repairs and maintenance of public utilities, social services benefiting children, or the mechanisms of electoral politics. What is at stake? What is the role attributed to race, class, economics, politics, and spiritual meaning in the way decisions are being made? In your opinion, are the issues under discussion, and any changes that have been made so far, adequate?

elevision is the prime mover of American culture. It is the foremost source of entertainment and news. More than any other medium, it regulates commerce, lifestyles, and social values. For many Americans television is the window of the world. In this chapter we will explore some of the various ways this extraordinary entity has become part of our lives—for better or worse.

By the age of 65, the average viewer will have spent nine years in front of the TV set. It's no wonder that a major complaint is how television takes kids away from creative play—reading, daydreaming, art, and sports. Yet another complaint is that with some 200 million TV sets in use in America today, television has intruded on family life. In our opening piece, "The Plug-In Drug," Marie Winn argues that television is replacing traditional family rituals while interfering in the formation of family bonds.

According to a 1993 report by the National Coalition on Television Violence, the average American child will have seen 200,000 violent acts on TV by the age of 18, including 40,000 murders. Since television shapes our behavior and attitudes, such heavy exposure to broadcast mayhem threatens to desensitize viewers, especially young ones, while prompting real violence. And that is the complaint of *Newsweek* columnist Meg Greenfield in "TV's True Violence."

And now for a look at the news—or, more precisely, the nonnews. The next piece, "Now . . . This," argues that the "entertainment values" of broadcast news have corrupted our knowledge of world affairs. With its heavy reliance on dynamic images and pleasing personalities, says Neil Postman, news has been packaged to suit the requirements of show biz, not the dissemination of information.

A byproduct of the television age is the creation of instant celebrities—personalities "to satisfy our primal need for gossip," says Christina Kelly in her essay, "Why Do We Need Celebrities?" Kelly wonders just what Luke Perry or Julia Roberts has done for humanity.

Black celebrities are the subject of the subsequent piece, "The Wrong Examples." According to David L. Evans, television viewers think the majority of successful black males are athletes or entertainers. Not only is that an unfortunate illusion, says Evans, but the medium is choked with poor role models for black children.

One of the most successful sitcoms ever is *Roseanne.* And, yet, for all the academic and popular articles written about television, very little has been said about Roseanne and her show, says Elayne Rapping in her piece, "In Praise of Roseanne." According to this media critic, one reason for the absence of serious discourse despite Roseanne's originality, talent, and "political *chutzpah*" is class. Roseanne is a blue-collar loudmouth with toughness, compassion, and a refreshing sense of humor.

So far, we have heard much about how bad television is with its dumb, low-grade shows; its violence; its deleterious effects on children; its undermining of the family. Some reviewers, however, have made peace with the tube. In "Don't Blame TV," ABC-TV commentator Jeff Greenfield contends that critics get carried away trying to pin all our social woes on television. Point-for-point he attempts to debunk their claims.

We close this chapter with a few chuckles from P. J. O'Rourke. "Why I Quit Watching Television" is the humorous confession of a man who decided to do something about all the grim reports of how TV has no artistic or social value, how it rots our brains, how it turns us into zombies. He got rid of his set. But as O'Rourke discovers, life without television was like . . . well, keep reading.

The Plug-In Drug

Marie Winn

For years, the harmful effects of television, particularly on children, have been the professional interest of social commentator and writer Marie Winn. She is author of The Plug-in Drug: TV *(1985), from which this essay has been adapted, and* Children Without Childhood *(1983). She says that home and family life have changed considerably—and in ways we may not care to imagine—since the invention of television. She makes a strong case against television, accusing it of being a prime force in the warping of children and in the disintegration of the American family.*

1   Less than forty years after the introduction of television into American society, a period that has seen the medium become so deeply ingrained in American life that in at least one state the television set has attained the rank of a legal necessity, safe from repossession in case of debt along with clothes, cooking utensils, and the like, television viewing has become an inevitable and ordinary part of daily life. Only in the early years of television did writers and commentators have sufficient perspective to separate the activity of watching television from the actual content it offers the viewer. In those early days writers frequently discussed the effects of television on family life. However, a curious myopia afflicted those early observers: almost without exception they regarded television as a favorable, beneficial, indeed, wondrous influence upon the family.

2   "Television is going to be a real asset in every home where there are children," predicts a writer in 1949.

3   "Television will take over your way of living and change your children's habits, but this change can be a wonderful improvement," claims another commentator.

4   "No survey's needed, of course, to establish that television has brought the family together in one room," writes *The New York Times'* television critic in 1949.

5   Each of the early articles about television is invariably accompanied by a photograph or illustration showing a family cozily sitting together before the television set, Sis on Mom's lap, Buddy perched on the arm of Dad's chair, Dad with his arm around Mom's shoulder. Who could have guessed that twenty or so years later Mom

would be watching a drama in the kitchen, the kids would be looking at cartoons in their room, while Dad would be taking in the ball game in the living room?

6   Of course television sets were enormously expensive in those early days. The idea that by 1982 more than half of all American families would own two or more sets seemed preposterous. The splintering of the multiple-set family was something the early writers could not foresee. Nor did anyone imagine the number of hours children would eventually devote to television, the changes television would effect upon child-rearing methods, the increasing domination of family schedules by children's viewing requirements—in short, the *power* of television to dominate family life.

7   After the first years, as children's consumption of the new medium increased, together with parental concern about the possible effects of so much television viewing, a steady refrain helped to soothe and reassure anxious parents. "Television always enters a pattern of influences that already exist: the home, the peer group, the school, the church and culture generally," wrote the authors of an early and influential study of television's effects on children. In other words, if the child's home life is all right, parents need not worry about the effects of all that television watching.

8   But television did not merely influence the child; it deeply influenced that "pattern of influences" everyone hoped would ameliorate the new medium's effects. Home and family life have changed in important ways since the advent of television. The peer group has become television-oriented, and much of the time children spend together is occupied by television viewing. Culture generally has been transformed by television. Therefore it is improper to assign to television the subsidiary role its many apologists (too often members of the television industry) insist it plays. Television is not merely one of a number of important influences upon today's child. Through the changes it has made in family life, television emerges as *the* important influence in children's lives today.

THE QUALITY OF FAMILY LIFE

9 Television's contribution to family life has been an equivocal one. For while it has, indeed, kept the members of the family from dispersing, it has not served to bring them *together.* By its domination of the time families spend together, it destroys the special quality that distinguishes one family from another, a quality that depends to a great extent on what a family *does,* what special rituals, games, recurrent jokes, familiar songs, and shared activities it accumulates.

10   "Like the sorcerer of old," writes Urie Bronfenbrenner, "the television set casts its magic spell, freezing speech and action, turning the living into silent statues so long as the enchantment lasts. The primary danger of the television screen lies not so much in the behavior it produces—although there is danger there—as in the behavior it prevents: the talks, the games, the family festivities and arguments through which much of the child's learning takes place and through which his character is formed. Turning on the television set can turn off the process that transforms children into people."

11   Yet parents have accepted a television-dominated family life so completely that they cannot see how the medium is involved in whatever problems they might be having. A first-grade teacher reports:

12   "I have one child in the group who's an only child. I wanted to find out more about her family life because this little girl was quite isolated from the group, didn't make friends, so I talked to her mother. Well, they don't have time to do anything in the evening, the mother said. The parents come home after picking up the child at the baby-sitter's. Then the mother fixes dinner while the child watches TV. Then they have dinner and the child goes to bed. I said to this mother, 'Well, couldn't she help you fix dinner? That would be a nice time for the two of you to talk,' and the mother said, 'Oh, but I'd hate to have her miss "Zoom." It's such a good program!'"

13   Even when families make efforts to control television, too often its very presence counterbalances the positive features of family life. A writer and mother of two boys aged 3 and 7 described her family's television schedule in an article in *The New York Times:*

>   We were in the midst of a full-scale War. Every day was a new battle and every program was a major skirmish. We agreed it was a bad scene all around and were ready to enter diplomatic negotiations. . . . In principle we have agreed on 2½ hours of TV a day, "Sesame Street," "Electric Company" (with dinner gobbled up in between) and two half-hour shows between 7 and 8:30 which enables the grown-ups to eat in peace and prevents the two boys from destroying one another. Their pre-bedtime choice is dreadful, because, as Josh recently admitted, "There's nothing much on I really like." . . . Clearly there is a need for first-rate children's shows at this time. . . .

14   Consider the "family life" described here: Presumably the father comes home from work during the "Sesame Street"—"Electric Company" stint. The children are either watching television, gobbling their dinner, or both. While the parents eat their dinner in peaceful privacy, the children watch another hour of television. Then there is only a half-hour left before bedtime, just enough time for baths, getting pajamas on, brushing teeth, and so on. The children's evening is regimented with an almost military precision. They watch their favorite programs, and when there is "nothing much on I really like," they watch whatever else is on—because *watching* is the important thing. Their mother does not see anything amiss with watching programs just for the sake of watching; she only wishes there were some first-rate children's shows on at those times.

15   Without conjuring up memories of the Victorian era with family games and long, leisurely meals, and large families, the question arises: isn't there a better family life available than this dismal, mechanized arrangement of children watching television for however long is allowed them, evening after evening?

16   Of course, families today still do *special* things together at times: go camping in the summer, go to the zoo on a nice Sunday, take various trips and expeditions. But their *ordinary* daily life together is diminished—that sitting around at the dinner table, that spontaneous taking up of an activity, those little games invented by children on the spur of the moment when there is nothing else to do, the scribbling, the chatting, and even the quarreling, all the things that form the fabric of a family, that

define a childhood. Instead, the children have their regular schedule of television programs and bedtime, and the parents have their peaceful dinner together.

17   The author of the article in the *Times* notes that "keeping a family sane means mediating between the needs of both children and adults." But surely the needs of the adults are being better met than the needs of the children, who are effectively shunted away and rendered untroublesome, while their parents enjoy a life as undemanding as that of any childless couple. In reality, it is those very demands that young children make upon a family that lead to growth, and it is the way parents accede to those demands that builds the relationships upon which the future of the family depends. If the family does not accumulate its backlog of shared experiences, shared *everyday* experiences that occur and recur and change and develop, then it is not likely to survive as anything other than a caretaking institution.

FAMILY RITUALS

18 Ritual is defined by sociologists as "that part of family life that the family likes about itself, is proud of and wants formally to continue." Another text notes that "the development of a ritual by a family is an index of the common interest of its members in the family as a group."

19   What has happened to family rituals, those regular, dependable, recurrent happenings that gave members of a family a feeling of *belonging* to a home rather than living in it merely for the sake of convenience, those experiences that act as the adhesive of family unity far more than any material advantages?

20   Mealtime rituals, going-to-bed rituals, illness rituals, holiday rituals—how many of these have survived the inroads of the television set?

21   A young woman who grew up near Chicago reminisces about her childhood and gives an idea of the effects of television upon family rituals:

22   "As a child I had millions of relatives around—my parents both come from relatively large families. My father had nine brothers and sisters. And so every holiday there was this great swoop-down of aunts, uncles, and millions of cousins. I just remember how wonderful it used to be. These thousands of cousins would come and everyone would play and ultimately, after dinner, all the women would be in the front of the house, drinking coffee and talking, all the men would be in the back of the house, drinking and smoking, and all the kids would be all over the place, playing hide and seek. Christmas time was particularly nice because everyone always brought all their toys and games. Our house had a couple of rooms with go-through closets, so there were always kids running in a great circle route. I remember it was just wonderful.

23   "And then all of a sudden one year I remember becoming suddenly aware of how different everything had become. The kids were no longer playing Monopoly or Clue or the other games we used to play together. It was because we had a television set which had been turned on for a football game. All of that socializing that had gone on previously had ended. Now everyone was sitting in front of the television

set, on a holiday, at a family party! I remember being stunned by how awful that was. Somehow the television had become more attractive."

24   As families have come to spend more and more of their time together engaged in the single activity of television watching, those rituals and pastimes that once gave family life its special quality have become more and more uncommon. Not since prehistoric times, when cave families hunted, gathered, ate, and slept, with little time remaining to accumulate a culture of any significance, have families been reduced to such a sameness.

REAL PEOPLE

25 It is not only the activities that a family might engage in together that are diminished by the powerful presence of television in the home. The relationships of the family members to each other are also affected, in both obvious and subtle ways. The hours that children spend in a one-way relationship with television people, an involvement that allows for no communication or interaction, surely affect their relationships with real-life people.

26 Studies show the importance of eye-to-eye contact, for instance, in real-life relationships, and indicate that the nature of one's eye-contact patterns, whether one looks another squarely in the eye or looks to the side or shifts one's gaze from side to side, may play a significant role in one's success or failure in human relationships. But no eye contact is possible in the child-television relationship, although in certain children's programs people purport to speak directly to the child and the camera fosters this illusion by focusing directly upon the person being filmed. (Mister Rogers is an example, telling the child, "I like you, you're special," etc.). How might such a distortion of real-life relationships affect a child's development of trust, of openness, of an ability to relate well to other *real* people?

27 Bruno Bettelheim writes:

> Children who have been taught, or conditioned, to listen passively most of the day to the warm verbal communications coming from the TV screen, to the deep emotional appeal of the so-called TV personality, are often unable to respond to real persons because they arouse so much less feeling than the skilled actor. Worse, they lose the ability to learn from reality because life experiences are much more complicated than the ones they see on the screen. . . .[†]

28 A teacher makes a similar observation about her personal viewing experiences:

29 "I have trouble mobilizing myself and dealing with real people after watching a few hours of television. It's just hard to make that transition from watching television to a real relationship. I suppose it's because there was no effort necessary while I was watching, and dealing with real people always requires a bit of effort.

[†]Bruno Bettelheim (1903–1991) was a world-renowned child psychologist and author of many books on the development of children's imaginations and identities. (Editor's note)

Imagine, then, how much harder it might be to do the same thing for a small child, particularly one who watches a lot of television every day."

30   But more obviously damaging to family relationships is the elimination of opportunities to talk, and perhaps more important, to argue, to air grievances, between parents and children and brothers and sisters. Families frequently use television to avoid confronting their problems, problems that will not go away if they are ignored but will only fester and become less easily resolvable as time goes on.

31   A mother reports:

32   "I find myself, with three children, wanting to turn on the TV set when they're fighting. I really have to struggle not to do it because I feel that's telling them this is the solution to the quarrel—but it's so tempting that I often do it."

33   A family therapist discusses the use of television as an avoidance mechanism:

34   "In a family I know the father comes home from work and turns on the television set. The children come and watch with him and the wife serves them their meal in front of the set. He then goes and takes a shower, or works on the car or something. She then goes and has her own dinner in front of the television set. It's a symptom of a deeper-rooted problem, sure. But it would help them all to get rid of the set. It would be far easier to work on what the symptom really means without the television. The television simply encourages a double avoidance of each other. They'd find out more quickly what was going on if they weren't able to hide behind the TV. Things wouldn't necessarily be better, of course, but they wouldn't be anesthetized."

35   The decreased opportunities for simple conversation between parents and children in the television-centered home may help explain an observation made by an emergency room nurse at a Boston hospital. She reports that parents just seem to sit there these days when they come in with a sick or seriously injured child, although talking to the child would distract and comfort him. "They don't seem to know *how* to talk to their own children at any length," the nurse observes. Similarly, a television critic writes in the *New York Times:* "I had just a day ago taken my son to the emergency ward of a hospital for stitches above his left eye, and the occasion seemed no more real to me than Maalot or 54th Street, south-central Los Angeles. There was distance and numbness and an inability to turn off the total institution. I didn't behave at all; I just watched. . . ."

36   A number of research studies substantiate the assumption that television interferes with family activities and the formation of family relationships. One survey shows that 78 percent of the respondents indicate no conversation taking place during viewing except at specified times such as commercials. The study notes: "The television atmosphere in most households is one of quiet absorption on the part of family members who are present. The nature of the family social life during a program could be described as 'parallel' rather than interactive, and the set does seem to dominate family life when it is on." Thirty-six percent of the respondents in another study indicated that television viewing was the only family activity participated in during the week.

37   In a summary of research findings on television's effect on family interactions James Garbarino states: "The early findings suggest that television had a disruptive

effect upon interaction and thus presumably human development. . . . It is not unreasonable to ask: 'Is the fact that the average American family during the 1950's came to include two parents, two children and a television set somehow related to the psychosocial characteristics of the young adults of the 1970's?'"

UNDERMINING THE FAMILY

38   In its effect on family relationships, in its facilitation of parental withdrawal from an active role in the socialization of their children, and in its replacement of family rituals and special events, television has played an important role in the disintegration of the American family. But of course it has not been the only contributing factor, perhaps not even the most important one. The steadily rising divorce rate, the increase in the number of working mothers, the decline of the extended family, the breakdown of neighborhoods and communities, the growing isolation of the nuclear family—all have seriously affected the family.

39   As Urie Bronfenbrenner suggests, the sources of family breakdown do not come from the family itself, but from the circumstances in which the family finds itself and the way of life imposed upon it by those circumstances. "When those circumstances and the way of life they generate undermine relationships of trust and emotional security between family members, when they make it difficult for parents to care for, educate and enjoy their children, when there is no support or recognition from the outside world for one's role as a parent and when time spent with one's family means frustration of career, personal fulfillment and peace of mind, then the development of the child is adversely affected," he writes.

40   But while the roots of alienation go deep into the fabric of American social history, television's presence in the home fertilizes them, encourages their wild and unchecked growth. Perhaps it is true that America's commitment to the television experience masks a spiritual vacuum, an empty and barren way of life, a desert of materialism. But it is television's dominant role in the family that anesthetizes the family into accepting its unhappy state and prevents it from struggling to better its condition, to improve its relationships, and to regain some of the richness it once possessed.

41   Others have noted the role of mass media in perpetuating an unsatisfactory *status quo*. Leisure-time activity, writes Irving Howe, "must provide relief from work monotony without making the return to work too unbearable; it must provide amusement without insight and pleasure without disturbance—as distinct from art which gives pleasure through disturbance. Mass culture is thus oriented towards a central aspect of industrial society: the depersonalization of the individual." Similarly, Jacques Ellul rejects the idea that television is a legitimate means of educating the citizen: "Education . . . takes place only incidentally. The clouding of his consciousness is paramount. . . ."

42   And so the American family muddles on, dimly aware that something is amiss but distracted from an understanding of its plight by an endless stream of television images. As family ties grow weaker and vaguer, as children's lives become more

separate from their parents', as parents' educational role in their children's lives is taken over by television and schools, family life becomes increasingly more unsatisfying for both parents and children. All that seems to be left is love, an abstraction that family members *know* is necessary but find great difficulty giving each other because the traditional opportunities for expressing love within the family have been reduced or destroyed.

43   For contemporary parents, love toward each other has increasingly come to mean successful sexual relations, as witnessed by the proliferation of sex manuals and sex therapists. The opportunities for manifesting other forms of love through mutual support, understanding, nurturing, even, to use an unpopular word, *serving* each other, are less and less available as mothers and fathers seek their independent destinies outside the family.

44   As for love of children, this love is increasingly expressed through supplying material comforts, amusements, and educational opportunities. Parents show their love for their children by sending them to good schools and camps, by providing them with good food and good doctors, by buying them toys, books, games, and a television set of their very own. Parents will even go further and express their love by attending PTA meetings to improve their children's schools, or by joining groups that are acting to improve the quality of their children's television programs.

45   But this is love at a remove, and is rarely understood by children. The more direct forms of parental love require time and patience, steady, dependable, ungrudgingly given time actually spent *with* children, reading to them, comforting them, playing, joking, and working with them. But even if parents were eager and willing to demonstrate that sort of direct love to their children today, the opportunities are diminished. What with school and Little League and piano lessons and, of course, the inevitable television programs, a day seems to offer just enough time for a goodnight kiss.

■ TOPICAL CONSIDERATIONS

1. According to Winn, in what specific ways does television destroy "the special quality that distinguishes one family from another" (paragraph 9)? What family behavior is dangerously "prevented"?
2. How does television threaten family unity and closeness, according to the author?
3. What does Winn say about the quality of television programs?
4. In what specific ways does television affect children's play and creativity?
5. What evidence does Winn present to support her claim that TV has endangered family rituals?
6. How can television adversely affect the way people—including children—relate to one another?
7. In paragraph 41, Irving Howe is quoted as saying that the mass media, including television, "must provide amusement without insight and pleasure without disturbance." Do you think this is a fair assessment of the nature of

network television? Do you think this is what the general American public wants? What it needs? What about public television? How would Howe assess PBS programs?

■ RHETORICAL CONSIDERATIONS

1. In what ways is television a "plug-in drug"? Is this a fair metaphor?
2. Winn says that people today are so dominated by the television set "that they cannot see how the medium is involved in whatever problems they might be having" (paragraph 11). How well does she illustrate that claim?
3. What would you say Winn's attitude is toward the American television public? Cite some passages in her essay to support your statement.
4. In paragraph 44, Winn speaks of love of children, stating that its expression has been reduced to material display. Do you think she oversimplifies? Does she offer much evidence? Need she do so?
5. Evaluate the kind and amount of evidence Winn summons to support her thesis in the essay. Is some of it excessive? Is it lacking in other places?

■ WRITING ASSIGNMENTS

1. Did television play a prominent role in your home? Did you and your family watch it regularly as you were growing up? If so, try to evaluate any negative effects television had on your family and your upbringing. Consider how it might have functioned as a babysitter for you and how it affected communication between family members, rituals, and creativity.
2. Winn calls television a "plug-in drug." The use of a drug often leads to some effort to shake the habit. Write a paper in which you explore the difficulties some people you know would have in adjusting to life without television. Consider the rigid patterns that might have evolved over the years with television.
3. Imagine what life might be like 20 years from now, given the rapid development and spread of cable television across America. Consider that television might someday have hundreds of channels broadcasting twenty-four hours a day. Consider also possible developments in interactive television where viewers can shop, order movies, or instantly be polled on political issues and candidates. Create a scenario of the total-television family of the future, extrapolating from some of Winn's observations.
4. In paragraph 13, Winn refers to the plight of a mother who tries to "control television" in her home. Write this woman a letter in which you suggest how she can creatively reorganize her family's day around activities other than television and still gets things accomplished.

TV's True Violence

Meg Greenfield

Perhaps the most common concern among critics of television is all the gratuitous violence. Some people worry about the effect of the mayhem and gore on viewers, especially children. Hundreds of studies have concluded that kids learn aggressive behavior from what they see on the screen. What bothers Meg Greenfield is that a steady "bombardment" of violent images will ultimately dull the response of children and adults to the real thing. Yet, she says there is some kind of TV violence she favors despite other critics' complaints.

Meg Greenfield is a columnist for *Newsweek* magazine where this piece appeared in June 1993.

1   Television violence is up for discussion again as yet another argument rages over whether and how much to curb it. I believe no subject in our society generates more hypocrisy and confusion, and that is saying something. Is there too much wanton, even obscene violence on TV, day in and day out? Of course there is, and it is disgusting, unless you are partial to the vivid, colorful sight of exploding heads and strung-out guts and guys endlessly careering around shooting other guys as a matter of mindless, pointless habit. Most of this stuff has long since abandoned any pretense to what the Supreme Court once called, in the context of an obscenity ruling, "redeeming social value." It is gore for gore's sake, drama based on violence as a first and only resort in conflict. Should the TV people who produce, market and broadcast this junk exercise restraint? Of course they should; I am not talking about the imposition of government codes or statutes here, of which I am eternally leery, but rather about the purveyors of this escalating mayhem having the taste and public spiritedness to do some necessary cutting back and toning down themselves.

2   When I say the subject has been a source of world-class hypocrisy I am referring in part to the fact that, although this is now changing, over the years it has generally been the liberals who objected to excessive violence on the tube and the conservatives who objected to the raw sexual stuff and that the two tended often to switch positions and use each other's arguments either pro or anti violence and pro or anti explicit sex. (Where sex and violence increasingly mix on the screen and in fact become a single phenomenon each chooses to see only what it wants to.) One side will tell you that the violence has a terrible seductive effect on the viewers who are coarsened by it and inspired to emulate the carefree aggression that they see. The same will be said of all the panting, pawing sex you witness on the tube—that it is corrupting viewers—only it will often be said this time by the same people who deny that violence has any effect on subsequent viewer behavior; it will, correspondingly, also tend to be denied by those who argue that violence does affect viewers' behavior.

3   Again, I think it's obvious that this bombardment has a coarsening impact on those people who watch faithfully, and especially where children are concerned, it is

surely giving many the idea that what they see portrayed on the screen as a matter of course is what they and others are expected to do in real life. Or, at a minimum, this coarsening involves making the unthinkable just a little less unthinkable, a little more OK.

4   My own objections, however, which are twofold, are somewhat different. First it is not the violence or shocking gore itself to which I object in TV fiction, but rather the volume, profligacy and undiscriminating nature of their presentation. You may read in the classics or observe in the theatrical production of Shakespeare, among others, episodes every bit as shaking and horrible as whatever it is that caused you to turn away from the TV screen the other night. I once saw one of Shakespeare's occasional but memorable onstage eye-gougings enacted in Cambridge, England, with the aid of suddenly popping out peeled grapes. It's the sort of thing you tend to remember long after you have forgotten the names of the characters in the play. Moreover, much Elizabethan theater and other works to which we now defer as classics had plenty of bloody hacking, slashing and related butchery to them designed to amuse an audience given to the enjoyment of bear-baiting, public hangings and assorted other fun.

5   But in the better of this literature anyway, the violence in the story meant something; it was singular; it was committed by a particularly cruel character; it had some purpose beyond its mere power to titillate, frighten and repel. Nor do I think any age has seen anything comparable to our own unending, daily inundation of the home by filmed, superrealistic closeup portrayals of human violence, of maiming and mutilation and slaughter. And although I also suspect that viewers, including kids, are probably better at keeping in mind the difference between art (if that's what it is) and life than some suppose, I do think there's a danger that a continuous diet of this sort of thing can eventually make us insensitive and impervious to the genuine article when we see it.

6   Here I come out for the only kind of TV violence I favor: the real stuff. This is my second worry about all the fictional violence on TV: that it will dull our reactions to the kind that is filmed not on a set but from Bosnia or Liberia or places in this country. I am not talking here of the kind of depiction of horrors that should be treated gingerly in the press, such as shockingly gruesome photographs of stricken or dead people whose living friends and relatives will be needlessly hurt all over again by the reproduction of this image. I am talking about those truly jarring, unsettling, very hard not to turn from images of the wounded kids in Sarajevo, murder victims in a dozen other massacres and wars, or screaming, limbless ones who committed no crime and caused no grievance but were merely unlucky enough to be in there when the terrorist group struck.

7   **_Different critics:_** There is, you understand, a whole school, different from the ordinary critics of TV violence, that thinks _this_ kind of violent or bloody or just plain scary TV representation should go, but for policy reasons. These are the people who maintain that such a large dose of ugly reality and pain will get us all riled up as individuals or as a society or a government and cause us to take some kind of a posi-

tion or think we have to do something or otherwise act in a way that they find troubling. There are people who say the filming of war scenes in Vietnam was wrong because of its impact on so much of the public, who believe that the horrors shown in Somalia or Sarajevo or Tiananmen are also something with which we cannot be trusted, that they tend to make us emotional and lead us away from the rigorous, coldhearted intellectual discipline required for policymaking. I grant that such sights on TV can be partial as to truth and in some ways misleading. But I think in an age of excessive governmental memoranda, autointoxication and blather, they are worth a thousand staged pictures of violence and a million political words. If we can't be trusted with the sight of violent reality or required to deal with it, we ought to go out of business. My main worry about TV violence of the senseless, mindless made-up kind is that it may, in time, render us incapable of recognizing and responding to the real thing.

■ TOPICAL CONSIDERATIONS

1. In her opening paragraph, Greenfield says that "no subject in our society generates more hypocrisy and confusion [than television violence]." How does she define this hypocrisy? Do you agree with her position here? Why or why not?

2. What is your position on the subject of television violence? What is your experience with it? Were you allowed to watch all programs at home, or did your parents impose limits? Have you ever felt personally uncomfortable with the content of a television program? Explain.

3. What kinds of television violence does Greenfield condone? What kinds does she disapprove of? Why? Where do you stand regarding this distinction?

4. Greenfield says that most television programming no longer has "redeeming social value." What do you take this phrase to mean? How might you define it? What are some potential problems with adherence to such a guiding principle?

5. Greenfield says that she is not in favor of the "imposition of government codes or statutes" in the service of controlling television violence. Instead, she places the responsibility for restraint upon television producers. Do you agree with this solution? Or do you think that government regulation is indeed necessary? Explain.

6. What is Greenfield's bottom-line argument against TV violence? Ultimately what might be the effect of bombarding the audience with staged violence? Do you agree with her?

7. Reread Greenfield's last paragraph. What is her critique of the government regarding images of "real" versus "staged" violence on television? How do you regard this critique?

■ RHETORICAL CONSIDERATIONS

1. How would you describe Greenfield's tone in this essay? Is it effective, given her topic? Why or why not?
2. In paragraph 4, Greenfield explains how violence is present in "classic" literature such as Shakespeare, noting a larger purpose for its use than the one it has in most TV programs. Does this comparison strengthen her argument for you? Why or why not?
3. Consider the structure of Greenfield's article. Locate where she directly states her argument. Do you find her format clear and effective? How does the structure of the piece affect the degree to which you are persuaded?
4. Reread Greenfield's conclusion. Do you find it satisfying? Does it provide sufficient closure? Explain your answer.

■ WRITING ASSIGNMENTS

1. Imagine that you are a policy maker in charge of writing a regulatory code regarding TV violence. Write a report outlining your proposals for controlling such violence. What guidelines would you use? Where would you draw the line as to what should be aired and what should not?
2. Write an essay in which you explore the different effects on you of "real" versus "staged" violence. Record your reactions to a program with dramatized violence versus news footage of actual violence (e.g., a recent crime, coverage of events in, say, a war-torn country, even historical footage from World War II or the Holocaust). What were your different responses? Do you feel desensitized in any way to the images of real violence? Do you feel called to action by these real images?
3. Greenfield notes that the principle of "redeeming social value" was determined by the Supreme Court in an obscenity ruling. Research recent legislation regarding the issue of "obscenity." (Recent examples might be the Helms Amendment on funding for the arts and humanities, the Mapplethorpe case in Cincinnati, or the highly publicized censorship cases of 2 Live Crew, Public Enemy and other rap groups). Come up with a working definition of "obscenity" regarding violence. When you have, write an essay analyzing the relationship between "obscenity" and TV violence.

"Now . . . This"

Neil Postman

Television is a visual medium whose fast-paced and dynamic images account for viewing pleasure. Consequently, discourse on television takes the form of entertainment. Simply put, the medium has little tolerance for argument, hypothesis, or explanation—it is all performance, Neil Postman says. And that includes broadcast news. In this essay he argues persuasively that the nightly news is a mindless entertainment package that creates the illusion of keeping the public informed. On the contrary, Postman says the news creates public ignorance by destroying critical faculties and the ability to process or evaluate all the information bits.

Neil Postman is a critic, writer, communication theorist, and professor of communication arts and sciences at New York University. He is editor of *Et cetera*, a journal of general semantics. His many books include *Teaching as a Subversive Activity, The Soft Revolution, The Disappearance of Childhood*, and *Amusing Ourselves to Death* (1985) from which this essay comes. His latest title is *Conscientious Objections* (1992).

1   The American humorist H. Allen Smith once suggested that of all the worrisome words in the English language, the scariest is "uh oh," as when a physician looks at your X rays and with knitted brow says, "Uh oh." I should like to suggest that the words which are the title of this chapter are as ominous as any, all the more so because they are spoken without knitted brow—indeed, with a kind of idiot's delight. The phrase, if that's what it may be called, adds to our grammar a new part of speech, a conjunction that does not connect anything to anything but does the opposite: separates everything from everything. As such, it serves as a compact metaphor for the discontinuities in so much that passes for public discourse in present-day America.

2   "Now . . . this" is commonly used on radio and television newscasts to indicate that what one has just heard or seen has no relevance to what one is about to hear or see, or possibly to anything one is ever likely to hear or see. The phrase is a means of acknowledging the fact that the world as mapped by the speeded-up electronic media has no order or meaning and is not to be taken seriously. There is no murder so brutal, no earthquake so devastating, no political blunder so costly—for that matter, no ball score so tantalizing or weather report so threatening—that it cannot be erased from our minds by a newscaster saying, "Now . . . this." The newscaster means that you have thought long enough on the previous matter (approximately forty-five seconds), that you must not be morbidly preoccupied with it (let us say, for ninety seconds), and that you must now give your attention to another fragment of news or a commercial.

3   Television did not invent the "Now . . . this" world view. . . . It is the offspring of the intercourse between telegraphy and photography. But it is through television that it has been nurtured and brought to a perverse maturity. For on television, nearly every half hour is a discrete event, separated in content, context, and emotional tex-

ture from what precedes and follows it. In part because television sells its time in seconds and minutes, in part because television must use images rather than words, in part because its audience can move freely to and from the television set, programs are structured so that almost each eight-minute segment may stand as a complete event in itself. Viewers are rarely required to carry over any thought or feeling from one parcel of time to another.

4   Of course, in television's presentation of the "news of the day," we may see the "Now . . . this" mode of discourse in its boldest and most embarrassing form. For there, we are presented not only with fragmented news but news without context, without consequences, without value, and therefore without essential seriousness; that is to say, news as pure entertainment.

5   Consider, for example, how you would proceed if you were given the opportunity to produce a television news show for any station concerned to attract the largest possible audience. You would, first, choose a cast of players, each of whom has a face that is both "likable" and "credible." Those who apply would, in fact, submit to you their eight-by-ten glossies, from which you would eliminate those whose countenances are not suitable for nightly display. This means that you will exclude women who are not beautiful or who are over the age of fifty, men who are bald, all people who are overweight or whose noses are too long or whose eyes are too close together. You will try, in other words, to assemble a cast of talking hairdo's. At the very least, you will want those whose faces would not be unwelcome on a magazine cover.

6   Christine Craft has just such a face, and so she applied for a co-anchor position on KMBC-TV in Kansas City. According to a lawyer who represented her in a sexism suit she later brought against the station, the management of KMBC-TV "loved Christine's look." She was accordingly hired in January 1981. She was fired in August 1981 because research indicated that her appearance "hampered viewer acceptance." What exactly does "hampered viewer acceptance" mean? And what does it have to do with the news? Hampered viewer acceptance means the same thing for television news as it does for any television show: Viewers do not like looking at the performer. It also means that viewers do not believe the performer, that she lacks credibility. In the case of a theatrical performance, we have a sense of what that implies: The actor does not persuade the audience that he or she is the character being portrayed. But what does lack of credibility imply in the case of a news show? What character is a co-anchor playing? And how do we decide that the performance lacks verisimilitude? Does the audience believe that the newscaster is lying, that what is reported did not in fact happen, that something important is being concealed?

7   It is frightening to think that this may be so, that the perception of the truth of a report rests heavily on the acceptability of the newscaster. In the ancient world, there was a tradition of banishing or killing the bearer of bad tidings. Does the television news show restore, in a curious form, this tradition? Do we banish those who tell us the news when we do not care for the face of the teller? Does television countermand the warnings we once received about the fallacy of the ad hominem argument?

8   If the answer to any of these questions is even a qualified "Yes," then here is an issue worthy of the attention of epistemologists. Stated in its simplest form, it is that

television provides a new (or, possibly restores an old) definition of truth: The credibility of the teller is the ultimate test of the truth of a proposition. "Credibility" here does not refer to the past record of the teller for making statements that have survived the rigors of reality testing. It refers only to the impression of sincerity, authenticity, vulnerability or attractiveness (choose one or more) conveyed by the actor/reporter.

9   This is a matter of considerable importance, for it goes beyond the question of how truth is perceived on television news shows. If on television, credibility replaces reality as the decisive test of truth-telling, political leaders need not trouble themselves very much with reality provided that their performances consistently generate a sense of verisimilitude. I suspect, for example, that the dishonor that now shrouds Richard Nixon results not from the fact that he lied but that on television he looks like a liar. Which, if true, should bring no comfort to anyone, not even veteran Nixon-haters. For the alternative possibilities are that one may look like a liar but be telling the truth; or even worse, look like a truth-teller but in fact be lying.

10   As a producer of a television news show, you would be well aware of these matters and would be careful to choose your cast on the basis of criteria used by David Merrick and other successful impresarios. Like them, you would then turn your attention to staging the show on principles that maximize entertainment value. You would, for example, select a musical theme for the show. All television news programs begin, end, and are somewhere in between punctuated with music. I have found very few Americans who regard this custom as peculiar, which fact I have taken as evidence for the dissolution of lines of demarcation between serious public discourse and entertainment. What has music to do with the news? Why is it there? It is there, I assume, for the same reason music is used in the theater and films—to create a mood and provide a leitmotif for the entertainment. If there were no music—as is the case when any television program is interrupted for a news flash— viewers would expect something truly alarming, possibly life-altering. But as long as the music is there as a frame for the program, the viewer is comforted to believe that there is nothing to be greatly alarmed about; that, in fact, the events that are reported have as much relation to reality as do scenes in a play.

11   This perception of a news show as a stylized dramatic performance whose content has been staged largely to entertain is reinforced by several other features, including the fact that the average length of any story is forty-five seconds. While brevity does not always suggest triviality, in this case it clearly does. It is simply not possible to convey a sense of seriousness about any event if its implications are exhausted in less than one minute's time. In fact, it is quite obvious that TV news has no intention of suggesting that any story *has* any implications, for that would require viewers to continue to think about it when it is done and therefore obstruct their attending to the next story that waits panting in the wings. In any case, viewers are not provided with much opportunity to be distracted from the next story since in all likelihood it will consist of some film footage. Pictures have little difficulty in overwhelming words and short-circuiting introspection. As a television producer, you would be certain to give both prominence and precedence to any event for which there is some sort of visual documentation. A suspected killer being brought into a

police station, the angry face of a cheated consumer, a barrel going over Niagara Falls (with a person alleged to be in it), the President disembarking from a helicopter on the White House lawn—these are always fascinating or amusing and easily satisfy the requirements of an entertaining show. It is, of course, not necessary that the visuals actually document the point of a story. Neither is it necessary to explain why such images are intruding themselves on public consciousness. Film footage justifies itself, as every television producer well knows.

12   It is also of considerable help in maintaining a high level of unreality that the newscasters do not pause to grimace or shiver when they speak their prefaces or epilogs to the film clips. Indeed, many newscasters do not appear to grasp the meaning of what they are saying, and some hold to a fixed and ingratiating enthusiasm as they report on earthquakes, mass killings and other disasters. Viewers would be quite disconcerted by any show of concern or terror on the part of newscasters. Viewers, after all, are partners with the newscasters in the "Now . . . this" culture, and they expect the newscaster to play out his or her role as a character who is marginally serious but who stays well clear of authentic understanding. The viewers, for their part, will not be caught contaminating their responses with a sense of reality, any more than an audience at a play would go scurrying to call home because a character on stage has said that a murderer is loose in the neighborhood.

13   The viewers also know that no matter how grave any fragment of news may appear (for example, on the day I write a Marine Corps general has declared that nuclear war between the United States and Russia is inevitable), it will shortly be followed by a series of commercials that will, in an instant, defuse the import of the news, in fact render it largely banal. This is a key element in the structure of a news program and all by itself refutes any claim that television news is designed as a serious form of public discourse. Imagine what you would think of me, and this book, if I were to pause here, tell you that I will return to my discussion in a moment, and then proceed to write a few words in behalf of United Airlines or the Chase Manhattan Bank. You would rightly think that I had no respect for you and, certainly, no respect for the subject. And if I did this not once but several times in each chapter, you would think the whole enterprise unworthy of your attention. Why, then, do we not think a news show similarly unworthy? The reason, I believe, is that whereas we expect books and even other media (such as film) to maintain a consistency of tone and a continuity of content, we have no such expectation of television, and especially television news. We have become so accustomed to its discontinuities that we are no longer struck dumb, as any sane person would be, by a newscaster who having just reported that a nuclear war is inevitable goes on to say that he will be right back after this word from Burger King; who says, in other words, "Now . . . this." One can hardly overestimate the damage that such juxtapositions do to our sense of the world as a serious place. The damage is especially massive to youthful viewers who depend so much on television for their clues as to how to respond to the world. In watching television news, they, more than any other segment of the audience, are drawn into an epistemology based on the assumption that all reports of cruelty and death are greatly exaggerated and, in any case, not to be taken seriously or responded to sanely.

14   I should go so far as to say that embedded in the surrealistic frame of a television news show is a theory of anticommunication, featuring a type of discourse that abandons logic, reason, sequence and rules of contradiction. In aesthetics, I believe the name given to this theory is Dadaism; in philosophy, nihilism; in psychiatry, schizophrenia. In the parlance of the theater, it is known as vaudeville.

15   For those who think I am here guilty of hyperbole, I offer the following description of television news by Robert MacNeil, executive editor and co-anchor of the "MacNeil-Lehrer Newshour." The idea, he writes, "is to keep everything brief, not to strain the attention of anyone but instead to provide constant stimulation through variety, novelty, action, and movement. You are required . . . to pay attention to no concept, no character, and no problem for more than a few seconds at a time." He goes on to say that the assumptions controlling a news show are "that bite-sized is best, that complexity must be avoided, that nuances are dispensable, that qualifications impede the simple message, that visual stimulation is a substitute for thought, and that verbal precision is an anachronism."

16   Robert MacNeil has more reason than most to give testimony about the television news show as vaudeville act. The "MacNeil-Lehrer Newshour" is an unusual and gracious attempt to bring to television some of the elements of typographic discourse. The program abjures visual stimulation, consists largely of extended explanations of events and in-depth interviews (which even there means only five to ten minutes), limits the number of stories covered, and emphasizes background and coherence. But television has exacted its price for MacNeil's rejection of a show business format. By television's standards, the audience is minuscule, the program is confined to public-television stations, and it is a good guess that the combined salary of MacNeil and Lehrer is one-fifth of Dan Rather's or Tom Brokaw's.

17   If you were a producer of a television news show for a commercial station, you would not have the option of defying television's requirements. It would be demanded of you that you strive for the largest possible audience, and, as a consequence and in spite of your best intentions, you would arrive at a production very nearly resembling MacNeil's description. Moreover, you would include some things MacNeil does not mention. You would try to make celebrities of your newscasters. You would advertise the show, both in the press and on television itself. You would do "news briefs," to serve as an inducement to viewers. You would have a weatherman as comic relief, and a sportscaster whose language is a touch uncouth (as a way of his relating to the beer-drinking common man). You would, in short, package the whole event as any producer might who is in the entertainment business.

18   The result of all this is that Americans are the best entertained and quite likely the least well-informed people in the Western world. I say this in the face of the popular conceit that television, as a window to the world, has made Americans exceedingly well informed. Much depends here, of course, on what is meant by being informed. I will pass over the now tiresome polls that tell us that, at any given moment, 70 percent of our citizens do not know who is the Secretary of State or the Chief Justice of the Supreme Court. Let us consider, instead, the case of Iran during the drama that was called the "Iranian Hostage Crisis." I don't suppose there has been a story in years that received more continuous attention from television. We

may assume, then, the Americans know most of what there is to know about this unhappy event. And now, I put these questions to you: Would it be an exaggeration to say that not one American in a hundred knows what language the Iranians speak? Or what the word "Ayatollah" means or implies? Or knows any details of the tenets of Iranian religious beliefs? Or the main outlines of their political history? Or knows who the Shah was, and where he came from?

19   Nonetheless, everyone had an opinion about this event, for in America everyone is entitled to an opinion, and it is certainly useful to have a few when a pollster shows up. But these are opinions of a quite different order from eighteenth- or nineteenth-century opinions. It is probably more accurate to call them emotions rather than opinions, which would account for the fact that they change from week to week, as the pollsters tell us. What is happening here is that television is altering the meaning of "being informed" by creating a species of information that might properly be called *disinformation*. I am using this word almost in the precise sense in which it is used by spies in the CIA or KGB. Disinformation does not mean false information. It means misleading information—misplaced, irrelevant, fragmented or superficial information—information that creates the illusion of knowing something but which in fact leads one away from knowing. In saying this, I do not mean to imply that television news deliberately aims to deprive Americans of a coherent, contextual understanding of their world. I mean to say that when news is packaged as entertainment, that is the inevitable result. And in saying that the television news show entertains but does not inform, I am saying something far more serious than that we are being deprived of authentic information. I am saying we are losing our sense of what it means to be well informed. Ignorance is always correctable. But what shall we do if we take ignorance to be knowledge?

20   Here is a startling example of how this process bedevils us. A *New York Times* article is headlined on February 15, 1983:

REAGAN MISSTATEMENTS GETTING LESS ATTENTION

The article begins in the following way:

> President Reagan's aides used to become visibly alarmed at suggestions that he had given mangled and perhaps misleading accounts of his policies or of current events in general. That doesn't seem to happen much anymore.
>
> Indeed, the President continues to make debatable assertions of fact but news accounts do not deal with them as extensively as they once did. In the view of White House officials, the declining news coverage mirrors a *decline in interest by the general public.* (my italics)

21   This report is not so much a news story as a story about the news, and our recent history suggests that it is not about Ronald Reagan's charm. It is about how news is defined, and I believe the story would be quite astonishing to both civil libertarians and tyrants of an earlier time. Walter Lippmann, for example, wrote in 1920: "There can be no liberty for a community which lacks the means by which to detect lies." For all of his pessimism about the possibilities of restoring an eighteenth- and nineteenth-century level of public discourse, Lippmann assumed, as did Thomas

Jefferson before him, that with a well-trained press functioning as a lie-detector, the public's interest in a President's mangling of the truth would be piqued, in both senses of that word. Given the means to detect lies, he believed, the public could not be indifferent to their consequences.

22   But this case refutes his assumption. The reporters who cover the White House are ready and able to expose lies, and thus create the grounds for informed and indignant opinion. But apparently the public declines to take an interest. To press reports of White House dissembling, the public has replied with Queen Victoria's famous line: "We are not amused." However, here the words mean something the Queen did not have in mind. They mean that what is not amusing does not compel their attention. Perhaps if the President's lies could be demonstrated by pictures and accompanied by music the public would raise a curious eyebrow. If a movie, like *All the President's Men,* could be made from his misleading accounts of government policy, if there were a break-in of some sort or sinister characters laundering money, attention would quite likely be paid. We do well to remember that President Nixon did not begin to come undone until his lies were given a theatrical setting at the Watergate hearings. But we do not have anything like that here. Apparently, all President Reagan does is *say* things that are not entirely true. And there is nothing entertaining in that. . . .

23   My point is that we are by now so thoroughly adjusted to the "Now . . . this" world of news—a world of fragments, where events stand alone, stripped of any connection to the past, or to the future, or to other events—that all assumptions of coherence have vanished. And so, perforce, has contradiction. In the context of *no context,* so to speak, it simply disappears. And in its absence, what possible interest could there be in a list of what the President says *now* and what he said *then?* It is merely a rehash of old news, and there is nothing interesting or entertaining in that. The only thing to be amused about is the bafflement of reporters at the public's indifference. There is an irony in the fact that the very group that has taken the world apart should, on trying to piece it together again, be surprised that no one notices much, or cares.

24   For all his perspicacity, George Orwell would have been stymied by this situation; there is nothing "Orwellian" about it. The President does not have the press under his thumb. *The New York Times* and *The Washington Post* are not *Pravda;* the Associated Press is not Tass. And there is no Newspeak here. Lies have not been defined as truth nor truth as lies. All that has happened is that the public has adjusted to incoherence and been amused into indifference. Which is why Aldous Huxley would not in the least be surprised by the story. Indeed, he prophesied its coming. He believed that it is far more likely that the Western democracies will dance and dream themselves into oblivion than march into it, single file and manacled. Huxley grasped, as Orwell did not, that it is not necessary to conceal anything from a public insensible to contradiction and narcoticized by technological diversions. Although Huxley did not specify that television would be our main line to the drug, he would have no difficulty accepting Robert MacNeil's observation that "Television is the *soma* of Aldous Huxley's *Brave New World.*" Big Brother turns out to be Howdy Doody.

25   I do not mean that the trivialization of public information is all accomplished *on* television. I mean that television is the paradigm for our conception of public information. As the printing press did in an earlier time, television has achieved the power to define the form in which news must come, and it has also defined how we shall respond to it. In presenting news to us packaged as vaudeville, television induces other media to do the same, so that the total information environment begins to mirror television.

26   For example, America's newest and highly successful national newspaper, *USA Today,* is modeled precisely on the format of television. It is sold on the street in receptacles that look like television sets. Its stories are uncommonly short, its design leans heavily on pictures, charts and other graphics, some of them printed in various colors. Its weather maps are a visual delight; its sports section includes enough pointless statistics to distract a computer. As a consequence, *USA Today,* which began publication in September 1982, has become the third largest daily in the United States (as of July 1984, according to the Audit Bureau of Circulations), moving quickly to overtake the *Daily News* and the *Wall Street Journal.* Journalists of a more traditional bent have criticized it for its superficiality and theatrics, but the paper's editors remain steadfast in their disregard of typographic standards. The paper's Editor-in-Chief, John Quinn, has said: "We are not up to undertaking projects of the dimensions needed to win prizes. They don't give awards for the best investigative paragraph." Here is an astonishing tribute to the resonance of television's epistemology: In the age of television, the paragraph is becoming the basic unit of news in print media. Moreover, Mr. Quinn need not fret too long about being deprived of awards. As other newspapers join in the transformation, the time cannot be far off when awards will be given for the best investigative sentence.

27   It needs also to be noted here that new and successful magazines such as *People* and *Us* are not only examples of television-oriented print media but have had an extraordinary "ricochet" effect on television itself. Whereas television taught the magazines that news is nothing but entertainment, the magazines have taught television that nothing but entertainment is news. Television programs, such as "Entertainment Tonight," turn information about entertainers and celebrities into "serious" cultural content, so that the circle begins to close: Both the form and content of news become entertainment.

28   Radio, of course, is the least likely medium to join in the descent into Huxleyan world of technological narcotics. It is, after all, particularly well suited to the transmission of rational, complex language. Nonetheless, and even if we disregard radio's captivation by the music industry, we appear to be left with the chilling fact that such language as radio allows us to hear is increasingly primitive, fragmented, and largely aimed at invoking visceral response; which is to say, it is the linguistic analogue to the ubiquitous rock music that is radio's principal source of income. As I write, the trend in call-in shows is for the "host" to insult callers whose language does not, in itself, go much beyond humanoid grunting. Such programs have little content, as this word used to be defined, and are merely of archeological interest in that they give us a sense of what a dialogue among Neanderthals might have been like. More to the point, the language of radio newscasts has become, under the influence of

television, increasingly decontextualized and discontinuous, so that the possibility of anyone's knowing about the world, as against merely knowing *of* it, is effectively blocked. In New York City, radio station WINS entreats its listeners to "Give us twenty-two minutes and we'll give you the world." This is said without irony, and its audience, we may assume, does not regard the slogan as the conception of a disordered mind.

29   And so, we move rapidly into an information environment which may rightly be called trivial pursuit. As the game of that name uses facts as a source of amusement, so do our sources of news. It has been demonstrated many times that a culture can survive misinformation and false opinion. It has not yet been demonstrated whether a culture can survive if it takes the measure of the world in twenty-two minutes. Or if the value of its news is determined by the number of laughs it provides.

■ **TOPICAL CONSIDERATIONS**

1. In your own words briefly summarize Postman's argument in this essay.
2. Why does the author find so "ominous" the two words that make up the title of this piece?
3. Has this reading changed your thinking? Has it affected your perception of broadcast news? If so, explain how. If not, why not?
4. Postman speaks of broadcast news as "pure entertainment." In what different ways is the news made to be entertaining? Do you agree with this claim?
5. How might "viewer credibility" replace "reality as the decisive test of truthtelling"? What dangers does Postman see in this? Do you share his concern?
6. Do you take for granted the "musical theme" of your favorite news show? Could you readily distinguish it from other networks' news themes? Do you like one over the others? If so, what are the reasons? Have you even wondered what music has to do with the news? Would you watch a news show if it had no music? Do you agree with the author's explanation of why news shows have musical themes?
7. "Viewers would be quite disconcerted by any show of concern or terror on the part of newscasters," says the author (paragraph 12). What does he mean by this? Do you agree with his explanation? Have you ever seen a newscaster do anything to violate the neutral approach to a story—for instance, "pause to grimace or shiver" or shake a head?
8. How does the "Now . . . this" structure of news programs reduce their seriousness according to Postman? Do you agree with this assessment? Do you agree with his claims of the damage done to young viewers? Would you restructure news shows if you could? Why or why not?
9. Do you agree or disagree that television "is altering the meaning of 'being informed'" (paragraph 19)? Can you give examples of your own?
10. How has television affected the format of other media? What other examples can you come up with? Going the other way, how has television

adopted magazine formats? What other examples can you come up with? Do Postman's observations here jive with your own? Explain how they do or do not.

■ RHETORICAL CONSIDERATIONS

1. Consider Postman's voice in this article. What sense do you get of him as an individual? Is he someone you'd like to spend some time with? Why or why not? Point to some details in the writing to support your answers.
2. Postman's vocabulary in places is quite sophisticated. Did any of the terms get in the way of your reading? Did you have to look up many? Which ones? What does the level of language here say about the intended audience for the essay?
3. In paragraph 10, Postman invites the reader to pretend he or she is a producer of a TV news show. In fact, he addresses the reader directly as "you." Trace how far this device is used in the essay. Why do you suppose he makes use of the second-person point of view? How effective is this strategy?
4. Explain the references to George Orwell and Aldous Huxley in paragraph 24. How are they used to support Postman's arguments? How effective are these references?
5. Writers at times have difficulty integrating outside sources into their discussion. Choose a paragraph in which Postman cites outside sources. Just how successfully does he incorporate these into the paragraph?

■ WRITING ASSIGNMENTS

1. In paragraph 19, Postman says that we Americans are "losing our sense of what it means to be well informed." Do you agree with this statement, or do you think that Postman is overstating the issue? Gather some evidence of your own and write an essay in which you present your own views on whether we are well informed by the media. You might consider, for instance, the TV coverage of the war with Iraq.
2. Although Postman does not include slogans as one of the features in the entertainment package of broadcast news, some shows make use of them. Consider the slogan for CNN's headline news: "Around the world in thirty minutes." How does this promo line capture Postman's contention that "television is altering the meaning of 'being informed'"? Write a paper stating your views; use supporting details.
3. Postman cites the "MacNeil-Lehrer Newshour" as a superior news program. Over the next few evenings tune in to that program and try to evaluate what makes it so different from network news shows. Consider the proportion of visual presentation to verbal, the level of language, the quality and depth of the coverage, the number and kinds of stories covered, the format and the

newscasters. How many "entertainment" features do you find? If you were not familiar with the program, would you now consider being a steady viewer? Why or why not?

4. Postman complains in paragraph 28 that the language of radio talk shows has declined to an "increasingly primitive, fragmented" level "aimed at invoking visceral response." Listen to some local talk shows. Does the language you hear warrant such complaints? Write an essay with your findings.

Why Do We Need Celebrities?

Christina Kelly

Before television, the public's fascination with cultural icons—from famous writers to movie stars—were satisfied by the gossip found in newspapers and fan magazines. But with the age of television, celebrity obsession was upon us. Not only were famous faces brought to us in our homes "up close and personal," but the medium created celebrities by the minute—all to satisfy an abnormal craving for star dirt. In the essay below, Christina Kelly questions our need for celebrities. Why do we find them fascinating? Why do we make them heroes? Are they appropriate role models for young people? For a reporter who covers teenage stars, her answers are quite unexpected.

In 1987, Christina Kelly started writing for *Sassy* magazine at which she is currently an editor. She has written articles for a variety of other publications including *Spin* and the *Utne Reader.*

1 I was in the shower, trying to think of a celebrity to interview, when I had a philosophical crisis. I wondered: Why do we need celebrities? Who even came up with the idea to make people into stars? And why do we idolize them? For what possible reason does a job like mine exist? Is it a sign of the decline of Western civilization?

2 People think what I do here is so glamorous, because I get to interview stars. And I have to admit that when I first started working at *Sassy* in 1987 I was really psyched about that part of my job. For the first couple of months, anyway. Then I noticed how celebrities (via their publicists) would jerk me around for months, rescheduling our interviews or completely backing out at the last minute. I could never get enough time with a celebrity to find out anything interesting, and some acted just plain rude to my face. I started getting resentful over the way I was treated, and was really disappointed to see that these people I had sort of worshiped from afar were pretty ordinary. So instead of perpetuating their myths, I decided I would just tell the truth. If the celeb was a jerk, I would say so. If he or she was different in person than what their press implied, I would say so. I still kissed a lot of butt, but if I thought anyone was stupid, a no-talent, pretentious or inane, I did not hold back that information.

3   I thought readers would appreciate that kind of honesty. Instead, many of them hated me for it. Even articles that I thought were fairly favorable pissed them off. I have gotten so many attacks on my character, like the over one-thousand-letter barrage of hate mail following my negative New Kids on the Block article almost three years ago, that I've become sort of immune to it by now. I've also received my share of positive fan mail, but it's mostly along the lines of the following: "You are *soooooo* lucky that you got to interview Johnny Depp! I love you!" A non sequitur, yes, but it also brings me to the point of this article: *Why* do people get so passionate over celebrities that they will not tolerate anything but wide-eyed, uncritical adoration? And, despite the fact that I am now really jaded about all this stuff, *why* did I recently dream that Keanu Reeves met me and thought I was so cool that we became best friends, even after I really had met him and decided he was about as articulate as a slug? I did a little scholarly research to find out.

4   A lot of times, fans will talk about Luke Perry or Julia Roberts or Kurt Cobain being their hero. But celebrities are not the same thing as heroes. Heroes existed way before celebrities ever did, even though celebrities now outshine heroes in the public consciousness. The traditional definition of a hero is someone who sacrifices him or herself for a higher purpose: to save other people or to support an idea. They are usually the founder of a new religion, nation, or way of life. Moses is the preeminent Judeo-Christian hero, because he took a journey up the mountain, and came back with the Ten Commandments. Jesus is the Christian hero, because he died for the redemption of humankind. Thomas Jefferson is an American hero, because he helped found a new order. Harriet Tubman risked her life to bring slaves north to freedom. Now, what has Luke Perry done to redeem humanity? At press time, nothing. Still, he is widely adored.

5   One of the little lessons I have learned in my job is that worshiping celebrities leaves you with a distinctly empty feeling. Experts say it's because celeb worship doesn't teach that you have to make sacrifices if you want to achieve anything worthwhile. But adulation of true heroes can inspire people to make sacrifices, both to help themselves and society at large. Now, in case you still doubt that celebrities are not heroes, let me convince you that achievement or even talent has little to do with celebrity. Even though talented people occasionally become celebrities, the easiest way to become one is to be marketed correctly. My friends New Kids on the Block are a perfect example: Impressario Maurice Starr created the group to make a lot of money off teenage girls. He found these five (supposedly cute) young guys, gave them singing and dancing lessons, wrote them some songs and got them a record deal. Publicists then set up interviews with lots of teen magazines (mindless pawns in the celebmaking game who went on and on about how hot they were), videos were made, promoters convinced radio stations to play the singles, and MTV to play the videos, and a phenomenon was created. They made a lot of money for themselves, Starr, and their record company, and they provided thousands of *Sassy* readers with a safe and distant focus for their hormonal longings. They had so many fans that *Rolling Stone* once ran an interview that actually took them seriously—I can only assume they did this because they wanted to sell magazines.

6   So, no-talents become celebrities all the time. The result is that no one in any walk of life seems to care about achievement or talent—the objective is fame.

Everyone wants to be famous, because in our society you are not really considered a success unless you are famous, no matter what your career. So doctors, lawyers, designers, politicians, magazine editors, writers, and artists all hire publicists as a matter of course. Even being famous for doing nothing, like Linda Evangelista or Vanna White, or just being related to someone famous, like Sean Lennon or LaToya Jackson, is more desirable than being truly creative and talented, but obscure.

7 Further proof that celebrities are not heroes: People who have been involved in some scandal or crime are treated like celebrities. Iran-contra flunky Oliver North was made into something of a national hero for his alleged involvement in clandestine activities that are violations of our Constitution. Alleged mafia boss John Gotti has kissed media butt so successfully that at his recent trial he was treated like a movie star rather than the criminal he is.

8 How did the above become celebrities? Like Luke, Johnny, Winona, Paula, Axl, and (your most beloved celebrity here), they satisfy our insatiable demand for something to talk about outside our own inconsequential little lives. Yes, inconsequential—to be human is to feel inconsequential; that's why religion was invented, to make us feel like we have a purpose. Now, with glamorous celebrities being crammed down our throats wherever we turn, we feel about as faceless as bees in a hive. I mean, this stream of famous, rich, powerful, perfectly airbrushed, implanted, and liposuctioned stars is so endless that you would have to be a powerhouse of self-esteem not to feel a little inferior. It's so dumb; we worship celebs because our lives are pointless, but doing that makes us feel even worse.

9 Let us briefly trace the history of the phenomenon that can make a perfectly wonderful high-school girl like yourself feel less worthy than, say, cross-eyed diamond ring-wearer Shannen Doherty. Before there was TV, before even newspapers, people loved to gossip—it is human nature to do this. At first it was confined to family, other people in their towns, and royalty. Then in the 1850s, printing innovations resulted in the first magazines. They published stories by people like Mark Twain and Charles Dickens, who became celebrities by virtue of reaching a big audience. Then when silent movies started in the 1890s, the first film actors became stars. Up on the screen, so much larger than life, these people seemed almost mythical, and audiences became fascinated by these projections of seeming perfection. People wanted to know all about them, and fanzines were started to satisfy that demand. Once TV started, the whole celeb-creation and -worship thing careened out of control, because information could come out instantly right into people's houses all over the world. TV gives you the false impression that celebrities are talking right to you, and you feel like they're your friends—so much so that some people will go right up to a star if they see one on the street.

10 So, in effect, the media created celebrities to satisfy our primal need for gossip. Over time, talking about people we have never met and are never likely to meet became an obsession. It's gotten to the point where some people are more interested in the personal lives of the stars than with the lives of their family and friends. No joke. That is why it is so ludicrous when a celeb wants to discuss only his or her work in an interview—like we care! We want the dirt on their personal lives.

11 Some people get off on all this attention. Madonna revels in exposure, is an absolute exhibitionist with her personal life. She knows we don't give a gosh darn

about her "work," and she keeps us happy with plenty of gossip. But many celebrities hate certain things about fame—like the fact that we own them. "I am public property," said Michelle Pfeiffer on the recent "Barbara Walters Academy Awards Special." "I am public domain." Celebrities like her are sick of the fact that their privacy has already been invaded in unthinkable ways: Tabloid journalists have searched their garbage, nude pictures they posed for ten years ago have been published, helicopters have swooped down on their weddings for photos.

12   As I write this I am painfully aware that because we, the staff of *Sassy,* put our pictures and personalities into the magazine, more people know who we are than we know who they are. We did it so you, the readers, would relate to our articles better, but it ended up making us into semicelebrities. We get fan mail and hate mail. Either we are part of the celeb worship problem, or we are making fun of the whole thing. It depends on how you look at it.

13   Anyway, readers will start getting sick of us soon, because the public is very fickle. People really get tired of hearing about celebrities after a while, and hunger for a new face to fixate on. Where, for example, are NKOTB or Debbie Gibson now? Where will poor little Lukeums be next year? The trendiest celebrities fade back into obscurity, while those who can update their image (Madonna, Cher) or who aren't tied to a single time period (Paul Newman) get to stick around a little longer. But even the celebrities with longevity get ripped apart by the media when they reach a certain point. Even though we helped create them, we can't help but resent that they're getting so much more attention than we are. Sometimes when celebrities have bad things happen to them, we feel vindicated. "We had to be obscure while they got to be famous, but look what happened to them," is our rationalization.

14   Besides the huge media machine in which I am but a cog, there's another reason we worship celebrities. As a whole, our society is not as religious as it once was. I don't pretend to have all the answers, but it seems like people need something to fulfill them the way organized religion once did—spirituality, art, some kind of life. Celebrity worship exists as a warped and unfulfilling substitute. True heroes often die for their people or their cause. That might be why we only feel vindicated when a celebrity dies, particularly if it's from self-destructive practices like drug or alcohol abuse. We made them stars, but then their fame made us feel insignificant—and we truly feel better about ourselves when they die. I am a part of this whole process. No wonder I feel soiled at the end of my workday.

■ **TOPICAL CONSIDERATIONS**

1. Kelly says that many of her readers "hated" her for her honesty in depicting stars as they are, rather than as they are portrayed in standard media. According to Kelly, why were these readers so angered by her portrayal? How might you react if you read a negative article about your favorite star?

2. In paragraph 4, Kelly makes a distinction between "celebrities" and "heroes." Does her definition here work for you? Is her conception of heroes

and celebrities—and the way in which ordinary folks seem to confuse the two—compatible with your own thinking on the subject? Why or why not?

3. In paragraph 5, Kelly states that ". . . achievement or even talent has little to do with celebrity. Even though talented people occasionally become celebrities, the easiest way to become one is to be marketed correctly." Analyze the connection Kelly makes here between marketing and celebrity. What are the economics of stardom, and how might they affect who becomes a star and how long they retain their celebrity status? Do you agree with Kelly that most celebrities are untalented?

4. Kelly claims that the New Kids on the Block "provided thousands of *Sassy* readers with a safe and distant focus for their hormonal longings." What do you take this to mean? Do you agree that the deflection of "dangerous" sexual desire is a function of teenage idols? Is this a positive or a negative phenomenon? Explain.

5. In paragraph 6, Kelly says that in our society "you are not really considered a success unless you are famous, no matter what your career." She goes on to say in paragraph 8 that celebrities satisfy our "insatiable demand for something to talk about outside our own inconsequential little lives." Do you agree that humans naturally feel inconsequential? That we need fame in order to feel successful? That we feel inferior to celebrities because "our lives are pointless"?

6. At the end of her essay, Kelly claims that the public resents the fame and fortune of celebrities. As a result, she says, many people feel "vindicated" when a celebrity dies, especially as a result of "self-destructive practices like drug or alcohol abuse." What is your opinion of this assertion? Do you agree with all or with any part of Kelly's statements? Explain.

■ RHETORICAL CONSIDERATIONS

1. Kelly opens her essay citing a "philosophical" crisis experienced while showering. Is this an effective introduction to her argument? In your opinion, does she sufficiently elaborate on the philosophical aspect of the issue throughout the piece? Explain.

2. Describe Kelly's voice in this piece, providing specific examples of language usage to support your answer. To what sort of audience is her essay projected? Do you feel that her tone is appropriate? How does her tone work to emphasize—or detract from—her argument? Explain your answer.

3. Throughout the essay Kelly examines her own complicity in the phenomenon of celebrity worship which she criticizes. How does such self-examination work in terms of the overall effectiveness of her argument? In your opinion, does she come to a satisfactory conclusion about her place in the media machine? Explain.

4. Kelly refers directly to particular celebrities as "evidence" to support her arguments—especially in paragraphs 5 and 6, where she "criticizes" some

stars by name. What effect does this naming have on her argument and its reception by readers? Do you think this is a useful rhetorical strategy? Why or why not?

5. In paragraphs 9 through 11, Kelly traces the history of celebrity worship. How does this part of the essay work in terms of the overall effectiveness of the piece? Would the argument have been as persuasive without it? Explain.

■ WRITING ASSIGNMENTS

1. Consider Kelly's claim that "we only feel vindicated when a celebrity dies. . . . We made them stars, but then their fame made us feel insignificant—and we truly feel better about ourselves when they die." Write an essay in which you respond to this statement, giving thought to all its implications. Do you agree with Kelly that the public feels vindicated by the death of a celebrity, especially from self-destructive practices? You might use recent or past examples of such deaths to explain your response.

2. Conduct biographical research on (a) someone you consider to be a hero and (b) someone you consider to be a star. Using the information you find, write an essay in which you compare the two, responding to Kelly's distinctions between heroes and celebrities. Are there similarities between the two figures you've researched? From your perspective, do the categories of "hero" and "celebrity" have anything in common?

3. In paragraph 9, Kelly says that "TV gives you the false impression that celebrities are talking right to you, and you feel like they're your friends." In a paper, explore your "relationship" with a celebrity with whom you especially identify. Be sure to address reasons for your identification, what it is you like or dislike about him or her, and how you feel about his or her celebrity.

4. Kelly refers to the role of the media in creating stars. Write an essay in which you outline your position on the role of the media in today's society. In your opinion, does it serve a useful purpose? Do journalists and reporters maintain high standards and integrity? Do the advantages of the services they provide outweigh the negative consequences—invasion of privacy, for example, or the mythology of celebrities?

The Wrong Examples

David L. Evans

In her essay, "Stolen Promise" (see Chapter 3, page 111), Patricia Raybon lamented the fact that her daughter could find few eligible black males to date at college. In part, she blamed the gender imbalance on the historic forces of poverty, crime, and social injustice. In this essay, a college admissions officer points to the influence of television. Because many black children do not have male role models in their daily lives, they look to TV. But, as his title announces, those images of black males are "slanted" toward successful athletes and entertainers.

David L. Evans is a senior admissions officer at Harvard. This essay first appeared in *Newsweek* magazine in March 1993.

1 As a college admissions officer I am alarmed at the dearth of qualified black male candidates. Often in high schools that are 90 percent black, *all* the African-American students who come to my presentation are female! This gender disparity persists to college matriculation where the black male population almost never equals that of the female.

2 What is happening to these young men? Who or what is influencing them? I submit that the absence of male role models and slanted television images of black males have something to do with it.

3 More than half of black children live in homes headed by women, and almost all of the black teachers they encounter are also women. This means that most African-American male children do not often meet black male role models in their daily lives. They must look beyond their immediate surroundings for exemplary black men to emulate. Lacking in-the-flesh models, many look to TV for black heroes.

4 Unfortunately, TV images of black males are not particularly diverse. Their usual roles are to display physical prowess, sing, dance, play a musical instrument or make an audience laugh. These roles are enticing and generously rewarded. But the reality is that success comes to only a few extraordinarily gifted performers or athletes.

5 A foreigner watching American TV would probably conclude that most successful black males are either athletes or entertainers. That image represents both success and failure. Success, because the substantial presence of blacks in sports, music and sitcoms is a milestone in the struggle begun almost 50 years ago to penetrate the racial barriers of big-league athletics and television. It is a failure because the overwhelming success of a *few* highly visible athletes, musicians and comedians has type-cast black males. Millions see these televised roles as a definition of black men. Nowhere is this more misleading than in the inner city, where young males see it as "the way out."

6 Ask a random sample of Americans to identify Michael Jordan, Bo Jackson, Magic Johnson, Hammer, Prince, Eddie Murphy or Mike Tyson. Correct responses would probably exceed 90 percent. Then ask them to identify Colin Powell, August

Wilson, Franklin Thomas, Mike Espy, Walter Massey, Earl Graves or the late Reginald Lewis and I doubt that 10 percent would respond correctly. The second group contains the chairman of the Joint Chiefs of Staff, a Pulitzer Prize–winning playwright, the president of the Ford Foundation, the secretary of agriculture, the director of the National Science Foundation, the publisher of Black Enterprise magazine and the former CEO of a multimillion-dollar business.

7   The Democratic National Convention that nominated Bill Clinton brought Ron Brown, Jesse Jackson, David Dinkins, Kurt Schmoke and Bernard Shaw into living rooms as impressive role models. Their relative numbers at the convention were in noticeable contrast to the black baseball players who made up nearly half of the All-Star teams on the Tuesday night of the convention.

8   This powerful medium has made the glamour of millionaire boxers, ballplayers, musicians and comedians appear so close, so tangible that, to naive young boys, it seems only a dribble or dance step away. In the hot glare of such surrealism, schoolwork and prudent personal behavior can become irrelevant.

9   Impressionable young black males are not the only Americans getting this potent message. *All* TV viewers are subtly told that blacks are "natural" athletes, they are "funny" and all of them have "rhythm." Such a thoroughly reinforced message doesn't lie dormant. A teacher who thinks every little black boy is a potential Bo Jackson or Eddie Murphy is likely to give his football practice a higher priority than his homework or to excuse his disruptive humor.

10   *Neck jewelry:*   Television's influence is so pronounced that one seldom meets a young black man who isn't wearing paraphernalia normally worn by athletes and entertainers. Young white men wear similar attire but not in the same proportion. Whites have many more televised role models from which to choose. There are very few whites in comparison to the number of blacks in the NBA. Black males are 12½ percent of the American male population but constitute 75 percent of the NBA and are thereby six times overrepresented. That television presents poor role models for *all* kids doesn't wash.

11   These highly visible men's influence is so dominant that it has redefined the place of neck jewelry, sneakers and sports apparel in our society. The yearning to imitate the stars has sometimes had dire consequences. Young lives have been lost over sneakers, gold chains and jackets. I dare say that many black prison inmates are the flotsam and jetsam from dreamboats that never made it to the NBA or MTV.

12   Producers of TV sports, popular music and sitcoms should acknowledge these "side effects" of the American Dream. More important are the superstars themselves. To a man, they are similar to lottery winners and their presence on TV is cruelly deceptive to their electronic protégés. Surely they can spend some of their time and resources to convince their young followers that even incredible talent doesn't assure fame or fortune. An athlete or performer must also be amazingly lucky in his quest for Mount Olympus.

13   A well-trained mind is a surer, although less glamorous, bet for success. Arthur Ashe spent his whole life teaching precisely this message. Bill Cosby and Jim Brown also come to mind as African-American superstars who use their substantial

influence to redirect young black males. At this time, when black men are finally making some inroads into the upper echelons of American society, we need more than ever to encourage the young to look beyond the stereotypes of popular culture.

■ TOPICAL CONSIDERATIONS

1. Evans says that the usual roles of black males on TV are designed to "display physical prowess, sing, dance, play a musical instrument or make an audience laugh" (paragraph 4). From your experience, do you agree with Evans? How do these roles compare with those of white males on television? According to Evans, and in your own analysis, what might be the outcome of such role allotment?

2. In Evans's opinion, television has made the glamour and riches of high-profile black athletes and musicians seem easily obtainable, whereas, statistically speaking, only a tiny percentage of the population will ever reach such goals. What are some consequences of the contradictions between such media images and the reality of socioeconomic conditions in America?

3. Some people propose that the recruitment of high school graduates or nongraduating college seniors by sports organizations be banned so as to encourage young athletes to fulfill their education. Do you agree with such proposals? Why or why not? How do you think Evans would respond to this idea?

4. According to Evans, how is television partly responsible for murders committed by black males for neck jewelry, sneakers, and sports apparel. Do you agree? Explain.

5. Evans describes the negative consequences of the unbalanced media images of black males as "'side effects' of the American Dream" (paragraph 12). What do you take this statement to mean? Do you agree with it? Why or why not?

6. In Evans's opinion, the producers of TV sports, music, and comedy shows, as well as the stars of these arenas, have a responsibility to counteract the deceptive nature of poor television role models upon viewers, especially young ones. Do you agree? How might this responsibility be practically manifested?

■ RHETORICAL CONSIDERATIONS

1. What is Evans's main argument? Where is the argument first presented in the essay? Do you feel that this essay presents it clearly and effectively? Why or why not?

2. Evans identifies his profession in the opening paragraph. How does this perspective affect your reception of his argument? Would it have helped had he identified himself as an African-American?

3. In paragraph 6, Evans provides a kind of pop quiz for readers to identify successful black Americans. How does this work within the larger contention of the essay? Do you find it an effective strategy, or does it seem out of place? Explain.

4. Throughout the essay, Evans names specific black individuals—some superstars, others high-profile blacks who have demonstrated a desire to "redirect black males." Does this identification of public figures add to the overall argument? Do you find this identification problematic in any way?

■ WRITING ASSIGNMENTS

1. Write a response to Evans's statement: "Impressionable young black males are not the only Americans getting this potent message [of unbalanced media images]" (paragraph 9). In your paper, explain the possible effects of stereotypical TV images of black males upon other viewers (females, non-Blacks, etc.).

2. Write an essay on your perception of the term *hero*. Who are your heroes, if any, and why? Do you feel that heroes (or role models) are necessary to healthy growth and development? What is the relationship between your idea of a hero (and your personal heroes) and media images? What role does the media play in developing and nurturing heroes, and what is your evaluation of that role?

3. Conduct a survey of television programs during five different prime-time slots (on five different evenings.) During each slot, "flip" through all the channels available on your set—including cable channels, if available. Keep track of the roles and images of black males—actors, sports figures, comedians, and musicians—during these time slots. After organizing your information, write a response to Evans's argument using your findings to support your position.

4. Write a letter to Evans from the point of view of either a television producer, a black male superstar, or a representative of a professional athletic organization. Regardless of whether your letter supports his argument or disagrees with it, be sure to address at least three main points made in his essay.

In Praise of Roseanne

Elayne Rapping

Whether or not Roseanne is the object of celebrity worship, her show *Roseanne* is one of the all-time most popular family sitcoms in television history. And, yet, according to Elayne Rapping, Roseanne has not been given the critical attention she deserves. While a number of books and countless academic articles have given attention to other pop culture icons in television history, Roseanne and her show, by comparison, have been snubbed. And the reason, Rapping explains, has to do with image and class. Roseanne is not the "liberal educated professional" found on *Murphy Brown* and *The Mary Tyler Moore Show* but a "fat, sloppy, foulmouthed, and bossy" matriarch of a blue-collar family. In this piece of long-overdue praise, Rapping explores Roseanne's unlikely stardom.

Elayne Rapping is a professor of communications at Adelphi University in Garden City, New York. She has written numerous articles about television and popular culture in a variety of magazines including *The Nation* and *The Progressive*. She is the author of two books, *The Looking Glass World of Nonfiction TV* (1987) and *The Movie of the Week: Private Stories, Public Events* (1992). This article first appeared in her column in *The Progressive* in July 1994.

1   The other night, while flipping among the three nightly network news broadcasts, I stopped—as I often do—to check out the *Roseanne* rerun Fox cleverly schedules during that time slot in New York. And, as often happens, I found myself sticking around longer than I intended, watching the Conners wiggle their way through whatever crisis had hit their Kmart window fan that day.

2   On the three more respectable networks, the Dow Jones averages rise and fall; Congress and the courts hand down weighty decisions in lofty prose; the official weapons of state are deployed, around the globe and in the inner cities, to preserve democracy and the American way. But in the Conner residence, where most things are either in disrepair or not yet paid for, it is possible to glimpse—as it rarely is on the newscasts themselves—how the fallout from such headlines might actually affect those who are relatively low in the pecking order.

3   On CBS, NBC, ABC, and CNN, the problems of the women who make headlines are not likely to sound familiar to most of us. Zoë Baird may be struggling with the servant issue. Hillary may have misplaced her capital-gains records. The Queen of England may be embroiled in royal-family dysfunction. But Roseanne, matriarch of the shabby Conner household, will be coping with less glamorous trauma—unemployment, foreclosure, job stress, marital power struggles, unruly and unmotivated kids—in a less dignified but more realistic style.

4   I am a big fan of Roseanne—Barr, Arnold, Conner, whatever. So are my female and working-class students, who invariably claim her as their own and hang on to her for dear life as they climb the ladder of class and professional achievement—an effort in which their parents have so hopefully invested everything they own. But it recently occurred to me that I have never—in the many years I've regularly analyzed

and commented on American popular culture—written a single word about her. Nor have I read many, outside the trashy tabloids, where her personal life and public persona are regularly recorded and described.

5   In the last year, I've read dozens of academic and popular articles, and two whole books, about *The Cosby Show*. Archie Bunker and *All in the Family* have been praised and analyzed endlessly. Even *Murphy Brown* and *The Mary Tyler Moore Show* are taken seriously in ever-broadening academic and journalistic circles. Not to mention the well-structured, post-structural Madonna, long the darling of feminist critics and academics.

6   What is it about these other media icons that makes them somehow more "respectable" subjects of intellectual analysis, more suitable to "serious" discourse? What is it about Roseanne that makes her so easy to ignore or write off, despite her (to me) obvious talent, originality, political *chutzpah,* and power? Gender and appearance are surely part of it; but I suspect that class—position as well as attitude—is the major factor. Bill Cosby's Cliff Huxtable, Mary Tyler Moore's Mary Richards, Candice Bergen's Murphy Brown are all well-turned out, well-educated liberal professionals. And the grungy, working-class Archie Bunker, far from scoring points for his class, is always beaten down by the liberal, professional mentality of everyone else on the show. As for Madonna, while she is certainly not respectable, she makes up for it by being blond, chic, and gorgeous, which, in our culture, covers a multitude of social sins.

7   But Roseanne is a different story, far more unassimilable into mainstream-media iconography than any of these others. Fat, sloppy, foul-mouthed, and bossy, she is just a bit too unrepentantly, combatively proud of her gender and class position and style to be easily molded into the "movin' on up" mode of American mass media. She isn't "movin' up" to anywhere. She is standing pat, week after week on her show—and a lot of the rest of the time in a lot of other places—speaking out for the dignity and the rights of those the media have set out to shame into invisibility or seduce into endless, self-hating efforts at personal transformation. With her bad hair and baggy pants and oversized shirts from the lower level of the mall, with her burned meat loaf and tuna casseroles and Malomars, with her rough language and politically incorrect child-rearing methods, with her dead-end minimum-wage jobs, Roseanne has gone further than Madonna or almost anyone else I can think of at turning the hegemonic norms of the corporate media on their heads. But few of the intellectual writing classes have seen fit to credit, much less celebrate, her for it. So I will.

8   To appreciate Roseanne's unlikely ascent into prime-time stardom, it's useful to place her within the generic traditions of the family sitcom. Roseanne is not a descendant of the pristine line of virginal wife/mothers who have set the norms for such characters from the days of June Cleaver to the present. No sweetly submissive smiles or politely helpful suggestions to hubby and kids for her. She is one of a rarer breed, the one invented and defined by Lucille Ball in *I Love Lucy,* in which the female protagonist is more Helpmeet from Hell than from Heaven.

9   The parallels between these two women are interesting, and reveal a lot about what has and hasn't changed for the women—white, working-class, and poor—who

make up the female majority in this country (although you'd never know it from watching TV). Both were, and are, popular and powerful beyond the dreams of almost any woman performer of their times. And yet both eschewed the traditional feminine, white, middle-class persona dictated by the norms of their days, preferring to present themselves as wild women, out of bounds, loud, funny, and noisy—all attributes which sexist culture beats out of most of us very early on. In a world in which females are enjoined not to take up too much space, not to make "spectacles" of ourselves, not to "disturb" but to contain "the peace," women like Roseanne and Lucy have always been frightening, repulsive, even indecent. That's why they so appall us even as, consciously or subconsciously, we are drawn to them.

10   I used to cringe when I watched *I Love Lucy* as a child. She filled me with embarrassment because she was so stereotypically "hysterical," so much a failure in her endless efforts to move out of the confines of traditional femininity and its many indignities (indignities otherwise kept hidden by the Stepford-like types of Donna Reed and June Cleaver).

11   I was far more comfortable, as a middle-class girl, with the persona created by Mary Tyler Moore—first as the frustrated dancer/wife in *The Dick Van Dyke Show* and later as the first real career woman in her own show. Unlike Lucy, Mary Richards was perfectly groomed and mannered. She was sweetly deferential in her apologetic efforts at assertiveness; embarrassingly grateful for every nod of respect or responsibility from her boss, "Mr. Grant." Ambitious, yes, but never forgetful of the "ladylike" way of moving up the corporate ladder, one dainty, unthreatening step at a time. Where Lucy embarrassed, Mary was soothing. No pratfalls or dumb disguises for her.

12   But through Roseanne, I've come to see the very improper Lucy differently. For her time, after all, she was a real fighter against those feminine constraints. She tried to *do* things and she tried to do them with other women, against the resistance of every man on the show. She was not well groomed, did not live in tasteful elegance, did not support and help her husband at business and social affairs—far from it. She was full of energy and rebelliousness and, yes, independence—to a point.

13   But of course she always failed, and lost, and made a fool of herself. Her show was pure slapstick fantasy, because, back then, the things she was trying to achieve were so far from imaginable that someone like her could only exist in a farcical mode. But, as Roseanne's very different way of playing this kind of woman shows, that is no longer true.

14   Like Lucy, Roseanne is loud, aggressive, messy, and ambitiously bossy. Roseanne, too, has close relationships with other women. And Roseanne, too, is larger than life, excessive, to many frightening and repulsive. But her show is no fantasy. It is the most realistic picture of gender, class, and family relations on television today. And that's because Roseanne herself is so consciously political, so gender- and class-conscious, in every detail of her show.

15   No more the harried husband rolling his eyes at his wife's antics. Where other sitcoms either ignore feminism and reproduce traditional relations or, perhaps worse, present perfectly harmonious couples—like the Huxtables—for whom gender equity comes as naturally as their good looks, Roseanne and Dan duke it out

over gender and power issues as equals who seem really to love, respect, and—not least—get angry at each other.

16   Nor does Roseanne need to think up crazy schemes for achieving the impossible—a project outside the home. Roseanne, like most of us, needs to work. The jobs she is forced to take—sweeping in a hair salon, waiting tables in malls and diners, working on an assembly line—are very like the ones Lucy nabbed and then messed up, to the wild laughter of the audience. But for Roseanne the humor is different. Roseanne fights with sexist, overbearing bosses, lashes out at her kids because she's stressed out at work, moonlights to get them through the rough days when Dan is out of work. And if these things are funny to watch, they are also deeply revealing of social and emotional truths in the lives of women and working-class families today.

17   The most touching and impressive thing about this series—and the main reason for its popularity—is its subtle presentation of progressive "messages" in a way that is neither preachy nor condescending to audiences. Much was made of the famous episode in which Roseanne was kissed by a lesbian character. (And it is surely a tribute to Roseanne's integrity and clout that this first lesbian kiss got past Standards and Practices because of her.) But the kiss itself was really no big deal. Lots of shows will be doing this kind of one minute/one scene "Wow, did you see that?" thing soon enough.

18   Sitcoms are, indeed, informed by liberal values, and they do, indeed, tend to preach to us about tolerance and personal freedom. Lesbianism, as an idea, an abstraction, a new entry on the now very long list of liberal tolerances to which the professional middle classes must pay lip service, was bound to hit prime time soon anyway. What made the Roseanne "lesbian episode" remarkable and radically different from the usual liberal sitcom style of tackling such issues was not the kiss itself but the startlingly honest discussions about homosexuality that followed the kiss, between Dan and his young son D.J.; and then between Dan and Roseanne, in bed.

19   This segment was politically audacious because it *did not* lecture the vast majority of Americans who are, yes, queasy about homosexuality. It presented them with a mirror image of their own confusion and anxiety, and led them to a position of relative comfort about it all, by sympathizing with their very real concern about radical social and sexual change.

20   This is how the show attacks all its difficult issues, sensational and mundane. Much has been made of Roseanne's way of yelling at her kids, even hitting them on at least one occasion. Clearly, this is not how parents, since Dr. Spock, have been told to behave, and for obvious and good reason. Nonetheless, we all do these things on occasion. (And those who don't, ever, probably have other serious parenting problems.) To pretend that parents don't do that—as most sitcoms do—is to condescend to viewers who know that this goes on everywhere, and who have, themselves, done it or at least fought the urge.

21   On *Roseanne,* such behavior is neither denied nor condemned; it is talked about and analyzed. After hitting her son, for example, Roseanne apologizes and confesses, heartbreakingly, that she was herself beaten as a child and that it was wrong

then and wrong now. It is this kind of honesty about negative feelings—especially when they are placed in the kind of social and economic context this show never slights—that makes the positive feelings of love and mutual respect within this battered, battling family so very believable.

22 Which brings me, unavoidably, to the issue of Roseanne Arnold herself, as a public persona—surely the major factor in the public unease about her. There are two "Roseannes"—both media images constructed cleverly and carefully by Arnold herself. "Roseanne Conner" is, as Arnold herself says, "much nicer." She is the sitcom version of how someone overcomes personal and economic difficulty and not only survives but thrives. She comes from a long line of show-business satirists whose humor was based on social and political truth. Like the Marx Brothers and Charlie Chaplin, she is the lovable outsider sneaking into the polite world to expose its hypocrisy and phoniness.

23 That is the fictional "Roseanne" of sitcom fame. The other persona, "Roseanne Barr Arnold"—the woman who appears in tabloids, talk shows, news shows, and comedy clubs—is far more outrageous, more dangerous. She is the ultimate bad girl, the woman who shouts out to the entire world every angry, nasty, shameful truth and emotion she feels about the lives of women, especially poor women, in America today.

24 Much of what Roseanne confesses to—about incest, wife abuse, mental illness, obesity, prostitution, lesbianism—makes people uncomfortable. It's tacky, embarrassing, improper, déclassé to discuss these issues in public. But so was much of what we Second Wave feminists and student activists and antiwar protesters and others insisted upon talking about and confessing to and doing in the 1960s. So is what Anita Hill insisted—in much classier style but to no less shock and outrage—on throwing at us from the Senate hearing rooms. So is almost every political statement and action that rocks the reactionary boats of institutionalized power and authority.

25 And like those other actions and statements, Roseanne's antics are inherently political, radical, salutary. For in speaking out about her hidden demons and ghosts and scars—as a woman, a working-class person, a victim of family and institutional abuse—she speaks *for* the myriad damaged and disempowered souls, mostly still silent and invisible, who also bear the scars of such class, gender, and age abuse.

26 My timing, as I write this, couldn't be worse, of course. The tabloids are currently ablaze with the latest, and most unfortunate, of Arnold brouhahas. Roseanne, having loudly accused her husband of infidelity and spousal abuse, filed for divorce, then almost immediately rescinded the statements and reconciled with her husband, only to file for divorce again a few weeks later.

27 I am neither shocked nor disillusioned by this. Every abused woman I have ever known has attempted, unsuccessfully, to leave her destructive relationship many times, before finally finding the strength and support to make the break. This, after all, is the very essence of the abuse syndrome. Only Roseanne, as usual, has chosen to play it out, in all its gory details, in the spotlight.

28 I'm a Roseanne fan. I like her show and marvel at her compassion and intelligence, at what she manages to get away with. I like her style—even when she offends me and makes me nervous (which she often does)—because the world needs

loud-mouthed unattractive women with brains, guts, a social conscience, and a sense of humor. There are few enough of them who make it through puberty with their spirits and energies intact.

■ TOPICAL CONSIDERATIONS

1. Are you a *Roseanne* fan? If so, do you agree with Rapping's reasons for liking the show? Explain.
2. How does Rapping perceive *Roseanne* to be different than other television programs—*The Cosby Show, Murphy Brown, The Mary Tyler Moore Show*—that have received critical attention from academics and journalists? What kinds of biases might this reveal on the part of these critics? Do you agree?
3. In comparing Roseanne to her forerunner, Lucille Ball, Rapping asserts in paragraph 9 that the qualities these women share—rebelliousness, loudness, funniness—are qualities that are "beaten out of" women early on in sexist U.S. culture. Instead, women are taught to be quiet, unaggressive peacemakers. Do you agree with this portrait of gender expectations in American culture? How might different media representations of women like Roseanne affect these expectations?
4. Rapping says that while Lucy tried to fight against gender constraints she failed because at the time her show was produced, the things she was trying to achieve were "so far from imaginable that someone like her could only exist in a farcical mode" (paragraph 13). How have gender roles and expectations changed so that a character like Roseanne is possible?
5. In paragrah 14, Rapping describes *Roseanne* as providing the "most realistic picture of gender, class, and family relations on television today." Do you agree? Why or why not?
6. Rapping makes the case that *Roseanne* is a politicized program, providing progressive "messages" to its public like the one sent by the famous lesbian-kiss episode. Do you agree that *Roseanne* is political in nature? Are the messages sent by the program palatable to a large viewing public? How so?

■ RHETORICAL CONSIDERATIONS

1. In her opening paragraph, Rapping compares *Roseanne* reruns—and the Fox network on which they appear—with the network news run on the "more respectable" networks. Why do you suppose she sets up this comparison so early on in the piece? Is this an effective element in her introduction?
2. In paragraphs 5 to 7, Rapping addresses the critical responses of journalists and academics to television programs like *The Cosby Show, Murphy Brown,* and *The Mary Tyler Moore Show,* stating that "few of the intellectual writing

classes have seen fit to credit" Roseanne for her brave portrayals of working class families. For what is she criticizing her fellow academics and journalists? How does this criticism work within the frame of the piece?

3. Rapping uses the first-person voice in this piece. Is this an effective strategy, or would a more distant third-person voice been more persuasive? Why or why not?

4. Why does Rapping include so much information about the *I Love Lucy Show,* as well as other shows portraying women, especially wives and mothers? Do you find this information to be useful, or does it seem tangential to the main argument? Explain.

■ WRITING ASSIGNMENTS

1. Write an essay in which you consider gender roles in modern American culture. How does the media represent gender, and how do these representations affect the ways in which people understand gender roles and conduct relationships? Provide at least three examples from television or film to support your argument.

2. Rapping argues that Roseanne provides a strong example for women. Write an essay in which you explore representations of men on TV. You might consider male characters on *Roseanne,* or on any other television shows or film. How are males represented? Are these representations consistent with your understanding of social gender expectations for males? How have representations and images of men on television changed over time?

3. Roseanne, while being enormously famous, is not a typical celebrity. In an editorial style similar to Rapping's, explore the phenomenon of Roseanne The Star. How did this woman, described by Rapping as "fat, sloppy, foulmouthed, and bossy" gain the status of celebrity? Think about the typical characteristics of celebrities, and consider how Roseanne does or does not meet them. (You might consult Christina Kelly's essay, "Why Do We Need Celebrities?") What does Roseanne's elevation to star status say about the general public and her audience?

4. Rapping claims that sitcoms are informed by liberal politics, and that *Roseanne* is famous largely because of its "subtle presentation of progressive messages." Write an essay in which you consider the political implications of sitcoms. Are these programs appropriate places for political messages to be presented? Why or why not? Can you think of other sitcoms that send out political messages? Be sure to use specific examples in your essay.

Don't Blame TV

Jeff Greenfield

Television has been indicted for nearly all our social ills—the rise in crime, increased divorce rate, lower voter turnout, falling SAT scores, the rise in sexual promiscuity, the collapse of family life. Indeed, television has been cited as the cause of the decline of Western civilization. Now a word from the defense: Jeff Greenfield, a correspondent for ABC's "Nightline" and "Evening News" and a syndicated columnist. What follows is some criticism of the critics of television—or, more exactly, an attack on their kneejerk assumptions that every American social and political ill can be blamed on television. This article first appeared in *TV Guide* in January 1986.

1 One of the enduring pieces of folk wisdom was uttered by the 19th-century humorist Artemus Ward, who warned his readers: "It ain't what you don't know that hurts you; it's what you know that just ain't so."

2 There's good advice in that warning to some of television's most vociferous critics, who are certain that every significant change in American social and political life can be traced, more or less directly, to the pervasive influence of TV.

3 It has been blamed for the decline of scores on scholastic achievement tests, for the rise in crime, for the decline in voter turnout, for the growth of premarital and extramarital sex, for the supposed collapse of family life and the increase in the divorce rate.

4 This is an understandable attitude. For one thing, television is the most visible, ubiquitous device to have entered our lives in the last 40 years. It is a medium in almost every American home, it is on in the average household some seven hours a day, and it is accessible by every kind of citizen from the most desperate of the poor to the wealthiest and most powerful among us.

5 If so pervasive a medium has come into our society in the last four decades, and if our society has changed in drastic ways in that same time, why not assume that TV is the reason why American life looks so different?

6 Well, as any philosopher can tell you, one good reason for skepticism is that you can't make assumptions about causes. They even have an impressive Latin phrase for that fallacy: *post hoc, ergo propter hoc.* For instance, if I do a rain dance at 5 P.M. and it rains at 6 P.M., did my dance bring down the rains? Probably not. But it's that kind of thinking, in my view, that characterizes much of the argument about how television influences our values.

7 It's perfectly clear, of course, that TV *does* influence some kinds of behavior. For example, back in 1954, *Disneyland* launched a series of episodes on the life of Davy Crockett, the legendary Tennessee frontiersman. A song based on that series swept the hit parade, and by that summer every kid in America was wearing a coonskin cap.

8 The same phenomenon has happened whenever a character on a prime-time television show suddenly strikes a chord in the country. Countless women tried to capture the Farrah Fawcett look a decade ago when *Charlie's Angels* first took flight. Schoolyards from Maine to California picked up—instantly, it seemed—on such

catch phrases as "Up your nose with a rubber hose!" (*Welcome Back, Kotter*), "Kiss my grits!" (*Alice*) and "Nanu-nanu!" (*Mork & Mindy*). Today, every singles bar in the land is packed with young men in expensive white sports jackets and T-shirts, trying to emulate the macho looks of *Miami Vice*'s Don Johnson.

9 These fads clearly show television's ability to influence matters that do not matter very much. Yet, when we turn to genuinely important things, television's impact becomes a lot less clear.

10 Take, for example, the decline in academic excellence, measured by the steady decline in Scholastic Aptitude Test scores from 1964 to 1982. It seemed perfectly logical to assume that a younger generation spending hours in front of the TV set every day with Fred Flintstone and Batman must have been suffering from brain atrophy. Yet, as writer David Owen noted in a recent book on educational testing, other equally impassioned explanations for the drop in scores included nuclear fallout, junk food, cigarette smoking by pregnant women, cold weather, declining church attendance, the draft, the assassination of President Kennedy and fluoridated water.

11 More significant, SAT scores stopped declining in 1982; they have been rising since then. Is TV use declining in the typical American home? On the contrary, it is increasing. If we really believed that our societal values are determined by new media, we might conclude that the birth of MTV in 1981 somehow caused the test scores to rise.

12 Or consider the frequently heard charge that the increase in TV violence is somehow responsible for the surge in crime. In fact, the crime rate nationally has been dropping for three straight years. It would be ludicrous to "credit" television for this; explanations are more likely to be found in the shift of population away from a "youth bulge" (where more crimes are committed) and improved tracking of career criminals in many big cities.

13 But why, then, ignore the demographic factors that saw in America an enormous jump in teen-agers and young adults in the 1960s and 1970s? Why *assume* that television, with its inevitable "crime-does-not-pay" morality, somehow turned our young into hoodlums? The same kind of problem bedevils those who argue that TV has triggered a wave of sexually permissive behavior. In the first place, television was the most sexually conservative of all media through the first quarter-century of its existence. While *Playboy* began making a clean breast of things in the mid-1950s, when book censorship was all but abolished in the "Lady Chatterly's Lover" decision of 1958, when movies began showing it all in the 1960s, television remained an oasis—or desert—of twin beds, flannel nightgowns and squeaky-clean dialogue and characters.

14 In fact, as late as 1970, CBS refused to let Mary Tyler Moore's Mary Richards character be a divorcee. The audience, they argued, would never accept it. Instead, she was presented as the survivor of a broken relationship.

15 Why, then, do we see so many broken families and divorces on television today? Because the networks are trying to denigrate the value of the nuclear family? Hardly. As *The Cosby Show* and its imitators show, network TV is only too happy to offer a benign view of loving husbands, wives and children.

16 The explanation, instead, lies in what was happening to the very fabric of American life. In 1950, at the dawn of television, the divorce rate was 2.6 per 1000

Americans. By 1983, it had jumped to five per thousand; nearly half of all marriages were ending in divorce. The reasons range from the increasing mobility of the population to the undermining of settled patterns of work, family, and neighborhood.

17   What's important to notice, however, is that it was not television that made divorce more acceptable in American society; it was changes in American society that made divorce more acceptable on television. (Which is why, in her new sitcom, Mary Tyler Moore can finally play a divorced woman.) In the mid 1980s, divorce has simply lost the power to shock.

18   That same argument, I think, undermines much of the fear that television has caused our young to become sexually precocious. From my increasingly dimming memory of youthful lust, I have my doubts about whether young lovers really need the impetus of *Dallas* or *The Young and the Restless* to start thinking about sex. The more serious answer, however, is that the spread of readily available birth control was a lot more persuasive a force in encouraging premarital sex than the words and images on TV.

19   We can measure this relative impotence of television in a different way. All through the 1950s and early 1960s, the images of women on TV were what feminists would call "negative"; they were portrayed as half-woman, half-child, incapable of holding a job or balancing a checkbook or even running a social evening. (How many times did Lucy burn the roast?) Yet the generation of women who grew up on television was the first to reject forcefully the wife-and-home-maker limitations that such images ought to have encouraged. These were the women who marched into law schools, medical schools and the halls of Congress.

20   The same was true of the images of black Americans, as TV borrowed the movie stereotypes of shiftless handymen and relentlessly cheerful maids. We didn't begin to see TV blacks as the equal of whites until Bill Cosby showed up in *I Spy* in 1966. Did the generation weaned on such fare turn out to be indifferent to the cause of black freedom in America? Hardly. This was the generation that organized and supported the civil-rights sit-ins and freedom rides in the South. Somehow, the reality of second-class citizenship was far more powerful than the imagery of dozens of television shows.

21   I have no argument with the idea that television contains many messages that need close attention; I hold no brief for shows that pander to the appetite for violence or smarmy sexuality or stereotyping. My point is that these evils ought to be fought on grounds of taste and common decency. We ought not to try and prove more than the facts will bear. Television, powerful as it is, has shown precious little power over the most fundamental values of Americans. Given most of what's on TV, that's probably a good thing. But it also suggests that the cries of alarm may be misplaced.

■ TOPICAL CONSIDERATIONS

1. What are some of the social ills television has been blamed for, according to the author? Why?
2. What does Greenfield say is wrong with the thinking of those critical of television?

3. How does Greenfield counter the argument that television was the main cause of the decline in SAT scores from 1964 to 1982?
4. How does Greenfield answer the charges that television violence is responsible for the rise in crime rates?
5. How does Greenfield seek to refute the claim that television is to blame for the rise in sexual promiscuity?
6. How does Greenfield answer the charge that television is responsible for the increased divorce rate?
7. According to Greenfield, how has television affected the image of women and black Americans?

■ RHETORICAL CONSIDERATIONS

1. How well does the Artemus Ward quotation in the opening paragraph establish Greenfield's line of argument?
2. Which of Greenfield's arguments seems the strongest and most convincing? Which seems the weakest and least convincing?
3. Paragraph 13 contains of two rhetorical questions. How effective are these questions in making Greenfield's point? Would straight statements have been more effective, given his argument?

■ WRITING ASSIGNMENTS

1. Do you agree with Greenfield that television gets too much of the blame for our social problems? Using your own knowledge of television, write a paper in which you answer this question.
2. Do you disagree with any of Greenfield's views here? In other words, do you feel that television contributes to social problems such as violence, sexual promiscuity, the divorce rate, and the collapse of family life? Write a paper in which you explain your feelings.
3. At the end of his essay, Greenfield admits that "television contains many messages that need close attention"—messages that "pander to the appetite for violence or smarmy sexuality or stereotyping." What problems of "taste and common decency" do you find with television? Specify by singling out certain shows.

Why I Quit Watching Television

P. J. O'Rourke

"Well, I was nuzzling her ear, making little kissy noises. . . . Then, all of a sudden, I experienced one of those devastating realizations: She was watching a *Star Trek* rerun over my shoulder." So laments P. J. O'Rourke, recalling when he decided that he had had it with television. Television was dumb. It was a waste of time. It kept him from more worthwhile activities. But as the author discovered in this humorous little essay, the lack of a television has severe aftereffects. P. J. O'Rourke was the editor of the *National Lampoon* during the late 1970s. His work has since appeared in a variety of magazines. Currently, he is "investigative humorist" for *Rolling Stone*. Collections of his essays include *Republican Party Reptile* (1987), *Parliament of Whores* (1991) and *All the Trouble in the World* (1994). This article first appeared in *Parade* magazine in December 1985.

1   I remember the exact moment I quit watching television. It was 10 years ago. I had a girlfriend who was a compulsive viewer. We were at her apartment on a Sunday afternoon, sitting on the couch, and I was . . . Well, I was nuzzling her ear, making little kissy noises, and generally acting like a boyfriend. Then, all of a sudden, I experienced one of those devastating realizations: She was watching a *Star Trek* rerun over my shoulder.

2   We had a big fight. I'm still wondering where our relationship went wrong. She's still wondering if Captain Kirk got beamed up in time to escape from the Klingons.

3   I was tired of watching television anyway. TV was too dumb. And TV was too much trouble. Not too much trouble to watch, of course, but there was too much trouble on the screen. Every show seemed to be about murder, theft, car chases or adultery. I was living in Manhattan at the time, and if I wanted to see those things, I could look out my window. Even comedy shows like *M*A*S*H* were about people getting blown apart. I figured there was enough real tragedy every day. Why get four more hours of it on TV every night? I gave my television set away.

4   TV is such a waste of time, I thought. I never considered how else I'd fill my evenings and weekends. It turns out there are worse things to do with time than waste it; more expensive things, anyway.

5   In my newfound leisure hours, I fixed up my apartment. This cost $12,000—$600 for the do-it-yourself remodeling and $11,400 for the carpenters, painters and plasterers to repair the damage I'd done. I also took up downhill skiing and paid $1500 for equipment when I probably could have gotten somebody to break my leg for free. And I began to read. This sounds worthwhile, but anyone who worries about the lewdness and mayhem on TV ought to peek into *The Satyricon* by Petronius or *Gargantua and Pantagruel* by Rabelais or some Shakespeare plays or even the Old Testament. Most of my reading, though, wasn't quite so brainy. I read paperbacks like *Murder for Brunch*. It's hard to call these more intellectual than *The Gong Show*.

6   Without a TV set (and with a new girlfriend), I had time for conversation. But a lot of conversations, if they go on long enough, turn into arguments. What's dumber—watching *Family Feud* or arguing about whether to get a TV so we *could* watch *Family Feud?*

7   Not having a TV is supposed to bring families closer together. I didn't have a family, so this didn't help me.

8   Not having a TV turns out to be more strange than virtuous. I don't see any trend-setting shows like *Miami Vice,* so I don't know what to wear. I still dress like John Cameron Swayze. Without TV advertising, I don't understand new consumer products. Styling mousse, for instance—is it edible? And since, as a spectator, I'm limited to home teams, I've lost interest in most professional sports. I'm honestly not sure what the Seattle Seagulls are. They may be a girls' field hockey team, for all I know. (Editor's note: They're the Sea*hawks*—a football team.)

9   *People* magazine, newspaper gossip columns and friends' conversations are filled with names that mean nothing to me—"Prince," "Sting," "Peewee," "Appollonia." Sounds like a litter of puppies. And the celebrities I do recognize are mystifying. Imagine Mr. T completely out of *The A-Team* context: What kind of character could he possibly play?

10   Lack of a television set has more severe effects too. No TV means no VCR. That is, I actually paid to see *Flashdance* and couldn't even fast-forward through the parts where Jennifer Beals has all her clothes on. Furthermore, I'm getting fat. When you don't have to wait for a commercial to get up and get a sandwich and a beer, you can get up and get a lot more beer and sandwiches.

11   So maybe television isn't so bad for us as it's supposed to be. To research this story, I borrowed my next-door neighbor's TV—or, rather, I borrowed his whole TV room, since televisions are connected to cables now, so you can get 100 silly channels instead of five or six. I watched some shows at the start of the new season: *Hell Town, Hometown, Crazy Like a Fox, Stir Crazy,* etc. There were a few surprises. On MTV, I saw the video of a song I thought was a tender love ballad. It turns out to be sung by guys in leather underwear chasing a girl through a sewer.

12   But, mostly, television was just the same. It was kind of comforting to see Johnny Carson again, a little grayer but with the same slack gags. Most of the shows are still violent, but I live in New Hampshire these days, and we don't have as much murder, theft or car-chasing (and not even as much adultery) as some might like. The shows are still dumb, but I'm 10 years older, and I've forgotten how perfect everything is in the television world. The people are all pretty. The pay phones all work. And all the endings are hopeful. That's not so bad. Most of us real people are a bit homely, and lots of our endings are hopeless. TV's perfect world was a relief. So I was sitting, comfortable as a pig, in my neighbor's armchair, punching remote-control buttons with my snout.

13   But I didn't enjoy it. No, sir. Not me. I've spent a whole decade acting superior to everybody because I don't watch television. I'm not about to back down and start liking it now. (Though I might drop in next door about 8 tonight. That's when *Amazing Stories* comes on.)

■ TOPICAL CONSIDERATIONS

1. Why did O'Rourke quit watching television?
2. The author complains that after giving up television what he did to fill his time turned out to be worse. What were some of those things, and why were they worse than watching television?
3. According to O'Rourke, what are some of the drawbacks of not having a television?
4. What changes in television does the author discover after a ten-year hiatus? What has stayed the same? Why does he say the "shows are still dumb"?
5. This essay is satirical, of course. What is O'Rourke mainly satirizing here? What does he actually suggest is wrong with television?
6. In paragraph 12, O'Rourke mentions "how perfect everything is in the television world." Then, he adds "That's not so bad." How does television create an illusion of a perfect world? Do you agree that such an illusion is "not so bad"? Can that illusion of a perfect world create problems for viewers?

■ RHETORICAL CONSIDERATIONS

1. One means of creating a humorous effect is irony. Find some examples of irony in this essay.
2. Consider the structure of this essay. Can you find a clear beginning, middle, and end? Where would you make the cuts, and why?
3. How well does the final paragraph illustrate the central point of this essay?

■ WRITING ASSIGNMENTS

1. Could you ever stop watching television? Write an essay in which you explore this possibility. Could you live without it? What might you miss? What could you afford to miss? What would you do to fill your leisure time (be realistic)?
2. O'Rourke humorously suggests that his girlfriend's addiction to television helped break up their relationship. Write a paper in which you describe how people's lives are governed by television schedules and how television intrudes on relationships.
3. "No TV means no VCR." So says the author who complains that he actually had to pay to see the movie *Flashdance* (paragraph 10). From your own perspective, what are the advantages and disadvantages of watching movies on VCRs instead of in movie houses? Do you think VCRs will be the death of movie houses?
4. O'Rourke says that coming back to TV after ten years he still finds the shows "dumb." Write a paper in which you talk about what's "dumb" about

television. You might consider analyzing a particular show—its characters and situations, its treatment of the real world and real people, and its messages, both subtle and obvious.

5. O'Rourke also says, "Most of the shows are still violent" (paragraph 12). Write a paper about television violence, analyzing a particular show or series. Is the violence realistic? Is it overdone? Do you think the violence is damaging to viewers?

The United States is "the most violent and self-destructive nation on earth," declared the Senate Judiciary Committee in a 1993 report. Americans are killing, raping, and robbing one another at a rate greatly surpassing every other country that keeps crime statistics. In 1995 there were nearly 25,000 murders committed in the United States, or nearly three an hour, as well as a record number of rapes, robberies, and assaults. While debates rage over issues of criminal justice and gun control, the violence increases and threatens the very nature of American life.

We open this chapter with a plea for nonviolence by one of this century's most courageous opponents of violence, Martin Luther King, Jr. Though "Pilgrimage to Nonviolence" was meant as an inspiration for black Americans struggling for racial equality during the most turbulent days of the civil rights movement, Dr. King's philosophy of nonviolence outlined here has universal appeal.

In the next piece, "The Culture of Violence," author Myriam Miedzian imagines what cultural anthropologists from a remote tribe in Australia might conclude about America were they to study various patterns of our culture: What, for instance, would they make of the headline-news roundup of daily murders, rapes, and assaults; or male movie idols Rambo, Chuck Norris, and Arnold Schwarzenegger; or all the mayhem on TV and cinema screens; or rock and rap songs advocating violence against women; or all the popular video games depicting street warfare? They would probably deduce that we are a culture bent on self-destruction.

The violence against women in America is truly shocking. The rape rate in the United States is 8 times higher than in France, 15 times higher than in England, 23 times higher than in Italy, and 26 times higher than in Japan, according to the Senate Judiciary report. Even more appalling, rape and assaults on women are rising faster than other crimes. The two pieces that follow address violence against women, the first from a personal perspective, the second from a socoideological one.

"An Incident in the Park" is not about the celebrated assault and rape of a Central Park jogger that filled the media in the early 1990s. In fact, this incident never made the papers. One reason is that the sexual assault on the author Aileen Hefferren did not result in physical injury. "It was no big deal," she was told. But that's just the point of her story: What kind of a society considers an assault on a woman an ordinary event?

Over the last few years considerable debate has raged over a problem on our college campuses and in society at large: acquaintance or "date" rape. Fueled by some famous cases, the debate has centered on the murky area where a man's advance is a woman's rape. The question comes down to "When is it rape?" The piece, "Date Rape's Other Victim," by Katie Roiphe raised considerable controversy when it first appeared because it dismisses claims of "rape-crisis feminists" that date-rape is an epidemic. Roiphe also questions victims' definitions of rape, alleging that their claims often rise out of regret and shame.

The next essay, written by an associate justice of the U.S. Supreme Court, Clarence Thomas, explores some fundamental questions about our criminal justice system. In "Crime and Punishment and Personal Responsibility," Thomas argues that for the system to work people must be held accountable for their acts no matter who they are or what their backgrounds. The question arises, can the poor and minorities of our society be blamed for their crimes when they themselves are victims of harmful circumstances—child abuse, poverty, poor education, racism? Clarence who is black and a product of childhood poverty himself says that if justice is to prevail there can be no excuses for one's actions.

Apparently Clarence's view is not shared by all jurors. According to Sophfronia Scott Gregory, author of the subsequent piece, many jurors have become sensitized to the motives and mindsets of those accused of violent crimes as the result of TV talk shows that every day give voice to people who claim to have committed violent crimes because they themselves were victims of abuse, incest, spousal battering, and posttraumatic stress. As "Oprah! Oprah in the Court" points out, the popularity of victimization has led to some "exotic arguments" and lighter sentences.

As its title indicates, the penultimate piece is a glimpse of the other side of our criminal justice system. "Life on the Shelf: What It's Like to Live in Prison" was written while its author George Dismukes serves a 16-year sentence for murder. Though he claims he is innocent, his essay is not his self-defense. Instead, his description of the bleakness and horror of confinement comes with the warning that the vast and growing underclass behind bars will be back on the streets as dangerous and depraved as ever unless some basic changes are made in the American judicial system.

Our final selection is "Why I Bought a Gun." As the title suggests, the author, Gail Buchalter, explains why a sensitive, intelligent woman from a liberal, upper-middle-class background would be driven to purchase a handgun.

Pilgrimage to Nonviolence

Martin Luther King, Jr.

We open this section with an essay by one of America's most prominent and charismatic opponents of violence, Dr. Martin Luther King, Jr. Written at a time when American blacks were suffering racial injustice, sometimes violently, this essay served as a call for social change through peaceful means. King was a clergyman and a prominent civil rights leader. In 1957, he organized the Southern Christian Leadership Conference to extend his nonviolent efforts toward equality and justice for his people. In 1964, he was awarded the Nobel Peace Prize. Four years later, while supporting striking sanitation workers in Memphis, King was shot and killed. The following statement comes from his *Stride Toward Freedom* (1958).

1 When I went to Montgomery as a pastor, I had not the slightest idea that I would later become involved in a crisis in which nonviolent resistance would be applicable. I nei-

ther started the protest nor suggested it. I simply responded to the call of the people for a spokesman. When the protest began, my mind, consciously or unconsciously, was driven back to the Sermon on the Mount, with its sublime teachings on love, and the Gandhian method of nonviolent resistance. As the days unfolded, I came to see the power of nonviolence more and more. Living through the actual experience of the protest, nonviolence became more than a method to which I gave intellectual assent; it became a commitment to a way of life. Many of the things that I had not cleared up intellectually concerning nonviolence were now solved in the sphere of practical action.

2   Since the philosophy of nonviolence played such a positive role in the Montgomery Movement, it may be wise to turn to a brief discussion of some basic aspects of this philosophy.

3   First, it must be emphasized that nonviolent resistance is not a method for cowards; it does resist. If one uses this method because he is afraid or merely because he lacks the instruments of violence, he is not truly nonviolent. This is why Gandhi often said that if cowardice is the only alternative to violence, it is better to fight. He made this statement conscious of the fact that there is always another alternative: no individual or group need submit to any wrong, nor need they use violence to right the wrong; there is the way of nonviolent resistance. This is ultimately the way of the strong man. It is not a method of stagnant passivity. The phrase "passive resistance" often gives the false impression that this is a sort of "do-nothing method" in which the resister quietly and passively accepts evil. But nothing is further from the truth. For while the nonviolent resister is passive in the sense that he is not physically aggressive toward his opponent, his mind and emotions are always active, constantly seeking to persuade his opponent that he is wrong. The method is passive physically, but strongly active spiritually. It is not passive nonresistance to evil, it is active nonviolent resistance to evil.

4   A second basic fact that characterizes nonviolence is that it does not seek to defeat or humiliate the opponent, but to win his friendship and understanding. The nonviolent resister must often express his protest through noncooperation or boycotts, but he realizes that these are not ends themselves; they are merely means to awaken a sense of moral shame in the opponent. The end is redemption and reconciliation. The aftermath of nonviolence is the creation of the beloved community, while the aftermath of violence is tragic bitterness.

5   A third characteristic of this method is that the attack is directed against forces of evil rather than against persons who happen to be doing the evil. It is evil that the nonviolent resister seeks to defeat, not the persons victimized by evil. If he is opposing racial injustice, the nonviolent resister has the vision to say that the basic tension is not between races. As I like to say to the people in Montgomery: "The tension in this city is not between white people and Negro people. The tension is, at bottom, between justice and injustice, between the forces of light and the forces of darkness. And if there is a victory, it will be a victory not merely for fifty thousand Negroes, but a victory for justice and the forces of light. We are out to defeat injustice and not white persons who may be unjust."

6   A fourth point that characterizes nonviolent resistance is a willingness to accept suffering without retaliation, to accept blows from the opponent without striking

back. "Rivers of blood may have to flow before we gain our freedom, but it must be our blood," Gandhi said to his countrymen. The nonviolent resister is willing to accept violence if necessary, but never to inflict it. He does not seek to dodge jail. If going to jail is necessary, he enters it "as a bridegroom enters the bride's chamber."

7   One may well ask: "What is the nonviolent resister's justification for this ordeal to which he invites men, for this mass political application of the ancient doctrine of turning the other cheek?" The answer is found in the realization that unearned suffering is redemptive. Suffering, the nonviolent resister realizes, has tremendous educational and transforming possibilities. "Things of fundamental importance to people are not secured by reason alone, but have to be purchased with their suffering," said Gandhi. He continues: "Suffering is infinitely more powerful than the law of the jungle for converting the opponent and opening his ears which are otherwise shut to the voice of reason."

8   A fifth point concerning nonviolent resistance is that it avoids not only external physical violence but also internal violence of spirit. The nonviolent resister not only refuses to shoot his opponent but he also refuses to hate him. At the center of nonviolence stands the principle of love. The nonviolent resister would contend that in the struggle for human dignity, the oppressed people of the world must not succumb to the temptation of becoming bitter or indulging in hate campaigns. To retaliate in kind would do nothing but intensify the existence of hate in the universe. Along the way of life, someone must have sense enough and morality enough to cut off the chain of hate. This can only be done by projecting the ethic of love to the center of our lives.

9   In speaking of love at this point, we are not referring to some sentimental or affectionate emotion. It would be nonsense to urge men to love their oppressors in an affectionate sense. Love in this connection means understanding, redemptive good will. Here the Greek language comes to our aid. There are three words for love in the Greek New Testament. First, there is *eros*. In Platonic philosophy *eros* meant the yearning of the soul for the realm of the divine. It has come now to mean a sort of aesthetic or romantic love. Second, there is *philia*, which means intimate affection between personal friends. *Philia* denotes a sort of reciprocal love; the person loves because he is loved. When we speak of loving those who oppose us, we refer to neither *eros* nor *philia*; we speak of a love which is expressed in the Greek word *agape*. *Agape* means understanding, redeeming good will for all men. It is an overflowing love which is purely spontaneous, unmotivated, groundless, and creative. It is not set in motion by any quality or function of its object. It is the love of God operating in the human heart.

10   *Agape* is disinterested love. It is a love in which the individual seeks not his own good, but the good of his neighbor (I Cor. 10:24). *Agape* does not begin by discriminating between worthy and unworthy people, or any qualities people possess. It begins by loving others *for their sakes*. It is entirely "neighbor-regarding concern for others," which discovers the neighbor in every man it meets. There, *agape* makes no distinction between friend and enemy; it is directed toward both. If one loves an individual merely on account of friendliness, he loves him for the sake of the benefits to be gained from the friendship, rather than for the friend's own sake.

Consequently, the best way to assure oneself that Love is disinterested is to have love for the enemy-neighbor from whom you can expect no good in return, but only hostility and persecution.

11   Another basic point about *agape* is that it springs from the *need* of the other person—his need for belonging to the best in the human family. The Samaritan who helped the Jew on the Jericho Road was "good" because he responded to the human need that he was presented with. God's love is eternal and fails not because man needs his love. St. Paul assures us that the loving act of redemption was done "while we were yet sinners"—that is, at the point of our greatest need for love. Since the white man's personality is greatly distorted by segregation, and his soul is greatly scarred, he needs the love of the Negro. The Negro must love the white man, because the white man needs his love to remove his tensions, insecurities, and fears.

12   *Agape* is not a weak, passive love. It is love in action. *Agape* is love seeking to preserve and create community. It is insistence on community even when one seeks to break it. *Agape* is a willingness to sacrifice in the interest of mutuality. *Agape* is a willingness to go to any length to restore community. It doesn't stop at the first mile, but it goes the second mile to restore community. It is a willingness to forgive, not seven times, but seventy times seven to restore community. The cross is the eternal expression of the length to which God will go in order to restore broken community. The resurrection is a symbol of God's triumph over all the forces that seek to block community. The Holy Spirit is the continuing community creating reality that moves through history. He who works against community is working against the whole of creation. Therefore, if I respond to hate with a reciprocal hate I do nothing but intensify cleavage in broken community. I can only close the gap in broken community by meeting hate with love. If I meet hate with hate, I become depersonalized, because creation is so designed that my personality can only be fulfilled in the context of community. Booker T. Washington was right: "Let no man pull you so low as to make you hate him." When he pulls you that low he brings you to the point of working against community; he drags you to the point of defying creation, and thereby becoming depersonalized.

13   In the final analysis, *agape* means a recognition of the fact that all life is interrelated. All humanity is involved in a single process, and all men are brothers. To the degree that I harm my brother, no matter what he is doing to me, to that extent I am harming myself. For example, white men often refuse federal aid to education in order to avoid giving the Negro his rights; but because all men are brothers they cannot deny Negro children without harming their own. They end, all efforts to the contrary, by hurting themselves. Why is this? Because men are brothers. If you harm me, you harm yourself.

14   Love, *agape,* is the only cement that can hold this broken community together. When I am commanded to love, I am commanded to restore community, to resist injustice, and to meet the needs of my brothers.

15   A sixth basic fact about nonviolent resistance is that it is based on the conviction that the universe is on the side of justice. Consequently, the believer in nonviolence has deep faith in the future. This faith is another reason why the nonviolent resister can accept suffering without retaliation. For he knows that in his struggle for jus-

tice he has cosmic companionship. It is true that there are devout believers in nonviolence who find it difficult to believe in a personal God. But even these persons believe in the existence of some creative force that works for universal wholeness. Whether we call it an unconscious process, an impersonal Brahman, or a Personal Being of matchless power and infinite love, there is a creative force in this universe that works to bring the disconnected aspects of reality into a harmonious whole.

■ TOPICAL CONSIDERATIONS

1. From reading King's essay, what kind of education would you say King had as a young man? How is this training reflected in the essay?
2. King was strongly influenced by Mahatma Gandhi, political activist and leader of the Indian people in the first half of this century. What do you know about Gandhi and his civil disobedience movement?
3. During the Vietnam War, thousands of young men fled to Canada and Europe to avoid being drafted. Would you call them nonviolent resisters? Consider the motives and aims of both types of protesters. Are conscientious objectors the same as nonviolent resisters, as described by Dr. King?
4. King refers to Jesus' Sermon on the Mount (recorded in the New Testament gospels of Matthew, chapters 5–7, and of Luke, Chapter 6, beginning at verse 20). What similarities do you see between its teachings and King's definition of nonviolent resistance? What differences do you see?
5. Is King's philosophy practical in today's world in which there is so much terrorism and violence? Give reasons for your answer.
6. When King defines *agape,* he discusses how it promotes community responsibility. Identify citizen groups in your community or on your campus that demonstrate the kind of love King defines here. What other evidence of *agape* do you find in our society?
7. Do you agree with King's philosophy? Could you practice it? Describe a situation in which you might find yourself wanting to resist. Explain how you would deal with the crisis. How would it be the same or different from King's approach?
8. King was a charismatic figure of the early sixties. Is there anything about this essay that would suggest why this was true?

■ RHETORICAL CONSIDERATIONS

1. Did King's opening capture your interest immediately? Was it an effective way to introduce his subject matter? Explain your reactions.
2. What is King's thesis? Is it stated explicitly or implicitly?
3. What primary rhetorical strategy does King use in developing his essay?
4. What transitional devices does King use when moving from one idea to another? How does he achieve variety so that he is not repeating the same words and phrases too often?

5. What do you think of King's conclusion? Does he need to summarize the points he made in his essay? Or has he successfully brought the essay to a close without the need for this? How would you have ended it?

■ WRITING ASSIGNMENTS

1. In paragraph 1, King remarks: "Many of the things I had not cleared up intellectually concerning nonviolence were now solved in the sphere of practical action." King's practical experiences molded his philosophy. In an essay, write about an experience you have had that taught you something about your own standards of behavior in society.

2. Were the young men who fled to Canada and Europe during the Vietnam War nonviolent resisters? In an essay, compare and contrast this type of resistance with the type King describes.

3. Identify a community action group in your community or on your campus that is involved in demonstrating *agape.* Write an essay describing the goals and actions of the group. Explain how the group demonstrates the kind of community responsibility King discusses in his essay.

4. At the beginning of his essay, King mentions Jesus' Sermon on the Mount (NT Mt 5–7 and Lk 6:20). Using your library's resources in theology, look up the opinions of three theologians on the Sermon on the Mount, on nonviolent resistance, on "liberation theology," or on similar subjects. Compare what you find to King's philosophy in this article. On what points does King agree with the theologians you have found? On what points does he disagree?

5. Using an African-American history source, identify one of the major civil rights campaigns with which King was associated between 1954 and 1968, and on which you would like to focus in this research project. Examine newspaper and news magazine coverage of the campaign. Try to find reports from different perspectives: (a) local white newspapers for the town in which the campaign took place; (b) the black press, such as the *Chicago Defender;* big-city newspapers, such as *The New York Times;* and different weekly or monthly news magazines. Contrast and compare the reports in your sources. How prominent is King's philosophy in the reporting? What differences in attitude do you find among your sources? How closely do protesters seem to conform to the principles King outlines in this article?

<table>
<tr><td></td><td>

The Culture of Violence

Myriam Miedzian

</td></tr>
</table>

Culture shapes behavior. Children learn what is acceptable and what is unacceptable behavior by watching the activities their culture sponsors. They imitate what they see in cultural forms—music, sports, games, drama, and so on—and reason out the principles by which their actions are accepted by their community. In an effort to explore the kind of culture we raise our children in today, Myriam Miedzian creates a hypothetical situation. She imagines what anthropologists from an isolated tribe in Australia would make of contemporary America were they to examine our popular role models, films, leisure time activities, music, sports, games, and toys among other components of our culture. Their conclusions would point to some "deep contradictions and absurdities" of our habits as they would ponder the root causes.

Myriam Miedzian is the author of *Boys Will Be Boys: How We Encourage Violence in Our Sons and What We Can Do to Stop It* (1991) from which this essay comes.

1   Anyone who has ever taken a cultural anthropology course is aware that different so-cieties weave different patterns of culture, and that the different threads—religion, music, sports, children's games, drama, work, relations between the sexes, commu-nal values, and so on—that make up the cultural web of a society are usually intri-cately related.

2   If a tribe's songs and dramas are centered on violence and warfare, if its young boys play war games and violently competitive sports from the earliest age, if its paintings, sculptures, and potteries depict fights and scenes of battle, it is a pretty sure bet that this is not a peaceful, gentle tribe.

3   Every child in the world is born into a particular culture and "from the moment of his birth the customs into which he is born shape his experience and behaviour," we are told by anthropologist Ruth Benedict.[1] Throughout history people have known this intuitively and so they have been careful to acculturate their children from the youngest age into a pattern of behavior that is acceptable to the group. We have in our own society some very clear and simple examples: Christian groups like the Hutterites and the Amish, or Jewish groups like the Hasidim want their children to grow up to be devoted primarily to religious rather than material values, to be sexually modest and completely chaste before marriage. They share a strong sense of community and commitment to taking responsibility for the well-being of all their members. Among the Hutterites and Amish there is a strong emphasis on non-violence. None of these groups allows their children to participate in the mainstream culture.

4   Sometimes societies develop customs that become highly detrimental to their members. A cultural trait that may be of considerable value in a limited form or that was of value at an earlier point of history is elaborated and continued in a form that is socially deleterious. Ruth Benedict refers to this as the "asocial elaboration of a cultural trait."

5   A prime example is the incest taboos and marital customs of the Kurnai tribe of Australia. Many a student of anthropology has laughed or at least chuckled at Benedict's descriptions. Benedict explains that all human societies have incest taboos, "but the relatives to whom the prohibition refers differ utterly among different peoples."[2] The Kurnai, like many other tribes, do not differentiate "lineal from collateral kin." Fathers and uncles, brothers and cousins, are not distinguished, so that "all relatives of one's own generation are one's brothers and sisters."[3]

6   The Kurnai also have an extreme horror of "brother-sister" marriage. Add to this their strict rules with respect to locality in the choice of a mate and the right of old men to marry the attractive young girls, and a situation is created in which there are almost no mates for young people, especially young men. This does not lead the Kurnai to change their incest taboos or rules of marriage. Quite to the contrary, "they insist upon them with every show of violence."[4]

7   As a result, the usual way for tribe members to marry is to elope. As soon as the villagers get wind of this crime, they set out in pursuit of the newlyweds with the intent to kill them if they catch them. That probably all the pursuers were married in the same way does not bother anyone. Moral indignation runs high. However, if the couple can reach an island traditionally recognized as a safe haven, the tribe may eventually accept them as husband and wife.

8   Cultural webs and irrationalities are simpler and easier to see in small, isolated tribes or small communities than in large industrial societies, but they exist in both.

9   Industrialized societies are made up of different socioeconomic classes, and often different ethnic groups. In a large country like ours, differences in geography and climate affect people. Nevertheless, there are certain aspects of our culture, besides a common language, that are widely shared. Children and adolescents from coast to coast play with the same toys, see many of the same films and TV shows, listen to the same rock music, play many of the same sports.

10   I suspect that if the Kurnai were to send a few anthropologists over to study contemporary American society, they would be as amused by our irrationalities as we are by theirs.

11   On the one hand, they would find in our Declaration of Independence a deep commitment to life, liberty, and the pursuit of happiness. An examination of the Constitution would reveal that the goals of our government include "justice," "domestic tranquility," and "the general welfare." An examination of contemporary society would reveal that we deplore murder, assault, wife- and child-battering, sexual abuse of children, and rape.

12   On the other hand, our newspaper headlines, our TV news with its daily roundups of murders and rapes, our crime statistics, and the fact that over six hundred thousand of our citizens—mostly male—are in prison would inform them just how deeply these problems afflict us. Having established this strong contradiction between our professed goals and beliefs, and our reality, our Kurnai anthropologists would begin to wonder what we teach our boys that makes them become such violent men. They would ask, "Who are your young boys' heroes, who are their role models?"

13   Rambo, Chuck Norris, Arnold Schwarzenegger, would be high on the list.

14   "Do your boys watch only violent adventure films?"

15   No. They like comedies too, but when they reach adolescence many of them become particularly fond of "slasher" films in which they can watch people being skinned, decapitated, cut up into chunks. Wanting to experience all aspects of our culture, the Kurnai anthropologists would undoubtedly watch a few slasher films. They would find out that the perpetrators are practically all male, and the films frequently center on the victimization of females.

16   "What about the rest of their leisure time, what do your boys do with it?"

17   Our young boys spend about twenty-eight hours a week watching TV. By the time they are eighteen, they have seen an average of twenty-six thousand TV murders, a vast majority of them committed by men.

18   "Do they listen to much music?"

19   They certainly do. They spend billions of dollars a year on records and tapes, not to mention radio and MTV. The Kurnai anthropologists might be advised to turn on MTV to see what the young boys like. They would find that the programming often consists of very angry-looking young men singing lyrics that are hard to make out, but the music sounds as angry as the men look. Women on the shows are often scantily clad, and sometimes it looks as if they are about to be raped.

20   "Can we see the texts of some of these lyrics?"

21   Samples of popular hits might include an album by Poison that reached number three on the Billboard pop charts and has sold over two million copies. Its lyrics include, "I want action tonight . . . I need a hot and I need it fast/*If I can't have her, I'll take her and make her* [my emphasis]."

22   Switching channels from MTV, the Kurnai would find that a considerable amount of American television is devoted to sports. Brawls and fistfights are common at these events, particularly in hockey but also in baseball and basketball. The main tactics in football, tackling and blocking, look exactly like bodily assault.

23   The anthropologists would find out that our high rates of violent crime have been exacerbated by an ever-growing drug problem. In light of this they would note that drug and alcohol abuse are common among athletes and the heavy metal musicians that many young people admire and emulate.

24   "What about your sons' toys?" the Kurnai might ask next.

25   A trip to the playground or a look under Christmas trees—religious symbols used to commemorate the birth of the deified founder of the nation's leading religion who preached a gospel of love and nonviolence—would reveal that while little girls get dolls and carriages and dollhouses; little boys get guns, "action figures" like GI Joe, and violent space-age toys and games.

26   By now the Kurnai would no doubt have discovered that rates of violence in our society are highest among boys and men raised by single mothers. Being anthropologists they would not be surprised since they would be aware of cross-cultural data indicating that the presence of a caring, involved father decreases the chances of a son being violent.

27   Delving deeper, they would find out that many boys who start out with fathers lose them along the way through divorce. They would hear divorced women, [as well as] social workers, psychiatrists, and other professionals complain bitterly that a large percentage of divorced fathers never or rarely see their children, nor do they make child support payments.

28   Increasingly stunned by the irrationalities of our society, they might inquire of these professionals: In light of the lack of interest of so many of your men in nurturing and taking responsibility for their children, and the subsequent increases in rates of violence and other social problems, why don't you encourage your little boys to become good fathers by buying them dolls and baby carriages and dollhouses? Why don't you encourage them to play house instead of training them to become warriors?

29   "Parents would never stand for that," professionals and parents would explain. "They are much too afraid that their sons might grow up to be gay if they played with 'wimpy' girls' toys."

30   At this point the visiting anthropologist might emit a cry of disbelief. Is it not obvious to these strange people who deplore violence, yet do everything possible to encourage it in their sons, that gay men do not have children? They don't push baby carriages, change diapers, or give bottles to their babies. Only heterosexual men become fathers and do these things. What could be more absurd than to think that little boys will become gay by rehearsing the quintessentially heterosexual role of being a father?[5]

31   Having established the deep contradictions and absurdities of our customs, the Kurnai would look for their origins. They would find that like many warrior societies, we have a long tradition of raising our boys to be tough, emotionally detached, deeply competitive, and concerned with dominance.

32   These traits, they would note, have gotten out of hand. The enormous escalation of violence that Americans are experiencing seems to coincide with the development of a vast system of communications technology that has led to the creation of a culture of violence of unprecedented dimensions, much of it directed toward or available to children. Instead of treasuring their children as a precious national resource to be handled with the utmost care, Americans have allowed them to be exploited as a commercial market.

33   How could they let this happen? the Kurnai would wonder. Surely they must understand that one of society's most important tasks, the socialization of the next generation, should not be left in the hands of people whose main concern is financial gain, people who will not hesitate to exploit the basest human tendencies for profit?

34   In their efforts to understand this puzzle they would be helped by their understanding of their own culture. The Kurnai would see that our "laissez-faire" attitude toward our children can be traced to the asocial elaboration of some of our most beneficial and admirable values, just as their absurd marital rules can be traced to originally useful taboos.

35   A system of largely unfettered free enterprise led to the extraordinary economic development of the nation. The subsequent commitment to free enterprise is so deep that the economic exploitation of children is taken for granted. Companies manufacture toys for six-year-olds that encourage reckless violence, sadism, and torture, and few people question their right to do so.

36   The Kurnai would turn next to the First Amendment, the embodiment of the national commitment to free speech.

37   It would not escape their attention that with respect to pornographic and "indecent" material, it has long been acknowledged that the First Amendment cannot apply equally to children and adults. Long-standing laws protect children from such material. That is why there are no Saturday morning pornographic TV programs.

38   For some strange reason, the Kurnai would conclude, these people have blinded themselves to the fact that what makes sense with respect to sex makes at least as much sense with respect to violence. And so they have allowed their children to be raised on tens of thousands of TV murders, detailed depictions of sadistic mutilations on the screen, and song lyrics that advocate rape.

39   What a perfect example of an asocial elaboration, they might exclaim! Everything is justified in terms of free enterprise and free speech, but this freedom as interpreted in present-day society contributes to the nation's enslavement!

40   Don't these Americans see that boys raised in a culture of violence are not free? Their basest, most destructive tendencies are reinforced from the youngest age to the detriment of their altruistic, pro-social tendencies. Then when they commit serious acts of violence they are sent to prison.

41   Don't they see that millions of Americans, especially women and elderly people, live in great fear of being mugged, raped, or murdered? Many are afraid to leave their homes after dark. ·

42   A survey of national crime statistics published by U.S. government agencies would inform the Kurnai that about twenty thousand Americans a year suffer the greatest loss of freedom. They are deprived of their lives through violent deaths. Their families and friends are permanently deprived of someone they love.

43   How long will it take these people, the exasperated anthropologists might wonder, until they realize that an interpretation of freedom that allows for no restraints with respect to the commercial exploitation of children is self-destructive?

44   The Kurnai would note that in other areas Americans acknowledge there is no such thing as absolute freedom. Ordinances prohibit people from playing loud music in the middle of the night if in doing so they deprive others of sleep. Laws restrict the freedom of chemical companies to dump pollutants into streams and rivers. But when it comes to producing a culture of violence that pollutes the minds of their young and encourages violence, these strange people act as if freedom were an absolute!

■ NOTES

1. Ruth Benedict, *Patterns of Culture* [New York: Mentor Books, 1946 (1934)], p. 18.
2. Ibid., p. 42.
3. Ibid., p. 43.
4. Ibid.
5. I owe this point to Letty Cottin Pogrebin in *Growing Up Free: Raising Your Child in the 80's* (New York: Bantam Books, 1981).

■ TOPICAL CONSIDERATIONS

1. In the first three paragraphs, what connections does Miedzian draw between culture and behavior? How does culture shape the behavior of young people as they learn to become adults in their society?

2. When or how do social customs become obsolete? Why are some customs which are not useful to a society's members still practiced?

3. Who are the Kurnai? How do the Kurnai define "brother-and-sister" relationships? Why does this definition force elopement among young people who wish to marry each other?

4. What kinds of questions do the Kurnai ask about American culture? How are their questions distinguished from the responses that Americans give them? What subjects or themes do they seem to be most interested in? Can you think of anything they may have forgotten to ask?

5. In paragraphs 32 and 33, Miedzian identifies a single source for America's problems with violence. What is that source? Do you agree with her explanation for the root cause of violence? Can you think of additional reasons?

6. In paragraphs 34 and 35, what explanation does Miedzian offer (through the Kurnai) about why this destructive attitude has been allowed to create a culture of violence? How does her reason illustrate the general principle she discussed in paragraph 4?

7. This article focuses almost completely on the socialization boys experience as they grow into men. How are girls and women presented in this article?

■ RHETORICAL CONSIDERATIONS

1. Miedzian's initial discussion of the Kurnai in paragraphs 5 through 7 makes them seem almost funny. How do her inclusion of a chuckling student and her word choices convey this tone? Why do you think she uses this tone to begin the article?

2. Why does the author use the Kurnai to investigate violence in America? How would her discussion have been different (more boring, more confrontational, perhaps even unpatriotic) without this storytelling touch? How does this device help a reader who does not know what a cultural anthropologist does?

3. Why does Miedzian have the Kurnai begin their investigation by reading the Declaration of Independence and the Constitution in paragraph 11? What function do these documents serve?

4. Do you think that the portrait of how American boys and girls are socialized is overstated? For example, can you think of films showing violent women and gentle men? male musicians who do not advocate rape? toys that teach men to love children? How do exceptions to Miedzian's observations help or hinder her argument?

5. What basic assumption does Miedzian make about human nature in paragraph 40? How likely is the average boy (and the average man) to commit a

violent act? How important is this assumption to her argument? Does she infer what it is that prevents all men from being insanely violent?

6. Miedzian makes a number of broad generalizations about American culture and behavior. List five examples of generalization. You might start by looking for places where she uses "often" or "usually," or where she refers to averages. Do these generalizations strengthen or weaken her argument?

■ WRITING ASSIGNMENTS

1. Identify a specific product available to young people today that you believe contributes to violence in America (e.g., a film, toy, or CD with objectionable lyrics). Write a letter to the manufacturer (or producer, or artist), explaining why this product is harmful, and why it should no longer be made available.

2. Following Miedzian's example of the Kurnai anthropologists, write a description of a social group of at least ten people that you know well. The group may consist of your dormitory mates, your family members, your church or temple congregation, or another set of people that thinks of itself as a unit with commonly held rules of conduct and values. Write as if you are a complete outsider, observing it for the first time, and not fully understanding the reasons for what you see. Be sure to look for customs that have outlived their usefulness.

3. Assume that you have been given as much money and as many skilled, thoughtful people as you need to make three specific changes within your community—your city, your college campus, or some other community you define as yours. Your goal is to eliminate or sharply reduce violence. What specific changes would you make, and why would you make them? Be sure to discuss what particular forms of violence you seek to eliminate.

| An Incident in the Park |
| Aileen C. Hefferren |

What follows is a very personal narrative of "an incident." No battering. No sexual assault. Not another senseless killing. Nothing that made the newspapers. Just a minor interlude between the author jogging in a park and a 12-year-old boy on a bike who touched her. But as small as the incident seems, the traumatic ramifications were large enough for the author to raise some tough questions about what our society has come to tolerate. Aileen Hefferren is assistant managing editor of the *National Interest*. This article first appeared in *Newsweek* in December 1990.

1 I realize that, with most U.S. cities awash in violent crime, my story will strike some readers as very mild. But I have learned the hard way that even a minor, unreported

incident can have profound effect. Early one evening last August, I was running on a well-used pathway in Washington, D.C.'s, Rock Creek Park. Finishing a six-mile run, I headed north from the P Street bridge toward Calvert Street when I heard a bicycle behind me. Suddenly, I felt a hand on my buttocks. Alongside rode a young male—I learned later he was only 12 years old—wearing a brightly colored jersey. I started to yell and reached out toward him. He skidded his bicycle into me, jumping aside as he did so. My hands, head, hip, elbow and shoulder hit the cement with great force; my leg hit his bicycle.

2   The boy, fists up, danced around me like a boxer. Crying and badly shaken, I shouted at him. People gathered. A woman on a bike said she saw the whole thing. Another boy, apparently his friend, stood aimlessly about, saying nothing.

3   Amid the confusion, my assailant rode off. A man on a 10-speed went after him. Several minutes later the boy returned and extended his hand to me. Sorry, he said, it was an accident. I couldn't shake his hand: it was not an accident. A runner said, "No, kid, it's not that easy." The runner signaled a Secret Service police car that was passing by. The boy promptly hopped on his bike again and rode away as we watched.

4   The Secret Service man, out of his jurisdiction, radioed for help. A fire chief, who happened to be driving by in one of those red station wagons, stopped to take my blood pressure and pulse, and cover my wounds. He asked over and over: "What day is today? Where are you? Did you lose consciousness?" My lower leg had begun to develop a contorted swelling. I was nauseated and shaking uncontrollably. The fire chief covered me with a blanket. District and Park police came and more people stopped. It began to get dark. My assailant's friend was taken in a police car, his bicycle in the trunk, to identify the assailant's house.

5   I was taken to the emergency room. Dehydrated and in shock, my body still shook. My leg was X-rayed for fractures; my head checked for concussion; my wounds cleaned and dressed. It was after midnight by the time I got home. During the next few days, I couldn't turn my head or raise my arms above waist level. I couldn't hold or lift anything with my hands. I could walk but only slowly and with great care. It was more than a month before I ran. Even now, every time I step off a curb pain shoots through my lower leg.

6   As a woman I have always been conscious of my surroundings, especially at night. To avoid or minimize risks, I have walked purposefully, carried house keys between my fingers, crossed the street when I saw a threatening person. But I was assaulted during the daylight with plenty of people around. My attacker was not a large man, he was not suspicious looking. The old rules no longer apply. Now I must fear boys. It is difficult to cope with this new vulnerability. When I see groups of kids, I find myself looking for my assailant among them. I am relieved when he is not there, but then I become anxious because other, unknown ones might be just like him.

7   Friends say, quite innocently, Why don't you run with someone, and only go during the daylight? But they don't understand what is lost. Running has always been an important part of my life. In school, I ran cross-country, even a marathon. As an adult I've run in road races. The long runs give me time to be alone, time to

think. Now I must find other people to run with—at mutually convenient times, for mutually convenient distances, at a mutually convenient pace or forgo it altogether. But when I run with another person, I still jump if my elbow touches a bush or if someone moves unexpectedly. Even a walk to the grocery store creates tension. Now I find myself looking away as people pass, trying to appear solemn, tough, never smiling. I have been forced to create a hard shell. Inside I am left compromised and insecure.

8   In the days following the assault I had to decide whether to press charges. Part of me wanted to settle the score, wanted the boy to be frightened, taken down to the station and fingerprinted. I also felt an obligation to other women and other runners to register his name with the police.

9   Of course, pressing charges might be a waste of time. My case was not unusual: one of the men who waited with me for the ambulance that night had been recently assaulted while running. The kid went unpunished.

10   In the end, I didn't have to decide. The detective told me he was going to go after the kid. The weeks went by and nothing happened. The few times the detective called I found myself expressing anger: how could it be taking so long? The police knew where the boy lived and that, as it turns out, he had a case pending from July, involving a stolen car. Finally the detective told me the prosecutor wouldn't sign an arrest warrant for "a case like this," meaning it was too minor to bother about.

11   As I said in the beginning, I know my story is no big deal the way things go these days. Compared to what happened to the Central Park jogger, I was lucky. That's why, it seems to me, my case is also significant. A 12-year-old boy touched a stranger in a sexual way in a public place during the daylight and then struck her when she protested. The boy goes unpunished. The woman is thought to be "lucky" to have "only" suffered bad cuts and bruises, humiliation and a shattering loss of confidence. That such a sequence of events barely merits public notice says more about the way we live now than does the occasional outrage evoked by more extreme events. Is not the measure of a society's condition what it accepts as ordinary and dismisses, rather than what it considers clearly exceptional?

■ TOPICAL CONSIDERATIONS

1. Have you or someone you know ever experienced a "minor" incident like the one Hefferren describes? How did it affect you?
2. In paragraph 6, Hefferren writes, "As a woman I have always been conscious of my surroundings." Why does she emphasize her gender? Is her "incident" limited by gender? Do you feel conscious of your surroundings? How does your answer make you feel?
3. What does Hefferren mean when she writes, "The old rules no longer apply" (paragraph 6)? Think of examples to back up or refute her point.
4. What are the consequences of Hefferren's attack? Does she lose or gain anything by it?
5. Have you ever been in a situation that made you feel vulnerable? What methods did you devise to overcome the vulnerability?

■ RHETORICAL CONSIDERATIONS

1. Hefferren's essay is very personal. Is this narrative method effective? Can you think of cases where such a style might not be effective?
2. In paragraph 11, why does Hefferren put the words *lucky* and *only* in quotation marks?
3. When is a rhetorical question effective? Consider the conclusion of Hefferren's essay. Why does she end her essay with such a question? Have you ever used this strategy?
4. Does the title of Hefferren's piece, "An Incident in the Park," prepare you for her narrative? Based on this title, what were your expectations of the piece?
5. Hefferren's piece reads like a story, but a main point is inferred throughout her narrative. In your own words, explain Hefferren's main idea.

■ WRITING ASSIGNMENTS

1. After witnessing Hefferren's attack, you write a letter to the editor of the local newspaper. What issues will you raise? What solutions will you offer?
2. You are the detective who took care of Hefferren's attack. Based on the information provided in Hefferren's piece, write an objective analysis of the incident for police files.

Date Rape's Other Victim

Katie Roiphe

In the last few years we have heard a lot about "date rape." In what seems a contradiction in terms, the label names an increasingly disturbing issue—and one that has raised a clamor on American college campuses. Women say date rape is a widespread yet hidden crime. Men claim it's difficult to prevent a crime they can't define. Where is the line between his date and her rape? According to Katie Roiphe, claims of a date-rape epidemic are simply an overstatement. In fact, she argues that there is no such crisis on campus, just a mood of "women as victims." And she faults feminists caught up with sexual harassment for redefining how men and women behave sexually. Ultimately, she claims, all the hype betrays feminism.

Katie Roiphe is a doctoral candidate in English literature at Princeton University. This article, which appeared in *The New York Times Magazine,* is adapted from her book, *The Morning After: Sex, Fear and Feminism on Campus* published in 1994.

1 One in four college women has been the victim of rape or attempted rape. One in four. I remember standing outside the dining hall in college, looking at a purple poster with this statistic written in bold letters. It didn't seem right. If sexual assault

was really so pervasive, it seemed strange that the intricate gossip networks hadn't picked up more than one or two shadowy instances of rape. If I was really standing in the middle of an "epidemic," a "crisis"—if 25 percent of my women friends were really being raped—wouldn't I know it?

2   These posters were not presenting facts. They were advertising a mood. Preoccupied with issues like date rape and sexual harassment, campus feminists produce endless images of women as victims—women offended by a professor's dirty joke, women pressured into sex by peers, women trying to say no but not managing to get it across.

3   This portrait of the delicate female bears a striking resemblance to that 50's ideal my mother and other women of her generation fought so hard to leave behind. They didn't like her passivity, her wide-eyed innocence. They didn't like the fact that she was perpetually offended by sexual innuendo. They didn't like her excessive need for protection. She represented personal, social and intellectual possibilities collapsed, and they worked and marched, shouted and wrote to make her irrelevant for their daughters. But here she is again, with her pure intentions and her wide eyes. Only this time it is the feminists themselves who are breathing new life into her.

4   Is there a rape crisis on campus? Measuring rape is not as straightforward as it might seem. Neil Gilbert, a professor of social welfare at the University of California at Berkeley, questions the validity of the one-in-four statistic. Gilbert points out that in a 1985 survey undertaken by Ms. magazine and financed by the National Institute of Mental Health, 73 percent of the women categorized as rape victims did not initially define their experience as rape; it was Mary Koss, the psychologist conducting the study, who did.

5   One of the questions used to define rape was: "Have you had sexual intercourse when you didn't want to because a man gave you alcohol or drugs." The phrasing raises the issue of agency. Why aren't college women responsible for their own intake of alcohol or drugs? A man may give her drugs, but she herself decides to take them. If we assume that women are not all helpless and naïve, then they should be held responsible for their choice to drink or take drugs. If a woman's "judgment is impaired" and she has sex, it isn't necessarily always the man's fault; it isn't necessarily always rape.

6   As Gilbert delves further into the numbers, he does not necessarily disprove the one-in-four statistic, but he does clarify what it means—the so-called rape epidemic on campuses is more a way of interpreting, a way of seeing, than a physical phenomenon. It is more about a change in sexual behavior. Whether or not one in four college women has been raped, then, is a matter of opinion, not a matter of mathematical fact.

7   That rape is a fact in some women's lives is not in question. It's hard to watch the solemn faces of young Bosnian girls, their words haltingly translated, as they tell of brutal rapes; or to read accounts of a suburban teen-ager raped and beaten while walking home from a shopping mall. We all agree that rape is a terrible thing, but we no longer agree on what rape is. Today's definition has stretched beyond bruises and

knives, threats of death or violence to include emotional pressure and the influence of alcohol. The lines between rape and sex begin to blur. The one-in-four statistic on those purple posters is measuring something elusive. It is measuring her word against his in a realm where words barely exist. There is a gray area in which one person's rape may be another's bad night. Definitions become entangled in passionate ideological battles. There hasn't been a remarkable change in the number of women being raped; just a change in how receptive the political climate is to those numbers.

8   The next question, then, is who is identifying this epidemic and why. Somebody is "finding" this rape crisis, and finding it for a reason. Asserting the prevalence of rape lends urgency, authority to a broader critique of culture.

9   In a dramatic description of the rape crisis, Naomi Wolf writes in "The Beauty Myth" that "Cultural representation of glamorized degradation has created a situation among the young in which boys rape and girls get raped *as a normal course of events.*" The italics are hers. Whether or not Wolf really believes rape is part of the "normal course of events" these days, she is making a larger point. Wolf's rhetorical excess serves her larger polemic about sexual politics. Her dramatic prose is a call to arms. She is trying to rally the feminist troops. Wolf uses rape as a red flag, an undeniable sign that things are falling apart.

10   From Susan Brownmiller—who brought the politics of rape into the mainstream with her 1975 best seller, "Against Our Will: Men, Women and Rape"—to Naomi Wolf, feminist prophets of the rape crisis are talking about something more than forced penetration. They are talking about what they define as a "rape culture." Rape is a natural trump card for feminism. Arguments about rape can be used to sequester feminism in the teary province of trauma and crisis. By blocking analysis with its claims to unique pandemic suffering, the rape crisis becomes a powerful source of authority.

11   Dead serious, eyes wide with concern, a college senior tells me that she believes one in four is too conservative an estimate. This is not the first time I've heard this. She tells me the right statistic is closer to one in two. That means one in two women are raped. It's amazing, she says, amazing that so many of us are sexually assaulted every day.

12   What is amazing is that this student actually believes that 50 percent of women are raped. This is the true crisis. Some substantial number of young women are walking around with this alarming belief: a hyperbole containing within it a state of perpetual fear.

13   "Acquaintance Rape: Is Dating Dangerous?" is a pamphlet commonly found at counseling centers. The cover title rises from the shards of a shattered photograph of a boy and girl dancing. Inside, the pamphlet offers a sample date-rape scenario. She thinks:

14   "He was really good looking and he had a great smile. . . . We talked and found we had a lot in common. I really liked him. When he asked me over to his place for a drink I thought it would be O.K. He was such a good listener and I wanted him to ask me out again."

15   She's just looking for a sensitive boy, a good listener with a nice smile, but un-fortunately his intentions are not as pure as hers. Beneath that nice smile, he thinks:

16   "She looked really hot, wearing a sexy dress that showed off her great body. We started talking right away. I knew that she liked me by the way she kept smiling and touching my arm while she was speaking. She seemed pretty relaxed so I asked her back to my place for a drink. . . . When she said 'Yes' I knew that I was going to be lucky!"

17   These cardboard stereotypes don't just educate freshmen about rape. They also educate them about "dates" and about sexual desire. With titles like "Friends Raping Friends: Could It Happen to You?" date-rape pamphlets call into question all rela-tionships between men and women. Beyond warning students about rape, the rape-crisis movement produces its own images of sexual behavior, in which men exert pressure and women resist. By defining the dangerous date in these terms—with this type of male and this type of female, and their different expectations—these pam-phlets promote their own perspective on how men and women feel about sex: men are lascivious, women are innocent.

18   The sleek images of pressure and resistance projected in rape education movies, videotapes, pamphlets and speeches create a model of acceptable sexual behavior. The don'ts imply their own set of do's. The movement against rape, then, not only dictates the way sex *shouldn't be* but also the way it *should be*. Sex should be gentle, it should not be aggressive; it should be absolutely equal, it should not involve domi-nation and submission; it should be tender, not ambivalent; it should communicate respect, it shouldn't communicate consuming desire.

19   In "Real Rape," Susan Estrich, a professor of law at the University of Southern California Law Center, slips her ideas about the nature of sexual encounters into her legal analysis of the problem of rape. She writes: "Many feminists would argue that so long as women are powerless relative to men, viewing a 'yes' as a sign of true consent is misguided. . . . Many women who say yes to men they know, whether on dates or on the job, would say no if they could. . . . Women's silence sometimes is the product not of passion and desire but of pressure and fear."

20   Like Estrich, most rape-crisis feminists claim they are not talking about sex; they're talking about violence. But, like Estrich, they are also talking about sex. With their advice, their scenarios, their sample aggressive male, the message projects a clear comment on the nature of sexuality: women are often unwilling partici-pants. They say yes because they feel they have to, because they are intimidated by male power.

21   The idea of "consent" has been redefined beyond the simple assertion that "no means no." Politically correct sex involves a yes, and a specific yes at that. According to the premise of "active consent," we can no longer afford ambiguity. We can no longer afford the dangers of unspoken consent. A former director of Columbia's date-rape education program told New York magazine, "Stone silence throughout an entire physical encounter with someone is not explicit consent."

22   This apparently practical, apparently clinical proscription cloaks retrograde as-sumptions about the way men and women experience sex. The idea that only an ex-plicit yes means yes proposes that, like children, women have trouble communicat-

ing what they want. Beyond its dubious premise about the limits of female communication, the idea of active consent bolsters stereotypes of men just out to "get some" and women who don't really want any.

23   Rape-crisis feminists express nostalgia for the days of greater social control, when the university acted in loco parentis and women were protected from the insatiable force of male desire. The rhetoric of feminists and conservatives blurs and overlaps in this desire to keep our youth safe and pure.

24   By viewing rape as encompassing more than the use or threat of physical violence to coerce someone into sex, rape-crisis feminists reinforce traditional views about the fragility of the female body and will. According to common definitions of date rape, even "verbal coercion" or "manipulation" constitute rape. Verbal coercion is defined as "a woman's consenting to unwanted sexual activity because of a man's verbal arguments not including verbal threats of force." The belief that "verbal coercion" is rape pervades workshops, counseling sessions and student opinion pieces. The suggestion lurking beneath this definition of rape is that men are not just physically but also intellectually and emotionally more powerful than women.

25   Imagine men sitting around in a circle talking about how she called him impotent and how she manipulated him into sex, how violated and dirty he felt afterward, how coercive she was, how she got him drunk first, how he hated his body and he couldn't eat for three weeks afterward. Imagine him calling this rape. Everyone feels the weight of emotional pressure at one time or another. The question is not whether people pressure each other but how our minds and our culture transform that pressure into full-blown assault. There would never be a rule or a law or even a pamphlet or peer counseling group for men who claimed to have been emotionally raped or verbally pressured into sex. And for the same reasons—assumption of basic competence, free will and strength of character—there should be no such rules or groups or pamphlets about women.

26   In discussing rape, campus feminists often slip into an outdated sexist vocabulary. But we have to be careful about using rape as metaphor. The sheer physical fact of rape has always been loaded with cultural meaning. Throughout history, women's bodies have been seen as property, as chaste objects, as virtuous vessels to be "dishonored," "ruined," "defiled." Their purity or lack of purity has been a measure of value for the men to whom they belonged.

27   "Politically, I call it rape whenever a woman has sex and feels violated," writes Catharine MacKinnon, a law professor and feminist legal scholar best known for her crusade against pornography. The language of virtue and violation reinforces retrograde stereotypes. It backs women into old corners. Younger feminists share MacKinnon's vocabulary and the accompanying assumptions about women's bodies. In one student's account of date rape in the Rag, a feminist magazine at Harvard, she talks about the anguish of being "defiled." Another writes, "I long to be innocent again." With such anachronistic constructions of the female body, with all their assumptions about female purity, these young women frame their experience of rape in archaic, sexist terms. Of course, sophisticated modern-day feminists don't use words like honor or virtue anymore. They know better than to say date-rape victims have been "defiled." Instead, they call it "post-traumatic stress syndrome." They tell the

victim she should not feel "shame," she should feel "traumatized." Within their overtly political psychology, forced penetration takes on a level of metaphysical significance: date rape resonates through a woman's entire life.

28   Combating myths about rape is one of the central missions of the rape-crisis movement. They spend money and energy trying to break down myths like "She asked for it." But with all their noise about rape myths, rape-crisis feminists are generating their own. The plays, the poems, the pamphlets, the Take Back the Night speakouts, are propelled by the myth of innocence lost.

29   All the talk about empowering the voiceless dissolves into the image of the naïve girl child who trusts the rakish man. This plot reaches back centuries. It propels Samuel Richardson's 18th-century epistolary novel, "Clarissa": after hundreds of pages chronicling the minute details of her plight, her seduction and resistance, her break from her family, Clarissa is raped by the duplicitous Robert Love-lace. Afterward, she refuses to eat and fades toward a very virtuous, very religious death. Over a thousand pages are devoted to the story of her fall from innocence, a weighty event by 18th-century standards. But did these 20th-century girls, raised on Madonna videos and the 6 o'clock news, really trust that people were good until they themselves were raped? Maybe. Were these girls, raised on horror movies and glossy Hollywood sex scenes, really as innocent as all that? Maybe. But maybe the myth of lost innocence is a trope—convenient, appealing, politically effective.

30   As long as we're taking back the night, we might as well take back our own purity. Sure, we were all kind of innocent, playing in the sandbox with bright red shovels—boys, too. We can all look back through the tumultuous tunnel of adolescence on a honey-glazed childhood, with simple rules and early bedtimes. We don't have to look at parents fighting, at sibling struggles, at casting out one best friend for another in the Darwinian playground. This is not the innocence lost; this is the innocence we never had.

31   The idea of a fall from childhood grace, pinned on one particular moment, a moment over which we had no control, much lamented, gives our lives a compelling narrative structure. It's easy to see why the 17-year-old likes it; it's easy to see why the rape-crisis feminist likes it. It's a natural human impulse put to political purpose. But in generating and perpetuating such myths, we should keep in mind that myths about innocence have been used to keep women inside and behind veils. They have been used to keep them out of work and in labor.

32   It's not hard to imagine Clarissa, in jeans and a sweatshirt, transported into the 20th century, at a Take Back the Night march. She would speak for a long time about her deception and rape, about verbal coercion and anorexia, about her ensuing post-traumatic stress syndrome. Latter-day Clarissas may worry more about their "self esteem" than their virtue, but they are still attaching the same quasi-religious value to the physical act.

33   "Calling It Rape," a play by Sonya Rasminsky, a recent Harvard graduate, is based on interviews with date-rape victims. The play, which has been performed at Harvard and may be taken into Boston-area high schools, begins with "To His Coy Mistress," by the 17th-century poet Andrew Marvell. Although generations of high-

school and college students have read this as a romantic poem, a poem about desire and the struggle against mortality, Rasminsky has reinterpreted it as a poem about rape. "Had we but world enough, and time, this coyness, lady, were no crime." But what Andrew Marvell didn't know then, and we know now, is that the real crime is not her coyness but his verbal coercion.

34   Farther along, the actors recount a rape that hinges on misunderstanding. A boy and girl are watching videos and he starts to come on to her. She does not want to have sex. As the situation progresses, she says, in an oblique effort to communicate her lack of enthusiasm, "If you're going to [expletive] me, use a condom." He interprets that as a yes, but it's really a no. And, according to this play, what happens next, condom or no condom, is rape.

35   This is a central idea of the rape-crisis movement: that sex has become our tower of Babel. He doesn't know what she wants (not to have sex) and she doesn't know what he wants (to have sex)—until it's too late. He speaks boyspeak and she speaks girlspeak and what comes out of all this verbal chaos is a lot of rapes. The theory of mixed signals and crossed stars has to do with more than gender politics. It comes in part, from the much-discussed diversity that has so radically shifted the social composition of the college class since the 50's.

36   Take my own Harvard dorm: the Adams House dining hall is large, with high ceilings and dark paneling. It hasn't changed much for generations. As soon as the students start milling around gathering salads, ice cream and coffee onto green trays, there are signs of change. There are students in jeans, flannel shirts, short skirts, girls in jackets, boys in bracelets, two pierced noses and lots of second-hand clothes.

37   Not so many years ago, this room was filled with boys in jackets and ties. Most of them were white, Christian and what we now call privileged. Students came from the same social milieu with the same social rules and it was assumed that everyone knew more or less how they were expected to behave with everyone else. Diversity and multiculturalism were unheard of, and if they had been, they would have been dirty words. With the shift in college environments, with the introduction of black kids, Asian kids, Jewish kids, kids from the wrong side of the tracks of nearly every railroad in the country, there was an accompanying anxiety about how people behave. When ivory tower meets melting pot, it causes tension, some confusion, some need for readjustment. In explaining the need for intensive "orientation" programs, including workshops on date rape, Columbia's assistant dean for freshmen stated in an interview in The New York Times: "You can't bring all these people together and say, 'Now be one big happy community,' without some sort of training. You can't just throw together somebody from a small town in Texas and someone from New York City and someone from a conservative fundamentalist home in the Midwest and say, 'Now without any sort of conversation, be best friends and get along and respect one another.'"

38   Catharine Stimpson, a University Professor at Rutgers and longtime advocate of women's studies programs, once pointed out that it's sometimes easier for people to talk about gender than to talk about class. "Miscommunication" is in some sense a word for the friction between the way we were and the way we are. Just as the idea

that we speak different languages is connected to gender—the arrival of women in classrooms, in dorms and in offices—it is also connected to class.

39   When the Southern heiress goes out with the plumber's son from the Bronx, when the kid from rural Arkansas goes out with a boy from Exeter, the anxiety is that they have different expectations. The dangerous "miscommunication" that recurs through the literature on date rape is a code word for difference in background. The rhetoric surrounding date rape and sexual harassment is in part a response to cultural mixing. The idea that men don't know what women mean when women say no stems from something deeper and more complicated than feminist concerns with rape.

40   People have asked me if I have ever been date-raped. And thinking back on complicated nights, on too many glasses of wine, on strange and familiar beds, I would have to say yes. With such a sweeping definition of rape, I wonder how many people there are, male or female, who haven't been date-raped at one point or another. People pressure and manipulate and cajole each other into all sorts of things all of the time. As Susan Sontag wrote, "Since Christianity upped the ante and concentrated on sexual behavior as the root of virtue, everything pertaining to sex has been a 'special case' in our culture, evoking peculiarly inconsistent attitudes." No human interactions are free from pressure, and the idea that sex is, or can be, makes it what Sontag calls a "special case," vulnerable to the inconsistent expectations of double standard.

41   With their expansive version of rape, rape-crisis feminists are inventing a kinder, gentler sexuality. Beneath the broad definition of rape, these feminists are endorsing their own utopian vision of sexual relations: sex without struggle, sex without power, sex without persuasion, sex without pursuit. If verbal coercion constitutes rape, then the word rape itself expands to include any kind of sex a woman experiences as negative.

42   When Martin Amis spoke at Princeton, he included a controversial joke: "As far as I'm concerned, you can change your mind before, even during, but just not after sex." The reason this joke is funny, and the reason it's also too serious to be funny, is that in the current atmosphere you *can* change your mind afterward. Regret can signify rape. A night that was a blur, a night you wish hadn't happened, can be rape. Since "verbal coercion" and "manipulation" are ambiguous, it's easy to decide afterwards that he manipulated you. You can realize it weeks or even years later. This is a movement that deals in retrospective trauma.

43   Rape has become a catch-all expression, a word used to define everything that is unpleasant and disturbing about relations between the sexes. Students say things like "I realize that sexual harassment is a kind of rape." If we refer to a whole range of behavior from emotional pressure to sexual harassment as "rape," then the idea itself gets diluted. It ceases to be powerful as either description or accusation.

44   Some feminists actually collapse the distinction between rape and sex. Catharine MacKinnon writes: "Compare victims' reports of rape with women's reports of sex. They look a lot alike. . . . In this light, the major distinction between in-

tercourse (normal) and rape (abnormal) is that the normal happens so often that one cannot get anyone to see anything wrong with it."

45   There are a few feminists involved in rape education who object to the current expanding definitions of sexual assault. Gillian Greensite, founder of the rape prevention education program at the University of California at Santa Cruz, writes that the seriousness of the crime "is being undermined by the growing tendency of some feminists to label all heterosexual miscommunication and insensitivity as acquaintance rape." From within the rape-crisis movement, Greensite's dissent makes an important point. If we are going to maintain an *idea* of rape, then we need to reserve it for instances of physical violence, or the threat of physical violence.

46   But some people want the melodrama. They want the absolute value placed on experience by absolute words. Words like "rape" and "verbal coercion" channel the confusing flow of experience into something easy to understand. The idea of date rape comes at us fast and coherent. It comes at us when we've just left home and haven't yet figured out where to put our new futons or how to organize our new social lives. The rhetoric about date rape defines the terms, gives names to nameless confusions and sorts through mixed feelings with a sort of insistent consistency. In the first rush of sexual experience, the fear of date rape offers a tangible framework to locate fears that are essentially abstract.

47   When my 55-year-old mother was young, navigating her way through dates, there was a definite social compass. There were places not to let him put his hands. There were invisible lines. The pill wasn't available. Abortion wasn't legal. And sex was just wrong. Her mother gave her "mad money" to take out on dates in case her date got drunk and she needed to escape. She had to go far enough to hold his interest and not far enough to endanger her reputation.

48   Now the rape-crisis feminists are offering new rules. They are giving a new political weight to the same old no. My mother's mother told her to drink sloe gin fizzes so she wouldn't drink too much and get too drunk and go too far. Now the date rape pamphlets tell us: "Avoid excessive use of alcohol and drugs. Alcohol and drugs interfere with clear thinking and effective communication." My mother's mother told her to stay away from empty rooms and dimly lighted streets. In "I Never Called It Rape," Robin Warshaw writes, "Especially with recent acquaintances, women should insist on going only to public places such as restaurants and movie theaters."

49   There is a danger in these new rules. We shouldn't need to be reminded that the rigidly conformist 50's were not the heyday of women's power. Barbara Ehrenreich writes of "re-making love," but there is a danger in re-making love in its old image. The terms may have changed, but attitudes about sex and women's bodies have not. Rape-crisis feminists threaten the progress that's been made. They are chasing the same stereotypes our mothers spent so much energy escaping.

50   One day I was looking through my mother's bookshelves and I found her old battered copy of Germaine Greer's feminist classic, "The Female Eunuch." The pages were dogeared and whole passages marked with penciled notes. It was 1971 when Germaine Greer fanned the fires with "The Female Eunuch" and it was 1971

when my mother read it, brand new, explosive, a tough and sexy terrorism for the early stirrings of the feminist movement.

51   Today's rape-crisis feminists threaten to create their own version of the desexualized woman Greer complained of 20 years ago. Her comments need to be recycled for present-day feminism. "It is often falsely assumed," Greer writes, "even by feminists, that sexuality is the enemy of the female who really wants to develop these aspects of her personality. . . . It was not the insistence upon her sex that weakened the American woman student's desire to make something of her education, but the insistence upon a *passive* sexual *role* [Greer's italics]. In fact, the chief instrument in the deflection and perversion of female energy is the denial of female sexuality for the substitution of femininity or sexlessness."

52   It is the passive sexual role that threatens us still, and it is the denial of female sexual agency that threatens to propel us backward.

■ TOPICAL CONSIDERATIONS

1. According to Roiphe in the first paragraph, how prevalent is rape on college campuses? What problems does she have with providing an exact set of statistics?

2. Why does Roiphe state that the "one in four" rape statistic is a matter of opinion, not a matter of fact? How can a statistic be an opinion? Who is responsible for this emotionally-charged opinion?

3. Roiphe complains that she is unable to trust statistics on rape reporting. Aside from the problem of defining what rape means, what additional problems might there be in collecting statistics? If you were a woman who had been raped, would you be willing to announce that fact to class members? To your family? In a public forum, such as a television report on rape? Would you want to file a police report on the incident? What might prevent your reporting a rape?

4. What images are portrayed in the counseling center pamphlet on acquaintance rape mentioned in paragraph 13? What does Roiphe think is wrong with those images?

5. What are the problems with making explicit consent the key issue in defining rape, according to Susan Estrich and other rape-crisis feminists? According to Roiphe, what is wrong with these objections?

6. According to Roiphe, what outmoded myths about women's sexuality are rape-crisis feminists using to make their case? Why does Roiphe believe these myths are so attractive to young women in college? Do you agree with Roiphe? Explain your reasoning.

7. According to feminists such as Sonya Rasminsky (paragraph 33–34), how do communication problems between men and women contribute to rape? Do you think the woman's request that the man use a condom was consent to sexual activity? Why does Roiphe disagree with discussions about rape based on miscommunication?

8. Why does Roiphe believe that it is wrong to expand our definition of rape "to include any kind of sex a woman experiences as negative"? How does she say this expanding definition is a step backward in terms of women's sexual and social equality?

9. How different does Roiphe think men and women are, especially in their desire for sex? Does she think most differences are inborn (natural, innate, programmed in with biological maleness or femaleness), or does she think most differences are social (due to training, socialization, custom, and tradition)? In a word, are men and women different mostly because of nature or nurture? What do you think?

10. In paragraphs 47 and 48, Roiphe describes some of the rules and codes of behavior which her mother followed in the mid- to late-1950s. What rules do young women follow now? Are the rules different now for women who are older—say, in their mid-20s or beyond? Do you think the rules women follow now have similar goals to the ones mentioned in Roiphe's article? What kinds of rules, if any, do men have?

■ RHETORICAL CONSIDERATIONS

1. Roiphe uses satire to make a number of her points. For example, she writes about a stereotype of "wide-eyed innocence" in paragraph 3, and then in paragraph 11 repeats the image by portraying a student whose opinion she disagrees with as having "eyes wide with concern." What other examples of satire can you find? Do you think Roiphe uses this device effectively?

2. Roiphe never defines date rape, or acquaintance rape, although that is the central issue in her article. How effective are the extended examples she supplies? Why does Roiphe never define it? How does this affect her argument?

3. In paragraphs 36 through 39, Roiphe debunks the idea that men and women have different ways of speaking that creates a climate for rape. Why does she discuss class and regional difference? How effective is this discussion in refuting male-female differences in communication? Do you agree with Roiphe?

4. Roiphe lampoons women she thinks would subscribe to the wrong ideas about rape: the wide-eyed innocent, or the prissy conformist of the 1950s. Why doesn't she spend any time describing women whose views about sex she would approve? Why are there no "sex-positive" women in this article? How does this omission affect her argument?

5. Roiphe thinks men and women are about the same in their desire for sex. How important is this assumption to her argument? That is, how would her argument have to be changed if scientists could prove that men have stronger sex drives (or, for that matter, that women do)?

6. Who is the "other victim" of date rape mentioned in the title—men, feminists, women? Why do you think Roiphe doesn't supply an answer and discuss this victimization thoroughly?

■ WRITING ASSIGNMENTS

1. From the comments and examples in this article, prepare a precise definition of rape that you think Roiphe would agree to. Do you accept this definition of rape? Why or why not? If you do not accept this definition, write a second definition and explain why it is better than Roiphe's.
2. How closely do Roiphe's ideas about men in this article agree with those in Myriam Miedzian's article "The Culture of Violence" earlier in this chapter? What ideas do you think Roiphe would agree with? disagree with? What do you think Miedzian's Kurnai anthropologists would say about contemporary rape-crisis feminism?
3. Find out what kind of rape-awareness, training, and prevention materials or programs your college or university offers. Do you think offerings are adequate? make realistic statements, and present appropriate images? Is there any way that you would recommend these materials be changed? Why or why not?
4. If possible, prepare a report on the prevalence of rape in your community or on your campus. Compare statistical information from at least four of the following local or campus resources: (a) newspapers; (b) college administrators or city government officials; (c) police, law enforcement, or justice system officials; (d) victim assistance programs; (e) women's advocacy groups; (f) battered women's shelters; (g) random surveys; (h) professional journals published for education or law enforcement professionals. Make sure you determine, if possible, how rape is defined by each source.

Crime and Punishment and Personal Responsibility

Clarence Thomas

What follows is a tightly constructed argument for a judicial system that is based on what people have done rather than who they are. Written by the conservative associate justice of the U.S. Supreme Court, Clarence Thomas, the essay takes on liberal judicial attitudes—what he calls the "rights revolution"—which question whether our minorities and poor can be blamed for their crimes since they themselves are victims of circumstances. For the criminal justice system to work, Thomas maintains, we cannot obviate individual responsibility. Otherwise Democracy and the individual will suffer.

This is an edited version of an address Mr. Thomas delivered in Washington D.C. at a symposium sponsored by the Federalist Society and the Manhattan Institute, "The Rights Revolution and America's Urban Poor: Victims or Beneficiaries?" It was originally published in the *Boston Sunday Globe* in May 1994.

1 I want to talk to you today about an aspect of the rights revolution—namely, how the current state of our criminal justice system has affected the ideal of personal responsibility. I am convinced that there can be no freedom and opportunity for many in our society if our criminal law loses sight of the importance of individual responsibility. Indeed, in my mind, the principal reason for a criminal justice system is to hold people accountable for the consequences of their actions. Put simply, it is to hold people's feet to the fire when they do something harmful to individuals or society as a whole.

2   Let's begin with the most practical reason for why we hold people accountable. The law cannot persuade where it cannot punish. Alexander Hamilton made this very point when he observed, "It is essential to the idea of a law that it be attended with a sanction . . . a punishment for disobedience." Most of us, I am sure, are regularly faced with the deterrent effect of the law, the incentive not to engage in conduct that might harm others. To be sure, we choose to honor speed limits because such behavior might well save our own lives. But we just as surely follow the rules because of the legal consequences of speeding—harsh fines and possible loss of our licenses.

3   Some underscore a different aspect of human nature in explaining why holding people responsible for their actions is central to our criminal justice system. Unlike any other living creature in the world, humans are moral, rational and thinking beings. We, therefore, expect one another to be able to distinguish between right and wrong and to act accordingly. Thus, when society punishes someone for breaking the law—when it holds him accountable for the consequences of his acts—we are recognizing that only mankind is capable of being moral or rational. We are, in short, acknowledging the human dignity of our fellow man. Indeed, people thrive in our society because of the expectations we all have regarding the capacity of the human will to do good. But to disregard this potential—to ignore the fact that someone has harmed others by breaking the law—treats our fellow man as beings that are incapable of determining right from wrong and controlling their behavior.

4   There are others who believe that the principal reason we hold people responsible for the consequences of their actions is because of our mutual political or social obligations in a civilized, democratic society. In accepting and benefiting from the wonderful opportunities of our free society, we each consent or agree to be bound by the rules and expect government to enforce them. When someone breaks the law, a fundamental trust has been violated. In effect, the lawbreaker is telling all of us that there can be no mutual expectation that society's rules will be followed and thereby protect all of us. On this view, we punish the criminal because he owes a debt to society for violating our trust. To do otherwise would cheat those who abide by law, and dilute the threat of force that the law is supposed to convey. And, if our government failed to remedy wrongs by holding people responsible for their acts, we would be faced with the prospect of vigilante justice and all the evils that accompany it.

5   For these and other reasons, then, I think most everyone agrees that we have a criminal justice system in order to hold people accountable. If properly administered, it stands to reason that the criminal law should help to ensure a greater degree of personal responsibility in our society. Put differently, the criminal law serves a

signaling function when we hold people accountable for their harmful acts. Punishing people is an expression of society's resolve that certain behavior will not be tolerated either because it hurts others, is counterproductive or is offensive to the sensibilities of our culture. In the absence of such a signal—if government does not punish harmful conduct—we send a dangerous message to society.

6   One must wonder, though, whether our criminal law is carrying out this signaling function. Why are so many of our streets rife with drug bazaars and other criminal enterprises? Why are so many of our schools devoid of the discipline that is necessary for a healthy learning environment and instead plagued by lawlessness? Why is there unprecedented fear of violence among so many of our fellow citizens?

7   One reason, I believe, is that the rights revolution worked a fundamental transformation in our criminal law. The very same ideas that prompted the judicial revolution in due process rights for the poor and that circumscribed the authority of local communities to set standards for decorum and civility on the streets or in the public schools also made it far more difficult for the criminal justice system to hold people responsible for the consequences of their harmful acts. I want to focus on one particular force behind the rights revolution that in my view had the most profound effect on the direction of the criminal law: namely, the idea that our society had failed to safeguard the interests of minorities, the poor and other groups; and, as a consequence, was, in fact, primarily at fault for their plight.

8   Much of the judicial revolution in individual rights was justified on the ground that the dignity and well-being of large segments of our population—minorities, women, the poor—were consistently ignored by our social and political institutions. As the victims of centuries of discrimination and oppression, blacks and other minorities could not enjoy the full benefits and opportunities that society had to offer. So too were the poor viewed as victims—uncontrollable forces contributed to their poverty, and yet their "stake" in welfare and other public benefits was not insulated from unregulated state power in the same way as the property interests of the more fortunate in society.

9   These concerns greatly influenced our courts in requiring that government hold hearings or comply with other procedural requirements before terminating public benefits received by minorities and the poorest of Americans. The view was that these entitlements were worth protecting because they aid the poor and underrepresented in achieving security and well-being.

10   Procedural protections also were viewed as necessary to ensure that government interference with public benefits was not arbitrary and unfair. Because minority and disadvantaged students are the most frequent objects of school discipline, for example, advocates of greater constitutional protections insisted that the absence of stringent procedural requirements for suspension could lead to racial discrimination and other forms of unequal treatment. Much the same arguments were made regarding limits on the power to evict tenants from public housing and to enforce broad vagrancy or anti-panhandling laws—government discretion had to be curbed in order to ensure that minorities or unpopular groups were not singled out for unfair and discriminatory treatment.

11   We can see, then, how the intellectual currents of the legal revolution in individual rights affected the management of community institutions such as schools and the civility of our streets, parks and other common spaces. But how did the ideas underlying this revolution affect the functioning of the criminal justice system?

12   Many began questioning whether the poor and minorities could be blamed for the crimes they committed. Our legal institutions and popular culture began identifying those accused of wrongdoing as victims of upbringing and circumstances. The point was made that human actions and choices, like events in the natural world, are often caused by factors outside of one's control. No longer was an individual identified as the cause of a harmful act. Rather, societal conditions or the actions of institutions and others in society became the responsible causes of harm. These external causes might be poverty, poor education, a faltering family structure, systemic racism or other forms of bigotry, and spousal or child abuse, just to name a few. The consequence of this new way of thinking about accountability and responsibility—or lack thereof—was that a large part of our society could escape being held accountable for the consequences of harmful conduct. The law punishes only those who are responsible for their actions; and in a world of countless uncontrollable causes of aggression or lawlessness, few will have to account for their behavior.

13   As a further extension of these ideas, some began challenging society's moral authority to hold many of our less fortunate citizens responsible for their harmful acts. Punishment is an expression of society's disapproval or reprobation. In other words, punishment is a way of directing society's moral indignation toward persons responsible for violating its rules. Critics insisted, though, that an individual's harmful conduct is not the only relevant factor in determining whether punishment is morally justified. The individual's conduct must be judged in relation to how society has acted toward that individual in the past. In this regard, many began appearing hesitant to hold responsible those individuals whose conduct might be explained as a response to societal injustice. How can we hold the poor responsible for their actions, some asked, when our society does little to remedy the social conditions of the ill-educated and unemployed in our urban areas? In a similar vein, others questioned how we could tell blacks in our inner cities to face the consequences for breaking the law when the very legal system and society which will judge their conduct perpetuated years of racism and unequal treatment under the law.

14   Once our legal system accepted the general premise that social conditions and upbringing could be excuses for harmful conduct, the range of causes that might prevent society from holding anyone accountable for his actions became potentially limitless. Do we punish a drunk driver who has a family history of alcoholism? A bigoted employer reared in a segregationist environment, who was taught that blacks are inferior? A thief or drug pusher who was raised in a dysfunctional family and who received a poor education? A violent gang member, rioter or murderer who attributes his rage, aggression and lack of respect for authority to a racist society that has oppressed him since birth? Which of these individuals, if any, should be excused for their conduct? Can we really distinguish among them in a principled way?

15   An effective criminal justice system—one that holds people accountable for harmful conduct—simply cannot be sustained under conditions where there are boundless excuses for violent behavior and no moral authority for the state to punish. If people know that they are not going to be held accountable because of a myriad of excuses, how will our society be able to influence behavior and provide incentives to follow the law? How can we teach future generations right from wrong if the idea of criminal responsibility is riddled with exceptions and our governing institutions and courts lack the moral self-confidence? A society that does not hold someone accountable for harmful behavior can be viewed as condoning—or even worse, endorsing—such conduct. In the long run, a society that abandons personal responsibility will lose its moral sense. And it is the urban poor whose lives are being destroyed the most by this loss of moral sense.

16   This is not surprising. A system that does not hold individuals accountable for their harmful acts treats them as less than full citizens. In such a world, people are reduced to the status of children or, even worse, treated as though they are animals without a soul. There may be a hard lesson here: In the face of injustice on the part of society, it is natural and easy to demand recompense or a dispensation from conventional norms. But all too often, doing so involves the individual accepting diminished responsibility for his future. Does the acceptance of diminished responsibility assure that the human spirit will not rise above the tragedies of one's existence? When we demand something from our oppressors—more lenient standards of conduct, for example—are we merely going from a state of slavery to a more deceptive, but equally destructive, state of dependency?

17   It also bears noting that contemporary efforts to rehabilitate criminals will never work in a system that often neglects to assign blame to individuals for their harmful acts. How can we encourage criminals not to return to crime if our justice system fosters the idea that it is society that has perpetuated racism and poverty—not the individual who engaged in harmful conduct—that is to blame for aggression and crime, and thus, in greatest need of rehabilitation and reform.

18   The transformation of the criminal justice system has had and will continue to have its greatest impact in our urban areas. It is there that modern excuses for criminal behavior abound—poverty, substandard education, faltering families, unemployment, a lack of respect for authority because of deep feelings of oppression.

19   I have no doubt that the rights revolution had a noble purpose: to stop society from threatening blacks, the poor and others—many of whom today occupy our urban areas—as if they were invisible, not worthy of attention. But the revolution missed a larger point by merely changing their status from invisible to victimized. Minorities and the poor are humans—capable of dignity as well as shame, folly as well as success. We should be treated as such.

■ TOPICAL CONSIDERATIONS

1. In paragraphs 1 through 4, Thomas explains why people must be held accountable for the consequences of their actions. What are the three main reasons that we must insist on such responsibility?

2. Thomas sums up his thoughts about criminal law in paragraph 5, by saying that it serves a "signaling function." What is a signal? Come up with some examples of signals. How is criminal law a signal? What evidence does Thomas supply in the following paragraph that the signal is no longer working well?

3. In paragraphs 7 through 11, what is the "rights revolution" (the "judicial revolution in due process rights") Thomas refers to? What groups benefited from this revolution? Why did these groups need protection from state governments in the form of lengthy, painstaking procedures?

4. Thomas, in paragraph 10, refers to "minorities or unpopular groups," and, in paragraph 12, to the effects of "popular culture." From your experience, what is an "unpopular group"? What is a "popular group"? (blacks? Korean shopkeepers in Los Angeles during the Rodney King riots? middle-class white men? Christians? left-handed people? others you can think of?) How does public opinion about popularity shape our perceptions about one group or another and our actions toward it? What is Thomas's attitude about popularity?

5. How does Thomas answer his question at the end of paragraph 11, "But how did the ideas underlying this revolution affect the functioning of the justice system?"

6. Which of the four individuals in paragraph 14 should be excused, according to Thomas—the drunk driver, the bigoted employer, the thief/drug pusher, or the gang member/murderer? Do you agree? Explain your answer.

7. Why does Thomas say that his argument is a "hard lesson" in paragraph 16? What is difficult or uncomfortable about his reasoning? In your opinion, is it really fair or compassionate for someone who has been victimized, oppressed, or discriminated against to be held responsible for breaking the law?

8. In paragraphs 15 through 19, what will eventually happen if the signaling function is not restored to criminal law? How and why will people who have benefited from the rights revolution, paradoxically, suffer most from this shift in judicial philosophy? Do you agree?

■ RHETORICAL CONSIDERATIONS

1. Thomas's argument has three main parts: (a) an overview of the criminal law; (b) discussion of a shift in legal decisions; and (c) discussion of effects and long-range consequences of this shift. For each of these three parts, identify the paragraphs in which Thomas presents it, and provide a one-sentence summary of his main idea.

2. Where does Thomas place the thesis statement for this article? How does this placement effect his argument?

3. The tone of this article is very formal or elevated. In what various ways does Thomas achieve that tone? Why do you think he uses such a tone? What expectations does he have about his readers or listeners?

4. Cite examples where Thomas plays upon readers' fears should society not follow his advice in administering the criminal justice system. How important are these fears in helping him make a compelling argument? In your opinion, does his use of fear make parts of his argument unfair?

5. Not until the final sentence of the article does Thomas identify himself as a member of a minority group. Why do you think he waits until this point to do so? Does this reference to his own identity play any part in his argument?

6. Why do you think Thomas spends so much time discussing the "rights revolution" in the middle of his article, since this is not his main point? What principles about responsibilities and benefits of citizens does he illustrate with this discussion? How does this historical background serve his main argument about punishing all lawbreakers equally, regardless of environment?

■ WRITING ASSIGNMENTS

1. In an essay, describe a time in your life when you broke a rule or a law, and you got caught. (It could be something as simple as turning in your paper for this class late, or violating your parents' curfew rules.) Did you make excuses? Were those excuses accepted? Do you think that your punishment (or the absence of punishment, if that was the case) served a "signaling function"?

2. In this article, Clarence Thomas refers only to lawbreaking that is prompted by anger caused by large, complicated social problems. The lawbreakers are lashing out at inappropriate targets, and harming innocent people. In your opinion, do the same standards of personal responsibility apply to those who break unjust laws, or who feel compelled to remedy a situation the law cannot or will not address? What about the following examples: women who kill abusive husbands or people who steal in order to feed their families? Martin Luther King who employed civil disobedience consisting of selectively breaking segregationist laws in order to bring about the rights revolution? Should these people be punished? You may want to use newspaper indexes to look up some sample cases to use in your discussion. Explore these questions in a paper.

3. Clarence Thomas is concerned that minority lawbreakers be punished just as harshly as any other lawbreaker who has committed a similar act. Using your school's government documents section, news indexes, and legal or criminal justice resources, find out whether minorities and nonminorities are punished equally. You may want to compare roughly similar cases (several case studies of people of different races who have committed similar crimes); or you might look for broader statistics on the numbers and proportions of crimes, conviction rates, and length of sentences for people of each race. What factors seem to influence the differences you find? Write up your research in a paper.

Oprah! Oprah in the Court!

Sophfronia Scott Gregory

For the last few years, courtroom trials have become the new show business, especially with such high-profile cases as O.J. Simpson's in 1995 and the Menendez brothers' the year before. Ironically, in spite of their crimes, many of the defendants have become cult heroes. According to the article below, one prime reason, as its title suggests, is television talk shows. As Sophfronia Scott Gregory explains, Americans are becoming more familiar with "the language of therapy and recovery" and more sympathetic with the motivations of abusers who themselves were abused.

Ms. Gregory is a staff writer for *Time*. This article first appeared in that magazine in June 1994.

1   In the quiet of suburban Los Angeles, Moosa Hanoukai picked up a pipe wrench and bludgeoned his wife Manijeh to death. When the businessman did not contest the facts, prosecutors assumed they had an easy second-degree murder conviction. But Hanoukai's attorney James Blatt mounted this defense: his client was a victim of husband battering and 25 years of abuse. Furthermore, because of the stringencies of an Iranian-Jewish culture, Hanoukai felt trapped: he killed Manijeh because he was not allowed to divorce her. The jury empathized and found Hanoukai guilty only of voluntary manslaughter. Instead of 15 years to life, he may serve as brief a prison term as 4½ years.

2   The Hanoukai verdict provoked little of the turmoil attending the acquittals of Lorena and John Bobbitt and the hung juries of the Menendez brothers. But critics charge that all these legal proceedings illustrate the same trend: juries are increasingly willing to make allowances for mitigating circumstances once considered largely irrelevant—abused spouses who kill, violated children who murder incestuous parents, victims of posttraumatic stress syndrome driven to violence by disturbing flashbacks.

3   Such tales are the daily stuff of talk shows, of course, leading some prosecutors to blame Oprah and company for making jurors more sympathetic to novel defense strategies that try to excuse the accused's behavior. "I call it the Oprahization of the jury pool," says Dan Lungren, attorney general of California. "It's the idea that people have become so set on viewing things from the Oprah view, the Geraldo view or the Phil Donahue view that they bring that into the jury box with them. And I think at base much of that tends to say, 'We don't hold people responsible for their actions because they've been the victim of some influence at some time in their life.'"

4   Thanks to the talk shows, Americans are increasingly familiar with the language of therapy and recovery—with new syndromes, with the fragility of the psyche and with the painful ways the abused can become abusive. Nan Whitfield, a Los Angeles public defender, believes media coverage of abuse has raised juror interest in the motives and mind-set of the accused. "I think juries have always been interested in *why* something happened," she says. "Once the defendant crosses the threshold and

does present that evidence [of his victimization], I do think the jurors' ears perk up and they become more interested." She speaks from some experience. She won the felony acquittal of Aurelia Macias, accused of cutting off her sleeping husband's testicles with a pair of scissors, by arguing that the California woman had been verbally and emotionally abused throughout her marriage and feared for her life. Macias now faces just one count of simple battery.

5   While authoritative studies have yet to be compiled, jury consultants are beginning to correlate TV habits with a juror's likely behavior during a trial and deliberations. Talk-show watchers, says Jo-Ellan Dimitrius, a jury consultant in Pasadena, California, are considered more likely to distrust the official version and to believe there are two sides to a story. At the same time, jurors who regularly watch such reality-based police shows as *America's Most Wanted* may harbor strong law-and-order beliefs. "We want to find out what drives a potential juror to watch the shows," says John Gilleland, a jury consultant with FTI Corp. in Chicago. "It's a signal to look at a person more closely."

6   Given the popularity of the victimization defense, attorneys have fewer qualms about taking a chance on exotic arguments that may, at the very least, bring their clients lighter sentences. The *American Bar Association Journal* this month cited a case in which a defense lawyer insisted that indulging in pornography was a form of intoxication—and thus reason to mitigate the sentence an Indiana man received for rape and murder. His client suffered from sexual sadism because of pornography, rendering him unable to gauge the wrongfulness of his conduct. Another lawyer in Milwaukee coined "cultural psychosis" to explain why an inner-city teenager killed another for her leather coat. The defense attorney sought to convince jurors that the girl's traumatic childhood in a violent inner-city neighborhood created a mental disorder similar to the posttraumatic stress syndrome that afflicts some Vietnam veterans.

7   The courts refused to admit those two arguments, but attorney Bill Lane had better luck with a legal strategy called urban survival syndrome. His client, Daimion Osby, 18, of Fort Worth, Texas, was accosted last year by two men who in the past had threatened him over a gambling debt. Osby pulled out a .38-cal. pistol and shot the unarmed men to death. The case ended last month in a mistrial. Though 11 of the 12 jurors voted for conviction, the foreman opted for acquittal. He agreed with the argument that Osby shot Willie Brooks, 28, and Marcus Brooks, 19, in part because the environment in which all three men lived—one of Fort Worth's most dangerous neighborhoods—heightened Osby's fear.

8   "Mr. Osby was threatened by young black men who fit the profile of the most dangerous men in America," says Jared Taylor, author of *Paved with Good Intentions: The Failure of Race Relations in Contemporary America* and an expert witness for the defense. "His decision to use his weapon when attacked is more understandable, since his assailants fit this profile." Urban survival, said Lane, "is an extension of the law of self-defense to try to make the jury understand the point of view of our client."

9   But African-American critics say the urban-survival defense harks back to a time when blacks were seen as an indistinguishable whole: volatile, angry and presumed guilty. "[The Osby mistrial] says 'these folks' can't help shooting each other,"

says the Rev. Ralph Waldo Emerson, a Fort Worth minister. "And it says to already nervous law-enforcement officials that they'd better be ready to draw when they stop someone in our community."

10   The criminal-justice system is "on the verge of a crisis of credibility," says Los Angeles District Attorney Gil Garcetti. He admits that in the Menendez brothers' cases, he and his team underestimated "the emotional pull" the abuse defense had on the jurors. Garcetti hopes to head off such tendencies among jurors by changing the system itself. At his initiative, a team of judges along with the heads of the state and county bar associations has formed a task force to study the possibility of altering rules about juries. Among ideas to be explored: broadening the pool of jurors to include a greater range of society, as well as judges stressing the importance of values and personal responsibility when they instruct jurors on how to deliberate.

11   Whitfield scoffs at such so-called reforms. "It is the very narrow-mindedness of some prosecutors that is always the best edge for a defense," she says. "They think they can just come into court, put on their evidence, and that will be the end of the story. They stop there. Well, thank God, juries don't." Legal scholars say juries have always been unpredictable, refusing to bend to controls the authorities hope to impress on them. "The tradition is that juries are the ultimate arbiter of law, not judges and not the state," says Anthony D'Amato, a law professor at Northwestern University. "And if they think the law is ridiculous, juries may ignore it. Instinctively, juries are getting it that they don't have to listen to the judge's instructions."

12   Are juries therefore influenced by the talk shows, or do talk shows merely cater to popular inquisitiveness? Talk-show host Montel Williams argues that "we reflect society—we don't create society." Rose Mary Henri, executive producer of the *Sally Jessy Raphaël* show, says: "I think we've helped the public awareness of domestic abuse and many of the abuse problems that exist, but I have no idea what kind of impact that has on someone who is serving on a jury."

13   And what does Oprah Winfrey have to say about Oprahization? The queen of talk is willing to concede some culpability. She says she and her colleagues have made society more sensitive to the idea that crimes are not committed in a vacuum. "What happened to you in the past is a part of who you are today," she says. However, she adds, "If, in the process, we have made people think that people are not responsible for their lives, then that is a fault." Ever the pioneer, she delivered that opinion last February on a segment entitled *Can You Get Away with Murder?*

■ **TOPICAL CONSIDERATIONS**

1. According to this article, why did the jury trials of Moosa Hanoukai, Lorena Bobbitt, and the Menendez brothers result in either a very light sentence, an acquittal ("not guilty"), or a hung jury ("couldn't find enough evidence")? What trend does the attorney general of California say these trials represent?

2. What nontelevision elements of popular culture are referred to in paragraphs 4 through 6? What trends in psychotherapy were used by Macias; in substance abuse, by the Indiana man, and in popular journalism, by the Milwaukee girl? What is your opinion of such defense strategies?

3. What defense for a lethal shooting was offered by Daimion Osby of Fort Worth? What do African-American community leaders have to say about defense strategies that emphasize blacks as victims of a poor environment? What are your own feelings about the kind of defense argued by Daimion Osby's lawyer?

4. What reforms of the criminal justice system have been proposed by Los Angeles District Attorney Gil Garcetti? Do those reforms seem reasonable to you? Why or why not? What objections were raised by Nan Whitfield, the Los Angeles public defender (first mentioned in paragraph 4), and Anthony D'Amato, a law professor at Northwestern University?

5. What do talk-show hosts have to say about the trend that they're being blamed for? In your opinion, are talk-show hosts responsible for problems in the criminal justice system, or are they simply offering entertainment?

6. Oprah Winfrey observes in the final paragraph that people's attitudes are shaped by individual experiences. In your opinion, how strong an influence does a person's experience have on attitude? Poll your classmates to see whether they approve of the acquittal of Lorena Bobbitt, or some case currently on the front page of your daily newspapers. Can you predict someone's opinions based on their gender, race, age, or other factors?

■ **RHETORICAL CONSIDERATIONS**

1. What is the tone of the first paragraph? How do you think Gregory wanted readers to respond? What strategies does she use to create this tone? How effective do you think this opening is to her article?

2. What is Gregory's thesis? Does she claim that talk shows are in fact responsible for trends in jurisprudence? Does she claim that criminals are not being held responsible for their actions?

3. When did you first realize that Daimion Osby of Fort Worth (see paragraphs 7–9) is African-American? What words tipped you off? What terminology does Gregory use as shorthand, code words, or synonyms for "black"? Do you think Gregory uses her terminology fairly?

4. Gregory consults two or three very different kinds of sources in this article. Do there seem to be differences in the kinds of material she draws from each source? Do you think that the specific way she uses each of these different groups biases her article in any way?

5. How does Gregory portray the professional scruples of defense attorneys in this article? What effect does her portrayal have on your willingness to believe that talk shows actually do have some effect on jury decisions?

6. Review the last sentence of the article again; the title of a planned Oprah show suggests that she will air a discussion of circumstantial excuses for murder, similar to the excuses documented in this article. Why do you think Gregory ends on this note? How do you think it changes the overall tone of the article?

■ WRITING ASSIGNMENTS

1. Select one episode of a talk show on which a criminal activity is discussed. If possible, make a videotape recording of it so you can analyze it at leisure. Record your responses to the initial announcement of the topic. How did you feel about the criminal? Sympathetic? Horrified? Angry? By the end of the show, had your feelings changed? What in the show swayed your opinion? Write up your findings and thoughts in a paper.

2. Using the videotape from the show described in question 1, prepare an objective statement about the show's topic, and a detailed, factual recounting of the crimes which were used as case studies. Be sure to include specific information, but not to slant your writing sympathetically. Share your case studies with another student in the class who has not seen that show, asking that classmate to judge "guilty" or "not guilty" based only on your written description. Do you agree with your classmate's judgment? If not, what additional information would you present to change his or her mind?

3. Research and select a well-publicized case such as that of O. J. Simpson, the Bobbitts, or the Menendez brothers. Locate several serious news articles about each one. Try to get as much information as possible about how the defense attorney made his or her case. Now, assume that you are a talk-show host. What questions would you ask the person who was tried for the crime? How would you keep your television audience interested? If your instructor agrees, you may want to prepare a script which allows you to dramatize your strategies as talk-show host for classmates.

4. Imagine that you could interview Clarence Thomas, author of the previous article. What do you think he would say about television talk shows and their influence on the criminal justice system? Write the questions that you would like to ask him, and the answers you think he would supply.

5. Using your library's resources, find out what kinds of instructions judges give to juries in criminal trials. If feasible, you may wish to supplement your readings with interviews—consider students in law school, interns working in neighborhood legal clinics, practicing criminal-law attorneys, or judges. Be certain, if you use live interviews, that you are well-enough acquainted with the issues and terminology. Write a paper on your findings.

6. Both Katie Roiphe in "Date Rape's Other Victim" and Gregory in this article make a brief mention of "post-traumatic stress disorder," or PTSD. Look up the disorder's symptoms and causes, using the American Psychiatric Association's standard reference work, the *Diagnostic and Statistical Manual of Mental Disorders*. Then research some professional journal literature in the fields of psychiatry, psychology, and social work for further discussion of symptoms, treatment, and the kinds of cases to which it is being applied. Based on your findings, is PTSD a sufficient excuse for a violent crime? Why or why not? Write up your findings and thoughts in a paper.

Life on The Shelf: What It's Like to Live in Prison

George Dismukes

This essay is a glimpse of what it is like to live in prison. It was written by a man who claims he was wrongly convicted of murder. His depiction of the dismal life on the inside serves as a deterrent to anyone, especially young people, who may take prison life lightly. But more than that, the essay is an explicit warning to the general readership that dumping money into bigger and more efficient prisons is not the answer to the problems of crime in America. It only makes things worse for all of us.

George Dismukes hopes to resume his career as an independent filmmaker once released from prison. This essay first appeared in *Newsweek*'s "My Turn" column in May 1994.

1   I speak to you from another world, that of the convicted criminal. I am in a minimum-security county holding unit. Do not be alarmed. Even were I not an innocent, 51-year-old grandfather jailed on circumstantial evidence, I'm in poor health and therefore not much of a threat. In addition, layers of steel and armed men separate you and me, not to mention time. My sentence is 16 years for murder two, wrongly convicted of shooting a man I was trying to help. I have served five months. Unless I am released on appeal bond this summer, the earliest I'll be considered for parole is in four years.

2   Many of my new colleagues are in here on minor charges such as petty theft or parole violation. There are a lot of small-time drug dealers who are repeat offenders. When I first arrived, I was placed in a cellblock that consisted of eight one-man night cells and a day room. There were a dozen of us altogether, meaning that those without seniority slept on the floor. The day room had a TV for our edification and amusement, two steel picnic tables with benches welded to the floor, a shower, a corner commode open to full view and a telephone. One wall of this place was bars, the others steel plates, as were the ceiling and floor. Here most of us watched the tube, read, played cards or squabbled about who would sit where and what shows we would watch.

3   At day's end we were returned to our night cells. Night is when the morons and neurotics holler and shake their bars, when the fanatics cry out entreaties to their God. One can shout obscenities at the neighbors with impunity. Those who would like to sleep are not permitted to have earplugs.

4   The jail also offers the pleasures of solitary confinement. That's where I am right now, in lockdown. One day they came and brought me here, without explanation. After the bedlam of where I had been, the quiet was a blessing, for I like to read and exercise my mind by filling yellow legal pads with introspection. That's me; solitary is tougher on those with little education or sense of contemplation. On the wall of my cell are graffiti left by former residents. One welcomes the newcomer to hell, others speak of the horrors of aloneness. I realize how fortunate I am that for me silence holds no terror.

5   I am curious about the way some of my neighbors in lockdown look through you, like zombies. This is not a pose. These men are not only defeated; they are utterly dehumanized, their personalities destroyed. Lying on my metal shelflike bunk, I hear hollow echoes of steel doors clanging and distant cries of pain or desperation. I have heard men completely wig out. They hurl themselves around their cells screaming, beating on the walls and themselves. This behavior is tolerated to a certain point, after which several guards will arrive and subdue the lunatic with force. Then he is dragged away. Where I don't know.

6   I am not like any of these men. I am experiencing my time here as a student, as if I were in the field, discovering an alien society. Within all bad lies good. The state is depriving me of freedom; I am repaid with time to survey this utterly banal world and a monk's cell in which to write.

7   Imagine yourself in this place. We are provided a fluorescent light fixture 4 feet long and 16 inches wide as a "sun." The solar pattern here is light 24 hours a day, for my keepers never turn it off. They need to peer in at me from time to time to make certain I am up to no mischief. A man can shave once a week when his razor is brought to his cell and left for an hour, the shaving done at a minute sink. Clothing is taken away for washing on an erratic schedule. We have mail service and phone access of a sort. All calls are long distance, collect. Long distance, appropriately, is anywhere outside the jail.

8   Most of my fellow incarcerates got here through acts of carelessness or stupidity. Some learned to steal and to oppose the greater society from the beginning. Others went to school but were unable to compete because of poverty or home environment. However they came, they're part of the vast and growing underclass that America is fostering as the distance between rich and poor widens, as the minority at the top gathers more and more of society's earnings to itself.

9   ***Out of sight:***   After their time inside, these men will go back to living the pointless, dangerous, deprived, depraved lives they lived before. The odds are very good that they will soon be caught in some misstep and resentenced. Whereupon citizen tax dollars will be used to invoke the petty callousness of life on the shelf. Society has no use for them outside, so it pays to lock them up out of sight, without opportunity or spiritual rehabilitation.

10   Perhaps you will be amused by what I, the intellectual con, feel about this. Let me say that we, the imprisoned, are America's shame. The real crime here is that of your folly. Millions of people in this land languish wasted, underachieving. From that group are plucked out thousands for special attention at high cost. They are forced to subsist in barbarous environments, written off as a total loss, human trash to be vilified and spoken of in clichés by men and women who ought to know better but lack imaginations.

11   I say to you, the smug and contented: watch out. As one return for your indifference, our numbers are enlarging, our costs are rising swiftly. Building bigger and better or, alternatively, more degrading prisons does not begin to start resolving the reasons behind the problems and madness. It only makes the gibbering louder and

the eventual consequences more awful for everyone when they finally occur. I find this situation to be humorous when I don't marvel.

12   Vengeful punishment is ethically maladroit and economically foolish. Guns, educational dysfunction and dissolved family structure lead most criminals to prison. Education should be insightful, not a blind lesson plan—more teachers, fewer administrators; youths should be aimed at support groups, not gangs. What about bonus plans for companies that try to help? That so few see any of this clearly is the real conundrum here.

■ TOPICAL CONSIDERATIONS

1. What does George Dismukes say he did to be put in prison? Where else in this article does Dismukes talk about himself, his family, his profession, or other personal qualities? How do these details help distinguish him from other inmates?

2. In paragraphs 2 through 7, Dismukes describes the behavior of his fellow inmates in response to ugly surroundings and overcrowding. What do his fellow inmates do? In general, how does he characterize prison life?

3. Can you at all identify with Dismukes's descriptions of prison life? In other words, have you ever spent time in an unpleasant surrounding that negatively affected your behavior? If so, describe the conditions and the kinds of behavior they fostered in you. How were the experiences similar to those described here?

4. Dismukes says that he is not like his fellow inmates. How does he say they got into prison? What social strata does he say they come from? What does he say will happen to them when they leave prison?

5. What problems of the present prison system does Dismukes discuss in his last three paragraphs? What dangers does Dismukes predict if the system is not changed? What are your reactions to his predictions? Do you agree with his suggestions about criminal justice?

6. What would you say is the chief motive behind Dismukes writing this article: philosophical, political, social, personal? Explain. Has this essay changed your views about prisons and criminal justice at all? Explain your answer.

■ RHETORICAL CONSIDERATIONS

1. Why does Dismukes tell us so little about himself? What effect do his sparse comments about his background, his history, or his personality traits have on his argument?

2. What pattern can you find in the behaviors of inmates that Dismukes describes in paragraphs 2 through 5? That is, in what order does he provide examples of what he has seen and heard? Why do you think he chose to structure his examples this way?

3. Dismukes claims in paragraph 10 that "millions of people" comprise the underclass. What are the implications that only a few unlucky, careless, or stupid people get convicted for crimes? That is, why should people seriously consider addressing problems outside of prisons? Why do you think Dismukes does not state these implications openly?

4. Who do you think Dismukes' audience is? Do you think Dismukes portrays himself as more like his readers, or more like his inmates? Where does he change his portrayal of himself in the article? Why do you think he creates this shift?

5. Why do you think Dismukes uses in the title of his piece the phase "life on the shelf"? Do you recognize it as having a special meaning that predates the article? How many different metaphoric meanings can you think of that Dismukes might have wanted readers to be aware of?

■ WRITING ASSIGNMENTS

1. In a paper describe a time in your life when you felt yourself "imprisoned." You might discuss a period when you were grounded by your parents; when you felt "trapped" in a relationship or a dead-end job; when a blizzard made going outdoors inadvisable; or another time when you could not come and go as you pleased. How did the experience feel? Did you think, say, or do anything that surprised you? Do you think you would respond differently today?

2. In paragraph 6, Dismukes presents himself "as a student . . . discovering an alien society." Miriam Miedzian, in her article "The Culture of Violence," also presents students of an alien society—the hypothetical Kurnai anthropologists. Compare and contrast Dismukes' activities with those of the Kurnai. In what ways are they the same? different? Do you think the differences you identify change their findings in some way? Or do you think that Dismukes would draw the same conclusions about American society, and the Kurnai would draw the same conclusions about prison? Write up your answers in a paper.

3. Dismukes says that he was unjustly imprisoned. Assume for the sake of argument that he is telling the truth. What do you think Clarence Thomas would have to say about such "mistakes" in the criminal justice system, based on his article appearing earlier in this chapter? If Thomas had a strong hunch that Dismukes were indeed innocent, but could not prove that hunch in a court of law, do you think he would advocate Dismukes' release? Or do you think that Thomas would say that some unfairness is the price we must pay for the "signaling function" of law? Write up your thoughts in a paper.

4. Dismukes suggests that crime-prevention efforts aimed at young people will be the most effective way to bring about permanent, beneficial social change. Research and report on outreach programs specifically designed to prevent young people from turning to criminal activities. You may work with library materials, or you may wish to investigate your community's church, social service agency, or school-related offerings.

5. Dismukes argues in his last few paragraphs that "guns, educational dysfunction and dissolved family structure lead most criminals to prison." Using materials from your library's news information sources, government documents, and professional criminal justice literature, find other opinions about what causes or contributes to a high rate of crime. Do experts and journalists agree with Dismukes and each other? What additional factors do other sources point to? What solutions do they offer? Write a paper with your findings.

Why I Bought a Gun
Gail Buchalter

Why would an intelligent, sensitive, liberal woman purchase a handgun? That was the question posed to writer Gail Buchalter, who after years of resistance bought a gun. Her article that follows is not intended to argue for or against any particular gun control legislation, or even to debate whether anyone should purchase a handgun. Rather, it is an attempt to understand why a person might feel the need to own a pistol and to explore the root causes of such a profound decision. Buchalter, who lives with her young son in a middle-class section of Los Angeles, is one of more than 12 million women in the United States who own guns. This essay was first published in *Parade* magazine in February 1988.

1 I was raised to wear black and cultured pearls in one of Manhattan's more desirable neighborhoods. My upper-middle-class background never involved guns. If my parents felt threatened, they simply put another lock on the door.

2 By high school, I had traded in my cashmere sweaters for a black arm band. I marched for Civil Rights, shunned Civil Defense drills and protested the Vietnam war. It was easy being 18 and a peacenik. I wasn't raising an 11-year-old child then.

3 Today, I am typical of the women whom gun manufacturers have been aiming at as potential buyers—and one of the millions who have succumbed: Between 1983 and 1986, there was a 53 percent increase in female gun-owners in the U.S.—from 7.9 million to 12.1 million, according to a Gallup Poll paid for by Smith & Wesson, the gun manufacturer.

4 Gun enthusiasts have created ad campaigns with such snappy slogans as "You Can't Rape a .38" or "Should You Shoot a Rapist Before He Cuts Your Throat?" While I was trying to come to a rational decision, I disliked these manipulative scare tactics. They only inflamed an issue that I never even dreamed would touch me.

5 I began questioning my beliefs one Halloween night in Phoenix, where I had moved when I married. I was almost home when another car nearly hit mine head-on. With the speed of a New York cabbie, I rolled down my window and screamed curses as the driver passed me. He instantly made a U-turn, almost climbing on my

back bumper. By now, he and his two friends were hanging out of the car windows, yelling that they were going to rape, cut and kill me.

6   I already had turned into our driveway when I realized my husband wasn't home. I was trapped. The car had pulled in behind me. I drove up to the back porch and got into the kitchen, where our dogs stood waiting for me. The three men spilled out of their car and into our yard.

7   My adrenaline was pumping faster than Edwin Moses' legs clearing a hurdle. I grabbed the collars of Jack, our 200-pound Irish wolfhound, and his 140-pound malamute buddy, Slush. Then I kicked open the back door—I was so scared that I became aggressive—and actually dared the three creeps to keep coming. With the dogs, the odds had changed in my favor, and the men ran back to the safety of their car, yelling that they'd be back the next day to blow me away. Fortunately, they never returned.

8   A few years and one divorce later, I headed for Los Angeles with my 3-year-old son, Jordan (the dogs had since departed). When I put him in preschool a few weeks later, the headmistress noted that I was a single parent and immediately warned me that there was a rapist in my new neighborhood.

9   I called the police, who confirmed this fact. The rapist had no *modus operandi*. Sometimes he would be waiting in his victim's house; other times he would break in while the person was asleep. Although it was summer, I would carefully lock my windows at night and then lie there and sweat in fear. Thankfully, the rapist was caught, but not before he had attacked two more women.

10   Over some time, at first imperceptibly, my suburban neighborhood became less secure. A street gang took over the apartment building across from my house, and flowers and compact cars gave way to graffiti and low-riders.

11   Daytime was quiet, but these gang members crawled out like cockroaches after dark. Several nights in a row they woke me up. It was one of the most terrifying times in my life. I could hear them talking and laughing as they leaned against our fence, tossing their empty beer cans into our front yard. I knew that they were drinking, but were they also using violence-inducing drugs such as PCP and crack? And if they broke in, could I get to the police before they got to me?

12   I found myself, to my surprise, wishing that I had a loaded pistol under my pillow. In the clear light of day, I found this reaction shocking and simply decided to move to a safer neighborhood, although it cost thousands of dollars more. Luckily, I was able to afford it.

13   Soon the papers were telling yet another tale of senseless horror. Richard Ramirez, who became known as "The Walk-In Killer," spent months crippling and killing before he was caught. His alleged crimes were so brutal and bizarre, his desire to inflict pain so intense, that I began to question my beliefs about the sanctity of human life—his, in particular. The thought of taking a human life is repugnant to me, but the idea of being someone's victim is worse. And how, I began to ask myself, do you talk pacifism to a murderer or a rapist?

14   Finally, I decided that I would defend myself, even if it meant killing another person. I realized that the one-sided pacifism I once so strongly had advocated could backfire on me and, worse, on my son. Reluctantly, I concluded that I had to insure the best option for our survival. My choices: to count on a cop or to own a pistol.

15   But still I didn't go out and buy a gun. Everything about guns is threatening. My only exposure to them had been in movies; owning one, I feared, would bring all that violence off of the screen and into my home.

16   So, instead, I called up my girlfriend (who has begged to remain nameless) and told her I had decided to buy a gun. We were both surprised that I didn't know she already had one. She was held up at gunpoint several years ago and bought what she said was a .37. We figured out it must be either a .38 or a .357. I was horrified when she admitted that not only had she no idea what type of gun she owned, but she also had never even shot it. It remains in her drawer, loaded and unused.

17   Upset, I hung up and called another friend. He was going to the National Rifle Association convention that was being held in Reno and suggested I tag along. My son's godmother lives there, so I figured I could visit her and kill two birds with one stone.

18   My first night in Reno, I attended the Handgun Hunters' Awards dinner and sat next to a contributing editor for one of the gun magazines. He bitterly complained that killing elephants had been outlawed, although there were thousands still running around Africa. Their legs, he explained, made wonderful trash baskets. I felt like Thumper on opening day of the hunting season, and my foot kept twitching under the table.

19   The next day at the convention center, I saw a sign announcing a seminar for women on handguns and safety. I met pistol-packing grandmas, kids who were into competitive shooting and law-enforcement agents. I listened to a few of them speak and then watched a video, "A Woman's Guide to Firearms." It explained everything from how guns worked to an individual's responsibilities as a gun owner.

20   It was my kind of movie, since everything about guns scares me—especially owning one. Statistics on children who are victims of their parents' handguns are overwhelming: About 300 children a year—almost a child a day—are killed by guns in this country, according to Handgun Control, Inc., which bases its numbers on data from the National Safety Council. Most of these killings are accidental.

21   As soon as I returned to Los Angeles, I called a man I had met a while ago who, I remembered, owned several guns. He told me he had a Smith & Wesson .38 Special for sale and recommended it, since it was small enough for me to handle yet had the necessary stopping power.

22   I bought the gun. That same day, I got six rounds of special ammunition with plastic tips that explode on impact. These are not for target practice; these are for protection.

23   For about $50, I also picked up the metal safety box that I had learned about in the video. Its push-button lock opens with a touch if you know the proper combination, possibly taking only a second or two longer than it does to reach into a night-table drawer. Now I knew that my son, Jordan, couldn't get his hands on it while I still could.

24   When I brought the gun home, Jordan was fascinated by it. He kept picking it up, while I nervously watched. But knowledge, I believe, is still our greatest defense. And since I'm in favor of education for sex, AIDS and learning to drive, I couldn't draw the line at teaching my son about guns.

25   Next, I took the pistol and my son to the target range. I rented a .22 caliber pistol for Jordan. (A .38 was too much gun for him to handle.) I was relieved when he put it down after 10 minutes—he didn't like the feel of it.

26   But that didn't prevent him from asking me if he should use the gun if someone broke into our house while I wasn't home. I shrieked "no!" so loud, we both jumped. I explained that, if someone ever broke in, he's young and agile enough to leap out the window and run for his life.

27   Today he couldn't care less about the gun. Every so often, when we're watching television in my room, I practice opening the safety box, and Jordan times me. I'm down to three seconds. I'll ask him what's the first thing you do when you handle a gun, and he looks at me like I'm a moron, saying for the umpteenth time: "Make sure it's unloaded. But I know I'm not to touch it or tell my friends about it." Jordan's already bored with it all.

28   I, on the other hand, look forward to Mondays—"Ladies' Night" at the target range—when I get to shoot for free. I buy a box of bullets and some targets from the guy behind the counter, put on the protective eye and ear coverings and walk through the double doors to the firing lines.

29   Once there, I load my gun, look down the sights of the barrel and adjust my aim. I fire six rounds into the chest of a life-sized target hanging 25 feet away. As each bullet rips a hole through the figure drawn there, I realize I'm getting used to owning a gun and no longer feeling faint when I pick it up. The weight of it has become comfortable in my hand. And I am keeping my promise to practice. Too many people are killed by their own guns because they don't know how to use them.

30   It took me years to decide to buy a gun, and then weeks before I could load it. It gave me nightmares.

31   One night I dreamed I woke up when someone broke into our house. I grabbed my gun and sat waiting at the foot of my bed. Finally, I saw him turn the corner as he headed toward me. He was big and filled the hallway—an impossible target to miss. I aimed the gun and froze, visualizing the bullet blowing a hole through his chest and spraying his flesh all over the walls and floor. I didn't want to shoot, but I knew my survival was on the line. I wrapped my finger around the trigger and finally squeezed it, simultaneously accepting the intruder's death at my own hand and the relief of not being a victim. I woke up as soon as I decided to shoot.

32   I was tearfully relieved that it had only been a dream.

33   I never have weighed the consequences of an act as strongly as I have that of buying a gun—but, then again, I never have done anything with such deadly repercussions. Most of my friends refuse even to discuss it with me. They believe that violence begets violence.

34   They're probably right.

■   **TOPICAL CONSIDERATIONS**

    1. How does Buchalter's decision to purchase a handgun contradict her upbringing and attitudes as a young woman?

2. What was the turning point for the author's attitude regarding handguns? What event or events made her question her pacifist beliefs? What finally convinced Buchalter to buy a gun?
3. Why had Buchalter's nameless woman friend purchased her handgun?
4. What does Buchalter learn at the National Rifle Association? How did her experience there make it easier for her to buy her own gun?
5. What reason does Buchalter give for teaching her young son about guns?
6. Do you sympathize with Buchalter's decision to purchase a gun? Would you have bought one if you were she?

■ RHETORICAL CONSIDERATIONS

1. Where does Buchalter state the thesis of her essay?
2. At the Handgun Hunters' Award dinner, Buchalter sits next to a man who complains about elephant-hunting laws. What is the function of this little detail? How does it comment on the change taking place in her? Explain her comment about feeling like "Thumper on opening day of the hunting season."
3. Comment on the effect of the concluding line of the article. What's the author's strategy behind making it a one-line paragraph? How do you interpret the meaning of this final comment?

■ WRITING ASSIGNMENTS

1. Do you or anyone you know own a handgun? If so, write a paper explaining how you feel about owning a handgun or how your friend feels about owning one.
2. Write a letter to Gail Buchalter in which you express your support for her decision to purchase a handgun.
3. Write a letter to Gail Buchalter in which you express your disappointment that she broke down and bought a handgun.
4. This essay brings up the question of gun control. What are your feelings on this issue? Do you think that there should be stronger gun control laws?

A pillar of Jeffersonian democracy is freedom of speech. It is a guarantee promised by the First Amendment of our Constitution—a guarantee designed to encourage the free exchange of ideas and beliefs and political debates. The fact that speech is protected by the First Amendment, however, does not necessarily mean that it is always right, proper, or civil. What happens when the right of one person to express him- or herself conflicts with the rights of another to be free from verbal abuse? What happens when free expression runs against community values? At what point does the degree of offensiveness of expression warrant censorship? And, at what point does censorship begin to rock the pillars of democracy? These are some of the questions that are inevitably raised in an open society such as ours—questions that are debated in a pro-and-con format in this chapter.

Over the last decade very real and conscious forces have worked to rid our language of offense. Born out of the recognition that America was rapidly becoming a multicultural society, efforts were aimed at making people more sensitive to built-in language prejudices against racial and ethnic minorities. Picking up momentum from the feminist movement, the new sensitivity grew to encompass language biases based on gender as well as sexual preference, age, class, and physical disability. By 1990 there were a dozen so-called politically correct or bias-free dictionaries offering alternatives to discriminatory language. One of the most popular and successful is Rosalie Maggio's *The Dictionary of Bias-Free Usage* whose introduction we've excerpted as the lead essay in this chapter. Examining how language subtly perpetuates prejudice, Maggio offers some simple guidelines for avoiding offensive stereotypes and exclusionary expressions. Not everybody, however, views such language-cleansing efforts as a good thing. To critics, such guides are just so much more hypersensitive political correctness (or PC) nonsense that squelches free expression while creating such awkward terms as "Chinaperson," banning words like "lady" and "Eskimo," and generally robbing English of its vitality, all in the name of gender and race neutrality. One critic is journalist Michiko Kakutani who specifically castigates the consciousness-raising efforts of Rosalie Maggio in "The Word Police." What bothers Kakutani is the Orwellian implications of a "PC police" hunting down users of "inappropriate" language and replacing it with a lot of "feel-good" doublespeak.

Next, we examine the issue of pornography, a matter that has for years tested the limits of the First Amendment. First, in "Let's Put Pornography Back in the Closet," Susan Brownmiller articulates major feminist objections to pornography: that it expresses an outright hatred for women, that its intent is to demean and dehumanize women for the sake of sexual stimulation, that it promotes sexual abuse of females. But not all women agree that obscene materials should be banned. In fact, this issue has divided feminists. While some call for censorship laws protecting the civil rights of women, others fear a threat to the broad protection of free expression found in the Constitution. One such woman is Susan Isaacs whose essay "Why We Must Put Up with Porn" takes the position that the selective abolishment of First Amendment protection would weaken its democratic intent.

Among the more sensational tests of free speech this decade are rap lyrics. In 1990, 2 Live Crew's album "Nasty as They Wanna Be" was declared obscene, and its members were arrested as were record store owners for selling the album. In 1992, Ice-T's single "Cop Killer" caused a national protest and boycott of parent company Time Warner, which eventually pulled the recording from the shelves. And in 1994, members of the National Political Congress of Black Women formally urged music stores to stop selling "gangsta rap" recordings by Dr. Dre and others who promote mayhem and killing. The following two pieces debate the value of such messages. In "Let's Stop Crying Wolf on Censorship," Jonathan Alter does not attack rappers but record executives. Not only do they peddle deadly messages to young black Americans, he argues, but they apply phony double standards whenever people lodge legitimate complaints—all in the name of profits. Taking the defense in "Bum Rap" is Michael Eric Dyson, the father of a teenage son, an ordained Baptist minister, and a professor of African-American studies. While acknowledging that gansta' rap is sometimes viciously sexist, homophobic, and violent, Dyson says that he is more disturbed by the way rap artists are scapegoated by white critics and black leaders. If people want to do something about the misogny, homophobia and violence that plagues black urban life, he argues, they should take a closer look at the social and political institutions that created such calamities instead of castigating those who narrate them.

One of the most difficult challenges to higher education has to do with the First Amendment. Does the right to freedom of expression prevent universities from curbing certain forms of speech—namely, racist, sexist, and other offensive discourse on campus? In "Regulating Racist Speech on Campus," Charles R. Lawrence III argues that allowing people to demean other members of a college community violates student-victims' rights to education. Taking the opposing side in "Free Speech on Campus," Nat Hentoff says that censorship of the language of hate threatens the very nature of a university and the spirit of academic freedom; at the same time, it makes more dangerous the forces of hate.

POLITICALLY CORRECT LANGUAGE—PRO

Why We Need Bias-Free Language

Rosalie Maggio

The growing reality of America's multiculturalism has produced in the last decade a heightened sensitivity to language that is offensive to members of minority groups. In response, a number of bias-free language guides have been produced—guides that caution against terms that might offend not only racial and ethnic groups but women, gays, senior citizens, the handicapped, animal lovers, and the overweight. One of the most successful guides is Rosalie Maggio's *The Dictionary of Bias-Free Usage: A Guide to Nondiscriminatory Language* (1991). In the following excerpt from that guide's introduction, the author discusses how to evaluate and recognize language bias, and why it should be avoided.

Rosalie Maggio is also the author of *The Nonsexist Word Finder* (1987), *How to Say It: Words, Phrases, Sentences, and Paragraphs for Every Situation* (1990), and *The Music Box Christmas* (1990). She has edited numerous college textbooks, and published hundreds of stories and articles in educational publications and children's magazines. She has won several literary honors and awards for her children's fiction and research on women's issues.

1   Language both reflects and shapes society. The textbook on American government that consistently uses male pronouns for the president, even when not referring to a specific individual (e.g., "a president may cast his veto"), reflects the fact that all our presidents have so far been men. But it also shapes a society in which the idea of a female president somehow "doesn't sound right."

2   Culture shapes language and then language shapes culture. "Contrary to the assumption that language merely reflects social patterns such as sex-role stereotypes, research in linguistics and social psychology has shown that these are in fact facilitated and reinforced by language" (Marlis Hellinger, in *Language and Power,* ed., Cheris Kramarae et al.).

3   Biased language can also, says Sanford Berman, "powerfully harm people, as amply demonstrated by bigots' and tyrants' deliberate attempts to linguistically dehumanize and demean groups they intend to exploit, oppress, or exterminate. Calling Asians 'gooks' made it easier to kill them. Calling blacks 'niggers' made it simpler to enslave and brutalize them. Calling Native Americans 'primitives' and 'savages' made it okay to conquer and despoil them. And to talk of 'fishermen,' 'councilmen,' and 'longshoremen' is to clearly exclude and discourage women from those pursuits, to diminish and degrade them."

4   The question is asked: Isn't it silly to get upset about language when there are so many more important issues that need our attention?

5   First, it's to be hoped that there are enough of us working on issues large and small that the work will all get done—someday. Second, the interconnections between the way we think, speak, and act are beyond dispute. Language goes hand-in-hand with social change—both shaping it and reflecting it. Sexual harassment was not a term anyone used twenty years ago; today we have laws against it. How could we have the law without the language; how could we have the language without the law? In fact, the judicial system is a good argument for the importance of "mere words"; the legal profession devotes great energy to the precise interpretation of words—often with far-reaching and significant consequences.

6   On August 21, 1990, in the midst of the Iraqi offensive, front-page headlines told the big story: President Bush had used the word *hostages* for the first time. Up to that time, *detainee* had been used. The difference between two very similar words was of possible life-and-death proportions. In another situation—also said to be life-and-death by some people—the difference between *fetal tissue* and *unborn baby* (in referring to the very same thing) is arguably the most debated issue in the country. So, yes, words have power and deserve our attention.

7 Some people are like George Crabbe's friend: "Habit with him was all the test of truth, / it must be right: I've done it from my youth." They have come of age using *handicapped, black-and-white, leper, mankind,* and pseudogeneric *he;* these terms must therefore be correct. And yet if there's one thing consistent about language it is that language is constantly changing; when the *Random House Dictionary of the English Language: 2nd Edition* was published in 1988, it contained 50,000 new entries, most of them words that had come into use since 1966. There were also 75,000 new definitions. (Incidentally, *RHD-II* asks its readers to "use gender-neutral terms wherever possible" and it never uses *mankind* in definitions where *people* is meant, nor does it ever refer to anyone of unknown gender as *he.*) However, few supporters of bias-free language are asking for changes; it is rather a matter of choice—which of the many acceptable words available to us will we use?

8 A high school student who felt that nonsexist language did demand some changes said, "But you don't understand! You're trying to change the English language, which has been around a lot longer than women have!"

9 One reviewer of the first edition commented, "There's no fun in limiting how you say a thing." Perhaps not. Yet few people complain about looking up a point of grammar or usage or checking the dictionary for a correct spelling. Most writers are very fussy about finding the precise best word, the exact rhythmic vehicle for their ideas. Whether or not these limits "spoil their fun" is an individual judgment. However, most of us accept that saying or writing the first thing that comes to mind is not often the way we want to be remembered. So if we have to think a little, if we have to search for the unbiased word, the inclusive phrase, it is not any more effort than we expend on proper grammar, spelling, and style.

10 Other people fear "losing" words, as though there weren't more where those came from. We are limited only by our imaginations; vague, inaccurate, and disrespectful words can be thrown overboard with no loss to society and no impoverishment of the language.

11 Others are tired of having to "watch what they say." But what they perhaps mean is that they're tired of being sensitive to others' requests. From childhood onward, we all learn to "watch what we say": we don't swear around our parents; we don't bring up certain topics around certain people; we speak differently to friend, boss, cleric, English teacher, lover, radio interviewer, child. Most of us are actually quite skilled at picking and choosing appropriate words; it seems odd that we are too "tired" to call people what they want to be called.

12 The greatest objection to bias-free language is that it will lead us to absurdities. Critics have posited something utterly ridiculous, cleverly demonstrated how silly it is, and then accounted themselves victorious in the battle against linguistic massacre. For example: "So I suppose now we're going to say: He/she ain't heavy, Father/Sister; he/she's my brother/sister." "I suppose next it will be 'ottoperson'." Cases have been built up against the mythic "woperson," "personipulate," and "personhole cover" (none of which has ever been advocated by any reputable sociolinguist). No grist appears too ridiculous for these mills. And, yes, they grind exceedingly small. Using a particular to condemn a universal is a fault in logic. But then ridicule, it is said, is the first and last argument of fools.

13   One of the most rewarding—and, for many people, the most unexpected—side effects of breaking away from traditional, biased language is a dramatic improvement in writing style. By replacing fuzzy, overgeneralized, cliché-ridden words with explicit, active words and by giving concrete examples and anecdotes instead of one-word-fits-all descriptions you can express yourself more dynamically, convincingly, and memorably.

14   "If those who have studied the art of writing are in accord on any one point, it is on this: the surest way to arouse and hold the attention of the reader is by being specific, definite, and concrete" (Strunk and White, *The Elements of Style*). Writers who talk about *brotherhood* or *spinsters* or *right-hand men* miss a chance to spark their writing with fresh descriptions; they leave their readers as uninspired as they are. Unthinking writing is also less informative. Why use the unrevealing *adman* when we could choose instead a precise, descriptive, inclusive word like *advertising executive, copywriter, account executive, ad writer,* or *media buyer?*

15   The word *manmade,* which seems so indispensable to us, doesn't actually say very much. Does it mean artificial? handmade? synthetic? fabricated? machine-made? custom-made? simulated? plastic? imitation? contrived?

16   Communication is—or ought to be—a two-way street. A speaker who uses *man* to mean *human being* while the audience hears it as *adult male* is an example of communication gone awry.

17   Bias-free language is logical, accurate, and realistic. Biased language is not. How logical is it to speak of the "discovery" of America, a land already inhabited by millions of people? Where is the accuracy in writing "Dear Sir" to a woman? Where is the realism in the full-page automobile advertisement that says in bold letters, "A good driver is a product of his environment," when more women than men influence car-buying decisions? Or how successful is the ad for a dot-matrix printer that says, "In 3,000 years, man's need to present his ideas hasn't changed. But his tools have," when many of these printers are bought and used by women, who also have ideas they need to present? And when we use stereotypes to talk about people ("isn't that just like a welfare mother/Indian/girl/old man"), our speech and writing will be inaccurate and unrealistic most of the time.

DEFINITION OF TERMS

Bias/Bias-Free

18 Biased language communicates inaccurately about what it means to be male or female; black or white; young or old; straight, gay, or bi; rich or poor; from one ethnic group or another; disabled or temporarily able-bodied; or to hold a particular belief system. It reflects the same bias found in racism, sexism, ageism, handicappism, classism, ethnocentrism, anti-Semitism, homophobia, and other forms of discrimination.

19 Bias occurs in the language in several ways.

1. Leaving out individuals or groups. "Employees are welcome to bring their wives and children" leaves out those employees who might want to bring husbands,

friends, or same-sex partners. "We are all immigrants in this country" leaves out Native Americans, who were here well before the first immigrants.

2. Making unwarranted assumptions. To address a sales letter about a new diaper to the mother assumes that the father won't be diapering the baby. To write "Anyone can use this fire safety ladder" assumes that all members of the household are able-bodied.

3. Calling individuals and groups by names or labels that they do not choose for themselves (e.g., *Gypsy, office girl, Eskimo, pygmy, Bushman, the elderly, colored man*) or terms that are derogatory (*fairy, libber, savage, bum, old goat*).

4. Stereotypical treatment that implies that all lesbians/Chinese/women/people with disabilities/teenagers are alike.

5. Unequal treatment of various groups in the same material.

6. Unnecessary mention of membership in a particular group. In a land of supposedly equal opportunity, of what importance is a person's race, sex, age, sexual orientation, disability, or creed? As soon as we mention one of these characteristics—without a good reason for doing so—we enter an area mined by potential linguistic disasters. Although there may be instances in which a person's sex, for example, is germane ("A recent study showed that female patients do not object to being cared for by male nurses"), most of the time it is not. Nor is mentioning a person's race, sexual orientation, disability, age, or belief system usually germane.

20   Bias can be overt or subtle. Jean Gaddy Wilson (in Brooks and Pinson, *Working with Words*) says, "Following one simple rule of writing or speaking will eliminate most biases. Ask yourself: Would you say the same thing about an affluent, white man?"

Inclusive/Exclusive

21   Inclusive language includes everyone; exclusive language excludes some people. The following quotation is inclusive: "The greatest revolution of our generation is the discovery that human beings, by changing the inner attitudes of their minds, can change the outer aspects of their lives" (William James). It is clear that James is speaking of all of us.

22   Examples of sex-exclusive writing fill most quotation books: "Man is the measure of all things" (Protagoras). "The People, though we think of a great entity when we use the word, means nothing more than so many millions of individual men" (James Bryce). "Man is nature's sole mistake" (W. S. Gilbert).

Sexist/Nonsexist

23   Sexist language promotes and maintains attitudes that stereotype people according to gender while assuming that the male is the norm—the significant gender. Nonsexist language treats all people equally and either does not refer to a person's sex at all when it is irrelevant or refers to men and women in symmetrical ways.

24   "A society in which women are taught anything but the management of a family, the care of men, and the creation of the future generation is a society which is on the

way out" (L. Ron Hubbard). "Behind every successful man is a woman—with nothing to wear" (L. Grant Glickman). "Nothing makes a man and wife feel closer, these days, than a joint tax return" (Gil Stern). These quotations display various characteristics of sexist writing: (1) stereotyping an entire sex by what might be appropriate for some of it; (2) assuming male superiority; (3) using unparallel terms (*man and wife* should be either *wife and husband/husband and wife* or *woman and man/man and woman*).

25   The following quotations clearly refer to all people: "It's really hard to be roommates with people if your suitcases are much better than theirs" (J. D. Salinger). "If people don't want to come out to the ball park, nobody's going to stop them" (Yogi Berra). "If men and women of capacity refuse to take part in politics and government, they condemn themselves, as well as the people, to the punishment of living under bad government" (Senator Sam J. Ervin). "I studied the lives of great men and famous women, and I found that the men and women who got to the top were those who did the jobs they had in hand, with everything they had of energy and enthusiasm and hard work" (Harry S. Truman).

Gender-Free/Gender-Fair/Gender-Specific

26 Gender-free terms do not indicate sex and can be used for either women/girls or men/boys (e.g., *teacher, bureaucrat, employee, hiker, operations manager, child, clerk, sales rep, hospital patient, student, grandparent, chief executive officer*).

27   Writing or speech that is gender-fair involves the symmetrical use of gender-specific words (e.g., *Ms. Leinwohl/Mr. Kelly, councilwoman/councilman, young man/young woman*) and promotes fairness to both sexes in the larger context. To ensure gender-fairness, ask yourself often: Would I write the same thing in the same way about a person of the opposite sex? Would I mind if this were said of me?

28   If you are describing the behavior of children on the playground, to be gender-fair you will refer to girls and boys an approximately equal number of times, and you will carefully observe what the children do, and not just assume that only the boys will climb to the top of the jungle gym and that only the girls will play quiet games.

29   Researchers studying the same baby described its cries as "anger" when they were told it was a boy and as "fear" when they were told it was a girl (cited in Cheris Kramarae, *The Voices and Words of Women and Men*). We are all victims of our unconscious and most deeply held biases.

30   Gender-specific words (for example, *alderwoman, businessman, altar girl*) are neither good nor bad in themselves. However, they need to be used gender-fairly; terms for women and terms for men should be used an approximately equal number of times in contexts that do not discriminate against either of them. One problem with gender-specific words is that they identify and even emphasize a person's sex when it is not necessary (and is sometimes even objectionable) to do so. Another problem is that they are so seldom used gender-fairly.

31   Although gender-free terms are generally preferable, sometimes gender-neutral language obscures the reality of women's or men's oppression. *Battered spouse* implies that men and women are equally battered; this is far from true. *Parent* is too often taken to mean *mother* and obscures the fact that more

and more fathers are very much involved in parenting; it is better here to use the gender-specific *fathers and mothers* or *mothers and fathers* than the gender-neutral *parents*.

Generic/Pseudogeneric

32 A generic is an all-purpose word that includes everybody (e.g., *workers, people, voters, civilians, elementary school students*). Generic pronouns include: *we, you, they.*

33   A pseudogeneric is a word that is used as though it included all people, but that in reality does not. *Mankind, forefathers, brotherhood,* and *alumni* are not generic because they leave out women. When used about Americans, *immigrants* leaves out all those who were here long before the first immigrants. "What a christian thing to do!" uses *christian* as a pseudogeneric for *kind* or *good-hearted* and leaves out all kind, good-hearted people who are not Christians.

34   Although some speakers and writers say that when they use *man* or *mankind* they mean everybody, their listeners and readers do not perceive the word that way and these terms are thus pseudogenerics. The pronoun *he* when used to mean *he and she* is another pseudogeneric.

35   Certain generic nouns are often assumed to refer only to men, for example, *politicians, physicians, lawyers, voters, legislators, clergy, farmers, colonists, immigrants, slaves, pioneers, settlers, members of the armed forces, judges, taxpayers.* References to "settlers, their wives, and children," or "those clergy permitted to have wives" are pseudogeneric.

36   In historical context it is particularly damaging for young people to read about settlers and explorers and pioneers as though they were all white men. Our language should describe the accomplishments of the human race in terms of all those who contributed to them.

SEX AND GENDER

37 An understanding of the difference between sex and gender is critical to the use of bias-free language.

38   Sex is biological: people with male genitals are male, and people with female genitals are female.

39   Gender is cultural: our notions of "masculine" tell us how we expect men to behave and our notions of "feminine" tell us how we expect women to behave. Words like *womanly/manly, tomboy/sissy, unfeminine/unmasculine* have nothing to do with the person's sex; they are culturally acquired, subjective concepts about character traits and expected behaviors that vary from one place to another, from one individual to another.

40   It is biologically impossible for a woman to be a sperm donor. It may be culturally unusual for a man to be a secretary, but it is not biologically impossible. To say "the secretary . . . she" assumes all secretaries are women and is sexist because the is-

sue is gender, not sex. Gender describes an individual's personal, legal, and social status without reference to genetic sex; gender is a subjective cultural attitude. Sex is an objective biological fact. Gender varies according to the culture. Sex is a constant.

41   The difference between sex and gender is important because much sexist language arises from cultural determinations of what a woman or man "ought" to be. Once a society decides, for example, that to be a man means to hide one's emotions, bring home a paycheck, and be able to discuss football standings while to be a woman means to be soft-spoken, love shopping, babies, and recipes, and "never have anything to wear," much of the population becomes a contradiction in terms—unmanly men and unwomanly women. Crying, nagging, gossiping, and shrieking are assumed to be women's lot; rough-housing, drinking beer, telling dirty jokes, and being unable to find one's socks and keys are laid at men's collective door. Lists of stereotypes appear silly because very few people fit them. The best way to ensure unbiased writing and speaking is to describe people as individuals, not as members of a set.

Gender Role Words

42   Certain sex-linked words depend for their meanings on cultural stereotypes: *feminine/masculine, manly/womanly, boyish/girlish, husbandly/wifely, fatherly/motherly, unfeminine/unmasculine, unmanly/unwomanly,* etc. What a person understands by these words will vary from culture to culture and even within a culture. Because the words depend for their meanings on interpretations of stereotypical behavior or characteristics, they may be grossly inaccurate when applied to individuals. Somewhere, sometime, men and women have said, thought, or done everything the other sex has said, thought, or done except for a very few sex-linked biological activities (e.g., only women can give birth or nurse a baby, only a man can donate sperm or impregnate a woman). To describe a woman as unwomanly is a contradiction in terms; if a woman is doing it, saying it, wearing it, thinking it, it must be—by definition—womanly.

43   F. Scott Fitzgerald did not use "feminine" to describe the unforgettable Daisy in *The Great Gatsby.* He wrote instead, "She laughed again, as if she said something very witty, and held my hand for a moment, looking up into my face, promising that there was no one in the world she so much wanted to see. That was a way she had." Daisy's charm did not belong to Woman; it was uniquely hers. Replacing vague sex-linked descriptors with thoughtful words that describe an individual instead of a member of a set can lead to language that touches people's minds and hearts.

NAMING

44   Naming is power, which is why the issue of naming is one of the most important in bias-free language.

Self-Definition

45 People decide what they want to be called. The correct names for individuals and groups are always those by which they refer to themselves. This "tradition" is not always unchallenged. Haig Bosmajian (*The Language of Oppression*) says, "It isn't strange that those persons who insist on defining themselves, who insist on this elemental privilege of self-naming, self-definition, and self-identity encounter vigorous resistance. Predictably, the resistance usually comes from the oppressor or would-be oppressor and is a result of the fact that he or she does not want to relinquish the power which comes from the ability to define others."

46 Dr. Ian Hancock uses the term *exonym* for a name applied to a group by outsiders. For example, Romani peoples object to being called by the exonym *Gypsies*. They do not call themselves Gypsies. Among the many other exonyms are: the elderly, colored people, homosexuals, pagans, adolescents, Eskimos, pygmies, savages. The test for an exonym is whether people describe themselves as "redmen," "illegal aliens," "holy rollers," etc., or whether only outsiders describe them that way.

47 There is a very small but visible element today demanding that gay men "give back" the word *gay*—a good example of denying people the right to name themselves. A late-night radio caller said several times that gay men had "stolen" this word from "our" language. It was not clear what language gay men spoke.

48 A woman nicknamed "Betty" early in life had always preferred her full name, "Elizabeth." On her fortieth birthday, she reverted to Elizabeth. An acquaintance who heard about the change said sharply, "I'll call her Betty if I like!"

49 We can call them Betty if we like, but it's arrogant, insensitive, and uninformed: the only rule we have in this area says we call people what they want to be called.

"Insider/Outsider" Rule

50 A related rule says that insiders may describe themselves in ways that outsiders may not. "Crip" appears in *The Disability Rag;* this does not mean that the word is available to anyone who wants to use it. "Big Fag" is printed on a gay man's T-shirt. He may use that expression; a non-gay may not so label him. One junior-high student yells to another, "Hey, nigger!" This would be highly offensive and inflammatory if the speaker were not African American. A group of women talk about "going out with the girls," but a co-worker should not refer to them as "girls." When questioned about just such a situation, Miss Manners replied that "people are allowed more leeway in what they call themselves than in what they call others."

"People First" Rule

51 Haim Ginott taught us that labels are disabling; intuitively most of us recognize this and resist being labeled. The disability movement originated the "people first" rule, which says we don't call someone a "diabetic" but rather "a person with diabetes." Saying someone is "an AIDS victim" reduces the person to a disease, a label, a statistic; use instead "a person with/who has/living with AIDS." The 1990 Americans with Disabilities Act is a good example of correct wording. Name the person as a person first, and let qualifiers (age, sex, disability, race) follow, but (and this is crucial) only if they are relevant. Readers of a magazine aimed at an older audience were asked what they wanted to be called (elderly? senior citizens? seniors? golden agers?). They rejected all the terms; one said, "How about 'people'?" When high school students rejected labels like kids, teens, teenagers, youth, adolescents, and juveniles, and were asked in exasperation just what they would like to be called, they said, "Could we just be people?"

Women as Separate People

52   One of the most sexist maneuvers in the language has been the identification of women by their connections to husband, son, or father—often even after he is dead. Women are commonly identified as someone's widow while men are never referred to as anyone's widower. Marie Marvingt, a French-woman who lived around the turn of the century, was an inventor, adventurer, stunt woman, superathlete, aviator, and all-around scholar. She chose to be affianced to neither man (as a wife) nor God (as a religious), but it was not long before an uneasy male press found her a fit partner. She is still known today by the revealing label "the Fiancée of Danger." If a connection is relevant, make it mutual. Instead of "Frieda, his wife of seventeen years," write "Frieda and Eric, married for seventeen years."

53   It is difficult for some people to watch women doing unconventional things with their names. For years the etiquette books were able to tell us precisely how to address a single woman, a married woman, a divorced woman, or a widowed woman (there was no similar etiquette on men because they have always been just men and we have never had a code to signal their marital status). But now some women are Ms. and some are Mrs., some are married but keeping their birth names, others are hyphenating their last name with their husband's, and still others have constructed new names for themselves. Some women—including African American women who were denied this right earlier in our history—take great pride in using their husband's name. All these forms are correct. The same rule of self-definition applies here: call the woman what she wants to be called.

■ TOPICAL CONSIDERATIONS

1. Maggio begins her article with a discussion of the ways language has real effects on people's attitudes and actions. What are some of the examples she supplies? How does language create desirable or undesirable consequences?
2. What are the four excuses people make to avoid using unbiased language? How does Maggio counter those excuses? What additional counterargument does she supply in defense of nonbiased language?
3. What main idea links all the different ways in which bias can occur (see paragraph 19)? Does biased language refer to individuals or to groups of people?

4. What are the categories Maggio specifically names as subject to biased language? Can you supply additional categories?

5. Maggio uses the term *symmetrical* several times (e.g., paragraphs 23 and 27). What does this term mean? Does Maggio want to encourage or discourage the use of symmetrical language? Does symmetry refer only to gender bias, or can it refer to other kinds of bias too?

6. What is the difference between gender-free, gender-fair, and gender-specific language in paragraphs 26 through 31? What examples does Maggio supply for each one? When is each kind of nonbiased language appropriate?

7. How can the principles of gender-free, gender-fair, and gender-specific language be applied to language that is biased about handicap, religion, race, age, or other group characteristics? Supply one example for each principle and include a phrase that contains biased language and a revision resolving the problem.

8. What does Maggio mean by a "generic" word? a "pseudogeneric" word? How might pseudogeneric references harm people?

9. What is an *exonym?* Are exonyms ever appropriate, according to Maggio's discussion? Did you recognize all the words Maggio lists in paragraph 46 as exonyms? Can you supply substitutes for all the exonyms? If not, what problems did you encounter? Can you supply examples of other exonyms from your own experience?

10. Why do you think Maggio considers *naming* "one of the most important [issues] in bias-free language" (paragraph 44)? What is so important about the ability to choose a name? What do you think the woman in paragraph 48 is communicating by choosing to be called Elizabeth? Why do you think Maggio links this announcement to the woman's fortieth birthday celebration?

■ RHETORICAL CONSIDERATIONS

1. What did the high-school student in paragraph 8 really mean to say? Why do you think Maggio includes this statement? What point is she trying to make? Do you think that this student was male or female? Would it make a difference? Why doesn't Maggio specify?

2. Which parts of this essay struck you as being the strongest? Which seemed to be the weakest? What would you say was the difference—the strength of the writing? the attitude? the tone? the number of examples? the quality of examples? Or was it a combination of each?

■ WRITING ASSIGNMENTS

1. In your experience, has anyone called you, or a member of a group to which you belong, a name you found offensive? How did that incident make you feel? Has anyone ever revealed to new friends a nickname or a middle name that you have but dislike? What was your response? Write a paper with your answer.

2. Locate a short piece of journalism in a contemporary newspaper. Select an article discussing one or more of the groups that Maggio says have suffered from biased language. First, rewrite it to reflect as many biases as you can think of. Then, discuss what strategies the author used to avoid the kinds of bias you have written in.

3. Locate an article in a contemporary newspaper that you think displays one or more of the biases Maggio describes. In a letter to the editor (no more than 500 words), persuade the newspaper editors to avoid such biased language in future articles. Remember that your writing will be more effective if you write in a calm, reasonable tone, use specific examples, and explain clearly the benefits of unbiased language.

4. How would you go about designing an advertising campaign for the magazine that Maggio says is "aimed at an older audience"? What words would you use to avoid offensive labeling and to avoid the vagueness of the broadly generic noun "people" (which is the same term the high school students ask to be designated by)?

POLITICALLY CORRECT LANGUAGE—CON

The Word Police

Michiko Kakutani

Not everybody applauds the efforts of those hoping to rid the language of offensive terms. To detractors, all such linguistic sensitivity is no more than a symptom of political correctness—a kind of be-sensitive-or-else campaign. They complain that unlike standard dictionaries, which are meant to help people use words, the so-called cautionary guides *warn* people against using them. Such is the complaint of Michiko Kakutani, who specifically targets Rosalie Maggio's *The Bias-Free Word Finder* as an example of the menace of hypersensitivity. She complains that in the name of the "politics of inclusion," proponents hunt down users of "inappropriate" language like the thought police from George Orwell's *1984*. And, claims Kakutani, they fill the English language with sloppy pious euphemisms.

Michiko Kakutani is a staff writer for *The New York Times,* where this article first appeared in January 1993.

1 This month's inaugural festivities, with their celebration, in Maya Angelou's words, of "humankind"—"the Asian, the Hispanic, the Jew/The African, the Native American, the Sioux,/The Catholic, the Muslim, the French, the Greek/The Irish, the Rabbi, the Priest, the Sheik,/The Gay, the Straight, the Preacher,/The privileged, the homeless, the Teacher"—constituted a kind of official embrace of multiculturalism and a new politics of inclusion.

2 The mood of political correctness, however, has already made firm inroads into popular culture. Washington boasts a store called Politically Correct that sells pro-whale, anti-meat, ban-the-bomb T-shirts, bumper stickers and buttons, as well as a local cable television show called "Politically Correct Cooking" that features interviews in the kitchen with representatives from groups like People for the Ethical Treatment of Animals.

3 The Coppertone suntan lotion people are planning to give their longtime cover girl, Little Miss (Ms?) Coppertone, a male equivalent, Little Mr. Coppertone. And even Superman (Super-person?) is rumored to be returning this spring, reincarnated as four ethnically diverse clones: an African-American, an Asian, a Caucasian and a Latino.

4 Nowhere is this P.C. mood more striking than in the increasingly noisy debate over language that has moved from university campuses to the country at large—a development that both underscores Americans' puritanical zeal for reform and their unwavering faith in the talismanic power of words.

5 Certainly no decent person can quarrel with the underlying impulse behind political correctness: a vision of a more just, inclusive society in which racism, sexism and prejudice of all sorts have been erased. But the methods and fervor of the self-appointed language police can lead to a rigid orthodoxy—and unintentional self-parody—opening the movement to the scorn of conservative opponents and the mockery of cartoonists and late-night television hosts.

6 It's hard to imagine women earning points for political correctness by saying "ovarimony" instead of "testimony"—as one participant at the recent Modern Language Association convention was overheard to suggest. It's equally hard to imagine people wanting to flaunt their lack of prejudice by giving up such words and phrases as "bull market," "kaiser roll," "Lazy Susan," and "charley horse."

7 Several books on bias-free language have already appeared, and the 1991 edition of the Random House Webster's College Dictionary boasts an appendix titled "Avoiding Sexist Language." The dictionary also includes such linguistic mutations as "womyn" (women, "used as an alternative spelling to avoid the suggestion of sexism perceived in the sequence m-e-n") and "waitron" (a gender-blind term for waiter or waitress).

8 Many of these dictionaries and guides not only warn the reader against offensive racial and sexual slurs, but also try to establish and enforce a whole new set of usage rules. Take, for instance, "The Bias-Free Word Finder, a Dictionary of Nondiscriminatory Language" by Rosalie Maggio (Beacon Press)—a volume often indistinguishable, in its meticulous solemnity, from the tongue-in-cheek "Official Politically Correct Dictionary and Handbook" put out last year by Henry Beard and Christopher Cerf (Villard Books). Ms. Maggio's book supplies the reader intent on using kinder, gentler language with writing guidelines as well as a detailed listing of more than 5,000 "biased words and phrases."

9 Whom are these guidelines for? Somehow one has a tough time picturing them replacing "Fowler's Modern English Usage" in the classroom, or being adopted by the average man (sorry, individual) in the street.

10 The "pseudogeneric 'he,'" we learn from Ms. Maggio, is to be avoided like the plague, as is the use of the word "man" to refer to humanity. "Fellow," "king," "lord"

and "master" are bad because they're "male-oriented words," and "king," "lord" and "master" are especially bad because they're also "hierarchical, dominator society terms." The politically correct lion becomes the "monarch of the jungle," new-age children play "someone on the top of the heap," and the "Mona Lisa" goes down in history as Leonardo's "acme of perfection."

11   As for the word "black," Ms. Maggio says it should be excised from terms with a negative spin: she recommends substituting words like "mouse" for "black eye," "ostracize" for "blackball," "payola" for "blackmail" and "outcast" for "black sheep." Clearly, some of these substitutions work better than others: somehow the "sinister humor" of Kurt Vonnegut or "Saturday Night Live" doesn't quite make it; nor does the "denouncing" of the Hollywood 10.

12   For the dedicated user of politically correct language, all these rules can make for some messy moral dilemmas. Whereas "battered wife" is a gender-biased term, the gender-free term "battered spouse," Ms. Maggio notes, incorrectly implies "that men and women are equally battered."

13   On one hand, say Francine Wattman Frank and Paula A. Treichler in their book "Language, Gender, and Professional Writing" (Modern Language Association), "he or she" is an appropriate construction for talking about an individual (like a jockey, say) who belongs to a profession that's predominantly male—it's a way of emphasizing "that such occupations are not barred to women or that women's concerns need to be kept in mind." On the other hand, they add, using masculine pronouns rhetorically can underscore ongoing male dominance in those fields, implying the need for change.

14   And what about the speech codes adopted by some universities in recent years? Although they were designed to prohibit students from uttering sexist and racist slurs, they would extend, by logic, to blacks who want to use the word "nigger" to strip the term of its racist connotations, or homosexuals who want to use the word "queer" to reclaim it from bigots.

15   In her book, Ms. Maggio recommends applying bias-free usage retroactively: she suggests paraphrasing politically incorrect quotations, or replacing "the sexist words or phrases with ellipsis dots and/or bracketed substitutes," or using "sic" "to show that the sexist words come from the original quotation and to call attention to the fact that they are incorrect."

16   Which leads the skeptical reader of "The Bias-Free Word Finder" to wonder whether "All the King's Men" should be retitled "All the Ruler's People"; "Pet Semetary," "Animal Companion Graves"; "Birdman of Alcatraz," "Bird-person of Alcatraz," and "The Iceman Cometh," "The Ice Route Driver Cometh"?

17   Will making such changes remove the prejudice in people's minds? Should we really spend time trying to come up with non-male-based alternatives to "Midas touch," "Achilles' heel," and "Montezuma's revenge"? Will tossing out Santa Claus—whom Ms. Maggio accuses of reinforcing "the cultural male-as-norm system"—in favor of Belfana, his Italian female alter ego, truly help banish sexism? Can the avoidance of "violent expressions and metaphors" like "kill two birds with one stone," "sock it to 'em" or "kick an idea around" actually promote a more harmonious world?

18   The point isn't that the excesses of the word police are comical. The point is that their intolerance (in the name of tolerance) has disturbing implications. In the first place, getting upset by phrases like "bullish on America" or "the City of Brotherly Love" tends to distract attention from the real problems of prejudice and injustice that exist in society at large, turning them into mere questions of semantics. Indeed, the emphasis currently put on politically correct usage has uncanny parallels with the academic movement of deconstruction—a method of textual analysis that focuses on language and linguistic pyrotechnics—which has become firmly established on university campuses.

19   In both cases, attention is focused on surfaces, on words and metaphors; in both cases, signs and symbols are accorded more importance than content. Hence, the attempt by some radical advocates to remove "The Adventures of Huckleberry Finn" from curriculums on the grounds that Twain's use of the word "nigger" makes the book a racist text—never mind the fact that this American classic (written in 1884) depicts the spiritual kinship achieved between a white boy and a runaway slave, never mind the fact that the "nigger" Jim emerges as the novel's most honorable, decent character.

20   Ironically enough, the P.C. movement's obsession with language is accompanied by a strange Orwellian willingness to warp the meaning of words by placing them under a high-powered ideological lens. For instance, the "Dictionary of Cautionary Words and Phrases"—a pamphlet issued by the University of Missouri's Multicultural Management Program to help turn "today's journalists into tomorrow's multicultural newsroom managers"—warns that using the word "articulate" to describe members of a minority group can suggest the opposite, "that 'those people' are not considered well educated, articulate and the like."

21   The pamphlet patronizes minority groups, by cautioning the reader against using the words "lazy" and "burly" to describe any member of such groups; and it issues a similar warning against using words like "gorgeous" and "petite" to describe women.

22   As euphemism proliferates with the rise of political correctness, there is a spread of the sort of sloppy, abstract language that Orwell said is "designed to make lies sound truthful and murder respectable, and to give an appearance of solidity to pure wind." "Fat" becomes "big boned" or "differently sized"; "stupid" becomes "exceptional"; "stoned" becomes "chemically inconvenienced."

23   Wait a minute here! Aren't such phrases eerily reminiscent of the euphemisms coined by the Government during Vietnam and Watergate? Remember how the military used to speak of "pacification," or how President Richard M. Nixon's press secretary, Ronald L. Ziegler, tried to get away with calling a lie an "inoperative statement"?

24   Calling the homeless "the underhoused" doesn't give them a place to live; calling the poor "the economically marginalized" doesn't help them pay the bills. Rather, by playing down their plight, such language might even make it easier to shrug off the seriousness of their situation.

25   Instead of allowing free discussion and debate to occur, many gung-ho advocates of politically correct language seem to think that simple suppression of a word or concept will magically make the problem disappear. In the "Bias-Free Word

Finder," Ms. Maggio entreats the reader not to perpetuate the negative stereotype of Eve. "Be extremely cautious in referring to the biblical Eve," she writes; "this story has profoundly contributed to negative attitudes toward women throughout history, largely because of misogynistic and patriarchal interpretations that labeled her evil, inferior, and seductive."

26   The story of Bluebeard, the rake (whoops!—the libertine) who killed his seven wives, she says, is also to be avoided, as is the biblical story of Jezebel. Of Jesus Christ, Ms. Maggio writes: "There have been few individuals in history as completely androgynous as Christ, and it does his message a disservice to overinsist on his maleness." She doesn't give the reader any hints on how this might be accomplished; presumably, one is supposed to avoid describing him as the Son of God.

27   Of course the P.C. police aren't the only ones who want to proscribe what people should say or give them guidelines for how they may use an idea; Jesse Helms and his supporters are up to exactly the same thing when they propose to patrol the boundaries of the permissible in art. In each case, the would-be censor aspires to suppress what he or she finds distasteful—all, of course, in the name of the public good.

28   In the case of the politically correct, the prohibition of certain words, phrases and ideas is advanced in the cause of building a brave new world free of racism and hate, but this vision of harmony clashes with the very ideals of diversity and inclusion that the multi-cultural movement holds dear, and it's purchased at the cost of freedom of expression and freedom of speech.

29   In fact, the utopian world envisioned by the language police would be bought at the expense of the ideals of individualism and democracy articulated in "The Gettysburg Address": "Fourscore and seven years ago our fathers brought forth on this continent a new nation, conceived in liberty and dedicated to the proposition that all men are created equal."

30   Of course, the P.C. police have already found Lincoln's words hopelessly "phallocentric." No doubt they would rewrite the passage: "Fourscore and seven years ago our foremothers and forefathers brought forth on this continent a new nation, formulated with liberty, and dedicated to the proposition that all humankind is created equal."

■ TOPICAL CONSIDERATIONS

1. What kinds of people are mentioned in the lines of Maya Angelou's inauguration poem? What do these people symbolize, according to Kakutani? How many of these groups are represented in your classroom right now?

2. What specific substitutions of words does Kakutani complain about in paragraph 10? Can you supply the "biased" term that the "politically correct" phrase has replaced in the second half of the paragraph?

3. What are the three "messy moral dilemmas" Kakutani points out in paragraphs 12 through 14? Why does she tag the examples she cites as dilemmas? Why does she object to following politically correct guidelines in each case?

4. What is wrong, according to Kakutani in paragraphs 15 and 16, with Maggio's recommendation that unbiased language be applied retroactively?

Rewrite one or two of the titles using Maggio's suggestions as quoted by Kakutani in paragraph 15—that is, use ellipses, brackets, and so on. How well do these suggestions work?

5. What examples of euphemism does Kakutani provide in paragraphs 22 through 24? What objections does she raise about these euphemisms? Why does she compare the new politically correct terms with terms from Watergate?

■ RHETORICAL CONSIDERATIONS

1. Describe the tone in Kakutani's first three paragraphs of the article. Do you think this piece is going to be serious, playful, or sarcastic? What evidence did you base your response on?

2. How do you think Kakutani would answer her own rhetorical question in paragraph 9? Why does she use a question there, rather than a declarative sentence such as "These guidelines do not seem to be useful to anyone"? Why does she think Maggio's book has no audience?

3. Why do you think Kakutani replaces the phrase "unbiased language" with the word "euphemism" in paragraph 22? What is the difference between the two terms. Do both make the same assumptions about the way language shapes our experiences? Does Kakutani use the word euphemism fairly?

4. Look closely at the wording of Kakutani's first sentence in paragraph 22. Why doesn't she say outright that political correctness *causes* "sloppy, abstract language"? What do you think Maggio would say about the cause-and-effect relationship of political correctness and language?

5. Kakutani interrupts herself twice to insert a "correction"—to substitute a politically correct term for an incorrect term she has inadvertently let slip. These appear in paragraphs 9 and 26. What's going on here—didn't she have enough time to edit her article?

6. Why do you think Kakutani entitles her article "The Word Police"? What does that title mean? What connections does it imply between the police and reformers promoting politically correct language? What attitude does Kakutani seem to have toward both groups?

■ WRITING ASSIGNMENTS

1. Compare the views about language of Rosalie Maggio in "Why We Need Bias-Free Language" and Kakutani in this article. What powers does each author believe language has? What power does language not have? Be sure to cite specific evidence from each author for your comparison.

2. Despite Kakutani's attack on Maggio's book, she agrees with at least some of Maggio's underlying assumptions—for example, about language and power, about the need to end prejudice, and other points. Identify and discuss at least three assumptions or values that both authors would agree on; then, discuss why they believe that different actions are appropriate to act on these values.

3. Examine some samples of your own writing earlier in the term, or from previous school terms. Where have you struggled with politically correct language use? Have you always been successful in using it? What substitutions or changes did you try that, on rereading, seem less than satisfactory?

4. Using your school's library, identify a national or major-city newspaper or news journal that is marketed for a group that sometimes suffers from biased language. Select an article you think is of special interest to that group. (For example, you might examine the African-American newspaper the *Chicago Defender* for coverage of the Rodney King beating or the O. J. Simpson Case; or the *Disability Rag* for coverage of legislation benefiting Americans with disabilities; or *Off Our Backs* for coverage of antigay and antilesbian legislation in Colorado). Then, select a major news source that is marketed for a general audience and find an article of similar length on the same event or issue. Compare the two articles. How did you feel about the issue after reading one? After reading the other? What differences do you see in the way language is used? What assumptions does each make about its readers' values and concerns? Do you think that the language each one uses makes a difference in the feeling you get about the issue? Or does the difference in tone have more to do with what is emphasized in the report than with what language is used to convey information?

OUTLAWING PORNOGRAPHY—PRO

Let's Put Pornography Back in the Closet

Susan Brownmiller

To the solace of some and the discomfort of others, the First Amendment is widely applied to protect free speech of many sorts: political dissent, unpopular ideas, art of "questionable" taste, and pornography. Some feel that such freedom of expression protects the very fiber of our democratic society, whereas others feel it erodes the rights of democratic citizens. In this piece Susan Brownmiller argues that First Amendment protection should not extend to pornography. She further argues that obscene material depicts "hatred of women" and is intended "to humiliate, degrade and dehumanize the female body." Summoning the interpretations of revered authorities, she challenges the current application of First Amendment protection.

Susan Brownmiller is the author of *Against Our Will* (1976), a study of the history of rape. This essay originally appeared in *Newsday* in 1979.

1 Free speech is one of the great foundations on which our democracy rests. I am old enough to remember the Hollywood Ten, the screenwriters who went to jail in the late 1940s because they refused to testify before a congressional committee about

their political affiliations. They tried to use the First Amendment as a defense, but they went to jail because in those days there were few civil liberties lawyers around who cared to champion the First Amendment right to free speech, when the speech concerned the Communist Party.

2 The Hollywood Ten were correct in claiming the First Amendment. Its high purpose is the protection of unpopular ideas and political dissent. In the dark, cold days of the 1950s, few civil libertarians were willing to declare themselves First Amendment absolutists. But in the brighter, though frantic, days of the 1960s, the principle of protecting unpopular political speech was gradually strengthened.

3 It is fair to say now that the battle has largely been won. Even the American Nazi Party has found itself the beneficiary of the dedicated, tireless work of the American Civil Liberties Union. But—and please notice the quotation marks coming up—"To equate the free and robust exchange of ideas and political debate with commercial exploitation of obscene material demeans the grand conception of the First Amendment and its high purposes in the historic struggle for freedom. It is a misuse of the great guarantees of free speech and free press."

4 I didn't say that, although I wish I had, for I think the words are thrilling. Chief Justice Warren Burger said it in 1973, in the United States Supreme Court's majority opinion in *Miller* v. *California.* During the same decades that the right to political free speech was being strengthened in the courts, the nation's obscenity laws also were undergoing extensive revision.

5 It's amazing to recall that in 1934 the question of whether James Joyce's *Ulysses* should be banned as pornographic actually went before the Court. The battle to protect *Ulysses* as a work of literature with redeeming social value was won. In later decades, Henry Miller's *Tropic* books, *Lady Chatterley's Lover* and the *Memoirs of Fanny Hill* also were adjudged not obscene. These decisions have been important to me. As the author of *Against Our Will,* a study of the history of rape that does contain explicit sexual material, I shudder to think how my book would have fared if James Joyce, D. H. Lawrence, and Henry Miller hadn't gone before me.

6 I am not a fan of *Chatterley* or the *Tropic* books, I should quickly mention. They are not to my literary taste, nor do I think they represent female sexuality with any degree of accuracy. But I would hardly suggest that we ban them. Such a suggestion wouldn't get very far anyway. The battle to protect these books is ancient history. Time does march on, quite methodically. What, then, is unlawfully obscene, and what does the First Amendment have to do with it?

7 In the Miller case of 1973 (not Henry Miller, by the way, but a porn distributor who sent unsolicited stuff through the mails), the Court came up with new guidelines that it hoped would strengthen obscenity laws by giving more power to the states. What it did in actuality was throw everything into confusion. It set up a three-part test by which materials can be adjudged obscene. The materials are obscene if they depict patently offensive, hard-core sexual conduct; lack serious scientific, literary, artistic or political value; and appeal to the prurient interest of an average person—as measured by contemporary community standards.

8 "Patently offensive," "prurient interest" and "hard-core" are indeed words to conjure with. "Contemporary community standards" are what we're trying to redefine.

The feminist objection to pornography is not based on prurience, which the dictionary defines as lustful, itching desire. We are not opposed to sex and desire, with or without the itch, and we certainly believe that explicit sexual material has its place in literature, art, science and education. Here we part company rather swiftly with old-line conservatives who don't want sex education in the high schools, for example.

9   No, the feminist objection to pornography is based on our belief that pornography represents hatred of women, that pornography's intent is to humiliate, degrade and dehumanize the female body for the purpose of erotic stimulation and pleasure. We are unalterably opposed to the presentation of the female body being stripped, bound, raped, tortured, mutilated and murdered in the name of commercial entertainment and free speech.

10   These images, which are standard pornographic fare, have nothing to do with the hallowed right of political dissent. They have everything to do with the creation of a cultural climate in which a rapist feels he is merely giving in to a normal urge and a woman is encouraged to believe that sexual masochism is healthy, liberated fun. Justice Potter Stewart once said about hard-core pornography "You know it when you see it," and that certainly used to be true. In the good old days, pornography looked awful. It was cheap and sleazy, and there was no mistaking it for art.

11   Nowadays, since the porn industry has become a multimillion dollar business, visual technology has been employed in its service. Pornographic movies are skillfully filmed and edited, pornographic still shots using the newest tenets of good design artfully grace the covers of *Hustler, Penthouse,* and *Playboy,* and the public—and the courts—are sadly confused.

12   The Supreme Court neglected to define "hard-core" in the Miller decision. This was a mistake. If "hard-core" refers only to explicit sexual intercourse, then that isn't good enough. When women or children or men—no matter how artfully—are shown tortured or terrorized in the service of sex, that's obscene. And "patently offensive," I would hope, to our "contemporary community standards."

13   Justice William O. Douglas wrote in his dissent to the Miller case that no one is "compelled to look." This is hardly true. To buy a paper at the corner newsstand is to subject oneself to a forcible immersion in pornography, to be demeaned by an array of dehumanized, chopped-up parts of the female anatomy, packaged like cuts of meat at the supermarket. I happen to like my body and I work hard at the gym to keep it in good shape, but I am embarrassed for my body and for the bodies of all women when I see the fragmented parts of us, so frivolously, and so flagrantly, displayed.

14   Some constitutional theorists (Justice Douglas was one) have maintained that any obscenity law is a serious abridgement of free speech. Others (and Justice Earl Warren was one) have maintained that the First Amendment was never intended to protect obscenity. We live quite compatibly with a host of free-speech abridgements. There are restraints against false and misleading advertising or statements—shouting "fire" without cause in a crowded movie theater, etc.—that do not threaten, but strengthen, our societal values. Restrictions on the public display of pornography belong in this category.

15   The distinction between permission to publish and permission to display publicly is an essential one and one which I think consonant with First Amendment principles. Justice Burger's words which I quoted above support this without question. We are not saying "Smash the presses" or "Ban the bad ones," but simply "Get the stuff out of our sight." Let the legislatures decide—using realistic and humane contemporary community standards—what can be displayed and what cannot. The courts, after all, will be the final arbiters.

■ TOPICAL CONSIDERATIONS

1. Has Brownmiller's article changed your opinion about free speech and pornography? If yes, in what ways? If no, where do you think Brownmiller's article failed?
2. Brownmiller is careful to furnish a definition of what she means by the term *pornography.* Do you think her definition is a clear one? A complete one? Why do you think she is so careful in defining her terms?
3. Brownmiller discusses a number of books that were nearly banned because they were considered "pornographic"—*Ulysses,* the *Tropic* books, *Lady Chatterley's Lover.* Why did people react negatively to these books? Can you think of other books (or movies, recordings, videos, etc.) that have caused a similar reaction in people?
4. Discuss Brownmiller's assertion that "the distinction between permission to publish and permission to display publicly is an essential one" (paragraph 15). What does Brownmiller mean by this? Do you agree or disagree with this statement?
5. Brownmiller acknowledges the power that the courts have in the debate about pornography. Do you think that she trusts the courts to comply with her opinion? Support your reasoning with evidence from the text.

■ RHETORICAL CONSIDERATIONS

1. "Free speech is one of the great foundations on which our democracy rests," opens Brownmiller. What is the effect of this introductory sentence on the reader? Does it point specifically to what the essay will discuss? If so, how? If not, why not?
2. Where does Brownmiller's argument begin? Do you think her thesis is in the most effective place in the essay?
3. What is the effect of paragraph 3, when Brownmiller says, "notice the quotation marks coming up"?
4. Why do you think that Brownmiller mentions *Lady Chatterley's Lover* and the *Tropic* books if she does not like them and does not find them accurate in depicting women's sexuality? Does this serve to strengthen or weaken her argument?

5. What is the effect of the last sentence in paragraph 12, when Brownmiller uses the language of the Supreme Court's obscenity standards to illustrate her viewpoint?

6. At the end of the essay, Brownmiller returns to Justice Burger's quotation and her admission that the courts "will be the final arbiters." Is this an effective conclusion to her argument? Why or why not?

■ WRITING ASSIGNMENTS

1. Imagine that you are a parent, and write a letter in which you urge a teacher to remove certain books from the school curriculum. Be specific about which books you want banned and why. Try to use a calm, informed tone, like the one in Brownmiller's essay.

2. As a teacher, respond to the parent who has written the letter objecting to the choice of certain books on the school's reading list. Defend the books, making sure to cite useful parts of the First Amendment to support your argument, as well as excerpts from the books themselves, if necessary.

3. Lately, much controversy in the movie business has centered around the NC-17 rating given to certain "explicit" films. Write an essay in which you analyze the usefulness of this rating (and, perhaps, of the movie rating system in general). Do you think that an NC-17 rating is given for sexually explicit material more than it is for violent material? Is that how it should be? Why or why not? Cite specific films to support your opinion.

OUTLAWING PORNOGRAPHY—CON

Why We Must Put Up with Porn
Susan Isaacs

As repugnant as some forms of free expression are, including pornography, Susan Isaacs is an absolutist when it comes to interpreting the First Amendment. Resorting to censorship, she claims, is an abdication of democratic freedom. Furthermore, "historically, censorship has often been the first step toward dictatorship." If pornography is banned today, what will be next?

Susan Isaacs is the author of several novels including *Almost Paradise* (1989), *The Magic Hour* (1992), and *After All These Years* (1993). She is a member of the National Coalition Against Censorship. This essay originally appeared in *Redbook* in August 1993.

1 If you and I were sitting together, listening to a little Vivaldi, sipping herbal tea, chatting about men and women, arguing about politics and art, we might get around to what to do about the porn problem—at which point you'd slam down your cup and

demand, How can you of all people defend smut-peddling slimeballs who portray women being beaten and raped?

2 Well . . .

3 You're the one (you'd be sure to remind me) who hates any kind of violence against women. You're the one who even gets upset when James Cagney, in *The Public Enemy,* the 1931 classic, smashes a grapefruit into Mae Clarke's face, for heaven's sake!

4 That's right, I'd say.

5 So? Don't you want to protect women? Why *not* ban books and films that degrade women?

6 Let's have another cup of tea and I'll tell you.

7 The problem is, who is going to decide what is degrading to women? If there were to be a blue-ribbon panel, who would select its members? Jerry Falwell of the religious right? Andrea Dworkin, who has written that all sexual intercourse is an expression of men's contempt for women? They certainly do not speak for me. Okay, what about a blue-ribbon panel of, say, Hillary Rodham Clinton, Sandra Day O'Connor, Jackie Joyner-Kersee, Katie Couric, Wendy Wasserstein, and Anne Tyler? A dream team, right?

8 Sure. But I'll be damned if I'd hand over my right to determine what I see and read to America's best and brightest any more than I would to my husband, my editor, my best friend, or my mother. And you, my tea-sipping companion, and you, out there in Salt Lake City, Sioux City, Jersey City: You also should decide for yourself.

9 But, you might say next, this sexually explicit garbage eggs people on to vicious criminal behavior.

10 The truth is, this remains unproven. While research has pointed to a correlation between both alcohol abuse and dysfunctional families and violent behavior, it has *not* established the same link between pornography and violence. When serial killer Ted Bundy was trying to get his death sentence commuted in 1989, he claimed that a lifetime of reading pornography made him the monster he was. And why shouldn't he? It was an easy out: It would clear him of responsibility for his evil deeds.

11 But, you say, proof or no proof, there is so much trash out there and I don't like it! Well, neither do I, but censorship is not the answer. The First Amendment gives you the right to picket a theater or start a letter-writing campaign against any work you consider loathsome. You do not have the right, however, to prevent others from seeing it.

12 Look, it's rarely easy being a defender of the First Amendment. More often than not, we wind up fighting for the right to burn the flag or burn a cross or say awful racist and sexist things. Or consider a movie like the upcoming *Boxing Helena.* It's about a doctor so obsessed with keeping a young woman all to himself that he amputates her legs and arms and keeps what's left of her in a box. Maybe it's art, maybe it's a disgusting, misogynistic piece of claptrap.

13 But if we want our great and beloved Constitution to work, we cannot abandon its principles when they don't suit us. To have speech we love, we have to defend speech we hate. Besides, most controversial material is open to more than one interpretation. To some, Robert Mapplethorpe's black-and-white photographs of nude men are breath-taking art; others think them immoral filth. In my own novel, *Almost Paradise,* the heroine, as a child, is sexually abused by her father. This criminal

betrayal colors her life. It was a nightmare for my character, and painful, even sickening, for me to write. Had some zealot been able to ban all references to incest—regardless of context or purpose—my novel would never have gotten written.

14   We can't hand over to anyone the power to decide what's appropriate for all. Because a year or a decade from now, someone might want to ban all depictions of career women or day-care centers, using the argument that they undermine family unity. Think that sounds extreme? Don't—historically, censorship has often been the first step toward dictatorship.

15   That's why we have to stand up for the First Amendment and not be moved, no matter how tempting it is to succumb to a just-this-once mentality. All of us, women and men, have to salute our Founding Fathers and say: Thanks for the legacy of freedom you gave us. And don't worry. We have the strength, the will, and yes, the guts to defend it.

■ TOPICAL CONSIDERATIONS

1. How does Isaacs define pornography? Do you agree with this definition? What terms, if any, might you add to it?
2. What, according to Isaacs, are the flaws of a so-called blue-ribbon panel to determine what books and films should or should not be banned? Is this a concept you would or would not support? Explain.
3. Why does Isaacs discount the relationship between pornography and violence. Can you offer an argument to support or refute her opinion?
4. Explain the author's statement, "To have speech we love, we have to defend speech we hate" (paragraph 13).
5. How does a "just-this-once mentality" endanger the Constitution according to Isaacs?

■ RHETORICAL CONSIDERATIONS

1. What tone is established in the opening paragraphs of the essay? What effect, if any, does Isaacs hope this tone will have on the readers? Does she maintain this tone throughout the piece? Explain your answer with specifics from the essay.
2. How does Isaacs use examples from her own writing and from the work of other artists to support her opposition to banning pornography? How thorough is her analysis?
3. Where in the essay does Isaacs anticipate her readers' objections to her argument? Give two examples.

■ WRITING ASSIGNMENTS

1. Assume you have been asked to form a "blue-ribbon panel" the task of which is to determine what is and what is not pornographic, and what should and should not be banned. Write a justification for such a panel and,

most importantly, explain who would be on the panel and why. Compare your panel members with those of your classmates. How, if at all, does this exercise influence your feelings about censorship?

2. As the introduction points out, this article originally appeared in *Redbook* magazine. Write a letter to the editor from Jerry Falwell or another member of the religious right responding to this essay.

3. Read a copy of the First Amendment, and use it as a basis for an argument either for or against censorship or freedom of speech. (Keep in mind this question: Are there ways that the First Amendment can be used to argue for both sides of this issue?)

4. Write an essay critiquing Brownmiller's and Issacs' essays. Try to be as objective as possible in assessing each article's strengths and weaknesses.

5. What are your own feelings about the First Amendment? Do you believe in absolute freedom of speech at all times, or do you think that there are some publications, movies or works of art that cross the line? Write an essay expressing your own views, making sure to cite specific examples of what should and should not be protected under the First Amendment.

CENSORING RAP MUSIC—PRO

Let's Stop Crying Wolf on Censorship

Jonathan Alter

If a rap song tells people to shoot blacks, is that art or a call for violence? If a radio station refuses to play such a song, is that censorship or editorial judgment? In this essay Jonathan Alter takes on these thorny questions. He argues that record company executives who produce "sociopathic entertainment" are more concerned with profit than moral responsibility. Furthermore, he claims, they wrap themselves in "phony" liberal pieties and cry censorship whenever radio stations ban recordings that are considered "socially irresponsible."

Jonathan Alter is a senior editor for *Newsweek*. This article first appeared in his "Between the Lines" column, in November 1993.

1 Imagine that a big record-company executive discovered a new skinhead band called Aryan Nation and distributed 2 million copies of a song with the lyrics: *Rat-a-tat and a tat like that / Never hesitate to put a nigga on his back.* This frank call for whites to kill blacks might run into a few problems around Hollywood. It's not likely, for instance, that Bill Clinton's advisers would recommend that their man appear at a gala fund-raiser at the executive's house. If radio stations declined to air Aryan Nation's songs advocating lynching, no one would scream "censorship."

2   Those lyrics in fact come from a rap song by Dr. Dre, whose label is Death Row/Interscope, which is part owned by Time Warner. Interscope is headed by Ted Field, a movie-and-record mogul who hosted Bill Clinton's big Hollywood fund-raiser last year. "A lot of this [criticism of rap] is just plain old racism," Field told the Los Angeles Times last month. "You can tell the people who want to stop us from releasing controversial rap music one thing: Kiss my ass."

3   Since Hollywood already has enough people who spend their days eagerly taking Ted Field up on that offer, I thought I'd try a different tack. It is Field and other phony liberals of his ilk, wrapping themselves in constitutional pieties, who are applying the racial double standards and devaluing legitimate civil-liberties concerns. It is they, more than the rappers themselves, who are responsible for spreading irresponsibility. And it is those who oppose them—private citizens rebuking or boycotting sociopathic entertainment—who are engaged in free expression in its best, most democratic sense.

4   That word—censorship—has been thrown around much too casually in recent years. If a record-company executive or an art-gallery owner or a book publisher declines to disseminate something, that's not censorship, it's judgment. It might be cowardly judgment or responsible judgment, but it is what they are paid to do. Garry Trudeau makes this point whenever some wimpy newspaper decides not to run a controversial "Doonesbury" strip: his fans say he was censored; he rightly calls it bad editing.

5   How did we get to a point where "art" became a code word for money? As record executive David Geffen said last year about Time Warner chief Gerald Levin's lame rationalizations for Ice-T's "Cop Killer," "To say that this whole issue is not about profit is silly. It certainly is not about artistic freedom." In other words, the Constitution guarantees all Americans the right to rap, but it says nothing about Dr. Dre's right to a record contract.

6   In fact, if censorship means companies like Sony and Time Warner and Capitol Records begin to think harder about the messages they're sending young African-Americans, then maybe we need more of it. If censorship means executives bear greater personal accountability for what their companies produce—if it means that when Ted Field walks into a Beverly Hills restaurant, the patrons turn around and say with disgust, "Hey, that's the guy who tells blacks to shoot each other"—then it could help.

7   But that's not what the word means. Real censorship is when the government—*the government*—bans books in school libraries, prosecutes artists and writers for their work, seizes pornography, exercises prior restraint. And there's the whiff of censorship when the government hints at future action, as Janet Reno did last month with the TV networks. The line here gets tricky. Tipper Gore was way ahead of her time, and she never advocated censorship, only voluntary labeling of albums. But as the wife of the vice president, she's probably wise to go light on the issue now. Otherwise it might begin to feel censorious. A few private institutions—like schools that try to punish offensive students speech—could also be categorized as engaging in real censorship.

8   Beyond that, let's give the word a rest. I was once a judge for a journalism contest sponsored by a group called Project Censored. The goal was to identify underreported or ignored stories, not officially censored ones. Such casual use of the word

demeans victims of real censorship, here and abroad. So does describing the battle over government funding of controversial art as a "censorship" issue. This is loopy. Declining to use taxpayer dollars to fund art is hardly the same as suppressing it. When Los Angeles radio station KACE-FM recently took the commendable step of banning "socially irresponsible" music from its format, this, too, was attacked by some other radio stations as censorship. These other stations routinely fail to play any folk music. Are they censoring Peter, Paul and Mary? Of course not. They're simply making a business assessment that folk is a ratings loser. What's annoying is the implicit assumption that choosing songs on the basis of what sells is somehow superior to choosing them on the basis of what's responsible.

9   If an editor wants to change the text of an article about ghetto life, that's editing. But if a rap producer wants to change sociopathic lyrics, that's seen as censorship. Even if you assume that rap is superior esthetically to journalism, is it really more worthy of protection? Is rap an inherently more valid form of expression than prose with no beat behind it? After all, they are both "voices of the community," waiting to be heard. So is Aryan Nation.

10   This is not an argument for applying a harsh moral standard to art, for easy listening everywhere on the dial, for record-company executives to sponsor nothing that they don't personally embrace. But even at its grimmest, music is meant to enhance life. Like tobacco executives, artists and record moguls who market death bear at least some responsibility for the consequences of their work. Let's confront that—and stop crying wolf on censorship.

■ TOPICAL CONSIDERATIONS

1. Why, according to Alter, would nobody cry censorship if radio stations refused to play the song quoted in paragraph 1, had it been recorded by a skinhead band called Aryan Nation instead of Dr. Dre?

2. Alter scorns rap promoters, such as Ted Field, who cry censorship when radio stations decide not to run songs because audiences might find the lyrics offensive. What distinctions does Alter draw between censorship and marketing? How does he make clear his position on the freedom of speech? Were you convinced by his argument?

3. Alter claims that the word *censorship* has been thrown around too casually in recent years. Do you agree? Can you think of examples when someone cried censorship when it didn't apply?

4. Find specific words or phrases in the essay that project Alter's low opinion of rap music. Do you think Alter's examples are a fair and accurate portrayal of the genre?

5. Did you find Alter's argument convincing? If so, which statements did you find the most persuasive, and why? If not, find claims that struck you as weak or unconvincing. Support your answers with specifics.

6. What is the message of Dr. Dre's lyrics: "Rat-a-tat and a tat like that / Never hesitate to put a nigga on his back"? Do you think they mean, as Alter

claims, that blacks should shoot each other? Do you find the words offensive? Or do you see a difference between the actual words and the message? Explain.

7. Is the message of rap music always violent? How do other performers use rap to communicate a different kind of message?

8. Think of art forms other than rap where an audience is challenged to consider whether or not the work is offensive. How did you feel about the performance (song, play, exhibit)? If you were in charge of producing or exhibiting the work, how would you decide what to do?

■ RHETORICAL CONSIDERATIONS

1. How does Alter redefine the word *censorship?* What conclusion does he make based on this definition?

2. Alter uses a number of illustrations to make his viewpoint clear. Find three of these and evaluate whether or not they work to persuade the reader of his views.

3. How does Alter use humor and exaggeration to his advantage in this essay? How does his style contrast with that of Lawrence and Hentoff in the subsequent essays?

4. What common ground would Alter find with Hentoff and with Lawrence? What differences?

5. Alter enjoys using rhetorical questions to highlight and clarify his views. Find two of the most effective rhetorical questions in this essay and discuss their significance.

■ WRITING ASSIGNMENTS

1. Imagine that you are Ted Field. Of course, you disagree with Alter. Write a letter to the editor responding to Alter's essay. Based on what you know from the essay about Ted Field, choose a tone that best impersonates him.

2. Do you advocate outright censorship of musical lyrics, or do you feel that people should be able to make informed purchasing decisions? In other words, would you argue for protective laws (censorship) or self-government on the part of the music industry? Do you think that warning labels on recordings are protection enough? Using specific examples and sound reasoning, write a paper in which you explore your thoughts on these questions.

3. Many people today claim that rock and rap lyrics are full of sexual violence against women. Do you agree? Do you think there is too much of this violence and that it should be banned? Explain your views in an essay.

4. Imagine that you are creating a new magazine devoted to popular culture. As editor you have to define editorial criteria. Write a statement on what your magazine will accept and what it will reject based on your cultural and

artistic values. Then write a statement on what your magazine will accept based on commercial values. How will you deal with advertisements?

5. Think of an art form you don't like and write an essay defending an artist's right to perform it.

Bum Rap

Michael Eric Dyson

Yes, gangsta' rap lyrics are disturbingly raw and violent. Yes, women and gays are sometimes viciously maligned. But for scholar and rap expert Michael Eric Dyson, some critics forget that rap is a reflection of its bleak inner city origins and the rage of afflicted people. He argues that if we want to do something about the social ills rappers narrate even in the nasty extreme, the answer is not censorship. Instead, we should try to understand the conditions that created such rage and bad attitudes.

Michael Eric Dyson is Director of the Institute of African-American Research and Professor of Communication Studies at the University of North Carolina at Chapel Hill. He is the author of *Reflecting Black: African-American Cultural Criticism* (1993), *Making Malcolm: The Myth and Meaning of Malcolm X* (1994), and *From God to Gangsta' Rap: Notes on Black Culture* (1995), from which this essay comes. His writing has appeared in *The New York Times, Washington Post, The Nation, Vibe* magazine, and *Rolling Stone.* In 1992 he won the Award of Excellence from the National Association of Black Journalists.

1   As a 35-year-old father of a 16-year-old son (yes, I was a teen father), and as a professor and ordained Baptist minister who grew up in Detroit's treacherous inner city, I am disturbed by some elements of gangsta' rap. But I'm even more anguished by the way many black leaders have scapegoated its artists. How can we avoid the pitfall of unfairly attacking black youth for problems that bewitched our culture long before they came on the scene? First, we should understand what forces drove the emergence of rap. Second, we should acknowledge that gangsta' rap crudely exposes harmful beliefs and practices that are often maintained with deceptive civility in many black communities.

2   If the 15-year evolution of hip-hop teaches us anything, its that history is made in unexpected ways by unexpected people with unexpected results. Rap is now safe from the perils of quick extinction predicted at its humble start. But its cesarian birth in the bitter belly of the seventies proved to be a Rosetta stone of black popular culture.

3   Afros, platforms, blunts, funk music and carnal eruptions define a "back-in-the-day" hip-hop aesthetic. But in reality, the severe seventies busted the economic

boom of the sixties. The fallout was felt in restructured automobile industries and collapsed steel-mills. It was extended in exported employment to foreign markets. Closer to home, there was the depletion of social services to reverse the material ruin of black life. Later, public spaces for black recreation were gutted by Reaganomics or violently transformed by lethal drug economies.

4   Hip-hop was born in these bleak conditions. Hip-hoppers joined pleasure and rage while turning the details of their difficult lives into craft and capital. This is the world hip-hop would come to "represent": privileged persons speaking for less visible or vocal peers. At their best, rappers shape the torturous twists of urban fate into lyrical elegies. They represent lives swallowed by too little love or opportunity. They represent themselves and their peers with aggrandizing anthems that boast of their ingenuity and luck in surviving. The art of "representin'" that is much ballyhooed in hip-hop is the witness of those left to tell the afflicted's story.

5   As rap expands its vision and influence, its unfavorable origins and its relentless quest to represent black youth are both a consolation and challenge to hip-hoppers. They remind rappers that history is not merely the stuff of imperial dreams from above. It isn't just the sanitizing myths of those with political power. Representing history is within reach of those who seize the opportunity to speak for themselves, to represent their own interests at all costs.

6   Even rap's largest controversies are about representation. Hip-hop's attitudes toward women and gays continually jolt in the unvarnished malevolence they reveal. But the sharp responses to rap's misogyny and homophobia signify its importance in battles over the cultural representation of other beleaguered groups. This is particularly true of gangsta' rap.

7   While gangsta' rap takes the heat for a range of social maladies from urban violence to sexual misconduct, the roots of our racial misery remain buried beneath moralizing discourse that is confused and sometimes dishonest.

8   There's no doubt that gangsta' rap is often sexist and that it reflects a vicious misogyny that has seized our nation with frightening intensity. For black women who are already beset by attacks from outside their communities, to feel the thrust of musical daggers to their dignity from within is doubly wounding. How painful it must be for black women, many of whom have fought valiantly for black pride, to hear the dissonant chord of disdain carried in the angry epithet "bitch."

9   But gangsta' rap often reaches higher than its ugliest, lowest common denominator. At its best, this music draws attention to complex dimensions of ghetto life ignored by many Americans. Of all the genres of hip-hop—from socially conscious rap to black nationalist expressions, from pop to hardcore—gangsta' rap has most aggressively narrated the pains and possibilities, the fantasies and fears, of poor black urban youth. Situated in the surreally violent climes of postindustrial Los Angeles and its bordering cities, gangsta' rap draws its metaphoric capital in part from the mix of myth and murder that gave the Western frontier a dangerous appeal a century ago.

10   Gangsta' rap is largely an indictment of bourgeois black cultural and political institutions by young people who do not find conventional methods of addressing personal and social calamity useful. When the leaders of those institutions, national

and local alike, castigate the excessive and romanticized violence of this music without trying to understand what precipitated its rise in the first place, they drive a greater wedge between themselves and the youth they so desperately want to help.

11   The recent attempts by black figures like C. Delores Tucker and Dionne Warwick, as well as national and local lawmakers, to have the sale of gangsta' rap censored, even outlawed, are surely misguided. When I testified before the U.S. Senate's Subcommittee on Juvenile Justice, as well as the Pennsylvania House of Representatives, I tried to make this point while acknowledging the need to responsibly confront gangsta' rap's problems. Censorship of gangsta' rap cannot begin to solve the problems of poor black youth; nor will it effectively curtail their consumption of music that is already circulated through dubbed tapes and without the benefit of significant air-play.

12   A crucial distinction needs to be made between censorship of gangsta' rap and edifying expressions of civic responsibility and community conscientiousness. The former seeks to prevent vulgar music from being sold that offends the moral sensibilities of particular groups by suppressing the First Amendment. The latter, however, is the admittedly more difficult but rewarding task of opposing—through protest and pamphleteering, through community activism and consciousness raising—the expression of misogynistic and sexist sentiments in rap lyrics and hip-hop culture. But we can't stop there.

13   If blacks really want to strike at the heart of sexism and misogyny in our communities, shouldn't we take a closer look at one crucial source of these blights? The central institution of black culture, the black church, which has given hope and inspiration to millions of blacks, has also given us an embarrassing legacy of sexism and misogyny.

14   Despite the great good it has achieved through a heroic tradition of emancipatory leadership, the black church continues to practice and justify *ecclesiastical apartheid.* More than 70 percent of black church members are female, yet they are generally excluded from the church's central station of power, the pulpit. And rarely are the few ordained female ministers elected to be pastors.

15   Yet black leaders, many of them ministers, excoriate rappers for their verbal sexual misconduct. It is difficult indeed to listen to civil rights veterans deplore the hostile depiction of women in gangsta' rap without mentioning the sexism of the movements for racial liberation of the 1960s. And of course the problem persists in many civil rights organizations today.

16   Sad, too, is the silence of most black leaders in the face of the vicious abuse of gay men and lesbians in gangsta' rap. "Fags," and "dykes" are prominent in the genre's vocabulary of rage, and black leaders' failure to make this an issue only reinforces the inferior, invisible status of gay men and lesbians in black cultural institutions, including the black church.

17   Gangsta' rap's greatest sin, in the eyes of many critics, is that it tells the truth about practices and beliefs that rappers hold in common with the black elite. This music has embarrassed black bourgeois culture and exposed its polite sexism and its disregard for gay men and lesbians. We should not continue to blame it for ills that existed long before hip-hop uttered its first syllable.

■ TOPICAL CONSIDERATIONS

1. According to Dyson, from what bleak economic conditions did gangsta' rap emerge?
2. What is the purpose of the art of "representin'" in rap music? At its best, what does "representin'" accomplish for black youth? In your opinion, does this effort at storytelling justify lyrics that are sometimes crude and "offensive"? Why or why not?
3. How, in Dyson's opinion, is the rap artist writing history? How is rap history different from traditional history? Do you consider rap music a kind of history?
4. What is Dyson's opinion about attempts to censor gangsta' rap? What approach does Dyson recommend in place of traditional censorship? Which approach do you favor? Explain your reasons.
5. Explain what Dyson calls "ecclesiastical apartheid."
6. In your opinion, does the sexism in the civil rights movement of the sixties disqualify contemporary black leaders from making charges of sexism in gangsta' rap?
7. Both Michael Dyson and Jonathan Alter find some rap lyrics disturbing and offensive. Do they take a similar or different stance toward the censorship of this music?

■ RHETORICAL CONSIDERATIONS

1. Explain the allusion to the Rosetta stone in paragraph 2.
2. In the opening of this essay, how does the author establish a personal affinity with the black youth who created gangsta' rap? Does this make the author's point of view more or less convincing?
3. At the end of paragraph 1, Dyson lists his two major ideas. Does he argue each of these points convincingly? Why or why not?

■ WRITING ASSIGNMENTS

1. At one point Dyson says, "At their best, rappers shape the torturous twists of urban fate into lyrical elegies" (paragraph 4). Write an essay supporting or disagreeing with this statement using contemporary rap lyrics.
2. Write an essay recommending that rap lyrics should or should not be censored.
3. Write a script in which Susan Brownmiller, Jonathan Alter, and Michael Eric Dyson debate whether or not rap lyrics that espouse violence against women should be banned. As much as possible, try to stay close to each author's voice.
4. Write a letter to someone in another country explaining Dyson's position in the debate about rap music and censorship. As best you can, describe the First Amendment rights and some of the socioeconomic forces that Dyson uses in his defense of rap.

REGULATING HATE SPEECH—PRO

Regulating Racist Speech on Campus

Charles R. Lawrence III

The last few years has seen a disturbing rise in racist and sexist language on college campuses. Some administrations have dealt with the problem by outright banning such offensive language on the grounds that racial slurs are violent verbal assaults that interfere with students' rights to an education. Others fear that putting sanctions on racist speech violates the First Amendment guarantee of free expression. In the following essay, a professor of law argues for the restricting of free speech by appealing to the U.S. Supreme Court's landmark decision in the case of *Brown* v. *Board of Education*. Charles R. Lawrence teaches law at Stanford University and the University of California at Los Angeles. He is the author of many articles on law and coauthor of the book, *The Bakke Case: The Politics of Inequality* (1979). A longer version of this article appeared in the February 1990 issue of *Duke Law*.

1 I have spent the better part of my life as a dissenter. As a high-school student, I was threatened with suspension for my refusal to participate in a civil-defense drill, and I have been a conspicuous consumer of my First Amendment liberties ever since. There are very strong reasons for protecting even racist speech. Perhaps the most important of these is that such protection reinforces our society's commitment to tolerance as a value, and that by protecting bad speech from government regulation, we will be forced to combat it as a community.

2 But I also have a deeply felt apprehension about the resurgence of racial violence and the corresponding rise in the incidence of verbal and symbolic assault and harassment to which blacks and other traditionally subjugated and excluded groups are subjected. I am troubled by the way the debate has been framed in response to the recent surge of racist incidents on college and university campuses and in response to some universities' attempts to regulate harassing speech. The problem has been framed as one in which the liberty of free speech is in conflict with the elimination of racism. I believe this has placed the bigot on the moral high ground and fanned the rising flames of racism.

3 Above all, I am troubled that we have not listened to the real victims, that we have shown so little understanding of their injury, and that we have abandoned those whose race, gender, or sexual preference continues to make them second-class citizens. It seems to me a very sad irony that the first instinct of civil libertarians has been to challenge even the smallest, most narrowly framed efforts by universities to provide black and other minority students with the protection the Constitution guarantees them.

4 The landmark case of *Brown* v. *Board of Education* is not a case that we normally think of as a case about speech. But *Brown* can be broadly read as articulating the principle of equal citizenship. *Brown* held that segregated schools were inherently unequal because of the *message* that segregation conveyed—that black children were an untouchable caste, unfit to go to school with white children. If we

understand the necessity of eliminating the system of signs and symbols that signal the inferiority of blacks, then we should hesitate before proclaiming that all racist speech that stops short of physical violence must be defended.

5   University officials who have formulated policies to respond to incidents of racial harassment have been characterized in the press as "thought police," but such policies generally do nothing more than impose sanctions against intentional face-to-face insults. When racist speech takes the form of face-to-face insults, catcalls, or other assaultive speech aimed at an individual or small group of persons, it falls directly within the "fighting words" exception to First Amendment protection. The Supreme Court has held that words which "by their very utterance inflict injury or tend to incite an immediate breach of the peace" are not protected by the First Amendment.

6   If the purpose of the First Amendment is to foster the greatest amount of speech, racial insults disserve that purpose. Assaultive racist speech functions as a preemptive strike. The invective is experienced as a blow, not as a proffered idea, and once the blow is struck, it is unlikely that a dialogue will follow. Racial insults are particularly undeserving of First Amendment protection because the perpetrator's intention is not to discover truth or initiate dialogue but to injure the victim. In most situations, members of minority groups realize that they are likely to lose if they respond to epithets by fighting and are forced to remain silent and submissive.

7   Courts have held that offensive speech may not be regulated in public forums such as streets where the listener may avoid the speech by moving on, but the regulation of otherwise protected speech has been permitted when the speech invades the privacy of the unwilling listener's home or when the unwilling listener cannot avoid the speech. Racist posters, fliers, and graffiti in dormitories, bathrooms, and other common living spaces would seem to clearly fall within the reasoning of these cases. Minority students should not be required to remain in their rooms in order to avoid racial assault. Minimally, they should find a safe haven in their dorms and in all other common rooms that are a part of their daily routine.

8   I would also argue that the university's responsibility for insuring that these students receive an equal educational opportunity provides a compelling justification for regulations that insure them safe passage in all common areas. A minority student should not have to risk becoming the target of racially assaulting speech every time he or she chooses to walk across campus. Regulating vilifying speech that cannot be anticipated or avoided would not preclude announced speeches and rallies— situations that would give minority-group members and their allies the chance to organize counter-demonstrations or avoid the speech altogether.

9   The most commonly advanced argument against the regulation of racist speech proceeds something like this: we recognize that minority groups suffer pain and injury as the result of racist speech, but we must allow this hate mongering for the benefit of society as a whole. Freedom of speech is the lifeblood of our democratic system. It is especially important for minorities because often it is their only vehicle for rallying support for the redress of their grievances. It will be impossible to formulate a prohibition so precise that it will prevent the racist speech you want to sup-

press without catching in the same net all kinds of speech that it would be unconscionable for a democratic society to suppress.

10 Whenever we make such arguments, we are striking a balance on the one hand between our concern for the continued free flow of ideas and the democratic process dependent on that flow, and, on the other, our desire to further the cause of equality. There can be no meaningful discussion of how we should reconcile our commitment to equality and our commitment to free speech until it is acknowledged that there is real harm inflicted by racist speech and that this harm is far from trivial.

11 To engage in a debate about the First Amendment and racist speech without a full understanding of the nature and extent of that harm is to risk making the First Amendment an instrument of domination rather than a vehicle of liberation. We have not known the experience of victimization by racist, misogynist, and homophobic speech, nor do we equally share the burden of the societal harm it inflicts. We are often quick to say that we have heard the cry of the victims when we have not.

12 The *Brown* case is again instructive because it speaks directly to the psychic injury inflicted by racist speech by noting that the symbolic message of segregation affected "the hearts and minds" of Negro children "in a way unlikely ever to be undone." Racial epithets and harassment often cause deep emotional scarring and feelings of anxiety and fear that pervade every aspect of a victim's life.

13 *Brown* also recognized that black children did not have an equal opportunity to learn and participate in the school community if they bore the additional burden of being subjected to the humiliation and psychic assault contained in the message of segregation. University students bear an analogous burden when they are forced to live and work in an environment where at any moment they may be subjected to denigrating verbal harassment and assault. The same injury was addressed by the Supreme Court when it held that sexual harassment that creates a hostile or abusive work environment violates the ban on sex discrimination in employment of Title VII of the Civil Rights Act of 1964.

14 Carefully drafted university regulations would bar the use of words as assault weapons and leave unregulated even the most heinous of ideas when those ideas are presented at times and places and in manners that provide an opportunity for reasoned rebuttal or escape from immediate injury. The history of the development of the right to free speech has been one of carefully evaluating the importance of free expression and its effects on other important societal interests. We have drawn the line between protected and unprotected speech before without dire results. (Courts have, for example, exempted from the protection of the First Amendment obscene speech and speech that disseminates official secrets, that defames or libels another person, or that is used to form a conspiracy or monopoly.)

15 Blacks and other people of color are skeptical about the argument that even the most injurious speech must remain unregulated because, in an unregulated marketplace of ideas, the best ones will rise to the top and gain acceptance. Our experience tells us quite the opposite. We have seen too many good liberal politicians shy away from the issues that might brand them as being too closely allied with us.

16 Whenever we decide that racist speech must be tolerated because of the importance of maintaining societal tolerance for all unpopular speech, we are asking

blacks and other subordinated groups to bear the burden for the good of all. We must be careful that the ease with which we strike the balance against the regulation of racist speech is in no way influenced by the fact that the cost will be borne by others. We must be certain that those who will pay that price are fairly represented in our deliberations and that they are heard.

17   At the core of the argument that we should resist all government regulation of speech is the ideal that the best cure for bad speech is good, that ideas that affirm equality and the worth of all individuals will ultimately prevail. This is an empty ideal unless those of us who would fight racism are vigilant and unequivocal in that fight. We must look for ways to offer assistance and support to students whose speech and political participation are chilled in a climate of racial harassment.

18   Civil rights lawyers might consider suing on behalf of blacks whose right to an equal education is denied by a university's failure to insure a nondiscriminatory educational climate or conditions of employment. We must embark upon the development of a First Amendment jurisprudence grounded in the reality of our history and our contemporary experience. We must think hard about how best to launch legal attacks against the most indefensible forms of hate speech. Good lawyers can create exceptions and narrow interpretations that limit the harm of hate speech without opening the floodgates of censorship.

19   Everyone concerned with these issues must find ways to engage actively in actions that resist and counter the racist ideas that we would have the First Amendment protect. If we fail in this, the victims of hate speech must rightly assume that we are on the oppressors' side.

■ TOPICAL CONSIDERATIONS

1. What reasons does Lawrence offer for protecting racist speech from governmental restrictions? Do you agree? How else can a community fight such speech?

2. According to the author, how in the debate over racist language does the fight against racism conflict with the fight for free speech? What fundamental problem does Lawrence have with this conflict? Are his reasons convincing to you? Why or why not?

3. According to the author, how can the case of *Brown* v. *Board of Education* be interpreted to cover protection of victims of racist speech?

4. Why, according to Lawrence, is racist speech "undeserving of First Amendment protection" (paragraph 6)? Do you agree? If not, why not? If so, can you think of any circumstances when racist speech should be protected?

5. What legal measures does Lawrence suggest for the protection of black students against hate speech?

6. Has this article affected your thinking on the subject of free speech and censorship? Has it changed your mind about the use of racially or sexually abusive language? Explain your answer.

7. Have you ever been the victim of abusive speech—speech that victimized you because of your race, gender, religion, ethnicity, or sexual preference? If so, do you agree with Lawrence's argument about the "psychic injury" (paragraph 12) such speech can cause? Did you experience such injury? Explain your answer.

8. Is there any racial tension on your campus? If so, do you see a link between racial tension and racist speech? What suggestions would you make to school officials to deal with such tension? Do you think that banning hate speech might lessen racial tension and violence? How about in society at large? Explain your reasoning.

■ RHETORICAL CONSIDERATIONS

1. Where in the essay do you get a clear focus on Lawrence's line of argument? What are the first signals that he sends to clue the reader? Can you point to a thesis statement?

2. Lawrence opens his essay saying that he has a long history as a "dissenter." What would you say is his strategy here? What kinds of assumptions does he make of his audience? What does his refusing to participate in a civil-defense drill have to do with the essay's central issues?

3. How convincingly does Lawrence argue that racist speech should not be protected by the First Amendment? What is the logic of his argument? What evidence does he offer as support?

4. Select one of Lawrence's arguments that you think is especially strong or especially weak, and explain why you regard it so.

5. Consider the author's voice in this essay. What sense do you get of Charles R. Lawrence III as an individual? In a paragraph, try to characterize him. Take into consideration his stand here as well as the style and tone of his writing.

■ WRITING ASSIGNMENTS

1. As Lawrence points out, many university officials—as well as legal scholars—view the outlawing of hate speech as contrary to the democratic spirit of pluralism and tolerance. Write a paper in which you argue that hate speech should be protected if we are to remain a legitimate democracy. In your discussion, explain just where you would draw the line on the protection, if at all.

2. Taking the opposite stand from above, and using some of your own ideas, write a paper in which you argue that racist (and/or sexist) speech should be outlawed because it can only contribute to the victimization of people and the already-tense social conditions in America. In your discussion, explain just what kinds of hate speech you would want to see banned, and why. Also explain why you think such speech could be controlled by regulation.

3. Suppose that a leader of a known hate group were invited to your campus, someone certain to speak in inflammatory racist language. Would you defend that person's right to address the student body? Why or why not? Should that person be protected under the First Amendment? Would you attend? Why or why not?

4. What if a condition of acceptance to your school was signing an agreement that you would refrain from using racist, sexist, or otherwise abusive language on campus—an agreement that could lead to suspension. Weighing the social benefits against the restrictions on freedom of expression, write a paper in which you explain why you would sign or not sign the agreement.

Free Speech on Campus

Nat Hentoff

Taking the opposing stand, First Amendment expert Nat Hentoff argues that instituting sanctions on hate speech seriously mocks the pluralistic nature of a university and academic freedom and inquiry. He warns that preventing or punishing offensive language could lead to Orwellian nightmares. Nat Hentoff is a staff writer for the *New Yorker* and the *Village Voice,* as well as a columnist for the *Washington Post.* Much of his writing focuses on the subject of freedom of expression including his book *The First Freedom: The Tumultuous History of Free Speech in America* (1989). He is also author of *American Heroes: In and Out of School* (1987), *Boston Boy: A Memoir* (1988), and *Free Speech for Me—But Not for Thee: How the American Left and Right Relentlessly Censor Each Other* (1992). This article first appeared in the May 1989 issue of the *Progressive.*

1 A flier distributed at the University of Michigan some months ago proclaimed that blacks "don't belong in classrooms, they belong hanging from trees."

2 At other campuses around the country, manifestations of racism are becoming commonplace. At Yale, a swastika and the words WHITE POWER! were painted on the building housing the University's Afro-American Cultural Center. At Temple University, a White Students Union has been formed with some 130 members.

3 Swastikas are not directed only at black students. The Nazi symbol has been spray-painted on the Jewish Student Union at Memphis State University. And on a number of campuses, women have been singled out as targets of wounding and sometimes frightening speech. At the law school of the State University of New York at Buffalo, several women students have received anonymous letters characterized by one professor as venomously sexist.

4   These and many more such signs of the resurgence of bigotry and know-nothingism throughout the society—as well as on campus—have to do solely with speech, including symbolic speech. There have also been physical assaults on black students and on black, white, and Asian women students, but the way to deal with physical attacks is clear: call the police and file a criminal complaint. What is to be done, however, about speech alone—however disgusting, inflammatory, and rawly divisive that speech may be?

5   At more and more colleges, administrators—with the enthusiastic support of black students, women students, and liberal students—have been answering that question by preventing or punishing speech. In public universities, this is a clear violation of the First Amendment. In private colleges and universities, suppression of speech mocks the secular religion of academic freedom and free inquiry.

6   The Student Press Law Center in Washington, D.C.—a vital source of legal support for student editors around the country—reports, for example, that at the University of Kansas, the student host and producer of a radio news program was forbidden by school officials from interviewing a leader of the Ku Klux Klan. So much for free inquiry on that campus.

7   In Madison, Wisconsin, the *Capital Times* ran a story in January about Chancellor Sheila Kaplan of the University of Wisconsin branch at Parkside, who ordered her campus to be scoured of "some anonymously placed white supremacist hate literature." Sounding like the legendary Mayor Frank ("I am the law") Hague of Jersey City, who booted "bad speech" out of town, Chancellor Kaplan said, "This institution is not a lamppost standing on the street corner. It doesn't belong to everyone."

8   Who decides what speech can be heard or read by everyone? Why, the Chancellor, of course. That's what George III used to say, too.

9   University of Wisconsin political science professor Carol Tebben thinks otherwise. She believes university administrators "are getting confused when they are acting as censors and trying to protect students from bad ideas. I don't think students need to be protected from bad ideas. I think they can determine for themselves what ideas are bad."

10   After all, if students are to be "protected" from bad ideas, how are they going to learn to identify and cope with them? Sending such ideas underground simply makes them stronger and more dangerous.

11   Professor Tebben's conviction that free speech means just that has become a decidedly minority view on many campuses. At the University of Buffalo Law School, the faculty unanimously adopted a "Statement Regarding Intellectual Freedom, Tolerance, and Political Harassment." Its title implies support of intellectual freedom, but the statement warned students that once they enter "this legal community," their right to free speech must become tempered "by the responsibility to promote equality and justice."

12   Accordingly, swift condemnation will befall anyone who engages in "remarks directed at another's race, sex, religion, national origin, age, or sex preference." Also forbidden are "other remarks based on prejudice and group stereotype."

13   This ukase is so broad that enforcement has to be alarmingly subjective. Yet the University of Buffalo Law School provides no due-process procedures for a student booked for making any of these prohibited remarks. Conceivably, a student caught playing a Lenny Bruce, Richard Pryor, or Sam Kinison album in his room could be tried for aggravated insensitivity by association.

14   When I looked into this wholesale cleansing of bad speech at Buffalo, I found it had encountered scant opposition. One protester was David Gerald Jay, a graduate of the law school and a cooperating attorney for the New York Civil Liberties Union. Said the appalled graduate: "Content-based prohibitions constitute prior restraint and should not be tolerated."

15   You would think that the law professors and administration at this public university might have known that. But hardly any professors dissented, and among the students only members of the conservative Federalist Society spoke up for free speech. The fifty-strong chapter of the National Lawyers Guild was on the other side. After all, it was more important to go on record as vigorously opposing racism and sexism than to expose oneself to charges of insensitivity to these malignancies.

16   The pressures to have the "right" attitude—as proved by having the "right" language in and out of class—can be stifling. A student who opposes affirmative action, for instance, can be branded a racist.

17   At the University of California at Los Angeles, the student newspaper ran an editorial cartoon satirizing affirmative action. (A student stops a rooster on campus and asks how the rooster got into UCLA. "Affirmative action," is the answer.) After outraged complaints from various minority groups, the editor was suspended for violating a publication policy against running "articles that perpetuate derogatory or cultural stereotypes." The art director was also suspended.

18   When the opinion editor of the student newspaper at California State University at Northridge wrote an article asserting that the sanctions against the editor and art director at UCLA amounted to censorship, he was suspended too.

19   At New York University Law School, a student was so disturbed by the pall of orthodoxy at that prestigious institution that he wrote to the school newspaper even though, as he said, he expected his letter to make him a pariah among his fellow students.

20   Barry Endick described the atmosphere at NYU created by "a host of watchdog committees and a generally hostile classroom reception regarding any student comment right of center." This "can be arguably viewed as symptomatic of a prevailing spirit of academic and social intolerance of . . . any idea which is not 'politically correct.'"

21   He went on to say something that might well be posted on campus bulletin boards around the country, though it would probably be torn down at many of them: "We ought to examine why students, so anxious to wield the Fourteenth Amendment, give short shrift to the First. Yes, Virginia, there are racist assholes. And you know what, the Constitution protects them, too."

22   Not when they engage in violence or vandalism. But when they speak or write, racist assholes fall right into this Oliver Wendell Holmes definition—highly unpopular among bigots, liberals, radicals, feminists, sexists, and college administra-

tors: "If there is any principle of the Constitution that more imperatively calls for attachment than any other, it is the principle of free thought—not free only for those who agree with us, but freedom for the thought we hate."

23   The language sounds like a pietistic Sunday sermon, but if it ever falls wholly into disuse, neither this publication nor any other journal of opinion—right or left— will survive.

24   Sometimes, college presidents and administrators sound as if they fully understand what Holmes was saying. Last year, for example, when the *Daily Pennsylvanian*—speaking for many at the University of Pennsylvania—urged that a speaking invitation to Louis Farrakhan be withdrawn, University President Sheldon Hackney disagreed.

25   "Open expression," said Hackney, "is the fundamental principle of a university." Yet consider what the same Sheldon Hackney did to the free-speech rights of a teacher at his own university. If any story distills the essence of the current decline of free speech on college campuses, it is the Ballad of Murray Dolfman.

26   For twenty-two years, Dolfman, a practicing lawyer in Philadelphia, had been a part-time lecturer in the Legal Studies Department of the University of Pennsylvania's Wharton School. For twenty-two years, no complaint had ever been made against him; indeed his student course evaluations had been outstanding. Each year students competed to get into his class.

27   On a November afternoon in 1984, Dolfman was lecturing about personal service contracts. His style somewhat resembles that of Professor Charles Kingsfield in *The Paper Chase*. Dolfman insists that students he calls on be prepared—or suffer the consequences. He treats all students this way—regardless of race, creed, or sex.

28   This day, Dolfman was pointing out that no one can be forced to work against his or her will—even if a contract has been signed. A court may prevent the resister from working for someone else so long as the contract is in effect but, Dolfman said, there can "be nothing that smacks of involuntary servitude."

29   Where does this concept come from? Dolfman looked around the room. Finally, a cautious hand was raised: "The Constitution?"

30   "Where in the Constitution?" No hands. "The Thirteenth Amendment," said the teacher. So, what does *it* say? The students were looking everywhere but at Dolfman.

31   "We will lose our liberties," Dolfman often told his classes, "if we don't know what they are."

32   On this occasion, he told them that he and other Jews, as ex-slaves, spoke at Passover of the time when they were slaves under the Pharaohs so that they would remember every year what it was like not to be free.

33   "We have ex-slaves here," Dolfman continued, "who should know about the Thirteenth Amendment." He asked black students in the class if they could tell him what was in that amendment.

34   "I wanted them to really think about it," Dolfman told me recently, "and know its history. You're better equipped to fight racism if you know all about those post-Civil War amendments and civil rights laws."

35   The Thirteenth Amendment provides that "neither slavery nor involuntary servitude . . . shall exist within the United States."

36   The black students in his class did not know what was in that amendment, and Dolfman had them read it aloud. Later, they complained to university officials that they had been hurt and humiliated by having been referred to as ex-slaves. Moreover, they said, they had no reason to be grateful for a constitutional amendment which gave them rights which should never have been denied them—and gave them precious little else. They had not made these points in class, although Dolfman—unlike Professor Kingsfield—encourages rebuttal.

37   Informed of the complaint, Dolfman told the black students he had intended no offense, and he apologized if they had been offended.

38   That would not do—either for the black students or for the administration. Furthermore, there were mounting black-Jewish tensions on campus, and someone had to be sacrificed. Who better than a part-time Jewish teacher with no contract and no union? He was sentenced by—George Orwell would have loved this—the Committee on Academic Freedom and Responsibility.

39   On his way to the stocks, Dolfman told President Sheldon Hackney that if a part-time instructor "can be punished on this kind of charge, a tenured professor can eventually be booted out, then a dean, and then a president."

40   Hackney was unmoved. Dolfman was banished from the campus for what came to be a year. But first he was forced to make a public apology to the entire university and then he was compelled to attend a "sensitivity and racial awareness" session. Sort of like a Vietnamese reeducation camp.

41   A few conservative professors objected to the stigmatization of Murray Dolfman. I know of no student dissent. Indeed, those students most concerned with making the campus more "sensitive" to diversity exulted in Dolfman's humiliation. So did most liberals on the faculty.

42   If my children were still of college age and wanted to attend the University of Pennsylvania, I would tell them this story. But where else could I encourage them to go?

■ TOPICAL CONSIDERATIONS

1. In your own words, summarize the argument Nat Hentoff is making here. What would you say his purpose is in the essay?
2. How are college and university administrators dealing with the recent rise in incidents of verbal abuse on American campuses? What is Hentoff's reaction to their handling of such problems?
3. With regard to the First Amendment, Hentoff distinguishes between physical assaults and those that are verbal and/or symbolic. What distinctions does he make? How does Charles R. Lawrence III in the previous essay distinguish between the two? Explain the different interpretations between the two authors.
4. If a leader of the Ku Klux Klan was barred from speaking at your school, would you protest? How about a member of the American Nazi party? The PLO? What about Louis Farrakhan? Explain your reasons.

5. In paragraph 9, the author quotes Professor Carol Tebben who states, "I don't think students need to be protected from bad ideas." Do you agree with Professor Tebben? Do you feel that students can "determine for themselves what ideas are bad"? What constitutes a bad idea to you? Can you imagine any bad ideas that you feel should be censored? What would they be, and under what circumstances?

6. Hentoff argues that many people who concur with sanctions on free speech do so to avoid being considered sexist or racist. Does this describe people you know? Do you think a person who opposes sexism and racism can still support freedom of speech? Or, do you think it's racist and sexist to be opposed to sanctions on racist and sexist speech? Explain your answers.

7. What problems does Hentoff have with University of Buffalo Law School's "Statement Regarding Intellectual Freedom, Tolerance, and Political Harassment"? What explanation does he offer for the wide acceptance of and "scant opposition" to that "ukase"? What are your feelings about such a Statement?

8. Would Hentoff agree that "sticks and stones will break my bones, but names will never hurt me?" What about Charles R. Lawrence III? What about you?

9. In paragraph 17, Hentoff cites the case of the UCLA student newspaper which ran an editorial cartoon satirizing affirmative action. From Hentoff's description, does the cartoon sound offensive to you? As described, how might it have been offensive to minority students? Do you think the administration was morally and legally justified in suspending the editor and art director? If this happened on your campus, how would you react? Explain why.

10. What do you make of the Dolfman case that Hentoff discusses in the last half of the essay? From what we're told, do you think that Dolfman was insensitive to the black students in his class? Do you think the black students were justified in their complaints? Do you think the administration was right in suspending Dolfman? Explain your answers.

■ RHETORICAL CONSIDERATIONS

1. Consider the title of this essay. What different meanings can it have? How does it forecast Hentoff's position in the essay? Do you think it's an effective title?

2. Where in the essay does Hentoff's line of argument begin to take focus? Is his line of argument carried clearly throughout the essay? Where does he state his thesis?

3. Consider the case of the editorial cartoon in the UCLA student newspaper (paragraphs 17 and 18). What about the cartoon does Hentoff want you to believe? Is his description of it satisfying to you? Would you prefer to actually see it before passing judgment on its offensiveness? Suppose you learned that Hentoff left out some particularly offensive details in the cartoon, say, a racist caricature of the rooster, how would that affect the impact of his argument?

4. Find two or three of Hentoff's sentences that you find particularly effective as examples of persuasive writing, then explain why they are effective.
5. Explain the meaning of the aside reference to George Orwell in paragraph 38. How is it an appropriate remark?
6. What do you make of the conclusion of this essay? What is the strategy of ending it with the question he asks? What's Hentoff's message here? Is his conclusion consistent with the development of his argument?

■ WRITING ASSIGNMENTS

1. In paragraph 10, Hentoff claims, "Sending such [bad] ideas underground simply makes them stronger and more dangerous." Explore this claim in a paper in which you try to imagine how certain "bad ideas" could become stronger and more dangerous were they censored.
2. Suppose your school had such a "Statement" as that at the University of Buffalo Law School (paragraph 11). Weighing the social benefits against the restrictions to the freedom of speech, would you be willing to sign a pledge of allegiance to it? Write a paper in which you explain your decision.
3. Where does *offensive* language end and *racist* and *sexist* language begin. Write a paper in which you try to determine these distinctions. Give clear examples to support your arguments.
4. Take another look at Charles Lawrence's essay. Which of the two arguments on the free speech issue seems the most persuasive? Explain exactly why you feel that way? Try to support your answer with specific evidence from each of the essays.
5. Write a letter to Nat Hentoff arguing that hate speech—racist, sexist and otherwise—should be regulated because it can only contribute to the already-tense social conditions in America.

Our magnificent planet has endured for 4.5 billion years of evolution, but its future is clouded by humankind's reckless ways: overpopulation, pollution, the depletion of resources, and the destruction of natural habitats. While some essays here celebrate the glories of nature others lament its redefinition.

Although brief, the opening piece grapples with universal questions about the natural world. Why do evil things happen? Why are there devastating earthquakes, floods, droughts, and wars? Is there an all-powerful, all-good God ruling creation, or is the universe a cold mechanistic system ruled by chance? In "A Cruel Universe, but the Only One Where Humans Could Exist," Gwynne Dyer explains why nature is nonmoral—why the universe does not seem to care about human life. If nature has been created by divinity, it could not be made any less cruel even if God had so wanted it.

Edward Hoagland, a naturalist and award-winning essayist who has the remarkable ability to draw profound insights from the most common scenes, in the essay that follows, "The Courage of Turtles," tightens the focus to a single remarkable species. In beautifully vivid descriptions, he captures the primitive majesty of these creatures. And, yet, he reminds us of their shrinking environment and numbers.

To many people, the shrinking of the environment and the frightening depletion of resources are sure signs that there is little time left to reverse the destruction. They argue that we must change our ways or life as we know it today will never be the same. This is the warning explicit in the final three selections.

"A Path of More Resistance" by naturalist Bill McKibben is a response to recent evidence that our world is becoming warmer. Called the *greenhouse effect,* the condition appears to be the result of the billions of tons of gases (methane, chlorofluorocarbons, and carbon dioxide) that are released into the atmosphere each year by industry and the burning of fossil fuels. If the warming trend continues, scientists fear cataclysmic environmental changes. To stop the trend, McKibben suggests a radical change in lifestyle—one stripped down to bare essentials. In order to live with nature he explains how he and his wife have pruned their desires, made sacrifices, and learned the pleasures of self-reliance.

While McKibben decries what we have done to the air and land, the next essay focuses on the seas of the world. In "The Cry of the Ocean," Peter Steinhart says that something is terribly wrong in the ocean and the fish are dying to tell us about it. No, it's not pollution but overfishing on a global scale. Fish populations are in rapid decline, Steinhart warns, and human survival is in the balance.

We close with a high-spirited and controversial call to save the environment, "Eco-Defense," by the late author and nature-activist Edward Abbey. Lamenting the assault on the American wilderness by developers and industry, and outraged that our government allows the pillage to continue, Abbey suggests that we fight back with hammers and nails. It's "illegal but ethically imperative." And, he adds, "it's good for the trees."

A Cruel Universe, but the Only One Where Humans Could Exist

Gwynne Dyer

Most of us have wondered at times why the natural universe seems so cruel and unjust a place. Just look at some of the brutal headlines over the past few years—the thousands of innocents lost to famine, earthquakes, volcanic eruptions, and diseases. Or consider the death of a child. As Gwynne Dyer says, even nonbelievers often wish the universe were a kinder, more forgiving environment. But, as he explains, it can't be and still be natural. Mr. Dyer is a columnist specializing in foreign affairs and creator of the 1985 PBS television series "War." This article first appeared in the *Boston Globe* in November 1985.

1 Why do babies die? Why do people starve to death in famines? Why is the universe so cruel, taking some people's lives away before they even had a chance to enjoy life, while others have long, happy lives and die peacefully in bed?

2 Religious people call it "the problem of evil." If God is all-powerful, why does he allow such horror and pain in his universe? A god who deliberately allowed Auschwitz and the killing fields of Cambodia to happen would not deserve our love, or even our respect—and if he couldn't prevent them, then he isn't all-powerful.

3 Cardinal Basil Hume, an English clergyman, was recently asked why God permitted such things by a journalist as they both stood in the middle of an Ethiopian refugee camp. Hume had the honesty to answer that he had "no idea." More sophisticated men of religion, whether Christian, Muslim or Jewish, might give longer answers that sounded plausible—but they are all answers that go round in circles.

4 If you don't believe in God, of course, then there is no philosophical problem. The universe is impersonal, human beings are on their own, and terrible things happen to them for the same reason they happen to fruit flies: no reason at all, except blind chance. But even non-believers often wish the universe were a kinder, more forgiving environment. And the answer is: it can't be.

5 It is an answer that applies equally to a universe created by a loving God and to a Godless universe which doesn't care about people at all. Any universe which could conceivably be a habitat for human beings must be one in which events have predictable consequences—even if those consequences include terrible tragedies for human beings.

6 Imagine, for a moment, a universe in which tragedies didn't happen. When the engines of a jet airliner fail on takeoff, it does not crash at the end of the runway and burn 150 people to death. Instead, it just wafts gently to the ground, because God loved the passengers and chose to save them.

7 But if that were all that happened when aircraft engines failed, there would be no need for aircraft maintenance. Indeed, there would be no need for engines, or even wings—and people could safely step off the edge of cliffs and walk on air. The law of gravity would be suspended whenever it endangered human lives.

8   So would all the other laws of nature. Whenever children's lives were at risk from disease, biochemistry would change its rules to save them. If an earthquake were going to kill thousands of people, continental drift would simply have to stop: so much for geology. And if someone tried to kill somebody else, the gun wouldn't work, or the bullet wouldn't fly straight, or it would turn into a marshmallow before it struck the victim.

9   In such a universe, there could be no science or technology, because there would be no fixed natural laws on which we could base them. The strength of steel and the temperature of boiling water would vary depending on whether human lives were threatened by a given value. There could not even be logic, since the same causes would not invariably have the same effects. It would be an entirely magical universe.

10   It is all a package, and quite indivisible. Either you have a magical Garden of Eden where non-human creatures closely resembling angels, with no hard choices to make and no penalties to pay, browse idly on lotus leaves. Or else you get the remorselessly logical universe we live in, where actions have consequences and you pay dearly for your own mistakes (and those of others).

11   I know there is little consolation in all this for those who have had to watch helplessly while their child died, or for the millions whose loves and hopes lie 40 years buried with the last world war. It is a cruel universe, and knowing why does not make it less cruel. But even God could not have made it any different if he wanted it to be an appropriate home for human beings.

12   It's cold comfort, but maybe there is some consolation to be had in the fact that we're extremely fortunate to have been able to visit the universe even briefly. At the instant of your conception and mine, a million other potential men and women lost their only chance to see the place at all.

■ TOPICAL CONSIDERATIONS

1. In paragraph 5, the author writes: "Any universe which could conceivably be a habitat for human beings must be one in which events have predictable consequences." In your own words explain what he means by this.
2. Why does Dyer say that "Hume had the honesty to answer that he had 'no idea'" (paragraph 3) when asked why God permits bad things to happen? What answer would you give?
3. If God prevented tragedies from happening in the universe, why would that mean there could be no science or technology?
4. According to Dyer, what consolation can we derive from recognizing that we live in a cruel universe?

■ RHETORICAL CONSIDERATIONS

1. What rhetorical strategy is Dyer using when he begins his essay with questions?
2. How well does Dyer illustrate his argument that the universe by necessity must be a cruel place for human habitation?

3. How does the final paragraph encourage appreciation of the universe as we know it? How does it reflect back on the opening paragraph?

■ WRITING ASSIGNMENTS

1. Write an essay supporting Dyer's thesis, using three examples from your own experience.
2. In paragraph 3, we are told that Cardinal Basil Hume, an English clergyman, said he had no idea why God permitted terrible things to occur. In a well-documented essay, write your own answer to the journalist's question.

	The Courage of Turtles
	Edward Hoagland

Edward Hoagland is one of the great essayists of our time. Although he has published novels and travel books, he is perhaps best known for his essays on nature. Here he evokes both the perseverance and the vulnerability of a creature of primordial majesty. Whether describing the turtle's appearance or diet or temperament, Hoagland displays an uncanny ability of making scenes come alive while drawing profound insights from the most common details. Here he captures some remarkable characteristics of turtles. And, yet, in his rich descriptions he sounds a darker note also, for like so many creatures turtles are suffering a loss of habitat. In an understated indictment of our callous age, Hoagland does not exclude himself as you will see in the haunting last lines of this essay. Edward Hoagland is the author of thirteen books, including *Cat Man, African Calliope: A Journey to the Sudan,* and *Walking the Dead Diamond River.* This essay comes from his collection, *The Courage of Turtles* (1985).

1 Turtles are a kind of bird with the governor turned low. With the same attitude of removal, they cock a glance at what is going on, as if they need only to fly away. Until recently they were also a case of virtue rewarded, at least in the town where I grew up, because, being humble creatures, there were plenty of them. Even when we still had a few bobcats in the woods the local snapping turtles, growing up to forty pounds, were the largest carnivores. You would see them through the amber water, as big as greeny wash basins at the bottom of the pond, until they faded into the inscrutable mud as if they hadn't existed at all.

2 When I was ten I went to Dr. Green's Pond, a two-acre pond across the road. When I was twelve I walked a mile or so to Taggart's Pond, which was lusher, had big water snakes and a waterfall; and shortly after that I was bicycling way up to the adventuresome vastness of Mud Pond, a lake-sized body of water in the reservoir

system of a Connecticut city, possessed of cat-backed little islands and empty shacks and a forest of pines and hardwoods along the shore. Otters, foxes and mink left their prints on the bank; there were pike and perch. As I got older, the estates and forgotten back lots in town were parceled out and sold for nice prices, yet, though the woods had shrunk, it seemed that fewer people walked in the woods. The new residents didn't know how to find them. Eventually, exploring, they did find them, and it required some ingenuity and doubling around on my part to go for eight miles without meeting someone. I was grown by now, I lived in New York, and that's what I wanted on the occasional weekends when I came out.

3   Since Mud Pond contained drinking water I had felt confident nothing untoward would happen there. For a long while the developers stayed away, until the drought of the mid-1960s. This event, squeezing the edges in, convinced the local water company that the pond really wasn't a necessity as a catch basin, however; so they bulldozed a hole in the earthen dam, bulldozed the banks to fill in the bottom, and landscaped the flow of water that remained to wind like an English brook and provide a domestic view for the houses which were planned. Most of the painted turtles of Mud Pond, who had been inaccessible as they sunned on their rocks, wound up in boxes in boys' closets within a matter of days. Their footsteps in the dry leaves gave them away as they wandered forlornly. The snappers and the little musk turtles, neither of whom leave the water except once a year to lay their eggs, dug into the drying mud for another siege of hot weather, which they were accustomed to doing whenever the pond got low. But this time it was low for good; the mud baked over them and slowly entombed them. As for the ducks, I couldn't stroll in the woods and not feel guilty, because they were crouched beside every stagnant pothole, or were slinking between the bushes with their heads tucked into their shoulders so that I wouldn't see them. If they decided I had, they beat their way up through the screen of trees, striking their wings dangerously, and wheeled about with that headlong, magnificent velocity to locate another poor puddle.

4   I used to catch possums and black snakes as well as turtles, and I kept dogs and goats. Some summers I worked in a menagerie with the big personalities of the animal kingdom, like elephants and rhinoceroses. I was twenty before these enthusiasms began to wane, and it was then that I picked turtles as the particular animal I wanted to keep in touch with. I was allergic to fur, for one thing, and turtles need minimal care and not much in the way of quarters. They're personable beasts. They see the same colors we do and they seem to see just as well, as one discovers in trying to sneak up on them. In the laboratory they unravel the twists of a maze with the hot-blooded rapidity of a mammal. Though they can't run as fast as a rat, they improve on their errors just as quickly, pausing at each crossroads to look left and right. And they rock rhythmically in place, as we often do, although they are hatched from eggs, not the womb. (A common explanation psychologists give for our pleasure in rocking quietly is that it recapitulates our mother's heartbeat *in utero.*)

5   Snakes, by contrast, are dryly silent and priapic. They are smooth movers, legalistic, unblinking, and they afford the humor which the humorless do. But they make challenging captives; sometimes they don't eat for months on a point of order—if the light isn't right, for instance. Alligators are sticklers too. They're like war-horses,

or German shepherds, and with their bar-shaped, vertical pupils adding emphasis, they have the *idée fixe* of eating, eating, even when they choose to refuse all food and stubbornly die. They delight in tossing a salamander up towards the sky and grabbing him in their long mouths as he comes down. They're so eager that they get the jitters, and they're too much of a proposition for a casual aquarium like mine. Frogs are depressingly defenseless: that moist, extensive back, with the bones almost sticking through. Hold a frog and you're holding its skeleton. Frogs' tasty legs are the staff of life to many animals—herons, raccoons, ribbon snakes—though they themselves are hard to feed. It's not an enviable role to be the staff of life, and after frogs you descend down the evolutionary ladder a big step to fish.

6   Turtles cough, burp, whistle, grunt and hiss, and produce social judgments. They put their heads together amicably enough, but then one drives the other back with the suddenness of two dogs who have been conversing in tones too low for an onlooker to hear. They pee in fear when they're first caught, but exercise both pluck and optimism in trying to escape, walking for hundreds of yards within the confines of their pen, carrying the weight of that cumbersome box on legs which are cruelly positioned for walking. They don't feel that the contest if unfair; they keep plugging, rolling like sailorly souls—a bobbing, infirm gait, a brave, sea-legged momentum—stopping occasionally to study the lay of the land. For me, anyway, they manage to contain the rest of the animal world. They can stretch out their necks like a giraffe, or loom underwater like an apocryphal hippo. They browse on lettuce thrown on the water like a cow moose which is partly submerged. They have a penguin's alertness, combined with a build like a Brontosaurus when they rise up on tiptoe. Then they hunch and ponderously lunge like a grizzly going forward.

7   Baby turtles in a turtle bowl are a puzzle in geometrics. They're as decorative as pansy petals, but they are also self-directed building blocks, propping themselves on one another in different arrangements, before upending the tower. The timid individuals turn fearless, or vice versa. If one gets a bit arrogant he will push the others off the rock and afterwards climb down into the water and cling to the back of one of those he has bullied, tickling him with his hind feet until he bucks like a bronco. On the other hand, when this same milder-mannered fellow isn't exerting himself, he will stare right into the face of the sun for hours. What could be more lionlike? And he's at home in or out of the water and does lots of metaphysical tilting. He sinks and rises, with an infinity of levels to choose from; or, elongating himself, he climbs out on the land again to perambulate, sits boxed in his box, and finally slides back in the water, submerging into dreams.

8   I have five of these babies in a kidney-shaped bowl. The hatchling, who is a painted turtle, is not as large as the top joint of my thumb. He eats chicken gladly. Other foods he will attempt to eat but not with sufficient perseverance to succeed because he's so little. The yellow-bellied terrapin is probably a yearling, and he eats salad voraciously, but no meat, fish or fowl. The Cumberland terrapin won't touch salad or chicken but eats fish and all of the meats except for bacon. The little snapper, with a black crenelated shell, feasts on any kind of meat, but rejects greens and fish. The fifth of the turtles is African. I acquired him only recently and don't know him well. A mottled brown, he unnerves the green turtles, dragging their food off to

his lairs. He doesn't seem to want to be green—he bites the algae off his shell, hanging meanwhile at daring, steep, head-first angles.

9   The snapper was a Ferdinand until I provided him with deeper water. Now he snaps at my pencil with his downturned and fearsome mouth, his swollen face like a napalm victim's. The Cumberland has an elliptical red mark on the side of his green-and-yellow head. He is benign by nature and ought to be as elegant as his scientific name (*Pseudemys scripta elegans*), except he has contracted a disease of the air bladder which has permanently inflated it; he floats high in the water at an undignified slant and can't go under. There may have been internal bleeding, too, because his carapace is stained along its ridge. Unfortunately, like flowers, baby turtles often die. Their mouths fill up with a white fungus and their lungs with pneumonia. Their organs clog up from the rust in the water, or diet troubles, and, like a dying man's, their eyes and heads become too prominent. Toward the end, the edge of the shell becomes flabby as felt and folds around them like a shroud.

10   While they live they're like puppies. Although they're vivacious, they would be a bore to be with all the time, so I also have an adult wood turtle about six inches long. Her shell is the equal of any seashell for sculpturing, even a Cellini shell; it's like an old, dusty, richly engraved medallion dug out of a hillside. Her legs are salmon-orange bordered with black and protected by canted, heroic scales. Her plastron—the bottom shell—is splotched like a margay cat's coat, with black ocelli on a yellow background. It is convex to make room for the female organs inside, whereas a male's would be concave to help him fit tightly on top of her. Altogether, she exhibits every camouflage color on her limbs and shells. She has a turtleneck neck, a tail like an elephant's, wise old pachydermous hind legs and the face of a turkey—except that when I carry her she gazes at the passing ground with a hawk's eyes and mouth. Her feet fit to the fingers of my hand, one to each one, and she rides looking down. She can walk on the floor in perfect silence, but usually she lets her shell knock portentously, like a footstep, so that she resembles some grand, concise, slow-moving lid. But if an earthworm is presented, she jerks swiftly ahead, poises above it and strikes like a mongoose, consuming it with wild vigor. Yet she will climb on my lap to eat bread or boiled eggs.

11   If put into a creek, she swims like a cutter, nosing forward to intercept a strange turtle and smell him. She drifts with the current to go downstream, maneuvering behind a rock when she wants to take stock, or sinking to the nether levels, while bubbles float up. Getting out, choosing her path, she will proceed a distance and dig into a pile of humus, thrusting herself to the coolest layer at the bottom. The hole closes over her until it's as small as a mouse's hole. She's not as aquatic as a musk turtle, not quite as terrestrial as the box turtles in the same woods, but because of her versatility she's marvelous, she's everywhere. And though she breathes the way we breathe, with scarcely perceptible movements of her chest, sometimes instead she pumps her throat ruminatively, like a pipe smoker sucking and puffing. She waits and blinks, pumping her throat, turning her head, then sets off like a loping tiger in slow motion, hurdling the jungly lumber, the pea vine and twigs. She estimates angles so well that when she rides over the rocks, sliding down a drop-off with her rugged front legs extended, she has the grace of a rodeo mare.

12　　But she's well off to be with me rather than at Mud Pond. The other turtles have fled—those that aren't baked into the bottom. Creeping up the brooks to sad, constricted marshes, burdened as they are with that box on their backs, they're walking into a setup where all their enemies move thirty times faster than they. It's like the nightmare most of us have whimpered through, where we are weighted down disastrously while trying to flee; fleeing our home ground, we try to run.

13　　I've seen turtles in still worst straits. On Broadway, in New York, there is a penny arcade which used to sell baby terrapins that were scrawled with bon mots in enamel paint, such as KISS ME BABY. The manager turned out to be a wholesaler as well, and once I asked him whether he had any larger turtles to sell. He took me upstairs to a loft room devoted to the turtle business. There were desks for the paper work and a series of racks that held shallow tin bins atop one another, each with several hundred babies crawling around in it. He was a smudgy-complexioned, serious fellow and he did have a few adult terrapins, but I was going to school and wasn't actually planning to buy; I'd only wanted to see them. They were aquatic turtles, but here they went without water, presumably for weeks, lurching about in those dry bins like handicapped citizens, living on gumption. An easel where the artist worked stood in the middle of the floor. She had a palette and a clip attached for fastening the babies in place. She wore a smock and a beret, and was homely, short and eccentric-looking, with funny black hair, like some of the ladies who show their paintings in Washington Square in May. She had a cold, she was smoking, and her hand wasn't very steady, although she worked quickly enough. The smile that she produced for me would have looked giddy if she had been happier, or drunk. Of course the turtles' doom was sealed when she painted them, because their bodies inside would continue to grow but their shells would not. Gradually, invisibly, they would be crushed. Around us their bellies—two thousand belly shells—rubbed on the bins with a mournful, momentous hiss.

14　　Somehow there were so many of them I didn't rescue one. Years later, however, I was walking on First Avenue when I noticed a basket of living turtles in front of a fish store. They were as dry as a heap of old bones in the sun; nevertheless, they were creeping over one another gimpily, doing their best to escape. I looked and was touched to discover that they appeared to be wood turtles, my favorites, so I bought one. In my apartment I looked closer and realized that in fact this was a diamondback terrapin, which was bad news. Diamondbacks are tidewater turtles from brackish estuaries, and I had no sea water to keep him in. He spent his days thumping interminably against the baseboards, pushing for an opening through the wall. He drank thirstily but would not eat and had none of the hearty, accepting qualities of wood turtles. He was morose, paler in color, sleeker and more Oriental in the carved ridges and rings that formed his shell. Though I felt sorry for him, finally I found his unrelenting presence exasperating. I carried him, struggling in a paper bag, across town to the Morton Street Pier on the Hudson. It was August but gray and windy. He was very surprised when I tossed him in; for the first time in our association, I think, he was afraid. He looked afraid as he bobbed about on top of the water, looking up at me from ten feet below. Though we were both accustomed to his resistance and rigidity, seeing him still pitiful, I recognized that I must have done the wrong thing. At least the river was salty, but it was also bottomless; the waves were too rough for him, and the tide was coming in, bumping him against the pilings underneath the pier. Too late, I realized that he wouldn't be able to swim to a peaceful inlet in New Jersey, even if he could figure out which way to swim. But since, short of diving in after him, there was nothing I could do, I walked away.

■ TOPICAL CONSIDERATIONS

1. What would you say is the main idea in Hoagland's essay? Is he trying to convince you of something? If so, what?
2. Why might Hoagland write, "I couldn't stroll in the woods and not feel guilty" (paragraph 3)? Have you ever felt a similar guilt involving animals or nature?
3. The author tells readers why he keeps turtles as pets. Can you summarize these reasons? Point to specific passages to explain your answer.
4. Why might Hoagland think that it is important to tell the reader what different kinds of turtles like to eat?
5. Hoagland describes turtles in a variety of ways. For example, he writes that they are "a puzzle in geometrics," "decorative," and "self-directed building blocks" (paragraph 7). Why might he choose these descriptions?
6. In paragraph 12, Hoagland describes the "nightmare most of us have whimpered through." Why does he describe this nightmare?
7. What is the purpose of the story about the penny arcade? What impression does Hoagland want you to take away after reading it? How does the description of the artist painting the turtles' shells contribute to the thesis of the essay?
8. What does Hoagland mean by the line, "They were aquatic turtles, but here they went without water, presumably for weeks, lurching about in those dry bins like handicapped citizens living on gumption" (paragraph 13)?
9. How does Hoagland's conclusion relate to his main point? Might it be a metaphor for something? What were your feelings as you finished the essay?

■ RHETORICAL CONSIDERATIONS

1. In paragraph 2 Hoagland writes, "though the woods had shrunk, it seemed that fewer people walked in the woods. The new residents didn't know how to find them." What does he mean by this remark? How would you describe the tone here?
2. Why might Hoagland have named this essay, "The Courage of Turtles"? What particularly courageous qualities of turtles does he point to?
3. What is the intended effect of the statement. "Turtles cough, burp, whistle, grunt and hiss, and produce social judgments" (paragraph 6)? What do all of these habits have in common?

4. Hoagland describes the shell of his adult wood turtle as an "old, dusty, richly engraved medallion dug out of a hillside" (paragraph 10). Analyze each element of the description—the modifiers, the dug-up engraved medal-lion analogy—and explain how the particular words contribute to the over-all image projected. Did the description successfully capture for you the turtle?

5. Hoagland, in paragraph 6, says that turtles "manage to contain the rest of the animal world." How does he back up this claim? Name some of the animals he compares turtles to. In what different ways does he say turtles are like human beings?

6. Why might Hoagland choose to write very specifically about his adult wood turtle (paragraphs 10 and 11)?

7. In paragraph 12, Hoagland echoes some of his introductory remarks about turtles "baked" into the bottom of Mud Pond. What is his purpose in returning to this image of "entombment" (paragraph 3)?

8. The first line of Hoagland's conclusion reads, "Somehow there were so many of them I didn't rescue one" (paragraph 14). What is the effect of this line? Do you think this conclusion is appropriate given what went before?

■ WRITING ASSIGNMENTS

1. Write an essay in which you develop thoughts about an animal in nature as Hoagland does. Include facts, details, and information about the habits and characteristics of the creature. What particular qualities, human or otherwise, do you attribute to the animal? Can your animal serve as a metaphor for something?

2. Hoagland makes some wonderfully vivid and insightful observations of turtles. Write your own observations but reverse the point of view. That is, describe humans through the eyes of a turtle or some other creature of the wild.

3. Would you have written a different ending to Hoagland's essay? If so, what would it have been? Write a letter to Mr. Hoagland explaining your changes and the reasons for them.

4. Write an essay in which you discuss the joys and rewards you've experienced exploring nature. Pick a particular experience you have had, and use specific details to make it come alive.

5. Write an essay in which you argue the need to protect endangered species even at the expense of industrial and economic growth.

6. Extinction is an irrefutable law of nature as evidenced by the thousands of different species preserved in fossils. Write an essay arguing that attempts to protect endangered species are costly and vain efforts to reverse a natural process.

A Path of More Resistance

Bill McKibben

Confronted with the sobering realization that the world of nature is endangered by a lifestyle of accumulation and growth, Bill McKibben offers a solution—a voluntary simplification of lifestyles. He sketches out a humble, simple alternative in which human happiness is secondary to the survival of the natural world. He suggests a life of reduced material possessions—a small wardrobe, few essentials, and almost no luxuries—of growing one's own food, and of burning as little fossil fuel as necessary. Could we conform to such a stripped-down life? Do we really have a choice? Bill McKibben has written many articles on nature which have appeared in *The New Yorker,* the *New York Review of Books* and *The New York Times.* He and his wife live in the Adirondack Mountains of New York. This piece was taken from his book *The End of Nature* published in 1989.

1   A half hour's hike brings my dog and me to the top of the hill behind my house. I know the hill well by now, each gully and small creek, each big rock, each opening around the edges. I know the places where the deer come, and the coyotes after them. It is no Bald Mountain, no unlogged virgin forest with trees ten feet around, but it is a deep and quiet and lovely place all the same.

2   Only the thought of what will happen as the new weather kicks in darkens my view: the trees dying, the hillside unable to hold its soil against the rainfall, the gullies sharpening, the deer looking for ever-scarcer browse. And, finally, the scrub and brush colonizing the slopes, clinging to what soil remains. Either that or the cemetery rows of perfect, heat-tolerant genetically improved pines.

3   From the top of the hill, if I stand on a certain ledge, I can see my house down below, white against the hemlocks. I can see my whole material life—the car, the bedroom, the chimney above the stove. I like that life, I like it enormously. But a choice seems unavoidable. Either that life down there changes, perhaps dramatically, or this life all around me up here changes—passes away.

4   That is a terrible choice. Two years ago, when I got married, my wife and I had the standard hopes and dreams, and their fulfillment seemed not so far away. We love to travel; we had set up our lives so that work wouldn't tie us down. Our house is nice and big—it seemed only a matter of time before it would fill with the racket of children.

5   As the consequences of the greenhouse effect have become clearer to us, though, we've started to prune and snip our desires. Instead of taking long vacation trips in the car, we ride our bikes on the road by the house. Instead of building a wood-fired hot tub for the backyard (the closest I've ever come to real decadence), we installed exciting new thermal-pane windows. Most of our other changes have been similarly small. We heat with our wood, and we try to keep the house at 55 degrees. We drive much less frequently; we shop twelve times a year, and there are weeks when we do not venture out at all. Though I'm a lousy gardener, I try to grow more and more of our food.

6 Still, those are the easy things, especially if you live in the country. And they're as much pleasure as sacrifice. It may be icy in most of the house but it's warm cuddled by the stove. I like digging in the garden, though it makes me more nervous than it did when it was pure hobby: if a storm knocks down a tomato plant, I feel slightly queasy. If we don't travel great distances and constantly see new sights, we have come to know the few square miles around us in every season and mood.

7 But there are harder changes, too, places where the constricting world has begun to bind and pinch. It is dawning on me and my wife that the world we inhabit is not the world we grew up in, the world where our hopes and dreams were formed. That responsibility may mean something new and sad. In other words, we try very hard not to think about how much we'd like a baby.

8 And it may take even more. Sometimes I stand on top of the hill and wonder if someday we'll need to move away, perhaps live closer to other people. Probably that would be more energy-efficient. Would I love the woods enough to leave them behind? I stand up there and look out over the mountain to the east and the lake to the south and the rippling wilderness knolls stretching off to the west—and to the house below with the line of blue smoke trailing out of the chimney. One world or the other will have to change.

9 And if it is the human world that changes—if this humbler idea begins to win out—what will the planet look like? Will it appeal only to screwballs, people who thrive on a monthly shower and no steady income?

10 It's hard to draw a detailed picture—it's so much easier to picture the defiant future, for it is merely the extension of our current longings. I've spent my whole life wanting more, so it's hard for me to imagine "less" in any but a negative way. But that imagination is what counts. Changing the way we think is at the heart of the question. If it ever happens, the actions will follow.

11 For example, to cope with the greenhouse problem, people may need to install more efficient washing machines. But if you buy such a machine and yet continue to feel that it's both your right and your joy to have a big wardrobe, then the essential momentum of our course won't be broken. For big wardrobes imply a world pretty much like our own, where people pile up possessions, and where human desire is the only measure that counts. Even if such a world somehow licks the greenhouse effect, it will still fall in a second for, say, the cornucopia of genetic engineering. On the other hand, you could slash your stock of clothes to a comfortable (or even uncomfortable) minimum and then chip in with your neighbors to buy a more efficient washing machine to which you would lug your dirty laundry. If we reached that point—the point where great closetfuls of clothes seemed slightly absurd, *unnatural*—then we might have begun to climb down from the tottering perch where we currently cling.

12 "Absurd" and "unnatural" are different from "wrong" or "immoral." This is not a moral argument. There are plenty of good reasons having to do with aesthetics or whimsy to own lots of sharp clothes. (And many more and much better reasons to, say, drive cars or raise large families.) But those reasons may be outweighed by the burden that such desires place on the natural world. And if we could see that clearly, then our thinking might change of its own accord.

13   In this particular example, the thinking is more radical than the action. If we decided against huge wardrobes (which is to say, against a whole way of looking at ourselves) and against every family's owning a washer (which is to say, against a pervasive individual consumerism), then taking your clothes down the street to wash them would be the most obvious idea in the world. If people *hadn't* changed their minds about such things, these would be obnoxious developments—you'd need to employ secret police to make sure they weren't washing in private. It wouldn't be worth it, and it wouldn't work. But if we had changed our minds, our current ways of life might soon seem as bizarre as the six thousand shoes of Imelda Marcos.

14   It's normal to imagine that this humbler world would resemble the past. Simply because the atmosphere was cleaner a century ago, though, there's no call to forget all that's been developed since. My wife and I just acquired a fax machine, for instance, on the premise that it makes for graceful, environmentally sound communication—an advanced way to do with less. But if communication prospered in a humbler world, transportation might well wither, as people began to live closer not only to their work but to their food supply. Oranges all year round—oranges at any season in the northern latitudes—might prove ambitious beyond our means, just as the tropics might have to learn to do without apples. We—or, at least, our grandchildren—might come to use the "appropriate technologies" of "sustainable development" that we urge on peasants through organizations like the Peace Corps—bicycle-powered pumps, solar cookstoves, and so on. And, as in a less developed country (a phrase that would probably turn into a source of some pride), more Westerners might find their work connected directly with their supper. That is to say, they would farm, which begins to sound a little quaint, a little utopian.

15   But conventional utopian ideas are not much help, either. Invariably they are designed to advance human happiness, which is found to be suffering as the result of crowding or stress or lack of meaningful work or not enough sex or too much sex. Machinery is therefore abolished, or cities abandoned, or families legislated against—but it's all in the name of man. Dirt under your nails will make you happier!

16   The humbler world I am describing is just the opposite. Human happiness would be of secondary importance. Perhaps it would be best for the planet if we all lived not in kibbutzes or on Jeffersonian farms, but crammed into a few huge cities like so many ants. I doubt a humbler world would be one big happy Pennsylvania Dutch colony. Certain human sadnesses might diminish; other human sadnesses would swell. But that would be beside the point. This is not an attempt at a utopia—as I said, I'm happy now. It's a stab at something else—an "atopia," perhaps—where our desires are not the engine.

17   The ground rules for such an atopia would be few enough. We would have to conquer the desire to grow in numbers; the human population would need to get gradually smaller, though how much smaller is an open question. Some deep ecologists say the human population shouldn't exceed a hundred million, others a billion or two—roughly our population a century ago. And those people would need to use

less in the way of resources—not just oil, but wood and water and chemicals and even land itself. Those are the essentials. But they are practical rules, not moral ones. Within them, a thousand cultures—vegetarian and hunter, communal and hermitic—could still exist.

18   A pair of California professors, George Sessions and Bill Devall, listed what they saw as some of the principles of deep ecology in a book (*Deep Ecology*) they published several years ago. Although the work shows its West Coast origins at times (there is some discussion of how this philosophy could give us "joyous confidence to dance with the sensuous harmonies discovered through spontaneous, playful intercourse with the rhythms of our bodies, the rhythms of flowing water"), it is frank about the sharp contrast between the current worldview and their proposed replacement: instead of material and economic growth, "elegantly simple" material needs; instead of consumerism, "doing with enough." It is frank, too, in its acknowledgment that deep ecology—that humility—is an infant philosophy, with many questions yet to be asked, much less answered: Exactly how much is enough? Or, what about poor people?

19   Those are hard questions—but perhaps not beyond our imagination. When we decided that accumulation and growth were our economic ideals, we invented wills and lending at interest and puritanism and supersonic aircraft. Why would we come up with ideas less powerful in an all-out race to do with less?

20   The difficulty is almost certainly more psychological than intellectual—less that we can't figure out major alterations in our way of life than that we simply don't want to. Even if our way of life has destroyed nature and endangered the planet, it is so hard to imagine living in any other fashion. The people whose lives may point the way—Thoreau, say, or Gandhi—we dismiss as exceptional, a polite way of saying there is no reason we should be expected to go where they pointed. The challenge they presented with the physical examples of their lives is much more subversive than anything they wrote or said: if they could live those simple lives, it's no use saying we could not. I could, I suppose, get by on half the money I currently spend. A voluntary simplification of life-styles is not beyond our abilities, but it is probably outside our desires.

21   And our desires count. Nothing is necessarily going to force us to live humbly; we are free to chance the other, defiant route and see what happens. The only thing we absolutely must do is cut back immediately on our use of fossil fuels. That is not an option; we need to do it in order to choose any other future. But there is no certainty we must simultaneously cut back on our material desires—not if we're willing to live in a world ever more estranged from nature. Both the defiant and the humble alternatives offer ways to adapt to the greenhouse effect, this total upheaval. They present us with a choice.

22   The obvious objection to this choice is that it does not exist: that man always pushes restlessly ahead, that it's inevitable, biological, part of "human nature." That is a cop-out, at least intellectually—that is, it may be true, but those of us who have thought about the question still have the moral burden of making a choice. Anyway, there are examples of civilizations, chiefly Eastern ones, that by choice spent cen

turies almost suspended in time. I *can* imagine a world in which we decide not to conduct genetic experiments or to build new dams, just as a few people in the late nineteenth century began to imagine forests that were not logged and so preserved the Adirondacks. As I said, I'm not certain what that world would look like. Probably it would have to develop an enormously powerful social taboo against "progress" of the defiant kind—a religious or quasi-religious horror at the thought of "improved chickens" and large families. And I'm not saying I see the path from here to any of the possible theres; my point is merely that, for the purpose of argument, I can imagine such a world. Possession of a certain technology imposes on us no duty to use it.

23   A second obvious objection is that perhaps we needn't decide now, that surely we can leave it for some future generation to figure out. That is an attractive idea and a traditional one; we have been putting off this particular question since at least 1864, when George Perkins Marsh, the first modern environmentalist, wrote that by our tree cutting and swamp draining we were "breaking up the floor and wainscotting and doors and window-frames of our dwelling for fuel to warm our bodies."

24   I have tried to explain, though, why it cannot be put off any longer. We just happen to be living at the moment when the carbon dioxide has increased to an intolerable level. We just happen to be alive at the moment when if nothing is done before we die the world's tropical rain forests will become a brown girdle around the planet that will last for millennia. It's simply our poor luck; it might have been nicer to have been born in 1890 and died in 1960, confident that everything was looking up. We just happen to be living in the decade when genetic engineering is acquiring a momentum that will soon be unstoppable. The comforting idea that we could decide to use such technology to, in the words of Lewis Thomas, cure "most of the unsolved diseases on society's agenda" and then not use it to straighten trees or grow giant trout seems implausible to me: we're already doing those things.

25   One needs, obviously, to be wary of millennialism. And it's perhaps not fair that those of us currently alive should have to deal with these developments. On the other hand, it wasn't fair that our fathers had to go fight Hitler. The American Methodist Church has just adopted a new hymnal, and, along with the usual wrangles over sexism and militarism and so on, there was a dispute over a marvelous Civil War–era hymn by James Russell Lowell. "Once to Every Man and Nation," it begins, "comes the moment to decide, / In the strife of truth with falsehood, for the good or evil side. / Some great cause, God's new messiah, offering each the bloom or blight, / And the choice goes by forever, / 'Twixt the darkness and the light." The hymnal committee reportedly decided against the tune on the grounds that it was unsound theology—that once was not enough, that it was never too late for a person to reform. But this was one of Martin Luther King's favorite hymns, and in terms of public policy, if not personal salvation, I fear it may be all too true.

26   Of these two paths which one will we choose? It's impossible to know for certain, but there's no question but that the momentum of our age ceaselessly hurries us ahead, making it horribly difficult to choose the humble path and incredibly easy to follow the defiant one.

27   I have a neighbor, a logger whom I'll call Jim Franklin. Jim honestly believes that the cause of acid rain in the Adirondacks is "too many trees," the result of environmentalists' setting too much land aside as wilderness. He has worked out a theory, something about the mat of pine needles accumulating on the ground, which I can't begin to repeat even though I have heard it several times. "I told it to the forest ranger and he just looked at me," says Jim, as if this were proof of the conspiracy. We believe things because we have a need to believe them. (That is not a novel insight, I realize.) Jim wants to log for economic reasons and for reasons that might be described as psychological or cultural, and he has constructed an idea to support his desire. But it is not a lie: he believes it to be true. Muir, on his thousand-mile stroll to the Gulf of Mexico, met a man in a particularly backward section of North Carolina who said to him: "I believe in Providence. Our fathers came into these valleys, got the richest of them, and skimmed the cream of the soil. The worn-out ground won't yield no roasting ears now. But the Lord foresaw this state of affairs and prepared something else for us. And what is it? Why, He meant us to bust open these copper mines and gold mines, so that we may have money to buy the corn we cannot raise." Though this argument has its obvious weaknesses, it is immensely appealing, just as the thought of a new genetically engineered cornucopia is appealing: it means we wouldn't have to change.

28   And we don't want to change. Jim wants to log as he always has. I want to be able to drive as I always have and go on living in the large house I live in and so on. The tidal force of biology continues to govern us, even when we realize (as no lemming can) that we're doing something stupid. This genetic inheritance from millions of years when it did make sense to grow and expand can't simply be shrugged off.

29   And the opposing forces are so weak. In a curious way, for example, some environmentalists have made it easier for people to ignore global threats. In the late 1960s and early 1970s, a spate of horror books came out—books filled with the direst predictions. "At the current rate of population increase, there will be a billion billion people on the face of the earth, or seventeen hundred for every square mile," wrote Paul Ehrlich. "Projecting this farther into the future, in about two thousand or three thousand years people would weigh more than the earth; in five thousand years everything in the visible universe would be converted into people, and their expansion would be at the speed of light." While this was technically true, it was also so unrealistic that we could safely ignore it. The greenhouse effect, he wrote, might raise ocean levels two hundred and fifty feet. "Gondola to the Empire State Building, anyone? he asked. "Lake Erie has died. . . . Lake Michigan will soon follow it into extinction."

30   But that didn't happen. Lake Erie rose again—still sick, of course, but not dead. The oil crisis eased and then turned into an oil glut. The greenhouse effect could realistically raise the sea level ten feet, which is plenty bad enough but sounds like nothing next to two hundred and fifty. With every unfulfilled apocalyptic projection, our confidence in the environmentalists has waned, our belief that we'll muddle through been bolstered.

31   We'll look for almost any reason not to change our attitudes; the inertia of the established order is powerful. If we can think of a plausible, or even implausible,

reason to discount environmental warnings, we will. If a solitary scientist says, as S. Fred Singer did in a recent issue of the *Wall Street Journal,* that the greenhouse effect is a "Mixture of fact and fancy," we read it to mean that the whole business is nonsense. And if we can imagine a plausible reason to believe that it will all be okay—if someone tells us that we can "manage" the planet, for instance—the temptation is to believe him. In 1980, when Ronald Reagan ran for the presidency, he made his shrillest attacks on the idea that we might be living in an "age of limits." This notion, perhaps the first necessary recognition on the road to a new relationship with the earth, a first baby step on a thousand-mile journey toward deep ecology, had gained some small currency with Carter administration officials. But Reagan attacked it mercilessly. Occasionally, as when he announced that trees pollute, he got in a little trouble. But the country forgave him, because it wanted to believe him— wanted to believe that, even though the shadows seemed to be lengthening, it was "morning in America." Unfortunately, optimism didn't aid the ozone layer.

■ TOPICAL CONSIDERATIONS

1. What is McKibben's main point? Is he trying to convince the reader of something? Did he convince you of anything? What is "the choice" that McKibben talks about in paragraphs 3 and 4?

2. In paragraph 4, McKibben talks about his "standard hopes and dreams." What are they? By whose standards is he weighing these "hopes and dreams"? Do you see certain assumptions from which he is writing the essay? Do your "hopes and dreams" differ from the standard? If so, how?

3. What are the positive and the negative aspects of the lifestyle that McKibben describes in paragraph 5? What parts of your current lifestyle would have to change? Would you be willing to make such "sacrifices"? Explain.

4. Why does McKibben write, "This is not a moral argument" (paragraph 12)? Does McKibben anticipate a counterargument?

5. What are the distinctions that McKibben makes between "utopia" and "atopia" (paragraphs 14–17)? Why are these important distinctions? What are his "ground rules for the 'atopia'" (paragraph 17)? Do you think that these are feasible goals? In your opinion, are any of them more feasible or more necessary than others?

6. McKibben admits the difficulty of carrying out his suggestions. Discuss his distinction between "ability" and "desire" that he discusses in paragraph 20.

7. In paragraph 22, McKibben writes, "Possession of a certain technology imposes on us no duty to use it." Do you agree or disagree with this statement? Can you think of particular technologies that McKibben might be referring to? Can you create your own list?

8. What technique does McKibben use to convince us to take action now?

9. Why might McKibben tell readers the story of "Jim Franklin" (paragraph 27)? How does the story contribute to his text? Did it change your attitude at all? Might it make you alter your behavior? Explain your answer.

10. McKibben writes, "some environmentalists have made it easier for people to ignore global threats" (paragraph 29). Why might he make this seemingly contradictory statement? Do you agree with him?

■ RHETORICAL CONSIDERATIONS

1. What is the effect of the repetition in paragraph 1: "I know . . . I know"?
2. In paragraph 3, McKibben changes the vocabulary he uses. He writes, "this life all around me up here changes—passes away." Why does he alter his words from *changes* to *passes away?*
3. Why does McKibben use words like "constricting," "bind," and "pinch" (paragraph 7)?
4. Does McKibben manage to keep an objective outlook? Can you find any lapses into subjectivity?
5. Why might McKibben put words like "absurd," "unnatural," "wrong," and "immoral" (paragraph 12) in quotation marks?
6. How would you characterize McKibben's tone throughout the essay? Does it change at all?
7. How does McKibben's conclusion affect how you react to his subject matter? Why might he invoke the examples of Jimmy Carter and Ronald Reagan?

■ WRITING ASSIGNMENTS

1. Try to imagine making some of the drastic changes in lifestyle that McKibben describes. Do you think you could adjust to the "sacrifices"—to the loss of luxuries, modern conveniences, and consumer commodities to which you have grown accustomed? Could you find satisfaction in growing your own food? Write up your ideas in a paper.
2. Do you think you could live the rest of your life without television and still be happy? Write an essay in which you explore that possibility. Examine whether you think your life would be changed for better or for worse.
3. For the good of the environment, would you be willing to switch from the automobile to a bicycle? Write a paper in which you answer this question. Try to imagine the circumstances that would so motivate you.
4. Consider the difference between a "utopia" and an "atopia." In a well-supported essay, discuss both of these ideas and describe the ideal human-centered world as opposed to the ideal world.
5. One of the major causes of environmental decline is the burning of fossil fuels. Raising the gasoline tax over the next five years would spur conservation of fuel. Would you be willing to pay an extra 50 cents for a gallon of gasoline if it would help save the environment? Write an essay in which you answer this question and explore the reasons.
6. Write a letter to your congressman (or to the president) in which you call for increased funding for research on alternate energy sources, including solar power and safe designs for nuclear reactors.

7. Write a paper in which you argue for or against laws requiring households to sort garbage into recyclable and nonrecyclable items.
8. Write a paper in which you argue for or against hypothetical tax laws penalizing married couples who have more than two children.

The Cry of the Ocean

Peter Steinhart

Many of us take the oceans of the world for granted. We see them as endless in time, space, and resources. Nevertheless, demand and high-tech efficiency are reducing marine life. According to a recent report of the United Nation's Food and Agriculture Organization, over 60 percent of fish populations they monitor were fully exploited or depleted. Such a mad mining of life, says Peter Steinhart, threatens the future of humanity—half of which "still lives within 50 miles of the coast." What can be done?

Peter Steinhart, author of *Tracks in the Sky* and *California's Wild Heritage,* writes about nature and environmental affairs. This essay first appeared in *Mother Jones* in August 1994.

1 Life on Earth began in the moonpull and seawind of the oceans. Human blood still has the salinity of seawater. We are, ourselves, miniature oceans, dressed in skin and gone exploring the arid world that rose out of ancient seas. We haven't gone far: Half the world's population still lives within 50 miles of the coast.

2 Nonetheless, our acquaintance with the sea generally ends at the first slap of ocean wave; what happens beyond the surf is hidden. But what is happening out there is something we should be angry about.

3 The signs are ominous. On a good day in the 1960s, an Atlantic fisherman could harpoon 30 large swordfish. Today, such swordfish are hardly ever seen; commercial fishermen on the East Coast set out a 15-to-30-mile line baited with 1,000 hooks. Even then, many they catch are immature.

4 What has happened to swordfish has happened to hundreds of marine species. In the last 15 years, New England cod, haddock, and yellowtail flounder have declined 70 percent; South Atlantic grouper and snapper, 80 percent; Atlantic bluefin tuna, 90 percent. More than 200 separate salmon spawning runs have vanished from the Pacific Northwest.

5 We are mining the seas of life. The number of fish caught in 11 of the world's 15 major fishing areas has declined from peak years, and four areas are at or near peak catch.

6 The human cost of this crisis is considerable. For many it means hunger, since in some countries more than half of the population's animal protein comes from the sea. Says Michael Sutton of the World Wildlife Fund, "Unlike rhinos, tigers, and bears, when you deplete fish populations, you're threatening the survival of humanity."

7   For others, it means the end of a way of life. The collapse of the Newfoundland cod fishery put 40,000 people out of work. In the Philippines, as traditional fishing by net and spear yields smaller and smaller returns, divers stay down 150 or 200 feet for hours, breathing air pumped through hoses, in hopes of spearing a profitable catch. In some villages, paralysis and brain damage caused by submersion at such depths is now a common affliction.

8   For centuries, people have gone to sea with heroic madness in their eyes. We went out to lift from the depths not just food but something mystical. We looked upon fish as castoffs from another world, as strange shapes and distant wills. We went to tempt the shimmering darkness and pull it into the light.

9   Even today, fish seem to us cold, silvery dreams to which we do not attribute a capacity for thought or feeling. We feel no remorse when the dazzle fades from their scales. We have never thought of fish as fellow creatures, and we do not—deep down—think of the sea as part of the living world.

10   In our technological age, such thinking has terrible consequences. Our ancient awe now floats in steel hulls, dragging multifilament net over miles of seabed to pull masses of life from the ocean. A modern North Pacific trawler can reportedly take in one million pounds of fish in a single day.

11   Since World War II, nation after nation has built fleets of such vessels, and as a result the world's finfish catch quadrupled between 1950 and 1990. It looked for a time as if the sea were an inexhaustible source of wealth.

12   But that was an illusion. Most of the increased catch came from a few distant water fisheries, whose limits were quickly reached. Meanwhile, coastal fishermen had to sail farther and farther from port to catch anything.

13   Large-scale fishing technologies have become less and less selective: Fish too small to be taken and species not legally fished are caught, and then thrown overboard to die. Lee Alverson of Seattle's Natural Resources Consultants estimates that in addition to the estimated 84 million metric tons of marine fish legally landed in the world each year, approximately 27 million metric tons are caught and dumped at sea. With an unreported catch that may be as high as 30 percent of the legal take, we are removing far more than the 100 million metric tons of marine fish that scientists estimate is the globe's maximum sustainable yearly harvest.

14   We like to think of the oceans as so vast and ancient as to be above greed or vanity. Byron wrote, "Man marks the earth with ruin—his control stops with the shore." But we now have the technological capacity to do to fish exactly what we did to the buffalo and the passenger pigeon.

15   We are reducing the oceans' productivity. We risk hunger, poverty, dislocation, and war. We destroy links to our evolutionary past and to the future. We turn our backs on the world and lose its kindness.

16   What can we do? Refusing to eat fish doesn't even begin to address the problem because others will assume our place. We must reduce the size of the world's fishing fleet, set new limits, and enforce them.

17   Government agencies are investigating restrictions on the gear fishermen may use, as one way to limit catch. More effective area limits and fishing quotas may also

be required. For these or other controls to work, however, we need international agreements binding all nations to a common set of rules.

18   Unless we find new ways to care for the sea, we will be its darkest legacy. Cast up from its depths millions of years ago, we may now be the agents of its destruction.

■ TOPICAL CONSIDERATIONS

1. What signs of the depletion of marine life does Steinhart see, and what are the consequences of this depletion for humanity?
2. According to Steinhart how does our non-anthropomorphic view of marine life fuel our depletion of the fishes of the sea? Does Steinhart share this non-anthropomorphic view or not? Cite passages to illustrate his perceptions.
3. In your opinion which paragraph offers the most potent indictment of modern fishing technologies?
4. Of the several recommendations to curb modern fishing technologies Steinhart makes, which do you think would be the most effective? The least? Why?
5. Recalling the previous essay, what kind of recommendations would Bill McKibben make to slow down or stop the overfishing of the seas? Read the next essay and consider what recommendations Edward Abbey would make. How would they differ, if at all, from Steinhart's recommendations?

■ RHETORICAL CONSIDERATIONS

1. In paragraph 1, what relationship is established between humans and the sea? How does this relationship differ with the one described in paragraph 2? Do these two paragraphs make an effective introduction to the essay? Why or why not?
2. Steinhart shifts tones in this essay from prophetic and biblical to straightforward and objective. Find examples of each of these styles. Explain Steinhart's purpose in shifting tone several times in the essay.
3. How does the last paragraph of the essay complete the thoughts expressed in the first and second paragraphs of the essay?

■ WRITING ASSIGNMENTS

1. Write a paragraph in which you elaborate on Byron's statement "Man marks the earth with ruin—his control stops with the shore." Demonstrate the truth or falsity of this statement with references to the state of the earth's oceans today.

2. Write an essay in which you compare the approaches that might be advocated by Peter Steinhart, Bill McKibben and Edward Abbey in response to the spoiling and depletion of the oceans.

3. Write a research paper on one of the following topics or a related topic of your own: government efforts to enforce limits on commercial fishing in U.S. waters; the effect of quotas on certain fishing communities; efforts to resupply reduced stock by commercial farming of certain fish species.

Eco-Defense
Edward Abbey

Edward Abbey was a sort of underground hero to the environmental movement. An impassioned environmentalist and irreverent writer, he dreamed of seeing "the whole American West made into a wilderness." He was born in Appalachia and worked off and on for both the National Park Service and the U.S. Forest Service. He wrote essays and seven novels, the most famous of which is *The Monkey Wrench Gang* (1976) which told of a group of environmentalists plotting to blow up Arizona's Glen Canyon Dam. He wrote, he once said, to make a difference: "to oppose injustice, to defy the powerful, to speak for the voiceless." Taken from *One Life at a Time, Please* (1988), this brief essay does all of that. It is at once an attack on the American government for selling out the American wilderness, as well as a call for defensive action by those so outraged. Other collections include *Slumgullion Stew: An Edward Abbey Reader* (1984) and *Down the River* (1982). Abbey died in 1989.

1 If a stranger batters your door down with an axe, threatens your family and yourself with deadly weapons, and proceeds to loot your home of whatever he wants, he is committing what is universally recognized—by law and in common morality—as a crime. In such a situation the householder has both the right and the obligation to defend himself, his family, and his property by whatever means are necessary. This right and this obligation is universally recognized, justified, and praised by all civilized human communities. Self-defense against attack is one of the basic laws not only of human society but of life itself, not only of human life but of all life.

2 The American wilderness, what little remains, is now undergoing exactly such an assault. With bulldozer, earth mover, chainsaw, and dynamite the international timber, mining, and beef industries are invading our public lands—property of all Americans—bashing their way into our forests, mountains, and rangelands and looting them for everything they can get away with. This for the sake of short-term profits in the corporate sector and multimillion-dollar annual salaries for the three-piece-suited gangsters (MBA—Harvard, Yale, University of Tokyo, et alia) who control

and manage these bandit enterprises. Cheered on, naturally, by *Time, Newsweek,* and *The Wall Street Journal,* actively encouraged, inevitably, by those jellyfish government agencies that are supposed to *protect* the public lands, and as always aided and abetted in every way possible by the compliant politicians of our Western states, such as Babbitt, DeConcini, Goldwater, McCain, Hatch, Garn, Simms, Hansen, Andrus, Wallop, Domenici and Co. Inc.—who would sell the graves of their mothers if there's a quick buck in the deal, over or under the table, what do they care.

3   Representative government in the United States has broken down. Our legislators do not represent the public, the voters, or even those who voted for them but rather the commercial-industrial interests that finance their political campaigns and control the organs of communication—the TV, the newspapers, the billboards, the radio. Politics is a game for the rich only. Representative government in the USA represents money, not people, and therefore has forfeited our allegiance and moral support. We owe it nothing but the taxation it extorts from us under threats of seizure of property, imprisonment, or in some cases already, when resisted, a violent death by gunfire.

4   Such is the nature and structure of the industrial megamachine (in Lewis Mumford's term) which is now attacking the American wilderness. That wilderness is our ancestral home, the primordial homeland of all living creatures including the human, and the present final dwelling place of such noble beings as the grizzly bear, the mountain lion, the eagle and the condor, the moose and the elk and the pronghorn antelope, the redwood tree, the yellow pine, the bristlecone pine, and yes, why not say it?—the streams, waterfalls, rivers, the very bedrock itself of our hills, canyons, deserts, mountains. For many of us, perhaps for most of us, the wilderness is more our home than the little stucco boxes, wallboard apartments, plywood trailer-houses, and cinderblock condominiums in which the majority are now confined by the poverty of an overcrowded industrial culture.

5   And if the wilderness is our true home, and if it is threatened with invasion, pillage, and destruction—as it certainly is—then we have the right to defend that home, as we would our private quarters, by whatever means are necessary. (An Englishman's home is his castle; the American's home is his favorite forest, river, fishing stream, her favorite mountain or desert canyon, his favorite swamp or woods or lake.) We have the right to resist and we have the obligation; not to defend that which we love would be dishonorable. The majority of the American people have demonstrated on every possible occasion that they support the ideal of wilderness preservation; even our politicians are forced by popular opinion to *pretend* to support the idea; as they have learned, a vote against wilderness is a vote against their own reelection. We are justified then in defending our homes—our private home and our public home—not only by common law and common morality but also by common belief. We are the majority; they—the powerful—are in the minority.

6   How best defend our homes? Well, that is a matter of the strategy, tactics, and technique which eco-defense is all about.

7   What is eco-defense? Eco-defense means fighting back. Eco-defense means sabotage. Eco-defense is risky but sporting; unauthorized but fun; illegal but ethically imperative. Next time you enter a public forest scheduled for chainsaw massacre by some timber corporation and its flunkies in the US Forest Service, carry a

hammer and a few pounds of 60-penny nails in your creel, saddlebag, game bag, backpack, or picnic basket. Spike those trees; you won't hurt them; they'll be grateful for the protection; and you may save the forest. Loggers hate nails. My Aunt Emma back in West Virginia has been enjoying this pleasant exercise for years. She swears by it. It's good for the trees, it's good for the woods, and it's good for the human soul. Spread the word.

■ TOPICAL CONSIDERATIONS

1. Explain the reasoning behind Abbey's eco-defense plan. What are its merits? What problems might it cause? Would you be willing to try his suggestions? Why or why not?
2. Why is it important for Abbey to emphasize that the "householder" has "both the right and the obligation" to protect his family and property (paragraph 1).
3. What does Abbey mean when he says, "Representative government in the USA represents money, not people" (paragraph 3).
4. Abbey writes that eco-defense is "illegal but ethically imperative" (paragraph 6). What does he mean by this? Do you agree with the weight of importance that Abbey puts on eco-defense? Can you think of other instances where people felt morally compelled to break the law?
5. Can you offer any other suggestions for eco-defense that might be more effective than what Abbey suggests?
6. Consider the previous arguments and suggestions of Hoagland, and McKibben. How does Abbey's suggestion for a better environment fit into the spectrum of advice from these other two men?

■ RHETORICAL CONSIDERATIONS

1. Consider the opening line of the essay. Was it an effective "hook?" Did it capture your attention? Did it make you want to read on? Do you think you might use such a strategy to open a paper?
2. How does the introductory paragraph set the tone and argument for the rest of the essay?
3. Consider Abbey's choice of words and how they shape the reader's response. Pay particular attention to phrases such as "batters . . . threatens . . . proceeds to loot" (paragraph 1) and his references to "three-piece-suited gangsters" and "jellyfish government agencies" (paragraph 2). Abbey writes of "the taxation" that the government "extorts" from us (paragraph 3). What is the connotation of *extort?* How does this word help color the reader's view of government?
4. Paragraph 6 is the shortest in the essay. From a rhetorical point of view, what is its function in the essay? What change in the discussion does it mark?

5. How would you describe the tone of Abbey's conclusion. How does it differ from the rest of the essay?

■ WRITING ASSIGNMENTS

1. You serve on a college committee that is investigating the implications of eco-defense. Draft a proposal offering suggestions for preserving local forests. Be certain to invoke Abbey's argument either positively or negatively. Would you recommend that a group of students follow Abbey's agenda?
2. You are a judge who is hearing the following case. The defendant is Abbey's Aunt Emma who is charged with criminal trespass to land and assault. The plaintiff is a logger who was seriously injured when his chain saw hit a nail. Draft a clear and well-supported decision in favor of the logger or Aunt Emma.
3. Write a letter to Abbey telling him what you think of his suggestion, and plan to offer additional suggestions to his eco-defense.
4. Write an essay in which you compare and contrast the methods of Abbey and those of Bill McKibben.

A mericans have a love affair with sports. Whether we're cheering from the stands or playing pickup ball on weekends, we crave the heat of competitive play. And, as each author here proclaims, that craving is healthy for the body and the collective psyche. In this chapter we explore the value of sports—what they do for us and what they mean.

We begin with an insightful interpretation of the two most American of sports in "Football Red and Baseball Green." As Murray Ross sees it, these games enact different ritual myths that fans are invited to become part of. Myths of pastoral harmony and heroic combat so fundamental to the American character.

We next turn to basketball, a sport dominated by black athletes. While Jeff Greenfield offers some explanations as to why two-thirds of professional players are African-Americans, his interest in "The Black and White Truth About Basketball" is to distinguish the principal differences between black and white styles of playing—styles, he says, that reflect "a fusion of cultures."

In the next selection, "Attitude," humorist Garrison Keillor lets us in on a basic secret to being a sport: Attitude. Focusing on softball, he gives some fine tips for any man or woman, young or old, who wants to pick up a bat and feel like the pros "without getting beaned or having to run too hard."

There was a time when sports were all-male experiences. But, as we see in the last two pieces, a rush of women into athletic competition has been taking place on every level—secondary schools, college, Olympic games, professional sports, and even Little League. In "Girls at Bat," Anna Quindlen celebrates liberated fields of play where girls and boys learn to handle a ball and competition equally. Women and basketball are the focus of "Playing to Win" in which Margaret A. Whitney describes how her daughter's inspiring intensity on the parquet court has overturned the forces of tradition.

Football Red and Baseball Green

Murray Ross

This opening piece serves as an overview of this chapter, each of whose essays views sports as something more than games. As Murray Ross explains, sports are rituals—the acting out of myths fundamental to American values. In his interpretation, baseball is a "pastoral" sport—it's played in a park and "creates an atmosphere in which everything exists in harmony." By contrast, football, which is played in an oval stadium, is a warrior spectacle.

Murray Ross is founder and director of a theater program at the University of Colorado at Colorado Springs. He has written articles on Elizabethan drama and film. His essay originally appeared in *Chicago Review* in 1971 and was updated in 1993.

1   Every Superbowl ever played has rated among the top television draws of its year. By now, after nearly three decades, we know the game has a more than fair chance of being not so hot, some sort of mismatched rout. Even so, everyone—and I mean just about *everyone*—watches. This revelation is just one way of indicating how popular and compelling spectator sports are in this country. Americans, or American men anyway, seem to care about the games they watch as much as the Elizabethans cared about their plays, and I suspect for some of the same reasons. There is, in sport, some of the rudimentary drama found in popular theater: familiar plots, type characters, heroic and comic action spiced with new and unpredictable variations. And common to watching both activities is the sense of participation in a shared tradition and in shared fantasies. If sport exploits these fantasies without significantly transcending them, it seems no less satisfying for all that.

2   It is my guess that sport spectating involves something more than the vicarious pleasures of identifying with athletic prowess. I suspect that each sport contains a fundamental myth which it elaborates for its fans, and that our pleasure in watching such games derives in part from belonging briefly to the mythical world which the game and its players bring to life. I am especially interested in baseball and football because they are so popular and so uniquely *American;* they began here and unlike basketball they have not been widely exported. Thus whatever can be said, mythically, about these games would seem to apply to our culture.

3   Baseball's myth may be the easier to identify since we have a greater historical perspective on the game. It was an instant success during the Industrialization, and most probably it was a reaction to the squalor, the faster pace, and the dreariness of the new conditions. Baseball was old-fashioned right from the start; it seems conceived in nostalgia, in the resuscitation of the Jeffersonian dream. It established an artificial rural environment, one removed from the toil of an urban life, which spectators could be admitted to and temporarily breathe in. Baseball is a *pastoral* sport, and I think the game can be best understood as this kind of art. For baseball does what all good pastoral does—it creates an atmosphere in which everything exists in harmony.

4   Consider, for instance, the spatial organization of the game. A kind of controlled openness is created by having everything fan out from home plate, and the crowd sees the game through an arranged perspective that is rarely violated. Visually this means that the game is always seen as a constant, rather calm whole, and that the players and the playing field are viewed in relationship to each other. Each player has a certain position, a special area to tend, and the game often seems to be as much a dialogue between the fielders and the field as it is a contest between the players themselves: Will that ball get through the hole? Can that outfielder run under that fly? As a moral genre, pastoral asserts the virtue of communion with nature. As a competitive game, baseball asserts that the team which best relates to the playing field (by hitting the ball in the right places) will win.

5   Having established its landscape, pastoral art operates to eliminate any reference to that bigger, more disturbing, more real world it has left behind. All games are to some extent insulated from the outside by having their own rules, but baseball has a circular structure as well which furthers its comfortable feeling of self-sufficiency. By this I mean that every motion of extention is also one of return—a ball hit outside is a *home* run, a full circle. Home—familiar, peaceful, secure—it is the beginning and end. You must go out but you must come back; only the completed movement is registered.

6   Time is a serious threat to any form of pastoral. The genre poses a timeless world of perpetual spring, and it does its best to silence the ticking of clocks which remind us that in time the green world fades into winter. One's sense of time is directly related to what happens in it, and baseball is so structured as to stretch out and ritualize whatever action it contains. Dramatic moments are few, and they are almost always isolated by the routine texture of normal play. It is certainly a game of climax and drama, but it is perhaps more a game of repeated and predictable action: the foul balls, the walks, the pitcher fussing around on the mound, the lazy fly ball to center field. This is, I think, as it should be, for baseball exists as an alternative to a world of too much action, struggle, and change. It is a merciful release from a more grinding and insistent tempo, and its time, as William Carlos Williams suggests, makes a virtue out of idleness simply by providing it:

> The crowd at the ball game
> is moved uniformly
> by a spirit of uselessness
> Which delights them. . . .

7   Within this expanded and idle time the baseball fan is at liberty to become a ceremonial participant and a lover of style. Because the action is normalized, how something is done becomes as important as the action itself. Thus baseball's most delicate and detailed aspects are often, to the spectator, the most interesting. The pitcher's windup, the anticipatory crouch of the infielders, the quick waggle of the bat as it poises for the pitch—these subtle miniature movements are as meaningful as the home runs and the strikeouts. It somehow matters in baseball that all the tiny rituals are observed: The shortstop must kick the dirt and the umpire must brush the plate with his pocket broom. In a sense baseball is largely a continuous series of small gestures, and I think it characteristic that the game's most treasured moment came when Babe Ruth pointed to where he subsequently hit a home run.

8   Baseball is a game where the little things mean a lot, and this, together with its clean serenity, its open space, and its ritualized action, is enough to place it in a world of yesterday. Baseball evokes for us a past which may never have been ours, but which we believe was, and certainly that is enough. In the Second World War, supposedly, we fought for "Baseball, Mom, and Apple Pie," and considering what baseball means, that phrase is a good one. We fought then for the right to believe in a green world of tranquility and uninterrupted contentment, where the little things would count. But now the possibilities of such a world are more remote, and it seems that while the entertainment of such a dream has an enduring appeal, it is no longer

sufficient for our fantasies. I think this may be why baseball is no longer our pre-eminent national pastime, and why its myth is being replaced by another more appropriate to the new realities (and fantasies) of our time.

9   Football, especially professional football, is the embodiment of a newer myth, one which in many respects is opposed to baseball's. The fundamental difference is that football is not a pastoral game; it is a heroic one. Football wants to convert men into gods; it suggests that magnificence and glory are as desirable as happiness. Football is designed, therefore, to impress its audience rather differently than baseball.

10   As a pastoral game, baseball attempts to close the gap between the players and the crowd. It creates the illusion, for instance, that with a lot of hard work, a little luck, and possibly some extra talent, the average spectator might well be playing, not watching. For most of us can do a few of the things the ball players do: catch a pop-up, field a ground ball, and maybe get a hit once in a while. As a heroic game, football is not concerned with a shared community of near-equals. It seeks almost the opposite relationship between its spectators and players, one which stresses the distance between them. We are not invited to identify with Thurman Thomas, Randall Cunningham, or any other of football's megaheroes any more than we are with Zeus. Football's heroes are systematically catapulted into Olympus; they are more than human. Commercial after commercial portrays them as giants of the earth, prodigies to be seen, properly, with awe. Most of us lesser beings could not begin to imagine ourselves playing their game without also imagining our instant humiliation and possible death. The players are that much bigger, that much faster than we are. Watching, we have enough problems figuring out what's going on. In baseball, most of what happens is what meets the eye, but in football each play involves twenty-two men acting simultaneously in combat: It's too much for a single pair of eyes to follow. So we now have two or three television commentators to explain the action as it unfolds, then another three at halftime to evaluate. Coaches have teams of spotters in the stands and hundreds of hours of videos to watch. There is a seemingly infinite proliferation of "meaningful" data; full comprehension remains on the horizon.

11   If football is distanced from its fans by its intricacy and "superhuman" play, it nonetheless remains a compelling and intense spectacle. Baseball, as I have implied, dissolves time and urgency in a green expanse, thereby creating a luxurious and peaceful sense of leisure. As is appropriate to a heroic enterprise, football reverses this procedure and converts space into time. The game is ideally played in an oval stadium, not in a "park," and the difference is the elimination of perspective. This makes football a perfect television game, because even at first hand it offers a flat, perpetually moving foreground (wherever the ball is). The eye in baseball viewing opens up; in football it zeroes in. There is no democratic vista in football, and spectators are not asked to relax, but to concentrate. You are encouraged to watch the drama, not a medley of ubiquitous gestures, and you are constantly reminded that this event is taking place in time. The third element in baseball is the field; in football this element is the clock. Traditionally heroes do reckon with time, and football players are no exceptions. Time in football is wound up inexorably until it reaches the breaking point in the last minutes of a close game. More often than not it is the clock which emerges as the real enemy, and it is the sense of time running out that regularly produces a pitch of tension uncommon in baseball.

12   A further reason for football's intensity is that the game is played like a war, with television putting the fans in the war room. The idea is to win by going through, around, or over the opposing team, and the battle lines, quite literally, are drawn on every play. Violence is somewhere at the heart of the game, and the combat quality is reflected in football's army language ("blitz," "trap," "zone," "bomb," "trenches," etc.). Coaches often sound like generals when they discuss their strategy. Woody Hayes, the legendary coach of Ohio State, explained his quarterback option play as if it had been conceived in the Pentagon: "You know," he said, "the most effective kind of warfare is siege. You have to attack on broad fronts. And that's all the option is—attacking on a broad front. You know General Sherman ran an option through the South."

13   Football like war is an arena for action, and like war football leaves little room for personal style. It seems to be a game which projects "character" more than personality, and for the most part football heroes, publicly, are a rather similar lot. They tend to become personifications rather than individuals, and, with certain exceptions, they are easily read emblematically as embodiments of heroic qualities such as "strength," "confidence," "grace," etc.—clichés really, but forceful enough when represented by the play of a Reggie White, a Troy Aikman, or a Jim Rice. Perhaps this simplification of personality results in part from the heroes' total identification with their mission, to the extent that they become more characterized by what they do than by what they intrinsically "are." At any rate football does not make as many allowances for the idiosyncrasies that baseball actually seems to encourage, and as a result there have been few football characters as eccentric and as recognizably human as, say, the pasta-loving Tommy Lasorda, the surly Jose Canseco, the exuberant Willie Mays.

14   A further reason for the underdeveloped qualities of football personalities, and one which gets us to the heart of the game's modernity, is that football is very much a game of modern technology. Football's action is largely interaction, and the game's complexity requires that its players mold themselves into a perfectly coordinated unit. The smoothness and precision of play execution are insatiable preoccupations, and most coaches believe that the team which makes the fewest mistakes will be the team that wins. Individual identity thus comes to be associated with the team or unit that one plays for to a much greater extent that in baseball. Yogi Berra was not so much a Yankee as a phenomenon unto himself, a man with his own language and a future as a cartoon character. But Mike Ditka, though personally forceful and particular, is mostly a Chicago Bear. Now, relieved of his stewardship, he's a publicly displaced identity, a lost man. The gods of football stand out not only because of their individual acts, but even more because they epitomize the style of the groups they belong to and represent. The archetypal ideal is Camelot, or what Camelot was advertised as: a group of men who function as equal parts of a larger whole, dependent on each other for total meaning.

15   The humanized machine as hero is something very new in sport, for in baseball anything approaching a machine has always been suspect. The famous Yankee teams of the fifties were almost flawlessly perfect, yet they never were especially popular. Their admirers took pains to romanticize their precision into something more natural

than plain mechanics—Joe DiMaggio, for instance, became the "Yankee Clipper." Even so, most people seemed to want the Brooklyn Dodgers (the "bums") to thrash them in the World Series. One of the most memorable triumphs in recent decades— the victory of the Amazin' Mets in 1969—was memorable precisely because it was the triumph of a random collection of inspired rejects over the superbly skilled, fully integrated, and almost homogenized Baltimore Orioles. In baseball, machinery seems tantamount to villainy, whereas in football this smooth perfection is part of the unexpected integration a championship team must attain.

16   It is not surprising, really, that we should have a game which asserts the heroic function of a mechanized group, since we have become a country where collective identity is a reality. Yet football's collective pattern is only one aspect of the way in which it seems to echo our contemporary environment. The game, like our society, can be thought of as a cluster of people living under great tension in a state of perpetual flux. The potential for sudden disaster or triumph is as great in football as it is in our own age, and although there is something ludicrous in equating interceptions with assassinations and long passes with moonshots, there is also something valid and appealing in the analogies. It seems to me that football does successfully reflect those salient and common conditions which affect us all, and it does so with the end of making us feel better about them and our lot. For one thing, it makes us feel that something can be released and connected in all this chaos; out of the accumulated pile of bodies something can emerge—a runner breaks into the clear or a pass finds its way to a receiver. To the spectator, plays such as these are human and dazzling. They suggest to the audience what it has hoped for (and been told) all along, that technology is still a tool and not a master. Fans get living proof of this every time a long pass is completed; they appreciate that it is the result of careful planning, perfect integration, and an effective "pattern," but they see too that it is human and that what counts as well is man, his desire, his natural skill, and his "grace under pressure." Football metaphysically yokes heroic action and technology by violence to suggest that they are mutually supportive. It's a doubtful proposition, but given how we live, it has its attractions.

17   Football, like the space program, is a game in the grand manner. Homer would have chronicled it; Beowulf would have played fullback. Baseball's roots are at least as deep; it's a variation of the Satyr play, it's a feast of fools. But today their mythic resonance has been eroded by commercial success. Like so much else in America, their character has been modified by money.

18   More and more, both baseball and football are being played indoors on rugs in multipurpose spaces. It doesn't make good business sense to play outside where it might rain and snow and do terrible things; it isn't really prudent to play on a natural field that can be destroyed in a single afternoon; and why build a whole stadium or park that's good for only one game? The fans in these stadiums are constantly diverted by huge whiz-bang scoreboards that dominate and describe the action, while the fans at home are constantly being reminded by at least three lively sportscasters of the other games, the other sports, and the other shows that are coming up later on the same stations. Both pro football and pro baseball now play vastly extended seasons, so that the World Series now takes place on chilly October nights

and football is well under way before the summer ends. From my point of view all this is regrettable, because these changes tend to remove the games from their intangible but palpable mythic contexts. No longer clearly set in nature, no longer given the chance to breathe and steep in their own special atmosphere, both baseball and football risk becoming demythologized. As fans we seem to participate a little less in mythic ritual these days, while being subjected even more to the statistics, the hype, and the salary disputes that proceed from a jazzed-up, inflated, yet somehow flattened sporting world—a world that looks too much like the one we live in all the time.

19   Still, there is much to be thankful for, and every season seems to bring its own contribution to mythic lore. Some people will think this nonsense, and I must admit there are good reasons for finding both games simply varieties of decadence.

20   In its preoccupation with mechanization, and in its open display of violence, football is the more obvious target for social moralists, but I wonder if this is finally more "corrupt" than the seductive picture of sanctuary and tranquility that baseball has so artfully drawn for us. Almost all sport is vulnerable to such criticism because it is not strictly ethical in intent, and for this reason there will always be room for puritans like the Elizabethan John Stubbes, who howled at the "wanton fruits which these cursed pastimes bring forth." As a longtime dedicated fan of almost anything athletic, I confess myself out of sympathy with most of this; which is to say, I guess, that I am vulnerable to those fantasies which these games support, and that I find happiness in the company of people who feel as I do.

21   A final note. It is interesting that the heroic and pastoral conventions which underlie our most popular sports are almost classically opposed. The contrasts are familiar: city versus country, aspirations versus contentment, activity versus peace, and so on. Judging from the rise of professional football, we seem to be slowly relinquishing that unfettered rural vision of ourselves that baseball so beautifully mirrors, and we have come to cast ourselves in a genre more reflective of a nation confronted by constant and unavoidable challenges. Right now, like the Elizabethans, we seem to share both heroic and pastoral yearnings, and we reach out to both. Perhaps these divided needs account in part for the enormous attention we as a nation now give to spectator sports. For sport provides one place where we can have our football and our baseball too.

■ TOPICAL CONSIDERATIONS

1. Ross claims that baseball and football each "contains a fundamental myth which it elaborates for its fans" (paragraph 2). What is a *myth?* If you are unfamiliar with the term, look it up in an encyclopedia or literary handbook. What is the usual relationship of myths to human culture? What specifically are the mythic functions of baseball and football, in Ross's view?

2. Consider Ross's analysis of the role time plays in baseball and football. What makes the function of the game clock *pastoral* in baseball? In what ways is time experienced in a typically *heroic* fashion in football? (Look up these literary terms if they are unfamiliar to you.)

3. Describe the influence of the physical playing field on the spectator at base-ball and football games. How does the spatial organization suggest to Ross elements of pastoral and heroic genres?
4. What different demands to these two sports make on their spectators?
5. What, in Ross's view, is causing baseball and football to become "demythol-ogized" (paragraph 18)? When and where have you experienced the sense Ross describes of a "somehow flattened sporting world" (paragraph 18)? In what ways have recent developments in these sports actually made them more enjoyable for fans and players?

■ RHETORICAL CONSIDERATIONS

1. Describe how Ross turns the methods of literary analysis onto sports in this essay. What did this approach illuminate for you about baseball and foot-ball? How did it alter your appreciation of literary analysis? What, if any-thing, did you find forced or contrived about Ross's analytical procedure?
2. Analyze Ross's tone at the opening of the essay. What words does he use to create a sense of his narrative personality? How appropriate is this tone to the subject matter?
3. Where does Ross acknowledge potential opposition to his argument? To what extent was he effective in dismissing these objections?
4. Consider the structure of paragraph 13. Where does Ross introduce the main point of this paragraph? How effectively does he support his claims with evidence? Where and how does Ross deflect potential opposition?
5. Who is Ross's target audience for this essay? How much knowledge of sports does Ross assume in his readers?
6. Evaluate the effectiveness of Ross's concluding paragraph. What tone is created by the opening phrase, "A final note"? Why is the paragraph's last sentence so catchy?

■ WRITING ASSIGNMENTS

1. Write a research paper about the social origins of football, baseball, or bas-ketball. Consider who first played the game; in what geographical areas it was most popular; what about it first captured the public imagination. Is the appeal of the sport different today than it was at first?
2. Write an essay describing the "fundamental myth" of a sport or athletic ac-tivity other than baseball and football—running, soccer, gymnastics, golf, or some other. Use Ross's essay to guide you in analyzing the activity in lit-erary terms.
3. Write a letter to Ross critiquing his work by offering examples that chal-lenge the "pastoral" and "heroic" model, such as colorful football players or baseball players whose identity seems wrapped up with a team image. You should also research Ross's own examples of players and elements of the game to determine when, if ever, he misrepresents his evidence.

The Black and White Truth About Basketball
Jeff Greenfield

As was aptly demonstrated in the previous piece, there is more to sports than just games. They ritualistically reflect all-American character and values. Likewise, in this essay a former sports reporter turns our attention to basketball and to some "truths" we may not have given thought to. Jeff Greenfield characterizes what he sees as distinctly different styles of black and white professional basketball players. But more than that, he looks to the social and historic circumstances that explain these contrastive styles on the court.

Jeff Greenfield served as a sportswriter for CBS TV for several years before moving to ABC TV news where he serves as political and media analyst. He is the author of several books including *A Populist Manifesto* (1972), *The World's Greatest Team* (a history of the Boston Celtics, 1976), *Television: The First 50 Years* (1977), and *The Real Campaign* (1982). This essay, which was updated in 1993, originally appeared in *Esquire* in 1975.

1   The dominance of black athletes over professional basketball is beyond dispute. Two-thirds of the players are black, and the number would be greater were it not for the continuing practice of picking white bench warmers for the sake of balance. Over the last two decades, no more than three white players have been among the ten starting players on the National Basketball Association's All-Star team, and in the last quarter century, only two white players—Dave Cowens and Larry Bird of the Boston Celtics—have ever been chosen as the NBA's Most Valuable Player.

2   And at a time when a baseball executive can lose his job for asserting that blacks lack "the necessities" to become pro sports executives and when the National Football League only in 1989 had its first black head coach, the NBA stands as a pro sports league that hired its first black head coach in 1968 (Bill Russell) and its first black general manager in the early 1970s (Wayne Embry of the Milwaukee Bucks). What discrimination remains—lack of equal opportunity for speaking engagements and product endorsements—has more to do with society than with basketball.

3   This dominance reflects a natural inheritance: Basketball is a pastime of the urban poor. The current generation of black athletes are heirs to a tradition more than half a century old. In a neighborhood without the money for bats, gloves, hockey sticks and ice skates, or shoulder pads, basketball is an eminently accessible sport. "Once it was the game of the Irish and Italian Catholics in Rockaway and the Jews on Fordham Road in the Bronx," writes David Wolf in his brilliant book, *Foul!* "It was recreation, status, and a way out." But now the ethnic names have been changed: Instead of the Red Holzmans, Red Auerbachs, and the McGuire brothers, there are the Michael Jordans and Charles Barkleys, the Shaquille O'Neals and Patrick Ewings. And professional basketball is a sport with national television exposure and million-dollar salaries.

4   But the mark on basketball of today's players can be measured by more than money or visibility. It is a question of style. For there is a clear difference between

"black" and "white" styles of play that is as clear as the difference between 155th Street at Eighth Avenue and Crystal City, Missouri. Most simply (remembering we are talking about culture, not chromosomes), "black" basketball is the use of superb athletic skill to adapt to the limits of space imposed by the game. "White" ball is the pulverization of that space by sheer intensity.*

5   It takes a conscious effort to realize how constricted the space is on a basketball court. Place a regulation court (ninety-four by fifty feet)—on a football field, and it will reach from the back of the end zone to the twenty-one-yard line; its width will cover less than a third of the field. On a baseball diamond, a basketball court will reach from home plate to first base. Compared to its principal indoor rival, ice hockey, basketball covers about one-fourth the playing area. Moreover, during the normal flow of the game, most of the action takes place on the third of the court nearest the basket. It is in this dollhouse space that ten men, each of them half a foot taller than the average man, come together to battle each other.

6   There is, thus, no room; basketball is a struggle for the edge: the half step with which to cut around the defender for a lay-up, the half second of freedom with which to release a jump shot, the instant a head turns allowing a pass to a teammate breaking for the basket. It is an arena for the subtlest of skills: the head fake, the shoulder fake, the shift of body weight to the right and the sudden cut to the left. Deception is crucial to success; and to young men who have learned early and painfully that life is a battle for survival, basketball is one of the few pursuits in which the weapon of deception is a legitimate tactic rather than the source of trouble.

7   If there is, then, the need to compete in a crowd, to battle for the edge, then the surest strategy is to develop the *unexpected:* to develop a shot that is simply and fundamentally different from the usual methods of putting the ball in the basket. Drive to the hoop, but go under it and come up the other side; hold the ball at waist level and shoot from there instead of bringing the ball up to eye level; leap into the air, but fall away from the basket instead of toward it. All these tactics, which a fan can see embodied in the astonishing play of the Chicago Bulls' Michael Jordan, take maximum advantage of the crowding on the court. They also stamp uniqueness on young men who may feel it nowhere else.

8   "For many young men in the slums," David Wolf writes, "the school yard is the only place they can feel true pride in what they do, where they can move free of inhibitions and where they can, by being spectacular, rise for the moment against the drabness and anonymity of their lives. Thus, when a player develops extraordinary 'school yard' moves and shots . . . [they] become his measure as a man."

9   So the moves that begin as tactics for scoring soon become calling cards. You don't just lay the ball in for an uncontested basket; you take the ball in both hands,

---

*This distinction has nothing to do with the question of whether whites can play as "well" as blacks. In 1987, the Detroit Pistons' Isiah Thomas quipped that the Celtics' Larry Bird was "a pretty good player," but would be much less celebrated and wealthy if he were black. As Thomas later said, Bird was one of the greatest pro players in history. Nor is this distinction about "smart," although the ex-Los Angeles Laker great Magic Johnson was right when he said that too many journalists attribute brilliant strategic moves by black players to "innate" ability.

leap as high as you can, and slam the ball through the hoop. When you jump in the air, fake a shot, bring the ball back to your body, and throw up a shot, all without coming back down, you have proven your worth in uncontestable fashion.

10   This liquid grace is an integral part of "black" ball, almost exclusively the province of the playground player. Some white stars like Bob Cousy, Billy Cunningham, Doug Collins, and Kevin McHale had it; John Stockton of the Utah Jazz has it now: the body control, the moves to the basket, the free-ranging mobility. Most of them also possessed the surface ease that is integral to the "black" style; an incorporation of the ethic of mean streets—to "make it" is not just to have wealth but to have it without strain. Whatever the muscles and organs are doing, the face of the "black" star almost never shows it. Magic Johnson of the Lakers could bring the ball downcourt with two men on him, whip a pass through an invisible opening, cut to the basket, take a return pass, and hit the shot all with no more emotion than a quick smile. So stoic was San Antonio Spurs' great George Gervin that he earned the nick-name "Ice Man." (Interestingly, a black coach like San Antonio's John Lucas exhibits far less emotion on the bench than a white counterpart like Portland's Rick Adelman.)

11   If there is a single trait that characterizes "black" ball it is leaping ability. Bob Cousy, ex-Celtic great and former pro coach, says that "when coaches get together, one is sure to say, 'I've got the one black kid in the country who can't jump.' When coaches see a white boy who can jump or who moves with extraordinary quickness, they say, 'He should have been born black, he's that good.'" This pervasive belief was immortalized by the title of the hit film: *White Men Can't Jump.*

12   Don Nelson, now a top executive with the Golden State Warriors, recalls that back in 1970, Dave Cowens, then a relatively unknown graduate of Florida State, prepared for his rookie pro season by playing in the Rucker League, an outdoor competition in Harlem playgrounds that pits pros against college kids and playground stars. So ferocious was Cowens's leaping ability, Nelson says, that "when the summer was over, everyone wanted to know who the white son of a bitch was who could jump so high." That's another way to overcome a crowd around the basket—just go over it.

13   Speed, mobility, quickness, acceleration, "the moves"—all of these are catch-phrases that surround the "black" playground athlete, the style of play. So does the most racially tinged of attributes, "rhythm." Yet rhythm is what the black stars themselves talk about: feeling the flow of the game, finding the tempo of the dribble, the step, the shot. It is an instinctive quality (although it stems from hundreds of hours of practice), and it is one that has led to difficulty between system-oriented coaches and free-form players. "Cats from the street have their own rhythm when they play," said college dropout Bill Spivey, onetime New York high school star. "It's not a matter of somebody setting you up and you shooting. You *feel* the shot. When a coach holds you back, you lose the feel and it isn't fun anymore."

14   When legendary Brooklyn playground star Connie Hawkins was winding up his NBA career under Laker coach Bill Sharman, he chafed under the methodical style of play. "He's systematic to the point where it begins to be a little too much. It's such an action-reaction type of game that when you have to do everything the same way, I think you lose something."

15   There is another kind of basketball that has grown up in America. It is not played on asphalt playgrounds with a crowd of kids competing for the court; it is played on macadam driveways by one boy with a ball and a backboard nailed over the garage; it is played in gyms in the frigid winter of the rural Midwest and on Southern dirt courts. It is a mechanical, precise development of skills (when Don Nelson was an Iowa farm boy, his incentive to make his shots was that an errant rebound would land in the middle of chicken droppings). It is a game without frills, without flow, but with effectiveness. It is "white" basketball: jagged, sweaty, stumbling, intense. Where a "black" player overcomes an obstacle with finesse and body control, a "white" player reacts by outrunning or overpowering the obstacle.

16   By this definition, the Boston Celtics have been classically "white" regardless of the pigmentation of the players. They have rarely suited up a player with dazzling moves; indeed such a player would probably have made Red Auerbach swallow his cigar. Instead, the Celtic philosophy has been to wear you down with execution, with constant running, with the same play run again and again and again. The rebound by Bill Russell (or Dave Cowens or Robert Parrish) triggers the fast break, as everyone races downcourt; the ball goes to Bob Cousy (or John Havlicek, or Larry Bird), who pulls up and takes the shot, or who drives and then finds Sam Jones (or Kevin McHale or M. L. Carr) free for an easy basket.

17   Perhaps the most definitively "white" position is that of the quick forward, one without great moves to the basket, without highly developed shots, without the height and mobility for rebounding effectiveness. So what does he do?

18   He runs. He runs from the opening jump to the final buzzer. He runs up and down the court, from base line to base line, back and forth under the basket, looking for the opening, the pass, the chance to take a quick step, the high-percentage shot. To watch Detroit's Bill Laimbeer or the Suns' Dan Majerle, players without speed or obvious moves, is to wonder what they are doing in the NBA—until you see them swing free and throw up a shot that, without demanding any apparent skill, somehow goes in the basket more frequently than the shots of many of their more skilled teammates. And to have watched the New York Knicks' (now U.S. Senator) Bill Bradley, or the Celtics' John Havlicek, is to have watched "white" ball at its best.

19   Havlicek or Laimbeer, or the Phoenix Suns' Danny Ainge, stand in dramatic contrast to Michael Jordan or to the Philadelphia 76ers' legend, Julius Erving. Erving had the capacity to make legends come true, leaping from the foul line and slam-dunking the ball on his way down; going up for a lay-up, pulling the ball to his body, and driving under and up the other side of the rim, defying gravity and probability with impossible moves and jumps. Michael Jordan of the Chicago Bulls has been seen by thousands spinning a full 360 degrees in midair before slamming the ball through the hoop.

20   When John Havlicek played, by contrast, he was the living embodiment of his small-town Ohio background. He would bring the ball downcourt, weaving left, then right, looking for a path. He would swing the ball to a teammate, cut behind the pick, take the pass, and release the shot in a flicker of time. It looked plain, unvarnished. But it was a blend of skills that not more than half a dozen other players in the league possessed.

21   To former pro Jim McMillian, a black who played quick forward with "white" attributes, "it's a matter of environment. Julius Erving grew up in a different environment from Havlicek. John came from a very small town in Ohio. There everything was done the easy way, the shortest distance between two points. It's nothing fancy; very few times will he go one-on-one. He hits the lay-up, hits the jump shot, makes the free throw, and after the game you look up and say, 'How did he hurt us that much?'"

22   "White" ball, then, is the basketball of patience, method, and sometimes brute strength. "Black" ball is the basketball of electric self-expression. One player has all the time in the world to perfect his skills, the other a need to prove himself. These are slippery categories, because a poor boy who is black can play "white" and a white boy of middle-class parents can play "black." Charles Oakley of the New York Knicks and John Paxson of the Chicago Bulls are athletes who seem to defy these categories.

23   And what makes basketball the most intriguing of sports is how these styles do not necessarily clash; how the punishing intensity of "white" players and the dazzling moves of the "blacks" can fit together, a fusion of cultures that seems more and more difficult in the world beyond the out-of-bounds line.

■ TOPICAL CONSIDERATIONS

1. In paragraph 13, Greenfield tells us that "the most racially tinged of attributes, 'rhythm,'" is one characteristic of "black" play. In what way is *rhythm* a racially tinged term? How does Greenfield defend his use of this term?

2. What does Greenfield mean when he insists that he is "talking about culture, not chromosomes" in this essay (paragraph 4)?

3. Consider the ways a disadvantaged urban childhood determines the "black" playing style, in Greenfield's analysis. What other court moves might result from the same environmental pressures? To what extent is this background typical of black basketball players? Do you think this is as prevalent as Greenfield indicates?

4. Analyze the relationship between the typical background of white basketball players and their court style. How effective did you find the evidence Greenfield uses to support his argument here?

5. Greenfield offers several examples of white players who play "black" basketball, and black players who play "white" basketball. If you are a basketball fan, what other players can you name who either break Greenfield's racial mold or do not have the kind of background "appropriate" to their racial category? Do these exceptions prove Greenfield's rule, or do they seriously weaken his argument?

6. Greenfield in his last paragraph compares the peaceful coexistence of races in basketball to "the world beyond the out-of-bounds line" (paragraph 23). Consider this statement alongside other references Greenfield makes to the racism of the world beyond basketball. To what extent do you agree with his depiction of race relations within the sport?

■ RHETORICAL CONSIDERATIONS

1. Evaluate the evidence Greenfield uses in paragraph 10. How convincing do you find his support here? To what extent is this kind of evidence typical of Greenfield's essay?
2. What is Greenfield's purpose in writing this essay? Where do you see evidence that he might be responding to other explanations of the relationship between black and white in basketball?
3. If Greenfield really is talking about "culture, not chromosomes," why does he use the terms *white* and *black* in this essay? What advantage does he gain by using this language? What might be the result of using different words? Why, when he uses these words, does he always place them in quotation marks?
4. How does Greenfield enhance his credibility as a sports commentator in this essay? Consider elements such as his apparent knowledge of the game, his sources, and the language he uses to make his argument.

■ WRITING ASSIGNMENTS

1. Research Greenfield's suggestion that basketball is not plagued by racism. Consider the percentage of blacks in management and coaching positions in both pro and major college teams, then write a paper that either supports or attacks Greenfield's claims about this issue.
2. Research the personal backgrounds of five or ten of the players that Greenfield uses as examples in his essay. To what extent are the black players products of the urban ghetto? To what extent do white players come from more affluent circumstances? Use the data you have gathered to critique Greenfield's argument.
3. Write an essay comparing the racial environment in college and pro basketball. Are things less or more harmonious in college basketball than in professional basketball?
4. Write a letter to Greenfield arguing that a player's position—point guard, forward, center—determines the style of play more than his race or socioeconomic background.

Attitude

Garrison Keillor

Garrison Keillor did a remarkable thing in this television age. In 1974, he managed to pull two million Americans to their radio sets each Saturday night. He did that for a dozen years since creating and hosting the live variety show "Prairie Home Companion," from Minneapolis. What made Keillor's National Public Radio production so popular is just the kind of warm wit and wisdom that characterize the following article. In the essay he gives some thoughts about playing softball—particularly about attitude and how it might be the most important part of the game. This essay is taken from a collection of Keillor's pieces—most published in *The New Yorker*— *Happy to Be Here* (1982). Keillor is also the author of two best-selling novels *Lake Wobegon Days* (1985) and *Leaving Home* (1987), as well as *The Book of Guys* (1993).

1 Long ago I passed the point in life when major-league ballplayers begin to be younger than yourself. Now all of them are, except for a few aging trigenarians and a couple of quadros who don't get around on the fastball as well as they used to and who sit out the second games of double-headers. However, despite my age (thirty-nine), I am still active and have a lot of interests. One of them is slow-pitch softball, a game that lets me go through the motions of baseball without getting beaned or having to run too hard. I play on a pretty casual team, one that drinks beer on the bench and substitutes freely. If a player's wife or girlfriend wants to play, we give her a glove and send her out to right field, no questions asked, and if she lets a pop fly drop six feet in front of her, nobody agonizes over it.

2   Except me. This year. For the first time in my life, just as I am entering the dark twilight of my slow-pitch career, I find myself taking the game seriously. It isn't the bonehead play that bothers me especially—the pop fly that drops untouched, the slow roller juggled and the ball then heaved ten feet over the first baseman's head and into the next diamond, the routine singles that go through outfielder's legs for doubles and triples with gloves flung after them. No, it isn't our stone-glove fielding or pussyfoot base-running or limp-wristed hitting that gives me fits, though these have put us on the short end of some mighty ridiculous scores this summer. It's our attitude.

3   Bottom of the ninth, down 18-3, two outs, a man on first and a woman on third, and our third baseman strikes out. *Strikes out!* In slow-pitch, not even your grandmother strikes out, but this guy does, and after his third strike—a wild swing at a ball that bounces on the plate—he topples over in the dirt and lies flat on his back, laughing. *Laughing!*

4   Same game, earlier. They have the bases loaded. A weak grounder is hit toward our second baseperson. The runners are running. She picks up the ball, and she looks at them. She looks at first, at second, at home. We yell, "Throw it! Throw it!" and she throws it, underhand, at the pitcher, who has turned and run to back up the catcher. The ball rolls across the third-base line and under the bench. Three runs

score. The batter, a fatso, chugs into second. The other team hoots and hollers, and
what does she do? She shrugs and smiles ("Oh, silly me"); after all, it's only a game.
Like the aforementioned strikeout artist, she treats her error as a joke. They have for-
given themselves instantly, which is unforgivable. It is *we* who should forgive them,
who can say, "It's all right, it's only a game." They are supposed to throw up their
hands and kick the dirt and hang their heads, as if this boner, even if it is their sixteenth of the afternoon—*this* is the one that really and truly breaks their hearts.

5   That attitude sweetens the game for everyone. The sinner feels sweet remorse.
The fatso feels some sense of accomplishment; this is no bunch of rumdums he
forced into an error but a team with some class. We, the sinner's teammates, feel
momentary anger at her—dumb! dumb play!—but then, seeing her grief, we sympathize with her in our hearts (any one of us might have made that mistake or
one worse), and we yell encouragement, including the shortstop, who, moments before, dropped an easy throw for a force at second. "That's all right! Come on! We
got 'em!" we yell. "Shake it off! These turkeys can't hit!" This makes us all feel
good, even though the turkeys now lead us by ten runs. We're getting clobbered, but
we have a winning attitude.

6   Let me say this about attitude: Each player is responsible for his or her own attitude, and to a considerable degree you can *create* a good attitude by doing certain
little things on the field. These are certain little things that ballplayers do in the Bigs,
and we ought to be doing them in the Slows.

1. When going up to bat, don't step right into the batter's box as if it were an elevator. The box is your turf, your stage. Take possession of it slowly and deliberately, starting with a lot of back-bending, knee-stretching, and torso-revolving
   in the on-deck circle. Then, approaching the box, stop outside it and tap the dirt
   off your spikes with your bat. You don't have spikes, you have sneakers, of
   course, but the significance of the tapping is the same. Then, upon entering the
   box, spit on the ground. It's a way of saying, "This here is mine. This is where I
   get my hits."
2. Spit frequently. Spit at all crucial moments. Spit correctly. Spit should be *blown,*
   not ptuied weakly with the lips, which often results in dribble. Spitting should
   convey forcefulness of purpose, concentration, pride. Spit down, not in the direction of others. Spit in the glove and on the fingers, especially after making a
   real knucklehead play; it's a way of saying, "I dropped the ball because my glove
   was dry."
3. At the bat and in the field, pick up dirt. Rub dirt in the fingers (especially after
   spitting on them). Toss dirt, as if testing the wind for velocity and direction.
   Smooth the dirt. Be involved with dirt. If no dirt is available (e.g., in the out-
   field), pluck tufts of grass. Fielders should be grooming their areas constantly
   between plays, flicking away tiny sticks and bits of gravel.
4. Take your time. Tie your laces. Confer with your teammates about possible
   situations that may arise and conceivable options in dealing with them.
   Extend the game. Three errors on three consecutive plays can be humiliating
   if the plays occur within the space of a couple of minutes, but if each error

is separated from the next by extensive conferences on the mound, lace-tying, glove adjustments, and arguing close calls (if any), the effect on morale is minimized.

5. Talk. Not just an occasional "Let's get a hit now" but continuous rhythmic chatter, a flow of syllables: "Hey babe hey babe c'mon babe good stick now hey babe long tater take him downtown babe . . . hey good eye good eye."

Infield chatter is harder to maintain. Since the slow-pitch is required to be a soft underhand lob, infielders hesitate to say, "Smoke him babe hey low heat hey throw it on the black babe chuck it in there back him up babe no hit no hit." Say it anyway.

6. One final rule, perhaps the most important of all: When your team is up and has made the third out, the batter and the players who were left on base do not come back to the bench for their gloves. *They remain on the field, and their teammates bring their gloves out to them.* This requires some organization and discipline, but it pays off big in morale. It says, "Although we're getting our pants knocked off, still we must conserve our energy."

7   Imagine that you have bobbled two fly balls in this rout and now you have just tried to stretch a single into a double and have been easily thrown out sliding into second base, where the base runner ahead of you had stopped. It was the third out and a dumb play, and your opponents smirk at you as they run off the field. You are the goat, a lonely and tragic figure sitting in the dirt. You curse yourself, jerking your head sharply forward. You stand up and kick the base. How miserable! How degrading! Your utter shame, though brief, bears silent testimony to the worthiness of your teammates, whom you have let down, and they appreciate it. They call out to you now as they take the field, and as the second baseman runs to his position he says, "Let's get 'em now," and tosses you your glove. Lowering your head, you trot slowly out to right. There you do some deep knee bends. You pick grass. You find a pebble and fling it into foul territory. As the first batter comes to the plate, you check the sun. You get set in your stance, poised to fly. Feet spread, hands on hips, you bend slightly at the waist and spit the expert spit of a veteran ballplayer—a player who has known the agony of defeat but who always bounces back, a player who has lost a stride on the base paths but can still make the big play.

8   This is *ball,* ladies and gentlemen. This is what it's all about.

■ **TOPICAL CONSIDERATIONS**

1. What does Keillor believe is the wrong attitude to have toward playing softball? What does he believe is the right attitude? If it's just a game, why is attitude so important?

2. Why does Keillor encourage his teammates to tap the dirt off their spikes when they are only wearing tennis shoes without spiked soles? What other apparently unnecessary acts does he insist they perform? Why does he feel these acts are so essential to the way the game is played?

3. How could Keillor's thesis and his comments about how to approach a game of softball be related to other activities? How could it help a student pass a course? Earn a promotion on a job? Get along better with a girlfriend or boyfriend?

4. How familiar is Keillor with professional baseball practices? Is he writing from firsthand or little, if any, experience? Cite specific passages to prove your point.

5. Suppose Murray Ross the author of "Football Red and Baseball Green," were to happen by one afternoon while Keillor and his team were playing a casual game of slow-pitch softball. While sitting on the bench with Ross, what comments might Keillor make about baseball as a reflection of American character?

■ RHETORICAL CONSIDERATIONS

1. Keillor introduces his thesis in installments. Where does he actually state it? Identify each of the stages that leads up to it.

2. Writers strive to use specifics to show their readers what they mean and to avoid speaking in vague generalities. Is Keillor successful in this? Cite specific passages that prove your point.

3. Keillor refers to the "Bigs" and the "Slows" (paragraph 6). He describes a member of the opposite team as a "fatso" and his team as "no bunch of rum-dums" (paragraph 5). Given these examples, how would you characterize the diction of this essay? Can you cite other examples?

4. Keillor often uses verbs that create a vivid word picture. In paragraph 4 he states: "The batter, a fatso, chugs into second." What image does "chugs" convey? What other interesting verbs does Keillor use?

5. What does Keillor's last sentence remind you of? Why is this a good concluding line?

■ WRITING ASSIGNMENTS

1. Write an essay in which you explain your own views on the proper attitude to take toward some other sport. Draw on ideas from Keillor's essay that you agree with. Select incidents and examples that illustrate the points you want to make.

2. Attitude is important for professional athletes, musicians, singers, actors, and other performers. Write an essay about the effect the right attitude has on a nonathletic activity such as playing a musical instrument, singing, or writing.

Girls at Bat

Anna Quindlen

Without a doubt today's women are beneficiaries of the considerable efforts made by the feminist movement begun nearly 30 years ago. Old stereotypes have faded as barriers to women's progress have fallen in most fields including sports. And that is the subject of this essay—the "girls of summer." Although Anna Quindlen had no option to play Little League as a girl, she is delighted that more girls today are at bat and more women are playing professionally. But will they ever cry, "Mighty Stacie has struck out"?

This essay first appeared in Quindlen's "Life in the 30's" column of the *New York Times* in June of 1988. Since its publication, she has become the mother of two sons and a daughter. Quindlen is also the author of the novels *Object Lesson* (1991) and *One True Thing* (1994) and the collection of essays, *Thinking Out Loud* (1993).

1 I can't tell you what a kick I get out of Little League these days. It's not that I'm a mother now, and can place my own stifled competitive spirit in the little mitts of my sons. They are too young for baseball, and who knows if they will have much interest when they grow older? It's not even that Little League seems to have improved greatly since my brothers played: back then, most coaches seemed to feel that the point of the exercise was to humiliate children and ram their shortcomings down their throats.

2 One of my brothers told me the other day that his oldest boy is playing this year, and that he was amazed and cheered by the emphasis on sportsmanship, on having a good time, on doing the best you can and giving everyone a turn. He said that during the games the children keep asking for the score, and the coach keeps telling them the score is not that important. In contrast, when my brother was in Little League, the score could be stated in three words: Win or die.

3 That's all great, but what I like about Little League today is simpler: those sweet moments when the batter makes a clean hit, and the shortstop fields it nicely, and he runs as fast as he can to second base but she tags him out, just in the nick of time. Or when the pitcher has to stop and readjust her hat to keep her bangs out of her eyes. Or when the left fielder catches a high pop fly and the batter mutters, "Stupid girl."

4 If I ever have a daughter, she will be able to play baseball. If my sons play baseball, they will play with girls as a matter of course. We're not talking about the Supreme Court here, or the White House, but, my goodness, for a former girl like me, what a difference a couple of decades makes.

5 When we were the girls of summer, our lives were different. Making plaques of plaster with our handprints in them to take home from day camp. Weaving endless chains out of elaborately folded chewing-gum wrappers (I cannot, for the life of me

now, remember the folding formula, or the point). Playing Baby in the Air and Monkey in the Middle in the street. Some nights the boys were there, and some nights they were at Little League practice, or even at actual games, proud as punch in their Central Plumbing or Downtown Hardware shirts and hats.

6   Strangely, I don't remember resenting it, unlike some women who are professional athletes now and who say they were galvanized by being excluded. Probably, secretly, I saw it as a blessing. I have the eye-hand coordination of a department-store dummy; I may be the only person who contrived to go to college in the 1970's and to never throw a Frisbee. When I compare notes with my husband, who was an indifferent athlete as a boy, I think his memories of not doing well are much more painful than my memories of not doing at all.

7   And I did play sports as a girl. I had no choice. But they were second-rate sports, it seemed to me; ephemeral sports; sports that were as important then in the real world as Baby in the Air was. Field hockey. Volleyball. Softball. Basketball was the exception and, not coincidentally, the sport I liked best, with its occasional suggestion of aggression and hostile body contact. But even that was girl's basketball. One summer I spent all my time playing on a park court with a group of tolerant boys— one or two thought the way to a girl's heart was to let her shoot from the outside—and I had to relearn all the rules. My teammates were stunned at the mishmash I had acquired from the women who coached me in gym. Still, I wasn't a half-bad guard.

8   But the boys played sports that were important: sports that people would show up to watch in the high school gym; sports that they would go on to play in college and, if they were terribly gifted, for large sums of money in professional athletics, which at some level passed for real life. The girls, of course, were cheerleaders, which required some athletic skill then and a good deal now, but which is really nothing more than a metaphor for traditional relationships between men and women, complete with short skirts and artificial smiles.

9   Perhaps my aspirations would have been different if I had grown up playing Little League, although I suspect not. I never think that if my life had not been blighted by lack of opportunity, a public-address system in the Bronx would be quavering, "Now playing third base for the New York Yankees. . . " with my husband and my father cheering in the spousal seats. Lots of other women managed to thrive despite the segregation: the tough-as-nails women who play volleyball in the Olympic Games, the ones who have tried and failed and tried again to make women's basketball as popular as men's, and the girls who have insisted on going out for the high school football team.

10   It's nice that girls in Little League have become commonplace now, so that many people don't think much about it. Except for me. I think about it a lot, fondly. I like to see the little girls go off, in their high socks and their hats and their Central Hardware shirts, doing something that I was not allowed to do. Who knows what they might grow up to be? Who knows what they might feel capable of doing? Who knows whether one of them might, incredibly, be publicly maligned by George Steinbrenner in the decades to come?

■ TOPICAL CONSIDERATIONS

1. According to Anna Quindlen, how do sports for children in the past contrast with sports for children today? From your own experience and observations, does her assessment ring true? Explain your answer.

2. Quindlen says that she does not remember resenting the fact that in her youth only boys played Little League. What reasons does she offer? By contrast, how did exclusion affect some of today's female professional athletes?

3. If you are a woman, did you experience exclusion from athletics as a girl? Or, do you know women who were excluded because of gender? If so, what were the effects? Do you know any women, yourself included, who play college or professional sports? How did their participation in, or exclusion from, athletics as girls affect their competition as adults?

4. If you are a male, did you play sports as a boy? If so, were there girls on the teams? Do you recall whether or not they participated equally or whether or not they were treated differently from boys? Explain.

5. Quindlen says that her husband's memories of not doing well are more painful than her memories of not playing sports at all. Do you think this is an accurate assessment of males and females today? Or, have times so changed since Quindlen's days?

6. Quindlen speaks of playing "second-rate sports" as a girl (paragraph 7). From you observation, are girl's sports today still "second-rate," "ephemeral," and ultimately unimportant? If so, what do you perceive are the problems? If not, what changes have been made, and why? What about on the collegiate level? Do women's athletics draw the same attention and support as do men's? What differences, if any, can you explain?

7. In paragraph 8, Quindlen says that girls' cheerleading "is really nothing more than a metaphor for traditional relationships between men and women." What does she mean by this statement? Do you agree with her? If so, why? If not, why not?

8. Did you ever play Little League? If so, do you recall active participation by girls? Were they treated the same as boys on the team? Were they excluded or treated differently by coaches and/or teammates?

9. Do you think that people's aspirations have anything to do with whether or not they played organized sports as kids? Do you think this is true for both males and females? Can you think of any individuals you know who bear out your observations?

■ RHETORICAL CONSIDERATIONS

1. At what point in the essay do you know Quindlen's focus? How does she cue her purpose?

2. Comment on the choice of pronouns in paragraph 3. What strategy is Quindlen using? Had the gender of the pronouns been switched, how would Quindlen's point have been altered?

3. What part of the essay did you find most interesting? Where was it less in-teresting? What are the differences between the two?

4. How would you characterize the style and tone of the writing here? (Consider, among other things, Quindlen's word choice, syntax, specific observations and evaluations.) What kind of a personality does the author project? Does she sound like somebody you would like to know? Explain your answer.

5. What do you remember best about the actual writing of this essay? Explain your answer.

6. Consider the concluding paragraph. Was this ending satisfying for you? Did it capture the tone, slant, and emphasis of the essay? Explain your answer.

■ **WRITING ASSIGNMENTS**

1. Throughout the essay, Quindlen reflects on her own experience, or lack of it, in sports. Try some reflection of your own. In a paper try to recall your own experiences and/or observations of organized sports from your youth. If you played, how would you assess your performance? What differences do you recall in the participation, performance, and encouragement of boys versus girls? What differences, if any, in sportsmanship? Did your participation, or lack of it, have any effect on your aspirations and/or competitiveness today? Cite some specific recollections to support your opinions.

2. If you attend a coed school, try to evaluate the differences between the men's and women's athletics in terms of sportsmanship and performance, as well as general support by the administration and student body. Try to ex-plain any differences you see. Do you find any discrimination that you would cite as sexist? Explain.

3. Write a paper in which you explore whether or not women's baseball— collegiate or professional—will eventually enjoy the same sponsorship, exposure, fan support, and training as does men's.

	Playing to Win
	Margaret A. Whitney

As Anna Quindlen points out in the previous piece, females are more active in athletics today than ever before. Girls on the Little League diamonds are a common sight. In high school and college, women's sports have experienced burgeoning growth. And across America millions of women swim, run, play golf, volleyball and do aerobics. But as women move onto playing fields traditionally ruled by men, questions of femininity, sexuality, power, and freedom arise. The following essay is an assessment of a young woman who as a high-school basketball player overcame family and the forces of tradition to sit still and be pretty. The essay was written by her mother who finds in the message of sports inspiration for her own midlife quest. Margaret A. Whitney is a writer and a doctoral candidate in technical communications at Rensselaer Polytechnic Institute. This article was first published in *The New York Times* Magazine in July 1988.

1 My daughter is an athlete. Nowadays, this statement won't strike many parents as unusual, but it does me. Until her freshman year in high school, Ann was only marginally interested in sport of any kind. When she played, she didn't swing hard, often dropped the ball, and had an annoying habit of tittering on field or court.

2 Indifference combined with another factor that did not bode well for a sports career. Ann was growing up to be beautiful. By the eighth grade, nature and orthodontics had produced a 5-foot-8-inch, 125-pound, brown-eyed beauty with a wonderful smile. People told her, too. And, as many young women know, it is considered a satisfactory accomplishment to be pretty and stay pretty. Then you can simply sit still and enjoy the unconditional positive regard. Ann loved the attention too, and didn't consider it demeaning when she was awarded "Best Hair," female category, in the eighth-grade yearbook.

3 So it came as a surprise when she became a jock. The first indication that athletic indifference had ended came when she joined the high-school cross-country team. She signed up in early September and ran third for the team within three days. Not only that. After one of those 3.1-mile races up hill and down dale on a rainy November afternoon, Ann came home muddy and bedraggled. Her hair was plastered to her head, and the mascara she had applied so carefully that morning ran in dark circles under her eyes. This is it, I thought. Wait until Lady Astor sees herself. But the kid with the best eighth-grade hair went on to finish the season and subsequently letter in cross-country, soccer, basketball and softball.

4 I love sports, she tells anyone who will listen. So do I, though my midlife quest for a doctorate leaves me little time for either playing or watching. My love of sports is bound up with the goals in my life and my hopes for my three daughters. I have begun to hear the message of sports. It is very different from many messages that women receive about living, and I think it is good.

5 My husband, for example, talked to Ann differently when he realized that she was a serious competitor and not just someone who wanted to get in shape so she'd look good in a prom dress. Be aggressive, he'd advise. Go for the ball. Be intense.

6 Be intense. She came in for some of the most scathing criticism from her dad, when, during basketball season, her intensity waned. You're pretending to play hard, he said. You like it on the bench? Do you like to watch while your teammates play?

7 I would think, how is this kid reacting to such advice? For years, she'd been told at home, at school, by countless advertisements, "Be quiet, Be good, Be still." When teachers reported that Ann was too talkative, not obedient enough, too flighty. When I dressed her up in frilly dresses and admonished her not to get dirty. When ideals of femininity are still, quiet, cool females in ads whose vacantness passes

for sophistication. How can any adolescent girl know what she's up against? Have you ever really noticed intensity? It is neither quiet nor good. And it's definitely not pretty.

8   In the end, her intensity revived. At half time, she'd look for her father, and he would come out of the bleachers to discuss tough defense, finding the open player, squaring up on her jump shot. I'd watch them at the edge of the court, a tall man and a tall girl, talking about how to play.

9   Of course I'm particularly sensitive at this point in my life to messages about trying hard, being active, getting better through individual and team effort. Ann, you could barely handle a basketball two years ago. Now you're bringing the ball up against the press. Two defenders are after you. You must dribble, stop, pass. We're depending on you. We need you to help us. I wonder if my own paroxysms of uncertainty would be eased had more people urged me—be active, go for it!

10   Not that dangers don't lurk for the females of her generation. I occasionally run this horror show in my own mental movie theater: an unctuous but handsome lawyer-like drone of a young man spies my Ann. Hmmm, he says unconsciously to himself, good gene pool, and wouldn't she go well with my BMW and the condo? Then I see Ann with a great new hairdo kissing the drone goodbyehoney and setting off to the nearest mall with splendid-looking children to spend money.

11   But the other night she came home from softball tryouts at 6 in the evening. The dark circles under her eyes were from exhaustion, not makeup. I tried too hard today, she says. I feel like I'm going to puke.

12   After she has revived, she explains. She wants to play a particular position. There is competition for it. I can't let anybody else get my spot, she says, I've got to prove that I can do it. Later we find out that she has not gotten the much-wanted third-base position, but she will start with the varsity team. My husband talks about the machinations of coaches and tells her to keep trying. You're doing fine, he says. She gets that I-am-going-to-keep-trying look on her face. The horror-show vision of Ann-as-Stepford-Wife fades.

13   Of course, Ann doesn't realize the changes she has wrought, the power of her self-definition. I'm an athlete, Ma, she tells me when I suggest participation in the school play or the yearbook. But she has really caused us all to rethink our views of existence: her younger sisters who consider sports a natural activity for females, her father whose advocacy of women has increased, and me. Because when I doubt my own abilities, I say to myself, Get intense, Margaret. Do you like to sit on the bench?

14   And my intensity revives.

15   I am not suggesting that participation in sports is the answer for all young women. It is not easy—the losing, jealousy, raw competition and intense personal criticism of performance.

16   And I don't wish to imply that the sports scene is a morality play either. Girls' sports can be funny. You can't forget that out on that field are a bunch of people who know the meaning of the word cute. During one game, I noticed that Ann had a blue ribbon tied on her ponytail, and it dawned on me that every girl on the team had an identical bow. Somehow I can't picture the Celtics gathered in the locker room of the Boston Garden agreeing to wear the same color sweatbands.

17   No, what has struck me, amazed me and made me hold my breath in wonder and in hope is both the ideal of sport and the reality of a young girl not afraid to do her best.

18   I watch her bringing the ball up the court. We yell encouragement from the stands, though I know she doesn't hear us. Her face is red with exertion, and her body is concentrated on the task. She dribbles, draws the defense to her, passes, runs. A teammate passes the ball back to her. They've beaten the press. She heads toward the hoop. Her father watches her, her sisters watch her, I watch her. And I think, drive, Ann, drive.

■ TOPICAL CONSIDERATIONS

1. How did Ann Whitney's beauty at first work against her sports career in high school?
2. Why did it come as a surprise to the author that her daughter became a jock?
3. What does the author mean by the statement, "I have begun to hear the message of sports" (paragraph 4). What is the "message of sports"? Do you agree the message "is good"?
4. What social forces were at work against Ann becoming a serious athlete? Do you see these forces working still? Have you ever had to confront such forces?
5. In paragraph 7, Whitney says that advertisements promote "quiet and cool" images of females "whose vacantness passes for sophistication." Do you find this observation to be generally true? Find some ads in magazines to support your answer. Can you find many ads in which such traditional female "ideals" are not projected—ads of active, competitive women?
6. The author says that she wishes when she was young she had been encouraged to be more active, to "go for it!" (paragraph 9). Why does she say this?
7. What "dangers" to her daughter's athletic career does Whitney fear? How does Ann allay her mother's fears?
8. This essay is more than just a celebration of the author's daughter. In your own words, what higher matters are celebrated?

■ RHETORICAL CONSIDERATIONS

1. How do the opening two lines forecast the central conflicts of the essay?
2. In paragraph 4, the author relates her daughter's athletic drive to her own "midlife quest" for a doctorate. How well does the author weave this issue into her essay? Does it ever take away from the story of her daughter? Does it add to it?
3. What is the rhetorical purpose and effect of the sudden switch to a direct address of Ann in the present tense in paragraph 9? Where else does this switch in perspective appear?

4. Explain the "Lady Astor" allusion in paragraph 3. Explain the "Ann-as-Stepford-Wife" allusion in paragraph 12.

■ **WRITING ASSIGNMENTS**

1. The author makes the point that female beauty works against female drive. Do you find this to be true? Do you think that women who are attractive are encouraged to be passive? Write an essay in which you explore this question. In it, address the same forces of school, family, and advertising.

2. Do you think females in sports receive the same quality of training as do males? Do they receive the same kind of encouragement? Write an essay examining any differences you have observed.

3. Do you see any difference in the athletic training females of your generation received and that of your parents? Talk to your parents about this, or someone from an older generation. Write an essay in which you compare the training of today's women with that of women from the past. Include personal experiences to illustrate the differences.

4. Write your own essay about "playing to win." Speak from either your own experience as an athlete or from the observation of athletes—male or female—you know or admire. Try to capture a sense of the drive and determination to excel in your essay.

Education in 1990s America is at a turning point. Educators argue that students aren't learning the way they used to while students and parents complain that teachers, professors, and curricula aren't measuring up to previous standards. What everybody agrees on is that changes from kindergarten through college better be made or we risk abandoning the future to chance. The essays in this chapter offer perspectives on what's wrong (and a little of what's right) with the state of education today.

Page Smith's "Killing the Spirit" looks critically at what you as students will come to know well in your college experience—the lecture. It has been estimated that almost 90 percent of all instruction at the university level is by the lecture method. Even if the lecturer is not dull, argues Professor Smith, without dialogue between student and instructor "there can be no genuine education."

The next piece, "A Liberating Curriculum," also by a college professor, grew out of a sorry realization that she has wasted over twenty years trying to educate students properly. As Roberta F. Borkat explains, instead of all those hours spent grading papers, explaining exams, holding conferences, conveying knowledge, she should have just passed out an A to everybody and saved herself and students hours of anxiety and concern. After all, isn't the reason for going to college to graduate with the highest gradepoint for the least effort?

"Why My Kids Hate Science" addresses the declining interest in science in American schools and colleges. It was written by scientist Robert M. Hazen who blames schools and scientists for this illiteracy that, he says, dulls the capacity to appreciate the elegant principles governing the universe.

The questionable state of history education is the subject of the essay that follows. According to Jonathan Alter and Lydia Denworth in "A (Vague) Sense of History," too few high-school graduates have mastered basic historic facts. The fear is that such national amnesia may affect our future as a democratic nation and as individuals. Unlike science or math, historical illiteracy cannot be linked to loss of international competitiveness. The problem is with the teaching of history. And, as reported, much is being done to reduce boredom and to incorporate multiculturalism in the curriculum.

On the theme of math education, we've taken a lighter approach. In "Can America be No. 1 in Math? You Bet Your Noogie," humorist Dave Barry recalls the formative experience of high-school math class to suggest how parents can do something about the "mathematical boneheadism" plaguing our nation.

Our final selection is an inspiring address on teaching and learning by best-selling author Robert Fulghum. In "A Bag of Possibles and Other Matters of the Mind," Fulghum calls on students to rediscover their natural creative talents and on educators to rekindle the self-esteem that kids lose between kindergarten and college.

	Killing the Spirit
	Page Smith

Drawing on some thirty years of college teaching, Page Smith scrutinizes that hallmark of the university experience: the lecture. Before reading this essay, consider the number of hours you've spent listening to lectures in your college career. Take a moment to evaluate those lectures making a list of strong and weak points. Ask yourself what makes a lecturer a success or a failure. Once you've done that, you'll be ready to react to Smith's contention that "the lecture system is the most inefficient way of transmitting knowledge ever devised." Mr. Smith is the author of fifteen books, the most recent of which is *Killing the Spirit* (1990) from which this essay was taken.

1   I came away from my years of teaching on the college and university level with a conviction that enactment, performance, dramatization are the most successful forms of teaching. Students must be incorporated, made, so far as possible, an integral part of the learning process. The notion that learning should have in it an element of inspired play would seem to the greater part of the academic establishment merely frivolous, but that is nonetheless the case. Of Ezekiel Cheever, the most famous schoolmaster of the Massachusetts Bay Colony, his onetime student Cotton Mather wrote that he so planned his lessons that his pupils "came to work as though they came to play," and Alfred North Whitehead, almost three hundred years later, noted that a teacher should make his/her students "glad they were there."

2   Since, we are told, 80 to 90 percent of all instruction in the typical university is by the lecture method, we should give close attention to this form of education. There is, I think, much truth in Patricia Nelson Limerick's observation that "lecturing is an unnatural act, an act for which providence did not design humans. It is perfectly all right, now and then, for a human to be possessed by the urge to speak, and to speak while others remain silent. But to do this regularly, one hour and 15 minutes at a time . . . for one person to drone on while others sit in silence? . . . I do not believe that this is what the Creator . . . designed humans to do."

3   The strange, almost incomprehensible fact is that many professors, just as they feel obliged to write dully, believe that they should lecture dully. To show enthusiasm is to risk appearing unscientific, unobjective; it is to appeal to the students' emotions rather than their intellect. Thus the ideal lecture is one crammed with facts and read in an uninflected monotone. Witness the testimony of the eminent sociologist Daniel Bell.

4   When Bell gave a talk to the faculty and staff and some graduate students at the Leningrad State University during a trip to Russia, he spoke extemporaneously (which professors seldom do) and with evident emotion, which clearly moved his listeners profoundly but which left Bell feeling "an odd turbulence. . . . For years," he writes, "I had fought within myself against giving emotional speeches. They were easy, cheap, sentimental, lachrymose. . . . In the lectures I usually give . . . I have tried to be expository, illustrative . . . resenting the cheap jibes to get a rise out of the

audience." Here, to his discomfort, he had let emotion get the best of him and, plainly, of his audience. I would only note that the kind of austerity and lack of emotion that Bell normally strove for is the classic mode of the American professor lecturing to his class.

5   The cult of lecturing dully, like the cult of writing dully, goes back, of course, some years. Edward Shils, professor of sociology and social thought at the University of Chicago, recalls the professors he encountered at the University of Pennsylvania in his youth. They seemed "a priesthood, rather uneven in their merits but uniform in their bearing; they never referred to anything personal. Some read from old lecture notes—one of them used to unroll the dog-eared lower corners of his foolscap manuscript and then haltingly decipher the thumb-worn last lines. Others lectured from cards that had served for years, to judge by the worn and furry edges. . . . The teachers began on time, ended on time, and left the room without saying a word more to their students, very seldom being detained by questioners. . . . Almost all male students wore suits, all wore neckties. . . . The classes were not large, yet there was no discussion. No questions were raised in class, and there were no office hours."

6   William Lyon Phelps described the Yale faculty in the 1890s thusly: "nearly all the members of the Faculty wore dark clothes, frock coats, high collars; in the classroom their manners had an icy formality. . . ." The clothes and manners have become informal, but the aloofness and impersonality, I fear, remain.

7   Karl Jaspers makes the point that the lecture, like research, must never become routine. It is the opportunity for the teacher to present in dramatic fashion, highlighted by his/her own insight and enthusiasm, material that cannot be conveyed with the same potency on the printed page. In the lecture the student must see *enacted* the power and excitement of ideas. The posture, gestures, and intonations of the lecturer carry as much force as the words themselves, words that, when reduced to notes, often lie quite inert on the page.

8   The lecture has a quasi-religious character about it, since exalted speech partakes of the sacred. Every lecture, listened to by dozens or hundreds of students, should partake of art (dramatic art being perhaps the closest). The lecturer who reads his notes dutifully is performing an act that the students can do better for themselves. Such an instructor gives up the very element of spontaneity which alone justifies the lecture as a form of teaching. The lecturer must *address* students. He/she is, after all, asking a good deal of them. If there are two hundred students in the class, the lecturer is saying to them, in effect: What I have to say is of such considerable consequence that I feel entitled to take up two hundred precious hours of your collective time in order to explain it to you, or, even better, in order to enlarge your sense of the possibilities of human existence in relation to this topic we are considering together. "Lectures which aim to sum up an entire subject are in a class by themselves," Jaspers writes. "Such lectures should be given only by the most mature professors drawing upon the sum total of their life's work. . . . Such lectures belong to what is irreplaceable in tradition. The memory of outstanding scholars lecturing, accompanies one throughout life. The printed lecture, perhaps even taken down word for word, is only a pale residue." The inspired lecture evokes, again in Jaspers'

words, "something from the teacher which would remain hidden without it. . . . He allows us to take part in his innermost intellectual being." The great lecture is thus a demonstration of something precious and essential in the life of the spirit and the mind, and the dramatic power that inheres in that unity. Such lectures link us with the sermons and political addresses that have played central roles in the "great chain of being" that links classes and generations and nations together in "the unity of spirit." Thus the casual, the perfunctory, the oft-repeated, the read lecture, the *dead* lecture, is a disservice both to the students and to the ideal of learning that presumably holds the whole venture together.

9   William Lyon Phelps at Yale was a "great teacher," in the classic tradition. "If a teacher wishes success with pupils, he must inflame their imagination," he wrote. "The lesson should put the classroom under the spell of an illusion, like a great drama." The abstract should be avoided. "If a pupil feels the reality of any subject, feels it in relation to actual life, half the battle is gained. Terms must be clothed in flesh and blood. . . ," Phelps wrote. The modern professor often takes a contrary turn. The real things are the abstractions; the personal, the individual, the anecdotal are all distractions and indulgences. A professor may give the same course, covering the same material, year in and year out (it is, after all, his "field," and he is actively discouraged from stepping outside it). He/she may go so far as to incorporate in the lectures the latest "researchers," to the degree that they are relevant to undergraduate students, but unless he/she rethinks each lecture, reanimates it, *reappropriates* it, and thereby makes evident to his listeners why they should take their valuable time to listen, the lecturer is discrediting the lecture system and the process of learning that the lecture system represents. The lecturer is putting forward a "negative stereotype," as we say, not just of himself and of lectures in general, but of the whole edifice of higher education. If the lecturer is bored by the constant repetition of familiar material, he may be sure that his auditors are even more bored. The comedian Professor Irwin Corey had a popular routine in which he fell asleep while lecturing; it was invariably greeted with enthusiastic applause.

10   In his fourteen-week survey of the great universities in 1910, the journalist Edwin Slosson attended more than a hundred classes. His strongest impression was "the waste of time and energy in the ordinary collegiate instruction." There was "no lack of industry, devotion, and enthusiasm on the part of the teachers, but the educational results," Slosson wrote, "are not commensurate with the opportunities afforded and the efforts expended." One's strongest impression was of "lost motion." There was "no general appreciation of the fact that the printing press had been invented in the years since the rise of the Medieval university." Most of the professors lectured poorly, and many did not "even take pains to speak distinctly enough so that they can be heard in their small classrooms without strained attention." Conveying information by ear was a strikingly inefficient way of transmitting it, especially to passive, note-taking students who often showed little comprehension of what they were hearing. "The lecture," Slosson concluded, "is useful for inspiration and demonstration, but not for information." It was apparent to Slosson that, despite its obvious and, in the main, undisputed shortcomings, the lecture was persisted in because it was the quickest and easiest way for a professor to discharge his nominal

obligations as a teacher of undergraduate students. One of the unfortunate consequences was that the professor commonly indulged himself in excessively detailed information in the field of his academic specialty, often scanting or ignoring issues of the greatest importance and interest to his captive auditors.

11   I must confess that my own attitude toward lecturing was deeply influenced by my experience in teaching Dante's *Divine Comedy* in a seminar. When I suggested to my students that they devise some modern hells for modern sins, two students in the seminar offered interesting hells for professors-who-neglected-their-students. They proposed that the professors be required to listen to lectures for all eternity. The only point of dispute between them was whether it would be worse torment for professors to have to listen to their own lectures or to those of an especially dull colleague. I have never been able to feel the same way about lecturing since. Every time in the intervening years that I have undertaken to lecture, I have suffered from posttraumatic stress syndrome.

12   I think it is fair to say that the lecture system is the most inefficient way of transmitting knowledge ever devised. It would be much more effective, in most instances, simply to print up a lecturer's notes and distribute them to the students at the beginning of the course. Or students might be given reading lists of important books to pursue on their own initiative. In many instances it would be more useful to let the students give the lectures. All this is not to say, of course, that particularly inventive and enterprising professors can't overcome the most negative aspects of the lecture system, but only to point out that very few do. Indeed, it is the nature of things that there are only a few great lecturers. In the thirty-some years in which I had contact with the academic world, I knew only five or six. They were individuals who had passionately held views of life as well as deep knowledge of their subjects. They took every lecture with the greatest seriousness and spoke as though they realized that to speak was both a privilege and a responsibility. Eugen Rosenstock-Huessy, William Hitchcock, Mary Holmes, Norman O. Brown, Donald Nichol, and Paul Lee all fell into that category.

13   The most conclusive argument against the lecture system is that all true education must involve response. If there is no dialogue, written or spoken, there can be no genuine education. The student must be lured out of his or her instinctive passivity. This can only be done properly if an atmosphere of trust is built in the classroom or seminar. The professor cannot ask his students to expose their innermost hopes and feelings unless he is equally candid with them and allows them to see him as a fallable, searching individual.

14   The best discussion of the relationship between professors and their students (which, of course, is at the heart of all true teaching) is, I am pleased to say, by a former student of mine, Patricia Nelson Limerick, a professor of history at the University of Colorado. After describing a number of imaginative ways to involve students in classroom exercises designed to break down the barriers between "aloof professors" and "shy students," Limerick writes: "In all these exercises, my goals have been the same; to bump students out of passivity, and to bump myself out of self-consciousness and sometimes out of complacency. . . . By contrast, the more conventional tensions of the classroom cause students and professors to fear making

fools of themselves. . . . The underlying reason for holding class, whatever the subject or the course, has to involve the project of inviting students to think for themselves, to ask their own questions, and to pursue the answers with both freedom of thought and discipline of argument." If a professor tries to promote such a notion in the conventional classroom, "there is such a disjunction between the medium and the message," Limerick writes, "that the project will work for only a few. . . . The trial and burden of adventurous teaching is that it never feels safe—you never sign a contract with the universe guaranteeing success in all your experiments."

15   That, of course, is the essence of teaching—taking chances. And you can only do that if you are willing to come down from your perch as a professor of this or that and be as vulnerable (or almost as vulnerable) as your students. No professional vulnerability, no real teaching.

16   Karl Jaspers wrote, "The reverence and love rendered to the master's person have something of worship in them," but Jaspers goes on to point out that the master must turn this "reverence and love" into the channels of learning in a manner perhaps akin to the analytic "transference," wherein the scrupulous analyst directs the patient's instinctive attachment to the analyst back toward the process of healing. Jaspers' ideal in the teaching relationship is the Socratic method, whereby teacher and student "stand on the same level. . . . No hard and fast educational system exists here, rather endless questioning and ultimate ignorance in the face of the absolute."

17   The geologist Israel C. Russell wrote in the journal *Science* in 1904: "In the school of research . . . professor and student should be co-workers and mutually assist each other. From such comradeship, that intangible something which is transmitted from person to person by association and contact, but cannot be written or spoken—we may term it 'inspiration,' or personal magnetism, or perhaps the radium of the soul—is acquired by the student to a greater degree than at any previous time in his life after leaving the caressing arms of his mother."

18   Alfred North Whitehead's wife, Evelyn, told Lucien Price: "When we first came to Harvard, Altie's [Whitehead's] colleagues in the department said, *'Don't let the students interfere with your work!'* Ten or fifteen minutes is long enough for any conference with them." Instead of following his colleagues' advice, Whitehead, who lectured three times a week, would give his students "a whole afternoon or a whole evening. . . . The traffic was two-way, for Whitehead felt that he needed contact with young minds to keep his own springs flowing. 'It is all nonsense,' he said, 'to suppose that the old cannot learn from the young.'"

19   Contacts between professors and their students outside the classroom, ideally in walks or sports or social occasions, are as important as or perhaps more important than classroom contacts, because they reveal something to the student about reality that can, I suspect, be learned no other way. Such contacts demonstrate that ideas are "embodied." They do not exist apart from a person, remote or near at hand, who enunciates, who takes responsibility for them by declaring them, by speaking about them. It is not only that ideas have consequences; they are held, passionately or perhaps frivolously, by individuals; otherwise they could not survive; they would die of inattention, and of course many do. We are all dependent, in the last analysis, on readers or listeners (and responders) who by responding remind us that we are talking to living souls.

20   In Woodrow Wilson's words: "The ideal college . . . should be a community, a place of close, natural, intimate association, not only of the young men who are its pupils and novices in various lines of study but also of young men with older men . . . of teachers with pupils, outside the classroom as well as inside. . . ."

21   When it became evident beyond question or cavil that professors were determined to ignore the "moral and spiritual" needs of their students, a new academic order called "counselors" was created. Counselors were in essence men and women employed to do what the traditional college education had professed to do (but which it had seldom done)—that is to say, care for what we would call today the psychological needs of the student, what, indeed, John Jay Chapman's ladies and bishops and teas had done at Harvard: provide some human contact, some counsel and advice. I suspect "ladies, Bishops and tea" were a sounder remedy for the distress of undergraduates not simply ignored but positively rebuffed by their instructors. The trouble was (and is) that most of the students who find their way to counselors are near the end of their rope. They have, as we say today, serious "problems." One can only speculate that there might be far fewer such "problems" if faculty members were willing to lend sympathetic ears to the trials and tribulations of the young men and women they are supposed to teach. Their defense, as one might suspect, is that they are not "experts" in matters pertaining to the psychological needs of students, they are only experts in Sanskrit, or economics or abnormal psychology or chemistry. I have long maintained that Ionesco's *The Lesson* should be performed each year for entering freshmen at our institutions of higher learning to prepare them for the years ahead. The reader may recall that in *The Lesson* the student arrives to interrupt the professor in his researches on the origin of ancient Spanish verbs. While he is lecturing on the subject, she experiences acute pain from a toothache. The professor ignores her cries until they become too obtrusive, at which point he strangles her. The play ends as another student arrives.

22   Testimony to the bad consciences of universities about the sorry state of the teaching function is the widespread practice of awarding, with much fanfare, cash prizes to the "teacher-of-the-year." This is supposed to demonstrate the institution's commitment to "excellence in teaching." What it does, in fact, is to distort and demean the true nature of teaching. It is also often the case that untenured winners of such awards soon disappear from the scene, victims of the publish-or-perish rule. So often has this been the case on some campuses that there has been pressure from the administration to make the award only to faculty who have already attained tenure, thus sparing the university the embarrassment of firing someone who has just been recognized as an outstanding teacher. Moreover, although the awards doubtless go, in the main, to deserving individuals, the winners are often those lecturers whom the students simply find the most entertaining. William Arrowsmith, the classics scholar, has written: "At present the universities are as uncongenial to teaching as the Mojave Desert to a clutch of Druid priests. If you want to restore a Druid priesthood you cannot do it by offering prizes for Druid-of-the-year. If you want Druids, you must grow forests. There is no other way of setting about it." In other words, if you want good teaching, you have to create an academic atmosphere where good teaching is encouraged, recognized, and rewarded with something more substantial than "prizes."

23   It should also be said that one of the greatest obstacles to effective teaching is
the grading system ("de-grading system" would be a better name for it). It treats the
students as isolated individuals. It pits them against each other and, in a sense,
against their teachers in a competitive struggle for survival. Only the fittest survive.
I have heard not a few professors boast of the severity of their grading. How many
students flunked a course was a measure of their tough-mindedness. In addition to
discouraging cooperation among students, grades falsify the relation between
teacher and student. The teacher's task is to win the student's confidence and to create an air of trust congenial to learning, but over this rather tender relationship there
hovers the cloud of that grade. Professors often fall into the habit of thinking of students less as people in need of help and guidance than as A students or C students, a
very bad frame of mind indeed.

■ TOPICAL CONSIDERATIONS

1. Do you think the author prefers the classic style of William Lyon Phelps or
   the modern one? Explain your answer using specific details. Which do you
   prefer? Which style have you seen more of in your school?
2. Do you agree with Smith's notion that 80 to 90 percent of all university
   instruction is lecture? In your response, discuss your own experience in
   college classes.
3. Smith begins with the point that "Students must be . . . an integral part of
   the learning process." Has this been true for you during your experience as a
   high-school and college student? Explain your answer.
4. Many students have difficulty taking lecture notes, especially if the lecture
   is dull. Do you find it easy or difficult to record the important information
   from a lecture? Describe your note-taking process during a lecture.
5. Has Smith's view of teaching changed your views, reinforced your views, or
   had no effect on your views of teaching? Explain your reasoning.
6. Alfred North Whitehead said, "It is all nonsense to suppose that the old cannot learn from the young" (paragraph 18). Do you agree or disagree? Why
   or why not?
7. Why does Smith think entering freshmen should view Ionesco's *The
   Lesson?* Do you agree? Why or why not?
8. Have you experienced classrooms where there is a dialogue between teacher
   and student? Describe how the class works and whether that method is advantageous. If you have not had such an experience, describe how you think
   it might work and whether that method would be advantageous.

■ RHETORICAL CONSIDERATIONS

1. At the beginning of the essay, Smith uses first-person point of view giving
   his opinion and backing it with several examples. After he gives a definition
   of lecturing, what change of tone does he use in the next three paragraphs?
   Is it effective? Explain why or why not.

2. The author interjects his personal feelings at several points. Give an example and explain whether you think it is effective or not.

3. When each of us writes an essay, we pull from our own experiences for examples. From where does Smith get his examples?

4. Is his use of past and present day examples effective? Use an example of each to agree or disagree.

5. Do you think this essay should end with paragraph 20, 21, or 22 rather than 23? Support your decision with valid reasoning.

6. Consider the voice of the author. Describe the author as a teacher based on his voice in this essay. Be sure to use specific examples.

■ WRITING ASSIGNMENTS

1. Has this essay influenced your view of college professors? If so, in a paper describe the influence of Smith's essay on your own views, attitudes and/or behavior.

2. We have all sat through lectures that bored us miserably. Think of a teacher or professor whose classes habitually put you to sleep or nearly so. In a paper try to analyze just what made that instructor's classes so dull. Aside from the material, consider his or her style of talking (i.e., intonation, volume, variation, accent), personal deportment, attitude, and the use or lack of anecdotes, humor, abstractions, specific details, visual aids, physical movement, gestures, facial expression, and so forth.

3. Design your own dull-lecturer's hell. In a paper try to describe what the experience should be like for outstandingly boring instructors. Try to come up with some original torments.

4. In a paper, describe a professor or teacher you have had who was truly an exception to the rule—one who was, in Smith's words (paragraph 9), a "'great teacher' in the classic tradition." In your paper, try to explain just what it was that made that person such an outstanding teacher.

A Liberating Curriculum

Roberta F. Borkat

Imagine taking courses where you didn't have to worry about grades. Better still, imagine a curriculum whereby you get an automatic grade of A in each course you enroll in. No more anxiety, no more burden of competition as you breeze through four obstacle-free years to graduation. Isn't that what college is all about? Such is the plan that Professor Roberta F. Borkat proposes after more than twenty years in the college classroom. Years, she says, of wasted efforts. Or were they?

Roberta F. Borkat is a professor of English and comparative literature at San Diego State University. Her essay first appeared in the "My Turn" column in *Newsweek* in April 1993.

1 A blessed change has come over me. Events of recent months have revealed to me that I have been laboring as a university professor for more than 20 years under a misguided theory of teaching. I humbly regret that during all those years I have caused distress and inconvenience to thousands of students while providing some amusement to my more practical colleagues. Enlightenment came to me in a sublime moment of clarity while I was being verbally attacked by a student whose paper I had just proved to have been plagiarized from "The Norton Anthology of English Literature." Suddenly, I understood the true purpose of my profession, and I devised a plan to embody that revelation. Every moment since then has been filled with delight about the advantages to students, professors and universities from my Plan to Increase Student Happiness.

2 The plan is simplicity itself: at the end of the second week of the semester, all students enrolled in each course will receive a final grade of A. Then their minds will be relieved of anxiety, and they will be free to do whatever they want for the rest of the term.

3 The benefits are immediately evident. Students will be assured of high grade-point averages and an absence of obstacles in their march toward graduation. Professors will be relieved of useless burdens and will have time to pursue their real interests. Universities will have achieved the long-desired goal of molding individual professors into interchangeable parts of a smoothly operating machine. Even the environment will be improved because education will no longer consume vast quantities of paper for books, compositions and examinations.

4 Although this scheme will instantly solve countless problems that have plagued education, a few people may raise trivial objections and even urge universities not to adopt it. Some of my colleagues may protest that we have an obligation to uphold the integrity of our profession. Poor fools, I understand their delusion, for I formerly shared it. To them, I say: "Hey, lighten up! Why make life difficult?"

5 Those who believe that we have a duty to increase the knowledge of our students may also object. I, too, used to think that knowledge was important and that we should encourage hard work and perseverance. Now I realize that the concept of re-

wards for merit is elitist and, therefore, wrong in a society that aims for equality in all things. We are a democracy. What could be more democratic than to give exactly the same grade to every single student?

6 One or two forlorn colleagues may even protest that we have a responsibility to significant works of the past because the writings of such authors as Chaucer, Shakespeare, Milton and Swift are intrinsically valuable. I can empathize with these misguided souls, for I once labored under the illusion that I was giving my students a precious gift by introducing them to works by great poets, play-wrights and satirists. Now I recognize the error of my ways. The writings of such authors may have seemed meaningful to our ancestors, who had nothing better to do, but we are living in a time of wonderful improvements. The writers of bygone eras have been made irrelevant, replaced by MTV and People magazine. After all, their bodies are dead. Why shouldn't their ideas be dead, too?

7 *Joyous smiles:* If any colleagues persist in protesting that we should try to convey knowledge to students and preserve our cultural heritage, I offer this suggestion: honestly consider what students really want. As one young man graciously explained to me, he had no desire to take my course but had enrolled in it merely to fulfill a requirement that he resented. His job schedule made it impossible for him to attend at least 30 percent of my class sessions, and he wouldn't have time to do much of the reading. Nevertheless, he wanted a good grade. Another student consulted me after the first exam, upset because she had not studied and had earned only 14 points out of a possible 100. I told her that, if she studied hard and attended class more regularly, she could do well enough on the remaining tests to pass the course. This encouragement did not satisfy her. What she wanted was an assurance that she would receive at least a B. Under my plan both students would be guaranteed an A. Why not? They have good looks and self-esteem. What more could anyone ever need in life?

8 I do not ask for thanks from the many people who will benefit. I'm grateful to my colleagues who for decades have tried to help me realize that seriousness about teaching is not the path to professorial prestige, rapid promotion and frequent sabbaticals. Alas, I was stubborn. Not until I heard the illuminating explanation of the student who had plagiarized from the anthology's introduction to Jonathan Swift did I fully grasp the wisdom that others had been generously offering to me for years— learning is just too hard. Now, with a light heart, I await the plan's adoption. In my mind's eye, I can see the happy faces of university administrators and professors, released at last from the irksome chore of dealing with students. I can imagine the joyous smiles of thousands of students, all with straight-A averages and plenty of free time.

9 My only regret is that I wasted so much time. For nearly 30 years, I threw away numerous hours annually on trivia: writing, grading and explaining examinations; grading hundreds of papers a semester; holding private conferences with students; reading countless books; buying extra materials to give students a feeling for the music, art and clothing of past centuries; endlessly worrying about how to improve my teaching. At last I see the folly of grubbing away in meaningless efforts. I

wish that I had faced facts earlier and had not lost years because of old-fashioned notions. But such are the penalties for those who do not understand the true purpose of education.

■ TOPICAL CONSIDERATIONS

1. Consider the main benefits Borkat says her "Plan to Increase Student Happiness" will have for students (paragraphs 2–3). Would you approve of such a plan? Why or why not?
2. In her last paragraph, Borkat describes how she wasted almost thirty years' time on teaching. Do you think this time was wasted or well spent? Why? Can you tell the difference between professors who put such effort into teaching, and those who do not? In general, do you believe you get a better education from harder-working teachers? Explain your answers.
3. Consider the students Borkat describes in her essay. What is their attitude toward school work? In what ways do the students in Borkat's essay accurately reflect today's college student? In what ways does Borkat misrepresent students?
4. Consider Borkat's attitude toward university administrators and her fellow professors. What, in Borkat's view, do these two groups believe is the goal of higher education? Does Borkat confirm your own observations, or do you have a different impression of university faculty and staff?
5. Borkat refers to the eighteenth century English writer Jonathan Swift twice. Why is Swift's work particularly relevant to this essay? If you know nothing about this writer, look him up in an encyclopedia or *The Norton Anthology of English Literature* mentioned in paragraph 1.
6. What do you think is Borkat's central point?

■ RHETORICAL CONSIDERATIONS

1. Carefully analyze the words Borkat uses in paragraph 1. What, for example, is the connotation of a word like "blessed" (in the first sentence)? Do you find other such connotations in her language? How does Borkat's word choice in this paragraph signal her real attitude toward her Plan?
2. Consider the organization of Borkat's essay by identifying the purpose of each of the nine paragraphs. What argumentative strategy does Borkat spend most time on? Why?
3. Analyze the logic Borkat uses in paragraph 5 to refute the idea that "we should encourage hard work and perseverance." Do you agree with Borkat's definition of democracy?
4. Do you think this essay could result in educational reform? Why or why not? If this is not its purpose, then what is?

■ WRITING ASSIGNMENTS

1. Using the same basic rhetorical strategy as Borkat, write an essay attacking some aspect of teacher belief or behavior.
2. Write a letter to Professor Borkat defending students against her criticism. Back up your argument with secondary research as well as personal interviews with other students, teachers, and members of the university administration.
3. Read Jonathan Swift's "A Modest Proposal" and write a paper in which you demonstrate how Borkat's own essay is similar in purpose, slant, tone, structure, and so forth.

Why My Kids Hate Science
Robert M. Hazen

From the White House to the corridors of academe, there is great concern over declining student interest in science. Fewer students are naming the sciences as college majors than in the past, and a diminishing number of graduates are science-literate. As the author argues here, this growing "illiteracy" is a threat to our survival as a nation. Without scientific knowledge, "informed decision can't be made about where we live, what we eat and how we treat our environment." In this essay, Robert M. Hazen, a scientist at the Carnegie Institution of Washington's Geophysical Laboratory and Robinson Professor at George Mason University, wants to know why our educational system is turning out scientifically illiterate graduates and who is to blame. He points a finger at professional scientists and offers ways to solve the problem. Hazen is the author of many scientific articles and eight books including *Science Matters: Achieving Scientific Literacy* (1991), coauthored with James Trefil.

1 Last year my sixth-grade daughter, Elizabeth, was subjected to science. Her education, week after week, consisted of mindless memorization of big words like "batholith" and "saprophyte"—words that an average Ph.D. scientist wouldn't know. She recited the accomplishments of famous scientists who did things like "improved nuclear fusion"—never mind that she hasn't the vaguest notion of what nuclear fusion means. Elizabeth did very well (she's good at memorizing things). And now she hates science. My eighth-grade son, Ben, was also abused by science education. Week after week he had to perform canned laboratory experiments—projects with preordained right and wrong answers. Ben figured out how to guess the right answers, so he got good grades. Now he hates science, too.

2 Science can provide an exhilarating outlet for every child's curiosity. Science education should teach ways to ask questions, and create a framework for seeking

answers. In elementary school, because of jargon and mathematical abstraction, my children got the mistaken impression that science is difficult, boring and irrelevant to their everyday interests. Year by year, class by class across America, the number of students who persevere with science education shrinks.

3   As a professional geologist who has tried to convey some of the wonder and excitement of science to nonscientists, I am saddened and angered to see "the great science turnoff." I know that science is profoundly important in our lives. Informed decisions can't be made about where we live, what we eat and how we treat our environment without basic knowledge about our physical world, the knowledge that constitutes scientific literacy. Yet studies and surveys prove that our educational system is turning out millions of scientifically illiterate graduates. What's gone wrong? Who is to blame?

4   Some people say the problem is too much TV, or lack of parental supervision, or the sometimes poor media image of scientists. Perhaps the fault lies in declining national standards of education, poorly trained teachers or inadequate resources. Maybe students are just too dumb. But I can't escape the truth. Blame for the scientific literacy crisis in America lies squarely at the feet of working scientists. Too often we have sacrificed general education for our own specialized interests. Why haven't children been taught the basics in science? Because most university scientists at the top of the educational hierarchy couldn't care less about teaching anyone but future scientists. To them, science education is a long process of elimination that weeds out and casts aside the unworthy. It's not surprising that scientists have guided science education in this way. All the good things in academic life—tenure, promotion, salary, prestige—hinge on one's reputation in specialized research. Educators focus on teaching advanced courses to students who are willing to run the laboratory. Time devoted to teaching, or even reading, general science is time wasted.

5   One amazing consequence of this emphasis is that working scientists are often as scientifically illiterate as nonscientists. I'm a good example. The last time I took a course in biology was in ninth grade, long before genetics had made it into the textbooks. In college I studied lots of earth science, even more in graduate school. But from that distant day in 1962 when I dissected a frog, to quite recently when as a teacher I was forced to learn about the revolution in our understanding of life, I was as illiterate in modern genetics as it was possible to be. The average Ph.D. scientist doesn't know enough to teach general science at any level.

6   Working physicists or geologists or biologists know a great deal about their specialties. That's why Americans win so many Nobel Prizes. But all that specialization comes at a price. National science leaders, who usually are the ones who have done the best playing the research game, have fostered an education policy more concerned with producing the next generation of specialized scientists than educating the average citizen. This policy has backfired by turning off students in unprecedented numbers.

7   The picture may seem bleak, but the solution is not all that difficult. First, we need to recognize that science can be shared without jargon and complex mathematics. You don't have to be a scientist to appreciate the overarching scientific principles that influence every action of our lives. The central ideas of science are simple and

elegant—together they form a seamless web of knowledge that ties together every aspect of our physical experience.

8   Then we need teachers who are able to convey this unified vision with confidence and enthusiasm. Teachers can't give students a vision if no one has ever given it to them, so every college and university needs to institute general science courses. These courses should be required of all future teachers. Administrators at institutions of higher learning should be as quick to reward the gifted teachers of general science with raises and tenure as they have been to reward the gifted science researcher.

9   The science classroom, at least through junior high school, should be a hands-on exploration of the universe. Textbooks that are daunting and boring should be burned. Standardized tests that bully teachers into creating a rigid curricula should be outlawed. Our children should be given the chance to explore backward in time, look outward through space and discover unity in the workings of the cosmos. Armed with that knowledge they will someday combat disease, create new materials and shape our environment in marvelous ways. Science will also give them the means to predict the consequences of their actions and perhaps, with wisdom, to save us from ourselves.

■ TOPICAL CONSIDERATIONS

1. Summarize why Hazen's own children hate science.
2. Do Hazen's descriptions of the way his children were taught science remind you of your own experience? How? If not, explain how your experience differed.
3. Whom does Hazen blame for the scientific literacy crisis? Do you agree or disagree with him? Explain your answer.
4. What solutions to the problem does he offer?
5. Describe the difference between general education and specialized interests in relation to the study of science.
6. Compare Hazen's view of teaching with Page Smith's ("Killing the Spirit"). Would they wish for similar teaching methods or not?

■ RHETORICAL CONSIDERATIONS

1. Hazen is critical of the scientific world. What gives him credibility as a critic? Do you think he practices what he preaches? Explain your answer.
2. What technique does the author use to develop his explanation of why "our" educational system is turning out millions of scientifically illiterate graduates?
3. Describe the changes in point of view in the essay and why you think he uses each.
4. Consider how this essay would work if it were written in third person rather than first person. Do you think it would be better or worse? Explain your answer.

5. When Hazen discusses the consequences of teaching specialized interest in science, he uses himself as an example. Can you relate to his own experience? If so, please explain. If not, explain how your experience differed.

6. Does the title of this essay prepare you for a discussion of how to handle scientific illiteracy? Explain your answer, referring to specific sections of the essay.

■ **WRITING ASSIGNMENTS**

1. Hazen's daughter memorized words like "batholith" and "saprophyte" (paragraph 1). Did you ever have to memorize something in school that you considered *mindless?* Describe the experience and results of it. If not, describe what you considered to be *mindful* memorization and why the experience was a good one.

2. Write a letter to Hazen from Page Smith. As Smith, describe how science could be kept alive in the classroom today.

3. You are a science teacher. Write a response to this essay. Be sure to deal with Hazen's specific comments on education.

4. Pretend you are a textbook publisher. What would you do to publish books that are not "daunting and boring" (paragraph 9). List and explain your plan.

A (Vague) Sense of History

Jonathan Alter and Lydia Denworth

Too many American high-school graduates are unfamiliar with the major events of the Civil War and World War I. Too many cannot name the countries the United States fought in World War II. Too many students see the study of history as plowing through a "dull data dump." As the authors here point out, ignorance of history is a danger to the very future of our nation and its individuals. The blame for the high degree of historical illiteracy, they say, is the way history has been taught in American schools. A cause for optimism, this essay offers many exciting suggestions to reform and revitalize the teaching of history. Instead of making it the rote memorization of dates and names, educators should fashion their courses as the study of real people with a more balanced approach to multiculturalism. This article first appeared in *Newsweek* magazine in September 1990.

1 Historians tend to tell the same joke when they're describing history education in America. It's the one about the teacher standing in the schoolroom door waving goodbye to students for the summer and calling after them, "By the way, we won World War II."

2   The problem with the joke, of course, is that it's not funny. The surveys on historical illiteracy are beginning to numb: nearly one third of American 17-year-olds cannot even identify which countries the United States fought against in that war. One third have no idea what *Brown* v. *Board of Education* accomplished. One third thought Columbus reached the New World after 1750. Two thirds cannot correctly place the Civil War between 1850 and 1900. Even when they get the answers right, some (many?) are just guessing.

3   Unlike math or science, ignorance of history cannot be directly connected to loss of international competitiveness. But it does affect our future as a democratic nation and as individuals. "People without a sense of history are amnesiacs," says Diane Ravitch, professor of history and education at Columbia University Teachers College. "They wake up and don't know who they are."

4   The good news is that there's growing agreement on what's wrong with the teaching of history and what needs to be done to fix it. The steps are tentative and yet to be felt in most classrooms. And the debate over "multiculturalism"—the latest buzzword in broadening history's scope—has politicized the subject in often distracting ways. But beneath the rhetoric lies some evidence that educators are beginning to paddle in the same direction, with California taking the lead.

5   In the spirit of consensus, here are a few paths for reform that sensible people should be able to agree on:

6   ***Recognize the boredom factor.***   History itself isn't boring; it's just taught that way. As in science, the natural curiosity of students is snuffed out at an early age. The reasons aren't hard to figure. "Kids see it as going through dull data dumps," says Francie Alexander, who oversees curriculum for California's Department of Education. The image of the teacher asking his students to read page 454, then answer the questions on page 506, is enough to induce a yawn without even being in the classroom. The natural human fascination with good stories, which the entertainment industry understands so well, is missing from history, where that fascination originated. Admitting this as a problem—avoiding the usual defensiveness of the educational establishment—is the first step toward doing something about it.

7   ***Rethink "social studies."***   Many educators now see the transformation of history into social studies as the root of what's wrong. Social studies began in the 1930s as an effort to make the subject more "relevant." Paul Hanna, its original champion, wrote that children were failing to "face the realities of this world in which we live—they escape, they retreat to a romantic realm of yesterday." Social studies flowered fully in the 1960s and 1970s, when such romantic stories and legends (for instance, King Arthur and the Round Table) were frequently replaced in the lower grades by studying family and neighborhood life. In higher grades, social studies came to mean an interdisciplinary approach that threw history into an academic stew with psychology, anthropology, ethnic studies, civics and other subjects.

8   The results have been discouraging. The "romantic realm" Hanna denigrated turns out to have a narrative thrust and natural appeal far more memorable than soupy sociology, which is what social studies—however noble in theory—so often

becomes. "Kids like history because it's the story of real people," says Elaine Reed of the Ohio-based Bradley Commission, which helps states reform their history programs. "There's some blood and gore in there, but also some love and caring."

9   Consider Arleen Chatman, a teacher at the 75th St. School in Los Angeles, who straps on an apron and takes her students on an imaginary covered-wagon ride across the country, complete with vivid first-person accounts of the arduous trip. The whole school (K-6) creates a time line by stringing a rope across the yard and attaching cards representing historical events. Chatman cites the fourth grade, which is usually the year that children study their state, as a good example of the differences between history and social studies. While the social-studies curriculum would focus that year on the (often dry) roles of various state offices, Chatman's fourth graders did a research project on William Mulholland, the "dream builder" who brought water to Los Angeles. A woman who had known Mulholland came to tea with the class. "This 90-year-old woman became so real to the kids," says Chatman. "She told them wonderful stories." Stories—the stuff of history—are what people of all ages crave. Properly told, they can bring any class alive.

10   As a practical matter in elementary school, there's just not enough time in the day to make history separate from civics, community issues and similar topics. But the aim should be for history and geography to play a larger role in that mix. And from junior high on, it makes more sense to define the subject as history instead of social studies. Otherwise schools are providing what Gilbert T. Sewall of the New York-based American Textbook Council calls "escape hatches for uninterested students to satisfy their diploma requirements." As of 1987, 15 percent of high-school graduates took no American history in high school, and 50 percent studied no world history. When psychology or anthropology or even driver's education classes count as social studies it's no wonder so many students don't know anything about the Civil War.

11   ***Expand history's place.***   One way to bridge the history gap is simply to teach more of it. Three years ago, California adopted a new History-Social Science Framework which strongly recommends that every student be required to take at least three years of American history and three years of world history between grades five and 12. (Most states currently mandate only one year of American history). In 1988, the Bradley Commission echoed California's plans, arguing that, properly taught, history would help develop certain "habits of the mind"—critical thinking, acceptance of uncertainty, appreciation of causation—that have been sadly lacking from many classrooms.

12   One of the obstacles to greater concentration on history is the National Council on Social Studies (NCSS), which often downplays history in favor of what NCSS executive director Fran Haley calls "a more integrated approach." Over the years, social studies has fallen prey to trends—ethnic, demographic, environmental, women's and "peace" studies—that are unobjectionable, even commendable in themselves. But these subject areas too often crowd out basic historical literacy. Instead of being included in the broad sweep of history, they tend to replace it. Only this year have

traditionalists organized to balance the NCSS with their own professional group, the National Council for History Education.

13   *Put "multiculturalism" in perspective.*   Even after arriving at a consensus on the importance of history, the debate still rages over *whose* history should be taught. In some ways, this is a diversion, like arguing calculus versus trigonometry when the students don't know how to add and subtract. But it is a passionate debate within the profession, and with minorities soon to make up one third of the public-school population, it will only grow in importance.

14   On one side are those who attack the traditional emphasis on American history and Western civilization as "Eurocentric." They argue that such curricula—which stress the centrality of the transfer of European values and traditions to America— are not meaningful for many minority students; in fact, they suggest that a tradi- tional approach can be downright harmful because it doesn't present positive enough views of nonwhite groups. This critique is fueled by a sense that curriculum is often too positive, downplaying, for instance, the horrors of slavery and the destruction of Indians. American history, these critics say, is often presented as a "parade of presi- dents." World history seems to be a story of Europe on top. "That's hard for kids attached to those nations that were subjugated," says Irene Segade, who teaches at San Diego High School.

15   The most extreme version of this view was contained in "A Curriculum of Inclusion," a highly controversial report issued last year by a New York task force assigned by Education Commissioner Thomas Sobol to review social studies. Sobol admits that he created the task force, which he says was preliminary and not respon- sible for curricular reform, essentially as a political gesture to minority groups upset by his appointment. (He is white.) He underestimated the potential for backlash. The report is a textbook case of what happens when education is treated as akin to a pork-barrel project, with bones thrown to constituency groups. Although the state's history curriculum was overhauled to make it more multicultural as recently as 1987, representatives of different ethnic groups each argued that their histories should be more heavily weighted.

16   The problem with the argument is that the contributions of different cultures have simply not been comparable. Like it or not, Europe has had the largest influence on this nation's values and institutions. "No one would say that Afro-Asian culture studies is not important. These parts of the world are relevant to us today," says Steve Houser, a history teacher at Horace Greeley High School in Chappaqua, N.Y. "But we have a problem with being [attacked as] 'Eurocentric.' We teach the good and the bad of European history—imperialism, world wars, the Holocaust. It's ridiculous to say that Europe hasn't had an inordinate influence over the modern world."

17   The "Europhobic" approach, says Diane Ravitch, "endorses the principle of col- lective guilt. It encourages a sense of rage and victimization in those who are the presumed descendants of victims and a sense of resentment in those who are the pre- sumed descendants of oppressors. Instead of learning from history about the dangers of prejudging individuals by their color or religion, students learn that it is appropri-

ate to think of others primarily in terms of their group identity." California Education Superintendent Bill Honig argues simply that the essential themes of history often transcend lines of race and national origin. He points to the Chinese students who raised the Statue of Liberty last year in Tiananmen Square. "They're quoting Montesquieu, Jefferson and Locke," he says. "In fact, they can quote [them] better than our people."

18 As bitter as this debate has become, there's a middle course between, say, portraying slavery as merely a minor episode and giving Benjamin Banneker equal weight to Benjamin Franklin. It is possible—even essential—to "step into the [minority group's] shoes, see it from their perspective" without letting that dominate a curriculum, as Sobol says. Primary source materials such as first-person accounts by slaves or Asian workers on the transcontinental railroad can achieve that end. So can classroom arguments about whether the West was "won" or "stolen." The creator of that exercise, Joseph Palumbo, a teacher at Stephens Junior High in Long Beach, Calif., also asks his students to view Columbus's landing in America from the Indians' point of view. This is multiculturalism with a human face, and it's easily achievable without harsh attacks and hand wringing.

19 **Demand good textbooks.** History textbooks are too often a crutch for teachers and a club over their students. They are almost always too long and boring. A 1987 study by Columbia University's American History Textbooks project found these texts "generally to be mere catalogues of factual material about the past, not sagas peopled with heroic and remarkable individuals engaged in exciting and momentous events." The insightful texts favored in Gilbert Sewall's report, such as "A History of the United States" *(Ginn and Co., Lexington, Mass.),* by Daniel Boorstin and Brooks Mather Kelly, all featured heavy participation by the distinguished authors.

20 Amazingly, this is rare in elementary and secondary history textbooks. Most are written—badly—by unknown and often professionally unqualified firms subcontracted by publishing houses. (The "authors" whose names appear on the cover often merely review and amend the turgid text.) Beyond placing less faith in textbooks in general, teachers should insist on texts that have strong narrative voices instead of those that make kaleidoscopic attempts at comprehensiveness. The whole historical establishment should worry less about battling over exactly which details are mentioned or missing from textbooks and more about making these books convey the wonder of history.

21 **Bring history alive.** This, after all, is the challenge. How to make Jefferson or Roosevelt or Gandhi inhabit the minds of students? Good teachers know it's possible. Use primary sources. Use literature. Tell a story. Relate historical events to current events. Insist that they write essays instead of merely answering multiple-choice questions. Make kids take sides in debate. Make them establish connections between different historical ideas. Make them *think.*

22 Joe Palumbo's eighth-grade students in Long Beach know more than when the Civil War took place. Last spring they spent class time using that war—and

others they had studied—to debate the morality and complexity of conflict. Was it right for Northern troops to burn Southern crops and leave the population hungry? Was it right for Confederates to hold Northerners in squalid POW camps? When do the ends justify the means? By the time the bell rang, the students were not yet finished arguing the issues with one another. The conversations continued out in the hall, almost making them late for their next class. Palumbo would not be one of those waving goodbye to his students with the words, "By the way, the North won."

■ TOPICAL CONSIDERATIONS

1. The authors bemoan the national problem of historical illiteracy in America. What specific examples do they offer as evidence?
2. Compare Robert A. Hazen's concern in "Why My Kids Hate Science" for the way science has been taught to Alter and Denworth's view of how history has been taught.
3. Have you ever taken a social studies course? If so, did your course have a "narrative thrust and natural appeal," or was it "soupy sociology" (paragraph 8)? Explain your answer. If you have never taken a social studies course, how do you think such a course should be taught?
4. The authors offer several suggestions to solve the problem of historical illiteracy. Mention each in a one-sentence description.
5. How would Page Smith ("Killing the Spirit") respond to the teaching methods of Joe Palumbo (paragraph 22)? Give specific examples.

■ RHETORICAL CONSIDERATIONS

1. Note the authors' use of envelope structure. That is, the beginning and end of the essay are tied neatly together. There are no loose ends. Explain how the authors do this in the essay.
2. Why do you suppose the authors of this essay chose to use the third person point of view while Robert A. Hazen uses first person in his essay? Which technique do you prefer, and why?
3. The authors deal with some controversial ideas but manage to offer both sides of these issues. Give an example of a controversial point and tell how the authors handle it tactfully.
4. Does the title prepare the reader for what follows? Please explain your answer.
5. With each path to reform (boldfaced words, paragraphs 6–21) the authors give specific examples to support their point. Which path to reform would you agree with based on your history education? Explain using your own experience as a student of history.

■ WRITING ASSIGNMENTS

1. Imagine that you are the supervisor of a history department in a high school. Write a letter to your teachers describing how they should teach history to their students. Base your ideas on those of Alter and Denworth.

2. Write a one-week lesson plan for the teaching of a particular unit of history—that is, American's entrance into World War II, the assassination of John Kennedy, civil rights reform. Explain how you would cover the subject by using the reform ideas of Alter and Denworth.

3. Think back to a history class that you had to take. Was the experience favorable or unfavorable? Write a letter to your high-school principal describing why you think this course was effectively or ineffectively taught. Be sure to use at least one specific example in your letter.

4. The integration of multicultural history is a controversial one. Write an essay in which you support a specific way of teaching multicultural history within the framework of the curriculum. You may refer to sources from this or other essays in your response.

Can America Be No. 1 in Math? You Bet Your Noogie
Dave Barry

Before reading this piece, recall that moment when a math problem rendered you apoplectic with humiliation and frustration. You'll be in the proper state of mind to appreciate Dave Barry's hilarious observations on mathematics—and the way it's taught in America.

Dave Barry has been described as "America's most preposterous newspaper columnist," a man "incapable of not being funny." He is the author of ten books and is a Pulitzer Prize–winning humorist whose *Miami Herald* column is syndicated in more than 200 publications. His books include *Babies and Other Hazards of Sex* (1984), *Dave Barry's Greatest Hits* (1989), and most recently *Dave Barry's Guide to Guys* (1995). The CBS sitcom "Dave's World" is based on Mr. Barry. This essay first appeared in his column in 1992.

1 Last week I witnessed a chilling example of what US Secretary of Education Arthur A. Tuberman was referring to in a recent speech when he said that, in terms of basic mathematics skills, the United States has become, and I quote, "a nation of stupids."

2 This incident occurred when my son and I were standing in line at Toys "R" Us, which is what we do for father-son bonding because it involves less screaming than Little League. Our immediate goal was to purchase an item that my son really needed, called the Intruder Alert. This is a battery-operated Surveillance Device that can be placed at strategic locations around the house; it makes an irritating elec-

tronic shriek when you, the intruder, walk past. This important technological break-through enables the child to get on your nerves even when he is not home.

3   The woman ahead of us wanted to buy four Teenage Mutant Ninja Turtle drinks, which come in those little cardboard drink boxes that adults cannot operate without dribbling on themselves, but which small children can instinctively transform into either drinking containers or squirt guns. The Toys "R" Us price was three drinks for 99 cents, but the woman wanted to buy *four* drinks. So the mathematical problem was: How much should the cashier charge for the fourth box?

4   Talk about your brain teasers! The cashier tried staring intently at the fourth box for a while, as if maybe one of the Ninja Turtles would suddenly blurt out the answer, but *that* didn't work. Then she got on the horn and talked to somebody in Management "R" Us, but *that* person didn't know the answer, either. So the cashier made another phone call, and then another. By now, I assumed she was talking to somebody in the highest echelon of the vast Toys "R" Us empire, some wealthy toy executive out on his giant yacht, which is powered by 176,485 "D" cell batteries (not included).

5   Finally, the cashier got the word: The fourth box should cost—I am not making this up—29 cents.

6   This is, of course, ridiculous. As anyone with a basic grasp of mathematics can tell you, if *three* drinks cost 99 cents, then a *fourth* drink would cost, let's see, four boxes, divided by 99 cents, carry your six over here and put it on the dividend, and your answer is . . . OK, your answer is definitely *not* 29 cents. And this is not an iso-lated incident of America's mathematical boneheadism. A recent study by the American Association of Recent Studies shows 74 percent of US high-school stu-dents—nearly half—were unable to solve the following problem:

7   "While traveling to their high-school graduation ceremony, Bill and Bob decide to fill their undershorts with Cheez Whiz. If Bill wears a size 32 brief and Bob wears a 40, and Cheez Whiz comes in an 8-ounce jar, how many times do you think these boys will have to repeat their senior year?"

8   Here is the ironic thing: America produces "smart" bombs, while Europe and Japan do not; yet our young people don't know the answers to test questions that are child's play for European and Japanese students. What should be done about this? The American Council of Mathematicians, after a lengthy study of this problem, re-cently proposed the following solution: "We tell Europe and Japan to give us the test answers, and if they don't, we drop the bombs on them."

9   Ha ha! Those mathematicians! Still bitter about not having prom dates! Seriously, though, this nation is a far cry from the America of the 1950s, when I was a student and we were No. 1 in math and science, constantly astounding the world with technical innovations such as color television, crunchy peanut butter and Sputnik. What was our secret? How did we learn so much?

10   The answer is that, back then, math was taught by what professional educators refer to as: The Noogie Method. At least this was the method used by Mr. O'Regan, a large man who taught me the times tables. Mr. O'Regan would stand directly be-hind you and yell: *"Nine times seven!"* And if you didn't state the answer immedi-ately, Mr. O'Regan would give you a noogie. You can easily identify us former

O'Regan students, because we have dents in our skulls large enough for chipmunks to nest in. Some of us also have facial tics: These were caused by algebra, which was taught by Mr. Schofield, using the Thrown Blackboard Eraser Method. But the point is that these systems worked: To this day, I can instantly remember that nine times seven is around 50.

11   It's good that I remember my math training, because I can help my son with his homework. He'll be sitting at the kitchen table, slaving over one of those horrible pages full of long-division problems, having trouble, and I'll say: "You know, Robert, this may seem difficult and boring now, but you're learning a skill that you'll probably never use again." If more parents would take the time to show this kind of concern, we Americans could "stand tall" again, instead of being a lazy, sloppy nation where—prepare to be shocked—some newspaper columnists, rather than doing research, will simply make up the name of the secretary of education.

■ TOPICAL CONSIDERATIONS

1. Even though Barry's essay is not serious and Robert A. Hazen's ("Why My Kids Hate Science") is, how does Barry's description in paragraph 11 of his son's "difficult and boring" math experience resemble the experience of Hazen's children learning science?
2. At several points in the essay the author presents statistics as if they were real. Give some examples of such made-up figures. How do these figures and Barry's calculations add to the humor? How do they illustrate the problem of declining math skills?
3. In the final paragraph, explain the logic in Barry's words of comfort to his son. Beneath the humor of it, what truth does his advice underscore about Robert's efforts? Do you agree with him? Do you think there is, nonetheless, good reason for the boy to continue in his efforts?
4. What part of this essay did you find to be most humorous? Why was it so funny to you? Did any jokes fall flat for you? If so, explain your answer.
5. Did any part of this essay make you rethink the math skills of Americans? Did it make you wonder about how we compare to other nations? Do you think there is any cause to worry about the state of math education in America? Explain your answer.

■ RHETORICAL CONSIDERATIONS

1. At what point in the essay do you know the author is not being serious?
2. How does Barry manipulate the reader into almost believing some of his points? Give specific examples.
3. How much truth do you see behind the humor here? Find an example of exaggeration that is funny but that points to a serious problem or issue.
4. Writers employ several strategies in creating various humorous effects. Try to find humorous passages whose effects were created by allusion, surprise,

irony, understatement, overstatement, a deliberate pretense to ignorance, and absurd logic. Can you find other comic devices?

5. Were you "shocked" when at the end Barry reveals that he made up the name of the Secretary of Education? What's the point of that confession? How is this deception consistent with other "deceptions" in the piece? Do you think this confession gives the essay good closure?

■ WRITING ASSIGNMENTS

1. Did you ever have an experience in a class which you could compare in an exaggerated, humorous way to the author's experiences with Mr. O'Regan and Mr. Schofield? If so, try your hand at capturing the experience.

2. Through satire and humor, Dave Barry is making fun of our educational system. Is there a message here? If so, what is it, and what are your feelings about the problem?

3. After stating the problems with math education in America, create satirical, humorous solutions. Draw from your years of experience and make up fictitious organizations, exaggerated statistics, interviews, quotations, examples, and so on for your report. Have fun.

4. Write a letter to a math teacher you've had explaining how a method he/she has used was or was not effective for your learning of math.

5. "'You're learning a skill that you'll probably never use again'" (paragraph 11); ". . . and this is not an isolated incident of America's boneheadism" (paragraph 6); ". . . which is what we do for father-son bonding" (paragraph 2). Select from Barry's essay a quotation such as one of these and use it as a thesis statement for an essay. You may be serious or humorous in your treatment.

A Bag of Possibles and Other Matters of The Mind

Robert Fulghum

In this piece, best-selling author Robert Fulghum explores the nature of learning. He introduces us to a group of students each of whom unabashedly claims to be a musician, a poet, an actor, and an artist—all in one! What separates these young, grade-school kids from college students, aside from a dozen or so years, is simply self-image. In this inspiring essay, the author exhorts us to rediscover and celebrate our innate ability to learn and our natural bent for creativity. At the same time, he offers a challenge to educators to consider doing something about "what went wrong between kindergarten and college." Robert Fulghum is the author of the extraordinarily popular book *All I Really Needed to Know I Learned in Kindergarten* (1990) and *Uh-Oh!* (1991). This article first appeared in *Newsweek* magazine in September 1990.

1   **1**   Since my apotheosis as Captain Kindergarten, I have been a frequent guest in schools, most often invited by kindergartens and colleges. The environments differ only in scale. In the beginners' classroom and on the university campuses the same opportunities and facilities exist. Tools for reading and writing and scientific experimentation are there—books and paper, labs and workboxes—and those things necessary for the arts—paint, music, costumes, room to dance—likewise available. In kindergarten, however, the resources are in one room, with access for all. In college, the resources are in separate buildings, with limited availability. But the most radical difference is in the self-image of the students.

2   Ask kindergartners how many can draw—and all hands shoot up. Yes, of course we draw—all of us. What can you draw? Anything! How about a dog eating a firetruck in a jungle? Sure! How big you want it?

3   How many of you can sing? All hands. Of course we sing! What can you sing? Anything. What if you don't know the words? No problem, we can make them up. Let's sing! Now? Why not!

4   How many of you dance? Unanimous again. What kind of music do you like to dance to? Any kind! Let's dance! Now? Sure, why not?

5   Do you like to act in plays? Yes! Do you play musical instruments? Yes! Do you write poetry? Yes! Can you read and write and count? Soon! We're learning that stuff now.

6   Their answer is Yes! Again and again and again, Yes! The children are large, infinite and eager. Everything is possible.

7   Try those same questions on a college audience. Only a few of the students will raise their hands when asked if they draw or dance or sing or paint or act or play an instrument. Not infrequently, those who do raise their hands will want to qualify their responses—I only play piano, I only draw horses, I only dance to rock and roll, I only sing in the shower.

8   College students will tell you they do not have talent, are not majoring in art or have not done any of these things since about third grade. Or worse, that they are embarrassed for others to see them sing or dance or act.

9   What went wrong between kindergarten and college? What happened to Yes! of course I can?

10   **2**   As I write I am still feeling exuberant from an encounter with the cast of Richard Wagner's opera "Die Walküre." Last night I watched a stirring performance of this classic drama. This morning I sat onstage with the cast and discussed just how the production happens. I especially wanted to know how they went about learning their parts—what strategies they used to commit all to memory.

11   The members of the cast are students in kindergarten and first grade. They did indeed perform "Die Walküre"—words, music, dance, costumes, scenery, the works. Next year they will do "Siegfried"—already in production—as part of a run through the entire "Ring" cycle. And no, this is not a special school of the performing arts for gifted children. It's the Spruce Street School in Seattle, Wash.

12   They are performing Wagner because they are not yet old enough to know they cannot. And they understand the opera because they make up stories and songs just like it out of their own lives.

13　　To answer the question, "How do children learn?", I did something schools never do: I asked children. Because they know. They have not been hanging in a closet somewhere for six years waiting for school to begin so they could learn. Half their mental capacity has developed before they come to the schoolhouse door. I repeat for emphasis—they know how to learn.

14　　Brünnhilde, still wearing her helmet, explains that it works best for her if she learns her lines in small sections and then pays careful attention to the first three words of a section and then learns those. In case she needs prompting, just a word or two will set off a chain reaction in her mind. She also switches around and sings the talking words and talks the singing words, doing all of this while she moves around instead of sitting still. Siegfried and Wotan have other methods of their own. All seem to know. All have different ways.

15　　The skeptical author is thinking maybe the children are just doing a trained-seal act—I mean Wagner is heavy stuff—surely they don't really get it. So I ask the young actress playing Brünnhilde to tell me how her character fits into the story. "Do you know about Little Red Riding Hood?" she asks. Yes. "Well it's kind of like that—there's trouble out there in the world for the girl and her grandmother and the wolf and everybody." And then, so I will understand better, she compared the role to that of Lady Macbeth. Yes. She knows about that, too. The school did "Macbeth" last fall. She also talks about "The Hobbit" and "Star Wars" and a radio play the class is writing that is a spoof on all this—"MacDude." "Do you understand?" she asks with concern. I do. And so does she.

16　　(By the way, the only significant deviation from the script came at the very end of "Die Walküre," where Wotan is supposed to take his sleeping daughter in his arms and kiss her eyelids. No way. Art may have its standards, but no 7-year-old boy is going to kiss a girl on her eyelids or anywhere else. There are limits.)

17　　**3**　　We are sent to school to be civilized and socialized. Why? Because we believe that knowledge is better than ignorance and that what is good for the group and what is good for the individual are intertwined.

18　　As a nation we have concluded that it is better for us all if all of us go to school.

19　　Thomas Jefferson first proposed, in 1779 to the Virginia Legislature, that all children be educated at public expense, but it was not until well into the next century that such a plan was put into place, and even then without enthusiasm on the part of the public. The idea was resisted by a substantial part of the population—sometimes with armed force. As late as the 1880s the law had to be enforced in some towns by militia who marched children to school under guard.

20　　In an aspiring nation in the age of the Industrial Revolution, it became a matter of political economy to have educated citizens.

21　　We still believe that it is important to be sent out of the home into the world to be initiated into society. We call that ritual ground "School." And when we get there we are required to learn the rules and regulations of community, to acquire certain skills and to learn something of human values and the long history of the reaching for light and dignity.

22　　Society puts its best foot forward in kindergarten and first grade.

23   **4**   Want to have an exciting conversation about education? Don't ask someone what they think of the schools. Never. Ask instead that they tell you about the best teacher they ever had. Ask instead that they tell you about the best learning experience they ever had. Ask them if they wish they could sing and dance and draw. Or ask what they are learning now or would like to learn soon. And ask them how they go about learning something. And then ask them if they were to design an educational system to support what they've just said, what would it be like.

24   **5**   There is no such thing as "the" human brain—no generic brain. What we know, how we know it, our strategies for learning and our idiosyncratic ways of being alive, differ significantly from person to person. The implications of this for education are almost overwhelming.

25   There are as many ways to learn something as there are learners.

26   There is no way to be human.

27   We achieve community with metaphors and consensus.

28   And this makes a teacher's task impossible.

29   Unless the teacher sees the task not as one of conveying prescribed information, but a way of empowering the student to continue doing what he came in the door doing pretty well—learning for himself. To do any less is to diminish his self-esteem.

30   **6**   As a teacher of drawing and painting and philosophy in a senior high school for 20 years, I offered a course the students called "drawing for turkeys." The prerequisites for the course, as described in the school catalog: "To qualify, you must think you have no talent or skill in drawing and wish otherwise, hoping that the art fairy will look you up someday. Further, you must be able to tie your shoelaces, write your name and be able to find your way to the studio regularly." The classes were always oversubscribed.

31   Every student learned to draw competently.

32   Because drawing is a matter of skill. Skills can be acquired with practice.

33   Because drawing is a matter of looking closely at something—carefully enough to translate what is seen three dimensionally into the language of two-dimensional line and shape and shadow.

34   To draw is to look. To look is to see. To see is to have vision. To have vision is to understand. To understand is to know. To know is to become. To become is to live.

35   And to the student who would acknowledge that she had acquired skills but still could not draw because she had no imagination, I would only say: "Tell me about your dreams at night." And she would—at length. And then I would ask, "Who is doing that inside your head?"

36   Now if drawing requires careful observation, the acquisition of skill, the application of visionary creative imagination—and that's exactly what graduate school, business, industry, government and these times need—then there is some reason to believe that the arts . . . etc. You take it from there.

37   After sharing this thinking with parents, they would say they wished they could do what their kids were doing in the drawing class (because they still half believed that all I had done was uncover their particular child's hidden talents). So I would

say come on to class. And we had night school for parents. And all the parents (except one) learned to draw competently, taking their drawings home to put in that place of artistic honor—the refrigerator door. (As for the one failure, she taught me humility and pushed my teaching skills and her learning skills as far as possible in the process. She's a good photographer now, though. She sees very well.)

38   **7**   On the occasion of his graduation from engineering college this June (*cum laude,* thank you very much), I gave my number-two son a gift of a "possibles bag."

39   The frontiersmen who first entered the American West were a long way from the resources of civilization for long periods of time. No matter what gear and supplies they started out with, they knew that sooner or later these would run out and they would have to rely on essentials. These essentials they called their "possibles"—with these items they could survive, even prevail, against all odds. In small leather bags strung around their necks they carried a brass case containing flint and steel and tinder to make fire. A knife on their belt, powder and shot and a gun completed their possibles.

40   But many survived when all these items were lost or stolen.

41   Because their real possibles were contained in a skin bag carried just behind their eyeballs. The lore of the wilderness won by experience, imagination, courage, dreams, self-confidence—these were what really armed them when all else failed.

42   I gave my son a replica of the frontiersmen's possibles bag to remind him of this spirit.

43   In a sheepskin sack I placed flint and steel and tinder that he might make his own fire when necessary: a Swiss Army knife—the biggest one with the most tools; a small lacquer box that contained a wishbone from a Thanksgiving turkey—my luck; a small, velvet pouch containing a tiny bronze statue of Buddha; a Cuban cigar in an aluminum tube; and a miniature bottle of Wild Turkey whisky in case he wants to bite a snake or vice versa. His engineering degree simply attests that he has come home from an adventure in the wilderness.

44   The possibles bag inside his head is what took him there, brought him back and sends him forth again and again and again.

45   **8**   I kept a journal during the years I taught. And in time I boiled my experience down into some one-line statements that became a personal litany to be said when school began and when school was not going well. You will have found some of these notions already expressed at length in the sections above; for emphasis, I restate them here:

46   Learning is taking place at all times in all circumstances for every person.

47   There are as many ways to learn something as there are people.

48   There is no one way to learn anything—learn how you learn—help the student do likewise.

49   There is nothing everyone must know.

50   All I have to do is accept the consequences of what I do not know.

51   There is no one way to be human.

52   Imagination is more important than information.

53   The quality of education depends more on what's going on at home than in the
school. And more on what is going on in the student than what is going on in the
teacher.

54   In learning, don't ask for food; ask for farming lessons. In teaching, vice versa.

55   If nobody learns as much as the teacher, then turn students into teachers.

56   Every student has something important to teach the teacher.

57   Discontent and ferment are signs the fires of education are burning well.

58   In education, look for trouble. If you can't find any, make some.

■ TOPICAL CONSIDERATIONS

1. What evidence does Fulghum offer to make his point that something "went
   wrong" between kindergarten and college? Can you recall something you
   were willing to try in kindergarten or first grade that you wouldn't do now?
   Explain your answer.

2. Why does Fulghum describe a presentation of Wagner's "Die Walküre?"
   What is his point here? Can you explain a learning method of your own? Is
   it similar to any of Brünnhilde's techniques?

3. Who first proposed public education? Was the idea favorably accepted? Do
   you agree or disagree with Fulghum that "society puts its best foot forward in kindergarten and first grade" (paragraph 22)? On what do you base
   your answer?

4. Does Fulghum advocate teacher-centered or student-centered learning?
   Why? Do you learn best in a teacher-centered or student-centered class?
   Describe a particular incident in your education that illustrates your point.

5. Fulghum explains in paragraph 30 how he taught "drawing for turkeys" in a
   senior high school. Explain his example and why you think he used it. Did
   you ever have an experience being a "turkey" before you mastered a skill? If
   so, describe it.

6. Summarize Fulghum's main points in this essay and tell how they relate to
   the title. Do you think it is a catchy title? Is it an effective one? Explain.

7. Did you learn something about education from this essay, and about the
   process of learning? If so, what exactly? Has Fulghum made you aware of
   some "trouble" in education? Has he inspired you to look for some trouble
   in education, or to make some? Explain.

■ RHETORICAL CONSIDERATIONS

1. Fulghum begins with an imaginary dialogue between teacher and kindergarten class and poses two questions in paragraph 9. Does the essay answer
   the two questions? If so, how?

2. The author gives both general and specific information in this essay. Do you think his personal examples are effective in proving his point? Why or why not?

3. Describe the tone of Fulghum's essay. Does it help to make his point, or would the essay be more effective using a different tone? Explain your answer.

4. Did you find any of this essay humorous? If so, point to an example of Fulghum's humor. Do you think the humor helps or hinders the essay? Explain.

5. What is the purpose of the author's digression into the history of public education from paragraphs 17 to 22? Is any of the information here new to you? How does this material relate to your own experience in public or private education?

6. Describe the author's use of the metaphor "possibles bag" (paragraphs 38–44). Does it work for you or not?

■ WRITING ASSIGNMENTS

1. At the end of his essay, Fulghum lists some "one-line statements" of self-advice. Select one of these as your theme and write an essay using specific examples from your own life and educational experience.

2. As a college student, describe how you would change things to provide a greater opportunity for student involvement in the arts. If you feel there are enough opportunities, or too many, explain why. Use specific examples from your own educational experience.

3. Write a letter to one of your professors telling him or her specifically how that course could be improved. In light of the importance of "empowering the student" to learn, consider the teacher's effectiveness, the presentation of material, and the amount learned in the course. You might also consider the workload; the degree of difficulty; the textbooks and readings; the syllabus, outlines, overviews; course organization; outside assignments, and so on. Is your professor the kind of person who would welcome such suggestions? Dare you send the letter signed?

·14·
On Death and Dying

Nobody wants to think about death. Nobody plans to die for a long time. Nevertheless, though it may seem morose, reading about death may make us better appreciate life while helping us come to terms with death's inevitability.

In the next hour 10,000 people will die. Some will be killed by fire, some by floods, some by famine, some by accident, some by another's hand. Whatever the circumstance, each person will have faced death in his or her own way. And each will have been one more reminder that dying is as natural as living. Such is the view of the first essay, "On Natural Death," by physician and biologist Lewis Thomas. In as grand a context as our planet's biosphere, death does not seem unreasonable or even cruel.

But accepting its naturalness will not eliminate one's fear of death—a fear that has long made the subject a taboo. The second piece explores the reasons why there is an increased fear of death in our society today. "On the Fear of Death" was written by Elisabeth Kübler-Ross, a psychiatrist who is renowned for her work with dying patients.

The next essay grew out of the sad and untimely death of a loved one. As Anne Ricks Sumers explains, doctors could do nothing to save her brother Rick's life. But as indicated by her article's title, "I Want to Die Home," he did have the option of spending his last days around family and friends—an option she was glad he took and one, she argues, more doctors and family should encourage.

The final piece is a cheerful personal reflection on death written by America's most famous baby doctor, Benjamin Spock. In "A Way to Say Farewell," the author spells out just the kind of funeral and memorial service he wants when he dies—and the cocktail party to follow. This upbeat view of such a dreadful subject is a good note on which to bid our own farewell.

On Natural Death
Lewis Thomas

Here, Dr. Lewis Thomas reflects on the subject of death from the viewpoint of a physician and biologist. When regarded in so grand a context as the natural world, dying might not seem the cruel and extraordinary phenomenon we have made of it. As he points out, dying is as "natural" as living. Thomas, who has served as chair of the Departments of Medicine and Pathology at New York University and Bellevue Medical Center and as dean of Yale Medical School, has also distinguished himself as a writer. His articles have appeared in both scientific and popular journals. His many books include *The Lives of the Cell* (1974), *Late Night Thoughts on Listening to Mahler's*

Ninth Symphony (1983), and his most recent work, *Fragile Species* (1992). The following article originally appeared in his column, "Notes of a Biology Watcher," for the *New England Journal of Medicine* in 1979.

1   There are so many new books about dying that there are now special shelves set aside for them in bookshops, along with the health-diet and home-repair paperbacks and the sex manuals. Some of them are so packed with detailed information and step-by-step instructions for performing the function that you'd think this was a new sort of skill which all of us are now required to learn. The strongest impression the casual reader gets, leafing through, is that proper dying has become an extraordinary, even an exotic experience, something only the specially trained get to do.

2   Also, you could be led to believe that we are the only creatures capable of the awareness of death, that when all the rest of nature is being cycled through dying, one generation after another, it is a different kind of process, done automatically and trivially, more "natural," as we say.

3   An elm in our backyard caught the blight this summer and dropped stone dead, leafless, almost overnight. One weekend it was a normal-looking elm, maybe a little bare in spots but nothing alarming, and the next weekend it was gone, passed over, departed, taken. Taken is right, for the tree surgeon came by yesterday with his crew of young helpers and their cherry picker and took it down branch by branch and carted it off in the back of a red truck, everyone singing.

4   The dying of a field mouse, at the jaws of an amiable household cat, is a spectacle I have beheld many times. It used to make me wince. Early in life I gave up throwing sticks at the cat to make him drop the mouse, because the dropped mouse regularly went ahead and died anyway, but I always shouted unaffections at the cat to let him know the sort of animal he had become. Nature, I thought, was an abomination.

5   Recently I've done some thinking about that mouse, and I wonder if his dying is necessarily all that different from the passing of our elm. The main difference, if there is one, would be in the matter of pain. I do not believe that an elm tree has pain receptors, and even so, the blight seems to me a relatively painless way to go even if there were nerve endings in a tree, which there are not. But the mouse dangling tail-down from the teeth of a gray cat is something else again, with pain beyond bearing, you'd think, all over his small body.

6   There are now some plausible reasons for thinking it is not like that at all, and you can make up an entirely different story about the mouse and his dying if you like. At the instant of being trapped and penetrated by teeth, peptide hormones are released by cells in the hypothalamus and the pituitary gland; instantly these substances, called endorphins, are attached to the surfaces of other cells responsible for pain perception; the hormones have the pharmacologic properties of opium; there is no pain. Thus it is that the mouse seems always to dangle so languidly from the jaws, lies there so quietly when dropped, dies of his injuries without a struggle. If a mouse could shrug, he'd shrug.

7   I do not know if this is true or not, nor do I know how to prove it if it is true. Maybe if you could get in there quickly enough and administer naloxone, a specific

morphine antagonist, you could turn off the endorphins and observe the restoration of pain, but this is not something I would care to do or see. I think I will leave it there, as a good guess about the dying of a cat-chewed mouse, perhaps about dying in general.

8   Montaigne had a hunch about dying, based on his own close call in a riding accident. He was so badly injured as to be believed dead by his companions, and was carried home with lamentations, "all bloody, stained all over with the blood I had thrown up." He remembers the entire episode, despite having been "dead, for two full hours," with wonderment:

> It seemed to me that my life was hanging only by the tip of my lips. I closed my eyes in order, it seemed to me, to help push it out, and took pleasure in growing languid and letting myself go. It was an idea that was only floating on the surface of my soul, as delicate and feeble as all the rest, but in truth not only free from distress but mingled with that sweet feeling that people have who have let themselves slide into sleep. I believe that this is the same state in which people find themselves whom we see fainting in the agony of death, and I maintain that we pity them without cause. . . . In order to get used to the idea of death, I find there is nothing like coming close to it.

Later, in another essay, Montaigne returns to it:

> If you know not how to die, never trouble yourself; Nature will in a moment fully and sufficiently instruct you; she will exactly do that business for you; take you no care for it.

9   The worst accident I've ever seen was on Okinawa, in the early days of the invasion, when a jeep ran into a troop carrier and was crushed nearly flat. Inside were two young MPs, trapped in bent steel, both mortally hurt, with only their heads and shoulders visible. We had a conversation while people with the right tools were prying them free. Sorry about the accident, they said. No, they said, they felt fine. Is everyone else okay, one of them said. Well, the other one said, no hurry now. And then they died.

10   Pain is useful for avoidance, for getting away when there's time to get away, but when it is end game, and no way back, pain is likely to be turned off, and the mechanisms for this are wonderfully precise and quick. If I had to design an ecosystem in which creatures had to live off each other and in which dying was an indispensable part of living, I could not think of a better way to manage.

■ TOPICAL CONSIDERATIONS

1. Thomas remarks on all the new literature about death and dying in the bookstores. How does he seem to regard this current fascination?
2. What exactly does Thomas mean by "natural" death (paragraph 2)? How, by implication, might death be *unnatural?*
3. What is the point of Thomas's anecdote about his elm tree dying? How does it connect to the central idea of the essay?

4. Observing the fate of the field mouse, Thomas decided that nature "was an abomination" (paragraph 4). Why might he have drawn this conclusion? Why, after reflecting upon the mouse's death, did Thomas change his view of nature?

5. What observations about dying does Montaigne make? How do they support Thomas's thesis?

■ RHETORICAL CONSIDERATIONS

1. This essay is a fine example of building a central thesis through the use of anecdotes. Explain how each of the anecdotes Thomas chose helps develop his thesis. What purpose does each serve? How are they thematically connected to each other?

2. Evaluate the tone of this essay. In your analysis, consider the use of language, in particular his mixture of colloquial expressions (for example, "Montaigne had a hunch about dying") and scientific terminology (see paragraph 6).

3. Where exactly does Thomas offer his thesis statement in the essay? What is the strategy for placing it here?

■ WRITING ASSIGNMENTS

1. Having read Lewis Thomas's reflections on death, have your own feelings about the subject changed any? Does death seem more "natural" to you now? In an essay, write your own reflections on the topic incorporating your response to Dr. Thomas's essay.

2. Have you ever had an experience with death? If so, write an essay on the loss of that person. Try to capture the feelings you experienced—anger, grief, and fear. Does Thomas's essay on the *naturalness* of death help you to come to terms with the experience?

On the Fear of Death

Elisabeth Kübler-Ross

Elisabeth Kübler-Ross, a Swiss-born American psychiatrist, is considered one of the world's foremost experts on the treatment of the terminally ill. She has conducted seminars and written widely about death and dying in order to help people better understand and cope with the process. Of her nine books on the subject her most famous is *On Death and Dying* (1969), from which this essay is taken. In 1988 she published *AIDS: The Ultimate Challenge* which describes her interaction with victims of this devastating disease.

Let me not pray to be sheltered from
dangers but to be fearless in facing them.
Let me not beg for the stilling of
my pain but for the heart to conquer it.
Let me not look for allies in life's
battlefield but to my own strength.
Let me not crave in anxious fear to
be saved but hope for the patience to win my freedom.
Grant me that I may not be a
coward, feeling your mercy in my
success alone; but let me find the grasp
of your hand in my failure.

RABINDRANATH TAGORE, FRUIT-GATHERING

1 Epidemics have taken a great toll of lives in past generations. Death in infancy and early childhood was frequent and there were few families who didn't lose a member of the family at an early age. Medicine has changed greatly in the last decades. Widespread vaccinations have practically eradicated many illnesses, at least in western Europe and the United States. The use of chemotherapy, especially the antibiotics, has contributed to an ever-decreasing number of fatalities in infectious diseases. Better child care and education has effected a low morbidity and mortality among children. The many diseases that have taken an impressive toll among the young and middle-aged have been conquered. The number of old people is on the rise, and with this fact come the number of people with malignancies and chronic diseases associated more with old age.

2 Pediatricians have less work with acute and life-threatening situations as they have an ever-increasing number of patients with psychosomatic disturbances and adjustment and behavior problems. Physicians have more people in their waiting rooms with emotional problems than they have ever had before, but they also have more elderly patients who not only try to live with their decreased physical abilities and limitations but who also face loneliness and isolation with all its pains and anguish. The majority of these people are not seen by a psychiatrist. Their needs have to be elicited and gratified by other professional people, for instance, chaplains and social workers. It is for them that I am trying to outline the changes that have taken place in the last few decades, changes that are ultimately responsible for the increased fear of death, the rising number of emotional problems, and the greater need for understanding of and coping with the problems of death and dying.

3 When we look back in time and study old cultures and people, we are impressed that death has always been distasteful to man and will probably always be. From a psychiatrist's point of view this is very understandable and can perhaps best be explained by our basic knowledge that, in our unconscious, death is never possible in regard to ourselves. It is inconceivable for our unconscious to imagine an actual ending of our own life here on earth, and if this life of ours has to end, the ending is always attributed to a malicious intervention from the outside by someone else. In simple

terms, in our unconscious mind we can only be killed; it is inconceivable to die of a natural cause or of old age. Therefore death in itself is associated with a bad act, a frightening happening, something that in itself calls for retribution and punishment.

4   One is wise to remember these fundamental facts as they are essential in understanding some of the most important, otherwise unintelligible communications of our patients.

5   The second fact that we have to comprehend is that in our unconscious mind we cannot distinguish between a wish and a deed. We are all aware of some of our illogical dreams in which two completely opposite statements can exist side by side—very acceptable in our dreams but unthinkable and illogical in our wakening state. Just as our unconscious mind cannot differentiate between the wish to kill somebody in anger and the act of having done so, the young child is unable to make this distinction. The child who angrily wishes his mother to drop dead for not having gratified his needs will be traumatized greatly by the actual death of his mother—even if this event is not linked closely in time with his destructive wishes. He will always take part of the whole blame for the loss of his mother. He will always say to himself—rarely to others—"I did it, I am responsible, I was bad, therefore Mommy left me." It is well to remember that the child will react in the same manner if he loses a parent by divorce, separation, or desertion. Death is often seen by a child as an impermanent thing and has therefore little distinction from a divorce in which he may have an opportunity to see a parent again.

6   Many a parent will remember remarks of their children such as, "I will bury my doggy now and next spring when the flowers come up again, he will get up." Maybe it was the same wish that motivated the ancient Egyptians to supply their dead with food and goods to keep them happy and the old American Indians to bury their relatives with their belongings.

7   When we grow older and begin to realize that our omnipotence is really not so omnipotent, that our strongest wishes are not powerful enough to make the impossible possible, the fear that we have contributed to the death of a loved one diminishes—and with it the guilt. The fear remains diminished, however, only so long as it is not challenged too strongly. Its vestiges can be seen daily in hospital corridors and in people associated with the bereaved.

8   A husband and wife may have been fighting for years, but when the partner dies, the survivor will pull his hair, whine and cry louder and beat his chest in regret, fear, and anguish, and will hence fear his own death more than before, still believing in the law of talion—an eye for an eye, a tooth for a tooth—"I am responsible for her death, I will have to die a pitiful death in retribution."

9   Maybe this knowledge will help us understand many of the old customs and rituals which have lasted over the centuries and whose purpose is to diminish the anger of the gods or the people as the case may be, thus decreasing the anticipated punishment. I am thinking of the ashes, the torn clothes, the veil, the *Klage Weiber**
of the old days—they are all means to ask you to take pity on them, the mourners,

---

Klage Weiber: wailing wives. [Ed.]

and are expressions of sorrow, grief, and shame. If someone grieves, beats his chest, tears his hair, or refuses to eat, it is an attempt at self-punishment to avoid or reduce the anticipated punishment for the blame that he takes on the death of a loved one.

10   This grief, shame, and guilt are not very far removed from feelings of anger and rage. The process of grief always includes some qualities of anger. Since none of us likes to admit anger at a deceased person, these emotions are often disguised or repressed and prolong the period of grief or show up in other ways. It is well to remember that it is not up to us to judge such feelings as bad or shameful but to understand their true meaning and origin as something very human. In order to illustrate this I will again use the example of the child—and the child in us. The five-year-old who loses his mother is both blaming himself for her disappearance and being angry at her for having deserted him and for no longer gratifying his needs. The dead person then turns into something the child loves and wants very much but also hates with equal intensity for this severe deprivation.

11   The ancient Hebrews regarded the body of a dead person as something unclean and not to be touched. The early American Indians talked about the evil spirits and shot arrows in the air to drive the spirits away. Many other cultures have rituals to take care of the "bad" dead person, and they all originate in this feeling of anger which still exists in all of us, though we dislike admitting it. The tradition of the tombstone may originate in the wish to keep the bad spirits deep down in the ground, and the pebbles that many mourners put on the grave are leftover symbols of the same wish. Though we call the firing of guns at military funerals a last salute, it is the same symbolic ritual as the Indian used when he shot his spears and arrows into the skies.

12   I give these examples to emphasize that man has not basically changed. Death is still a fearful, frightening happening, and the fear of death is a universal fear even if we think we have mastered it on many levels.

13   What has changed is our way of coping and dealing with death and dying and our dying patients.

14   Having been raised in a country in Europe where science is not so advanced, where modern techniques have just started to find their way into medicine, and where people still live as they did in this country half a century ago, I may have had an opportunity to study a part of the evolution of mankind in a shorter period.

15   I remember as a child the death of a farmer. He fell from a tree and was not expected to live. He asked simply to die at home, a wish that was granted without question. He called his daughters into the bedroom and spoke with each one of them alone for a few moments. He arranged his affairs quietly, though he was in great pain, and distributed his belongings and his land, none of which was to be split until his wife should follow him in death. He also asked each of his children to share in the work, duties, and tasks that he had carried on until the time of the accident. He asked his friends to visit him once more, to bid goodbye to them. Although I was a small child at the time, he did not exclude me or my siblings. We were allowed to share in the preparations of the family just as we were permitted to grieve with them until he died. When he did die, he was left at home, in his own beloved home which he had built, and among his friends and neighbors who went to take a last look at him where he lay in the midst of flowers in the place he had lived in and loved so

much. In that country today there is still no make-believe slumber room, no embalming, no false makeup to pretend sleep. Only the signs of very disfiguring illnesses are covered up with bandages and only infectious cases are removed from the home prior to the burial.

16   Why do I describe such "old-fashioned" customs? I think they are an indication of our acceptance of a fatal outcome, and they help the dying patient as well as his family to accept the loss of a loved one. If a patient is allowed to terminate his life in the familiar and beloved environment, it requires less adjustment for him. His own family knows him well enough to replace a sedative with a glass of his favorite wine; or the smell of a home-cooked soup may give him the appetite to sip a few spoons of fluid which, I think, is still more enjoyable than an infusion. I will not minimize the need for sedatives and infusions and realize full well from my own experience as a country doctor that they are sometimes life-saving and often unavoidable. But I also know that patience and familiar people and foods could replace many a bottle of intravenous fluids given for the simple reason that it fulfills the physiological need without involving too many people and/or individual nursing care.

17   The fact that children are allowed to stay at home where a fatality has struck and are included in the talk, discussions, and fears gives them the feeling that they are not alone in their grief and gives them the comfort of shared responsibility and shared mourning. It prepares them gradually and helps them view death as part of life, an experience which may help them grow and mature.

18   This is in great contrast to a society in which death is viewed as taboo, discussion of it is regarded as morbid, and children are excluded with the presumption and pretext that it would be "too much" for them. They are then sent off to relatives, often accompanied by some unconvincing lies of "Mother has gone on a long trip" or other unbelievable stories. The child senses that something is wrong, and his distrust in adults will only multiply if other relatives add new variations of the story, avoid his questions or suspicions, shower him with gifts as a meager substitute for a loss he is not permitted to deal with. Sooner or later the child will become aware of the changed family situation and, depending on the age and personality of the child, will have an unresolved grief and regard this incident as a frightening, mysterious, in any case very traumatic experience with untrustworthy grownups, which he has no way to cope with.

19   It is equally unwise to tell a little child who lost her brother that God loved little boys so much that he took little Johnny to heaven. When this little girl grew up to be a woman she never solved her anger at God, which resulted in a psychotic depression when she lost her own little son three decades later.

20   We would think that our great emancipation, our knowledge of science and of man, has given us better ways and means to prepare ourselves and our families for this inevitable happening. Instead the days are gone when a man was allowed to die in peace and dignity in his own home.

21   The more we are making advancements in science, the more we seem to fear and deny the reality of death. How is this possible?

22   We use euphemisms, we make the dead look as if they were asleep, we ship the children off to protect them from the anxiety and turmoil around the house

if the patient is fortunate enough to die at home, we don't allow children to visit their dying parents in the hospital, we have long and controversial discussions about whether patients should be told the truth—a question that rarely arises when the dying person is tended by the family physician who has known him from delivery to death and who knows the weaknesses and strengths of each member of the family.

23   I think there are many reasons for this flight away from facing death calmly. One of the most important facts is that dying nowadays is more gruesome in many ways, namely, more lonely, mechanical, and dehumanized; at times it is even difficult to determine technically when the time of death has occurred.

24   Dying becomes lonely and impersonal because the patient is often taken out of his familiar environment and rushed to an emergency room. Whoever has been very sick and has required rest and comfort especially may recall his experience of being put on a stretcher and enduring the noise of the ambulance siren and hectic rush until the hospital gates open. Only those who have lived through this may appreciate the discomfort and cold necessity of such transportation which is only the beginning of a long ordeal—hard to endure when you are well, difficult to express in words when noise, light, pumps, and voices are all too much to put up with. It may well be that we might consider more the patient under the sheets and blankets and perhaps stop our well-meant efficiency and rush in order to hold the patient's hand, to smile, or to listen to a question. I include the trip to the hospital as the first episode in dying, as it is for many. I am putting it exaggeratedly in contrast to the sick man who is left at home—not to say that lives should not be saved if they can be saved by a hospitalization but to keep the focus on the patient's experience, his needs and his reactions.

25   When a patient is severely ill, he is often treated like a person with no right to an opinion. It is often someone else who makes the decision if and when and where a patient should be hospitalized. It would take so little to remember that the sick person too has feelings, has wishes and opinions, and has—most important of all—the right to be heard.

26   Well, our presumed patient has now reached the emergency room. He will be surrounded by busy nurses, orderlies, interns, residents, a lab technician perhaps who will take some blood, an electrocardiogram technician who takes the cardiogram. He may be moved to X-ray and he will overhear opinions of his condition and discussions and questions to members of the family. He slowly but surely is beginning to be treated like a thing. He is no longer a person. Decisions are made often without his opinion. If he tries to rebel he will be sedated and after hours of waiting and wondering whether he has the strength, he will be wheeled into the operating room or intensive treatment unit and become an object of great concern and great financial investment.

27   He may cry for rest, peace, and dignity, but he will get infusions, transfusions, a heart machine, or tracheotomy if necessary. He may want one single person to stop for one single minute so that he can ask one single question—but he will get a dozen people around the clock, all busily preoccupied with his heart rate, pulse, electrocardiogram or pulmonary functions, his secretions or excretions but not with him as a

human being. He may wish to fight it all but it is going to be a useless fight since all this is done in the fight for his life, and if they can save his life they can consider the person afterwards. Those who consider the person first may lose precious time to save his life! At least this seems to be the rationale or justification behind all this— or is it? Is the reason for this increasingly mechanical, depersonalized approach our own defensiveness? Is this approach our own way to cope with and repress the anxieties that a terminally or critically ill patient evokes in us? Is our concentration on equipment, on blood pressure, our desperate attempt to deny the impending death which is so frightening and discomforting to us that we displace all our knowledge onto machines, since they are less close to us than the suffering face of another human being which would remind us once more of our lack of omnipotence, our own limits and failures, and last but not least perhaps our own mortality?

28   Maybe the question has to be raised: Are we becoming less human or more human? . . . it is clear that whatever the answer may be, the patient is suffering more— not physically, perhaps, but emotionally. And his needs have not changed over the centuries, only our ability to gratify them.

■ TOPICAL CONSIDERATIONS

1. To what does Kübler-Ross attribute the increased fear of death and related emotional problems in our society?
2. What point is Kübler-Ross illustrating in her anecdote of the farmer? How does the farmer's dying differ from the way most people die today?
3. According to the author, what are the potential dangers of excluding children from the experience of another's death?
4. What is the thrust of Kübler-Ross's argument regarding the treatment of terminally ill patients? Do you agree with her view? Do you think that there is some justification for this kind of treatment?
5. To what does the author attribute the "depersonalized approach" (paragraph 27) to a patient's dying?

■ RHETORICAL CONSIDERATIONS

1. Where in the essay does Kübler-Ross move from explanation to argument?
2. Where does the author give the thesis statement in this piece?
3. Divide this essay into three parts. Which paragraphs constitute the beginning? Which constitute the middle? Which constitute the end? Briefly explain how each of the parts is logically connected to the others.

■ WRITING ASSIGNMENTS

1. The author opens her essay with a quotation. Write a paper in which you discuss the appropriateness of this quotation to the essay.
2. Do you recall your fear of death as a child? If so, try to describe it and any experiences that might have contributed to it.

3. Has anyone close to you ever died? If so, in a paper try to describe how you dealt with that person's death. In the process of grief did you feel conflicting emotions of shame, guilt, and anger?

4. Kübler-Ross recalls the memory of a farmer who took charge of his own dying. What would you do if you were so critically wounded?

5. The author criticizes the impersonal treatment of emergency-room patients. Did you ever find yourself in an emergency room? Did you think the treatment you received was "lonely, mechanical, and dehumanized"? Try to recapture the experience, whether you were the patient or someone you accompanied.

6. In a paper, try to explain what it means to "die with dignity." You may choose to refer to the Kübler-Ross essay or other readings. Try to make your discussion concrete, even personal if possible.

7. Toward the end of this essay Kübler-Ross criticizes the "well-meant efficiency" of medical people. Do you think that cool efficiency of medical care is sometimes needed in order to save lives? Explore this question in a paper.

I Want to Die at Home

Anne Ricks Sumers

This essay chronicles a personal encounter with death. But as the title suggests, Anne Ricks Sumers turns the experience of her brother's dying into an argument for last rights. Hospitals, she says, are "great places . . . to have surgery. . . . But not to die." People should be a able to spend their last days with family and friends, not dying prolonged deaths under sedation in hospital beds.

Sumers is an ophthalmologist practicing in New Jersey. Her essay first appeared in *Newsweek* magazine in April 1994.

1 Last week my brother Rick died at home. I am so proud that we helped him die at home. Everyone should have as beautiful a death. Don't get me wrong—it is tragic and wrong that he should be dead. Rick was only 40, a nice, funny guy, a good husband, a dedicated lawyer, a father of a little boy who needs him. He didn't "choose death"; he wanted desperately to live, but a brain tumor was killing him and the doctors couldn't do a thing. He had only one choice: die in the hospital or die at home.

2 Three months ago, doctors discovered cancer in both of Rick's kidneys. The kidneys were removed and he and his wife coped well with home dialysis. He returned to work, took care of his son, remodeled his kitchen and went to a Redskins game.

3 Then disaster struck. It all happened so quickly. On a Tuesday his wife noticed Rick was confused. By Wednesday he was hallucinating and an MRI showed that his brain was studded with inoperable cancer. Doctors said chemotherapy or radiation

might buy him a few more weeks of life, but they couldn't predict whether he would become more lucid. When Rick was coherent, his only wish was to go home.

4   "Where are you, Rick?" said the intern, testing Rick's mental status.

5   "I don't know," he answered politely, "but I want to go home."

6   Rick was confused and disoriented, but he was fully aware that he was confused and disoriented. I showed him pictures of my children I keep on my key chain; he shook my keys and gently put them back in my hand: "You better drive. I'm too f—ed up to drive."

7   My brother was a strong guy. He kept getting up out of bed. The hospital staff tied him down. He was furious, humiliated, embarrassed, enraged, confused and frightened.

8   A hospital is no place to die. It's noisy and busy and impersonal; there's no privacy anywhere for conversation or a last marital snuggle; there's no place for the family to wait and nap; only one or two people can be with the dying person. The rest of the family hovers unconnected in a waiting room, drinking bad coffee, making long phone calls on pay phones in lobbies. It was exhausting.

9   Please don't misunderstand me; I like hospitals. Hospitals are great places to live, to struggle for life, to undergo treatments, to have surgery, to have babies. But not to die. If it's at all possible, people should die in familiar surroundings in their own beds.

10   Rick begged to go home. The doctors could offer us nothing more. Hospice care wasn't available on such short notice. We all knew it would be an enormous responsibility to take him home.

11   But Rick's wife is the most determined person I know. He wanted to go home and she wanted to take him home. Rick's doctor was empathetic and efficient; in less than two hours after we came to this decision, we were on the road in an ambulance, heading to his house.

12   Rick's last evening was wild, fun, tragic and exhilarating. Rick walked from room to room in his house, savoring a glass of red wine, eating a cookie, talking with his best friend, our mother and dad, our sisters and brothers. Neighbors stopped in with food and stayed for the conversation. Friends from the Quaker Meeting House stopped by. Cousins arrived.

13   It was like a Thanksgiving—good food, lots of conversation, but the guest of honor would be dead in a few days, or hours.

14   Although Rick was confused he wasn't frightened. Rick knew he was in his home, surrounded by friends and family. He was thrilled to be there. He ate. He cleaned. He was busy all evening, reminiscing, telling fragments of stories, neatening up, washing dishes, giving advice and eating well.

15   At the end of the evening he brushed his teeth, washed his face, lay down in his wife's arms in his own bed and kissed her goodnight. By morning he was in a deep coma.

16   All that long Saturday my family was together and we grieved. We watched over Rick. My father planted bulbs, daffodils and tulips, to make the spring beautiful for his grandson. My mother washed Rick's hair. My brothers and sisters and in-laws

painted the porch banisters. Family, friends and neighbors came by to see him sleeping in his bed. Sometimes as many as 10 people were in his bedroom, talking, crying, laughing or telling stories about him, or just being with him—other times it was just his wife.

17 He took his last breath with his wife and his best friend beside him, his family singing old folk songs in the living room. He was peaceful, quiet, never frightened or restrained. Rick died far too young. But everyone should hope to die like this; not just with dignity, but with fun and love, with old friends and family.

18 Over the past week I have told friends about my brother's death. A few friends shared with me their regret about their parents dying prolonged and painful deaths alone in the hospital, sedated or agitated, not recognizing their children. Other people express fear of a dead body in the house—"Wasn't it ugly?" they ask. No, it looked like he was sleeping.

19 Rick's death was as gentle as a death can be. It worked because all parties—doctors, family, Rick and Rick's wife—were able to face facts and act on them. His doctors had the sense to recognize that no more could be done in the way of treatment and had the honesty to tell us. Rick's wife was determined to do right by him, whatever the burden of responsibility she was to bear. Our families were supportive of all her decisions and as loving and helpful as we could be.

20 Doctors must learn to let go—if there's nothing more to offer the patient then nothing more should be done—let patients go home. We all should plan for this among ourselves—preparing our next of kin. Families, husbands, wives need not be fearful. If a family member is dying in a hospital and wants to return home, try to find the means to do it.

21 And to all of the nurses, doctors and social workers in hospices: continue to do your good work. You have the right idea.

■ **TOPICAL CONSIDERATIONS**

1. What is Sumers' argument? Can you locate a thesis statement? Have you encountered similar arguments before? If so, in what ways did her essay confirm or alter your thinking?

2. Consider what Rick's family does on the day of his death (paragraph 16). How are these activities unusual for a death-bed vigil?

3. How was the last night of Rick's life "like a Thanksgiving" (paragraph 13)? Consider the adjectives and imagery used to describe this gathering.

4. Compare Rick's brief stay in the hospital to his experience at home. How can you generalize about the differences between the two places? If you have spent time in a hospital (either as patient or visitor), consider whether the depiction of hospital life rings true.

5. How would you describe the economic and social background of Sumers and her family? Evaluate the clues about their professions, tastes, lifestyles, or belief systems. Does your sense of their social position make the argument more or less compelling to you?

■ RHETORICAL CONSIDERATIONS

1. How does Sumers create a sense of immediacy in this essay? Describe how this atmosphere of urgency affected you as a reader.
2. How does Sumers create an emotional bond between Rick and the reader? What details about Rick's life and death did you identify with? Consider how your response to Rick increases the effectiveness of Sumers' argument.
3. Rick's death is the only example Sumers uses to support her thesis. How would you evaluate this case as evidence in an argument? Is it typical and representative? Is Sumers justified in generalizing from this particular incident?
4. Consider the implied audience for this argument. Does it include more than one group? Has Sumers effectively anticipated and addressed potential opposition from her audience? What opposition can you think of not successfully acknowledged here?

■ WRITING ASSIGNMENTS

1. Write a condolence letter to Sumers sympathizing with her loss while criticizing her argument.
2. Write an essay arguing that hospitals and other institutions are the best places for people to die in many circumstances. Support your argument with information about the way death comes in a variety of illnesses—cancer, heart disease, Alzheimer's disease, and so on. Include in your research both printed sources and personal testimony; interviewing local hospital staff and acquaintances who have recently lost family members may be helpful.
3. Would you bring a member of your family home to die? Take a position on this issue and write an essay based on your personal circumstances and beliefs, supporting your case with family interviews if appropriate.

	A Way to Say Farewell
	Benjamin Spock

The subject of human death does not readily lend itself to upbeat reflections. However, we have found one that at least regards the matter in a positive spirit. Appropriately, it was written by America's most famous baby doctor who reflects on the end of a life—his own. "I don't want tiptoers around me. I want cheerful people who will look me in the eye." Dr. Spock, who was born in 1904 and who still actively writes on children, is the author of *Baby and Child Care*, which has sold more than 40 million copies since it was first published in 1943. His latest book is *A Better World for Our Children* (1995). This article originally appeared in *Parade* magazine in 1985.

1 Being in good health and of sound mind, except for absentmindedness and a poor memory for names, I'm not expecting to die for a long time—not if I can help it. But, at 81, I'd like to give some guidelines to my relatives. As far as I know, and one never knows for sure until his time comes, I don't fear the dying as long as it's not very painful or lonely or lacking in dignity.

2 I say "one never knows" because I've been surprised by the behavior of some physicians as they've died; by my own behavior when a patient died; and by the behavior of an old friend during a fatal illness.

3 It is a fairly common occurrence for a physician, who should know better, to ignore obvious symptoms of cancer in himself until it is too late for treatment, apparently preferring to hope against hope that his suspicion is not correct.

4 The mother of a patient of mine long ago called me in dismay at 7 A.M. to say that she had just found her infant son dead in his crib. I told her to rush him to a hospital that was close to their home, much closer than I was. If he was dead, I suggested she ask for an autopsy that would reassure her and her husband that there had been no neglect on their part. It was clear to me that they wanted me to meet with them—sooner or later—but I could not face them. I gave excuses. Years later, when I read that some staff people in hospitals tend to avoid, and thereby neglect, a patient who is dying, I understood. The fear of facing death is truly powerful.

5 A close, wise friend and colleague of mine (not a physician) died slowly and painfully of inoperable cancer. She was the sole support of three young children and should have been making careful plans for their future and discussing this with them. But she never asked anyone about her diagnosis. And, respecting her apparent wish to remain in ignorance, nobody ever volunteered the information. Each time I visited, I expected her finally to ask, and each time I was flabbergasted that she did not. Now, years later, I realize that she might have preferred a frank discussion with her doctor but had been put off by his reluctance to raise the issue. Perhaps she only was following his cue.

6 I'm reminded of an episode in Elisabeth Kübler-Ross's book *On Death and Dying,* in which she was asked by a physician to talk with his patient, whom he confidently believed did not know his diagnosis. She didn't want to shock the patient; on the other hand, she wanted to make it easy for him to communicate with her. So she simply asked, "How sick are you?" and he replied, "I am full of cancer."

7 This case made me realize that I would want a physician and a spouse who were, on the one hand, cheerful but who would not pretend that everything was lovely. I don't want around me solemn, whispering tiptoers. But I also don't want hearty, loud-voiced types who keep asking me, in a routine way, how I feel or whether there is anything I want. I want people, preferably attractive ones, who will look me in the eye in a friendly or even loving manner, discuss openly any of my concerns and ask only those questions that apply to my actual situation.

8 I would want my doctor to give any treatment available if it had a chance of curing me or keeping me alive and lively for a number of years. But I would not want to be kept alive with antibiotics, infusions, transfusions, anticancer drugs or radiation if they were just to postpone my death for a few months—especially if I had lost my marbles.

9   Having been brought up with a strong emphasis on the importance of appearances, I have a real dread of going visibly senile without realizing it.

10   I remember my distress when, some years ago, I happened to descend in a Plaza Hotel elevator with a famous architect. Though he was old, he still maintained a dashing appearance: a broad-brimmed but flat-topped cowboy hat such as Gary Cooper wore in *High Noon,* an expensive-looking suit and a flowing silk bow tie. His jacket, however, was dotted with food spots. He seemed carefree, but I felt deeply embarrassed for him. Since then, I've inspected my jacket carefully each morning, though I realized at that time that, if senility sets in, I will have forgotten this precaution.

11   Of course, the reason that physicians often will go to such extremes to keep a hopelessly ill patient alive is because their job, their training and their ethics direct them to do so. Besides, they can be sued by a disgruntled relative for not having done everything conceivable.

12   When I wonder what directions to leave, I realize that, in addition to my own wishes, there will be my wife's feelings and my doctor's ethics to consider. For instance, even though I've decided in advance that I want to be put out of my misery if the pain proves unbearable, will my doctor be willing to give the necessary dose of medication—or to leave it handy—and will Mary have the nerve to jab the needle?

13   The omission of artificial life-support systems is only one aspect of being allowed to die naturally. I would want to be at home, if that wasn't too burdensome, or in a hospice, rather than in a hospital. I have been a frequent patient in hospitals, and I am grateful for having had excellent doctors and nurses. But hospitals are nothing like home. They are more like factories—clean, modern factories to produce diagnoses and treatments. A stream of staffers barges in, as if from outer space: history taker, physical examiners, temperature and pulse takers, meal servers, bath givers, stretcher pushers, X-ray technicians, bed makers, pill pushers, specimen takers. Not one of them is primarily interested in the person, of course.

14   In recent years, the hospice movement, which began in England, has spread over the U.S. The aim is to let the person die as pleasantly as possible in a homelike setting, surrounded by family and some familiar possessions and spared pain by regular, heavy medication—without any fussing that is not provided solely for comfort. That's the departure for me.

15   I'd also like to have something to say about my memorial service, though I don't expect to be looking down from heaven at the time of the event. I don't like to think of myself as being unceremoniously buried or burned up without some kind of service to mark my passage from person to memory.

16   I dislike intensely the atmosphere of the conventional funeral: the darkened room, the solemn people, silent or whispering or sniffling, the funeral director's assistants pretending to feel mournful. My ideal would be the New Orleans black funeral, in which friends snake-dance through the streets to the music of a jazz band. But a satisfactory compromise would be a church service for my friends to think of me together for an hour and say farewell.

17   I would like the people to be normally noisy and cheerful. The music might consist of the ragtime and jazz to which I love to dance in order to liberate myself from

my puritanical upbringing, lively hymns, and such tunes as "The Battle Hymn of the Republic" and "America the Beautiful," which always choke me up, not with sorrow but with exultation. I like the service for the dead delivered in the rich cadences that have come down to us through the centuries. I'd like the minister, preferably William Sloane Coffin Jr., who enjoys life and with whom I was put on trial for our opposition to the Vietnam war, to speak of our hope that the peacemakers really will prevail. And some child-development person or parent could speak of my belief in the infinite perfectibility of children and of my agreement with Jesus' words: "Suffer little children, and forbid them not, to come unto me: for of such is the kingdom of heaven."

18   Then there could be a cheerful cocktail party somewhere nearby.

■ TOPICAL CONSIDERATIONS

1. What three examples does Spock give to show that one never knows what his own reaction to death will be?
2. Spock says in paragraph 7 that he doesn't want "solemn, whispering tiptoers" at his deathbed. What type of person does he want?
3. Why would Spock prefer hospice care to hospital care in the event of a long terminal illness?
4. What kind of memorial service does Spock say he would like for himself? What kind of service would you design for yourself? Consider your choice of place, guests, music, speakers, and readings.

■ RHETORICAL CONSIDERATIONS

1. What single detail makes Dr. Spock's description of the aging architect poignant?
2. Find examples where Spock concludes a very serious, potentially grim series of sentences with a short, clipped, and cheerful remark. Why does he do this?
3. Why does Spock begin the piece with the phrase, "being in good health and of sound mind"? What is the effect?

■ WRITING ASSIGNMENTS

1. Write an essay describing the way someone you know dealt with death.
2. Reread Elisabeth Kübler-Ross's essay, "On the Fear of Death," in this chapter, then write an essay expressing your reaction to her ideas in light of Dr. Spock's thoughts on his own death.
3. Write a mock will in which you lay down the guidelines for your own funeral. Design the kind of service you would like to have specifying the guests, location, music, readings, and so forth.

Acknowledgments

From *One Life at a Time, Please* by Edward Abbey. Copyright © 1988 by Edward Abbey. Reprinted by permission of Henry Holt and Co., Inc.

"What Do Men Really Want?" by Sam Allis. Copyright © 1990 Time Inc. Reprinted by permission.

"Let's Stop Crying Wolf on Censorship" by Jonathan Alter. From *Newsweek,* 11/29/93. Copyright © 1993, Newsweek, Inc. All rights reserved. Reprinted by permission.

"A Vague Sense of History" by Jonathan Alter and Lydia Denworth. From *Newsweek,* 9/90. Copyright © 1990, Newsweek, Inc. All rights reserved. Reprinted by permission.

From *I Know Why the Caged Bird Sings* by Maya Angelou. Copyright © 1969 by Maya Angelou. Reprinted by permission of Random House, Inc.

"Money for Morality" by Mary Arguelles. Reprinted by permission of the author.

"Hard Sell" and "As Busy as We Wanna Be" by Deborah Baldwin. Reprinted by permission of the author.

"Customer's Always Right" and "You Have to be a Real Stud Hombre Cybermuffin" by Dave Barry. Reprinted by permission of the author.

"Why I Quit Practicing Law" by Sam Benson. Reprinted by permission of the author.

"A Liberating Curriculum" by Roberta F. Borkat. From *Newsweek*, 4/12/93. Copyright © 1993, Newsweek, Inc. All rights reserved. Reprinted by permission.

"Let's Put Pornography Back in the Closet" by Susan Brownmiller. Reprinted by permission of the author.

"Older Children and Divorce" by Barbara Cain. Copyright © 1990 by The New York Times Company. Reprinted by permission.

"A Clack of Tiny Sparks" and "Remembrance of Gay Boyhood" by Bernard Cooper. Copyright © 1990 by Harper's Magazine. All rights reserved. Reprinted from the Jan. 1991 issue by special permission.

"Life on the Shelf: What It's Like to Live in Prison" by George Desmukes. From *Newsweek,* 5/2/ 94. Copyright © 1994, Newsweek, Inc. All rights reserved. Reprinted by permission.

"On Keeping a Notebook" from *Slouching Towards Bethlehem* by Joan Didion. Copyright © 1966, 1968 by Joan Didion. Reprinted by permission of Farrar, Straus & Giroux, Inc.

"Come, Let Me Offend You" by Eve Drobot. From *Newsweek,* 9/28/93. Copyright © 1993, Newsweek, Inc. All rights reserved. Reprinted by permission.

Excerpt from "The American Family vs. The American Dream" by Barbara Ehrenreich. Reprinted by permission of the author.

"The Wrong Examples" by David L. Evans. From *Newsweek* 3/1/93. Copyright © 1993, Newsweek, Inc. All rights reserved. Reprinted by permission.

Excerpt from *Channels of Desire* by Stuart Ewen and Elizabeth Ewen. 2nd edition copyright © 1992 by the Regents of the University of Minnesota. Published by the University of Minnesota Press. 1982 original publication by McGraw-Hill; copyright © 1982 by Ewen and Ewen.

Warren Farrell, "Why Men Are the Way They Are," *Family Therapy Network,* November/December 1988. Reprinted by permission.

"The Selling of Pain: We Writhe, Therefore We Are" by George Felton. Reprinted by permission of the author.

"A New Twist on Lost Youth: The Mall Rats" by William Glaberson. Copyright © 1992 by The New York Times Company. Reprinted by permission.

"The Black and White Truth about Basketball." Reprinted by permission of Sterling Lord Literistic, Inc. Copyright © 1993 by Jeff Greenfield.

"TV's True Violence" by Meg Greenfield. From *Newsweek,* 6/21/93. Copyright © 1993, Newsweek, Inc. All rights reserved. Reprinted by permission.

From *Nigger: An Autobiography* by Dick Gregory. Copyright © 1964 by Dick Gregory Enterprises, Inc. Used by permission of Dutton Signet, a division of Penguin Books USA Inc.

"Oprah! Oprah in the Court" by Sophronia Scott Gregory. Copyright © 1994 Time Inc. Reprinted by permission.

"About Men; A Father's Rite" by Chester Higgins, Jr. Copyright © 1992 by The New York Times Company. Reprinted by permission.

"The Courage of Turtles." Copyright © 1968 by Edward Hoagland.

"Sex is for Adults" by Ellen Hopkins. Copyright © 1992 by The New York Times Company. Reprinted by permission.

"Salvation" from *The Big Sea* by Langston Hughes. Copyright © 1940 by Langston Hughes and copyright renewed © 1968 by Arna Bontemps and George Houston Bass. Reprinted by permission of Hill and Wang, a division of Farrar, Straus & Giroux, Inc.

"The Word Police" by Michiko Kakutani. Copyright © 1993 by The New York Times Company. Reprinted by permission.

Reprinted with the permission of Simon & Schuster from *Happy to Be Here* by Garrison Keillor. Copyright © 1982 by Garrison Keillor.

"Why Do We Need Celebrities" by Christina Kelly. First appeared in *Sassy* June 1992. Written by Christina Kelly. Reprinted with the permission of *Sassy* Magazine. Copyright © 1992 by *Sassy* Publishers, Inc.

"Pilgrimage to Nonviolence." Reprinted by arrangement with The Heirs to the Estate of Martin Luther King, Jr., c/o Joan Daves Agency as agent for the proprietor. Copyright © 1958 by Martin Luther King, Jr., copyright renewed 1986 by Coretta Scott King.

Reprinted with the permission of Macmillan Publishing Company from *On Death and Dying* by Elisabeth Kubler-Ross. Copyright © 1969 by Elisabeth Kubler-Ross, M. D.

"Houses and Streets, but No Neighborhood" by Alan Lupo. Reprinted courtesy of The Boston Globe.

From *The End of Nature* by William McKibben. Copyright © 1989 by William McKibben. Reprinted by permission of Random House, Inc.

Excerpt from *The Dictionary of Bias-Free Usage: A Guide to Nondiscriminatory Language* by Rosalie Maggio. Reprinted from *The Dictionary of Bias-Free Usage: A Guide to Nondiscriminatory Language* by Rosalie Maggio. Copyright © 1991 by Rosalie Maggio. Published by the Oryx Press. Used by permission of Rosalie Maggio and the Oryx Press, 800-279-6799.

From *Boys Will Be Boys* by Myriam Miedzian. Copyright © 1991 by Myriam Miedzian. Used by permission of Doubleday, a division of Bantam Doubleday Dell Publishing Group, Inc.

Twelve page excerpt of Chapter 7, "Sex, Sin, and Suggestion" from *Are They Selling her Lips?* by Carol Moog. Copyright © 1990 by Carol Moog. By permission of William Morrow and Company, Inc.

"What's In a Name?" by Itabari Njeri. Reprinted by permission of the author.

"Conan and Me" by Bill Persky. Reprinted by permission of the author.

"Now...This" from *Amusing Ourselves to Death* by Neil Postman. Copyright © 1985 by Neil Postman. Used by permission of Viking Penguin, a division of Penguin Books USA Inc.

"Life in the 30's; Girls at Bat" by Anna Quindlen. Copyright © 1988 by The New York Times Company. Reprinted by permission.

"In Praise of Roseanne" by Elayne Rapping. Reprinted by permission from *The Progressive,* 409 East Main Street, Madison, WI 53703

"Hers; Stolen Promises" by Patricia Raybon. Copyright © 1992 by The New York Times Company. Reprinted by permission.

Reprinted with the permission of Simon & Schuster from *Writin' Is Fightin': Seven Years of Boxing on Paper* by Ishmael Reed. Copyright © 1988 by Ishmael Reed.

From *The Morning After* by Katie Roiphe. Copyright © 1993 by Katherine Anne Roiphe. By permission of Little, Brown and Company.

"Football Red and Baseball Green" by Murray Ross. Reprinted by permission of the author.

"My Brother, Myself" by Dick Schaap. Reprinted by permission of the author.

"The Cult of Ethnicity, Good and Bad" by Arthur Schlesinger, Jr. Copyright © 1991 Time Inc. Reprinted by permission.

"Getting to Know About You and Me" by Chana Schoenburger. From *Newsweek,* 9/20/93. Copyright © 1993, Newsweek, Inc. All rights reserved. Reprinted by permission.

Excerpt from pages 117-125 from *The Overworked American: The Unexpected Decline of Leisure* by Juliet Schor. Copyright © 1991 by BasicBooks, a division of HarperCollins Publishers Inc. Reprinted by permission of BasicBooks, a division of HarperCollins Publishers Inc.

From *Killing the Spirit* by Page Smith. Copyright © 1990 by Page Smith. Used by permission of Viking Penguin, a division of Penguin Books USA Inc.

"The Cry of the Ocean" by Peter Steinhart. Reprinted with permission from *Mother Jones* Magazine, © 1994, Foundation for National Progress.

"Eye of the Beholder" by Grace Suh. Reprinted by permission of the author.

"I Want to Die at Home" by Anne Rick Sumners. From *Newsweek,* 4/4/ 94, Copyright © 1994, Newsweek, Inc. All rights reserved. Reprinted by permission.

"Wears Jumpsuit. Sensible Shoes. Uses Husband's Last Name" by Deborah Tannen. Copyright © 1993 by The New York Times Company. Reprinted by permission.

"Crime and Punishment & Personal Responsibility" by Clarence Thomas. Reprinted by permission of the author.

"On Natural Death," copyright © 1979 by Lewis Thomas, from *The Medusa and the Snail* by Lewis Thomas. Used by permission of Viking Penguin, a division of Penguin Books USA Inc.

"A Word From Our Sponsor" by Patricia Volk. Copyright © 1987 by The New York Times Company. Reprinted by permission.

"In Search of Our Mothers' Gardens" from *In Search of Our Mothers' Gardens: Womanist Prose,* copyright © 1974 by Alice Walker, reprinted by permission of Harcourt Brace & Company.

"Women" from *Revolutionary Petunias and Other Poems,* copyright © 1970 by Alice Walker, reprinted by permission of Haroucrt Brace & Company.

From *Race Matters* by Cornel West. Copyright © 1993 by Cornel West. Reprinted by permission of Beacon Press .

"Hers; Playing to Win" by Margaret A. Whitney. Copyright © 1988 by The New York Times Company. Reprinted by permission.

"Daddy Tucked the Blanket" by Randall Williams. Copyright © 1975 by The New York Times Company. Reprinted by permission.

From *The Plug-In Drug, Revised Edition* by Marie Winn. Copyright © 1977, 1985 by Marie Winn Miller. Used by permission of Viking Penguin, a division of Penguin Books USA Inc.

The first chapter, pp. 9-19, "The Beauty Myth" from *The Beauty Myth* by Naomi Wolf. Copyright © 1991 by Naomi Wolf. By permission of William Morrow and Company, Inc.

Cover Illustration

We extend our thanks to all the people who provided buttons for the cover photograph. In all cases, reproduction rights to the buttons remain with the company that produced them.

"All One People"/Nutritech; "No Condoms? Get Outta My House"/GMHC.

We are particularly grateful to Donnelly/Colt for providing the following buttons: "Celebrate Diversity," "Health Care is a Right not a Privilege," "Kids Need Praise Everyday," "Child Care Not War Fare," "Choice," "If You Think Education is Expensive, Try Ignorance," "Meat is Dead," "Vegetarian Peace For All Who Live," "Justice Does Not Prevail Where Prejudice Exists," "Your Hate Becomes You," "Rebel With a Cause," "Silence is the Voice of Complicity," "Attitudes are the Real Disability," "Stop Domestic Violence," "If You Can't Change Your Mind Are You Sure You've Still Got One?," "Refuse to Be Abused," and "Please Don't Give Me War Toys."

Instructor's Manual
to accompany
The Contemporary Reader

FIFTH EDITION

Gary Goshgarian

Northeastern University

with assistance from
Catherine Anderson
Paul Crumbly
Phebe Jensen
Jeanne Phoenix Laurel
Elizabeth Swanson

Contents

•4•
Consumer Culture

•5•
Advertising

•6•
Male/Female

•7•
Multicultural America

•8•
Television

•9•
Crime and Punishment

•10•
Censorship Versus Free Speech

•11•
Nature and the Environment

•12•
Sports

•13•
Education

•14•
On Death and Dying

Preface

This instructor's manual provides answers to the questions asked after each selection in *The Contemporary Reader,* Fifth Edition. Such answers do not presume to do the work for the instructor; they are just meant to help. Certainly these answers are not exhaustive nor the only ones appropriate, and I hope that students and instructors will conspire to provide others.

GARY GOSHGARIAN

Personal Discoveries

On Keeping a Notebook
Joan Didion

TOPICAL CONSIDERATIONS

1. Didion begins with a quotation, probably overheard, of a woman lamenting a breakup with her lover. The place and date are recorded, along with a description of a "dirty crepe-de-Chine wrapper" the woman was wearing. Didion assumes that because she wrote it down, the scene must have significance to her. In the next three paragraphs she explores her memory and fills in other details, including a description of another woman who also is leaving her lover and who doesn't look forward to a summer of loneliness. Didion imagines the two women meeting, and sharing their stories.

   In some ways, the paragraphs are confusing because Didion seems hesitant about the accuracy of her own memory but willing to comment on the feelings of irritation and depression the scene recalls. She is more interested in remembering why she recorded the scene, and in exploring its meaning, rather than what may have actually occurred. As she states later in the essay, her prime concern is with how she feels about a remembered event and not its factual accuracy. The meaning of the entry seems to come clear by the end of the third paragraph when Didion concludes that the second woman "is afflicted by a little self-pity, and she wants to compare Estelles. That is what that was all about." Didion seems to identify with this feeling of self-pity.

2. Didion's mother gave her a Big Five Tablet (paragraph 5) on which she wrote a fantasy of woman who was freezing to death in the Arctic one night then walking in the Sahara heat the next day. Didion claims that this entry was an early indication of her love of exaggeration, irony, and the exotic—something she finds more revealing than a typical entry of ordinary childhood life. Students might remember what kind of paper they first wrote on, what pen or pencils they used; also, the kinds of stories, poems and fantasies they recorded. They might even explore what these early habits revealed about their own thinking and learning processes.

3. Didion was very unsuccessful at keeping a conventional diary. She writes that she was so bored by the task that she abandoned it altogether and started writing what most people would call "lies" (paragraph 7). Often, her family members disagree with her memories of a shared event, and she admits they may be right. Although these scenes may be fictitious, Didion claims, they preserve a kernel

of truth which she says is more significant than factual accuracy: how an experience felt. Students may recall how their memories of important events conflict with others' versions, and the tension this created. They can discuss why their version was closer to their own personal insight.

4. Didion believes that our society teaches us to regard what others think as more important than our own thoughts. Only the young and the old are permitted to indulge their dreams and fantasies, while everyone else must pay attention to others' needs and preferences. Didion writes that this kind of thinking never succeeds. Although we may be dutifully recording what is happening around us, our deepest self, our personal view, comes through in our private writing. This private writing is not a *pensée* or essay written for the public. A private notebook is more personal, erratic, rougher, and, Didion implies, more truthful than an essay written for the public. Students' opinions of Didion's belief may differ.

5. The entry "He was born the night the Titanic went down" brings Didion back to an interview she had with a rich and famous woman who made that remark in reference to her husband. After the interview which left Didion hung over and disoriented, she felt envious of the woman's luxurious home and her successful children. Her anxiety is heightened by what follows the interview: she runs over a black snake, then overhears a woman in the check-out line talking about an affair with a man whose wife recently had a baby. She ascribes her depression to her yearning for children at the time. For Didion it is important to keep in touch with the darkest parts of the self, to "keep on nodding terms with the people we used to be, whether we find them attractive company or not." (Paragraph 16) If we neglect to do that, then we easily forget who we are, and we lose touch with the betrayals and conflicts we have caused or witnessed.

RHETORICAL CONSIDERATIONS

1. By using so many illustrations of personal scenes, impressions, or dialogs, Didion's essay models the kind of notebook she keeps. She can explore ideas or ask questions in much the same way you would when writing in a personal notebook.

   Reactions to Didion's style will vary, but you may want to discuss how Didion often details a notebook entry, then steps back to explain it. In paragraphs 1 through 3, for instance, she describes the scene of one lonely woman talking to the bartender, and another woman, equally lonely, sitting near-by. In the third paragraph, Didion concludes that the point of the scene is to remember what self-pity feels like. These first three paragraphs, don't seem to have a connection with Didion's theme until she brings the readers attention to personal nature of the entry, and its private meaning to her.

   It may be useful to point out to students that Didion may be *telling* the reader too much instead of *showing* us her meaning through this scene. An example that works better in the essay is paragraph 12. In exploring how a writer may fail to understand why she records a certain detail, Didion notes that she has listed many seemingly trivial entries as "FACT." Only later does she realize that her record of a sign claiming that a mandarin coat was once worn by a woman who gave lectures on a teapot collection could bring back a vivid childhood memory of her own household, cluttered with teapots and souvenirs.

2. Use of the present tense makes Didion's writing more immediate and interesting. She conveys the feeling that she is looking over her old notebook entries, commenting on them one at time, and gaining insights into her own mind as she moves along.

3. These sentences are bold, striking summations, and often conclusions of illustrations and scenes from the preceding paragraphs. Many times, Didion will offer an illustration of a notebook entry, or a memory connected with the entry and explore it with questions, or by using conditional such as "might" and "would." Her straightforward declarative sentences (e.g., "How it felt to me: that is getting closer to the truth about a notebook" and, "In fact I have abandoned altogether that kind of pointless entry; instead I tell what some would call lies") give her essay more definition, more authority, in contrast to the tentative questions and the conditional verb tense used elsewhere in the essay.

Shame
Dick Gregory

TOPICAL CONSIDERATIONS

1. This is really up to the students. They need to draw on their own insights and experiences.

2. Gregory describes Helene as light-complexioned, clean, well-mannered, popular, and smart in school. His choice of adjectives suggests that success to him means being socially acceptable. It seems fairly obvious that he felt this way because of the extreme poverty of his home. Students can answer the rest of the questions on their own.

3. The first question is more for students to consider based on what they perceive happened with Gregory as a child. It is possible to argue that Gregory's own actions prompted the teacher to make a scene, but outward circumstances deserve, perhaps, a larger share of the blame. The teacher's lack of sensitivity intensified Gregory's embarrassment instead of easing or removing it. On a deeper level, his home environment was perhaps the real culprit.

4. Your students can discuss whether any of us *need* to feel shame when the circumstances are beyond our control. Shame to Gregory meant not being clean, having to wipe his nose on his hand because he didn't have a handkerchief, wearing clothes that didn't fit, being on relief, not having a Daddy—all of which added up to not "belonging," being different, being an outcast. Gregory's refusal to go to school after this incident, of course, is not the only way he could have handled the situation. But returning to school might have demanded more courage and been more difficult than could be expected of a 7-year-old.

5. Helene Tucker symbolized all that Gregory lacked in order to be socially accept-able. His attempt to impress her that day in the classroom was motivated by his desire to hide or overcome this lack. When he failed, his shame was intensified. Achieving goals that would be impressive enough to win Helene's approval would mean erasing the sense of failure this incident had created. Although this was obviously a successful motivational device, students can no doubt suggest others from their own experience.

6. Gregory doesn't tell us exactly how he was finally able to get Helene Tucker out of his system, but that he was married and making money are significant clues. Obviously, once he had become successful and socially acceptable, he no longer felt the need to prove himself to anyone. He had passed the test.

7. From Gregory's account, the teacher appears to have been extremely insensi-tive. It might be useful to have students consider whether they feel his point of view is biased or objective. They might discuss how the teacher would have described the incident. It is up to the students to decide how else the teacher might have handled the situation. One answer might be that she could have allowed Gregory to pledge an amount of money and then spoken to him about it afterward.

8. This is really up to the students.

RHETORICAL CONSIDERATIONS

1. In the first two sentences, it is a succinct, attention-getting opening that leads logically into the narrative.

2. Light-complexioned, clean, smart. These are useful adjectives. They give clues as to why Gregory was in love with Helene and, more importantly, why he felt inferior. It's a good number of adjectives—more would overdo it. It might be useful to point out to students that adjectives should be used sparingly and with a distinct purpose.

3. NARRATIVE: Several of the paragraphs are developed by example. The last paragraph is a good sample passage.

4. The first paragraph is a good example of how Gregory tells and shows how he feels about Helene. He tells us he was in love with her. He then gives sev-eral narrative examples of how he acted, which shows that he was in love with her. He explains that he brushed his hair before going to school, got a hand-kerchief so that he wouldn't have to wipe his nose on his hand, and washed his only shirt and socks out every night so that he could be clean. He mentions that the latter often made him sick because they were sometimes wet when he put them on for school.

5. Gregory introduces his narrative by telling us that school taught him what shame is. But it isn't until his conclusion that he fully *explains* what shame meant to him. Yes, this is effective. Because of the narrative incident that pre-cedes this explanation, the reader understands better what Gregory means. The conclusion gives a perspective on the incident while avoiding any redundancy or unnecessary repetition. The last sentence is a succinct reminder of the crux of the problem.

Graduation

Maya Angelou

TOPICAL CONSIDERATIONS

1. Angelou remarks that all the children had "graduation epidemic" and "trembled visibly with anticipation." She remembers that graduating students frequently forgot their books, tablets, and pencils; the younger children fell all over themselves to lend them theirs. Everyone was involved in the preparations: Small children rehearsed their songs. Older girls prepared refreshments, and older boys made sets and stage scenery. Parents ordered new shoes and clothes from Sears and Roebuck or Montgomery Ward. Seamstresses were hired to make graduation dresses and alter secondhand pants. Even the subject for the minister's sermon on the preceding Sunday was graduation. Apparently Stamps did not have many important occasions. The people were poor, and many of their children did not continue on to college. Graduation was the high point of their educational career.

2. Booker T. Washington was a black leader who discouraged political dissent or rebellion and promoted the idea that the blacks' interests could be better served by improving their education than by political agitation. Black political activists have criticized Washington's views as promoting an attitude of subservience. Such an attitude seemed inherent in the response of the principal and assembly to Mr. Donleavy's speech. In his introduction, the principal mumbled something about "the friendship of kindly people to those less fortunate than themselves" and spoke of gratitude for Mr. Donleavy's being able to make time in his busy schedule to speak at the graduation ceremony. Angelou comments, too, that during the speech, "Amens and Yes sir's began to fall around the room like rain through a ragged umbrella."

3. Angelou remarks that she felt something unrehearsed and unpleasant was about to occur when the choir director and principal unexpectedly signaled for everyone to be seated for the prayer after the singing of the American National Anthem and the Pledge of Allegiance. She noticed, too, that the principal's voice had changed when he returned to the dais following the prayer. Angelou comments that the Amens and Yes sir's became fewer and fewer as Mr. Donleavy's speech progressed. Those which could be heard "lay dully in the air with the heaviness of habit." Later, she comments that "the man's dead words fell like bricks around the auditorium." Mr. Donleavy's speech implied that black children could aspire only to be maids and farmers, handymen and washerwomen. He praised the nearby white school graduates for the academic achievements but held up black athletes as the only models for the black students. As Angelou points out, "The white kids were going to have a chance to become Galileos and Madame Curies and Edisons and Gauguins, and our boys (the girls weren't even in on it) would try to be Jesse Owenses and Joe Louises."

4. Angelou resents the condescension in Mr. Donleavy's remarks. Numerous historical and literary allusions suggest that there was more academic excellence

than Mr. Donleavy was aware of. Angelou could say the preamble to the Constitution faster than her brother, Bailey, and knew the names of the presidents in chronological and alphabetical order. The title of Henry Reed's valedictory speech quoted Hamlet's famous line: "To Be or Not to Be." Bailey gave Angelou a book of poems by Edgar Allen Poe, and they both walked through the rows of dirt in the garden reciting "Annabel Lee." The daughter of the Baptist minister recited "Invictus" at the graduation exercises. Historical allusions include Galileo, Madame Curie, Edison, and Gauguin. Angelou mentions, too, that students had drawn "meticulous maps," learned how to spell decasyllabic words, and memorized "The Rape of Lucrece."

5. Just as the assembly was about to sing the Negro National Anthem, the graduation ceremony was interrupted so that Mr. Donleavy could be introduced to give his speech. Questions 3 and 4 illustrate what happened after this Mr. Donleavy's speech left everyone feeling despondent and defeated. Very few could appreciate the idealistic philosophizing about future aspirations in Henry Reed's speech "To Be or Not to Be." It wasn't until Henry Reed, sensing the despondency, abruptly stopped speaking and began leading the graduating class in the singing of the Negro National Anthem that Angelou and the rest of the assembly were able to regain their pride and confidence in themselves. The Anthem inspired them to forge ahead in spite of the implications in Mr. Donleavy's remarks. If they had sung the anthem earlier, it would not have meant as much and would have been lost in Mr. Donleavy's talk.

6. Gregory, too, as a child had felt the shame of being considered not good enough or smart enough. He, too, had been made to feel that the was inferior and must take a back seat to those with more money and better advantages. He could have told them about his moment of shame and how he had overcome it. He could have inspired them to become not just athletes but Galileos, Madame Curies, Edisons, or Gauguins, if that was what they chose to be.

7. Given Angelou's later achievements, you could say that she began her life that day when the entire graduating class sang the Negro National Anthem and gained renewed inspiration to forge ahead in response to Henry Reed's challenging speech "To Be or Not to Be."

RHETORICAL CONSIDERATIONS

1. Children "trembled with anticipation" and adults were "excited." They all had "graduation epidemic." Junior students were "anxious" to help. Graduating students were "travelers with exotic destinations" who "strutted" around school like "nobility." Younger students "fell all over themselves" to lend them forgotten school supplies. Angelou's word choices emphasize the excitement everyone felt in preparing for graduation. Such an emphasis, in turn, accentuates the heaviness of the atmosphere when Mr. Donleavy gave his speech.

2. Angelou describes the incident from the point of view of a graduating eighth grader much involved in the preparation and ceremony. Her immediate, firsthand account creates for the reader a sense of closeness to the events and promotes empathy for the black students and their families. Although Angelou

writes from a distinct point of view, her account seems fairly accurate. Bailey, being older and no longer directly involved with graduation, might have told the incident with more detachment. He might have compared his own graduation to Angelou's or discussed what could be expected to take place after graduation. The minister, too, would have brought a more detached point of view to the occasion. He might have offered a philosophical discussion of the moral implications of the event. Mr. Donleavy might have remarked on the respectful sobriety of the audience, emphasized the problems involved with his even being able to attend the ceremony, and continued the essay with a discussion of more significant items on his agenda for that day.

3. Rain falling through a ragged umbrella suggests a dejected, defenseless, neglected condition. Angelou uses numerous figures of speech: In preparing for graduation, former years of isolation were left behind as "hanging ropes of parasitic moss." The morning of graduation was like young childhood, whereas the hours that followed resembled the maturity of an adult. Children dressed in crepe-paper dresses and butterfly wings dashed about on the evening of graduation "like fireflies." The principal's voice introducing Mr. Donleavy's was "like a river diminishing to a stream and then to a trickle." Mr. Donleavy's "dead words fell like bricks." Professor Parsons sat like a "sculptor's reject." At the end of the ceremony, the echoes of the Negro National Anthem "shivered" in the air. The assembly had been in "icy," "dark" waters but had risen to the surface to a "bright sun" that "spoke to our souls."

4. Angelou uses numerous specific, concrete details. This is a good opportunity to point out to students that specific words are more effective than general ones. Instead of saying that it never hurt younger students to call older students nicknames. Angelou remarks: "It never hurt a sixth grader to have a play sister in the eighth grade, or a tenth-year student to be able to call a twelfth grader Bubba." Instead of stating generally that a nearby Negro school trained students for agricultural and mechanical jobs, Angelou refers to "South's A & M (Agricultural and Mechanical) schools, which trained Negro youths to be carpenters, farmers, handymen, masons, maids, cooks, and baby nurses." She doesn't say simply that parents ordered new clothes from a mail-order store but instead: "Parents . . . had ordered new shoes and ready-made clothes for themselves from Sears and Roebuck and Montgomery Ward." The younger children weren't just rehearsing their skit. They were "practicing their hops and their little songs that sounded like silver bells."

Salvation
Langston Hughes

TOPICAL CONSIDERATIONS

1. The first sentence refers to his having gone through the motions of being saved—how he is regarded by the rest of the congregation. However, from inside—from where Hughes narrates this piece—he felt no salvation; he felt and saw no Jesus come.

2. Hughes's motivation was nearly all group pressure—his aunt, the preacher, his friend Westley, and the rest of the congregation. Ironically, the very promise of his elders—that Jesus would enter his life—prevents him from going forth until the very end. Hughes says that he sat there dutifully waiting for Jesus to come as expected. It was only out of pressure, the tearful pleading of his aunt in particular and his shame for holding things up, that he rose to his feet. Westley, on the other hand, is much more practical, less gullible than young Hughes. "'God damn!'" he whispers (his words ringing with irony). "'I'm tired o' sitting here. Let's get up and be saved.'" Westley is more realistic about "salvation." It has more to do with getting the ceremony over with than saving his soul.

3. Hughes says that he cried for three reasons: that he had lied to his aunt about seeing Jesus, that he "had deceived-everybody in church," and that he "didn't believe there was a Jesus any more, since he didn't come." His aunt says that it was because the Holy Ghost had come into his life, and because he had seen Jesus. In reality, just the opposite is true for the boy. Neither Jesus nor the Holy Ghost entered his life. What young Hughes learns is that he has been deceived by the adult world and the promise of "salvation." Also, that "faith is the substance of things hoped for, the evidence of things not seen." It might be said that the only "salvation" he experiences is that from religious conformity.

4. I suppose I would tell the young boy that some people believe that there is a God and a Jesus, and that salvation comes to those who practice their belief. Also that there are others who don't believe, that to them life on earth is it and there is nothing beyond the grave. I would say that belief should and could not be based on "proof" or miracles, that just because Hughes did not see Jesus, that does not mean Jesus didn't exist or that there was no God or afterlife as promised in the scriptures.

5. See above. In many ways this essay describes not simply a rite of passage, a coming of age experience for Hughes. It represents the dilemma of modern man and woman—religious belief in our highly rational world. Religious teachings, particularly Judeo-Christian, hold up ancient miracles as evidence of the supernatural, of the existence of God. That miracles apparently don't occur today points to the necessity of religious faith to come from within, to rise above the need for scientific evidence and the empirical world. No doubt, this question should raise some interesting responses among the students. It would be interesting to see which students have been made cynical by a society so lacking in myths and mysticism and which have sustained their faith.

RHETORICAL CONSIDERATIONS

1. Hughes wisely chose to recreate the flashback rather than simply tell the reader about the events in church. A writer's best hope of achieving the truth is not talking about emotions, but the things that cause them. If the writer gets it *right* the reader will reduplicate the writer's emotions, therefore experiencing what the writer experienced. Of course, the things that matter greatly to a writer are often intangible—love, fear, disappointment, hatred, pride, and passion—and they

cannot be described well. One cannot successfully describe love or fear; one must describe a person in love or a frightening event. In other words, one must embody the indescribable in the describable, the abstract in the concrete. Hughes cannot exactly articulate the feelings he had about not finding Jesus, about doubt and the sense of shame sitting there in the church. However, Hughes can recreate the circumstances that helped produce such feelings— feelings that the reader can perhaps experience reading about the event. One can explain ideas, but emotions have to be illustrated. Hughes does it very well here.

2. In a short time, Hughes creates a vivid scene in the church and uses words that help to create a boy's perspective. Paragraph 4 is particularly descriptive as is paragraph 7, where an anxious congregation "in a mighty wail of moans and voices" surround the boy all alone with his doubts.

3. Hughes's choice of words are accurately chosen to create a 12-year-old's perspective. Occasionally, the language sounds more sophisticated than that of a child. In paragraph 4, "old men with work-gnarled hands" is a phrase beyond most boys of 12. But in most of the other places the language is in line with the boy's point of view. The last line in particular has the breathless catalog of a child, especially "and that now I didn't believe there was a Jesus any more, since he didn't come to help me." Even the self-centered logic has the ring of a child's mind.

The Eye of the Beholder
Grace Suh

TOPICAL CONSIDERATIONS

1. Students will pinpoint any number of Suh's themes. Among them: Beauty originates from a person's sense of integrity, not from a commercial product. Western ideas of beauty warp our sense of self-esteem and self-worth. We have internalized American, commercialized ideas of beauty so much that we cannot see our own true worth.

2. Suh catches a glimpse of her unkempt, unmade-up reflection in the window of an office tower. Even though she had renounced so-called suburban values with the emphasis on appearance, she concluded that she had gone too far, and that her appearance was not just natural any longer, but unattractive. She decides "to fight back" vigorously and envisions a total "reclamation project" that would not just repair her looks, but turn her into a beauty.

3. Suh trusts the Estée Lauder woman because she seems less imperious and judgmental than those from the Chanel counter. Suh willingly consents to being scrubbed, masqued, and treated with astringent. Suh relaxes in the woman's care, imagining how all the products used on her face will transform her. The Estée woman is not working in vain, she tells herself, because Suh will buy the products.

4. While the beautician is pleased with the results, Suh is horrified by the even shade of her face and sharp contrast of her lips. However, Suh puts up a good

front, believing the beautician didn't have much to work with anyway. Students should see that Suh has been manipulated by a very convincing marketing campaign that plays into some women's sensitivity about their looks. You may discuss the feelings of powerlessness a woman (or man) may feel at the cosmetics counter in the hands of gorgeously made-up beauticians who seem possessed by special knowledge of natural beauty lacking in us mere customers.

5. Suh at first passively consents to having her eyelids made over, believing the beautician knows best; but when she sees the results, she is horrified because the re-drawn eyelid has totally distorted her face. She feels negated by this woman in whose hands she had so completely trusted her face. And she is angered when the woman says, "At least now you have an eyelid." The comment is an insult to Suh's ethnicity, because it implies that only women with large eyelids can be beautiful. At this point, she imagines the woman's life as pathetic and meaningless, but she keeps quiet and coolly walks away. Students may have various responses, but many may understand Suh's sense of powerlessness in the cosmetics chair. She gets her revenge by leaving the Estée products on the train and vowing never to use them.

6. Suh quickly washes off the makeup, then boards a subway train. In the reflection, she notices her scrubbed face and concludes that she does have an eyelid, and that her face "wasn't pretty. But I was familiar and comforting. I was myself." A few hours earlier she hated that reflection; but the beauty makeover insulted her integrity. And she discovered her true face—one she prefers to the painted one. Her leaving the products kit on the subway is a sign of her acceptance of herself as she is—a contrast to her attitude at the beginning of the essay when Suh described her face as a "reclamation project."

7. When Suh looks into the mirror at the white beautician's handiwork, she says: "I felt negated; I had been blotted out and another face drawn in my place." Similarly, In Angelou's essay after Henry Reed had given his "To Be Or Not To Be" speech, Angelou describes the irony of the situation: "the world didn't think we had minds, and they let us know it. . . . Not 'rub,' Henry, 'erase.' 'Ah there's the erase.' US." Both Maya Angelou and Grace Suh have been strongly rubbed out by the actions of unthinking white individuals.

At the end of the essay, Suh reaffirms her self-worth by washing off the makeup and leaving the cosmetics on the subway. She finds comfort in recognizing her own Asian face again, not the painted-on image of a Western, white model. Angelou's community breaks into the "Negro National Anthem" in response to the indifference of the white visitor. The anthem affirms the community's pride in being African-American.

RHETORICAL CONSIDERATIONS

1. The Shakespearian phrase "Beauty lies in the eye of the beholder" directly reflects the central theme of the essay: that beauty is relative. Not only does the title point to the physical difference between Asian and Western eyes, but

to differences in how society views beauty, and how Suh views herself. The Asian eye may not uphold the same beauty standards as does the Western eye.

At first, when the author caught her own reflection in the office window, she saw someone unkempt and ugly. After she went through an insulting beauty makeover, then washed off its evidence out of horror, Suh came to accept the final reflection. She concluded that her face may not be pretty, but it was her own, not the dominant culture's ideal. Suh's theme is that self-respect is more valuable than a commercial idea of beauty.

2. Suh's tone is very up front, honest and self-aware. Students may be struck by how freely she admits personal flaws in her appearance and thinking. In the first sentence she confesses that she "made up her mind to become beautiful," and in the next few she comes down hard on her looks. She also confesses being taken in by the promises of cosmetics marketing and beauty products (paragraphs 5 and 9). When she realizes what the counter-worker has done to her eyes, she is horrified and angry. Suh's honest innocence and anger help convince us of the truth of her argument: that beauty is more than skin deep.

3. Suh is quite visually descriptive when she juxtaposes her own image with that of models and beauticians. And the contrast immediately establishes her sense of inferiority. Right off she describes herself as having "ragged hair," "dark circles," "facial blemishes," and "shapeless, wrinkled clothes." In contrast, the beauty mavens at the cosmetics counters are "priestesses of beauty in their sacred smocks." The makeup unguents have an almost magical potency: "bright blue mud masque," "clear, tingling astringent." The Estée Lauder beautician violently contrasts Suh's own looks: "her gleaming, polished features, her lacquered nails, the glittering mosaic of her eye shadow, the complex red shimmer of her mouth, her flawless, dewy skin. . . ." These strong descriptions prepare the reader for an inevitable letdown when Suh beholds her own reflection.

4. In paragraph 12, the beautician announces that she will work on the "biggie"— Suh's eyes. Up until that moment, the narrative has emphasized the magic of the experience, and Suh's desire to be totally transformed by the almost goddesslike Estée Lauder beautician. By including a dialog between the counter worker and Suh (paragraphs 11–23), the reader watches the drama unfold, while revealing the woman's personality and prejudices. She snaps at Suh with words such as "Oriental," implying that Suh had no eyelids. The dialog more dramatically captures the conflict than straight narrative.

5. One example is the following statement in paragraph 25: "The fact of the matter was that she was pretty, and I was not. Her blue eyes were recessed and in an intricate pattern of folds and hollows. Mine bulged out." In the preceding paragraph, Suh is angry at the counter woman who has negated her Asian identity by drawing a large eyelid on her face. She imagines that the woman has nothing to look forward to but soap operas while Suh had her whole young life to live. But, ironically Suh realizes that it doesn't matter if this middle-aged woman has nothing to do in her life, she has what is admired in our culture: deep eyelids. But the implication here (and the source of irony) reaches beyond beauty. Suh

could have also said, "The fact of the matter was, the woman is white, and I am not." Or, "The woman has the kinds of looks that are admired by the majority culture, and I do not."

The Ambivalence of Abortion
Linda Bird Francke

TOPICAL CONSIDERATIONS

1. A new baby would preclude her husband's option of changing his career at the same time as it would put the author "right back in the nursery," just when her youngest child was finally in school and when she had taken on a full-time job after so many years of part-time freelancing.
2. They are nervous, ill at ease. The men do not speak to each other, knowing that they "had to be there, wishing they weren't." She notices a depressed embarrassment for being at the clinic.
3. Francke says that shame links the rather disparate group of women. Those pregnant women were "losing life that day, not giving it" (paragraph 10).
4. She panicked because of a crisis of conscience. There she was, a woman who cherished life, now in an abortion clinic. Her political convictions about a woman's right to have an abortion are stripped away as she suddenly faces the reality of what she is about to do. She adds that she would still defend a woman's right to have an abortion, but for her there is a moral crisis.
5. She had always supported a woman's right to have an abortion. I do not think she experienced any change of heart.
6. By "modern" she means "liberated," "enlightened" by the principles espoused by the women's movement in the last decade, particularly that right "to exercise the option of motherhood." But "modern" also carries the kind of political cold mindedness that comes from adherence to abstractions, which crumble for her when she herself faces the termination of the fetus growing inside her.
7. This might suggest female conventionality—a stereotypical need to be saved from a bad decision by a man. But I think her fantasy goes beyond rigid sexual roles of heroic rescuer and helpless damsel in distress. She is close to the edge of turning back, and she seems to want her husband—whom she treats as an equal throughout—to convince her by bursting into the operating room and pulling her back.
8. She will be haunted for a long time by that little ghost of the last paragraph.

RHETORICAL CONSIDERATIONS

1. Ambivalence is the state of having contradictory thoughts or feelings about a particular matter. In this case, the contradiction that besets the author is both wanting to have an abortion and not wanting to have one. The ambivalence is illustrated immediately when the pregnancy is "heralded" with "shocked silence

and Scotch" instead of with "champagne and hope." She begins to discuss her ambivalence directly in paragraph 13.

2. The repetition signals that they are trying to convince themselves that there was no room in their lives for another baby. She repeats herself twice in paragraph 27: the first occasion, like that in paragraph 3, shows how much they are trying to convince themselves that "it certainly does make more sense not to be having a baby right now"; the second emphasizes the persistent ambivalence, "Of course, we have room," "Of course, we do," which perhaps comes closer to the truth.

3. She is never sentimental, that is why this is so powerful a piece of writing.

4. The change, a euphemistic one, conceals the fact that abortions are performed there—a change that reflects a conflict with antiabortion attitudes of the community.

5. Her seemingly neutral stance is a way of highlighting the irony that the procedure of abortion is so simple and easy in contrast with the anxiety she suffers.

6. She is fairly neutral in describing the other women in the clinic, although her description of the youngest Puerto Rican girl with head lowered in shame while refusing birth control options is a pathetic one.

7. The smiling aide is responding to the woman's fear of physical pain. The image of the woman doing a jig later on that day counters the potentially crippling effect of the operation on the spirit—one the author experiences.

8. She is being sardonic here. Women suffer most during abortion.

9. The image is a powerful metaphor of the aborted baby as a flower wrapped in a wet towel like a diaper, with the plastic bag functioning as both the placental sac and a suffocation chamber. The image captures the ambivalence at once.

10. The switch to the present tense demonstrates how even now—years later—she has not overcome the emotional anguish of her decision and perhaps never will. The paragraph will always be in the present tense.

Why I Quit Practicing Law

Sam Benson

TOPICAL CONSIDERATIONS

1. Benson says that he left his practice because he was becoming increasingly uncomfortable with the "misery" his profession caused other people; and throughout the essay he explores how the law profession does more harm than good. Students may be surprised by the bluntness of Benson's confession, and may want to discuss how other respected professions such as medicine and education are losing their popularity.

2. Adversarial law requires that attorneys vigorously represent their clients, even if it means defending people who are unethical. Students could explore the justice system in European countries that frequently employ the Napoleonic code, which generally assumes a person is guilty until proven innocent.

3. Because of the adversarial nature of the law, attorneys are required to use any means available to win, similar to fighting a war. As in war, also, the truth of a situation is often "the first casualty." For instance, people paying attorneys in personal injury cases, malpractice cases, and the like expect them to do heavy battle—to vigorously accumulate evidence in their favor, while overlooking that which conflicts with their interests. In trial cases, Benson criticizes the pretrial "discovery" in which attorney interrogation often intimidates and harasses opponents. In the end, the winner may not be the truly deserving client or justice, but the one who can hold out the longest emotionally or financially. In short, the system encourages attorneys to be dishonest and disagreeable, which is how the public views them.

4. Lawyers who try to act ethically often cannot compete with those who approach every case as if doing combat. It is also difficult for a lawyer to explain the ethical side of a case to a client who wants to win, Benson writes. Students may turn to the medical profession and the pressures to prescribe medication when not needed or to perform an unnecessary operation for the high fee, or to avoid a necessary operation out of fear of a malpractice suit.

5. This quote from Richard Burke refers to Benson's point that many lawyers, under pressure, are taking shortcuts and coming up with false evidence and exaggerations to win their case.

6. Benson is not optimistic. Our problems will remain as long we maintain the adversarial system of justice. Student opinions will differ, but most will conclude that he is not hopeful.

RHETORICAL CONSIDERATIONS

1. Outside his office, Benson sees "fancy landscaping" and an "immaculately kept brick driveway," revealing that his office is far removed from the trappings of ordinary life and people's suffering. His blunt confessional statements: "I was tired of the chicanery. I was tired of the deceit," reveal his strong repugnance toward the profession and his realization that it causes misery.

2. Benson's use of "hired gun" dramatically expresses the role of an attorney as someone paid to do combat against an enemy. Throughout he relies on combat imagery to evoke the sense of battle. In paragraphs 2 through 4 he refers to Desert Storm, "a warlike setting," and "the old warring axiom."

3. The author's tone could be described as one of quiet moral outrage. In some respects, it sounds like a legal brief. He is clearly appalled by what he sees in the justice system, but he also deftly explains the reasons why the system works as it does.

4. Benson clearly explains the problems with our adversarial justice system, and gives good examples of why the system does not deliver justice. Even though he claims that no one personal experience pushed him over the edge, the reader may be left wondering if there isn't something Benson is holding back. His first paragraph, so personally revealing, hints that he might launch into a personal narrative, revealing a turning-point episode. But he does not.

A Clack of Tiny Sparks: Remembrance of a Gay Boyhood

Bernard Cooper

TOPICAL CONSIDERATIONS

1. When Cooper first invites Grady over for a swim, he admires how at home Grady is with his body and begins to wonder, after Theresa Sanchez's question, if what he feels might be love—a very difficult admission for him. He also believes that Grady's quiet, understated Hollywood family must be socially superior to his Jewish one, "a dark and vociferous people who ate with abandon." He decides to keep his distance from Grady because he believes his feelings are not "normal." Gregory's crush on Helene is equally intense and distant. He details how carefully he had to wash his socks in water melted down from ice in order to appear presentable to Helene. Like Cooper, Gregory's object of affection is someone he imagines as far above him, unattainable. Helene's father is a paperhanger; Gregory had no father. Cooper thinks of himself as an uncomfortable misfit in school because of his homosexual feelings, while Grady is self-confident and athletic—qualities that Cooper envies.

2. At the age of fourteen, Theresa Sanchez reads exotic books behind her algebra text. Her hair is streaked with blond, much "higher than the flaccid bouffant of the other girls." She is clearly superior to others in the school and strikingly different, in Cooper's view. She also represents someone who welcomes difference, and who is comfortable with herself, and not afraid to be different. Her frank and accepting inquiry as to Cooper's gayness leads him to explore the possibility. She also admits nonchalantly to having friends who are gay. Later in the essay, Cooper regrets that he had not known more about himself and his sexual identity to answer her more truthfully. He would have been much happier in high school, he says, and he could have met some of her friends.

3. Cooper's family has variable moods: sometimes they are brooding and obsessively preoccupied, other times they are garrulous and expansive. Their range of moods made it difficult for Cooper to talk about his feelings as a gay person. He could never be sure of their reaction. At one point Cooper recalls the "mistake" he made in asking his mother what the word "fag" meant. She responded to his question by grabbing him by the shoulders and demanding to know if someone had called him a fag. Cooper lied and his mother's relief made Cooper feel all the more isolated. Her judgment was all important to him: "My longing was wrong in the eyes of my mother, whose hazel eyes were the eyes of the world, and if that longing continued unchecked, the unwieldy shape of my fate would be cast, and I'd be subjected to a lifetime of scorn."

   While gay students may not be willing to discuss their own personal experiences coming out, they may admit to the difficulties of revealing details of their sexual lives to parents. You may discuss how our sexual selves might be the most essential expression of our personality; when our sexual lives are judged, the criticism has implications for the kind of people we will be our whole life, "the shape of our fate," as Cooper writes.

4. Following his mother's extreme reaction to his question about the meaning of fag, Cooper tries to force himself to like women and to forget Grady or other men. He convinced himself that his yearning was like a bad habit, and that with self-discipline he could vanquish his longings by kissing a girl. When he is invited to a makeout party, he gladly accepts; but when he attempts to kiss a girl, he is distracted by thoughts of Grady. The class may be aware of therapies that try to condition someone who is gay to love the opposite sex. You may want to explore why these therapies often backfire and make the person feel worse about himself or herself. The class might discuss what happens to an individual who tries to repress love for someone who is unavailable or unaccepting.

5. When Cooper is asked by his art teacher to deliver a note to a literature teacher, he meets up with Theresa Sanchez in the hallway, packing her books to leave the school. In the course of their goodbyes, Theresa implies that the note Cooper is delivering is a love note between two men. Although Cooper writes that he doesn't remember the literature teacher's reaction to the note, he imagines the pain the two may have felt in being forced to keep their love lives hidden. Cooper writes of the teacher as a "lone man mouthing an epic, his gestures ardent in empty air." But he says he saw no signs of the love of the two men at school. The author includes this scene to further demonstrate how much he was looking for guidance and direction as he was coming to terms with his own sexuality. If Cooper had been exposed to a positive model for a gay relationship, he implies, he may have had an easier time coming out.

6. Cooper learns that other students have a store of superstitious beliefs about gays: they wear green, can't whistle, and try to hypnotize young boys. His friend Grady tells him that gays have a marked gesture when looking at their hands. His friend Theresa who has gay friends also believes in telling gay characteristics. Cooper wonders about these signs and himself. He also wonders if his classmates will discover his secret and expose him. In discussing stereotypes, it might be useful to point out that Cooper's examples reveal a belief that gay people aren't normal—a belief that might underscore some people's concern about their own sexuality.

RHETORICAL CONSIDERATIONS

1. The author is happily content with his life as a gay man, and has a stable relationship. His declaration of happiness and love is an affirmation of his gay identity, while demonstrating a resolution to the difficulties experienced in high school. His ending is purposefully celebratory to reinforce the idea that gay identity can be a positive experience. The author implies that if he had known he could be so happy, he would have come out a long time ago.

2. In paragraph 37, after recounting all his efforts to squelch his growing attraction to men, Cooper returns to the image of Grady in the swimming pool: "I swam up behind him, encircled his shoulder's, astonished by his taut flesh. The two of us

flailed, pretended to drown. Beneath the heavy press of water, Grady's orange hair wavered, a flame that couldn't be doused." Cooper's choice of language reveals a strong passion that won't go out. He realizes that he has been unsuccessful in trying to repress these feelings. Cooper's tone in this passage is tender and erotic, a foreshadowing of the upbeat ending to come in the next two paragraphs.

3. Cooper came to understand his sexuality indirectly, and only through small signals gleaned from his classmates' hints, his parents' fears, and clues from the relationship between two male teachers. The title's image is from Cooper's description of the makeout party at the end of paragraph 25: "All the shuffling across the carpet charged everyone's arms and lips with static, and eventually, between low moans and soft osculations, I could hear the clack of tiny sparks and see them flare here and there in the dark like meager, short-lived stars." Cooper is a distant bystander to this party, one who longs to have a sexual experience, but finds himself far removed from this social climate that demands he participate as a heterosexual.

·2·
Family Matters

In Search of Our Mothers' Gardens
Alice Walker

TOPICAL CONSIDERATIONS

1. Toomer is speaking of the black women of the twenties whose spirituality was stronger than the sexual and racial abuse they suffered. "To the men who used them . . . they became 'Saints'" (paragraph 1). They were the women who suffered these inequities in the only way they knew how—acting like lunatics or resorting to suicide. Walker states that these women Toomer described did not know the richness they held. "Some . . . were our mothers and grandmothers" (paragraph 1). They were waiting to be recognized as real people, individuals.

2. The author speaks of these women as creators whose creativity found no release. Their spirituality "which is the basis of Art" (paragraph 10) suffered under the strain of abuse and stifled talent. They were emotional, physical and spiritual slaves. The sculptors, painters, and writers were prevented from expressing themselves; only the creativity of the singer was not thwarted. Walker laments that many writers suffered the agony of dying "with their real gifts stifled within them" (paragraph 13).

3. Wheatley did try to use her gift of poetry even though she was a slave. She made time to write her poetry before or after her many chores, and she held onto her dreams through her poetry. Her gift became her escape and she "kept alive, in so many of our ancestors, the notion of song" (paragraph 26). That is, Phillis Wheatley kept the spirit of the early black American alive for future generations.

4. The author discovers that in researching the history of creative black women, she found "the truest answer . . . can be found very close" (paragraph 29). She discovers that the essay is a personal account but also an historical account of the world of creative black women. That is, the two accounts share theme and meaning. Alice Walker "went in search of the secret of what has fed that muzzled and often mutilated, but vibrant, creative spirit that the black woman has inherited, and that pops out in wild and unlikely places to this day" (paragraph 32).

5. Her mother's stories became the stories the author wrote and published. She discovered only recently that the manner in which she writes her stories models the way her mother told them. Also, her characters model real-life people that she

had heard about from her mother. In her creativity with flowers. Walker's mother becomes an artist, too. As Walker says, "She has handed down respect for the possibilities—and the will to grasp them" (paragraph 45).

6. Walker has discovered the creativity she inherited from her mother. She had identified her mother's artistic gift and, through it, has found her own.

RHETORICAL CONSIDERATIONS

1. The language of Walker is packed with emotion much like the emotion of the women she is describing. From the first paragraph to the end, Walker uses examples of emotional language and students will select different passages as examples. Most will indicate the effectiveness in portraying the stifled creativity in the women. Some examples of the language include: "They dreamed dreams no one knew" and "the mule of the world" (paragraph 5), "who died under some ignorant and depraved white overseer's lash" (paragraph 12), or the description of Phillis Wheatley "suffering from malnutrition and neglect and who knows what mental agonies" (paragraph 22). Students should have no trouble finding emotional language in this essay. Its effectiveness depends on their point of view and how they relate it to the main points of the essay.

2. The excerpt establishes the hidden nature and temperament of black women in Toomer's time. It speaks of the hope for future generations of black women and tells "about an art that would be born, an art that would open the way for women the likes of her." The prostitute represents all the black women who were abused and "considered themselves unworthy even of hope." Walker continues the essay explaining how these women created their "gardens" of hope for the future generations of black women.

3. Walker establishes the irony of Woolf's comment that a woman must have her own room "and enough money to support herself" (paragraph 17) if she is to write fiction. In contrast, Walker offers the squalid, slave life of Phillis Wheatley. Once she has established this contrast, then she is able to insert editorial comments in the Woolf quotation to deepen the contrast between the life of a white female writer and that of a black female writer. She also uses the phrase "contrary instincts" to describe the conflicts within such black writers as Wheatley, Nella Larsen, and Zora Neale Hurston.

4. Again, the contrast between the white women and black women becomes obvious. Wheatley, a black woman, associates freedom with the golden hair of the goddess. Walker adds italics to the word golden to emphasize the contrast.

5. Walker ends the paragraph with a strong, defiant stand that no one can deny a black woman's right to be an artist. There is a sense that not only will black women be artists but they will prevail. This leads to the next paragraph where she states, "[We will] fearlessly pull out of ourselves . . . and identify with our lives the living creativity some of our great-grandmothers were not allowed to know." This paragraph leads into the thesis paragraph (29).

6. Here Walker uses the insertions to give examples of black writers and their struggles. She also uses the quotation to reinforce her idea that women of previous generations "handed on the creative spark."

A Father's Rite
Chester Higgins, Jr.

TOPICAL CONSIDERATIONS

1. Higgins's personal experience with fathers and fatherhood is characterized by physical and emotional distance. He did not meet his biological father until he was nineteen, and then only at his own instigation; his stepfather was present physically but "a distant man" emotionally (paragraph 3). As a father himself, divorce put Higgins up against New York State laws that threatened to "reduce his relationship with his children to that of an uncle" (paragraph 4).

   These experiences left Higgins with two, conflicting attitudes toward parenting. He is determined to "take the role of a father seriously" (paragraph 3) and to "maintain as much contact with my children as the law would allow" (paragraph 4). At the same he has no model for how to become a loving and responsible father: he is "an impostor" who feels that fatherhood "seems to require skills never taught to [him]" (paragraph 3).

2. Damani is 20; Higgins was also in his 20s when he first went to Africa (paragraph 1). Damani "shares [Higgins's] love of His Majesty and of reggae, the music of the Rastafarians who worship Selassie" (paragraph 5). Such similarities are important because Higgins is trying to create a sense of identity and ancestral continuity between himself and his son.

3. The three religions of Africa mentioned in the essay all inspire Higgins to create his "father's rite." The reinternment of Haile Selassie provides the trip with its original purpose; even though that ceremony is postponed, its place is, in a sense, ultimately filled by the ritual between Higgins and Damani. The idea of the ritual comes to Higgins in a dream-vision in the "sacred city of Lalibala" (paragraph 6), and it is finally performed in the Valley of the Kings approached from "the heavenly perch of ancient Egyptian gods," in front of the "wall painting of Osiris, the god of resurrection."

4. In the ritual, Higgins defines Africa as a kind of ancestral spirit that exists apart from the material reality of the continent. Higgins tells his son that they are Africans "not because we were born in Africa, but because Africa was born in us" (paragraph 14). Students might note that Higgins is working on a book of photographs of people of African descent whose title—*Feeling the Spirit: The Family of Africa*—further suggests the continent is, in Higgins's view, a spirit as well as a place.

5. The merging of past and present is central to the ritual, in which Damani is blessed and encouraged by the spirits of his ancestors. Elsewhere in the essay,

both the Selassie reinternment and the mural of the God Osiris thematically suggest the return (or resurrection) of past lives. The journey into the past is repeated in the essay's organization. The three religions described consecutively recede chronologically: Selassie was born a hundred years ago; the churches in Lalibala were built in the twelfth century; the most ancient Temple of Karnak is "one of the largest, oldest stone temples in the world" (paragraph 11).

6. Here students should recognize the central claim of the essay. Higgins has discovered that fatherhood is not only an individual relationship, but the avenue through which a child connects to a larger cultural heritage. As African-Americans, Higgins and his son had to travel together to their ancestral roots to make this discovery.

RHETORICAL CONSIDERATIONS

1. Students might have noticed the image of the boat "slipping along the water in a dark night without a lamp or a lighthouse" (paragraph 3) which describes Higgins's sense of inadequacy as a father. The picture of Damani in dreadlocks, blending into the Ethiopian population, is a visual expression of the idea that Africa has been born in him. The idea for the ritual comes to Higgins initially in a dream vision; the actual words he would use took "six days" more to arrive (paragraph 7). Students might also have been struck by the elaborately visual description of the Valley of the Kings (paragraph 12).

2. Even though Africa is ultimately a spiritual concept, the physical earth and stone of the continent is symbolically significant throughout. In the ritual, Higgins tells Damani that "This piece of earth is a symbol of the lives of your ancestors. It is a bonding of their lives to yours" (paragraph 14). The earth is also important in the other African religions described here. Selassie is awaiting reinterment in the earth; in Lalibala, "churches were hewn out of the surrounding mountains." The "tombs of the Pharaohs are hewn into the lower part of the mountains. . . . Inside each tomb, 12-foot-square passageways lead down several thousand feet into the solid rock" (paragraph 12). All the religions seem literally grounded in the soil, and the ritual in fact takes place underground, inside the African continent.

3. The Valley of the Kings brings together several central themes: the merging of past and present, the importance of the African land and the greatness of Africa, the spirituality of its people. The description of the towering mountains visually emphasizes Africa's greatness. As students will already have noted, the site allows the ritual to take place underground, literally within Africa. Inside the "sacred chambers" vivid wall paintings bring the past to life by recreating the "real and imaginary lives of Pharaonic Egyptians" (12). Finally, the ritual is performed before the painting of Osiris, the God of Resurrection, who here seems to symbolize the return of the African past to bless Damani.

4. Students—particularly female ones—may have noticed that, although the essay claims to be about fathers, it seems rather to be more specifically about fathers and sons. We know that Higgins has a daughter, two years older than Damani, but there is no mention of any ritual trip to Africa for her.

5. The delay in giving us this information not only creates a sense of urgency and suspense in the last half of the essay, but it also fittingly puts the ritual in the essay's climactic position, right before the end.

Daddy Tucked the Blanket
Randall Williams

TOPICAL CONSIDERATIONS

1. He says that he found his freedom and "was getting out." His escape was from the poverty and the humiliation of it. Throughout the essay, Williams stresses how painful poverty is, particularly for young people who want to be accepted by peers, who want to have the things other kids have, things they see on television. Thus his breaking out, his escape, is a way of looking for more. At the same time, it is an escape from the humiliation of being poor—the same humiliation that kept him from bringing a friend to his house while in high school.
2. The house was apparently not large enough to comfortably accommodate the Williams family, which, the author says, was large. Several young people slept in one room. The house was old, hot in summer and cold in winter, and in disrepair. Plaster kept falling from the ceiling above his bed and the walls also crumbled when they tried to paint them. The kitchen had no counter space and no hot water; also, the house had no closets. The windows were broken, the hallway was dirty, and the wallpaper was peeling.
3. He characterizes his parents as hardworking, caring, unselfish, kind, and frustrated by their impoverished status. His father worked hard at a full-time job outside the home as his mother did inside the home. But no matter how much his father made, they never got out of their economic rut. Williams says he got out because of scholarships to college.
4. According to Williams the anger between his parents was really displaced from the economic "trap their lives were in. It ruined their marriage because they had no one to yell at but each other."
5. He is grateful for that moment of humiliation, probably because it made him determine not to be poor when he grew up. Perhaps it helped him decide to go after scholarships so that he could go to college and thus into a profession that would afford him escape from the poverty of his past.

RHETORICAL CONSIDERATIONS

1. The first sentence of paragraph 5 serves as William's thesis statement.
2. All the details pointing to the uncomfortable and ruinous conditions of the houses they lived in certainly illustrate their plight. In particular, his reference to the plaster falling on his face at night; trying to paint a crumbling wall: how bright paint emphasized the holes in the walls; the reference to the dirty hallway, broken windows, and cracked ceiling that would greet a prospective date for his

sisters. The most moving detail is his illustration of his father's using wire to tie his boots in winter because any money he had went for the kids' clothes.

3. He talks about his parents' frustrations and anger. He first introduces the potential ruin in paragraph 12, where he says his father used to yell at his mother because she couldn't keep the house clean. Williams observes that his father probably knew his yelling was an outlet for his rage at being poor. He mentions that again in paragraph 16. Then in the following paragraph Williams says that the anger climaxed in a "particularly violent argument" about the washing machine that broke down. In an aside we learn that the only water faucet was outside on the porch; we also learn that his mother had to do their school clothes in a washtub.

4. He uses illustrative details through the essay, although it is not particularly descriptive. Paragraphs 11 and 15 are the most descriptive. I would have liked more descriptive details.

5. The style of William's essay probably is closer to that of most composition students than to the style of many essays in the text. It is simple and direct, achieved by simple vocabulary and short declarative sentences with few modifiers. Many of William's sentences, particularly at the beginning, open with "I" or "we" followed by a simple verb. He even opts for clichés instead of fresh expressions: "We lived like hell" (paragraph 8), "my father worked his head off" (paragraph 6). And, as indicated by the brief paragraphs, he does not go into much detail or analysis but keeps on the surface or impression level pretty much throughout.

6. The title carries a touching suggestion of how, despite the awful conditions of their lives, the home had love and caring. The specific reference is in paragraph 18, where the author describes his father's tucking the blanket around his sleeping mother on the night they had a violent argument. Again, the message is that there was loving and caring in the family; however, even that broke down under the stress of poverty.

7. "Sentimental" implies exploitation of the reader's emotions. I do not find the essay sentimental, although it is touching in places. In fact, I sense Williams holding back, consciously avoiding the sound of sentimentality, even in describing his father's tucking in his mother while tears fell from his eyes. He applies the same control at the end when he describes the classroom humiliation. He could have exaggerated the scene or dramatized it for greater emotional appeal, but he chose not to.

My Brother, My Self

Dick Schaap

TOPICAL CONSIDERATIONS

1. Schaap's relationship with his brother is marked by similar interests, loyalty, love, and—paradoxically—an apparently unbridgeable distance. They live in the same city and are both journalists; on the other hand, they rarely see each

other, hardly ever consult on professional matters, and Schaap says he does "not really know" his brother. Nevertheless, Schaap takes "fierce pride" in his brother's work and claims to "love him very much" (paragraph 1). Students can discuss whether this peculiar kind of closeness is characteristic of family intimacy. They may also note gender distinctions that characterize the sorts of topics likely to come up with mothers as opposed to fathers, or sisters as opposed to brothers.

2. Studying these passages should help students see the irony of Schaap's claim that they "always were" different, for the brothers essentially changed roles in their twenties. Dick Schaap was the more socially conscious and politically radical one in college, working on a paper known as "the upstate *Daily Worker*," and attending a school of Industrial and Labor Relations that was "sometimes called the Little Kremlin" (paragraph 4); after college, he began his career as an editor at *Newsweek* and the New York *Herald Tribune.* Attending the same college a few years later, Bill Schaap "was a disc jockey on the campus radio station and the social chairman of his fraternity"; he then went to a prestigious law school, married a wealthy woman, joined a "Wall Street law firm," and bought real estate (paragraph 7). Now, Dick Schaap is the sportswriter and mainstream journalist, and Bill the "radical" (paragraph 3).

3. This exercise should give students a sense of the political climate of this period, one which will help them understand the ideological divisions between the Schaap brothers. Bill Schaap has identified himself with the radical student movement, opposition to the Vietnam War, black power, and other leftist causes.

4. Students might disagree on this point. The remark that politics intrudes on the relationship is actually facetious, since it refers to the literal intrusion of three right-of-center journalists at the Schaaps' restaurant table; the incident seems more to embarrass Bill (and amuse Dick) than to drive a wedge between the brothers. Elsewhere, Schaap explicitly says their different political values have not divided them: "I do not think I have to be protected from my brother, and his beliefs" (paragraph 13). Although he may not always agree with Bill, Dick says he has not "lost all my liberalism, all my idealism." Nevertheless, students might argue that their lack of personal and professional closeness is inevitably tied to their different political beliefs.

5. By giving us a basis for comparison, the list of writing brothers highlights certain aspects of the Schaaps' relationship. For example, we see how much Dick Schaap values loyalty between brothers in his admiring description of John Lardner, a sports writer who refused to denounce his radical brother, Ring, during the McCarthy era (paragraph 14). The Vecsey brothers are, like the Schaaps, mirror images of each other: though both sportswriters, they are opposites stylistically and psychologically. The inevitability of jealousy among two brothers in the same profession is clear in the example of the famous Neil Simon and his little-known brother Danny.

RHETORICAL CONSIDERATIONS

1. Students can analyze the parallel structure used throughout this paragraph to compare the two brothers. In the first two sentences, for example, Schaap says "I work for ABC. My brother works against the CIA," repeating the use of an acronym at the end of the sentence to further stress the opposition. Later, Schaap writes, "I cover the American League. He covers American imperialism." Such repetition and word play stresses not only the differences between the Schaaps but, simultaneously, their common activities as professional journalists whose work is shaped by political interests, the demands of research, and institutional affiliations.

2. Students may have been confused and irritated by the numerous, possibly unfamiliar topical references. Cumulatively, these references provide the reader with the picture of a very public world—odd in an essay that is supposedly about a personal relationship. The impression the citations create rhetorically is thematically significant, since it underlines the distance between the Schaaps: They relate to each other not in private or intimate contexts, but on a public stage.

3. The underlying purpose of this essay may have been for Schaap to tell his brother explicitly that he loves and honors him. That Schaap would make this pronouncement first in a national magazine simply confirms everything he has told us about their relationship, since we know they are incapable of intimate communication even though they are linked in other, more public ways.

4. Here we see Dick and Bill Schaap in a family context for the first time. Not only is their trip to the funeral parlor the most personal moment in the essay, but the anecdote allows us to see in action what Schaap has been describing throughout the essay: their essential similarity. With the mention of the funeral director's name (Lazarus) "without a word, without even a glance, every conceivable pun and joke about rising from the dead raced, uninvited, into my head and my brother's" (paragraph 20). The fact that their minds work so similarly is one source of their strange kind of closeness.

My Grandmother, The Bag Lady

Patsy Neal

TOPICAL CONSIDERATIONS

1. The transformation of Neal's grandmother to bag lady was gradual, not sudden. Once moved to a nursing home, she visited her own home less frequently as she became more infirm. Much of each visit was spent walking about the house touching beloved objects and browsing through closets and drawers. As periods of confinement in the nursing home lengthened, she took to hiding her few possessions under mattresses and chair cushions while complaining that her things were being stolen. Finally, she placed her things in a bag attached to her walker. As Neal eventually comes to realize, "that walker and her purse . . . [became] her home."

2. For the family, security meant meeting physical needs; a safe environment, regular medication, bodily warmth and well-rounded meals. For the grandmother, on the other hand, security was tied to her possessions, to things she could call her own. Over the years she lost possessions—her car, dogs, and, finally, her home—and with these her security and sense of control over life.

3. The note underscores for Neal the traits of quiet dignity, courage, and caring that the grandmother still possesses. Though lonely the grandmother does not wake her family, but takes pleasure in their comfort and rest.

4. The grandmother controls her few material possessions by keeping them by her side, tucked in bags, and in her purse. In a greater sense, she still exerts great control over her character. The tiny note reveals how she subordinates her own need for companionship to her daughter's and granddaughter's need for rest. It also reveals what pleasure and comfort she takes in this protectiveness.

RHETORICAL CONSIDERATIONS

1. In the first paragraph the author describes the bag ladies found on today's city streets. When she confirms that her own grandmother "had become one of them," the reader is shocked, immediately curious, and involved. We associate bag ladies with poverty and abandonment while grandmothers conjure up Norman Rockwell images of white-haired old women making cookies and telling children stories. The conjunction of the two is at once provocative and disturbing.

2. The author writes, "over the years my grandmother's space for living had diminished *like melting butter.* . . " (paragraph 12). And later, ". . . over the years those possessions had dwindled away *like sand dropping through an hourglass.* . . " (paragraph 14). Both similes are quite effective. Each underscores the notion of a slow, almost imperceptible diminishing of space and possessions. The second simile has the added poignancy of time running out for the old woman. Though not highly original these figures of speech are in keeping with the straightforward account.

3. To be sentimental, something must evoke an excess of emotion. It must elicit a reaction out of proportion to the subject discussed. I found this conclusion touching. It does evoke a strong reaction of pity and sorrow. However, it underscores a theme established early in the piece, namely that of loss—loss of place, possessions, and independence. This last sentence is a hope that on some level Neal's elderly grandmother can have back what she has lost.

Older Children and Divorce

Barbara S. Cain

TOPICAL CONSIDERATIONS

1. More divorces are occurring during midlife when greater numbers of offspring are college age. There has been little research in this area, so the author presents the results of a 1984 study at University of California at San Diego and

University of Michigan at Ann Arbor which she reported in the May 1989 issue of *Psychiatry*. Students may agree or disagree with what is presented, but it would be hard for them to disagree with the fact that there are more midlife divorces affecting college-age offspring. The reasons will differ.

2. Again, responses will be based on personal experience. Cain's study showed that many did make that assumption about marriages of 20 years or more based on their parents' and their friends' parents' relationships.

3. The three most common reactions were to withdraw from romantic relationships, plunge into hedonism daring their parents to complain, or take refuge in protective nihilism. Student choices will differ but should reflect some strong responses.

4. College-age children of divorce do not blame themselves for their parents' separation; younger children do. College students wish they could have prevented the separation, but face the fact that their parents probably stayed together for their sake until they went off to college. The other variance is that the college-age children do not have a loyalty conflict; they clearly see one parent "worthy of blame, the other worthy of compassion" (paragraph 24). Younger children do not know who to side with and cannot deal with mixed loyalties.

5. Answers will vary but students will probably refer to nurturing or supportive roles they have had to play with their parents. Others will indicate that they would be supportive if their parents needed them or cannot imagine having to play such a role.

RHETORICAL CONSIDERATIONS

1. The purpose is to present a scenario as an example of the prevailing attitude. That is, many couples who divorce consider the welfare of younger children while assuming college-age students can handle a divorce. The scenario is used to grab the reader's attention through a specific example before paragraph 2 clearly states the point of the example and the purpose of the essay.

2. This essay is the report of a clinical psychologist. The author uses the language of an educated professional presenting a report in an article. Students may find the vocabulary difficult or distracting from the informal quotations of the students participating in the study. On the other hand, the contrast of the informal language from real respondents and the formal language of the researcher makes the distinction between the two more obvious.

3. The author refers to the sense of loss these college-age children of divorce experience. They long for the family unit they had in childhood, "the one in the photo album, the one whose members shared the same history. . ." (paragraph 9). In the last paragraph, Cain mentions that most of the students in the study really want to marry and have children "to recapture the family of childhood. . ." (paragraph 48). In other words, the author repeats the phrase to point out that the students want to recapture what they lost when their parents divorced.

4. The rhythm and variety make what could be a dull report of a study interesting. The quotations bring the report to life and give it more credibility. Most students will think the quotations help the reader wade through a lengthy report.

5. The physical dismantling of the house means the loss of the place where the members of the family had shared happy and sad experiences. Those memories plus the physical objects associated with those memories would no longer be together. The shared history, photo albums, family rituals will no longer occur. The splitting of material possessions symbolically splits the family, too.

Changing Times

The Terrible Twenties
Daniel Smith-Rowsey

TOPICAL CONSIDERATIONS

1. In Smith-Rowsey's essay, "erotic fantasies" (paragraph 8) stem from "slim-and-trim MTV bimbos" (paragraph 5) and "fleshy beer commercials" (paragraph 5); "Aggressive tendencies" are the result of the older generation's starting "the fire of selfishness and indulgence, building it up until every need or desire was immediately appeased" (paragraph 8); "Evanescent funds of youth" (paragraph 8) are now evanescent funds of adulthood caused by the "get-rich-quick ethos" (paragraph 7) and our reduction to "12-year-olds who want everything now." He substantiates this statement effectively in this essay, but students will probably disagree with this bleak assessment.

2. Smith-Rowsey's sweeping claim is curious. His intention is to blame the stupidity of his generation on the mistakes of the previous generation, but he risks alienating his peers by calling them stupid. Smith-Rowsey measures intelligence using traditional methods: SAT scores, knowledge of geography, foreign language ability, competency in basic math, and love of books. And he makes a good case for his assumption. But his reasoning seems to make a more subtle indictment of the national education system than of his generation. However, his generation does "understand and worry about racism, the environment, abortion, the homeless, nuclear policy" (paragraph 4). This requires a different kind of awareness that cannot be gained in geography class. Therefore, his mention of the "street smarts" of 1990s youth might be seen to undercut his assertion of 20-year-olds' stupidity.

3. Smith-Rowsey seems to suggest that valuing pop culture over education is wrong. He reveals the emptiness of twentysomethings in order to blame the fortysomethings for their lack of values and the damage. However, students may agree that many 20-year-olds place pop culture higher than education as necessary to their development: It is youths' way of making space for themselves in the world, of gaining independence and a separate generational identity for themselves, of learning about things that their parents can't teach them.

4. Paragraph 7 implies that the former generation committed to the civil rights, equal rights, and gay rights movements has forsaken them for the dollar. Those movements were supposed to serve as the generation's "major re-evaluation of its identity." Instead, the majority took on a new identity devoted to the "get-rich-quick-ethos." As a result, none of the movements save, perhaps, gay rights,

has the support they once had. The mainstream has abandoned these causes, pushing them to societal margins. Smith-Rowsey seems to care little about social causes. He says his only concern is that those who chose capitalism over social justice will usurp "the system" before he gets a chance at the "get-rich-quick" economy. He writes, "It's not that I'm angry at you for selling out to the system. It's that there won't be a system for me to sell out to."

5. The essay disproves the Billy Joel line. Smith-Rowsey says the former generation has consumed too much and given too little to enable their children the chance to achieve what they have. He expresses his fear of finding that one day "the money isn't there anymore," (paragraph 7), that there will be a "bankrupt economy," (paragraph 7), that "pretty soon we won't have youth or money" (paragraph 8), and that the older generation "will have robbed us of the skills and money" (paragraph 9) to change the world. He is also concerned that his generation will not have the character to survive: "the whole mall culture has reduced us all to 12-year-olds who want everything now" (paragraph 8); "all we've been left with are the erotic fantasies, aggressive tendencies, and evanescent funds of youth" (paragraph 8); "Perhaps you really have created a nation of mush-heads who always prefer style over substance" (paragraph 9); "our kids will be even dumber, poorer, and more violent than us" (paragraph 9). Many students will probably disagree with this assessment.

6. According to Smith-Rowsey, the younger generation has inherited "MTV bimbos, fleshy beer commercials," "David Letterman," "Nintendo," "Cable TV," "BMWs," "cellular phones," and "the mall culture" from their parents—and none too positive. Students might mention such technological advances as gene splicing, superconductivity, and artificial intelligence, and such social advances as the strides in civil rights and political freedom.

RHETORICAL CONSIDERATIONS

1. "This is an open letter to the baby boomers of the next generation," he writes (paragraph 3), although the second-person address is for his parents' generation—for example, "Did you think we wouldn't care?" (paragraph 2). The "you" works as a finger-pointing device: "You did this to us." Smith-Rowsey uses the "we" to increase support for his somewhat whiny cries of injustice. Students may resent being included in Smith-Rowsey's lament.

2. A "latchkey" child is one who unlocks the door and lets him- or herself in the house after school each day. The word reflects the dual-income household that grew prevalent in the 1980s. Other new words include "twentysomethings," a variation of the once-popular TV show "Thirtysomething" that featured baby-boom consumers. Also, MTV, David Letterman, Nintendo, Cable TV, and cellular phones—all of which are part of the 1980s and 1990s consumer America lexicon that underscore the preoccupation with image.

3. Smith-Rowsey's lead is the most effective part of the essay. Many people of his generation look at growing housing costs, high unemployment rates, and so on and cannot even imagine being able to afford what their parents had. Thoughts

of a single-income household are almost unheard of. The paragraph begins with one complete sentence, then continues with two fragments, pieces of a time that cannot be repeated. Unlike the rest of the essay, this paragraph shows longing without being whiny.

4. To some, Smith-Rowsey may seem to whine his way through the essay. He blames his parents' generation for everything and assumes no responsibility for his own development. He pleads, "If there's any part of you left that still loves us enough, we could really use it" (paragraph 9). While it is true that the older generation has consumed too much, a stronger less complaining self-obsessed voice from the twentysomething generation might earn more respect.

As Busy As We Wanna Be

Deborah Baldwin

TOPICAL CONSIDERATIONS

1. Students raised in a time marked by the hyperactivity of MTV will probably relate well to the idea of time as perpetually in short supply, especially given the demands placed upon them by college life. Discussion might take up cultural determinants of "time management"—Baldwin's term is, after all, the Great American Time Crunch. Is it true that in other parts of the world time is savored in ways uncommon in the United States? Would we feel less of a Time Crunch if the siesta, say, were part of our cultural heritage, or if we were accustomed to lingering for two to three hours over dinner?

2. The media has produced the *global village*. Not only are people exposed to images from all over the world, but the development of satellite communication has shortened the distance between "us" and the world "out there." Additionally, the power of advertising and reportage on different lifestyles has created the desire for material goods, travel, and other living opportunities that were largely inconceivable before media exposure.

3. Baldwin points out that with so many options, the ability to focus on one task for an extended period of time is lessened. The media makes things worse with its sound bites and flashing images. Baldwin implicitly yearns for a past when time was less cluttered and choices were fewer.

4. This is an important statement leading to Baldwin's discussion of work and consumption in America. Literally this says that the more one produces, the more meaningfully one's time has been spent. This touches upon the American work ethic, the competition-based market, and the American dream. Baldwin also notes that the measure of meaning according to productivity has seeped into leisure time: People want leisure that can be "clocked" on the treadmill or in goods purchased at the mall. Unfortunately, according to Baldwin, this attitude precludes meaningful activities with less tangible results such as relationships, helping others, or private meditation, prayer, and learning.

5. This discussion should address how our consumer culture has made time a commodity, and how people must work overtime to finance that new house or to buy the appliances, clothes, and vacations marketed in the media. To change this situation requires we change habits fundamental to our economy.

6. Again, this statement points to the work ethic going back to pioneer ideals of building the strength of the country. The issue becomes moral in a country that preaches lifting oneself up by the bootstraps—if you're not working hard enough you won't be able to support yourself, your family, or others. The argument could be made that this attitude is so embedded in U.S. culture that it is now common for self-esteem and ethical codes to be based upon it.

7. Open for discussion, though clearly Baldwin is referring to change on a macro, rather than a micro, level. That is, she recommends a change in attitude and in habitual activity, not in daily scheduling detail.

8. This discussion will probably take shape around nostalgic visions of pre–Industrial Revolution America, before technology, the media, and consumerism complicated daily life in ways described by Baldwin. Simplicity may be interpreted as making things by hand, growing one's own food, making one's own clothes—and accompanying this simplicity may be a vision of a time characterized by a greater sense of community than the fragmented technoculture marking contemporary American life. On the other hand, it is important to note, as Baldwin does early on, the irony that most industrial and technical innovations were created in order to simplify life, as well as to increase the number of leisure hours that a person might spend with his or her family.

RHETORICAL CONSIDERATIONS

1. Baldwin gets a lot of mileage out of this image. First, escalators are technical innovations created for the express purpose of helping people arrive more quickly—symbols of the shift to machine efficiency from human power. Second, escalators are generally used by people on their way to work, shopping centers, or cultural and sporting events—all of which Baldwin identifies as major time consumers in American life. Students might think about making use of metaphors in their writing.

2. Baldwin's essay is packed with information, and she employs effective devices to make that information palatable. Her paragraphs are relatively short and quick, packaging ideas and parcels of information in easily digestible portions. Spatial breaks are used as markers announcing shifts in focus. This technique allows her to develop the different aspects of her argument without having to develop a continuous narrative thread which might be limiting to the multifaceted nature of her topic. Some students might find the lack of transitions jarring. You might use this objection to point out that the arrangement of information on a page, using spatial breaks or subheadings, is a common organizational technique in many kinds of professional writing, including business, legal, and technical writing.

3. The first-person plural point of view creates an author-reader complicity. This inclusiveness mirrors a nationalistic identification—that is, *we* Americans. When she shifts to the first-person singular near the end, Baldwin positions herself by speaking for her own experience of time management. Had she retained the plural perspective, she could not have spoken of ideas for change with the same force as she does by saying, "this is what I have done."

4. Baldwin's use of supporting detail is one of the great strengths of this piece. Rather than speaking in generalizations, she is careful to bolster her arguments with vividly drawn details. These specifics follow on the heels of general statements and serve to illustrate that statement. For example, in paragraph 5, Baldwin follows the assertion that "many of us also are dabbling in a rich stew of options, identities, ways of life" with a string of specific examples of such options. (See also paragraphs 10, 23, and 26 for similar instances.) The middle section of her essay is loaded with statistics and citations from experts to support her more assertive claims here. These seem appropriate given that Baldwin has moved from basic information about time management to interpretive assertions which require "reliable" support rather than details.

A Child of Crack
Michele L. Norris

TOPICAL CONSIDERATIONS

1. Addie and Dooney Waters's home is an "apartment in Washington Heights, a federally subsidized complex . . . where people congregated to buy and use drugs" (paragraph 4)—in short, a crack house. Drug paraphernalia replaces ketchup and mustard; boiling water is used for scalding people, not cooking food; the toilet overflows with human waste. Dooney wets his bed every night, gets himself up and dressed for school, cannot bathe, and never has a meal cooked for him. The Waters's apartment is a horrendous perversion of a home.

2. Dooney has witnessed his mother's neck and shoulders scalded by boiling water thrown by a 15-year-old boy; he has seen his half-brother shot by a "family friend" (paragraph 13); he was present when a pot of bleach and boiling water was tossed at a 19-year-old (paragraph 11); and he himself was burned by boiling water and singed by a Coke can being heated for crack. These incidents are shocking because they involve people maiming and scarring their neighbors and families. The weapons are mostly innocent domestic items.

3. Prince George's County Department of Social Services was ineffectual. Although it sent letters to the inhabitants of the crack house threatening to take their children from them, the Department lacked power to take action. Social workers investigated charges but were caught up in the red tape that binds children to their natural mothers, regardless of their situation; also, they were too

"'yellow' to visit Washington Heights." The most serious indictment of the system is that case workers "rarely had time to bring cases to court, even after they had corroborated charges of abuse and neglect." Although the Department of Social Services was well aware that Waters's apartment was a crack house, they could do little about it.

4. In 1977, the Washington Heights complex was listed as "luxury apartments" (paragraph 27). Addie Waters described it as "'a nice, clean place full of working class folks'" (paragraph 27) even though recreational drug use including "marijuana, speed, and powder cocaine" was common in the community. However, "the introduction of crack swept in another era." Crack marked the beginning of the "War on Drugs" scenario that now pervades the media. Norris writes, "Not all Washington Heights residents are involved in the drug trade. Many families take pains to shield themselves and their families from drugs and violence" (paragraph 29). Here students may relate stories of their own cities in which drug violence is rampant and the innocent are murdered.

5. For Dooney, Nancy Reagan's "Just Say No" to drugs campaign was a farce. From the time when he learned to talk, he begged his mother with Reagan rhetoric: "'Mommy say no to drugs.'" In paragraph 48, Norris writes that Dooney "scoffed at school programs designed to teach pupils to 'just say no' to drugs." Dooney says in paragraph 49, "'The Drug Avengers ain't real. . . . They couldn't stop my mother from doing drugs.'" White middle-class students may believe that Just Say No campaigns and public awareness wiped drugs out of their suburban environments. But inner-city black children of crack addicts need more powerful weapons.

6. Dooney Waters's teachers were surrogate parents. His principal and teachers created "an after-school counseling and tutorial program" (paragraph 8). They also fed him. More and more teachers are being called upon to attend physical and emotional needs of children that are ignored at home. As the instructional aide says. "'You do more parenting than teaching nowadays'" (paragraph 52). Dooney's teachers visited his home several times, pushed for a Department of Social Services investigation, and placed him in a transitional first grade with special tutoring. Dooney's teachers and the Greenbelt Center's program are the only hopeful signs in the report.

RHETORICAL CONSIDERATIONS

1. Ketchup and mustard are staples of a fast-food restaurant. Pipes, spoons, and needles are staples of a crack house. Like ketchup and mustard, the drug paraphernalia was always restocked. Also like ketchup and mustard, they were the extras. The crack was the meat. The analogy is sobering.

2. The essay is journalistically responsible because Norris compiled her facts from several sources over a substantial period of time. Along with a photographer, she visited the Washington Heights apartment several times and established a relationship with her two main sources, Addie and Dooney Waters. She gives direct quotes from members of the public school department, a social worker for the

Department of Social Services, a spokeswoman for the National Education Association, a police officer, and crack house residents.

3. Norris's introduction captures the reader's interest because of its incongruity with the title. The essay begins, "Dooney Waters, a thickset six-year-old missing two front teeth, sat hunched over a notebook drawing a family portrait." It's the portrait of normalcy; yet the title promises a sordid story. The second line is deeply ironic as the family portrait expands to a mother smoking crack and a son crying. This twist draws the reader into a look at society's underbelly.

4. Dooney's vocabulary is never precocious, but his subject matter reveals that he has seen too much too soon. In paragraph 3 he says, "Drugs have wrecked a lot of mothers and fathers and children and babies. If I don't be careful, drugs are going to wreck me too." Dooney's cause-and-effect assumptions are all rooted in drug violence—for instance, "Russell was shot 'cause of drugs." His view of law enforcement is foreign to most middle-class white children: He says, "[the police know] about the drugs at my house . . . but they don't do nothing about it." As a very young child Dooney says, "Mommy, say no to drugs"; by 6 years of age he is already disillusioned: "The Drug Avengers ain't real. . . . They couldn't stop my mother from doing drugs." His vocabulary and speech are on a par with any 6-year-old. Yet there are signs of the psychological toll: he sucks his thumb, clings onto his teachers, and wets his bed.

5. The conclusion of the essay dramatically parallels Dooney's struggle to get his mother to stop using drugs. He believes that asking his mother to "Just Say No" to drugs will make her quit; then he realizes it doesn't. He believes in the educational cartoon Drug Avengers, but then sees they have no power in the real war against drugs. He knows that police are supposed to represent law and order, yet he only knows them as people who raided his mother's closet, who called her names, who would shoot her. It is logical that Dooney finally concedes to the likelihood of a future in drugs. His short six years of life have been a long series of disappointments and concessions to harsh survival.

Sex Is for Adults

Ellen Hopkins

TOPICAL CONSIDERATIONS

1. Students will probably feel invested in this issue and will vary widely in their positions. The issues of pregnancy, abortion, sex education, and AIDS are relevant to this discussion, which might address the idea implicit in Hopkins's introduction that teenage sex is more or less preventable depending upon educational approaches to the issue. Students might not agree that their sexual practices are or should be preventable through education.

2. Hopkins uses the terms uncritically. By implication "right-wing crazies" represent conservative religious groups advocating abstinence on the grounds of orthodox Christian prescriptions against "fornication" and sex before marriage,

using scare tactics as enforcement. The category "liberal feminist" here refers to a left-leaning agenda primarily concerned with the rights of women and children. Importantly, Hopkins identifies herself as part of the latter community, thereby influencing the perspective of the essay.

3. Open for discussion.

4. Students can think of all the different ways they have come into contact with information about AIDS—formal education programs, health center posters and brochures at school, media programming and public service announcements, billboards, music, and so on—and to compare and contrast the relative effectiveness of these different approaches.

5. In paragraphs 10 through 13, Hopkins lists statistics that seem to support the argument that there is little to the idea of "safer" sex. This is both because condoms are notoriously ineffective and because, as Hopkins claims, teenagers often use condoms improperly.

6. Discussion might take up the idea of learned (environmental) versus essential (biological) traits; that is, since teenagers are biologically equipped for sexual activity it may be argued that they are therefore "ready" for it, and that their sexual activity is determined by their biological makeup and their choice. On the other hand, as Hopkins argues, sexual activity at young ages may be a function of socially determined factors—peer pressure, lack of education, and the like—and therefore may be controlled by educational programs advocating abstinence. Most likely the reality falls somewhere in the middle.

7. The conclusion that "sex is for grown-ups" follows from the evidence on erratic birth control use and disease protection, and from her statement that teenagers should experience a "longing" for what they aren't yet "ready to have." Statistically speaking, Hopkins is correct in asserting that adults experience nowhere near the rates of birth control failure experienced by teenagers. Students might disagree with the notion that teenagers are not "ready" (emotionally) to be engaged in sexual relationships, resenting the implication that physical expression of their love is less "valid" than that of adults.

8. These statistics are often cyclical. Children of single-parent households are likely to become single parents. There are many "indirect" consequences of the breakdown of the two-parent family through divorce or teenage pregnancy. As single parents are generally sole supporters of the family, kids are often left on their own after school, subject to the influences of television, drugs, alcohol, and sex.

RHETORICAL CONSIDERATIONS

1. There are problems with this comparison. Contrary to Hopkins's claim that presently only "losers swerve off into the night," drunk driving, despite massive education programs and increasingly strict laws, is still rampant, especially among teenagers. Also, drunk driving offenders are subject to state law (carrying financial penalties, required education and service hours, and even jail time) while sexually active teenagers will never be subject to such penalties. Finally, while Hopkins's piece leads up to the idea of an "abstinence education" program

in schools, such programs are light years behind work against drunk driving by, among others, groups such as MADD and SADD (Mothers/Students Against Drunk Driving) which have launched massive educational, advertising, and legislative campaigns—and waited years before beginning to see results.

2. Hopkins's use of these labels is uncritical, without explanation or clarification, coming off as a kind of name-calling. Clearly she favors the "liberal feminist" point-of-view. In paragraphs 18 and 19 she contrasts the attempts at abstinence education of the "religious right" with the more "intelligent, effective" efforts of liberal groups. The use of these categories is tricky: She will obviously gain the support of a "liberal" readership, while alienating more conservative readers. Ultimately, regardless of readership, using labels in this way widens the ground upon which opposed groups battle. Rather than working to help educate teenagers about the dangers of sex, these "activists" fight one another.

3. The italicized passages allow Hopkins in essence to carry on a conversation with herself. Each italicized passage contains an assertion in the argument against current sex education programs. Hopkins then provides evidence and elaboration of these assertions in regular typeface in the paragraphs following them. This format also imitates a common format of sex education brochures and pamphlets distributed to students, which often bullet a "fact" in bold or italic typeface as an attention-getter, using regular type to elaborate upon or provide evidence for that fact, eventually building to an overall argument or conclusion.

4. The majority of Hopkins's supporting evidence takes the form of statistics on teenage pregnancy, sexually transmitted disease, and the long-term effects of early sexual activity, providing, in the weight of their numbers, convincing evidence of the overwhelming risks taken by sexually active teenagers.

5. Some students may feel that the piece would be stronger with more personal "evidence" such as "true" stories or anecdotes. As it is, these personal references are effective in bringing all the statistics to life. They are also powerful in that they directly follow Hopkins's discussion of abstinence education in the schools, providing examples from real life of both the tragic results of teenage sex and her concern for a youngster with whom Hopkins herself faces the difficult process of abstinence education.

On Kids and Slasher Movies

Michael Ventura

TOPICAL CONSIDERATIONS

1. According to Ventura, the boy's choosing to be a "maniac killer" reflects a world that is terrifying, overwhelming, and filled with "killer-maniac energy" (paragraph 7). The costume is a way to arm himself against the pointless violence. However, to the boy the slasher costume may have little real-world significance; instead, it may be a change from the usual hobo costume. As kids, your male students might have costumed themselves as cowboys, Indians, pirates, ghosts, hobos, Superman, E.T., or Luke Skywalker. It can be argued that most choices

say more about pop culture than society. Most children do not consciously connect their costume to its symbolism; they simply choose from what's popular. Choice of a killer mask may reveal nothing more than an older kid's recommendation. It can be said that Ventura imposes more meaning on the choice than is warranted.

2. Ventura believes that the boy needs the power of the killer "for his very survival" (paragraph 7). It's a kind of self-inoculating against the world's poison. (The costume is also attractive because the boy will outclass the four-time hobos and five-time ghosts.) Students may agree with Ventura's assertion that in a world so full of senseless violence one option is to psychologically arm ourselves against it.

3. For Ventura's stand, see subsequent answer for Rhetorical Consideration 1. For discussion, you might consider some of these topics: whether horror movies contribute to violence; whether said movies feed viewers' own dark impulses; how horror movies are mysogynistic; how a steady diet of horror can desensitize people's morals to real horror; how habitual viewing of such adrenalin-pumping films mutes interest in other kinds of movies.

4. If one physically feels horror, it seems more real than if one intellectualizes it. Because Ventura's knees, chest and intestines reacted so violently, his realization of wrong was instinctual, primal, and, therefore, sincere.

5. Ventura says that because of its awesomely devastating power, the atomic bomb can arrange the world through threats to weaker powers of usage. With the political and economic shifts worldwide, the term "superpower" may become obsolete. Although in Operation Desert Storm, the United States used 1990s Star Wars technology to defeat the Iraqis, the world has developed alternatives to war to rearrange the world. With communism dead, arsenals diminishing through arms reduction treaties, and an economically stronger Europe emerging, the world may be rearranged by people, not devastating fetish objects.

6. Daniel Smith-Rowsey would agree that a world ruined by the "new technologies and the turn toward cutthroat capitalism" ("The Terrible Twenties," paragraph 7) would spawn children who want to be "unstoppable murderers." He would blame the desire to be an "unstoppable murderer" on his parents' generation—the generation that made the slasher film in the first place. Smith-Rowsey would argue that the child has been "fed on the video culture" and finds pop culture "more attractive than education" ("The Terrible Twenties," paragraph 5). The child's desire would prove Smith-Rowsey's challenge to the older generation: "And then you really will be the last modern smart generation because our kids will be even dumber, poorer, and more violent than us" ("The Terrible Twenties," paragraph 8).

RHETORICAL CONSIDERATIONS

1. The essay's title suggests that slasher movies do cause children to act violently. But the title misleads, since Ventura states that slasher movies have little or nothing to do with children's and the world's violence. In paragraph 5 he writes:

"Nor would I be too quick to blame the boy's desire on television and slasher films." He adds, "the worst atrocities from the pharaohs to Vietnam were committed quite ably before the first slasher film was made." Finally, he says, "Keeping your child away from TV may make you feel better, but can any child be protected from the total weight of Western history?"

2. A fetish can be an object believed to have magical powers, an object that one is irrationally devoted to, or a nonsexual item that arouses sexual feelings. The bomb-as-fetish object fits all three definitions: (1) because of its immense power, the bomb was thought of in World War II as an instrument of unfathomable power; (2) world leaders, scientists, and madmen irrationally worship it; (3) a nuclear-tipped missile has phallic appeal.

3. Ventura's conclusion asks for the reader's sympathy in somewhat melodramatic terms. He calls for no practical action, only to "stand by his choice, and pray for the play of his struggling soul." The conclusion suggests that the damage that has affected the boy is irreversible given the "three thousand years of Judeo-Christian culture" (paragraph 4). Ventura's strategy is effective if he wants someone to commiserate with him.

4. Paragraph 6 describes how the snake sheds its skin like the century sheds its years. As the layers have peeled away, so have order and traditions in the world. What remains is a "dancing, varicolored snake of a century." This reflects the chaotic, frenzied world in which "pointless violence is evident everywhere, on every level."

5. The boy wants the murderer's costume because of the weight of "three thousand years of Judeo-Christian culture"—a culture from which children cannot escape (paragraph 5). The phrase is ironic because of the religious denotations. The violence that has wracked the centuries violates Jewish and Christian doctrine.

Stolen Promise

Patricia Raybon

TOPICAL CONSIDERATIONS

1. Raybon refers to young black men, oftentimes involved with drugs and gangs, who drop out of school or who die young. She is also referring implicitly to the unbalanced power structures that keep these conditions in place. The metaphor of *war* is apt, as the problem she describes has all of its trappings: death, destruction, loss, pain. She says that no one in power is fighting this war meaning that those who are fighting it are the racial minority and, therefore, reflect the uneven distribution of power in this country. Discussion might focus on why a disproportionate number of young black men die each year; why the number of people living in poor inner city neighborhoods is disproportionately composed of blacks or Hispanics; how money, power, education, goods, and services are distributed in this country; and who "controls" these circumstances. How do all these relate to the phenomena described by Raybon?

2. Earlier Raybon describes her family as "privileged" and "advantaged." In part, she's referring to material terms. Students might consider their own sense of privilege or advantage—or lack thereof—and its consequences. Students who have not personally experienced the conditions Raybon describes may empathize with her claim that for those who live in relative comfort the 6 o'clock news seems like another world. You could attempt to stimulate a debate about complacency or the idea of "complicity"—how we all contribute to the problem, willingly or unwillingly. As Raybon states, "the inner city's chaos and the neglect that cause it aren't somebody else's problems, they're mine" (paragraph 13).

3. Among young people living in dangerous urban conditions a recurring theme is the devaluation of life. Many don't expect to see the age of 30. Such an outlook allows little room for dreams or the kind of romance to which Raybon refers, especially the long-term commitment of marriage and family.

4. Raybon is afraid that her college-educated daughter who, by virtue of her upbringing and education, will have to marry someone less educated and less prosperous. There are other ways, however, to "marry down" in this culture, and this brings up the question of how American culture is stratified. It is less acceptable for an older woman to marry a younger man than it is the other way around. People can "marry down" racially, too—minority person marrying a white is thought to be marrying "up"; the reverse is also true.

5. Discussion can flesh out what Raybon leaves unsaid: the history of race relations in this country, beginning with slavery and touching on segregation, the civil rights movement, the development of urban living conditions. It might be helpful to look at contemporary expressions of the "pain and history" to which Raybon refers, for example, by analyzing lyrics of rap songs with which students may be familiar. Students will probably have differing opinions regarding interracial relationships.

6. Raybon is surprisingly honest about her feelings. At a time when the word "hate" in relation to race is deeply vexed she uses it without apology. Importantly, she expresses her hatred not toward people but the "forces" that allow discrimination to continue. (It may be noted, however, that these forces are not disembodied. Behind them are people making decisions and enforcing rules.

RHETORICAL CONSIDERATIONS

1. Raybon's choice to position herself as a mother in making her argument determines the angle of the piece as well as what information is included. It is a unique angle in addressing the issue of the high death rates of young black men. Rather than reeling off statistics and writing in the third person or writing an editorial style piece, Raybon takes the very specific position of someone who is both directly and indirectly affected by the issue: directly, in that she can speak on behalf of all the mother's who have lost sons in this "war"; indirectly because she is speaking from a position of sorrow resulting from the difficulty her

daughter faces in dating and marriage. Speaking from the position of a mother makes her perspective specific and accessible for readers.

2. Each of these paragraphs contains information that comes at us straight on: All the young men are gone. Dead. Besides dramatic effect, the short fast punches reflect the lives of young black men.

3. The essay is sharply lacking in foundational information. She probably feels that the media has familiarized us enough. Still, she refers to power structures without specificity and describes problems of the inner city without exploration of causes or contexts. There are no quotations from other writers on the subject, nor statistics to support her statements on the widespread deaths of young black men. Further, she does not explain the "painful history" behind her father's aversion to interracial relationships in paragraph 21. This lack of detail weakens her argument.

4. Direct dialogue provides a sense of immediacy as well as some liveliness to the argument. It also creates a sense of truth to the essay—that the reader is privy to the real-life experience of a "representative" black mother and daughter.

5. The essay, while deeply charged politically, is mediated by its rhetorical vehicle: the language of romance accompanying Raybon's focus on the issue of declining marriage possibilities for young black women. While many of her assertions are deeply politicized and controversial, they are made easily palatable for a general readership by their submersion in a narrative about a mother's concerns for her daughter.

Houses and Streets, but No Neighborhood

Alan Lupo

TOPICAL CONSIDERATIONS

1. The word "neighborhood" might be explored here, as it may have different connotations for students than it did for Lupo.

2. Lupo identifies television, the suburban boom, advanced home technology, such as computers, and a "new American" philosophy of isolation as factors responsible for the loss of old-fashioned neighborhoods..

3. Certainly malls and franchising have created a deep homogeneity in American culture, largely erasing regional differences or individuality in goods for sale. At the same time, students might perceive benefits in mall culture that Lupo does not address—a certain community formed around and sustained by the mall itself. See Glaberson's essay, "Mall Rats."

4. Demographic information supports Lupo's claim; the trend in real estate is to move away from the city for the safety of the suburbs. In fact, a discussion of the changing nature of inner-city neighborhoods, about which Lupo seems particularly nostalgic, might be appropriate, given the increased incidence of drugs,

crime, and violence. To Lupo the oldtime neighborhood spontaneity is preferable to today's organized community activities.

RHETORICAL CONSIDERATIONS

1. The title clearly delineates the distinction between a physical neighborhood and a community. His descriptions of current streets and cul-de-sacs still retain the physical likeness of neighborhoods but clearly lack the spirit of community. It is this distinction which carries his sense of loss.
2. This might seem like an odd phrase with which to bracket his argument; however, it works in that both "somebody" and "something" are responsible for the changes. The "something" points to demographic; the "somebody" implies the human forces who both create and tolerate these changes. Using the words "somebody" and "something" also work nicely in setting up the closing metaphor of the missing child on the milk carton—a metaphor which would not work had Lupo not described the forces behind the changes.
3. Interestingly, the narrator is not the man through whose eyes the reader views the passing streets but another who is apparently watching the man walking, referring to him in the third person. This device works to provide distance: the reader is encouraged to see the man walking, and to see what the man sees. The scene is brought to life in a different way than if Lupo had written the piece in the first-person, narrating his own journey through the city. Many readers will also be able to relate to the man who is described as feeling compelled to walk because of the "new" fitness craze, and who seems to have come from a generation before all the changes.

You Have to Be a Real Stud Hombre Cybermuffin to Handle "Windows"
Dave Barry

TOPICAL CONSIDERATIONS

1. For discussion. However, for students who claim they happily avoid computers, the difficulty to completely elude them in everyday life might be pointed out—bank machines and grocery store checkout payment devices are two examples.
2. Most students will have grown up during the mass-market computer boom. Thus, they will be familiar with computer games (Barry, in paragraph 11, mentions the computer "F-117A Stealth Fighter") and with the transition from typewriters to word processors with endless graphic options. The advantages of computers are overwhelming in terms of what they can do and how fast they can do it. At the same time, Barry humorously dramatizes the widespread fear of user-unfriendly computers—programs so complex they scare off the average customer. The move toward massive computer use also sets off Brave-New-

World alarms—that is, the possibility of a machine-dominated world where labor is of little or no value.

3. Internet is one of many information superhighways, offering thousands of options, interconnections, and activities. For instance, electronic mail where you have an address from which you can send and receive messages—all in the ethereal realm of "cyberspace." Literally anyone with a computer and a modem can hook up and communicate with folks around the world. Many people see this as a revolution in communication, a prophesy of the death of the printed word (books, letters, newspapers) in the next century and of unfathomable revolutions in media and communications. Internet is already having an effect on people's lives. Behind all of Barry's good fun lurks a confession of many computer enthusiasts who spend lots of time at their computers, physically alone but in the company of countless faceless Internet friends. Students might feel that this phenomenon will eventually add to the fragmented nature of contemporary technoculture, marked by a loss of community and personal communication.

4. Barry's humorous description of computers is compatible with Baldwin's more serious discussion of the irony that, despite the technology developed since the Industrial Revolution for the purpose of decreasing labor hours, people are working more hours than ever. As Barry points out, computers—the ultimate in labor-reducing technology—seem to increase work hours for users trying to navigate difficult programs, or losing themselves in all the on-line activities.

5. While Barry acknowledges the solitary nature of a "social life" on the Internet, he also points out that folks who have no interest in computers are just as isolated in that they are cordoned off in their living rooms, devouring whatever the television has to offer. He also seems to enjoy his computer lifestyle, calling himself a "happy nerd in cyberspace." Even satirically he doesn't touch upon the loss of community Lupo discusses. Students may not ever have experienced the kind of neighborhood Lupo misses; however, they may still feel some impact of computer activities on their lives and relationships.

RHETORICAL CONSIDERATIONS

1. Beneath the humor, Barry touches on the issue of changing lifestyles and work habits: the difficulties and rewards of making computers a regular part of the workplace; the economics of the computer boom, for example, with reference to computer wizard Bill Gates; and the odd conditions of "social" contact in cyberspace.

2. In general, Barry's irony works on foiled expectations. He will lead the reader in one direction then suddenly change course in the opposite direction. For instance, he begins with a broad assertion about how efficient his computer has made pumping out his column, then details just how clumsy it is in carrying out small tasks (paragraph 3). His funny transcription of a telephone conversation between Bill Gates and a frantic business executive is a wonderfully ironic spoof

of the baffled computer user with a ridiculously simple solution to his problem, known only to the ludicrously expensive cyber-guru (paragraphs 5–10). Barry's roast of the whole computer explosion is done in such a way that his irony is not lost on any reader regardless of his or her level of computer literacy.

3. Barry's attitude is something like that of the average Joe—somewhere between love and hate for the boons and pitfalls of computers. It's an attitude most readers should find suitable to the piece.

4. Barry's title works to set up the irony characterizing his essay. It also mixes its metaphors in a way that captures the changing times evident in the piece: the "stud hombre" of stereotypical macho days and the "cybermuffins" of the new generation masters of cyberspace.

5. Barry's movement from first-person anecdote to second-person direct address increases reader identification.

·4·
Consumer Culture

Work and Spend
Juliet B. Schor

TOPICAL CONSIDERATIONS

1. Schor says that the view of human nature as naturally acquisitive is wrong, since many societies, such as the common people in medieval Europe and in nineteenth- and early twentieth-century United States, "exhibited a restricted appetite for material goods." Consumerism, according to her, is a "specific product of capitalism." Students will decide for themselves which view of human nature is true.

2. Again, students will have to make up their own minds about modern consumer discontent. Schor gives evidence that the "American dream" of improving each generation's standard of living was always a mirage. She cites statistics from a 1928 Yale faculty study and a 1922 Berkeley faculty study. She also includes examples from advertising in the 1920s when ads were first used as psychological warfare or scare techniques.

   Agreeing with Galbraith, she finds that manufacturers did attempt to "create the wants [they] attempt[ed] to satisfy," and succeeded in creating a dissatisfied customer. Business made this customer "discontented with what he or she already had," and led to the "consumption ethic."

3. Trade unions and social reformers, including religious groups, attempted to stop this "consumption ethic," which led to working long hours by offering the enticement of leisure time instead. However, labor and reformers lost the battle for increases in free time and decreases in consumption to business which prefers long working hours and vigorous consumption.

   Consumerism still is the victor over leisure time in the 1990s. Labor groups seem more interested in health care and retirement benefits than in working shorter hours. Social reformers and religious groups spend more energy in trying to get people jobs and decent housing than in worrying about the length of the working day.

4. Students' answers will vary.

5. The authority is John Maynard Keyes (1883–1946), whose chief work is *The General Theory of Employment, Interest, and Money* (1936). Instead of a free economy, Keyes advocated active government intervention in the market, and influenced nations to adopt spending programs such as the New Deal in the United States in the 1930s. In spite of Keyes' favoring a governmental

planned economy and wide control of economic life by democratic public-service corporations, his faith in the capitalistic system led him to accept business' domination over labor and social groups, therefore accepting the consumer ethic.

6. For the students.

7. Native American cultures originally placed little value on material goods and practiced public disposal of wealth in ceremonies such as the potlatch, a ceremonial feast in which the host gives away articles of value to his guests. This communal culture would not place much value on "keeping up with the Joneses."

   Those who practice alternative cultures, such as the New Age individuals, strive for greater leisure and fewer material goods. This group scorns the consumer mentality and considers consumers spoilers of the environment.

RHETORICAL CONSIDERATIONS

1. Schor's main purpose is stated in paragraph 27. "My purpose is to add a dimension to this analysis of consumption which has heretofore been neglected—its connection to the incentive structure operating in labor markets. The consumer traps I have described are just the flip side of the bias toward long hours embedded in the production system." Even though the claim appears in the final paragraph, the argument is an inductive one. All preceding material leads up to this conclusion.

2. The tone of this essay (or chapter) is formal, structured, and serious. It seems to be written for an academic audience, with all the scholarly paraphernalia such as lengthy quotations and footnotes this audience requires. Presumably the audience is made up of scholars knowledgeable in economics, because most of the references to people well-known in that field are unknown to the general reader.

3. *Super helerodynes* simply means radios. *Asymptote* refers to a straight line, always approaching, but never meeting a curve. Although Schor does not clarify an "asymptote culture," its consumers assume that they will reach a state of complete satisfaction with purchase of the newest luxury, but they never get there, just as the straight line never meets the curve. Students may wish the terms were defined.

4. Schor is trying to prove her side of the argument by painting a black picture of business and a white picture of labor and social reformers. The focus of her book is after all, the overworked American. In this excerpt she blames the advertising industry for creating dissatisfied consumers who must work more in order to buy things they really don't need. To show the weaknesses of the labor unions and social reformers would be counterproductive to her contentions, so she stacks the deck by quoting only those economic authorities who agree with her. She also quotes an ILGWU pamphlet in paragraph 12 and a prominent Catholic spokesman in paragraph 13, but no one from the business world.

5. Many students find the use of the feminine pronoun somewhat disconcerting at first, since they are used to the universal *he*. However, many authors of textbooks and magazine articles now use *she* and female names instead of male. Students can look in their textbooks for examples.

Spend and Save
Barbara Ehrenreich

TOPICAL CONSIDERATIONS

1. The "puritanical" message is to "'Work hard, save, defer gratification, curb your impulses'" (paragraph 3); it comes "from school, from church, often from parents, and every so often from political figures" (paragraph 4). The "permissive" message, which comes from advertising, says "'Buy, spend, get it now, indulge yourself'" (paragraph 3). Student assessment of the power of these "spend and save" messages will vary.

2. Most of the products Ehrenreich uses to define advertising's "underlying message" are either luxury items or expensive versions of necessities, including Michelob beer, "silky Hanes pantyhose," BMWs, and cigarettes. Many other products and services—such as life insurance, pickup trucks, vacuum cleaners, even airline travels—are often sold by appealing to the kind of traditional values Ehrenreich identifies with the puritanical message: responsibility, hard work, family, fiscal prudence, self-restraint. Students might now begin to ponder whether the puritanical and permissive messages are as fundamentally opposed as Ehrenreich claims. They might also wonder whether "traditional values" are not also created, or at the very least exploited, by the advertising media which Ehrenreich claims only communicates the permissive message.

3. Ehrenreich's purpose here is apparently to encourage family therapists to "devote more attention" (paragraph 5) to consumer culture in considering psychological problems. The main point of her essay is that the conflicting messages of consumer culture create "psychological consequences" (paragraph 8) that include "anxiety, fear, a nameless dread" (paragraph 10). Noting the essay's original forum should help students see that Ehrenreich is not, as some might at first have thought, simply arguing that the conflicting "spend and save" messages exist in our culture; instead, their existence is technically part of the evidence to support her call for a new therapeutic approach.

4. Some students will probably be able to clarify these terms for the class by supplementing Ehrenreich's definitions with their own knowledge. The "superego" is the part of the moral makeup of personality which makes the individual "play by the rules" (paragraph 8). In a self-denying context it would explain staying in an unhappy marriage or responsibly complete meaningless or unsatisfying work, and so forth. In contrast, the "id" operates on the pleasure principle, always encouraging instant gratification no matter what the consequences. To

Ehrenreich, Freud's theory suggest why the spend and save messages are both powerful: they appeal to different parts of the human psyche which are internally conflicted to begin with.

5. The Cold War increased the power of the "puritanical" message because it fed into fears that overindulgence would have ominous consequences, perhaps enabling America's rivals on the world stage to gain the upper hand. The evidence offered for this argument is sketchy. Ehrenreich claims that "softened" was "the word they used" to described the effect of affluence on American competitiveness, but she never clarifies who *they* might be. Though she is discussing a phenomenon of the 1980s, part of Ehrenreich's "evidence" is a book title from the 1950s—a very different chapter in Cold War history. In fact, the 1980s seem like an unlikely decade about which to make this claim. For one thing, the Cold War began to defrost in the latter part of that decade, certainly by 1987. For another, the 1980s were anything but a puritanical decade, economically speaking; "spend and spend" could perhaps best describe the prevailing financial wisdom. Because of hasty generalizations, vague references, and misrepresentations, Ehrenreich's cultural analysis of the Cold War and the 1980s seems flawed.

RHETORICAL CONSIDERATIONS

1. Ehrenreich creates a common ground with her reader by opening her essay with two personal anecdotes. Many readers will relate to the stories of the billboard and—especially—the American Express bill. At the same time, Ehrenreich bridges the distance between herself and her reader by using an informal tone, describing the recent calls for Americans to save more as having happened "only 10 minutes ago, historically speaking" (paragraph 1), for example, and paraphrasing American Express's request for payment as "'You miserable wretch, pay up or die'" (paragraph 2). Ehrenreich also makes herself appealing by becoming somewhat confessional, admitting, for example, that the general American inability to save money "certainly is my problem" (paragraph 1).

   Both anecdotes reflect the underlying claim of the essay by illustrating the quick alternation between spend and save messages. The example of the billboard describes the rapid historical shift in national economic policy, from a "save" to a "spend" mandate. The American Express anecdote captures the apparently contradictory pressure on credit card holders to be fiscally cavalier in running up bills, but fiscally responsible in paying them. Some students may note that these examples, though germane, are anecdotal—and not necessarily representative of the culture as a whole.

2. In our culture, the word *puritanical* implies an old-fashioned, somewhat pointless moral rigidity. *Permissive* has equally negative connotations, implying a lazy lack of discipline, usually on the part of parents. Thinking up alternative words—*frugal* or *responsible* for puritanical, say; or *carefree* or *fun-loving* for permissive—should help students see how word choice affects meaning. The use of such censorious words increases the sense, central to Ehrenreich's claim, that the conflicts between these messages constitute a serious cultural problem.

3. Though many students may find Ehrenreich's description of the values promoted by family, church and school unobjectionable, they should notice that absolutely no evidence supports this assertion; instead, the essay simply states it. It could be argued that an equally powerful cultural message suggests, for example, that American families stand for love, charity, and increased buying power; after all, one provision of the American dream is that each generation should be better off materially than the last. In this sense the American family could be seen as broadcasting the permissive as well as the puritanical message. Besides, as students will already have discussed, it is perfectly possible that supposedly "typical" family values could themselves be, at least in part, the creation of advertising media. Students can discuss other values traditionally emanating from church and school.

4. The essay offers little concrete evidence to support this claim, though astute students will have noticed that Ehrenreich apparently makes her argument at book length in *Fear of Falling* (paragraph 10); perhaps there her evidence is more persuasive. Ehrenreich uses inductive logic to suppose, from the "existence" (itself a theory) of two conflicting spend and save messages, that the tension created has psychological consequences in individuals who are necessarily "torn between the contradictory personality types that our society seems to require of us" (paragraph 10). The theory is plausible, perhaps probable, but it is only a theory.

5. Bell's book upholds Ehrenreich's belief in the existence of two conflicting spend and save messages, since he apparently argues "that our consumer-based economy makes two absolutely contradictory psychological demands on its members" (paragraph 7). While Ehrenreich's main concern is the psychological effect of these clashing cultural messages, Bell seems to have been more interested in broader social analysis. Like other theoretical writers, Ehrenreich uses Bell's authority to support and second her own claim. There are hints of a problem with Ehrenreich's use of Bell, however, when Ehrenreich calls Bell's book "one of the best—in fact one of the only—books dealing with [the] paradox" between permissive and puritanical messages (paragraph 7). Since these two seem the only promoters of this theory, the reader might wonder whether Bell's and Ehrenreich's theories are well received in the larger scholarly community.

Mall Rats
William Glaberson

TOPICAL CONSIDERATIONS

1. Responses will vary. Discussion on this topic should help students see that, in Glaberson's view, the mall has simply replaced "the malt shop or the diner" (paragraph 6) as the "backdrop to all the usual themes of adolescence" (paragraph 8).

2. Though Glaberson allows for the possibility of a "special starkness in the lives of the mall's teen-agers," he clearly finds their antics no different from those of adolescents of the past or rural America: Loves and heartbreaks, experiments with drugs and liquor, romantic encounters in the back seats of cars, shop-lifting "for those in search of a rebellious image" (paragraphs 8–9), teenagers who are "flirting with different identities" (paragraph 11)—all could be found as easily on the small-town streets of *American Graffiti* as in the malls of the 1990s, though the fashions have changed ("nose rings and beepers constitute current chic," paragraph 10). Feeling hollow might itself be an occupational hazard of adolescence, though not all students may agree with Glaberson here.

3. In Riverdale, Christine was shot at by a stranger on her way home from school. In contrast, the mall seems like a safe place, indeed; it is no more dangerous to be a teenager there than anywhere else. The "hurts" which can come to her in the mall are emotional, not physical (paragraph 32).

4. Scooby supposedly personifies "the dark side of the mall-rat world" (paragraph 14), but students will quickly see that he is really just a mixed up suburban kid with a substance abuse problem. Scooby is apparently an ineffective crook; though he wears a black leather jacket "bought with a stolen credit card" (paragraph 13) he is soon jailed for credit card fraud. His criminal record barely advances in seriousness beyond the "usual themes of adolescence" (paragraph 8): he was "jailed for car theft," "arrested for smoking marijuana," and he ran what he himself terms, perhaps self-aggrandizingly, a "black market" in shop-lifted items (paragraph 17). He even smokes light, mentholated cigarettes.

   Scooby's status comes simply from logging more hours in front of "Time Out," and knowing more people, than anyone else. But most of the other teenagers do not grant him the status he tries to confer on himself (paragraph 22); Jon Bourque denies that "Scooby was the leader," and Christine Tako "made a face at the mention of the full-timers in the food court" (paragraph 30). Scooby may ultimately seem more pathetic than threatening, especially if students have seen firsthand or in the media more serious teenage criminal activity—hard drugs, gang violence, weapons, grand larceny.

5. Though Bourque denies Scooby's leadership, he immediately seems to claim the status of mall-rat king himself. Glaberson creates this impression in part through the juxtaposition of the three sentences in paragraph 29. After claiming there is no mall leader, Bourque points out that he had logged as many hours as anyone outside Time Out. "'I'm here every day of the week all day,' he said." Bourque, here, seems to be stating his own credentials for the mall-rat king role. This kind of jockeying for social position within and between cliques might spark some memories among students, further demonstrating how typical mall-rat life is of most adolescent life.

RHETORICAL CONSIDERATIONS

1. Using this rather dramatic phrase to describe Tako's quandary about whether to introduce herself to a cute boy creates a tone of affectionate irony that some students might find condescending. The phrase captures the adolescent sense that

such decisions are indeed of historic magnitude; at the same time, the inappropriateness of the language jokingly reveals the actual triviality of this "decision." Glaberson repeats this tone throughout the essay, for example when he describes teenagers at the mall joining "in that ancient teen-age conviction that there is nothing else to do" (paragraph 5), and when he says, melodramatically, that Christine Tako's "parents wanted to protect her. But there are some hurts, she learned at the mall, for which there is no protection" (paragraph 32).

2. The "story" of Tako's decision gives a kind of miniature plot to the article, which begins by stating her dilemma and ends at the moment of her decision. The incident creates a mild sort of suspense that might keep a reader interested throughout. Tako is not only a fine example of mall-rat culture, but also a kind of native guide who can lead Glaberson through her world. Her story of the "boy in the suit" who betrayed her for "a wiry 14-year-old girl with black hair" (paragraph 35), for example, allows a glimpse into mall romance which Glaberson, as a grown man and professional journalist, might not otherwise have seen.

3. The teenagers who are described with nicknames or personal accoutrements are by and large less individualized than the named mall-rats like Jon Bourque, Christine Tako, and Michelle Sell. Scooby is a possible exception, though his "cartoon canine" (paragraph 16) name makes him ultimately a little cartoonish himself. By including so many nameless adolescents, Glaberson furthers the impression that the experience here is universal. The names of the individual actors may change, but the cast of adolescent characters—the 14-year-old girl who will "do anything to be part of the group" (paragraph 35), the irresistible boy with blue eyes, the other boy who seems (ironically) somehow not "typical" (paragraph 33)—remains the same, in many different times and places.

4. The language of the "round-faced teen-ager" is completely mono- and disyllabic. She uses the present tense almost exclusively, and is repetitive, especially of the verb *to say* ("I'm at home saying . . . [M]y friends call me up and say . . . And I say . . . And they say . . . And I say. . . ."). Certain slang terms—*cool* and *OK*—apparently carry enormous amounts of meaning not readily identifiable to the uninitiated. Glaberson gives us Michelle's speech verbatim in order to capture the character of teenage communication skills and the atmosphere of adolescence.

Money for Morality

Mary Arguelles

TOPICAL CONSIDERATIONS

1. Responses will vary. Many readers will at least initially side with the teachers in this case; the reward may seem like an insufficient barometer (to use Arguelles's imagery) of gratitude or appreciation. Whether readers' minds are changed by Arguelles's argument is a test of the article's effectiveness. If students do disagree with Arguelles about this case, teachers might point out that their response in a sense supports Arguelles's argument, since it suggests that readers lack their

own "ethical thermostat" and can only measure honesty in terms of external, in this case monetary, rewards.

2. Open for discussion.

3. The situations are similar, in Arguelles's estimation, because both teach children that moral principles—honesty, hard work, or integrity—have not an intrinsic but a monetary value. Children given this message will never learn that virtue is its own reward; rather, they will be motivated to do "good" only because it can lead to material gain.

Students may disagree about how apt this parallel is. It could be argued that returning $600 cash untouched means, for an 8-year-old, successfully resisting extraordinary temptation. The teachers' attempt to recognize this successful moral battle appropriately records how hard it is to be "good" in such an unusual circumstance. On the other hand, doing school work well—like doing any job well—should not be considered an extraordinary act worthy of special commendation. Whatever the extent of disagreement among students on this question, discussion should help them see that Arguelles's interpretation is just that—one interpretation that is vulnerable to criticism, even from readers who share Arguelles's basic values.

4. The golden rule is to do unto others as you would have them do unto you—or, in more vernacular terms, one good turn deserves another. "The promise of the golden rule" is that good deeds will be ultimately rewarded when someone does "a good turn for you" (paragraph 3). Arguelles claims that the fast pace of today's world means that no one can wait patiently for that good turn to come around; instead, people want prompt repayment on their moral debts, preferably in cash: "With the world racing by us, we have no patience for a rain check on good deeds" (paragraph 3).

5. Arguelles regrets the deterioration of "the simple virtues of honesty, kindness and integrity" (paragraph 7); these are the primary virtues illustrated in her examples. Defining integrity as the sense of satisfaction that comes from doing your best, Arguelles values the integrity and honesty of the 8-year-old boy. Integrity is also the virtue undermined when parents bribe students to get good grades (paragraph 4) and when "pizza is given as a reward for reading" (paragraph 5). Other virtues might include the belief that money can't buy happiness, suggested when Arguelles tries to teach her daughter by example that "there are some simple pleasures that don't require a purchase" (paragraph 7). The example of the teenage mothers offered $10 for every week they do not get pregnant suggests that personal responsibility, or perhaps even chastity, is another value Arguelles holds.

RHETORICAL CONSIDERATIONS

1. A thermostat automatically measures and controls internal temperature—of a person, architectural space, or machine. It works without external stimulus or manipulation. An "ethical thermostat," then, would automatically measure and respond to the ethics of any given situation. The image nicely illustrates one of

Arguelles's main points: "As a society, we seem to be losing a grip on our internal control. . . . Instead, we rely on external 'stuff' as a measure of our worth" (paragraph 5). As Arguelles sees it, most of our ethical thermostats are in bad need of repair.

2. In this analogy, spinach "represents" the virtues (honesty, integrity, kindness) while "ice cream" represents the spoils (cash rewards, pizza, $10 a week). Just as eating lots of ice cream makes spinach seem less tasty, so "our moral taste buds have been dulled by an endless onslaught of artificial sweeteners" (paragraph 6). The "endless parade of incentives," like a too-steady diet of "candy bars and banana splits," has made us incapable of appreciating the joys of "good behavior"—the joys of spinach.

   Students may disagree about the effectiveness of the analogy. On the one hand, it effectively puts abstract principles into concrete terms. But even if students find the comparison clever or appropriate, they should recognize that it does not constitute concrete, objective support; it is argument by analogy, an always impressionistic form of support.

3. Arguelles's evidence for this crisis is anecdotal. The opening story of the 8-year-old boy is only one isolated incident; it is also, as students will already have seen, subject to differing interpretations than the one Arguelles chooses. However, the several "outraged" teachers and contributors to the $150 "good Samaritan" award suggest a widespread like-mindedness. It is impossible to tell how widespread the practice of rewarding students for grades actually is. Though it may seem weak, Arguelles offers as added "proof" her 13-year-old son, who has told her "many times" about money rewards for good grades (paragraph 4). Since her son may be angling for such rewards himself, he might well be exaggerating the extent of the practice. Rewarding pizza for reading is done in only "one national reading program" (paragraph 5). Citations from researchers in education and sociology, interviews with teachers, even an informal survey of parents in her son's class all might have lent more credibility to her argument. Of course, such documentation in an essay of such limited space may not be possible.

   The use of anecdotal evidence does not destroy Arguelles's argument; however, it should demonstrate to students the difficulty of making generalized values arguments. Though the values Arguelles honors are above reproach—who would weigh in against "honesty, kindness and integrity"?—her belief that these virtues "suffer from an image problem" (paragraph 7) is arguable. Had she more room, perhaps, her anecdotes could have been bolstered with more evidence.

4. Arguelles works hard to avoid being sanctimonious here, an important—and difficult—strategy in a values argument. She is at times humorous, such as when she suggests her son might be telling her about his classmates' rewards for grades "hinting that I should do the same for him should he ever receive an A (or maybe he was working on $5 for a B)" (paragraph 4). Her discussion of spinach is also done with a light touch: "While some may say spinach doesn't need any help looking bad, I submit it's from years of kowtowing to ice cream" (paragraph 6).

5. Arguelles increases her credibility largely by describing herself as a mother. She is apparently a thoughtful and responsible one. Her attitude toward her son in paragraph 4 is firm (she has no intention of rewarding him for good grades) but affectionately nonjudgmental (she does not seem to care whether he earns A's or not). She takes her role as a mother seriously, reading "countless child-care books" when pregnant. She tries to teach her children not by preaching, but by example (paragraph 7). Students can discuss the extent to which motherhood, fairly or not, automatically confers moral authority on women in our society.

The Ends Justify the Jeans

Stuart Ewen and Elizabeth Ewen

TOPICAL CONSIDERATIONS

1. In the Ewens' analysis, designer jeans promise two kinds of "freedom," sexual and financial. In paragraph 3, we are told that over the "rainbow" of "female backsides" in the Gloria Vanderbilt advertisement "lies the promise of perpetual pleasure." The "signature of an heiress" (paragraph 1) on the back pocket of each jean also suggests that in purchasing blue jeans, buyers associate themselves with a world free of monetary concerns.

   "Calvin Klein makes a similar promise" of both sexual ecstasy and worry-free leisure (paragraph 4). Despite the "image of wear" manufactured into the jean's mottled seams "all evidence of toil" is erased from the picture in the advertisement. Not only does the Calvin Klein model wear a spotless satin shirt, but she also represents animalistic sexual passion: "She purrs; she growls" (paragraph 4). Bon Jour jeans similarly promise freedom from economic concerns, but they assuage Protestant work ethic guilt by creating the illusion of toil: they "look like you're moving even when you're idle" (paragraph 5).

   The word "promise" is central to this essay's argument. As the Ewens attempt to prove, when people buy certain fashions they identify themselves with whatever the fashion represents at that historical moment: with James Dean in *Rebel Without a Cause* in the 1950s; with the "tenant farmers and share-croppers" in the civil rights struggles of the 1960s (paragraph 14); with the purring, satin-clad Calvin Klein model in the 1980s. For this reason, analyzing the promise of whatever is in fashion can tell us much about the wishes, regrets, and desires of the culture at a particular historical moment. In this sense, fashion is "a complex world of history, promise, and change" (paragraph 22).

2. In several ways, the invention of blue jeans marked the increased dehumanization of American workers during the westward expansion of the mid-nineteenth century. A "newly mobile work force" (paragraph 6) was suddenly cut off from the female kin who traditionally made their clothes; this domestic vacuum was filled by mass-produced clothing manufactured by large corporations such as Levis. First constructed using a "technology borrowed from the construction of

horse blankets," blue jeans reified the idea that laboring men were little more than pack animals: "Cloth for beasts of burden was translated to the needs of men of burden" (paragraph 6). The clothing of these men offered no food for imagination or desire; they "held little promise. . . , save the promise that they would be ready for the next day's labors" (paragraph 6).

    In contrast, the fashions of the upper classes represented superfluity, wealth, and leisure. For women, the "mark of prosperity" was "to wear enough material on one's back to clothe many of a more common caste" (paragraph 7). Upper-class men's clothes were similarly designed to expose the excess fabric used in their creation: "The display of cloth was the mark of substance and, most certainly, profit" (paragraph 9). The clothes of the upper class, then, expressed the "promise" of prosperity: of disposable income, material possession, and excess.

3. In the Ewens' analysis, blue jeans provide one example of how "opposite worlds collide violently and then mesh in fashion" (paragraph 22). This sort of collision can be seen in the way blue jeans bring together various incongruous elements in American culture. For example, the growth of the cowboy myth in the early twentieth century brought to an increasingly urbanized population the image of rural expanse and simplicity so central to the myth of America. In the newly created movie cowboys "the range hands of the early cattle industry were reborn as icons of a noble, rural simplicity; rugged individualism; primal morality and law" (paragraph 12). These icons created "new and different meanings" for blue jeans, which became "emblems of a simpler and uncorrupted life" (paragraph 12). Soon jeans were worn even by the "well-heeled" as "a symbolic escape" (paragraph 12) from an increasingly restrictive world.

    In the 1950s, "blue denim became part of a statement, a rejection of post-war suburban society and the tyrannies of . . . fashion-conscious consumerism" (paragraph 13). Overworked businessmen, women and girls oppressed by the feminine mystique, even "suburban gardeners" wore blue jeans to express various degrees of "contempt" toward the complacencies of "cold-war suburbia." This phenomenon seems to have harmlessly channelled a low-level dissatisfaction: Those suburban gardeners who "slipped into their Levis for their moments of casual comfort," for example, do so for a nap on the porches of their presumably comfortable homes made possible through conformity to the "priorities of the business world" (paragraph 13).

    In the 1960s, mostly Northern college students who went to the south to help "overturn the deeply embedded centuries of segregation and race hatred" began to wear denim as a symbolic representation of solidarity with the black "tenant farmers and sharecroppers, grandchildren of slaves" who they came to help (paragraph 14). During this period, the "garb of toil was sanctified by the dignity of struggle"

    Students can discuss the question the Ewens leave open at the end of their essay: whether blue jeans have been a "meaningful component of social change" (paragraph 26). Aside from the civil rights and anti-war movements of the 1960s, in the examples given here blue jeans seem more like a social safety valve than the vehicle for significant social change.

4. For feminists blue jeans were a way of "rejecting the sex roles of convention," making a statement "against restrictive fashion, sexual objectification, passive femininity" (paragraph 16). Ironically, by the 1980s blue jeans had come to represent the absolute opposite image of women: The Calvin Klein ad, for example, apparently appeals to women who would like to imagine themselves in a "moment of submission" (paragraph 4).

5. Although designer jeans promise "fantasies of freedom," both sexual and financial, their economic existence depends on the oppression of the "weavers and dyers and cutters and sewers and finishers . . . in the sweatshops of Hong Kong" (paragraph 18). Though jeans advertisements promise freedom, it is an "exploitative labor system that underwrites these fantasies of freedom" (paragraph 18).

6. Students may understandably have trouble finding a single thesis statement, since the Ewens' thesis is complex and multilevelled. The broadest argument made here is that fashion is "a keystone in the shifting architectures of class, sexuality, national identity" (paragraph 24). Not only does fashion represent broad historical developments (such as social and demographic change, shifts in the economic base or means of production, and political upheaval) but it is a medium in which culture works through such conflicts: "Opposite worlds collide violently and then mesh in fashion. Social conflict and contradiction are displayed . . . and diffused" (paragraph 22). The Ewens are interested not in fashion for its own sake, but in what fashion can tell us about American cultural history. Blue jeans are simply an example of the cultural importance of fashion.

RHETORICAL CONSIDERATIONS

1. Students might disagree on the effectiveness of articulating the argument last. This strategy allows the Ewens to capture the readers' imagination with fascinating historical detail before putting the data into a larger interpretive frame. Some students might have felt that, without a clearer thesis up front, they were drifting through the first 21 paragraphs, unsure of the essay's purpose.

2. The essay opens like a news account, situating the reader in present time (July 14, 1980) but also in Western history (it is the anniversary of Bastille Day) and in physical place (Broadway, at Seventy-second). These three elements are necessary for critics like the Ewens who situate the meaning of a cultural artifact in its historical and cultural context. Bastille Day—the French equivalent of the Fourth of July, and so symbolic of the birth of Western democracy—is ironically marked by freedom's current contortion, in the Gloria Vanderbilt models "hobbled in the finery of freedom" (paragraph 2).

Stylistically, the paragraph puts the reader in the narrator's shoes in two ways: by using the first person, and by withholding information so that readers receive it in an approximation of real time, in the same sequence as the curbside viewer. First, a "blur of color . . . invades the corridor of vision"; the advertisement then comes into focus as narrator and reader look up. After pausing at its stop throughout the second paragraph, the bus "moves along" at the start of paragraph three. With the narrators, we see the colors of the jeans advertisement, described with adjectives that stress their visual qualities: "bright red, orange, shocking saffron, lavender blue, marine, livid, purplescent, raven."

3. The short sentences in the second paragraph superimpose historical images of female subjection onto the Gloria Vanderbilt advertisement. The images on the bus become part of a list of other emblems of women's physical oppression: "the *Grecian bend*. The bustle. Foot-bound women of China. Corsets. High heels. Hobble skirts" (paragraph 2). The style telescopes history to stress the way that "today's freedom" (paragraph 3) actually repeats the physical subjection of women across human history.

4. Horatio Alger was an American author whose name became synonymous with the story of young men pulling themselves up by their bootstraps; Ragged Dick is only the most famous of a series of Alger books chronicling this rags-to-riches journey. The example nicely illustrates the way absolute divisions between classes in the nineteenth century were marked by a sartorial line: "a neat gray suit of clothes . . . signals Dick's impending metamorphosis from a ragged bootblack to 'Richard Hunter, Esq.,' a gentleman of substance." As a tale about bridging class boundaries, Ragged Dick also anticipates the blurring of such once-firm lines in the fashion of the twentieth century.

5. Examining these paragraphs closely should help students see how secondary sources can provide raw data for analysis without overwhelming an original argument. Here the Ewens use facts found from earlier writers in their field, then interpret them in order to integrate the material into their own argument. So the "fact" that dresses of European royal attendants "contained "1,100 yards of material" is interpreted by the Ewens to mean that "the mark of prosperity" for rich nineteenth century women was "to wear enough material on one's back to clothe many of a more common caste" (paragraph 7). In paragraph 9, the description of nineteenth century American business attire, "'trimmed with dark braid accenting the lapels and cuffs,'" or comprising "'a black satin vest with a collar and a black cravat on his high shirt collar'" is interpreted to mean that "the display of cloth was the mark of substance and, most certainly, profit" (paragraph 9).

The Customer's Always Right
Dave Barry

TOPICAL CONSIDERATIONS

1. Open for discussion.
2. Responses will vary. Most students will have some experience, through part-time jobs or school activities, with being on the customer service side of the

consumer divide. Questions 1 and 2 could be useful in illuminating, through students' own experiences, Barry's underlying claim: that everyone shifts sides in the consumer wars, sometimes being in the position of the hapless consumer, other times forced to deal with the imbecilic public in a service capacity.

3. In recounting this anecdote, Barry temporarily sides with the people in customer service, justifying their hatred of the public in general. Like all service workers, Barry became "convinced" of the public's stupidity after a long day of customer complaints. The newspaper readers do not come off well in this incident. None of them seem to care "about, say, the quality of the schools," but they are "RABID" when the paper erroneously calls a goose a duck (paragraph 4). The public's interests are apparently always this trivial: The most popular part of the paper is the horoscope (paragraph 4).

   Of course, Barry also pokes fun at himself here. A goose is certainly not "just a big duck" (paragraph 5); and he was himself at fault for mislabeling the photograph in the first place.

   This story is funny not only because everyone involved behaves absurdly, but also because of the connotative associations of its main protagonists—ducks and geese being somewhat silly (and silly-sounding) birds to begin with. Barry's incredulous response to the suggestion that the paper publish a correction—"For whom? The geese?" (paragraph 5)—humorously illustrates the seriousness with which the public wants to defend the honor of these birds. Barry also slyly suggests a less than complimentary attitude toward his readers when he alerts us that condescension toward the public is "the underlying assumption of journalism" (paragraph 5).

4. Even though the "duck vs. goose" issue mainly illustrates the public's idiocy, Barry also suggests the absurdity of the paper—and by extension, of the companies and customer service representatives (including himself) who condemn them. As if confessing to criminal behavior, Barry tells us sheepishly that he "used to be—I am not proud of this—a newspaper editor. This was at a paper in West Chester, Pa., called—I am not proud of this, either—the 'Daily Local News.'" Just as consumers may have always suspected, this particular company (the paper) cares not a jot about its "public's" actual interests. Instead, the newspaper imposes its point of view on innocent citizens simply trying to "find the right bedsheets" in the shopping mall. The absurdity of the paper's single angle—local response to all news—is suggested in two examples of typical headlines: "LOCAL RESIDENTS REACT TO NIXON RESIGNATION" and "LOCAL RESIDENTS REACT TO DISCOVERY THAT CLAMS MATE FOR LIFE."

   Of course, the "public" in this paragraph is equally ridiculous. They are poor excuses for citizens, being evidently oblivious to an event of such historic magnitude as Nixon's resignation. This paragraph, then, illustrates the back-and-forth rhythm of the entire article, which finds absurd the actions of both consumers and customer service representatives.

5. The story provides a fantasy solution to the feelings of powerlessness experienced by consumers up against monopolies like electric companies. The Russian army commander's resolution of the "billing dispute" has the virtues of all successful solutions: It is simple, direct, and produces instantaneous results.

The placement of this incident in Russia is significant for several reasons. The Russian army is paradigmatic of large, impersonal, bureaucratic machines, but here it takes on the role of the wronged consumer, further illustrating Barry's point about the situational nature of consumerhood. Placing the dispute in Russia universalizes the problems of consumers. That such a typically capitalist problem could occur in a country that until quite recently had a communist economy increases the humor: No one, apparently, is safe from electric companies anymore, even the Russian army—who presumably did not even have electric bills until the overthrow of the Soviet Union.

Barry fittingly never tells us who is right in this "billing dispute"; his article has throughout shown us that right and wrong reside, simultaneously, on both sides in disputes between "the public" and customer service people. This incident reconceptualizes consumer-customer service relations as a kind of war, where all's fair in the pursuit of equitable bill settlements.

6. Students by now should recognize that the answer to this question will depend entirely on where in American culture the answerer is standing: whether he or she, at that moment, is identifying with the consumer or the beleaguered service personnel. Throughout our lives, Barry's essay shows us, we inhabit these two subject positions alternately.

RHETORICAL CONSIDERATIONS

1. On the one hand, the cliché confirms that pleasing the customer is the single most important component of a consumer-based business. At the same time, it implies a certain intractableness on the part of customers: no matter how belligerent, thick-headed, or unreasonable, they must be humored, though perhaps through gritted teeth. Because of this complex tone, Barry's title manages to side both with the customer's grievances—the title does proclaim that he or she is "right"—and with the customer service representatives who must tolerate the average idiot.

The Russian tank incident gives new meaning to the title, since in that story the customer is "right" only because the threat he poses to the electric company is greater than the common threat of all electric companies, namely, that "1. They have a bunch of electricity. 2. You need it. 3. So shut up" (paragraph 7).

2. Obviously, Barry uses capitalization to emphasize some words. The quotations from the "Automated Answering System in paragraph 8," for example, stress the bullying aspects of that machine. More importantly, the use of capitalization gives this essay the quality of spoken speech. By graphically stressing some words over others the essay creates a sense of Barry's voice, which readers can almost "hear" shouting in disgust at the "RABID" readers of his newspaper, for example, or screaming with glee about "what a GREAT concept" the Russian army commander has hit on. Capitalization, then, increases both the informality of the essay and our sense of the individual writing it.

3. Barry's essay shifts back and forth between the perspectives of the consumer and the customer service representatives. The first two paragraphs address themselves directly to the "typical consumer." Paragraphs 3 to 6 illustrate the

frustrating experiences of people who must cope with dissatisfied customers. Paragraphs 7 and 8 demonstrate the belligerence of some large companies; then paragraphs 9 to 14 offer a solution (of sorts) to the problem posed in paragraph 1: how "you, the lowly consumer, can gain the serious attention of a large and powerful business" (paragraph 9). Though each paragraph internally suggests the simultaneous absurdity of both consumers and customer service representatives, the larger organization of the essay supports, in broader strokes, Barry's main claim that we all identify with these two groups alternatively.

4. Barry's ending brings the essay in a tidy circle. In the first paragraph, Barry defined the "typical consumer" as one "whose mail consists mainly of offers for credit cards that he or she already has." The ending suggests a new, more effective use for those credit cards: Purchase a tank from which to launch complaints against intransigent customer service departments. Consumers need not concern themselves with how to pay the credit card company for this multimillion dollar purchase: "You have a tank, right?" (paragraph 14). The most effective way to deal with customer service departments, then, is to declare openly the metaphorical war that is already underway. The customer who ends the essay—threatening to reduce "the entire 'Customer Service' department to tiny smoking shards" (paragraph 10), safe in his tank from pesky billing disputes—will certainly be accorded the respect promised in the essay's title.

5

Advertising

The Hard Sell
Deborah Baldwin

TOPICAL CONSIDERATIONS

1. Baldwin wants to sensitize her readers to "round-the-clock commercialism" (paragraph 8). She quotes Michael Jacobson and Ronald Collins of the Center for Science in the Public Interest, "Omnipresent commercialism is wrecking America . . . (paragraph 12). Her audience is comprised of the kind of people she describes as the Urbane family—middle-class liberal urbanites. Although students may not include themselves in this audience, they probably will agree with some of Baldwin's points.

2. Today's ads, the author argues, are more about personal empowerment than the pleasures of society and the senses—ideas which sold products in previous eras, according to Baldwin in paragraph 21. Also, current TV ads must be as entertaining as regular programs to get consumers' attention. Some advertisers on TV increase the volume and intensity of their ads to steal attention from other ads. Other ads satirize advertising itself, such as those bragging that their announcer is the worst, even if their product is the best. Advertisers want us to think we *can* solve all of our problems in life by buying their products, even if this is not possible. Death and taxes continue inexorably, in spite of advertising.

3. Corporations buy time on public broadcasting where they are mentioned twice a day, six days a week, for a year—for $250,000. Corporations donate money to art galleries and museums and get, in addition to good public relations, their names emblazoned on banners and posters. Students may argue that in a recession corporate sponsors make possible a special museum exhibit or sporting event. Or they may argue that when art and sports become commercialized, freedom of expression is threatened.

4. Since the average consumer is unaware of how his or her life is filled with commercials, most students will become aware of this saturation only after reading about it. As Kilbourne continues in paragraph 32, ads "sell images, values, goals, concepts of who we are and who we should be. . . ."

5. The Center for the Study of Commercialism is a Washington-based group that "wants to raise awareness of commercialism's costs" and to change single-minded consumers into civic-minded individuals. Michael Jacobson, a nutrition activist, founder and head of the center, wants to make the public aware of the glut of advertising. Cofounder Ronald Collins joins Jacobson in warning how consumerism is destroying America. The members of the board include critic

Mark Crispin Miller who states that life today can be lived as a theme park because of the blend of commercial and noncommercial messages in our existence. Another board member George Gerbner, former dean of a communication school, worries about TV commercials' effect on children, as does Neil Postman who also is concerned about TV's influence on the learning process. Jean Kilbourne studies the power of advertising as a socializing force. Students should agree with some of these warnings.

6. Some parallels between political advertising and commercial advertising are found in paragraph 15. "Both involved simplistic plots, with beginnings, middles, and ends, and both made heavy use of emotional images and sound bites." Students could discuss political ads for the 1992 election campaign.

7. Gerbner is afraid that our children are being brought up in a culture dictated, not by the child's home, family, community, or country, but by a "transnational corporation with something to sell." Students may agree that children are very vulnerable to the advertisers' ploys.

RHETORICAL CONSIDERATIONS

1. Baldwin begins her article with a day in the life of the Urbanes to show how advertising has become an integral part of our existence. She gives many examples of this phenomenon, such as corporations mentioned on "non-commercial" radio, clothing displaying manufacturers' names, and popular singers who turn their songs into commercials.

2. "Advertorial," in paragraph 4, means an advertising section in *The New Yorker* that looks like part of the magazine's regular content but is really one long commercial travelogue devised to lure tourists and business people. The neologism "advertorial" is made up of "advertisement" and "editorial," and sounds better than "ad."

3. In paragraph 7, Baldwin states her thesis: "While our forefathers and mothers rose with the sun to labor in the fields, we rise with the radio and TV, immersed every waking hour in nonstop nudges from corporate America to Just Say Yes." The essay is supported by statements, which enlarge it with specific examples from various authorities and published sources. The essay does not drift from the main point.

4. In paragraph 36 Baldwin refers to the Reagan administration's actions toward institutions that were "robbed of government support." In paragraph 37 she discusses President Bush's ballyhooed education initiative. Both *robbed* and *ballyhooed* have very negative connotations, which show Baldwin's feelings towards these presidents' treatments of institutions.

5. Baldwin's humor can be seen in her examples of ads placed, at the bottom of golf cups and in public restrooms; in the plugging of beer and cigarettes to armchair athletes; teachers rounding up students to watch Burger King ads on classroom Channel One; and Liberty Bell earrings sold at national historic sites. The "ad nauseums" are the funniest sections. The final irony of the essay is Baldwin's statement that her daughter prefers the vibrant Saturday morning ads to the insipid children's cartoons.

Delectable Materialism

Michael Schudson

TOPICAL CONSIDERATIONS

1. Schudson does not find that advertising has the strong influence on our lives that Baldwin claims. In spite of the fact that advertising is pervasive in our society, Schudson says that consumers buy because they desire the convenience and the pleasure conferred by products, not because of the irresistible allure of advertising. In paragraph 5 he says, "The consumer culture is sustained socially not by manufactured images but by the goods themselves as they are used." In other words, people purchase items for practical purposes (mowing the lawn and washing dishes) and sometimes for simple pleasure as in the purchase of a cashmere coat. He also disagrees with Baldwin regarding the influence TV has on children, saying that school is much more influential than TV because children are a captive audience when they attend school.

2. As stated above, he does not agree that TV influences children to the extent maintained by George Gerbner and Neil Postman in Baldwin's article. Schudson says that children have the choice of watching TV or leaving the room and of paying attention to the ads or letting their minds wander, without being caught by a teacher.

3. In paragraph 4, Schudson first agrees with then contradicts Baldwin in the parenthetical statement, "television is turned on in the average American household seven hours a day but no individual member of the family watches it for that length of time." Since Schudson gives no evidence for this statement, students may disagree with him, citing their own experiences.

4. Schudson finds nothing wrong with "wanting more," "aping the neighbors," and "seeking to be fashionable." He maintains that consuming is so pleasant that material goods do not have to be "force fed" to customers by advertisers. Students will give their own reasons for buying products.

5. Schudson claims that advertising has a Quaker quality; some ads emphasize price and, thus, "keep in mind economy as a chief criterion in buying." Advertising has a Puritan quality in that many ads stress simple function and practicality—for example, ads for detergents and other cleaning products.

6. Eastern European refugees probably want stable governments more than consumer goods. They need the basic necessities of life, beginning with an end to the ethnic wars in their countries, and continuing with food and shelter. Only when these necessities have been taken care of, will the Eastern Europeans be able to emulate the Western consumer societies.

7. Students should be encouraged to weigh the authors' evidence before making up their own minds about the contradictory opinions.

RHETORICAL CONSIDERATIONS

1. Throughout the article Schudson states opinions of authorities, then corrects them according to his own beliefs. He begins by contradicting contemporary social critics and calling them "confused." Then he refutes the findings of histo-

rian David Potter, stating that Potter "got it wrong 40 years ago"—that is, that advertising cannot be considered an institution of social control. Schudson also disagrees with advertising critics Galbraith, Packard, and Ewen in their belief that "people have to learn to desire more and more," because, as he says, in a materialistic society, Americans want more and more naturally. At the end of the article he agrees that advertising has some negative qualities such as its not being republican, but refutes these qualities by saying that advertising "unifies us around a belief in difference, variety, abundance, pluralism, choice, democracy." The tactic is particularly effective because Schudson contradicts the ideas of well-established if not eminent authorities in the field of economics and social science.

2. In paragraph 7, all of Schudson's rhetorical questions require affirmative answers. He expects his readers to agree with him that material goods do not require force feeding, that consumerism is pleasant, that aping the neighbors or seeking to be fashionable is not unheard of, that we don't need a multibillion-dollar enterprise to coax us into buying, that desire for possessions is not rare, and that pleasure in goods is not so unusual. The structure of this paragraph carries out the same overall structure of the entire article, that is, he contradicts statements to affirm his own argument.

3. Although Schudson quotes many authorities in this article, he only quotes them to refute their arguments. His arguments are not backed up by any evidence except his own experience and contentions. He may be guilty of several fallacies in logic. For instance, he cites only his own son to support his argument that children are not influenced as much by television as by school. This is an example of a "hasty generalization." He also may be making an *ad populum* argument by assuming that his audience are inveterate consumers who would applaud his insights.

4. In the last paragraph of her article, Baldwin describes how her young daughter would rather watch ads on the Saturday children's programs because they are more vivid and immediate than the regular cartoons. Schudson's personal experience is watching his son go to kindergarten in paragraph 4 of his article. Their firsthand experiences help to illustrate their points, but, as mentioned above, this is Schudson's only positive example to back up his case, while Baldwin's entire article is filled with evidence to prove her case.

5. Baldwin is probably liberal, and Schudson is probably conservative. Baldwin's authorities, particularly the Center for Science in the Public Interest, seem liberal and she agrees with them. Schudson disagrees with all of his authorities, some of whom are known liberals (David Potter and John Kenneth Galbraith).

The Selling of Pain: We Writhe, Therefore We Are
George Felton

TOPICAL CONSIDERATIONS

1. The bottom line of Felton's argument is that in current consumer health obsessions—reflected in advertising campaigns—less is actually excess. That is, our compulsions to asceticism, self-denial, and a painful concern with health are ac-

tually signs of hedonism. In Felton's opinion, we have taken "healthism" beyond the limit.

2. Advertising is certainly a reflection of societal concerns. Felton's example of healthism is a good one; it is no surprise that in the age of AIDS, advertising has moved from the idea of "sex sells" to "health sells." However, one of the strengths of advertising is that it tends to feed on itself: picking up on a trend such as health, it then enforces and reinforces that trend in the public mind, shaping our conscious and unconscious needs, activities, and spending decisions. This discussion might emphasize the ubiquity of media advertising and its power over the public.

3. Students may experience healthism in their lives in the very forms Felton cites: eating, exercise, and sexual activity. While students may resist the association of their lifestyle choices with advertising campaigns, discussion might highlight advertising-produced guilt around eating and exercise—for example, soda pop and cereal that Felton refers to.

4. For discussion.

5. One side of the debate claims that the proliferation of the waif look in ads and fashion magazines makes young women feel inadequate if they aren't poker thin, contributing to the already rampant epidemic of anorexia and bulimia in this country. On the other hand, many critics argue that by using superthin models, advertisers and editors are simply celebrating a different female body type, moving away from traditional notions of the "ideal woman" which are arguably just as dangerous.

RHETORICAL CONSIDERATIONS

1. Felton's attitude here is made clear in his introduction, when he says that advertising eventually starts telling consumers what to think. Clearly he feels that the healthism campaign is a marketing ploy to which the public has fallen. He is also highly cynical toward the content of healthism ads. For instance, in paragraph 13, at the end of long descriptions of fitness-related ads, he comes to the conclusion that, according to these ads, we are meant to "exist like this, whirling round and round, elegant gerbils in elegant cages." While the ads themselves preach that healthism is for our own good, Felton takes a very cynical stand.

2. The label is quite apt. First, it gives a sense of authority to Felton's argument—the *ism* suffix has the weight of a "scientific" phenomenon. Second, it also aptly describes the issue discussed in paragraph 2. Third, it contrasts nicely with the concept of hedonism and works well when he illustrates, in his conclusion, how these two seeming opposites are really just facets of the same trick in the million dollar mass-marketing game.

3. Felton's descriptions are well executed, and, rather than simply presenting straight observations of the ad content, they employ language that supports his overall argument. For instance, the description of the Nike print ad analyzes the slogan "Just Do It" from a very different angle than the creators of the campaign

would likely take, emphasizing the apparent superiority complex of the people in the ad as opposed to the "sloppiness" of the ordinary people reading it (paragraph 1). According to Felton, the Quaker Oats guy, Wilford Brimley, casts a "baleful" eye upon the consumer (paragraph 3), and the pristine quality of Calvin Klein Eternity ads subliminally urges us to "sidestep passion" (paragraph 8). In particular, the passage on Eternity and the description of the Kate Moss ads (paragraph 9) are vividly drawn.

A Word from Our Sponsor

Patricia Volk

TOPICAL CONSIDERATIONS

1. As Volk illustrates, the language of advertising violates rules of grammar in, for example, its use of double negatives and its lack of parallelism. But more serious is the fact that advertising also violates "rules" of truth. Big, simple claims such as "Coke Is It" are made without question, without substantiation, without clear meaning. And that is Volk's major point, that the message of advertising has little to do with truth. Even legal protection of the truth can be circumvented, as she illustrates in the way *new* becomes *improved* after six months.

2. As Charles O'Neill says in the next essay, "The Language of Advertising," one of the familiar charges against advertising is that it sells daydreams. Volk is making a similar claim. The power of the ad writer's word is "virtually limitless." *New* is a powerful buzzword and always has been simply because it appeals to our desire to have the latest thing, to be *au courant*.

    What is interesting is that although O'Neill deflects the blame away from advertisers to the uncritical consumer, Volk seems to express some guilt at bending the truth.

3. Much of the effectiveness of the essay is in the cynical humor. One might even feel some of Volk's regret at being part of an industry that best succeeds where it best deceives (as in paragraph 12, where the author exclaims, "What if the world is not waiting for Mega-Bran, the cereal that tastes like Styrofoam pellets and gets soggy in the bowl?").

4. There are only a couple of options, according to Volk, open to ad writers whose product has no unique selling point. They can "make it sing"—that is, come up with catchy jingles or songs—or buy celebrity endorsement.

5. It illustrates how advertisers can create consumer anxiety—as well as the products to cure it.

6. Volk says that the talent to write great ad copy is almost genetic. One has to have an instinct to "twist and twiddle words." Her point is consistent with her initial claim that the language of advertising has no rules. And "rulelessness" can't be taught.

RHETORICAL CONSIDERATIONS

1. She gives several good examples in the first two paragraphs: lack of parallelism, double negatives, and outright deception (*creme* and *virtually*).
2. She's cynical.
3. Her use of industry jargon does several things. First, it introduces us to advertising lingo—the "inside" argot that identifies the copywriting profession while it excludes nonmembers. Second, it creates some of the humorous tension in the piece, some of the cynicism, since Volk wants to distance herself from the silliness of expressions. Third, it illustrates how professional jargon serves as a kind of linguistic fig leaf—for example, making a bad product "sing" its way into the consumer's life.
4. The suggestion that FDR would have made a great adman for detergent is very amusing and effective—and is also cynically consistent with her attitude throughout. As she says early on, hope is what advertising sells best. And such was the message of Roosevelt's mighty line.

The Language of Advertising
Charles A. O'Neill

TOPICAL CONSIDERATIONS

1. Open for discussion. Many students will recall the efforts of many to have Joe Camel banned from advertising.
2. Open for discussion.
3. O'Neill says that writers "must glamorize the superficial differences" when product differences do not exist, or they must create differences by getting the audience involved in the action in the ad, not the product itself. For discussion, consider the recent Taster's Choice instant coffee series of ads that present a courting sequence between two neighbors who meet as strangers on an elevator then several commercials later go flying off to Paris in a still-evolving story.
4. O'Neill cites six charges that have been made against advertising. He quotes critics who think that advertising debases English; that it downgrades or underestimates the intelligence of the public; that it warps our vision of reality; that it sells us daydreams—distracting, purposeless visions of lifestyles beyond our reach; that it feeds on human weaknesses; and that it encourages unhealthy habits. In support of advertising, O'Neill's primary argument is simply that advertising language is only a reflection of the society around it, and that "slaying the messenger would not alter the fact—if it is a fact—that 'America will be the death of English'." On the positive side, he also offers the thought that advertising is an acceptable stimulus for the natural evolution of language. Furthermore, he says that advertising does not *force* us to buy anything, but

rather stimulates the development of new products in the marketplace and conveys useful information.

5. According to O'Neill, the language used in advertising has special characteristics that separate it from other languages; it is edited and purposeful, rich and arresting, calculated to involve those exposed to the advertising message, and usually simple in structure. In addition to these general characteristics, which O'Neill examines in some detail, he suggests that advertising language is different from other languages because it often carries its own special rules of grammar. For example, most of the statements in the Winston Lights ad cited in paragraph 30, are incomplete thoughts and, therefore, do not meet the requirements of a formal English sentence.

6. Proper English—that is, English that follows the rules from Strunk and White's *Elements of Style* and consists of word meanings from the gargantuan *Oxford English Dictionary*—prescribes the correct grammar, usage, and spelling. Colloquial or substandard English describes what most people, particularly college students, use in their own correspondence and in general conversation, even if they write their papers in standard English. Students will decide for themselves which usage they prefer for advertisements.

7. Any number of symbols may be suggested. O'Neill refers to the use of the color red in the depiction of autumn and fire to suggest warmth, experience, and wisdom. Other symbols could include the strong-armed man on the Mr. Clean detergent bottle, the giant of Jolly-Green fame, or BMWs. Are symbols effective? O'Neill believes they are, because with repeated exposure they acquire the power to call up in the consumer's mind a host of ideas and images that could not be communicated as effectively in any other way.

8. Even if a famous person endorses a product, he or she is not an expert in that particular field, so it does not follow that the product is especially good or even any better than the competition's product. That boxing champ Marvin Haggler has recently pushed Oscar Mayer franks doesn't make for a better hot dog, since he is not an expert on processed meats. But we might think that if Oscar Mayer is good enough for Mr. Haggler, it's good enough for us.

RHETORICAL CONSIDERATIONS

1. O'Neil hooks the reader's interest immediately with a kind of guessing game, teasing us with descriptions of a nameless celebrity who turns out to be Old Joe, the cartoon camel. O'Neill likening of Old Joe's image to that of a rock star reveals the author's awareness of his college audience—which is also that of R. J. Reynolds. His use of Old Joe also reveals the author's attitude toward advertising—one that is neither damning nor naive. He makes the point in paragraph 4 that the clamor over Old Joe underscores America's ambivalence about advertising. The reference to the ad campaign serves as a springboard to the rest of the discussion about how advertising mirrors society's values and expectations. He does not commit himself to either side of the Joe Camel debate.

2. O'Neill's style could be described as "advertising" style. In his own writing, he makes use of some of the techniques he describes. First, he personalized his writing, involving the reader in the communication process. Several times, especially up front, he addresses the reader as *you*. To emphasize his point about the simplicity of ad language, he supports his narrative with the most effective kind of testimonial available, an invitation for the reader to conduct fog index calculations on ads. A second feature of advertising language found in O'Neill's essay is the simplicity of language. O'Neill's own language is direct and simple. In a sense, he is selling the language of advertising in his discussion, without raising his vocabulary or voice. Finally, he carefully engineers his own language as do ad writers, selecting his words. You can see this in his discussion of Joe Camel at the beginning and the very end.
3. Open for discussion.

Sex, Sin, and Suggestion

Carol Moog

TOPICAL CONSIDERATIONS

1. According to the author, every man and woman needs to feel sexually viable and desirable. And every man and woman wants to feel loved and able to express love. Yet most men and women are plagued by insecurities, about their sexuality and ability to love. Playing off these insecurities, sexual imagery in advertising holds an immediate and powerful attraction for the viewer.
2. The symbolic or indirect sexual message appeals directly to the unconscious. The viewers are most likely not aware that they are getting a message. A symbolic sexual message is not filtered out or consciously identified by rational or logical thought, nor discriminated by those antennae that tell us what is and is not culturally appropriate.
3. Moog analyzes a Newport ad in which cigarettes are associated with themes of sexual dominance and submission thus connecting cigarettes with sexual excitement and pleasure. In the ad, two young men carry a pole from which hangs their female "prey," in deer-bounty fashion. The woman is positioned so her head is near one man's crotch and her bottom is exposed to the man in the rear. The tag line of the ad is, "After all, if smoking isn't a pleasure, why bother?" The ad copy and the visuals connect and extol the pleasure of Newports and the pleasure of sexuality. The image is symbolic and the unconscious doesn't separate the product from the passion. The idea being promoted is that sex and cigarettes are both fun so why not indulge oneself. Students might mention that everything from perfume to jeans to Madonna is promoted on themes of dominance and submission.
4. Moog says that women can look at ads with a great deal of sexual content and still remember what is being promoted. On the other hand, Moog claims that

when men are confronted by an ad with a great deal of sexual imagery, they cannot remember what is being advertised—some can't even remember what was in the ad. In paragraph 17 Moog says, "Sexy ads do rivet a man's attention, but the intellectual circuits can get overloaded fast and, at that point, all that gets marketed is food for fantasies." Moog does not offer statistics or quote studies to support this assertion. One could wonder how accurate her observation is or if it's a stereotyped notion of men as so rattled and undone by sex that they can't think straight. This old notion is not a harmless one; it's been used to justify unwarranted sexual advances by men—even rape. It would be interesting to note if students think this generalization is justified. Are young men today more aware and sensitive and less prone to this kind of knee-jerk reaction?

5. The ads described in this article usually involve a young, fragile, porcelain-skinned girl in an encounter with a salacious older man. The man, looking old enough to be the girl's father, is often in a menacing or dominating stance and seems about to make a sexual demand. The author demonstrates that this sexual imagery creates the "illusion that being possessed by a powerful, older man can be a glamorous identity for a confused, angry adolescent girl . . . a daring walk on the rebel side of the tracks" (paragraph 23). Thus, sex becomes a way to reject parental restraints and control.

6. For the students.

7. Moog uses the ad for Calvin Klein fragrance for men to illustrate the Narcissus myth. Here a man stares into a mirror mesmerized by his own image. Moog argues that at the root of this narcissism is a feeling of worthlessness, the need to reach unattainable goals, and a craving for the admiration of others. These ads appeal to a person with such psychological flaws; and buying the product only reinforces these negative character traits.

8. For the students.

9. There are several psychological ramifications of the sexual sell, none of them positive. At the beginning of the essay Moog says, "When advertisers link products with sexuality, they lock in with people's deepest fears of being unlovable; they offer their products and images as the tickets to love, when what they're really providing are more masks for people to hide behind." Later, referring to the Newport ad which focuses on male prowess achieved through sexuality, Moog points out in paragraph 17 that "For men in this culture trying to grow up, to move from sexual preoccupations into committed relationships, advertisers' sexual preoccupations help keep them stuck in the crippling quicksand of adolescence." Thus, the messages in the ads contribute to stunted psychological development. Moog's analysis of the Narcissus ad reveals a campaign that glamorizes self-absorption and isolation. This same theme is picked up and developed further in the Obsession ads. Akin to self-absorption is psychological detachment as evidenced by totally indifferent models who seem devoid of feeling or thought. As Moog says, "The real obsession is again with the self, which is certainly one way of pulling back from messy, possibly even disease-carrying relationships, with no expectations of closeness that counts." Clearly, Moog feels that such imagery does not contribute to healthy psychological development.

RHETORICAL CONSIDERATIONS

1. For copyright reasons, we could not reproduce the visuals. However, the article works nicely even without them. Ms. Moog does a fine job describing the salient points of the ads in a lively and detailed fashion. Her descriptions should engage the student's imagination sufficiently.

2. Throughout the essay Moog effectively balances these two levels of expertise to show us how sex sells. Her familiarity with ads and the way they work comes through in virtually every analysis. And her deft explanation of the psychological factors draws on her background as a psychologist. Her analysis of Guess Jeans nicely demonstrates these skills.

3. Ms. Moog is very objective in her analysis. She raises questions about ethical issues in a tactful rather than confrontational manner. She is direct, she does not mince words, nor is she shrill. Hers is a good example of strong criticism that does not sound like an Old Testament prophet. There are several occasions when she poses what might be uncomfortable questions for the ad industry—for example, the sexual entanglements in Guess Jeans and Trouble perfume ads. In paragraph 25 she asks, "Hasn't anyone told advertisers about AIDS?" And when discussing the Narcissus theme she points out that "People in desperate need of validation from others are caught in a media avalanche of narcissistic images of people who essentially feel empty and unlovable beneath their grandiose postures" (paragraph 31). She concludes with a forceful statement about the advertising and the collective memory of a culture: "Because these portraits reflect essentially insecure identities, the images promoted point the way toward more, rather than less, emotional emptiness" (paragraph 43).

4. For the students. In my mind, the analysis seems right on target. But this question could stimulate an interesting class discussion about "hidden meaning" among other issues.

6

Male/Female

Masculine/Feminine
Prudence Mackintosh

TOPICAL CONSIDERATIONS

1. Seven-year-old Jack comes home singing, "Farrah Fawcett, Farrah Fawcett, I love you" and threatens to give his brother a bloody nose. A friend's daughter hesitates about being a lawyer like Daddy when she learns that no one wears blue tutus in the courtroom. In another friend's family with two sons and a daughter, only the daughter is interested in keeping her room neat and setting the table. A little girl baby sits quietly looking at a blade of grass while Mackintosh's son, William, uproots the grass by handfuls and eats it. The rest is up to the student.

2. It illustrates Mackintosh's thesis: "Certain inborn traits seem to be immune to parental and cultural tampering." It seems fairly obvious, though, that nurturing qualities do not belong exclusively to girls and aggression is not typical only of boys. You might point to the increase in male nurses and in fathers who seek and win custody of their children, as well as to the presence of women leaders in Congress, in the military, and in corporations, as evidence.

3. This is up to the student.

4. It seems fair to say that there are qualities that both men and women share. Some of these are intelligence, creativity, strength, dominion, consideration, thoughtfulness. As question 2 implies, even sensitivity, compassion, and aggressiveness cannot be thought of as exclusively belonging to boys or girls.

5. No. Men sometimes choose to be male nurses or secretaries and are good at what they do. Mackintosh simply argues that parents shouldn't try to ignore the fact that there are some innate behavioral differences between boys and girls.

RHETORICAL CONSIDERATIONS

1. Mackintosh's initial sentence implies a question: *Can* the aggressive tendencies in boys be tempered with sensitivity and compassion? She reintroduces this question toward the end of the paragraph: "In such an environment, surely they would grow up free of sex-role stereotypes. At the very least wouldn't they pick up their own socks?" Implicit in this remark is the broader question: *Can* children be raised free of sex-role stereotypes? Mackintosh's answer to the question is explicitly stated in paragraph 14: "Certain inborn traits seem to be immune to parental and cultural tampering."

2. Although Mackintosh's essay is primarily expository, she mixes other rhetorical strategies to develop her exposition. A number of paragraphs (2,3,4, and 5) are developed by example. She links paragraphs with a narrative sentence or two. In paragraph 6, Mackintosh begins an analysis of cause and effect that turns out also to be a persuasive strategy that continues to the last paragraph.

3. Any five of Mackintosh's sentences could be cited. One example from paragraph 2: "They know moms *and dads* do dishes and diapers." A general version might be: "They know parents do household chores." An example from paragraph 3: "These moms looked on Barbie with disdain and bought trucks and science kits." A general version might be: "These mothers shunned feminine toys." The general statements are less colorful and interesting and don't show as vividly what Mackintosh means.

4. The first paragraph explains what she originally intended to do in raising her boys. Throughout the essay she shows what caused her to modify her views. In the last paragraph, she states her new position.

Wears Jump Suit. Sensible Shoes. Uses Husband's Last Name
Deborah Tannen

TOPICAL CONSIDERATIONS

1. The styles Tannen describes are coherent in that all aspects of each woman's appearance—from hair to clothing to makeup to shoes—are aligned to provide a unified overall effect. The woman in sensible shoes, for instance, does not have wild, sexy, frosted hair. Tannen's descriptions serve to illustrate the danger of stereotyping, the human tendency to associate certain *styles* with certain *personality types.* Based on Tannen's observations, each woman fits a common stereotype: the sensible no-frills woman, the sophisticate, the slut. Discussion calls for critical thought about the validity of unconscious judgments based solely upon the messages sent by appearances.

2. According to Tannen, women's fashion choices make statements about them—"marking" them—while men have the option of remaining "unmarked" by wearing standard attire such as a suit or shirt and slacks. Men who choose unmarked clothes are not subject to judgments based upon their appearances; women, on the other hand, are always subject to character inferences drawn from their appearance.

3. In paragraph 17, Tannen writes, "The range of women's hairstyles is staggering, but a woman whose hair has no particular style is perceived as not caring about how she looks, which can disqualify her for many positions, and will subtly diminish her as a person in the eyes of some." Class discussion might touch on job requirements of airline stewardesses, who must maintain a certain weight, or TV journalists who are let go because of their appearance, or hiring decisions based

upon a woman's appearance. Documented cases of such discrimination are fewer for men for whom age and even weight are often culturally seen as signs of wisdom and authority rather than of physical deterioration.

4. In biological terms, women are "unmarked" while men are "marked"—for example, males have nonfunctional nipples. The point illustrates that the construct of male as the neutral, unmarked term and female as the marked is cultural and political rather than biological.

5. As Tannen points out in paragraph 28, "the female was declared by grammarians to be the marked case." This was a decision with specific motivations and consequences. Tannen uses the notion of marking to move from the topic of appearance, to language, and back again. The relationship she builds between the two illustrates her argument about how widespread gender marking is for women, and how relatively absent it is for men. Discussion might focus on student experience with gender marking.

6. Marking women who discuss gender issues as feminist is further evidence of the phenomenon. In Tannen's experience, male colleagues conducting similar kinds of research are not labeled feminist. Tannen has problems with being marked feminist by virtue of her research since her work is not slanted toward a specific political position on gender. It simply records her observations and draws conclusions from those observations which, according to Tannen, are strictly objective and undeserving of markings.

RHETORICAL CONSIDERATIONS

1. This introduction might seem inordinately long and detailed to students at first. However the descriptions in these paragraphs provide an explicit visual foundation for Tannen's argument about marked and unmarked dress—which, in turn, lead to her argument about gender marking in our culture.

2. Paragraph 9 marks the first change in focus from the style markings to linguistic markings. The transition is marked by additional space between the lines; the same device is used in paragraph 24 to mark a similar shift. Tannen deftly relates the two issues, emphasizing the illogic of gendered marking. Her argument moves from describing contemporary gender marking in paragraphs 1 through 8, making the link with linguistic theory in paragraph 9, and providing biological evidence to refute the logic of the female as a marked case in paragraph 24. Ultimately she proves that the marking of the female originates in decisions reflecting the historical power imbalance between men and women rather than from some essential or biological "fact." This method of argument might be used as a model for students writing persuasive essays.

3. Tannen's essay is largely written in the first person, which allows her to personalize the gender marking phenomenon and, thus, establish reader identification. The first-person perspective also establishes her own position on the subject, rather than writing from behind the screen of the third person, or "objective," voice. She shifts into a third-person voice when providing background information to her argument—for example, in paragraphs 9 through 11 where in

an informative, impersonal tone she explains the marking in linguistic theory. Similarly, Tannen assumes the third-person voice in paragraphs 24 through 28 when summarizing Ralph Fasold's arguments on biological gender differences in language. Note that in both cases this shift of tone into the third person is followed by a reversion to the first person, which allows Tannen to relate the third-person "evidence" to her first hand experience, each "voice" supplementing the other while strengthening the overall argument. Again, this technique might be useful as a model for students experimenting with voice and point-of-view in narrative or persuasive essays.

4. Tannen has provided three different types of evidence: information based on personal experience (paragraphs 1–8), information based on "common knowledge" (paragraphs 17–23), and information derived from the findings of outside sources (paragraphs 9, 10, 24–28). These different kinds of evidence provide layers of support to her argument. Personal experience alone might leave readers feeling a lack of credibility. An argument based upon common knowledge might likewise seem thin or obvious, while an article whose authority was derived solely from the words of experts might lack vitality and appear boring or removed from the practicality of real life.

The Failure of Feminism
Kay Ebeling

TOPICAL CONSIDERATIONS

1. Ebeling blames feminism for convincing her that she could "make it on [her] own," as a divorced mother. She also thinks that feminism "gave men all the financial and personal advantages over women" (paragraph 5). She resents that women often must work long hours for little pay while trying to raise the children on their own. This does not feel like "liberation" to her.

2. Ebeling states that the "Experimental Generation" values "'actively pursuing new ways for men and women to interact now that old traditions no longer exist'" (paragraph 2). This generation wants to invent new ways for men and women to relate to one another because they feel that the old ways no longer serve society's changing needs. Ebeling wants everything to be "the way it was, pre-feminism" (paragraph 9). She wants men to be the primary breadwinners and women to be the primary caretakers of the children. She is frustrated with her minimal economic achievements and thinks that a return to "old traditions" (paragraph 2) will make her and her child more economically secure.

3. The "Yuppie" is very much concerned with his own individual happiness and not much concerned with hers. His treatment of her is indicative of a contemporary movement away from the values of social responsibility and toward individualism. Ebeling sees his attitude as representative of a society that does not care about the welfare of the women and children who have suffered as a result of divorce.

4. Ebeling argues that because women are "child-bearers," they are naturally respon- sible for the raising of those children. She feels duped by feminism because the message she got from it was that women did not need the support of a husband in order to be happy and fulfilled. However, single mothers like Ebeling have found it difficult to be both full-time mothers and career women. Mothering takes up a great deal of time and energy, and so, single mothers cannot put as much into a ca- reer as single fathers can. Students may argue that fathers could do all of the things that Ebeling says mothers must do for children. An interesting debate could be prompted by listing the things students think mothers do and then discussing which of these tasks are biologically impossible for fathers to perform.

5. Ebeling wants to return to "traditional" roles for men and women. She wants women to focus more on raising their children and less on having a career. If women wish to work outside the home, they should get jobs ["start small busi- nesses, do consulting, write freelance out of the home" (paragraph 9)] that don't take them away from their children for too long a time. She wants men to focus more on providing economic security for mothers and children. Students will come up with other solutions as well.

6. Answers will vary. Push students to say more than just "Divorce stinks." or "Divorce is great." Students should explore the reasoning behind their thinking and connect it to what Ebeling is saying.

RHETORICAL CONSIDERATIONS

1. Feminists are often accused of being man-haters. By writing about dating, Ebeling makes it clear that she is not angry with men so much as she is upset about the feminist arguments that have not worked for her. This framing device separates the two issues.

2. Answers will vary from student to student.

3. Capitalizing "Yuppie," "Experimental Generation," "Great Experiment that Failed," and "Brainless Betty" lend a sarcastic tone to Ebeling's article. This tech- nique conveys her disdain for these ideas without having to specifically state it.

The Beauty Myth
Naomi Wolf

TOPICAL CONSIDERATIONS

1. The beauty myth, in Wolf's words, is a "violent backlash against feminism that uses images of female beauty as a political weapon against women's advance- ment" (paragraph 5). It's purpose is to control the amount of power women have and to keep women from advancing too much. The beauty myth subverts the gains made in the women's movement by creating new, image-based controls to replace the discriminatory practices that feminism has abolished.

2. Students will come up with a variety of examples, but their primary ones will probably come from television. See if you can push them to come up with more subtle, harder-to-see examples.

3. The beauty myth works by convincing both men and women that there is such a thing as an attainable version of beauty that all women should aspire to. Men are encouraged to desire women who try to be beautiful, so this puts even more pressure on women to conform to standards of beauty. The beauty myth is a form of social control in that it creates "fictions" (paragraph 20) and calls them values so that everyone will want to attain them.

4. It is likely that specific physical attributes of women will be the topic here. Breast size, hair color, and weight are just some of the ideals that have changed in valuation over the years.

5. Wolf means that the beauty myth is a tool men's institutions use to retain power over women. There is no natural, aesthetic, or religious basis to the beauty myth; it is the creation of a society that depends on the devaluation of women (and other groups) for its survival.

6. Answers to this question will vary.

7. In the mid-1800s, when advancements in technology made it possible, through images reproduced in "fashion plates, daguerrotypes, tintypes, and roto-gravures" (paragraph 16), women were bombarded with pictures of the proper domestic wife. These images helped to support industrial capitalism's need to keep women in the domestic sphere, tending to the comforts of industry's workers. Today, much more advanced kinds of image technology are used to support the beauty myth.

8. Many of these "social fictions" (paragraph 18) still hold their ground. It remains widely held that children require supervision exclusively by their mothers, and that women should be happy to keep their houses spotlessly clean, despite major feminist efforts to establish such other alternatives as day care and shared household responsibility. Some modern-day "social fictions" include the myth of the Supermom who is able to have a successful full-time career; raise a happy family; keep her house clean, her husband happy, and herself beautiful all at the same time. There is also a growing trend to encourage successful career women to find staying home and raising children much more satisfying than having a career. Women who do succeed in business must not make more money than their husbands, or they will ruin these husbands' self-esteem. All of these "fictions" work to keep women out of positions of power in society or, if they are already in positions of power, try to convince them that assuming more "feminine" tasks instead will be more rewarding.

9. Answers to this question will vary.

10. Answers to this question will vary.

11. Wolf contends that women as well as men are "stunned and disoriented" (para-graph 21) by all of the rapid changes in gender role expectations, and so they seek solace in traditional, comforting ways of being. Also, "powerful industries" like the diet, cosmetics, and cosmetic surgery industry have become so large that they depend on the existence of the beauty myth for their economic sur-

vival. Accordingly, these industries add to the barrage of voices constantly creating "unconscious personal anxieties" (paragraph 22) in women by clamoring for them to be beautiful.

12. Wolf contends that because our society is "dependent now on the continued underpayment of women" (paragraph 25), there is an economic as well as psychological reason for maintaining the beauty myth.

13. Students may conclude that women do more of the daily, domestic buying but that men do more large-purchase buying. This in itself is an extension of the power relations in the beauty myth and would be interesting to discuss.

14. Answers to this question will vary.

RHETORICAL CONSIDERATIONS

1. It is because Wolf's thesis is so controversial that she must first pull us into her argument by explaining how the women's movement accomplished new freedoms for women but then was seriously undercut by the beauty myth. She is trying to win support for her side before she actually states her argument by first pointing out the injustices at work in the beauty myth.

2. Answers to this question will vary.

3. Answers to this question will vary.

4. She uses the Iron Maiden as a metaphor for how women exist within the confines of the beauty myth. They are forced to be beautiful on the outside, like the famous German torture device, while psychologically, they are cruelly censored.

5. To colonize is to go into a foreign land and establish your own form of government there. Wolf contends that the beauty myth is the "private reality" that has forced its way into the foreign land of female consciousness and set up its own government there. Wolf is seeing this colonization of female consciousness in a negative sense.

Why Men Are the Way They Are

Warren Farrell

TOPICAL CONSIDERATIONS

1. According to Farrell, women who used to benefit from men's higher salaries because they were married to them now want those same high salaries for themselves. Also, women now have more choices about what to do with their lives— enter the workplace, be a wife and mother, or do both. Men still have the same pressures to make enough money to support their families, but now they must compete with women as well as men for their incomes.

2. Ebeling sees divorce's effect on men and women differently. She thinks divorce benefits men because they very often keep their already high salaries while women have to take low-paying jobs and support the children at the same time. Ebeling's views on the effects of divorce are based on personal experience, whereas Farrell's views are generalizations he has made from observing society. These two different points of reference help to shape each author's viewpoint.

3. Answers to this question will vary.

4. Farrell states that women now have to decide whether to have a full-time career, a full-time family, or some combination of career and family. Men only have the option of working full-time their whole lives. Students whose primary caregivers are single mothers working full-time *and* raising a family full-time may see women's choices as somewhat more limited than Farrell makes them out to be.

5. Answers to this question will vary.

6. Farrell seems to want to get across the idea that there is just as much inequality against men as there is against women. He wants his readers to develop some compassion for the pressures and anxieties men experience because they are goaded into being success objects by society. Students can choose from any number of examples from the article to support their answers.

RHETORICAL CONSIDERATIONS

1. Farrell makes good use of valid statistics to support points he is making—an analysis of 1000 commercials in 1987 proves man's "bad guy" image, a Census Bureau statistic proves men work more on their full-time jobs than women do. But, too much of his article relies on personal sampling to "prove" his points. For instance, he goes into a card shop and a book store, peruses the products, and discovers a preponderance of male-bashing going on. He relies on informal surveys of women who have spoken with him to back up his point that women have three options today while men only have one. When he explains how high-school students choose dates, he hypothesizes that "chances are almost 100 percent" that the girls want good-looking *and* successful partners while men are only interested in good-looking partners. His reliance on these informal types of sampling weakens the thrust of his argument.

2. Farrell says feminism is "like fluoride in water—we drink it without being aware of its presence" (paragraph 4). He contends that feminism has stimulated a "bad guy" (paragraph 4) image of men and has lauded the working mother while neglecting the working father. Farrell seems to be berating feminism for its one-sided focus on the rights of women.

3. Farrell takes a confidently informative stance in order to convey his information. It is as if he is the comforting therapist assuring men that they, too, have been pressured into roles they may not want to accept. He tries to explain what

those pressures have been, to bring them out into the open, so men can begin to take control of their own lives.

What Do Men Really Want?
Sam Allis

TOPICAL CONSIDERATIONS

1. First there was the "strong, stoic John Wayne–type" (paragraph 5). Then came the sensitive, nurturing types like Alan Alda. Now, the author laments, the male role model must be "the devoted family man with terrific triceps" (paragraph 6) and a wallet to match those muscles. Allis argues (and you could extend this argument to the other types as well) that the sensitive man was so overemphasized, that Americans grew tired with such a narrowly defined role model. I think you could say the same about the John Wayne–type and even today's new role models.

2. Allis says that men have reacted to these changes with increasing anxiety. He thinks that too much pressure is put on men to achieve financial success through these role models. Although, according to Allis, men have tried to become stoic or sensitive or muscle-bound as the roles dictate, they have done so at the expense of their own emotional well-being.

3. Student answers to this question will vary.

4. It is most likely that students, in explaining why they agree or disagree with this statement, will draw on examples of men who are very close to them—fathers, relatives, friends. It might also be interesting for students to compare answers with one another to see how their conceptions about this subject differ from one another.

5. Student answers to this question will vary.

6. Allis contends that men need role models who value consciousness-raising, without having to be financially successful in the bargain. He longs for a movement with the momentum that the women's movement had, and laments that, so far, men's groups are small and too primally focused. He also argues that men need to start supporting one another and accepting each other's diverse natures. He says that before men can face up to the dilemmas of living in an ever-changing world, they must become comfortable with themselves.

7. Student answers to this question will vary.

8. Student answers to this question will vary.

RHETORICAL CONSIDERATIONS

1. John Wayne gets to be "strong" and "stoic," while the Alan Alda types are "hollow-chested" men who "bawl" at the drop of a hat (paragraph 5). Sounds as if Allis is lamenting the demise of the John Wayne–type and celebrating the demise of the Alan Alda type. In paragraph 6, the role model that supplants the sensitive man is sarcastically portrayed. Allis goes on to say that women

only liked Alan Alda and Mel Gibson because they were rich. Couldn't the same argument be made for John Wayne as well?

2. Both articles have an undercurrent tone of anger at the pressures society puts on its male or female members. Neither article entones much sympathy for the gender it is not focusing on. Allis's article is different from Ebeling's in that he uses more humorous language to get his point across. Ebeling's article relies on more personal experiences to get her point across; perhaps for her the issue is too close to home to be joked about.

3. Allis uses a question and answer format to organize his material. The essay begins and ends with the question "What do men really want?" The student must decide how effective a device this is for her or him.

Conan and Me

Bill Persky

TOPICAL CONSIDERATIONS

1. Persky's essay has to do with the reality of one's "self," and how to shed cultural affectations in order to get to that reality. In his opening, Persky cites "feelings of inadequacy" as the reason for adopting an affected accent—that is, if one speaks with a cultured British accent, one is assumed to be *cultured,* leaving those around him feeling less so. Some students might concede that a crisp British accent makes them feel inferior; yet the inverse might be true also: that they feel superior to people speaking with a dialect considered less cultured than their own. Ask students if they have ever taken on affectations—in dress, accent, or social or economic position—and how societal expectations contributed to the need for such.

2. Persky sets up a standard for a heroic male response to crisis earlier in the paragraph by describing an *ideal* male reaction. His actual confrontation with the intruder juxtaposes the desire to play that ideal with his actual reaction to real-life fear and terror. This says something about gender stereotypes and their effect on the behavior and attitudes of people in everyday life, as well as the reinforcement of these stereotypes in the media. Discussion might expose the difficulty of living up to such expectations—and the resultant need for hiding traits that do not jive with gender stereotypes.

3. Persky attributes his fear and hysteria (screaming in a high-pitched voice, hitting the intruder with a pillow) to his mother, while claiming to resemble Schwarzenegger when he barks his macho commands and engages in "hand to hand combat" (paragraph 5). This dichotomy illustrates archetypal feminine and masculine traits found in most people. At the same time, however, such models of behavior serve to perpetuate those stereotypes.

4. Mackintosh is positioned in the middle of the debate, noting that her boys seem to have some inherent traits different from those of girls, while at the same time their cultural conditioning contributes strongly to their development in terms of

gender roles. Persky seems to emphasize the pervasive cultural conditioning which leaves men feeling compelled to hide their "real" selves underneath layers of constructed macho. It's important to point out the dangers of attributing sex-role differences wholly to either biology or environment.

RHETORICAL CONSIDERATIONS

1. Persky's introduction is an apt way of getting at the complicated issue of cultural affectation and concealed identities. The anecdote is also a good way to set the tone for the piece, which is informal, chatty, occasionally bemused, and written as a first-person narrative. Persky makes himself accessible to his reader as just a guy telling a story, and he starts off with another guy telling a story in order to set the chummy mood.

2. Persky's narrator consistently makes himself vulnerable to his reader, encouraging empathy and identification. This is a strategy which is particularly suitable to the piece. In paragraph 2, Persky surprises the reader with a particularly revealing statement: "I have some images of myself that I'd like to think are real." It's a courageous confession identifying the author as an uncertain individual striving to know his "self" despite the pervasive cultural forces that insist he act like a film hero. Similarly, the author's admitted fear of fighting (paragraph 9) has the same effect. Persky continues with this honest—at times self-deprecating—tone throughout the piece.

3. Again, these clues serve to improve reader identification: Persky uses them to position himself as a man, just like any other, an active participant in pop culture, vulnerable to the pains and triumphs of cultural sex-role conditioning. The first clues are the most obvious: his comparison with a combination of Arnold Schwarzenegger and his mother. Next, Persky says that he is currently reading *The Bonfire of the Vanities,* a popular book representing the lives of hard-hitting lawyers and businessmen ("Masters of the Universe," Wolfe calls them) in the Big Apple. Next, he considers drawing upon the "new, upper-body strength" developed at the "Vertical Club," implying a kind of artificiality in the current mania for health clubs. Each of these clues is familiar enough to allow for reader recognition and identification.

4. In paragraphs 11 and 12, Persky shifts gears into the issue of right and wrong. Persky uses the anecdote of the intruder to illustrate a moment of purity in self-knowledge. Some might feel that this equation of a morally clear-cut situation with a person's ability to "be himself" is somewhat unclear, and introduced too late in the argument to be effective.

7

Multicultural America

Ethnic Identity

Getting to Know About You and Me

Chana Schoenberger

TOPICAL CONSIDERATIONS

1. Schoenberger designs the exchanges to elicit laughter, as one error compounds another. One student confuses Mormons with Mennonites; another assumes that Jews unilaterally followed Jesus at the beginnings of the Christian church, simply because Jesus' origins were Jewish; another has knowledge of Jewish customs only through Bible stories over two thousand years old, that have apparently been watered down through Sunday School lessons. The question about Mormonism is even more amusing, because it comes from a Mormon girl's stereotype that her own people have extraordinary numbers of offspring.

2. Schoenberger's friends seem tolerant of each other's lack of information; in fact, their candor in questioning and answering is remarkably free of snipes and jibes. Depending on your class's demographics, you may get a variety of responses—possibly even some reminiscences that are still hurtful, open wounds.

3. Schoenberger is shocked at her professor's use of the word "Jew" as a verb, meaning to cheat, swindle, or shortchange. For one thing, he is the central authority figure, a mentor leading and directing this group of teenagers in a rite of passage from the kid-stuff experiments of a high-school class into a world where real science is happening. Because he plays an elevated role, Schoenberger expects better of him. More importantly, the professor's comment is different from her friends' questions, which resulted from benign ignorance. The professor makes a statement!

4. Of course Schoenberger wants us to see that ice cream and grilled cheese sandwiches are personal choices, rather than religious mandates or cultural preferences. Yet, both Schoenberger and the only other Jewish student in the program share these particular tastes, so Schoenberger worries that her friends will make wrong generalizations. Of course, she's worried about more than food.

5. Schoenberger discusses the importance of her participation in paragraphs 12 through 14. She isn't worried that her high-school peers will lack for information if she does not help with such presentations. However, the summer experience

has shown her a mild version of the consequences of ignorance. Because of this experience, she feels a call to community service in fighting ignorance about Jews; the high school's offerings are an appropriate outlet for her at this point.

RHETORICAL CONSIDERATIONS

1. Schoenberger arranges her material in three parts: First, she begins with comments that are not only silly, but childlike. They do capture the students' ignorance of various religions, but do an equally deft job at portraying young people building up their store of knowledge about the world by exchanging information directly with each other (rather than learning about other religions from books and lectures). Older folks may be just as profoundly ignorant, but they probably wouldn't ask these questions. Next, she discusses the professor. He is a more serious problem who seems to stand as an object lesson, an example of what these young scholars could turn into if they don't learn about other religious groups. His own knowledge of others is ossified, and there's a good chance that he transmits his prejudices to uninquisitive young. Finally, Schoenberger mentions the "really vicious anti-Semite" and the "malignantly prejudiced person" as types she's never met. This triptych is a spectrum of ignorance.

2. Schoenberger isn't interested in perceptions of the rightness or wrongness of religious observances and beliefs, except as beliefs manifest in "contact zones." Religious intolerance these days does not delve into practices conducted behind closed doors. Only when religious practice violates broadly, held values—for example, "animal sacrifice" (paragraph 6)—do we get our hackles up. However, when a group's practices become visible to outsiders—when they occur in a cultural contact zone—intolerance may rise sharply. For example, if Mennonites dressed "normally" in public, then the girl in paragraph 4 would probably not have commented. Schoenberger suggests this slant when she advocates respect for "each other's traditions" in paragraph 11, which is a (misleading?) conflation of religious with ethnic groups that places her discussion in the context of multiculturalism as named in paragraph 12. Her focus on cultural manifestations also helps her make a broader point than she could if she focused solely on explicating Jewish religious observances. She speaks of anti-Semitism because it is within her own immediate experience, but by implication she opposes prejudice against other groups, too.

3. Schoenberger makes good use of her friends' prestige. Given the sponsorship of this program by the National Science Foundation, candidates are the *crème de la crème* of their age-group. By implication, they were also trained by good schools, and nurtured by families with high ambitions. Yet despite their squeaky-clean appeal for adults, their grousing about cafeteria food makes them appealing for young people as well. Schoenberger uses these implications to make a point: Anyone can hold, mistaken stereotypes and prejudicial beliefs about another group. Had her friends been tagged as troublemakers, it would be much easier to write them off with a shrug of expectation. Instead, readers probably admire and identify with the group, and will have less of a step to make in attending to their own ignorance.

4. Most of Schoenberger's article (paragraphs 2–9) is personal narrative about her summer experience; it's framed by another narrative, about her decision to work with the school's Diversity Committee in presenting Jewish religious celebrations (paragraphs 1 and 14). The remaining material (paragraphs 10–13) contains the most thesis-oriented potential. The strength of the piece rests on the interrelationship between the two narratives, rather than on either one by itself. Furthermore, the most memorable aspect of the piece is not what Schoenberger preaches, but what she and her friends actually do. Rather than didactically advocating a particular course of action, she has shown herself engaged in specific action.

Your Parents Must Be Very Proud
Richard Rodriguez

TOPICAL CONSIDERATIONS

1. Rodriguez admits in the second paragraph, "I had such contradictory feelings." The essence of his conflict is that he wishes to be like everyone else, to erase cultural differences. While he could reject much of his native heritage, his parents could not. That Rodriguez wants to be American is evident in his assertion: "Simply, what mattered to me was that they [his parents] were not like my teacher." Rodriguez is ashamed of his parents' accents, "then guilty for the shame." He admits that his parents were always behind him. Nevertheless, he still feels "nervous," "resentful," "protective."

   Most students regardless of their cultural backgrounds have, at one time or another, been embarrassed by their parents. Discuss this universal feeling and the complications added when parents and children grow up in different cultures.

2. The common bond among the two sets of parents is that each is "proud" of their children. However, each set of parents deals differently with their children's entrance into a predominantly white American society. The essays feature an Hispanic family and an Asian family. These essays revolve more around class issues than race issues and grapple with the generation gap and the bicultural complications of it.

   Rodriguez's parents understand intelligence in the concrete: "It was my father again who wondered why I didn't display my awards on the wall of my bedroom" (paragraph 13). They have not entered Rodriguez's world of ideas; the strain in their relationship is caused less by race than by intellectual pursuits.

   Rodriguez's parents remark "[we are] proud of all our children!" They are trying to maintain a relationship with their children that is threatened by American culture that emphasizes independence over family. His mother wonders why the "family wasn't close anymore," "more in the Mexican style" (paragraph 14).

   In the Elizabeth Wong essay, "To Be an All-American Girl," the cultural difference between mother and daughter is strong. The parent-child relationship in this essay is close to Rodriguez's as it revolves around the "cultural divorce" that Elizabeth seeks and her mother tries to prevent. Wong's mother wants her to go to Chinese school, while Wong's father inhibits his wife's assimilation into American culture by calling her Ruth, a name which she cannot pronounce. Part of Elizabeth's rejection of the Chinese culture may stem from her mother's difficulty with the English language, a source of embarrassment for Elizabeth and her brother. Her brother says to his mother, "'You set a bad example'" (paragraph 10). Again, Elizabeth is so concerned about fitting into American culture that she tells the American reader, "I was one of you" (paragraph 14).

"Grown up" is a significant phrase in the two essays. Each author experiences his or her fears during adolescence when every degree of difference between them and their American schoolmates is magnified.

3. Education means opportunity to both Rodriguez and his parents. Mrs. Rodriguez "saw in education the opportunity for job advancement" (paragraph 5). Mr. Rodriguez saw that education "could enable a person to escape from a life of mere labor" (paragraph 9). However, American education failed both his parents. His mother was awarded a high-school diploma when she could hardly speak English, and his father was denied the chance to study for his diploma.

His parents' experience jaded their views of higher education. While his father "despised the trivialization of higher education . . . the half education that so often passed as mass education" (paragraph 12), his mother wondered, "'Why aren't the colleges in Sacramento good enough for you?'" (paragraph 15). They believed the purpose of education was to earn a ticket to a better life. They enjoyed the tangible side of education: Rodriguez's sixth grade trophy, his high-school diploma.

Rodriguez had been admitted to Stanford. What he wanted from education surpassed his parents' understanding. He writes, "My departure would only make physically apparent the separation that had occurred long before." While Rodriguez would contemplate the world of ideas, the "universality of Shakespeare's appeal" (paragraph 16), his parents would contemplate "what might have been" if they had received a real education.

4. Rodriguez's mother wants the family to be close "more in the Mexican style." American culture has broken the family apart. Because American ideals are rooted in the American, "be all that you can be" philosophy, the power of the individual is valued over the power of the family. To succeed in America often requires people to venture alone, to leave family behind. Rodriguez has done this physically and intellectually.

RHETORICAL CONSIDERATIONS

1. Rodriguez subtly contradicts his statement, "Your parents must be very proud" with phrases tucked into the narrative. In paragraph 1 he writes, "though stupidly I took for granted their enormous native intelligence." As "the scholarship boy," he has not yet acquired respect for unschooled intelligence. A sentence in paragraph 3 reads simply, "They made success possible."

In paragraph 11, Rodriguez admits that his parents "endured [his] precocious behavior." The essay is painful; part of the pain comes through admitting his and his parents' differences which, at the end of the essay, they do not reconcile. What is unwritten in the essay is more important than what is written. The strength of the essay lies in the irony tightened "into a knot" between his pride in his parents and their pride in him and their mutual inability to communicate.

2. "There is no simple roadmap through the heart of the scholarship boy" is not unlike Frost's "The Road Not Taken." By being a scholarship boy, Rodriguez has already deviated from class and familial expectations. He is choosing to go a different way, not a direct route. The road is complicated by family loyalty and class struggle.

3. The "Universality of Shakespeare's appeal" is ironic because it suggests that Shakespeare is accessible to everyone. Perhaps the feelings conveyed in the plays are universal, but for Rodriguez's parents to participate in this discussion and understanding of Shakespeare's universality, they would have had to be far more educated.

4. Rodriguez began hearing "Your parents must be very proud" from age 12. This statement drives the essay and Rodriguez's guilt. The word "pride" (or some form of it) is used nine times in the essay. It is a voice from the past haunting Rodriguez and reminding him of the irony of his conflicting feelings for his parents.

5. As in all centuries but our own, "soft hands" were the sign of a gentleman, and one that didn't have to work for a living. Mr. Rodriguez, mostly a laborer and mostly of the old school, believed that "some great achievement of leisure was implied by [the author's] papers and books." To Mr. Rodriguez, the high-school diploma is "Nice," a tangible sign of accomplishment.

   Perhaps the father, like the son, has contradictory feelings toward his children's education. A "diploma" was a sign of accomplishment, "soft hands" a sign of privilege. He received neither; his son received both.

6. The conclusion of the essay is universal (far more so than Shakespeare). Familial communication has completely broken down. Parents who sacrificed much for their son cannot even hold a conversation with him. This is the final irony of the title; how can his parents be proud of him when they can no longer understand him?

Black Men and Public Space
Brent Staples

TOPICAL CONSIDERATIONS

1. The encounter with the fleeing woman, which happened when he was ten years younger, made Staples realize how as a black man he could "alter public space in ugly ways." In particular, how at night he was indistinguishable from one of the muggers who "occasionally seeped into the area from the surrounding ghetto." The realization, says Staples, "surprised, embarrassed, and dismayed" him "all at once." He adds, "Her flight made me feel like an accomplice in tyranny."

2. In paragraph 2, Staples says that were he to stumble upon somebody armed and threatened, he could easily be shot just for being black. Further on he mentions how he was once mistaken for a burglar in the office of the magazine for which

he wrote. Also, how a jewelry store proprietor feeling the same apprehension brought out her Doberman pinscher only because he was black.

3. Part of his explanation is that he was one of the few "good boys" growing up in a neighborhood of gang warfare, knifings, and murder. He says he chose to be noncombatant and timid as the result of having seen too many young men killed including family members and friends.

4. After his story about another black journalist being mistaken for a murderer, Staple's own smothering of rage seems wise. In paragraph 11, he explains that not doing so "would surely have led to madness."

5. He lists several strategies: giving "wide berth to nervous people on subway platforms," trying not to appear as if he's following people, remaining "calm and extremely congenial" when questioned by police. He also says he has taken to whistling classical tunes to reduce tension of nighttime pedestrians.

6. For the student. This question might generate some lively discussion since some students might argue that Staples goes too far not to intimidate—for example, why should a nonviolent black man have to go out of his way to make others feel at ease with his presence? Others might find his strategies socially responsible. There are still others who might be able to identify with the threat Staples poses, whether they are black or white. A large male, no matter what his race, is aware of the threat he poses to a lone woman walking on a deserted street. Of course, the key issue here is race, and black men are aware of the burden of the urban mugger stereotype.

RHETORICAL CONSIDERATIONS

1. The opening line is provocative. It makes the reader want to go on. Victim is a charged word, yet the woman is simply a victim of Staples's blackness.

2. Staples is trying to delineate the image from which the woman fled—a large, young black man with "a beard and billowing hair" and wearing a military jacket with his hands shoved into the pockets. The image in context of the deserted night streets of affluent, predominantly white Hyde Park at the edge of a black ghetto is menacing particularly, as Staples sadly learns, because he is black.

3. There are some mildly humorous places, mostly ironic in intent. For instance, in paragraph 2 the author says how he is "scarcely able to take a knife to a raw chicken—let alone hold one to a person's throat." Most of the humor resides in the final paragraph in images of him whistling Beethoven and Vivaldi. In particular, the final two lines are amusing in a darkly ironic way.

To Be an All-American Girl

Elizabeth Wong

TOPICAL CONSIDERATIONS

1. The last line of the essay, "Sadly, I still am" (paragraph 15), quietly suggests that Wong regrets her divorce from Chinese culture. The whole essay is filled with childhood memories of the unpleasantries of leftover Chinese culture being

forced on a young American girl. The essay is not at all nostalgic. In her descriptions, she emphasizes the negative; she imagined her Chinese teacher as a "repressed maniacal child killer" (paragraph 3), the Chinese language was "a source of embarrassment" (paragraph 8). Only from the last line can the reader gather that she has learned from her Chinese experiences.

2. In the essay, language is power—and one that separates child from parent and Chinatown from America. The Chinese language is first, "a source of embarrassment." It is also "unbeautiful." Elizabeth believes she will be "thought of as mad, as talking gibberish" (paragraph 9) if she speaks Chinese. The English language is the key out of Chinatown. Measures of success come in odd doses: "'My, doesn't she move her lips fast,' they would say, meaning that I'd be able to keep up with the world outside Chinatown" (paragraph 9).

   Elizabeth's brother and father use the English language to torment and thereby oppress Mrs. Wong. Elizabeth's father "had played a cruel joke on Mom by assigning her an American name that her tongue wouldn't allow her to say" (paragraph 11). Her brother "was especially hard on his mother," and, when he spoke incorrectly, "He'd blame it on her: 'See Mom, it's all your fault. You set a bad example'" (paragraph 10).

3. The grandmother's voice was "loud," "nagging," "rhythmless," "patternless," "quick," and "unbeautiful" (paragraph 8). Elizabeth gets no comfort from this voice because it is the voice of another culture. She has been severed from her grandmother by culture. Her grandmother's voice is threatening; perhaps she represents China and all that is un-American.

4. "Ancient mothballs or dirty closets" (paragraph 4) symbolize old, unwanted things. Wong's preference for "new scents" reflects her need to adopt the culture of America which represents a new language, new customs, new ethnic foods. Her "raunchy" grandmother and "chaotic, frenzied" Chinatown are like old mothballs and dirty closets.

5. Wong cannot simply write, *Sing san ho,* the Chinese for "How are you?" because the alphabets are completely different. The thousands of characters in the Chinese-alphabet make the language incredibly difficult to learn. Writing "the phonetic" emphasizes not only the difference in the alphabets but also symbolizes the difference in culture.

6. Wong's definition of culture involves tracing one's race back to its origins. Her culture is Chinese including its "unbeautiful" language and Chinatown. Though she is beginning to make American culture her own, she does not yet consider it a part of her.

7. Wong's feelings toward Chinese school are cross-cultural. Chinese school is not unlike Hebrew school, or any religious or other afterschool education that cuts out children's play time.

8. There is much rejection in the essay. Throughout the essay Wong rejects her Chinese culture, including even Chinese New Year; her brother rejects the language; and her father rejects his wife's feelings by giving her a name which she cannot pronounce. There is little warmth to the essay because Wong's acceptance of American culture comes at a high price.

RHETORICAL CONSIDERATIONS

1. The reader is not aware that Wong feels any regret about her cultural divorce until the last line of the essay. This is effective because the reader leaves the essay with the one sentiment that she is sad to be "all-American." However, there is no buildup to this statement and little evidence to show that she yearns for any part of Chinese culture.

2. "Pedestrian" and "public" carry negative connotations in the essay. In her childhood Wong held the "lilting romance of French and the gentle refinement of the American South" above the Chinese language. Pedestrian and public are common, crass—like rhythmless, patternless Chinese.

3. Making errors such as "What it is" reveals that English is not a person's native language. Wong's brother's incentive to speak perfect English is not to score well on a test, but to fit into American society.

   For class discussion consider the importance of perfect grammar in one's native language. If foreigners strive to perfect it, should citizens also?

4. A divorce implies there was a marriage. It was not easy to obtain a divorce from Chinese culture because Elizabeth was once married to it. Her marriage ties to China included the language, her family, its history, customs, food, and so on. Once she has abandoned the language and left her family, she still has the memories and her physical appearance to remind her of her roots.

5. Pidgin speech implies that her mother's attempt at English was a mix of Chinese and English, creating a jargon that can convey only the most elementary message. The chop suey analogy suggests that Chinese had spread throughout her English, perhaps overwhelming it. Though damning, the chop suey analogy is an effective one.

What's in a Name?

Itabari Njeri

TOPICAL CONSIDERATIONS

1. For student discussion. You might ask about women who marry keeping their birth-names, hyphenating, or making some other decision about a surname. You might also ask whether any of your students' forebears changed their names (or had their names changed by others) as part of the immigration process, or had their names miscopied by a careless or malicious official. Or you might ask how they would feel if an unmarried sibling, or even a divorcing parent, were to change his or her name so that it became something different from the student's own surname.

2. Njeri details questions from many different kinds of people. People in Greenville "snarl" and mangle the name, with a number of responses having derogatory connotations; these people seem narrow-minded and provincial. Others shorten the name, deciding (against Njeri's wishes) the name is "too

long" to be convenient. Whites hope they're meeting an "exotic," or "smile knowingly" with false understanding, or cringe when Njeri mentions that her name sounds unusual because slavery obliterated African names. These whites come across as naive, smugly liberal, or guilty. Blacks, along with whites, demand her real name, as if the name she has carefully chosen and legally secured is a fake. Some people, like her mother, recalcitrantly insist upon using her real name (Jill) once they've pried it out of her. This range of responses suggests a personality too willing to arbitrate others' reality, and to dismiss whatever does not fit preconceived notions. Njeri would probably pryer a simple acknowledgement of her name as if she'd been introduced as "Mary Smith."

3. Njeri's term *slave name* refers to names imposed on people of African descent by their owners in the New World, people who frequently imposed an arbitrary or cruelly whimsical Anglicized first name on slaves, and their own surnames as a mark of ownership. In paragraph 24, Njeri alludes to illegitimate children—products of rape, concubinage, or consensual unions which could not be legalized under the laws of the time—who took their fathers' names. Chronologically last in her sequence are newly freed slaves who chose names other than ones imposed by former masters. (Njeri's comment that their choices were motivated by a wish to assimilate sounds a bit like an accusation, and may not be entirely historically accurate.) Njeri considers all English-language names to be products in one way or another of slavery; without the dynamics of this peculiar institution, African peoples would have retained African names.

4. The only synonym for "people of African descent living in the United States" Njeri seems to dislike is "Negro," given the context of its use in paragraph 9. She presents the rest of the terms as roughly interchangeable, with minor shadings of meaning she alludes to in paragraph 36, but doesn't explain. Njeri uses Sterling Stuckey's comments about pan-Africanism (a philosophy which understands that the political, cultural and economic well-being of peoples of African descent everywhere are linked) as a springboard into her most important point in this discussion. That is, African-Americans should be seen as an ethnic group, with rich, valuable cultural resources which have considerably enriched the United States. To see people as a color is merely to observe outward physiological distinctions. To see people as a race is merely to accept quasi-scientific nomenclature based on superficial differences observed by the label-imposing group. (More familiar to most white Americans might be the egregious errors of lumping Chinese, Japanese, and Korean people into a single racial category *Oriental,* or of insisting that people of Mexican and Puerto Rican descent are both *Hispanic.*

5. Africans are as prejudiced as white Americans because they have access to images of African-American people through the same media distortions as white Americans. A Kenyan man's marriage is scratched when his mother protests the bride is a "low-down, ignorant, drug-dealing, murderous" (paragraph 46) African-American. A Tanzanian chides Njeri that her name doesn't or shouldn't belong to her. Africans observing her light skin see a mongrel, and assume that she will have something in common with local "half-castes"—and even the lat-

ter group looks down on her. (Paragraphs 53 and 54 might help students who had problems with race as a pseudo-scientific concept. Her "racial" category is black in the United States, but white in Tanzania.) Njeri's responses run from annoyance to delight, although she's well prepared for the range of responses through her African studies minor in college. Only being called a "white woman" catches her completely off guard.

RHETORICAL CONSIDERATIONS

1. Njeri comes close to discussing her motivations in paragraphs 15 and 16, with the discussion of slave names; the peer pressure of black nationalism in paragraph 21; and the detail that her name is Kikuyu in paragraph 47. However, she does not offer an extended rationale of her own choice, but rather focuses on reactions. One effect is to invest her decision with dignity; she holds the reader at arm's length, out of intimacy range. Another effect is to focus attention on the very real effect that her name has (and by extension, the effect of names for people of African descent). The issue of naming provides Njeri an opportunity to discuss and educate on much broader issues, such as entertainment-media images of black people, race and racial designation, and the African diaspora.

2. The question posed in paragraph 26 comes closest to a thesis: "The loss of our African culture . . . poses a profound [conflict] that has divided blacks many times since Emancipation: do we accept the loss and assimilate totally or do we try to reclaim our culture and synthesize it with our present reality?" To some extent, Njeri answers this question with novelist Trey Ellis's praise for syncretic African-American culture in paragraph 28, and again in paragraph 38 with references to transformation as an enriching interchange between disparate cultures. She does not wish to assimilate, but to synthesize. The thesis has little to do with names and naming, except tangentially, or as a vehicle. It's an effective strategy for crafting an issue fraught with psychological and scholarly weight into something manageable, even pleasantly amusing to read.

3. Njeri's meditation on the history of surnames in paragraphs 22 and 23 forms the bridge between her own personal choice and the larger question of what a group of people shall be called. The two issues are, of course, related in a number of ways. For example, both are legacies of slavery and the diaspora (the forcible dispersion of a people from their homeland). Both involve conscious, deliberate efforts at self-determination. Both assume that specific names resonate with connotations, which shape the way people are perceived by others, and the way they feel about themselves. Njeri's strategy is an effective counter to the most common objections against either kind of naming.

4. Her choice at first glance needs no extrinsic justification; she's defined the scope of her essay. Nor, one assumes, does she want to become caught up in comparative oppression. She consistently focuses on a feature of the black experience that distinguishes it from that of any other group in the so-called American melting pot: slavery and natal alienation.

5. The final anecdote is a light-hearted echo of the recalcitrant Americans' insistence on trying to shorten Njeri's name (paragraph 5). In terms of formal structure, it brings the article full circle, creating closure with a sort of rhetorical shrug—"the more things change, the more they stay the same." This device also echoes Njeri's sensibility that Africa is "the motherland" (paragraph 54). That is, despite her college-minor wisdom, and the historical dissociation of African-Americans from a completely African identity, the visit to Africa seems to carry the psychological weight of a return for Njeri. Thematically, the anecdote reinforces the alienation that pulses through the article; as an African-American, Njeri suggests that she can never quite be "at home" anywhere in the world.

Taking a Stand

America: The Multinational Society
Ishmael Reed

TOPICAL CONSIDERATIONS

1. At the beginning of paragraph 5, Reed states his thesis: "Such blurring of cultural styles occurs in everyday life in the United States to a greater extent than anyone can imagine and is probably more prevalent than the sensational conflict between people of different backgrounds that is played up and often encouraged by the media." Reed proves this statement with anecdotes (visiting an African-American seminar conducted by a white professor, noting Dallas's bilingual airport), by uncovering history (Benjamin Franklin's being influenced by Iroquois government, the cubists' and surrealists' derivation from African and Native American art, the not-so-pure Puritans), and an appeal to authority (Yale professors). The essay, which pushes its agenda evenly, is a fine teaching tool for composition studies. The piece proves its thesis thoroughly, holds the reader's interest, at the same time it is objective and intellectually appealing. Also, it is a rare positive piece that deemphasizes cultural conflict and shows America emerging as a truly multicultural society.

2. "Cultural bouillabaisse" suggests America at its best. Superior to the older term "melting pot," this label projects multiculturalism that subsumes bilingualism, ethnic foods, a McDonald's with African art on the wall, and outcasts from "monocultural intellectual circles" (paragraph 3). The term also transcends the more exclusionary "Western civilization" which denies the past and continuing contribution of African, Native American, Middle Eastern, and Asian cultures on the "vaguely defined entity" (paragraph 5).

3. Art shows how Western, Eastern, and African cultures are inextricably bound. Reed cites "late nineteenth- and twentieth-century French paintings" that were "influenced by Japanese art"; the "cubists, through whom the influence of

African art changed modern art"; the surrealists who were moved by the Pacific Northwest Indians (paragraph 5). Additionally, he mentions Beethoven's inclusion of Turkish marches in his Ninth Symphony and the paintings of African mythological symbols in a Milwaukee McDonald's (paragraph 4). All these citations lend validity to his argument, for by revealing objective influences of what is considered "Western art," Reed demonstrates the need for redefinition.

4. Reed's definition of *monoculturalist* can be gleaned from his description of Hitler: "for wasn't Adolf Hitler the archetypal monoculturalist who, in his pigheaded arrogance, believed that one way and one blood was so pure that it had to be protected from alien strains at all costs" (paragraph 8). A monoculturalist, then, is one who desires a society of a single culture alone. Monoculturalists, for instance, would deny as unfit the influence of African cultures upon those of the Americas. From the essay one gathers that monoculturalism is prevalent in American society; presidents of universities, television networks, and school teachers preach its monodoctrine (paragraphs 12–13). However, Reed sees multiculturalism as a powerful force. Deciding whether multiculturalism or monoculturalism shapes America in the nineties is a subject for class discussion.

5. The "street level scribbles" in paragraph 8 include "White Power," "Niggers and Spics Suck," and "Hitler was a prophet." Thematically, the three suggest the continuation of white supremacy as a belief. Textually, they are more damaging. Graffiti, or "street scribbles," are texts for the masses. Because they are public documents, their existence suggests a wide acceptance. They are doubly effective because their message is damaging as is the physical marring of property. Also, because graffiti is public, in the open, it reaches a far broader audience than text between the covers of a book.

6. In paragraph 9, Reed deflates American schoolbooks' definition that the founding of America occurred because of the Puritans, frequently considered "a 'hardy band' of no-nonsense patriarchs whose discipline razed the forest and brought order to the New World." Reed builds up his argument by introducing the Puritans in their ideal history book image: "industrious, responsible," with plenty of "Yankee ingenuity." Then he undercuts the definition with understated sarcasm: "They worshipped in churches whose colors blended in with the New England snow"—that is, white churches, white people, maybe even a white God.

Reed begins paragraph 10 subtly: "The Puritans were daring people, but they had a mean streak." The descriptions of Puritans' murdering children, hating Christmas, exacting cruel punishment is shocking. They also reveal the extent to which American school children have been exposed only to the white side of the story. Once again Reed demonstrates that though America has a multicultural makeup, education about America's multiculturalism is slanted.

Students can discuss the schoolbook concept of the discovery of the New World in light of Reed's and the other essays in this chapter. Also, how to find truth in history, and whether the term *historical fact* is an oxymoron.

7. Reed envisions a North America that is neither "humdrum" nor "homogeneous" (paragraph 14). He wants a continent with people who are not "bereft of imagi-

nation" or "of culture." He doesn't want a world that has "all brains and no heart, no fiction, no poetry." In short, Reed wants North America "to become a place where the cultures of the world crisscross." Reed subtly warns against monoculturalism. His description of a homogeneous people without imagination is a haunting reminder of Hitler's Germany.

RHETORICAL CONSIDERATIONS

1. The "Elect" comes from early American Protestants' belief that certain people were chosen by God for eternal life, and certain people were not. The "Elect" suggests the "privileged" in society. In the seventeenth century, the Elect were white Anglo-Saxon Protestants; in the twentieth century, they are also white Anglo-Saxon Protestants.

2. Without knowing Reed's background, the thoroughness of his prose marks him an authority. He attends seminars, interviews people, researches art history and American history, and includes the voices of teachers, television networks, politicians, poets, and McDonald's managers, thereby covering a wide spectrum of American society. Reed presents the voices of people who disagree with him as well as evidence that agrees with him.

3. The essay proves that the "world is here" through its mention of North America today and the international strands that helped shaped it. The essay's thesis (first sentence of paragraph 5) is quite effective, as are the historical revelations. The imagery of the cultural bouillabaisse is woven throughout the essay beginning with the epigraph. The only spot of the essay that is ineffective is the last sentence of paragraph 12: "A modern up-tempo state of complex rhythms that depends upon contacts with an international community can no longer behave as if it dwelled in a 'Zion Wilderness' surrounded by beasts and pagans." While clever and complex, the sentence seems an abrupt rebuttal to the two preceding statements and gets lost at the tail end of the paragraph.

4. The places Reed mentions include a college seminar, a McDonald's restaurant, the Islamic section of Detroit, a snow white church and a humdrum homogeneous world. Reed juxtaposes the church (a monocultural place of the past), the threat of a monocultural future, with the vibrancy of the present's multiculturalism. Reed demonstrates that multiculturalism is pervasive, healthy, and necessary for a North American destiny. Reed mentions these places by name so the reader can identify with them and recognize their multiculturalism.

The Cult of Ethnicity, Good and Bad
Arthur M. Schlesinger, Jr.

TOPICAL CONSIDERATIONS

1. To Schlesinger *race* seems to connote slightly more noticeable differences between peoples than *ethnicity.* (Indeed, the quote from Crèvecoeur in paragraph 5 uses *race* to refer to European groups we would now barely recognize as distin-

guishable ethnicities.) As an aggregate, *race-ethnicity* refers to distinctions based on (geographical) origin, language, and religion. *Diversity* means the mixing of peoples—the voluntary, peaceable coexistence of two or more different racial or ethnic groups within a single geopolitical unit.

2. In the beginning of his article, Schlesinger sees mobility as part and parcel of human nature. Its effects are greatly augmented by modern technology since people today can move with relatively less inconvenience and danger, than ever before. In paragraphs 5 and 6, Schlesinger cites immigrants attracted by the promise and bounty of a new world. In paragraphs 7 and 8, he gestures toward groups whose opportunities were limited by racism and prejudice. Finally, he identifies education as a cause of ethnic diversity.

3. Schlesinger begins supporting his claim that the United States is "a multiethnic country" with quotes from eighteenth-century writer Hector St. John de Crèvecoeur and George Washington. Both stress intermixture and a leveling of differences as the way that the United States was to create or attain a culture of its own, distinct from its status as a colony of Britain. Israel Zangwill's 1908 play finally coined the analogy of the United States to a "melting pot." Yet multiethnic is an ideal and a goal for Schlesinger only as a starting point, and not a final result. As exhilarating and gratifying as differences can be, the goal of all immigrants must be to assimilate: to lose their ethnic distinctiveness, and become more like all other Americans. It is desirable that a multiethnic country, then, be one in which people of all ethnicities have become more like one another than they are like their country (or ethnic-racial heritage) of origin. This is how Americans have "succeeded in pulling off this almost unprecedented trick" (paragraph 4), the trick of avoiding the murderous ethnic unrest that plagues so much of the rest of the world.

4. A *cult* is a religious group, numerically a minority; the term carries additional connotations of members' adhering to beliefs or worship practices considered unusual, bizarre, or dangerous. The cult of ethnicity began, according to Schlesinger, at the beginning of the twentieth century when non-Anglo whites and nonwhite minorities had attained sufficient critical mass, because of changes in immigration laws, to begin demanding recognition and rights. Initially, the results were positive. Schlesinger admits that their lack of earlier recognition was shameful, particularly in light of achievements. A second positive result was that Americans, particularly those of European stock, were forced to relinquish provincial, isolationist attitudes. However, we've taken a good thing too far today. The cult of ethnicity encourages individuals to look to their own ethnic and racial groups as having "inviolable" boundaries—as self-contained units of interest, all but guaranteed to develop at some point an agenda that conflicts with the nationwide interest of America.

5. At the end of paragraph 6, Schlesinger observes that "no institution was more potent . . . than the American public school" in helping forge a sense of national unity and identity by teaching immigrant children the common language, cus-

toms, political rights and responsibilities, and values. However, Schlesinger says that well-meaning but wrong-headed people have derailed this venerable historical function by "promoting, celebrating, and perpetuating separate ethnic origins and identities" (paragraph 9). The results can only be growing fragmentation and hostility. The basic problem is that students are made to feel they have more in common with their own ethnic or racial group than with the nation as a whole. One contributing problem is that the curriculum has warped into therapy sessions, with students being given feel-good fairy tales, whittled out of the national identity, based on each student's own ethnicity. A second contributing problem is that European culture, which forms the base for American culture (according to Schlesinger, the "unique source" of our highest ideas), has been vilified to the extent that nobody would want to admit a European intellectual heritage. The big problem with such multiculturalism, says Schlesinger, is in the public schools. Colleges and universities seem to have far less impact in Schlesinger's opinion, presumably because those attending do so voluntarily, are already adults capable of thinking for themselves, and will probably be exposed to several competing versions rather than a single authoritative lesson plan.

6. Open for discussion.
7. Schlesinger seems to follow Crèvecoeur in the statement that "all nations are melted into a new race [or ethnicity, in modern parlance] of men" (paragraph 5). Americans comprise an ethnicity unto themselves in that they are different from any other people in the world. As new immigrants continue to join us, the newcomers will undoubtedly transform us in ways suggested by paragraph 8; but only newcomers should highlight or promote or retain their own sensibility of "difference." Students who have traveled in groups that Americans consider "integrated" to a completely different area of the world will probably understand this.

RHETORICAL CONSIDERATIONS

1. The first section (paragraphs 1–4) provides a world overview of diversity. Schlesinger's long list of countries in paragraph 3 suggests the universality of his subject; it also reinforces his claim that the United States is unique in its relative tranquility. The second section (paragraphs 5–8) focuses on U.S. history. Schlesinger establishes that the country has been diverse from its inception, and that public figures have endorsed diversity as a strength. However he makes clean that some groups were not fully embraced by the melting pot at first. Finally, Schlesinger points out how we have gone astray from the original vision. Particularly through education, we are promoting a divisive agenda rather than one that unifies the nation, a step backward from an almost-accomplished ideal, if interethnic marriages are an indicator.

The shape of the essay as a whole is an inverted triangle. His thesis is best captured in the final sentence. In each section, Schlesinger discusses a progressively narrower scope of location and chronology; each section serves as backdrop to the next. This strategy allows him to build reader consensus for an argument that may be considered reactionary. He keeps readers in agreement with broad, innocuous statements as long as possible, hoping the momentum will carry readers through less fashionable parts of the argument. Had he begun with a thesis that is bound to set some readers' teeth on edge, his tone might have been more defensive; he might feel obliged to fend off objections before he has had a chance to make his case.

2. Whether students perceive the article as rife with generalizations will probably depend on their grounding in history. His list of countries experiencing ethnic troubles, for example, assumes that readers are up on current events, as well as the major ethnic groups and their histories in each nation. Paragraphs 7 and 8 make gestures toward nineteenth and early twentieth century American history, and assumes that readers know exactly how black, yellow, red, and brown Americans were "put . . . outside the pale." He assumes that readers know what Afrocentrism is.

   Broad, abstract statements are meaningless unless there is a compact of understanding between author and reader for each word. On the one hand, Schlesinger writes with admirable economy, and he writes specifically for a well-educated reader. He is not really interested in providing a history lesson but in making an argument. To spell out every gesture would add cumbersome detail. On the other hand, his very breadth of language allows him some questionable assumptions. For example, George Washington's use of the verb *assimilate*, (paragraph 6), is quite different from Schlesinger's own use of the noun form *assimilation* in paragraph 9. The former means to become habituated to, familiar with; the latter means to internalize mainstream standards and judgments as a replacement for a foreign, ethnic identity.

3. Schlesinger's "ethnic" and Reed's "national" are pretty much synonyms, but despite their roughly interchangeable terminology, each author means something completely different. Schlesinger promotes assimilation, integration, the melting pot, and an "American nationality . . . inescapably English in language, ideas, and institutions" (paragraph 7). Reed, on the other hand, does not see the infrastructural base of U.S. culture remaining so identifiably monolithic, nor does he see that as a desirable goal. Where Schlesinger sees change by a simple process of addition to and subtraction from Anglo institutions, Reed sees a far more radical transformation more amenable to comparisons with alchemy. Schlesinger would seem to be addressing Reed's complaints directly in paragraph 8, when he says that the "achievements" of "non-Anglo whites and . . . nonwhite minorities" were shamefully neglected. Again, the two authors' terms are analogous, but their meanings completely different. By *achievements*, Schlesinger probably means inventions or contributions that took place after a group was nominally assimilated into Anglo-based culture, and measurable by Anglo cultural standards. Reed, on the other hand, looks to a culture's preexisting art, music, politics, and so on for contributions. Despite some surface use of similar language, the two would probably agree on very little.

Come, Let Me Offend You

Eve Drobot

TOPICAL CONSIDERATIONS

1. Drobot mentions a handful of potentially lethal discussion topics and terms. A "raging vegetarian" could be offended by someone waxing rhapsodic over a recent veal dinner. A Muslim who believes that Salman Rushdie deserves to die for his *The Satanic Verses* (which is either satiric or blasphemous, depending on your politics) could disagree with civil-libertarian views on censorship. A lesbian might be offended by a heterosexual joke. And the hypothetical environmentalist can't participate in that time-honored Geneva of small-talk, the weather, without raving on about hairspray.

   It's possible Drobot has had one such experience, but scarcely likely that these are all real anecdotes, much less typical. They're exaggerations in the proactive vehemence of the person supposedly offended. Probably a more typical response would be for the offended person to change the subject, or fail to laugh heartily, or make a less aggressive bow out of that particular topic.

2. The expression comes from "wearing your heart on your sleeve," an indicator that the state of one's romantic entanglements is unusually obvious through words or gestures. The connotation is that the individual so-described is vulgarly pursuing some hapless object of affection, or tastelessly making loud laments about his or her lovelorn status. Drobot has generalized the meaning to suggest that we all make our sensitivities blatantly visible in a system of pins or badges. She points to the precedent of Christians wearing crosses, and Jews either a Star of David or Hebrew letter, and suggests a system of icons with examples including sexual orientation, details about family of origin, religion, and musicality.

3. Of course, half the humor of this article is that most of us, even in this abbreviated list, couldn't wear just one, nor do the symbols have unambiguous meanings. The broccoli stickpin could just as easily represent anti–George Bush politics (Bush loathed broccoli); most pagans do not worship golden calves; the historically correct symbol for lesbians, since Drobot refers to their origin in Nazi Germany, would be a black triangle rather than a pink one; and the bunny head could just as easily refer to a zero-population advocacy group as an animal rights sensibility. If you have time, you might invite students to list (if not draw) an assortment of icons—and how they'll affix them so they're legible.

4. The poetry editor submitted selections without stopping to consider that the publisher wanted to include representatives of various groups—"gays, third-generation Americans, Native Americans, refugees, Young Republicans, and those who use wheelchairs." In other words, the editor was asked to affix the appropriate stickers to each poem before his selection would pass muster with the publisher. While Drobot doesn't explicitly mention it, one thing wrong with this scenario is that the publisher did not communicate the request initially. Drobot does remind us, however, of a goal that she says used to be commonly held, and

which most of us still probably believe in: that the quality of poetry isn't determined by identity politics. Taking pains to represent each group isn't, according to Drobot, going to result in an anthology that contains higher-quality poetry. In fact, she implies, the quota system may force out some perfectly wonderful poetry just because the poet's identity is overrepresented elsewhere, to make room for lesser-quality poetry by an author whose group isn't adequately represented.

5. No, Drobot doesn't think insulting people is okay. In paragraph 4, she emphatically understands, and applauds, taboos on racist and sexist jokes (although she's willing to flirt with this taboo by turning the tables on the usual connotation of the word "sexist," by starting a joke that one feminist might tell another). In paragraph 12, her statement of principle for this article highlights a desire to see the world transformed so that discrimination is eliminated. And finally, in the last paragraph, she briefly mentions the similarity of her own playful suggestion that people wear identifying icons to Hitler's labeling people in order to exterminate them; racial prejudice is inexcusable.

6. Open for discussion, though I think she protesteth too much.

RHETORICAL CONSIDERATIONS

1. A few surface similarities exist behind the people Drobot mentions: They're all people whose hypersensitivities aren't immediately visible. These people are likely to turn up anywhere, in any group—it's impossible to tell, for example, whether the vegetarian is a surfing instructor, a truck driver, or an accountant. (On second thought, probably none work in a pork sausage factory.) All hold minority viewpoints, views which a statistical majority of Americans don't agree with. But probably a more important reason Drobot assembled this list, rather than another, is that all these minority stances are considered popular or chic. They all have a certain glamour, or have recently enjoyed 15 minutes of fame in a national news broadcast or two as the "human interest" spot. As her apology for being a "Pollyanna" in paragraph 12 suggests, Drobot isn't critiquing people for sensitivity at real slights or insults with genuine malice behind them. Rather, she's exasperated that people have let their sense of dignity become so overdetermined by media hype and trendiness. And politically speaking, these groups unanimously espouse a liberal sensibility.

2. Drobot inserts an exception to the taboo on sexist jokes, hypothesizing that if she and the reader (the "you" addressed throughout) discover they are both feminists, then it's okay to make jokes about men. Presumably her second feminist shares the view that men are not a particularly endangered or dumped-on species. The two women have sufficient knowledge about each other to assure that neither will be offended by this joke. Her point is that the potential for insult is to some degree relative to the identities of the people sharing the comment. Drobot uses this opportunity to heighten the sense of absurdity throughout her article, by momentarily assuming the role of a stand-up comic. By framing the anecdote in the subjunctive, and further distancing it with parentheses, her argument is not muddied.

3. Drobot probably doesn't believe that the world can be made perfect, although she seems to believe that the goal is worth continued striving for. That she does have high ideals makes her opinion more credible; she's not just carping about something that grates on her nerves personally, but sees hypersensitivity as an obstacle to improvements worth making. It doesn't seem likely that we'll be able to stop running afoul of each other's sensitivities. Still, just what is the correct, centrist position is hard to determine. The Muslim who believes that Rushdie's novel was blasphemous operates from a position that is fundamentally different from American belief that religious principles should have very little to do with civil law. The ethics of the vegetarian do not accord with majority notions that the ontological status of beings on the food chain is rigidly compartmentalized. In a diverse culture, where there is likely to be so little consensus on basic principles, it's difficult to imagine that an insult-free world can exist. The best we can hope for is more thoughtful responses than gritted teeth, grinding halts, and deliberately embarrassing pauses in conversation.

4. Despite the whimsical language about an "insane fellow with a ridiculous mustache," Drobot's parting shot is sobering. Most of the rest of her article focuses on inconsequential kinds of insult, clashes that don't have nearly this potential for harm. One effect of this closing is that Drobot takes her tongue out of cheek momentarily, urging readers not to confuse the trivial kinds of insults and bickering she describes with real hatred. Inconsequential, trendy identity politics and their discontents can keep us from tackling real problems like Hitler.

   This reference seems to bring to a point the undertone throughout her article, "haven't these people got anything better to do?" In addition, it keeps readers from taking seriously her suggestion about clusters of symbols. If we go on making sharp us-and-them divisions among ourselves, we're setting ourselves up for even greater antagonism and scapegoating. Finally, Drobot seems to suggest that as human beings we're more than just a single quality, or a single group's member. If her proliferation of little badges didn't make that clear enough, then reference to Hitler might. To flatten an individual's whole worth and range of potential into a single category, or even a handful of categories, is the ultimate insult.

5. From its title onward, Drobot assumes that she is talking to an individual reader. She addresses that reader as *you* in asides—for example, the tag question "you see?" She also words transitions between ideas to sound as if she is thinking off-the-cuff, so the new idea seems like a spontaneous, tangential veer from the main subject—just as informal conversations leap around spontaneously with a more amorphous shape than the academic essay.

   Her rhetorical questions not only prompt the reader to think, or provide information in the guise of a question, but also sound as if she's genuinely asking readers to hold up their end of the conversation by responding. Finally, she backtracks, apologizes, and adds the kind of conversational responses to a listener's body language or facial expression: "God forbid, I tell a good, old-fashioned heterosexual joke . . . " (paragraph 2); "Now, I realize I am probably dating myself . . . " (paragraph 12).

One effect of Drobot's style is to keep her argument breezy and non-serious. She seems to want readers to lighten up, and gives us an example in her playful, almost self-mocking style. She also establishes intimacy with the conversational tone. Because she builds a rapport with readers by playing the role of a loquacious friend, it's less likely that any of her comments will insult readers' sensitivities.

Why I Dread Black History Month
Wayne M. Joseph

TOPICAL CONSIDERATIONS

1. Black History Month is "a national observance" celebrated in February, in which the history, achievements, cultural contributions, and "firsts" of African-Americans are made visible through school programs, media offerings, and public events. Celebrations emphasize pride in African heritage though they tend to spotlight high-profile celebrities such as Martin Luther King and sometimes feel a bit frenetic. Student involvement in activities will probably vary, as may their responses to events. As Joseph's tone suggests, not all organizers' approaches are completely successful at bringing creative inspiration to bear year after year. Yet not all Black History Month celebrations are moribund lesson plans and mealy-mouthed recitations about "greatness" as Joseph suggests.

2. First, it's impossible to cram all of the contributions of black people into four weeks. Any attempt to do so must necessarily trivialize, because it must take procrustean measures to oversimplify. Second, having a separate month in which black history is discussed tends to isolate black history and its American context; "both" histories will inevitably suffer. To write a history of the Civil War and its aftermath without discussing its single most important issue—slavery, emancipation, and provisions for assisting newly freed slaves—is an exercise in absurdity. To discuss the development of an autonomous, vibrant American culture without any reference to black people's contributions is also absurd. Third and finally, black history celebrations in America should focus on black Americans—not on Africans. Black Americans were radically transformed by the middle passage (literally, the route slave ships took through the mid-Atlantic; figuratively, the emotionally wrenching dislocation from all familiar cultural institutions). The heroism, courage, and perseverance of everyday black individuals in America is far more accessible and pertinent to all Americans' sense of history than distant historic superstars.

3. Joseph says that Black History Month's superficial, hackneyed programs cannot "fill that void" in a black child who is looking for a sense of identity and self-worth. The history of family members will provide a much more satisfying set of precedents and role models, probably because they are more demonstrably "like" the child than the distant celebrities, whose personal circumstances and background may be very different from the child's own (except for the variable

of race). Black people are not cookie-cutter replicas of each other. Furthermore, emphasis on family members provides attainable models for success, by stressing everyday responses and values in response to everyday challenges—rather than the outstanding accomplishments of extraordinary people. Your students' sense of how much inspiration they get from relatives may vary, especially if they are college-age students who are still struggling to differentiate themselves from their parents.

4. Joseph believes that in a multicultural society, people's achievements should not earn "more or less recognition based solely on heritage." It's true that black Americans have had a hard time gaining access to fields and positions that our nation finds especially prestigious. But if we think of ourselves as a multicultural society, then it's inappropriate to single out someone only because of race. Quite likely, then, Joseph takes a dim view of fanfare for Bessie Coleman or Thurgood Marshall simply because they are black. Of course, nothing Joseph has said implies that their courage or integrity should be ignored, or that their contributions to aviation and law should be slighted. Rather, he would want their personal qualities and triumphs to be recorded alongside those of Charles Lindbergh and Benjamin Franklin—who of course are not singled out for their whiteness, but for their accomplishments.

5. Joseph complains that the limitations imposed by a single month are insulting because it makes of black history a momentary spectacle rather than an ongoing process. If students have a difficult time understanding this, you might offer as an analogy the allegation that some people are Sunday-only or Christmas-and-Easter-only Christians—that is, they are reverential and kind only on designated cue. Joseph's suggested alternative: "Celebrate the contributions of *all* Americans *every* month of the school year." Joseph is clearly a man with high levels of idealism and energy. His school no doubt thrives under his attentive, thoughtful principalship. But a lazy, or overworked, or even bigoted principal in another school could create a very different kind of atmosphere. Do we need an institutionalized month to circumvent the vagaries of personal character?

RHETORICAL CONSIDERATIONS

1. Joseph's language hums with sarcasm in the first two paragraphs. He uses hyperbole when he says he is "overcome with a feeling of dread" as February approaches, and when he presents his thesis as his "humble estimation." Calling Black History Month a "thriving monument to tokenism" is a damning stroke; by implication, those misguided African-Americans who embrace it are handkerchief-headed fools lauding their own denigration. He offers a pileup of media tributes (PBS specials, newspaper "special sections," radio features, performing and visual arts offerings); his verb suggests aggressive violence. Teachers who "dust off last year's lesson plans" have put together a dog-and-pony show they perform year after year; attendees who wear African garb and speak Swahili appear affected and ditsy rather than noble and proud.

2. Joseph's examples of the Civil War and Reconstruction, American music and dance, and American culture generally all see American history as deficient without a discussion of black people's contributions. His examples show a one-way movement: Black contributions to mainstream America. Of course, cultural synthesis was and is a two-way street, but white influences on black culture have been historically exaggerated. Until the 1940s, it was widely accepted that Africans came to the new world as cultural blanks, ready and willing to have an American cultural identity inscribed upon them. Black history—whether taught year-round, or only in February—insists upon black people as active shapers and doers in history, acting from a preexisting cultural base, rather than passive recipients of their first dose of "real" culture through the unfortunate mechanism of the slave trade. But unless black people are shown acting in a broader context, instead of in a vacuum, they might as well be portrayed as passive recipients.

   Joseph is writing for an audience of all races and ethnicities. Hence he needs to make black history an issue that is important to everyone. If he shows that all history is damaged, deficient, distorted when information about black Americans is omitted, then he has established an adequately broad scope. If he focuses on ways that the history of black people only has been misshapen, then he risks losing some of his audience who don't think it's all that important.

3. Joseph's suggestions that children talk about their own family members, and that black people's contributions to American history be celebrated year-round are crucial parts of his argument. If his article were to end with paragraph 7, then he could be misunderstood as saying that black people don't have anything to celebrate, or at least don't have enough to fill up an entire month. He has observed the repetition and superficiality of some Black History Month offerings, and has at this point done little to show what's lacking to round out the picture. In short, he has dwelled on the negative. And his audience is probably pretty depressed or angry by this point. In paragraph 8, however, he sets about regaining readers' faith by offering them some solutions to the problems he has catalogued. Black people do have heroism and courage and accomplishments to celebrate. They have strong families and a vibrant role in the whole of American's hopes and dreams, none of which should be denied or covered up. It's the showcase that's all wrong—not the talent. By allowing his argument to sink to its nadir at midpoint, and then pulling it back up out of a nosedive, Joseph has taken a big risk. Readers could get disgusted at midpoint and quit reading. However, because the piece is relatively short and energetic, it's unlikely they'll do so.

4. Joseph's use of the passive voice is echoed in the judgment that this treatment is "condescending," and in the second passive construction, "the past of black Americans is handled. . . ." Arrogance is implied by the word condescending; and great power is apparent in the celebrants demeaningly awaiting permission. Just as Joseph believes that history is an important determinant of our future, he believes that it is our responsibility as citizens to decide what's in that history. Joseph might also be disguising a stance that readers might find too bitter, indeed seems on the verge of erupting here and elsewhere in his article. That is,

his language comes close to suggesting that the encapsulation and trivialization of black Americans' history in the institution of Black History Month is not completely accidental. What better way to weaken a people and their resolve than to bore everyone to tears with this endless rehash of "Dr. King, Malcolm X, Jackie Robinson, et al." (paragraph 8)?

5. Joseph might have made one or two more references to multiculturalism elsewhere, although his references seem sincere rather than gratuitous. He might, for example, have mentioned that other minority groups have contributed to American history in paragraph 5 (since his carefully quote-marked "'American' history" seems to refer exclusively to material focusing on white people). Likewise, he might have diversified his list in paragraph 7 beyond German, Italian, and Jewish immigrants. However, his reference to a multicultural society in paragraph 10 suggests that his revisionist history would include more groups than black and white. His reference to all Americans in the final line assures us that he does not understand black history's relationship to the rest of American history as an isolated problem. In fact, it tangentially raises the spectre of what would happen if many other minority groups were to demand equitable treatment. Given that March is already Women's History Month, and the school year is only nine, maybe ten months long, we would run out of months very quickly if we tried to partition out the calendar.

Race Matters
Cornel West

TOPICAL CONSIDERATIONS

1. West says the riots were neither "race riots" nor "class rebellion." Instead, West calls the events in Los Angeles a "display of justified social rage" at the inability of Americans and their national leaders to discuss complex intersections of race, economics, culture, and politics. He says that race may be the symptom, or the scapegoat, but its role has been far overestimated. As evidence of this claim, West notes that the events in Los Angales disappeared far too quickly from public forums; once "our truncated public discussions of race" had been aired, we were too scared or too paralyzed to grapple with the real, underlying issues.

2. To West, a liberal is someone who believes that "more government programs can solve racial problems." By throwing money at such problems, liberals relieve their guilty consciences. However, their solution elides constructive criticism and expectations of personal responsibility from black people. Conservatives, on the other hand, are behavioralists and moralists. They blame black men for shortcomings in willpower and moral integrity, conveniently ignoring the immorality of the social structure that promotes and even rewards destructive behavior. Conservatives blame the victim; based on that blame, they deny assistance because the victim is either not worthy or is incapable of benefiting. In sum, liberals focus only on structure, ignoring the individual; conservatives focus only on the individual, ignoring the structure.

3. West says liberals and conservatives both view black people as "problems" to be solved, rather than as people human beings who are integral to both the polity and the welfare of the nation as a whole. Liberals want black people "to be 'included' and 'integrated' into 'our' society and culture" (paragraph 6)—as if black people began from an outsider status in the first place. Liberals implicitly believe that black people can learn to behave appropriately if they are provided with sufficient resources to change their deficient beliefs, values, and lifestyles. Conservatives demand that blacks be "'well behaved' and 'worthy of acceptance'" before they are admitted to "'our' way of life." Like liberals, they arrogate unto themselves the privilege of defining what our way of life is, acting as gatekeepers. Unlike liberals, they expect black people to change their deficient lifestyles voluntarily, with no assistance, as an assay of worthiness.

4. Black nationalism, according to West, is a response against this pressure to conform to a set of standards black people had no hand in shaping. It will thrive as long as race continues to play a significant role in the way that Americans are treated by legal, economic, media, and popular opinion systems. West does not dismiss *all* black nationalism, nor does he dismiss it as inherently wrong or flawed. In fact, Afrocentrism is "gallant" because it insists that black "doings and sufferings" be central to discussions about black people. But his sense that it "thrives" under adverse conditions makes much of it seem a defensive, secondhand posture rather than a perspective possessed of freestanding integrity. More openly, he criticizes Afrocentrism as silent or retrograde on any issue except race—including class, feminism, sexuality, and multiculturalism. West approves of black nationalism which does not hobble itself with narrow-minded constraints to coalition-building, but he doesn't see it as a complete answer to America's racial problems either.

5. Factors aren't as discrete as the list mentioned in the Topical Considerations suggests, hence the material students include under each category may vary slightly. (a) Economics: Part of the rage vented in the L.A. riots was despair created by the "'silent' depression." Although dollar amounts and inflation rates can be jostled around to prove almost anything, most Americans can purchase 20 percent less than they could 20 years ago with the wages they earn. Furthermore, this is an average; "wealth has been upwardly distributed," so low-wage earners' purchasing power has fallen even more sharply. (b) Class: Many white Americans have ensconced themselves in the suburbs, at the same time that their organized political clout controls policies within cities. Populations and labor markets have shifted to such an extent that the affluent residents and businesses that used to pay the lion's share of city taxes have fled. But while the tax base shrinks, demand for programs and services increases. With less money spread ever more thinly, the result can only be "unemployment, hunger, homelessness, and sickness for millions." (c) Politics: At a micro level, black people are not treated equitably by law enforcement or legal systems. At a macro level, politicians spend most of their time fund raising to win elections with platforms based on will-o'-the-wisp images rather than on conscientious debate.

6. Spiritual: People are disconnected from one another, and from family and small-community bonds that can provide a sense of meaning and stability in a healthy life, and can be a resource for emotional support in times of trouble. Cultural: People do not have a sense of connection to others or to the consequences of their own actions; they live in "random nows." Culture has become a mechanism for selling, rather than mode for celebrating. Our frustrations with this insatiable cycle of "pleasure, property, and power" has led to sexual and homicidal violence. West doesn't really distinguish spiritual decay and cultural decay as either causes or effects of the more tangible public-sector problems discussed in question 4; perhaps it's safest to say the two clusters of problems are interrelated.

7. A *public square* is literally the square located in the center of a community's cluster of buildings, and can be found throughout nearly every culture that makes the distinction between public and private space. Usually, it's an open plot of land, surrounded by local-government offices and businesses, which enjoy high-traffic, high-priority status. It is a place where people may meet for organized celebrations or simply to enjoy one another's presence. Most of West's attention can be phrased in terms of this metaphor. In paragraph 18, he says that we must acknowledge that we are our own best resources; we cannot look elsewhere for help or guidance. In paragraph 19, he makes the public square the explicit equivalent of the public infrastructure—the systems of transportation and utility services that make everyday transactions and life possible. Implicit in paragraph 20 is the notion that children are not privatized property, nor are they a benefit and joy only to their parents—they are resources whose welfare a community can ill-afford to neglect. In paragraph 21, West warns that despite the pressing need to "ensure access to basic social goods," he does not advocate mindless change for the sake of change alone. We must avoid making "a fetish of the public square," or avoid sacrificing individual choice and welfare to the good of the whole.

8. Although West doesn't say so overtly, he looks askance at traditional party politics; the good of the party tends to become a self-justifying end, with the good of the people, or at least the electing constituents, too often being sacrificed. His emphasis on grassroots organizing, and on cutting out elites and television personalities, indicate that he doesn't have much hope for finding such a person in the traditional avenues of political careerism. He says he doesn't want a saint; yet the qualifications necessary for the job are the education and wisdom to grasp complex dynamics, realism tempered by visionary insight, and personal courage tempered by the ability to inspire people to act from highest principle.

RHETORICAL CONSIDERATIONS

1. The central question for West is, "What is to be done?" America is falling apart and urgently needs to address serious problems. The 1992 riots give West immediate access to the sense of urgency he feels, far more so than if he had used a conventional thesis that stated the whole of his vision of the problem, for a conventional thesis would have to be abstract, allowing readers to distance them-

selves. The 1992 riots were a jarring landmark in national consciousness. The next two sections, on predictable liberal-conservative responses and on the inadequacy of black nationalism as a response, are enactments of a judgment West has already pronounced: that the problems are not about race. If we agree with the broad outlines of his dismissal of these three approaches, then we should agree with the assumption in his next section—that race isn't the problem. Since race isn't the problem, West provides a comprehensive discussion of what is—and then provides his central question, the main idea of his essay.

West's structure is pretty traditional: (a) something is wrong; (b) traditional definitions and solutions to the problem haven't worked; (c) let's redefine the problem; (d) now that we've adequately redefined the problem, here are some better places to look for solutions. West lets readers linger on looming problems before he provides us a focused analysis and a range of solutions. By the time we get to paragraph 17, we're relieved to see the main idea emerge; and are more likely to embrace his solutions.

2. West uses a common belletristic device, the epigraph: a passage from a well-known, often revered author. Generally epigraphs aren't directly referenced within the text proper; they establish a mood or introduce a problem that resonates with the author's purpose by juxtaposition. They provide a jumping-off point. The Ellison passage begins by observing that the well-acknowledged American identity crisis among European immigrants was mitigated when they were able to define themselves as not-black. Blackness gave them a reference point for an otherwise disorganized unity as American, rather than as European. Yet Ellison concludes with a point that West leaves as a tease: that there is "something indisputably American about Negroes," and something indisputably Negro about Americans. The Gordian knot of black and white Americans' identities provides the jumping-off point for West's own essay.

3. Other examples of personification: the 1992 riots had "ugly, xenophobic resentment" (paragraph 1); predictable schisms in public debate result in "paralysis" (paragraph 2); white America is "weak-willed" (paragraph 8); Afrocentrism is "gallant" (paragraph 9); jobs have undergone an "exodus" (paragraph 12); policies on infrastructure are "myopic" (paragraph 19). West also tends to use reverse anthropomorphism, attributing inhuman characteristics to people, when he wants to heighten despair. People are "rootless and dangling" (paragraph 13); urban dwellers are "deracinated" and "denuded" (paragraph 13); politicians who should behave like "thermostats" function as "thermometers" (paragraph 15). The cumulative effect is to enliven West's prose, since he is writing about a large, abstract set of ideas.

4. West's use of quotation marks provides an opportunity to discuss stylistic finesse. At first, he appears to be quoting the typical liberal and conservative view. But his quoted words represent intent of the words, rather than the words such an individual would actually use. Thus his quoted words serve as parodic translation of underlying discourse. Quotes also place an ironic spin on meaning. The way he uses the pronoun *our* indicates that its meaning is anything but an inclusive possessive for "all Americans"; rather, it designates ownership by a

self-appointed, patronizing elite set of gatekeepers. One possible translation of the first part of the sentence: "Hence, liberals misguidedly believe that black people are to be included and integrated into society and culture, an idea that is not possible in the first place because black people are already part of society and culture, and in the second place because society and culture are not owned by liberals. . . ."

5. West does seem optimistic that people are fundamentally good enough and wise enough to halt their ride down the "slippery slope toward economic strife, social turmoil, and cultural chaos" (paragraph 10). If he were not, then there would be little cause for him to issue such a rousing call to action. Still, West does not sound entirely convinced that he will be heeded. By his own admission, black people alone cannot (and should not have to) resolve the problems he has outlined.

Has he convinced the people who are not "landless, propertyless, and luckless" (paragraph 22)—the small minority controlling so much wealth and power—that the changes he advocates are really in their best interest? Has he overcome the objection that best interests are a long-run proposition, rather than short-term gratification? In addition, has he provided solutions that we can not only agree to in theory, but find a way to put into practice? For student discussion.

6. Baldwin, as the full epigraph passage explains, is himself quoting from a Negro Spiritual, which encodes a folk belief: that God not only set up the rainbow as visible sign of his love for and promises to humanity after the great flood, but threatened the next clean-slate catastrophe would come by fire. When the world becomes too wicked, God will step in once again as the fierce judge, but in a judgment by fire, it's hard to think of any way that some would find or be given a way to escape. The immediate effect of this ending is to intensify West's urgency that we begin to act on changes right away. Whether through eschatological agency or sociological empiricism, a crisis seems imminent. In term of his long-range strategy, West's final allusion to Baldwin places him, along with directly cited references to Ellison and DuBois, in good company. He is not a lone voice crying in the wilderness, but is reiterating something that black intellectuals have been pointing out for a hundred years and beyond: that race matters to all Americans.

·8·
Television

The Plug-In Drug
Marie Winn

TOPICAL CONSIDERATIONS

1. Television consumes the time families would otherwise spend together in their special rituals, games, jokes, songs, and other shared activities. What it prevents—and Winn finds this dangerous—is interaction among members of the family.
2. Family closeness and unity are threatened by the presence of television because one-way involvement with it reduces communication and interaction among family members. Television often is a way to avoid confronting family problems.
3. Winn says nothing about the quality of television in her essay. Her worry is simply the powerful presence of television in the household and its adverse effects on the quality of family life.
4. If children turn on the television during those hours when they could be inventing little games or drawing or chatting with others, their ability to create, play, and interact might be threatened, says Winn. Games offer a means for a child to learn how to think and socialize.
5. I think Winn presents sufficient evidence. She cites a variety of authors of television studies, including Urie Bronfenbrenner and Bruno Bettelheim; she also refers to people she has interviewed, such as the Chicago woman in paragraph 22.
6. Because television is a one-way relationship, it lacks eye-contact, response, real interplay, and argument—it means no communication. For children, in particular, that artificial relationship could condition people to inadequate responsiveness to real people. As Bettelheim says (paragraph 27), real people arouse much less feeling than the skilled actor, who creates an illusion of intimacy. And real-life relationships are far more complicated than those among television personalities.
7. Some network documentaries and news specials are exceptions, I think. Most network television falls under Howe's assessment. The PBS channels offer more depth, variety, and culture. I think Howe would favor many of the offerings on PBS television.

RHETORICAL CONSIDERATIONS

1. "Plug-in drug" is an appropriate metaphor for television because it suggests both the electronic nature of the medium and the addictive, mind-numbing effects.
2. Her example in paragraph 13 is a powerfully convincing illustration.

3. I would say that Winn feels American television audiences are vulnerable to the powerful presence of television. See paragraphs 11 and 14.
4. I think she is accurate in her observation about the way some parents demonstrate their love for their kids—supplying them with "material comforts, amusements and educational opportunities."
5. Her evidence is adequate support for her thesis.

TV's True Violence

Meg Greenfield

TOPICAL CONSIDERATIONS

1. Greenfield draws this "hypocrisy" down party lines; that is, "liberals" object to television violence and "conservatives" object to explicit sexual material. For Greenfield there can be no real separation of sex and violence on television; that each group objects to one and not the other, using the same basic arguments as evidence, is hypocritical.
2. To focus discussion you might ask students to identify currently popular shows or television movies and to think about their own reactions to them.
3. The only kind of television violence Greenfield favors is "the real stuff"; that is, documentation of real-life struggles, crises, and traumas. Two notes for discussion: (1) Clearly the kinds of "real" violence Greenfield finds tenable are strictly political. She would not find acceptable the current spate of cop shows despite their verisimilitude. (2) Students should consider ways in which the line between "real" and "unreal" violence is clouded by the proliferation of "reality" television—shows that recreate emergency situations, from accidents and medical emergencies to crime control, complete with drug busts, highway pursuits, and shoot-outs.
4. Some might argue that "redeeming social value" varies with people and their contexts. Also, the word "redeeming" is ambiguous. Just how much social value must be added to the recipe for a violent program in order to redeem it in the minds of an ever-shifting public audience?
5. This question might speak to those students familiar with recent efforts to regulate rock and rap music. You might ask them to consider how government regulation of the television industry might work: How much regulation is enough? Who decides what is acceptable? What are the standards? In terms of self-censorship, you might ask what is at stake for television producers given the fact that sex and violence sell.
6. Greenfield says her main worry "is that it may, in time, render us incapable of recognizing and responding to the real thing." In short, it will desensitize us and dull our horror.
7. Greenfield makes a rather subtle critique of government control here. Her point is that policy makers have an investment in regulating images of international violence and struggle so as not to provoke organized protest by viewers. She is

also critical of excessive bureaucracy—"excessive governmental memoranda, autointoxication and blather."

RHETORICAL CONSIDERATIONS

1. Greenfield writes in the first person, but rather than writing a narrative piece, she engages the reader in an editorial tone appropriate to the seriousness with which she approaches the subject. Her tone fits the thoughtful analysis; as in all good editorials, she states the problem as she sees it in forthright terms then offers possible solutions. She is always logical and judiciously avoids emotionalism.

2. The point that violence in cultural works ought not to be characterized by "volume, profligacy and [an] undiscriminating nature" is well taken. Not only does television reproduce violent images, but it does so without a purpose "beyond its mere power to titillate, frighten and repel." Some might argue, however, that the comparison reinforces a cultural superiority of "classics" over "pop" works—a hierarchy that seems of waning value in contemporary society. Some potentially good discussions here.

3. The bottom-line argument is repeated three times (paragraphs 3, 5, and 7) following reinforcement of her points. This strategy is quite successful, for each point builds to a statement of the basic argument, thus reinforced itself in the reader's mind.

4. The structure of her essay builds upon the basic argument. Thus, students might not be prepared for the conclusion with its focus upon governmental policy. However, it may be argued that the conclusion does more work than the conventional "restatement of the thesis" formula. While it does restate the argument (for the third and last time), it also adds another dimension.

"Now . . . This"
Neil Postman

TOPICAL CONSIDERATIONS

1. Because television is a visual medium made up of fast-moving and dramatic images, news takes on the form of entertainment. But as Postman warns us, such entertainment value creates public ignorance by dulling our ability to process and evaluate all the information bits.

2. He finds "Now . . . This" an ominous metaphor of the discontinuities that pass for "public discourse in America." The phrases underscore the perception of the media that the world has "no order or meaning and is not to be taken seriously."

3. Open for discussion. One hopes that students will be enlightened.

4. Postman says broadcast news is packaged entertainment. First, broadcast news teams have faces that are "likable" and "credible"—"talking hairdos" with celebrity status; second, each show has a "musical theme"; third, the news provides the viewer no time to process a story to avoid distraction from the next

story; fourth, heavy use of visual documentation keeps us fascinated; fifth, news shows advertise to attract more viewers; finally, weatherforecasters would serve as "comic relief" just as sportscasters talk a little like Joe Sixpack. One might add all the mindless happy banter exchanged by the anchor-desk personalities—all part of the design to keep us feeling good about those awful reports of mayhem.

5. He warns that politicians need not worry about their behavior as long as their appearance before the camera is good.

6. Open for discussion.

7. Postman says that in order to maintain "a high level of unreality," newscasters never show emotion or any sign they "grasp the meaning of what they are saying." Since we are by the medium cast in a role of complicity with newscasters, we expect them to be "marginally serious" though impervious to implications. An emotional response would only invite our own reality to be "contaminated" thereby reducing the theatrical sense of unreality and making us feel vulnerable.

8. Postman makes the point that the way commercials are built into the news programs "refutes any claim that television news is designed as a serious form of public discourse." A sudden shift from the report of a major disaster to a Burger King commercial reduces the seriousness and reality of the report. For young viewers, the message is that such reports are exaggerated. This is a keen observation that might make students reassess their favorite news shows.

9. Yes. Open for discussion.

10. Postman cites the highly popular *USA Today* whose stories are very short and whose design is very visual and multicolored. One might point to the recent change in the *Christian Science Monitor,* now stripped down and more graphic than its traditional form. There are several TV news programs that even call themselves "news magazines" or "journals." Network examples—"20/20," "Prime Time Live," "Nightline," "48 Hours," and the progenitor of them all, "60 Minutes."

RHETORICAL CONSIDERATIONS

1. Postman comes across as a very intelligent and concerned individual. Open for discussion.

2. The vocabulary is rather refined. Postman was clearly aiming at an educated and, perhaps, postgraduate audience.

3. The use of the second person is very effective as it makes a participant of the reader. Though not intrusive, the technique runs through paragraph 17 where he completes his discussion of the several ways you can turn your news show into an entertaining package.

4. These are potent references since we associate them with dystopian nightmare worlds (Orwell's *1984* and Huxley's *Brave New World*) in which people are either conditioned by fear to accept an unreality ("Newspeak") or seek drugs ("soma") to escape the one they've created. Postman says that television news is nothing so insidious as Newspeak; but nearly so bad, we have "adjusted to incoherence and been amused into indifference." Huxley would not be shocked. He

predicted it in *Brave New World.* Orwell, on the other hand, gave us a society in which Big Brother government revised history, truth, and reality. Revisionism and lies made up the fabric of things in *1984.* Postman says that he need not have gone so far in his speculations, that people could be conditioned to accept incoherence, inconsistencies, and disinformation without all the dark deception.

5. A good example is paragraph 15. Here he smoothly integrates the support of Robert MacNeil.

Why Do We Need Celebrities?

Christina Kelly

TOPICAL CONSIDERATIONS

1. Kelly's assertion rests on the case she is building about the "mythology" of stars. According to her, average people are so invested in the mythology of perfection surrounding their favorite celebrities that they cannot accept less-than-favorable perceptions of them.

2. To Kelly a hero is someone who "sacrifices him or herself for a higher purpose"—say, saving other people or supporting high ideals (paragraph 4). Kelly feels that many—if not most—celebrities are famous as a result of marketing strategies rather than talent or achievement, let alone personal sacrifice. The implication that the majority of celebrities have no talent or that they never use their star-status, time, or money for social good are generalizations that could be refuted. Also, Kelly neglects to address ways in which "stars" *are* heroes in terms of contemporary culture; that is, they represent people who have achieved the American dream so widely marketed in the United States. As such, celebrity myth has much deeper cultural roots and implications than the inferiority complexes to which Kelly attributes stargazing.

3. Kelly cites New Kids on the Block as a group of no-talent boys used to make "a lot of money off teenage girls." She argues that this group, rather than being naturally talented, was created and groomed from the ground up by their agent, then sold to radio stations, MTV, and video companies around the country for huge profits. Kelly is right that without the media and publicity machines there could be no "stars" as we know them. This discussion might focus on a critical analysis of the politics of profit in the entertainment field. Students might think about the fact that everything from programming choices on television to the current rising star in Hollywood is economically driven.

4. This statement carries a couple of difficult implications. First, *Sassy* readers (ranging in age from 18 to 24 years) might take offense at their portrayal as mindless teenyboppers, pouring their "hormonal" longings into media creations. Second, while Kelly has a point that teen idols, known and "loved" through media images alone, are a safe alternative to the dangers of actual sexual activity— especially given that teenagers are experiencing the fastest rate of HIV transmission—she does not address the flip side of this argument, which is that the

marketing of teen sex symbols serves to increase desire for romance and intimacy. Many teenage-oriented television programs and movies depict stars engaged in intimate activity, creating a sense of comfort for many young viewers who emulate their favorite celebs.

5. Rhetorically speaking, Kelly attempts to plug into some real philosophical problems with the argument that our instability of purpose, a natural part of the human condition, causes us to crave celebrity contact. Unfortunately, Kelly's treatment of the large philosophical construct she raises is rather shallow.

6. To some readers, Kelly's logic may seem twisted, even frightening. It is conceivable that the illusionary media images of fame and fortune may create the kind of envy and resentment to which Kelly refers. Yet, her argument that we feel better about ourselves when someone dies—*especially* as the result of drug or alcohol abuse—may strike many students as unjustified, even vicious. You might consider whether her claims would include Kurt Cobain in the category of empty sex symbols. Cobain committed suicide in 1994.

RHETORICAL CONSIDERATIONS

1. Given the tone, voice, and topic of this piece, opening on a philosophical crisis is a bit jarring, if not ironic (especially given that the "crisis" occurred while in the shower: how long could it have lasted?). Kelly, however, makes an effort to uphold the philosophical strand in her argument by comparing the current trend of celebrity worship to the need for religion and art—to fill our "inconsequential little lives" (see paragraphs 8 and 14). Still, her invocation of philosophy, and of the problem of the "decline of Western civilization" is like invoking the mountain to discuss the molehill: It is given a somewhat cursory treatment in the frame of her argument.

2. Kelly's tone is decidedly informal. Clearly her projected audience—the readership of *Sassy* magazine—is young, trendy, and hip. Her vernacular targets an audience in their late teens or early twenties. See paragraphs 2 and 3, for example: "I was really psyched. . . "; "celebrities . . . would jerk me around. . . "; "I still kissed butt. . . "; "Even articles I thought were favorable pissed them off." This voice is effective as a point of identification between Kelly and her readers.

3. See paragraph 3, where Kelly relates a dream in which, despite having met and disliked him in real life, "Keanu Reeves thought I was so cool that we became best friends"; paragraph 12, wherein Kelly examines *Sassy's* practice of publishing staff photos in the masthead, thereby lending a star quality to their images; and, most importantly, paragraph 14, in which Kelly says that "I am a part of this whole process. No wonder I feel soiled at the end of my workday." While acknowledgment of her participation in the phenomenon is admirable—even crucial in terms of making an honest, persuasive argument—Kelly does not follow through on her self-examination. That is, she does not offer possible solutions or ideas as to how she might help change the problem given her strategic position in the system that creates it. Instead, she comes off sounding hypocritical. Then again, what can Kelly realistically do but write articles such as this one on occasion.

4. This naming has several effects. First, it serves as a sort of self-test for readers; that is, Kelly asks readers to question their own response to her attacks on celebrities. (Of course, reader identification with the celebrities in question is requisite here.) Second, such references give the article specificity and liveliness, though these limit its shelf life. Finally, she demonstrates her courage and daring in naming names, as grating and judgmental as it may strike some.

5. This history is useful in that it allows readers a context for understanding her argument. Kelly, in paragraph 10, comes to the conclusion that "the media created celebrities to satisfy our primal need for gossip." It may be vague, but this conclusion seems to connect to her earlier pronouncement that celebrity worship is attributable to the "inconsequentiality" of human life. That is, so uneventful are the lives of some that they find satisfaction in star dirt. If that's the case, then the O. J. Simpson case in 1994 would indict the lives of most Americans over the age of 14.

The Wrong Examples
David L. Evans

TOPICAL CONSIDERATIONS

1. Evans makes the point that high-profile black males are most often athletes, singers, or comedians. He's fairly accurate. Even sitcoms are filled with the same roles. It may be useful to turn discussion to racial stereotyping (paragraph 9) and how these roles have grown out of generations-old views of black males' physical (often read *sexual*) prowess, musical ability, or comic talent. (For a discussion of the origin and perpetuation of these stereotypes, see Michelle Wallace, *Black Macho and the Myth of the Superwoman*.) By contrast, Evans points out the diversity of media roles for white men: politicians, executives, critics, authors, and so forth. Evans is right, I think, about the subtle effects of such images.

2. Evans feels that all television viewers are vulnerable to the seductive power of media images of wealth and glamour; however, young black males, statistically lacking in positive adult role models, are particularly susceptible. He adds that, these images send the message that schoolwork, career training, and prudent personal behavior are irrelevant to success, which depends solely upon talent in athletics or performance.

3. Open for discussion—though it seems that this proposal does not really get to the heart of the matter, which is the lack of positive black male role models on television. And Evans would probably agree. You might encourage students to examine the larger issues here: the social and political inequities between blacks and whites in America, the economic realities for a large proportion of black families, and the absence of black men and women in top, decision-making positions in the media.

4. Evans finds that television images of superstars in chains or sports paraphernalia feed into the consumer mentality in the United States. As viewers are bom-

barded with images of "heroes" with lifestyles unattainable to most people, the status of such material goods—for example, jewelry and sneakers—and the craving for them is inflated to a level that sometimes results in violence. In short, kids kill to wear Michael Jordan's shoes.

5. This statement gets at the heart of the idea of the American "good life"—the dream of opportunity rooted in colonial and immigrant history but that can be criticized as mythical for certain sectors of the population given socioeconomic conditions. Students might analyze the power of the American dream in their own experience and how that dream might be attained. Discussion might also address for whom the American dream is a viable goal, and which sectors of society are generally denied access.

6. Many students may feel that while television producers have such a responsibility, the superstars who have "earned" their status do not. Still, they may feel that, responsibility or no, stars might donate their time to counteracting destructive images—by using television to broadcast public service messages regarding the values of education, hard work, and team-play; by donating money to community youth organizations, scholarship funds, or career incentive programs, and so on.

RHETORICAL CONSIDERATIONS

1. Evans's argument is clearly stated in the second paragraph of his piece: "I submit that the absence of male role models and slanted television images of black males have something to do with [the dearth of qualified black male college candidates and graduates]." The directness of the statement concisely focuses the reader's attention to the issue. The essay is well ordered, with step-by-step elaboration of the problem and presentation of possible solutions.

2. Evans positions himself at the opening of his essay as a college admissions officer. In this way, he both locates his stake in this issue and maintains an authoritative perspective on statistical information about young black males. This stance, in turn, provides a strong foundation from which to critique television for its lack of black male role models. Writing from the perspective of an educator also strengthens his advocacy of higher education as an alternative to fly-by-night careers in television, music, or athletics—that is, he's a good role model.

3. Evans's strategy is effective. His audience takes a quiz as they read, thus achieving a concrete illustration of his point—that readers among the estimated 90 percent are unable to identify the lower-profile (but equally successful) black Americans in the second group.

4. Some students may find this identification effective in that it provides concrete illustration of Evans's argument. There is, however, a problem with his rhetorical construction of such identifications: He identifies some stars as the sort of negative role models perpetuating stereotypical images in impressionable young minds (e.g., Bo Jackson and Eddie Murphy) while identifying others as responsible men who "use their substantial influence to redirect young black males" (e.g., the late Arthur Ashe, Bill Cosby, and Jim Brown.) Such identifications seem to pass judgment on the persons in question; this might be unfounded. Is

Evans correct in his implication that Jackson and Murphy don't take any responsibility for redirecting black youth? Also, this dichotomy might serve to pit public figures against one another in the reader's imagination—good guys and bad guys.

In Praise of Roseanne

Elayne Rapping

TOPICAL CONSIDERATIONS

1. Open for discussion. Students might be drawn to the show more by the "surface" qualities—for example, Roseanne's loud, funny manner—which Rapping identifies as signs of its deeper political engagement with issues of class and gender.

2. For Rapping, critics have paid more attention to shows such as "The Cosby Show" and "Murphy Brown" because they are somehow considered more intellectually respectable because of their representations of "well-turned out, well-educated liberal professionals," Rapping says in paragraph 6. Her argument is that Roseanne is harder for critics to digest because of her image as a loud, bossy, working-class female—an image that they take less seriously than what is projected on shows depicting mainstream professionals.

3. Whether or not students agree with these formulations of gender roles, it is important for them to think critically about the impact of television representations of women and men. These representations, disseminated on a mass level, often act as behavioral models or standards for viewers to emulate. Depictions of women who break the boundaries of gender expectations could have a wide impact on female viewers who might find such representations empowering. Such representations could ultimately play a part in changing social norms and prescriptions regarding gender roles.

4. A large part of Lucy's schtick came from trying to secure employment outside of the home—at which she inevitably failed. There was little talk of money, and, of course, Ricky was the wage earner as well as controller of his wife's activities. With the rise of women in the workplace, a space was carved for a Roseanne who provides an image of a woman who works and is involved with the financial maintenance of her family. Her husband does not have the final word on things, and she successfully asserts her needs within the framework of her marriage. It might also be interesting to note that audiences were shocked to see bedroom scenes with Lucy and Ricky who were forced by the networks to sleep in twin beds. Not so Roseanne!

5. Students from different socioeconomic classes might disagree on what is a realistic representation of gender, class and family relations. However, whether or not students identify with Roseanne, she clearly provides images of gender, class, and family that are not typical to the little screen, and that might be a window onto a different world. In either case, the images are positive and productive.

6. Roseanne helps her audience to digest "difficult" issues and messages with her sharp sense of humor. In this way things like the lesbian kiss episode are "easy"

to watch because they are funny, but still arouse enough interest and controversy to be the topic of much conversation—proof that a message is indeed being sent and considered.

RHETORICAL CONSIDERATIONS

1. In an essay preoccupied with representations of economics and class, this opening is appropriate, especially given that Rapping goes on to compare "Roseanne" with other critically acclaimed programs that take as their focus "liberal professionals" of the upper-middle class. She is, in a sense, rescuing "Roseanne" from critical oblivion resulting from class biases. She also makes the point that the "news" presented in reruns of "Roseanne" is much more realistic and easier to identify with than the news on The News, which covers the big, the rich, and the powerful without addressing how these people and events affect "ordinary" folks.

2. Rapping's critique is appropriate since the very class bias that Roseanne sends up in her show is evident in the critical and media apparatuses in this country. The media, she claims, refuse to celebrate Roseanne for her work on behalf of working class people, praising instead programming that reinforces the "hegemonic norms" of gender and class in this country, and revealing in the process their own class biases. This critique serves to underscore her basic argument regarding the need for critically conscious television representations of gender and class biases.

3. The first person works well in this essay because it allows Rapping to position herself as an average viewer rather than as a distanced intellectual critic—the kind she disparages for their biases. It is also appropriate since the piece centers on identification with media representations, especially on the part of women. The first person allows Rapping to illustrate her own identifications in a progression from Lucille Ball to Roseanne. This provides a point of identification for the reader.

4. This information places Roseanne in the context of other television women, such as Lucy, Mary, June, and so forth, a strategy that illustrates why certain models of femininity were ineffective (Mary, June) while others (Lucy, Roseanne) are strong and positive representation.

Don't Blame TV
Jeff Greenfield

TOPICAL CONSIDERATIONS

1. Greenfield says that critics have blamed television for what amounts to the decline of Western civilization, including falling SAT scores, growing sexual promiscuity, lower voter turnout, increasing divorce rates, rising crime, and col-

lapsing family life. The reason for all the blame is that television is the most visible and pervasive medium we have. Nearly every American family has one or more television sets.

2. Greenfield says it seems reasonable to assume that television is behind all our social ills. He argues, however, that "you can't make assumptions about causes" (paragraph 6). And he brings up the fallacy of *post hoc, ergo propter hoc* reasoning.

3. Greenfield continues his line of argument that the cause is not clear. He says in paragraph 10 that studies (from the David Owen book) show that the drop in SAT scores can be attributed to "nuclear fallout, junk food, cigarette smoking by pregnant women, cold weather, declining church attendance, the draft, the assassination of President Kennedy and fluoridated water." He also points out that scores since 1982 have been on the rise.

4. Greenfield points out that for the last few years the crime rate has, in fact, dropped. The explanation for the drop, he says, is most likely to be the shift of population away from the "youth bulge" and improved criminal justice methods. He wonders how critics can assume that television, with its crime-does-not-pay morality, still manages to turn young people into criminals.

5. On the question of sexual promiscuity, Greenfield says that television "was the most sexually conservative of all media through the first quarter-century of its existence" (paragraph 13). While movies and magazines such as *Playboy* became more explicit and literary censorship was all but abolished, television "remained an oasis" of propriety. Greenfield adds that it isn't television that has caused young people to become "sexually precocious"; it is probably the "spread of readily available birth control" that encourages premarital sex.

6. He argues that television did not make divorce more acceptable in American society; it was changes in American society that made divorce more acceptable on television.

7. His argument once again is that television is not a cause of social changes but a mirror of them. On the images of women and blacks, Greenfield says that in the early years television borrowed limiting stereotypical images from movies. But despite these images, he argues, women and blacks brought up with television forcefully rejected these images and organized successfully for their civil rights. His point is that television is a relatively impotent social force, for a major social revolution such as civil rights took place even though blacks on television were being depicted as second-class citizens.

RHETORICAL CONSIDERATIONS

1. The Ward quotation is essentially the gist of Greenfield's argument. He never strays from the idea that critics base all their criticism of television on unfounded assumptions—"what you know that just ain't so" (paragraph 1).

2. I think Greenfield's most convincing argument is the way in which the civil rights and women's movements were set in motion even though television aired

shows in which women and blacks were negatively portrayed. His weakest argument, I think, is his defense of television on the issue of declining SAT scores. He resorts to "writer David Owen" in a "recent book on educational testing" and lists other causes, but without documentation. I would have liked to see more evidence linking these other culprits to the drop in scores.

3. Throughout the essay Greenfield argues against unfounded assumptions that television is behind the decline in our society. Although statements ordinarily have rhetorically greater potency in making an argument, Greenfield is not trying to get to the root of social problems as much as he is trying to expose fallacies in criticism. Thus, the rhetorical questions effectively put down the assumptions by implying the answers. Also, the reasonable tone of the questions is more ingratiating to the reader than a loud, defensive declaration.

Why I Quit Watching Television
P. J. O'Rourke

TOPICAL CONSIDERATIONS

1. O'Rourke says he quit watching television the day he realized his girlfriend was more interested in a "Star Trek" rerun than in him. Undoubtedly, he's exaggerating for humorous effect, although his message is that television has a "plug-in drug" effect, as Marie Winn points out in her essay, "the Plug-In Drug." Also, he says, television is dumb, violent, and a waste of time; and it keeps you from doing more important things.

2. He is being ironic in his complaints here. In paragraph 4, he says that not watching television turned out to be expensive—$1,500 for ski equipment (not to mention the broken leg) and $12,000 for deciding to fix his apartment in his leisure time. He also complains that his reading turned out to be dumber, more violent, and lewder than television. He also says that conversation in his spare time turned into arguments with his new girlfriend about getting a television set. O'Rourke adds that being off television caused him to get fat and put him out of touch with fashions, sports, and personalities.

3. The major drawback is being out of touch with the world of television—the fashions, the personalities, the shows, the sports events.

4. The medium itself has changed somewhat since cable, MTV, and VCRs were introduced. Yet the substantive changes are minimal—just some new shows with new faces. The violence and dumbness have stayed the same. And it's dumb "how perfect everything is in the television world," O'Rourke says in paragraph 12.

5. O'Rourke is satirically poking fun at television and the viewer. But, of course, beneath the irony and exaggeration lie some very real messages. He makes fun of the viewer's addiction to television (his first girlfriend's attention to "Star Trek," his second girlfriend's craving for shows such as "Family Feud," his

neighbor's cable and "television room," and his own readdiction at the end); our inability to fill our time with more worthwhile activities; the way television keeps us *au courant* and "cultural"; the bizarreness of MTV videos.

6. Despite the violence on television, O'Rourke observes in paragraph 12 that "the people are all pretty. The pay phones all work. And all the endings are hopeful." His point is that much of television is not about real people in realistic situations. It might be a good idea for students to discuss a show or series in which "television perfection" is analyzed for the messages. Some critics have complained that relationships among characters, particularly in comedy series, are idealized and romanticized and thus create unrealistic expectations for the viewer. Others complain that some people's behavior is modeled on that of television characters.

RHETORICAL CONSIDERATIONS

1. Some examples of irony: (1) the $11,400 that he had to pay carpenters, painters, and plasterers "to repair the damage" he had done when he decided on the "do-it-yourself remodeling" of his apartment; (2) his feuding with his girl-friend over getting a television set so that they could watch "Family Feud"; (3) his first impression of the MTV song video he saw; the parenthetical last two lines of the essay.

2. Beginning: paragraphs 1 through 3 (his getting rid of television) Middle: para-graphs 4 through 10 (what went wrong when he did) End: paragraphs 11 to the end (his reassessment of television after ten years and his return to it)

3. The final paragraph humorously stresses his ambivalence. He swears he doesn't like the television he sees; he sounds adamant about not returning to the tube. Yet, parenthetically, that subversive other impulse suggests that despite his con-victions he'll start watching and liking it all again. He sounds like a reformed al-coholic dangerously testing himself—or a drug addict slipping back to his habit.

9

Crime and Punishment

Pilgrimage to Nonviolence
Martin Luther King, Jr.

TOPICAL CONSIDERATIONS

1. King was trained in the ministry. His essay hints that he is intimately acquainted with the Bible. He points out, for example, that in the Greek translation of the New Testament, three words are used for love that have different root meanings. (He builds a major portion of the essay on this fact.) King also refers to Paul and the Samaritan who helped the Jew on the road to Jericho.
2. As a young man, Gandhi studied law in London. This training prepared him first for his fight against legal discrimination in South Africa and later for his leadership in India's struggle for political independence. His success as India's leader resulted mainly from his practice of civil disobedience (a term he borrowed from Henry David Thoreau's essay by that name). This form of social protest demands not only that its advocates actively resist injustice and discrimination, but that they do so without resorting to physical violence and without fleeing. It demands instead that they submit to any violence that may be inflicted upon them because of their resistance. Implicit in such nonviolent resistance is the conviction that it will eventually cause the perpetrators of the injustice and violence to see the lack of common humanity and injustice in their acts and cease doing them voluntarily.
3. The first point in King's explanation of his philosophy indicates that there is a difference. King emphasizes that nonviolent resisters are not passive. They don't run away or avoid facing an issue. Instead, they actively protest against injustice or social wrongs by confronting them and by accepting whatever punishment may result from their refusal to submit. Those who fled to Canada did so not only to avoid and protest against the Vietnam War but also to escape punishment. This is passive nonviolent resistance. Also, by fleeing, they were expressing an attitude that could appear to be cowardice. King explains that cowardice is no part of nonviolent resistance. Because conscientious objectors agree to perform noncombative services in lieu of combat duty, they don't actually protest against or resist war but only their own active involvement in it.
4. King's philosophy requires not just physical courage but moral stamina. The qualities of character needed to express such moral stamina are taught in the Sermon on the Mount: poorness of spirit, sorrow for present wrongs, meekness, mercy, hunger for righteousness, desire to be a peacemaker, and rejoicing in the face of persecution.

5. There are obviously no easy answers to this question. World events reveal that returning evil for evil or hatred for hatred results in escalation of terrorism and violence. It is obvious that nations, court systems, and individuals can't sit back and allow acts of violence and terrorism to go unpunished and unchecked. But perhaps as individuals practice the teachings of the Sermon on the Mount and King's philosophy of nonviolent resistance, this action can go far toward lessening the tensions that result in terrorism and violence.

6. YMCA and YWCA. Girl and Boy Scouts. Rotary Club. Elks. Masons. Shriners. Eastern Star. Salvation Army. Local charity organizations. United Fund. Good Will. American Red Cross. Human and social service organizations. Government-sponsored welfare programs.

7. For the students.

8. He speaks of redemption and reconciliation and reveals an intelligent, wise, practical love for humanity that can be emotionally as well as intellectually appealing.

RHETORICAL CONSIDERATIONS

1. This is up to the students. Many would probably say yes. The pronoun *I* and personal experiences can be attention-getting, especially at the beginning of an essay.

2. In paragraph 2, King indicates that his purpose in writing is to discuss the basic points in his philosophy. But also, in his narrative introduction, he mentions that when the Montgomery movement began, he was reminded of the Sermon on the Mount and Gandhi's method of nonviolent resistance. He seems to imply here that his philosophy is derived from these two earlier sources.

3. King's is an expository essay developed primarily by definition. A narrative pattern opens the essay.

4. Notice the variety of words King chooses to achieve a smooth transition when he explains the six basic points in his philosophy: First, a basic fact, second basic fact, a third characteristic, a fourth point, a fifth point, a sixth basic fact.

5. Because King's essay is short and he clearly delineates the six points of his philosophy, he doesn't need to summarize these points in the end. In fact, to do so would be unnecessarily repetitious. Also, the last point is appropriate for a conclusion because it points to the underlying reason nonviolent resisters are convinced that their efforts will count for something.

The Culture of Violence
Myriam Miedzian

TOPICAL CONSIDERATIONS

1. Culture shapes behavior. Children learn what behavior is acceptable and what's unacceptable by watching and participating in the activities their culture sponsors. They imitate what they see in cultural forms (Miedzian lists religion, mu-

sic, sports, etc.). Inevitably, they generalize and reason out the principles for acceptable behavior and judgments about how their own actions will be received by their community.

2. In paragraph 4, Miedzian draws support from anthropologist Ruth Benedict for the contention that dysfunctional customs are holdovers from an earlier time. At one time, the trait or behavior encoded into the obsolete custom was useful. For example, if a tribe like that in paragraph 2 is not in imminent danger and, thus, doesn't need customs promoting readiness for war, then an anthropologist would assume that its war customs are holdovers from an earlier era when violence was necessary.

3. The Kurnai are a tribe of people in Australia. They define brothers and sisters as "all relatives of one's own generation." The Kurnai would thus be as disgusted by the marriage of distant cousins as Americans would be at the marriage of two people who have the same two biological parents. Since regulations about locality and the rights of old men further limit the options, any two young people who wish to marry are almost bound to be forbidden by one rule or another. If they wish to exercise individual choice, they must elope.

4. The Kurnai questions are indicated by separate paragraphs, with quotation marks designating their words and a lack of quotation marks designating American responses. They ask about role models, film, leisure time, music, sports, toys, and content of play activity; they also apparently ask about religion and parenting. These themes correspond roughly with the components of culture Miedzian identifies in paragraph 1. However, they are pretty heavily loaded toward popular culture and leisure; the Kurnai apparently never ask about the arts, education, or work; and their questions about religion and parenting are tangential to more pressing concerns about leisure.

5. Miedzian identifies consumer capitalism as the root of America's violence. Capitalism values profit above all else. Through television advertising, children contribute to the profit of large corporations. An unspoken assumption here is that corporations have discovered children will generate more profit from violence-oriented goods than from goods that promote healthy character development. Whether or not students accept capitalism as the scapegoat will depend in part on the sophistication of their understanding of economic theory. Some students may see racism, misogyny, or other forms of intolerance, either as root or contributing causes alongside consumer capitalism; others may see basic human depravity causing both intolerance and capitalism. Others may simply believe that buying lots of stuff at the mall is a good thing unto itself.

6. Miedzian says that "unfettered free enterprise" was initially beneficial for the United States because it led to "the extraordinary economic development of the nation." That is, it played a very positive role in the past, so cultural attitudes and customs about free enterprise developed a supportive mentality in the people whom it benefited. However, in paragraph 4, Miedzian explains that when conditions change, customs and values may not change as quickly. Implicitly, the United States no longer needs economic development, at least not at such a rapid pace. Yet we still venerate the profit motive at the expense of other values that presently may be more useful to us. Attitudes have not yet caught up.

7. Girls are, of course, socialized into their own gender roles. Nor would the relationship between female socialization and male violence be an easy one to elucidate, since female parenting for all children, including boys, is the social norm. But Miedzian is here presenting a schematic for the nonacademic audience. Still, the women in this article are a passive lot. They are active neither in their roles as mothers nor as full human entities. Inevitably they are victims of male violence. When the violence is specified, it is rape. Mothering behavior serves no function in Miedzian beyond a role model for "wimpiness" in men. (And the Kurnai, our "authorities" on American culture, then conflate male wimpiness with gentleness.) The most active women appear in paragraph 27—divorcees complaining about their lack of child support. Finally, all the "people" who shape and consume "our culture" seem to be exclusively male.

RHETORICAL CONSIDERATIONS

1. Miedzian focuses on the illogical and potentially lethal results of Kurnai kinship definitions and marriage customs. Paragraph 5 introduces humor with the (presumably Western) anthropology student chuckling. While the Kurnai express "extreme horror" in paragraph 6, to us outsider-readers the horror seems excessive. The denouement comes in paragraph 7, where word choices transform Kurnai outrage into a primitive Keystone Cops sequence. "Villagers" (not elders, or parents, or relatives) "get wind of" (rather than discover, or find out—as if something smelled bad) an event which causes "moral indignation" (hypocrisy, since the elopement is an instant replay of nearly everyone else's marriage circumstances). Given the number of indignant villagers who are still around after their own elopements, the implication is that their "intent to kill" is not serious, or is even a mockery. The tone would seem disrespectfully ethnocentric if Miedzian were not to turn the anthropologist's mirror around so quickly to ridicule American customs. Laughter here hinges on paradox. It allows us to recognize the disparity between the goal or ideal (marriage, and the perpetuation of the species) and the behavior surrounding it (death or extinction of the species). Because we are prepared to accept the Kurnai's illogic, we can more readily see our own contradictions.

2. Student answers may differ widely. First, the Kurnai's own customs have already given readers permission to laugh at someone else's foibles. Hence laughter at one's own customs may come more easily. Second, the Kurnai help readers attain an objective perspective. Because the Kurnai are so different from us, they can reasonably ask questions about customs and cultural practices we take for granted. Third, Miedzian gets to avoid playing "the heavy" in pointing out the stupidities of American culture. Nobody has to trash Americans and risk being disloyal to everything we stand for; our own answers to the Kurnai questions damn us with little additional comment. Fourth, Miedzian gets to slide in methodologies of cultural anthropology without cumbersome lectures on what exactly a professional in the field looks for. She need merely add "as a cultural anthropologist, the Kurnai would already know that. . . ." Finally, the Kurnai are

probably most effective because they pose no threat to our way of life. As aboriginals, they may have the wisdom to pass judgment on us, but they cannot impose negative trade sanctions or threaten military intervention.

3. The documents play a number of functions: They establish a specifically American context for the comments that follow. They establish a baseline of our ideals and goals more concretely and specifically than other material might. They are incorporated into all American laws and institutions, therefore, Miedzian is not obliged to prove consensus for these ideals. Finally, since they also contrast starkly with the portrait of what we really do (rather than what we say we want), these documents may also function as a quiet plea for our culture's intrinsic value.

4. Student responses will vary. Hollywood has recently brought us Thelma and Louise, Mrs. Doubtfire, and Sigourney Weaver's Ripley in the *Alien* films; also, Alan Alda. Of course, one might argue that these films and stars succeed precisely through the novelty of reversing gender stereotypes, without substantively affecting the stereotype itself. Romantic ballads and "she left me so I'm cryin' in my beer" laments by male singers remain popular. And while frilly pink ponies and grimacing masked turtles also remain popular, more gender-neutral toys seem to be available—although cuddly dolls for posttoddler boys aren't much in evidence. The more examples students can generate, the more problems they will see with Miedzian's argument: Her generalizations tend to be overstatements.

5. The article's basic assumption is articulated clearly here: that human nature is heavily (if not completely) conditioned by environment. Anyone is capable of violence. As an infant, the boy's "destructive" qualities are in equilibrium with his "altruistic" qualities. Development of his personality depends on culture. A boy learns to become a man based on what he sees reinforced through images, sanctioned activities, and institutions—in a word, through culture. But if American culture is as violent as Miedzian implies it is, and if the response to cultural conditioning is so mindlessly knee-jerk, then it would seem that no man can escape it. Of course, what holds our society in check are those formative "good" influences in our environment—love, compassion, moral rightness.

6. Five possibilities: (1) "Many" adolescent boys like slasher films (paragraph 15). (2) They see "an average" of 26,000 television murders by age 18 (paragraph 17). (3) All girls receive "dolls and carriages and dollhouses" as Christmas presents (paragraph 25). (4) "A large percentage of divorced fathers" are deadbeat dads (paragraph 27). (5) Apparently all toys that manufacturers produce for boys "encourage reckless violence, sadism, and torture." In addition, she defines American culture as crossing regional boundaries. From there on, her statements seem to apply almost exclusively to middle-class, white, heterosexual Christians. Generalization is essential to the argument, since adequate discussion of exceptions would clutter it with irrelevant material. But the aggregate weight of the generalizations here might strike some as excessive and, thus, a weakness.

An Incident in the Park

Aileen C. Hefferren

TOPICAL CONSIDERATIONS

1. Student answers will vary.
2. Hefferren emphasizes gender to heighten the vulnerability women feel in certain situations. Students should be able to point out where cases of race, class, or age would make a person more vulnerable depending on the particular situation.
3. Traditionally, people are aware of stereotypically "dangerous" situations. For example, Hefferren writes, "I have walked purposefully, carried house keys between my fingers, crossed the street when I saw a threatening person" (paragraph 6). According to Hefferren, expectations and guidelines are now disrupted; crimes occur during the day on crowded streets. These, to Hefferren, are "new rules."
4. Hefferren faces a new vulnerability. She is no longer able to live the life she chooses, in the manner she chooses. Some decisions are now made for her: She can no longer run when and where she wants. In this way she looses some freedom. Students may also suggest that Hefferren "gains" insight into the violence that prevails in our society.
5. Student answers will vary, but it might be beneficial to encourage them to see Hefferren's piece, her making the incident and her feelings about the incident public, as an attempt to overcome her own vulnerability. By publishing her story, Hefferren may, in some way, take control of a situation in which she feels powerless.

RHETORICAL CONSIDERATIONS

1. Hefferren's narrative style may appeal to students' personal emotions. Such a narrative would not be very effective for a police report or any objective representation of the event.
2. Hefferren puts these words in quotes to highlight her questioning tone. Students should recognize that this device calls attention to how ridiculous it is to call an assault victim "lucky."
3. Rhetorical questions leave the readers with something to think about. They also suggest a lack of closure to the piece, and consequently, the issue remains unsolved. In this case, the question points not to the attack, but to the reactions to the attack. She questions the standards by which we judge certain behaviors and their consequences.
4. The title, "An Incident in the Park," calls attention to the downplaying of violence in America. A reader might expect a less dramatic scenario than the one Hefferren offers us because of traditional associations with "parks." Since *incident* is such a neutral word, Hefferren's story might surprise some readers.

5. Hefferren's main point is that "even an unreported incident can have a profound effect" (paragraph 1). This effect is Hefferren's realization that the theory of "relative" violence is problematic, and the cycle continues. If some assaults are not "serious" enough to prosecute, these assaults will continue because there are no real consequences to deter the attackers. She sees no solutions in sight.

Date Rape's Other Victim
Katie Roiphe

TOPICAL CONSIDERATIONS

1. Roiphe begins her discussion with a poster stating that one in four college women has been the victim of rape, or of attempted rape. But the number seems high to her, based on her personal network of women friends.
2. Roiphe cites a critique by Neil Gilbert of a survey performed by psychologist Mary Koss. Gilbert notes that 73 percent of the respondents labeled as rape victims did not think of themselves as such. The label was imposed by the researcher. According to Gilbert (with whom Roiphe agrees), Koss skewed her questions and the way she compiled responses in order to "prove" what she already believed to be true: a high incidence of rape. Roiphe assures us that rape does indeed occur, and that it is a serious problem. But far too many kinds of events are being lumped into the category. Hence, because the definition of rape has been stretched so far, the statistic has become an opinion, and one that Roiphe does not share. According to her, feminists are responsible for this egregious half-truth, deliberately manipulating information to build support for their goals and movements.
3. Collecting accurate rape statistics is difficult for a number of reasons. Women who identify themselves as having been raped are labeled as victims. A *victim* becomes fair game for any psychologist who wishes to insist that her opinions and behavior are an effect of the rape, no matter how contrived the connection. Because women are held responsible for saying no, a woman who is raped may be led to feel shame that she provoked, invited, or caused the incident in some way. A woman who speaks up in the presence of her attacker may well feel vulnerable to reprisal, even if she doesn't identify him by name. While the rape crisis movement has led to medical, law enforcement, and judiciary reforms, women still experience insensitive responses through official reporting channels.
4. The cover is a shattered photograph of a boy and a girl dancing. Inside, monologues indicate moderate attraction ("good looking"), reasonable caution ("I thought it would be O.K."), and desire for low-intimacy friendship ("ask me out again"). The boy's thoughts make him seem obsessed with sex from first glance ("really hot . . . sexy dress"), calculating the girl's every gesture as a sexual message ("touching my arm . . . seemed pretty relaxed"), and "scoring" mentality ("going to be lucky!") Roiphe calls these "cardboard images." She complains

that far from educating young people about rape, the pamphlet actually promotes a brand of heterosexuality that is remote from reality or desirability. She says than an honest portrayal might show sex as aggressive, involving domination and submission, less than tender, and more about passion than respect.

5. Roiphe objects that talk of explicit consent wrongly turns the discussion into one of sexuality. Her three major objections are summarized in paragraph 25: First, making rules or laws about explicit consent assumes that women are incompetent to communicate their own wishes. Second, the rules assume that women do not have free will because they never want to have sex; they can only choose to say no to someone else's propositions. Finally, the rules assume that women lack "strength of character," as well as physical strength, and therefore need rules as an equalizer to use against men who have greater physical, emotional, and intellectual strength.

6. By using language such as "innocence," "shame," and "defilement" Roiphe says feminists hearken back to Victorian notions that women possess spiritual, intangible "purity" that sets them apart from men. Purity can be "lost" through rape—or, possibly, through any act of assertive, joyful sexuality. In paragraphs 31 and 32, Roiphe connects this Victorian ideology explicitly with the life stage of a young woman leaving home for the first time to attend college. While this wrenching out-of-the-sandbox, into-the-rat-race transition is a normal part of growing up, young women are encouraged by rape-crisis feminists to sublimate their angst by recasting it in terms of sexuality.

7. Feminists like Sonya Rasminsky, in her play *Calling It Rape*, suggest that rape frequently hinges on misunderstanding. In the rape (which is recounted, rather than enacted), a woman has asked that a man use a condom. Students may disagree about whether or not her request constitutes consent—it's especially difficult to tell, since the drama has actors discussing rather than acting out the event, and since readers are at one more remove through Roiphe's retelling. The woman might have wanted to prevent pregnancy, disease, or AIDS infection—she need not have been giving consent for sex. Roiphe mocks the notion that there are separate discourses of "boyspeak" and "girlspeak." Instead, she believes that colleges have become far more diverse in terms of class, regional, cultural, ethnic, religious, and political backgrounds—as well as in terms of gender. Differences other than gender are responsible for misunderstandings.

8. First, Roiphe does not believe that sex can be made free from manipulation, coercive persuasion, or contests of the will. Second, expanding the definition of rape dilutes the power of the word when applied to cases of "real" rape. Third, overuse of the word has led some feminists to "collapse the distinction between rape and sex." To avoid rape, women must refrain from sex. Fourth, indiscriminate use of the word oversimplifies our lives. Finally, the confluence of these problems creates an ethos much like "the rigidly conformist 50's," hardly "the heyday of women's power."

9. Roiphe's argument assumes that men and women are pretty similar. She would probably concede that men have the edge in physical strength, since she is willing to admit in paragraph 7 that some women actually do suffer from rape—

although for Roiphe to consider it real, it seems that "bruises and knives, threats of death or violence" must always be present. But in paragraphs 22 through 25, she decries education campaigns that make women seem more asexual, stupid, and emotionally fragile than men. Most differences for Roiphe, then, seem to stem from women's socialization into archaic codes of behavior and ways of talking about sexuality. Perhaps these customs once held some justification; that is, perhaps they are social holdovers like the ones Miedzian ("The Culture of Violence") discusses. But they make no sense in the twentieth century.

10. Discussion will depend on the demographics of your classroom. It might be interesting to have students jot down, say, the five most important rules they believe women follow, and have them compare notes.

RHETORICAL CONSIDERATIONS

1. Some examples: The poster in paragraph 1 is purple—a color usually associated with inflated prose, exaggerated claims. In paragraph 7, "one person's rape may be another's bad night"—some things labeled rape are about as significant as a bad hair day. The man claiming he's been raped, in paragraph 25 looks pretty silly. Clarissa's transposition into the twentieth century, in paragraph 32, also looks silly, and recycles the wide-eyed innocent again. The "kinder, gentler sexuality" in paragraph 41 is a poke at former president George Bush's call for a "kinder and gentler nation." How well the satire does or doesn't work probably depends on the reader's agreement with Roiphe's article in the first place.

2. Roiphe doesn't define acquaintance rape because she doesn't think it exists. She offers some examples, but each one is a fiction. Discussion may be split on how effective her withholding a definition is. On the one hand, if you agree that date rape doesn't exist, then a definition is, of course, impossible. But, on the other hand, Roiphe didn't come up with the term *date rape* herself—and surely somewhere she must have found a definition or two that she could have picked apart as inadequate to cover actual incidents or as marred by faulty reasoning. Without a definition, Roiphe risks appearing to tilt at windmills.

3. Roiphe points out that miscommunication is inevitable on many campuses, because schools today seek students from a much broader range of class, regional, cultural, ethnic, religious, and political backgrounds. The shifts she sketches coincide roughly with women's being accepted into colleges and professions that had been male bastions for years. To the extent that she is able to contextualize feminists' claims about differences in the way men and women speak about sex, she makes a pretty strong case that miscommunication isn't always the reason for rape. That is, a man and a woman sharing the same background may have more in common than two women or two men whose backgrounds differ extensively. But Roiphe overstates, perhaps even slings a red herring, when she makes the blanket claim in paragraph 39 that the "'miscommunication' that recurs through the literature on date rape is a code word for difference in background."

4. Student responses might vary, but women who have a healthy sense of their own sexuality are conspicuously missing from this article. Her main point, of course, is to refute an argument that she does not agree with, not to offer a primer on human sexuality for college women. She might also have omitted the portrait of healthy female sexuality because one simple definition cannot suffice; Roiphe wants to avoid being boxed into a corner.

5. Roiphe assumes any differences in sexual drive or desire can be attributed to socialization, rather than biology. This fundamental similarity is an important cornerstone in her argument: If men and women desire sex equally, then it is no more likely that one will initiate a sexual advance than the other. If scientists could prove men desire sex more than women, then men would have more incentive to coerce or deceive women to obtain sex. In that case, Roiphe would have to work harder to establish that women were participating in sex voluntarily.

6. It is easy to think that the "other victim" here is men, laboring under a blanket accusation of nearly uncontrollable lust. But with the exception of the satire in paragraph 25, Roiphe says very little about how men are affected by the problematic redefinition of rape. Feminists appear to be victims of their own hysteria. Moreover, women, whether feminist or not, are at least potential victims of straitjacket moral codes that prevent them from having any fun. By leaving the "other victim" unspecified, Roiphe effectively generates an air of hyped-up paranoia that mimics the atmosphere generated by stretching the definition of rape too far. With rape so ambiguous, women college students are kept in "a state of perpetual fear" (paragraph 12), any sane heterosexual man would think twice about even holding hands on a date, and feminists are shooting their movement in the foot. Everyone loses in Roiphe's analysis.

Crime and Punishment and Personal Responsibility
Clarence Thomas

TOPICAL CONSIDERATIONS

1. The first reason is deterrence. Although we may voluntarily comply with laws, such as speed limits, because they are in our own best interests, Thomas is unwilling to trust either self-interest or altruism for compliance. We obey laws because we do not want to be punished. The second reason is respect for human dignity. By insisting that lawbreakers be punished, we implicitly acknowledge their humanity—their capacity for knowing right from wrong, and their capacity for self-control. The third reason is the social compact. In order to think of ourselves as members of a social unit, we must be able to trust each other. When that trust is violated by an individual lawbreaker, the trust among other members of society can only be maintained if the lawbreaker is punished.

2. A signal is a mark, a flag, a sign that distinguishes one kind of thing from another kind of thing. Some examples: somebody waving flags in the middle of the road is signaling danger or need of assistance. A Post-It note in a book sig-

nals that a specific reading or passage in that book is important. Criminal law serves a signaling function by marking certain kinds of behavior as harmful, offensive, counterproductive, or otherwise inappropriate. In paragraph 6, Thomas points out that the prevalence of harmful behavior suggests that the signaling function no longer works well. If it worked, we would have fewer examples of lawlessness to contend with.

3. Thomas refers to the civil rights movement, women's liberation, and the war on poverty from the 1960s and 1970s; also, to the resultant belief that some individuals need protection from discriminatory enforcement of existing laws. The groups who benefited were (racial and ethnic) minorities, women, and the poor. Federal interventions were seen as necessary because the chain of court appeals was liable to be saturated with prejudice against these "unpopular groups," barring fair decisions. Procedural protections—specific guidelines for decision making—often spell out steps in nit-picking mechanical or statistical detail. The object of these protections was to assure that uniform standards were applied to each and every case, to assure that personal whim was minimized in decisions, and to make the whole process visible to outside enforcement agencies.

4. An "unpopular group" is one that may be fair game for discriminatory treatment. Defined narrowly, any group can be made into a disadvantaged minority, as Bakke demonstrated. Clearly, disadvantaged groups' rights may overlap and conflict. However, Thomas might be read as ambivalent on popular culture, and popularity generally. On the one hand, he is scornful of the effects of popularity in paragraph 12, where he finds popularity partly to blame for looser standards of personal responsibility. On the other hand, he approves of at least two effects of the rights revolution: the "judicial revolution in due process rights" and the circumscribed authority "of local communities to set standards for decorum and civility" (paragraph 7). His ambivalence comes when he fails to admit that popularity was instrumental in creating the rights revolution. Had blacks or women or the poor not been able to make a compelling public case of their injustice, then no remedies would have been offered them.

5. First, Thomas says that the poor and minorities were themselves perceived as victims of society. They were unable to obtain equitable treatment because of racism, classism, or sexism. Second, he reasons, that this victim status created excuses for individual lawbreakers. Victims are by definition harmed sufficiently so that they lose some of their capacity for free choice. Finally, in order to function effectively, criminal law must assume that lawbreakers are responsible for their actions; yet social ills were perceived to have removed the individual's capacity to choose to act responsibly. In effect, "society" is blamed for the individual's wrongdoing. Paragraphs 12 and 13 are key to Thomas's argument.

6. Thomas must answer that none of these individuals should be excused. While Thomas supplies a social-ills "excuse" for each individual's behavior, his point is that no such excuse is valid. Each one has made a choice to perform a wrongful act, and each one must be punished if the signaling function of the law is to remain intact.

7. This is a "hard lesson" because it will be painful to enforce. If we are compassionate, caring human beings, then it will (and should be, Thomas seems to imply) very difficult to inflict the additional pain of punishment on someone who has already been harmed by the system. But two wrongs don't make a right. Even if we extend compassion to one individual—even if we could be assured that compassion would benefit our one "oppressed" lawbreaker far more than punishment—the larger social consequences must outweigh the personal considerations. The law's signaling function must remain paramount, or our society will disintegrate into chaos, says Thomas.

8. If we fail to punish lawlessness, Thomas says, then we signal to young people that we condone such behavior, no matter what rhetoric we write into law. The poor and minorities suffer most with this shift in philosophy for several reasons. First, if lawlessness is thus condoned among minorities, then there will be no effective deterrent against lawbreakers in minority communities. Second, obviating personal responsibility treats people as if they were children or animals. Third, if we fail to hold people accountable for their actions, then people can never take pride in their accomplishments, either. Without reason for pride, people will cease to strive to overcome their bad environments, because they will have no reason to do so.

RHETORICAL CONSIDERATIONS

1. (a) The overview of criminal law is presented in paragraphs 1 through 5. Students' summaries may vary, but one sample might be: *Criminal law is necessary for a safe society that acknowledges human dignity.* (b) The discussion of a shift in legal decisions runs from paragraphs 6 to 13, with paragraph 6 serving as a transition. The main idea here might be as follows: *The rights revolution has wrongly allowed lawbreakers to blame society, rather than themselves, for their actions.* (c) The part on effects and consequences for society runs from paragraph 14 to the end of the article. It may be summarized as: *If we continue to accept social ills as excuses for breaking the law, then we will suffer from a chaotic, violent breakdown of society.*

2. Probably the best candidate for thesis statement appears at the beginning of the article: ". . . there can be no freedom and opportunity for many in our society if our criminal law loses sight of the importance of individual responsibility." Not only is the statement brisk and straightforward setting forth the businesslike, thoughtful tone, but its early placement forecasts the reasoning to come.

3. Students may cite a number of devices contributing to the formal tone. Thomas uses no humor, no hooks to snare reader attention, no cute devices or engaging anecdotes. He does address readers from time to time, such as "Let's begin" in paragraph 2, and he does prompt audience reflection with rhetorical questions inviting disciplined, careful thought. He is sparing with figures of speech, and those he uses tend to be lofty. For example, "rife with drug bazaars" in paragraph 6. The structure of his sentences is complex. His prose is carefully crafted and balanced—no undigested globs of thought, no tongue twisters, with enough long-short variations in sentence length to avoid tedium.

Yet, craft is subordinate to purpose. Thomas is not seeking to entertain, but to inform with scalpel-like precision. He assumes his audience is highly educated, either as lawyers or as well-informed professionals. He also assumes that his audience has more than passing knowledge of the "rights revolution," and that they come to his article with an intrinsic interest in what he has to say. Finally, he assumes that they know he is the Supreme Court justice appointed upon Justice Thurgood Marshall's retirement, with heated debates during nominating procedures about whether he was appointed specifically because he is an African-American.

4. Thomas conjures up a number of nightmarish fears throughout his argument. He begins small, with traffic laws in paragraph 2, but quickly moves to drugs, street crime, and violence in schools in paragraph 6. Throughout the remainder of the article, he is concerned with serious personal crime rather than "victimless" crimes such as prostitution or tax evasion. While Thomas takes as his province "the law" as a whole, his examples have a narrow breadth. Fear does make his argument more compelling, since the clincher at the end is that failure to follow his advice will cause an increase in violent, personal crime.

5. After the stormy 1991 Supreme Court appointment hearings, few readers would be unaware of Thomas's race. There was strong speculation, although Anita Hill's charges of sexual harassment overshadowed it, that Thomas was chosen because he is African-American rather than someone possessed of the best legal mind among the candidates. At first glance, his reference seems ingenuous. Yet his use of *we* in that final sentence reverses his use of the pronoun throughout the rest of the article. Thomas has consistently identified himself as one with an undifferentiated group of law-abiding American citizens—"we choose to honor speed limits" in paragraph 2, "our schools" in paragraph 6, and numerous instances of "how can we hold responsible. . . ." The intended effect of this pronoun switch seems to be surprise. Throughout the article, Thomas has let readers identify "the poor" and "minorities" as criminals weaseling through the legal system. However in this eloquent and logical article Thomas offers himself as living proof that being poor and black does not make human dignity or success impossible.

6. At first, the rights revolution section (paragraphs 7–11) seems to be an unnecessarily long digression. However, Thomas is concerned throughout with identifying various kinds of cause-and-effect sequences, and with refuting specious reasoning. It makes sense, then, for him to chart historical causes. By using the rights revolution as the start of the problem, Thomas avoids blaming any one group for current errors in legal logic. The driving principle of the rights revolution was that everyone should have equal privileges, protections, and shares in the nation's wealth, along with equal responsibilities. This principle was violated when minorities and the poor did not have access to the benefits; the rights revolution sought to restore those benefits. Those who took the wrong turn, discussed beginning in paragraph 12, are shown to have noble intentions. However, the wrong turn did occur when the judicial system began waiving equal responsibilities to offset lack of equal benefits. The two things (responsibilities and benefits) are not interchangeable—presumably because the concept of a rational

human being assumes that we always have choices about whether or not to be responsible, even when we have no control over our receipt of benefits. Thomas discusses the rights revolution at such length in order to set up the major building blocks in his argument in historical context and to show good faith in the intentions of contemporary legal theorists.

Oprah! Oprah in the Court!
Sophfronia Scott Gregory

TOPICAL CONSIDERATIONS

1. In each case, the juries were swayed to sympathy for the defendants because of "mitigating circumstances." Each one claimed that domestic violence was a contributing factor in his or her violent action. Lorena Bobbitt, accused of mutilating her husband, claimed that he had been a physically and emotionally abusive husband. The Menendez brothers, accused of murdering their parents, also claimed their parents had been abusive. Dan Lundgren, attorney general of the state of California calls a legal defense that invokes such an excuse based on vivid or even lurid testimony "Oprahization."

2. First, Macias' defense drew upon the recent focus on victimization and abuse cycles in the fields of psychotherapy and social work, and in the burgeoning, self-help publishing. The Indiana man's defense refers to his "intoxication" with pornography. A number of behavioral treatment programs take their cues from Alcoholics Anonymous, often with little change from the AA strategies of a 12-step program, and a philosophy stressing the behavior as disease that individuals are not responsible for contracting. (That is, they are no more responsible for getting the disease than is a diabetic; but they are responsible for controlling it—a fine distinction sometimes lost.) Finally, the girl who killed to obtain a leather coat brings together two popular foci of white middle-class obsessions: a post-Reaganomics fascination with the "plight" of the "inner-city poor," and the aftershocks of Vietnam.

3. Daimion Osby's defense was "urban survival syndrome." Osby and his victims lived in a poor, predominantly black, crime-ridden neigborhood. The two men who threatened him "fit the profile of the most dangerous men in America." Therefore, Osby usually lived in a state of abnormally heightened fear, and he had every reason to become even more fearful when black men threatened him. Critics are divided. Jared Taylor (not specifically identified as black, but as an "expert witness") seems to think this defense is a good idea—that is, it's a jungle out there! On the other hand, Rev. Emerson (whose comment "our community" identifies him as black) deplores this defense.

4. Garcetti, who tried the Menendez brothers, was surprised at the "emotional pull" that vivid discussions of abuse had on the jury. He believes jurists' emotions either are an inappropriate source of bias or must be carefully constrained. Nan

Whitfield, however, expresses relief that jurors are subject to emotion, which she valorizes as an important human quality in contrast to prosecutors' narrow-minded insistence on facts. D'Amato points out that juries have historically operated with a will of their own, no matter what their instructions have been. If they believe that a law is unfair, they may even return a verdict that flies in the face of immediate logic, but reaches "instinctively" for higher justification.

5. Montel Williams, in paragraph 12, refuses to acknowledge any responsibility for legal trends, observing that the cause-and-effect sequence has been turned around—that is, television is simply a mirror for contemporary trends; by itself, it creates nothing. Rose Mary Henri, the executive producer for Sally Jessy Raphaël, is unsure what her show's direct effect on criminal law has been. However, she does credit her show with increased public awareness of various kinds of abuse. Finally, Oprah Winfrey herself agrees with Henri when she comments that her talk show has increased public awareness. But unlike Williams, she frets about the possible impact of her show on court decisions; specifically, she's concerned about whether or not the show adequately stresses personal responsibility. Student discussion on who's right will vary. It will depend to some extent on their personal views of the media.

6. Student discussion will vary. Those who aren't newspaper-readers might need to see a few clips on an issue in order to become involved. You might have students conduct a random campus poll—asking for information on the respondent's gender, race, age, and so on, and trying to correlate it with an opinion on a current issue.

RHETORICAL CONSIDERATIONS

1. The tone of the first paragraph, an enticing hook, is sensational, almost as if Gregory were emulating one of the talk shows. She achieves the tone with at least three devices. First, she emphasizes dramatic contrasts. The violence of the pipe-wrench murder is placed against a backdrop of a quiet suburban neighborhood. The prosecuting attorneys assumed the case would be easy, but it became extremely difficult. Second, she selects powerfully vivid words: *bludgeon, mount, battering.* Finally, she uses stock turns of phrase that smack of tabloid journalism: "in the quiet of suburban Los Angeles," "battering and 25 years of abuse," "Hanoukai felt trapped." This introduction presents in capsule version the sort of dramatic tension that Gregory suggests is part of daytime talk shows. If Gregory were attempting a more serious cause-and-effect argument, then the histrionics might seem out of place.

2. Gregory's thesis appears in paragraph 2: that "critics charge . . . juries are increasingly willing to make allowances," and that their willingness has something to do with daytime talk shows. The article is more a report of trends in public opinion than a watertight argument. Although she seems sympathetic to the idea that some influence exists, Gregory never tells us her own opinions.

3. The earliest clue appears in the first sentence of paragraph 7: the word "urban." This topic sentence compares Osby's case to that of the Milwaukee girl who was

called "an inner-city teenager," another synonym for people of color. The next overt clue appears at the end of the paragraph: his neighborhood was "dangerous," a reinforcement of the "inner-city" connotations. Jared Taylor's comments in the paragraph that follows identifies the dead men as black, but is silent on Osby's race. Finally, Rev. Emerson comments that "'these folks' can't help shooting each other." He explicitly includes Osby in the category "these folks," where the quote marks indicate Rev. Emerson's disdain for the categorization of all black people as "volatile, angry, and presumed guilty." Nowhere, however, do Gregory or her sources outright say "Osby is African-American." Is Gregory squeamish about race? Is she trying to playdown race in the Osby case? Is she relying on journalistic code words to save space? It's difficult to tell.

4. In order, Gregory has used (1) Dan Lungren, attorney general of California; (2) Nan Whitfield, an L.A. public defender; (3) Jo-Ellan Dimitrius, a jury consultant in Pasadena; (4) John Gilleland, a jury consultant in Chicago; (5) an Indiana defense lawyer, indirectly through the *American Bar Association Journal;* (6) another defense lawyer in Milwaukee; and (7) defense lawyer Bill Lane in Texas. Up to this point, sources have been exclusively legal. (8) Jared Taylor's role as "expert witness for the defense" in the Osby case suggests weighty albeit nonlegal credentials; and (9) Rev. Ralph Waldo Emerson is a Fort Worth minister and community activist. Following this nonlegal interlude, Gregory again cites legal experts: (10) L.A. district attorney Gil Garcetti; Whitfield (mentioned earlier); and (11) law professor Anthony D'Amato. In the last two paragraphs, she obtains comments from (12) Montel Williams, talk-show host; (13) Rose Mary Henri, executive producer of a talk show; and (14) Oprah Winfrey. The sheer number of sources is impressive. However, it's an odd assembly. Since Gregory's focus is on the effect of talk shows, it does make some sense for her to give more weight to the legal experts (sources 1–7 and 10–11 noted previously), as well as to social commentators (sources 8–9). These are the folks more likely to have thought deeply about Gregory's main subject; for talk-show professionals who seem more interested in recovery and ratings, it's a peripheral issue.

5. Gregory's defense attorneys seem slick, willing to go to any length to win acquittal—even if clients are guilty. In all of the cases cited, Gregory assumes that the defendant actually committed the act described, and that the defendant's lawyer believed he or she had committed the act. Descriptions of defense strategies connote gleeful gamesmanship. Attorneys have "fewer qualms" about "exotic arguments"; they coin terms like "cultural psychosis" to solidify concepts favorable to their cases; and one, Whitfield, "scoffs" at questions about credibility. Courts are exasperated, refusing to admit the worst arguments; nevertheless, the clever, conniving defense attorney merely formulates another silly argument in a war of attrition. The aggregate picture is so unsavory that one is almost willing to hope talk-show hosts do have an influence, because anyone short of the devil himself is likely to be less pernicious than a defense attorney.

6. With this parting shot, Gregory introduces a sour note of cynicism about the willingness of even the best-hearted talk-show host to pander to her audience's taste for cheap thrills. Her characterization of Oprah Winfrey herself in the final para-

graph seems to be the most sympathetic of all the hosts mentioned. Although she's dubbed the "queen of talk," Oprah seems to be genuinely concerned about the effects her show might have. Yet the title for the new show suggests that Oprah's humane ambivalence is tainted in her quest for high Nielsen ratings.

Life on the Shelf: What It's Like to Live in Prison

George Dismukes

TOPICAL CONSIDERATIONS

1. If Dismukes is being honest with us, then he did nothing to cause his imprisonment. He was jailed "on circumstantial evidence" for shooting and murdering a man whom he was trying to help. Dismukes further identifies himself as 51 years old, a grandfather, and "in poor health." Beyond these facts, Dismukes says nothing about himself directly, and precious little indirectly. His comments, in paragraph 4, about his response to solitary confinement suggest that he is well educated, an obvious fact from his command of the language. He also states in the beginning of paragraph 6, "I am not like any of these men," suggesting that he has enjoyed middle-class privilege most of his life; but the exact contours of his background remain vague.

2. Daytime activities included petty squabbling about trivial matters. During the night, Dismukes lost sleep because of the noise of men shouting, hollering, or praying. He sums it up as "bedlam," akin to a premodern facility for confining the insane. He describes lockdown, or solitary confinement, without direct contact with fellow inmates. The graffiti on his walls speak of terror, loneliness, and despair. Dismukes can also hear other lockdown inmates, although apparently at more of a distance; some seem to have completely lost their sanity. As a grace note, he describes the erratic laundry schedule, curtailed shaving and telephone privileges, and lack of sunlight in lockdown. Prison sounds like hell.

3. Student responses will vary. The comparison of prison to a college dorm is perhaps invidious, but should prompt students to make the connection that Dismukes clearly wants them to make: environment can shape behavior in even the strongest, most well-balanced personality. Unaesthetic or noxious surroundings.

4. Dismukes says that most of the men in the prison did something careless or stupid. In paragraph 2, he has characterized their crimes as petty theft, parole violation, and small-time drug-dealing. He generally assumes they are guilty of the crimes which landed them inside. They became involved in criminal activity because poverty and lack of class privilege left them few other options. In paragraph 12, he names a symbolic trio of contributing factors: "guns, educational dysfunction and dissolved family structure." When they leave, Dismukes believes that their poverty and lack of options will remain unchanged. Before and after their prison experience, they live "pointless, dangerous, deprived, depraved lives."

5. The current problem Dismukes focuses on in paragraph 10 is that "Millions of people in this land languish wasted, underachieving." The prison system contains only a small proportion of these millions. By implication, these millions could be making productive, thoughtful contributions to America's social, economic, political, and cultural fabric. Instead, they are "written off as . . . human trash." In paragraph 11, he examines what will happen if we don't change this system, especially the trend to pump more money into prisons, and to jail more people. Rather than remedying any problems, this trend makes them worse. Finally, in paragraph 12, he suggests some root causes of crime that should be addressed. Most of his ideas here are directly or indirectly focused on young people, suggesting that training and early intervention are far more effective than punishment after the fact of a crime.

6. Philosophical and social. See above. Some students might argue that he is trying to create pity for himself. But I don't see that. See answer 1 in Rhetorical Considerations that follow.

RHETORICAL CONSIDERATIONS

1. Students may come up with a number of reasons for the sparse self-commentary. One might be that Dismukes does not want to focus attention on himself, but on the social arguments he presents. Given the article's initial appearance in *Newsweek,* Dismukes had a limited amount of space. Another important and related effect is that Dismukes avoids wallowing in self-pity. There's very little he can say about his wrongful conviction or prison conditions that would not seem calculated, perhaps even whining. Therefore he deflects attention away from himself. Also, this strategy makes him seem stoically controlled, detached, and therefore a credible witness to prison conditions. Finally, the absence of personal detail makes him seem as dehumanized as the prison system would wish to make him; he is one among many, undifferentiated. That anonymous quality, coupled with his affable, almost genial tone throughout the article, may also be calculated to get readers to understand "there but for the grace of God go I."

2. Dismukes provides examples of irrational behavior that begins at a minor, almost benign, level and rapidly degenerates into wretched, nearly incomprehensible behavior. He also moves from external descriptions to a more intimate view of the psychological states that motivate the behavior. First, he mentions petty squabbles. Next, he details nighttime hollering. Following that, he becomes more psychologically intimate. The graffiti mention feelings that prompt irrational behavior: fear, loneliness, the solipsism of ignorance. Finally, he describes someone who has lost all rational control, to the extent that behavior becomes self-destructive (hurling himself against walls, beating himself). It's an effective string for pulling readers into gradual empathetic understanding. Had he described the extreme-case first, readers would have had little to identify with.

3. The implications that millions suffer but only a few thousand are caught are chilling. Millions remain who have at the very least the same prompts and tempta-

tions to criminal action. Given Dismukes' behaviorist leanings about human nature, it is highly probable that he believes a good number of those millions actually engage in crime. Furthermore, the ones who remain outside of prison are lucky—or more careful, or more intelligent—than prison inmates. It's as if he sees contemporary social structure as a vast Darwinist machine, patiently weeding out the lesser crooks so the more vicious ones remain alive and well, not only functioning but teaching the next generation. Once they recognize this implication, students may not agree on whether his soft-pedaling is effective. Dismukes could have pounded us over the head with it, in a dramatic fire-and-brimstone "reform now, the end is near" jeremiad. But then, he probably would have turned off many of his readers. The main appeal of the piece is that it remains modest and quasi-personal in its claims. And if that is indeed his strategy, then the unspoken implications contribute to the haunting quality of his observations.

4. Dismukes is writing for white middle-class readers, people who need to be shown in detail the consequences of being found "guilty" of a serious crime. In the first 6 paragraphs, Dismukes notes various ways he is different from other inmates, and more like his readers: intellectual, reflective, curious. From paragraphs 7 through 9, he is not so different from the inmates. Any man would feel dehumanized by once-a-week shaves. Any office worker would wince at the complete replacement of sunlight by a fluorescent fixture. Anybody can act carelessly or stupidly. Anybody can feel his or her life at a stalemate. In paragraph 10, Dismukes' stance changes again. He insults readers, apostrophizing them directly as "men and women who . . . lack imaginations." In effect, he has cut himself off from either inmates or readers, standing alone.

At one time, Dismukes too was among "the smug and contented," oblivious to the looming problem he describes. But now, by a fluke, he finds himself the beneficiary of sudden insight. This movement is problematic. It does make him sound rather wise and heroic by the end of the article; certainly the wisdom, at least, is necessary for him to get his message across. But it also makes him sound bitter and cynical, Cassandra-like in his last paragraph. He speaks with the voice of prophecy, but is pretty sure nobody is listening because people are too stupid. They're just as much zombies as the inmates in lockdown.

5. To be "left on the shelf" is a metaphor for an old maid, a woman past marriageable age, who has failed to attract a man to marry her. Hence she is doomed to a life of playing "odd woman out"—an awkward social encumbrance in a society dominated by coupleism. Dismukes doesn't seem to be referring to his marital status. However, he does present himself as occupying an odd location in the social scheme: neither part of the underclass, nor any longer eligible for ruling-class privileges. Just as some "odd women" leveraged their social awkwardness into subversive freedom, Dismukes feels himself freed from the blinders of conventional social caste (albeit not without compromised freedom elsewhere).

A second meaning might be literal. Something that is left on the shelf is at a better vantage point than if it were off the shelf. It is above, or at least to one side of the main action, rather than being a participant, and thus may have a more complete or objective view. Additionally, do note in paragraph 5 the reference to Dismukes' "shelflike bunk" in lockdown, perhaps gesturing toward his sense of enforced passivity, as if he were sleeping—or confined to a small, precarious place.

Why I Bought a Gun
Gail Buchalter

TOPICAL CONSIDERATIONS

1. Buchalter's purchase of a gun stands in sharp contrast to her cultured upbringing and liberal-minded ideals. Buchalter says that there was no place for guns in her upper-middle-class background. When threatened, her parents "simply put another lock on the door." In high school, Buchalter says she underwent a transformation of values, from cashmere sweaters to black arm band. As with so many young people of the late 1960s and early 1970s, the author says she became an active pacifist marching for civil rights and against the Vietnam War.

2. The turning point came one Halloween night in Phoenix when Buchalter was pursued by three men threatening "to rape, cut and kill" her. What saved her, no doubt, was the sight of her two large dogs whose protection helped make her daringly aggressive. "I was so scared that I became aggressive," she writes. The men ran off but not without promising to return to kill her. That awful episode taught Buchalter not only to fear the mindless, random violence in our society, but to consider doing something about it. By the time she moved to Los Angeles she had a 3-year-old son to worry about. What convinced her to purchase her Smith & Wesson .38 was the gradual takeover of her neighborhood by drug-dealing street gangs. Moreover, the threat of Richard Ramirez, "the Walk-In Killer" whose "crimes were so brutal and bizarre" compelled her to defend herself despite her pacifism. Reluctantly she concluded that to insure her survival and that of her son's she needed a gun.

3. She was held up at gunpoint years before. This discovery no doubt encourages the author to follow the same path before she too became a victim to violence.

4. Buchalter cites two important features of her experience at the National Rifle Association convention: that lots of ordinary people from grandmas to kids were buying guns; and, from the video seminars for women she learns the function and care of firearms.

5. In paragraph 24, Buchalter says that "knowledge . . . is still our greatest defense," a justification fortified by her belief in educating the young about sex and AIDS. In the next two paragraphs she describes how persistent she was in teaching her son how to handle the gun—how to check that it was unloaded and how not to use it if someone broke into their house.

6. In her situation with a young son and gangs infesting the neighborhood, I think I might have done the same. Student reaction here should be interesting.

RHETORICAL CONSIDERATIONS

1. The opening sentence of paragraph 3 is her thesis statement.
2. This detail does several things. First, sitting next to a contributing editor for a gun magazine puts her next to the kind of people she previously would not have associated with. A one-time pacifist and political liberal, Buchalter would probably have avoided NRA men. Here she's a stranger in a strange land. The man's bitter complaint about the outlawing of elephant hunting says something about the kinds of people the NRA attracts, men who are insensitive to killing animals that are high on the endangered species lists. Also, his comment about elephant legs making "wonderful trash baskets" characterizes him as something short of barbaric. Feeling like Thumper, the rabbit friend of Bambi, on "opening day of the hunting season" suggests how vulnerable she feels next to the man. And her twitching foot confirms her lack of ease.
3. By assigning the final comment its own paragraph gives it special emphasis and dramatic impact. The line functions as commentary to the author's friends who are dismayed that she owns a gun and who "believe that violence begets violence." Sitting alone, the comment carries a note of sad resignation and inevitability. In other words, her friends are "probably right" that someday that nightmare two paragraphs back might come true. The line also rhetorically rounds out the essay as it sadly reflects on how far from the innocence and idealism Buchalter has come since the reflections in the first two paragraphs.

10

Censorship Versus Free Speech

Politically Correct Language—Pro

Why We Need Bias-Free Language

Rosalie Maggio

TOPICAL CONSIDERATIONS

1. Maggio introduces her article with concrete examples rather than with abstract generalizations. In her first example, she points out that generic use of masculine pronouns (the generic *he*) to refer to the United States president makes it difficult to think about a woman holding that office. Her second example, in paragraphs 2 and 3, concerns racist language; when Caucasians have used derogatory labels to refer to other racial and ethnic groups, they have found it easier to inflict violent harm on those groups. When the term *sexual harassment* came into currency, legislators were able to formulate laws to help in eliminating that behavior. People who are described as *detainees* are experiencing a private inconvenience that is not the business of international politics. When those same people are *hostages,* their problem attains global significance. *Fetal tissue* is subject to far fewer moral and legal restraints upon what may be done with it than is an *unborn baby.* In all cases, the specific language leads to fairly dramatic decisions and actions.

2. The first excuse Maggio lists, in paragraph 9, is lack of "fun"—enjoyment of spontaneous, playful use of language. She counters this objection by pointing out that careful speakers and writers edit their words for accuracy all the time; unbiased language does not detract any further than does routine attention to "proper grammar, spelling, and style." The next excuse is that the language will be deprived of richness of expression (paragraph 10). Maggio contends that human imagination is more than adequate to offset any perceived losses. The third excuse is a reluctance to be overly self-conscious about avoiding offense (paragraph 11). Here Maggio becomes impatient, snapping that people who advance such an objection are insensitive and lazy. Just as we edit our spoken and written words for mechanical precision, we similarly adapt our choices to make the words appropriate for a specific audience. The greatest objection, she says, is also the one that sounds most foolish (paragraph 12): that efforts at unbiased language will lead to absurd phrases. She dismisses this argument as unfounded nit-picking. Maggio adds one more reason for using unbiased language: It will improve writing style by removing clichés and generalized language, replacing them with precise, specific terms.

3. Maggio states, in paragraph 18, that "biased language communicates inaccurately." Biased language is fundamentally about groups, or about individuals in the

context of group membership; it is not about the individual separate from all components of his or her social identity. Biased language makes assumptions about individuals based on their membership in a group. Those assumptions may or may not hold true for the individual instance. A speaker who carelessly assumes that one individual conforms completely to conventionally accepted or normative behaviors, attitudes, and abilities associated with a group is guilty of stereotyping.

4. The categories Maggio supplies are sex, race, age, sexual orientation, ethnicity, disability status, and religious belief. However, she tends to lean heavily on illustrations from sexism alone. Students may not be able to come up with new categories—or, if they've just had a run-in with a landlord who "doesn't rent to students," they might. The difficulty is that our sense of who needs (or doesn't need) protection from biased language changes over time.

5. In paragraph 23, Maggio uses the term to refer to language that "treats all people equally"; in paragraph 27, she says that symmetrical language "promotes fairness to both sexes." Clearly, it's a quality she means to encourage. Symmetry refers to equal or balanced treatment; it means using terms that convey equivalent amounts of information about different groups of people, when the difference between the groups isn't important.

   Maggio and other writers commonly use symmetry to discuss only gender-bias, but it has important implications for other forms of biased language. Minorities complain, for example, of journalism that somehow never fails to point out that a criminal was African-American, Hispanic, or Native American—but when the criminal is white, reference to race is omitted.

6. Gender-free language omits all reference to gender by using neutral terms. It is appropriate when gender is irrelevant to the subject under discussion. Gender-fair language uses symmetry: equivalent terms to refer to men and women. Maggio extends the concept in paragraphs 28 and 29, when she warns us not to draw generalizations about a group based only on its male participants, and not to interpret identical behavior with language that conveys different connotations based on gender stereotype. Gender-specific language seems to contradict the first principle—that we not mention gender if at all possible. However, this principle functions as a safeguard against faulty generalizations. If a vast majority of people who suffer from a particular kind of oppression are women (or men), then the language should reflect that preponderance so that we can observe it and correct it.

7. Student responses will vary. A brilliant politician who happens to be blind need not be referred to as "the blind politician" in most cases, following the principle of gender-free language. A name (perhaps followed by a title in the initial reference) would suffice. Following the gender-fair principle, reportage of an ecumenical meeting should not refer to "nine members of the clergy and a rabbi," drawing undue attention to the one Jewish participant. Solutions might include reference to "ten religious leaders," placing all on equal footing, or could offer a more specific breakdown of the other nine individuals' religious affiliation. Gender-specific language seeks to draw attention where attention can help bring about a resolution of attitudes and problems. Hence a reference to "those who would be affected by a reduction in Social Security benefits" might well be followed by the parenthetical

addition, "most of whom are over 65." The solution isn't as elegant or simple as changing "battered spouse" to "battered wife," but it follows the same idea.

8. A generic word is a noun or pronoun that refers to a group of people (or, presumably, other entities) based on shared characteristics. A pseudogeneric term is one that purports to refer to a range of people, but which contains internal contradictions that restrict its meaning more narrowly. The contradiction can occur in a compound word such as *mankind* (in which women are excluded) or in a word that has acquired a conventional meaning, such as *immigrants* to refer to United States citizens (omitting Native Americans and African-Americans).

   Pseudogeneric words cause harm by making it difficult to imagine members of the group who do not belong to the word's more restrictive meaning. From Maggio's example, the harm is especially evident when young, impressionable minds are impressed with erroneous limitations.

9. An exonym is a group label—a generic noun—imposed on a group of people by someone outside of that group. Maggio implies that exonyms are always to be avoided since the people so designated do not refer to themselves that way. Exonyms offend because they deny the individual's or group's right to decide on a satisfying form of self-reference.

   Students might not recognize some of the words Maggio lists, or they might have problems coming up with appropriate substitutes. Recognition calls for knowledge of the history, etymology, and sensitivity of such words so as not to come up with a worse substitute. Part of the problem is that some groups may not have reached a consensus on what they want to be called. A new generation may spurn the usage of a former generation, resulting in a confusing sedimentation of terms. In order to know whether Negro, colored, black, Afro-American, or African-American is acceptable, for example, a speaker must know something about the context in which the word will be used. "Negro" would usually be inappropriate in conversation with younger Americans of African descent; but it would be mandatory in certain historical references (the 1920s as the era of the "New Negro"), and is still used as a neutral, preferred term by some older Americans of African descent.

   Furthermore, some terms are being actively "reclaimed" by their constituent groups—that is, they are being used consciously and repeatedly as appropriate labels as a way to affirm identity and group solidarity. Of the terms Maggio lists, *gay* and *pagan* are undergoing this process now.

10. Maggio says simply that "naming is power," but this may not be discursive enough for students. A name is important because it is the piece of language most intimately associated with identity. The name substitutes for the person or group; thus, if it has any near-homonyms in the language in which it is used, it can generate consequences. Someone with a name like "Suzy Bright," for example, may be treated differently in school than someone named "Bertha Gray."

    By linking the woman's name to a milestone birthday—a decade-marker well into adult maturity—Maggio is emphasizing that the decision calls attention to dignity and maturity. If students have trouble understanding the import, you might try going around the room and asking for the first association that pops into their heads with "Betty" (Betty Crocker? Betty and Veronica?), and a similar run-through for "Elizabeth" (Queen Elizabeth? Elizabeth Taylor?).

RHETORICAL CONSIDERATIONS

1. The student who claimed that the English language had "been around a lot longer than women" probably meant to say *feminists* rather than "women." At a superficial level, the comment is funny. Taken literally, the student's comment implies that speakers of English were, for a long time, exclusively men—women simply did not exist. The student's comment also implies that all women are feminists, whose desired changes would be chaotically disruptive, and that language is and should remain static, unchanging, timeless, and hermetically sealed from human tampering.

    Maggio suggests that language insidiously shapes our perceptions about who has the authority to make decisions. Even if the student's comment had not contained unintentional humor, it reveals stubborn resistance to the notion that women have a right to change language. The only legitimate speakers and actors are men, with that sense of legitimacy conveyed and reinforced by each use of "the generic 'he'" and other sexist language Maggio here seeks to remedy.

    Students may decide that the student was a young man. But entertaining the possibility that the student was a young woman suggests more potently the power language has to shape experience. If the student was a woman, then she has ironically negated her right to speak English.
2. Open for discussion. Some students may comment on the essay's predominant attention to sexist language.

Politically Correct Language—Con

The Word Police
Michiko Kakutani

TOPICAL CONSIDERATIONS

1. The Whitmanesque litany of different kinds of people juxtaposes a broad range of people from different races, religions, ethnic origins, sexual orientations, and professions. It's hard to imagine that any one classful of students would contain such a representation; yet, this is only a small sampling of the kinds of people who comprise the population of the United States. The range of people listed, according to Kakutani, sought to represent "a new politics of inclusion." That is, Bill Clinton's successful presidential campaign was based in part on constructing an image that promised to acknowledge the needs and claims of a full spectrum of the country's citizens instead of a dominant, narrowly defined elite corps.
2. In the first half of the paragraph, Kakutani complains about the pseudogeneric *he.* She not only objects to avoiding the word *man* but to replacing words that either are male or invoke hierarchical organization. The "nonbiased" term *monarch of the jungle* replaces king of the jungle, *someone on top of the heap* replaces king of the hill (with the substitution of "hill" seeming a bit gratuitous), and *acme of perfection* replaces masterpiece.

3. The messy dilemmas begin with the problem of contradictions to a specific rule. Maggio's directive to use gender-specific language contradicts her directive to use gender-free language. A second dilemma is the contradictory edict issued by Francine Wattman Frank and Paula Treichler, that sometimes using inclusive pairs of pronouns, "he and she," is appropriate, but that sometimes using the pseudogeneric *he* to emphasize wrongful exclusion of women is appropriate (paragraph 13). The problem with both examples is that the decision about what terms to use is based on a value system that either is not shared by all speakers or is inaccessible to those earnestly trying to make the right choice.

   The final dilemma is one of fairness, a contradiction in principle rather than in rule. Speech codes restrict the use of a word by one group, while allowing its use by another group. However, if laws are supposed to be blind to bias-prone conditions like race or sexual preference, then they cannot extend any privilege to a group based on those conditions.

4. Kakutani does not agree that the titles of well-known literary works (or any works at all, for that matter) should be changed or edited to conform to the bias-free guidelines Maggio recommends. Her examples, in paragraph 16, are chosen to sound silly and lack euphony; the substitutions disrupt carefully crafted rhythms and interplays of sound. Furthermore, as the substitute title "Animal Companion Graves" contrives to illustrate, changes can damage the connotative resonances of an original title so badly that the title becomes gibberish. Finally, if students were to employ brackets and ellipses, they would end up with cumbersome overpunctuated messes. This seems to be Kakutani's point—although it might make a good object lesson in proper citation procedures, too.

5. Kakutani lists *big boned* and *differently sized* as replacements for fat; *exceptional* for stupid; *chemically inconvenienced* for stoned; *the underhoused* for the homeless; and *the economically marginalized* for the poor. She compares these newly coined politically correct terms to obfuscating lingo used during Watergate—*pacification* for military aggression, and *inoperative statement* for lie—in order to draw attention to the way both kinds of language try to deceive readers about the referential subject of this language.

   She objects that these terms are deceptive, merely drawing our attention away from the real problems the original terms designated. As a result, the substitute terms are at best clumsy. Worse yet, they may actually impair our abilities to solve the problems they name, because they help make the seriousness of the problems invisible.

RHETORICAL CONSIDERATIONS

1. Kakutani begins with a solemn moment: President Bill Clinton's inauguration. She seems to laud the event, which for many signified an "official embrace of multiculturalism and a new politics of inclusion." Her second paragraph shifts slightly in tone, but for those readers who would shop at the Politically Correct store, or who agree that animals should not be tortured in the name of cuisine,

little seems out of joint here. Kakutani seems merely to be commenting on the belatedness of this official recognition.

Only in paragraph 3 does her sarcasm become evident. She questioningly "corrects" designations for the Coppertone girl and for Superman in parentheses, and by the time she has applied the term *clones* to revisionist cartoon characters, her disapproval has become apparent.

2. Kakutani would probably answer her question with a resounding "Nobody!" Her strategy of using a rhetorical question here (and throughout the piece) functions to invite readers to mull over just who would use these guidelines, and to get a sense of the futility of searching for an answer. Those who are concerned with politically correct language, she implies, will already know most of the rules in the book, while those who don't know the rules probably don't care or are hostile to them.

The rhetorical question also functions as a sarcastic device, and as a way to vary sentence structure. Kakutani is probably not a good role model for students trying to master a straightforward academic prose style, however; it may be well to warn them away from such a peppering of questions.

3. Kakutani seems to be switching the terms of the debate when she slips in the word "euphemism." Note that she does not explicitly equate this term with "unbiased language"; she lets the reader draw that connection. The two are, of course, very different. A euphemism is a word that seeks to cover up an unpleasant truth, but its final goal is mere disguise in the name of politeness rather than an effort to bring about conceptual change. Efforts to create unbiased language, on the other hand, do not just cover up an unpleasant truth, although this may be their immediate effect. The long-term goal of unbiased language is to change "truth" (not the underlying phenomenon, but the significance we attach to that phenomenon). This being the case, Kakutani uses the word euphemism unfairly.

4. Kakutani avoids drawing an exact connection between the two. It seems like a sneaky maneuver, although it's hard to tell just why she waffles here—unless she's deliberately obscuring a weak point in her argument. All she says is that the two have occurred simultaneously. The reader is left with an impression of causality, but Kakutani can't really be blamed for the false connection.

Maggio would probably agree that there is a cause-and-effect relationship between the two, but she would reverse them. That is, Kakutani apparently wants us to believe that PC reform efforts *cause* sloppy language. Maggio would probably tag sloppy language as the cause, rather than the effect; for Maggio, sloppy language carrying outmoded biases has created a need for PC reform efforts as antidote and cure.

5. Kakutani's lapses and immediate corrections are, of course, not the results of haste, but an effort to illustrate how time consuming and nit-picking the effort of conforming to these guidelines can become. In the first instance, "man (sorry, individual) in the street," she interrupts a clichéd term to insert a new, genuinely generic word. This instance demonstrates how "forgivable" biased language is, because it is so deeply embedded in well-worn phrases.

In the second, "Bluebeard, the rake (whoops!—the libertine)," she uses a conventionally masculine description, "rake," which she replaces with the more neutral "libertine." The irony in the second example is that Bluebeard's story is to be avoided, because its portrayal is too stereotypically masculine.

6. Kakutani assumes that her audience experiences the police as vaguely threatening and disruptive, possibly with an added element of irrational brutality. Kakutani seems resentful, even defiant of language reformers' efforts. Like the police, they seem to have some power to enforce their demands (although Kakutani never spells out the consequences for failing to comply with the word police). Like the police, they may operate within a reasonably orderly lawful system but may sometimes end up enforcing nothing but their own prejudices and whims. Like the police, their ostensible purpose is to make the world a kinder, gentler place for everyone, but they sometimes cause far more destructive problems than they ameliorate.

Outlawing Pornography—Pro

Let's Put Pornography Back in the Closet

Susan Brownmiller

TOPICAL CONSIDERATIONS

1. Students' answers will vary.
2. Yes, Brownmiller's definition (which occurs mainly in paragraph 9) is clear and easily understood. She is careful to define her terms so that what she is saying has less of a chance of being misconstrued. It's very important when writing, and especially when writing persuasive discourse, to stipulate exactly what you mean by certain "key" terms (especially those that do have multiple shades of meaning). This way, opponents cannot base counterattacks on semantics alone.
3. Students' opinions will vary, though most will probably have a hard time thinking of literature (and especially literature now valorized by the academy) as potentially pornographic.
4. Brownmiller means that people can publish or print whatever kinds of work they want to, but that putting that work on a shelf (in a drug store, in a magazine or book store, or in a grocery store, for example) where the general public has ready and easy access to it should be controlled. Students' opinions on this will vary.
5. Since Brownmiller argues with an extremely assured voice, and since she does invoke the Supreme Court so often (in a manner which suggests that she agrees with certain decisions), she most likely does trust the court to agree with her stance on this issue.

RHETORICAL CONSIDERATIONS

1. This is a very forceful opening statement because it seems absolute and confidently put forth. However, it does not necessarily concur with the rest of Brownmiller's argument, which focuses on the "fact" that free speech can indeed go too far. (She says it does as far as pornography is concerned.)

2. The slant of Brownmiller's argument is apparent in paragraph 3; and her thesis is in that same paragraph—at the end. What is interesting, however, is the fact that Brownmiller's thesis is not stated in her own words; rather, the words of Chief Justice Warren Burger supply her thesis. This is an effective maneuver, because she lends authority to her own voice (and to her argument) by quoting from a respected source.

3. By telling the reader to notice the quotation marks around a sentence, Brownmiller calls attention to (or highlights) the statement, while also letting the reader know that she is borrowing from another authority on the matter of free speech and pornography. She is also letting us know that she already has supporters for her argument.

4. She mentions these books as evidence of a time when claims of "pornography" went too far—and to explain that, had these works been deemed pornographic, some of her writing might have been. This does not necessarily function to help her argument because, first of all, she shows how time changes the notion of what is and what isn't acceptable. (We can assume that her argument, too, might weaken with time.) Also, this passage serves to show exactly how subjective these kinds of judgments can be.

5. As she does throughout this essay, Brownmiller uses quotation marks to highlight certain parts of her argument (to give these ideas emphasis), as well as to invoke an authority within her writing, which illustrates the "powerful" support that her position has.

6. This is a safe and fair way to end her argument, although it tends to lack punch. By the end of her essay, Brownmiller seems to have given up all rights to her opinions to the court; this, some readers might find off-putting—"If the courts just decide anyway, why the argument?"

Outlawing Pornography—Con

Why We Must Put Up with Porn

Susan Isaacs

TOPICAL CONSIDERATIONS

1. In the context of this article, Isaacs defines pornography as material such as books or films that degrades women. One could say that this is not an inclusive definition. It does not mention men or children, who are also victims of pornography.

2. A problem of a blue-ribbon panel is twofold. First, definitions of pornography differ among people and groups. Thus, what a right-wing religious group claims as pornographic might differ from what a left-wing secular group defines as pornographic. Second, adhering to such a panel's recommendation requires suspending one's own judgments and beliefs.

3. Isaacs states that research has not established a link between pornography and violence. However, this assertion is not elaborated or specified, thus requiring the reader to simply take Isaacs' word on faith. The lack of any specificity weakens her argument.

4. We must support the right of those espousing opinions we may find noxious to express such views. Censorship is typically a precursor of dictatorship.

5. Once censorship is allowed, it can easily be applied to any and all ideas even those we think could never be threatened by such restrictions. For instance, says Isaacs, ". . . someone might want to ban all depictions of career women or day-care centers, using the argument that they undermine family unity" (paragraph 14).

RHETORICAL CONSIDERATIONS

1. Isaacs uses a chatty, intimate tone, as though she is talking with an acquaintance. The effect is to take the reader into her confidence and to assume she and the reader share the same values and experiences. Examples abound.

2. Isaacs talks of her own novel, *Almost Paradise,* and explains how a zealot could have decided that incest, a theme in her book, must be deleted. She speaks, too, of Robert Mapplethorpe's work considered beautiful by some and obscene by others. Let the viewer not the censors decide, she seems to say.

3. Paragraphs 9 and 11 contain good examples.

Censoring Rap Music—Pro

Let's Stop Crying Wolf on Censorship

Jonathan Alter

TOPICAL CONSIDERATIONS

1. The suggestion is that liberals would decry censoring African-American rap artists but not racist skinheads. Essentially, Alter decries a double standard: that it's permissible for blacks to call for violence against blacks, but not for whites. Of course, the argument can be made that Dr. Dre's lyrics are bitterly ironic, whereas the same by a racist skinhead band called Aryan Nation would be an ugly battle cry.

2. Alter claims that a decision against a rap song is not censorship, but sound business judgment. He defends the right of record companies, radio station managers, and editors to reject what they think their audiences don't want to hear. This is neither a freedom of speech nor a censorship issue says Alter, but a marketing decision: ". . . the Constitution guarantees all Americans the right to rap,

but it says nothing about Dr. Dre's right to a record contract." Alter accuses Field and others like him of falsely invoking First Amendment rights and paying a disservice to legitimate civil liberty concerns. According to Alter, those who boycott offensive entertainment are the ones practicing true freedom of expression.

3. Answers will depend on the class, but it would be useful to remind students of freedom-of-speech abuses in other countries—that is, the confiscation of material deemed as antigovernment and the prosecution of its producers.

4. More than once, Alter refers to the "sociopathic lyrics" of rap music, quoting the lines from Dr. Dre as an illustration. He states that executives should be worried about the "messages they're sending young African Americans," thereby implying that rap inspires violence and that its audience only includes blacks. At the end of his essay, he states that "even at its grimmest, music is meant to enhance life" and compares rap marketers to tobacco executives who "market death." Nowhere does Alter distinguish between "good" and "bad" rap, leading readers to conclude that his general opinion is negative.

5. Alter is most convincing when analyzing *censorship*—in particular, when he points out that real censorship entails government repression, not business or editorial decisions. By clarifying the word, Alter reveals the ulterior motives of rap promoters and others who want to profit by selling what many believe is offensive. For these promoters, who Alter finds more offensive than the singers, the issue is not freedom of speech, but freedom to make a buck.

Some might see Alter's argument weakened by an obvious oversight regarding governmental censorship. He says that although foreign governments ban books and prosecute artists, in America the role of judging what is offensive is left to book publishers, gallery owners, communities, radio stations and so on. But what happens when the government intervenes on decisions of public institutions such as art galleries, or funding sources such as the National Endowment for the Arts? While our government doesn't out right ban exhibits or performances, it has in the past exercised the same authority as a business by denying monies to the artist or threatening to close shows. The result is the same as censorship: no show. (The Robert Mapplethorpe photography exhibits a few years ago caused a storm of controversy.)

6. Opinions will vary. Literally, the words mean *don't think twice about killing a black person.* However, listeners may hear a different message all together. Enhanced by the beat and, in video, the clothes and gestures, there is a strong undercurrent of satire and mimicry that the gray words in an article don't show. For example, the word *nigga* is racist language, snatched from white culture and thrown back in the shape of a Southern redneck slur. In context of the violent imperative, Dr. Dre might be said to parody white culture and its history of abuse. Of course, some students may agree with Alter that the words do call for violence rather than scorn.

7. Some students may include Queen Latifah as an example of a female singer who counters the antifemale lyrics of some rap songs. Other performers communicate their ideas on peace, solidarity, and racial unity through rap.

8. Answer will vary, but instructors could provide examples from recent performances and exhibits from around the country: the Mapplethorpe show in Boston a few years ago; David Lynch's movies, and others.

RHETORICAL CONSIDERATIONS

1. In Paragraph 4, Alter claims that what rap stars and their promoters are calling censorship, producers and editors call an editorial or business judgment not to produce the song or run it on radio. The decision may not be courageous, but it doesn't interfere with artistic expression. The issue at hand is not whether rappers have the right to express themselves, but whether they will get paid to do so. According to Alter, real censorship occurs when the government bans books in libraries, seizes pornography, or prosecutes artists. One of Alter's conclusions is, if censorship means that producers think twice about messages they're sending young African-Americans, then we need more of it.

2. *Example 1:* In the opening paragraph, Alter offers an imaginary situation—a band called Aryan Nation selling a song with racist lyrics—and he concludes no one would be surprised if radio stations declined to run it. He then reveals that the offensive lines are really lyrics from a rap song, and reports how outraged the producer was when radio stations refused it. The analogy is attention-grabbing but not convincing because a black rap group and a white racist band are not interchangeable. The difference is tone: the rappers are being ironic, while the hypothetical skinheads would be calling for racist violence.

   Example 2: In the same paragraph, Alter imagines the kind of predicament the White House would be in if it permitted Aryan Nation's producers to appear there at a benefit. An irony is revealed in the second paragraph when Alter relates that the producer of the offensive rap song once held a Hollywood benefit for President Clinton. Alter's point is amusing, but the illustration doesn't connect to his main argument.

   Example 3: Alter states in paragraph 4, "Garry Trudeau makes his point whenever some wimpy newspaper decides not to run a controversial 'Doonesbury' strip: his fans say he was censored; he rightly calls it bad editing." This is a good illustration because it further draws the distinction between censorship and business judgment. It clarifies vividly his previous declaration that record company executives, art gallery owners, or book publishers who refuse to disseminate material are within their rights to make decisions based on what they know about their audiences. This illustration also draws attention to another one of Alter's points: the misuse of the word censorship.

3. Alter has fun quoting Ted Field to his own advantage: "You can tell the people who want to stop us from releasing controversial rap music one thing: Kiss my ass." He then adds his own rejoinder: "Since Hollywood already has enough people who spend their days eagerly taking Ted Field up on that offer, I thought I'd try a different tack." He also suggests kiddingly that Tipper Gore is presently "going light" on her record labeling campaign for fear of seeming too "censorious." Even Alter's harsh judgment of rap music is conveyed with a light touch:

"It is Ted Field and other phony liberals of his ilk, wrapping themselves in constitutional pieties. . . ."

Alter's choice to approach the issue of censorship by looking at rap already separates him from the more serious and academic concerns of Lawrence. By comparison to the scholarly and measured tone of Lawrence, Alter is straight-talking, and direct. He uses slang (e.g., in paragraph 8, "This is loopy"). He also uses more humor. Hentoff is less scholarly and formal than Lawrence, and nearly as hard-hitting and sharp-edged as Alter.

4. In paragraph 7, Alter concedes that censorship may exist in private schools where officials have tried to punish offensive speech, a claim Hentoff makes in his essay. Like Hentoff, he is clarifying what is true censorship and what others claim it is, yet Alter may part company with Hentoff over issues of what is offensive and what is not. Like Lawrence, Alter is concerned about the effects of offensive speech, and he pleas for those distributing messages to take responsibility for their actions.

5. Paragraph 5: "How did we get to the point where 'art' became a code word for money?" This question is the heart of the essay, Alter's critique of how rap promoters use claims of censorship to draw attention and sympathy. According to Alter, their claims belittle those who suffer real censorship.

Paragraph 8: "These other stations routinely fail to play any folk music. Are they censoring Peter, Paul and Mary?" This question points out the absurd reasoning of those who cry censorship when radio stations refuse to play their songs. He makes the point that responsible judgment is the prerogative of radio station managers who choose one form of music over another.

Censoring Rap Music—Con

Bum Rap

Michael Eric Dyson

TOPICAL CONSIDERATIONS

1. The seventies was a time of economic collapse for black communities. According to Dyson the job markets offering economic stability to many blacks families eroded when the automobile industry reorganized and the steel industry weakened. In tandem, social services supportive of black families and community funding for public recreational areas were cut back.

2. The art of "representin'" tells the story of those living in poverty and chaos. These stories validate the lives, the suffering, and the joys and the rage of those who face annihilating social/economic hardships. Rap music is a way to give voice to the voiceless, to acknowledge their experiences. At its best, Dyson says rappers "shape the torturous twists of urban fate into lyrical elegies."

3. Rap in its "relentless quest to represent black youth" writes a history of the common man immersed in the urban world of today which can hold both wonder

and horror. Dyson feels this delineation of life is history, history free from the political or sanitizing interpretations of conventional historians.

4. Dyson cites recent attempts by black figures such as C. Dolores Tucker and Dionne Warwick to have gangsta' rap censored, possibly even outlawed. He opposes this because it will not solve the problems of black youth, it will not curtail the consumption of this music, and it is a suppression of First Amendment rights. He does, however, feel that one can express moral objections to the content of these lyrics, sometimes misogynistic and sometimes homophobic. Such protest, according to Dyson, should take the form of pamphleteering, community activism, and consciousness raising.

5. Dyson uses the term "ecclesiastical apartheid" to describe black churches in which a population 70 percent female rarely includes female ministers.

6. Open for discussion.

7. Dyson is opposed to censorship. He feels that citizens objecting to rap lyrics should protest by pamphleteering or by disseminating their point of view. He is opposed to any arm of the entertainment industry, whether record producers or radio stations, censoring rap music. Alter, on the other hand, takes pains to narrowly define censorship. He sees censorship as government intervention in the production and distribution of art. He does not consider the decision of a record company executive, a radio producer, or a funding agency not to play or support rap music, for instance, as censorship. He sees that as reasonable discretion. Alters and Dyson define censorship differently. But while Dyson recommends no interference with the distribution of rap lyrics, Alter approves of such interference.

RHETORICAL CONSIDERATIONS

1. The Rosetta stone is an archaeological treasure discovered in Egypt in 1799. Its parallel inscriptions in Greek and ancient Egyptian provided a key to the deciphering of ancient Egyptian writing. Similarly gangsta' rap, according to Dyson, provides an aid in understanding the lives of the poor and disempowered young of the inner city.

2. The author's connectedness to today's inner city black youth is shored up when he mentions that he grew up in "Detroit's treacherous inner city," that he was a teen father. This suggests a familiarity with the background and culture that rap music deals with.

3. An understanding of the "forces that drove the emergence of rap" is explored in paragraphs 3 and 4. A brief discussion of the economic underpinnings of the evolution of rap is included in paragraph 3, while a discussion of the form and function of rap can be found in paragraph 4. The last third of the essay illuminates Dyson's more subtle but equally important point that some black leaders condemning rap for being sexist and homophobic can be accused of holding similar attitudes. For example, Dyson sees "ecclesiastical apartheid" in today's black church as well as in the civil rights movement of the sixties. Whether students

feel that attitudes held three decades ago can legitimately undercut the moral authority of today's black leaders, as Dyson seems to say, should be discussed.

Regulating Hate Speech—Pro

Regulating Racist Speech on Campus
Charles R. Lawrence III

TOPICAL CONSIDERATIONS

1. Lawrence says that the protection of racist speech from government regulation "reinforces our society's commitment to tolerance as a value, and that . . . we will be forced to combat it as a community." An alternative means of combating racist speech might be public protests and demonstrations.
2. Lawrence says that by so framing the issue, the racial bigot ends up being morally elevating while "the rising flames of racism" are fanned. Lawrence says that racist language is an assault on its victim, not an invitation to dialogue. Also, by allowing unrestricted rights to those who practice hate language, we allow both psychic injury and racial victimization of minority people to continue.
3. Any "system of signs and symbols" that suggests the inferiority of blacks would fall under the legislation of the *Brown* v. *Board of Education* case, says Lawrence, since that case articulates "the principle of equal citizenship" (paragraph 4).
4. Lawrence argues that racist speech functions as a "preemptive strike" against its victim. "The invective is experienced as a blow" (paragraph 6) that is intended to hurt not to "discover truth or initiate dialogue."
5. Lawrence suggests that civil rights lawyers might sue on behalf of black students "whose right to an equal education is denied by a university's failure to insure a non-discriminatory educational climate or conditions of employment." Such threats would move many academic administrations to take action.
6. Open for discussion.
7. Open for discussion.
8. Open for discussion.

RHETORICAL CONSIDERATIONS

1. In paragraph 2, Lawrence's line of argument begins to take focus as he explains his apprehension about the rise in racial incidents and racist speech. The first clue to his opposition is the opening word, "But," which has been clearly prepared for by the whole first paragraph. Probably the clearest thesis statement is the last sentence of paragraph 4.
2. Right off Lawrence establishes himself as one who questions authority and who ardently defends individual rights, including his refusal to participate in a civil-

defense drill in high school. His strategy is to set himself up a seemingly inflexible on such issues to underscore the dangerous consequences of unrestricted racist speech to which, in the next paragraph, he concedes strong opposition.

3. Lawrence's argument is clearly syllogistic: The First Amendment does not protect utterances that "inflict injury or tend to incite an immediate breach of peace"; racist speech injures and incites violence; thus, the First Amendment does not protect racist speech.

4. Open for discussion.

5. For the students.

Regulating Hate Speech—Con

Free Speech on Campus

Nat Hentoff

TOPICAL CONSIDERATIONS

1. Hentoff is arguing that instituting sanctions on speech poses a serious threat to the very idea of the university and the spirit of academic freedom and free inquiry.

2. According to the author, more and more colleges are handling the problem by "preventing or punishing speech." Hentoff is strongly opposed to such measures.

3. Hentoff makes a clear distinction between racially motivated physical attacks and racist or sexist speech, "however disgusting, inflammatory, and rawly divisive." Lawrence, on the other hand, argues that verbal abuse "functions as preemptive strike" that is "experienced as a blow" and that causes "psychic injury." By categorizing it as such, Lawrence makes a case that racist speech falls within the "fighting words" exception to First Amendment protection.

4. Open for discussion.

5. Open for discussion.

6. Open for discussion.

7. Hentoff is troubled by a few things: first, the ironic deception of the very title of the Statement; second, he is appalled at the "scant opposition" by faculty and students who would rather "go on record as vigorously opposing racism and sexism than to expose [themselves] to charges of insensitivity to these malignancies." Hentoff finds such "politically correct" silence frightening. He also finds frightening the implications of the Statement—that a student who opposes affirmative action could be "branded a racist." Or somebody caught playing a Lenny Bruce album could be "tried for aggravated insensitivity by association."

8. Open for discussion.

9. Open for discussion.

10. Open for discussion.

RHETORICAL CONSIDERATIONS

1. The title has two possible meanings: (1) the state of free speech on campus; and (2) the imperative, "You must free speech on campus!" It's a clever and apt choice.

2. Hentoff's argument does not begin to take focus until paragraph 5, where he also gives his thesis statement in the last line. Up to this point, he establishes the background—that is, the recent surge in racist incidents on college campuses.

3. Hentoff wants the reader to believe that the cartoon was not particularly offensive. Some students might not want to pass judgment without having seen the cartoon. Though there is no way to tell from the essay, it is quite possible that Hentoff leaves out details that would weaken his argument.

4. For the student.

5. The Orwell reference is aptly ironic. You might remind students that Orwell was a novelist, essayist, and one of the most important social critics of this century. In 1949, he published the novel *1984,* which painted a nightmare vision of a totalitarian state in which free speech and free thought were capital crimes.

6. The concluding line is ominously appropriate; it brings to a head the fear underlying Hentoff's argument that the trend toward sanctioning free speech may be universal. Whether or not students buy his arguments, they must recognize the implications and impact of the closing question.

11

Nature and the Environment

A Cruel Universe, but the Only One Where Humans Could Exist
Gwynne Dyer

TOPICAL CONSIDERATIONS

1. Because we are reasoning beings, the only universe we could possibly inhabit would have to be one in which events were predictable. Without predictability all experience would be chaotic and random; likewise, there would be no science or natural laws.
2. Dyer says Hume was honest because he did not offer some long, circular answer that came to the same conclusion: simply, that no one knows why God permits terrible things to occur in our universe.
3. There could be no science in a universe of divine favoritism. The laws of nature and all logic would not exist. And all that occurred would be "magical" and unpredictable. Man could not exist in such a "Garden of Eden."
4. Actually, Dyer offers us two consolations. In paragraph 11, he says that even God could not have made the universe any different than it is if he wanted it to be an appropriate home for human beings. And in the final paragraph he says that we can derive consolation from knowing that we are fortunate to be alive, because at our conception "a million other potential men and women lost their only chance to see the place at all."

RHETORICAL CONSIDERATIONS

1. The questions that open the essay are some of our oldest and hardest. Consequently, they are guaranteed to capture our attention and make us read on in the hope that the author will offer some answers.
2. In the central paragraphs—7 through 9—Dyer briefly illustrates why the universe must be a cruel one, why it must be nonselective. He speculates on a universe that would not allow air crashes, diseases, earthquakes, or murder. The result would be a magical realm in which the laws of nature and logic did not work.
3. Dyer ends his essay with a reminder of the miracle of life and how fortunate we are to have visited the universe, cruel as it is, instead of the "million other potential men and women" who could have been conceived by our parents instead of us. This paragraph rounds off the essay by returning to the theme of the questions in the first paragraph—human life is marked by both impersonal cruelty and luck.

The Courage of Turtles

Edward Hoagland

TOPICAL CONSIDERATIONS

1. The main idea of Hoagland's essay is to call attention to the horror that faces the earth's wildlife. By focusing on the courage or, as he puts it, "the gumption" of turtles, Hoagland shows the possibility in our need to survive. But by the end of the essay, even he loses hope and walk away. This departure parallels the fact that most people now walk away from impending environmental disaster. To some, the problem may seem too far away. To others, it may be too overwhelming to confront.

2. Hoagland feels guilty strolling in the woods because of the many animals that are uprooted by human attempts to "develop" nature. In this development, turtles are entombed in mud, and ducks are driven from their natural and comfortable habitats. Hoagland's guilt probably arises from the simple connection he has to these "developers." Some students may express the same emotions in relation to animals kept in captivity by zoos or aquariums. Others may move away from animal examples and raise issues like homelessness or "Third World" countries. These examples can be useful in understanding Hoagland's final remarks about walking away.

3. Hoagland says he likes turtles for a variety of reasons (no fur, minimal care, and the fact that they are personable beasts). He also compares them to other animals, but eventually, readers discover that Hoagland really admires their diversity and how much like people they are (paragraphs 4–6).

4. Hoagland tells us various turtles' menus to reinforce his personification of them. This technique helps sentimentalize the animals—make them seem more like us.

5. Hoagland uses these descriptions to broaden his audience. If people reading don't particularly care for other animals or people (to which the turtles are compared), then they must be convinced of the merits of turtles on another level. These descriptions appeal to the lover of objects, of art, of games and amusement.

6. The description of this nightmare allows the reader to empathize with the turtle. By comparing the turtle's situation to the common, if not collective, nightmare of being trapped, Hoagland summons our sympathy. Every reader has had nightmares about being chased and trapped.

7. The story of the penny arcade serves to exemplify the warped standards that humans have created for their comforts and amusements. Hoagland wants us to read this narrative and feel saddened, certainly; but, it also points to the overwhelming complexity of the problem: sad and almost pathetic. We admire the turtles as we see them within the structure of victim and victimizer, or oppressed and oppressor.

8. This is the key of Hoagland's essay. These turtles survive regardless of their situations and terrible conditions because they want to live, and this is the ultimate courage.

9. Hoagland's conclusion is very disheartening. It illuminates the point that turtles have courage, but it also illuminates the point that humans have no idea how to readjust nature now that they have disrupted it. Giving up hope, the narrator speaks to all of us—we walk away in a variety of ways. Perhaps Hoagland means to imply that we, as humans, do not have the courage of turtles, and in the face of this realization, we feel hopeless: "But since short of diving in after him, there was nothing I could do, I walked away" (paragraph 14). The conclusion also serves as a metaphor for humanity's treatment of nature. No matter how well-intentioned our actions might have been, the simple act of altering the ecosystem has been an unfortunate mistake. We have driven animals out of their natural habitat, and then we destroyed their habitats for our benefit. Even if we try to put them back into their habitats, the damage is irreparable.

RHETORICAL CONSIDERATIONS

1. Some of Hoagland's tone in this piece is, understandably, sneering and misanthropic. He comments here on the inability of people to connect with nature even though they are bulldozing over it—and destroying it—to live on top of it.

2. There are many metaphors for courage in this essay. Hoagland tells us that turtles are "lionlike," (paragraph 7) and he points to the situation in the penny arcade to tell readers that even out of water the aquatic turtles were "living on gumption" (paragraph 13). Even in the conclusion, Hoagland implies that turtles had the courage to trust humans.

3. The statement personifies the turtle. Such "socially unacceptable" habits attributed to turtles draws an unflattering parallel to humans. However, the more "sophisticated" human is also able to produce social judgments. Thus, the parallel ranks the turtle with humans on a mental as well as physical level. The effect is to endear the turtle to the reader. If we see us in the turtle we might make the effort to do what it takes to save the creature.

4. For the students.

5. Hoagland compares turtles to—or differentiates them from—many different species in the animal kingdom: "birds" (paragraph 1), "snakes . . . alligators . . . frogs" (paragraph 5), "giraffe . . . hippo . . . cow moose . . . penguin . . . Brontosaurus" (paragraph 6), "lion" (paragraph 7), "puppies . . . elephant . . . turkey . . . hawk . . . mongoose" (paragraph 10), "tiger . . . and . . . rodeo mare" (paragraph 11). In addition, Hoagland compares turtles to humans throughout the piece. For instance, Hoagland writes, "They're personal beasts. They see the same colors we do . . . they unravel the twists of a maze with the hot-blooded rapidity of a mammal. Though they can't run as fast as a rat, they improve on their errors just as quickly, pausing at each crossroads to look left and right. And they rock rhythmically in place, as we often do" (paragraph 4). In addition, they "burp, whistle, grunt and hiss, and produce social judgments" (paragraph 6). They can be arrogant (paragraph 7), and they enjoy different foods (paragraph 8). Finally, they breathe "the way we breathe" (paragraph 11). Hoagland also sees turtles as games or art: "a puzzle in geometrics . . . decorative . . . and self-

directed building blocks" (paragraph 7). These wonderful metaphors are in part what makes this essay so magical a piece of writing.

6. Unlike baby turtles, the wood turtle is not boring. His description of it, rich in both animal and human references, succeeds in making the creature an individual. It's a fine example of personification—a key strategy of his writing throughout.

7. Hoagland returns to Mud Pond to begin his conclusion. After describing the pond, he creates in the reader an attachment and an admiration for the turtles he describes so vividly. The return to Mud Pond and the entombed turtles reminds us of the dangers of fooling with nature. Such a species rich in so many ways is dying because we have wittingly or unwittingly changed its habitat.

8. The statement serves to demonstrate the overwhelming complexity of the situation and how powerless a lone person may feel. When there is so much to do, often nothing gets done. Students should identify with this experience—too much school work, for instance. Perhaps you could steer discussion to social or political causes and the sense of being overwhelmed that Hoagland yields to at the end.

A Path of More Resistance

Bill McKibben

TOPIC CONSIDERATIONS

1. McKibben's main point is that we must make a choice in regard to nature: "One world or the other will have to change" (paragraph 8). McKibben warns that we either continue altering the planet further in potentially dangerous ways or make some sacrifices in the ways we live in order to save the planet.

2. "Standard hopes and dreams," according to McKibben, include marriage, travel, a large home, and children (paragraph 4). These "standards" show a certain cultural bias. Students might have different hopes and dreams to compare. For example, McKibben's standards show a rural, middle- to upper-middle-class heterosexual culture. Not everyone wants to marry, own homes, travel, or have children. To some, the order might be different. To others, the content of these standards might be entirely different. Whatever the standards, McKibben implies in paragraph 10, all humans need to restructure their priorities not to make sacrifices, but to see the world in a new and different way. As he writes, "I've spent my whole life wanting more, so it's hard for me to imagine 'less' in any but a negative way. But that imagination is what counts. Changing the way we think is at the heart of the question" (paragraph 10).

3. The suggestions that McKibben makes in paragraph 5 seem simple enough, but encourage students to actively engage these issues. Are they willing to compromise the car, the hot tub, the grocery store, and gas or oil heat when the choices are a colder house, long bike rides, and serious gardening? The immediate benefits—on a traditional hierarchy of what's best—would deny any of McKibben's

examples, but encourage students to practice what he suggests in paragraph 10: stop imagining "less" in only negative ways. Once we consider this possibility, students might see the health benefits of bike riding and keeping a garden.

4. McKibben tells readers that "'Absurd' and 'unnatural' are different from 'wrong' or 'immoral'" (paragraph 12). By clarifying these terms, McKibben is able to lay down his central argument. As he goes on to explain, there may be plenty of good reasons to keep living the way we are; we are not "wrong" in our actions, nor are we being judged for them in any moral way, but they may not be the best reasons to continue. As McKibben writes, "those reasons may be outweighed by the burden that such desires place on the natural world" (paragraph 12). McKibben does consider the counterargument quite well. He writes, "It's normal to imagine that this humbler world would resemble the past. Simply because the atmosphere was cleaner a century ago, though, there's no call to forget all that's been developed since" (paragraph 14). This argument, that we will all revert to primitivism, is ridiculous to McKibben. By anticipating this counterargument, he strengthens his own argument.

5. Utopias according to McKibben are "quaint" (paragraph 14). "Invariably they are designed to advance human happiness, which is found to be suffering as the result of crowding or stress or lack of meaningful work or not enough sex or too much sex . . . but it's all in the name of man" (paragraph 15). "Atopia," on the other hand is not human-centered. "Human happiness would be of secondary importance" (paragraph 16). The issue would be what is "best for the planet" (paragraph 16). The ground rules, McKibben writes, are a call for a smaller human population that uses fewer resources, "not just oil, but wood and water and chemicals and even land itself" (paragraph 17). These seem like easy enough ground rules, especially when McKibben continues, "they are practical rules, not moral ones. Within them, a thousand cultures—vegetarian and hunter, communal and hermitic—could still exist" (paragraph 17). What step could students make toward accomplishing the goal that McKibben suggests? Encourage them to consider the negative effects of suggestions such as the curbing of reproductive rights and the possible loss of jobs as a result of a cutback in resources.

6. McKibben illuminates this point by saying that "The difficulty is almost certainly more psychological than intellectual—less that we can't figure out major alterations in our way of life than we simply don't want to" (paragraph 20). This might be a common attitude among many students. Even McKibben is willing to admit that "our desires count" (paragraph 21). But beyond abilities and desires is our need to "cut back immediately on our use of fossil fuels" (paragraph 21). McKibben anticipates our desires without dismissing them, and this is the choice he discusses at the beginning of the essay.

7. McKibben makes this comment to anticipate those who will accuse him of trying to stall "human advances." McKibben acknowledges that we needn't stop "advancing," but we also needn't continue to press onward. Students may think of examples as extreme as the atom bomb. We have developed it, and it exists for better or for worse, but we might not use it again. Consider also VCRs, microwave ovens, plastic shopping bags, the power lawn mower, television.

8. McKibben tries to convince us that we should take action now by drawing some parallels. First he explains that "we just happen to be living at the" wrong moment. In addition, he acknowledges that we might not want to deal with it, that it might not be "fair," but he also writes that it "wasn't fair that our fathers had to go fight Hitler" (paragraph 25). This analogy might be very effective in continuing a discussion on ability versus desire.

9. McKibben tells readers the Jim Franklin story to point to a crucial idea: "We believe things because we need to believe them" (paragraph 27). Encourage students to respond to this comment. In addition, you might want to relate it's echo in McKibben's conclusion: "We'll look for almost any reason not to change our attitudes; the inertia of the established order is powerful. If we can think of a plausible, or even implausible, reason to discount environmental warnings, we will" (paragraph 31).

10. This final comment is a reminder that some environmentalists have been dramatically wrong, or they exaggerated so much in their predictions that no one will believe them anymore.

RHETORICAL CONSIDERATIONS

1. McKibben repeats this phrase to emphasize his point that he "knows" the nature that surrounds his house. The repetition lends both a poetic and an emphatic effect to the introduction.

2. Certainly students will make the connection between "passes away" and death. The word, "changes," is not as connotative. In addition, it is not as judgmental. McKibben is trying to convince his readers to do something; thus he needs language that is persuasive.

3. These words with their negative connotations serve to illustrate the "passing away" of the nature we inhabit. McKibben's descriptive language is often similarly charged.

4. McKibben's outlook, at times, seems quite objective: He anticipates the counterargument, so he appears to be considering both sides. In this way, students may see this piece as a fine example of argumentation. Underneath this objectivity, however, are the very real "sacrifices" or changes that McKibben is making in his own life. These changes point to his biases, and ultimately, he is trying to convince readers to realize that there is a choice, and to make it.

5. In quotes these words call attention to the nature of judgments. Instead of constructing the world in terms of binary oppositions like *right* and *wrong*, McKibben suggests that there are more than two sides to an argument, thus, readers might not feel passing judgments on their individual lifestyles.

6. McKibben's tone varies throughout the essay. At times, when he is relating stories to the reader, it is meditative and sad. At other times, he argues with the qualities of a politician—for example, when explaining the necessary steps for the necessary choice. At other moments, his tone is philosophical.

7. McKibben's conclusion appeals to the axiom that "we believe what we want to believe." In this way, McKibben is manipulating how readers construct envi-

ronmental problems. Carter and Reagan serve in illuminating these points. We elect our public officials to tell us how smart we are, how right we are; but when they begin to tell us what we might not want to hear, we don't listen—we change leaders.

The Cry of the Ocean
Peter Steinhart

TOPICAL CONSIDERATIONS

1. Paragraphs 3, 4, 5, and 13 catalogue a variety of ways in which marine life is being depleted. Paragraphs 6, 7, and 15 cite some of the catastrophic consequences for humanity. In general, the depletion of marine life would result in great economic disasters for many communities and countries that depend upon fishing as livelihood. But, worse, the disaster in terms of human lives could be catastrophic. As Steinhart points out in paragraph 1, fifty percent of the world's population lives within 50 miles of a coastline and, presumably, depends upon seafood for part of its survival.

2. Our nonanthropomorphic view of the sea enables us to exclude the sea from our vision of the natural, living world. The urge to protect and preserve does not easily extend to life with which we feel no affinity, life with which we do not identify. Steinhart tries to jog our awareness of our bond with the sea and the life in it. This is demonstrated in the opening paragraphs where he shows human life emerging from the sea and talks of humans as "miniature oceans" whose blood has the "salinity of seawater."

3. The students may choose paragraphs 10, 11, 12, or 13.

4. For the student. Probably the only hope is a combination of a cutback on commercial fishing through bans and mass farming of certain species such as the Atlantic salmon and cod.

5. Bill McKibben would probably emphasize alterations in lifestyle as a way of combating this problem. He seems to believe that what happens in the microcosm can have impact on the macrocosm, especially if people *en masse* alter their attitudes and behavior. Edward Abbey, on the other hand, would probably call for radical and individual action. He might recommend, for instance, the sabotaging of fishing vessels and nets. Steinhart's recommendations seem more middle-of-the-road than those of McKibben or Abbey. He recommends working for the implementation of restrictions by governmental agencies and international agreements.

RHETORICAL CONSIDERATIONS

1. Paragraph 1 demonstrates that humans are one with the sea, that we have a biological, evolutionary bond with marine life. In sharp contrast, paragraph 2 implies that our lack of awareness of this bond is contributing to the demise of the

seas. These introductory paragraphs quite effectively underscore the irony of humanity's indifference to its own spawning grounds.

2. Paragraphs 8 and 9 are good examples of a tone that is prophetic and Biblical. Paragraph 13 is objective and straightforward. The shifting of these tones reminds readers of their intimacy and affinity with the sea as well as their role in its destruction.

3. The last paragraph picks up the theme of humanity's responsibility to the sea from which it evolved.

Eco-Defense

Edward Abbey

TOPICAL CONSIDERATIONS

1. Abbey's main point is that we are obliged to defend the wilderness—as our home—by any means necessary. He writes, "not to defend that which we love would be dishonorable" (paragraph 5). Abbey goes about bolstering his point with a discussion of the wilderness as our home. Once he completes this task— "For many of us . . . the wilderness is more our home" (paragraph 4)—he explains our obligation to defend it (paragraph 5). Many people would be unwilling to join Abbey in his actions for a variety of reasons. In addition to its illegality is the bodily harm posed to loggers. Some students, however, may equate the life of trees with the life of humans. In this case, as Abbey suggests, the loggers' attempt to saw down a tree is met with self-defense: the 60 penny nails.

2. This notion of having an "obligation" to defend one's home is an American tradition—one that is the crucial premise to Abbey's argument.

3. This statement is closely related to his claim that "Representative government has broken down" (paragraph 3). Abbey says that instead of listening to their constituents, government representatives listen to the money of big business which often promote practices that are antienvironment.

4. Abbey's remark that eco-defense is "ethically imperative" recalls his comments that defending our home is "an obligation" (paragraphs 1, 5). By grouping illegality with ethical imperatives, he makes an appeal outside of the law to our own personal laws. Direct students to talk about this distinction. Consider people who have broken the law for ethical reasons: Henry David Thoreau, Mahatma Gandhi, and Martin Luther King, Jr. Some students may not see the distinction between personal law and government law, but it has been the basis for many grassroots rebellions.

5. Students answers will vary, but many may see more legal ways to approach the issue.

6. Students should be able to identify the fact that Abbey's suggestion is the most radical, but it is also the most specific and concrete of all those offered in the essays in Chapter 11. Hoagland never suggests to take any action; he tries to save

a few turtles, but the task overwhelms him so much that he gives up. McKibben's atopia is too ambiguous and abstract; he even fails to name the problem, though he does offer various suggestions. Abbey's suggestion, while radical, is specific, and it is a concrete form of action.

RHETORICAL CONSIDERATIONS

1. Abbey's introduction is a very effective hook intended to elicit a strong response. His word choice and references to violence put readers on the defensive and thus create the analogy that logically leads to his conclusion that the only way to stop the destruction of the wilderness is to spike trees.

2. Abbey sets up his introduction to draw the reader into his argument. He uses the attack on home and family as an analogy to the current attack on the environment. By intriguing his reader in the first paragraph, he hopes to carry the reader through the same argument in terms of the wilderness. Some students may not be willing to follow Abbey's transitions. Some may fail to accept his initial analogy. In this case, students are not likely to follow the remainder of his argument. His strength is in the language he uses to move the reader through his transitions. For example, in paragraph 5, he writes, "if the wilderness is our true home, and if it is threatened . . . then we have the right to defend that home." His weakness is in the initial assumptions he makes.

3. Abbey's use of language tends to put us on the defensive. The violence of his language and the negative connotations of "gangsters" and "jellyfish" negate the validity of any counterargument. There is much evidence throughout the piece of such charged language. For example, you might point students to the description of the congressmen who "would sell the graves of their mothers" (paragraph 3). The connotation of extortion is theft. By using such a word, Abbey follows through on his metaphor of the "three-piece suited gangsters" (paragraph 2). In addition, this word shows the government participating in illegal acts; thus, Abbey's methods become justified in their illegality.

4. This is the turning point of Abbey's essay; it serves as an introduction to his concrete suggestion. It is an effective technique because it captures our attention, and it holds it for what comes after.

5. Abbey's tone in his conclusion is leading. His reference to Aunt Emma appeals to a wider audience. His "defense" cannot appear as violent as the introduction so he directly addresses the audience and includes them in his plans. Encourage your students to discuss Abbey's suggestion as an invitation.

·12·
Sports

Football Red and Baseball Green
Murray Ross

TOPICAL CONSIDERATIONS

1. As most students will know, myths are stories that express in imaginary form the dominant wishes, fears, and beliefs of a people. Ross's use of the term is sociological (rather than archetypal or religious) in that he sees represented in baseball and football the social and demographic change, and accompanying cultural anxieties, of twentieth-century America.

   Baseball developed at the time of "the Industrialization, and most probably it was a reaction to the squalor, the faster pace, and the dreariness of the new conditions" (paragraph 3). Baseball was "old-fashioned right from the start" (paragraph 3); it expressed fears about the changes brought on by industrialization and nostalgia for a simpler, more rural time. Football, on the other hand, "asserts the heroic function of a mechanized group, since we have become a country where collective identity is a reality. . . . The game, like our society, can be thought of as a cluster of people living under great tension in a state of perpetual flux" (paragraph 16). So football tries to make sense of "those salient and common conditions which affect us all, and it does so with the end of making us feel better about them and our lot" (paragraph 16).

2. Just as pastoral takes place in "a timeless world of perpetual spring," so in baseball time is measured in "repeated and predictable action," stressing the eternal rather than quotidian nature of Time—the continuity of natural, cyclical repetition rather the limitations of mortal time indicated by the relentless ticking of a game clock. Baseball creates a sense of "expanded and idle time" (paragraph 7) that defines spectator, as well as player, experience.

   In contrast, as heroes "traditionally . . . reckon with time," so time is the crucial third element in football, being "wound up inexorably until it reaches the breaking point in the last minutes of a close game" (paragraph 11). Time is a major source of football's intensity.

3. Pastoral "asserts the virtue of communion with nature"; similarly, "baseball asserts that the team which best relates to the playing field (by hitting the ball in the right places) will win" (paragraph 4). Visually, the open field presents to the viewer's gaze "a constant, rather calm whole" that suggests to Ross the dominant sense in pastoral that things fit harmoniously together in "a timeless world of perpetual spring" (paragraph 6).

   In football, there is no such lazy, "democratic vista"; the game instead "offers a flat, perpetually moving foreground" (paragraph 11). Fans "are not asked to relax, but to concentrate." Whereas "the third element in baseball is the field; in football this element is the clock" (paragraph 11).

4. Baseball "attempts to close the gap between the players and the crowd"; football "seeks almost the opposite relationship between its spectators and players, one which stresses the distance between them" (paragraph 10). Such a distance is appropriate to a heroic form that "wants to convert men into gods" (paragraph (9).

5. Ross argues that the "commercial success" these sports enjoy has forced them from their original milieu, robbing the sports of their "special atmosphere" (paragraph 18). By extending the season, by moving the games inside multipurpose stadiums, and by replacing grass with more durable arificial surfaces owners and managers have increased the profit margin but divorced the games from their original contexts.

Students might note a certain nostalgia in Ross's dislike of these innovations. While Ross's argument centers on the experience of attending live games in person, the "pure" experience of professional sports has traditionally been available only to a select few. On the other hand, both games have been regularly broadcast for years; many of the changes Ross complains of here will do little to alter the experience of fans who usually "attend" the games through television and radio. Some changes will make life easier for fans, who need not be inconvenienced by rain delays and cancellations; surely some football players, for example, appreciate a having a roof over their heads in the snows of December. Besides, for purists there are still plenty of old-fashioned venues in which to see these games—in the farm leagues of baseball, and at the college, high school, junior high, even little-league levels.

RHETORICAL CONSIDERATIONS

1. Ross presents what might be called textual evidence, including descriptions of the spatial, temporal, and mechanical elements of each game. He then interprets his data, analyzing the effect these elements have on the reader/spectator.

Students who are usually more interested in sports than literature might see the point of this kind of analysis when it is turned on a topic such as baseball or football. Others may launch the objection that Ross is reading too much into his text.

2. Throughout the essay, but most importantly at its very start, Ross associates himself rhetorically with the reader, creating a tone that implies informal discussion rather than formal argument. In the first paragraph, Ross uses the first and third person to narrow the distance between himself and his readers; he also stresses the provisional nature of his argument by qualifying almost every statement. The opening of the paragraph's fifth sentence is characteristic: "Americans, or American men anyway, seem to care about the games they watch as much as the Elizabethans cared about their plays, and I suspect for some of the same reasons." Even before finishing this assertion Ross limits it, making it less sweeping and hence less controversial as "Americans" become "American men." Instead of insisting on his observation about the similarity between Elizabethan theater and twentieth century sports Ross describes it only as a *suspicion*. It is, similarly, only his "guess" that "sport spectating involves some-

thing more than the vicarious pleasures of identifying with athletic prowess" (paragraph 2).

Despite the use of technical terms and quite detailed analysis, Ross's tone is casual and provisional throughout the essay in a way that is appropriate both to the topic and to interpretive argument. In the absence of any hard evidence except common knowledge and conclusions produced by his wits, Ross wisely does not lean too hard on his assertions; instead, he encourages readers to relax, give him the benefit of the doubt, hear him out, and leisurely consider the merits of what he has to say.

3. Ross most thoroughly addresses opposition in paragraphs 19 and 20 when he notes those readers who might "think this nonsense." One way of deflecting opposition is simply to tolerate it: "I must admit," Ross says, "there are good reasons for finding both games simply varieties of decadence" (paragraph 19). Ross defends his own point of view gently, largely by reserving for himself the right to differ in opinion from those who would attack all sport "because it is not strictly ethical in intent" (paragraph 20). Ross feels "out of sympathy" with this argument and admits: "I am vulnerable to those fantasies which these games support, and . . . I find happiness in the company of people who feel as I do."

4. As analysis of this paragraph will reveal, Ross's paragraphs are extremely coherent, well developed, and tightly constructed. The first sentence transitions the reader from the subject of the previous paragraph (football's similarity to war); the second elaborates on the first in stating the topic sentence: "[Football] seems to be a game which projects 'character' more than personality, and for the most part football heroes, publicly, are a rather similar lot." Both this and the succeeding three sentences begin with words indicating that the argument is only provisional ("It seems," "They tend," "Perhaps," "At any rate"); in this way Ross deflects a certain amount of opposition by not pushing his point too strenuously. The third sentence illustrates the paragraph's argument with three football players who are balanced at the end of the paragraph with three baseball players. The language used to describe these six players subtly supports the paragraph's main argument. The football players are "a Reggie White, a Troy Aikman, or a Jim Rice"; the addition of an article ("a") before each name depersonalizes the men even as Ross names them individually. In contrast, each of the baseball players are distinguished by a colorful modifier: "the pasta-loving Tommy Lasorda, the surly Jose Canseco, the exuberant Willie Mays." Although Ross's evidence is anecdotal, his tone, effective use of language, and clarity manipulate the reader quite effectively, diminishing the need for more objective evidence that would be hard to muster in this kind of interpretive argument.

5. Ross's essay will probably appeal to fans of both sports and literature. Although he assumes his reader will have basic knowledge of football and baseball, Ross's analysis could be followed by almost all readers. The essay would be more interesting to sports fans, however, because so much of the evidence is in the form of player's names. Readers without a mental picture of Thurman Thomas or Randall Cunningham, for example, may not appreciate how these men are "catapulted into Olympus" (paragraph 10) by the hoopla surrounding football. Such

references might be more convincing—but could also prove more controversial—to readers who can imagine the men behind the names.

6. With the phrase "A Final note," Ross indicates that his last paragraph will perform a typical concluding function: It will not reiterate the previous argument, but speculate about the larger meaning of the discussed phenomenon. Here, Ross suggests that football and baseball are both currently popular because they allow Americans to reconcile "that unfettered rural vision of ourselves that baseball so beautifully mirrors," with an anticipated future made up of "constant and unavoidable challenges." The words "A final note" continue the casual atmosphere of the entire essay: Ross bequeaths his thoughts only the status of a "note," adding a bit of grammatical informality with the use of an incomplete sentence. The last sentence rewrites the cliché about having a cake and eating it too; not only does it end the essay on a mildly ringing note, but it further indicates the importance of sports which, in Ross's view, provide impossible, fantasy solutions to real and imagined social problems.

The Black and White Truth About Basketball
Jeff Greenfield

TOPICAL CONSIDERATIONS

1. Greenfield tries to avoid the kind of "essentializing biologism" that has often been used to claim the racial inferiority of African-Americans. The idea that all black people have "rhythm" is a powerful, long-standing racist stereotype that defines the talents of the black race as both "natural" and inherently physical—not the result of application or intellectual talent. This kind of observation originally justified the exploitation of African muscle power in the cotton fields and kitchens of slave owners; later it supported the cultural oppression of African-Americans, particularly their exclusion from positions of public authority and prestige. In a footnote in the essay (page 495), Magic Johnson illustrates how such ideas are used to denigrate black athletes when he observes that "too many journalists attribute brilliant strategic moves by black players to 'innate' ability."

   Greenfield defends his use of the term *rhythm* here by saying that "rhythm is what the black stars themselves talk about" (paragraph 13). Though he says that rhythm is an "instinctive quality," he qualifies this observation by claiming that such instinct "stems from hundreds of hours of practice" (paragraph 13). Seen in the context of his larger argument, Greenfield apparently attempts to redefine this usually racist term by understanding it as the result of socioeconomic and cultural, not biological, factors.

2. As the "rhythm" passage should already have alerted students, Greenfield wants to avoid potentially racist essentialism by proposing a cultural explanation about why blacks predominate in basketball. Black play is different from white not

because African-American people are biologically different, but because the socioeconomic position of American blacks has formed their social expectations—and hence their playing style—differently.

3. Since this essay's definition of the black style of basketball depends on the sense that a deprived, inner-city childhood is the shared background of almost all black players, Greenfield mentions no other possible alternative—though, of course, others do exist. Although a disproportionate number of African-American men do grow up in urban ghettos, many also grow up in rural areas, playing ball in suburban driveways, midwestern gyms, perhaps especially on those "Southern dirt courts" that Greenfield defines as the exclusive territory of young white players (paragraph 15).

Greenfield's assessment of the way the mean streets of the city translate into a distinctive basketball style is also debatable. According to Greenfield, growing up in poor and troubled neighborhoods instills black players with "the need to compete in a crowd, to battle for the edge" (paragraph 7). For this reason, "'black' ball is the basketball of electric self-expression" (paragraph 22). Since "'the school yard is the only place they can feel true pride in what they do'" (Greenfield is quoting David Wolf's book *Foul!* here), black players have evolved a "'spectacular'" style, which allows them to "'rise for the moment against the drabness and anonymity of their lives'" (paragraph 8). Deception, supposedly a central skill in the urban "battle for survival," can be turned to good use in basketball, "one of the few pursuits in which the weapon of deception is a legitimate tactic rather than the source of trouble" (paragraph 6). In considering the persuasiveness of this analysis, students might consider whether these socioeconomic factors might just as easily have produced a white style of basketball, in which sheer physical force and speed are used to transcend obstacles.

4. White basketball "is played on macadam driveways by one boy with a ball and a backboard nailed over the garage; it is played in gyms in the frigid winter of the rural Midwest and on Southern dirt courts" (paragraph 15). The rural and suburban milieus result in games played "without frills, without flow, but with effectiveness. . . . Where a 'black' player overcomes an obstacle with finesse and body control, a 'white' player reacts by outrunning or overpowering the obstacle" (paragraph 15).

The only evidence Greenfield offers for this assessment is the analysis of "former pro Jim McMillian," who explains the style of the white player (who is also a "'white'" player) John Havlicek: "John came from a very small town in Ohio. There everything was done the easy way, the shortest distance between two points. It's nothing fancy" (paragraph 21).

Students may be struck by the vague generalizations of both Greenfield and McMillian on the relationship of the white style to rural and suburban American life. Do all midwesterners really live a simple life? What exactly is "the easy way," and what is the "everything" done by it—cooking, shopping, working? Havlicek's play may certainly be "plain" and "unvarnished" (paragraph 20), but is it as "easy" as he makes it seem? And isn't it possible that small-town midwestern youth might feel the same urge to "rise for the moment against the drabness and anonymity of their lives" that urban city kids feel (paragraph 8)?

Questions 3 and 4 should help students see that Greenfield makes broad generalizations about the backgrounds of both black and white players in order to present a convincing case for the opposition between black and white styles of basketball.

5. Open for discussion. Sports-literate students will be able to think of many exceptions to Greenfield's rule, and in the process provide some relevant education for fellow students (and teachers) less well-informed about the game. However, such examples do not necessarily debilitate Greenfield's argument, since one of his goals is to get his readers to reconceptualize the categories of "white" and "black," to see them not in terms of skin color but of socioeconomic background. The dominance of basketball by various groups has changed as the racial composition of the "urban poor" has changed; once "'the game of the Irish and Italian Catholics in Rockaway and the Jews on Fordham Road in the Bronx'" (paragraph 3), basketball at the moment is the game of inner-city urban blacks, according to Greenfield. Black, in Greenfield's use of the word, becomes almost a simple synonym for the urban poor. Given this new definition of black, exceptions to Greenfield's rule could be said to prove his point—if, that is, the white players who play black-style bsketball also come from deprived, urban backgrounds.

6. Greenfield has a relatively idealized sense of racial equality in basketball. He believes the two styles of basketball together create "a fusion of cultures that seems more and more difficult in the world beyond the out-of-bounds line" (paragraph 23). In the essay's second paragraph Greenfield has claimed that blacks are much more heavily represented in the front offices of basketball than in either baseball or football: "What discrimination remains—lack of equal opportunity for speaking engagements and product endorsements—has more to do with society than with basketball." Students can dispute whether basketball is quite the model of social justice that Greenfield seems to think. Considering that he has deconstructed the terms *white* and *black* by this point in this article, Greenfield seems unjustified in claiming that the two styles together create any kind of meaningful cultural fusion, since they no longer directly represent white people and black people, but rather a socioeconomic abstraction.

RHETORICAL CONSIDERATIONS

1. Here, as throughout the essay, Greenfield relies entirely on anecdotal evidence. Greenfield cites one or two players and coaches who certainly prove his point that black-style basketball includes a kind of "surface ease" as well as "liquid grace." But other black players—including one of Greenfield's own examples, Michael Jordan—are anything but unemotional on the court. Students who know basketball will be able to think of many black players and coaches who display as much or more emotion as white players.

Analyzing this passage should help students see that Greenfield is vulnerable to the charge of not providing representative evidence.

2. The barely spoken assumption, which this essay seems designed to refute, is the racial explanation of black dominance in the sport: that black men simply have the chromosomes that make success possible. The essay's first sentence notes that "the dominance of black athletes over professional basketball is beyond dispute." The prevalence of the biological explanation for this disparity is indicated, for example, in Magic Johnson's already cited comment about journalists who chalk the skill of black players up to innate ability, and Bob Cousy's observation that "When coaches see a white boy who can jump or who moves with extraordinary quickness, they say, 'He should have been born black, he's that good?'" (paragraph 11). Greenfield seems to want to replace the biological explanation with one based on the social and cultural determinants of human behavior.

3. Greenfield's use of these terms is directly connected to the purpose identified in the previous answer to question 2. Since he wants to explain the "dominance of black athletes over professional basketball," he must use the terms *white* and *black* to explain that phenomenon: his conclusion is that black players are better because, originating in urban ghettos, they are hungrier for success and recognition and as a result evolve more creative, explosive play. But because he wants to avoid biological essentialism Greenfield places these terms in quotation marks, indicating that they refer to something other than skin color. Using other, purely descriptive terms (perhaps "urban," "lower-class," or "electric" for *black* style; "rural," "suburban," "middle-class" or "powerful" for the *white* style) would have made the argument less effective at describing the phenomenon of black dominance and robbed the essay of much of its polemical power, since by using these terms Greenfield takes on a charged racial issue head-on. Whatever the ultimate success or failure of Greenfield's argument—and it has several problems of logic and evidence—it does productively attempt to make readers rethink the terms *black* and *white* in less essentializing ways.

4. Greenfield is clearly proficient with basketball rules and lingo, a fact that will be most evident to readers not themselves knowledgeable about the game. In paragraph 6, for example, he uses standard basketball terms ("a layup," "a jump shot" "the head fake, the shoulder fake"). Greenfield also increases his credibility by creating the sense that he has talked personally to almost all the players and managers cited, although these quotations could feasibly have come from printed sources. Greenfield always introduces the comments of players, coaches, and other authorities with language that allows for verbal transmission; examples include Bob Cousy in paragraph 11; Don Nelson in paragraph 12; Bill Spivey in paragraph 13; and Bill Sharman in paragraph 14. In this way Greenfield rhetorically solidifies the impression that he is a basketball insider, intimate not only with the game but with its major players.

Attitude

Garrison Keillor

TOPICAL CONSIDERATIONS

1. Keillor believes that the wrong attitude is to laugh off mistakes as if they were only a joke. It's his view that even amateur ballplayers should act like professionals and take themselves and the game seriously.

2. He believes it is important for them to signal to each other and to anyone who may be watching their game that they can conduct themselves as professionally as any ballplayers in the Bigs. Spit correctly, frequently, and at all crucial moments. Pick up dirt, rub it in the fingers, toss it, smooth it, be involved with it. If no dirt is available, pluck grass. Maintain a continuous, rhythmic chatter. Keillor apparently believes such behavior builds morale and encourages team members to play a better and more enjoyable game.

3. Although Keillor points to some of the more absurd mannerisms of professional players, his remarks drive home a valid point. Taking a serious professional attitude toward any worthwhile endeavor would certainly ensure greater success for an individual than if he were to laugh at the challenge and shrug his shoulders at his mistakes.

4. Keillor's close observation of some of the more laughable idiosyncracies of ballplayers suggests that he has been a frequent spectator.

5. If Keillor and Ross were on a bench together, they might lean back and reminisce about the time when baseball was the national pastime, when people were less in a hurry, less eager for aggressive, tension-filled clashes on the football field, and more interested in a quiet visit to the ballpark, where they could watch individual players exhibit their talents on the ballfield.

RHETORICAL CONSIDERATIONS

1. In the first paragraph, Keillor describes his own and his teammates' freewheeling approach to the game, explains that no one agonizes over mistakes, and then remarks: "Except me. This year." At the end of this paragraph, he identifies the problem: attitude. In paragraphs 3 through 5, he contrasts what he feels is the right and wrong attitude toward playing the game. Then, in paragraph 6, he establishes his thesis: he proposes to map out the steps even amateur ballplayers should follow in order to adopt a professional attitude toward the game.

2. Yes. Keillor is very successful in his use of specifics. The first paragraph is a good example to cite. Keillor doesn't just talk about older players who can't play very well any more. He refers to "aging trigenarians and quadros who don't get around on the fastball as well as they used to and who sit out the second games of double-headers." Instead of simply remarking that slow-pitch baseball lets him play baseball without getting hurt, he states specifically that he can play "without getting beaned or having to run too hard." He doesn't stop with a vague reference to a "pretty casual team," but specifies that they are a team that

"drinks beer on the bench and substitutes freely," a team that watches a wife or girlfriend let a "pop fly drop six feet in front of her," without agonizing over it.

3. For the most part, his diction is informal and conversational. The other team members are "turkeys." One of Keillor's teammates makes a "dumb! dumb play!" A batter is "this guy." The opposing team "hoots and hollers." His team gets "clobbered."

4. "Chugs" suggests a slow-moving locomotive pulling a heavy weight into second base. A player "*topples* over in the dirt." The right attitude "*sweetens* the game." Their team gets "*clobbered.*" Fielders should "*groom* their areas" and "*flick away* tiny sticks and bits of gravel." A player might have "*bobbled* two fly balls."

5. This last sentence sounds like a broadcaster's comment over the loudspeaker during a professional major league ballgame. In effect, Keillor is saying: "Now that we have the proper professional attitude, let's play ball." It's a way to bring the essay to an end while suggesting a new beginning.

Girls at Bat
Anna Quindlen

TOPICAL CONSIDERATIONS

1. Sports for children have changed in two ways, according to Quindlen. First, and most obvious, is that girls play more sports today, especially Little League. Also, coaching style has eased up with a greater emphasis on sportsmanship. In the past, the point of Little League was "Win or die"; likewise, coaches were very hard on their players, humiliating them and ramming "their shortcomings down their throats."

2. Unfortunately, Little League was not an option for Quindlen in her girlhood. She says she didn't even resent the policy since she was not very coordinated. By contrast, some women who are professionals today were galvanized, she says, by being excluded. Some of that same galvanization is addressed directly and indirectly in the next few essays.

3. Open for discussion.

4. Open for discussion.

5. I think things are somewhat different since more young women today played sports in their youth. Students might argue whether or not performance is more important to male than female egoes. You might also have them read the next two essays for elucidation. Personally, I think ego in sports is gender-free.

6. I don't think they are second-rate insomuch as the coaching and competition. Nevertheless, men's teams, both collegiate and professional, get more financial and spiritual support still.

7. Metaphorically, this fits the traditional male-female relationship: men aggressively pursuing victory in life's many arenas, whether it be employment, war,

sports, and the like, while women remain on the sidelines boosting male egoes with cheers of encouragement and flashing thighs.

8. Open for discussion.

9. It could be argued that organized athletic competition in childhood would encourage the same in adulthood, regardless of gender.

RHETORICAL CONSIDERATIONS

1. The opening line of paragraph 3 establishes Quindlen's focus. She cues her purpose both by direct statement (". . . but what I like about Little League today is simpler. . . ") and by the subtle alternation of male and female pronouns in her reflection of girls at play.

2. Quindlen is subtly alternating the traditional use of male with female for the anonymous third-person pronoun. But, more importantly, it is the girl players who are central to the descriptions: the second base player tagging out the male batter, the pitcher adjusting her hat, and the left fielder catching the pop fly.

3. Open for discussion.

4. The essay is very readable and very accessible, made so by Quindlen's nearly person-to-person chattiness. Consider the direct address to the reader of the opening line and its colloquialism ("I can't tell you what a kick I get out of Little League.") Also, an occasional cliché ("I can't for the life of me. . . " and "proud as punch" in paragraph 5). Her vocabulary is never difficult; yet, she uses familiar words in precise, fresh ways—for example, "my own stifled competitive spirit" (paragraph 1); and the witty self-deprecation of "I have the eye-hand coordination of a department-store dummy" (paragraph 6). Quindlen's wise and gentle manner and her warm humor project an affable personality.

5. Open for discussion.

6. Students should find the conclusion nicely satisfying. The whole paragraph captures the warm reflective style of the piece. Also, it echoes the pleasure she speaks of in the opening line of the piece—that is, of seeing girls as commonplace in today's Little League. She also returns to her speculation on how early competition in sports will affect girls when they grow up—a speculation that succinctly and cleverly is wrapped up in her final question about George Steinbrenner.

Playing to Win

Margaret A. Whitney

TOPICAL CONSIDERATIONS

1. Ann's statuesque beauty summoned traditional attitudes toward female pulchritude. If you're pretty, you don't have to be active to win approval.

2. Having been voted "Best Hair" in her eighth-grade yearbook, Ann was expected to succumb to the passive beauty syndrome. However, the young woman found that athletic competition was far more rewarding than merely being good looking.

3. The message of sports is to be aggressive and intense. Whitney recognizes in her daughter's drive a reflection of her own determination in winning her doc-

torate despite the demands of home and parenting. Self-definition is the message and goal of sports. Yes, it is good.

4. In paragraph 7, Whitney says that at home and school her daughter had been told to be still, be quiet, be good. The message: female passivity was a virtue. The same is true in "countless advertisements," complains the author. Many ads promote women as nurturers, passive, and noncompetitive.

5. The majority of ads with women in them project the very cool, passive "ideals" Whitney speaks of.

6. She says her own "paroxysms of uncertainty [regarding her pursuit of a doctorate] would be eased" (paragraph 9). She is from an older generation that did not encourage women to aim high and play to win.

7. Whitney says she fears that her daughter—and other females of her generation—might be lured off course by the enticements of men. In her dark fantasies, she imagines a predatory young lawyer trapping her in marriage, motherhood, and a material world.

8. More than just a celebration of Ann's drive and accomplishments, the essay is applause for today's young women who "are not afraid to do . . . [their] best." It celebrates the liberation of women on fields and courts of play—a liberation that comes with "paroxysms of uncertainty" for Whitney and other women of her generation.

RHETORICAL CONSIDERATIONS

1. The central issues in this essay have to do with how today's women have broken out of yesterday's molds. The first sentence bespeaks the case. And although the second sentence underscores how common the situation is, it ends with an expression of the author's dismay—a dismay that unifies the essay. Throughout the piece, Whitney measures her daughter's accomplishments and determination against the forces of tradition.

2. Whitney's discussion of Ann's playing to win is not a springboard to her own self-examination. On the contrary, her daughter's story is a central inspiration, occasionally serving to remind the author of the handicaps she must overcome in pursuing her goal as a doctoral student.

3. The sudden switch to a direct, interior dialogue with Ann has the effect of putting the author in the stands of a game and the reader in the head of a proud mother. A sense of immediacy is created—as if the rest of the piece is a reflection made while at a game. This perspective is returned to at the end as Whitney cheers her daughter on. I think the effect is wonderful, even moving at the end.

4. Lady Astor (1879–1964), or Viscountess Astor, an American born Nancy Langhorne, was the first woman member of the British House of Commons. Extremely wealthy, Lady Astor's name became synonymous with elegance and sophistication. *The Stepford Wives,* named after the Ira Levin novel, is a sardonic science fiction movie about men whose ideals of female beauty, submissiveness, and subservience lead to the forced transformation of women into android wives.

·13·
Education

Killing the Spirit
Page Smith

TOPICAL CONSIDERATIONS

1. Smith would prefer the classic tradition of the great lecturer because that style encourages the lecturer to avoid the abstract, inflame the imagination of the pupils, and relate the subject matter to real life. The modern lecturer presents the "negative stereotype" by repeating the same lecture merely by adding the latest research without considering his or her listeners.
2. Students will agree or disagree. The examples they use from their own experiences will vary.
3. Answers will vary depending upon the students' individual experiences.
4. Students will describe a variety of note-taking methods which may lead to an interesting classroom discussion.
5. Again the answers will vary, but this question may lead to an active classroom discussion.
6. Students will agree or disagree. Their specific reasons will vary.
7. The play would prepare students for the way most of their professors will treat them, in Smith's view. In the play the professor refuses to stop lecturing when the student suffers a toothache. When she interrupts his lecture by crying out in pain, he strangles her. Another student arrives as the curtain comes down.
8. Students will either describe an experience that they have had or they will describe how they think a student-teacher dialogue might work. All students should explain whether they think the experience would be advantageous.

RHETORICAL CONSIDERATIONS

1. Smith gives the professional point of view of lectures with a tongue-in-cheek tone mocking seriousness. The first paragraph is statement, followed by an example, then he extends this tone with further examples.
2. In paragraph 2, he interjects, "we are told," as if this may or may not be true. He also inserts an "I think" for emphasis. In the last sentence of paragraph 5, Smith adds "I fear," indicating his displeasure that professors are still aloof and impersonal. In the opening sentence of paragraph 14, Smith says, "I am pleased to say" to reinforce his pride in a former student.

3. Smith's examples come from the history of education, contemporary works on education, television comedians, his own experience as an educator for over thirty years, and his former students.

4. Use of historical and contemporary examples help to reinforce Smith's points and add credibility.

5. Answers will vary. Students may feel that the essay should end with paragraph 20 because it has closure with the relationship between professors and students, and because it reinforces the ideas of the first paragraph. Students may choose paragraph 21 because it ends with good information and with a powerful example. Some may choose 22 because of the reinforcement with another example and the use of a strong ending.

6. Some students may consider Smith a braggart using his own success stories—that is, teaching Dante and using Limerick's words. They may also see Smith as a realistic teacher who practices what he preaches (i.e., the same examples compared to examples from historical and contemporary educators).

A Liberating Curriculum
Roberta F. Borkat

TOPICAL CONSIDERATIONS

1. Borkat says her plan to award the grade of A to all students in the second week of the semester will relieve anxiety, free students up "to do whatever they want," and assure them of "high grade-point averages and an absence of obstacles in their march toward graduation" (paragraph 3). Students may find this amusingly appealing, though they will also notice that the absurd plan would make a mockery of education and render their degrees useless.

2. This question should provoke an interesting discussion; responses will vary.

3. Students will probably have noticed Borkat's deeply cynical opinion of students; they may or may not think this opinion is justified. The student in paragraph 1 (who returns in paragraph 8) is a plagiarizer; the young man in paragraph 7 wants the assurance of a good grade even though he plans neither to do the reading nor attend class regularly; another student wants to be guaranteed a B after failing the first exam. All want good grades without working for them.

4. In paragraph 3, Borkat suggests her plan will relieve professors of "useless burdens," enabling them time to "pursue their real interests"; universities "will have achieved the long-desired goal of molding individual professors into interchangeable parts of a smoothly operating machine." In paragraph 8, Borkat imagines the "happy faces of university administrators and professors, released at last from the irksome chore of dealing with students." These passages suggest that university administrators want simply to create an efficient bureaucracy, and that professors are more interested in their personal and professional devel-

opment than in teaching. Students should also note the "one or two forlorn colleagues" who have more idealistic aims. By and large, Borkat is as cynical about these groups as she is about students.

5. Some students will probably know the essay that provides the model for this one: Swift's "A Modest Proposal." There, Swift attacks contemporary social practices by making a shockingly outlandish proposal with an absolutely straight face. Students familiar with Swift's work can describe the similarity between Swift's satire and Borkat's: In both, the author consistently states the exact opposite of what he or she actually believes.

6. Students may still not find Borkat's main point absolutely clear—and with good reason, since satire almost always works obliquely. Though never directly stated, Borkat clearly believes that some people involved in higher education—students, faculty, and university administrators—have no real commitment to learning. Instead, education has become merely a troublesome obstacle blocking the path to what these people really want: graduation; "professorial prestige, rapid promotion and frequent sabbaticals" (paragraph 8); and a "smoothly operating" bureaucratic machine (paragraph 3).

RHETORICAL CONSIDERATIONS

1. Borkat sardonically relates her new belief in her "Plan" to a kind of religious conversion; the diction is so patently inappropriate to the topic at hand that it helps signal her ironic intent. Once students have seen the pseudoreligious connotations of the word "blessed" in the first sentence they should be able to identify its appearance in subsequent words and phrases: the suggestion that knowledge has been "revealed" to her; that "Enlightenment came to me in a sublime moment of clarity"; that her conversion was effected by a "revelation."

2. After introducing her plan in paragraphs 1 and 2, Borkat suggests potential benefits in paragraph 3. She then spends four paragraphs (4, 5, 6, and 7) addressing the opposition to her argument. Paragraph 8 suggests that her plan will satisfy not only students, but university administrators; paragraph 9 facetiously regrets she wasted almost thirty years trying to help students learn. Borkat spends most of her time presenting—and facetiously addressing—opposition to her proposal. This strategy allows Borkat to express her real view at some length, since she actually concurs with her opposition.

3. Here Borkat uses faulty reasoning to promote a point with which she actually disagrees. Borkat falsely defines democracy as a system "that aims for equality in all things"; students should see a conflict between this notion of democracy and the concept as they know it. The inaccuracy of the definition debilitates this part of Borkat's argument.

4. Borkat's purpose does not seem to be educational reform, primarily because she makes little or no effort to achieve common ground with the villains in the story—the students, teachers, and university administrators whose ideas need reforming. This is, of course, a central characteristic of satire, which is almost by definition critical rather than constructive. Borkat's satire, like Swift's, iden-

tifies and attacks a problem with withering wit but makes little or no effort to win over the people who might reform the abuse in question. Since the essay first appeared in *Newsweek,* a general interest periodical, Borkat's audience is not necessarily academic; rather, the piece seems designed for the public at large, who it invites to scorn academic folly.

Why My Kids Hate Science
Robert M. Hazen

TOPICAL CONSIDERATIONS

1. His children hate science because it has been taught to them through "mindless memorization" and "canned laboratory experiments." In other words, the children learned how to play the game to get good grades but learned nothing about the concepts of science.
2. Answers will vary.
3. Hazen blames the scientific-literacy crisis on working scientists. Some students may agree because they feel they have not been taught the basics in science or may have had science teachers who directed their lectures to science majors only. Others may disagree because they see the need for future scientists, or they are successful science majors, or they enjoy taking advanced science courses involving laboratory experimentation.
4. Hazen offers the following solutions:
   a. Teach the central ideas of science in a simple, elegant manner.
   b. Train teachers to convey the central ideas of science with confidence and enthusiasm.
   c. Involve students in hands-on exploration of the universe in science classrooms.
5. General education involves a basic knowledge of our physical world. Specialized interests involve teaching advanced courses and doing specific laboratory research.
6. Yes. Smith wants lectures to bring the reality of any subject alive in the classroom. Hazen wants science to come alive for students in the classroom.

RHETORICAL CONSIDERATIONS

1. He is a geologist and a member of the scientific community that he criticizes. He does describe some of his own experiences (i.e., his learning by teaching genetics). Answers for the second part may vary.
2. Hazen presents many possible reasons: too much television, lack of parental supervision, poor media image of scientists, declining national standards

of education, poorly trained teachers, inadequate resources, or dumb students. Then, he gives his reason and includes himself as a working scientist.

3. First, he gives the point of view of a parent to establish the problem, then he takes the view of a working scientist to give the reason, and finally the view of a member of society to offer a solution.

4. Third person would distance the author from the reader and from the topic. He could not use his personal experience as a father, nor could he gain credibility as a scientist criticizing scientists. The tone would lack the personal informality that helps to make his argument strong.

5. Answers will vary.

6. For the student.

A (Vague) Sense of History

Jonathan Alter and Lydia Denworth

TOPICAL CONSIDERATIONS

1. Nearly one-third of American 17-year-olds do not know which countries fought against the United States in World War II. One-third do not know what *Brown* v. *Board of Education* accomplished. One-third thought Columbus reached the New World after 1750. Two-thirds cannot correctly place the Civil War between 1850 and 1900.

2. Both essays discuss the rote memorization and lectures that dull a student's interest. Alter and Denworth say, "The natural curiosity of students is snuffed out at an early age." Hazen talks about "mindless memorizations" and "canned laboratory experiments" that turn students off. They both say bringing the subjects to life is the answer. Science should use real life experience in experiments and history should be taught as the narrative of real people.

3. Some students may describe how the teaching of history as a story about real people made it interesting. Others may tell how they never got the real history because of studies of anthropology, civics, psychology, family, and neighborhood life. Those who have not taken a social studies course may describe what they would like to learn or never did learn.

4. Recognize the boredom factor means to encourage students' curiosity by telling good stories. Rethink social studies to focus on a "narrative thrust and natural appeal." Expand history's place by requiring more courses for high-school graduation. Put multiculturalism in perspective by using primary source materials and first-person accounts. Demand good textbooks by selecting insightful ones with distinguished authors. Bring history alive by making students think through a variety of teaching methods.

5. Page Smith believes "students must be . . . an integral part of the learning process." He also thinks lectures should inflame the imagination of the pupils.

He would like Palumbo's using classroom arguments, stepping into the shoes of minority groups, and questioning issues of historical and contemporary times. These techniques fulfill Smith's beliefs by inflaming students' imaginations and involving them in the learning process.

RHETORICAL CONSIDERATIONS

1. The authors connect the beginning and end through the example which refers to the "joke" at the beginning, then the Palumbo example at the end refutes the "joke" at the beginning.
2. This essay in third person is written in a more formal tone using historical information and subheadings similar to a history text. For instance, the authors use detailed statistics in relation to historical information (i.e., "Nearly ⅓ of American 17 year olds cannot . . . ") to prove the historical illiteracy in America. They also cite noted authorities such as Diane Ravitch and use case studies like Joe Palumbo.

   Hazen's essay, written in first person, uses personal experiences. Also, the author takes the blame for the poor teaching by science educators because he is one. Student answers will vary.
3. The integration of multiculturalism into the teaching of history is a controversial issue which will probably be the first one mentioned by many students. The authors explain the side of putting too much emphasis on American history and Western civilization. Then, they go from the extreme of that side to the opposite side before offering a middle course. They also deal with the controversial issue of social studies versus history by presenting the views of two organizations, NCSS and NCHE.
4. The title with the word "vague" in parentheses indicates that the sense of history is limited. Some students may sense that it does not indicate that ways of correcting the problem of historical illiteracy do not naturally follow from making one aware of the problem.
5. Student answers will reflect individual experience in history class. Most students will probably select recognition of the boredom factor, use of good textbooks, or bringing history alive.

Can America Be No. 1 in Math? You Bet Your Noogie
Dave Barry

TOPICAL CONSIDERATIONS

1. Both men complain that their children find their respective subjects difficult and boring. Hazen speaks of "mindless memorization" and "canned laboratory experiments" while Barry depicts Robert as "slaving order . . . horrible pages full of long-division problems" that teach him a skill he'll never need in life.

2. Barry mixes made-up statistics with botched calculations to create the humor while demonstrating his own poor math skills. He cites the price of drinks, the absurd 176,485 "D" cell battery powering the executive's yacht, and the fagure of 74 percent of high school students who couldn't figure out the problem in paragraph 7. He also facetiously cannot figure out how much the fourth drink costs; and he says "nine times seven is around fifty." Barry is having fun, but beneath it he touches upon the declining math skills.

3. Barry's advice to Robert is funny because its structure is logical while its content is contradictory. The expectation is that after the "but" Barry will offer warm consolation to make what seems "difficult and boring" all worthwhile. But the humor spins on the surprise paradox that not only is the homework what Robert suspects, but it's essentially useless. And there is some truth to his point. Aside from the purist notion that knowing is better than not knowing, Robert's slaving *is* a waste of time since in life most people never have to long divide. If they're in a profession that uses numbers, they will surely do such comutations on calculators or computers.

4. Depending on the students' sense of humor, they may respond by describing a whole incident such as figuring out the cost of the fourth drink at Toys "R" Us or the classroom experiences with Mr. O'Regan or Mr. Schofield. On the other hand, they may select a small description such as a secretary of education calling America "a nation of stupids," Barry's creation of the American Association of Recent Studies, or the response of the American Council of Mathematicians to the European and Japanese superiority in testing.

5. Open for discussion.

RHETORICAL CONSIDERATIONS

1. The title itself tells the reader it is not serious, no matter what a "noogie" is. In the first paragraph he mentions a real position, U.S. Secretary of Education, even though he makes up the name of the person filling the position. Students who do not know who is currently the secretary of education may believe this first sentence until the quotation, "a nation of stupids."

2. He uses real brand names (see answer 1 in Topical Considerations), places (Toys "R" Us, Japan, Europe) and statistics ("74 percent of U.S. high school students . . . ") to lead the reader into an exaggerated response. He also follows a statement with "Seriously, though" as if he will stop making jokes, but he doesn't.

3. Students may respond in two ways to this question. Those who think there is truth in the essay may state that the overall feeling toward U.S. students is that their math ability is inferior to the ability of European and Japanese students. They may also see truth in the idea that you really don't use math that much in life because of calculators and computers. On the other hand, those who feel there is no truth to this essay may say that all semblance of credibility is destroyed because nothing he says should be taken seriously. Therefore, responses may differ according to slight differences in the tone readers sense.

4. Some will prefer the quotations which include the one in the opening paragraph and the one by the American Council of Mathematicians. These are downright silly and some students will select them for that reason. Others will prefer the complicated intricacies of the price of the fourth cardboard drink box and the Cheez Whiz problem because they involve a more sustained and detailed kind of absurdity.

5. Answers will vary according to how much students liked the essay. Few will be surprised at his admission, some will say that he destroys the tone by suddenly being honest, others will point out the use of the secretary of education at the beginning and end to tie the essay together. The appropriateness may depend on the involvement of the reader in the essay.

A Bag of Possibles and Other Matters of the Mind

Robert Fulghum

TOPICAL CONSIDERATIONS

1. He describes the access in kindergarten to all resources in one room as opposed to limited availability to resources spread across the campus in college. He then uses several questions asked kindergarten children and gives their enthusiastic, positive response to try whatever is asked of them. For instance, can they dance, draw, sing? In contrast, he describes how college students restrict and qualify their responses. Personal examples will vary.

2. Kindergarten children performed this difficult opera and he shares their method of learning. The young students differ in their methods of learning, and they learn on their own. Responses on personal learning methods will differ. Brünnhilde creates her own method by learning small sections of the opera and dialogue at a time and focusing on the first three words of each section. Also, she sings the talking parts and talks the singing parts while moving around the room instead of sitting still.

3. Thomas Jefferson proposed public education in 1779 but it took over one hundred years to enforce. No, it was not favorably accepted. Individual responses will differ.

4. He advocates student-centered learning because the teacher must empower the student to learn for him- or herself.

5. He taught only students who thought they had no talent or skill. All learned to draw competently because "drawing is a matter of skill. Skills can be acquired with practice (paragraph 32)." Personal responses will vary.

6. Students in kindergarten and first grade know how to learn on their own. He suggests teachers must be aware of individual ways of learning because all minds differ. His explanation of the possibles bag describes the possibilities in

each person's mind. The title reflects the ideas mentioned above, plus the one-line statements at the end.

7. For the student; answers will vary according to personal experience.

RHETORICAL CONSIDERATIONS

1. Yes. He explains how public education encourages students to be "civilized and socialized." He says that if teachers try to convey prescribed information without empowering students to learn for themselves, teachers will diminish the students' self-esteem.

2. Students will determine whether they think the examples are effective or not. Personal examples include his encounter with the cast of Wagner's "Die Walküre," his description of teaching "drawing for turkeys," the explanation of the possibles bag he gave his son for graduation, and the list of his one-line statements from his journal.

3. The tone is informal, conversational, almost talking aloud. He wants the reader to feel involved in a conversation with the writer. Answers will differ as to whether students like this tone or not.

4. Some examples of Fulghum's use of humor include describing how the kindergarten students stay true to "Die Walküre" except at the end when the boy must kiss the girl's eyelids. "No 7-year-old boy is going to kiss a girl's eyelids or anywhere else." He refers to himself as Captain Kindergarten and uses the parenthetical comment about his son's graduation "cum laude, thank you very much." Students will give personal responses to whether or not they thought the humor was funny or appropriate for this essay.

5. The purpose of his digression is to inform the reader of the background of public education to send children to school to become "civilized and socialized." Personal responses may vary.

6. Frontiersmen's "possibles bags" enabled them to survive just as what is inside a person's head enables him or her to survive today. Fulghum's possibles inside the head include experience, imagination, courage, dreams, and self-confidence.

On Death and Dying

On Natural Death
Lewis Thomas

TOPICAL CONSIDERATIONS

1. Thomas finds all the current fascination with dying and death remarkable, as if learning how to die properly is reserved for "the specially trained." His point is that even though human beings have been dying since the beginning, people today need to be instructed on how to perceive, prepare for, and cope with the subject. Perhaps because past generations were closer to the natural world, people regarded dying a phenomenon as natural as living. What Thomas does in this essay is put the experience in context of the natural order of things.

2. Thomas defines "natural" by association here. His reference to the elm tree and the "cat-chewed" field mouse creates a context for the death of the two young MPs and, by association, all of humanity. All dying is "natural." "Unnatural" death refers to an attitude of those who cannot grapple with the subject matter, who regard human death as a higher phenomenon. The author's focusing on the subject of pain makes clear how the body contains natural mechanisms for the preparation of death. Like the elm feeling no pain, both mice and men are suspended painlessly in the jaws of death. In short, as Montaigne says, "Nature will in a moment fully and sufficiently instruct" (paragraph 9) us on how to die.

3. We see trees dying and being cut down all the time. Therefore, we might regard such deaths as automatic and trivial, more "natural" than our own. But our own dying is part of the same ecological cycles, cruel as they might seem. See above for more.

4. His first reaction to the sight of the mouse dangling from the jaws of the cat was outrage. The creature, no doubt, was suffering "pain beyond bearing." Nature's cruelty was the "abomination" he could not accept. However, after medically reconsidering the event, Thomas deduced that the endorphins released by the creature's hypothalamus and pituitary glands most likely spared it pain. There is no way of knowing for sure that the mouse died without struggle. But Thomas finds consolation in the speculation. Not unnecessarily cruel, nature rescued the animal's final moments from agony. Likewise, similar mechanisms are natural components of our own bodies as witnessed by Montaigne and the two dying soldiers.

5. Montaigne records the experience of nearly dying. In the first passage Thomas quotes, the philosopher makes death seem like drifting off to sleep. He uses gentle images of floating and "growing languid" and "letting go." His point is that

nature adjusts us to our dying by setting us free gently. Although Montaigne does not say this, nor Thomas directly, the dying experience is the wonderful result of millions of years of evolution, a process that favors the organism—a "death right," perhaps.

RHETORICAL CONSIDERATIONS

1. Thomas gives us three anecdotes. The first, the death and removal of his elm tree, illustrates several things: the sudden, unexpected quality of death; the naturalness of the process (it "caught the blight this summer"); and the casual regard of the "natural" process of trees dying, "done automatically and trivially" (the crew "took it down . . . and carted it off. . . , everyone singing"). This anecdote used in paragraph 5 connects to the second anecdote about the mouse specifically on the matter of pain. Just as the elm, lacking "pain receptors," did not suffer its end, so the mouse dying in the cat's teeth went without struggle. The point is that in the "end game," as Thomas calls death, nature spares its creatures. The third anecdote climbs the chain of being to humans at the moment of death. That the mortally wounded MPs could chat casually dramatically illustrates the extraordinary response the body has to its own death—a response that is common to mice and men and is as natural as life.

2. The tone of this piece is reflective, lightly philosophical, and friendly. Although the essay was written for the *New England Journal of Medicine,* Thomas writes less for his medical colleagues than he does for the general reader. His profession obviously comes through in paragraphs 6 and 7 with several technical terms that lend credibility to his speculations. However, balancing the scientific terminology are occasional colloquialisms: "dropped stone dead" and "went ahead and died anyway" (paragraph 4), "a hunch about dying" and "close call" (paragraph 8), and "end game" (paragraph 11). The overall tone might be considered "reader-friendly." His language is accessible and his discussion of the subject matter is positive without being frivolous, and insightful without being heavy or moribund.

3. The clearest statement of his thesis is the last sentence in the final paragraph. It is a statement that he builds up to from the first line. And coming where it does following the anecdotes, references to Montaigne and his own reflections, the statement has the impact of Q.E.D.

On the Fear of Death
Elisabeth Kübler-Ross

TOPICAL CONSIDERATIONS

1. The increased attention to the subject of death really has something to do with the increasing population of older people in the country. The median age in America is rising, so more and more people are concerned with the realities of

coping with their own mortality and that of peers. But even more important, dying today is more frightening because it has been made "more lone, mechanical, and dehumanized" by increased technology.

2. When the author was a child she, along with others, was invited to visit the dying farmer. By so doing, she shared in the preparations of his death. The anecdote illustrates her point that both the dying and the survivors need to accept the inevitability of death and the eventual loss. It also illustrates how children in particular need to share in death so as to better accept its reality and the fact that they are not alone in their grief. By contrast to dying in a hospital bed hooked up to machines and surrounded by strangers in medical whites, the farmer dying at home is far less lonely and impersonal.

3. Children who are excluded from death sense that "something is wrong" and end up distrusting adults. They will sense the loss and, "depending on the age and personality of the child" (paragraph 18), may develop "an unresolved grief." Kübler-Ross says that these children might also regard the particular death as "frightening, mysterious," and too traumatic to cope with successfully.

4. Toward the end of the essay, Kübler-Ross advocates that severely ill patients be regarded as persons not things, that their emotional needs be addressed not just their medical needs. Dying today, she observes, is made all the more lonely and dehumanized because patients are removed from their homes to hospitals where they find themselves surrounded by machines and impersonal technicians more concerned with treatment than the patient as a person. His or her feelings, opinions, or wishes may be disregarded; and when asserted, they are often met with "infusions, transfusions, a heart machine, or tracheotomy if necessary." In short, Kübler-Ross argues for death with dignity.

5. It is clear that the "we" at the end of the essay refers to people in the medical profession—physicians, nurses, and technicians. In paragraph 27, Kübler-Ross wonders if the increased "mechanical, depersonalized approach" might be medics' "defensiveness" against their helplessness in the face of death as well as their own mortality. Instead of taking time to hold a dying patient's hand, they fill their attention with numbers and equipment thereby emotionally detaching themselves from the event of any human identity with the patient.

RHETORICAL CONSIDERATIONS

1. Up to paragraph 18, the essay is essentially explanatory in nature—mostly regarding the fear of death and how societies cope with it. Although paragraph 17 is mostly analytical in nature, Kübler-Ross begins her criticism of making death a taboo for children. The first clear statement of an argument comes at the beginning of the next paragraph where she says "It is equally unwise to tell a little child who lost her brother that God loved little boys so much that he took little Johnny to heaven." From here to the end her argument is loud and clear: that despite all the advancements in medical science, we are moving further away from the days when people died "in peace and dignity."

2. The last sentence in paragraph 2 serves as a thesis statement for the essay.

3. Paragraphs 1 through 10 serves as a beginning: Despite the advancements in medical science, humans suffer a universal fear of death. The middle, paragraphs 11 through 17, deals with older customs of dealing with death. The end of the essay, from paragraph 18, talks about today's fear of death and the way we attempt to deflect the anxiety and turmoil.

I Want to Die at Home
Anne Ricks Sumers

TOPICAL CONSIDERATIONS

1. Sumers' thesis is "If it's at all possible, people should die in familiar surroundings in their own beds" (paragraph 9). Students might point to other, related claims, such as "If a family member is dying in a hospital and wants to return home, try to find the means to do it" (paragraph 20) and "Doctors must learn to . . . let patients go home" (paragraph 20). A secondary point is one Sumers shares with Elizabeth Kübler-Ross and Benjamin Spock: the belief that death should be treated as a natural part of life, not sequestered away behind closed doors.

    Students might consider whether they would like to die at home, or whether they would be willing to nurse their parents, brothers, sisters, or significant others at home. By considering the level of their own opposition to this proposal, students might begin to see that Sumers both over- and underestimates her opposition: The idea of death at home is appealing to many; the reality is not always as ideal as in the case of Sumers' brother.

2. While Rick is dying, his family participates in activities symbolically associated with renewal: They plant flowers; they paint the porch (paragraph 16). Since the images stress life, continuity, and community instead of death, finality, and separation, they vividly support Sumers' claim that death is a natural part of living.

3. Analyzing Rick's last night should further clarify the reconceptualization of death Sumers calls for here. The last night is Thanksgiving-like because it focuses on food and togetherness. Sumers tells us several times that Rick eats well; specifically, we see him "savoring a glass of red wine" and "eating a cookie" (paragraph 12). Since the usual purpose of eating (maintaining life) is irrelevant to Rick now, food is serving primarily its festive, ritualistic purpose.

    The togetherness extends beyond the immediate family to a larger community that includes neighbors, friends from church, and cousins (paragraph 12). Instead of being a somber death watch, the evening is "wild, fun, tragic and exhilarating" (paragraph 12), with Rick the liveliest of them all: "He was busy all evening, reminiscing, telling fragments of stories, neatening up, washing dishes, giving advice and eating well" (paragraph 14). Though hours from death, Rick is very much at the center of life.

4. The opposition of hospital and home is a central structuring principle of the essay; in addition, all the parallels support Sumers' contention that death is an extension of life. So, in the hospital only two people can be with Rick at

a time, and the family "hovers unconnected in a waiting room" (paragraph 8); at home they are all together. At the hospital there is no real privacy for "a last marital snuggle" (paragraph 8); at home, Rick falls asleep in his wife's arms. Communication with the larger circle of friends and acquaintances can only be made through "long phone calls on pay phones" in the hospital (paragraph 8); at home, members of the extended family casually stop by. While at the hospital Rick is "furious, humiliated, embarrassed, enraged, confused and frightened," at home he is "confused" but benignly so. Rick is tied down in his bed in the hospital (paragraph 7); at home, he "walked from room to room in his house" (paragraph 12). Students might also discuss the connotative contrast between the drink at the hospital ("bad coffee") and the drink at home ("a glass of red wine").

5. The bits of information about this family's socioeconomic background construct a picture of relative privilege. Rick was a lawyer (paragraph 1) who had enough financial resources to remodel his kitchen when recovering from kidney surgery (paragraph 2); we see him "savoring" wine (paragraph 12). Sumers herself is an ophthalmologist. The family are Quakers (paragraph 12), a religion (as some students might know) associated with individuality and liberal politics. Theirs is an apparently intact nuclear family that is well established in the community as well (visitors include neighbors and cousins as well as friends from church). Medical expenses do not seem to be a problem.

     This family's apparent prosperity may affect students differently. Some might find this knowledge increases the family's appeal, since they seem such responsible, upstanding citizens. Others may recognize how the family's socioeconomic status makes home death more feasible than it would be, say, in a low-income home with two children, one wage earner, and no health insurance.

RHETORICAL CONSIDERATIONS

1. Throughout the essay, Sumers stresses both the recentness of Rick's death and the speed with which it occurred. Immediacy is created in the first sentence: "Last week, my brother Rick died at home" (paragraph 1); we also learn Sumers has had only "the past week" to process the death (and write this article). Sumers also stresses the rapidity of her brother's sudden decline, which "all happened so quickly" (paragraph 3): She shifts from measuring time in months (Rick's first diagnosis was "three months ago," paragraph 2) to days: on a Tuesday he is confused, by Wednesday he is hallucinating (paragraph 3), on Saturday he is dead (paragraphs 16–17). Such immediacy increases both the drama of the story and its emotional effectiveness by drawing the readers closer to this tragic death.

2. Sumers' characterization of Rick increases her argument's emotional effect, since it encourages readers to identify with her dying brother. Students will, of course, point to different details. Some might remember that he was a Redskins fan (paragraph 2), others might have been struck by him brushing his teeth and lying down "in his wife's arms" (paragraph 15) before slipping into a coma. Students might relate to the episode of the key chain (paragraph 6), where Rick's final loss of control is associated, lightly, with the willed delirium of a

wild night of drinking. Such details both universalize Rick (making him into a kind of Everyman) and individualize him, increasing the emotional effect of his loss on readers who do not know him personally.

3. Students at this point should recognize the difficulty of generalizing from one example in argument. The argument is based largely on an emotional appeal. Moving as the story is, Rick's death is not necessarily representative, being atypical in both speed and relative cleanliness—as at least some students should know from experience. He dies the day after returning from the hospital, instead of lingering for weeks or months; he is not violent or dangerously irrational; he can feed himself, brush his teeth, and wash his face until he slips into a coma. Despite his being the terminal patient, he cleans up after others (paragraph 14), reversing usual circumstances. The physical details of dying are not always so easy to cope with.

4. These questions should help students recognize the rather fuzzy sense of audience here. In the last paragraph, Sumers addresses "nurses, doctors and social workers in hospices" (paragraph 21), but since these health-care professionals are already involved in keeping the terminally ill out of hospitals they cannot be the essay's main audience. Sumers implies her argument is meant to convince doctors who "must learn to let . . . patients go home" (paragraph 20), but she herself never encountered opposition to home death from that quarter: "Rick's doctor was empathetic and efficient" and let Rick go "less than two hours" after the family decided to take him home (paragraph 11).

The only real opposition Sumers identifies comes from potential family members, friends of Sumers who "express fear of a dead body in the house" (paragraph 18). This group seems more clearly to be Sumers' target audience, as the essay's first appearance in the general-interest periodical *Newsweek* would suggest. The purpose of the essay, then, is not so much to influence public policy as to encourage the culture to reconceptualize death and take it into their home, as Rick's family did. In fact, Sumers' audience seems more narrowly defined still as middle- and upper-middle-class families for whom home death is an option. The opposition not refuted—or even identified—is mostly socio-economic. Home death might not work for families who lack the resources, human or financial, of the Sumers clan; nor would it work in long-term, debilitating illness, when jobs, care of young children, and other family responsibilities could not be deferred.

A Way to Say Farewell
Benjamin Spock

TOPICAL CONSIDERATIONS

1. Dr. Spock cites three examples, all expressing denial and avoidance. The first is that of physicians, who often ignore symptoms of cancer. Instead of seeking treatment, doctors prefer to "hope against hope" that their suspicions are un-

founded. They deny signs of their disease until their conditions are inoperable. The second example comes from Spock's own experience—that of the mother who called him to say that she had found her infant son dead in his crib. Clearly she wished Spock's immediate presence. Instead, Spock directed her to rush the child to a hospital. At a later time, Spock says he realized that his directives were his way of avoiding the situation of death. The third example emphasizes the difficulty of talking about imminent death—the mother of three who was dying of cancer yet who never asked her doctor for a diagnosis. Apparently she wished to remain ignorant, fearing the worst. Similarly, the attending physicians, including Spock, never spoke bluntly to her about her condition. Years later Spock realized that perhaps the patient had wished for a frank discussion but was discouraged by her physician's reluctance. "Perhaps she was only following his cue." Though Spock begins his essay saying, "I don't fear the dying as long as it's not very painful or lonely or lacking in dignity," these examples give him pause. He knows he cannot predict with certainty what his reaction to death will be.

2. Spock wants cheerful, straightforward types around him, he says—people who would discuss openly any concerns he might have but who would avoid gratuitous inquiries.

3. Spock compares hospitals to clean factories designed to produce diagnoses and treatments. He stresses the impersonality of hospitals in paragraph 13, "A stream of staffers barges in, as if from outer space: history taker, physical examiners, temperature and pulse takers, meal servers, bath givers, stretcher pushers, X-ray technicians, bed makers, pill pushers, specimen takers." The catalogue makes the patient sound like an item on a production line, and reveals the impersonality of the hospital environment.

On the other hand, Spock feels that a hospice offers a far more humane alternative. The goal of the hospice is to let a person die as comfortably as possible in a homelike setting, surrounded by family and familiar possessions. Medical attention, in the form of heavy medication, is provided only to ease pain and not to prolong life.

4. Spock's ideal send off would be a cheerful funeral, New Orleans style, but he would settle for a sedate church service. For the student to discuss.

RHETORICAL CONSIDERATIONS

1. Clearly, the architect is a man of style. His dashing appearance is emphasized by his broad-brimmed hat, expensive suit, and flowing silk bow tie. A single detail destroys his urbane image: "His jacket, however, was dotted with food spots" (paragraph 10). That detail conveys the embarrassing onset of senility.

2. In paragraph 8, Spock discusses his aversion to treatments designed not to cure illness but to postpone death. He writes, "But I would not want to be kept alive with antibiotics, infusions, transfusions, anticancer drugs or radiation if they were just to postpone my death for a few months. . . ." He concludes this solemn reflection with "especially if I had lost my marbles." The colloquial surprise at

the end jolts the reader and reduces the solemnity. Similarly, at the end of paragraph 12 he wonders, if he were in unbearable pain would his doctor be willing to provide him a terminal dose of medication? He concludes with "and will Mary have the nerve to jab the needle?" Again the colloquial aside softens the somber subject matter. Spock uses this blunting technique at the end of paragraph 14, where a discussion of death in a hospice is followed by "That's the departure for me." The most effective use of this technique occurs in the last sentence of the essay. Following a description of his self-designed memorial service and the biblical passage about children, he cannot resist the upbeat conclusion: "Then there could be a cheerful cocktail party somewhere nearby."

3. The opening phrase sounds like the beginning of a will. It alerts us to Spock's intention of addressing the issue of his own death. Instead of giving directives about the dispersal of his worldly goods, he directs people how to say farewell to him.